D0203385

ADVANCED ACCOUNTING

ADVANCED ACCOUNTING

Fourth Edition

Debra C. Jeter
Vanderbilt University

Paul K. Chaney
Vanderbilt University

John Wiley & Sons, Inc.

VICE PRESIDENT & EXECUTIVE PUBLISHER	George Hoffman
ASSOCIATE PUBLISHER	Chris DeJohn
SENIOR PRODUCTION EDITOR	Patricia McFadden
SENIOR MARKETING MANAGER	Julia Flohr
CREATIVE DIRECTOR	Harry Nolan
SENIOR DESIGNER	Madelyn Lesure
PROJECT EDITOR	Ed Brislin
EDITORIAL ASSISTANT	Kara Taylor
MARKETING ASSISTANT	Laura Finley
EXECUTIVE MEDIA EDITOR	Allison Morris
MEDIA EDITOR	Greg Chaput
PRODUCTION MANAGEMENT SERVICES	Ingrao Associates
COVER IMAGE:	Linda & Colin Mckie/iStockphoto
COVER DESIGNER:	Madelyn Lesure
TEXT DESIGNER:	Lee Goldstein

This book was set in 8/10 New Baskerville by Preparé and printed and bound by RRD/Jefferson City. The cover was printed by RRD/Jefferson City.

This book is printed on acid free paper. ∞

ISBN-13 9780470506981

ISBN-10 0470506989

Printed in the United States of America

10 9 8 7 6 5 4 3 2

ABOUT THE AUTHORS

Debra Jeter is an Associate Professor of Management in the Owen Graduate School of Management at Vanderbilt University. She received her Ph.D. in accounting from Vanderbilt University. Dr. Jeter has published articles in *The Accounting Review, the Journal of Accounting and Economics, Auditing: A Journal of Practice and Theory, Contemporary Accounting Research,* and *Accounting Horizons,* as well as in popular magazines including *Working Woman* and *Savvy*. She has co-authored one previous book, "Managerial Cost Accounting: Planning and Control," and has written chapters in others. She has taught at both the graduate and undergraduate levels and is currently teaching financial accounting to masters' level students.

Dr. Jeter has also taught financial accounting in the Executive International MBA program for the Vlerick School of Management in Ghent and has served as a Visiting Research Professor at the University of Auckland. Debra Jeter has served on the editorial boards of *The Accounting Review, Accounting Enquiries, Issues in Accounting Education,* and *International Journal of Accounting, Auditing and Performance Evaluation,* and as an ad hoc associate editor for *Auditing: A Journal of Practice & Theory.* She is currently an associate editor of *Issues in Accounting Education.* She won a Dean's Award for Teaching Excellence in 1998 and the Webb Teaching Award in 2002. She won the Outstanding Alumnus Award in 2006 from her undergraduate university, Murray State University. Her research interests extend to financial accounting and auditing, including earnings management, components of earnings, audit opinions, and the market for audit services. She practiced as a CPA in Columbus, Ohio before entering academia.

Paul Chaney is the E. Bronson Ingram Professor of Accounting in the Owen Graduate School of Management at Vanderbilt University. He has been at the Owen Graduate School since obtaining his Ph.D. from Indiana University in 1983. He has taught both undergraduate and graduate students, and currently teaches the core financial accounting class for both the MBA and Executive MBA programs. He has taught extensively in executive programs, including courses in Accounting and Finance for the Non-Financial Executive and specialized courses for specific businesses.

Dr. Chaney has published articles in the *Accounting Review,* the *Journal of Accounting Research,* the *Journal of Public Economics,* the *Journal of Business, Contemporary Accounting Research,* the *Journal of Accounting and Economics,* and *Accounting Horizons.* He has won three teaching awards and serves on the editorial board for several academic journals.

PREFACE

Convergence with international accounting standards has played an important role in virtually every project entered into by the Financial Accounting Standards Board (FASB) in recent years. Accounting for business combinations is no exception. In the 4th edition of Advanced Accounting, we compare and contrast U.S. standards and international principles throughout the book, drawing the readers' attention to remaining differences with an IFRS icon. The reader is made aware of important changes, both present and expected future ones. We also incorporate the FASB's new codification system for referencing standards.

This book is designed for advanced courses dealing with financial accounting and reporting in the following topical areas: business combinations, consolidated financial statements, international accounting, foreign currency transactions, accounting for derivative instruments, translation of financial statements of foreign affiliates, segment reporting and interim reporting, partnerships, fund accounting and accounting for governmental units, and accounting for nongovernment–nonbusiness organizations. The primary objective of this book is to provide a comprehensive treatment of selected topics in a clear and understandable manner. The changes related to *SFAS No. 141R* [ASC 805] and *160* [ASC 810] are integrated throughout the edition. As in previous editions, we strive to maintain maximum flexibility to the instructor in the selection and breadth of coverage for topics dealing with consolidated financial statements and other advanced topics.

The effects of alternative concepts of consolidation, such as the parent company and the entity concepts, are presented in Chapter 1, along with FASB's decision to change from the past hybrid approach to the economic entity concept for consolidations. This change has been fully incorporated in this edition. We also expand our discussion of the FASB's conceptual framework in Chapter 1. We discuss the deferred income tax consequences in appendices to various consolidations chapters. Thus, such topics as the effects of undistributed subsidiary income and unrealized intercompany profit, as well as differences between the assigned values and tax bases of assets and liabilities of an acquired company, may be omitted or included as desired by the instructor.

All chapters have been updated where appropriate to reflect the most recent pronouncements of the Financial Accounting Standards Board and the Governmental Accounting Standards Board.

In teaching consolidation concepts, a decision must be made about the recording method that should be emphasized in presenting consolidated workpaper procedures. The three major alternatives for recording investments in subsidiaries are the (1) cost method, (2) partial equity (or simple equity) method, and (3) complete equity (or sophisticated equity) method. A brief description of each method follows.

1. *Cost method.* The investment in subsidiary is carried at its cost, with no adjustments made to the investment account for subsidiary income or dividends. Dividends received by the parent company are recorded as an increase in cash and as dividend income.

2. *Partial equity method.* The investment account is adjusted for the parent company's share of the subsidiary's reported earnings or losses, and dividends received from the subsidiary are deducted from the investment account. Generally, no other adjustments are made to the investment in subsidiary account.
3. *Complete equity method.* This method is the same as the partial equity method except that additional adjustments are made to the investment in subsidiary account to reflect the effects of (a) the elimination of unrealized intercompany profits, (b) the amortization (depreciation) of the difference between cost and book value, (c) the additional stockholders' equity transactions undertaken by the subsidiary that change the parent company's share of the subsidiary's stockholders' equity.

We have elected to present all three methods, using generic icons to distinguish among the three. The instructor has the flexibility to teach all three methods, or to instruct the students to ignore one or two. If the student is interested in learning all three methods, he can, even if the instructor only focuses on one or two. Also, we believe this feature makes the book an excellent reference for the student to keep after graduation, so that he or she can adapt to any method needed.

Our decision to include all three methods was influenced in part by surveys of practitioners and professors. In a survey of corporate controllers of Fortune 500 companies who were asked to indicate the method used on their books for investments in subsidiaries that are consolidated, more than 71 percent indicated that they used the cost method. In contrast, in surveys of professors teaching advanced accounting courses, the most popular method was either the partial or complete equity method. Also, in reviewing the response of users and reviewers to our previous editions (which took the same approach), we found that while one user recommended reducing the attention to the complete equity method and a few others recommended expanding it and reducing the other two, most seemed pleased with the balance.

The coverage on changes in ownership interests in Chapter 8, which was limited to a summary of the proposed and existing standards in the previous edition, is now presented fully.

Important Features of This Edition

1. We introduce a discussion of international accounting standards on each topic where such standards exist, and compare and contrast U.S. GAAP and IFRS. An IFRS icon is presented in the margins of these pages.
2. We incorporate a discussion of the joint projects of the FASB and the IASB throughout the textbook where appropriate, with an expanded discussion in Chapter 11. In Chapter 11, we pay particular attention to the three major joint projects of the two Boards: revenue recognition, accounting for leases, and financial statement presentation.
3. We expand our discussion of the FASB's conceptual framework as it relates to Advanced Accounting in Chapter 1, and we include marginal references to ***Related Concepts*** throughout the book. The GASB's conceptual framework is discussed in Chapters 17 and 18.
4. We include questions or problems related to ***Business Ethics*** in the end of chapter materials for every chapter.
5. We include a real-company annual report (or excerpts) with related questions (***Analyzing Financial Statements***) in the end of chapter materials for several chapters, including Chapters 4, 14, 17, and 18.

6. In chapter 9 of the 4th edition, we expand the homework material to include the effective interest, in addition to the straight-line, method for amortization of bond premiums and discounts. In chapters 6 and 7, the 4th edition includes appendices on deferred taxes related to the topics in those chapters. (These changes were made at the request of users of the book, something we try to do whenever feasible.)
7. We update many of our ***in-the-news*** boxes that appear in each chapter to reflect recent business and economic events that are relevant to the subject matter.
8. We integrate ***goodwill impairment*** into some illustrations in the body of Chapter 5, as well as in several homework problems.
9. We have made some materials available for users online, including an expanded discussion of the ***accounting for investments*** (an expansion of the summary in Chapter 4).
10. ***Learning objectives*** are included in the page margins of the chapters, and relevant learning objective numbers are provided with the end of chapter materials.
11. We introduce ***graphical illustrations*** in some chapters.
12. We describe and integrate the changes in the accounting for business combinations approved by the FASB in its pronouncements, both in 2001 and in 2007. The new standards are integrated throughout Chapters 1 through 9, with particular focus in Chapters 2 and 5.
13. We illustrate the goodwill impairment test described in *SFAS No. 142* [ASC 350], discussing its frequency, the steps laid out in the new standard, and some of the likely implementation problems. We include exercises on this test in Chapters 2 and 5.
14. We include a few short-answer questions (and solutions) periodically throughout each chapter to enable the student to test his or her knowledge of the content covered up to that point in the chapter before moving on.
15. The organization of the worksheets applies a format that separates accounts to the income statement, the statement of retained earnings, and the balance sheet in distinct sections. Also, the placement of the worksheets near the relevant text is important to readers.
16. All illustrations are printed upright on the page and labeled clearly for convenient study and reference.
17. Entries made on consolidated statements workpapers are also presented in general journal form and are shaded in blue to distinguish them from book entries, to facilitate exposition and study.
18. We include a thorough discussion at the beginning of Chapter 4 on the three methods of accounting for investments, and the importance of the complete equity method for certain investments that are not consolidated, or in the parent-only statements.
19. We include learning objectives and end of chapter summaries in each chapter and a glossary of terms at the end of the book.
20. To distinguish among parent company entries and workpaper entries, we present parent entries in gray and workpaper entries in blue.
21. Chapters 17 through 19 reflect the latest GASB and FASB pronouncements related to fund accounting.

Clearly there are more topics in this text than can be covered adequately in a one-semester or one-quarter course. We believe that it is generally better for both students and instructors to cover a selected number of topics in depth rather than to undertake a superficial coverage of a larger number of topics. Modules of material that an instructor may consider for exclusion in any one semester or quarter include the following:

- Chapters 7–9. An expanded analysis of problems in the preparation of consolidated financial statements.
- Chapter 10. Insolvency—liquidation and reorganization.
- Chapters 11–14. International accounting, foreign currency transactions and translation, and segment and interim reporting.
- Chapters 15 and 16. Partnership accounting.
- Chapters 17 through 19. Fund accounting, accounting for governmental units, and accounting for nongovernment–nonbusiness organizations (NNOs).

Supplements

Supplements for this edition include a Solutions Manual, Test Bank, PowerPoint slides, Instructor Manual, Computerized Test Bank, and Study Guide. The supplements will be available online at *www.wiley.com/college/Jeter*. The authors of the Solutions Manual and Instructor's Manual are Debra C. Jeter and Paul K. Chaney. Other supplement authors include: Coby Harmon (University of California, Santa Barbara) – PowerPoint slides; Elizabeth Stanny (Sonoma State University) – Study Guide; and Kelly Ann Ulto (Fordham University) – Test Bank.

Cover Photo

The cover photograph features the skyline of Auckland, New Zealand, where Professor Jeter has conducted research for several years with colleagues at the University of Auckland. It symbolizes the growing globalization of business and accounting.

Acknowledgements

We wish to thank the following individuals for their suggestions and assistance in the preparation of this edition

Thank you also goes to Steve Anderson, Matthew Baker, Douglas Barney (Indiana University Southeast), Gene Bryson (University of Alabama in Huntsville), Cordy Cates, Cindy Chaney, Lori Holder-Webb (University of Wisconsin), Suzanne Ingrao, Marianne James (California State University—Los Angeles), Nicole Jenkins, Norman Jeter, Betsy Johnson, Eldon Kuhns (Lycoming College), Daniel P. Mahoney (University of Scranton), Ron Mano (Weber State University), Norman Meonske (Kent State University), Bruce Michelson (University of Maryland), Anahit (Anya) Mkrtchyan, Sarah Opfer (Portland University), David Pearson (Case Western Reserve University), Joe Pollaro, Jerry Purtell (Linfield College), Kathleen Sobieralski (University of Maryland University College), Kris Stratten, Leslie Turner (Northern Kentucky University), Kelly Ulto (Fordham University), Zhemin Wang (University of Wisconsin—Parkside), and Matthew White.

Thank you also goes to Coby Harmon (University of California, Santa Barbara) for preparing the PowerPoint slides, to Elizabeth Stanny (Sonoma State University) for preparing the Study Guide, to Kelly Ann Ulto (Fordham University) for preparing the Test Bank, and to Larry Falcetto (Emporia State University), Dick Wasson (San Diego State University), Bernie Weinrich (Lindenwood University), Barbara Muller, Lynn Stallworth, LuAnn Bean, and Jim Emig for their helpful textbook, solutions manual, and test bank accuracy review comments. Finally we would like to acknowledge a few individuals at Wiley who helped all this come together: Jeff Howard, Chris DeJohn, Ed Brislin, and Julia Flohr.

BRIEF CONTENTS

ACCOUNTING FOR MERGERS, ACQUISITIONS, AND LIQUIDATIONS

1 Introduction to Business Combinations and the Conceptual Framework, 1
2 Accounting for Business Combinations, 44
3 Consolidated Financial Statements—Date of Acquisition, 83
4 Consolidated Financial Statements after Acquisition, 132
5 Allocation and Depreciation of Differences Between Implied and Book Values, 217
6 Elimination of Unrealized Profit on Intercompany Sales of Inventory, 301
7 Elimination of Unrealized Gains or Losses on Intercompany Sales of Property and Equipment, 358
8 Changes in Ownership Interest, 414
9 Intercompany Bond Holdings and Miscellaneous Topics—Consolidated Financial Statements, 452
10 Insolvency—Liquidation and Reorganization, 515

ACCOUNTING IN THE INTERNATIONAL MARKETPLACE

11 International Financial Reporting Standards, 552
12 Accounting for Foreign Currency Transactions and Hedging Foreign Exchange Risk, 591
13 Translation of Financial Statements of Foreign Affiliates, 639
14 Reporting for Segments and for Interim Financial Periods, 687

PARTNERSHIP ACCOUNTING

15 Partnerships: Formation, Operation, and Ownership Changes, 724
16 Partnership Liquidation, 771

FUND AND NONPROFIT ACCOUNTING

17 Introduction to Fund Accounting, 802
18 Introduction to Accounting for State and Local Governmental Units, 851
19 Accounting for Nongovernment Nonbusiness Organizations: Colleges and Universities, Hospitals and Other Health Care Organizations, 928

CONTENTS

I ACCOUNTING FOR MERGERS AND ACQUISITIONS

INTRODUCTION TO BUSINESS COMBINATIONS AND THE CONCEPTUAL FRAMEWORK 1

Learning Objectives, 1
Planning M&A in a Changing Environment and under Changing Accounting Requirements, 4
Nature of the Combination, 5
Business Combinations: Why? Why not?, 7
Business Combinations: Historical Perspective, 11
Terminology and Types of Combinations, 14
Takeover Premiums, 17
Avoiding the Pitfalls before the Deal, 19
Determining Price and Method of Payment in Business Combinations, 21
Alternative Concepts of Consolidated Financial Statements, 25
FASB's Conceptual Framework, 30
Summary , 37
Appendix: FASB Codification Project, 38
Standards Issued by Standard Setters Other than the SEC , 40
Standards Issued by the SEC , 40
Questions, 41
Exercises, 41

ACCOUNTING FOR BUSINESS COMBINATIONS 44

Learning Objectives, 44
Historical Perspective on Business Combinations, 44
Pro Forma Statements and Disclosure Requirement, 53
Explanation and Illustration of Acquisition Accounting, 56
Contingent Consideration in an Acquisition, 61
Leveraged Buyouts, 65
IFRS versus U.S. GAAP, 66
Summary, 67

Appendix A: Deferred Taxes in Business Combinations, 69
Questions, 71
Exercises, 72
Problems, 78

3 CONSOLIDATED FINANCIAL STATEMENTS—DATE OF ACQUISITION 83

Learning Objectives, 83
Definitions of Subsidiary and Control, 85
Requirements for the Inclusion of Subsidiaries in the Consolidated Financial Statements, 88
Reasons for Subsidiary Companies, 89
Consolidated Financial Statements, 89
Investments at the Date of Acquisition, 91
Consolidated Balance Sheets: the Use of Workpapers, 92
A Comprehensive Illustration—More than One Subsidiary Company, 108
Limitations of Consolidated Statements, 110
Summary, 113
Appendix A: Deferred Taxes on the Date of Acquisition, 114
Accounting for Uncertain Tax Positions, 115
Appendix B: Consolidation of Variable Interest Entities, 117
Questions, 119
Exercises, 120
Problems, 125

4 CONSOLIDATED FINANCIAL STATEMENTS AFTER ACQUISITION 132

Learning Objectives, 132
Accounting for Investments by the Cost, Partial Equity, and Complete Equity Methods, 133
Consolidated Statements after Acquisition—Cost Method, 141
Recording Investments in Subsidiaries—Equity Method (Partial or Complete), 153
Elimination of Intercompany Revenue and Expense Items, 163
Interim Acquisitions of Subsidiary Stock, 165
Consolidated Statement of Cash Flows, 177
Illustration of Preparation of a Consolidated Statement of Cash Flows: Year of Acquisition, 180
Compare U.S. GAAP and IFRS Regarding Equity Method, 184
Summary, 185
Appendix A: Alternative Workpaper Format, 186
Appendix B: Deferred Tax Consequences When Affiliates File Separate Income Tax Returns—Undistributed Income, 188

Consolidated Tax Returns—Affiliated Companies (80% or More Ownership Levels), 189
Separate Tax Returns—Deferred Tax Consequences Arising Because of Undistributed Subsidiary Income, 189
The Cost Method—Separate Tax Returns, 190
Undistributed Income Is Expected To Be Realized When the Subsidiary Is Sold, 192
The Partial and Complete Equity Methods—Separate Tax Returns, 192
Questions, 194
Exercises, 196
Problems, 203

ALLOCATION AND DEPRECIATION OF DIFFERENCES BETWEEN IMPLIED AND BOOK VALUES 217

Learning Objectives, 217
Allocation of the Difference Between Implied and Book Values to Assets and Liabilities of Subsidiary: Acquisition Date, 219
Effect of Allocation and Depreciation of Differences Between Implied and Book Values on Consolidated Net Income: Year Subsequent to Acquisition, 226
Consolidated Statements Workpaper—Investment Recorded Using The Cost Method, 231
Cost Method Analysis of Controlling and Noncontrolling Interests in Consolidated Net Income and Retained Earnings, 240
Consolidated Statements Workpaper—Investment Recorded Using Partial Equity Method, 242
Partial Equity Method Analysis of Controlling and Noncontrolling Interests in consolidated Net Income and Retained Earnings, 250
Consolidated Statements Workpaper—Investment Recorded Using Complete Equity Method, 252
Complete Equity Method Analysis of Controlling Interest in Consolidated Net Income and Retained Earnings, 260
Additional Considerations Relating to Treatment of Difference Between Implied and Book Values, 261
Push Down Accounting, 270
IFRS Vs. U.S. GAAP on Research & Development Costs, 275
Summary, 276
Questions, 277
Exercises, 279
Problems, 284

ELIMINATION OF UNREALIZED PROFIT ON INTERCOMPANY SALES OF INVENTORY 301

Learning Objectives, 301
Effects of Intercompany Sales of Merchandise on the Determination of Consolidated Balances, 302

Cost Method: Consolidated Statements Workpaper—Upstream Sales, 312
Cost Method—Analysis of Consolidated Net Income and Consolidated Retained Earnings, 318
Consolidated Statements Workpaper—Partial Equity Method, 321
Partial Equity Method—Analysis of Consolidated Net Income and Consolidated Retained Earnings, 325
Consolidated Statements Workpaper—Complete Equity Method, 326
Complete Equity Method—Analysis of Consolidated Net Income and Consolidated Retained Earnings, 331
Summary of Workpaper Entries Relating to Intercompany Sales of Inventory, 331
Intercompany Profit Prior To Parent–Subsidiary Affiliation, 332
Summary, 333
Appendix: Deferred Tax Consequences Arising Because of Unrealized Intercompany Profit, 334
Intercompany Sales of Inventory—Cost and Partial Equity Method, 335
Undistributed Subsidiary Income—The Impact of Unrealized Intercompany Profit on the Calculation of Deferred Taxes, 337
Questions, 340
Exercises, 341
Problems, 344

ELIMINATION OF UNREALIZED GAINS OR LOSSES ON INTERCOMPANY SALES OF PROPERTY AND EQUIPMENT **358**

Learning objectives, 358
Intercompany Sales Of Land (Nondepreciable Property), 359
Intercompany Sales Of Depreciable Property (Machinery, Equipment, and Buildings), 362
Consolidated Statements Workpaper—Cost and partial Equity Methods, 370
Calculation of Consolidated Net Income and Consolidated Retained Earnings, 379
Consolidated Statements Workpaper—Complete Equity Method, 382
Calculation and Allocation of Consolidated Net Income; Consolidated Retained Earnings: Complete Equity Method, 389
Summary of Workpaper Entries Relating to Intercompany Sales of Equipment, 389
Intercompany Interest, Rents, and Service Fees, 389
Summary, 393
Appendix: Impact of Unrealized Intercompany Profit on the Calculation of Deferred Tax Consequences Related to Undistributed Subsidiary Income, 396
Calculations (And Allocation) of Consolidated Net Income and Consolidated Retained Earnings, 397
Questions, 399

Exercises, 399
Problems, 403

CHANGES IN OWNERSHIP INTEREST 414

Learning Objectives, 414
Parent Acquires Subsidiary Stock Through Several Open-Market Purchases—Cost Method, 416
Parent Sells Subsidiary Stock Investment on the Open Market, 420
Equity Method—Purchases and Sales of Subsidiary Stock By the Parent, 424
Parent Sells Subsidiary Stock Investmenton the Open Market, 428
Subsidiary Issues Stock, 430
Summary, 438
Questions, 439
Exercises, 440
Problems, 443

INTERCOMPANY BOND HOLDINGS AND MISCELLANEOUS TOPICS—CONSOLIDATED FINANCIAL STATEMENTS 452

Learning Objectives, 452
Intercompany Bond Holdings, 453
Accounting for Bonds—A Review, 454
Constructive Gain or Loss on Intercompany bond Holdings, 455
Accounting for Intercompany Bonds Illustrated, 458
Book Entry Related To Bond Investment, 459
Interim Purchase of Intercompany Bonds, 475
Notes Receivable Discounted, 476
Stock Dividends issued by A Subsidiary Company, 478
Dividends From Preacquisition Earnings, 482
Subsidiary with both Preferred and Common Stock Outstanding, 483
Consolidating a Subsidiary with Preferred stock Outstanding, 486
Summary, 497
Questions, 498
Exercises, 499
Problems, 504

INSOLVENCY—LIQUIDATION AND REORGANIZATION 515

Learning Objectives, 515
Contractual Agreements, 516
Bankruptcy, 518
Liquidation (Chapter 7), 521

Reorganization Under the Reform Act (Chapter 11), 522
Trustee Accounting and Reporting, 532
Realization and Liquidation Account, 535
Summary, 539
Questions, 540
Exercises, 540
Problems, 545

II ACCOUNTING IN THE INTERNATIONAL MARKETPLACE

INTERNATIONAL FINANCIAL REPORTING STANDARDS 552

Learning Objectives, 552
The Increasing Importance of International Accounting Standards, 552
The Road to Convergence—U.S. GAAP and IFRS, 553
Significant Similarities and Differences Between U.S. GAAP and IFRS, 557
GAAP Hierarchy—U.S. Versus IFRS, 558
Long-Term Convergence Issues FASB and IASB, 567
Lease Accounting Convergence, 568
Revenue Recognition Convergence, 570
Financial Statement Presentation, 572
How the Financial Statements Might Change, 573
International Convergence Issues, 576
American Depository Receipts (ADRS): An Overview, 580
Summary, 582
Appendix A: List of Current International Financial Reporting Standards, Issued By IASC and IASB, 583
Questions, 584
Exercises, 585
Problems, 586

ACCOUNTING FOR FOREIGN CURRENCY TRANSACTIONS AND HEDGING FOREIGN EXCHANGE RISK 591

Learning Objectives, 591
Exchange Rates—Means of Translation, 592
Measured Versus Denominated, 594
Foreign Currency Transactions, 595
Using Forward Contracts as a Hedge, 605
Summary, 623

Questions, 624
Exercises, 625
Problems, 632

TRANSLATION OF FINANCIAL STATEMENTS OF FOREIGN AFFILIATES 639

Learning Objectives, 639
Accounting for Operations in Foreign Countries, 640
Translating Financial Statements of Foreign Affiliates, 641
Objectives of Translation—SFAS No. 52, 642
Translation Methods, 643
Identifying the Functional Currency, 645
Translation of Foreign Currency Financial Statements, 646
Translation of Foreign Financial Statements Illustrated, 650
Financial Statement Disclosure, 660
Historical Developments of Accounting Standards, 661
Summary, 663
Appendix: Accounting for a Foreign Affiliate and Preparation of Consolidated Statements Workpaper Illustrated, 664
Date of Acquisition, 664
Accounting for an Investment in a Foreign Affiliate—After Acquisition, 665
Consolidation When the Temporal Method of Translation is Used, 666
Remeasurement and Translation of Foreign Currency Transactions, 668
Intercompany Receivables and Payables, 669
Elimination of Intercompany Profit, 669
Liquidation of a Foreign Investment, 670
Questions, 671
Exercises, 671
Problems, 678

REPORTING FOR SEGMENTS AND FOR INTERIM FINANCIAL PERIODS 687

Learning Objectives, 687
Need for Disaggregated Financial Data, 688
Standards of Financial Accounting and Reporting, 688
International Accounting Standards Board (IASB) Position on Segment Reporting, 699
Interim Financial Reporting, 701
Summary, 709
Appendix: Operating Segments, 711
Basis for Presentation, 712

Our Businesses, 713
Questions, 714
Exercises, 715
Problems, 719

III PARTNERSHIP ACCOUNTING

PARTNERSHIPS: FORMATION, OPERATION, AND OWNERSHIP CHANGES 724

Learning Objectives, 724
Partnership Defined, 726
Reasons for Forming a Partnership, 726
Characteristics of a Partnership, 727
Partnership Agreement, 730
Accounting for a Partnership, 731
Special Problems in Allocation of Income and Loss, 739
Financial Statement Presentation, 741
Changes in the Ownership of the Partnership, 742
Section A: Admission of a New Partner, 744
Section B: Withdrawal of a Partner, 751
Summary, 755
Questions, 756
Exercises, 757
Problems, 763

16 PARTNERSHIP LIQUIDATION 771

Learning Objectives, 771
Steps in the Liquidation Process, 772
Priorities of Partnership and Personal Creditors, 774
Simple Liquidation Illustrated, 776
Installment Liquidation, 778
Incorporation of a Partnership, 787
Summary, 789
Questions, 790
Exercises, 790
Problems, 796

IV FUND AND NONPROFIT ACCOUNTING

INTRODUCTION TO FUND ACCOUNTING 802

Learning objectives, 802
Classifications of Nonbusiness Organizations, 803
Distinctions Between Nonbusiness Organizations and Profit-Oriented Enterprises, 803
Financial Accounting and Reporting Standards for Nonbusiness Organizations, 805
Fund Accounting, 807
Reporting Inventory and Prepayments in the Financial Statements, 832
Summary, 834
Appendix: City of Atlanta Partial Financial Statements, 836
Questions, 837
Exercises, 839
Problems, 843

INTRODUCTION TO ACCOUNTING FOR STATE AND LOCAL GOVERNMENTAL UNITS 851

Learning Objectives, 851
The History of Generally Accepted Governmental Accounting Standards, 853
The Structure of Governmental Accounting, 855
Governmental Fund Entities, 857
Proprietary Funds, 875
Fiduciary Funds, 878
Capital Assets and Long-Term Debt, 879
External Reporting Requirements (GASB Statement No. 34), 884
Government Fund-Based Reporting, 885
Government-Wide Reporting, 888
Management's Discussion and Analysis (MD&A), 893
Special Assessments, 894
Interfund Activity, 897
Summary, 900
Appendix A: Questions, 906
Analyzing Financial Statements (AFS), 907
Exercises, 908
Problems, 915

ACCOUNTING FOR NONGOVERNMENT NONBUSINESS ORGANIZATIONS: COLLEGES AND UNIVERSITIES, HOSPITALS AND OTHER HEALTH CARE ORGANIZATIONS 928

Learning Objectives, 928
Sources of Generally Accepted Accounting Standards for Nongovernment Nonbusiness Organizations, 929
Fund Accounting, 933

Accrual Basis of Accounting, 934
Classification of Revenue and Expense, 935
Accounting for Current Funds, 936
Contributions, 940
Accounting for Plant Funds, 943
Accounting for Endowment Funds, 948
Accounting for Investments, 950
Accounting for Loan Funds, 951
Accounting for Agency (Custodial) Funds, 952
Accounting for Annuity and Life Income Funds, 952
Issues Relating to Colleges and Universities, 953
Issues Relating to Hospitals, 953
Summary, 954
Appendix: Sample Financial Statements for Private Educational Institutions, 956
Questions, 960
Exercises, 960
Problems, 968

Glossary, 977
Appendix, 985
Index, 989

1

INTRODUCTION TO BUSINESS COMBINATIONS AND THE CONCEPTUAL FRAMEWORK

LEARNING OBJECTIVES

1. Describe historical trends in types of business combinations.
2. Identify the major reasons firms combine.
3. Identify the factors that managers should consider in exercising due diligence in business combinations.
4. Identify defensive tactics used to attempt to block business combinations.
5. Distinguish between an asset and a stock acquisition.
6. Indicate the factors used to determine the price and the method of payment for a business combination.
7. Calculate an estimate of the value of goodwill to be included in an offering price by discounting expected future excess earnings over some period of years.
8. Describe the two alternative views of consolidated financial statements: the economic entity and the parent company concepts.
9. List and discuss each of the seven *Statements of Financial Accounting Concepts (SFAC)*.
10. Describe some of the current joint projects of the FASB and the International Accounting Standards Board (IASB), and their primary objectives.

Growth through mergers and acquisitions (M&A) has become a standard in business not only in America but throughout the world. In the new millennium, the most recent in a series of booms in merger activity was sparked by cheaper credit and by global competition, in addition to the usual growth-related incentives predominant during the boom of the 1990s. By the end of 2008, however, uncertainty in the commercial credit markets had led to anxiety about whether merger transactions could continue to be achieved successfully in the current environment, and by the middle of 2009 M&A activity had nearly come to a halt. With plunging market values and tightened credit, the mix and nature of the financing components were clearly in flux, and major adaptations needed to consummate any new deals.

Merger activity seems to be highly correlated with the movement of the stock market. Increased stock valuation increases a firm's ability to use its shares to acquire other companies and is often more appealing than issuing debt. During the merger cycle of the 1990s, equity values fueled the merger wave. The slowing of merger activity in the early years of the 21st century provided a dramatic contrast to this preceding period. Beginning with the merger of Morgan Stanley and Dean Witter Discover and ending with the biggest acquisition to that date—WorldCom's bid for MCI—the year 1997 marked the third consecutive year of record mergers and acquisitions activity.[1] The pace accelerated still further in 1998 with unprecedented merger activity in the banking industry, the auto industry, financial services, and telecommunications, among others. This activity left experts wondering why and whether bigger was truly better. It also left consumers asking what the impact would be on service. A wave of stock swaps was undoubtedly sparked by record highs in the stock market, and stockholders reaped benefits from the mergers in many cases, at least in the short run. Regulators voiced concern about the dampening of competition, and consumers were quick to wonder where the real benefits lay. Following the accounting scandals of 2001 (WorldCom, Enron, Tyco, etc.), merger activity lulled for a few years.

Also in 2001, the *Financial Accounting Standards Board* (*FASB*) voted in two major accounting changes related to business combinations. The first met with vehement protests that economic activity would be further slowed as a result and the second with excitement that it might instead be spurred. Both changes are detailed in Chapter 2.

By the middle of 2002, however, these hopes had been temporarily quelled. Instead of increased earnings, many firms active in mergers during the 1990s were forced to report large charges related to the diminished value of long-lived assets (mainly goodwill). Merger activity slumped, suggesting that the frenzy had run its course. Market reaction to the mergers that did occur during this period typified the market's doubts. When ***Northrop Grumman Corp.*** announced the acquisition of ***TRW Inc.*** for $7.8 billion, the deal was praised but no market reaction was noted. In contrast, when Vivendi Universal admitted merger-gone-wrong woes, investors scurried.

By the middle of the first decade of the 21st century, however, the frenzy was returning with steady growth in merger activity from 2003 to 2006. In 2005, almost 18% of all M&A (mergers & acquisitions) deals were in the services sector. In a one-week period in June of 2006, $100 billion of acquisitions occurred, including Phelps Dodge's $35.4 billion acquisition of Inco Ltd. and Falconbridge Ltd. In addition, because of the economic rise in China and India, companies there were looking to increase their global foothold and began acquiring European companies. Thus cross-border deals within Europe accounted for a third of the global M&A deals.

However, by the end of 2008, a decline in overall merger activity was apparent as the U.S. economy slid into a recession, and some forecasters were predicting the next chapter in mergers and acquisitions to center around bankruptcy-related activity. Data from Thomson Reuters revealed that in 2008, bankruptcy-related merger activity increased for the first time in the last six years. For example, the number of Chapter 11 M&A purchases rose from 136 for the entire year of 2007 to 167 for the first ten months of 2008, with more to come. Overall mergers, on the other hand, decreased from $87 billion in the United States ($277 billion globally) during October 2007 to $78 billion in the United States ($259 billion globally) during October 2008, based on the Reuters data.

[1] *WSJ Europe*, "U.S. Merger Activity Marks New Record," by Steven Lipin, 1/2/98, p. R9.

INTERNATIONAL ACCOUNTING STANDARDS BOARD

Consolidated Financial Statements[1]

In June 2003, the International Accounting Standards Board (IASB) initiated a project on reporting consolidated financial statements. These statements present an entity's assets, liabilities, equity, revenues, and expenses with those of other entities it controls as if they were a single economic entity. The project's objective is to publish a single International Financial Reporting Standard (IFRS) on the topic of consolidation to replace two previous international standards (IAS 27, Consolidated and Separate Financial Statements, and an Interpretation SIC-12, Consolidation—Special Purpose Entities).

The project is intended to: (1) revise the definition of control in an effort to apply the same criteria to all entities with a focus on (but not limited to) the consolidation of structured entities, and (2) enhance the disclosures about consolidated and nonconsolidated entities.

The IASB proposes the following definition of control of an entity:

> *A reporting entity controls another entity when the reporting entity has the power to direct the activities of that other entity to generate returns for the reporting entity.*

The Board believes that the power to govern the financial and operating policies is one means of having power to direct another entity's activities, but not the only means. Power can be achieved in a variety of ways, including having voting rights, having options or convertible instruments, having an agent with the ability to direct the activities for the benefit of the controlling entity, by means of contractual arrangements, or some combination of the above. The Board further indicates that it is not necessary for an entity to have actually *exercised* its power to direct the activities in order for it to have control over the other entity. For example, it may not have exercised its voting rights or its options to acquire voting rights, or may not be actively directing the activities.

The proposed definition retains the concept from a prior international standard (IAS 27) that control conveys the right to obtain benefits from another entity. The exposure draft uses the term "returns" rather than "benefits," which was used in the prior standard, to eliminate confusion over whether "benefits" implied only positive returns. The Board believes that "returns" indicates more explicitly that such returns may be positive or negative.

The Board clarifies its position with respect to an entity that holds less than half the voting stock of another entity by stating that it can still have control in some situations. Guidance to making this determination includes: (a) options and convertible instruments to obtain voting rights of an entity, and (b) how to assess whether an entity has control if it holds voting rights both directly and on behalf of other parties as an agent.

Status of International Project

An exposure draft was issued in December 2008, with comments to be received by March 20, 2009. The Board plans to issue a revised standard by the end of 2009.

Comparison to U.S. GAAP on Business Combinations

Completely replacing *FASB Statement No. 141,* the new standard (*FASB Statement No. 141R,* Topic 805) expands the scope of the definition of business combinations. Previously, the term applied only to combinations in which control was obtained by transferring consideration. The new standard redefines a "business combination" as "a transaction or other event in which an acquiring entity obtains control of one or more businesses." The statement applies to all business entities, including mutual entities that previously applied the pooling of interests method. However, it excludes entities that are already under common control and mergers of not-for-profit entities.

IFRS

[1] "Consolidated Financial Statements," Exposure Draft (ED) 10 of the International Accounting Standards Board, December 2008, Copyright IASCF.

On December 4, 2007, FASB released two new standards, *FASB Statement No. 141 R,* Business Combinations, and *FASB Statement No. 160,* Noncontrolling Interests in Consolidated Financial Statements [ASC 805, "Business Combinations" and ASC 810, "Consolidations," based on FASB's new codification system]. These standards have altered the accounting for business combinations dramatically.

Both statements became effective for years *beginning after December 15, 2008,* and are intended to improve the relevance, comparability and transparency of financial information related to business combinations, and to facilitate the convergence with international standards. They represent the completion of the first major joint project of the FASB and the IASB (International Accounting Standards Board), according to one FASB member, G. Michael Crooch. The FASB also believes the new standards will reduce the complexity of accounting for business combinations. These standards are integrated throughout this text.

"If we are going to ride the IASB and the IFRS [International Financial Reporting Standards] horse, we want to make sure that it's as good as it can be. We want to make sure that the IASB is strong, is independent, is well resourced, and is properly funded in a broad-based and secure way."[2]

IFRS

PLANNING M&A IN A CHANGING ENVIRONMENT AND UNDER CHANGING ACCOUNTING REQUIREMENTS

1. The timing of deals is critical. The number of days between agreement or announcement and deal consummation can make a huge difference.
2. The effects on reporting may cause surprises. More purchases qualify as business combinations than previously. Income tax provisions can trigger disclosures.
3. Assembling the needed skill and establishing the needed controls takes time. The use of fair values is expanded, and more items will need remeasurement or monitoring after the deal.
4. The impact on earnings in the year of acquisition and subsequent years will differ from that in past mergers, as will the effects on earnings of step purchases or sales.
5. Unforeseen effects on debt covenants or other legal arrangements may be lurking in the background, as a result of the changes in key financial ratios.[3]

"By 2006, the percentage of the mergers and acquisitions market accounted for by private-equity firms had increased to approximately 15 percent from around 4 percent in 1990."[4]

[2] "Change Agent: Robert Hertz discusses FASB's priorities, the road to convergence and changes ahead for CPAs," Journal of Accountancy, February 2008, p. 31.

[3] BDO Seidman, LLP, "Client Advisory," No. 2008-1, January 31, 2008.

[4] *The New York Post,* "Money to Burn," by Suzanne Kapner, March 28, 2006, p. 33.

In part due to demand for energy assets, as well as easy access to capital and a record amount of private equity fund raising, merger and acquisition volume worldwide soared to over $2.7 trillion in 2005, marking a 38.4% increase from 2004 (which was previously the best year for M&A since 2000 and one of the best years ever for deal making). In the U.S., M&A volume rose 33.3% to more than $1.1 trillion from $848.7 billion in 2004. These results mark the first time U.S. M&A proceeds exceeded the trillion dollar mark since 2000.[5]

Growth is a major objective of many business organizations. Top management often lists growth or expansion as one of its primary goals. A company may grow slowly, gradually expanding its product lines, facilities, or services, or it may skyrocket almost overnight. Some managers consider growth so important that they say their companies must "grow or die." In the past hundred years, many U.S. businesses have achieved their goal of expansion through business combinations. A **business combination** occurs when *the operations of two or more companies are brought under common control.*

AT&T Corporation announced its intentions to buy BellSouth Corporation for $67 billion. This action was a direct result of increased competition against low-cost rivals in the phone, wireless, and television markets. This is considered an interesting move because if approved, it would reunite another of the Baby Bells with AT&T. AT&T was required to spin off its local exchange service operating units in 1982. At that time, seven companies were created, and these companies were known as the Baby Bells. Since then, AT&T has reacquired three of the Baby Bells, and BellSouth would be the fourth Baby Bell acquired. Only two other Baby Bells remain at this time: Qwest and Verizon. The merger ranks as one of the dozen largest deals ever.[6]

NATURE OF THE COMBINATION

A business combination may be friendly or unfriendly. In a **friendly combination**, *the boards of directors of the potential combining companies negotiate mutually agreeable terms of a proposed combination.* The proposal is then submitted to the stockholders of the involved companies for approval. Normally, a two-thirds or three-fourths positive vote is required by corporate bylaws to bind all stockholders to the combination.

An **unfriendly (hostile) combination** results when *the board of directors of a company targeted for acquisition resists the combination.* A formal ***tender offer*** enables the acquiring firm to deal directly with individual shareholders. The tender offer, usually published in a newspaper, typically provides a price higher than the current market price for shares made available by a certain date. If a sufficient number of shares are not made available, the acquiring firm may reserve the right to withdraw the offer. Because they are relatively quick and easily executed (often in about a month), tender offers are the preferred means of acquiring public companies.

[5] Thompson Financial, "Fourth Quarter 2005 Mergers & Acquisitions Review."

[6] *The New York Times,* "Huge Phone Deal Seeks to Thwart Smaller Rivals," by Ken Belson, 3/6/06, p. A1.

BASF AG, the transnational chemical company based in Germany, will file an unsolicited $4.9 billion takeover bid for Engelhard Corp., the New Jersey–based specialty chemicals maker. The disclosure of BASF's all-cash tender offer for Engelhard comes as it tries to become a market leader in the fast-expanding catalyst industry. If successful, the tender would represent the biggest German hostile takeover of a U.S. corporation and BASF's largest acquisition ever.[7]

Although tender offers are the preferred method for presenting hostile bids, most tender offers are friendly ones, done with the support of the target company's management. Nonetheless, hostile takeovers have become sufficiently common that a number of mechanisms have emerged to resist takeover.

A friendly bid by Germany's Bayer AG for fellow German drug maker Schering AG tops a hostile bid by Merck KGaA and could create a pharmaceutical behemoth capable of competing with U.S. and European rivals. Schering's executive board backed Bayer's €16.34 billion ($19.73 billion) offer, making it unlikely another bidder will emerge. If approved by Schering's shareholders, the two companies plan to combine their prescription drug businesses into a new firm called Bayer-Schering Pharmaceuticals with anticipated sales of more than €9 billion a year and headquarters in Berlin. Revenue of the new company would exceed that of Schering-Plough Corp. of the U.S., which is unrelated to the German Schering.[8]

Defense Tactics

Resistance often involves various moves by the target company, generally with colorful terms. Whether such defenses are ultimately beneficial to shareholders remains a controversial issue. Academic research examining the price reaction to defensive actions has produced mixed results, suggesting that the defenses are good for stockholders in some cases and bad in others. For example, when the defensive moves result in the bidder (or another bidder) offering an amount higher than initially offered, the stockholders benefit. But when an offer of $40 a share is avoided and the target firm remains independent with a price of $30, there is less evidence that the shareholders have benefited.

A certain amount of controversy surrounds the effectiveness, as well as the ultimate benefits, of the following defensive moves:

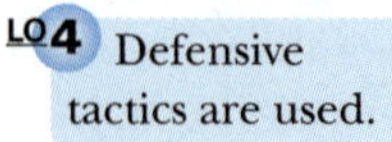
LO4 Defensive tactics are used.

1. *Poison pill:* Issuing stock rights to existing shareholders enabling them to purchase additional shares at a price below market value, but exercisable only in the event of a potential takeover. This tactic has been effective in some instances, but bidders may take managers to court and eliminate the defense. In other instances the original shareholders benefit from the tactic. Chrysler Corp. announced that it was extending a poison pill plan until February 23, 2008, under

[7] *WSJ*, "BASF Aims to Bulk Up Globally," by Mike Esterl, 1/5/06, p. A14.

[8] *WSJ*, "Bayer Joins Race to Build German Drug Titan," by Jeanne Whalen, Jason Singer, and Mike Esterl, 3/24/06, p. A3.

which the rights become exercisable if anyone announces a tender offer for 15% or more, or acquires 15%, of Chrysler's outstanding common shares. Poison pills are rarely triggered, but their existence serves as a preventative measure.

In its attempt to ward off investors calling for new management, health-club operator Bally Total Fitness Holding Corp. stated that its two largest shareholders may be conspiring, which could trigger the company's poison pill and effectively reduce the investors' ownership stakes. The shareholders, Liberation Investments and Pardus Capital Management, have called for new members on Bally's board and the firing of CEO Paul Toback. The Chicago-based company said it was considering petitioning a court to determine whether its shareholder-rights plan was triggered as a result of Liberation and Pardus acting together.[9]

2. *Greenmail:* The purchase of any shares held by the would-be acquiring company at a price substantially in excess of their fair value. The purchased shares are then held as treasury stock or retired. This tactic is largely ineffective because it may result in an expensive excise tax; further, from an accounting perspective, the excess of the price paid over the market price is expensed.
3. *White knight or white squire:* Encouraging a third firm more acceptable to the target company management to acquire or merge with the target company.
4. *Pac-man defense:* Attempting an unfriendly takeover of the would-be acquiring company.
5. *Selling the crown jewels:* The sale of valuable assets to others to make the firm less attractive to the would-be acquirer. The negative aspect is that the firm, if it survives, is left without some important assets.
6. *Leveraged buyouts:* The purchase of a controlling interest in the target firm by its managers and third-party investors, who usually incur substantial debt in the process and subsequently take the firm private. The bonds issued often take the form of high-interest, high-risk "junk" bonds. Leveraged buyouts will be discussed in more detail in Chapter 2.

BUSINESS COMBINATIONS: WHY? WHY NOT?

LO2 Reasons firms combine.

A company may expand in several ways. Some firms concentrate on **internal** expansion. A firm may expand internally by engaging in product research and development. Hewlett-Packard is an example of a company that relied for many years on new product development to maintain and expand its market share. A firm may choose instead to emphasize marketing and promotional activities to obtain a greater share of a given market. Although such efforts usually do not expand the total market, they may redistribute that market by increasing the company's share of it.

For other firms, **external** expansion is the goal; that is, they try to expand by acquiring one or more other firms. This form of expansion, aimed at producing relatively rapid growth, has exploded in frequency and magnitude in recent years. A

[9] *WSJ*, "Bally Examines Poison Pill Move to Fight Pressures," Reuters News Service, 12/27/05, p. A6.

company may achieve significant cost savings as a result of external expansion, perhaps by acquiring one of its major suppliers.

In addition to rapid expansion, the business combination method, or external expansion, has several other potential advantages over internal expansion:

1. ***Operating synergies*** may take a variety of forms. Whether the merger is **vertical** (*a merger between a supplier and a customer*) or **horizontal** (*a merger between competitors*), combination with an existing company provides management of the acquiring company with an established operating unit with its own experienced personnel, regular suppliers, productive facilities, and distribution channels. In the case of vertical mergers, synergies may result from the elimination of certain costs related to negotiation, bargaining, and coordination between the parties. In the case of a horizontal merger, potential synergies include the combination of sales forces, facilities, outlets, and so on, and the elimination of unnecessary duplication in costs. When a private company is acquired, a plus may be the potential to eliminate not only duplication in costs but also unnecessary costs.

Chiron Corp. agreed to be acquired by Novartis AG for $45 per share, or $5.1 billion. Swiss pharmaceutical giant Novartis already owned 42% of Chiron, the biotechnology pioneer. Novartis's reason for acquiring Chiron is the fast-growing flu vaccine market, Chiron's focus, as well as its production of other inoculations for meningitis and polio. Novartis predicts that the market for all vaccines worldwide will more than double from $9.6 billion in 2004 to in excess of $20 billion in 2009 as prevention becomes a bigger element of healthcare.[10]

Management of the acquiring company can draw upon the operating history and the related historical database of the acquired company for planning purposes. A history of profitable operations by the acquired company may, of course, greatly reduce the risk involved in the new undertaking. A careful examination of the acquired company's expenses may reveal both expected and unexpected costs that can be eliminated. On the more negative (or cautious) side, be aware that the term "synergies" is sometimes used loosely. If there are truly expenses that can be eliminated, services that can be combined, and excess capacity that can be reduced, the merger is more likely to prove successful than if it is based on growth and "so-called synergies," suggests Michael Jensen, a professor of finance at the Harvard Business School.

Views on whether synergies are real or simply a plug figure to justify a merger that shouldn't happen are diverse. Time Warner, for example, has fluctuated back and forth on this issue in recent years. President Jeffrey Bewkes recently was quoted as saying, "No division should subsidize another." When queried about the message his predecessors sent to shareholders, he said, "It's bull—"[11]

[10] *WSJ*, "Novartis Agrees to Acquire the Rest of Chiron for $5.1 Billion," by David P. Hamilton, 11/1/05, p. A6.

[11] *WSJ*, "After Years of Pushing Synergy, Time Warner Inc. Says Enough," by Matthew Karnitschnig, 6/2/06, p. A1.

GAINS FROM BULKING UP[12]

Industry	*Key Benefit of Consolidation*
Antenna towers	Frees up capital and management time for wireless communications operators
Funeral homes	Yields greater discounts on coffins, supplies, and equipment
Health clubs	Spreads regional marketing and advertising costs over more facilities
Landfill sites	Lets operators cope with the new environmental and regulatory demands
Physician group practices	Reduces overhead and costs of medical procedures

2. Combination may enable a company to compete more effectively in the **international marketplace**. For example, an acquiring firm may diversify its operations rather rapidly by entering new markets; alternatively, it may need to ensure its sources of supply or market outlets. Entry into new markets may also be undertaken to obtain cost savings realized by smoothing cyclical operations. Diminishing savings from cost-cutting *within* individual companies makes combination more appealing. The financial crisis in Asia accelerated the pace for a time as American and European multinationals competed for a shrinking Asian market. However, a combination of growing competition, globalization, deregulation, and financial engineering has led to increasingly complex companies and elusive profits.
3. Business combinations are sometimes entered into to take advantage of **income tax** laws. The opportunity to file a consolidated tax return may allow profitable corporations' tax liabilities to be reduced by the losses of unprofitable affiliates. When an acquisition is financed using debt, the interest payments are tax deductible, creating a **financial synergy** or "tax gain." Many combinations in the past were planned to obtain the advantage of significant operating loss carryforwards that could be utilized by the acquiring company. However, the Tax Reform Act of 1986 limited the use of operating loss carryforwards in merged companies. Because tax laws vary from year to year and from country to country, it is difficult to do justice to the importance of tax effects within the scope of this chapter. Nonetheless, it is important to note that tax implications are often a driving force in merger decisions.
4. **Diversification** resulting from a merger offers a number of advantages, including increased flexibility, an internal capital market, an increase in the firm's debt capacity, more protection from competitors over proprietary information, and sometimes a more effective utilization of the organization's resources. In debating the tradeoffs between diversification and focusing on one (or a few) specialties, there are no obvious answers.

---

[12] *Business Week*, "Buy 'Em Out, Then Build 'Em Up," by Eric Schine, 5/18/95, p. 84.

More than a third of bankruptcy merger activity in 2008 took place in financial services, with the sale of assets by Lehman Brothers (New York investment bank) and the $2.8 billion acquisition by a consortium of Ashikaga Bank (Japan). Others included Thornwood Associates' $900 million purchase of Federal-Mogul, Mendecino Redwood's $600 million acquisition of Pacific Lumber, and NBTY's $371 million purchase of Leiner Health Products.[13]

5. **Divestitures** accounted for over 30% of the merger and acquisitions activity in each quarter from 1995 into mid-1998. Shedding divisions that are not part of a company's core business became common during this period. In some cases the divestitures may be viewed as "undoing" or "redoing" past acquisitions. A popular alternative to selling off a division is to "spin off" a unit. Examples include AT&T's spin-off of its equipment business to form ***Lucent Technologies Inc.***, Sears Roebuck's spin-off of ***Allstate Corp.*** and ***Dean Witter Discover & Co.***, and Cincinnati Bell's proposed spin-off of its billing and customer-management businesses to form ***Convergys Corp.***

As Verizon Communications seeks to focus more on its wireless business and high-growth areas such as Internet services and television, the company said it plans to shed its phone directories business in a transaction that could be valued at more than $17 billion. The divestiture should lighten Verizon's debt load, an essential step as it moves forward with a $20 billion effort to replace its copper network with fiber-optic strands and starts offering television to subscribers.[14]

Notwithstanding its apparent advantages, business combination may not always be the best means of expansion. An overriding emphasis on rapid growth may result in the pyramiding of one company on another without sufficient management control over the resulting conglomerate. Too often in such cases, management fails to maintain a sound enough financial equity base to sustain the company during periods of recession. Unsuccessful or incompatible combinations may lead to future divestitures.

In order to avoid large dilutions of equity, some companies have relied on the use of various debt and preferred stock instruments to finance expansion, only to find themselves unable to provide the required debt service during a period of decreasing economic activity. The junk bond market used to finance many of the mergers in the 1980s had essentially collapsed by the end of that decade.

Business combinations may destroy, rather than create, value in some instances. For example, if the merged firm's managers transfer resources to subsidize money-losing segments instead of shutting them down, the result will be a suboptimal allocation of capital. This situation may arise because of reluctance to eliminate jobs or to acknowledge a past mistake.

Some critics of the accounting methods used in the United States prior to 2002 to account for business combinations argued that one of the methods did not hold

[13] "Water Cooler: What Players in the Mid Market Are Talking About," Mergers & Acquisitions, December 2008.

[14] *WSJ*, by Ionne Searcy, Dennis K. Berman, and Almar Latour, 12/5/05, p. A3.

executives accountable for their actions if the price they paid was too high, thus encouraging firms to "pay too much." Although opinions are divided over the relative merits of the accounting alternatives, most will agree that the resulting financial statements should reflect the economics of the business combination. Furthermore, if and when the accounting standards and the resulting statements fail even partially at this objective, it is crucial that the users of financial data be able to identify the deficiencies. Thus we urge the reader to keep in mind that an important reason for learning and understanding the details of accounting for business combinations is to understand the economics of the business combination, which in turn requires understanding any possible deficiencies in the accounting presentation.

BUSINESS COMBINATIONS: HISTORICAL PERSPECTIVE

LO1 Historical trends in types of M&A.

In the United States there have been three fairly distinct periods characterized by many business mergers, consolidations, and other forms of combinations: 1880–1904, 1905–1930, and 1945–present. During the first period, huge holding companies, or trusts, were created by investment bankers seeking to establish monopoly control over certain industries. This type of combination is generally called **horizontal integration** because it involves the combination of companies within the same industry. Examples of the trusts formed during this period are J. P. Morgan's U.S. Steel Corporation and other giant firms such as Standard Oil, the American Sugar Refining Company, and the American Tobacco Company. By 1904, more than 300 such trusts had been formed, and they controlled more than 40% of the nation's industrial capital.

The second period of business combination activity, fostered by the federal government during World War I, continued through the 1920s. In an effort to bolster the war effort, the government encouraged business combinations to obtain greater standardization of materials and parts and to discourage price competition. After the war, it was difficult to reverse this trend, and business combinations continued. These combinations were efforts to obtain better integration of operations, reduce costs, and improve competitive positions rather than attempts to establish monopoly control over an industry. This type of combination is called **vertical integration** because it involves the combination of a company with its suppliers or customers. For example, Ford Motor Company expanded by acquiring a glass company, rubber plantations, a cement plant, a steel mill, and other businesses that supplied its automobile manufacturing business. From 1925 to 1930, more than 1,200 combinations took place, and about 7,000 companies disappeared in the process.

The third period started after World War II and has exhibited rapid growth in merger activity since the mid-1960s, and even more rapid growth since the 1980s. The total dollar value of mergers and acquisitions grew from under $20 billion in 1967 to over $300 billion by 1995 and over $1 trillion in 1998, and $3.5 trillion by 2006. Even allowing for changes in the value of the dollar over time, the acceleration is obvious. By 1996, the number of yearly mergers completed was nearly 7,000. Some observers have called this activity **merger mania**, and most agreed that the mania had ended by mid-2002. However, by 2006, merger activity was soaring once more. Illustration 1-1 presents two rough graphs of the level of merger activity for acquisitions over $10 million from 1972 to 2008 in number of deals, and from 1979 to 2008 in dollar volume. Illustration 1-2 presents summary statistics on the level of activity for the year 2008 by industry sector for acquisitions with purchase prices valued in excess of $10 million.

ILLUSTRATION 1-1 PART A

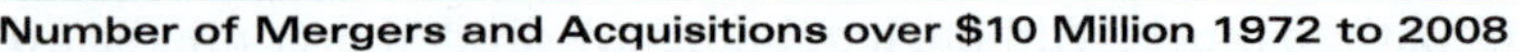

Number of Mergers and Acquisitions over $10 Million 1972 to 2008

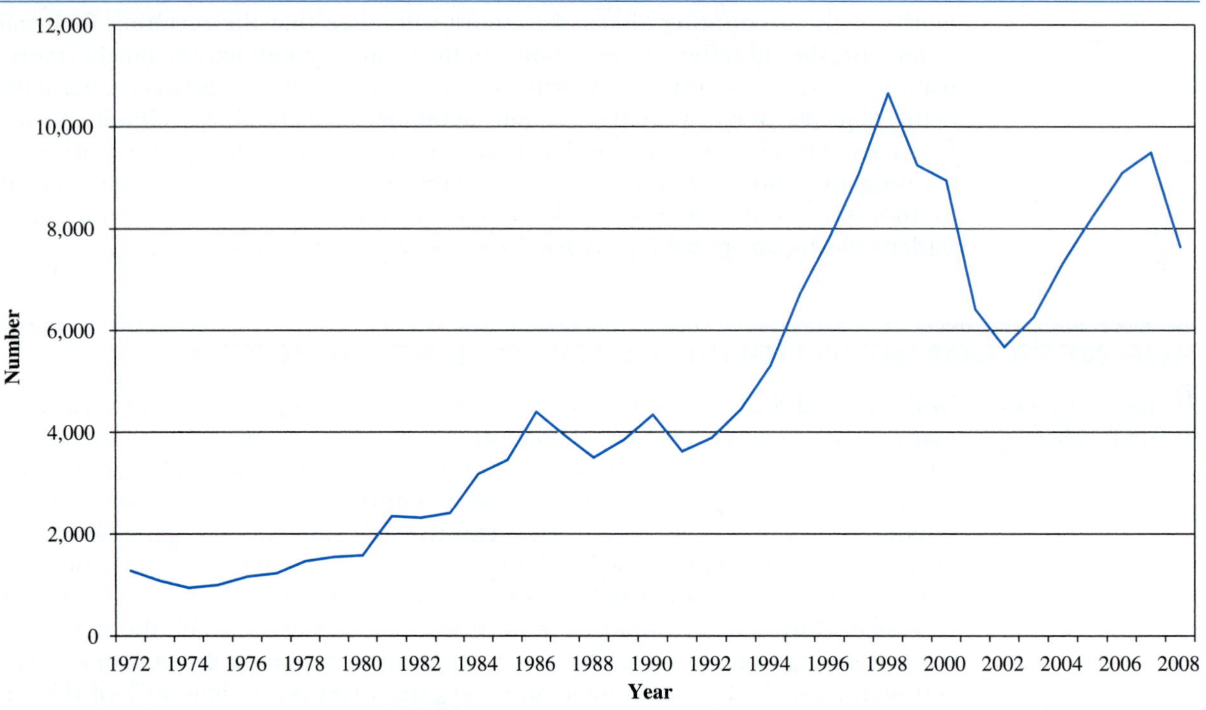

Adapted from *Mergers and Acquisitions,* February 2002, 2004, 2006, 2009, March/April 1999, May/June 1989, 1982.

ILLUSTRATION 1-1 PART B

Value of Mergers and Acquisitions over $10 Million 1979 to 2008

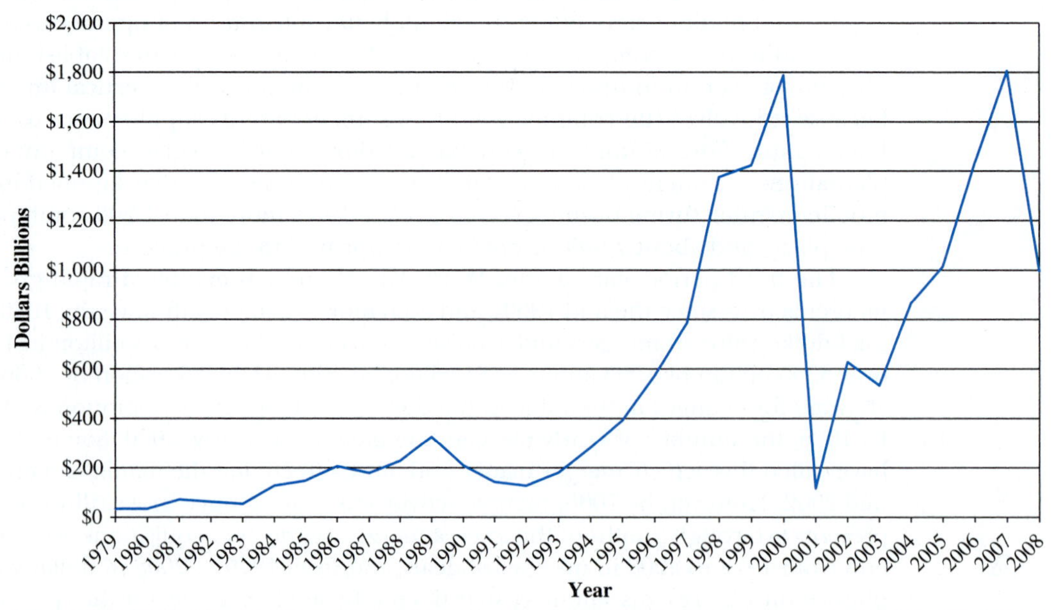

Adapted from *Mergers and Acquisitions,* February 2009, 2006, 2004, 2002, March/April 1999, May/June 1989, 1982 Almanac & Index.

ILLUSTRATION 1-2

10 Most Active Industries by Number of Transactions in 2008 over $10 Million

Rank	*Industry*	*Number of Deals*	*% of All M&A Deals*
1	Business Services	1,426	18.7%
2	Software	687	9.0%
3	Insurance	284	3.7%
4	Durable Goods Wholesaling	273	3.6%
5	Health Services	258	3.4%
6	Investment & Commodity Firms	246	3.2%
7	Measuring, Medical & Photographic Equipment	242	3.2%
8	Oil & Gas	240	3.1%
9	Insurance	230	3.0%
10	Hotels & Casinos	225	3.0%

10 Most Active Industries by Dollar Volume in 2008

Rank	*Industry*	*Value ($ billions)*	*% of Total M&A Value*
1	Telecommunications	101.8	10.2%
2	Metal & Metal Products	88.5	8.9%
3	Oil & Gas	66.9	6.7%
4	Real Estate Firms	54.4	5.5%
5	Business Services	54.4	5.5%
6	Software	54.0	5.4%
7	Investment & Commodity Firms	53.3	5.3%
8	General Merchandise & Apparel Retailing	44.7	4.5%
9	Hotels & Casinos	43.7	4.4%
10	Insurance	41.6	4.2%

Adapted from *Mergers & Acquisitions*, February 2009 p. 59.

This most recent period can be further subdivided to focus on trends of particular decades or subperiods. For example, many of the mergers that occurred in the United States from the 1950s through the 1970s were **conglomerate** mergers. Here the primary motivation for combination was often to diversify business risk by combining companies in different industries having little, if any, production or market similarities, or possibly to create value by lowering the firm's cost of capital. One conjecture for the popularity of this type of merger during this time period was the strictness of regulators in limiting combinations of firms in the same industry. One conglomerate may acquire another, as Esmark did when it acquired Norton-Simon, and conglomerates may spin off, or divest themselves of, individual businesses. Management of the conglomerate hopes to smooth earnings over time by counterbalancing the effects of economic forces that affect different industries at different times.

In contrast, the 1980s were characterized by a relaxation in antitrust enforcement during the Reagan administration and by the emergence of high-yield junk bonds to finance acquisitions. The dominant type of acquisition during this period and into the 1990s was the **strategic acquisition**, claiming to benefit from **operating synergies**. These synergies may arise when the talents or strengths of one of the firms complement the products or needs of the other, or they may arise simply because the firms were former competitors. An argument can be made that the dominant form of acquisition shifted in the 1980s because many of the conglomerate mergers of the 1960s and 1970s proved unsuccessful; in fact, some of the takeovers of the 1980s were of a disciplinary nature, intended to break up conglomerates.

Deregulation undoubtedly played a role in the popularity of combinations in the 1990s. In industries that were once fragmented because concentration was forbidden, the pace of mergers picked up significantly in the presence of deregulation. These industries include banking, telecommunications, and broadcasting. Although recent years have witnessed few deals blocked due to antitrust enforcement, an example of a major transaction dropped in 1996 because of a planned FTC (Federal Trade Commission) challenge was in the drugstore industry. The FTC challenged the impact of a proposed merger between ***Rite Aid Corp.*** and ***Revco D.S. Inc.*** on market power in several sectors of the East and Midwest. Nonetheless, subsequent deals in the industry saw both companies involved: Rite Aid acquired ***Thrifty PayLess Holdings Inc.***, and ***CVS Inc.*** purchased Revco in February 1997.

Later, the Justice Department sued to block Primestar's acquisition of a satellite slot owned by ***MCI*** and ***News Corp.*** The department claimed the deal would thwart competition by giving the companies the last direct competition to cable: a direct-broadcast satellite service using 18-inch dish receivers.[15] Other deals were dropped in the face of possible intervention, including a planned merger between CPA firms KPMG Peat Marwick and Ernst & Young in 1998, although other factors undoubtedly played a role as well. Nonetheless, over time the group of large CPA firms once referred to as the Big 8 has blended into the Big 4, raising concerns about a possible lack of competition in the audit market for large companies.

With Barack Obama winning the presidential election, dealmakers have a few months to prepare for some likely effects on the deal community. A Democratic White House is expected to translate into tighter antitrust policies, as seen in the Clinton Administration. Also, Obama's win could impact certain sectors adversely, according to some sources, including investment banks, oil and gas companies, credit card companies, and big pharmaceuticals. More positive outcomes are predicted for alternative energy providers, healthcare and IT firms, and sizeable manufacturers who maintain large unionized workforces.[16]

TERMINOLOGY AND TYPES OF COMBINATIONS

LO5 Stock versus asset acquisitions.

From an accounting perspective, the distinction that is most important at this stage is between an **asset acquisition** and a **stock acquisition**. In Chapter 2, we focus on the acquisition of the assets of the acquired company, where only the acquiring or new

[15] *WSJ*, "Antitrust Suit Filed to Block Primestar Purchase," by John Wilke, 5/13/98, p. A3 (Eastern Edition).

[16] "Sizing Up the Candidates," Mergers & Acquisitions, March 2008.

FIGURE 1-1

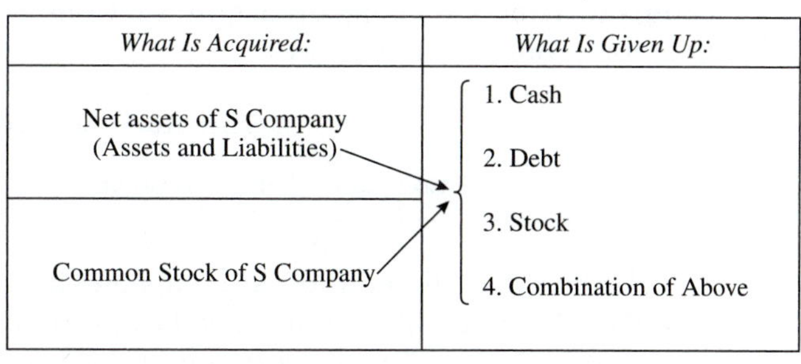

company survives. Thus the books of the acquired company are closed out, and its assets and liabilities are transferred to the books of the acquirer. In subsequent chapters, we will discuss the stock acquisition case where the acquired company and its books remain intact and consolidated financial statements are prepared periodically. In such cases, the acquiring company debits an account "Investment in Subsidiary" rather than transferring the underlying assets and liabilities onto its own books.

What Is Acquired:
What Is Given Up:
Net assets of S Company (Assets and Liabilities)
Common Stock of S Company
1. Cash
2. Debt
3. Stock
4. Combination of Above

Note that the distinction between an asset acquisition and a stock acquisition does not imply anything about the medium of exchange or consideration used to consummate the acquisition. Thus a firm may gain control of another firm in a stock acquisition using cash, debt, stock, or some combination of the three as consideration. Alternatively, a firm may acquire the total assets of another firm using cash, debt, stock, or some combination of the three. There are two independent issues related to the consummation of a combination: what is acquired (assets or stock) and what is given up (the consideration for the combination). These are shown in Figure 1-1.

In an asset acquisition, a firm must acquire 100% of the assets of the other firm. In a stock acquisition, a firm may obtain control by purchasing 50% or more of the voting common stock (or possibly even less). This introduces one of the most obvious advantages of the stock acquisition over the asset acquisition: a lower total cost in many cases. Also, in a stock acquisition, direct formal negotiations with the acquired firm's management may be avoided. Further, there may be advantages to maintaining the acquired firm as a separate legal entity. The possible advantages include liability limited to the assets of the individual corporation and greater flexibility in filing individual or consolidated tax returns. Finally, regulations pertaining to one of the firms do not automatically extend to the entire merged entity in a stock acquisition. A stock acquisition has its own complications, however, and the economics and specifics of a given situation will dictate the type of acquisition preferred.

Other terms related to mergers and acquisitions merit mention. For example, business combinations are sometimes classified by method of combination into three types—statutory mergers, statutory consolidations, and stock acquisitions. However, the distinction between these categories is largely a technicality, and the terms **mergers**, **consolidations**, and **acquisitions** are popularly used interchangeably.

A **statutory merger** results when *one company acquires all the net assets of one or more other companies through an exchange of stock, payment of cash or other property, or issue of debt instruments (or a combination of these methods)*. The acquiring company survives, whereas the acquired company (or companies) ceases to exist as a separate legal entity, although it may be continued as a separate division of the acquiring company. Thus, if A Company acquires B Company in a statutory merger, the combination is often expressed as

Statutory Merger

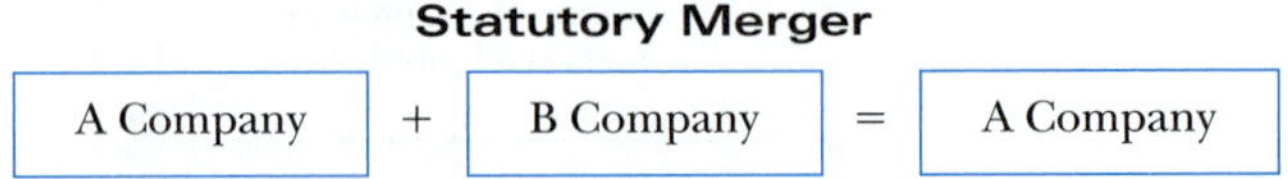

The boards of directors of the companies involved normally negotiate the terms of a plan of merger, which must then be approved by the stockholders of each company involved. State laws or corporation bylaws dictate the percentage of positive votes required for approval of the plan.

A **statutory consolidation** results when *a new corporation is formed to acquire two or more other corporations through an exchange of voting stock; the acquired corporations then cease to exist as separate legal entities.* For example, if C Company is formed to consolidate A Company and B Company, the combination is generally expressed as

Statutory Consolidation

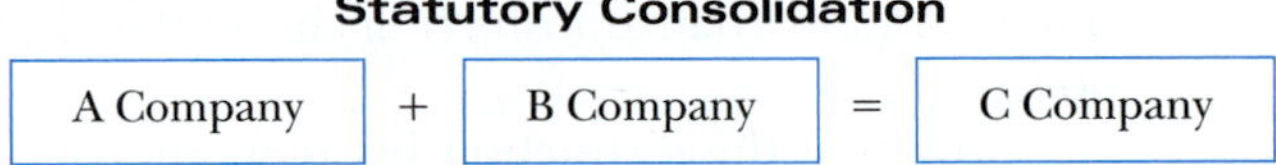

Stockholders of the acquired companies (A and B) become stockholders in the new entity (C). The combination of ***Chrysler Corp.*** and ***Daimler-Benz*** to form ***DaimlerChrysler*** is an example of this type of consolidation. The acquired companies in a statutory consolidation may be operated as separate divisions of the new corporation, just as they may under a statutory merger. Statutory consolidations require the same type of stockholder approval as do statutory mergers.

Synergistic deals may be viable even in the current environment, given adequate flexibility and preparation. Although the successful financing of large deals depends largely on capital markets, local middle market deals—say, less than $20 million—more often rely on a combination of commercial loans, seller financing, and equity from private sources or a private equity group.[17]

A **stock acquisition** occurs when *one corporation pays cash or issues stock or debt for all or part of the voting stock of another company, and the acquired company remains intact as a separate legal entity.* When the acquiring company acquires a controlling interest in the voting stock of the acquired company (for example, if A Company acquires 50% of the voting stock of B Company), a parent–subsidiary relationship results. Consolidated financial statements (explained in later chapters) are prepared and the business combination is often expressed as

Consolidated Financial Statements

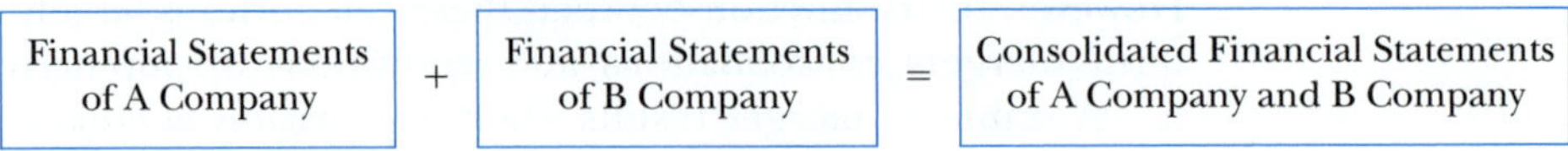

[17] "The Credit Puzzle," by Lou Banach and Jim Gettel, Mergers & Acquisitions, December 2008.

TEST
YOUR KNOWLEDGE

NOTE: Solutions to ***Test Your Knowledge*** questions are found at the end of each chapter before the end-of-chapter questions.

Short Answer

1. Name the following takeover defense tactics:
   a. Issuing stock rights to existing shareholders, enabling them to purchase additional shares at a price below market value, but exercisable only in the event of a potential takeover. _______
   b. The purchase of a controlling interest in the target firm by its managers and third-party investors, who usually incur substantial debt in the process and subsequently take the firm private. _______
   c. Encouraging a third firm, more acceptable to the target company management, to acquire or merge with the target company. _______

Multiple Choice

2. Which one of the following statements is ***incorrect***?
   a. In an asset acquisition, the books of the acquired company are closed out, and its assets and liabilities are transferred to the books of the acquirer.
   b. In many cases, stock acquisitions entail lower total cost than asset acquisitions.
   c. Regulations pertaining to one of the firms do not automatically extend to the entire merged entity in a stock acquisition.
   d. A stock acquisition occurs when one corporation pays cash, issues stock, or issues debt for all or part of the voting stock of another company; and the acquired company dissolves and ceases to exist as a separate legal entity.
3. Which of the following can be used as consideration in a stock acquisition?
   a. Cash
   b. Debt
   c. Stock
   d. Any of the above may be used

TAKEOVER PREMIUMS

A **takeover premium** is *the term applied to the excess of the amount offered, or agreed upon, in an acquisition over the prior stock price of the acquired firm.* It is not unusual for the takeover premium to be as high as 100% of the target firm's market share price before the acquisition, and the average hovered around 40% to 50% into the late 1990s. In the face of the already high stock prices of this period, speculation was mixed as to the future of takeover premiums. Some experts predicted the premiums would shrink, leading to "takeunders" in some cases where companies are acquired below the listed stock prices. These predictions found some subsequent fulfillment as premiums in 2006 declined to around 20%.

During March of 2006, the Capital One Financial Corporation agreed to acquire the North Fork Bancorporation for about $14.6 billion in cash and stock. North Fork shareholders will receive a mix of cash and Capital One shares, representing a 22.8% premium over the closing price of North Fork shares.[18]

[18] *The New York Times,* "Capital One Reported in Deal for North Fork," by Andrew Ross Sorkin and Eric Dash, March 13, 2006, p. A18.

Possible reasons acquirers are willing to pay high premiums vary. One factor is that the acquirers' own stock prices may be at a level which makes it attractive to issue stock (rather than cash) to consummate the acquisition. Another factor is the availability of relatively cheap credit for mergers and acquisitions.

Bidders may have private information about the target firm suggesting that it is worth more than its current market value or has assets not reported on the balance sheet (such as in-process research and development). Alternatively, companies desperate to boost earnings may believe that growth by acquisitions is essential to survive in the global marketplace and that the competition necessitates the premiums. At the other end of the spectrum, a final possibility, which cannot be entirely ruled out, is that managers eager for growth may simply pay too much.

One research study presented evidence that higher premiums were offered for firms with high cash flows, relatively low growth opportunities, and high tax liabilities relative to their equity values.[19] Another study suggested that the bigger the ego of the acquiring firm's CEO, the higher the takeover premium, while still another suggested that any premium over 25% is extremely risky.[20] Some compensation analysts argue that the massive options payouts to executives combined with golden parachutes provide an unhealthy incentive for executives to negotiate mergers, citing Chrysler's merger with Daimler-Benz as an example.[21]

Takeover premiums have attracted so much attention that some strategists (e.g., Paine Webber's Edward Kerschner) have advised clients looking for investments to choose stocks that might get taken over. Cautious financial advisors point out that lofty stock prices are a double-edged sword for financial buyers because they mean high prices for both companies' stocks and costlier acquisitions. Also, when stock prices fluctuate, the agreed-upon purchase price may suddenly appear more or less attractive than it did at the time of agreement. For example, a proposed acquisition of ***Comsat Corp.*** by Lockheed Martin Corp. was announced in September 1998, with the acquisition valued at $2.6 billion, of which 49% was to be paid in cash and the rest in Lockheed stock. When Lockheed Martin's stock price subsequently faltered enough to suggest a 16% drop in the total value of the transaction, Comsat shareholders questioned whether the consideration for the transaction was fairly priced.[22]

Some statistics suggest that of "6000 acquisitions, only 900 return the cost of capital. It is easy to do deals. It is very difficult to make them succeed."[23]

---

[19] The study, entitled "Free Cash Flow and Stockholder Gains in Going Private Transactions," was conducted by Lehn and Poulsen (***Journal of Finance***, July 1989, pp. 771–787). Also see "The Case against Mergers," by Phillip Zweig, ***Business Week***, 10/30/95, pp. 122–130.

[20] "Acquisition Behavior, Strategic Resource Commitments and the Acquisition Game: A New Perspective on Performance and Risk in Acquiring Firms," by Mark Sirower, doctoral dissertation, Columbia University, 1994.

[21] *WSJ*, "Chrysler Executives May Reap Windfall," by Gregory White, 5/13/98, p. A3.

[22] *WSJ*, "Lockheed Bid for Comsat Hits Obstacles," by Anne Marie Squeo, 6/11/99, p. A3.

[23] *M&A*, "How Acquirers Can Be Blindsided by the Numbers," May/June 1997, p. 29.

AVOIDING THE PITFALLS BEFORE THE DEAL

In a survey of 101 corporations that completed a merger or acquisition transaction of at least $100 million, KPMG found that 93% of companies queried believed that their deal enhanced shareholder value and over a third said they would not do anything different in subsequent deals. However, KPMG's objective examination of the deals showed that only 31% of these deals improved value. KPMG concluded that many companies may not be prepared to make an honest assessment of the success of their deals in order to avoid making mistakes in future deals.[24]

LO3 Factors to be considered in due diligence.

To consider the potential impact on a firm's earnings realistically, the acquiring firm's managers and advisors must exercise **due diligence** in considering the information presented to them. The factors to beware of include the following:

1. Be cautious in interpreting any **percentages** presented by the selling company. For example, the seller may be operating below capacity (say, at 60% of capacity), but the available capacity may be for a product that is unprofitable or that is concentrated at a specific location, while the desirable product line (which the acquirer wishes to expand) is already at capacity.
2. Don't neglect to include **assumed liabilities** in the assessment of the cost of the merger. The purchase price for a firm's assets is the sum of the cash or securities issued to consummate the merger **plus** any liabilities assumed. This is equivalent to viewing the purchase price for a firm's **net** assets (assets **minus** liabilities assumed) as the sum of the cash or securities issued to consummate the merger.

An important part of a buyer's preparation involves the development of a due diligence report (sometimes by a public accounting firm) for the purpose of uncovering "skeletons in the closet" (like vendor reliance or customer concentrations). These reports offer a fairly objective perspective of the business, so sharing them with potential lenders is one way of building trust and confidence in the collateral and cash flow. Most lenders prefer a 1 to 1 loan-to-collateral ratio in any deal, and regular monitoring through a monthly borrowing base. A lot of the scrutiny by senior lenders gets directed to the buyer's credentials and familiarity with the industry.[25]

In addition to liabilities that are on the books of the acquired firm, be aware of the possibility of less obvious liabilities. Accounting standards require an acquiring firm to recognize at fair value all assets acquired and liabilities assumed, whether or not shown in the financial statements of the acquired company.[26]

Furthermore, a recent pronouncement of the Financial Accounting Standards Board, "Business Combinations," *FASB Statement No. 141R* [ASC 805], issued December 4, 2007, states that any *contingent* assets or liabilities that are acquired or assumed as part of a business combination must be measured and

[24] *KPMG Transaction Services*, "The Morning After—Driving for Post Deal Success," January 31, 2006.

[25] "The Credit Puzzle," by Lou Banach and Jim Gettel, Mergers & Acquisitions, December 2008.

[26] Accounting Principles Board, *Opinion No. 16*, ***Business Combinations***, Paragraphs 87 and 88.

recognized at their fair values (provided they satisfy the definition of assets or liabilities), **even if they do not meet the usual recognition criteria for recording contingent items (detailed in *FASB Statement No. 5*, "Accounting for Contingencies"** [paragraph 450–20–25–2]).[27]

FASB Statement No. 141R [ASC 805] also states that any costs associated with restructuring or exit activities should not be treated as liabilities at the acquisition date unless they meet the criteria for recognition laid out in *FASB Statement No. 146*, "Accounting for Costs Associated with Exit or Disposal Activities [ASC 420-10-15-2]."[28] Instead, costs not meeting these criteria should be expensed in the period in which they are incurred. For example, future costs expected with regard to exiting an activity of the target, terminating the employment of the acquiree's employees, or relocation of those employees are not accounted for as part of the business combination.[29]

3. Watch out for the impact on earnings of the **allocation of expenses** and the effects of production increases, standard cost variances, LIFO liquidations, and byproduct sales. For example, a firm that is planning to be acquired may grow inventory levels in order to allocate its fixed costs over more units, thus decreasing the cost of goods sold and increasing the bottom line. However, the inventory level that is acquired may be excessive and ultimately costly.
4. Note any **nonrecurring items** that may have artificially or temporarily boosted earnings. In addition to nonrecurring gains or revenues, look for recent **changes in estimates, accrual levels, *and* methods.** While material changes in method are a required disclosure under GAAP, the rules on materiality are fuzzy, and changes in estimates and accruals are frequently not disclosed.

"While everything in the offering memorandum may very well be true, although not necessarily, the facts are designed to make the company look better than it would if an analyst were to dig into those facts."[30]

5. Be careful of **CEO egos**. Striving to be number one may make business sense, but not everyone can hold that spot. One CEO drew both praise and criticism with his deal-of-the-month style. He stated, "There are the big dogs, there are the

[27] *FASB Statement No. 5* [ASC 450–20–25–2] states that, in general, contingent liabilities (and related losses) should be accrued if they are both probable and reasonably estimable while contingent assets (and gains) should usually not be reflected to avoid misleading implications about their realizability. These conditions still apply for noncontractual contingent liabilities unless it is *more likely than not* that an asset or liability exists. The number of deals with contingent payments nearly doubled between 1997 and 2006, while the dollar value of those deals more than doubled (with the earn-out value portion rising from 3.3 billion dollars in 1997 to a high of 6.1 billion dollars in 2001 and leveling back to 5.3 billion dollars in 2006). See Chapter 2 for further details.

[28] *FASB Statement No. 146* [ASC 420–10–25–2] reiterates the definition of a liability and states that only present obligations to others are liabilities. It clarifies by specifying that an obligation becomes a present obligation when a past transaction or event leaves little or no discretion to avoid settlement, and that an exit or disposal plan, by itself, does not create a present obligation.

[29] FASB's new Codification system, referenced here, is discussed in the Appendix.

[30] *M&A*, "How Acquirers Can Be Blindsided by the Numbers," May/June 1997, p. 29.

ILLUSTRATION 1-3
Mode of Payment in M&A Deals

	Cash		*Stock*		*Combination*	
Year	#	%	#	%	#	%
2002	1260	63.8%	402	20.4%	313	15.8%
2003	1535	74.2%	311	15.0%	224	10.8%
2004	1734	73.9%	288	12.3%	326	13.9%
2005	1988	76.0%	282	10.8%	346	13.2%
2006	2014	78.9%	212	8.3%	328	12.8%

Source: Mergers & Acquistions January 2007.

ankle-biters, and then there are those caught in the middle." The midsize firms have to combine, he claimed.[31]

DETERMINING PRICE AND METHOD OF PAYMENT IN BUSINESS COMBINATIONS

LO6 Factors affecting price and method of payment.

Whether an acquisition is structured as an asset acquisition or a stock acquisition, the acquiring firm must choose to finance the combination with cash, stock, or debt (or some combination). The cash-financed portion of acquisition prices dropped from 42.3% in 1994 to 13.4% in 1998, according to Securities Data Co. of Newark, New Jersey. This represented the lowest share of cash in over ten years.[32] Note that the dollar volume of cash used in 1998 acquisitions was not down, but rather the percentage of cash included in the total acquisition price. The proportion of cash included in the total cost increased again in the deals of the early part of the 21st century. The number of cash deals rose by 60% from 2002 to 2006, while the number of stock-only deals dropped by about 47% and the number of combination deals remained relatively flat.[33]

The trends are often explained by fluctuating stock valuations. The higher the acquiring firm's stock valuation, the fewer shares are needed to pay for the acquisition. This means less dilution to existing shareholders, a frequent concern in the planning stages of a proposed acquisition. When stock prices slumped in the middle of 2001, merger activity slowed as well. But by the middle of the decade, both were booming once more. Then, merger activity rose steadily from 2002 to 2006, remained approximately the same in 2007 as in 2006, and then fell off by the end of 2008 as stock prices plunged and the economy slid into a recession.

[31] *WSJ*, "In the New Mergers Conglomerates Are Out, Being No. 1 Is In," by Bernard Wysocki Jr., 12/31/97, p. A1.

[32] *WSJ*, "Mergers Reached This Year Are Using the Lowest Share of Cash in Ten Years," by Greg Ip, 4/16/98, p. C1.

[33] Mergers & Acquisitions, January 2007, page 57.

In the latest merger run in 2005, the number of deals using stock decreased to about 11% of total deals, while in 2000, the percentage of deals using all stock averaged around 27%. Stock-for-stock swaps are more common when stock prices are increasing.[34]

When a business combination is effected through an open-market acquisition of stock, no particular problems arise in connection with determining price or method of payment. Price is determined by the normal functioning of the stock market, and payment is generally in cash, although some or all of the cash may have to be raised by the acquiring company through debt or equity issues. Effecting a combination may present some difficulty if there are not enough willing sellers at the open-market price to permit the acquiring company to buy a majority of the outstanding shares of the company being acquired. In that event, the acquiring company must either negotiate a price directly with individuals holding large blocks of shares or revert to an open tender offer.

When a business combination is effected by a stock swap, or exchange of securities, both price and method of payment problems arise. In this case, the price is expressed in terms of a **stock exchange ratio**, which is generally defined as *the number of shares of the acquiring company to be exchanged for each share of the acquired company*, and constitutes a **negotiated price**. It is important to understand that each constituent of the combination makes two kinds of contributions to the new entity—net assets and future earnings. The accountant often becomes deeply involved in the determination of the values of these contributions. Some of the issues and the problems that arise are discussed in the following section.

Net Asset and Future Earnings Contributions

Determination of an equitable price for each constituent company, and of the resulting exchange ratio, requires the valuation of each company's net assets as well as their expected contribution to the future earnings of the new entity. The accountant is often called upon to aid in determining net asset value by assessing, for example, the expected collectibility of accounts receivable, current replacement costs for inventories and some fixed assets, and the current value of long-term liabilities based on current interest rates. To estimate current replacement costs of real estate and other items of plant and equipment, the services of appraisal firms may be needed.

Estimation of the value of goodwill to be included in an offering price is subjective. A number of alternative methods are available, usually involving the discounting of expected future cash flows (or free cash flows), earnings, or excess earnings over some period of years. Generally, the use of free cash flows or earnings yields an estimate of the entire firm value (including goodwill), whereas the use of excess earnings yields an estimate of the goodwill component of total firm value. We next describe the steps in the excess earnings approach and then follow with an illustration.

[34] *WSJ*, "Year-End Review of Markets & Finance 2005," by Dennis Berman, 1/3/06, p. R1.

EXCESS EARNINGS APPROACH TO ESTIMATING GOODWILL

1. Identify a normal rate of return on assets for firms similar to the company being targeted. Statistical services are available to provide averages, or a normal rate may be estimated by examining annual reports of comparable firms. The rate may be estimated as a return on either total assets or on ***net*** identifiable assets (assets other than goodwill minus liabilities).
2. Apply the rate of return identified in step 1 to the level of identifiable assets (or net assets) of the target to approximate what the "normal" firm in this industry might generate with the same level of resources. We will refer to the product as "normal earnings."
3. Estimate the expected future earnings of the target. Past earnings are generally useful here and provide a more objective measure than management's projections, although both should be considered. Exclude any nonrecurring gains or losses (extraordinary items, gains and losses from discontinued operations, etc.) from past earnings if they are used to estimate future earnings.
4. Subtract the normal earnings calculated in step 2 from the expected target earnings from step 3. The difference is "excess earnings." If the normal earnings are greater than the target's expected earnings, then no goodwill is implied under this approach.
5. To compute estimated goodwill from "excess earnings," we must assume an appropriate time period and a discount rate. The shorter the time period and the higher the discount rate, the more conservative the estimate. If the excess earnings are expected to last indefinitely, the present value of a perpetuity may be calculated simply by dividing the excess earnings by the discount rate. For finite time periods, use present-value tables or calculations to compute the present value of an annuity. Because of the assumptions needed in step 5, a range of goodwill estimates may be obtained simply by varying the assumed discount rate and/or the assumed discount period.
6. Add the estimated goodwill from step 5 to the fair value of the firm's net identifiable assets to arrive at a possible offering price.

LO7 Estimating goodwill.

Estimating Goodwill and Potential Offering Price Wanna Buy Company is considering acquiring ***Hot Stuff Inc.*** and is wondering how much it should offer. Wanna Buy makes the following computations and assumptions to help in the decision.

a. Hot Stuff's identifiable assets have a total fair value of $7,000,000. Hot Stuff has liabilities totalling $3,200,000. The assets include patents and copyrights with a fair value approximating book value, buildings with a fair value 50% higher than book value, and equipment with a fair value 25% lower than book value. The remaining lives of the assets are deemed to be approximately equal to those used by Hot Stuff.

b. Hot Stuff's pretax income for the year 2006 was $1,059,000, which is believed by Wanna Buy to be more indicative of future expectations than any of the preceding years. The net income of $1,059,000 included the following items, among others:

Amortization of patents and copyrights	$50,000
Depreciation on buildings	360,000
Depreciation on equipment	80,000
Extraordinary gain	250,000
Loss from discontinued operations	175,000
Pension expense	59,000

c. The normal rate of return on net assets for the industry is 14%.

d. Wanna Buy believes that any excess earnings will continue for seven years and that a rate of return of 15% is required on the investment.

Based on the assumptions above and ignoring tax effects, we will first calculate an estimation of the implied goodwill, and then use that estimate to arrive at a reasonable offering price for Hot Stuff.

Normal earnings for similar firms: ($7,000,000 − $3,200,000) × 14% = $532,000

Expected earnings of target:		
Pretax income of Hot Stuff		$1,059,000
Add: Losses on discontinued operations	175,000	
Reduced depreciation on equipment	20,000	195,000
Subtotal		1,254,000
Subtract: Additional depreciation on building	180,000	
Extraordinary gain	250,000	430,000
Target's expected future earnings		824,000

Excess earnings of target: $824,000 − $532,000 = $292,000 per year

Present value of excess earnings (ordinary annuity) for seven years at 15% (see Table A2 in Appendix at back of textbook):

Estimated goodwill: $292,000 × 4.16042 = $1,214,843

Implied offering price = Fair value of assets − Fair value of liabilities + Estimated goodwill
= $7,000,000 − $3,200,000 + $1,214,843 = $5,014,843.

In the illustration above, in arriving at the target's expected future earnings, we ignored the items that are expected to continue after the acquisition, such as the amortization of the patents and copyrights and the pension expense. We backed out nonrecurring gains and losses on extraordinary items or discontinued operations. We adjusted the prior reported earnings for the expected increase in depreciation on the building (50% higher than in the past), leading to a decrease in projected earnings. In contrast, we increased projected earnings for the decrease in equipment depreciation (25% lower than in the past). In practice, more specific information should be available as to which components of earnings are expected to continue at the same level, which might be reduced because of economies or cost-cutting plans, and which might increase because of transition costs. The better the information used in the computation, the better the estimate of goodwill and offering price.

Where the constituent companies have used different accounting methods, the accountant will often need to reconstruct their financial statements on the basis of agreed-upon accounting methods in order to obtain reasonably comparable data. Once comparable data have been obtained for a number of prior periods, they are analyzed further to project future contributions to earnings. The expected contributions to future earnings may vary widely among constituents, and the exchange ratio should reflect this fact. The whole process of valuation, of course, requires the careful exercise of professional judgment. Ultimately, however, the exchange ratio is determined by the bargaining ability of the individual parties to the combination.

Once the overall values of relative net asset and earnings contributions have been agreed on, the types of securities to be issued by the new entity in exchange for those of the combining companies must be determined. In some cases a single class of stock will be issued; in other cases equity may require the use of more than one class of security.

The concepts of earnings **dilution** and **accretion** are critical to the valuation of a merger. Does the merger increase or decrease expected earnings performance of the acquiring institution? From a financial and shareholder perspective, the price paid for a firm is hard to justify if earnings per share declines. When this happens, the acquisition is considered **dilutive**. Conversely, if the earnings per share increases as a result of the acquisition, it is referred to as an **accretive** acquisition.

Upon the agreement to purchase Creo, Inc. for $900 million in cash, Eastman Kodak Company's CEO Daniel Carp stated that the "acquisition will result in some modest earnings dilution for the remainder of 2005." However, Carp expects that the Creo transaction will be accretive in 2006, adding "at least 5 cents to per-share operational earnings, driven by cost savings and revenue growth available to the combined entity."[35]

Many deals lower earnings per share initially but add significantly to value in later years. While initial dilution may not be a deal killer, however, many managers feel that they cannot afford to wait too long for a deal to begin to show a positive return. Opinions are divided, however, on what drives the market in relation to mergers and acquisitions, nor do research studies offer conclusive evidence on the subject. Bart Madden, a partner in a valuation advisory firm in Chicago, remarked, "I totally disagree that the market is EPS driven. From the perspective of the owner or manager of capital, what matters is cash in, cash out, not reported earnings."[36] He acknowledges, however, that CFOs, who "live in a world of accounting rules," are concerned about reported earnings.

Build-A-Bear Workshop, the teddy-bear-stuffing retailer, purchased U.K.-based rival Bear Factory for $41.4 million in cash to help solidify Build-A-Bear's global position. Build-A-Bear expected the acquisition to be accretive to earnings per share by 2007.[37]

ALTERNATIVE CONCEPTS OF CONSOLIDATED FINANCIAL STATEMENTS

LO8 Economic entity and parent company concepts.

As mentioned previously, business combinations may take the form of asset acquisitions or stock acquisitions. When the combination is consummated as an asset acquisition, the books of the acquired company are closed out and the accounting takes place on the books of the acquirer, as illustrated in Chapter 2. When the combination is consummated as a stock acquisition, both companies continue to prepare journal and ledger entries separately through future periods. Periodically the two sets of books are combined into one through a procedure sometimes referred to as the **consolidating process** to produce a set of consolidated financial statements. Chapters 3 through 9 deal with many of the technical procedures needed to carry out this process. Here we present a brief introduction to the more theoretical concepts involved in accounting for the consolidated entity. The question that arises relates to the primary purpose of the consolidated financial statements and to the relationships between the affiliated companies and their shareholders, keeping

[35] *Business Wire*, "Kodak Announces Agreement to Acquire Creo Inc," 1/31/05.

[36] *CFO*, "Say Goodbye to Pooling," by Ian Springsteel, February 1997, p. 79.

[37] *MSNBC.com*, "When Bears Collide," by Rick Aristotle Munarriz, 3/6/06.

in mind that a certain group of shareholders may own a portion of the acquired company (often referred to as the **subsidiary**) but none of the acquiring company (or **parent**).

Historically, practice in the U.S. has reflected a compromise between two general concepts of consolidation given various designations in the accounting literature. However, in *FASB Statement No. 141-R* and *No. 160* [ASC 805 and 810], the FASB indicates that the economic entity concept is now to be embraced more fully. Next, let us review the basic differences between the alternative concepts. For our purposes, we will refer to them as the **parent company concept** and the **economic entity concept** (sometimes called the **economic unit concept**). A third concept, **proportionate consolidation**, was rejected by the FASB.

Although only one of these—the economic entity concept—is embraced by current GAAP and thus integrated throughout this text, the two more popular concepts are described below (as defined by the Financial Accounting Standards Board).[38]

Parent Company Concept

The parent company concept emphasizes the interests of the parent's shareholders. As a result, the consolidated financial statements reflect those stockholder interests in the parent itself, plus their undivided interests in the net assets of the parent's subsidiaries. The consolidated balance sheet is essentially a modification of the parent's balance sheet with the assets and liabilities of all subsidiaries substituted for the parent's investment in subsidiaries. The stockholders' equity of the parent company is also the stockholders' equity of the consolidated entity. Similarly, the consolidated income statement is essentially a modification of the parent's income statement with the revenues, expenses, gains, and losses of subsidiaries substituted for the parent's income from investment in subsidiaries. These multi-line substitutions for single lines in the parent's balance sheet and income statement are intended to make the parent's financial statements more informative about the parent's total ownership holdings.

Economic Entity Concept

The economic entity concept emphasizes control of the whole by a single management. As a result, under this concept, consolidated financial statements are intended to provide information about a group of legal entities—a parent company and its subsidiaries—operating as a single unit. The assets, liabilities, revenues, expenses, gains, and losses of the various component entities are the assets, liabilities, revenues, expenses, gains, and losses of the consolidated entity. Unless all subsidiaries are wholly owned, the business enterprise's proprietary interest (assets less liabilities) is divided into the controlling interest (stockholders or other owners of the parent company) and one or more noncontrolling interests in subsidiaries. Both the controlling and the noncontrolling interests are part of the proprietary group of the consolidated entity, even though the noncontrolling stockholders' ownership interests relate only to the affiliates whose shares they own.

---

[38] *FASB Discussion Memorandum*, "Consolidation Policy and Procedures" FASB (Norwalk, CT: September 10, 1991), pars. 63 and 64.

The parent company concept represents the view that the primary purpose of consolidated financial statements is to provide information relevant to the controlling stockholders. The parent company effectively controls the assets and operations of the subsidiary. Noncontrolling stockholders do not exercise any ownership control over the subsidiary company or the parent company. Thus, the parent company concept places emphasis on the needs of the controlling stockholders, and the noncontrolling interest is essentially relegated to the position of a claim against the consolidated entity. Thus, the noncontrolling, or minority, interest should be presented as a liability in the consolidated statement of financial position under the parent company concept or, as described in the next section, as a separate component before stockholders' equity.

The economic entity concept represents the view that the affiliated companies are a separate, identifiable economic entity. Meaningful evaluation by any interested party of the financial position and results of operations of the economic entity is possible only if the individual assets, liabilities, revenues, and expenses of the affiliated companies making up the economic entity are combined. The economic entity concept treats both controlling and noncontrolling stockholders as contributors to the economic unit's capital. Thus, the noncontrolling, or minority, interest should be presented as a component of equity in the consolidated financial statement under the economic entity concept.

The FASB stated that it had considered and rejected the concept of proportionate consolidation for subsidiaries. This concept, although not used in current or past practice, has been advocated by some as an alternative to full consolidation. Under proportionate consolidation, the consolidated statements would include only a portion, based on the parent's ownership interest, of the subsidiary's assets, liabilities, revenues, expenses, gains, and losses. The FASB stated that because the consolidated entity has the power to direct the use of all the assets of a controlled entity, omitting a portion of those assets from the statements would not be representationally faithful. Similarly, omitting part of the revenues and expenses from the consolidated income statement would not be representationally faithful.

Differences between the concepts are relevant only to less than wholly owned subsidiaries; they center on conflicting views concerning answers to three basic questions:

1. What is the nature of a noncontrolling interest?
2. What income figure constitutes consolidated net income?
3. What values should be reported in the consolidated balance sheet?

A related issue concerns the percentage (total or partial) of unrealized intercompany profit to be eliminated in the determination of consolidated balances.

Noncontrolling Interest

Under the **economic entity concept**, *a noncontrolling interest is a part of the ownership equity in the entire economic unit.* Thus, a noncontrolling interest is of the same general nature and is accounted for in essentially the same way as the controlling interest (i.e., as a component of owners' equity). Under the ***parent company concept***, the nature and classification of a noncontrolling interest are unclear. The parent company concept views the consolidated financial statements as those of the parent company.

From that perspective, the noncontrolling interest is similar to a liability; but because the parent does not have a present obligation to pay cash or release other assets, it is not a liability based on the FASB's technical definition of a "liability." Nor is it a true component of owners' equity since the noncontrolling investors in a subsidiary do not have an ownership interest in the subsidiary's parent. Consequently, the parent company concept theoretically supports reporting the noncontrolling interest below liabilities but above stockholders' equity in the consolidated balance sheet.

Consolidated Net Income

Under the **parent company concept**, *consolidated net income consists of the realized combined income of the parent company and its subsidiaries after deducting noncontrolling interest in income*; that is, the noncontrolling interest in income is deducted as an expense item in determining consolidated net income. This view emphasizes that the parent company stockholders are directly interested in their share of the results of operations as a measure of earnings in relation to their investment and dividend expectations.

Under the ***economic entity concept***, consolidated net income consists of the total realized combined income of the parent company and its subsidiaries. The total combined income is then allocated proportionately to the noncontrolling interest and the controlling interest. Noncontrolling interest in income is considered an allocated portion of consolidated net income, rather than an element in the determination of consolidated net income. The concept emphasizes the view that the consolidated financial statements represent those of a single economic unit with several classes of stockholder interest. Thus, noncontrolling interest in net assets is considered a separate element of stockholders' equity, and the noncontrolling interest in net income reflects the share of consolidated net income allocated to the noncontrolling stockholders.

Consolidated Balance Sheet Values

In the case of less than wholly owned subsidiaries, the question arises as to whether to value the subsidiary assets and liabilities at the ***total*** fair value implied by the price paid for the controlling interest, or at their book value adjusted only for the excess of cost over book value paid by the parent company. For example, assume that P Company acquires a 60% interest in S Company for $960,000 when the book value of the net assets and of the stockholders' equity of S Company is $1,000,000. The implied fair value of the net assets of S Company is $1,600,000 ($960,000/.6), and the difference between the implied fair value and the book value is $600,000 ($1,600,000 − $1,000,000). For presentation in the consolidated financial statements, should the net assets of S Company be written up by $600,000 or by 60% of $600,000?

Application of the ***parent company concept*** in this situation restricts the write-up of the net assets of S Company to $360,000 (.6 × $600,000) on the theory that the write-up should be restricted to the amount actually paid by P Company in excess of the book value of the interest it acquires [$960,000 − (.6 × $1,000,000) = $360,000]. In other words, the value assigned to the net assets should not exceed cost to the parent company. Thus, the net assets of the subsidiary are included in the consolidated financial statements at their book value ($1,000,000) plus the

parent company's share of the difference between fair value and book value (.6 × $600,000) = $360,000, or at a total of $1,360,000 on the date of acquisition. Noncontrolling interest is reported at its percentage interest in the **reported book value** of the net assets of S Company, or $400,000 (.4 × $1,000,000).

Application of the ***economic entity concept*** results in a write-up of the net assets of S Company in the consolidated statements workpaper by $600,000 to $1,600,000 on the theory that the consolidated financial statements should reflect 100% of the net asset values of the affiliated companies. On the date of acquisition, the net assets of the subsidiary are included in the consolidated financial statements at their book value ($1,000,000) plus **the entire difference** between their fair value and their book value ($600,000), or a total of $1,600,000. Noncontrolling interest is reported at its percentage interest in the **fair value** of the net assets of S Company, or $640,000 (.4 × $1,600,000).

Regardless of the concept followed, the controlling interest in the net assets of the subsidiary reported in the consolidated financial statements is the same and is equal to P Company's cost, as demonstrated here:

	Parent Company Concept	*Economic Unit Concept*
Net assets of S Company included in consolidation	$1,360,000	$1,600,000
Less: Noncontrolling interest	400,000	640,000
Controlling interest (cost)	$ 960,000	$ 960,000

While U.S. standards have, in the past, been more consistent with the parent company concept with respect to write-up of net assets, the implementation of *FASB Statements No. 141R* and *160* [ASC 805 and 810] results in a shift to the economic entity concept in this regard, among others.

Intercompany Profit

There are two alternative points of view as to the amount of intercompany profit that should be considered unrealized in the determination of consolidated income. The elimination methods associated with these two points of view are generally referred to as **total** (100%) **elimination** and **partial elimination**.

Proponents of total elimination regard all the intercompany profit associated with assets remaining in the affiliated group to be unrealized. Proponents of partial elimination regard only the parent company's share of the profit recognized by the selling affiliate to be unrealized. Under total elimination, the entire amount of unconfirmed intercompany profit is eliminated from combined income and the related asset balance. Under partial elimination, only the parent company's share of the unconfirmed intercompany profit recognized by the selling affiliate is eliminated.

Past and Future Practice

Past practice has viewed noncontrolling interest in income neither as an expense nor as an allocation of consolidated net income, but as a special equity interest in the consolidated entity's combined income that must be recognized when all the earnings of a less than wholly owned subsidiary are combined with the earnings of the parent company. Noncontrolling interest in net assets has been viewed neither as a liability nor as true stockholders' equity, but rather as a special interest in the combined net assets that must be recognized when all the assets and liabilities of a less than wholly owned subsidiary are combined with those of the parent company.

In contrast, under the new standards, the noncontrolling interest in income is viewed as an allocation of consolidated net income on the income statement, and the noncontrolling interest in net assets as a component of equity in the balance sheet.

Past and future accounting standards are, however, consistent in requiring the total elimination of unrealized intercompany profit in assets acquired from affiliated companies, regardless of the percentage of ownership.

FASB'S CONCEPTUAL FRAMEWORK

The Financial Accounting Standards Board (FASB) began the process of developing a conceptual framework for financial reporting in 1976, a process that continues to the present. The much-needed objective of providing a basis for standard setting and controversy resolution has, as expected, proved to be challenging. The statements of concepts issued to date are summarized in Figure 1-2. The reader should be aware, however, that some changes have been proposed by the FASB, in a joint project with the IASB, with respect to the objective of financial reporting and the qualitative characteristics.

FIGURE 1-2

Conceptual Framework for Financial Accounting and Reporting*

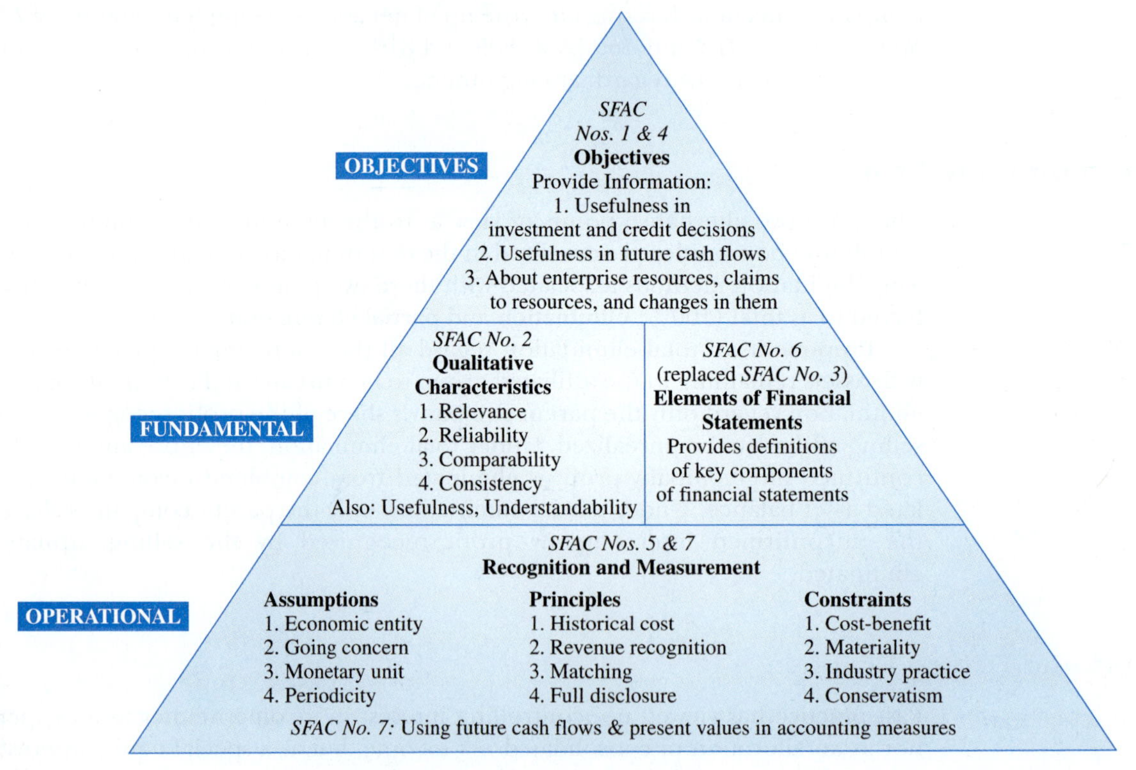

*Adapted from "Accounting for Financial Analysis" by W. C. Norby, *Financial Analysts Journal*, March–April 1982, p. 22.

In May 2008, as part of a joint project with the IASB, the FASB issued an exposure draft addressing possible changes in the framework with respect to the objectives, qualitative characteristics, and constraints of financial information that is useful for decision-making.

In relating the previous discussion to the FASB's conceptual framework, we will initially focus on one principle—historical cost—and one assumption—economic entity—both from *SFAC No. 5*. We next proceed to provide an overview of the conceptual framework, our focus being on the areas most relevant to topics in this textbook.

Advanced accounting, as a discipline, has been particularly vulnerable in recent years to fairly drastic changes in generally accepted accounting principles (GAAP) as prescribed by the FASB. In particular, the area of accounting for business combinations and consolidations has received much attention both from the FASB and from constituents affected by the proposed changes. These changes will be discussed and integrated throughout the next nine chapters. The purpose of our discussion here is to draw the readers' attention to the role played by the FASB's conceptual framework in these changes and discussions, as well as in other pending or potential changes that may affect GAAP in the future.

Joint Project of FASB and IASB on Conceptual Framework The objective of the joint project is to develop an improved common conceptual framework that provides a sound foundation for developing future standards. Such a framework is believed to be essential to the two Boards' goal of developing standards that are principles-based, internally consistent, and internationally converged. The new framework is expected to deal with a wide range of issues, and will build on the existing IASB and FASB frameworks, while also considering developments subsequent to the issuance of those frameworks.

One of the goals of the Boards, which is shared by their constituents, is for the standards to be clearly based on consistent principles that are rooted in fundamental concepts rather than a collection of conventions. The objective is for the body of standards taken as a whole, as well as the application of those standards, to be based on a sound, comprehensive, and internally consistent framework. Another important goal is to converge the standards of the two Boards. As the Boards strive to more closely align their agendas to achieve standard convergence, they will be hampered unless they are basing decisions on the same basic framework.

Economic Entity vs. Parent Concept and the Conceptual Framework

The parent concept, discussed in the preceding section, was the essential approach used in the U.S. until 2008 for accounting for business combinations (although there were some exceptions to a wholly-applied parent concept, as previously addressed). The parent company concept is tied to the *historical cost* principle, which suggests that the best measure of valuation of a given asset is the price paid. Historical cost thus suggests that the purchase price of an acquired firm should be relied on in assessing the value of the acquired assets, including goodwill. One problem that arises from a theoretical perspective is how to value the noncontrolling interest, or the portion of the acquired firm's assets which did not change hands in an arm's length transaction. The historical cost perspective would suggest that those assets (or portions thereof) remain at their previous book values. This approach might be argued to produce more "*reliable*" or "representationally faithful" values, addressed in the FASB's conceptual framework as a desirable attribute and, in fact, one of the primary qualitative characteristics of accounting information (*SFAC No. 2*).

In contrast, the economic entity concept is itself an integral part of the FASB's conceptual framework and is named specifically in *SFAC No. 5* as one of the basic assumptions in accounting. The economic entity assumption views economic activity as being related to a particular unit of accountability, and the standard indicates that a parent and its subsidiaries represent *one economic entity* even though they may include *several legal entities*. Thus, the recent shift to the economic entity concept seems to be entirely consistent with the assumptions laid out by the FASB for GAAP.

The economic entity concept might also be argued to produce more *relevant*, if not necessarily more reliable, information for users. The two primary characteristics of relevance and reliability (or representational faithfulness)often find themselves in conflict in any given accounting debate. For example, the view of many users is that *market value accounting* would provide far more *relevant* information for users than continued reliance on historical cost in general. Proponents of historical cost, however, argue that market valuations suffer from too much subjectivity and vulnerability to bias, and are much *less* representationally faithful.

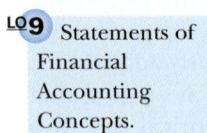

In the joint project of the FASB and the IASB on the conceptual framework, the conclusion was reached that the entity perspective is more consistent with the fact that the vast majority of today's business entities have substance distinct from that of their capital providers. As such, the proprietary perspective does not reflect a realistic view of financial reporting. The Boards have not yet considered the effect that adoption of the entity perspective will have on phases of their project that have not yet been deliberated, and decisions related to those phases are being deferred.

IN THE NEWS

Embedded in many of FASB's recent pronouncements have been a number of indicators of a shift away from historical cost accounting in the direction of fair value accounting. This shift drew a great deal of attention, much of it negative, when the financial crisis of 2008 became apparent. Critics claimed that values were dropping to artificially low values, forcing banks to take large write-downs, launching a desperate cycle from which they might not recover. Dennis Beresford, an accounting professor at the University of Georgia and chairman of the FASB from 1987 to 1997, explained, "It's intended to be more or less for orderly markets. But we don't have orderly markets these days. It's not so much that mark to market has people complaining, but marking to a particular market. Today it's more of fire-sale prices."[39]

Overview of FASB's Conceptual Framework

LO9 Statements of Financial Accounting Concepts.

The *Statements of Financial Accounting Concepts* issued by the FASB include the following:

SFAC No. 1: Objectives of Financial Reporting by Business Enterprises,

SFAC No. 2: Qualitative Characteristics of Accounting Information,

SFAC No. 3 (replaced by SFAC No. 6): Elements of Financial Statements of Business Enterprises,

SFAC No. 4: Objectives of Financial Reporting by Nonbusiness Organizations

[39] "Wall St. Points to Disclosure As Issue," by Carrie Johnson, Washingtonpost.com, September 23, 2008.

SFAC No. 5: Recognition and Measurement in Financial Statements of Business Enterprises,

SFAC No. 6 (replaces SFAC No. 3): Elements of Financial Statements, and

SFAC No. 7: Using Cash Flow Information and Present Value in Accounting Measurements.

Please refer to Figure 1-2 for a brief summation of these statements. Our focus is on *SFAC No. 1, No. 2, No. 6*, and *No. 5*. The remaining statements of concept include one which was subsequently replaced by *SFAC No. 6 (SFAC No. 3)*, one which relates primarily to the last three chapters of our textbook (*SFAC No. 4*), and the newest *FASB Statement of Concept, No. 7*, which provides some information on the use of discounted cash flows and present values as a measurement approach. *SFAC No. 7* might be viewed as an expansion of *SFAC No. 5*, and is thus included in the same level in Figure 1-2.

Under current GAAP, the *Statements of Financial Accounting Concepts (SFAC)* do not hold the same level of authoritative support as the FASB's *Statements of Financial Accounting Standards (SFAS)*. However, the FASB has expressed an intent to incorporate the new conceptual framework (resulting from the joint project with the IASB) into the codification in the future, thus elevating the status of Concepts.

It is widely known that the GAAP hierarchy sets forth the level of authority attributed to a given accounting pronouncement or document. For example, an SFAS pronouncement, which is in category (a) of the GAAP hierarchy, has a higher authority than a FASB Technical Bulletin, which is in category (b). Preparers of financial statements will look to category (a) GAAP in selecting and applying appropriate accounting principles, and turn to categories (b), (c), and (d), in that order, only if the accounting for a transaction or event is not specified in category (a). Where there might be conflicting guidance between two categories, the more authoritative category will prevail.

SFAS 162 comes in response to an SEC study in July 2003, which, in part, endorsed an improvement to the SAS 69 GAAP hierarchy ("old GAAP hierarchy"). The old GAAP hierarchy has been described as complex, directed to the auditor, and ranks the Concepts Statements too low in the chain of command. Indeed, it is in the Concepts Statements that some of the most fundamental terms of our profession are defined: assets, liabilities, equity, income, expense, accrual basis of accounting and materiality, along with a profound discussion of the often-quoted "objectives of financial reporting."[40]

Linking the Conceptual Framework to Advanced Accounting Issues

We begin with a brief discussion of the two *Statements of Concepts* which receive the least attention in the following paragraphs (*SFAC No. 4 and SFAC No. 7*). With respect to *SFAC No. 4*, the Board believes that the objectives of reporting for government-sponsored entities should be, in general, similar to those of business enterprises engaged in similar activities. Please see Chapters 17 through 19 for further discussion. Moving to *SFAC No. 7*, the use of present values is clearly relevant in the accounting for business combinations as it impacts the estimated valuation of goodwill (previously illustrated in Chapter 1), as well as other intangible assets acquired

[40] "Home at Last," by Christine Davis and Michael McPartlan, *California CPA*, July 1, 2008.

in a business combination. Just as clearly, the use of present values is hampered by issues of uncertainty, both about estimated cash flows and about appropriate discount rates. As stated in *SFAC No. 7*, the objective of using present values in an accounting measurement is to capture, to the extent possible, the economic difference between sets of estimated future cash flows. The standard provides some guidance in this regard.

Referring to Figure 1-2, note that the secondary qualities laid out in *SFAC No. 2* are *consistency* and *comparability*. (The primary qualities are reliability and relevance.) These are distinguished from each other in that comparability refers primarily to being able to compare one company with another, knowing that they are using the same general accounting techniques to produce their numbers, while consistency refers mainly to within-company comparisons, such as the comparison of the third quarter of 2007 to the third quarter of 2008, again knowing the same general principles have been adhered to in both quarters.

The quality of *comparability* was very much at stake in FASB's decision in 2001 to eliminate the *pooling of interests* method for business combinations. This method was also argued to violate the *historical cost* principle as it essentially ignored the value of the consideration (stock) issued for the acquisition of another company. Of even greater concern was the potential for two nearly identical acquisitions to yield very different balance sheets, merely because one was accounted for under the pooling of interests method while the other used purchase accounting.

The issue of *consistency* plays a role in the recent shift from the parent concept to the economic entity concept, as the former method valued a portion (the noncontrolling interest) of a given asset at prior book values and another portion (the controlling interest) of that same asset at exchange-date market value. The result was a piecemeal valuation of assets on the consolidated balance sheet.

Distinguishing between Earnings and Comprehensive Income

Opponents of the change to the economic entity view of consolidated financial statements may argue that the economic entity concept is less *conservative*, as it often revalues assets—in the case of a less than 100% acquisition—to a higher amount than has been reflected in an arm's length transaction by relying on the valuation *implied* by the purchase price. However, the constraint of conservatism, as defined in *SFAC No. 5*, only applies to situations where there is *doubt* about the proper valuation and encourages the choice, in such situations, of the solution least likely to overstate earnings or assets. One example of conservatism in current GAAP is the use of the *lower of cost or market* to value inventories. See Chapter 6 for a discussion of this method in the context of consolidations. Proper application of conservatism does not suggest that assets or net income should ever be deliberately understated.

Turning now to the elements of financial statements, see Illustration 1-4 for a summary of definitions. We might note that earnings is not defined as one of the elements included in *SFAC No. 6*. In fact, the FASB explicitly stated that it reserved the term earnings for possible use to designate a significant intermediate measure or component of comprehensive income. In *SFAC No. 5*, FASB states that "it is important to avoid focusing attention almost exclusively on the bottom line, earnings per share, or other highly simplified condensations." *SFAC No. 5* goes on to state that "statements of earnings and of comprehensive income together reflect the extent to which, and the ways in which, the equity of an entity increased or

ILLUSTRATION 1-4

Definitions of Financial Statement Elements**

Assets. Probable future economic benefits obtained or controlled by a particular entity as a result of past transactions or events.

Liabilities. Probable future sacrifices of economic benefits arising from present obligations of a particular entity to transfer assets or provide services to other entities in the future as a result of past transactions or events.

Equity. Residual interest in the assets of an entity that remains after deducting its liabilities, or the claims of the owners of the entity's assets.

Investments by Owners. Increase in net assets of a particular enterprise resulting from transfers to it from other entities of something of value to obtain or increase ownership interests (equity) in it.

Distributions to Owners. Decrease in net assets of a particular enterprise resulting from transferring assets, rendering services, or incurring liabilities by the enterprise to its owners (dividends or Draws).

Comprehensive Income. Change in equity (net assets) of an entity during a period from transactions and other events and circumstances from nonowner sources, i.e., all changes in equity during a period except from investments by owners and distributions to owners.

Revenues. Inflows or other enhancements of assets of an entity or settlement of its liabilities (or a combinations of both) during a period from delivering or producing goods, rendering services, or other activities that constitute the entity's ongoing major or central operations.

Expenses. Outflows or other using up of assets or incurrences of liabilities (or a combination of both) during a period of delivering or producing goods, rendering services, or carrying out other activities that constitute the entity's ongoing major or central operations.

Gains. Increases in equity (net assets) from peripheral or incidental transactions of an entity and from all other transactions and other events and circumstances affecting the entity during a period except from revenues or investments by owners.

Losses. Decreases in equity (net assets) from peripheral or incidental transactions of an entity and from all other transactions and other events and circumstances affecting the entity during a period except from expenses or distributions to owners.

** "Elements of Financial Statements," *Statement of Financial Accounting Concepts No. 6* (Stamford, Conn.: FASB, December 1985), pp. ix and x.

decreased from all sources other than transactions with owners during a period." The statement further expresses an expectation that the concept of earnings will evolve or develop over time. *SFAC No. 5* does, however, provide a working definition of earnings as follows:

> Earnings is a measure of entity performance during a period. It measures the extent to which asset *inflows* (revenues and gains) associated with cash-to-cash cycles substantially completed during the period exceed asset *outflows* (expenses and losses) associated, directly or indirectly, with the same cycles.

In other words, earnings is essentially revenues and gains minus expenses and losses, with the exception of any losses or gains explicitly stated by FASB to bypass earnings and, instead, to be reported as a component of *other comprehensive income.*

What are examples of these "odd" gains and losses that bypass earnings under current GAAP? *SFAC No. 5* describes them as "principally certain holding gains or losses that are recognized in the period but are excluded from earnings such as some changes in market values of investments ... and foreign currency translation adjustments."

Not all changes in market values of investments are excluded from earnings, however. For example, the gains or losses recognized upon marking Trading Securities to market values *are* reported in earnings, while those on Available-for-Sale securities generally are not. Similarly, the gains or losses on foreign currency translation may or may not be reported in earnings, depending on whether the firm is using the temporal method (restatement) or the current method (translation) for its subsidiaries. In one case, the gain or loss appears in earnings. In the other, it appears as a component of *other comprehensive income.* This distinction is elaborated upon in Chapter 13, Translation of Financial Statements of Foreign Affiliates.

In short, these distinctions seem rather arbitrary and are thus, not surprisingly, confusing to students as well as to users of financial statements. The FASB's choices in this regard appear to be affected by: (a) the volatility that a particular gain or loss might introduce into earnings, and whether that volatility is reflective of true economic performance (in which case it should be reported in earnings) or is reflective of something else (in which case it is more likely to fall into other comprehensive income); and (b) the attitude of various constituents, or the effect of lobbying, which is in turn largely related to (a).

In this text, we use the term *net income* to refer to *earnings*, and we do not focus on comprehensive income in most chapters. In the absence of gains or losses designated to bypass earnings, earnings and comprehensive income are the same. However, if the firm has foreign subsidiaries or has available-for-sale securities or other investments that are being marked to market at the balance sheet date, the reader should be aware that current GAAP distinguishes between net current income and comprehensive income. Other items that may arise include certain gains or losses related to a firm's net pension liability; these too may bypass retained earnings and be reported instead as a component of *other comprehensive income.*

Be aware that any item which bypasses earnings will not appear in retained earnings (by definition, the accumulated earnings since incorporation minus dividends declared). Thus, other comprehensive income appears on the balance sheet as a separate component of stockholders' equity, labeled "Accumulated Other Comprehensive Income."

The FASB has issued a discussion paper (October 16, 2008) on financial presentation, in which it proposes that entities should present comprehensive income and its components in a single ***statement of comprehensive income.*** This statement would still display net income as a subtotal, and continue on to display total comprehensive income on the same statement. Like most other current projects, this project reflects the joint efforts of the FASB and the IASB.

Asset Impairment and the Conceptual Framework

SFAC No. 5 provides the following guidance with respect to expenses and losses:

> *Consumption of benefit.* Earnings are generally recognized when an entity's economic benefits are consumed in revenue earnings activities (or matched to the period incurred or allocated systematically); or
>
> *Loss or lack of benefit.* Expenses or losses are recognized if it becomes evident that previously recognized future economic benefits of assets have been reduced or eliminated, or that liabilities have increased, without associated benefits.

In 2001, the FASB abandoned its long-held position that all intangible assets must be amortized over their useful lives, not to exceed 40 years. In the place of this position was born a new standard. If the asset has a finite life, amortize it, as before, over its useful life. However, if the life is deemed indefinite, then do not amortize the asset. Instead, review it periodically (at least once a year) for impairment or decreased value. The former approach (that of amortization) illustrates a *consumption or benefit* approach to measuring expenses while the impairment standard illustrates a *loss or lack of benefit* approach.

Another of the principles laid out by the FASB in *SFAC No. 5* is that of ***matching*** expenses to revenues (see Illustration 1-3; see also query on p. 33). The *consumption of benefit* approach emphasizes a more direct matching of expenses to revenues, while the *loss or lack of benefit* represents an example of those types of expenses that are most difficult, if not impossible, to match adequately to the generation of revenue. Thus, such losses as the impairment of goodwill reflect an attempt to recognize the loss of benefit in the period in which that loss is first identified.

Chapters 2 and 5 illustrate the impact of the impairment of goodwill (deemed to have an indefinite life) on the financial statements of the acquiring company and the consolidated entity, respectively.

SUMMARY

1. *Describe historical trends in types of business combinations.* Horizontal integration involving the combination of companies within the same industry was popular from 1880 to 1904. Vertical integration involving the combination of a company with its customers or suppliers became more prevalent from 1905 through 1930. The period beginning after World War II has been called merger mania. From the 1950s through the 1970s, conglomerate mergers between companies in different industries occurred in the face of antitrust regulation restricting combinations within a particular industry. A relaxation of antitrust regulation in the 1980s and the emergence of high-yield junk bonds led to a number of strategic acquisitions claiming to benefit from operating synergies. High stock prices in the 1990s created a wealth of mergers using stock as the medium of exchange.
2. *Identify the major reasons firms combine.* Firms combine to achieve growth goals or mandates, to obtain operating synergies, to compete more effectively in the international marketplace, to take advantage of tax laws in some cases, and to diversify or alternatively to eliminate competition.
3. *Identify the factors that managers should consider in exercising due diligence in business combinations.* Managers should be aware of unrecorded liabilities; take care in interpreting percentages quoted by the selling company; examine the impact on earnings from allocated expenses, changes in LIFO reserves and inventory levels, and product sales; note any nonrecurring items, changes in estimates, accruals, or methods; and be careful of CEO egos.
4. *Identify defensive tactics used to attempt to block business combinations.* Defensive tactics employed by target companies to avoid potential takeover include poison pills, greenmail, white knights or white squires, pac-man defense, selling the crown jewels, and leveraged buyouts.
5. *Distinguish between an asset and a stock acquisition.* An asset acquisition involves the purchase of all of the acquired company's net assets, whereas a stock acquisition involves the attainment of control via purchase of a controlling interest in the stock of the acquired company.
6. *Indicate the factors used to determine the price and the method of payment for a business combination.* Factors to be considered include the effect the acquisition is expected to have on future earnings performance, referred to as dilution or accretion, and the value of the firm's identifiable net assets as well as the estimated value of its implied goodwill. The method of payment is affected by the liquidity position of the purchasing firm, the willingness of the sellers to accept alternative forms of financing (stock, debt, cash, or a combination), and tax issues.

7. *Calculate an estimate of the value of goodwill to be included in an offering price by discounting expected future excess earnings over some period of years.* Identify a normal rate of return for firms similar to the company being targeted. Apply the rate of return to the level of identifiable assets (or net assets) of the target to approximate what the "normal" firm in this industry might generate with the same level of resources (normal earnings). Estimate the expected future earnings of the target. Subtract the normal earnings from the expected target earnings. The difference is "excess earnings." Assume an appropriate time period and a discount rate to calculate the discounted value of the excess earnings, or the estimated goodwill.
8. *Describe the two alternative views of consolidated financial statements: the economic entity and the parent company concepts.* Under the parent company concept, the consolidated financial statements reflect the stockholders' interests in the parent, plus their undivided interests in the net assets of the parent's subsidiaries. Thus the focus is on the interests of the parent's shareholders. In contrast, the economic entity concept emphasizes control of the whole by a single management. As a result, under this concept, consolidated financial statements are intended to provide information about a group of legal entities—a parent company and its subsidiaries—operating as a single unit.
9. *List and discuss each of the seven Statements of Financial Accounting Concepts (SFAC).* *SFAC No. 1*: Objectives of Financial Reporting by Business Enterprises—discusses the purposes of financial reporting, with the emphasis on the needs of creditors and investors. *SFAC No. 2*: Qualitative Characteristics of Accounting Information—identifies reliability and relevance as primary qualities of accounting information, consistency and comparability as secondary qualities, usefulness to decision makers as the overriding determinant of value, and understandability as the communications link. *SFAC No. 3 (replaced by SFAC No. 6):* Elements of Financial Statements of Business Enterprises. *SFAC No. 4:* Objectives of Financial Reporting by Nonbusiness Organizations—identifies objectives similar to *SFAC No. 1*. *SFAC No. 5*: Recognition and Measurement in Financial Statements of Business Enterprises—recognizes principles, assumptions, and constraints of accounting. *SFAC No. 6 (replaces SFAC No. 3)*: Elements of Financial Statements—provides definitions of the components of financial statements. *SFAC No. 7:* Using Cash Flow Information and Present Value in Accounting Measurements—provides some guidance for these challenging measures.
10. *Describe some of the current joint projects of the FASB and the International Accounting Standards Board (IASB), and their primary objectives.* Among the current joint projects of the FASB and the International Accounting Standards Board (IASB) are projects on business combinations, on the conceptual framework, and on financial presentation. Objectives include the development of standards that are principles based, internally consistent, and internationally converged; for the standards to be clearly based on consistent principles that are rooted in fundamental concepts rather than a collection of conventions; for the body of standards taken as a whole, as well as the application of those standards, to be based on a sound, comprehensive, and internally consistent framework; and convergence of the standards of the two Boards.

APPENDIX: FASB CODIFICATION PROJECT

On July 1, 2009, the Financial Accounting Standards Board (FASB) launched the *FASB Accounting Standards Codification* as the single source of authoritative nongovernmental U.S. generally accepted accounting principles (GAAP). The Codification is effective for interim and annual periods ending after September 15, 2009. All existing accounting standards documents are integrated into the new codification (and thus superseded), as described in *FASB Statement No. 168*, "The FASB Accounting Standards Codification and the Hierarchy of Generally Accepted Accounting Principles." All other accounting literature not included in the Codification is nonauthoritative.

While not intended to change existing U.S. GAAP, the purpose of the Codification is to integrate existing accounting standards by multiple standard-setters within levels A through D of the current GAAP hierarchy. Cross-references are provided to link the Codification to the original standards. The Codification also contains relevant portions of authoritative content issued by the Securities and Exchange Commission as well as selected SEC staff interpretations and administrative guidelines.

It does not include SEC staff speeches, testimony, or Current Issues and Rulemaking Projects (CIRPs), nor does it include pronouncements of the IASB. Nonetheless, one expectation of the Codification's implementation is that it will ease the convergence of U.S. GAAP and international standards (IFRS); and the material correlates at the topic and section levels to IFRS. As we move forward, future U.S. accounting standards will be issued in the form of an update to the appropriate topic or subtopic within the Codification.

The FASB had been working on this project to codify by topic the body of U.S. GAAP for several years. The codification is intended to simplify the classification of existing and future standards by restructuring all authoritative U.S. GAAP (other than that for governmental entities) into one online database under a common referencing system. The codification is organized in a tiered structure consisting of a framework of topics, subtopics, sections, subsections, and paragraphs on each subject. The Codification does not codify all GAAP since the GAAP hierarchy also includes items such as practice, textbooks, articles, and other similar content. Thus referencing the Codification will be used instead of referring to specific FASB statements. In fact, the FASB will no longer issue statements, but will instead issue updates to the Codification. The Codification will replace the GAAP hierarchy.

GAAP pronouncements are divided into roughly 90 accounting topics, and all topics are displayed using a consistent structure. In order to apply or search the Codification, one must understand the structure of the Codification. References to the Codification will contain four groupings of numbers. These four numbered items refer to (1) the topic, (2) the subtopic, (3) the section, and (4) the paragraph number for the appropriate accounting. Thus the code 450-20-25-2 refers to topic 450 (which is 'contingencies'); subtopic 20 (which is loss 'contingencies'); section 25 (which is recognition); and 2 (refers to the second paragraph).

Topics are organized in four main areas:

1. Presentation (Topic Codes 205–299). These Topics relate only to presentation matters and do not address recognition, measurement, and derecognition matters. Topics include Income Statement, Balance Sheet, Earnings per Share, etc.
2. Financial Statement Accounts (Topic Codes 305–700). The Codification organizes Topics in financial statement order including Assets, Liabilities, Equity, Revenue, and Expenses. Topics include Receivables, Revenue Recognition, Inventory, etc.
3. Broad Transactions (Topic codes 805–899). These Topics relate to multiple financial statement accounts and are generally transaction-oriented. Topics include Business Combinations, Derivatives, Nonmonetary Transactions, etc.
4. Industries (Topic codes 905–999). These Topics relate to accounting that is unique to an industry or type of activity. Topics include Airlines, Software, Real Estate, etc.

Throughout this textbook, we reference the codification using topic number only on occasion (i.e., ASC 810 "Consolidations") or in many instances using up to four groupings of numbers (i.e., ASC 810-20-25-4).

The Codification includes the following literature issued by various standard setters that apply to all entities (other than governmental entities).

Standards Issued by Standard Setters Other than the SEC

a. Financial Accounting Standards Board (FASB)
   1. Statements (FAS)
   2. Interpretations (FIN)
   3. Technical Bulletins (FTB)
   4. Staff Positions (FSP)
   5. Staff Implementation Guides (Q&A)
   6. Statement No. 138 Examples

b. Emerging Issues Task Force (EITF)
   1. Abstracts
   2. Topic D

c. Derivative Implementation Group (DIG) Issues

d. Accounting Principles Board (APB) Opinions

e. Accounting Research Bulletins (ARB)

f. Accounting Interpretations (AIN)

g. American Institute of Certified Public Accountants (AICPA)
   1. Statements of Position (SOP)
   2. Audit and Accounting Guides (AAG)—only incremental accounting guidance
   3. Practice Bulletins (PB), including the Notices to Practitioners elevated to Practice Bulletin status by Practice Bulletin 1
   4. Technical Inquiry Service (TIS)—only for Software Revenue Recognition

Standards Issued by the SEC

To increase the utility of the Codification for public companies, relevant portions of authoritative content issued by the SEC and selected SEC staff interpretations and administrative guidance have been included for reference in the Codification, such as:

(a) Regulation S-X (SX)

(b) Financial Reporting Releases (FRR)/Accounting Series Releases (ASR)

(c) Interpretive Releases (IR)

(d) SEC Staff guidance in
   1. Staff Accounting Bulletins (SAB)
   2. EITF Topic D and SEC Staff Observer comments.

TEST YOUR KNOWLEDGE SOLUTIONS

1. a. poison pill
   b. leveraged buyout (LBO)
   c. white knight
2. d
3. d

QUESTIONS

LO2 1. Distinguish between internal and external expansion of a firm.

LO2 2. List four advantages of a business combination as compared to internal expansion.

LO1 3. What is the primary legal constraint on business combinations? Why does such a constraint exist?

LO2 4. Business combinations may be classified into three types based upon the relationships among the combining entities (e.g., combinations with suppliers, customers, competitors, etc.). Identify and define these types.

LO5 5. Distinguish among a statutory merger, a statutory consolidation, and a stock acquisition.

LO4 6. Define a tender offer and describe its use.

LO6 7. When stock is exchanged for stock in a business combination, how is the stock exchange ratio generally expressed?

LO4 8. Define some defensive measures used by target firms to avoid a takeover. Are these measures beneficial for shareholders?

LO5 9. Explain the potential advantages of a stock acquisition over an asset acquisition.

LO6 10. Explain the difference between an accretive and a dilutive acquisition.

LO8 11. Describe the difference between the economic entity concept and the parent company concept approaches to the reporting of subsidiary assets and liabilities in the consolidated financial statements on the date of the acquisition.

LO8 12. Contrast the consolidated effects of the parent company concept and the economic entity concept in terms of:

(a) The treatment of noncontrolling interests.

(b) The elimination of intercompany profits.

(c) The valuation of subsidiary net assets in the consolidated financial statements.

(d) The definition of consolidated net income.

LO8 13. Under the economic entity concept, the net assets of the subsidiary are included in the consolidated financial statements at the total fair value that is implied by the price paid by the parent company for its controlling interest. What practical or conceptual problems do you see in this approach to valuation?

LO9 14. Is the economic entity or the parent concept more consistent with the principles addressed in the FASB's conceptual framework? Explain your answer.

LO9 15. How does the FASB's conceptual framework influence the development of new standards?

LO9 16. What is the difference between net income, or earnings, and comprehensive income?

Business Ethics

From 1999 to 2001, Tyco's revenue grew approximately 24% and it acquired over 700 companies. It was widely rumored that Tyco executives aggressively managed the performance of the companies that they acquired by suggesting that before the acquisition, they should accelerate the payment of liabilities, delay recording the collections of revenue, and increase the estimated amounts in reserve accounts.

1. What effect does each of the three items have on the reported net income of the acquired company before the acquisition and on the reported net income of the combined company in the first year of the acquisition and future years?
2. What effect does each of the three items have on the cash from operations of the acquired company before the acquisition and on the cash from operations of the combined company in the first year of the acquisition and future years?
3. If you are the manager of the acquired company, how do you respond to these suggestions?
4. Assume that all three items can be managed within the rules provided by GAAP but would be regarded by many as pushing the limits of GAAP. Is there an ethical issue? Describe your position as: (A) an accountant for the target company and (B) as an accountant for Tyco.

EXERCISES

EXERCISE 1-1 **Estimating Goodwill and Potential Offering Price** LO7

Plantation Homes Company is considering the acquisition of Condominiums, Inc. early in 2008. To assess the amount it might be willing to pay, Plantation Homes makes the following computations and assumptions.

A. Condominiums, Inc. has identifiable assets with a total fair value of $15,000,000 and liabilities of $8,800,000. The assets include office equipment with a fair value approximating book value, buildings with a fair value 30% higher than book value, and land with a fair value 75% higher than book value. The remaining lives of the assets are deemed to be approximately equal to those used by Condominiums, Inc.

B. Condominiums, Inc.'s pretax incomes for the years 2005 through 2007 were $1,200,000, $1,500,000, and $950,000, respectively. Plantation Homes believes that an average of these earnings represents a fair estimate of annual earnings for the indefinite future. However, it may need to consider adjustments to the following items included in pretax earnings:

Depreciation on buildings (each year)	960,000
Depreciation on equipment (each year)	50,000
Extraordinary loss (year 2007)	300,000
Sales commissions (each year)	250,000

C. The normal rate of return on net assets for the industry is 15%.

Required:

A. Assume further that Plantation Homes feels that it must earn a 25% return on its investment and that goodwill is determined by capitalizing excess earnings. Based on these assumptions, calculate a reasonable offering price for Condominiums, Inc. Indicate how much of the price consists of goodwill. Ignore tax effects.

B. Assume that Plantation Homes feels that it must earn a 15% return on its investment, but that average excess earnings are to be capitalized for three years only. Based on these assumptions, calculate a reasonable offering price for Condominiums, Inc. Indicate how much of the price consists of goodwill. Ignore tax effects.

EXERCISE 1-2 Estimating Goodwill and Valuation LO7

Alpha Company is considering the purchase of Beta Company. Alpha has collected the following data about Beta:

	Beta Company Book Values	*Estimated Market Values*
Total identifiable assets	$585,000	$750,000
Total liabilities	320,000	320,000
Owners' equity	$265,000	

Cumulative total net cash earnings for the past five years of $850,000 includes extraordinary cash gains of $67,000 and nonrecurring cash losses of $48,000.

Alpha Company expects a return on its investment of 15%. Assume that Alpha prefers to use cash earnings rather than accrual-based earnings to estimate its offering price, and that it estimates the total valuation of Beta to be equal to the present value of cash-based earnings (rather than excess earnings) discounted over five years. (Goodwill is then computed as the amount implied by the excess of the total valuation over the identifiable net assets valuation.)

Required:

A. Compute (a) an offering price based on the information above that Alpha might be willing to pay, and (b) the amount of goodwill included in that price.

B. Compute the amount of goodwill actually recorded, assuming the negotiations result in a final purchase price of $625,000 cash.

EXERCISE 1-3 Estimated and Actual Goodwill LO7

Passion Company is trying to decide whether or not to acquire Desiree Inc. The following balance sheet for Desiree Inc. provides information about book values. Estimated market values are also listed, based upon Passion Company's appraisals.

	Desiree Inc. Book Values	*Desiree Inc. Market Values*
Current assets	$260,000	$ 260,000
Property, plant & equipment (net)	650,000	740,000
Total assets	$910,000	$1,000,000
Total liabilities	$400,000	$ 400,000
Common stock, $10 par value	160,000	
Retained earnings	350,000	
Total liabilities and equities	$910,000	

Passion Company expects that Desiree will earn approximately $150,000 per year in net income over the next five years. This income is higher than the 12% annual return on tangible assets considered to be the industry "norm."

Required:

A. Compute an estimation of goodwill based on the information above that Passion might be willing to pay (include in its purchase price), under each of the following additional assumptions:

(1) Passion is willing to pay for *excess* earnings for an expected life of five years (undiscounted).

(2) Passion is willing to pay for *excess* earnings for an expected life of five years, which should be capitalized at the industry normal rate of return.

(3) Excess earnings are expected to last indefinitely, but Passion demands a higher rate of return of 20% because of the risk involved.

B. Comment on the relative merits of the three alternatives in part (A) above.

C. Determine the amount of goodwill to be recorded on the books if Passion pays $800,000 cash and assumes Desiree's liabilities.

2

ACCOUNTING FOR BUSINESS COMBINATIONS

LEARNING OBJECTIVES

1. Describe the major changes in the accounting for business combinations passed by the FASB in December 2007, and the reasons for those changes.
2. Describe the two major changes in the accounting for business combinations approved by the FASB in 2001, as well as the reasons for those changes.
3. Discuss the goodwill impairment test described in ***SFAS No. 142*** **[ASC 350-20-35]**, including its frequency, the steps laid out in the new standard, and some of the likely implementation problems.
4. Explain how acquisition expenses are reported.
5. Describe the use of pro forma statements in business combinations.
6. Describe the valuation of assets, including goodwill, and liabilities acquired in a business combination accounted for by the acquisition method.
7. Explain how contingent consideration affects the valuation of assets acquired in a business combination accounted for by the acquisition method.
8. Describe a leveraged buyout.
9. Describe the disclosure requirements according to ***SFAS No. 141R*** **[ASC 805-10-50]**, "Business Combinations," related to each business combination that takes place during a given year.
10. Describe at least one of the differences between U.S. GAAP and IFRS related to the accounting for business combinations.

HISTORICAL PERSPECTIVE ON BUSINESS COMBINATIONS

In response to possible changes to the tax code by the IRS, which could greatly alter how changes in the value of intangible assets affect a company's tax liability, Selva Ozelli, a CPA and international tax expert, stated that intangibles are "the main drivers of economic value creation and economic growth in American multinational companies...[and] contribute significantly to an enterprise's competitive advantage. They often have the potential to yield above-average profits, while physical and financial assets are rapidly becoming commoditized."[1]

[1] *Accounting Today*, "New Regs Would Change the Landscape for Intangibles," by Roger Russell, 9/26/05, p. 3.

LO1 FASB's two major changes for business combinations.

What's New? FASB shook up the accounting community in the area of business combinations in December of 2007 by releasing two new standards. The first, ***SFAS No. 141R*** **[ASC 805]**, "Business Combinations," completely replaced ***FASB Statement No. 141***. This pronouncement supports the use of a single method in accounting for business combinations, and uses the term "acquisition method" in place of the previous term, "purchase method," to describe the preferred approach. Most of the primary conclusions reached in ***SFAS No. 141*** (and elaborated upon in the following paragraph) are carried forward without reconsideration. The differences addressed in the newer standard related to a number of criticisms that have haunted the accounting for business combinations for some time.

One of the criticisms is that the standards of accounting for business combinations differ significantly between U.S. GAAP and International Financial Reporting Standards (IFRS). In 2002 the two principal standard setting boards, the FASB and the IASB (International Accounting Standards Board), agreed to reconsider the topic jointly with the objective of convergence, or finding a common and comprehensive standard that could be used both domestically and in cross-border situations. Nonetheless, the standards are not identical. Those differences are described at the end of this chapter.

The objective of the change was to recommend a single method that should result in more comparable and transparent financial statements. The essence of the change is that the acquired business should be recognized at its fair value on the acquisition date rather than its cost, regardless of whether the acquirer purchases all or only a controlling percentage (even if the combination is achieved in stages). In the past, when a business combination was achieved in stages (for example, a company purchases 20% of another company at one date, purchases an additional 20% a number of years later, and then achieves control by purchasing 12% at a still later date), the cost amounts from prior purchases (which might have occurred decades earlier) were combined with current values to create an accumulated total that reflected a mix of fair values and old book values being carried forward. This combination of amounts has long been criticized as lacking consistency, understandability, and usefulness. **Under *SFAS No. 141R* [ASC 805], the fair values of all assets and liabilities on the acquisition date, defined as the date the acquirer obtains control of the acquiree, are reflected in the financial statements**. This change has the potential to affect the timing and the structure of deals.

The amendment to business combinations, put forward jointly by the International Accounting Standards Board (IASB) and U.S. Financial Accounting Standards Board (FASB), has its share of opponents. Various parties, including companies, analysts, accountants and regulatory bodies, tried to block the change, which they claimed was an effort by the standard setters to implement new rules rather than fine-tune the existing ones. The new standard places emphasis on fair values in a business combination, even in cases where less than 100% of the equity interests in the acquiree are purchased. Opponents state that the outcome of placing more goodwill on a company's financial statement is to produce artificial figures that fail to reflect the true value of a takeover transaction.[2]

[2] *Finance Week*, "Analysis: New Merger Rules to Increase Scrutiny in Deal-Making," 11/16/05, p. 14.

CHANGES IN GAAP [TOPIC 805] WITH SIGNIFICANT IMPLICATIONS FOR DEALS

Issue	*Prior GAAP*	*Current GAAP*
Measurement date for securities issued	Use a reasonable period of time before and after the terms are agreed to and announced.	Use the fair value on the acquisition date.
Acquisitions costs	Capitalize the costs.	Expense as incurred.
Acquisition of control but less than 100%	Minority interest is recorded at historical cost.	Non-controlling interest is recorded at fair value along with 100% of the goodwill.
In-process R&D	Included as part of purchase price, but then immediately expenses.	Included as part of purchase price, treated as an asset.
Negative goodwill	Reduction of certain noncurrent assets with the remained as extraordinary gain.	No reduction of assets is recorded, record as a gain on the income statement.
Contingent consideration	Record when determinable and reflect subsequent changes in the purchase price.	Record at fair value on the acquisition date with subsequent changes recorded on the income statement.
Business definition	A business is defined as a self-sustaining integrated set of activities and assets conducted and managed for the purpose of providing a return to investors. The definition would exclude early-stage development entities.	A business or a *group of assets* no longer must be self-sustaining. The business or group of assets must be capable of generating a revenue stream. This definition would include early-stage development entities.
Decreases in ownership interest	Include gains and losses on decreases in ownership interest in income.	Decreases in ownership (if control is still maintained) are capital transactions. Decreases in ownership accompanied by a loss of control result in a gain or loss. The gain or loss is realized on the portion of interest sold an unrealized on the equity interests retained.

SFAS No. 141R [topic 805] also broadens the scope of the standard to apply to business combinations involving only mutual entities, those achieved by contract alone, and the initial consolidation of variable interest entities (VIEs). Variable interest entities are discussed in Chapter 3.

The second standard, also issued on December 4, 2007, "Noncontrolling Interests in Consolidated Financial Statements," **[ASC 810]** amended *Accounting Research Bulletin (ARB) No. 51*. This pronouncement established standards for the reporting of the noncontrolling interest when the acquirer obtains control without purchasing

100% of the acquiree. A noncontrolling (or minority) interest does not exist in net asset acquisitions, which are the focus of this chapter. Thus most of the discussion of this issue is deferred to Chapter 3.

Previous Change In a unanimous vote in 2001, the *Financial Accounting Standards Board (FASB)* reaffirmed a decision that had drawn strong opposition from businesses and had led some members of Congress to propose legislative intervention. But opposition softened when the Board voted to change the alternative method of accounting for mergers, purchase accounting, to make it less onerous. Companies had often tried to avoid 'purchase accounting' because it required them to add the intangible asset goodwill to their balance sheets and then write off the goodwill over 20 years or more, lowering profits. But the Board decided that it would no longer require, or even allow, the write-off of goodwill until the company concluded that its value was impaired. This could mean higher profits.[3]

RELATED CONCEPTS

Requiring one method for all acquisitions makes financial statements more *comparable* across firms than allowing two methods for similar events.

Historically, two distinct methods of accounting for business combinations were permitted in the United States: purchase and pooling of interests. Although the majority of mergers were accounted for by the purchase method, in cases where the stock of one company was being exchanged for all the assets or most of the stock (90% or more) of the other, firms sometimes went to great lengths to satisfy an elaborate set of pooling criteria laid out by the U.S. standard setters. Today all mergers in the United States must be accounted for by the acquisition (or purchase) method.

With the issuance of ***SFAS No. 141***, "Business Combinations," **[ASC 805]** and ***SFAS No. 142***, "Goodwill and Other Intangible Assets," **[ASC 810]** in June 2001, the FASB culminated a project on business combinations brought to its agenda in August 1996 to reconsider ***APB Opinion No. 16***, "Business Combinations," and ***APB Opinion No. 17***, "Intangible Assets." Although some companies' management and even analysts responded initially with rosy predictions that the earnings numbers would look a lot ***better*** for companies with large amounts of goodwill, less than a year later many of these same firms were writing off large chunks of goodwill under the new impairment rules.

LO2 FASB's two major changes of 2001.

In a pronouncement issued in June 2001, **the Board reaffirmed its proposal to prohibit the popular method referred to as the pooling of interests and decided that goodwill would no longer be amortized and would instead be tested periodically for impairment in a manner different from other assets.** Specifically, use of the pooling method has been prohibited for business combinations initiated since June 30, 2001. Goodwill acquired in a business combination completed since June 30, 2001, should not be amortized.

The Board included the following statements in justifying the changes: Analysts and other users of financial statements indicated that it was difficult to compare the financial results of entities because different methods of accounting for business combinations were used. Users of financial statements also indicated a need for better information about intangible assets because those assets are an increasingly important economic resource for many entities and are an increasing proportion of the assets acquired in many business combinations. Company managements indicated that the differences between the pooling and purchase methods of accounting for business combinations affected competition in markets for mergers and acquisitions.

[3] *New York Times*, "Board Ends Method of Accounting for Mergers," by Floyd Norris, 1/25/01, p. C9.

As might be predicted, responses to the changes ranged from complaints that the FASB had "given away the store"[4] to praise that the combined changes would yield enhanced flexibility for businesses.

Others, such as Morgan Stanley Dean Witter's Trevor Harris, argued from the onset that there should be no long-term effect on stock prices and that any initial price effect from the changed accounting standards was merely a momentum play.[5]

While fans of the standards regarding goodwill accounting applauded their flexibility, critics questioned whether the goodwill impairment test opens the door for manipulation of earnings via the timing of write-offs, and some suggested an increase in hostile activity.

Goodwill Impairment Test

LO3 Goodwill impairment assessment.

SFAS No. 142 **[ASC 350–20–35]** requires that goodwill impairment be tested annually and that—for all significant ***prior*** acquisitions—a benchmark goodwill assessment be conducted within six months of adoption of the new standard. Transitional rules for impairment of previously recognized goodwill allowed firms taking impairment losses on adoption to treat those items as below-the-line charges shown after extraordinary items on the income statement. This option, however, was not available in subsequent years.

Robert Willens of Lehman Brothers predicted that most companies facing impaired goodwill would prefer to take the charges soon rather than later. "If an impairment is indicated," said Willens, "you want to do this in 2002. You can explain it more easily now as part of adopting new rules. That's because, during the first year after the treatment goes into effect, goodwill impairment charges show up as the cumulative effect of a change in accounting principles."[6]

For purposes of the goodwill impairment test, all goodwill must be assigned to a reporting unit. Goodwill impairment for each reporting unit should be tested in a two-step process. In the first step, the fair value of a reporting unit is compared to its carrying amount (goodwill included) at the date of the periodic review. The fair value of the unit may be based on quoted market prices, prices of comparable businesses, or a present value or other valuation technique. If the fair value at the review date is less than the carrying amount, then the second step is necessary. In the second step, the carrying value of the goodwill is compared to its implied fair value. See Figure 2-1 for a visual illustration of this process.

What is a reporting unit? A reporting unit is the level at which management reviews and assesses the operating segment's performance—in other words, discrete business lines or units that can be grouped by geography and can produce stand-alone financial statements (for example, four operating divisions reporting to the corporate parent). A company can use a reporting unit one level below the operating segment for impairment testing if components of an operating segment engage in business activities for which discrete financial information is available, have economic characteristics different from the other components of the operating segments, and are at the level at which goodwill benefits are realized.

---

[4] *WSJ*, "FASB Backs Down on Goodwill-Accounting Rules," 12/7/00, page A2.

[5] *WSJ*, "Goodwill Hunting: Accounting Change May Lift Profits, but Stock Prices May Not Follow Suit," by Jonathan Weil, 1/25/01, p. C1.

[6] *WSJ Online*, "Study Sees Hundred of Companies Writing Down Goodwill This Year," by Henny Sender, 4/24/02, *wsj.com*.

FIGURE 2-1
Goodwill Impairment Tests

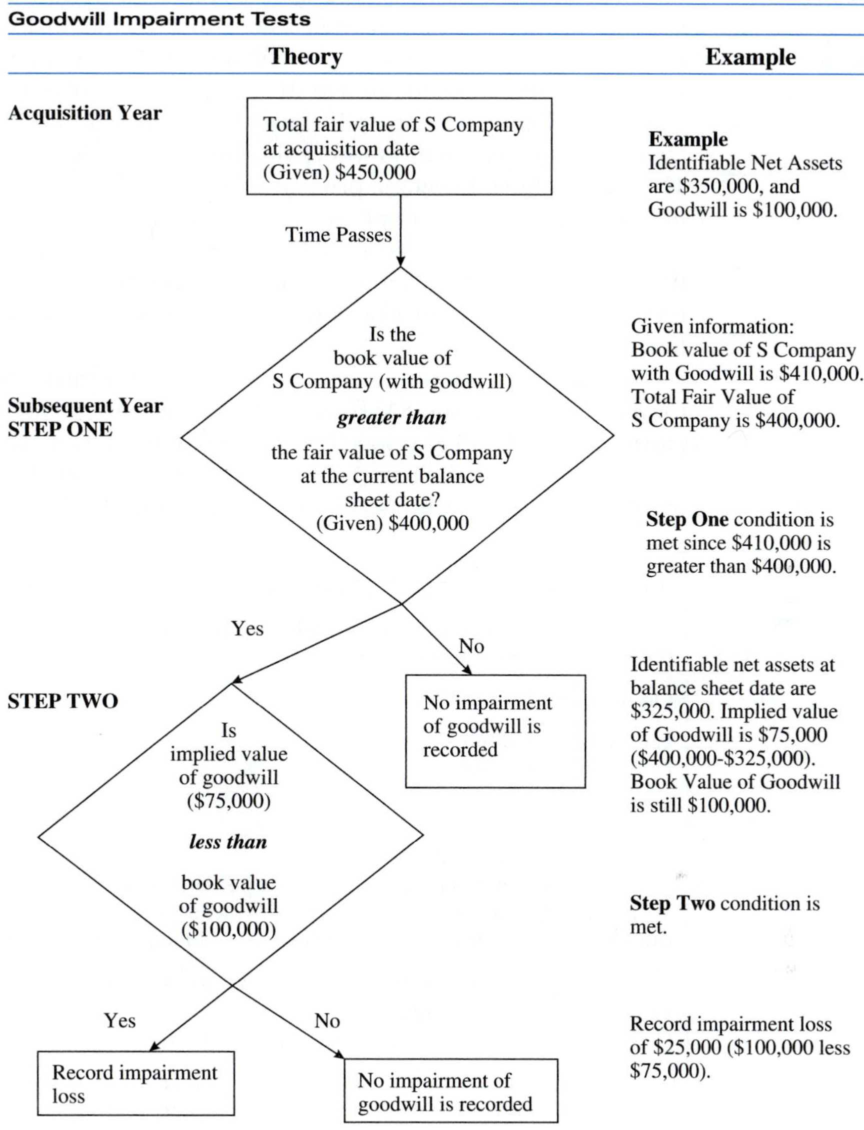
Theory
Example
Acquisition Year
Total fair value of S Company at acquisition date (Given) $450,000
Example
Identifiable Net Assets are $350,000, and Goodwill is $100,000.
Time Passes
Subsequent Year
STEP ONE
Is the book value of S Company (with goodwill) greater than the fair value of S Company at the current balance sheet date? (Given) $400,000
Given information:
Book value of S Company with Goodwill is $410,000.
Total Fair Value of S Company is $400,000.
Step One condition is met since $410,000 is greater than $400,000.
Yes
No
STEP TWO
No impairment of goodwill is recorded
Is implied value of goodwill ($75,000) less than book value of goodwill ($100,000)
Identifiable net assets at balance sheet date are $325,000. Implied value of Goodwill is $75,000 ($400,000-$325,000). Book Value of Goodwill is still $100,000.
Step Two condition is met.
Yes
No
Record impairment loss
No impairment of goodwill is recorded
Record impairment loss of $25,000 ($100,000 less $75,000).

IN THE NEWS

How tough is it to establish a value for the reporting unit? Businesses may not like the impairment rules because of the difficulty they have determining the fair value of the segment. However, if the reporting unit is a whole company, the current stock price will represent fair value. Although many finance managers object that current trading price doesn't always reflect fair value, CPAs like this measure because it is objective and verifiable.[7]

[7] *Journal of Accountancy*, "Say Goodbye to Pooling and Goodwill Amortization," by S. R. Moehrle and J. A. Reynolds-Moehrle, September 2001, p. 31.

RELATED CONCEPTS

Objectivity and verifiability are specified in *SFAC No. 2* as attributes of *reliability*.

The calculation of the implied fair value of goodwill used in the impairment test is similar to the method illustrated later in this chapter for valuing the goodwill at the date of the combination. The FASB specifies that an entity should allocate the fair value of the reporting unit at the review date to all of its assets and liabilities (including unrecognized intangible assets other than goodwill) as if the unit had been acquired in a combination where the fair value of the unit was the purchase price. The excess of that purchase price over the fair value of identifiable net assets (assets minus liabilities) is the implied fair value of the goodwill.

After a goodwill impairment loss is recognized, the adjusted carrying amount of the goodwill becomes its new accounting basis. Subsequent reversal of a previously recognized impairment loss is prohibited once the measurement of that loss has been completed.

If an impairment test for goodwill occurs at the same time as an impairment test for any other asset, the FASB instructs that the other asset should be tested for impairment first. FASB also specifies that intangible assets other than goodwill should be amortized over their useful lives (if finite lives exist) and reviewed for impairment in accordance with ***SFAS No. 142*** **[ASC 350–30–35–17, 18]**.

ILLUSTRATION OF DETERMINING GOODWILL IMPAIRMENT

There are two steps in determining whether the value of goodwill has been impaired. Assume the following information

On the date of acquisition:

Fair value of the reporting unit	$450,000
Fair value of identifiable net assets	350,000
Goodwill	$100,000

On the first periodic review date:

The first step determines if there is a potential impairment. Step two will be needed only if the carrying value of the reporting unit (including goodwill) is larger than the fair value of the reporting unit. If the carrying value is less, no impairment is considered.

Step One: Does potential impairment exist (i.e., is step two needed)?

Fair value of the reporting unit	$400,000
Carrying value of reporting unit (includes goodwill)	410,000

Potential goodwill impairment must be further considered if the carrying value of the reporting unit is larger than $400,000, in this example. If this occurs, then proceed to step two.

Step two determines the amount of the impairment (if any). In step two, the fair value of goodwill is determined by comparing the fair value of the reporting unit at the periodic review date to the fair value of the identifiable net assets at this time. (The difference is the implied value of goodwill on this date.)

Step Two: What is the amount of goodwill impairment (if any)?

Fair value of the reporting unit	$400,000
Fair value of identifiable net assets at review date	325,000
Fair value of goodwill (implied)	$ 75,000

Since the carrying value of goodwill is $100,000 and the remaining fair value of goodwill is $75,000, goodwill impairment of $25,000 must be reported.

Carrying value of goodwill	$100,000
Fair value of goodwill	75,000
Goodwill impairment loss	$ 25,000

Disclosures Mandated by FASB

SFAS No. 141R **[ASC 805]** requires the following disclosures for goodwill:

RELATED CONCEPTS

***Full disclosure* suggests that all important aspects of acquisitions should be revealed to readers of the financial statements. This includes the reasons for subsequent impairment losses.**

1. The total amount of acquired goodwill and the amount expected to be deductible for tax purposes.
2. The amount of goodwill by reporting segment (if the acquiring firm is required to disclose segment information in accordance with *SFAS No. 131* **[ASC 280]**, "Disclosures about Segments of an Enterprise and Related Information"), unless not practicable.

SFAS No. 142 **[ASC 350–20–45]** specifies the presentation of goodwill in the balance sheet and income statement (if impairment occurs) as follows:

a. The aggregate amount of goodwill should be a separate line item in the balance sheet.
b. The aggregate amount of losses from goodwill impairment should be shown as a separate line item in the operating section of the income statement unless some of the impairment is associated with a discontinued operation (in which case it is shown net-of-tax in the discontinued operations section).

In a period in which an impairment loss occurs, *SFAS No. 142* **[ASC 350–20–50–2]** mandates the following disclosures in the notes:

1. A description of the facts and circumstances leading to the impairment.
2. The amount of the impairment loss and the method of determining the fair value of the reporting unit.
3. The nature and amounts of any adjustments made to impairment estimates from earlier periods, if significant.

CBS Corp. announced that it wrote down the goodwill value of its television and radio assets by $9.5 billion to $13.5 billion, resulting in a sizable fourth quarter loss. It is the second consecutive year CBS has taken a goodwill write-down under the accounting rule that requires an annual test for impairment of intangible assets. The most recent write-down is reflective of continued challenges and slow growth in the radio and broadcast television industries.[8]

LO9 New disclosure requirements for business combinations.

Other Required Disclosures *SFAS No. 141R* **[ASC 805–10–50–2]** states that to meet its objectives, the acquirer should disclose pertinent information for each material business combination that takes place during the reporting period, to include the following:

- The name and a description of the acquiree.
- The acquisition date.
- The percentage of voting equity instruments acquired.
- The primary reasons for the business combination, including a description of the factors that contributed to the recognition of goodwill.

[8] *WSJ*, "CBS Posts $9.14 Billion Loss on Hefty Asset Write-Downs," Brooks Barnes, 2/23/06.

- The fair value of the acquiree and the basis for measuring that value on the acquisition date.
- The fair value of the consideration transferred, including the fair value of each major class of consideration.
- The amounts recognized at the acquisition date for each major class of assets acquired and liabilities assumed in the form of a condensed balance sheet.
- The maximum potential amount of future payments the acquirer could be required to make under the terms of the acquisition agreement.

A portion of auditors' testimony in the case against former Enron Corp. Chairman Kenneth Lay focused on the "alleged downward manipulation of charges for goodwill expenses." Prosecutors argued that Mr. Lay misled the company's auditors in October 2001 regarding Enron's plans for a water-distribution unit in order to avoid big charges to earnings. The accounting rules introduced in 2001 require a company to write-down an asset if it doesn't meet certain standards, which in the water-distribution's case included whether the company had a costly growth plan. Without such a plan, Enron would have been forced to recognize impairment in an amount in the hundreds of millions of dollars. At the time of the audit, Lay claimed the company planned to spend over $1 billion on the unit; this statement contradicted earlier claims that the company was going to sell the water operation, a non-core business.[9]

Other Intangible Assets

An acquired intangible asset other than goodwill should be amortized over its useful economic life if the asset has a limited useful life. Such assets should be reviewed for impairment in accordance with ***SFAS No. 144*** **[ASC 350–30–35–10]**, "Accounting for the Impairment or Disposal of Long-Lived Assets." However, if an acquired intangible asset other than goodwill has an indefinite life, it should not be amortized until its life is determined to be finite. Instead it should be tested annually (at a minimum) for impairment.

FASB recognized the possible impact of the standard on earnings volatility in the following statements: Because goodwill and some intangible assets are no longer amortized, the reported amounts of goodwill and intangible assets (as well as total assets) do not decrease at the same time and in the same manner as under previous standards. There may be more volatility in reported income than under previous standards because impairment losses are likely to occur irregularly and in varying amounts.

Treatment of Acquisition Expenses

LO4 Reporting acquisition expenses.

Under ***SFAS No. 141R*** **[ASC 805–10–25–23]**, acquisition-related costs are excluded from the measurement of the consideration paid, because such costs are not part of the fair value of the acquiree and are not assets. This is a change from past GAAP

[9] *WSJ*, "Enron Former Auditors Testify on Charges, Reserve Accounts," by Gary McWilliams and John R. Emshwiller, 3/21/06, p. C3.

where the purchase method required only indirect costs to be expensed, while direct costs were capitalized as part of the purchase price. ***Direct expenses*** *incurred in the combination include finder's fees, as well as advisory, legal, accounting, valuation, and other professional or consulting fees.* ***Indirect****, ongoing costs include the cost to maintain a mergers and acquisitions department, as well as other general administrative costs such as managerial or secretarial time and overhead that are allocated to the merger but would have existed in its absence.* ***SFAS No. 141R*** **[ASC 805–20]** requires that both direct and indirect costs be expensed, and that the cost of issuing securities also be excluded from the consideration and accounted for separately from the business combination accounting. Expected restructuring costs (with no obligation at the acquisition date) are also accounted for separately from the business combination. In the absence of more explicit guidance, we assume that ***security issuance costs*** are *assigned to the valuation of the security*, thus reducing the additional contributed capital for stock issues or adjusting the premium or discount on bond issues.

ACQUISITION COSTS—AN ILLUSTRATION

Suppose that SMC Company acquires 100% of the net assets of Bee Company (net book value of $100,000) by issuing shares of common stock with a fair value of $120,000. With respect to the merger, SMC incurred $1,500 of accounting and consulting costs and $3,000 of stock issue costs. SMC maintains a mergers department that incurred a monthly cost of $2,000. The following illustrates how these direct and indirect merger costs and the security issue costs are recorded.

ACQUISITION ACCOUNTING:

Professional Fees Expense (Direct)	1,500	
Merger Department Expense (Indirect)	2,000	
Other Contributed Capital (Security Issue Costs)*	3,000	
Cash		$6,500

* *SFAS No. 141R* [paragraph 805-10-25-23] states that the costs to issue debt or equity securities shall be recognized in accordance with other applicable GAAP.

PRO FORMA STATEMENTS AND DISCLOSURE REQUIREMENT

LO5 Use of pro forma statements.

Pro forma statements, sometimes called **"as if"** statements, are prepared to show the effect of planned or contemplated transactions by showing how they might have affected the historical financial statements if they had been consummated during the period covered by those statements. Pro forma statements serve two functions in relation to business combinations: (1) to provide information in the ***planning*** stages of the combination and (2) to ***disclose*** relevant information subsequent to the combination.

First, pro forma statements are often prepared before the fact for combinations under consideration. When management is contemplating the purchase price offer, for example, a number of pro forma statements may be produced, using different assumed purchase prices and projecting one or more years into the future, or alternatively restating a past period as though the firms had been combined. After the boards of directors of the constituents have reached tentative agreement on a combination proposal, pro forma statements showing the effects of the proposal may be prepared for distribution to the stockholders of the constituents for their consideration prior to voting on the proposal. If the proposed combination involves the issue of new securities under *Securities and Exchange Commission (SEC)* rules, pro forma statements may be required as part of the registration statement.

When a pro forma statement is prepared, the tentative or hypothetical nature of the statement should be clearly indicated, generally by describing it as "pro forma" in the heading and including a description of the character of the transactions given effect to. Further description of any other adjustments should be clearly stated on the statement or in related notes. A pro forma balance sheet (based on data presented in Illustration 2-2) that might be prepared for use by the companies' stockholders is presented in Illustration 2-1. The normal procedure is to show the audited balance sheet as of a given date, individual adjustments for the proposed transaction, and resulting account balances.

Second, pro forma presentation is a valuable method of disclosing relevant information to stockholders and other users subsequent to the combination. Some types of pro forma presentation are required by ***SFAS No. 141R*** **[ASC 805–10–50]** if the combined enterprise is a public business enterprise.

If a material business combination (or series of combinations material in the aggregate) occurred during the year, ***notes*** to financial statements should include on a pro forma basis:

1. Results of operations for the current year as though the companies had combined at the beginning of the year, unless the acquisition was at or near the beginning of the year.
2. Results of operations for the immediately preceding period as though the companies had combined at the beginning of that period if comparative financial statements are presented.

ILLUSTRATION 2-1

P Company Pro Forma Balance Sheet
Giving Effect to Proposed Issue of Common Stock for All the Net Assets of S Company January 1, 2009

Assets	*Audited Balance Sheet*	*Adjustment*	*Pro Forma Balance Sheet*
Cash and receivables	$ 250,000	$ 170,000	$ 420,000
Inventories	260,000	140,000	400,000
Land	600,000	400,000	1,000,000
Buildings & equipment	800,000	1,000,000	1,800,000
Accumulated depreciation	(300,000)		(300,000)
Goodwill	—0—	230,000	230,000
Total assets	$1,610,000		$3,550,000
Liabilities and Equity			
Current liabilities	$ 110,000	150,000	260,000
Bonds payable	—0—	350,000	350,000
Common stock	750,000	450,000	1,200,000
Other contributed capital	400,000	990,000	1,390,000
Retained earnings	350,000		350,000
Total equities	$1,610,000		$3,550,000

At a minimum, ***SFAS No. 141R*** **[ASC 270–10–S99–1]** requires that the supplemental pro forma information include:

a. Revenue.

b. Income before extraordinary items.

c. Net income.

d. Earnings per share.

e. Nature and amounts of any material, nonrecurring items included in the pro forma amounts.

In determining pro forma amounts, income taxes, interest expense, preferred dividends, and depreciation and amortization of assets should be adjusted to reflect the accounting base used for each in recording the business combination.

TEST YOUR KNOWLEDGE

NOTE: Solutions to ***Test Your Knowledge*** questions are found at the end of each chapter before the end-of-chapter questions.

Multiple Choice

1. Which of the following statements is *true* with respect to the accounting for business combinations under U.S. GAAP?
   a. Incomparability of financial statements under the previous rules permitting two distinct methods of accounting for business combinations (purchase and pooling) was corrected by making amortization of goodwill optional.
   b. Under the current standards, impairment of goodwill is not accounted for because it does not affect the actual profit of the company.
   c. The acquired business should be recognized at its fair value on the acquisition date, regardless of whether the acquirer purchases all or only a controlling percentage.
   d. Any goodwill acquired in previous acquisitions should continue to be amortized after the year 2001 for the continuity of the accounting practice.
2. Goodwill impairment exists only if the fair value of the business unit:
   a. Equals the carrying value of the reporting unit (including goodwill).
   b. Is greater than the carrying value of the reporting unit (including goodwill).
   c. Is less than the carrying value of the reporting unit (including goodwill).
   d. None of the above.
3. Which of the following is *incorrect*?
   a. Under acquisition accounting, direct acquisition costs are recorded by decreasing goodwill as a contra account.
   b. Under acquisition method accounting, indirect acquisition costs (such as expenses incurred by a firm's permanent M&A department) are expensed.
   c. Security issue costs, such as brokerage fees, reduce the Excess Paid In Capital account (i.e., are recorded as a debit to that account).
   d. Accounting and consulting fees incurred in a business combination are expenses under the current standards for acquisitions.

EXPLANATION AND ILLUSTRATION OF ACQUISITION ACCOUNTING

As the term implies, the acquisition method treats the combination as the acquisition of one or more companies by another. The Exposure Draft specifies four steps in the accounting for a business combination:

1. Identify the acquirer.
2. Determine the acquisition date.
3. Measure the fair value of the acquiree.
4. Measure and recognize the assets acquired and liabilities assumed.

Bank of New York will swap its retail banking business for J.P. Morgan Chase's corporate trust unit plus $150 million in cash. The Bank of New York's retail and regional middle-market businesses were valued at $3.1 billion while J.P. Morgan Chase's corporate trust business was valued at $2.8 billion. The difference results in a net cash payment, after negotiations, to Bank of New York.[10]

Assets acquired by issuing shares of stock of the acquiring corporation are recorded at the fair values of the stock given or the assets received, whichever is more clearly evident. If the stock is actively traded, its quoted market price, after making allowance for market fluctuations, additional quantities issued, issue costs, and so on, is normally better evidence of fair value than are appraisal values of the net assets of an acquired company. Thus, an adjusted market price of the shares issued is commonly used. Where the issued stock is of a new or closely held company, however, the fair value of the assets received must generally be used. Any security issuance costs, whether bonds or stocks, incurred to consummate the merger are deducted from the value assigned to the debt or equity.

LO6 Valuation of acquired assets and liabilities assumed.

Identifiable assets acquired (including intangibles other than goodwill) and liabilities assumed should be recorded at their fair values at the date of acquisition. Any excess of total cost over the sum of amounts assigned to identifiable assets and liabilities is recorded as goodwill. Goodwill should not be amortized but should be adjusted downward only when it is "impaired" as described in the preceding section.

In the past, managers seeking to reduce the amount of goodwill recorded as a result of the acquisition sometimes found creative ways to avoid or reduce goodwill prior to the issuance by increasing the amounts allocated to other accounts. One tactic involved identifying *in-process research and development (R&D)* in the acquired company. FASB standards require that R&D costs be expensed as incurred, not capitalized. In an interpretation of the standard on R&D, FASB stated that some forms of R&D, including a specific research project in progress, which transferred in an acquisition, should also be expensed. Furthermore, the amount to be expensed was to be determined not by the original cost of the actual R&D but by the amount paid by the acquiring company. **However, under *SFAS No. 141R* [ASC 805–20],**

[10] *MarketWatch.com*, "Bank of New York, J.P. Morgan Swap Assets," by Kathie O'Donnell, 4/8/06.

in-process R&D is measured and recorded at fair value as an asset on the acquisition date. This requirement does not extend to R&D in contexts other than business combinations. In any event, the importance of maintaining supporting documentation for any amounts assigned to R&D is clear.

St. Jude Medical, Inc. announced that it will acquire Irvine Biomedical, Inc. (IBI), an Irvine, California-based company that develops electrophysiology (EP) catheter products used by physician specialists to diagnose and treat cardiac rhythm disorders. St. Jude foresees recording an in-process R&D charge of $8 to $10 million at closing in connection with this acquisition. Apart from this in-process R&D charge, the transaction will not impact St. Jude's existing EPS guidance for 2004.[11]

When the net amount of the fair values of identifiable assets less liabilities ***exceeds the total cost*** of the acquired company, the acquisition is sometimes referred to as a **bargain**. When a bargain acquisition occurs, either some of the acquired assets must be adjusted downward or a gain must be recognized to balance the accounts. Because of its reluctance to recognize income in a purchase or acquisition (where the usual facets of revenue recognition are absent), the FASB had, in the past, required that most long-lived assets be written down on a pro rata basis in such a situation before recognizing any gain. The Exposure Draft differs markedly. It advises that the fair values be considered carefully, and adjustments made as needed. It does not, however, require that any asset be marked down *below* its fair value. Once that determination is established, then **the excess of acquisition-date fair value of net assets over the consideration paid is recognized in income.**

Acquisition Example Assume that on January 1, 2009, P Company, in a merger, ***acquired the assets*** and assumed the liabilities of S Company. P Company gave one of its $15 par value common shares to the former stockholders of S Company for every two shares of the $5 par value common stock they held. Throughout this text, the company names P and S are frequently used to distinguish a parent company from a subsidiary. In an asset acquisition, these terms are inappropriate because the books of the acquired firm are dissolved at the time of acquisition. Nonetheless, the distinction is useful to avoid confusion between the acquirer and the acquired.

P Company common stock, which was selling at a range of $50 to $52 per share during an extended period prior to the combination, is considered to have a fair value per share of $48 after an appropriate reduction is made in its market value for additional shares issued and for issue costs. The total value of the stock issued is $1,440,000 ($48 × 30,000 shares). Balance sheets for P and S companies (along with relevant fair value data) on January 1, 2009, are presented in Illustration 2-2. Because the book value of the bonds is $400,000, bond discount in the amount of $50,000 ($400,000 − $350,000) must be recorded to reduce the bonds payable to their present value.

[11] *Business Wire*, "St. Jude Medical Announces Agreement to Acquire Irvine Biomedical, Inc.," 8/10/04.

ILLUSTRATION 2-2

Balance Sheets of P and S Companies January 1, 2009

	P Company	*S Company*	
	Book Value	*Book Value*	*Fair Value*
Cash and receivables	$ 250,000	$ 180,000	$ 170,000
Inventories	260,000	100,000	140,000
Land	600,000	120,000	400,000
Buildings & equipment	800,000	900,000	1,000,000
Accumulated depreciation—buildings & equipment	(300,000)	(300,000)	
Total assets	$1,610,000	$1,000,000	$1,710,000
Current liabilities	$ 110,000	$ 110,000	$ 150,000
Bonds payable, 9%, due 1/1/2015, interest payable semiannually on 6/30 and 12/31*	—0—	400,000	350,000
Total liabilities	$ 110,000	$ 510,000	$ 500,000
Stockholders' Equity			
Common stock, $15 par value, 50,000 shares	750,000		
Common stock, $5 par value, 60,000 shares		300,000	
Other contributed capital	400,000	50,000	
Retained earnings	350,000	140,000	
Total Stockholders' equity	1,500,000	490,000	
Total liabilities and stockholders' equity	$1,610,000	$1,000,000	
Net assets at book value (Assets minus liabilities)	$1,500,000	$ 490,000	
Net assets at fair value			$1,210,000

* Bonds payable are valued at their present value by discounting the future payments at the current market rate.

To record the exchange of stock for the net assets of S Company, P Company will make the following entry:

Cash and Receivables	170,000	
Inventories	140,000	
Land	400,000	
Buildings & Equipment (net)	1,000,000	
Discount on Bonds Payable	50,000	
Goodwill (1,440,000 − 1,210,000**)	230,000	
Current Liabilities		150,000
Bonds Payable		400,000
Common Stock* (30,000 × $15)		450,000
Other Contributed Capital* (30,000 × [$48 − $15])		990,000

* The sum of common stock and other contributed capital is $1,440,000.

** Fair value of net assets = $1,710,000 − $500,000 = $1,210,000.

After the merger, S Company ceases to exist as a separate legal entity. Note that under the acquisition method the cost of the net assets is measured by the fair value (30,000 shares × $48 = $1,440,000) of the shares given in exchange. Common stock is credited for the par value of the shares issued, with the remainder credited to other contributed capital. Individual assets acquired and liabilities assumed are recorded at their fair values. Plant assets are recorded at their fair values in their current depreciated state (without an initial balance in accumulated depreciation), the customary procedure for recording the purchase of new or used assets. Bonds

ILLUSTRATION 2-3

P Company Balance Sheet after Acquisition, January 1, 2009

Cash and receivables		$ 420,000
Inventories		400,000
Land		1,000,000
Buildings & equipment	1,800,000	
Accumulated depreciation—buildings & equipment	(300,000)	1,500,000
Goodwill		230,000
Total assets		$3,550,000
Current liabilities		$ 260,000
Bonds payable	$400,000	
Less: Bond discount	50,000	350,000
Total liabilities		610,000
Common stock, $15 par value, 80,000 shares outstanding	1,200,000	
Other contributed capital	1,390,000	
Retained earnings	350,000	
Stockholders' equity		2,940,000
Total liabilities and equity		$3,550,000

payable are recorded at their fair value by recognizing a premium or a discount on the bonds. After all assets and liabilities have been recorded at their fair values, an excess of cost over fair value of $230,000 remains and is recorded as goodwill.

A balance sheet prepared after the acquisition of S Company is presented in Illustration 2-3.

If an acquisition takes place within a fiscal period, GAAP requires the inclusion of the acquired company's revenues and expenses in the purchaser's income statement only from the date of acquisition forward. Income earned by the acquired company prior to the date of acquisition is considered to be included in the net assets acquired.

Income Tax Consequences in Business Combinations

The fair values of specific assets acquired and liabilities assumed in a business combination may differ from the income tax bases of those items. ***SFAS No. 109* [ASC 805–740]** requires that a deferred tax asset or liability be recognized for differences between the assigned values and tax bases of the assets and liabilities recognized in a business combination. The treatment of income tax consequences is addressed in Appendix A.

Bargain Acquisition Illustration (Purchase Price Below Fair Value of Identifiable Net Assets)

When the price paid to acquire another firm is lower than the fair value of identifiable net assets (assets minus liabilities), the acquisition is referred to as a ***bargain***. Although less common than acquisitions involving goodwill, bargain acquisitions do occur and require the application of specific rules to conform to generally accepted accounting principles. In the past (under *FASB Statement No. 141*), those rules were fairly complex. However, ***SFAS No. 141R* [ASC 805–30]** simplified this issue.

Chicago-based Abbott Laboratories completed its $4.1 billion cash acquisition of Guidant Corp.'s vascular-device business. Abbott originally agreed to the purchase during the bidding war between Johnson & Johnson and Boston Scientific over cardiac-device maker Guidant. Abbott's vascular operations generated just $253 million in revenues in 2005 while Guidant's had more than $1 billion in 2005. Abbott said it expects the combined vascular group to have revenue of $3 billion in 2006. Experts consider Abbott to have obtained a solid bargain in its purchase.[12]

- Any previously recorded goodwill on the seller's books is eliminated (and no new goodwill recorded).
- A **gain** is reflected in current earnings of the acquiree to the extent that the fair value of net assets exceeds the consideration paid.

RELATED CONCEPTS

Because a gain incurred on purchase of assets, or a related firm, does not meet the conceptual view of appropriate *revenue recognition* (no earnings process has occurred), FASB continues to strive to find the best approach for bargain acquisitions.

In the past (and under *SFAS No. 141*), the excess of fair value over cost was allocated to reduce long-lived assets (with certain specified exceptions) in proportion to their fair values in determining their assigned values. If the long-lived assets were reduced to zero, and still an excess remained, an extraordinary gain was recognized under *SFAS No. 141.* Prior to *SFAS No. 141,* negative goodwill was recorded as a deferred credit and amortized. ***SFAS No. 141R*** **[ASC 805–30–25–2]** does not permit the recording of negative goodwill in this manner nor is the recognized gain to be treated as extraordinary.

Example of a Bargain Purchase Assume that Payless Company pays $17,000 cash for all the net assets of Shoddy Company when Shoddy Company's balance sheet shows the following book values and fair values:

	Book Value	*Fair Value*
Current Assets	$ 5,000	$ 5,000
Buildings (net)	10,000	15,000
Land	3,000	5,000
Total Assets	$18,000	$25,000
Liabilities	$ 2,000	$ 2,000
Common Stock	9,000	
Retained Earnings	7,000	
Total Liabilities and Equity	$18,000	
Net Assets at Book Value	$16,000	
Net Assets at Fair Value		$23,000

Cost of the acquisition ($17,000) minus the fair value of net assets acquired ($23,000) produces a bargain, or an excess of fair value of net assets acquired over cost of $6,000.

The entry by Payless Company to record the acquisition is then:

Current Assets	5,000	
Buildings	15,000	
Land	5,000	
Liabilities		2,000
Cash		17,000
Gain on acquisition of Shoddy (ordinary)		6,000

[12] *Chicago Tribune,* "Abbott Completes Vascular Purchase," James P. Miller, 4/22/06.

CONTINGENT CONSIDERATION IN AN ACQUISITION

LO7 Contingent consideration and valuation of assets.

Purchase agreements sometimes provide that the purchasing company will give additional consideration to the seller if certain specified future events or transactions occur. The contingency may require the payment of cash (or other assets) or the issuance of additional securities. ***SFAS No. 141R* [ASC 450]** requires that all contractual contingencies, as well as non-contractual liabilities for which it is **more likely than not** that an asset or liability exists, be measured and recognized at fair value on the acquisition date.* This includes contingencies based on earnings, guarantees of future security prices, and contingent payouts based on the outcome of a lawsuit. For example, if the acquirer agrees to transfer additional equity interests, cash or other assets to the former owners of the acquiree at some future date if *specified targets are met,* the acquirer should measure and recognize the fair value of the *contingent consideration* as of the acquisition date. That consideration would be classified as either debt or equity on the basis of other generally accepted accounted principles.

As discussed in Chapter 1, the expected contribution by the acquired company to the future earnings of the acquiring company is an important element in determining the price to be paid for the acquired company. Because future earnings are unknown, the purchase agreement may contain a provision that the purchaser will give additional consideration to the former stockholders of the acquired company if the combined company's earnings equal or exceed a specified amount over some specified period. In essence, the parties to the business combination agree that the total price to be paid for the acquired company will not be known until the end of the contingency period. Nonetheless, the fair value must be estimated and recognized on the acquisition date. Subsequent adjustments usually result from events or changes in circumstances that take place after the acquisition date and, thus, should not be treated as adjustments to the consideration paid.

As an example, assume that P Company acquired all the net assets of S Company in exchange for P Company's common stock. P Company also agreed to pay an additional $150,000 to the former stockholders of S Company if the average postcombination earnings over the next two years equaled or exceeded $800,000. Assume that the contingency is expected to be met, and goodwill was recorded in the original acquisition transaction. To complete the recording of the acquisition, P Company will make the following entry:

Goodwill	150,000	
Liability for Contingent Consideration		150,000

Assuming that the target is met, P Company will make the following entry:

Liability for Contingent Consideration	150,000	
Cash		150,000

On the other hand, assume that the target is not met. The position taken in *SFAS No. 141R* **[ASC 805–30–35–1]** is that the conditions that kept the target from being met occurred in a subsequent period, and that P Company had the

* Otherwise, non-contractual liabilities are recorded under other applicable GAPP, such as *SFAS No. 5* [topic 450].

information to measure the liability at the acquisition date based on circumstances that existed at that time. Thus the adjustment will flow through the income statement in the subsequent period, as follows:

Liability for Contingent Consideration	150,000	
Income from Change in Estimate		150,000

If the contingent consideration took the form of stock instead of cash, it would be classified as Paid-in-Capital from Contingent Consideration Issuable. *SFAS No.141R* **[ASC 805–30–35–1]** states that contingent consideration classified as equity shall not be remeasured. For example, suppose that P Company acquired all the net assets of S Company in exchange for P Company's common stock. P Company also agreed to issue additional shares of common stock to the former stockholders of S Company if the average postcombination earnings over the next two years equalled or exceeded $800,000. Assume that the contingency is expected to be met, and goodwill was recorded in the original acquisition transaction. Based on the information available at the acquisition date, the additional 10,000 shares (par value of $1 per share) expected to be issued are valued at $150,000. To complete the recording of the acquisition, P Company will make the following entry:

Goodwill	150,000	
Paid-in-Capital for Contingent Consideration		150,000

Assuming that the target is met, but the stock price has increased from $15 per share to $18 per share at the time of issuance, P Company will not adjust the original amount recorded as equity. Thus, P Company will make the following entry:

Paid-in-Capital for Contingent Consideration	150,000	
Common Stock ($1 par)		10,000
Paid-in-Capital in Excess of Par		140,000

Adjustments During the Measurement Period

SFAS No. 141R **[ASC 805–10–25]** defines the **measurement period** as the period after the initial acquisition date during which the acquirer may adjust the provisional amounts recognized at the acquisition date. This period allows a reasonable time to obtain the information necessary to identify and measure the fair value of the acquiree's assets and liabilities, as well as the fair value of the consideration transferred. If some of the measurements can only be determined provisionally by the end of the period in which the business combination occurs, the acquirer should report those provisional determinations in the financial statements.

During the measurement period, the acquirer can adjust the provisional amounts initially recorded (usually an increase or decrease in goodwill, unless the new information relates to a specific asset or liability) to reflect new information that surfaces during this period that would have altered the measurement if it had been known on the acquisition date. **The measurement period ends as soon as the acquirer has the needed information about facts and circumstances (or learns that the information is unobtainable), not to exceed one year from the acquisition date.**

Contingency Based on Outcome of a Lawsuit

To illustrate, assume that P Company acquires S Company on December 31, 2008, for cash plus contingent consideration depending on the assessment of a lawsuit against S Company assumed by P Company. The initial provisional assessment includes an estimated liability for the lawsuit of $250,000, an estimated contingent liability to the shareholders of $25,000, and goodwill of $330,000. The acquisition contract specifies the following conditions: So long as the lawsuit is settled for less than $500,000, S Company shareholders will receive some additional consideration. If the lawsuit results in a settlement of $500,000 or more, then S Company shareholders will receive no additional consideration. If the settlement is resolved with a smaller (larger) outlay than anticipated ($250,000), the shareholders of S Company will receive additional (reduced) consideration accordingly, thus adjusting the contingent liability above or below $25,000. Suppose that during the measurement period, new information reveals the estimated liability for the lawsuit to be $275,000, and the estimated contingent liability to the shareholders to be $22,500. **Because the new information was (a) obtained during the measurement period, and (b) related to circumstances that existed at the acquisition date, the following journal entry would be made to complete the initial recording of the business combination:**

Goodwill	22,500	
Liability for Contingent Consideration	2,500	
Estimated Liability for Lawsuit		25,000

In some cases, consideration contingently issuable may depend on both future earnings and future security prices. In such cases, an additional cost of the acquired company should be recorded for all additional consideration contingent on future events, based on the best available information and estimates at the acquisition date (as adjusted by the end of the measurement period for facts that existed at the acquisition date).

In a deal that would represent a significant step in connecting railway systems in the United States and Mexico, Kansas City Southern agreed to acquire full control of Mexico's most important railroad, Grupo Transportacion Ferroviaria Mexicana SA, known as Grupo TFM. The cash-and-stock deal is currently valued at $555.1 million and could rise to $665.1 million if contingent payments are paid. KC Southern will pay the $110 million in contingency payments if Grupo TFM is able to repurchase the Mexican government's 20% financial stake in the company in exchange for Grupo TFM dropping a tax lawsuit against the Mexican government.[13]

Contingent payments based on earnings appear in only a small fraction of deals, accounting for an even smaller percentage of total dollar value overall. Although they may be helpful in getting past negotiating obstacles and possibly in reducing up-front payouts for buyers, they suffer from drawbacks in implementation. In particular, they are very difficult to administer and may trigger post-deal conflicts

[13] *WSJ*, "Kansas City Southern to Buy Mexican Railroad," by Daniel Machalaba and Joel Millman, 12/16/04, p. A9.

ILLUSTRATION 2-4

Deals with Contingent Payments 2000 to 2006 ($ Billions)

Year	*No. of Deals*	*Value*	*Earn-out Value*
2000	140	32.2	5.9
2001	120	20.7	6.1
2002	118	9.8	2.5
2003	92	20.2	5.0
2004	123	13.9	4.5
2005	127	19.5	4.6
2006	175	29.2	5.3

Source: *Mergers & Acquisitions*, February 2007.

between buyers and sellers. Their primary niche is in the acquisition of private companies where management retention is a key issue. Other places where they are used include cross-border deals and deals where corporate sellers wish to maintain a share in future performance. Illustration 2-4 summarizes recent trends related to the use of contingent payments.

TEST YOUR KNOWLEDGE

NOTE: Solutions to ***Test Your Knowledge*** questions are found at the end of each chapter before the end-of-chapter questions.

Multiple Choice

1. In the year of a material business combination, pro forma disclosures must include all of the following except:
   a. Revenue
   b. Net income
   c. Tax expenses
   d. Nonrecurring items
2. Which of the following statements best describes the current authoritative position with regard to the accounting for contingent consideration?
   a. If contingent consideration depends on both future earnings and future security prices, an additional cost of the acquired company should be recorded only for the portion of consideration dependent on future earnings.
   b. The measurement period for adjusting provisional amounts always ends at the year-end of the period in which the acquisition occurred.
   c. A contingency based on security prices has no effect on the determination of cost to the acquiring company.
   d. The purpose of the measurement period is to provide a reasonable time to obtain the information necessary to identify and measure the fair value of the acquiree's assets and liabilities, as well as the fair value of the consideration transferred.
3. Which of the following statements concerning bargain purchases (purchase price below fair value of identifiable assets) is *correct*?
   a. Any previously recorded goodwill on the seller's books is eliminated and no new goodwill is recorded.
   b. Long-lived assets, including in-process R&D and excluding marketable securities, are recorded at fair market value minus an adjustment for the bargain, under current GAAP.

c. An extraordinary gain is recorded in the event that all long-lived assets other than marketable securities are reduced to the original purchase price, under current GAAP.

d. Current assets, long-term investments in marketable securities (other than those accounted for by the equity method), assets to be disposed by sale, deferred tax assets, prepaid assets relating to pension or other post-retirement benefit plans, and assumed liabilities are the only accounts that are always recorded at fair market value, under current GAAP.

LEVERAGED BUYOUTS

LO8 Leveraged buyouts.

A *leveraged buyout (LBO)* occurs when a group of employees (generally a management group) and third-party investors create a new company to acquire all the outstanding common shares of their employer company. The management group contributes whatever stock they hold to the new corporation and borrows sufficient funds to acquire the remainder of the common stock. The old corporation is then merged into the new corporation. The LBO term results because most of the capital of the new corporation comes from borrowed funds. The LBO market rose dramatically from 1997 to 2007, as evidenced in Illustration 2-5, before dropping off in 2008.

Kohlberg Kravis Roberts & Co. (KKR) agreed to purchase Flextronics Software Systems for $900 million, making the deal India's biggest leveraged buyout ever. Under the agreement, Singapore-based Flextronics International Ltd., the world's largest producer of electronics for other companies, will sell 85% of the unit to KKR. The investment in Flextronics Software surpasses General Electric Co.'s 2004 sale of its Indian call-center group to buyout firms General Atlantic Partners LLC and Oak Hill Capital Partners LP for $500 million.[14]

ILLUSTRATION 2-5

The Leveraged Buyout Market (LBO) 2000–2008

Year	*No. of Deals*	*% of all Deals*
2000	311	3.5%
2001	159	2.5%
2002	175	3.1%
2003	182	2.9%
2004	351	4.8%
2005	496	6.0%
2006	698	7.7%
2007	764	8.1%
2008	519	6.8%

Source: *Mergers and Acquisitions*, February 2009.

[14] *Bloomberg.com*, "KKR Acquires Flextronics Software in India's Biggest Buyout," by Vivek Shankar, 4/17/06.

The basic accounting question relates to the net asset values (fair or book) to be used by the new corporation. Accounting procedures generally followed the rules advocated by the Emerging Issues Task Force in *Consensus Position No. 88–16,* which did not view LBOs as business combinations. *FASB Statement No. 141R* did not comprehensively address this issue but did indicate that this position was no longer applicable. The essence of the change suggests that the economic entity concept should be applied here as well; thus leveraged buyout (LBO) transactions are now to be viewed as business combinations.

IFRS VERSUS U.S. GAAP

As mentioned in Chapter 1, the project on business combinations was the first of several joint projects undertaken by the FASB and the IASB in their move to converge standards globally. Nonetheless, complete convergence has not yet occurred. Most significantly the international standard currently allows the user a choice between writing all assets, including goodwill, up fully (100% including the noncontrolling share), as required now under U.S. GAAP, or continuing to write goodwill up only to the extent of the parent's percentage of ownership. This difference will be illustrated more fully in subsequent chapters in the context of stock (rather than asset) acquisitions. Other differences and similarities are summarized in Illustration 2-6.

ILLUSTRATION 2-6

Comparison of Business Combinations and Consolidations under U.S. GAAP and IFRS*

U.S. GAAP	*IFRS*
1. Fair value of **contingent consideration** recorded at acquisition date, with subsequent adjustments recognized through earnings if contingent liability (no adjustment for equity).	1. IFRS 3R uses the same approach.
2. **Contingent assets and liabilities** assumed (such as warranties) are measured at fair value on the acquisition date if they can be reasonable estimated. If not, they are treated according to *SFAS No. 5.*	2. Under IFRS 3R a contingent liability is recognized at the acquisition date if its fair value can be reliably measured.
3. **Noncontrolling interest** is recorded at fair value and is presented in equity.	3. Noncontrolling interest can be recorded either at fair value or at the proportionate share of the net assets acquired. Also presented in equity.
4. **Special purpose entities** (SPEs) are consolidated if the most significant activities of the SPE are controlled. Qualified SPEs (QSPEs) are no longer exempted from consolidation rules.	4. Special purpose entities (SPEs) are consolidated if controlled. QSPEs are not addressed.
5. **Direct acquisition costs** (excluding the costs of issuing debt or equity securities) are expensed.	5. IFRS 3R uses the same approach.
6. **Goodwill** is not amortized, but is tested for impairment using a two-step process.	6. Goodwill is not amortized, but is tested for impairment using a one-step process.
7. **Negative goodwill** in an acquisition is recorded as an ordinary gain in income (not extraordinary).	7. IAS 36 uses the same approach.

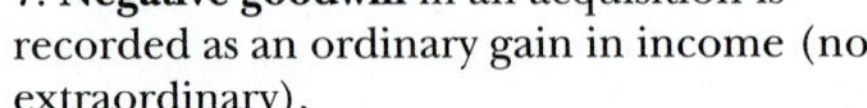

(continued)

ILLUSTRATION 2-6 *(continued)*

U.S. GAAP	IFRS
8. **Fair value** is based on exit prices, i.e. the price that would be received to sell an asset or paid to transfer a liability in an orderly transaction between market participants at the measurement date.	8. Fair value is the amount for which an asset could be exchanged or a liability settled between knowledgeable, willing parties in an arm's length transaction.
9. **Purchased in-process R&D** is capitalized with subsequent expenditures expensed. The capitalized portion is then amortized.	9. Purchased in-process R&D is capitalized with the potential for subsequent expenditures to be capitalized. The capitalized portion is then amortized.
10. Parent and subsidiary **accounting policies** ***do not need*** to conform.	10. Parent and subsidiary accounting policies ***do need*** to conform.
11. **Restructuring plans** are accounted for separately from the business combination and generally expensed (unless conditions in ***SFAS No. 146*** **[ASC 420]** are met).	11. Similar accounting under IFRS 3 and amended IAS 27.
12. **Measurement period** ends at the earlier of a) one year from the acquisition date, or b) the date when the acquirer receives needed information to consummate the acquisition.	12. Similar to U.S. GAAP.
13. For **step acquisitions**, all previous ownership interests are adjusted to fair value, with any gain or loss recorded in earnings.	13. Similar to U.S. GAAP.
14 . **Reporting dates** for the parent and subsidiary can be different up to three months. Significant events in that time must be *disclosed.*	14. Permits a three-month difference if impractical to prepare the subsidiary's statements on the same date; however, *adjustments are required* for significant events in that period.
15. Potential voting rights are generally not considered in determining **control**.	15. Potential voting rights are considered if currently exercisable.

* For complete coverage of the differences between IFRS and U.S. GAAP, see *IFRS 2009, Interpretation and Application of International Financial Reporting Standards*, by Epstein and Jermakowicz, 2009 (John Wiley and Sons, Inc.).

SUMMARY

1. *Describe the changes in the accounting for business combinations approved by the FASB in 2007, and the reasons for those changes.* Under *SFAS No. 141R* [ASC 805], the fair values of all assets and liabilities on the acquisition date, defined as the date the acquirer obtains control of the acquiree, are reflected in the financial statements, even if control is obtained with less than 100% ownership and even if control is achieved in stages rather than all at once. *SFAS No. 141R* [ASC 805] also broadens the scope from that of *SFAS No. 141* to apply to business combinations involving only mutual entities, those achieved by contract alone, and the initial consolidation of variable interest entities (VIEs). *SFAS No. 160* [ASC 810-10-45-15 and 16] establishes standards for the reporting of the noncontrolling interest when the acquirer obtains control without purchasing 100% of the acquiree.

2. *Describe the two major changes in the accounting for business combinations approved by the FASB in 2001, as well as the reasons for those changes.* Of the two methods of accounting historically used in the United States—***purchase*** (now called acquisition)and ***pooling of interests***—pooling is now prohibited. In addition, the goodwill often recorded under the acquisition method is no longer amortized but instead is reviewed periodically for impairment. The standard setters believe that virtually all business combinations are acquisitions and thus should be accounted for in the same way that other asset acquisitions are accounted for, based on the fair values exchanged. Furthermore, users need better information about intangible assets, such as the goodwill that was not recorded in a pooling. The decision to discontinue the amortization of goodwill appears to be largely the result of pressure applied to the FASB and a fear that economic activity and competitive position internationally might otherwise be injured.

3. *Discuss the goodwill impairment test described in SFAS No. 142 [ASC 350–20–35], including its frequency, the steps laid out in the standard, and some of the implementation problems.* Goodwill impairment for each reporting unit should be tested in a two-step process at least once a year. In the first step, the fair value of a reporting unit is compared to its carrying amount (goodwill included) at the date of the periodic review. If the fair value at the review date is less than the carrying amount, then the second step is necessary. In the second step, the carrying value of the goodwill is compared to its implied fair value (and a loss recognized when the carrying value is the higher of the two). To arrive at an implied fair value for the goodwill, the FASB specifies that an entity should allocate the fair value of the reporting unit at the review date to all of its assets and liabilities as if the unit had been acquired in a combination with the fair value of the unit as its purchase price. The excess of that fair value (purchase price) over the fair value of identifiable net assets is the implied fair value of the goodwill. Determining the fair value of the unit may prove difficult in cases where there are no quoted market prices. See Figure 2-1 for an illustration of the goodwill impairment rules.

4. *Explain how acquisition expenses are reported.* Under *FASB Statement No 141R* [ASC 805–10–25–23], acquisition-related costs are excluded from the measurement of the consideration paid, because such costs are not part of the fair value of the acquiree and are not assets. This is a change from past GAAP where the purchase method required only indirect costs to be expensed, while direct costs were capitalized as part of the purchase price. Current GAAP requires that both direct and indirect costs be expensed, and that the cost of issuing securities is also excluded from the consideration and accounted for separately from the business combination accounting.

5. *Describe the use of pro forma statements in business combinations.* Pro forma statements, sometimes called "as if" statements, are prepared to show the effect of planned or contemplated transactions by estimating how they might have affected the historical financial statements if they had been consummated during the period covered by those statements. Pro forma statements serve two functions in relation to business combinations: (1) to provide information in the ***planning*** stages of the combination and (2) to ***disclose*** relevant information subsequent to the combination.

6. *Describe the valuation of assets, including goodwill, and liabilities acquired in a business combination accounted for by the acquisition method.* Assets and liabilities acquired are recorded at their fair values. Any excess of cost over the fair value of net assets acquired is recorded as goodwill.

7. *Explain how contingent consideration affects the valuation of assets acquired in a business combination accounted for by the acquisition method.* If certain specified future events or transactions occur, the purchaser must pay additional consideration. The purchaser records the additional consideration at its fair value as an adjustment to the original purchase transaction. This entry is made to complete the recording of the business combination on the date of acquisition, based on the best information available at that time. Adjustments to provisional amounts may be made throughout the measurement period only if they reveal additional information about conditions that existed at the acquisition date. After the measurement date, subsequent adjustments for any contingent consideration recorded as a liability are recognized in the income statement; contingent consideration recorded as equity is not remeasured.

8. *Describe a leveraged buyout.* A leveraged buyout (LBO) occurs when a group of employees (generally a management group) and third-party investors create a new company to acquire all the outstanding common shares of their employer company. The LBO term results because most of the capital of the new corporation comes from borrowed funds.

9. *Describe the disclosure requirements according to current GAAP related to each business combination that takes place during a given year.* Required disclosures include: the name and a description of the acquiree; the acquisition date; the percentage of voting equity instruments acquired; the primary reasons for the business

combination; the fair value of the acquiree and the basis for measuring that value on the acquisition date; the fair value of the consideration transferred; the amounts recognized at the acquisition date for each major class of assets acquired and liabilities assumed; and the maximum potential amount of future payments the acquirer could be required to make under the terms of the acquisition agreement.

10. *Describe at least one of the differences between U.S. GAAP and IFRS related to the accounting for business combinations.* When a noncontrolling interest exists, IFRS allows a choice between recognizing goodwill fully or only to the extent of the acquired percentage, while U.S. GAAP requires full (100%) recognition of implied goodwill, even when a non-controlling interests remains.

APPENDIX A

Deferred Taxes in Business Combinations

A common motivation for the selling firm in a business combination is to structure the deal so that any gain is tax-free at the time of the combination. To the extent that the seller accepts common stock rather than cash or debt in exchange for the assets, the sellers may not have to pay taxes until a later date when the shares accepted are sold. In this situation, the acquiring firm inherits the book values of the assets acquired for ***tax*** purposes. When the acquirer has inherited the book values of the assets for tax purposes but has recorded market values for reporting purposes, a deferred tax liability needs to be recognized.

For example, suppose that Taxaware Company has net assets totaling $700,000 (market value), including fixed assets with a market value of $200,000 and a book value of $140,000. The book values of all other assets approximate market values. Taxaware Company is acquired by Blinko in a combination that qualifies as a *nontaxable exchange* for Taxaware shareholders. Blinko issues common stock valued at $800,000 (par value $150,000). First, if we disregard tax effects, the entry to record the acquisition would be:

Assets	$700,000	
Goodwill	100,000	
Common Stock		$150,000
Additional Contributed Capital		650,000

Now consider tax effects, assuming a 30% tax rate. First, the excess of market value over book value of the fixed assets creates a deferred tax liability because the excess depreciation is not tax deductible. Thus, the deferred tax liability associated with the fixed assets equals 30% × $60,000 (the difference between market and book values), or $18,000. The inclusion of deferred taxes would increase goodwill by $18,000 to a total of $118,000. The entry to include goodwill is as follows:

Assets	700,000	
Goodwill	118,000	
Deferred Tax Liability (.3 × [200,000 − 140,000])		18,000
Common Stock		150,000
Additional Contributed Capital		650,000

The reader may be aware that in recent years in the United States, *the amortization of goodwill is often deductible on the tax return of the acquirer over a period of 15 years.* This, however, is **not the case in a nontaxable exchange, where the goodwill is not subject to amortization on either the tax return or the books under current GAAP.** Thus, in a nontaxable exchange, there is no obvious temporary difference related to the goodwill. In *FASB Statement No. 141R* [ASC 805–740] the FASB addressed the issue of deferred taxes in business combinations, stating its decision not to require deferred taxes be measured at fair value. The statement amends *FASB Statement No. 109*, and states that a deferred tax liability or asset should be recognized for differences between the recognized values of assets acquired and liabilities assumed in a business combination (except the portion of goodwill for which amortization is not deductible for tax purposes). Thus, we do not record a deferred tax liability on goodwill in this illustration.

Note, however, that in a *taxable exchange*, the excess amount of tax-deductible goodwill over the goodwill recorded in the books *does* meet the definition of a temporary difference. Further, *FASB Statement No. 141R* [ASC 805–740] addresses this issue explicitly, stating that the tax benefit in such a case should be recognized at the date of the business combination.

In *FASB Statement No. 141R* [ASC 805–740–45–20], FASB also addressed changes in the valuation allowance on deferred tax assets. *FASB Statement No. 109* [paragraph 740–10–45–20] requires that such an allowance be recognized when it is deemed more likely than not that some or all of the deferred tax asset will not be realized. *FASB Statement No. 141R* [ASC 805–740] states that a change in the valuation allowance resulting from changed circumstances due to a business combination should be accounted for separately from the business combination. In other words, the change in the valuation allowance would be shown as income or expense in the period of the combination. FASB stated that this position was in line with the goal of convergence toward international standards. See Figure 2-2 for a summary of the changes in deferred taxes resulting from *FABS Statement No. 141R* [ASC 805].

"Together, these statements [ASC 805] and [ASC 740] can affect acquisitions past, present, and future—dramatically changing the way companies account for future business combinations and minority interests (now noncontrolling interests). In some cases, they can affect the tax accounting for transactions completed prior to the effective date." Examples of potential changes from the prior standard include: the handling of tax uncertainties and their effect on the valuation allowance; the recording of a deferred tax asset when goodwill for tax is greater than book goodwill; the effect of contingent consideration on the purchase price, deferred tax assets, and the tax provision; and transaction costs that are now expensed for book as well as tax purposes (thus no deferred taxes).[15]

[15] Deloitte Tax Services, "Mergers and acquisitions: why tax accounting will never be the same again," 2008 Deloitte Development LLC.

Figure 2-2

Summary of Selected Income Tax Changes: Old vs. New Application

	Old	*New*
Changes in the valuation allowance resulting from the business combination.	Decreases in the acquirer's valuation allowance are included in the business combination accounting.	Changes would be reflected in the income statement or in some cases, equity.
Subsequent changes in the valuation allowance related to the target's recorded tax attributes or the tax positions acquired.	All changes would first reduce goodwill to zero, then reduce other noncurrent intangibles to zero and lastly reduce income tax expense.	Changes would be reflected in the income statement or, in some cases, equity (not for measurement period adjustments). Accounting depends on whether the new information relates to conditions that existed at the acquisition date.
Excess of the tax-deductible amount over accounting goodwill.	No deferred tax asset recognized in the business combination; when the tax deduction is realized on the tax return, reduce goodwill to zero, then reduce other noncurrent intangibles to zero and finally reduce income tax expense.	Recognize a deferred tax asset.

TEST YOUR KNOWLEDGE SOLUTIONS

2-1 1. c
2. c
3. a

2-2 1. c
2. d
3. a

QUESTIONS

(The letter A after a question, exercise, or problem means that the question, exercise, or problem relates to Chapter Appendix A.)

LO7 **1.** When contingent consideration in an acquisition is based on security prices, how should this contingency be reflected on the acquisition date? If the estimate changes during the measurement period, how is this handled? If the estimate changes after the end of the measurement period, how is this adjustment handled? Why?

LO5 **2.** What are pro forma financial statements? What is their purpose?

LO3 **3.** How would a company determine whether goodwill has been impaired?

LO3 **4.** AOL announced that because of an accounting change (*FASB Statements Nos. 141R* [ASC 805] *and 142* [ASC 350]), earnings would be increasing over the next 25 years by $5.9 billion a year. What change(s) required by FASB (in *SFAS Nos. 141R and 142*) resulted in an increase in AOL's income? Would you expect this increase in earnings to have a positive impact on AOL's stock price? Why or why not?

Business Ethics

There have been several recent cases of a CEO or CFO resigning or being ousted for misrepresenting academic credentials. For instance, during February 2006, the CEO of RadioShack resigned by 'mutual agreement' for inflating his educational background. During

2002, Veritas Software Corporation's CFO resigned after claiming to have an MBA from Stanford University. On the other hand, Bausch & Lomb Inc.'s board refused the CEO's offer to resign following a questionable claim to have an MBA.

Suppose you have been retained by the board of a company where the CEO has 'overstated' credentials. This company has a code of ethics and conduct which states that the employee should always do "the right thing."

(a) What is the board of directors' responsibility in such matters?

(b) What arguments would you make to ask the CEO to resign? What damage might be caused if the decision is made to retain the current CEO?

EXERCISES

EXERCISE 2-1 **Asset Purchase** LO6

Preston Company acquired the assets (except for cash) and assumed the liabilities of Saville Company. Immediately prior to the acquisition, Saville Company's balance sheet was as follows:

	Book Value	*Fair Value*
Cash	$ 120,000	$ 120,000
Receivables (net)	192,000	228,000
Inventory	360,000	396,000
Plant and equipment (net)	480,000	540,000
Land	420,000	660,000
Total assets	$1,572,000	$1,944,000
Liabilities	$ 540,000	$ 594,000
Common stock ($5 par value)	480,000	
Other contributed capital	132,000	
Retained earnings	420,000	
Total equities	$1,572,000	

Required:

A. Prepare the journal entries on the books of Preston Company to record the purchase of the assets and assumption of the liabilities of Saville Company if the amount paid was $1,560,000 in cash.

B. Repeat the requirement in (A) assuming that the amount paid was $990,000.

EXERCISE 2-2 **Acquisition Method** LO6

The balance sheets of Petrello Company and Sanchez Company as of January 1, 2011, are presented below. On that date, after an extended period of negotiation, the two companies agreed to merge. To effect the merger, Petrello Company is to exchange its unissued common stock for all the outstanding shares of Sanchez Company in the ratio of $\frac{1}{2}$ share of Petrello for each share of Sanchez. Market values of the shares were agreed on as Petrello, $48; Sanchez, $24. The fair values of Sanchez Company's assets and liabilities are equal to their book values with the exception of plant and equipment, which has an estimated fair value of $720,000.

	Petrello	*Sanchez*
Cash	$ 480,000	$ 200,000
Receivables	480,000	240,000
Inventories	2,000,000	240,000
Plant and equipment (net)	3,840,000	800,000 720,000
Total assets	$6,800,000	$1,480,000
Liabilities	$1,200,000	$ 320,000
Common stock, $16 par value	3,440,000	800,000
Other contributed capital	400,000	—0—
Retained earnings	1,760,000	360,000
Total equities	$6,800,000	$1,480,000

Required:

Prepare a balance sheet for Petrello Company immediately after the merger.

EXERCISE 2-3 **Asset Purchase, Cash and Stock** LO6

Pretzel Company acquired the assets (except for cash) and assumed the liabilities of Salt Company on January 2, 2012. As compensation, Pretzel Company gave 30,000 shares of its common stock, 15,000 shares of its 10% preferred stock, and cash of $50,000 to the stockholders of Salt Company. On the acquisition date, Pretzel Company stock had the following characteristics:

PRETZEL COMPANY

Stock	*Par Value*	*Fair Value*
Common	$ 10	$ 25
Preferred	100	100

Immediately prior to the acquisition, Salt Company's balance sheet reported the following book values and fair values:

SALT COMPANY
Balance Sheet
January 2, 2012

	Book value	*Fair value*
Cash	$ 165,000	$ 165,000
Accounts receivable (net of $11,000 allowance)	220,000	198,000
Inventory—LIFO cost	275,000	330,000
Land	396,000	550,000
Buildings and equipment (net)	1,144,000	1,144,000
Total assets	$2,200,000	$2,387,000
Current liabilities	$ 275,000	$ 275,000
Bonds Payable, 10%	450,000	495,000
Common stock, $5 par value	770,000	
Other contributed capital	396,000	
Retained earnings	309,000	
Total liabilities and stockholders' equity	$2,200,000	

Required:

Prepare the journal entry on the books of Pretzel Company to record the acquisition of the assets and assumption of the liabilities of Salt Company.

EXERCISE 2-4 **Asset Purchase, Cash** LO6

P Company acquired the assets and assumed the liabilities of S Company on January 1, 2010, for $510,000 when S Company's balance sheet was as follows:

S COMPANY
Balance Sheet
January 1, 2010

Cash	$ 96,000
Receivables	55,200
Inventory	110,400
Land	169,200
Plant and equipment (net)	466,800
Total	$897,600
Accounts payable	$ 44,400
Bonds payable, 10%, due 12/31/2015, Par	480,000
Common stock, $2 par value	120,000
Retained earnings	253,200
Total	$897,600

Fair values of S Company's assets and liabilities were equal to their book values except for the following:

1. Inventory has a fair value of $126,000.
2. Land has a fair value of $198,000.
3. The bonds pay interest semiannually on June 30 and December 31. The current yield rate on bonds of similar risk is 8%.

Required:

Prepare the journal entry on P Company's books to record the acquisition of the assets and assumption of the liabilities of S Company.

EXERCISE 2-5 **Asset Purchase, Contingent Consideration** LO7

Pritano Company acquired all the net assets of Succo Company on December 31, 2010, for $2,160,000 cash. The balance sheet of Succo Company immediately prior to the acquisition showed:

	Book value	*Fair value*
Current assets	$ 960,000	$ 960,000
Plant and equipment	1,080,000	1,440,000
Total	$2,040,000	$2,400,000
Liabilities	$ 180,000	$ 216,000
Common stock	480,000	
Other contributed capital	600,000	
Retained earnings	780,000	
Total	$2,040,000	

As part of the negotiations, Pritano agreed to pay the stockholders of Succo $360,000 cash if the postcombination earnings of Pritano averaged $2,160,000 or more per year over the next two years.

Required:

Prepare the journal entries on the books of Pritano to record the acquisition on December 31, 2010. It is expected that the earnings target is likely to be met.

EXERCISE 2-6 **Asset Purchase, Contingent Consideration** LO7

On January 1, 2010, Platz Company acquired all the net assets of Satz Company by issuing 75,000 shares of its $10 par value common stock to the stockholders of Satz Company. During negotiations Platz Company agreed to issue additional shares of common stock to the stockholders of Satz if the average postcombination earnings over the next three years equaled or exceeded $2,500,000. On January 1, 2010 the market value of Platz stock was $50 per share. Based on the information available at the acquisition date, the additional 10,000 shares are expected to be issued.

Required:

A. Prepare the journal entry on Platz Company's books on January 1, 2010. It is expected that the earnings target is likely to be met. Platz Company records goodwill on acquisition.

B. Prepare the journal entry on Platz Company's books on January 1, 2014, when the additional shares are issued. On this date the market value of Platz stock is valued at $60 per share.

EXERCISE 2-7 **Multiple Choice** LO6

Price Company issued 8,000 shares of its $20 par value common stock for the net assets of Sims Company in a business combination under which Sims Company will be merged into Price Company. On the date of the combination, Price Company common stock had a fair value of $30 per share. Balance sheets for Price Company and Sims Company immediately prior to the combination were:

	Price	*Sims*
Current assets	$ 438,000	$ 64,000
Plant and equipment (net)	575,000	136,000
Total	$1,013,000	$200,000
Liabilities	$ 300,000	$ 50,000
Common stock, $20 par value	550,000	80,000
Other contributed capital	72,500	20,000
Retained earnings	90,500	50,000
Total	$1,013,000	$200,000

Required:

Select the letter of the best answer.

1. If the business combination is treated as a purchase and Sims Company's net assets have a fair value of $228,800, Price Company's balance sheet immediately after the combination will include goodwill of
   (a) $10,200.
   (b) $12,800.
   (c) $11,200.
   (d) $18,800.

2. If the business combination is treated as a purchase and the fair value of Sims Company's current assets is $90,000, its plant and equipment is $242,000, and its liabilities are $56,000, Price Company's balance sheet immediately after the combination will include
   (a) Negative goodwill of $36,000.
   (b) Plant and equipment of $817,000.
   (c) Gain of $36,000.
   (d) Goodwill of $36,000.

EXERCISE 2-8 **Purchase** LO6

Effective December 31, 2010, Zintel Corporation proposes to issue additional shares of its common stock in exchange for all the assets and liabilities of Smith Corporation and Platz Corporation, after which Smith and Platz will distribute the Zintel stock to their stockholders in complete liquidation and dissolution. Balance sheets of each of the corporations immediately prior to merger on December 31, 2010, follow. The common stock exchange ratio was negotiated to be 1:1 for both Smith and Platz.

	Zintel	*Smith*	*Platz*
Current assets	$1,600,000	$ 350,000	$ 12,000
Long-term assets (net)	5,700,000	1,890,000	98,000
Total	$7,300,000	$2,240,000	$110,000
Current liabilities	$ 700,000	$ 110,000	$ 9,000
Long-term debt	1,100,000	430,000	61,000
Common stock, $5 par value	2,500,000	700,000	20,000
Retained earnings	3,000,000	1,000,000	20,000
Total	$7,300,000	$2,240,000	$110,000

Required:

Prepare journal entries on Zintel's books to record the combination. Assume the following:

The identifiable assets and liabilities of Smith and Platz are all reflected in the balance sheets (above), and their recorded amounts are equal to their current fair values except for long-term assets. The fair value of Smith's long-term assets exceed their book value by $20,000, and the fair value of Platz's long-term assets exceed their book values by $5,000. Zintel's common stock is traded actively and has a current market price of $15 per share. Prepare journal entries on Zintel's books to record the combination. *(AICPA adapted)*

EXERCISE 2-9 **Allocation of Purchase Price to Various Assets and Liabilities** LO6

Company S has no long-term marketable securities. Assume the following scenarios:

Case A

Assume that P Company paid $130,000 cash for 100% of the net assets of S Company.

S Company

	Assets			
	Current Assets	*Long-lived Assets*	*Liabilities*	*Net Assets*
Book Value	$15,000	$85,000	$20,000	$80,000
Fair Value	20,000	130,000	30,000	120,000

Case B

Assume that P Company paid $110,000 cash for 100% of the net assets of S Company.

S Company

	Assets			
	Current Assets	*Long-lived Assets*	*Liabilities*	*Net Assets*
Book Value	$15,000	$85,000	$20,000	$80,000
Fair Value	30,000	80,000	20,000	90,000

Case C

Assume that P Company paid $15,000 cash for 100% of the net assets of S Company.

S Company

	Assets			
	Current Assets	*Long-lived Assets*	*Liabilities*	*Net Assets*
Book Value	$15,000	$85,000	$20,000	$80,000
Fair Value	20,000	40,000	40,000	20,000

Required:

Complete the following schedule by listing the amount that would be recorded on P's books.

	Assets				*Retained Earnings*
	Goodwill	*Current Assets*	*Long-lived Assets*	*Liabilities*	*(Gain in Income Statement)*
Case A					
Case B					
Case C					

EXERCISE 2-10 **Goodwill Impairment Test** LO3

On January 1, 2010, Porsche Company acquired the net assets of Saab Company for $450,000 cash. The fair value of Saab's identifiable net assets was $375,000 on this date. Porsche Company decided to measure goodwill impairment using the present value of future cash flows to estimate the fair value of the reporting unit (Saab). The information for these subsequent years is as follows:

Year	*Present Value of Future Cash Flows*	*Carrying Value of Saab's Identifiable Net Assets**	*Fair Value Saab's Identifiable Net Assets*
2011	$400,000	$330,000	$340,000
2012	$400,000	$320,000	345,000
2013	$350,000	$300,000	325,000

* Identifiable net assets do not include goodwill.

Required:

Part A: For each year determine the amount of goodwill impairment, if any.

Part B: Prepare the journal entries needed each year to record the goodwill impairment (if any) on Porsche's books from 2011 to 2013.

Part C: How should goodwill (and its impairment) be presented on the balance sheet and the income statement in each year?

Part D: If goodwill is impaired, what additional information needs to be disclosed?

EXERCISE 2-11 **Relation between Purchase Price, Goodwill, and Negative Goodwill** LO6

The following balance sheets were reported on January 1, 2011, for Peach Company and Stream Company:

	Peach	*Stream*
Cash	$ 100,000	$ 20,000
Inventory	300,000	100,000
Equipment (net)	880,000	380,000
Total	$1,280,000	$500,000
Total Liabilities	$ 300,000	$100,000
Common stock, $20 par value	400,000	200,000
Other contributed capital	250,000	70,000
Retained earnings	330,000	130,000
Total	$1,280,000	$500,000

Required:

Appraisals reveal that the inventory has a fair value of $120,000, and the equipment has a current value of $410,000. The book value and fair value of liabilities are the same. Assuming that Peach Company wishes to acquire Stream for cash in an asset acquisition, determine the following cutoff amounts:

A. The purchase price above which Peach would record goodwill.

B. The purchase price below which the equipment would be recorded at less than its fair market value.

C. The purchase price below which Peach would record a gain.

D. The purchase price below which Peach would obtain a "bargain."

E. The purchase price at which Peach would record $50,000 of goodwill.

EXERCISE 2-12A Acquisition Entry, Deferred Taxes

Patel Company issued 100,000 shares of $1 par value common stock (market value of $6/share) for the net assets of Seely Company on January 1, 2011, in a statutory merger. Seely Company had the following assets, liabilities, and owners' equity at that time:

	Book Value Tax Basis	*Fair Value*	*Difference*
Cash	$ 20,000	$ 20,000	$—0—
Accounts receivable	112,000	112,000	—0—
Inventory (LIFO)	82,000	134,000	52,000
Land	30,000	55,000	25,000
Plant assets (net)	392,000	463,000	71,000
Total assets	$636,000	$784,000	
Allowance for uncollectible accounts	$ 10,000	$ 10,000	$—0—
Accounts payable	54,000	54,000	—0—
Bonds payable	200,000	180,000	20,000
Common stock, $1 par value	80,000		
Other contributed capital	132,000		
Retained earnings	160,000		
Total equities	$636,000		

Required:

Prepare the journal entry to record the assets acquired and liabilities assumed. Assume an income tax rate of 40%.

PROBLEMS

PROBLEM 2-1 Consolidation LO6

Condensed balance sheets for Phillips Company and Solina Company on January 1, 2010, are as follows:

	Phillips	*Solina*
Current assets	$180,000	$ 85,000
Plant and equipment (net)	450,000	140,000
Total assets	$630,000	$225,000
Total liabilities	$ 95,000	$ 35,000
Common stock, $10 par value	350,000	160,000
Other contributed capital	125,000	53,000
Retained earnings (deficit)	60,000	(23,000)
Total liabilities and equities	$630,000	$225,000

On January 1, 2010, the stockholders of Phillips and Solina agreed to a consolidation. Because FASB requires that one party be recognized as the acquirer and the other as the acquiree, it was agreed that Phillips was acquiring Solina. Phillips agreed to issue 20,000 shares of its $10 par stock to acquire all the net assets of Solina at a time when the fair value of Phillips' common stock was $15 per share.

On the date of consolidation, the fair values of Solina's current assets and liabilities were equal to their book values. The fair value of plant and equipment was, however, $150,000. Phillips will incur $20,000 of direct acquisition costs and $6,000 in stock issue costs.

Required:

Prepare the journal entries on the books of Phillips to record the acquisition of Solina Company's net assets.

PROBLEM 2-2 **Merger and Consolidation, Goodwill Impairment** LO3 LO6

Stockholders of Acme Company, Baltic Company, and Colt Company are considering alternative arrangements for a business combination. Balance sheets and the fair values of each company's assets on October 1, 2011, were as follows:

	Acme	*Baltic*	*Colt*
Assets	$3,900,000	$7,500,000	$ 950,000
Liabilities	$2,030,000	$2,200,000	$ 260,000
Common stock, $20 par value	2,000,000	1,800,000	540,000
Other contributed capital	—0—	600,000	190,000
Retained earnings (deficit)	(130,000)	2,900,000	(40,000)
Total equities	$3,900,000	$7,500,000	$ 950,000
Fair values of assets	$4,200,000	$9,000,000	$1,300,000

Acme Company shares have a fair value of $50. A fair (market) price is not available for shares of the other companies because they are closely held. Fair values of liabilities equal book values.

Required:

A. Prepare a balance sheet for the business combination. Assume the following: Acme Company acquires all the assets and assumes all the liabilities of Baltic and Colt Companies by issuing in exchange 140,000 shares of its common stock to Baltic Company and 40,000 shares of its common stock to Colt Company.

B. Assume, further, that the acquisition was consummated on October 1, 2011, as described above. However, by the end of 2012, Acme was concerned that the fair values of one or both of the acquired units had deteriorated. To test for impairment, Acme decided to measure goodwill impairment using the present value of future cash flows to estimate the fair value of the reporting units (Baltic and Colt). Acme accumulated the following data:

Year 2012	*Present Value of Future Cash Flows*	*Carrying Value of Identifiable Net Assets**	*Fair Value Identifiable Net Assets*
Baltic	$6,500,000	$6,340,000	$6,350,000
Colt	$1,900,000	1,200,000	1,000,000

* Identifiable Net Assets do not include goodwill.

Prepare the journal entry, if needed, to record goodwill impairment at December 31, 2012.

PROBLEM 2-3 **Purchase of Net Assets Using Bonds** LO6

On January 1, 2011, Perez Company acquired all the assets and assumed all the liabilities of Stalton Company and merged Stalton into Perez. In exchange for the net assets of Stalton, Perez gave its bonds payable with a maturity value of $600,000, a stated interest rate of 10%, interest payable semiannually on June 30 and December 31, a maturity date of January 1,

2021, and a yield rate of 12%. Balance sheets for Perez and Stalton (as well as fair value data) on January 1, 2011, were as follows:

	Perez	*Stalton*	
	Book Value	*Book Value*	*Fair Value*
Cash	$ 250,000	$114,000	$114,000
Receivables	352,700	150,000	135,000
Inventories	848,300	232,000	310,000
Land	700,000	100,000	315,000
Buildings	950,000	410,000	54,900
Accumulated depreciation—buildings	(325,000)	(170,500)	
Equipment	262,750	136,450	39,450
Accumulated depreciation—equipment	(70,050)	(90,450)	
Total assets	$2,968,700	$881,500	$968,350
Current liabilities	$ 292,700	$ 95,300	$ 95,300
Bonds payable, 8% due 1/1/2016, Interest payable 6/30 and 12/31		300,000	260,000
Common stock, $15 par value	1,200,000		
Common stock, $5 par value		236,500	
Other contributed capital	950,000	170,000	
Retained earnings	526,000	79,700	
Total equities	$2,968,700	$881,500	

Required:

Prepare the journal entry on the books of Perez Company to record the acquisition of Stalton Company's assets and liabilities in exchange for the bonds.

PROBLEM 2-4 **Cash Acquisition, Contingent Consideration** LO6 LO7

Pham Company acquired the assets (except for cash) and assumed the liabilities of Senn Company on January 1, 2011, paying $720,000 cash. Senn Company's December 31, 2010, balance sheet, reflecting both book values and fair values, showed:

	Book Value	*Fair Value*
Accounts receivable (net)	$ 72,000	$ 65,000
Inventory	86,000	99,000
Land	110,000	162,000
Buildings (net)	369,000	450,000
Equipment (net)	237,000	288,000
Total	$874,000	$1,064,000
Accounts payable	$ 83,000	$ 83,000
Note payable	180,000	180,000
Common stock, $2 par value	153,000	
Other contributed capital	229,000	
Retained earnings	229,000	
Total	$874,000	

As part of the negotiations, Pham Company agreed to pay the former stockholders of Senn Company $135,000 cash if the postcombination earnings of the combined company (Pham) reached certain levels during 2011 and 2012.

Required:

A. Record the journal entry on the books of Pham Company to record the acquisition on January 1, 2011. It is expected that the earnings target is likely to be met.

B. Assuming the earnings contingency is met, prepare the journal entry on Pham Company's books to settle the contingency on January 2, 2013.

C. Assuming the earnings contingency is not met, prepare the necessary journal entry on Pham Company's books on January 2, 2013.

PROBLEM 2-5 **Asset Acquisition, Pro forma** LO5

Balance sheets for Salt Company and Pepper Company on December 31, 2010, follow:

	Salt	*Pepper*
ASSETS		
Cash	$ 95,000	$ 180,000
Receivables	117,000	230,000
Inventories	134,000	231,400
Plant assets	690,000	1,236,500
Total assets	$1,036,000	$1,877,900
EQUITIES		
Accounts payable	$ 180,000	$ 255,900
Mortgage payable	152,500	180,000
Common stock, $20 par value	340,000	900,000
Other contributed capital	179,500	270,000
Retained earnings	184,000	272,000
Total equities	$1,036,000	$1,877,900

Pepper Company tentatively plans to issue 30,000 shares of its $20 par value stock, which has a current market value of $37 per share net of commissions and other issue costs. Pepper Company then plans to acquire the assets and assume the liabilities of Salt Company for a cash payment of $800,000 and $300,000 in long-term 8% notes payable. Pepper Company's receivables include $60,000 owed by Salt Company. Pepper Company is willing to pay more than the book value of Salt Company assets because plant assets are undervalued by $215,000 and Salt Company has historically earned above-normal profits.

Required:

Prepare a pro forma balance sheet showing the effects of these planned transactions.

PROBLEM 2-6 **Purchase, Decision to Accept** LO5

Spalding Company has offered to sell to Ping Company its assets at their book values plus $1,800,000 representing payment for goodwill. Operating data for 2010 for the two companies are as follows:

	Ping Company	*Spalding Company*
Sales	$3,510,100	$2,365,800
Cost of goods sold	1,752,360	1,423,800
Gross profit	1,757,740	942,000
Selling expenses	$ 632,500	$ 292,100
Other expenses	172,600	150,000
Total expenses	805,100	442,100
Net income	$ 952,640	$ 499,900

Ping Company's management estimates the following operating changes if Spalding Company is merged with Ping Company through a purchase:

A. After the merger, the sales volume of Ping Company will be 20% in excess of the present combined sales volume, and the sale price per unit will be decreased by 10%.

B. Fixed manufacturing expenses have been 35% of cost of goods sold for each company. After the merger the fixed manufacturing expenses of Ping Company will be increased by 70% of the current fixed manufacturing expenses of Spalding Company. The current variable manufacturing expenses of Ping Company, which is 70% of cost of goods sold, is expected to increase in proportion to the increase in sales volume.

C. Selling expenses of Ping Company are expected to be 85% of the present combined selling expenses of the two companies.

D. Other expenses of Ping Company are expected to increase by 85% as a result of the merger.

Any excess of the estimated net income of the merged company over the combined present net income of the two companies is to be capitalized at 20%. If this amount exceeds the price set by Spalding Company for goodwill, Ping Company will accept the offer.

Required:

Prepare a pro forma (or projected) income statement for Ping Company for 2011 assuming the merger takes place, and indicate whether Ping Company should accept the offer.

PROBLEM 2-7A Acquisition Entry and Deferred Taxes

On January 1, 2012, Pruitt Company issued 30,000 shares of its $2 par value common stock for the net assets of Shah Company in a statutory merger accounted for as a purchase. Pruitt's common stock had a fair value of $28 per share at that time. A schedule of the Shah Company assets acquired and liabilities assumed at book values (which are equal to their tax bases) and fair values follows:

Item	*Book Value/Tax Basis*	*Fair Value*	*Excess*
Receivables (net)	$125,000	$ 125,000	$ —0—
Inventory	167,000	195,000	28,000
Land	86,500	120,000	33,500
Plant assets (net)	467,000	567,000	100,000
Patents	95,000	200,000	105,000
Total	$940,500	$1,207,000	$266,500
Current liabilities	$ 89,500	$ 89,500	$—0—
Bonds payable	300,000	360,000	60,000
Common stock	120,000		
Other contributed capital	164,000		
Retained earnings	267,000		
Total	$940,500		

Additional Information:

1. Pruitt's income tax rate is 35%.
2. Shah's beginning inventory was all sold during 2012.
3. Useful lives for depreciation and amortization purposes are:

Plant assets	10 years
Patents	8 years
Bond premium	10 years

4. Pruitt uses the straight-line method for all depreciation and amortization purposes.

Required:

A. Prepare the entry on Pruitt Company's books to record the acquisition of the assets and assumption of the liabilities of Shah Company.

B. Assuming Pruitt Company had taxable income of $468,000 in 2012, prepare the income tax entry for 2012.

3

CONSOLIDATED FINANCIAL STATEMENTS—DATE OF ACQUISITION

LEARNING OBJECTIVES

1. Understand the concept of control as used in reference to consolidations.
2. Explain the role of a noncontrolling interest in business combinations.
3. Describe the reasons why a company acquires a subsidiary rather than its net assets.
4. Describe the valuation and classification of accounts in consolidated financial statements.
5. List the requirements for inclusion of a subsidiary in consolidated financial statements.
6. Discuss the limitations of consolidated financial statements.
7. Record the investment in the subsidiary on the parent's books at the date of acquisition.
8. Prepare the consolidated workpapers and eliminating entries at the date of acquisition.
9. Compute and allocate the difference between implied value and book value of the acquired firm's equity.
10. Discuss some of the similarities and differences between U.S. GAAP and IFRS with respect to the preparation of consolidated financial statements at the date of acquisition.

Berkshire Hathaway Inc. agreed to purchase an 80% stake in Iscar Metalworking Cos., a privately held Israeli company, for $4 billion. Iscar's shareholders will retain ownership of the remaining 20% of the company. Berkshire's chairman, Warren Buffett, stated that he does not intend to make major changes at Iscar and that the company will remain headquartered in Tefen, Israel. Iscar is a world leader in the tools industry, exporting and fabricating its products around the globe for industries including aerospace and automotive. Many speculate that Berkshire may use Iscar as a base for consolidating other players in the tools industry, such as U.S.-based Kennametal, Inc.[1]

[1] *WSJ*, "Berkshire Buys 80% of Tool Maker for $4 Billion," by Karen Richardson and Dennis K. Berman, 5/6/06, p. A3.

1. Why would Berkshire not purchase the entire company and instead only purchase a majority stake?
2. What reasons would cause Buffett to not implement major changes at Iscar?

The 1990s and start of the next century saw merger activity sweeping the service industries with unparalleled enthusiasm, if not always with equal success. A move to merge health-maintenance organizations, for example, was followed by the consolidation of group physicians' practices. Small companies were often targeted, where the big investors were less interested, helping to keep the acquisition price more affordable (e.g., five times cash flows, rather than six times cash flows). A technique called "platform investing" enables a buyer to start with one acquisition and to follow it with others until the company is large enough to take public. Examples of service-sector industries where this technique has proven sometimes successful include funeral homes, golf resorts, landfill sites, and antenna towers. Among the less-successful efforts to date are restaurants, service stations, and dry cleaners.[2] From the mom-and-pop stores to the largest service organizations in the country, business combinations appeared to be a way of life for American business.

"Few things in banking are as ho-hum as the back-office operations that handle billions of deposits, withdrawals, and other transactions every day. But with acquisition activity intensifying such systems are about to face a huge test." J.P Morgan Chase & Co., Wells Fargo & Co. and PNC Financial Services Group Inc. will need to spend hundreds of millions of dollars over the next several years to integrate recent acquisitions of Washington Mutual's banking operations, Wachovia Corp. and National City Corp. Combining two banks is notoriously expensive, risky, and complicated. It took J.P. Morgan about seventeen years after its 1988 acquisition to merge the operations fully of Texas Commerce Banc-shares Inc.[3]

The merger mania slacked in 2002, as many former acquisitions proved unprofitable, but surged again by the middle of the decade before slacking off in late 2008.

Recall that business combinations may be negotiated either as **asset acquisitions** or as **stock acquisitions**. In Chapter 2 the procedural focus was on business combinations arising from ***asset acquisitions***. In those situations the acquiring company survived, and the acquired company or companies ceased to exist as separate legal entities. The focus in this chapter is on accounting practices followed in ***stock acquisitions***, that is, when one company **controls** the activities of another company through the direct or indirect ownership of some or all of its voting stock.

When this occurs, the acquiring company is generally referred to as the **parent** and the acquired company as a **subsidiary**. Those holding any remaining stock in a subsidiary are referred to as the **noncontrolling (minority) interest**. Any joint relationship is termed an **affiliation**, and the related companies are called **affiliated companies**. Each of the affiliated companies continues its separate legal existence, and the investing company carries its interest as an investment. The affiliated companies continue to account individually for their own assets and liabilities, with the parent company reflecting the investment on its books in a single account,

LO2 Noncontrolling interest (NCI).

[2] *Business Week*, "Buy 'Em Out, Then Build 'Em Up," by Eric Schine, 5/8/95, p. 85.

[3] *Wall Street Journal*, "Next Crisis for U.S. Banks? Integration," by Robin Sidel, p. C1, January 9, 2009.

Investment in Subsidiary. This account will ultimately be eliminated in the consolidating process to produce a set of consolidated financial statements. However, the investment account will be maintained in the "parent" records. Thus, an important distinction is noted between the ***consolidated*** statements and the ***parent only*** records or statements in the case of stock acquisitions.

A corporate affiliation may, of course, consist of more than two companies. A parent may obtain a controlling interest in the voting stock of several subsidiaries. If one or more of the subsidiaries owns a controlling interest in one or more other companies, a chain of ownership is forged by which the parent company controls, either directly or indirectly, the activities of the other companies. Many large American conglomerates have been formed by a variety of indirect ownerships.

In a stock-for-stock deal valued at $1.46 billion, Houston-based Plains Exploration & Production Co. will acquire Stone Energy Corp. of Lafayette, Louisiana. The purchase price is based on Plains' closing stock price on April 21 and the assumption of $483 million of Stone's debt. Shareholders of Stone will receive 1.25 shares of Plains per share of Stone common. Upon the deal's closing, Plains shareholders will own 70% of the combined company while Stone shareholders will own 30%.[4]

1. What risks do the shareholders of Stone take on by accepting only stock in this transaction?
2. Discuss reasons why Plains' shareholders would rather use its stock than cash to purchase Stone.

DEFINITIONS OF SUBSIDIARY AND CONTROL

LO1 Meaning of control.

Although the term **subsidiary** takes on varied meanings in practice, in this text it refers to *the situation wherein a parent company (and/or the parent's other subsidiaries) owns a controlling financial interest in another company, whether that company is incorporated or not (such as a trust or partnership).*[5] Both the IASB and the FASB have indicated their opinion that the definition of control should not be limited to the common presumption in practice of a 50% cutoff but should instead include an indirect ability to control another entity's assets. In February 1999, the FASB issued a revised Exposure Draft, focusing on another entity's **policies and management** rather than its assets; in December 2008 the IASB issued an Exposure Draft ***Consolidated Financial Statements***, and in June 2009 FASB issued two new standards related to the consolidation of certain special entities that had formerly been exempted.

Controlling interest is defined as the portion of the equity of the consolidated group attributable to the parent and the parent's owners. One of the sources of contention or

[4] *Houston Business Journal*, "Plains E&P to Acquire Stone Energy," 4/24/06.

[5] The SEC distinguishes majority-owned, totally held, and wholly owned subsidiaries. The term **majority-owned** means *a subsidiary more than 50% of whose outstanding voting shares are owned by its parent and/or the parent's other majority-owned subsidiaries.* The term **totally held** means *a subsidiary (1) substantially all of whose outstanding equity securities are owned by its parent and/or the parent's other totally held subsidiaries, and (2) which is not indebted to any person other than its parent and/or the parent's other totally held subsidiaries, in an amount that is material in relation to the particular subsidiary.* The term **wholly owned** means *a subsidiary all of whose outstanding voting shares are owned by its parent and/or the parent's other wholly owned subsidiaries.*

uncertainty involves the *special rules that allowed special purpose entities (SPEs)* to remain unconsolidated when certain criteria were met until November 2009. The accounting for these types of entities came under fire in the last quarter of 2001 when the Enron debacle became everyday news.

By March 2002, the Enron controversy had threatened to inflict political damage on the White House, and President Bush proposed an SEC plan to tighten oversight of the accounting profession. Critics were quick to dismiss his proposal as too light or "toothless," and by July 2002 a number of other accounting scandals had followed on the heels of Enron.

Profits rose 20% in Walt Disney Co.'s fiscal third quarter as revenue at its parks and resorts and studio-entertainment businesses doubled. Revenue at parks and resorts climbed 32% to $2.29 billion as the financial statements of Euro Disney and Hong Kong Disneyland were consolidated, contributing $332 million to the revenue increase. Disney adopted an accounting rule pertaining to the consolidation of variable interest entities or VIEs. In implementing this rule, Disney consolidated the balance sheets of Euro Disney and Hong Kong Disneyland as of March 31, and the income and cash flow statements beginning April 1.[6]

1. Prior to the adoption of the accounting rule, where in Disney's financial statements would the financial results from the VIEs appear?
2. Why might Disney choose separate dates to consolidate the balance sheets and income and cash flow statements?

The FASB abandoned its original exposure draft on the accounting for special-purpose entities in favor of an Interpretation (*FASB Interpretation No. 46*) on the accounting for *variable interest entities*, or *VIEs*. This Interpretation was subsequently revised in December 2003, and *FASB Interpretation 46-R* took effect for most companies in 2004 or 2005. Then, in June 2009, the FASB concluded its deliberations on the subject and issued *SFAS No. 166* and *SFAS No. 167*. *SFAS No. 166* eliminates the exemption from consolidation for certain SPEs that previously "qualified." *SFAS No. 167* requires a company to perform a qualitative analysis to determine whether it must consolidate a VIE. This standard assumes that companies that control another entity through interests other than voting interests should consolidate the controlled entity, ***requiring existing unconsolidated VIEs to be consolidated by their primary beneficiaries if the entities do not disperse risks effectively among involved parties.*** The ***primary beneficiary*** of a VIE is the party that absorbs a majority of the entity's expected losses, receives a majority of its expected residual returns, or both. ***Variable interests*** are the ownership, contractual or other pecuniary interests in an entity that change with changes in the fair value of the entity's net assets other than variable interests.

FASB's objective **[ASC 810–10–05–8 to 810–10–05–13]** was stated as improving financial reporting by those firms involved with VIEs. The conclusion of the FASB is that the assets, liabilities, and activities of these entities should be included in the consolidated financial statements of the firms with a controlling interest in them. Both new standards require additional disclosures related to risk exposure. More details are presented in APPENDIX B of this chapter. International standards do not address VIEs.

[6] *Dow Jones Business News*, "Disney's 3Q Net Rose 20% on Parks, Studio Revenue Growth," by Rose K. Manzo, 8/10/04.

The question of how to handle *qualifying special purpose entities (QSPEs)* had been particularly troublesome. According to *FASB Statement No. 140*, a QSPE was a separate structure that held passive financial assets for the benefit of the investors and was so passive, and its actions and decisions so limited, that control (and thus consolidation) was not an issue. International accounting standards (IFRS, or International Financial Reporting Standards), in contrast, did not contain provisions that allow for the idea of a QSPE, and they require all "controlled" SPEs to be consolidated. With the issuance of *FASB Statement No. 166*, FASB removed the exemption from consolidation for QSPEs. As a result, many QSPEs that were off-balance sheet became subject to the revised consolidation guidance for VIEs (*FASB Statement No. 167*). *FASB Statement No. 156*, "Accounting for Servicing of Financial Assets—another amendment of *FASB Statement No. 140* **[ASC 860–50–35]**" addresses the recognition of transfers to a QSPE with respect to separately recognized servicing assets and liabilities. When a firm transfers financial assets to a QSPE in a guaranteed mortgage securitization (in which the transferor retains the resulting securities and classifies them either as available-for-sale securities or trading securities), the firm is required under *Statement No. 156* to recognize a servicing asset or servicing liability. The Statement also requires that such assets and liabilities be initially measured at fair value, if practicable.

IFRS

On July 30, 2002, President Bush signed into law an Accounting Industry Reform Act, requiring chief executive officers to certify the validity of their firms' financial statements beginning August 14, 2002. Other aspects of the act included the following: the establishment of an oversight board for the accounting industry and the auditing sector in particular (the PCAOB or Public Companies' Accounting Oversight Board); restrictions on the types of consulting services allowed to be performed by auditors, such as bookkeeping, financial systems design, and personnel and legal services; bans on personal loans from companies to their top officials and directors; and the creation of new penalties for corporate fraud.

The Public Company Accounting Oversight Board announced that the upcoming scheduled inspections of public accounting firms will focus on whether firms heed PCAOB warnings concerning rigid and overreaching audits and guidance provided by the board. "A key emphasis of the 2006 inspections will be the efficiency of the firms' performance of audits of internal control over financial reporting," said PCAOB Acting Chairman Bill Gradison in a statement. Inspectors will also examine whether auditors used a "top-down" approach by beginning the audit by focusing on company-level controls instead of utilizing checklists without considering what areas were critical to a client's specific business.[7]

FASB has defined control as the "ability of an entity to direct the policies and management that guide the ongoing activities of another entity so as to increase its benefits and limit its losses from that other entity's activities. For purposes of consolidated financial statements, control involves decision-making ability that is not shared with others." It stressed the need to prepare consolidated financial statements whenever **control** exists, even in the absence of a majority ownership, and provided a list of indicators of presumed control, noting that the proposed definition is similar to the explicit definitions recommended by the International Accounting Standards Board.

[7] *CFO.com Magazine*, "PCAOB: Auditor Judgment under Scrutiny," by Tim Reason, 5/3/06.

Consolidation of entities that are not majority-owned is opposed by some companies, particularly biotechnology and pharmaceutical concerns, whose financial strength could be hurt by reporting consolidated financials. Accounting professionals have argued that some firms deliberately avoid consolidating results by owning less than 50% of the voting stock in an entity, even though they effectively control it by hiring and firing management.[8]

1. In what instances would a company *want* to consolidate an entity of which the company owns less than 50%?
2. Discuss ways that a company can control another with less than majority ownership.

In this chapter we focus on situations where the control is evidenced by a majority ownership. The same procedures would apply, however, in the case where a smaller percentage ownership exists concurrently with evidence of effective control (for example, the parent owns 40% of the voting stock, and no other party has a significant interest, or the parent controls the board).

The Securities and Exchange Commission defines a subsidiary as an affiliate controlled by another entity, directly or indirectly, through one or more intermediaries. Control means the possession, direct or indirect, of the power to direct or cause the direction of the management and policies of another entity, whether through the ownership of voting shares, by contract, or otherwise. The debate arises because such a definition is less clear cut than majority ownership. It is, however, consistent with the stated objective of the IASB and the FASB to move away from rules-based accounting in favor of principles-based accounting.

REQUIREMENTS FOR THE INCLUSION OF SUBSIDIARIES IN THE CONSOLIDATED FINANCIAL STATEMENTS

LO5 Requirements regarding consolidation of subsidiaries.

The purpose of consolidated statements is to present the operating results and the financial position of a parent and all its subsidiaries as if they are one economic entity. Given this purpose and problems related to off-balance-sheet financing, the FASB has taken the position that essentially all controlled corporations should be consolidated. In general, the objective of consolidation is to provide the most meaningful financial presentation possible in the circumstances. The FASB has reemphasized the basic position that parent-company -only financial statements are unacceptable for general purpose distribution; that is, the consolidated financial statements are the primary statements of the economic entity. It notes that parent-company-only statements may be needed in addition to consolidated financial statements for the interests of such parties as bondholders, other creditors, and preferred shareholders of the parent. Consolidating statements, with columns for different subsidiaries or groups of subsidiaries and one column for the parent, are one effective way to present such information.

Under some circumstances, majority-owned subsidiaries should be excluded from the consolidated statements. Those circumstances include those where:

1. Control does not rest with the majority owner. For example, a subsidiary in legal reorganization or bankruptcy should not be consolidated.
2. The subsidiary operates under governmentally imposed uncertainty so severe as to raise significant doubt about the parent's control. For example, a foreign

[8] *WSJ*, "FASB Seeks More Disclosure in Minor Stakes," by Elizabeth MacDonald, 3/3/99, p. C12.

subsidiary is domiciled in a country with foreign exchange restrictions, controls, or other governmentally imposed uncertainties so severe that they cast significant doubt on the parent's ability to control the subsidiary.

A difference in fiscal year-ends between the parent and a subsidiary does not justify the exclusion of the subsidiary from the consolidation financial statements. It is generally viewed as feasible for the subsidiary to prepare financial statements to coincide, or nearly coincide, with the parent's fiscal period. When the difference between year-ends is greater than three months, it is usually acceptable to use the subsidiary's statements for its fiscal period, giving recognition by disclosure notes or other means of intervening events that materially affect the results of operations or financial position.

REASONS FOR SUBSIDIARY COMPANIES

LO3 Acquiring assets or stock.

There are several advantages to acquiring a controlling interest in the voting stock of another company rather than its assets or all its voting stock. For example:

1. Stock acquisition is relatively simple. Stock can be acquired by open market purchases or by cash tender offers to the subsidiary's stockholders. Such acquisitions avoid the often lengthy and difficult negotiations that are required in an exchange of stock for stock in a complete takeover.
2. Control of the subsidiary's operations can be accomplished with a much smaller investment, since not all of the stock need be acquired.
3. The separate legal existence of the individual affiliates provides an element of protection of the parent's assets from attachment by creditors of the subsidiary. A parent may sometimes establish a subsidiary by forming a new corporation rather than simply adding a division to the existing company. The limited liability characteristic of the corporate form of business organization is often the primary reason for doing so.

CONSOLIDATED FINANCIAL STATEMENTS

RELATED CONCEPTS

The *economic entity* assumption suggests that a parent and its subsidiaries be viewed as one economic entity, even if several separate legal entities exist.

The statements prepared for a parent company and its subsidiaries are called **consolidated financial statements**. They include the full complement of statements normally prepared for a separate entity and represent essentially the sum of the assets, liabilities, revenues, and expenses of the affiliates after eliminating the effect of any transactions among the affiliated companies. Accountants recognize that the unconsolidated financial statements of the parent company, the **legal entity**, are *insufficient to present the financial position and results of operations of the* ***economic entity*** *controlled by the parent company.*

Consider for a moment the unconsolidated financial statements of the parent company. When the parent acquires a controlling interest in the subsidiary, the parent makes an entry debiting **Investment in Subsidiary** and crediting either cash, debt, or stock (or some combination), depending on the medium of exchange. Assume that the acquisition relies on a cash purchase price of $5 million. The entry on the parent's books would be:

Investment in Subsidiary	$5,000,000	
Cash		$5,000,000

The parent's investment account represents the parent's investment in the different asset and liability accounts of the subsidiary and often includes a significant amount of goodwill. However, it is recorded in a single account entitled Investment. The subsidiary, in contrast, continues to keep its detailed books based on historical book values. These values are not as current as the market values assessed by the parent at the date of acquisition, but they are detailed as to classification. One way of looking at the process of consolidating is to consider the following table.

LO4 Valuation and classification of subsidiary assets and liabilities.

	Investment Account on the Parent's Books	*Asset and Liability Accounts on the Subsidiary's Books*
Valuation	Market Value	Historical Value
Classification	One Account	Multiple Accounts

From the table above, we see that neither the parent's Investment account nor the subsidiary's detailed asset and liability accounts serves to provide ***both*** the valuation and classification desired in the consolidated financial statements. The process of preparing consolidated financial statements aims to achieve the desirable characteristics in the diagonal by showing the detailed asset and liability accounts on the consolidated balance sheet, but using the valuation established by the acquisition price. Further, this valuation provides the basis needed to measure earnings, reflecting all necessary charges.[9]

The purpose of consolidated statements is to present, primarily for the benefit of the owners and creditors of the parent, the results of operations and the financial position of a parent company and all its subsidiaries as if the consolidated group were a single economic entity.[10] Consolidated statements ignore the legal aspects of the separate entities but focus instead on the economic entity under the "control" of management. The presumption is that most users of financial statements prefer to evaluate the economic entity rather than the legal entity. Thus, the preparation of consolidated statements is an example of focusing on substance rather than form.

Although consolidated statements for the economic entity are considered to be more appropriate for use by the stockholders and creditors of the parent company (and are the only general-purpose financial statement acceptable under GAAP for companies with one or more subsidiaries), they are not substitutes for the statements prepared by the separate subsidiaries. Creditors of the subsidiaries must look to the statements of the individual legal entities in assessing the degree of protection related to their claims. Likewise, noncontrolling stockholders need the statements of the individual companies to determine the degree of investment risk involved and the amounts available for dividends. Also, regulatory agencies are often concerned with the net resources and results of operations of the individual subsidiaries.

[9] *Statement of Financial Accounting Standards No. 94,* "Consolidation of All Majority-Owned Subsidiaries" (Norwalk, CT: FASB, 1987) [ASC 810].

[10] This position was expressed by the FASB in *FASB Statement No. [160]* [ASC 810–10–10–1], December 2007.

INVESTMENTS AT THE DATE OF ACQUISITION

LO7 Recording of investment at acquisition.

The general principles used to record business combinations effected as asset acquisitions were discussed in Chapter 2. ***In this chapter and throughout*** Chapters 4 ***through*** 9, ***we will concentrate on accounting for the acquisition of another company's voting stock.*** APPENDIX A to this chapter presents issues related to deferred taxes at the date of acquisition.

Recording Investments at Cost (Parent's Books)

The basic guidelines for valuation discussed in Chapter 2 pertaining to business combinations apply equally to the acquisition of voting stock in another company. Under the purchase or acquisition method, the stock investment is recorded at its cost as measured by the fair value of the consideration given or the consideration received, whichever is more clearly evident. Recall that the consideration given may consist of cash, other assets, debt securities, stock of the acquiring company, or a combination of these items. Under *SFAS No. 141R* **[ASC 805–10–25–23]**, both the direct costs of acquiring the stock and the indirect costs relating to acquisitions (such as the costs of maintaining an acquisitions department) should be expensed as incurred.

If cash is used for the acquisition, the investment is recorded at its cash cost, excluding broker's fees and other direct costs of the investment. For example, assume that P Company acquires all 10,000 shares of the common stock of S Company for $25 per share and pays acquisition fees of $10,000. The entry to record the investment on P Company's books is:

Investment in S Company	250,000	
Cash (10,000) ($25)		250,000

The acquisition fee would be recorded in a separate entry as an expense. If P Company acquired only 50% of the 10,000 shares at $25 per share and paid an acquisition fee of $8,000, the acquisition entry would be:

Investment in S Company	125,000	
Cash (5,000) ($25)		125,000

If P Company issues stock in the acquisition, the investment is recorded at the fair value of the stock issued, giving effect to any costs of registering the stock issue. Assume, for example, that P Company issues 20,000 of its $10 par value common shares with a fair value of $13 per share for the 10,000 shares of S Company, and that registration costs amount to $5,000, paid in cash. The entries to record the investment on P Company's books are:

Investment in S Company (20,000) ($13)	260,000	
Common Stock (20,000) ($10)		200,000
Other Contributed Capital (20,000) ($3)		60,000
Other Contributed Capital	5,000	
Cash (registration costs)		5,000

If P Company paid an additional $10,000 as a finder's fee, the entry would be:

Professional Fees Expense	10,000	
Cash		10,000

TEST YOUR KNOWLEDGE

NOTE: Solutions to ***Test Your Knowledge*** questions are found at the end of each chapter before the end-of-chapter questions.

Multiple Choice

1. Stock given as consideration is valued at:
   (A) Fair market value
   (B) Par value
   (C) Historical cost
   (D) None of the above
2. Which of the following advantages and/or disadvantages of stock acquisitions relative to asset acquisitions (and subsequent consolidated financial statements) is *misstated*?
   (A) *FASB Statement No. 141R* **[ASC 805]** indicates that consolidated statements need not be produced as long as a parent company owns less than 50% of the voting shares of the subsidiary.
   (B) Stock can be acquired by open-market purchases or by cash tender offers to the subsidiary's stockholders.
   (C) Control of the subsidiary's operation can be accomplished with a much smaller investment, since not all of the stock need be acquired.
   (D) The separate legal existence of the individual affiliates provides an element of protection of the parent's assets from attachment by creditors of the subsidiary.
3. Which of the following is not (generally) an advantage of stock acquisitions over asset acquisitions?
   (A) Speed
   (B) Majority of ownership not required
   (C) Liability protection
   (D) Anonymity
4. In its conceptual framework, the FASB set out a number of principles to be adhered to in standard setting and in interpreting financial statements. The decision to require a consolidated statement, rather than separate financial statements, for a parent firm and its subsidiary best illustrates which of the following principles or concepts?
   (A) Periodicity
   (B) Going concern
   (C) Materiality
   (D) Economic entity

CONSOLIDATED BALANCE SHEETS: THE USE OF WORKPAPERS

LO8 Preparing consolidated statements using a workpaper.

Affiliated companies should prepare a full set of financial statements (balance sheet, or statement of position; statement of income and comprehensive income; statement of cash flows; statement of stockholders' equity (or retained earnings); and notes to the financial statements). As of the **date of acquisition** of one company by another, however, the most relevant statement is the consolidated balance sheet. Preparation of the other consolidated financial statements becomes important with the passage of time and is discussed in later chapters.

The consolidated balance sheet reports ***the sum*** of the assets and liabilities of a parent and its subsidiaries as if they constituted a single company. Assets and liabilities are summed in their entirety, regardless of whether the parent owns 100% or a smaller controlling interest. In the latter case, the noncontrolling interests are reflected as a component of owners' equity. This interest may be referred to as either the noncontrolling interest in net assets or as the noncontrolling interest in equity (these terms are identical), and is sometimes abbreviated as NCI.

Since the parent and its subsidiaries are being treated as a single entity, eliminations must be made to cancel the effects of transactions among them. Intercompany receivables and payables, for example, must be eliminated to avoid double counting and to avoid giving the impression that the consolidated entity owes money to itself. Likewise, any intercompany profits in assets arising from subsequent transactions must be eliminated, since an entity cannot profit on transactions with itself. A **workpaper** is frequently used to summarize the effects of the various additions, eliminations, and so forth. Among the types of transactions that necessitate eliminating entries are the following:[11]

RELATED CONCEPTS

The *revenue recognition* principle indicates that revenue should be recognized only when transactions with entities *outside* the consolidated economic unit are completed.

Intercompany Accounts to Be Eliminated

Parent's Accounts		*Subsidiary's Accounts*
Investment in subsidiary	Against	Equity accounts
Intercompany receivable (payable)	Against	Intercompany payable (receivable)
Advances to subsidiary (from subsidiary)	Against	Advances from parent (to parent)
Interest revenue (interest expense)	Against	Interest expense (interest revenue)
Dividend revenue (dividends declared)	Against	Dividends declared (dividend revenue)
Management fee received from subsidiary	Against	Management fee paid to parent
Sales to subsidiary (purchases of inventory from subsidiary)	Against	Purchases of inventory from parent (sales to parent)

The process of eliminating these and other types of items (such as the profit or loss on intercompany sales of assets not realized in transactions with outsiders) will be discussed in detail in this and later chapters. This chapter will focus on balance sheet accounts, while later chapters will focus on both balance sheet and income statement accounts.

Investment Elimination

LO8 Investment is eliminated for consolidated statements.

An important basic elimination in the preparation of consolidated statements is the elimination of the investment account and the related subsidiary's stockholders' equity. The investment account represents the investment by the parent company in the net assets of the subsidiary and is, therefore, reciprocal to the subsidiary company's stockholders' equity. Since the subsidiary company's assets and liabilities are combined with those of the parent company in the consolidated balance sheet, it is necessary to eliminate the investment account of the parent company against the related stockholders' equity of the subsidiary to avoid double counting of these net assets. In effect, when the parent company's share of the subsidiary company's equity is eliminated against the investment account, the subsidiary company's net assets are substituted for the investment account in the consolidated balance sheet.

[11] The account used by the parent to record dividends received from the subsidiary will differ if the parent uses the equity method, described in Chapter 4, to account for its investment.

The process of combining the individual assets and liabilities of a parent company and its subsidiary at the date of acquisition is discussed next. To start the consolidating process, a useful first step is to prepare a *"Computation and Allocation of Difference between Implied Value and Book Value"* schedule (CAD). Preparation of this schedule requires us to address three basic issues.

LO9 Computing and allocating the difference between implied and book value (CAD).

1. Determine the percentage of stock acquired in the subsidiary. (Is it a 100% acquisition, or a smaller percentage?)
2. Use the purchase price (cost) to compute the ***implied value*** of the subsidiary. Simply divide the purchase price by the percentage acquired to calculate this value. If the percentage is 100%, the implied value will equal the purchase price.
3. Compare the implied value from step (2) to the book value of the subsidiary's equity. If a difference exists, we must then allocate that difference to adjust the underlying assets and/or liabilities of the acquired company.

The book value of the equity is the sum of all equity accounts (common stock, additional contributed capital, retained earnings, etc.), which equals the book value of the acquired firm's assets minus liabilities at the date of acquisition.

Implied Value of Subsidiary Equity = (Acquisition Price)/(Percentage Acquired)

Note that the comparison is between implied value and ***book*** value. This comparison is appropriate because the subsidiary company's accounts are recorded at book value amounts, and the trial balance of the subsidiary company (along with the trial balance of the parent company) provides the starting point for the consolidation process. Thus, although market values are crucial in determining the numbers that are eventually reported in the consolidated financial statements, we use book values to establish a starting point. When the implied value exceeds the book value, the difference will be distributed to adjust net assets upward. See Figure 3-1 for a graphic illustration of this principle. When the implied value is less than the book value, the difference may be distributed to adjust net assets downward, or a gain may be recognized for a "bargain," as dictated by the facts of the acquisition.

The steps above lead to the following possible cases:

Case 1. The implied value (IV) of the subsidiary (purchase price divided by percentage acquired) is **equal** to the book value of the subsidiary company's equity (IV = BV), and

- **a.** The parent company acquires 100% of the subsidiary company's stock; or
- **b.** The parent company acquires less than 100% of the subsidiary company's stock.

Case 2. The implied value of the subsidiary **exceeds** the book value of the subsidiary company's equity (IV > BV), and

- **a.** The parent company acquires 100% of the subsidiary company's stock; or
- **b.** The parent company acquires less than 100% of the subsidiary company's stock.

Case 3. The implied value of the subsidiary is **less** than the book value of the subsidiary company's equity (IV < BV), and

- **a.** The parent company acquires 100% of the subsidiary company's stock; or
- **b.** The parent company acquires less than 100% of the subsidiary company's stock.

FIGURE 3-1

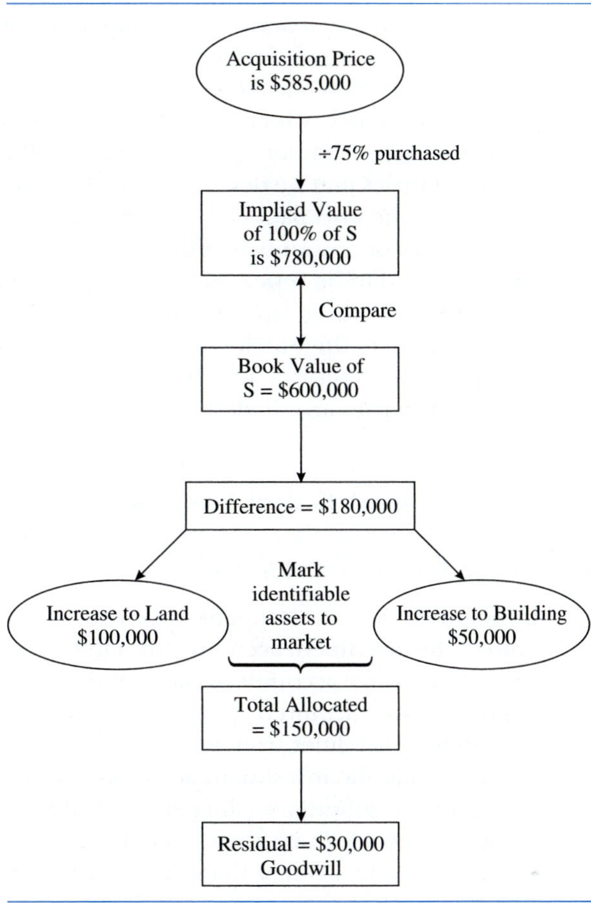

We next illustrate the alternatives above in the order listed, with the exception that we omit illustrations of Cases 2(a) and 3(a), which should be readily apparent after reading the others. Examples are based on the balance sheets as of January 1, 2007, for P Company and S Company as shown in Illustration 3-1.

ILLUSTRATION 3-1

Balance Sheets for P Company and S Company
January 1, 2010

	P Company	*S Company*
Cash	$100,000	$ 20,000
Other current assets	140,000	50,000
Plant and equipment (net)	120,000	40,000
Land	40,000	20,000
Total assets	$400,000	$130,000
Liabilities	$ 60,000	$ 50,000
Common stock, $10 par value	200,000	50,000
Other contributed capital	40,000	10,000
Retained earnings	100,000	20,000
Total Liabilities and Equity	$400,000	$130,000

It is important to distinguish between **actual entries** that are *recorded in the books of one of the two companies* and **workpaper-only entries**. The entries *presented in the preceding section to record the Investment in S Company were actual entries, which would be recorded in the accounts of P Company*. These types of entries would already be reflected in the trial balance, which constitutes the first column of the workpapers presented throughout this chapter (see, for example, Illustration 3-2 or Illustration 3-3).

The entries that we develop next, and which appear in the middle "elimination" columns of the workpapers, are ***workpaper-only entries***. As such, they are never posted to the books or accounts of either company's general ledger. Consequently, the entries will need to be repeated each year in the consolidating process. In some cases a number of entries from prior years may be combined to simplify the process; but, in essence, the entries are being repeated each year. Throughout this book, workpaper-only entries will be presented **shaded in blue**. Parent company and subsidiary entries are shaded in **gray**.

Case 1 (a): Implied Value of Subsidiary Is Equal to Book Value of Subsidiary Company's Equity (IV = BV)—Total Ownership (100% of Subsidiary Stock Acquired)

If the purchase price happens to be exactly equal to the book value of the equity acquired, the investment account (from the parent's trial balance) will eliminate cleanly against the equity accounts of the subsidiary. If we assume further that the market values of the assets acquired approximate their book values, then there is no need to adjust assets or liabilities from their recorded values. The end result of the eliminating process is that the investment account is completely eliminated, as are the equity accounts of the subsidiary (since it is a 100% acquisition). In essence the investment account is replaced with the underlying assets and liabilities of the subsidiary.

To illustrate, assume that on January 1, 2010, P Company acquired all the outstanding stock (5,000 shares) of S Company for a cash payment of $80,000. P Company would record an actual journal entry as follows:

Investment in S Company	$80,000	
Cash		$80,000

Immediately after the acquisition, P Company has $20,000 in cash ($100,000 shown in Illustration 3-1, immediately prior to acquisition, minus $80,000 spent to acquire Company S) and $80,000 in an Investment in S Company account. These amounts appear in the first column of the workpaper presented in Illustration 3-2. In the case of a 100% acquisition, the implied value of the subsidiary equals the purchase price. The Computation and Allocation of Difference Between Implied and Book Values Schedule reveals no difference, as shown below.

Computation and Allocation of Difference (between Implied and Book Values) Schedule

	Parent Share	*NonControlling Share*	*Total Value*
Purchase price and implied value	$80,000	—0—	$80,000
Less: Book value of equity acquired	80,000	—0—	80,000
Difference between implied and book values	$ —0—	$—0—	$ —0—

Note that the $80,000 paid equals the recorded value of S Company's stockholders' equity. Data for the preparation of formal consolidated statements are normally accumulated on a workpaper, on which any required adjusting and eliminating entries are made prior to combining remaining balances. **Adjusting entries** are *those needed to correct any accounts of the affiliates that may be incorrect or to recognize the unrecorded effect of transactions that have been recorded by one party, but not by the other.* Adjusting entries must be made ultimately on the books of one or more of the affiliates. **Eliminating entries** are *made to cancel the effects of intercompany transactions and are made on the workpaper only.* In all illustrations throughout this book, **letter notation** is *used to identify related parts of adjusting entries,* and **number notation** to *identify related parts of eliminating entries.* Note, however, that some of the eliminating entries will involve "adjustments" to accounts, particularly when there is a difference between implied and book values. Thus, it is technically more accurate to think of eliminating entries as eliminating/adjusting entries or as workpaper entries. These entries will be our focus throughout the next several chapters, and adjusting entries are used only rarely.

The workpaper entry to eliminate S Company's stockholders' equity against the investment account, in general journal form, is:

(1)	Common Stock—S Company	50,000	
	Other Contributed Capital—S Company	10,000	
	Retained Earnings—S Company	20,000	
	Investment in S Company		80,000

Remember, although it is expressed in general journal form, this is a **workpaper-only entry**. No entry is made on the books of either company. As mentioned previously, ***all workpaper entries are shaded in blue*** to distinguish them clearly from book entries.

A workpaper for the preparation of a consolidated balance sheet for P and S Companies on January 1, 2010, the date of acquisition, is presented in Illustration 3-2.

Acquisition Accounting
Implied Value Equals Book Value
Wholly Owned Subsidiary
Date of Acquisition

ILLUSTRATION 3-2
Consolidated Balance Sheet Workpaper
P Company and Subsidiary
January 1, 2010

			Eliminations		
	P Company	*S Company*	*Dr.*	*Cr.*	*Consolidated Balances*
Cash	20,000	20,000			40,000
Other Current Assets	140,000	50,000			190,000
Plant and Equipment	120,000	40,000			160,000
Land	40,000	20,000			60,000
Investment in S Company	80,000			(1) 80,000	
Total Assets	$400,000	$130,000			$450,000
Liabilities	60,000	50,000			110,000
Common Stock					
P Company	200,000				200,000
S Company		50,000	(1) 50,000		
Other Contributed Capital					
P Company	40,000				40,000
S Company		10,000	(1) 10,000		
Retained Earnings					
P Company	100,000				100,000
S Company		20,000	(1) 20,000		
Total Liabilities and Equity	$400,000	$130,000	$80,000	$80,000	$450,000

(1) To eliminate investment in S Company.

Note the following on the workpaper:

1. The investment account and related subsidiary's stockholders' equity have been eliminated, and the subsidiary company's net assets substituted for the investment account.
2. Consolidated assets and liabilities consist of the sum of the parent and subsidiary assets and liabilities in each classification.
3. Consolidated stockholders' equity is the same as the parent company's equity. This is as it should be, since the subsidiary company's stockholders' equity has been eliminated against the parent company's investment account. The consolidated balance sheet is that of the ***economic*** entity, and the only ownership interest is that represented by P Company's stockholders; that is, P Company owns all of S Company's stock.

Case 1 (b): Implied Value of Subsidiary Is Equal to Book Value of Subsidiary Company's Stock (IV = BV)—Partial Ownership (Less Than 100% of Subsidiary Stock Acquired)

Next we introduce a noncontrolling interest. In this situation, the consolidated balance sheet will nonetheless reflect the combined assets and liabilities of parent and subsidiary ***in their entirety***. To balance, the equity interests will then be separated into the noncontrolling interest's equity in net assets and the usual controlling interest equity accounts.

Assume that on January 1, 2010, P Company acquired 90% (4,500 shares) of the stock of S Company for $72,000. Since P Company owns less than 100% of S Company's stock, consideration must be given to the existence of a noncontrolling interest (minority interest) in the net assets of S Company. The purchase price of $72,000 for 90% of S Company implies a total valuation for S Company of $72,000/90%, or $80,000. The noncontrolling interest is, thus, implied to be valued at 10% × $80,000 or $8,000. In this illustration the implied and book values are equal, both for the controlling and noncontrolling interests. A Computation and Allocation of Difference (CAD) Schedule would appear as follows:

Computation and Allocation of Difference (between Implied and Book Values) Schedule

	Parent Share	*Noncontrolling Share*	*Total Value*
Purchase price and implied value	**$72,000**	**8,000**	80,000
Less: Book value of subsidiary equity:			
Common stock	45,000	5,000	**50,000**
Other contributed capital	9,000	1,000	**10,000**
Retained earnings	18,000	2,000	**20,000**
Total book value	72,000	8,000	80,000
Difference between implied and book value	—0—	—0—	—0—

Note that the amounts in bold in the CAD Schedule provide the entries in the following workpaper investment elimination entry:

(1)	Common Stock—S Company	50,000	
	Other Contributed Capital—S Company	10,000	
	Retained Earnings—S Company	20,000	
	Investment in S Company		72,000
	Noncontrolling Interest in Equity		8,000

The entire 100% of S Company's equity is eliminated, 90% against the investment account with the remaining 10% of S Company's equity constituting the noncontrolling interest. The purpose of the consolidated balance sheet is to report the net resources under the control of a single management, and the management of P Company effectively controls all S Company's resources. Thus, all S Company's assets and liabilities are combined with those of P Company on the consolidated balance sheet, and the noncontrolling interest representing the noncontrolling shareholders' interest in the net assets is a separate component of stockholders' equity.

A workpaper for the preparation of a consolidated balance sheet at the date of acquisition in this situation is presented in Illustration 3-3. A separate column is added to the workpaper in this illustration between the eliminations columns and the consolidated balances to compute the noncontrolling interest in equity. The total in this column represents the percentage of equity of S Company ***not*** acquired by P Company and recorded at the fair value implied by P Company's acquisition price. The total noncontrolling interest is transferred to the consolidated balance sheet column.

Acquisition Accounting
Implied Value Equals Book Value
90% Owned Subsidiary
Date of Acquisition

ILLUSTRATION 3-3
Consolidated Balance Sheet Workpaper
P Company and Subsidiary
January 1, 2010

	P Company	*S Company*	*Eliminations Dr.*	*Eliminations Cr.*	*Noncontrolling Interest*	*Consolidated Balances*
Cash	$ 28,000	$ 20,000				$ 48,000
Other Current Assets	140,000	50,000				190,000
Plant and Equipment	120,000	40,000				160,000
Land	40,000	20,000				60,000
Investment in S Company	72,000			(1) 72,000		
Total Assets	$400,000	$130,000				$458,000
Liabilities	60,000	50,000				110,000
Common stock						
P Company	200,000					200,000
S Company		50,000	(1) 50,000			
Other Contributed Capital						
P Company	40,000					40,000
S Company		10,000	(1) 10,000			
Retained Earnings						
P Company	100,000					100,000
S Company		20,000	(1) 20,000			
Noncontrolling Interest				(1) 8,000	$8,000	8,000
Total Liabilities and Equity	$400,000	$130,000	$80,000	$80,000		$458,000

(1) To eliminate investment in S Company and create noncontrolling interest account.

Although it is listed last on the workpaper, the noncontrolling interest on the actual consolidated balance sheet should appear as the ***first component of stockholders' equity*** (because it is the nearest, from the perspective of the controlling interest, to a liability).

In comparing Illustration 3-2 and Illustration 3-3, it might be noted that: (1) consolidated assets are $8,000 greater in Illustration 3-3 since it took $8,000 less cash to acquire a 90% investment, and (2) an $8,000 noncontrolling interest exists (the remaining 10%). Noncontrolling interest is accumulated on the consolidated workpaper in a separate column.

The proper classification of the noncontrolling interest has been a subject of debate. From the perspective of the controlling interest, it is similar to a liability. It is not, however, a liability because it does not require a future payment by the parent company or the consolidated entity. The shareholders who represent the noncontrolling interest are indeed stockholders, but only of the subsidiary company and not the parent. Some companies, in the past, presented this interest after liabilities and before stockholders' equity on the balance sheet to convey the "hybrid" nature of the noncontrolling interest. According to ***FASB Statement No. 160*** [ASC 810–10–45–16], the noncontrolling interest should be presented as a part of stockholders' equity of the consolidated entity, but clearly labeled to distinguish it from the other equity accounts.[12]

Case 2 (b): Implied Value Exceeds Book Value of Subsidiary Company's Equity (IV > BV)—Partial Ownership (Less Than 100% of Subsidiary Stock Acquired)

Next, we continue to allow for a noncontrolling interest, and we introduce a difference between the cost and the book value acquired, and thus between the implied value and the book value of the subsidiary. In Case 2, we illustrate the common situation where the purchase price is higher than the book value of equity acquired.

Assume that on January 1, 2010, P Company acquired 4,000 shares (80%) of the outstanding common stock of S Company for $74,000 cash, after which P Company has $26,000 in cash and $74,000 in an Investment in S Company. The purchase price of $74,000 for 80% of S Company implies a total value of $74,000/80% or $92,500. The implied value of the noncontrolling interest is $92,500 × 20% or $18,500. The total implied value of $92,500 exceeds the book value of equity of $80,000 by $12,500. A Computation and Allocation of Difference (CAD) Schedule for this situation *begins* as follows:

Computation and Allocation of Difference (between Implied and Book Values) Schedule

	Parent Share	*Noncontrolling Share*	*Total Value*
Purchase price and implied value	**$74,000**	**18,500**	92,500
Less: Book value of equity acquired:			
Common stock	40,000	10,000	**50,000**
Other contributed capital	8,000	2,000	**10,000**
Retained earnings	16,000	4,000	**20,000**
Total book value	64,000	16,000	80,000
Difference between implied and book value	10,000	2,500	**12,500**

[12] The term "**minority interest**" may not reflect clearly the actual nature of some items. For example, a parent company may own 25% of its subsidiary's outstanding preferred stock. In this case, the use of the term "minority interest" to represent the 75% interest held by noncontrolling shareholders is not representative of the circumstances. Also, a parent may have control of a subsidiary with less than 50% of its common stock. The term "noncontrolling interest" is recommended by FASB and is used throughout this text.

In this case, because there is a difference between implied and book values, we must not only ***compute*** the difference but also ***allocate*** that difference to the appropriate accounts. If we assume that the entire difference is attributable to land with a current market value higher than its historical recorded cost, we would complete the CAD schedule as follows:

Computation and Allocation of Difference (between Implied and Book Values) Schedule

	Parent Share	*Noncontrolling Share*	*Total Value*
Purchase price and implied value	**$74,000**	**18,500**	92,500
Less: Book value of equity acquired:			
Common stock	40,000	10,000	**50,000**
Other contributed capital	8,000	2,000	**10,000**
Retained earnings	16,000	4,000	**20,000**
Total book value	64,000	16,000	80,000
Difference between implied and book value	10,000	2,500	**12,500**
Adjust land upward (mark to market)	(10,000)	(2,500)	**(12,500)**
Balance	—0—	—0—	—0—

The difference must be allocated to specific accounts. In this example, the adjustment to increase land to its market value is a debit, and is shown in parentheses. The popular phrase "mark to market" may be used here. In no case would the asset be marked higher than its market value. The amounts are then summed (treating debit adjustments as negative amounts) to yield a balance. The correct distribution of the difference between implied and book values depends on the market values of the underlying assets and liabilities. If the difference is ***larger than the amount*** needed to adjust all net assets, then, ***the excess is goodwill.***

In the past, firms looking for creative ways to avoid recording goodwill sometimes wrote off a portion of the purchase price as an immediate expense under the guise of in-process R&D. This issue has been a controversial one, and *FASB Statement No. 141R* **[paragraph 805–20–35–5]** now requires that in-process R&D be capitalized ***if it is acquired in a business combination.***

Johnson & Johnson (J&J) agreed to acquire privately owned TransForm Pharmaceuticals for $230 million in 2005. The transaction resulted in a one-off $50 million after-tax charge relating to the acquisition of in-process R&D. The deal was aimed at enhancing J&J's ability to leverage existing elements in its pipeline. Under the new FASB position (*SFAS No. 141R* [805–20–35–5]), this treatment of in-process R&D is no longer allowed.[13]

By adjusting all net assets to their market value, a negative balance could result. This situation, referred to as a ***bargain acquisition***, occurs when the ***acquisition price is less than the market value of identifiable net assets acquired.*** After eliminating any previously recorded goodwill on the books of the acquiree, *SFAS No. 141R* **[paragraph 805–30–25–2]** requires that ***this negative balance be recognized in its entirety as an ordinary gain in the income statement in the period of the acquisition.*** We will illustrate bargain acquisitions, which were initially introduced in Chapter 2, again in Chapter 5.

[13] *World Markets Research Center*, "J&J Seeks R&D Boost Through Acquisition of TransForm Pharmaceuticals," by Henry Dummett, 3/10/05.

The treatment of bargain purchase reflects a significant change from prior GAAP, which required that negative goodwill be allocated as a reduction of acquired assets below their fair value. Such a reduction is no longer allowed.

Textbook problems (including those at the end of this chapter) will often make simplifying assumptions, such as "Assume that any difference between implied and book values is attributable solely to land," or "Assume that any difference between implied and book values is attributable to goodwill." This latter assumption is equivalent to stating that book values approximate fair market values. It is important, however, to be aware that more complex adjustments are often needed, and may include a variety of asset and liability accounts (as illustrated in detail in Chapter 5).

Returning to the example above, in which a difference of $12,500 is attributed to land, a workpaper for a consolidated balance sheet at the date of acquisition in this situation is presented in Illustration 3-4.

Acquisition Accounting
Implied Value Equals Book Value
80% Owned Subsidiary
Date of Acquisition

ILLUSTRATION 3-4
Consolidated Balance Sheet Workpaper
P Company and Subsidiary
January 1, 2010

	P Company	*S Company*	*Eliminations Dr.*	*Eliminations Cr.*	*Noncontrolling Interest*	*Consolidated Balances*
Cash	26,000	20,000				46,000
Other Current Assets	140,000	50,000				190,000
Plant and Equipment	120,000	40,000				160,000
Land	40,000	20,000	(2) 12,500			72,500
Investment in S Company	74,000			(1) 74,000		
Difference between implied and book value			(1) 12,500	(2) 12,500		
Total Assets	$400,000	$130,000				$468,500
Liabilities	60,000	50,000				110,000
Common Stock						
P Company	200,000					200,000
S Company		50,000	(1) 50,000			
Other Contributed Capital						
P Company	40,000					40,000
S Company		10,000	(1) 10,000			
Retained Earnings						
P Company	100,000					100,000
S Company		20,000	(1) 20,000			
Noncontrolling Interest				(1) 18,500	18,500	18,500
Total Liabilities and Equity	$400,000	$130,000	$105,000	$105,000		$468,500

(1) To eliminate investment in S Company and create noncontrolling interest account.
(2) To distribute the difference between implied and book value.

The first workpaper investment elimination entry is:

(1)	Common Stock—S Company	50,000	
	Other Contributed Capital—S Company	10,000	
	Retained Earnings—S Company	20,000	
	Difference between Implied and Book Values	12,500	
	Investment in S Company		74,000
	Noncontrolling Interest in Equity		18,500

Elimination entry (1) serves to eliminate the investment account against the equity accounts of the subsidiary and to recognize the difference between implied and book values. A new account entitled "Difference between Implied and Book Values" is created in this entry. This account is a temporary account, which will be immediately eliminated in the very next entry.

Elimination entry (2) (below) serves to allocate the Difference between Implied and Book Values to the appropriate accounts, in this case land:

(2)	Land	12,500	
	Difference between Implied and Book Values		12,500

Clearly entries (1) and (2) could be collapsed into one entry, and the account Difference between Implied and Book Values avoided. It becomes useful, however, to separate the two entries in situations involving a number of accounts with more complex adjustments. As this account will be used in future chapters, it is helpful to become acquainted with it at this point.

Reasons an Acquiring Company May Pay More Than Book Value The parent company often pays an amount in excess of the book value of the subsidiary company's stock acquired. Although we have assumed here that it relates to the undervaluation of the subsidiary company's land, any one, or a combination, of the following conditions might exist:

1. The fair, or current, value of one or more specific tangible or intangible assets of the subsidiary company may exceed its recorded value because of appreciation. Sometimes the application of conservative accounting procedures under generally accepted accounting principles results in book values that are lower than fair values for assets. Examples are:
   - **a.** The current expensing of some costs that may contain future benefits (for example, research and development expenditures),
   - **b.** The use of accelerated depreciation methods,
   - **c.** The use of the LIFO inventory method, and
   - **d.** The general prohibition against recognizing unrealized gains.
2. The excess payment may indicate the existence of unrecorded goodwill of the subsidiary company as reflected by its above-normal earning capacity.
3. Liabilities, generally long-term ones, may be overvalued. For example, the subsidiary company may have 8% bonds payable outstanding when acquired by the parent company even though the market rate of interest is 12% at that time.
4. A variety of market factors may affect the price paid for the stock. The mere entry of another large buyer of stock into the market would generally have the effect of increasing the stock's market price. In essence, the parent company is willing to pay a premium for the right to acquire control and the related economic advantages it expects to obtain from integrated operations.

Golden West Financial Corp. agreed to a purchase by Charlotte-based Wachovia Corp. for roughly $26 billion in stock-and-cash. In the agreement, each shareholder of Golden West will receive 1.051 shares of Wachovia stock, valued at $62.42 based on Friday's closing prices, plus $18.65 in cash for each share of Golden West. The price represents roughly a 15% premium over Golden West's current market value. The move will allow Wachovia to stretch its brand across 285 branches in 10 states where Golden West currently operates under the name World Savings Bank.

Wachovia will become the sixth-largest holder of deposits in the much-coveted California market, though its market share will continue to trail Bank of America Corp., Washington Mutual and Wells Fargo & Co[14].

1. Explain why shareholders of Golden West would accept both cash and stock from Wachovia in this acquisition.
2. Discuss integration issues that could arise in this purchase.

Case 3 (b): Implied Value of Subsidiary Is Less Than Book Value (IV < BV)—Partial Ownership (Less Than 100% of Subsidiary Stock Acquired)

Finally, we illustrate the less common situation where the purchase price is below the book value of the acquired equity, still assuming the existence of a noncontrolling interest. In this case, the implied value of the subsidiary is below its book value as well.

Assume that on January 1, 2010, P Company acquired 4,000 shares (80%) of the outstanding common stock of S Company for $60,000, after which P Company has $40,000 in cash and $60,000 in an Investment in S Company. The implied value of the subsidiary is thus $60,000/80% or $75,000. The noncontrolling interest is $75,000 × 20% or $15,000. The book value of S Company equity of $80,000 exceeds its implied value of $75,000 by $5,000. We assume that the difference between implied and book values is attributable to plant and equipment, in this case an overvaluation of $5,000. The Computation and Allocation of Difference (CAD) Schedule would appear as follows:

Computation and Allocation of Difference (between Implied and Book Values) Schedule

	Parent Share	*Noncontrolling Share*	*Total Value*
Purchase price and implied value	**$60,000**	**$15,000**	$75,000
Less: Book value of equity acquired:			
Common stock	40,000	10,000	**50,000**
Other contributed capital	8,000	2,000	**10,000**
Retained earnings	16,000	4,000	**20,000**
Total book value	$64,000	$16,000	$80,000
Difference between implied and book value	(4,000)	(1,000)	**(5,000)**
Adjust Plant & Equipment downward	4,000	1,000	**5,000**
Balance	—0—	—0—	—0—

In this instance the difference is negative and is shown in parentheses, and the adjustment is a credit to plant & equipment. When the difference between cost and book value is negative (i.e., purchase price is below book values), it generally reflects one or a combination of the following:[15]

1. One or more of the subsidiary company's assets is overvalued,
2. One or more of the subsidiary company's liabilities is undervalued or unrecognized, or
3. The parent company simply made a bargain purchase.

---

[14] *WSJ*, "Wachovia Strikes $26 Billion Deal for Golden West," by Dennis K. Berman, Carrick Mollenkamp, and Valerie Bauerlein, 5/8/05, p. A1.

[15] Chapter 5 elaborates on these alternatives, with illustrations.

As usual, the Computation and Allocation Schedule yields two eliminating/adjusting entries. The investment elimination entry is:

(1)	Common Stock—S Company	50,000	
	Other Contributed Capital—S Company	10,000	
	Retained Earnings—S Company	20,000	
	Difference between Implied and Book Values		5,000
	Investment in S Company		60,000
	Noncontrolling Interest in Equity		15,000

Note that when the difference is negative, it appears in the journal entry as a credit in order to balance the entry. In the second workpaper entry, this account will be debited to eliminate it, and the appropriate underlying asset and/or liability accounts will be adjusted to reflect a net downward adjustment of net assets, in this case plant & equipment. The second elimination entry is:

(2)	Difference between Implied and Book Values	5,000	
	Plant and Equipment		5,000

A workpaper for a consolidated balance sheet at date of acquisition in this situation is presented in Illustration 3-5.

Acquisition Accounting
Book Value Exceeds Implied Value
80% Owned Subsidiary
Date of Acquisition

ILLUSTRATION 3-5
Consolidated Balance Sheet Workpaper
P Company and Subsidiary
January 1, 2010

			Eliminations			
	P Company	*S Company*	*Dr.*	*Cr.*	*Noncontrolling Interest*	*Consolidated Balances*
Cash	40,000	20,000				60,000
Other Current Assets	140,000	50,000				190,000
Plant and Equipment	120,000	40,000		(2) 5,000		155,000
Land	40,000	20,000				60,000
Investment in S Company	60,000			(1) 60,000		
Difference between implied and book value			(2) 5,000	(1) 5,000		
Total Assets	$400,000	$130,000				$465,000
Liabilities	60,000	50,000				110,000
Common Stock						
P Company	200,000					200,000
S Company		50,000	(1) 50,000			
Other Contributed Capital						
P Company	40,000					40,000
S Company		10,000	(1) 10,000			
Retained Earnings						
P Company	100,000					100,000
S Company		20,000	(1) 20,000			
Noncontrolling Interest				(1) 15,000	15,000	15,000
Total Liabilities and Equity	$400,000	$130,000	$85,000	$85,000		$465,000

(1) To eliminate investment in S Company and create noncontrolling interest account.
(2) To distribute the difference between implied and book value.

Subsidiary Treasury Stock Holdings

A subsidiary may hold some of its own shares as treasury stock at the time the parent company acquires its interest. Recall that treasury stock is a contra-equity account, which has a debit balance on the books of the subsidiary. The computation of the percentage interest acquired, as well as the total equity acquired, is based on shares outstanding and should, therefore, exclude treasury shares.

For example, assume that P Company acquired 18,000 shares of S Company common stock on January 1, 2010, for a payment of $320,000 when S Company's stockholders' equity section appeared as follows:

Common Stock, $10 par, 25,000 shares issued	$250,000
Other Contributed Capital	50,000
Retained Earnings	125,000
	425,000
Less: Treasury Stock at Cost, 1,000 Shares	20,000
Total Stockholders' Equity	$405,000

P Company's interest in S Company is 75% (18,000 shares/24,000 shares), and the total implied value of S Company is $320,000/75% or $426,667. The implied value of the noncontrolling interest is $426,667 × 25% or $106,667. This results in a difference between implied and book values of $426,667 − $405,000 or $21,667.

Because the treasury stock account represents a contra stockholders' equity account, it must be eliminated by a credit when the investment account and subsidiary company's equity accounts are eliminated on the workpaper. Thus, the workpaper eliminating entry is:

Common Stock—S Company	250,000	
Other Contributed Capital—S Company	50,000	
Retained Earnings—S Company	125,000	
Difference between Implied and Book Values	21,667	
Investment in S Company		320,000
Noncontrolling Interest in Equity		106,667
Treasury Stock—S Company		20,000

Other Intercompany Balance Sheet Eliminations

Up to this point we have discussed the elimination of the subsidiary equity against the related investment account, with recognition in the consolidated accounts of the noncontrolling interest in equity. Balance sheet eliminations of a variety of intercompany receivables and payables are also often required. Intercompany accounts receivable, notes receivable, and interest receivable, for example, must be eliminated against the reciprocal accounts payable, notes payable, and interest payable. Cash advances among affiliated companies constitute receivables and payables and must be eliminated. Eliminations also must be made for all types of intercompany accruals for such items as rent and other services. The full amount of all intercompany receivables and payables is eliminated without regard to the percentage of control held by the parent company.

For example, to eliminate a $25,000 cash advance made by P Company and received by S Company, the following entry would be made:

Advance from P Company	$25,000	
Advance to S Company		$25,000

Similarly, to eliminate a $100,000 intercompany account receivable/payable, this entry would be made:

Accounts Payable (to S)	$100,000	
Accounts Receivable (from P)		$100,000

Adjusting Entries Prior to Eliminating Entries

At times, workpaper adjustments to accounting data may be needed before appropriate eliminating entries can be accomplished. The need for adjustments generally arises because of in-transit items where only one of the affiliates has recorded the effect of an intercompany transaction. For example, the parent company may have recorded a cash advance to one of its subsidiaries near year-end but the subsidiary has not yet recorded the receipt of the advance. Thus, the Advances to Subsidiary account on the parent company's books has no reciprocal account on the subsidiary company's books. An adjusting workpaper entry debiting Cash and crediting Advances from Parent is required so that the asset (cash) can be appropriately included in consolidated assets and a reciprocal account established that permits the elimination of intercompany advances. The workpaper eliminations columns may be used to enter these adjusting entries. Alternatively, it is possible simply to adjust the subsidiary company's statements prior to their entry on the workpaper.

TEST YOUR KNOWLEDGE

NOTE: Solutions to ***Test Your Knowledge*** questions are found at the end of each chapter before the end-of-chapter questions.

Multiple Choice

1. Which of the following adjustments do not occur in the consolidating process?
   (A) Elimination of parent's retained earnings
   (B) Elimination of intra-company balances
   (C) Allocations of difference between implied and book values
   (D) Elimination of the investment account
2. The noncontrolling interest in the subsidiary is reported as:
   (A) Asset
   (B) Liability
   (C) Equity
   (D) Expense

True or False

3. ________ a. In computing the difference between the implied and book values, the implied value of the acquired entity will always equal the purchase price to the parent.

   ________ b. In the Computation and Allocation of Difference (between Implied Value and Book Value) schedule for a stock acquisition, the implied value of subsidiary equity is computed as: (purchase price) divided by (percentage acquired by parent).

________ c. Once the eliminating/adjusting entry columns of the worksheet are completed, the entries are posted to the books of the company's general ledger and therefore need not be repeated in the following year in the consolidating process.

________ d. In allocating the difference between implied and book values, if the difference is more than needed to adjust all net assets to market values, then the excess is goodwill.

A COMPREHENSIVE ILLUSTRATION—MORE THAN ONE SUBSIDIARY COMPANY

No particular problem exists where the parent company owns a direct controlling interest in more than one subsidiary company. The balance sheet of each affiliate is entered on the workpaper, any adjustments needed are prepared, and all related intercompany accounts, including those between subsidiary companies, are eliminated. The remaining balances are combined, and they constitute the consolidated balance sheet.

It is useful at this point to look at an illustrative workpaper and consolidated balance sheet for a parent company, P Company, and its two subsidiaries, S Company and T Company. Assume that on January 1, 2010, P Company acquired 90% and 80% of the outstanding common stock of S Company and T Company for $250,200 and $115,000, respectively. Immediately after the stock acquisition, balance sheets of the affiliates were:

January 1, 2010

	P Company	*S Company*	*T Company*
Cash	$ 81,800	$ 36,000	$ 4,000
Accounts receivable (net)	68,000	59,000	10,000
Inventories	76,000	64,000	15,000
Advances to T Company	20,000		
Investment in S Company	250,200		
Investment in T Company	115,000		
Plant and equipment (net)	200,000	241,000	130,000
Land	24,000	10,000	6,000
Total assets	$835,000	$410,000	$165,000
Accounts payable	$ 85,000	$ 40,000	$ 25,000
Notes payable	—0—	100,000	—0—
Common stock, $10 par value	500,000	200,000	100,000
Retained earnings	250,000	70,000	40,000
Total liabilities and equity	$835,000	$410,000	$165,000

Other information

1. On the date of acquisition, P Company mailed a cash advance of $20,000 to T Company to improve T Company's working capital position. T Company had not yet received and, therefore, had not yet recorded the advance.
2. On the date of acquisition, P Company owed S Company $6,000 for purchases on open account, and S Company owed T Company $5,000 for such purchases. All these items had been sold by the purchasing companies prior to the date of acquisition.
3. The difference between implied and the book values of equity relates to the undervaluation of subsidiary plant and equipment.

Since the Investments are carried in two separate accounts, it is best to prepare two separate CAD Schedules, one for each investment, as follows:

Computation and Allocation of Difference (between Implied and Book Values) Schedule (Investment in S Company)

	Parent Share	*Noncontrolling Share*	*Total Value*
Purchase price and implied value	**$250,200**	**27,800**	278,000
Less: Book value of subsidiary equity:			
Common stock	180,000	20,000	**200,000**
Retained earnings	63,000	7,000	**70,000**
Total book value	243,000	27,000	270,000
Difference between implied and book value	7,200	800	**8,000**
Adjust plant assets upward	(7,200)	(800)	**(8,000)**
Balance	—0—	—0—	—0—

Computation and Allocation of Difference (between Implied and Book Values) Schedule (Investment in T Company)

	Parent Share	*Noncontrolling Share*	*Total Value*
Purchase price and implied value	**$115,000**	**28,750**	143,750
Less: Book value of subsidiary equity:			
Common stock	80,000	20,000	**100,000**
Retained earnings	32,000	8,000	**40,000**
Total book value	112,000	28,000	140,000
Difference between implied and book value	3,000	750	**3,750**
Adjust Plant Assets upward	(3,000)	(750)	**(3,750)**
Balance	—0—	—0—	—0—

A workpaper for the preparation of a consolidated balance sheet on January 1, 2010, for P, S, and T companies is presented in Illustration 3-6. Several items on the workpaper should be noted. The cash in transit from P Company to T Company was picked up through an adjusting entry; if not, $20,000 cash would have been excluded from the consolidated balance sheet. The adjustment also provided a reciprocal account, Advance from P Company, that permitted the elimination of the intercompany transaction for advances. (The perceptive reader will have already noticed that the same net effect could have been accomplished by a combined adjusting and eliminating entry with a debit to Cash and a credit to Advance to T.)

The elimination of all intercompany accounts receivable and accounts payable, including those between subsidiary companies, was accomplished through one entry. There is no need to eliminate them individually. Notice also that the equity in each subsidiary company was eliminated against each individual investment account, with a corresponding amount recorded for the noncontrolling interest in each.

The formal consolidated balance sheet is prepared from the detail in the consolidated balance sheet columns of the workpaper and is presented in Illustration 3-7. Note the agreement between the common stock and retained earnings balances in the consolidated balance sheet and those in the final column of the workpaper (Illustration 3-6) for P Company. The balance sheet data are classified according to normal balance sheet arrangements. As discussed earlier,

Acquisition Accounting
Two Partially Owned Subsidiaries
Date of Acquisition

ILLUSTRATION 3-6
Consolidated Balance Sheet Workpaper
P Company and Subsidiary
January 1, 2010

	P Company	S Company	T Company	Eliminations Dr.	Eliminations Cr.	Noncontrolling Interest	Consolidated Balances
Cash	81,800	36,000	4,000	(a) 20,000			141,800
Accounts Receivable (net)	68,000	59,000	10,000		(2) 11,000		126,000
Inventories	76,000	64,000	15,000				155,000
Advance to T Company	20,000				(1) 20,000		
Investment in S Company	250,200				(3) 250,200		
Investment in T Company	115,000				(4) 115,000		
Plant and Equipment (net)	200,000	241,000	130,000	(5) 8,000			
				(6) 3,750			582,750
Land	24,000	10,000	6,000				40,000
Difference between implied and book value				(3) 8,000	(5) 8,000		
				(4) 3,750	(6) 3,750		
Total Assets	835,000	410,000	165,000				1,045,550
Accounts Payable	85,000	40,000	25,000	(2) 11,000			139,000
Notes Payable		100,000					100,000
Common Stock							
P Company	500,000						500,000
S Company		200,000		(3) 200,000			
T Company			100,000	(4) 100,000			
Retained Earnings							
P Company	250,000						250,000
S Company		70,000		(3) 70,000			
T Company			40,000	(4) 40,000			
Advance from P Company				(1) 20,000	(a) 20,000		
Noncontrolling Interest					(3) 27,800		
					(4) 28,750	56,550	56,550
Total Liabilities and Equity	835,000	410,000	165,000	484,500	484,500		1,045,550

(a) To adjust for cash advance in transit from P Company to T Company.
(1) To eliminate intercompany advances.
(2) To eliminate intercompany accounts payable and receivable.
(3) To eliminate investment in S Company and create noncontrolling interest account.
(4) To eliminate investment in T Company and create noncontrolling interest account.
(5) To allocate the implied over book value for S Company to plant and equipment.
(6) To allocate the implied over book value for T Company to plant and equipment.

noncontrolling interest in consolidated net assets or equity should be shown as a component of stockholders' equity (preferably the first component of equity listed in the balance sheet).

LIMITATIONS OF CONSOLIDATED STATEMENTS

LO6 Limitations of consolidated statements.

As noted earlier, consolidated statements may have limited usefulness for noncontrolling stockholders, subsidiary creditors, and some regulatory agencies. These groups may find little information of value to them in the consolidated statements

ILLUSTRATION 3-7

Consolidated Balance Sheet
P Company and Subsidiaries
January 1, 2010

Assets		
Current assets:		
Cash		$ 141,800
Accounts receivable (net)		126,000
Inventories		155,000
Total current assets		423,000
Plant and equipment (net)		582,750
Land		40,000
Total assets		$1,045,550
Liabilities and Stockholders' Equity		
Current liabilities:		
Accounts payable		$ 139,000
Notes payable		100,000
Total liabilities		239,000
Stockholders' equity:		
Noncontrolling interest in consolidated net assets	$ 56,550	
Common stock, $10 par value	500,000	
Retained earnings	250,000	806,550
Total liabilities and stockholders' equity		$1,045,550

because they contain insufficient detail about the individual subsidiaries. For example, creditors of a specific company have claims only against the resources of that company unless the parent guarantees the claims.

In addition, financial analysts have criticized consolidated statements on several counts. For example, highly diversified companies operating across several industries, often the result of mergers and acquisitions, are difficult to analyze or compare. For instance, *General Electric* (*GE*) reports consolidated financial statements that include its credit corporation. The combining of a financial company with a manufacturing company makes interpreting the statements more difficult. In an attempt to make the statements more readable, GE reports three columns with each statement: one showing the total consolidated statements, a column for GE, and a column for the credit corporation. Consolidated operating results for such companies cannot be compared with industry standards, nor can one conglomerate be compared with another. Both the SEC and the FASB have developed requirements for segmental reporting in an effort to address these concerns. Determining what constitutes a segment is not easy, however, and the standards have met criticism and subsequent revision. Segmental reporting is discussed in Chapter 14.

Regardless of these limitations, however, consolidated statements continue to grow in importance. The vast majority of publicly held companies own one or more subsidiaries and report on a consolidated basis. Thus, consolidated statements have assumed the position of primary statements, and the separate statements of individual subsidiaries are considered supplementary. The recent attention by both the FASB and international standards board reaffirm this role.

ILLUSTRATION 3-8

Comparison of Business Combinations and Consolidations under U.S. GAAP and IFRS*

U.S. GAAP	IFRS
1. Fair value of **contingent consideration** recorded at acquisition date, with subsequent adjustments recognized through earnings if contingent liability (no adjustment for equity).	1. IFRS 3R uses the same approach.
2. **Contractual contingent liabilities** assumed (such as warranties) are measured at fair value on the acquisition date. **Non-contractual contingent liabilities** (such as patent infringement) are measured at fair value only if it is more likely than not that a liability exists.	2. Under IFRS 3R a contingent liability is recognized at the acquisition date if its fair value can be reliably measured.
3. **Noncontrolling interest** is recorded at fair value and is presented in equity.	3. Noncontrolling interest can be recorded either at fair value or at the proportionate share of the net assets acquired. Also presented in equity.
4. **Special purpose entities** (SPEs) are consolidated if the most significant activities of the SPE are controlled. Qualified SPEs (QSPEs) are no longer exempted from consolidation rules.	4. Special purpose entities (SPEs) are consolidated if controlled. QSPEs are not addressed.
5. **Direct acquisition costs** (excluding the costs of issuing debt or equity securities) are expensed.	5. IFRS 3R uses the same approach.
6. **Goodwill** is not amortized, but is tested for impairment using a two-step process.	6. Goodwill is not amortized, but is tested for impairment using a one-step process.
7. **Negative goodwill** in an acquisition is recorded as an ordinary gain in income (not extraordinary).	7. IAS 36 uses the same approach.
8. **Fair value** is based on exit prices, i.e. the price that would be received to sell an asset or paid to transfer a liability in an orderly transaction between market participants at the measurement date.	8. Fair value is the amount for which an asset could be exchanged or a liability settled between knowledgeable, willing parties in an arm's length transaction.
9. **Purchased in-process R&D** is capitalized with subsequent expenditures expensed. The capitalized portion is then amortized.	9. Purchased in-process R&D is capitalized with the potential for subsequent expenditures to be capitalized. The capitalized portion is then amortized. 
10. Parent and subsidiary **accounting policies** ***do not need*** to conform.	10. Parent and subsidiary accounting policies ***do need*** to conform.
11. **Restructuring plans** are accounted for separately from the business combination and generally expensed (unless conditions in *SFAS No. 146* **[ASC 420]** are met).	11. Similar accounting under IFRS 3 and amended IAS 27.
12. **Measurement period** ends at the earlier of a) one year from the acquisition date, or b) the date when the acquirer receives needed information to consummate the acquisition.	12. Similar to U.S. GAAP.
13. For **step acquisitions**, all previous ownership interests are adjusted to fair value, with any gain or loss recorded in earnings.	13. Similar to U.S. GAAP.
14 . **Reporting dates** for the parent and subsidiary can be different up to three months. Significant events in that time must be *disclosed.*	14. Permits a three-month difference if impractical to prepare the subsidiary's statements on the same date; however, *adjustments are required* for significant events in that period.
15. Potential voting rights are generally not considered in determining **control**.	15. Potential voting rights are considered if currently exercisable.

*For complete coverage of the differences between IFRS and U.S. GAAP, see *IFRS 2009, Interpretation and Application of International Financial Reporting Standards*, by Epstein and Jermakowicz, 2009 (John Wiley and Sons, Inc.).

SUMMARY

1. *Understand the concept of control as used in reference to consolidations.* When one firm (referred to as the parent) effectively controls the activities of another firm (the subsidiary) through the direct or indirect ownership of some or all of its voting stock or by some other means, consolidated financial statements are required.
2. *Explain the role of a noncontrolling interest in business combinations.* The noncontrolling interest in a consolidated entity refers to the stock of the subsidiary firm, if any, which is not controlled by the parent. This interest appears as a component of equity in the consolidated balance sheet.
3. *Describe the reasons why a company acquires a subsidiary rather than its net assets.* A firm may acquire stock by open market purchases or by cash tender offers to the subsidiary's stockholders, thus avoiding the often lengthy and difficult negotiations that are required in a complete takeover. Control of the subsidiary's operations can be accomplished with a much smaller investment, since not all of the stock need be acquired. Also, the separate legal existence of the individual affiliates provides an element of protection of the parent's assets from attachment by creditors of the subsidiary.
4. *Describe the valuation and classification of accounts in consolidated financial statements.* In the consolidated balance sheet, the assets and liabilities of the subsidiary are combined with those of the parent on an item-by-item basis. Assets and liabilities are reflected at their fair market values, as determined at the date of acquisition, including goodwill, if any (and as subsequently depreciated, amortized, or adjusted for impairment).
5. *List the requirements for inclusion of a subsidiary in consolidated financial statements.* Essentially all controlled corporations should be consolidated with the controlling entity. Exceptions include those situations where: the subsidiary is in legal reorganization or bankruptcy, or a foreign subsidiary operates in an environment that casts significant doubt about the parent's effective control.
6. *Discuss the limitations of consolidated financial statements.* Consolidated financial statements are of limited use to noncontrolling stockholders, to subsidiary creditors, and possibly to regulatory agencies (e.g., if only the subsidiary is regulated). Also, when highly diversified companies operate across several industries, the aggregation of dissimilar data makes analysis difficult.
7. *Record the investment in the subsidiary on the parent's books at the date of acquisition.* On the books of the parent company, the investment is recorded as a debit to Investment in Subsidiary and a credit to the appropriate account(s) based on the consideration used in the exchange (cash, debt, stock, or a combination). Any stock issued is recorded at its fair market value, and the investment is thus also recorded at the fair value of consideration paid. Direct and indirect acquisition costs, if any, are recorded (expensed) separately from the acquisition.
8. *Prepare the consolidated workpapers and eliminating entries at the date of acquisition.* The consolidated workpapers serve to sum the assets and liabilities of the parent and subsidiary, with adjustments made to assets and liabilities of the subsidiary to "mark" their values to market values, based on the acquisition price and the value this implies for the entire subsidiary. These adjustments are accomplished via "eliminating and adjusting" entries, which also serve to eliminate the investment account against the subsidiary's equity accounts, and to recognize the noncontrolling interest in equity. Thus, the consolidated balance sheet reflects only the equity of the controlling shareholders (in the parent firm) and the noncontrolling shareholders (in the subsidiary).
9. *Compute and allocate the difference between implied value and book value of the acquired firm's equity.* The difference between implied and book values of the acquired firm's equity is the amount by which the subsidiary's assets and liabilities must be adjusted in total (including the recognition of goodwill, if any). The use of an account by this name (difference between implied and book values) facilitates this process in the eliminating entries, and the differential account itself is eliminated as well.
10. *Discuss some of the similarities and differences between U.S. GAAP and IFRS with respect to the preparation of consolidated financial statements at the date of acquisition.* Both U.S. GAAP and IFRS now require that all controlled SPEs (special purpose entities) be consolidated, but U.S. GAAP still recognize variable interest entities (VIEs), while IFRS do not. IFRS allow a choice in the valuation of the noncontrolling interest in equity and related goodwill, while FASB requires the implied fair valuation (as evidenced by the acquisition price) for both. IFRS require that parent and subsidiary accounting policies conform; U.S. GAAP do not. Both now require the capitalization of purchased in-process R&D.

APPENDIX A

Deferred Taxes on the Date of Acquisition

If a purchase acquisition is tax-free to the seller, the tax bases of the acquired assets and liabilities are carried forward at historical book values. However, the assets and liabilities of the acquired company are recorded on the consolidated books at adjusted fair value. Under current guidelines, the tax effects of the difference between consolidated book values and the tax bases must be recorded as deferred tax liabilities or assets (*SFAS No. 109* and *SFAS No. 141R* **[ASC 805 and ASC 740]**).

Consider the following example. Suppose that Purchasing Company acquires 90% of Selling Company by issuing stock valued at $800,000. The only difference between book value and fair value relates to depreciable plant and equipment. Plant and equipment has a market value of $400,000 and a book value of $250,000. All other book values approximate market values. Assume that the combination qualifies as a nontaxable exchange. On the date of acquisition, Selling Company's book value of equity is $600,000, which includes $150,000 of common stock and $450,000 of retained earnings. Assume a 30% tax rate. Consider the following Computation and Allocation Schedule with and without considering deferred taxes.

Computation and Allocation of Difference Schedule (without Consideration of Deferred Taxes)

	Parent Share	*Noncontrolling Share*	*Total Value*
Purchase price and implied value	**$800,000**	**88,889**	888,889
Less: Book value of subsidiary equity	540,000	60,000	600,000
Difference between implied and book value	260,000	28,889	**288,889**
Adjust plant and equipment upward	(135,000)	(15,000)	**(150,000)**
Balance	125,000	13,889	138,889
Goodwill	(125,000)	(13,889)	**(138,889)**
Balance	—0—	—0—	—0—

Computation and Allocation of Difference Schedule (with Consideration of Deferred Taxes)

	Parent Share	*Noncontrolling Share*	*Total Value*
Purchase price and implied value	**$800,000**	**88,889**	888,889
Less: Book value of subsidiary equity	540,000	60,000	600,000
Difference between implied and book value	260,000	28,889	**288,889**
Adjust plant and equipment upward	(135,000)	(15,000)	**(150,000)**
Deferred tax liability on plant and equipment (400,000 − 250,000) (30%)	40,500	4,500	**45,000**
Balance	165,500	18,389	183,889
Goodwill	(165,500)	(18,389)	**(183,889)**
Balance	—0—	—0—	—0—

Notice that goodwill is increased when deferred taxes are computed on the timing difference related to the depreciable bases of plant and equipment. This occurs because the additional future depreciation from the write-up of plant and equipment is reported on the consolidated income statement but is nondeductible for tax purposes, creating a timing difference between book and tax. Recall that deferred taxes are classified in the balance sheet according to the item that gave rise to them. Since plant and equipment are long-term assets, the deferred tax liability would also be ***long-term***.

ACCOUNTING FOR UNCERTAIN TAX POSITIONS

Reasons for Change

In June 2006, the FASB issued Interpretation No. 48, *Accounting for Uncertain Tax Positions—an Interpretation of FASB Statement No. 109* [ASC 740–10]. The main reason FASB stated for the issuance of this interpretation was to clarify the accounting for uncertain tax positions and reduce diverse accounting practices, which had developed due to the lack of an explicitly defined confidence level to be met before recognizing benefits from an uncertain tax position.

For example, some enterprises recognize all tax positions taken or anticipated to be taken in a tax return and include the effects of any uncertainty about the detection and sustainability of the positions in the deferred tax asset valuation allowance, or in their analysis of the adequacy of the income tax liability. Other enterprises use a predetermined confidence threshold for initial recognition of benefits from tax positions and a probable loss threshold to provide for contingent losses related to uncertain tax positions. Still other enterprises have identified uncertain tax positions based on certain attributes, and then applied the guidance for gain contingencies in paragraph 17 of *FASB Statement No. 5, Accounting for Contingencies* [ASC 320–10–45].

According to FASB, this diversity in practice results in non-comparability in reporting income tax expense; thus the issues addressed in their interpretation should improve financial reporting by defining a criterion that an individual tax position must meet before the benefit is recognized in an enterprise's financial statements. The IASB has acknowledged similar diversity in the application of international standards on this topic.

The issued Interpretation has been criticized by power companies, as well as by the Edison Electric Institute, who claimed that the new rule is likely to result in overstated tax liabilities and a greater workload, while not improving financial reporting.[16]

Main Issues and Changes

Initial Recognition Under the Interpretation, the recognition of a tax benefit would occur when it is "more likely than not" that the position would be sustained upon audit by the relevant taxing authority, including final resolution of any related

[16] Electric Utility Week, 26 September 2005, **Power commenters question need for FASB 'uncertain tax positions' rule**.

litigation or appeals process. The 'more-likely-than-not' criterion means a likelihood of more than 50 percent.

Classification In general, the Board concluded that the liability arising from the difference between the tax position and the amount recognized and measured should be classified as a current liability if anticipated to be paid within one year or the operating cycle. Only a liability related to a taxable temporary difference, as defined in *SFAS No. 109* [ASC 740–10–45] should be classified as a deferred liability.

Subsequent Recognition Under the Interpretation, a tax position that fails to meet the "more-likely-than-not" threshold for initial recognition can be recognized in the first interim period that meets any one of the following conditions: a) the more-likely-than-not recognition threshold is met by the reporting date, b) the tax position is effectively settled, or c) the statue of limitations for the relevant taxing authority to examine and challenge the tax position has expired.

Derecognition Previously recognized tax benefits from positions that no longer meet the more-likely-than-not threshold would be derecognized by recording an income tax liability or eliminating a deferred tax asset.

Use of a valuation allowance as described in *SFAS No. 109* [ASC 740–10–30], or a valuation account as described in *SFAC No. 6, Elements of Financial Statements,* is not an appropriate substitute for the derecognition of a tax position when the derecognition threshold is met.

Interest and Penalties The Interpretation notes that if the payment of interest on the underpayment of income taxes is required by the relevant tax law, the accrual of interest should be based on the difference between the tax benefit recognized in the financial statements and the tax position. Interest should be accrued in the period the interest is incurred. If a penalty applies to a tax position, the liability for the penalty should be recognized in the period the penalty is deemed to have been incurred.

Disclosures The Board also concluded that liabilities recognized in financial statements pursuant to this Interpretation for tax positions for which it is reasonably possible that the total amounts of unrecognized tax benefits will significantly increase or decrease within 12 months of the reporting date should be disclosed (i.e., the nature of the uncertainty, the nature of the event that might cause the event to change, and an estimate of the range of the reasonably possible change).

The workpaper entry to eliminate the investment account is as follows:

(1)	Common Stock—Selling Company	150,000	
	Retained Earnings—Selling Company	450,000	
	Difference between Implied and Book Values	288,889	
	Investment in S Company		800,000
	Noncontrolling Interest in Equity		88,889

The entry to allocate the difference between implied and book values is affected by the deferred tax amounts. The following entries show the allocation with and without deferred taxes.

		Without Deferred Taxes		With Deferred Taxes	
(2)	Plant and Equipment	150,000		150,000	
	Goodwill	138,889		183,889	
	Deferred tax liability (Long-term)				45,000
	Difference between Implied and Book Values		288,889		288,889

Of the two entries above, only the entry ***with*** deferred taxes is complete, according to *SFAS No. 109 and SFAS No. 141R* **[topic 805]**. Thus a deferred tax liability or asset should be recorded for each adjustment in the Computation and Allocation Schedule that creates a timing difference. For instance, if inventory value is increased, a ***current*** deferred tax liability would be created.

APPENDIX B

Consolidation of Variable Interest Entities

FASB has issued guidance for the consolidation of special-purpose entities (SPEs) through Interpretation No. 46(R) "Consolidation of Variable Interest Entities" and *SFAS No. 167,* "Amendments to FASB Interpretation No. 46(R) [ASC 810–10–30]."

An enterprise shall consolidate a variable interest entity (VIE) when that enterprise has a variable interest (or combination of variable interests) that provides the enterprise with a controlling financial interest on the basis of the certain provisions (listed below). The enterprise that consolidates a variable interest entity is called the primary beneficiary of that entity.

FASB Statement No. 167 requires ongoing reassessments of whether an enterprise is the primary beneficiary of a variable interest entity. Previously, Interpretation 46(R) required reconsideration of whether an enterprise is the primary beneficiary of a variable interest entity only when specific events occurred. *SFAS No. 167* eliminates the quantitative approach previously required for determining the primary beneficiary of a variable interest entity, which was based on determining which enterprise absorbs the majority of the entity's expected losses, receives a majority of the entity's expected residual returns, or both. *SFAS No. 167* requires enhanced disclosures that will provide users of financial statements with more transparent information about an enterprise's involvement in a variable interest entity.

An enterprise with a variable interest in a variable interest entity shall assess whether the enterprise has a controlling financial interest in the entity and, thus, is the entity's primary beneficiary. An enterprise shall be deemed to have a *controlling financial interest* in a variable interest entity *if* it has *both* of the following characteristics:

a. The power to direct the activities of a variable interest entity that most significantly impact the entity's economic performance.

b. The obligation to absorb losses of the entity that could potentially be significant to the variable interest entity or the right to receive benefits from the entity that could potentially be significant to the variable interest entity.

The primary beneficiary of a VIE is required to disclose the following:

- The carrying amounts and classification of the variable interest entity's assets and liabilities in the statement of financial position that are consolidated in accordance with this Interpretation, including qualitative information about the relationship(s) between those assets and liabilities. For example, if the variable interest entity's assets can be used only to settle obligations of the variable interest entity, the enterprise shall disclose qualitative information about the nature of the restrictions on those assets.
- Lack of recourse if creditors (or beneficial interest holders) of a consolidated variable interest entity have no recourse to the general credit of the primary beneficiary.
- Terms of arrangements, giving consideration to both explicit arrangements and implicit variable interests that could require the enterprise to provide financial support (for example, liquidity arrangements and obligations to purchase assets) to the variable interest entity, including events or circumstances that could expose the enterprise to a loss.

In addition to disclosures required by other pronouncements, an enterprise that holds a variable interest in a variable interest entity, but is not the variable interest entity's primary beneficiary, shall disclose:

(a) The carrying amounts and classification of the assets and liabilities in the enterprise's statement of financial position that relate to the enterprise's variable interest in the variable interest entity.

(b) The enterprise's maximum exposure to loss as a result of its involvement with the variable interest entity, including how the maximum exposure is determined and the significant sources of the enterprise's exposure to the variable interest entity. If the enterprise's maximum exposure to loss as a result of its involvement with the variable interest entity cannot be quantified, that fact shall be disclosed.

(c) A tabular comparison of the carrying amounts of the assets and liabilities, as required by (a) above, and the enterprise's maximum exposure to loss, as required by (b) above. An enterprise shall provide qualitative and quantitative information to allow financial statement users to understand the differences between the two amounts.

(d) Information about any liquidity arrangements, guarantees, and/or other commitments by third parties that may affect the fair value or risk of the enterprise's variable interest in the variable interest entity is encouraged.

TEST YOUR KNOWLEDGE

3.3

NOTE: Solutions to ***Test Your Knowledge*** questions are found at the end of each chapter before the end-of-chapter questions.

Multiple Choice

1. Parent Company P purchased 90% of Subsidiary Company S for stock worth $100,000. Subsidiary Company S had a net book value of $50,000

including: "bonds payable" at a book value of $10,000 and a fair value of $15,000; "inventory" with a book value of $5,000 and a fair value of $7,000; and "PP&E" with a book value of $10,000 and a fair value of $20,000. Assuming the tax rate is 40% (and ignoring any deferred taxes on goodwill), net deferred taxes are:
(A) $2,520
(B) $2,800
(C) $6,120
(D) $6,800

2. Assuming an acquisition is not a bargain, the impact of reflecting a net deferred tax liability account is that the firm will also reflect an increased amount of:
(A) Land
(B) Difference between Implied and Book Value
(C) Common Stock
(D) Goodwill

TEST YOUR KNOWLEDGE SOLUTIONS

3-1. 1. a
2. a
3. d
4. d

3-2. 1. a
2. c
3. a F
3. b T
3. c F
3. d T

3-3. 1. b
2. d

QUESTIONS

(The letter A or B indicated for a question, exercise, or problem refers to a related appendix.)

LO3 **1.** What are the advantages of acquiring the *majority* of the voting stock of another company rather than acquiring *all* its voting stock?

LO1 **2.** What is the justification for preparing consolidated financial statements when, in fact, it is apparent that the consolidated group is not a legal entity?

LO6 **3.** Why is it often necessary to prepare separate financial statements for each legal entity in a consolidated group even though consolidated statements provide a better economic picture of the combined activities?

LO5 **4.** What aspects of control must exist before a subsidiary is consolidated?

LO8 **5.** Why are consolidated workpapers used in preparing consolidated financial statements?

LO2 **6.** Define noncontrolling (minority) interest. List three methods that might be used for reporting the noncontrolling interest in a consolidated balance sheet, and state which is preferred under the ***SFAS No. 160*** [topic 810].

LO8 **7.** Give several reasons why a parent company would be willing to pay more than book value for subsidiary stock acquired.

LO8 8. What effect do subsidiary treasury stock holdings have at the time the subsidiary is acquired? How should the treasury stock be treated on consolidated workpapers?

LO8 9. What effect does a noncontrolling interest have on the amount of intercompany receivables and payables eliminated on a consolidated balance sheet?

10A. ***SFAS No. 109*** and ***SFAS No. 141R*** [ASC 740 and 805] require that a deferred tax asset or liability be recognized for likely differences between the reported values and tax bases of assets and liabilities recognized in business combinations (for example, in exchanges that are nontaxable to the selling shareholders). Does this decision change the amount of consolidated net income reported in years subsequent to the business combination? Explain.

Business Ethics

Part I. You are working on the valuation of accounts receivable, and bad debt reserves for the current year's annual report. The CFO stops by and asks you to reduce the reserve by enough to increase the current year's EPS by 2 cents a share. The company's policy has always been to use the previous year's actual bad debt percentage adjusted for a specific economic index. The CFO's suggested change would still be within acceptable GAAP. However, later, you learn that with the increased EPS, the CFO would qualify for a significant bonus. What do you do and why?

Part II. Consider the following:

Accounting firm KPMG created tax shelters called BLIPS, FLIP, OPIS, and SOS that were based largely in the Cayman Islands and allowed wealthy clients (there were 186) to create $5 billion in losses, which were then deducted from their income for IRS tax purposes. BLIPS (Bond Linked Issue Premium Structures) had clients borrow from an offshore bank for purposes of purchasing currency. The client would then sell the currency back to the lender for a loss. However, the IRS contends the losses were phony and that there was never any risk to the client in the deals. The IRS has indicted eight former KPMG partners and an outside lawyer alleging that the transactions were shams, illegal methods for avoiding taxes. KPMG has agreed to pay a $456 million fine, no longer to do tax shelters, and to cooperate with the government in its prosecution of the nine individuals involved in the tax shelter scheme.

Many argue that the courts have not always held that such tax avoidance schemes show criminal intent because the tax laws permit individuals to minimize taxes. However, the IRS argues that these shelters evidence intent because of the lack of risk.

Question

In this case, the IRS contends that the losses generated by the tax shelters were phony and that the clients never incurred any risk. Do tax avoidance schemes indicate criminal intent if the tax laws permit individuals to minimize taxes? Justify your answer.

EXERCISES

EXERCISE 3-1 Workpaper Elimination Entries: 3 Cases LO8

Prepare in general journal form the workpaper entries to eliminate Prancer Company's investment in Saltez Company in the preparation of a consolidated balance sheet at the date of acquisition for each of the following independent cases:

			Saltez Company Equity Balances		
Cash	*Percent of Stock Owned*	*Investment Cost*	*Common Stock*	*Other Contributed Capital*	*Retained Earnings*
a.	100%	$351,000	$160,000	$92,000	$43,000
b.	90	232,000	190,000	75,000	(29,000)
c.	80	159,000	180,000	40,000	(4,000)

Any difference between book value of net assets and the value implied by the purchase price relates to subsidiary property plant and equipment except for case (c). In case (c) assume that all book values and fair values are the same.

EXERCISE 3-2 **Stock Purchase Entries** LO7 LO8

On January 1, 2011, Polo Company purchased 100% of the common stock of Save Company by issuing 40,000 shares of its (Polo's) $10 par value common stock with a market price of $17.50 per share. Polo incurred cash expenses of $20,000 for registering and issuing the common stock. The stockholders' equity section of the two companies' balance sheets on December 31, 2010, were:

	Polo	*Save*
Common stock, $10 par value	$350,000	$320,000
Other contributed capital	590,000	175,000
Retained earnings	380,000	205,000

Required:

A. Prepare the journal entry on the books of Polo Company to record the purchase of the common stock of Save Company and related expenses.

B. Prepare the elimination entry required for the preparation of a consolidated balance sheet workpaper on the date of acquisition.

EXERCISE 3-3 **Consolidated Balance Sheet, Stock Purchase** LO7 LO8

On January 2, 2011, Prunce Company acquired 90% of the outstanding common stock of Sun Company for $192,000 cash. Just before the acquisition, the balance sheets of the two companies were as follows:

	Prunce	*Sun*
Cash	$260,000	$ 64,000
Accounts receivable (net)	142,000	23,000
Inventory	117,000	54,000
Plant and equipment (net)	386,000	98,000
Land	63,000	32,000
Total asset	$968,000	$271,000
Accounts payable	$104,000	$ 47,000
Mortgage payable	72,000	39,000
Common stock, $2 par value	400,000	70,000
Other contributed capital	208,000	20,000
Retained earnings	184,000	95,000
Total equities	$968,000	$271,000

The fair values of Sun Company's assets and liabilities are equal to their book values with the exception of land.

Required:

A. Prepare a journal entry to record the purchase of Sun Company's common stock.

B. Prepare a consolidated balance sheet at the date of acquisition.

EXERCISE 3-4 **Purchase, Date of Acquisition** LO7 LO8 LO9

On January 1, 2010, Peach Company issued 1,500 of its $20 par value common shares with a fair value of $60 per share in exchange for the 2,000 outstanding common shares of Swartz

Company in a purchase transaction. Registration costs amounted to $1,700, paid in cash. Just prior to the acquisition, the balance sheets of the two companies were as follows:

	Peach Company	*Swartz Company*
Cash	$ 73,000	$ 13,000
Accounts receivable (net)	95,000	19,000
Inventory	58,000	25,000
Plant and equipment (net)	95,000	43,000
Land	26,000	22,000
Total assets	$347,000	$122,000
Accounts payable	$ 66,000	$ 18,000
Notes payable	82,000	21,000
Common stock, $20 par value	100,000	40,000
Other contributed capital	60,000	24,000
Retained earnings	39,000	19,000
Total equities	$347,000	$122,000

Any difference between the book value of equity and the value implied by the purchase price relates to goodwill.

Required:

A. Prepare the journal entry on Peach Company's books to record the exchange of stock.

B. Prepare a Computation and Allocation Schedule for the difference between book value and value implied by the purchase price.

C. Prepare a consolidated balance sheet at the date of acquisition.

EXERCISE 3-5 **Treasury Stock Held by Subsidiary** LO8

Pool Company purchased 90% of the outstanding common stock of Spruce Company on December 31, 2011, for cash. At that time the balance sheet of Spruce Company was as follows:

Current assets	$1,050,000
Plant and equipment	990,000
Land	170,000
Total assets	$2,210,000
Liabilities	$ 820,000
Common stock, $20 par value	900,000
Other contributed capital	440,000
Retained earnings	150,000
Total	2,310,000
Less treasury stock at cost, 5,000 shares	100,000
Total equities	$2,210,000

Required:

Prepare the elimination entry required for the preparation of a consolidated balance sheet workpaper on December 31, 2011, assuming:

(1) The purchase price of the stock was $1,400,000. Assume that any difference between the book value of net assets and the value implied by the purchase price relates to subsidiary land.

(2) The purchase price of the stock was $1,160,000. Assume that the subsidiary land has a fair value of $180,000, and the other assets and liabilities are fairly valued.

EXERCISE 3-6 **Elimination Entry, Consolidated Balance Sheet** LO8

On December 31, 2010, Price Company purchased a controlling interest in Shipley Company. The balance sheet of Price Company and the consolidated balance sheet on December 31, 2010, were as follows:

	Price Company	*Consolidated*
Cash	$ 22,000	$ 37,900
Accounts receivable	35,000	57,000
Inventory	127,000	161,600
Investment in Shipley Company	212,000	—0—
Plant and equipment (net)	190,000	337,000
Land	120,000	220,412
Total	$706,000	$813,912
Accounts payable	$ 42,000	$112,500
Note payable	100,000	100,000
Noncontrolling interest in Shipley Company	—0—	37,412
Common stock	300,000	300,000
Other contributed capital	164,000	164,000
Retained earnings	100,000	100,000
Total	$706,000	$813,912

On the date of acquisition, the stockholders' equity section of Shipley Company's balance sheet was as follows:

Common stock	$ 90,000
Other contributed capital	90,000
Retained earnings	56,000
Total	$236,000

Required:

A. Prepare the investment elimination entry made to complete a consolidated balance sheet workpaper. Any difference between book value and the value implied by the purchase price relates to subsidiary land.

B. Prepare Shipley Company's balance sheet as it appeared on December 31, 2010.

EXERCISE 3-7 **Intercompany Receivables and Payables** LO8

Polychromasia, Inc. had a number of receivables from subsidiaries at the balance sheet date, as well as several payables to subsidiaries. Of its five subsidiaries, four are consolidated in the financial statements (Green Company, Black Inc., White & Sons, and Silver Co.). Only the Brown Company is not consolidated with Polychromasia and the other affiliates. The following list of receivables and payables shows balances at 12/31/10.

Interest receivable from the Brown Company	$ 50,000
Interest payable to Black Inc.	75,000
Intercompany payable to Silver Co.	105,000
Long-term advance to Green Company	150,000
Long-term payable to Silver Co.	450,000
Long-term receivable from Brown Company	500,000

Required:

A. Show the classification and amount(s) that should be reported in the consolidated balance sheet of Polychromasia, Inc. and Subsidiaries at 12/31/10 as receivable from subsidiaries.

B. Show the classification and amount(s) that should be reported in the consolidated balance sheet of Polychromasia, Inc. and Subsidiaries at 12/31/10 as payable to subsidiaries.

EXERCISE 3-8 **Stock Acquisition, Journal Entry by Parent** LO7

Peep Inc. acquired 100% of the outstanding common stock of Shy Inc. for $2,500,000 cash and 15,000 shares of its common stock ($2 par value). The stock's market value was $40 on the acquisition date.

Required:

Prepare the journal entry to record the acquisition.

EXERCISE 3-9 **Acquisition Costs** LO7

Assume the same information from Exercise 3–8. In addition, Peep Inc. incurred the following direct costs:

Accounting fees for the purchase	$15,000
Legal fees for registering the common stock	30,000
Other legal fees for the acquisition	45,000
Travel expenses to meet with Shy managers	5,000
SEC filing fees	2,000
	$97,000

Before the acquisition consummation date, $90,000 of the direct costs was charged to a deferred charges account pending the completion of the acquisition. The remaining $7,000 has not been accrued or paid.

Required:

Prepare the journal entry to record both the acquisition and the direct costs.

EXERCISE 3-10A **Deferred Tax Effects, Acquisition Entry and Eliminating Entries**

Patel Company issued 95,000 shares of $1 par value common stock (market value of $6/share) for 95% of the common stock of Seely Company on January 1, 2011. Seely Company had the following assets, liabilities, and owners' equity at that time:

	Book Value/Tax Basis	*Fair Value*	*Difference*
Cash	$ 20,000	$ 20,000	$—0—
Accounts receivable	112,000	112,000	—0—
Inventory (LIFO)	82,000	134,000	52,000
Land	30,000	55,000	25,000
Plant assets (net)	392,000	463,000	71,000
Total assets	$636,000	$784,000	$148,000
Allowance for uncollectible accounts	$ 10,000	$ 10,000	$—0—
Accounts payable	54,000	54,000	—0—
Bonds payable	200,000	180,000	20,000
Common stock, $1 par value	80,000		
Other contributed capital	132,000		
Retained earnings	160,000		
Total equities	$636,000		

Required:

A. Prepare the stock acquisition entry on the books of Patel Company, taking into account tax effects. Assume an income tax rate of 40%.

B. Prepare eliminating entries for the preparation of a consolidated balance sheet workpaper on January 1, 2011.

EXERCISE 3-11A **Deferred Tax Effects at Date of Acquisition**

Profeet Company purchased the Starless Company in a nontaxable combination consummated as a stock acquisition. Profeet issued 10,000 shares of $5 par value common stock, with a market value of $70, in exchange for all the stock of Starless. The following information about Starless Company is available on the combination date.

STARLESS COMPANY

Book value of net assets	$600,000	
Deferred tax liability from using Modified Accelerated Cost Recover System (MACRS) depreciation for tax purposes	24,000	
Other Items	*Book Value*	*Fair Value*
Fixed assets	$410,000	$490,000
Long-term debt	450,000	500,000

The current and future tax rate is expected to be 40%.

Required:

Prepare the journal entry to record the acquisition, taking into account tax effects.

PROBLEMS

PROBLEM 3-1 **Consolidated Workpaper: Two Cases** LO8 LO9

The two following separate cases show the financial position of a parent company and its subsidiary company on November 30, 2011, just after the parent had purchased 90% of the subsidiary's stock:

	Case I		*Case II*	
	P Company	*S Company*	*P Company*	*S Company*
Current assets	$ 880,000	$260,000	$ 780,000	$280,000
Investment in S Company	190,000		190,000	
Long-term assets	1,400,000	400,000	1,200,000	400,000
Other assets	90,000	40,000	70,000	70,000
Total	$2,560,000	$700,000	$2,240,000	$750,000
Current liabilities	$ 640,000	$270,000	$ 700,000	$260,000
Long-term liabilities	850,000	290,000	920,000	270,000
Common stock	600,000	180,000	600,000	180,000
Retained earnings	470,000	(40,000)	20,000	40,000
Total	$2,560,000	$700,000	$2,240,000	$750,000

Required:

Prepare a November 30, 2011, consolidated balance sheet workpaper for each of the foregoing cases. In Case I, any difference between book value of equity and the value implied by the purchase price relates to subsidiary long-term assets. In Case II, assume that any excess of book value over the value implied by purchase price is due to overvalued long-term assets.

PROBLEM 3-2 **Consolidated Balance Sheet Workpaper** LO8 LO9

On January 1, 2011, Perry Company purchased 8,000 shares of Soho Company's common stock for $120,000. Immediately after the stock acquisition, the statements of financial position of Perry and Soho appeared as follows:

Assets	*Perry*	*Soho*
Cash	$ 39,000	$ 19,000
Accounts receivable	53,000	31,000
Inventory	42,000	25,000
Investment in Soho Company	120,000	
Plant assets	160,000	110,500
Accumulated depreciation—plant assets	(52,000)	(19,500)
Total	$362,000	$166,000
Liabilities and Owners' Equity		
Current liabilities	$ 18,500	$ 26,000
Mortgage notes payable	40,000	
Common stock, $10 par value	120,000	100,000
Other contributed capital	135,000	16,500
Retained earnings	48,500	23,500
Total	$362,000	$166,000

Required:

A. Calculate the percentage of Soho acquired by Perry Company. Prepare a schedule to compute the difference between book value of equity and the value implied by the purchase price. Any difference between the book value of equity and the value implied by the purchase price relates to subsidiary plant assets.

B. Prepare a consolidated balance sheet workpaper as of January 1, 2011.

PROBLEM 3-3 **Intercompany Bond Holdings at Par, 90% Owned Subsidiary** LO8 LO9

Balance sheets for P Company and S Company on August 1, 2011, are as follows:

	P Company	*S Company*
Cash	$ 165,500	$106,000
Receivables	366,000	126,000
Inventory	261,000	108,000
Investment in bonds	306,000	—0—
Investment in S Company stock	586,500	—0—
Plant and equipment (net)	573,000	320,000
Land	200,000	300,000
Total	$2,458,000	$960,000
Accounts payable	$ 174,000	$ 58,000
Accrued expenses	32,400	26,000
Bonds payable, 8%	—0—	200,000
Common stock	1,500,000	460,000
Other contributed capital	260,000	60,000
Retained earnings	491,600	156,000
Total	$2,458,000	$960,000

Required:

Prepare a workpaper for a consolidated balance sheet for P Company and its subsidiary on August 1, 2011, taking into consideration the following:

1. P Company acquired 90% of the outstanding common stock of S Company on August 1, 2011, for a cash payment of $586,500.
2. Included in the Investment in Bonds account are $40,000 par value of S Company bonds payable that were purchased at par by P Company in 2002. The bonds pay interest on April 30 and October 31. S Company has appropriately accrued interest expense on August 1, 2011; P Company, however, inadvertently failed to accrue interest income on the S Company bonds.

3. Included in P Company receivables is a $35,000 cash advance to S Company that was mailed on August 1, 2011. S Company had not yet received the advance at the time of the preparation of its August 1, 2011, balance sheet.
4. Assume that any excess of book value over the value implied by purchase price is due to overvalued plant and equipment.

PROBLEM 3-4 Parent and Two Subsidiaries, Intercompany Notes LO8

On January 2, 2011, Phillips Company purchased 80% of Sanchez Company and 90% of Thomas Company for $225,000 and $168,000, respectively. Immediately before the acquisitions, the balance sheets of the three companies were as follows:

	Phillips	*Sanchez*	*Thomas*
Cash	$400,000	$ 43,700	$ 20,000
Accounts receivable	28,000	24,000	20,000
Note receivable	—0—	10,000	—0—
Interest receivable	—0—	300	—0—
Inventory	120,000	96,000	43,000
Equipment	60,000	40,000	30,000
Land	180,000	80,000	70,000
Total	$788,000	$294,000	$183,000
Accounts payable	$ 28,000	$ 20,000	$ 18,000
Note payable	—0—	—0—	10,000
Common stock	300,000	120,000	75,000
Other contributed capital	300,000	90,000	40,000
Retained earnings	160,000	64,000	40,000
Total	$788,000	$294,000	$183,000

The note receivable and interest receivable of Sanchez relate to a loan made to Thomas Company on October 1, 2010. Thomas failed to record the accrued interest expense on the note.

Required:

Prepare a consolidated balance sheet workpaper as of January 2, 2011. Any difference between book value and the value implied by the purchase price relates to subsidiary land.

PROBLEM 3-5 Determining Balance Sheet Prior to Consolidation LO8

On January 1, 2011, Pat Company purchased 90% of the outstanding common stock of Solo Company for $236,000 cash. The balance sheet for Pat Company just before the acquisition of Solo Company stock, along with the consolidated balance sheet prepared at the date of acquisition, follows.

	Pat Company December 31, 2010	*Consolidated January 1, 2011*
Cash	$ 540,000	$ 352,000
Accounts receivable	272,000	346,000
Advances to Solo Company	10,000	
Inventory	376,000	451,000
Plant and equipment	622,000	820,000
Land	350,000	421,000
Total	$2,170,000	$2,390,000
Accounts payable	$ 280,000	$ 386,000
Long-term liabilities	520,000	605,500
Noncontrolling interest in subsidiary		28,500
Common stock	890,000	890,000
Other contributed capital	300,000	300,000
Retained earnings	180,000	180,000
Total	$2,170,000	$2,390,000

One week before the acquisition, Pat Company had advanced $10,000 to Solo Company. Solo Company had not yet recorded the transaction on the date of acquisition. In addition, on the date of acquisition, Solo Company owed Pat Company $4,000 for purchases of merchandise on account. The merchandise had been sold to outside parties prior to the date of acquisition.

Required:

A. Determine the amount of cash that appeared on Solo Company's balance sheet immediately prior to the acquisition of its stock by Pat Company.

B. Determine the amount of total stockholders' equity on Solo Company's separate balance sheet at the date of acquisition.

C. Determine the amount of total assets appearing on Solo Company's separate balance sheet on the date of acquisition.

PROBLEM 3-6 **In-Transit Items** LO8

On July 31, 2011, Ping Company purchased 90% of Santos Company's common stock for $2,010,000 cash. Immediately after the acquisition, the two companies' balance sheets were as follows:

	Ping	*Santos*
Cash	$ 320,000	$ 150,000
Accounts receivable	600,000	300,000
Note receivable	100,000	—0—
Inventory	1,840,000	400,000
Advance to Santos Company	60,000	—0—
Investment in Santos Company	2,010,000	—0—
Plant and equipment (net)	3,000,000	1,500,000
Land	90,000	90,000
Total	$8,020,000	$2,440,000
Accounts payable	$ 800,000	$ 140,000
Notes payable	900,000	100,000
Common stock	2,400,000	900,000
Other contributed capital	2,200,000	680,000
Retained earnings	1,720,000	620,000
Total	$8,020,000	$2,440,000

Santos Company has not yet recorded the $60,000 cash advance from Ping Company. Ping Company's accounts receivable include $20,000 due from Santos Company. Santos Company's $100,000 note payable is payable to Ping Company. Neither company has recorded $7,000 of interest accrued on the note from January 1 to July 31. Any difference between book value and the value implied by the purchase price relates to land.

Required:

Prepare a consolidated balance sheet workpaper on July 31, 2011.

PROBLEM 3-7 **Purchase Using Cash and Using Stock** LO8

Balance sheets for Prego Company and Sprague Company as of December 31, 2010, follow:

	Prego Company	*Sprague Company*
Cash	$ 700,000	$111,000
Accounts receivable (net)	892,000	230,000
Inventory	544,000	60,000
Property and equipment (net)	$1,927,000	$468,000
Land	120,000	94,000
Total assets	$4,183,000	$963,000
Accounts payable	$ 302,000	$152,000
Notes payable	588,000	61,000
Long-term debt	350,000	90,000
Common stock	1,800,000	500,000
Other contributed capital	543,000	80,000
Retained earnings	600,000	80,000
Total equities	$4,183,000	$963,000

The fair values of Sprague Company's assets and liabilities are equal to their book values.

Required:

Prepare a consolidated balance sheet as of January 1, 2011, under each of the following assumptions:

A. On January 1, 2011, Prego Company purchased 90% of the outstanding common stock of Sprague Company for $594,000.

B. On January 1, 2011, Prego Company exchanged 11,880 of its $20 par value common shares with a fair value of $50 per share for 90% of the outstanding common shares of Sprague Company. The transaction is a purchase.

PROBLEM 3-8 **Intercompany Items, Two Subsidiaries** LO7 LO8 LO9

On February 1, 2011, Punto Company purchased 95% of the outstanding common stock of Sara Company and 85% of the outstanding common stock of Rob Company. Immediately before the two acquisitions, balance sheets of the three companies were as follows:

	Punto	*Sara*	*Rob*
Cash	$165,000	$ 45,000	$17,000
Accounts receivable	35,000	35,000	26,000
Notes receivable	18,000	—0—	—0—
Merchandise inventory	106,000	35,500	14,000
Prepaid insurance	13,500	2,500	500
Advances to Sara Company	10,000		
Advances to Rob Company	5,000		
Land	248,000	43,000	15,000
Buildings (net)	100,000	27,000	16,000
Equipment (net)	35,000	10,000	2,500
Total	$735,500	$198,000	$91,000
Accounts payable	$ 25,500	$ 20,000	$10,500
Income taxes payable	30,000	10,000	—0—
Notes payable	—0—	6,000	10,500
Bonds payable	100,000	—0—	—0—
Common stock, $10 par value	300,000	144,000	42,000
Other contributed capital	150,000	12,000	38,000
Retained earnings (deficit)	130,000	6,000	(10,000)
Total	$735,500	$198,000	$91,000

The following additional information is relevant.

1. One week before the acquisitions, Punto Company had advanced $10,000 to Sara Company and $5,000 to Rob Company. Sara Company recorded an increase to Accounts Payable for its advance, but Rob Company had not recorded the transaction.
2. On the date of acquisition, Punto Company owed Sara Company $12,000 for purchases on account, and Rob Company owed Punto Company $3,000 and Sara Company $6,000 for such purchases. The goods purchased had all been sold to outside parties prior to acquisition.
3. Punto Company exchanged 13,400 shares of its common stock with a fair value of $12 per share for 95% of the outstanding common stock of Sara Company. In addition, stock issue fees of $4,000 were paid in cash. The acquisition was accounted for as a purchase.
4. Punto Company paid $50,000 cash for the 85% interest in Rob Company.
5. Three thousand dollars of Sara Company's notes payable and $9,500 of Rob Company's notes payable were payable to Punto Company.
6. Assume that for Sara, any difference between book value and the value implied by the purchase price relates to subsidiary land. However, for Rob, assume that any excess of book value over the value implied by the purchase price is due to overvalued buildings.

Required:

A. Give the book entries to record the two acquisitions in the accounts of Punto Company.
B. Prepare a consolidated balance sheet workpaper immediately after acquisition.
C. Prepare a consolidated balance sheet at the date of acquisition for Punto Company and its subsidiaries.

PROBLEM 3-9 **Intercompany Notes, 90% Acquisition** LO8 LO9

On January 1, 2009, Pope Company purchased 90% of Sun Company's common stock for $5,800,000 cash. Immediately after the acquisition, the two companies' balance sheets were as follows:

	Pope	*Sun*
Cash	$ 297,000	$ 165,000
Accounts receivable	432,000	468,000
Notes receivable	90,000	
Inventory	1,980,000	1,447,000
Investment in Sun Company	5,800,000	
Plant and equipment (net)	5,730,000	3,740,000
Land	1,575,000	908,000
Total	$15,904,000	$6,728,000
Accounts payable	$ 698,000	$ 247,000
Notes payable	2,250,000	110,000
Common stock ($15 par)	4,500,000	5,250,000
Other contributed capital	5,198,000	396,000
Treasury stock held		(1,200,000)
Retained earnings	3,258,000	1,925,000
Total	$15,904,000	$6,728,000

Sun Company's note payable includes a $90,000 note payable to Pope Company, plus $20,000 payable to a bank. Any difference between book value and the value implied by the purchase price relates to subsidiary property and equipment.

Required:

A. Prepare a Computation and Allocation Schedule for the difference between book value of equity and the value implied by the purchase price.
B. Prepare a consolidated balance sheet workpaper on January 1, 2009.

PROBLEM 3-10A Deferred Tax Effects

On January 1, 2012, Pruitt Company issued 25,500 shares of its common stock in exchange for 85% of the outstanding common stock of Shah Company. Pruitt's common stock had a fair value of $28 per share at that time (par value of $2 per share). Pruitt Company uses the cost method to account for its investment in Shah Company and files a consolidated income tax return. A schedule of the Shah Company assets acquired and liabilities assumed at book values (which are equal to their tax bases) and fair values follows.

Item	*Book Value/ Tax Basis*	*Fair Value*	*Excess*
Receivables (net)	$125,000	$ 125,000	$ —0—
Inventory	167,000	195,000	28,000
Land	86,500	120,000	33,500
Plant assets (net)	467,000	567,000	100,000
Patents	95,000	200,000	105,000
Total	$940,500	$1,207,000	$266,500
Current liabilities	$ 89,500	$ 89,500	$ —0—
Bonds payable	300,000	360,000	60,000
Common stock	120,000		
Other contributed capital	164,000		
Retained earnings	267,000		
Total	$940,500		

Additional Information:

1. Pruitt's income tax rate is 35%.
2. Shah's beginning inventory was all sold during 2012.
3. Useful lives for depreciation and amortization purposes are:

Plant assets	10 years
Patents	8 years
Bond premium	10 years

4. Pruitt uses the straight-line method for all depreciation and amortization purposes.

Required:

A. Prepare the stock acquisition entry on Pruitt Company's books.

B. Prepare the eliminating entries for a consolidated statements workpaper on January 1, 2012, immediately after acquisition.

Note: See Chapter 5, Problem 5–18 for an expanded version of this problem on the effects of deferred taxes in subsequent periods.

4

CONSOLIDATED FINANCIAL STATEMENTS AFTER ACQUISITION

LEARNING OBJECTIVES

1. Describe the accounting treatment required under current GAAP for varying levels of influence or control by investors.
2. Prepare journal entries on the parent's books to account for an investment using the cost method, the partial equity method, and the complete equity method.
3. Understand the use of the workpaper in preparing consolidated financial statements.
4. Prepare a schedule for the computation and allocation of the difference between implied and book values.
5. Prepare the workpaper eliminating entries for the year of acquisition (and subsequent years) for the cost and equity methods.
6. Describe two alternative methods to account for interim acquisitions of subsidiary stock at the end of the first year.
7. Explain how the consolidated statement of cash flows differs from a single firm's statement of cash flows.
8. Understand how the reporting of an acquisition on the consolidated statement of cash flows differs when stock is issued rather than cash.
9. Describe some of the differences between U.S. GAAP and IFRS in accounting for equity investments.

Capital One Financial agreed to its second deal in a year to acquire a regional bank, continuing a rash of consolidations in the credit card industry. The independent credit card issuer will acquire North Fork Bancorp of Melville, NY, for $14.5 billion and in doing so will expand into the desirable Northeastern U.S. retail banking market. The deal follows Capital One's purchase of Hibernia Bank of New Orleans last fall for $5 billion. The combined Capital One-North Fork puts the company in the top 10 largest banks in the U.S. based on deposits and managed loans. It will also be the third-largest retail bank in the New York region.[1]

Investments in voting stock of other companies may be consolidated, or they may be separately reported in the financial statements at cost, at fair value, or at equity. The

[1] *Forbes.com*, "Capital Consolidation," by Liz Moyer, 3/13/06.

method of reporting adopted depends on a number of factors including the size of the investment, the extent to which the investor exercises control over the activities of the investee, and the marketability of the securities. **Investor** refers to a *business entity that holds an investment in voting stock of another company.* **Investee** refers to *a corporation that issued voting stock held by an investor.*

ACCOUNTING FOR INVESTMENTS BY THE COST, PARTIAL EQUITY, AND COMPLETE EQUITY METHODS

LO1 Varying levels of ownership are accounted for differently.

Generally speaking, there are three levels of influence or control by an investor over an investee, which determine the appropriate accounting treatment. There are no absolute percentages to distinguish among these levels, but there are guidelines. The three levels and the corresponding accounting treatment are summarized as follows:

RELATED CONCEPTS

When available for sale securities are adjusted to market, the unrealized gain or loss is recorded as *other comprehensive income* rather than a component of net income.

Level	*Guideline Percentages*	*Usual Accounting Treatment*
No significant influence	Less than 20%	Investment carried at fair value at current year-end (trading or available for sale securities)—method traditionally referred to as *cost* method with an adjustment for market changes.
Significant influence (no control)	20 to 50%[a]	Investment measured under the equity method; may be elected to be carried at fair value under an irrevocable option.[b]
Effective control	Greater than 50%	Consolidated statements required (investment eliminated, combined financial statements): investment recorded under *cost, partial equity*, or *complete equity* method.

[a] The IASB issued an exposure draft in December 2008 entitled 'Consolidated Financial Statements,' in which control is defined as 'the ability of an entity to direct the activities of another entity to generate returns for the reporting entity.'

[b] This election may be made when *FASB Statement No. 159* is adopted or when the investment becomes subject to the equity method. *FASB Statement No. 159* **[ASC 825–10–25–4]**.

The focus in this chapter is on presenting financial statements for consolidated entities (i.e., those in the third category above). Nonetheless, the parent company must account for its investment income from the subsidiary in its own books by one of the methods used for accounting for investments. Investment income will subsequently be eliminated, as will the investment account itself, when the two sets of books are merged into one consolidated set of financial data. Thus, so long as the eliminating process is carried out accurately, the parent has a certain amount of discretion in choosing how it accounts for its investment. This discretion exists because the consolidated financial statements will be identical, regardless of which method is used. However, ***if the parent issues parent-only financial statements for any purpose, the***

complete equity method should be used on those statements for investees over which the parent has either significant influence or effective control.

To understand the effect of the earnings of the subsidiary on the consolidated entity, and on the noncontrolling interest, the reader needs to understand the mechanics that lead to the blending of two sets of books (income statement, retained earnings statement, and balance sheet) into one. Thus, we begin this chapter with a general discussion of accounting for investments, keeping in mind that our purpose is to prepare consolidated financial statements where appropriate.

In distinguishing among the three levels of influence/control, an investor is generally presumed not to have significant influence if the percentage owned is less than 20% of the investee's outstanding common stock. Exceptions are possible; for example, the investor might own only 18% but be the single largest investor, with the remaining 82% spread among a large number of very small investors, in which case the 18% would represent significant influence, and the equity method would be appropriate. In general, however, an investor owning less than 20% of the investee's stock accounts for the investment account at its fair value, under a method traditionally referred to as the "cost" method but with adjustments for changes in the fair value over time.

When a company owns a sufficient amount of another company's stock to have significant influence (usually at least 20%), but not enough to effectively control the other company (less than 50% in most cases), the equity method is required. Under *FASB Statement No. 159* **[ASC 825–10–25–2]**, these equity investments may alternatively be carried at fair value under an irrevocable election to do so. Once the investor is deemed to have effective control over the other company (with or without a majority of stock ownership), consolidated statements are required.

In Chapter 3, we focused on the preparation of the consolidated balance sheet at the date of acquisition. With the passage of time, however, consolidating procedures are needed to prepare not only the consolidated balance sheet, but also a consolidated income statement, a consolidated statement of retained earnings, and a consolidated statement of cash flows. In this chapter we address the preparation of these statements subsequent to the date of acquisition.

When consolidated financial statements are appropriate (the investor has effective control over the investee), then the investment account, which is carried on the books of the parent company, will be eliminated in the consolidation process. Thus, it is not relevant to the consolidated statements whether the investor measures the investment account using the cost method or using the equity method, so long as the eliminating entries are properly prepared. When prepared correctly, the resulting consolidated financial statements will be identical, regardless of how the investment was carried in the books of the parent company (investor). At least three possible methods exist and are used in practice on the books of the parent company: the cost method, the partial equity method, and the complete equity method. Recognition of which of these methods is being used is important because the appropriate eliminating entries will vary depending on that choice. Further, because all three are used in practice, it is worthwhile to compare and contrast the three briefly at this point.

Of the three methods, only the complete equity method is acceptable for those investments where ***significant influence but not control*** is present. Our focus, however, is on investments that will be consolidated (for example, majority ownership). *Nonetheless, from an internal decision-making standpoint, if the parent firm relies upon the unconsolidated statements for any purposes, the complete equity method might be considered superior to the other two in terms of approximating the operating effects of the investment.* In contrast, the cost method is the simplest of the three to prepare on the books of the parent and is the most commonly used method in practice. The partial equity method might be viewed as a compromise, being somewhat easier to prepare on the books of the parent than the complete equity method but also providing a rough approximation of the operating effects of the investment. When decisions are based solely on the consolidated statements, the primary consideration is ease and cost of preparation; this may explain why many companies choose the simplest method (cost method).

Under all three methods, the investment account is initially recorded at its cost. The differences among the three methods then lie in subsequent entries. If the cost method is used, the investment account is adjusted only when additional shares of stock in the investee are purchased or sold (or in the event of a liquidating dividend).[2] Fair value adjustments will be made periodically as needed, but these are generally accomplished using a separate account, Fair Value Adjustment, thus preserving historical cost in the investment account. (The Fair Value Adjustment account has a debit balance when fair value is higher than historical cost, and a credit balance when fair value is lower than historical cost.) Since these fair value adjustments have no impact on the consolidated financial statements (they would have to be reversed if made), we do not make such adjustments in this text.

Under the equity method, more frequent entries appear in the investment account on the books of the parent. Under the partial equity method, the investor adjusts the investment account upward for its share of the investee's earnings and downward for its share of the investee's dividends declared. Under the complete equity method, additional adjustments are made to the investment account for the effects of unrealized intercompany profits, the depreciation or amortization of any differences between market and book values, and possible impairment losses on any goodwill implied in the acquisition price. ***Remember, the cost method and various forms of the equity method are methods to record investments after acquisition.*** All acquisitions reflect cost at the date of acquisition.

Because all three methods have advantages and disadvantages, and because individual preferences will vary as to which method(s) are most important to the student, book entries and workpaper eliminating entries assuming the use of each of the three methods are discussed and illustrated in separate sections throughout this text. In *some* portions of this chapter, however, partial equity and complete equity methods are indistinguishable given the assumptions of the example, in which case they are illustrated only once to conserve space. Icons in the margin of the pages are used to distinguish between the cost and equity methods. To distinguish between

[2] A liquidating dividend occurs when the investee has paid cumulative dividends in excess of cumulative earnings (since acquisition). Such excess dividends are treated as a return of capital and, upon their receipt, are recorded by the investor as a decrease in the investment account under the cost method.

partial and complete equity, the word "complete" or "partial" appears on the icon when needed. In addition, blue print is used to help identify those sections of text that distinguish the equity method from the cost method.

First, though, every student should have a basic understanding of the differences among the three methods in accounting for the investment on the books of the parent. These are illustrated below, and are also summarized in Figure 4-1, presented at the end of this section.

Cost Method on Books of Investor

To illustrate the accounting for an investment in a subsidiary accounted for by the **cost method**, assume that P Company acquired 90% of the outstanding voting stock of S Company at the beginning of Year 1 for $800,000. As mentioned previously, icons in the margin of the pages are used to distinguish between the cost and equity methods. Income (loss) of S Company and dividends declared by S Company during the next three years are listed below. During the third year, the firm pays a liquidating dividend (i.e., the cumulative dividends declared exceeds the cumulative income earned).

Year	*Income (Loss)*	*Dividends Declared*	*Cumulative Income over (under) Dividends*
1	$90,000	$30,000	$60,000
2	(20,000)	30,000	10,000
3	10,000	30,000	(10,000)

Journal entries on the books of P Company to account for the investment in S Company during the three years follow:

LO2 Journal entries for Parent using cost method.

Year 1—P's Books		
Investment in S Company	800,000	
Cash		800,000
To record the initial investment.		
Cash	27,000	
Dividend Income		27,000
To record dividends received .9($30,000).		

Year 2—P's Books		
Cash	27,000	
Dividend Income		27,000
To record dividends received .9($30,000).		

Year 3—P's Books		
Cash	27,000	
Dividend Income		18,000
Investment in S Company		9,000
To record dividends received, $9,000 of which represents a return of investment.		

After these entries are posted, the investment account will appear as follows:

Investment in S Company (Cost Method)

Year 1 Cost	800,000		
		Year 3 Liquidating dividend	9,000
Year 3 Balance	791,000		

Year 1 entries record the initial investment and the receipt of dividends from S Company. In year 2, although S Company incurred a $20,000 loss, there was a $60,000 excess of earnings over dividends in Year 1. Consequently, the dividends received are recognized as income by P Company. In year 3, however, a **liquidating dividend** occurs. From the point of view of a parent company, a purchased subsidiary is deemed to have distributed a liquidating dividend when the cumulative amount of its dividends declared exceeds its cumulative reported earnings after its acquisition. Such excess dividends are treated as a return of capital and are recorded as a reduction of the investment account rather than as dividend income. The liquidating dividend is 90% of the excess of dividends paid over cumulative earnings since acquisition (90% of $10,000).

Partial Equity Method on Books of Investor

Next, assume that P Company has elected to use the partial equity method to record the investment in S Company above. The entries for the first three years would appear as follows:

Year 1—P's Books

Investment in S Company	800,000	
Cash		800,000
To record the initial investment.		
Investment in S Company	81,000	
Equity in Subsidiary Income .9($90,000)		81,000
To record P's share of subsidiary income.		
Cash	27,000	
Investment in S Company		27,000
To record dividends received .9($30,000)		

Note: The entries to record equity in subsidiary income and dividends received may be combined into one entry, if desired.

Year 2—P's Books

Equity in Subsidiary Loss	18,000	
Investment in S Company		18,000
To record equity in subsidiary loss .9($20,000).		
Cash	27,000	
Investment in S Company		27,000
To record dividends received .9($30,000).		

Year 3—P's Books

Investment in S Company	9,000	
Equity in Subsidiary Income		9,000
To record equity in subsidiary income .9($10,000).		
Cash	27,000	
Investment in S Company		27,000
To record dividends received .9($30,000).		

LO2 Journal entries for Parent using partial equity method.

After these entries are posted, the investment account will appear as follows:

Investment in S Company (Partial Equity Method)

Year 1 Cost	800,000		
Year 1 Equity in subsidiary income	81,000	Year 1 Share of dividends declared	27,000
Year 1 Balance	854,000		
		Year 2 Equity in subsidiary loss	18,000
		Year 2 Share of dividends declared	27,000
Year 2 Balance	809,000		
Year 3 Equity in subsidiary income	9,000	Year 3 Share of dividends declared	27,000
Year 3 Balance	791,000		

Complete Equity Method on Books of Investor

"BlackRock, a U.S.-based investment management firm with approximately $342 billion in assets under management, will acquire Merrill Lynch's investment management business in exchange for a 49 percent ownership interest. Upon the closing of this transaction, PNC Financial Services will continue to own 44.5 million shares of BlackRock, representing an ownership interest of approximately 34 percent. Thereafter, BlackRock will be deconsolidated from PNC's financial statements and will be accounted for using the equity method."[3]

1. Although Merrill Lynch will not own more than 50% of BlackRock, would you consider Merrill to have "control" of BlackRock? Why or why not?
2. Does PNC have "control" of BlackRock, as defined by FASB?

LO2 Journal entries for Parent using complete equity method.

The complete equity method is usually required to report common stock investments in the 20% to 50% range, assuming the investor has the ability to exercise significant influence over the operating activities of the investee and does *not* have effective control over the investee. In addition, a parent company may use, in its own books, the complete equity method to *account for* investments in subsidiaries that will be consolidated. This method is similar to the partial equity method up to a point, but it requires additional entries in most instances.

Continuing the illustration above, assume additionally that the $800,000 purchase price exceeded the book value of the underlying equity of S Company by $100,000; and that the difference was attributed half to goodwill ($50,000) and half to an excess of market over book values of depreciable assets ($50,000). Under current FASB regulations, goodwill would be capitalized and not amortized. The additional depreciation expense implied by the difference between market and book values, however, must still be accounted for. The depreciation of the excess, if spread over a remaining useful life of 10 years, would result in a charge to earnings of $5,000 per year. This charge has the impact of lowering the equity in subsidiary income, or increasing the equity in subsidiary loss, recorded by the parent.

[3] *PNC Financial Services Group press release,* "PNC to Report $1.6 Billion Gain on the Merger of BlackRock and Merrill Lynch Investment Managers," 2/15/06.

The entries for the first three years under the complete equity method are as follows:

Year 1—P's Books

Investment in S Company	800,000	
Cash		800,000
To record the initial investment.		
Investment in S Company	81,000	
Equity in Subsidiary Income .9($90,000)		81,000
To record equity in subsidiary income.		
Equity in Subsidiary Income	5,000	
Investment in S Company ($50,000/10 years)		5,000
To adjust equity in subsidiary income for the excess depreciation		
Cash	27,000	
Investment in S Company		27,000
To record dividends received .9($30,000).		

Note: The entries to record equity in subsidiary income and dividends received may be combined into one entry, if desired.

Year 2—P's Books

Equity in Subsidiary Loss	18,000	
Investment in S Company		18,000
To record equity in subsidiary loss .9($20,000).		
Equity in Subsidiary Loss ($50,000/10 years)	5,000	
Investment in S Company		5,000
To adjust equity in subsidiary loss for the excess depreciation.		
Cash	27,000	
Investment in S Company		27,000
To record dividends received .9($30,000).		

Year 3—P's Books

Investment in S Company	9,000	
Equity in Subsidiary Income		9,000
To record equity in subsidiary income .9($10,000).		
Equity in Subsidiary Income ($50,000/10 years)	5,000	
Investment in S Company		5,000
To adjust equity in subsidiary income for the excess depreciation.		
Cash	27,000	
Investment in S Company		27,000
To record dividends received .9($30,000).		

After these entries are posted, the investment account will appear as follows:

Investment in S Company (Complete Equity Method)

Year 1 Cost	800,000		
Year 1 Equity in subsidiary income	81,000	Year 1 Excess depreciation	5,000
		Year 1 Share of dividends declared	27,000
Year 1 Balance	849,000		
		Year 2 Equity in subsidiary loss	18,000
		Year 2 Excess depreciation	5,000
		Year 2 Share of dividends declared	27,000
Year 2 Balance	799,000		
Year 3 Equity in subsidiary income	9,000	Year 3 Excess depreciation	5,000
		Year 3 Share of dividends declared	27,000
Year 3 Balance	776,000		

The additional entry to adjust the equity in subsidiary income for the additional depreciation in Year 1 may be viewed as reversing out a portion of the income recognized; the result is a net equity in subsidiary income for Year 1 of $76,000 ($81,000 minus $5,000). In Year 2, however, since the subsidiary showed a loss for the period, the additional depreciation has the effect of increasing the loss from the amount initially recorded ($18,000) to a larger loss of $23,000.

A solid understanding of the entries made on the books of the investor (presented above) will help greatly in understanding the eliminating entries presented in the following sections. In some sense these entries may be viewed as "undoing" the above entries. It is important to realize, however, that the eliminating entries are not "parent-only" entries. In many cases an eliminating entry will affect certain accounts of the parent and others of the subsidiary. For example, the entry to eliminate the investment account (a parent company account) against the equity accounts of the subsidiary affects both parent and subsidiary accounts. Some accounts do not need eliminating because the effects on parent and subsidiary are offsetting. For example, in the entries above, we saw that the parent debited cash when dividends were received from the subsidiary. We know that cash on the books of the subsidiary is credited when dividends are paid. The net effect on cash of the consolidated entry is thus zero. No entry is made to the cash account in the consolidating process. See Figure 4-1 for a comparison of the three methods on the books of the parent.

FIGURE 4-1

Comparison of the Investment T Accounts (Cost vs. Partial Equity vs. Complete Equity Method)

Investment in S Company—Cost Method

Year 1 Acquisition cost	800,000		
Year 1 and 2 Balance	800,000		
		Year 3 Subsidiary liquidating dividend	9,000
Year 3 Balance	791,000		

Investment in S Company—Partial Equity Method

Year 1 Acquisition cost	800,000		
Year 1 Equity in subsidiary income	81,000	Year 1 Share of dividends declared	27,000
Year 1 Balance	854,000		
		Year 2 Equity in subsidiary loss	18,000
		Year 2 Share of dividend declared	27,000
Year 2 Balance	809,000		
Year 3 Equity in subsidiary income	9,000	Year 3 Share of dividend declared	27,000
Year 3 Balance	791,000		

Investment in S Company—Complete Equity Method

Year 1 Acquisition cost	800,000		
Year 1 Equity in subsidiary income adjusted for excess depreciation	76,000	Year 1 Share of dividend declared	27,000
Year 1 Balance	849,000		
		Year 2 Equity in subsidiary loss, adjusted	23,000
		Year 2 Share of dividend declared	27,000
Year 2 Balance	799,000		
Year 3 Equity in subsidiary income adjusted for excess depreciation	4,000	Year 3 Share of dividend declared	27,000
Year 3 Balance	776,000		

TEST
YOUR KNOWLEDGE

NOTE: Solutions to ***Test Your Knowledge*** questions are found at the end of each chapter before the end-of-chapter questions.

True or False

1. __________ a. Under the cost method for recording investments, dividends are recorded by reducing the Investment in Subsidiary asset account.

   __________ b. Under current GAAP additional depreciation due to market values in excess of book values no longer necessitates a reduction in the equity in subsidiary income (on the books of the parent) under the complete equity method.

Multiple Choice

2. Assuming that the acquisition price of Company S includes some differences between market and book values of depreciable assets, differences arise between the complete equity method and the partial equity method in how the accounts of the parent reflect:
   (A) Dividends
   (B) Income
   (C) Retained Earnings
   (D) Both B and C
3. Which of the following statements regarding methods to record investments after acquisition is incorrect?
   (A) It is not relevant to the consolidated financial statements whether the parent company measures its investment account using the cost method or using one of the equity methods so long as the eliminating entries are properly prepared.
   (B) Initial recording of the investment (at its cost) is identical in all three methods, i.e., cost, partial equity, or complete equity method.
   (C) Under the partial equity method, the investor adjusts the investment account upward for its share of the investee's earnings and dividends declared.
   (D) For periods subsequent to acquisition, both the investment account and the equity in subsidiary income will be larger under the partial equity method than under the complete equity method if the subsidiary carries depreciable assets with market values greater than book values.

CONSOLIDATED STATEMENTS AFTER ACQUISITION—COST METHOD

The preparation of consolidated financial statements after acquisition is not materially different in concept from preparing them at the acquisition date in the sense that reciprocal accounts are eliminated and remaining balances are combined. The process is more complex, however, because time has elapsed and business activity has taken place between the date of acquisition and the date of consolidated statement preparation. On the date of acquisition, the only relevant financial statement is the consolidated balance sheet; after acquisition, a complete set of consolidated financial statements—income statement, retained earnings statement, balance sheet, and statement of cash flows—must be prepared for the affiliated group of companies. Deferred tax issues are presented in Appendix B to this chapter.

Workpaper Format

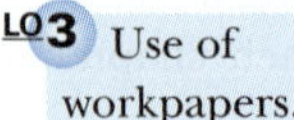
LO3 Use of workpapers.

Accounting workpapers are used to accumulate, classify, and arrange data for a variety of accounting purposes, including the preparation of financial reports and statements. Although workpaper style and technique vary among firms and individuals, we have adopted a three-section workpaper for illustrative purposes in this book. The format includes a separate section for each of three basic financial statements—income statement, retained earnings statement, and balance sheet. In some cases the input to the workpaper comes from the individual financial statements of the affiliates to be consolidated, in which case the three-section workpaper is particularly appropriate. At other times, however, input may be from affiliate trial balances, and the data must be arranged in financial statement form before the workpaper can be completed. Organizing the data provides a useful review for students, however, and emphasizes the linkages among these three financial statements. An alternative format to preparing the workpaper is provided in Appendix A in this chapter (using the information in Illustration 4-4).

COST

The fourth statement, the statement of cash flows, is prepared from the information in the consolidated income statement and from two comparative consolidated balance sheets. It will be presented later in this chapter.

The discussion and illustrations that follow are based on trial balances at December 31, 2010, for P Company and S Company given in Illustration 4-1. Throughout this chapter, any difference between the cost of the investment and the book value of the equity interest acquired is assumed to relate to the under- or overvaluation of subsidiary goodwill or to land and is, therefore, assigned to goodwill or land in the second eliminating entry. Because neither goodwill nor land is subject to depreciation or amortization under current GAAP, this serves to defer at least one complication to Chapter 5. More realistic assumptions, and the resulting complications, will be dealt with fully in Chapter 5.

ILLUSTRATION 4-1

P Company and S Company Trial Balances
December 31, 2010

	P Company		*S Company*	
	Dr.	*Cr.*	*Dr.*	*Cr.*
Cash	$ 79,000		$ 18,000	
Accounts Receivable (net)	64,000		28,000	
Inventory, 1/1	56,000		32,000	
Investment in S Company	165,000			
Property and Equipment (net)	180,000		165,000	
Goodwill	35,000		17,000	
Accounts Payable		$ 35,000		$ 24,000
Other Liabilities		62,000		37,000
Common Stock, $10 par value		200,000		100,000
Other Contributed Capital		40,000		50,000
Retained Earnings, 1/1		210,000		40,000
Dividends Declared	20,000		10,000	
Sales		300,000		160,000
Dividend Income		8,000		
Purchases	186,000		95,000	
Expenses	70,000		46,000	
	$855,000	$855,000	$411,000	$411,000
Inventory, 12/31	$ 67,000		$ 43,000	

Year of Acquisition—Cost Method

Assume that P Company purchased 80% of the outstanding shares of S Company common stock on January 1, 2010, for $165,000. The underlying book value of S company's net assets on that date was $190,000. P Company made the following entry:

P's Books		
Investment in S Company	165,000	
Cash		165,000

On June 6, 2010, S Company paid a $10,000 dividend and made the following entry:

S's Books		
Dividends Declared	10,000	
Cash		10,000

(Recall that the Dividends Declared account is a temporary account that is closed to retained earnings at year-end. An alternative is to debit retained earnings directly when dividends are declared.) Since P Company owns 80% of S Company's common stock, the receipt of the dividend was recorded by P Company as follows:

P's Books		
Cash	8,000	
Dividend Income (80% × $10,000)		8,000

LO4 Preparing Computation and Allocation Difference (CAD) Schedule.

Note that the trial balance data in Illustration 4-1 reflect the effects of both the investment and dividend transactions. Also note that the existing balances in goodwill on the books of both companies indicate that both firms have been involved in previous net asset acquisitions (as discussed in Chapter 2).

Begin the consolidating process, as always, by preparing a Computation and Allocation Schedule, as follows:

Computation and Allocation of Difference Schedule

	Parent Share	*Noncontrolling Share*	*Total Value*
Purchase price and implied value	**$165,000**	**41,250**	206,250
Less: Book value of equity acquired:			
Common stock	80,000	20,000	**100,000**
Other contributed capital	40,000	10,000	**50,000**
Retained earnings	32,000	8,000	**40,000**
Total book value	152,000	38,000	190,000
Difference between implied and book value	13,000	3,250	**16,250**
Record new goodwill	(13,000)	(3,250)	**(16,250)**
Balance	—0—	—0—	—0—

RELATED CONCEPTS

The *historical cost* principle allows for the recording of goodwill only when a purchase transaction occurs. Whether or not the total value implied by the purchase price should extend to the NCI is a subject of much debate.

Because the difference between implied and book values is established only at the date of acquisition, ***this schedule will not change in future periods.*** Thus, there will be $16,250 to distribute each year, although the makeup of that distribution may shift over time. Since it is attributed to goodwill in this example, the distribution will not change unless the goodwill is subsequently impaired.

A workpaper for the preparation of consolidated financial statements at December 31, 2010, the end of the year of acquisition, is presented in Illustration 4-2.

Data from the trial balances are arranged in statement form and entered on the workpaper. Consolidated financial statements should include only balances resulting from transactions with outsiders. Eliminating techniques are designed to accomplish this end. The consolidated income statement is essentially a combination of the revenue, expense, gain, and loss accounts of all consolidated affiliates after elimination of amounts representing the effect of transactions among the affiliates. The combined income of the affiliates, after eliminating any intercompany transactions, is referred to as **consolidated net income**. This amount is allocated to the controlling and noncontrolling interests. In the workpaper, consolidated net income is reduced by the noncontrolling interest's share (if any) of the net income of the subsidiaries to arrive at the **controlling interest in consolidated net income**. Note that in the past, the controlling interest has often been referred to as consolidated net income. The terminology used here and by the FASB in *FASB Statement No. 160* **[ASC 810–10–10–1]** reflects the change from the parent concept to the economic entity concept for consolidated financial statements. The controlling interest in consolidated net income consists of parent company net income plus (minus) its share of the affiliate's income (loss) resulting from transactions with outside parties. The consolidated retained earnings statement consists of beginning consolidated retained earnings plus the controlling interest in consolidated net income (or minus the interest in a consolidated loss), minus parent company dividends declared. The net balance represents consolidated retained earnings at the end of the period. The noncontrolling interest in net assets is reflected as a separate component of equity.

Workpaper Observations

LO5 Workpaper eliminating entries.

Several observations should be noted concerning the workpaper presented in Illustration 4-2.

1. *Each section of the workpaper represents one of three consolidated financial statements*: Note that the ***entire bottom line*** of the income statement, which represents net income, is transferred to the Net Income line on the retained earnings statement. Similarly, the ***entire bottom line*** of the retained earnings statement, which represents ending retained earnings, is transferred to the Retained Earnings line on the balance sheet.
2. *Elimination of the investment account*: The elimination of the investment account at the end of the first year is the same one that would be made at the date of acquisition for the preparation of a consolidated balance sheet. One exception is that S Company's beginning retained earnings is eliminated in the ***retained earnings section*** of the workpaper, rather than in the balance sheet section. In subsequent years, the debit to Retained Earnings–S Company will always be for the subsidiary retained earnings balance at the ***beginning of the current year***. Changes in retained earnings during the current year are always reflected in the retained earnings statement section of the workpaper. Also note that in subsequent years, there will be an additional entry preceding the elimination of the investment account, and this entry will arise from changes in the Retained Earnings account of the subsidiary from the date of acquisition to the beginning of the current year. This entry is not needed in year 1 because no such change has occurred yet.

Cost Method | **ILLUSTRATION 4-2**

80% Owned | **Consolidated Statements Workpaper—Cost Method**

Year of Acquisition | **P Company and Subsidiary for the Year Ended December 31, 2010**

Income Statement	P Company	S Company	Eliminations Dr.	Eliminations Cr.	Noncontrolling Interest	Consolidated Balances
Sales	300,000	160,000				460,000
Dividend Income	8,000		(3) 8,000			
Total Revenue	308,000	160,000				460,000
Cost of Goods Sold:						
Inventory, 1/1	56,000	32,000				88,000
Purchases	186,000	95,000				281,000
	242,000	127,000				369,000
Inventory, 12/31	67,000	43,000				110,000
Cost of Goods Sold	175,000	84,000				259,000
Expenses	70,000	46,000				116,000
Total Cost and Expense	245,000	130,000				375,000
Consolidated Net Income	63,000	30,000				85,000
Noncontrolling Interest in Income					6,000	(6,000)*
Net Income to Retained Earnings	63,000	30,000	8,000	—0—	6,000	79,000
Retained Earnings Statement						
1/1 Retained Earnings						
P Company	210,000					210,000
S Company		40,000	(1) 40,000			
Net Income from above	63,000	30,000	8,000	—0—	6,000	79,000
Dividends Declared						
P Company	(20,000)					(20,000)
S Company		(10,000)		(3) 8,000	(2,000)	
12/31 Retained Earnings to Balance Sheet	253,000	60,000	48,000	8,000	4,000	269,000
Balance Sheet						
Cash	79,000	18,000				97,000
Accounts Receivable (net)	64,000	28,000				92,000
Inventory, 12/31	67,000	43,000				110,000
Investment in S Company	165,000			(1) 165,000		
Difference between Implied and Book Value			(1) 16,250	(2) 16,250		
Property and Equipment (net)	180,000	165,000				345,000
Goodwill	35,000	17,000	(2) 16,250			68,250
Total	590,000	271,000				712,250
Accounts Payable	35,000	24,000				59,000
Other Liabilities	62,000	37,000				99,000
Common Stock						
P Company	200,000					200,000
S Company		100,000	(1) 100,000			
Other Contributed Capital						
P Company	40,000					40,000
S Company		50,000	(1) 50,000			
Retained Earnings from above	253,000	60,000	48,000	8,000	4,000	269,000
1/1 Noncontrolling Interest in Net Assets				(1) 41,250	41,250	
12/31 Noncontrolling Interest in Net Assets					45,250	45,250
Total	590,000	271,000	230,500	230,500		712,250

* .2($30,000) = $6,000

(1) To eliminate the investment in S Company and create noncontrolling interest account.
(2) To allocate the difference between implied and book value to goodwill.
(3) To eliminate intercompany dividends.

It is useful to formulate eliminating entries in ***general journal entry form***, even though they are not recorded in the general journal, to be sure that they balance before entering them in the workpaper. Be sure to number each entry as it is entered in the workpaper. This helps to keep the eliminating entries in balance as well. It may also be helpful to think of each entry by a shortened name, as indicated in quotation marks after the following entries.

		Debit	Credit
(1)	Common Stock—S Company	100,000	
	Other Contributed Capital—S Company	50,000	
	1/1 Retained Earnings—S Company	40,000	
	Difference between Implied and Book Values	16,250	
	Investment in S Company		165,000
	Noncontrolling Interest in Equity		41,250
	"The investment entry"		

RELATED CONCEPTS

When control is achieved with a relatively low percentage ownership (55% for example), a *conservative* view might question whether it is appropriate to record the entire (100%) implied value of $16,250 of goodwill.

3. *Allocation of the difference between implied and book value*: The second elimination entry is also identical to that which would have been made at the date of acquisition. It serves to distribute the difference between implied and book values of subsidiary equity to the appropriate account(s), in this case to goodwill.

		Debit	Credit
(2)	Goodwill	16,250	
	Difference between Implied and Book Value		16,250
	"The differential entry"		

It is worth noting that the recording of goodwill is one of the more controversial of the topics addressed by FASB in its decisions regarding business combinations. Some respondents during the comment period expressed a preference to conform to the International Accounting model used in the past for business combinations, which has marked the identifiable net assets entirely to their fair value at the date of the acquisition (as here), but has recorded goodwill only to the extent of the parent's percentage of the subsidiary. In other words, goodwill would be recorded for only 80% × $16,250, or $13,000, and the noncontrolling interest would be lowered by $3,250 if the choice allowed under IFRS, which permits recognition of goodwill using either the "full" goodwill method or "parent-only" goodwill method, were followed.

4. *Intercompany dividends*: The elimination of intercompany dividends is made by a debit to Dividend Income and a credit to Dividends Declared. In placing this entry into the Eliminations columns of the workpaper, note that the Dividend Income debit appears in the ***Income Statement*** section, while the Dividends *Declared credit appears* in the ***Retained Earnings Statement*** section. It is commonly the case that an eliminating entry will affect more than one of the three statements, as here (and also in entry (1)).

		Debit	Credit
(3)	Dividend Income	8,000	
	Dividends Declared—S Company		8,000
	"The dividend entry"		

This eliminating entry also serves to prevent the double counting of income, since the subsidiary's individual income and expense items are combined with the parent's in the determination of consolidated income.

5. *Noncontrolling interest in consolidated net income*: There is one number on the workpaper that is calculated and then inserted directly into the income statement, and does not flow from the trial balance columns. That number is the ***noncontrolling interest in consolidated net income.*** To facilitate the calculation of the noncontrolling and controlling interests in consolidated income, a t-account approach is helpful. In later chapters, the presence of intercompany profits and other complications will make the calculation more complex than it is at this point. It is, therefore, useful to form the habit of using the t-accounts now.

COST

Noncontrolling Interest in Consolidated Net Income

	Internally generated income of S Company	$30,000
	Any needed adjustments (see Chapter 5)	0
	Adjusted income of subsidiary	30,000
	Noncontrolling percentage owned	20%
	Noncontrolling interest in income	6,000

The first t-account (above) calculates the distribution of consolidated net income to the noncontrolling interest. This number can be inserted directly into the next-to-bottom line of the ***Income Statement*** Section. When this amount is subtracted from the consolidated income of $85,000, the resulting amount of $79,000 represents the **controlling interest in consolidated net income.** ($30,000).8

The parent company t-account serves as a useful check of the controlling interest in consolidated net income. The 80% controlling percentage in the adjusted income of subsidiary ($30,000 from t-account above) will appear in P Company's t-account as part of the controlling interest. For the parent company, the internally generated income represents the amount from the first column of the trial balance ($63,000) minus any income which came from the subsidiary (dividend income, in this case, of $8,000), or $55,000 income from P Company's independent operations.

Controlling Interest in Consolidated Net Income

	Internally generated income of P Company ($63,000 income minus $8,000 dividend income from subsidiary)	$55,000
	Any needed adjustments (see Chapter 5)	0
	Percentage of subsidiary adjusted income (80%)($30,000)	24,000
	Controlling interest in income	$79,000

6. *Consolidated retained earnings*: Consolidated retained earnings on December 31, 2010, of $269,000 can be determined as follows:

P Company's reported retained earnings, 1/1	$210,000
Plus: controlling interest in consolidated net income for 2010	79,000
Less: P Company's dividends declared during 2010	(20,000)
Consolidated Retained Earnings, 12/31	$269,000

The calculation above appears in the final column of the workpaper in the Retained Earnings Statement section. Alternatively, or as a check, consolidated retained earnings may be determined as:

P Company's reported retained earnings, 12/31	$253,000
Plus P Company's share of the increase in S Company's retained earnings from the date of acquisition to the end of 2010: .8($60,000 − $40,000)	16,000
Consolidated Retained Earnings, 12/31	$269,000

7. The eliminations columns in each section do not balance, since individual eliminations made involve more than one section. The total eliminations for all three sections, however, must be in balance.
8. Noncontrolling interest in consolidated net assets or equity at the beginning of the year ($41,250) can be obtained from the first line of the CAD schedule, or can be determined directly by multiplying the noncontrolling interest percentage times the implied value of the subsidiary at acquisition. Thus, noncontrolling interest in consolidated net assets can be computed as $206,250 × 20% at this date. To calculate the noncontrolling interest at year-end, sum the following components:

COST

Total Noncontrolling Interest	
$41,250	Noncontrolling interest at the date of acquisition, representing 20% of the implied value of the subsidiary.
6,000	A $6,000 (20% × $30,000) interest in the amount of S Company income that is included in consolidated net income. The $6,000 is considered an allocation of consolidated net income to the noncontrolling shareholders.
(2,000)	A $2,000 (20% × $10,000) decrease for dividends distributed to the noncontrolling stockholders during the year. The other $8,000 in dividends represents parent company dividend income and is, therefore, eliminated.
$45,250	Total Noncontrolling Interest

The sum of the noncontrolling interest column is transferred to the consolidated balance sheet as one amount since it reflects the noncontrolling stockholders' interest in the net assets of the consolidated group.

After Year of Acquisition-Cost Method

LO5 Workpaper eliminating entries after acquisition (cost method).

For illustrative purposes, assume continuation of the previous example with data updated to the following year. Trial balances for P Company and S Company at December 31, 2011, are given in Illustration 4-3. Because we are using the cost method, the Investment in S Company account still reflects the cost of the investment, $165,000. The beginning retained earnings balances for P and S Companies on January 1, 2011, are the same as the ending retained earnings balances on December 31, 2010 (confirmed in Illustration 4-2, first two columns). Although the trial balance is dated December 31, 2011, the retained earnings balance is dated January 1, 2011, because the income statement and Dividends Declared accounts are still open.

A workpaper for the preparation of consolidated financial statements for P and S Companies for the year ended December 31, 2011, is presented in Illustration 4-4. Note that the detail comprising cost of goods sold is provided in Illustration 4-2 (beginning inventory plus purchases minus ending inventory). In Illustration 4-4 and subsequent illustrations in this chapter, the detail will be collapsed into one item, Cost of Goods Sold. In later chapters, however, we will use the detailed accounts when the focus is more directly upon inventory and the calculation of cost of goods sold (in the presence of intercompany profit, for instance).

ILLUSTRATION 4-3
P Company and S Company Trial Balances
December 31, 2011

	P Company		S Company	
	Dr.	*Cr.*	*Dr.*	*Cr.*
Cash	$ 74,000		$ 41,000	
Accounts Receivable (net)	71,000		33,000	
Inventory, 1/1	67,000		43,000	
Investment in S Company	165,000			
Property and Equipment (net)	245,000		185,000	
Goodwill	35,000		17,000	
Accounts Payable		$ 61,000		$ 30,000
Other Liabilities		70,000		45,000
Common Stock, $10 par value		200,000		100,000
Other Contributed Capital		40,000		50,000
Retained Earnings, 1/1		253,000		60,000
Dividends Declared	30,000		10,000	
Sales		350,000		190,000
Dividend Income		8,000		
Purchases	215,000		90,000	
Expenses	80,000		56,000	
	$982,000	$982,000	$475,000	$475,000
Inventory, 12/31	$ 82,000		$ 39,000	

The workpaper entries in years after the year of acquisition are essentially the same as those made for the year of acquisition (Illustration 4-2) with one major exception. Before the elimination of the investment account, a workpaper entry, (1) in Illustration 4-4, is made to the investment account and P Company's beginning retained earnings to recognize P Company's share of the cumulative undistributed income or loss of S Company from the ***date of acquisition to the beginning of the current year*** as follows:

(1)	Investment in S Company	16,000	
	1/1 Retained Earnings—P Company (Consolidated Retained Earnings) [80% × ($60,000 − $40,000)]		16,000

This entry may be viewed as either ***the entry to convert from the cost method to the equity method or the entry to establish reciprocity***. The following two points explain these essentially complementary views of the entry.

1. The reciprocity entry adjusts P Company's beginning retained earnings balance on the workpaper to the appropriate beginning consolidated retained earnings amount. As indicated earlier, consolidated retained earnings on January 1, 2011, consists of P Company's reported retained earnings plus P Company's share of the undistributed earnings (income less dividends) of S Company from the date of stock acquisition to the beginning of 2011. Note that, after the reciprocity entry is made, the beginning (1/1/11) consolidated retained earnings of $269,000 (Illustration 4-4) equals the ending (12/31/10) consolidated retained earnings amount (Illustration 4-2).
2. If this entry is viewed as a conversion to the equity method, the following question might well arise: Why should we convert to the equity method if all methods

Cost Method
80% Owned
Subsequent to Year of Acquisition

ILLUSTRATION 4-4
Consolidated Statements Workpaper
P Company and Subsidiary
for the Year Ended December 31, 2011

	P Company	S Company	Eliminations Dr.		Eliminations Cr.		Noncontrolling Interest	Consolidated Balances
Income Statement								
Sales	350,000	190,000						540,000
Dividend Income	8,000		(4)	8,000				
Total Revenue	358,000	190,000						540,000
Cost of Goods Sold	200,000	94,000						294,000
Expenses	80,000	56,000						136,000
Total Cost and Expense	280,000	150,000						430,000
Consolidated Net Income	78,000	40,000						110,000
Noncontrolling Interest in Income							8,000	(8,000)*
Net Income to Retained Earnings	78,000	40,000		8,000		—0—	8,000	102,000
Retained Earnings Statement								
1/1 Retained Earnings								
P Company	253,000				(1)	16,000		269,000
S Company		60,000	(2)	60,000				
Net Income from above	78,000	40,000		8,000		—0—	8,000	102,000
Dividends Declared								
P Company	(30,000)							(30,000)
S Company		(10,000)			(4)	8,000	(2,000)	
12/31 Retained Earnings to Balance Sheet	301,000	90,000		68,000		24,000	6,000	341,000
Balance Sheet								
Cash	74,000	41,000						115,000
Accounts Receivable (net)	71,000	33,000						104,000
Inventory, 12/31	82,000	39,000						121,000
Investment in S Company	165,000		(1)	16,000	(2)	181,000		
Difference between Implied and Book Value			(2)	16,250	(3)	16,250		
Property and Equipment (net)	245,000	185,000						430,000
Goodwill	35,000	17,000	(3)	16,250				68,250
Total	672,000	315,000						838,250
Accounts Payable	61,000	30,000						91,000
Other Liabilities	70,000	45,000						115,000
Common Stock								
P Company	200,000							200,000
S Company		100,000	(2)	100,000				
Other Contributed Capital								
P Company	40,000							40,000
S Company		50,000	(2)	50,000				
Retained Earnings from above	301,000	90,000		68,000		24,000	6,000	341,000
1/1 Noncontrolling Interest in Net Assets					(2)	45,250**	45,250	
12/31 Noncontrolling Interest in Net Assets							51,250	51,250
Total	672,000	315,000		266,500		266,500		838,250

* .2($40,000) = $8,000.
** $41,250 + ($60,000 − $40,000) × .2 = $45,250.
(1) To recognize P Company's share (80%) of S Company's undistributed income from date of acquisition to beginning of the current year. (Also referred to as "To establish reciprocity" or "to convert to equity method".)
(2) To eliminate the investment in S Company and create noncontrolling interest account.
(3) To allocate the difference between implied and book value to goodwill.
(4) To eliminate intercompany dividends.

are acceptable and all yield the same final results? Recall that under the equity method, the parent records its equity in the subsidiary income in its income statement and thus ultimately in its retained earnings. If we consider the two accounts in the conversion entry, it is true that the investment is going to be eliminated to zero anyway; but the retained earnings account of the parent company, which must ultimately reflect the equity in subsidiary income, will not be eliminated. Instead, it needs to be adjusted if the cost method is used.

Although it is true that the investment account must be eliminated after it is adjusted, the reciprocity (conversion) entry facilitates this elimination. The amount needed for the workpaper entry to establish reciprocity can be most accurately computed by multiplying the parent company's percentage of ownership times the increase or decrease in the subsidiary's retained earnings from the date of stock acquisition to the beginning of the current year. This approach adjusts for complications that might arise where the subsidiary may have made direct entries to its retained earnings for prior period adjustments.

This approach is also the most efficient because it provides a shortcut in lieu of making separate entries for each year's income and each year's dividend declarations. Recall that the workpaper entries are just that, workpaper only, and as such they do not get posted to the accounts of either the parent or subsidiary company. Hence entries that were made on a previous year's workpaper must be "caught up" in subsequent periods. If income and dividend entries were made separately for each year, imagine the number of entries in year 9 or year 20!

After the investment account is adjusted by workpaper entry (1), P Company's share of S Company's equity is eliminated against the **adjusted investment account** in entry (2) below:

COST

(2)	Common Stock—S Company	100,000	
	Other Contributed Capital—S Company	50,000	
	1/1 Retained Earnings—S Company	60,000	
	Difference between Implied and Book Value	16,250	
	Investment in S Company [$165,000 + .8(60,000 − 40,000)]		181,000
	Noncontrolling Interest in Equity [$41,250 + .2(60,000 − 40,000)]		45,250

Entry (3) distributes the difference between implied and book values, as follows:

(3)	Goodwill	16,250	
	Difference between Implied and Book Values		16,250

Next, intercompany dividend income is eliminated as follows:

(4)	Dividend Income	8,000	
	Dividends Declared—S Company		8,000

Consolidated balances are then determined in the same manner as in previous illustrations. Remember that the entry to establish reciprocity (convert to equity) is a cumulative one that recognizes the parent's share of the change in the subsidiary's retained earnings from the date of acquisition to the beginning of the current year. Thus, for example, the reciprocity entry for the ***third year*** in the December 31, 2012, workpaper is as follows:

ILLUSTRATION 4-5

P Company and Subsidiary
Consolidated Statement of Income and Retained Earnings
for the Year Ended December 31, 2011

Sales	$540,000
Cost of goods sold	294,000
Gross margin	246,000
Expenses	136,000
Consolidated net income	110,000
Noncontrolling interest in income	8,000
Controlling interest in income	102,000
Retained earnings, 1/1/2011	269,000
Total	371,000
Dividends declared	30,000
Retained earnings, 12/31/2011	$341,000

P Company and Subsidiary
Consolidated Balance Sheet
December 31, 2011

Assets		
Current Assets:		
Cash		$115,000
Accounts Receivable (net)		104,000
Inventories		121,000
Total current assets		340,000
Property and Equipment (net)		430,000
Goodwill		68,250
Total assets		$838,250
Liabilities and Stockholders' Equity		
Accounts payable		$ 91,000
Other liabilities		115,000
Total liabilities		206,000
Stockholders' equity:		
Noncontrolling interest in net assets	51,250	
Common Stock, $10 par value	200,000	
Other contributed capital	40,000	
Retained earnings	341,000	632,250
Total liabilities and stockholders' equity		$838,250

Investment in S Company	40,000	
1/1 Retained Earnings—P Company .8($90,000 − $40,000)		40,000
"The reciprocity/conversion entry for year three"		

An example of a consolidated statement of income and retained earnings and a consolidated balance sheet (based on Illustration 4-4) is presented in Illustration 4-5. Notice that ***all (100%) of S Company's revenues and expenses*** are included in the consolidated income statement. The noncontrolling interest's share of the subsidiary's income is shown as a separate component of consolidated net income and is deducted from consolidated net income (NI) to arrive at the controlling interest. Likewise, ***all of S Company's assets and liabilities*** are included with those of P Company in the consolidated balance sheet. The noncontrolling interest's share of the net assets is then included as a separate item within the stockholders' equity section of the consolidated balance sheet.

TEST YOUR KNOWLEDGE

NOTE: Solutions to ***Test Your Knowledge*** questions are found at the end of each chapter before the end-of-chapter questions.

Multiple Choice

1. The entry to establish reciprocity or convert from the cost to the equity method usually involves a debit to Investment in Subsidiary and a credit to what account?
   (A) Subsidiary's end-of-the-year Retained Earnings
   (B) Parent's end-of-the-year Retained Earnings
   (C) Parent's beginning-of-the-year Retained Earnings
   (D) Subsidiary's beginning-of-the-year Retained Earnings

RECORDING INVESTMENTS IN SUBSIDIARIES—EQUITY METHOD (PARTIAL OR COMPLETE)

Companies may elect to use the equity method to record their investments in subsidiaries to estimate the operating effects of their investments for internal decision-making purposes. As with the cost method, the investment is recorded initially at its cost under the equity method. Subsequent to acquisition, the major differences between the cost and equity methods pertain to the period in which subsidiary income is formally recorded on the books of the parent company and the amount of income recognized. Under the assumptions of this chapter, partial and complete equity methods are indistinguishable. Thus, the differences between the two do not become important until Chapter 5. In Chapter 5, we will explore alternative assumptions regarding the disposition of the difference between implied value and book value, which will necessitate amortization, depreciation, or impairment adjustments. In subsequent chapters, we will explore other complications that may arise under the complete equity method. **To facilitate an understanding of the differences among the methods, the sections of text that differ depending on the method choice are presented in blue for the equity method.**

One frequent complication occurs when the parent and subsidiary have different year-ends. The SEC allows the parent to use a different year-end for its subsidiary provided the subsidiary data are not more than 93 days old. The parent simply combines the data for the subsidiary's 12 months with its own, just as though the year-ends were the same. The SEC requirement has become broadly accepted in practice. In some cases, firms find it desirable for the subsidiary's year to end earlier to facilitate the adjusting, closing, and consolidating procedures in a timely fashion. However, the preference is to use the "best available data," weighing the tradeoffs between reliability and timeliness. Thus, in some cases, the best alternative may be to combine the subsidiary's interim data with the parent's year-end data.

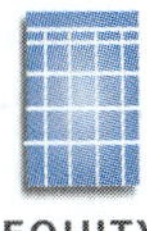

EQUITY

As illustrated in previous sections of this chapter, no income from the subsidiary is recorded by the parent company under the cost method until it is distributed as dividends. When distributed, the parent records its share of the dividends as dividend income. Under the equity method, income is recorded in the books of the parent company in the same accounting period that it is reported by the subsidiary company, whether or not such income is distributed to the parent company.

Assume that P Company purchased 80% of the outstanding shares of S Company common stock on January 1, 2010, for $165,000. The underlying book value of S Company's net assets (100%) on that date was $190,000. P Company made the following entry:

P's Books		
Investment in S Company	165,000	
Cash		165,000

EQUITY

P Company would record income in the first year based not on dividends received, but on its share of the subsidiary's income. Under the partial equity method, this amount will be based on income ***reported*** by the subsidiary. Under the complete equity method, the subsidiary's reported income will be adjusted under certain circumstances, as illustrated at the beginning of this chapter. Throughout the remainder of this chapter, however, we assume that those adjustments will not be needed. Hence adjusted income will equal reported income. The "adjustments" concept will be introduced very briefly in this chapter and developed in later chapters.

Assuming a current period income of $30,000 reported by S Company, P Company would make the following entry on its books:

P's Books		
Investment in S Company	24,000	
Equity in subsidiary income .8($30,000)		24,000

Dividends received from the subsidiary (parent's share assumed to be $8,000) are then ***credited*** to the Investment account, as follows:

P's Books		
Cash (or Dividends Receivable)	8,000	
Investment in S Company		8,000

Consequently, the parent company's share of the ***cumulative undistributed income (income less dividends)*** of the subsidiary is accumulated over time as an addition to the investment account. In this example, the parent's share of undistributed income for the year was $16,000 (i.e., the same amount as the reciprocity entry for firms using the cost method!).

Investment Carried at Equity—Year of Acquisition

LO5 Workpaper eliminating entries (equity method).

In this section we illustrate the consolidated workpaper used to prepare consolidated financial statements under the equity method. Keep in mind that workpapers are just that, a means to an end, with the real goal being the preparation of correct financial statements. Regardless of whether the parent's books are kept using the cost method or one of the equity methods, the consolidated financial statements should be identical. The eliminating entries needed to achieve the correct balances, however, are not identical.

Assume that at the end of the first year, the trial balances of P Company and S Company appear as shown in Illustration 4-6. Begin the consolidating process, as always, by preparing a Computation and Allocation (CAD) Schedule, as follows:

EQUITY

Computation and Allocation of Difference Schedule

	Parent Share	*Noncontrolling Share*	*Total Value*
Purchase price and implied value	**$165,000**	**41,250**	206,250
Less: Book value of equity acquired:			
Common stock	80,000	20,000	**100,000**
Other contributed capital	40,000	10,000	**50,000**
Retained earnings	32,000	8,000	**40,000**
Total book value	152,000	38,000	190,000
Difference between implied and book value	13,000	3,250	**16,250**
Record new goodwill	(13,000)	(3,250)	**(16,250)**
Balance	—0—	—0—	—0—

Because the difference between implied and book values is established only at the date of acquisition, this schedule will not change in future periods.

Note that the trial balance data in Illustration 4-6 reflect the effects of the investment, equity in subsidiary income, and dividend transactions presented above. These balances are next arranged into ***income statement, retained earnings statement***, and ***balance sheet statement*** sections as they are entered into the first two columns of the consolidated workpaper presented in Illustration 4-7.

When the investment account is carried on the Equity basis, it is necessary first to make a workpaper entry reversing the effects of the parent company's entries to the Investment account for subsidiary income and dividends during the current year. Here the entry differs from that under the Cost Method.

To eliminate the account "equity in subsidiary income" from the consolidated income statement, the following workpaper entry, presented in general journal form, is made:

ILLUSTRATION 4-6

P Company and S Company Trial Balances
December 31, 2010

	P Company		*S Company*	
	Dr.	*Cr.*	*Dr.*	*Cr.*
Cash	$ 79,000		$ 18,000	
Accounts Receivable (net)	64,000		28,000	
Inventory, 1/1	56,000		32,000	
Investment in S Company	181,000			
Property and Equipment (net)	180,000		165,000	
Goodwill	35,000		17,000	
Accounts Payable		$ 35,000		$ 24,000
Other Liabilities		62,000		37,000
Common Stock, $10 par value		200,000		100,000
Other Contributed Capital		40,000		50,000
Retained Earnings, 1/1		210,000		40,000
Dividends Declared	20,000		10,000	
Sales		300,000		160,000
Equity in Subsidiary Income		24,000		
Purchases	186,000		95,000	
Expenses	70,000		46,000	
	$871,000	$871,000	$411,000	$411,000
Inventory, 12/31	$ 67,000		$ 43,000	

Equity Method
80% Owned Subsidiary
Year of Acquisition

ILLUSTRATION 4-7
Consolidated Statements Workpaper
P Company and Subsidiary for the Year Ended December 31, 2010

Income Statement	*P Company*	*S Company*	*Eliminations Dr.*	*Eliminations Cr.*	*Noncontrolling Interest*	*Consolidated Balances*
Sales	300,000	160,000				460,000
Equity in Subsidiary Income	24,000		(1) 24,000			
Total Revenue	324,000	160,000				460,000
Cost of Goods Sold	175,000	84,000				259,000
Expenses	70,000	46,000				116,000
Total Cost and Expense	245,000	130,000				375,000
Consolidated Net Income	79,000	30,000				85,000
Noncontrolling Interest in NI					6,000*	(6,000)
Net Income to Retained Earnings	79,000	30,000	24,000	—0—	6,000	79,000
Retained Earnings Statement						
1/1 Retained Earnings						
P Company	210,000					210,000
S Company		40,000	(3) 40,000			
Net Income from above	79,000	30,000	24,000	—0—	6,000	79,000
Dividends Declared						
P Company	(20,000)					(20,000)
S Company		(10,000)		(2) 8,000	(2,000)	
12/31 Retained Earnings to Balance Sheet	269,000	60,000	64,000	8,000	4,000	269,000
Balance Sheet						
Cash	79,000	18,000				97,000
Accounts Receivable (net)	64,000	28,000				92,000
Inventory, 12/31	67,000	43,000				110,000
Investment in S Company	181,000		(2) 8,000	(1) 24,000 (3) 165,000		
Difference between Implied and Book Value			(3) 16,250	(4) 16,250		
Property and Equipment (net)	180,000	165,000				345,000
Goodwill	35,000	17,000	(4) 16,250			68,250
Total	606,000	271,000				712,250
Accounts Payable	35,000	24,000				59,000
Other Liabilities	62,000	37,000				99,000
Common Stock						
P Company	200,000					200,000
S Company		100,000	(3) 100,000			
Other Contributed Capital						
P Company	40,000					40,000
S Company		50,000	(3) 50,000			
Retained Earnings from above	269,000	60,000	64,000	8,000	4,000	269,000
1/1 Noncontrolling Interest in Net Assets				(3) 41,250	41,250	
12/31 Noncontrolling Interest in Net Assets					45,250	45,250
Total	606,000	271,000	254,500	254,500		712,250

* 20% × $30,000 = $6,000.
(1) To reverse the effect of parent company entry during the year for subsidiary income.
(2) To reverse the effect of parent company entry during the year for subsidiary dividends.
(3) To eliminate the investment in S Company and create noncontrolling interest.
(4) To allocate the excess of implied over book value to goodwill.

		Debit	Credit
(1)	Equity in Subsidiary Income	24,000	
	Investment in S Company		24,000

Next, to eliminate intercompany dividends under the equity method, this workpaper entry is made:

		Debit	Credit
(2)	Investment in S Company	8,000	
	Dividends Declared		8,000

Alternatively, these two entries may be collapsed into one entry, as follows:

		Debit	Credit
(1)–(2)	Equity in Subsidiary Income	24,000	
	Investment in S Company		16,000
	Dividends Declared		8,000

EQUITY

This reversal has two effects. First, it eliminates the equity in subsidiary income and dividends recorded by P Company. Second, it returns the investment account to its balance as of the beginning of the year. This is necessary because it is the parent company's share of the subsidiary's retained earnings at the ***beginning of the year*** that is eliminated in the investment elimination entry.

A third eliminating entry must then be made to eliminate the Investment account against subsidiary equity, and the fourth entry distributes the difference between implied and book values of equity, as follows:

		Debit	Credit
(3)	Common Stock—S Company	100,000	
	Other Contributed Capital—S Company	50,000	
	1/1 Retained Earnings—S Company	40,000	
	Difference between Implied and Book Values	16,250	
	Investment in S Company		165,000
	Noncontrolling Interest in Equity		41,250
	"*The investment entry*"		

		Debit	Credit
(4)	Goodwill	16,250	
	Difference between Implied and Book Value		16,250
	"*The differential entry*"		

The next few paragraphs relate to basic workpaper concepts that do not differ between the cost and equity methods. Thus, for those who have already read the section of the chapter on the cost method, this will serve as a review.

To complete the worksheet, the account balances are extended from left to right. Two lines merit attention. First, the ***entire bottom line*** of the income statement, which represents net income, is transferred to the Net Income line on the retained earnings statement. Similarly, the ***entire bottom line*** of the retained earnings statement, which represents ending retained earnings, is transferred to the retained earnings line on the balance sheet. Throughout this and future chapters on consolidation, we will see that *any eliminating entries to the account Retained Earnings will be entered in the Beginning Balance on the retained earnings statements (not on the balance sheet, ending balance).* Because the Current Year Income and Dividends Declared accounts are still open, current year changes in Retained Earnings will be adjusted through those accounts (or in the retained earnings section of the workpaper).

There is one number on the workpaper that is calculated and then inserted directly into the income statement, and does not flow from the trial balance columns. That number is the ***noncontrolling interest in consolidated net income.*** To facilitate the calculation of the noncontrolling and controlling interests in consolidated net income, a t-account approach is helpful. In later chapters, the presence of intercompany profits and other complications will make the calculation more complex than it is at this point. It is, nonetheless, useful to form the habit of using the t-accounts now.

The first t-account (below) calculates the distribution of consolidated net income to the noncontrolling interest. This number can be inserted directly into the next-to-bottom line of the Income Statement section. When this amount is subtracted from the consolidated income of $85,000, the resulting amount of $79,000 represents the ***controlling interest in consolidated net income.*** It is interesting to note that this is the very same amount that the parent reported in its trial balance originally. In future chapters, we will see that this is the case only if the parent uses the complete equity method. For example, if profit or loss on intercompany sales between parent and subsidiary must be eliminated at the balance sheet date, an adjustment will be required to reconcile the two numbers under the partial equity method. Similarly, if any difference between implied and book values is attributed to depreciable assets, an adjustment will also be needed under the partial equity method. Hence it is useful to check the calculation of the controlling interest in consolidated net income.

EQUITY

Noncontrolling Interest in Consolidated Net Income

	Internally generated income of S Company	$30,000
	Any needed adjustments (see Chapter 5)	0
	Adjusted income of subsidiary	30,000
	Noncontrolling percentage owned	20%
	Noncontrolling interest in income	6,000

The next t-account serves as a check of the controlling interest in consolidated income. The 80% controlling percentage in the adjusted income of subsidiary ($30,000 from t-account above) will appear in P Company's t-account as part of the controlling interest. For the parent company, the internally generated income represents the amount from the first column of the trial balance ($79,000) minus any income which came from the subsidiary (equity in subsidiary income, in this case, of $24,000), or $55,000 income from P Company's independent operations.

($30,000).8

Controlling Interest in Consolidated Net Income

	Internally generated income ($79,000 income minus $24,000 equity in subsidiary income)	$55,000
	Any needed adjustments (see Chapter 5)	0
	Percentage of subsidiary adjusted income (80%)($30,000)	24,000
	Controlling interest in income	$79,000

EQUITY

Consolidated retained earnings on December 31, 2010, of $269,000 can be determined as follows:

P Company's reported retained earnings, 1/1	$210,000
Plus controlling interest in consolidated net income for 2010	79,000
Less P Company's dividends declared during 2010	(20,000)
Consolidated Retained Earnings, 12/31	$269,000

The calculation above appears in the final column of the workpaper in the Retained Earnings Statement section.

Under the complete equity method (or the partial equity method if there are no complicating adjustments, as here), the ending Consolidated Retained Earnings equals Retained Earnings—P at the end of the year as shown in the first column of the workpaper.

Note that the eliminations columns in each section do not balance, since individual eliminations often involve more than one section. The total eliminations for all three sections, however, must be in balance.

Noncontrolling interest in consolidated net assets or equity at the beginning of the year ($41,250) can be obtained from the first line of the CAD schedule, or can be determined directly by multiplying the noncontrolling interest percentage times the implied value of the subsidiary at acquisition. Thus, noncontrolling interest in consolidated net assets can be computed as $206,250 × 20% at this date. To calculate the noncontrolling interest at year-end, sum the following components:

Total Noncontrolling Interest

$41,250	Noncontrolling interest at the date of acquisition, representing 20% of the implied value of the subsidiary.
6,000	A $6,000 (20% × $30,000) interest in the amount of S Company income that is included in consolidated net income. The $6,000 is considered an allocation of consolidated net income to the noncontrolling shareholders.
(2,000)	A $2,000 (20% × $10,000) decrease for dividends distributed to the noncontrolling stockholders during the year. The other $8,000 in dividends represents parent company dividend income and is, therefore, eliminated.
$45,250	Total Noncontrolling Interest

Comparison of Illustration 4-2 and Illustration 4-7 brings out an important observation. ***The consolidated column of the workpaper is the same under the cost and equity methods. Thus, the decision to use the cost or equity method to record investments in subsidiaries that will be consolidated has no impact on the consolidated financial statements. Only the elimination process is affected.***

Note once more that P Company's reported net income of $79,000 (Illustration 4-7) and consolidated net income are identical. Likewise, P Company's December 31, 2010, retained earnings equal consolidated retained earnings at that date. In later chapters we will see that this will always be true under the complete equity method, but not under the partial equity method. We obtain this result here because P Company has recorded its share of S Company's earnings, and because of the absence of complicating assumptions.

Investment Carried at Equity—After Year of Acquisition

To illustrate the preparation of a consolidated workpaper for years after the year of acquisition under the equity method, assume the data given in Illustration 4-8, and the use of the equity method rather than the cost method. After P Company has recorded its share of S Company's income ($32,000) and dividends declared ($8,000), the Investment in S Company account appears as follows:

EQUITY

ILLUSTRATION 4-8

P Company and S Company Trial Balances
(Year after Acquisition)
December 31, 2011

	P Company		*S Company*	
	Dr.	*Cr.*	*Dr.*	*Cr.*
Cash	$ 74,000		$ 41,000	
Accounts Receivable (net)	71,000		33,000	
Inventory, 1/1	67,000		43,000	
Investment in S Company	205,000			
Property and Equipment (net)	245,000		185,000	
Goodwill	35,000		17,000	
Accounts Payable		$ 61,000		$ 30,000
Other Liabilities		70,000		45,000
Common Stock		200,000		100,000
Other Contributed Capital		40,000		50,000
Retained Earnings, 1/1		269,000		60,000
Dividends Declared	30,000		10,000	
Sales		350,000		190,000
Equity in Subsidiary Income		32,000		
Purchases	215,000		90,000	
Expenses	80,000		56,000	
	$1,022,000	$1,022,000	$475,000	$475,000
Inventory, 12/31	$ 82,000		$ 39,000	

Investment in S Company

12/31/10	Balance	181,000	Dividends	8,000
	Subsidiary income	32,000		
12/31/11	Balance	205,000		

The preparation of the Computation and Allocation (CAD) Schedule is the same as it was in the year of acquisition; that is, it does not need to be prepared again. The elimination process also follows the same procedures as in the year of acquisition (with current year amounts). A consolidated statements workpaper in this case is presented in Illustration 4-9. We next review the workpaper entries in general journal entry form. Note that although the CAD Schedule does not change, the third eliminating entry (to eliminate the Investment account against the equity accounts of the subsidiary) will change to reflect the Retained Earnings balance of the subsidiary at the ***beginning of the current year*** and the corresponding change in the Investment account ($60,000 − $40,000) × 80% and in the noncontrolling interest ($60,000 − $40,000) × 20%.

LO5 Workpaper eliminating entries after acquisition (equity method).

As in the year of acquisition, the Equity in Subsidiary account must be eliminated against the Investment in Subsidiary account. The amount of this entry is obtained from the trial balance column for P Company, and it equals the parent's percentage (80%) of S Company's reported net income ($40,000):

(1) Equity in Subsidiary Income	32,000	
Investment in S Company		32,000

Next, to eliminate intercompany dividends under the equity method, this workpaper entry is made:

(2)	Investment in S Company	8,000	
	Dividends Declared		8,000

Alternatively, these two entries may be collapsed into one entry, as follows:

(1)–(2)	Equity in Subsidiary Income	32,000	
	Investment in S Company		24,000
	Dividends Declared		8,000

As in the year of acquisition, these entries eliminate the equity in subsidiary income and dividends recorded by P Company, and return the investment account to its balance as of the beginning of the year. This is necessary because it is the subsidiary's retained earnings at the ***beginning of the year*** that is eliminated in the third or investment elimination entry.

The third eliminating entry eliminates the Investment account against subsidiary equity and recognizes the noncontrolling interest as of the beginning of the current year. The fourth entry distributes the difference between implied and book values of equity, as follows:

(3)	Common Stock—S Company	100,000	
	Other Contributed Capital—S Company	50,000	
	1/1 Retained Earnings—S Company	60,000	
	Difference between Implied and Book Value	16,250	
	Investment in S Company \$165,000 + .8(60,000 − 40,000) or (\$205,000 − \$24,000, from entries (1) and (2))		181,000
	Noncontrolling Interest in Equity \$41,250 + .2(60,000 − 40,000)		45,250

(4)	Goodwill	16,250	
	Difference between Implied and Book Values		16,250

The only differences in the affiliates' account data as compared to the cost method workpaper appear in P Company's statements. The Investment account in P Company's balance sheet shows a balance of \$205,000 rather than \$165,000; and equity in subsidiary income of \$32,000, rather than dividend income of \$8,000, is listed in P Company's income statement. In addition, P Company's beginning and ending retained earnings are \$16,000 and \$40,000 larger, respectively, which reflects the effect of recording its share (80%) of S Company's income in 2010 and 2011 rather than recording only its share of dividends distributed by S Company.

EQUITY

Also, observe that the consolidated columns in Illustration 4-4 and Illustration 4-9 are the same; regardless of the method used (cost or equity), the consolidated results are unaffected.

Investment Carried at Complete Equity

LO5 Workpaper eliminating entries (complete equity method).

Under the assumptions of the preceding illustration, the complete equity method and the partial equity method are identical, not only in the end result but also in the steps to consolidate. Under other assumptions, however, the two may differ in the steps (though not in the end result).

Equity Method
80% Owned Subsidiary
Subsequent to Year of Acquisition

ILLUSTRATION 4-9
Consolidated Statements Workpaper
P Company and Subsidiary for the Year Ended December 31, 2011

	P Company	S Company	Eliminations Dr.	Eliminations Cr.	Noncontrolling Interest	Consolidated Balances
Income Statement						
Sales	350,000	190,000				540,000
Equity in Subsidiary Income	32,000		(1) 32,000			
Total Revenue	382,000	190,000				540,000
Cost of Goods Sold	200,000	94,000				294,000
Expenses	80,000	56,000				136,000
Total Cost and Expense	280,000	150,000				430,000
Net/Consolidated Income	102,000	40,000				110,000
Noncontrolling Interest in Income					8,000	(8,000)*
Net Income to Retained Earnings	102,000	40,000	32,000	—0—	8,000	102,000
Retained Earnings Statement						
1/1 Retained Earnings						
P Company	269,000					269,000
S Company		60,000	(3) 60,000			
Controlling Interest in Net Income from above	102,000	40,000	32,000	—0—	8,000	102,000
Dividends Declared						
P Company	(30,000)					(30,000)
S Company		(10,000)		(2) 8,000	(2,000)	
12/31 Retained Earnings to Balance Sheet	341,000	90,000	92,000	8,000	6,000	341,000
Balance Sheet						
Cash	74,000	41,000				115,000
Accounts Receivable (net)	71,000	33,000				104,000
Inventory, 12/31	82,000	39,000				121,000
Investment in S Company	205,000		(2) 8,000	(1) 32,000 (3) 181,000		
Difference between Implied and Book Value			(3) 16,250	(4) 16,250		
Property and Equipment (net)	245,000	185,000				430,000
Goodwill	35,000	17,000	(4) 16,250			68,250
Total	712,000	315,000				838,250
Accounts Payable	61,000	30,000				91,000
Other Liabilities	70,000	45,000				115,000
Common Stock						
P Company	200,000					200,000
S Company		100,000	(3) 100,000			
Other Contributed Capital						
P Company	40,000					40,000
S Company		50,000	(3) 50,000			
Retained Earnings from above	341,000	90,000	92,000	8,000	6,000	341,000
1/1 Noncontrolling Interest in Net Assets				(3) 45,250**	45,250	
12/31 Noncontrolling Interest in Net Assets					51,250	51,250
Total	712,000	315,000	282,500	282,500		838,250

* 20% × $40,000 = $8,000.
** $41,250 + ($60,000 − $40,000) × .2 = $45,250.
(1) To reverse the effect of parent company entry during the year for subsidiary income.
(2) To reverse the effect of parent company entry during the year for subsidiary dividends.
(3) To eliminate the investment in S Company and create noncontrolling interest account.
(4) To allocate the excess of implied over book value to goodwill.

Recall that the complete equity method is quite similar to the partial equity method, but involves additional entries to the investment account on the books of the parent. These additional adjustments are made to the investment account for the amortization, depreciation, or impairment of differences between market and book values, for the effects of unrealized intercompany profits, and for stockholders' equity transactions undertaken by the subsidiary.

In the absence of these types of transactions, the complete equity method is identical to the partial equity method, both on the books of the parent and in the workpaper eliminating entries, as in the preceding illustration.

Let us assume that no unrealized intercompany profits are involved (neither the parent nor the subsidiary made sales to the other party), and the subsidiary did not participate in any stockholders' equity transactions. In this situation we need only consider the possible amortization, depreciation, or impairment of differences between market and book values, in addition to the concepts presented in the preceding illustration. In that illustration, we assumed that any difference between purchase price and the book value of equity acquired related to goodwill. Under generally accepted accounting principles, we do not amortize, depreciate, or appreciate goodwill over time. Instead it is reviewed for impairment. In Chapter 5, we will explore alternative assumptions regarding the disposition of the difference between implied value and book value, which will necessitate amortization or depreciation adjustments. In subsequent chapters, we will explore other complications that may result in differences between the partial and complete equity methods.

Summary of Workpaper Eliminating Entries

Basic workpaper consolidating (eliminating/adjusting) entries depend on whether (1) the cost method or equity method is used to record the investment on the books of the parent company, and (2) the workpaper is being prepared at the end of the year of acquisition or at the end of periods after the year of acquisition. Workpaper eliminating entries for the alternatives are summarized in Illustration 4-10.

ELIMINATION OF INTERCOMPANY REVENUE AND EXPENSE ITEMS

Discussion and illustrations to this point have emphasized the procedures used to eliminate the parent company's interest in subsidiary equity against the investment account at the end of the year of stock acquisition and for subsequent periods. Before proceeding with a discussion of some special topics relating to consolidated statements in succeeding chapters, it should be noted that several types of intercompany revenue and expense items must be eliminated in the preparation of a consolidated income statement.

Affiliates often engage in numerous sale/purchase transactions with other affiliates, such as the sale of merchandise or equipment by a subsidiary to its parent, or vice versa. Procedures used to eliminate these intercompany sales (purchases), as well as any unrealized profit remaining in inventories, are discussed and illustrated

ILLUSTRATION 4-10

Summary of Basic Workpaper Eliminating Entries

Cost Method	*Partial Equity Method*	*Complete Equity Method*
End of Year of Acquisition		
Dividend Income **Dividends Declared—S** To eliminate intercompany dividend income.	**Equity in Subsidiary Income** **Dividends Declared—S** **Investment in S Company** To eliminate equity in subsidiary *reported* income and dividends and return the investment account to its cost at date of acquisition.	**Equity in Subsidiary Income** **Dividends Declared—S** **Investment in S Company** To eliminate equity in subsidiary *adjusted* income and dividends and return the investment account to its cost at date of acquisition. (Adjustments are addressed in Chapter 5.)
Capital Stock—S **Other Contributed Capital—S** **Retained Earnings—S** **Difference Between Implied and Book Value** **Investment in S Company** **NCI**	**Same as Cost Method**	**Same as Cost Method**
To eliminate P Company's share of S Company's stockholders' equity against the investment account, and create an account for the noncontrolling interest, if any.		
End of Periods Subsequent to Year of Acquisition		
Investment in S Company **Retained Earnings—P**	**No Entry Needed**	**No Entry Needed**
To recognize P Company's share of S Company's undistributed income from the date of acquisition to beginning of the current year (reciprocity or conversion entry).		
Dividend Income **Dividends Declared—S** To eliminate intercompany dividend income.	**Equity in Subsidiary Income** **Dividends Declared—S** **Investment in S Company** To eliminate equity in subsidiary *reported* income and dividends and return the investment account to its balance as of beginning of the current year.	**Equity in Subsidiary Income** **Dividends Declared—S** **Investment in S Company** To eliminate equity in subsidiary *adjusted* income and dividends and return the investment account to its balance as of beginning of the current year. (Adjustments are addressed in Chapter 5.)
Capital Stock—S **Other Contributed Capital—S** **Retained Earnings—S** **Difference Between Implied and Book Value** **Investment in Company** **NCI**	**Same as Cost Method**	**Same as Cost Method**
To eliminate P Company's share of S Company's stockholders' equity against the investment account, and recognize NCI.		

in Chapters 6 and 7. Eliminating workpaper entries are also needed for such intercompany revenue and expense items as interest, rent, and professional services. For example, the workpaper entry to eliminate intercompany interest revenue and expense takes the following form:

Interest Revenue	8,000	
Interest Expense		8,000

TEST YOUR KNOWLEDGE

NOTE: Solutions to ***Test Your Knowledge*** questions are found at the end of each chapter before the end-of-chapter questions.

Multiple Choice

1. In periods subsequent to acquisition and in *the absence of intercompany profits or other complicating transactions,* the noncontrolling interest (as shown in the consolidated balance sheet) can be determined by summing the noncontrolling interest in equity at acquisition *and*:
   (A) The noncontrolling percentage of the book value of the subsidiary's net assets.
   (B) The noncontrolling percentage of the fair value of the subsidiary's net assets.
   (C) The noncontrolling percentage of the subsidiary's year-end retained earnings.
   (D) The noncontrolling percentage of the change in subsidiary retained earnings from acquisition to the end of the current year.

INTERIM ACQUISITIONS OF SUBSIDIARY STOCK

LO 6 Two approaches for interim acquisitions.

Discussion and illustrations to this point have been limited to situations in which the parent company acquired its interest in a subsidiary at the beginning of the subsidiary's fiscal period. That condition is unrealistic because many stock acquisitions are made during the subsidiary's fiscal period. Thus, the proper treatment in consolidated financial statements of the subsidiary's revenue and expense items for the partial period ***before*** acquisition must be considered.

For example, suppose that P Company acquires 90% of the outstanding common stock of S Company on April 1, 2010. Both companies close their books on December 31. Consider S's income statement in Illustration 4-11. In this illustration, the revenues and expenses for S Company are presented in total, and also separately for the periods before and after the acquisition. S Company earns $36,000 of income for the entire year. P Company is entitled to 90% of the income earned since April (90% of $27,000 or $24,300). As mentioned earlier, ***under acquisition***

ILLUSTRATION 4-11
S Company
Income Statement and Allocation to Various Interests
for the Year Ended December 31, 2010

Income Statement	*(1) Entire Year*	*(2) January to April*	*(3) April to December*
Sales	160,000	40,000	120,000
Dividend Income			
Total Revenue	160,000	40,000	120,000
Cost of Goods Sold	80,000	20,000	60,000
Other Expenses	44,000	11,000	33,000
Total Cost and Expense	124,000	31,000	93,000
Net Income	36,000	9,000	27,000
Noncontrolling Interest in Income (10%) after Purchase			2,700
Controlling Interest in Consolidated Net Income (after Purchase)			24,300

Note: P acquires S Company on April 1, 2010.

accounting, revenues and expenses of the acquired company are included with those of the acquiring company only from the date of acquisition forward. In essence, the amounts to be combined with the parent in the year of acquisition are shown in the third column of Illustration 4-11. However, the totals from column 1 are often shown as the starting point for two reasons: (1) the revenue and expense accounts in the books of the subsidiary are likely to reflect the entire year, and (2) users may be interested in preacquisition information.

Therefore two acceptable alternatives for presenting the subsidiary's revenue and expense items in the consolidated income statement in the year of acquisition are allowed under current generally accepted accounting principles. Although the authoritative standard[4] expresses a preference for one of the two, this preference is not a requirement; thus, we present both. Both alternatives result in the same consolidated income; the difference lies in the detail included in the statement.

One alternative, the ***full-year reporting alternative***, is to include the subsidiary's revenues and expenses in the consolidated income statement for the entire year (as though S has been acquired at the beginning of the year). These revenues and expenses are shown in the first column of Illustration 4-11. Then a deduction is needed at the bottom of the consolidated income statement for the applicable preacquisition earnings of \$9,000 (\$36,000 $\times \frac{1}{4}$) earned by S prior to April 1. This amount is subtracted from combined income to arrive at ***consolidated net income***. Then, the noncontrolling interest in income subsequent to acquisition (.10 $\times$ \$36,000 $\times \frac{3}{4}$, or \$2,700) is subtracted to arrive at the ***controlling interest in consolidated net income***. These adjustments reduce S's net income from \$36,000 to \$24,300, the amount of income earned since acquisition by the *controlling interest*. The amounts used in calculating the controlling interest are reflected in Illustration 4-11.

This alternative is particularly practical when the subsidiary does not close its books on the date of acquisition. Since closing procedures normally occur only at the end of the fiscal year, this is usually the case with an interim acquisition. Hence the revenue and expense accounts of the subsidiary are accumulated throughout the year, and their totals in the trial balance include both the partial period preceding the acquisition and the partial period following the acquisition.

The second alternative, ***the partial-year reporting alternative***, includes presentation of the subsidiary's revenue and expenses from the date of acquisition only. To accomplish this, the subsidiary closes the books on the date of acquisition (i.e., preacquisition income is closed to retained earnings). In Illustration 4-11, the third column shows the revenues and expenses to be reported under this alternative. Both alternatives are presented next.

Interim Acquisition under the Cost Method—Full-Year Reporting Alternative

Assume that P Company acquired 90% of the outstanding common stock of S Company on April 1, 2010, for a cash payment of \$290,700. The difference between implied and book value relates to the undervaluation of S Company land. Trial balances at December 31, 2010, for P and S companies are as on the next page.

[4] *Accounting Research Bulletin No. 51*, "Consolidated Financial Statements" (New York: AICPA, 1959), par. 11. [paragraph 810–10–45–4]

COST

	P Company		S Company	
	Dr.	Cr.	Dr.	Cr.
Current Assets	$ 145,300		$ 71,000	
Investment in S Company	290,700			
Plant and Equipment (net)	326,000		200,000	
Land	120,000		90,000	
Liabilities		$ 100,000		$ 65,000
Common Stock		500,000		200,000
Retained Earnings, 1/1		214,000		80,000
Dividends Declared, 11/1	50,000		20,000	
Sales		600,000		160,000
Dividend Income		18,000		
Cost of Goods Sold	380,000		80,000	
Other Expense	120,000		44,000	
	$1,432,000	$1,432,000	$505,000	$505,000

As always, the first step is to prepare a CAD Schedule. For an interim acquisition, this schedule will include one or two additional amounts in the calculation of equity acquired: one for the income purchased, and one for dividends declared (if any) by the subsidiary during the current year prior to acquisition.

Computation and Allocation of Difference Schedule

	Parent Share	*Noncontrolling Share*	*Total Value*
Purchase price and implied value	**$290,700**	**32,300**	323,000
Less: Book value of equity acquired:			
Common stock	180,000	20,000	**200,000**
Retained earnings, January 1	72,000	8,000	**80,000**
Income from 1/1–4/1	8,100	900	**9,000**
Dividends from 1/1–4/1	(—0—)	(—0—)	**(—0—)**
Total book value	260,100	28,900	289,000
Difference between implied and book value	30,600	3,400	**34,000**
Adjust land upward (mark to market)	(30,600)	(3,400)	**(34,000)**
Balance	—0—	—0—	—0—

Note that the new amount(s) included in the Computation and Allocation Schedule relate to income and dividends of the subsidiary for the period from the beginning of the current year (1/1) to the date of acquisition (4/1). In essence these are amounts that would have been included in retained earnings of the subsidiary if closing procedures (to zero out the temporary accounts) had been performed on April 1 (as in the partial-year alternative we present next). April 1, however, is not the usual date for closing entries. Note, also, that dividends declared by the subsidiary for the period from 1/1 to 4/1 are listed as zero in our example because the subsidiary's dividends were not declared until 11/1. A workpaper for the preparation of consolidated statements on December 31, 2010, is presented in Illustration 4-12.

COST

S Company's entire income statement account balances are included on the workpaper, and S Company's net income earned before acquisition is deducted as

Cost Method

Interim Purchase of Stock

90% Owned Subsidiary

Alternative One: Full-Year Reporting

ILLUSTRATION 4-12

Consolidated Statements Workpaper

P Company and Subsidiary

for the Year Ended December 31, 2010

	P	S	Eliminations		Noncontrolling	Consolidated
Income Statement	*Company*	*Company*	*Dr.*	*Cr.*	*Interest*	*Balances*
Sales	600,000	160,000				760,000
Dividend Income	18,000		(3) 18,000			
Total Revenue	618,000	160,000				760,000
Cost of Goods Sold	380,000	80,000				460,000
Other Expenses	120,000	44,000				164,000
Total Cost and Expense	500,000	124,000				624,000
Net/Combined Income	118,000	36,000				136,000
Subsidiary Income before Acquisition			(1) 9,000			(9,000)
Consolidated Net Income						127,000
Noncontrolling Interest in Net Income					2,700*	(2,700)
Net Income to Retained Earnings	118,000	36,000	27,000	—0—	2,700	124,300
Retained Earnings Statement						
1/1 Retained Earnings						
P Company	214,000					214,000
S Company		80,000	(1) 80,000			
Net Income from above	118,000	36,000	27,000	—0—	2,700	124,300
Dividends Declared						
P Company	(50,000)					(50,000)
S Company		(20,000)		(3) 18,000	(2,000)	
12/31 Retained Earnings to Balance Sheet	282,000	96,000	107,000	18,000	700	288,300
Balance Sheet						
Current Assets	145,300	71,000				216,300
Investment in S Company	290,700			(1) 290,700		
Difference between Implied and Book Value			(1) 34,000	(2) 34,000		
Property and Equipment (net)	326,000	200,000				526,000
Land	120,000	90,000	(2) 34,000			244,000
Total	882,000	361,000				986,300
Liabilities	100,000	65,000				165,000
Common Stock						
P Company	500,000					500,000
S Company		200,000	(1) 200,000			
Retained Earnings from above	282,000	96,000	107,000	18,000	700	288,300
1/1 Noncontrolling Interest in Net Assets				(1) 32,300	32,300	
12/31 Noncontrolling Interest in Net Assets					33,000	33,000
Total	882,000	361,000	375,000	375,000		986,300

* .1($36,000) × 3/4 = $2,700 noncontrolling interest in income after acquisition.
(1) To eliminate the investment in S Company and create noncontrolling interest account.
(2) To allocate the difference between implied and book value to land.
(3) To eliminate intercompany dividends.

"subsidiary income before acquisition." Thus, the workpaper eliminating entry for the investment account, in general journal form, is:

(1)	Common Stock—S Company	200,000	
	1/1 Retained Earnings—S Company	80,000	
	Subsidiary Income Before Acquisition	9,000	
	Difference between Implied and Book Values	34,000	
	Investment in S Company		290,700
	Noncontrolling Interest in Equity		32,300
	"The investment entry"		

There is no need for a reciprocity/conversion entry in Year 1 because the retained earnings account has not changed on the books of the subsidiary since acquisition. Also note that if there were any dividends declared by the subsidiary between 1/1 and 4/1, they would have appeared in entry (1) above as a credit.

In the computation of subsidiary income before acquisition, it is assumed that S Company's income of $36,000 was earned evenly throughout the year. Because one-fourth of the year had expired by April 1, the date of acquisition, net income prior to the acquisition date was $36,000 × $\frac{1}{4}$ or $9,000, as reflected in the CAD Schedule. The noncontrolling interest for the entire year amounts to $36,000 × 10% or $3,600. Of the $3,600, $900 was already included in the implied value of the subsidiary equity of the noncontrolling interest at April 1 (10% × $323,000, or $32,300). Thus, the increase in the noncontrolling interest in equity after acquisition is only $2,700, which is reflected as the noncontrolling interest in consolidated net income for the year of acquisition.

If S Company earns its income unevenly throughout the year, because of the seasonal nature of its business, for example, this should be taken into consideration in estimating the amount of net income earned before April 1. In the event the subsidiary incurs a net loss for the year, a "subsidiary loss prior to acquisition" is credited in the elimination entry and added to combined income in determining consolidated net income. Similarly, the noncontrolling interest in a net loss of a subsidiary is shown as a deduction in the noncontrolling interest *column* and an addition in computing the ***controlling interest*** in consolidated net income.

In subsequent years, the establishment of reciprocity is based on the parent company's share of the change in subsidiary retained earnings from the date of acquisition, April 1, 2010, to the beginning of the appropriate year. S Company's retained earnings on the acquisition date, April 1, 2010, were $89,000, consisting of the 1/1/10 balance of $80,000 plus the $9,000 income earned from January 1 to April 1, 2010. If retained earnings on December 31, 2011, are $96,000, the December 31, 2011, workpaper entry to establish reciprocity, for example, is:

Investment in S Company	6,300	
1/1 Retained Earnings—P Company .9($96,000 − $89,000)		6,300

Consolidated net income and consolidated retained earnings can be verified as follows:

Consolidated Net Income

P Company income from its independent operations ($118,000 − $18,000 dividend income from S Company)	$100,000
P Company's share of S Company's income since acquisition (.9 × $27,000)	24,300
Controlling Interest in Consolidated Net Income	$124,300
Noncontrolling Interest in Consolidated Net Income (.1 × $27,000)	2,700
Consolidated Net Income (Total)	$127,000

Consolidated Retained Earnings

P Company's reported retained earnings	$282,000
P Company's share of the *undistributed* income of S Company since date of acquisition [($27,000 − $20,000) × .9]	6,300
Consolidated Retained Earnings	$288,300

Interim Acquisition under the Cost Method—Partial-Year Reporting Alternative

Another method of prorating income is to include in the consolidated income statement only the subsidiary's revenue and expenses after the date of acquisition. Thus, assuming the interim purchase situation discussed earlier, in which the purchase of stock took place on April 1, only three-fourths of S Company's sales, cost of goods sold, and other expense are included in the consolidated income statement as if S Company's books had been closed on April 1, 2010. These are the amounts shown in column 3 of Illustration 4-11.

If the books are actually closed on April 1, 2010, this alternative is facilitated. The following entry should be made on S's books:

S's Books		
Income Summary	9,000	
Retained Earnings		9,000

If this occurs, the balance in the retained earnings account on the books of the subsidiary (after closing entries on 4/1) is: $80,000 (balance at 1/1) + $9,000 (income for first three months of the year, column 2 of Illustration 4-11), or $89,000.

Computation and Allocation of Difference Schedule

	Parent Share	*Noncontrolling Share*	*Total Value*
Purchase price and implied value	**$290,700**	**32,300**	323,000
Less: Book value of equity:			
Common stock	180,000	20,000	**200,000**
Retained earnings, 4/1	80,100	8,900	**89,000**
Total book value	260,100	28,900	289,000
Difference between implied and book value	30,600	3,400	**34,000**
Adjust land upward (mark to market)	(30,600)	(3,400)	**(34,000)**
Balance	—0—	—0—	—0—

COST

A workpaper for the preparation of consolidated financial statements on December 31, 2010, is presented in Illustration 4-13.

Cost Method
Interim Purchase of Stock
90% Owned Subsidiary
Alternative Two—Partial-Year Reporting

ILLUSTRATION 4-13
Consolidated Statements Workpaper
P Company and Subsidiary
for the Year Ended December 31, 2010

Income Statement	P Company	S Company	Eliminations Dr.	Eliminations Cr.	Noncontrolling Interest	Consolidated Balances
Sales	600,000	120,000				720,000
Dividend Income	18,000		(3) 18,000			
Total Revenue	618,000	120,000				720,000
Cost of Goods Sold	380,000	60,000				440,000
Other Expenses	120,000	33,000				153,000
Total Cost and Expense	500,000	93,000				593,000
Net/Consolidated Income	118,000	27,000				127,000
Noncontrolling Interest in Income					2,700*	(2,700)
Net Income to Retained Earnings	118,000	27,000	18,000	—0—	2,700	124,300
Retained Earnings Statement						
Retained Earnings						
P Company	214,000					214,000
S Company		89,000	(1) 89,000			
Net Income from above	118,000	27,000	18,000	—0—	2,700	124,300
Dividends Declared						
P Company	(50,000)					(50,000)
S Company		(20,000)		(3) 18,000	(2,000)	
2/31 Retained Earnings to Balance Sheet	282,000	96,000	107,000	18,000	700	288,300
Balance Sheet						
Current Assets	145,300	71,000				216,300
Investment in S Company	290,700			(1) 290,700		
Difference between Implied and Book Value			(1) 34,000	(2) 34,000		
Property and Equipment (net)	326,000	200,000				526,000
Land	120,000	90,000	(2) 34,000			244,000
Total	882,000	361,000				986,300
Liabilities	100,000	65,000				165,000
Common Stock						
P Company	500,000					500,000
S Company		200,000	(1) 200,000			
Retained Earnings from above	282,000	96,000	107,000	18,000	700	288,300
4/1 Noncontrolling Interest in Net Assets				(1) 32,300	32,300	
12/31 Noncontrolling Interest in Net Assets					33,000	33,000
Total	882,000	361,000	375,000	375,000		986,300

*.1 ($27,000) = $2,700.
(1) To eliminate the investment in S Company and create noncontrolling interest account.
(2) To allocate the difference between implied and book value to land.
(3) To eliminate intercompany dividends.

The workpaper entry to eliminate the investment account is:

		Dr.	Cr.
(1)	Common Stock—S Company	200,000	
	4/1 Retained Earnings—S Company	89,000	
	Difference between Implied and Book Values	34,000	
	Investment in S Company		290,700
	Noncontrolling Interest in Equity		32,300

Note that S Company's beginning retained earnings is $9,000 greater than it is in Illustration 4-12, reflecting the effect of the closing to retained earnings of income earned during the first three months. Noncontrolling interest in net income included in consolidated net income is 10% of $27,000, or $2,700 earned subsequent to acquisition. Note that consolidated net income, consolidated retained earnings, and the consolidated balance sheet are identical to those in Illustration 4-12. Only the detail included in the consolidated income statement is different.

Interim Acquisition: The Equity Method—Full-Year Reporting Alternative

The preceding discussion assumed that the parent company recorded its investment using the cost method. If the equity method had been used, P Company would have recognized (in actual entries posted to the general ledger) its share of subsidiary income earned ***after*** acquisition. On the books of the parent company, dividends would be treated as usual as a reduction in the investment account. Thus, still using the example introduced in Illustration 4-11, P Company would make the following dividend and earnings entries relative to its investment in S Company for the year 2010.

EQUITY

P's Books

Investment in S Company	24,300	
Equity in Subsidiary Income .9($27,000)		24,300
To record equity in subsidiary income.		
Cash	18,000	
Investment in S Company		18,000
To record dividends received .9($20,000).		

For an interim acquisition assuming the use of the full-year reporting alternative, the Computation and Allocation Schedule will include one or two additional amounts in the calculation of equity: one for the partial-period income of S prior to acquisition, and one for dividends declared (if any) by the subsidiary during the current year prior to acquisition.

Computation and Allocation of Difference Schedule

	Parent Share	*Noncontrolling Share*	*Total Value*
Purchase price and implied value	**$290,700**	**32,300**	323,000
Less: Book value of equity:			
Common stock	180,000	20,000	**200,000**
Retained earnings, January 1	72,000	8,000	**80,000**
Income from 1/1–4/1	8,100	900	**9,000**
Dividends from 1/1–4/1	(0)	(0)	**(0)**
Total book value	260,100	28,900	289,000
Difference between implied and book value	30,600	3,400	**34,000**
Adjust land upward (mark to market)	(30,600)	(3,400)	(34,000)
Balance	—0—	—0—	—0—

The new amount(s) included in the Computation and Allocation Schedule are for income and dividends of the subsidiary for the period from the beginning of the current year (1/1) to the date of acquisition (4/1). These are amounts that would have been included in retained earnings of the subsidiary if closing procedures had been performed on April 1 (not a normal date for closing entries, which usually are made at year-end). Note, also, that dividends declared by the subsidiary for the period from 1/1 to 4/1 are listed as zero because the subsidiary's dividends were not declared until 11/1 in our example.

A workpaper for the preparation of consolidated statements on December 31, 2010, is presented in Illustration 4-14. S Company's entire income statement account balances are included in the workpaper, and P Company's share of S Company's net income earned before acquisition is deducted as "subsidiary income before acquisition."

Workpaper eliminating entries at the end of 2010 under the equity method would be:

EQUITY

(1)	Equity in Subsidiary Income	24,300	
	Investment in S Company		24,300
(2)	Investment in S Company	18,000	
	Dividends Declared—S Company		18,000
	To adjust investment account to beginning of year balance and to eliminate equity in subsidiary income and intercompany dividends.		
(3)	Common Stock—S Company	200,000	
	1/1 Retained Earnings—S Company	80,000	
	Subsidiary Income before Acquisition	9,000	
	Difference between Implied and Book Values	34,000	
	Investment in S Company		290,700
	Noncontrolling interest in equity		32,300
	To eliminate investment account and establish noncontrolling interest in equity.		
(4)	Land	34,000	
	Difference between Implied and Book Value		34,000

Interim Acquisition under the Equity Method—Partial-Year Reporting Alternative

If the partial-year reporting alternative is used in conjunction with the equity method, P Company would recognize its share of S Company's income after acquisition in its general ledger accounts (as always with the equity method). S Company would, however, close its revenue and expense accounts at 4/1 into retained earnings. The 12/31 trial balance includes only the period from 4/1 to 12/31, or three-fourths of S Company's revenue and expense items for the year. These amounts are reflected in the third column of Illustration 4-11. This is the portion to itemize in the consolidated income statement under the partial-year reporting alternative as well. Thus, there is no need to subtract any "subsidiary income prior to acquisition" at the bottom of the consolidated income statement.

Computation and Allocation of Difference Schedule

	Parent Share	*Noncontrolling Share*	*Total Value*
Purchase price and implied value	**$290,700**	**32,300**	323,000
Less: Book value of equity acquired:			
Common stock	180,000	20,000	**200,000**
Retained earnings, 4/1	80,100	8,900	**89,000**
Total book value	260,100	28,900	289,000
Difference between implied and book value	30,600	3,400	**34,000**
Adjust land upward (mark to market)	(30,600)	(3,400)	**(34,000)**
Balance	—0—	—0—	—0—

Equity Method
Interim Purchase of Stock
90% Owned Subsidiary
Alternative One: **Full-Year Reporting**

ILLUSTRATION 4-14
Consolidated Statements Workpaper
P Company and Subsidiary
for the Year Ended December 31, 2010

	P	S	*Eliminations*		Noncontrolling	Consolidated
Income Statement	*Company*	*Company*	*Dr.*	*Cr.*	*Interest*	*Balances*
Sales	600,000	160,000				760,000
Equity in Subsidiary Income	24,300		(1) 24,300			
Total Revenue	624,300	160,000				760,000
Cost of Goods Sold	380,000	80,000				460,000
Other Expenses	120,000	44,000				164,000
Total Cost and Expense	500,000	124,000				624,000
Net/Combined Income	124,300	36,000				136,000
Subsidiary Income before Acquisition			(3) 9,000			(9,000)
Consolidated Net Income						127,000
Noncontrolling Interest in Income					2,700*	(2,700)
Net Income to Retained Earnings	124,300	36,000	33,300	—0—	2,700	124,300
Retained Earnings Statement						
1/1 Retained Earnings						
P Company	214,000					214,000
S Company		80,000	(3) 80,000			
Net Income from above	124,300	36,000	33,300	—0—	2,700	124,300
Dividends Declared						
P Company	(50,000)					(50,000)
S Company		(20,000)		(2) 18,000	(2,000)	
12/31 Retained Earnings to Balance Sheet	288,300	96,000	113,300	18,000	700	288,300
Balance Sheet						
Current Assets	145,300	71,000				216,300
Investment in S Company	297,000		(2) 18,000	(1) 24,300 (3) 290,700		
Difference between Implied and Book Value			(3) 34,000	(4) 34,000		
Property ad Equipment (net)	326,000	200,000				526,000
Land	120,000	90,000	(4) 34,000			244,000
Total	888,300	361,000				986,300
Liabilities	100,000	65,000				165,000
Common Stock						
P Company	500,000					500,000
S Company		200,000	(3) 200,000			
Retained Earnings from above	288,300	96,000	113,300	18,000	700	288,300
4/1 Noncontrolling Interest in Net assets				(3) 32,300	32,300	
12/31 Noncontrolling Interest in Net Assets					33,000	33,000
Total	888,300	361,000	399,300	399,300		986,300

*.1($36,000) × 3/4 = $2,700 noncontrolling interest in earnings subsequent to acquisition.
(1) To reverse the effect of parent company entry during the year for subsidiary income.
(2) To reverse the effect of parent company entry during the year for subsidiary dividends.
(3) To eliminate the investment in S Company and create noncontrolling interest account.
(4) To allocate the excess of implied over book value to land.

A workpaper for the preparation of consolidated financial statements on December 31, 2010, is presented in Illustration 4-15. Workpaper elimination entries are then as follows:

(1)	Equity in Subsidiary Income	24,300	
	Investment in S Company		24,300
(2)	Investment in S Company	18,000	
	Dividends Declared—S Company		18,000
(3)	Common Stock—S Company	200,000	
	4/1 Retained Earnings—S Company	89,000	
	Difference between Implied and Book Values	34,000	
	Investment in S Company		290,700
	Noncontrolling Interest in Equity		32,300
(4)	Land	34,000	
	Difference between Implied and Book Value		34,000

To verify the amount of income reported, prepare t-accounts for the nonconcontrolling and controlling interests as follows:

Noncontrolling Interest in Consolidated Net Income

	Internally generated income of S Company (after acquisition)	$27,000
	Any needed adjustments (Chapter 5)	0
	Adjusted income of subsidiary	27,000
	Noncontrolling percentage owned	10%
	Noncontrolling interest in income	2,700

(90%) (27,000)

Controlling Interest in Consolidated Income

	Internally generated income of P Company (entire year: $124,300 – $24,300)	$100,000
	Any needed adjustments (Chapter 5)	0
	Percentage of subsidiary adjusted income (90%) ($27,000)	24,300
	Controlling interest in income	$124,300

TEST YOUR KNOWLEDGE

NOTE: Solutions to ***Test Your Knowledge*** questions are found at the end of each chapter before the end-of-chapter questions.

Multiple Choice

1. Cash spent or received in consummating an acquisition should be reflected in which of the following sections of the statement of cash flows:
   (A) Operating
   (B) Investing
   (C) Financing
   (D) Notes to the statement of cash flows

Equity Method
Interim Purchase of Stock
90% Owned Subsidiary
Alternative Two: **Partial-Year Reporting**

ILLUSTRATION 4-15
Consolidated Statements Workpaper
P Company and Subsidiary
for the Year Ended December 31, 2010

Income Statement	P Company	S Company	Eliminations Dr.	Eliminations Cr.	Noncontrolling Interest	Consolidated Balances
Sales	600,000	120,000				720,000
Equity in Subsidiary Income	24,300		(1) 24,300			
Total Revenue	624,300	120,000				720,000
Cost of Goods Sold	380,000	60,000				440,000
Other Expenses	120,000	33,000				153,000
Total Cost and Expense	500,000	93,000				593,000
Net/Consolidated Income	124,300	27,000				127,000
Noncontrolling Interest in Income					2,700*	(2,700)
Net Income to Retained Earnings	124,300	27,000	24,300	—0—	2,700	124,300
Retained Earnings Statement						
Retained Earnings						
P Company	214,000					214,000
S Company		89,000	(3) 89,000			
Net Income from above	124,300	27,000	24,300	—0—	2,700	124,300
Dividends Declared						
P Company	(50,000)					(50,000)
S Company		(20,000)		(2) 18,000	(2,000)	
12/31 Retained Earnings to Balance Sheet	288,300	96,000	113,300	18,000	700	288,300
Balance Sheet						
Current Assets	145,300	71,000				216,300
Investment in S Company	297,000		(2) 18,000	(1) 24,300 (3) 290,700		
Difference between Implied and Book Value			(3) 34,000	(4) 34,000		
Property and Equipment (net)	326,000	200,000				526,000
Land	120,000	90,000	(4) 34,000			244,000
Total	888,300	361,000				986,300
Liabilities	100,000	65,000				165,000
Common Stock						
P Company	500,000					500,000
S Company		200,000	(3) 200,000			
Retained Earnings from above	288,300	96,000	113,300	18,000	700	288,300
4/1 Noncontrolling Interest in Net Assets				(1) 32,300	32,300	
12/31 Noncontrolling Interest in Net Assets					33,000	33,000
Total	888,300	361,000	399,300	399,300		986,300

*.10($27,000) = $2,700.
(1) To reverse the effect of parent company entry during the year for subsidiary income.
(2) To reverse the effect of parent company entry during the year for subsidiary dividends.
(3) To eliminate the investment in S Company and create noncontrolling interest account.
(4) To allocate the excess of implied over book value to land.

CONSOLIDATED STATEMENT OF CASH FLOWS

LO7 Peculiarities of Consolidated Statement of Cash Flows.

The procedures followed in the preparation of a statement of cash flows are discussed in most intermediate accounting texts. When the company is reporting on a consolidated basis, the statement of cash flows must also be presented on a consolidated basis. The starting point for the consolidated cash flow statement is the consolidated income statement and comparative consolidated balance sheets (beginning and end of current year). Thus the preparation of the consolidated statement of cash flows will be the same, regardless of how the parent accounts for its investment (cost method, partial equity method, or complete equity method). This is true because the final product (the consolidated financial statements) is always the same if the consolidating procedures are done correctly.

We will first discuss years subsequent to the year of acquisition, and then the preparation of the consolidated statement of cash flows in the year of acquisition. In years subsequent to the year of acquisition, a consolidated balance sheet should be available for both the beginning and end of the current year. The consolidated statement of cash flows reflects all cash outlays and inflows of the consolidated entity except those between parent and subsidiary. Therefore, we are interested in explaining 100% of the changes in balance sheet accounts of parent and subsidiary (not just the portion of the subsidiary controlled by the parent). Because the consolidated balance sheet reflects 100% of the assets and liabilities of both parent and subsidiary, the preparation of a consolidated statement of cash flows is quite similar in most respects to that of a single (unconsolidated) firm. At least three aspects of the statement do, however, differ (or require modification). They are:

1. *Noncontrolling interest in consolidated net income.* Accounting standards require the disclosure of cash flows from operating activities for the reporting period. Like the consolidated balance sheet and the consolidated income statement, the consolidated statement of cash flows presents ***combined*** information for the parent and its subsidiaries (i.e., combined cash flows). Cash flows from operating activities may be presented by either the direct or the indirect method. Under the indirect method, we begin with net income for the period and add back (or deduct) any items recognized in determining that net income that did not result in an outflow (or inflow) of cash. These adjustments normally include such items as depreciation and amortization. ***If the statement of cash flows starts with consolidated net income, then the noncontrolling interest is already included and need not be added back.*** However, if the starting amount (net income) reflects only the ***controlling interest*** in consolidated net income (often the "bottom line" on the consolidated income statement), an additional adjustment for a consolidated statement of cash flows is the ***add-back of the noncontrolling interest in consolidated net income*** (or deduction of the noncontrolling interest's share of a loss).
2. *Subsidiary dividends paid*: Because we are interested in reflecting 100% of cash outlays and inflows between the consolidated entity and outsiders, any subsidiary dividends ***paid to the noncontrolling stockholders*** must be included with dividends paid by the parent company when calculating cash outflow from financing activities. The dividends paid by the subsidiary to the parent do not involve cash flows to or from outsiders and thus are not reported on the consolidated statement of cash flows.

3. *Parent company acquisition of additional subsidiary shares:* The cost of the acquisition of additional shares in a subsidiary by the parent company may or may not constitute a cash outflow from investing activities. If the acquisition is an open market purchase, it does represent such an outflow.

Illustration of Preparation of a Consolidated Statement of Cash Flows: Year after Acquisition

As an illustration of the preparation of a consolidated statement of cash flows, a consolidated income statement and comparative consolidated balance sheets for P Company and its 90% owned subsidiary, S Company, along with other information, are presented in Illustration 4–16.

ILLUSTRATION 4-16

P Company and Subsidiary
Consolidated Income Statement
for the Year Ended December 31, 2011

Sales	$540,000
Cost of goods sold	294,000
Gross profit	246,000
Operating expenses	136,000
Income from operations	110,000
Equity in income of Zorn Company	6,000
Consolidated net income	116,000
Noncontrolling interest in consolidated net income	4,000
Controlling interest in consolidated net income	$112,000

P Company and S Company Comparative
Consolidated Balance Sheets

	December 31	
Assets	*2010*	*2011*
Cash	$ 60,000	97,000
Accounts receivable (net)	92,000	120,000
Inventories	110,000	101,000
Plant and equipment (net)	245,000	404,000
Investments	152,000	158,000
Goodwill	20,000	20,000
Total assets	$679,000	$900,000
Liabilities and Equity		
Accounts payable	$ 60,000	$ 93,000
Accrued expenses payable	99,000	89,000
Total liabilities	159,000	182,000
Stockholders' equity:		
Noncontrolling interest in net assets	20,000	22,000
Common stock, $2 par value	2000,000	220,000
Other contributed capital	40,000	140,000
Retained earnings	260,000	336,000
Total stockholders' equity	520,000	718,000
Total Liabilities and Equity	$679,000	$900,000

Other Information:

1. Depreciation expense of $26,000 is included in operating expenses.
2. Manufacturing equipment was acquired during 2011 for cash of $185,000.
3. Investments include a 30% common stock investment in Zorn Company on which $6,000 of equity in investee income was recognized. No dividends were received during the year.
4. Noncontrolling interest in consolidated net income was $4,000. However, $2,000 was distributed to noncontrolling stockholders as dividends during the year. Thus noncontrolling interest in net assets on the balance sheet increased by only $2,000.
5. Ten thousand shares of common stock were issued by P Company on the open market for cash at $12 per share.
6. Dividend payments totaled $38,000, of which $36,000 were to P Company stockholders (thereby reducing consolidated retained earnings), and $2,000 were to S Company noncontrolling stockholders.

A consolidated statement of cash flows, using the indirect method of presenting cash flows from operating activities, is shown in Illustration 4-17.

ILLUSTRATION 4-17

P Company and Subsidiary
Consolidated Statement of Cash Flows
for the Year Ended December 31, 2011

Cash flows from operating activities:		
Controlling interest in consolidated net income		$112,000
Noncontrolling interest in consolidated net income		4,000
Consolidated Net Income		$116,000
Adjustments to convert net income to net cash flow from operating activities:		
Depreciation expense		26,000
Increase in accounts receivable		(28,000)
Decrease in inventories		9,000
Increase in accounts payable		33,000
Decrease in accrued expenses payable		(10,000)
Equity in income of Zorn Company		(6,000)
Net cash flow from operating activities		$140,000
Cash flows from investing activities:		
Payments for purchase of plant assets		(185,000)
Cash flows from financing activities:		
Proceeds from the issuance of common stock	$120,000	
Cash dividends declared and paid	(38,000)	
Net cash flow from financing activities		82,000
Increase in cash		$37,000
Cash Balance, beginning		60,000
Cash Balance, ending		$97,000

If the direct method is used to report cash from operations on the consolidated statement of cash flows, the statement would be identical to Illustration 4-17 with one exception. The "cash flows from operating activities" would be replaced with the following:

Cash flows from operating activities:		
Cash received from customers (1)		$512,000
Less cash paid for:		
Purchases of merchandise (2)	$252,000	
Operating expenses (3)	120,000	372,000
Net cash flow from operating activities		$140,000
(1) Beginning accounts receivable		$ 92,000
Sales		540,000
Ending accounts receivable		(120,000)
Cash received from customers		($512,000)
(2) Cost of goods sold		$294,000
Beginning inventory		(110,000)
Ending inventory		101,000
Accrual basis purchases		285,000
Beginning accounts payable		60,000
Ending accounts payable		(93,000)
Cash basis purchases		$252,000
(3) Operating expenses		$136,000
Depreciation expense		(26,000)
Beginning accrued expenses		99,000
Ending accrued expenses		(89,000)
Cash paid for operating expenses		$120,000

ILLUSTRATION OF PREPARATION OF A CONSOLIDATED STATEMENT OF CASH FLOWS: YEAR OF ACQUISITION

LO8 Stock issued as Consideration in Statement of Cash Flows.

The preparation of the consolidated statement of cash flows in the year of acquisition is complicated slightly because the comparative balance sheets at the beginning and end of the current year are dissimilar. Specifically, the balance sheet at the ***end*** of the year of acquisition reflects consolidated balances, while the beginning of the year reflects parent-only balances. Thus the net change in cash that investors wish to interpret is the change from the parent's beginning-of-year balance to the combined (consolidated) end-of-year cash balance. To accomplish this reconciliation, two realizations are important.

1. Any cash spent or received in the acquisition itself should be reflected in the ***Investing*** activities section of the consolidated statement of cash flows. For example, if the parent paid total cash of $1,000,000 to acquire a subsidiary, which brought $300,000 cash to the consolidated entity, the net decrease in cash would appear as a $700,000 outlay. On the other hand, if the parent issued only stock or debt (no cash) to acquire the same subsidiary, the net increase would appear as a $300,000 cash inflow. The issuance of stock or debt would appear in the notes to the financial statements as a significant noncash investing and financing activity.
2. To explain the change in cash successfully, the assets and liabilities of the subsidiary ***at the date of acquisition*** must be added to those of the parent at the beginning of the current year. For example, assume that P Company had $1,500,000 in long-term notes payable at the beginning of the year, S Company had $500,000 in long-term notes payable at the date of acquisition, and the consolidated entity had $3,000,000 in long-term notes payable at the end of the year. To explain the net change, the ***Financing*** section of the statement of cash flows might reflect a cash inflow of $1,000,000 from borrowing activities.

To illustrate the preparation of a consolidated statement of cash flows in the year of acquisition, consider the information in Illustration 4-18. In this problem, P Company acquires 80% of S Company on April 1, 2011 for $200,000 cash. In this illustration the last six columns are the familiar columns used to prepare the consolidated balance sheet and income statement at the end of 2011. However, two additional columns have been added: one showing the beginning-of-year balances (January 1, 2011) for the balance sheet accounts for P Company and one showing the balances on the date of acquisition (April 1, 2011) for S Company. The information in these columns is needed to prepare the consolidated statement of cash flows for 2011, but does not affect any of the extensions or calculations needed to complete the worksheet in Illustration 4-18. Other information used in the example includes the following:

1. Total consolidated depreciation expense is $30,000.
2. The companies issued $205,000 of debt.
3. The companies purchased $95,000 of property, plant, and equipment.
4. The excess of implied over book value is attributable to land ($200,000 − .8($160,000 + $80,000) = $8,000).
5. The partial-year alternative is used for presenting subsidiary income and expense accounts.

The comparative consolidated balance sheet, prepared from Illustration 4-18, is shown in Illustration 4-19. Notice that the beginning of the year balance sheet amounts are the same as P Company's beginning of the year balance sheet (or the first column in the workpaper in Illustration 4-18). Therefore, the change in cash in the consolidated statement of cash flows is an increase of $35,000, calculated as the $115,000 ending consolidated balance less the $80,000 beginning balance.

Now consider the two points made above. How is the $200,000 cash acquisition reported on the statement of cash flows? The acquisition is listed in the investing activities section and represents the net assets acquired. But since S Company had $28,000 cash on hand on the date of acquisition, the net effect on cash from the acquisition is the $200,000 paid less the $28,000 acquired or $172,000. Hence, on the statement of cash flows, the acquisition is listed as a $172,000 cash outflow. The consolidated statement of cash flows is shown in Illustration 4-20.

Second, all calculations of changes in balance sheet accounts require that assets and liabilities acquired from S Company be added to the beginning P Company balances. For instance, on the comparative balance sheets shown in Illustration 4-19, accounts receivable has a beginning balance of $65,000 and an ending balance of $123,000. Because accounts receivable of $38,000 were acquired on April 1, 2011, the change in receivables is the ending consolidated amount of $123,000 less the beginning balance of $65,000 and the amount purchased in the acquisition of $38,000. (See Illustration 4-18.) This gives the correct increase in accounts receivable of $20,000. As a result, in published annual reports, the changes in the working capital accounts from the previous year's balance sheet do not reconcile to the amounts shown on the statement of cash flows in the year of acquisition. Similar reasoning is used for all the remaining changes in balance sheet accounts, such as property, plant, and equipment.

Another point about the consolidated statement of cash flows concerns the $12,000 dividends paid by S Company. Since P Company purchased 80% of S Company, $9,600 of the dividends must be eliminated. However, the $2,400 remaining dividends paid by S Company to the noncontrolling shareholders must be subtracted as a financing item. We have shown this separately on the cash flow statement in Illustration 4-20 even though in practice the dividend amounts paid by P Company and S Company are often combined.

Cost Method
Interim Purchase of Stock
80% Owned Subsidiary
Partial-Year Reporting

ILLUSTRATION 4-18

Consolidated Statement of Cash Flows for the Year Ended December 31, 2011

Income Statement	*P Company*	*S Company*	*P Company 1/1 to 12/31*	*S Company 4/1 to 12/31*	*Eliminations Dr.*	*Eliminations Cr.*	*Noncontrolling Interest*	*Consolidated Balances*
Sales			350,000	200,000				550,000
Dividend Income .8($12,000)			9,600		(3) 9,600			
Total Revenue			359,600	200,000				550,000
Cost of Goods Sold			200,000	95,000				295,000
Other Expenses			80,000	65,000				145,000
Total Cost and Expense			280,000	160,000				440,000
Consolidated Net Income			79,600	40,000				110,000
Noncontrolling Interest in Income							8,000*	(8,000)
Net Income to Retained Earnings			79,600	40,000	9,600	—0—	8,000	102,000
Retained Earnings								
P Company, 1/1			90,000					90,000
S Company, 4/1				80,000	(1) 80,000			
Net Income from above			79,600	40,000	9,600	—0—	8,000	102,000
Dividends Declared								
P Company			(30,000)					(30,000)
S Company				(12,000)		(3) 9,600	(2,400)	
12/31 Retained Earnings to Balance Sheet			139,600	108,000	89,600	9,600	5,600	162,000
Balance Sheet	*At 1/1/2011*	*At 4/1/2011*	*At 12/31/11*	*At 12/31/11*				
Cash	80,000	28,000	75,000	40,000				115,000
Accounts Receivable 65,000	65,000	38,000	70,000	53,000				123,000
Inventory	70,000	53,000	86,600	40,000				126,600
Investment in S Company			200,000			(1) 200,000		
Difference between Implied and Book Value					(1) 10,000	(2) 10,000		
Property and Equipment (net)	180,000	175,000	245,000	175,000				420,000
Land	35,000	27,000	35,000	27,000	(2) 10,000			72,000
Total	430,000	321,000	711,600	335,000				856,600
Accounts Payable	35,000	34,000	60,000	22,000				82,000
Other Liabilities	65,000	47,000	272,000	45,000				317,000
Common Stock								
P Company	240,000		240,000					240,000
S Company		160,000		160,000	(1) 160,000			
Retained Earnings	90,000	80,000	139,600	108,000	89,600	9,600	5,600	162,000
4/1 Noncontrolling Interest in Net Assets						(1) 50,000	50,000	
12/31 Noncontrolling Interest in Net Assets							55,600	55,600
Total	430,000	321,000	711,600	335,000	269,600	269,600		856,600

* .2 ($40,000) = $8,000
(1) To eliminate the investment in S Company and create noncontrolling interest account.
(2) To allocate the difference between implied and book value to land.
(3) To eliminate intercompany dividends.

ILLUSTRATION 4-19

P Company and S Company (S Company Included from 12/31/11 Only)
Comparative Consolidated Balance Sheets

	December 31	
Assets	*2010*	*2011*
Cash	$80,000	$115,000
Accounts receivable (net)	65,000	123,000
Inventories	70,000	126,600
Plant and equipment (net)	180,000	420,000
Land	35,000	72,000
Total assets	$430,000	$856,600
Liabilities and Equity		
Accounts payable	$ 35,000	$ 82,000
Other Liabilities	65,000	317,000
Total liabilities	100,000	399,000
Stockholders' equity:		
Noncontrolling interest in net assets		55,600
Common stock, $2 par value	240,000	240,000
Retained earnings	90,000	162,000
Total stockholders' equity	330,000	457,600
Total Liabilities and Equity	$430,000	$856,600

ILLUSTRATION 4-20

P Company and Subsidiary
Consolidated Statement of Cash Flows
for the Year Ended December 31, 2011

Cash flows from operating activities:		
Controlling interest in Net Income	$102,000	
Noncontrolling interest in consolidated Net Income (.2) ($40,000)	8,000	
Consolidated Net Income	110,000	
Adjustments to convert net income to net cash flow from operating activities:		
Depreciation expense	30,000	
Increase in accounts receivable ($123,000 – 65,000 – 38,000)	(20,000)	
Increase in inventories ($126,600 – 70,000 – 53,000)	(3,600)	
Increase in accounts payable ($82,000 – 35,000 – 34,000)	13,000	
Net cash flow from operating activities		$129,400
Cash flows from investing activities:		
Payments for purchase of plant assets	(95,000)	
Cash paid (net) for acquisition of S ($200,000 less cash acquired of $28,000)	(172,000)	
Net cash flow from investing activities		($267,000)
Cash flows from financing activities:		
Proceeds from the issuance of debt	$205,000	
Cash dividends declared and paid by P Company	(30,000)	
Cash dividends declared and paid by S Company to noncontrolling shareholders (.2) ($12,000)	(2,400)	
Net cash flow from financing activities		$172,600
Increase in cash ($115,000 – $80,000)		35,000
Cash Balance, beginning		80,000
Cash Balance, ending		$115,000

Finally, the preparation of the consolidated statement of cash flows is the same regardless of whether the parent uses the cost method, partial equity method, or complete equity method to account for its investment in any subsidiaries that are consolidated. This is true because the preparation is based on the consolidated income statement and consolidated balance sheets, and these are identical under the three methods.

COMPARE U.S. GAAP AND IFRS REGARDING EQUITY METHOD

In the following table, we provide a comparison of the similarities and differences between the equity method used for investments in the United States and the accounting for associates (IASB term for equity investments) under IFRS.

Application of the Equity Method

Issue	*U.S. GAAP*	*IFRS*
Relevant standards	*APB No. 18* **[ASC 323]** *and SFAS No. 159* **[ASC 825]**	*IAS 28*
Terminology	Equity method investments.	Investments in associates.
Requirement to apply equity method	Corporate entities that exert significant influence (but not control) must use the equity method (unless the investor has elected the fair value option).	An **associate** is an entity in which the investor has significant influence (excluding subsidiaries and joint ventures). Investments in associates are accounted for using the equity method.
Significant influence	Presumed if the investor has 20% or more of the voting rights in a corporate investee.	Same as in the United States.
Potential voting rights	Generally not considered.	Consider the existence and effects of potential voting rights on currently exercisable or convertible instruments.
Joint ventures	Equity method is required for jointly controlled entities.	Use proportionate consolidation. The equity method may be used, but is not recommended (there is a current proposal to eliminate proportionate consolidation).
Limited partnerships	The equity method is generally applied to investments of more than 3 to 5%.	Equity method is applied to investments using the "significant influence" principle.
Carrying value of the investment	Increased (decreased) with the investor's share of profit (loss) of the investee after the date of acquisition.	Same as in the United States.
Uniform accounting policies	Not required.	Uniform accounting policies are required (use top-side adjustments when policies are different).
Different reporting dates	Permits a three-month difference (and disclose significant events)	Permits a three-month difference if it is impractical to change; however, investors must adjust for significant events.
Exemptions from the equity method	*SFAS No. 159* **[ASC 825–10– 25–1]** gives entities the option to account for equity investments at fair value.	Associates classified as held for sale.

SUMMARY

1. *Describe the accounting treatment required under current GAAP for varying levels of influence or control by investors.* With few exceptions, all ***subsidiaries*** (investments in which the investor has a controlling interest) must be consolidated and may not be reported as separate investments in the consolidated financial statements. The parent may use any of at least three methods (cost, partial equity, or complete equity) to account for investments during the year that are going to be consolidated, provided the consolidating process is carried out properly. The equity method ***must*** be used to account for investments in investees in which the investor has significant influence but not control (usually 20%–50%). For investments in investees where the investor does not have significant influence (normally less than 20%), the investment should be reported at its fair value.

2. *Prepare journal entries on the parent's books to account for an investment using the cost method, the partial equity method, and the complete equity method.* The most important difference between the cost and equity methods pertains to the period in which the parent recognizes subsidiary income on its books. If the cost method is in use, the parent recognizes its share of subsidiary income only when dividends are declared by the subsidiary. If the partial equity method is in use, the investor will recognize its share of the subsidiary's income when reported by the subsidiary, regardless of whether dividends have been distributed. A debit to cash and a credit to the investment account record the receipt of dividends under the partial equity method. The complete equity method differs from the partial equity method only in that the share of subsidiary income to be recognized is adjusted in certain cases from the amount reported by the subsidiary (for example, for depreciation on the excess of market over book values of depreciable assets).

3. *Understand the use of the workpaper in preparing consolidated financial statements.* Accounting workpapers are helpful in accumulating, classifying, and arranging data for the preparation of consolidated financial statements. The three-section workpaper format used in this text includes a separate section for each of three basic financial statements—income statement, retained earnings statement, and balance sheet. In some cases the input to the workpaper comes from the individual financial statements of the affiliates to be consolidated, in which case the three-section workpaper is particularly appropriate. At other times, however, input may be from affiliate trial balances, and the data must be arranged in financial statement form before the workpaper can be completed.

4. *Prepare a schedule for the computation and allocation of the difference between implied and book values.* The schedule begins with the cost (or purchase price) and divides this amount by the percentage acquired to compute the implied value of the subsidiary. Next the book value of the subsidiary's equity at the date of acquisition is subtracted from the implied value. This difference is then allocated to adjust the assets and/or liabilities of the subsidiary for differences between their book values and fair values. Any remaining excess is labeled as goodwill. Special rules apply for bargain purchases.

5. *Prepare the workpaper eliminating entries for the year of acquisition (and subsequent years) for the cost and equity methods.* Under the cost method, dividends declared by the subsidiary are eliminated against dividend income recorded by the parent. The investment account is eliminated against the equity accounts of the subsidiary, and an account is created for the noncontrolling interest in equity. The difference between implied and book values is recorded in a separate account by that name. The difference is then allocated to adjust underlying assets and/or liabilities, and to record goodwill in some cases. Under the equity method, the dividends declared by the subsidiary are eliminated against the investment account, as is the equity in subsidiary income. The investment account is eliminated in the same way as under the cost method. In subsequent years, the cost method requires an initial entry to establish reciprocity or convert to equity. This entry, which is not needed under the equity method, debits the investment account and credits retained earnings of the parent (for the change in retained earnings of the subsidiary from the date of acquisition to the beginning of the current year multiplied by the parent's percentage).

6. *Describe two alternative methods to account for interim acquisitions of subsidiary stock at the end of the first year.* If an investment in the common stock of a subsidiary is made during the year rather than on the first day, there are two methods available to

treat the preacquisition revenue and expense items of the subsidiary. The first method includes the subsidiary in consolidation as though it had been acquired at the beginning of the year, and then makes a deduction at the bottom of the consolidated income statement for the preacquisition subsidiary earnings. The second method includes in the consolidated income statement only the subsidiary revenue and expense amounts for the period after acquisition.

7. *Explain how the consolidated statement of cash flows differs from a single firm's statement of cash flows.* In the preparation of a consolidated statement of cash flows, the starting point under the indirect approach should be ***consolidated net income*** (including the noncontrolling interest). Alternatively, the statement can begin with the ***controlling interest in consolidated net income***, in which case the noncontrolling interest in income must be added to the controlling interest just as depreciation and amortization expenses are added. Subsidiary dividend payments to noncontrolling shareholders represent a ***Financing*** outflow of cash. Subsidiary dividend payments to the parent company represent an intercompany transfer and thus are not reflected on the consolidated statement of cash flows. The cost of acquiring additional subsidiary shares of common stock is an ***Investing*** outflow of cash if the purchase is made from outsiders, but not if made directly from the subsidiary.

8. *Understand how the reporting of an acquisition on the consolidated statement of cash flows differs when stock is issued rather than cash.* Any cash spent or received in the acquisition itself should be reflected in the ***Investing*** activities section of the consolidated statement of cash flows. The issuance of stock or debt would appear in the ***Notes to the Financial Statements*** as a significant noncash investing and financing activity.

9. *Describe some of the differences between IFRS and U.S. GAAP in the accounting for equity investments.* In the United States, the investments are referred to as "equity investments"; under international standards, the investments are referred to as "investments in associates." Potential voting rights are considered under international standards in determining significant influence, while potential voting rights are not explicitly considered under U.S. GAAP.

APPENDIX A

Alternative Workpaper Format

A variety of workpaper formats may be used in the preparation of consolidated financial statements. They may be classified generally into two categories, the three-division workpaper format used in this text, and the trial balance format. In the three-divisional format the account balances of the individual firms are first arranged into financial statement format. In contrast, in the trial balance format, columns are provided for the trial balances, the elimination entries, and normally, each financial statement to be prepared, except for the statement of cash flows.

The consolidated balances derived in a workpaper are the same regardless of the format selected. The statement preparer with a sound understanding of consolidation principles should be able to adapt quite easily to alternative workpaper formats. However, the reader may want to develop a familiarity with the trial balance format, since this format may be used by some companies.

To illustrate the trial balance workpaper format, and at the same time to verify that the results are the same as they would be if the three-divisional format were used, the same facts used in the preparation of Illustration 4-4 are assumed in Illustration 4-21.

Cost Method

80% Owned Subsidiary

Trial Balance Format

ILLUSTRATION 4-21

Consolidated Statements Workpaper Based on Illustration 4-4

P Company and Subsidiary for the Year Ended December 31, 2011

Debits	P Company	S Company	Eliminations Dr.	Eliminations Cr.	Consolidated Income Statement	Consolidated Retained Earnings Statement	Noncontrolling Interest	Consolidated Balance Sheet
Cash	74,000	41,000						115,000
Accounts Receivable	71,000	33,000						104,000
Inventory 1/1	67,000	43,000			110,000			
Investment in S Company	165,000		(1) 16,000	(2) 181,000				—0—
Difference between implied and book value			(2) 16,250	(3) 16,250				
Other Assets	280,000	202,000	(3) 16,250					498,250
Dividends Declared								
P Company	30,000					(30,000)		
S Company		10,000		(4) 8,000			(2,000)	
Purchases	215,000	90,000			305,000			
Other Expense	80,000	56,000			136,000			
Total	982,000	475,000						
Inventory 12/31 (Asset)	82,000	39,000						121,000
Total Assets								838,250
Credits								
Liabilities	131,000	75,000						206,000
Capital Stock								
P Company	240,000							240,000
S Company		150,000	(2) 150,000					
1/1 Retained Earnings								
P Company	253,000			(1) 16,000		269,000		
S Company		60,000	(2) 60,000					
Sales	350,000	190,000			(540,000)			
Dividend Income	8,000		(4) 8,000		—0—			
Totals	982,000	475,000						
Inventory 12/31 (COGS)	82,000	39,000			(121,000)			
Consolidated Net Income					110,000			
Noncontrolling Interest in Income .2($40,000)]					(8,000)		8,000	
Controlling Interest in Net Income					102,000	102,000		
Consolidated Retained Earnings						341,000		341,000
1/1 Noncontrolling Interest in Net Assets				(1) 45,250			45,250	
12/31 Noncontrolling Interest in Net Assets							51,250	51,250
Total Liabilities and Equity			266,500	266,500				838,250

(1) To establish reciprocity as of 1/1/2011 [($60,000 − $40,000) × .80].
(2) To eliminate the investment account and create noncontrolling interest account.
(3) To allocate the difference between implied and book value to land.
(4) To eliminate intercompany dividends.

The steps in the preparation of the workpaper are: (1) The trial balances of the individual affiliates are entered in the first two columns. In this case, the debit account balances are separated from the credit account balances. Or the accounts can be listed as they appear in the ledger. A debit column and a credit column may be provided for each firm or one column may be used and the credit balances identified by parentheses. (2) The account balances are analyzed, and the required adjustments and eliminations are entered in the next two vertical columns. (3) The net adjusted balances are extended to the appropriate columns. Separate columns are provided to accumulate the account balances needed for the preparation of the consolidated income statement, retained earnings statement, and balance sheet. In addition, an optional column is provided for the identification of the noncontrolling interest. (4) Once the accounts are extended, the consolidated net income is computed from the income statement column and allocated between the noncontrolling and controlling interests. (5) The consolidated retained earnings balance and total noncontrolling interest in equity can now be computed. The amounts are extended to the final column and should balance the liabilities and equities with the total assets. The reader will observe that these procedures are similar to the preparation of an eight-column worksheet developed to facilitate the preparation of financial statements for an individual firm.

A comparison of the elimination entries in Illustration 4-21 with those of Illustration 4-4 will reveal that the entries are the same, regardless of the form of workpaper used to accumulate the consolidated balances.

APPENDIX B

Deferred Tax Consequences When Affiliates File Separate Income Tax Returns—Undistributed Income

When a parent company owns at least 80% of a domestic subsidiary, the companies generally elect to file a consolidated income tax return. If they do not elect to file a joint return or own less than 80%, the companies file separate tax returns. In these cases, the parent includes the amount of dividends received from the investment on its own tax return. In the main body of this text, we have assumed that the affiliates (80% or more ownership levels) file a consolidated income tax return. Deferred tax issues are discussed in the appendices.

What happens when the companies do not file consolidated tax returns and file separate tax returns? Deferred tax consequences can arise since differences usually exist between the time income is reported in the consolidated financial statements and the time such income is included in the taxable income of the separate affiliates. Two major topics require attention in addressing the treatment of deferred income tax consequences when the affiliates each file separate income tax returns:

1. Undistributed subsidiary income (Appendix B of Chapter 4).
2. Elimination of unrealized intercompany profit (discussed in the appendices to Chapters 6 and 7).

Consolidated Tax Returns—Affiliated Companies (80% or More Ownership Levels)

When affiliated companies elect to file one consolidated return, the tax expense amount is computed on the consolidated workpapers rather than on the individual books of the parent and subsidiary. The amount of tax expense attributed to each company is computed from combined income and allocated back to each company's books.

When consolidated income tax returns are filed, temporary differences generally do not arise in the preparation of consolidated financial statements. For example, unrealized intercompany profit is generally treated the same way in calculating both consolidated taxable income and consolidated net income on the consolidated income statement. Thus, no timing differences arise because of the elimination of unrealized intercompany profit.

Separate Tax Returns—Deferred Tax Consequences Arising Because of Undistributed Subsidiary Income

When separate tax returns are filed, the parent company will include dividends received from the subsidiary in its taxable income, while the subsidiary's reported income is included in **consolidated net income**. Thus the difference between the subsidiary's income and dividends paid represents a temporary difference because eventually this undistributed amount will be realized through future dividends or upon sale of the subsidiary. Deferred taxes must be recorded on the books of the parent or in the consolidating workpaper for the economic entity in the amount of undistributed income to the **consolidated entity**. Whether the deferred taxes are recorded by the parent company or are only recorded in the workpaper consolidated entries depends on how the parent accounts for its investment in the subsidiary—cost versus equity. Both methods are illustrated in the following sections of this appendix.

The measurement of the deferred tax consequences of the undistributed income of a subsidiary depends on assumptions as to the nature of the transaction(s) that result in the future taxation of the undistributed income. If the parent company's equity in the undistributed income is expected to be realized in the form of a taxable dividend, the deferred tax amount is computed considering all available tax credits and exclusions. Federal income tax rules permit a portion of the dividends received from a domestic subsidiary to be excluded from taxable income. Under current federal income tax rules, the following amount of dividends can be excluded from taxable income for a given level of ownership:

Ownership Percentage in Subsidiary	*Amount of Dividends Excluded from Taxable Income*
80% or more	100% of Dividends Excluded
20% up to 80%	80% of Dividends Excluded
Less than 20%	70% of Dividends Excluded

Thus, when the undistributed income of the subsidiary is expected to be received in the form of future dividend distributions, the dividends-received exclusion must be considered. On the other hand, if the undistributed earnings of the subsidiary is not expected to be realized until the subsidiary is sold, the dividends-received exclusion is not used in computing deferred taxes. In this case, the capital gains tax rate is used to compute deferred taxes.

APB (Accounting Principles Board) ***Opinion No. 23*** allowed firms to demonstrate that undistributed subsidiary earnings are permanently reinvested and no timing differences are created. This indefinite reversal rule was eliminated by ***SFAS No. 109***, which requires deferred taxes to be recorded for undistributed income.

The Cost Method—Separate Tax Returns

Assume that the parent uses the cost method to account for the investment and that both the parent and the subsidiary file separate tax returns. This means each company records a tax provision based on the items reported on its individual books. Tax consequences relating to undistributed income are not recorded on the books of the parent company when the investment in the subsidiary is recorded using the cost method. This is because dividends are recognized as income on the parent's income statement and tax return. Therefore, no timing differences occur. However, for consolidated purposes, equity income is recognized on the income statement, while dividends are included on the tax return, creating a timing difference for consolidated purposes. Thus, **workpaper** entries are necessary each year to report the income tax consequences of past and current undistributed income.

COST

To illustrate, assume that P Company owns 75% of the voting stock of S Company. The stock was acquired on January 1, 2011, when S Company's retained earnings amounted to $150,000. In the year of acquisition (2011), S Company reported net income of $90,000 and paid dividends of $30,000. Since P Company is filing a separate tax return, P Company reports $22,500 of dividend income (75% of S Company's dividends of $30,000) as income on its tax return. However, on the consolidated income statement, 75% of S Company's income, or $67,500, is reported as income. Assume that the undistributed income of $45,000 (75% of $90,000 less $30,000) is expected to be paid as a future dividend and is expected to be included on the tax return in some future years. Because the $45,000 will become future income, deferred taxes must be computed using this amount after considering the dividend exclusion rules (80% of dividends are excluded for 75% ownership).[5] The tax rate is assumed to be 40%, and the capital gains rate is assumed to be 25% in this example.

[5] Note that P Company pays taxes of $1,800 on the $22,500 of dividends received from S Company (40% × 20% not excluded × $22,500). Therefore, combining the taxes paid on the dividend income of $1,800 and the tax expense of $3,600 recognized on the undistributed income totals a tax amount of $5,400. This equals the amount of taxes that would be owed if the entire amount of S Company's income was paid in dividends during the year ($90,000 × 75% × 20% × 40%).

The following workpaper entry is needed at the end of 2011:

Workpaper Entry—Cost Method—Year of Acquisition (2011)		
Undistributed Income Expected to Be Received as Future Dividend		
Tax Expense*	3,600	
Deferred Tax Liability		3,600

**Undistributed Income Expected to Be Received as Future Dividends*

P Company's share of undistributed income expected to be received as a future dividend (75% × $60,000)	$45,000
Percent of future dividends that are taxed	20%
Future dividends that will be taxed	$ 9,000
Income tax rate	40%
Deferred tax liability	$ 3,600

At the end of the next year (2012), suppose that S Company's ending retained earnings is $320,000. Total undistributed earnings since acquisition are $170,000, or $320,000 less $150,000. P Company's share of undistributed earnings is $127,500 (or 75% of $170,000), including $45,000 from year 2011 and $82,500 from year 2012. Therefore, the amount of total deferred tax liability at the end of the second year can be computed as follows:

Undistributed Income Expected to Be Received as Future Dividends

	Year 2011	*Year 2012*	*Total*
P Company's share of undistributed income expected to be received as dividends	$45,000	$82,500	$127,500
Percent of future dividends that are taxed	20%	20%	20%
Future dividends that will be taxed	$ 9,000	$16,500	$ 25,500
Tax rate	40%	40%	40%
Deferred tax liability	$ 3,600	$ 6,600	$ 10,200

The workpaper entry for the subsequent year is as follows:

Workpaper Entry—Cost Method—Year Subsequent to Acquisition (2012)		
Undistributed Income Expected to Be Received as Future Dividend		
Beginning Retained Earnings—P Company (prior year deferred taxes)	3,600	
Tax Expense (current year deferred taxes)	6,600	
Deferred Tax Liability		10,200

The debit to the beginning balance of P Company's retained earnings for each subsequent year reflects the sum of the debits from the ***prior year's*** deferred tax workpaper entry to tax expense and beginning retained earnings, if any. This is the estimated tax on P Company's share of the undistributed income of S Company from the date of acquisition to the beginning of the current year. If tax rates change, the adjustment to the deferred tax liability flows through the current deferred tax expense. Thus, the debit to beginning retained earnings is still the same as the credit made to the deferred tax liability in the prior year's workpaper.

Undistributed Income Is Expected To Be Realized When the Subsidiary Is Sold

If the undistributed income is not expected to be received as a future dividend but is expected to be realized when the investment is sold, the undistributed income is taxed at the capital gains rate as shown below:

Undistributed Income Expected to Be Received as Future Capital Gain

	Year 2011	*Year 2012*	*Total*
P Company's share of undistributed income expected to be realized in the future as a capital gain	$45,000	$82,500	$127,500
Capital Gains Tax rate	25%	25%	25%
Deferred tax liability	$11,250	$20,625	$ 31,875

Note that the 80% dividend exclusion is ignored. In addition, the appropriate tax rate to use is the capital gains tax rate.

The workpaper entries at the end of 2011 and 2012 to report the income tax consequences are as follows:

Workpaper Entry—Cost Method—Year of Acquisition and Year Subsequent to Acquisition (2011 and 2012)
Undistributed Income Expected to Be Received as Gain upon Sale of Subsidiary

Year 2011

Tax Expense	11,250	
Deferred Tax Liability		11,250

Year 2012

Beginning Retained Earnings 1/1—P Company (prior year)	11,250	
Income Tax Expense (current year)	20,625	
Deferred Tax Liability		31,875

A similar workpaper entry is needed every year.

The Partial and Complete Equity Methods—Separate Tax Returns

If the equity method is used to account for the investment, there is a timing difference between books and tax on the books of the parent. Equity income is reported on the parent's income statement while dividends are included on the tax return. Therefore, deferred taxes on the parent's books must reflect the amount of undistributed income in the subsidiary. Generally, the parent will only make deferred tax entries if less than 80% of the subsidiary is owned since there is a 100% dividend exclusion for higher ownership percentages (regardless of whether the undistributed income is expected to be realized as a dividend or as a capital gain).

Consider the following example. P Company owns 75% of the voting stock of S Company. The stock was acquired on January 1, 2011, when S Company's retained earnings amounted to $150,000. In the year of acquisition (2011), S Company reported net income of $90,000 and paid dividends of $30,000. Since P Company is filing a separate tax return, P Company's income earned from the investment reported on the tax return is not the equity income but the amount of dividends received, $22,500 (75% of S Company's dividends of $30,000).

However, on the consolidated income statement, 75% of S Company's income, or $67,500, is reported as equity income. Assume that the undistributed income of $45,000 (75% of $90,000 less $30,000) is expected to be paid as a future dividend and will be included on the tax return in some future years. Because the $45,000 is reported as current period equity income and is expected to be included on future tax returns when received either as a dividend or a capital gain, deferred taxes on this timing difference must be computed. If expected as a future dividend, the timing difference is computed after considering any dividend exclusion rules (80% excluded for 75% ownership). The current tax rate is assumed to be 40% and the capital gains tax rate to be 25%.

The entries on P Company's books for equity income and the receipt of dividends are as follows:

P Company Books—Partial and Complete Equity Methods		
Investment in S Company	67,500	
Equity in S Company Income		67,500
To record 75% of S Company income ($90,000).		
Cash	22,500	
Investment in S Company		22,500
To record the receipt of 75% of S Company's dividends paid ($30,000).		

Because P Company prepares its own tax return, the undistributed earnings of $45,000 (the $67,500 income less the dividends of $22,500) represents a timing difference. The following entry assumes that the undistributed income is expected to be received as a future dividend and only 20% is taxable (80% dividend exclusion). This entry adjusts tax expense and the deferred tax liability on P Company's books:

P Company Books—Partial and Complete Equity Methods		
Undistributed Income Expected to Be Received as a Future Dividend		
Tax expense (45,000 × .2 × .4)	3,600	
Deferred Tax Liability		3,600

Note that this entry is an adjustment of P Company's tax expense and not the equity income account. Because of this, no special workpaper entries are needed for deferred taxes if the equity method is used to account for the investment.

If the undistributed income is expected to be realized as a capital gain when the subsidiary is sold, the following entry would be made on P Company's books:

P Company Books—Partial and Complete Equity Methods		
Undistributed Income Expected to Be Received as a Capital Gain		
Tax Expense (45,000 × .25)	11,250	
Deferred Tax Liability		11,250

In this case, the 80% dividend exclusion is ignored. Because the entry is made on the books of P Company, again no workpaper entry is needed for deferred taxes in this instance under the equity method.

TEST YOUR KNOWLEDGE SOLUTIONS

4-1. 1. a. F
b. F
2. d
3. c

4-2. 1. c

4-3. 1. d

4-4. 1. b

QUESTIONS

(The letter A or B indicated for a question, exercise, or problem refers to a related appendix.)

LO1 1. How should nonconsolidated subsidiaries be reported in consolidated financial statements?

LO2 2. How are liquidating dividends treated on the books of an investor, assuming the investor uses the cost method? Assuming the investor uses the equity method?

LO5 3. How are dividends declared and paid by a subsidiary during the year eliminated in the consolidated workpapers under each method of accounting for investments?

LO2 4. How is the income reported by the subsidiary reflected on the books of the investor under each of the methods of accounting for investments?

LO2 5. Define: Consolidated net income; consolidated retained earnings.

LO5 6. At the date of an 80% acquisition, a subsidiary had common stock of $100,000 and retained earnings of $16,250. Seven years later, at December 31, 2010, the subsidiary's retained earnings had increased to $461,430. What adjustment will be made on the consolidated workpaper at December 31, 2011, to recognize the parent's share of the cumulative undistributed profits (losses) of its subsidiary? Under which method(s) is this adjustment needed? Why?

LO5 7. On a consolidated workpaper for a parent and its partially owned subsidiary, the noncontrolling interest column accumulates the noncontrolling interests' share of several account balances. What are these accounts?

LO5 8. If a parent company elects to use the partial equity method rather than the cost method to record its investments in subsidiaries, what effect will this choice have on the consolidated financial statements? If the parent company elects the complete equity method?

LO6 9. Describe two methods for treating the preacquisition revenue and expense items of a subsidiary purchased during a fiscal period.

LO1 10. A principal limitation of consolidated financial statements is their lack of separate financial information about the assets, liabilities, revenues, and expenses of the individual companies included in the consolidation. Identify some problems that the reader of consolidated financial statements would encounter as a result of this limitation.

LO7 11. In the preparation of a consolidated statement of cash flows, what adjustments are necessary because of the existence of a noncontrolling interest? *(AICPA adapted)*

LO9 12. What do potential voting rights refer to, and how do they affect the application of the equity method for investments under IFRS? Under U.S. GAAP? What is the term generally used for equity method investments under IFRS?

13B. Is the recognition of a deferred tax asset or deferred tax liability when allocating the difference between book value and the value implied by the purchase price affected by whether or not the affiliates file a consolidated income tax return? *(Appendix)*

14B. What assumptions must be made about the realization of undistributed subsidiary income when the affiliates file separate income tax returns? Why? *(Appendix)*

15B. The FASB elected to require that deferred tax effects relating to unrealized intercompany profits be calculated based on the income tax paid by the selling affiliate rather than on the future tax benefit to the purchasing affiliate. Describe circumstances where the amounts calculated under these approaches would be different. *(Appendix)*

16B. Identify two types of temporary differences that may arise in the consolidated financial statements when the affiliates file separate income tax returns. *(Appendix)*

Business Ethics

On April 5, 2006, the New York State Attorney sued a New York online advertising firm for surreptitiously installing spyware advertising programs on consumers' computers. The Attorney General claimed that consumers believed they were downloading free games or 'browser' enhancements.

The company claimed that the spyware was identified as 'advertising-supported' and that the software is easy to remove and doesn't collect personal data.

Is there an ethical issue for the company? Comment on and justify your position.

ANALYZING FINANCIAL STATEMENTS

AFS4-1 In the following table, General Electric's Balance Sheet from its 2005 annual report is shown. There are six columns of numbers. In the first two columns, GE's consolidated balance sheets for 2004 and 2005, respectively, are reported. The middle set of columns (listed under GE) represents GE's unconsolidated balance sheet, which treats all controlled subsidiaries as investments. Finally, the last two columns, listed under GECS (General Electric Credit Services), represent the balance sheet for GE's 100% owned subsidiary, GECS.

General Electric (GE) 2005 Balance Sheet

	Consolidated		*GE*		*GECS*	
Assets	*2005*	*2004*	*2005*	*2004*	*2005*	*2004*
Cash and equivalents	$ 9,011	$ 12,152	$ 2,015	$ 3,155	$ 7,316	$ 9,191
Investment securities	53,144	56,923	461	413	52,706	56,539
Current receivables	14,851	14,233	15,058	14,533		
Inventories	10,474	9,778	10,315	9,589	159	189
Financing receivables—net	287,639	282,699			287,639	282,699
Other GECS receivables	14,767	11,340			19,060	14,965
Property, plant and equipment—net	67,528	63,103	16,504	16,756	51,024	46,347
Investment in GECS			50,815	54,292		
Intangible assets—net	81,726	78,456	57,839	54,720	23,887	23,736
All other assets	87,446	89,557	36,752	38,123	52,058	52,572
Assets of discontinued operations	46,756	132,266			46,756	132,266
Total assets	$673,342	$750,507	$189,759	$191,581	$540,605	$618,504
Liabilities and Equity						
Short-term borrowings	$158,156	$157,195	$ 1,127	$ 3,409	$157,672	$154,292
Accounts payable, principally trade accounts	21,273	19,137	11,870	11,013	13,133	11,374
Progress collections and price adjustments accrued	4,456	3,937	4,456	3,937		
Dividends payable	2,623	2,329	2,623	2,329		
All other current costs and expenses accrued	18,419	17,539	18,436	17,569		
Long-term borrowings	212,281	207,871	9,081	7,625	204,397	201,209
Investment contracts, insurance liabilities, and insurance annuity benefits	45,432	48,076			45,722	48,393
All other liabilities	40,632	42,779	23,273	23,561	17,453	19,300
Deferred income taxes	16,330	15,285	3,733	3,616	12,597	11,669
Liabilities of and minority interest in discontinued operations	36,332	112,935			36,568	113,073
Total liabilities	555,934	627,083	74,599	73,059	487,542	559,310
Minority interest in equity of consolidated affiliates	8,054	12,603	5,806	7,701	2,248	4,902
Common stock (10,484,268,000 and 10,586,358,000 shares outstanding at year-end 2005 and 2004, respectively)	669	669	669	669	1	1
Accumulated gains (losses)—net						
Investment securities	1,831	2,268	1,831	2,268	1,754	2,345
Currency translation adjustments	2,532	6,850	2,532	6,850	2,287	5,104
Cash flow hedges	(822)	(1,223)	(822)	(1,223)	(813)	(1,354)
Minimum pension liabilities	(874)	(657)	(874)	(657)	(179)	(150)
Other capital	25,227	24,265	25,227	24,265	12,386	12,370
Retained earnings	98,117	91,411	98,117	91,411	35,379	35,976
Less common stock held in treasury	(17,326)	(12,762)	(17,326)	(12,762)		
Total shareowner' equity	109,354	110,821	109,354	110,821	50,815	54,292
Total liabilities and equity	$673,342	$750,507	$189,759	$191,581	$540,605	$618,504

Required:

A. Examine the middle set of columns showing GE's unconsolidated numbers. GE reports $50,815 as the investment in GECS. Which method does GE use to account for this investment, cost or equity method? Explain your answer.

B. Compare the consolidated totals for assets, liabilities, and equity to the totals for GE's numbers unconsolidated. Which totals are different between the consolidated and the unconsolidated numbers? Explain why some numbers are the same when consolidated and why some numbers are different.

C. The minority interest amount (FASB prefers the term noncontrolling interest) reported for 2005 on the consolidated statement is $8,054. Is any of this related to GECS? Explain your answer. Under the new exposure drafts, predict whether minority interest will increase, decrease, or stay the same (keep in mind that GE has a large amount of goodwill reported in intangible assets).

D. In addition to reporting the consolidated numbers, GE also reports separate information on GE and GECS. What do we learn from this increased disclosure beyond what we might learn if only the consolidated numbers were reported? Suppose that GE reported on GECS using the equity method and did not consolidate the subsidiary. Would this be misleading to the users of the financial statements? Why, or why not?

EXERCISES

EXERCISE 4-1 **Parent Company Entries, Liquidating Dividend** LO2

Percy Company purchased 80% of the outstanding voting shares of Song Company at the beginning of 2009 for $387,000. At the time of purchase, Song Company's total stockholders' equity amounted to $475,000. Income and dividend distributions for Song Company from 2009 through 2011 are as follows:

	2009	*2010*	*2011*
Net income (loss)	$63,500	$52,500	($55,000)
Dividend distribution	25,000	50,000	35,000

Required:

Prepare journal entries on the books of Percy Company from the date of purchase through 2011 to account for its investment in Song Company under each of the following assumptions:

A. Percy Company uses the cost method to record its investment.

B. Percy Company uses the partial equity method to record its investment.

C. Percy Company uses the complete equity method to record its investment. The difference between book value of equity acquired and the value implied by the purchase price was attributed solely to an excess of market over book values of depreciable assets, with a remaining life of 10 years.

EXERCISE 4-2 **Workpaper Eliminating Entries, Cost Method** LO5

Park Company purchased 90% of the stock of Salt Company on January 1, 2009, for $465,000, an amount equal to $15,000 in excess of the book value of equity acquired. This excess payment relates to an undervaluation of Salt Company's land. On the date of purchase, Salt Company's retained earnings balance was $50,000. The remainder of the stockholders' equity consists of no-par common stock. During 2013, Salt Company declared dividends in the amount of $10,000, and reported net income of $40,000. The retained earnings balance of Salt Company on December 31, 2012, was $160,000. Park Company uses the cost method to record its investment.

Required:

Prepare in general journal form the workpaper entries that would be made in the preparation of a consolidated statements workpaper on December 31, 2013.

EXERCISE 4-3 Workpaper Eliminating Entries, Equity Method LO5

At the beginning of 2009, Presidio Company purchased 95% of the common stock of Succo Company for $494,000. On that date, Succo Company's stockholders' equity consisted of the following:

Common stock	$300,000
Other contributed capital	100,000
Retained earnings	120,000
Total	$520,000

During 2017, Succo Company reported net income of $40,000 and distributed dividends in the amount of $19,000. Succo Company's retained earnings balance at the end of 2016 amounted to $160,000. Presidio Company uses the equity method.

Required:

Prepare in general journal form the workpaper entries necessary in the compilation of consolidated financial statements on December 31, 2017. Explain why the partial and complete equity methods would result in the same entries in this instance.

EXERCISE 4-4 Workpaper Eliminating Entries, Losses by Subsidiary LO5

Poco Company purchased 85% of the outstanding common stock of Serena Company on December 31, 2009, for $310,000 cash. On that date, Serena Company's stockholders' equity consisted of the following:

Common stock	$240,000
Other contributed capital	55,000
Retained earnings	50,000
	$345,000

During 2012, Serena Company distributed a dividend in the amount of $12,000 and at year-end reported a net loss of $10,000. During the time that Poco Company has held its investment in Serena Company, Serena Company's retained earnings balance has decreased $29,500 to a net balance of $20,500 after closing on December 31, 2012. Serena Company did not declare or distribute any dividends in 2010 or 2011. The difference between book value and the value implied by the purchase price relates to goodwill.

Required:

A. Assume that Poco Company uses the equity method. Prepare in general journal form the entries needed in the preparation of a consolidated statements workpaper on December 31, 2012. Explain why the partial and complete equity methods would result in the same entries in this instance.

B. Assume that Poco Company uses the cost method. Prepare in general journal form the entries needed in the preparation of a consolidated statements workpaper on December 31, 2012.

EXERCISE 4-5

Eliminating Entries, Noncontrolling Interest LO2

On January 1, 2009, Plate Company purchased a 90% interest in the common stock of Set Company for $650,000, an amount $20,000 in excess of the book value of equity acquired. The excess relates to the understatement of Set Company's land holdings.

Excerpts from the consolidated retained earnings section of the consolidated statements workpaper for the year ended December 31, 2009, follow:

	Set Company	*Consolidated Balances*
1/1/09 retained earnings	190,000	880,000
Net income from above	132,000	420,000
Dividends declared	(50,000)	(88,000)
12/31/09 retained earnings to the balance sheet	272,000	1,212,000

Set Company's stockholders' equity is composed of common stock and retained earnings only.

Required:

A. Prepare the eliminating entries required for the preparation of a consolidated statements workpaper on December 31, 2009, assuming the use of the cost method.

B. Prepare the eliminating entries required for the preparation of a consolidated statements workpaper on December 31, 2009, assuming the use of the equity method.

C. Determine the total noncontrolling interest that will be reported on the consolidated balance sheet on December 31, 2009. How does the noncontrolling interest differ between the cost method and the equity method?

EXERCISE 4-6

Parent Entries and Eliminating Entries, Equity Method, Year of Acquisition LO2 LO5

On January 1, 2009, Pert Company purchased 85% of the outstanding common stock of Sales Company for $350,000. On that date, Sales Company's stockholders' equity consisted of common stock, $100,000; other contributed capital, $40,000; and retained earnings, $140,000. Pert Company paid more than the book value of net assets acquired because the recorded cost of Sales Company's land was significantly less than its fair value.

During 2009 Sales Company earned $148,000 and declared and paid a $50,000 dividend. Pert Company used the partial equity method to record its investment in Sales Company.

Required:

A. Prepare the investment-related entries on Pert Company's books for 2009.

B. Prepare the workpaper eliminating entries for a workpaper on December 31, 2009.

EXERCISE 4-7

Equity Method, Year Subsequent to Acquisition LO2 LO5

Continue the situation in Exercise 4-6 and assume that during 2010 Sales Company earned $190,000 and declared and paid a $50,000 dividend.

Required:

A. Prepare the investment-related entries on Pert Company's books for 2010.

B. Prepare the workpaper eliminating entries for a workpaper on December 31, 2010.

EXERCISE 4-8 **Interim Purchase of Stock, Full-Year Reporting Alternative, Cost Method** LO6

On May 1, 2010, Peters Company purchased 80% of the common stock of Smith Company for $50,000. Additional data concerning these two companies for the years 2010 and 2011 are:

	2010		*2011*	
	Peters	*Smith*	*Peters*	*Smith*
Common stock	$100,000	$25,000	$100,000	$25,000
Other contributed capital	40,000	10,000	40,000	10,000
Retained earnings, 1/1	80,000	10,000	129,000	53,000
Net income (loss)	64,000	45,000	37,500	(5,000)
Cash dividends (11/30)	15,000	2,000	5,000	—0—

Any difference between book value and the value implied by the purchase price relates to Smith Company's land. Peters Company uses the cost method to record its investment.

Required:

A. Prepare the workpaper entries that would be made on a consolidated statements workpaper for the years ended December 31, 2010 and 2011 for Peters Company and its subsidiary, assuming that Smith Company's income is earned evenly throughout the year. (Use the full-year reporting alternative.)

B. Calculate consolidated net income and consolidated retained earnings for 2010 and 2011.

EXERCISE 4-9 **Interim Purchase, Partial-Year Reporting Alternative, Cost Method** LO6

Using the data presented in Exercise 4-8, prepare workpaper elimination entries for 2010 assuming use of the partial-year reporting alternative.

EXERCISE 4-10 **Interim Purchase, Partial-Year Reporting Alternative, Equity Method** LO2 LO6

On October 1, 2010, Para Company purchased 90% of the outstanding common stock of Star Company for $210,000. Additional data concerning Star Company for 2010 follows:

Common stock	$70,000
Other contributed capital	30,000
Retained earnings, 1/1	70,000
Net income	60,000
Dividends declared and paid (12/15)	10,000

Any difference between book value and the value implied by the purchase price relates to goodwill. Para Company uses the partial equity method to record its investment in Star Company.

Required:

A. Prepare on Para Company's books journal entries to record the investment-related activities for 2010.

B. Prepare workpaper eliminating entries for a workpaper on December 31, 2010. Star Company's net income is earned evenly throughout the year. (Use alternative two—the partial-year reporting alternative.)

C. Repeat part B, but use the full-year reporting alternative.

EXERCISE 4-11 **Cash Flow from Operations** LO7

A consolidated income statement and selected comparative consolidated balance sheet data for Palano Company and subsidiary follow:

Palano Company and Subsidiary
Consolidated Income Statement
for the Year Ended December 31, 2010

Sales		$701,000
Cost of sales		263,000
Gross profit		438,000
Operating expenses:		
Depreciation expense	$ 76,000	
Selling expenses	122,000	
Administrative expenses	85,000	283,000
Consolidated net income		155,000
Less noncontrolling interest in consolidated net income		38,750
Controlling interest in consolidated net income		$116,250

	December 31	
	2009	*2010*
Accounts receivable	$229,000	$318,000
Inventory	194,000	234,000
Prepaid selling expenses	26,000	30,000
Accounts payable	99,000	79,000
Accrued selling expenses	96,000	84,000
Accrued administrative expenses	56,000	39,000

Required:

Prepare the cash flow from operating activities section of a consolidated statement of cash flows assuming use of the:

A. Direct method.

B. Indirect method.

EXERCISE 4-12 **Allocation of Difference between Book Value and the Value Implied by the Purchase Price, Parent Company Entries, Three Methods** LO2 LO4 LO5

On January 1, 2012, Plutonium Corporation acquired 80% of the outstanding stock of Sulfurst Inc. for $268,000 cash. The following balance sheet shows Sulfurst Inc.'s book values immediately prior to acquisition, as well as the appraised values of its assets and liabilities by Plutonium's experts.

	Sulfurst Inc.'s Book Values	*Sulfurst Inc.'s Market Values*
Current assets	$ 90,000	$ 90,000
Property, plant & equipment:		
Land	80,000	100,000
Building & machinery (net)	170,000	170,000
Total assets	$340,000	
Total liabilities	$100,000	$100,000
Common stock, $5 par value	100,000	
Additional paid-in-capital	20,000	
Retained earnings	120,000	
Total liabilities and equities	$340,000	

Required:

A. Prepare a Computation and Allocation Schedule for the Difference between Book Value and the Value Implied by the Purchase Price.

B. Prepare the entry to be made on the books of Plutonium Corporation to record its investment in Sulfurst Inc.

Assume that during the first two years after acquisition of Sulfurst Inc., Sulfurst reports the following changes in its retained earnings:

Retained earnings, January 1, 2012	$120,000
Net income, 2012	40,000
Less: dividends, 2012	(24,000)
Net income, 2013	45,000
Less: dividends, 2013	(21,600)
Retained earnings, December 31, 2013	$159,400

C. Prepare journal entries under each of the following methods to record the information above on the books of Plutonium Corporation for the years 2012 and 2013, assuming that all depreciable assets have a remaining life of 20 years.

(1) Plutonium uses the cost method to account for its investment in Sulfurst.

(2) Plutonium uses the partial equity method to account for its investment in Sulfurst.

(3) Plutonium uses the complete equity method to account for its investment in Sulfurst.

EXERCISE 4-13 Subsidiary Loss LO5

The following accounts appeared in the separate financial statements at the end of 2014 for Pressing Inc. and its wholly-owned subsidiary, Stressing Inc. Stressing was acquired in 2009.

	Pressing Inc.	*Stressing Inc.*
Investment in subsidiary	660,000	
Dividends receivable	5,000	
Dividends payable	20,000	$5,000
Common stock	300,000	20,000
Additional paid-in-capital	500,000	380,000
Retained earnings, 12/31/14	500,000	260,000
Dividends declared	(75,000)	(24,000)
Equity in net loss of subsidiary	$(55,000)	
Retained earnings at 1/1/14	380,000	

Requsired:

1. How can you determine whether Pressing is using the cost or equity method to account for its investment in Stressing?
2. Compute controlling interest in consolidated income.
3. How much income did Pressing Inc. earn from its own independent operations?
4. Compute consolidated retained earnings at 12/31/14.
5. What are consolidated dividends?
6. Compute retained earnings at 1/1/14 for Stressing Inc.
7. Was there any difference between book value and the value implied by the purchase price at acquisition? Prepare workpaper entries needed at the end of 2014.
8. If Pressing used the cost method instead of the equity method, how would Pressing Inc's retained earnings change at the end of 2014? Describe in words.
9. If Pressing uses the cost method instead of the equity method, what workpaper entries would be required at the end of 2014? Describe in words.

EXERCISE 4-14 **Cash Flow Statement, Year of Acquisition** LO7

Badco Inc. purchased a 90% interest in Lazytoo Company for $600,000 cash on January 1, 2011. Any excess of implied over book value was attributed to depreciable assets with a 15-year remaining life (straight-line depreciation). To help pay for the acquisition, Badco issued $300,000, 20-year, 12% bonds at par value. Lazytoo's balance sheet on the date of acquisition was as follows:

Assets		*Liabilities and Equity*	
Cash	$ 10,000	Accrued payables	$ 90,000
Inventory	140,000	Bonds payable	100,000
Fixed assets (net)	540,000	Common stock ($10 par)	200,000
		Retained earnings	300,000
Total assets	$690,000	Total liabilities and equity	$690,000

Consolidated net income for 2011 was $155,889. Badco declared and paid dividends of $10,000 and Lazytoo declared and paid dividends of $5,000. There were no purchases or sales of property, plant, and equipment during the year.

At the end of 2011, the following information was also available:

	Badco Company 12/31/10		*Consolidated 12/31/11*	
	Debits	*Credits*	*Debits*	*Credits*
Cash	$ 390,000		$ 63,500	
Inventory	190,000		454,000	
Fixed Assets	750,000		1,385,555	
Accrued payables		150,000		111,000
Bonds payable		200,000		600,000
Noncontrolling interest				73,055
Common Stock, ($10 par)		200,000		200,000
Additional paid-in-capital		550,000		550,000
Retained earnings		230,000		369,000
Total	$1,330,000	$1,330,000	$1,903,055	$1,903,055

Required:

Prepare a consolidated statement of cash flows using the indirect method for Badco and its subsidiary for the year ended December 31, 2011.

EXERCISE 4-15B **Entries for Deferred Taxes from Undistributed Income, Cost and Equity (Appendix)**

On January 1, 2009, Plenty Company purchased a 70% interest in the common stock of Set Company for $650,000, an amount $20,000 in excess of the book value of equity acquired. The excess relates to the understatement of Set Company's land holdings.

Excerpts from both company's financial statements for the year ended December 31, 2009, follow:

	Set Company	*Plenty Company*
1/1/09 retained earnings	190,000	880,000
Income from independent operations	132,000	420,000
Dividends declared	(50,000)	(88,000)

Set Company's stockholders' equity is composed of common stock and retained earnings only. Both companies file separate tax returns, and the expected tax rate is 40%. The capital gains tax rate is 20%, and there is an 80% dividend exclusion rate.

Required:

A. Prepare the entry(s) needed at the end of 2009 to report the income tax consequences of undistributed income assuming the use of the cost method, under each of the following assumptions. Indicate whether the entry is recorded on the books of Set, Plenty, or worksheet only.

(1) Plenty expects the undistributed income will be realized in the form of future dividends.

(2) Plenty expects the undistributed income will be realized only when the stock is sold, in the form of capital gains.

B. Prepare the entry(s) needed at the end of 2009 to report the income tax consequences of undistributed income assuming the use of the partial equity method, under each of the following assumptions. Indicate whether the entry is recorded on the books of Set, Plenty, or worksheet only.

(1) Plenty expects the undistributed income will be realized in the form of future dividends.

(2) Plenty expects the undistributed income will be realized only when the stock is sold, in the form of capital gains.

C. Prepare the entry(s) needed at the end of 2009 to report the income tax consequences of undistributed income assuming the use of the complete equity method, under each of the following assumptions. Indicate whether the entry is recorded on the books of Set, Plenty, or worksheet only.

(1) Plenty expects the undistributed income will be realized in the form of future dividends.

(2) Plenty expects the undistributed income will be realized only when the stock is sold, in the form of capital gains.

PROBLEMS

PROBLEM 4-1 Parent Company Entries, Three Methods LO2

On January 1, 2009, Perelli Company purchased 90,000 of the 100,000 outstanding shares of common stock of Singer Company as a long-term investment. The purchase price of $4,972,000 was paid in cash. At the purchase date, the balance sheet of Singer Company included the following:

Current assets	$2,926,550
Long-term assets	3,894,530
Other assets	759,690
Current liabilities	1,557,542
Common stock, $20 par value	2,000,000
Other contributed capital	1,891,400
Retained earnings	1,621,000

Additional data on Singer Company for the four years following the purchase are:

	2009	*2010*	*2011*	*2012*
Net income (loss)	$1,997,800	$476,000	$(179,600)	$(323,800)
Cash dividends paid, 12/30	500,000	500,000	500,000	500,000

Required:

Prepare journal entries under each of the following methods to record the purchase and all investment-related subsequent events on the books of Perelli Company for the four years, assuming that any excess of purchase price over equity acquired was attributable solely to an excess of market over book values of depreciable assets (with a remaining life of 15 years). (Assume straight-line depreciation.)

A. Perelli uses the cost method to account for its investment in Singer.

B. Perelli uses the partial equity method to account for its investment in Singer.

C. Perelli uses the complete equity method to account for its investment in Singer.

PROBLEM 4-2 **Determine Method, Consolidated Workpaper, Wholly-Owned Subsidiary** LO5

Parry Corporation acquired a 100% interest in Sent Company on January 1, 2009, paying $140,000. Financial statement data for the two companies for the year ended December 31, 2009 follow:

Income Statement	*Parry*	*Sent*
Sales	$476,000	$154,500
Cost of goods sold	285,600	121,000
Other expense	45,500	29,500
Dividend income	3,500	—0—
Retained Earnings Statement		
Balance, 1/1	76,000	19,500
Net income	148,400	4,000
Dividends declared	17,500	3,500
Balance Sheet		
Cash	84,400	29,000
Accounts receivable	76,000	56,500
Inventory	49,500	36,500
Investment in Sent Company	140,000	—0—
Land	4,000	12,000
Accounts payable	27,000	14,000
Common stock	120,000	100,000
Retained earnings	206,900	20,000

Required:

A. What method is being used by Parry to account for its investment in Sent Company? How can you tell?

B. Prepare a workpaper for the preparation of consolidated financial statements on December 31, 2009. Any difference between the book value of equity acquired and the value implied by the purchase price relates to subsidiary land.

PROBLEM 4-3 **Consolidated Workpaper, Wholly-Owned Subsidiary**

Perkins Company acquired 100% of Schultz Company on January 1, 2010, for $161,500. On December 31, 2010, the companies prepared the following trial balances:

	Perkins	*Schultz*
Cash	$ 25,000	$ 30,000
Inventory	105,000	97,500
Investment in Schultz Company	222,000	—0—
Land	111,000	97,000
Cost of Goods Sold	225,000	59,500
Other Expense	40,000	40,000
Dividends Declared	15,000	10,000
Total Debits	$743,000	$334,000
Accounts Payable	$ 72,500	$ 17,500
Capital Stock	160,000	75,000
Other Contributed Capital	35,000	17,500
Retained Earnings, 1/1	25,000	54,000
Sales	380,000	170,000
Equity in Subsidiary Income	70,500	—0—
Total Credits	$743,000	$334,000

Required:

A. What method is being used by Perkins to account for its investment in Schultz Company? How can you tell?

B. Prepare a workpaper for the preparation of consolidated financial statements on December 31, 2010. Any difference between the book value of equity acquired and the value implied by the purchase price relates to goodwill.

PROBLEM 4-4 **Consolidated Workpaper, Partially-Owned Subsidiary, Cost Method** LO5

Place Company purchased 92% of the common stock of Shaw, Inc. on January 1, 2010, for $400,000. Trial balances at the end of 2010 for the companies were:

	Place	*Shaw*
Cash	$ 80,350	$ 87,000
Accounts and Notes Receivable	200,000	210,000
Inventory, 1/1	70,000	50,000
Investment in Shaw, Inc.	400,000	—0—
Plant Assets	300,000	200,000
Dividends Declared	35,000	22,000
Purchases	240,000	150,000
Selling Expenses	28,000	20,000
Other Expenses	15,000	13,000
	$1,368,350	$752,000
Accounts and Notes Payable	$ 99,110	$ 38,000
Other Liabilities	45,000	15,000
Common Stock, $10 par	150,000	100,000
Other Contributed Captital	279,000	149,000
Retained Earnings, 1/1	225,000	170,000
Sales	550,000	280,000
Dividend Income	20,240	—0—
	$1,368,350	$752,000

Inventory balances on December 31, 2010, were $25,000 for Place and $15,000 for Shaw, Inc. Shaw's accounts and notes payable contain a $15,000 note payable to Place.

Required:

Prepare a workpaper for the preparation of consolidated financial statements on December 31, 2010. The difference between book value of equity acquired and the value implied by the purchase price relates to subsidiary land, which is included in plant assets.

PROBLEM 4-5 **Consolidated Workpaper, Partially-Owned Subsidiary—Subsequent Years** LO5

On January 1, 2010, Perez Company purchased 90% of the capital stock of Sanchez Company for $85,000. Sanchez Company had capital stock of $70,000 and retained earnings of $12,000 at that time. On December 31, 2014, the trial balances of the two companies were:

	Perez	*Sanchez*
Cash	$ 13,000	$ 14,000
Accounts receivable	22,000	36,000
Inventory, 1/1	14,000	8,000
Advance to Sanchez Company	8,000	—0—
Investment in Sanchez Company	85,000	—0—
Plant and equipment	50,000	44,000
Land	17,800	6,000
Dividends declared	10,000	12,000
Purchases	84,000	20,000
Other expense	10,000	16,000
Total debits	$313,800	$156,000
Accounts payable	$ 6,000	$ 6,000
Other liabilities	37,000	—0—
Advance from Perez Company	—0—	8,000
Capital stock	100,000	70,000
Retained earnings	50,000	30,000
Sales	110,000	42,000
Dividend income	10,800	—0—
Total credits	$313,800	$156,000
Inventory, 12/31	$ 40,000	$ 15,000

Any difference between book value and the value implied by the purchase price relates to goodwill.

Required:

A. What method is being used by Perez to account for its investment in Sanchez Company? How can you tell?

B. Prepare a workpaper for the preparation of consolidated financial statements on 12/31/14.

PROBLEM 4-6 **Consolidated Workpaper, Partially-Owned Subsidiary—Subsequent Years** LO5

On January 1, 2009, Plank Company purchased 80% of the outstanding capital stock of Scoba Company for $53,000. At that time, Scoba's stockholders' equity consisted of capital stock, $55,000; other contributed capital, $5,000; and retained earnings, $4,000. On December 31, 2013, the two companies' trial balances were as follows:

	Plank	*Scoba*
Cash	$ 42,000	$ 22,000
Accounts Receivable	21,000	17,000
Inventory	15,000	8,000
Investment in Scoba Company	61,000	—0—
Land	52,000	48,000
Dividends Declared	10,000	8,000
Cost of Goods Sold	85,400	20,000
Other Expense	10,000	12,000
	$296,400	$135,000

	Plank	*Scoba*
Accounts Payable	$ 12,000	$ 6,000
Other Liabilities	5,000	4,000
Capital Stock	100,000	55,000
Other Contributed Capital	20,000	5,000
Retained Earnings, 1/1	40,000	15,000
Sales	105,000	50,000
Equity in Subsidiary Income	14,400	—0—
	$296,400	$135,000

The accounts payable of Scoba Company include $3,000 payable to Plank Company.

Required:

A. What method is being used by Plank to account for its investment in Scoba Company? How can you tell?

B. Prepare a consolidated statements workpaper at December 31, 2013. Any difference between book value and the value implied by the purchase price relates to subsidiary land.

PROBLEM 4-7 **Consolidated Workpaper, Partially-Owned Subsidiary—Subsequent Years, Cost Method** Price Company purchased 90% of the outstanding common stock of Score Company on January 1, 2009, for $450,000. At that time, Score Company had stockholders' equity consisting of common stock, $200,000; other contributed capital, $160,000; and retained earnings, $90,000. On December 31, 2013, trial balances for Price Company and Score Company were as follows:

	Price	*Score*
Cash	$ 109,000	$ 78,000
Accounts Receivable	166,000	94,000
Note Receivable	75,000	—0—
Inventory	309,000	158,000
Investment in Score Company	450,000	—0—
Plant and Equipment	940,000	420,000
Land	160,000	70,000
Dividends Declared	70,000	50,000
Cost of Goods Sold	822,000	242,000
Operating Expenses	250,500	124,000
Total Debits	$3,351,500	$1,236,000
Accounts Payable	$ 132,000	$ 46,000
Notes Payable	300,000	120,000
Common Stock	500,000	200,000
Other Contributed Capital	260,000	160,000
Retained Earnings, 1/1	687,000	210,000
Sales	1,420,000	500,000
Dividend and Interest Income	52,500	—0—
Total Credits	$3,351,500	$1,236,000

Price Company's note receivable is receivable from Score Company. Interest of $7,500 was paid by Score to Price during 2013. Any difference between book value and the value implied by the purchase price relates to goodwill.

Required:

Prepare a consolidated statements workpaper on December 31, 2013.

PROBLEM 4-8 **Consolidated Workpapers, Two Consecutive Years, Cost Method** LO5

On January 1, 2010, Parker Company purchased 95% of the outstanding common stock of Sid Company for $160,000. At that time, Sid's stockholders' equity consisted of common stock, $120,000; other contributed capital, $10,000; and retained earnings, $23,000. On December 31, 2010, the two companies' trial balances were as follows:

	Parker	*Sid*
Cash	$ 62,000	$ 30,000
Accounts Receivable	32,000	29,000
Inventory	30,000	16,000
Investment in Sid Company	160,000	—0—
Plant and Equipment	105,000	82,000
Land	29,000	34,000
Dividends Declared	20,000	20,000
Cost of Goods Sold	130,000	40,000
Operating Expenses	20,000	14,000
Total Debits	$588,000	$265,000
Accounts Payable	$ 19,000	$ 12,000
Other Liabilities	10,000	20,000
Common Stock	180,000	120,000
Other Contributed Capital	60,000	10,000
Retained Earnings, 1/1	40,000	23,000
Sales	260,000	80,000
Dividend Income	19,000	—0—
Total Credits	$588,000	$265,000

Required:

A. Prepare a consolidated statements workpaper on December 31, 2010.

B. Prepare a consolidated statements workpaper on December 31, 2011, assuming trial balances for Parker and Sid on that date were:

	Parker	*Sid*
Cash	$ 67,000	$ 16,000
Accounts Receivable	56,000	32,000
Inventory	38,000	48,500
Investment in Sid Company	160,000	—0—
Plant and Equipment	124,000	80,000
Land	29,000	34,000
Dividends Declared	20,000	20,000
Cost of Goods Sold	155,000	52,000
Operating Expenses	30,000	18,000
Total Debits	$679,000	$300,500
Accounts Payable	$ 16,000	$ 7,000
Other Liabilities	15,000	14,500
Common Stock	180,000	120,000
Other Contributed Capital	60,000	10,000
Retained Earnings, 1/1	149,000	29,000
Sales	240,000	120,000
Dividend Income	19,000	—0—
Total Credits	$679,000	$300,500

PROBLEM 4-9 **Consolidated Workpaper, Treasury Stock, Cost Method** LO5

December 31, 2012, trial balances for Pledge Company and its subsidiary Stom Company follow:

	Pledge	*Stom*
Cash and Marketable Securities	$ 184,600	$ 72,000
Receivables (net)	182,000	180,000
Inventory	214,000	212,000
Investment in Stom Company	300,000	—0—
Plant and Equipment (net)	309,000	301,000
Land	85,000	75,000
Cost of Goods Sold	460,000	185,000
Operating Expenses	225,000	65,000
Dividends Declared	50,000	30,000
Treasury Stock (10,000 shares at cost)	—0—	20,000
Total Debits	$2,009,600	$1,140,000
Accounts Payable	$ 96,000	$ 79,000
Accrued Expenses	31,000	18,000
Notes Payable	100,000	200,000
Common Stock, $1 par value	300,000	100,000
Other Contributed Capital	150,000	80,000
Retained Earnings, 1/1	422,000	320,000
Sales	880,000	340,000
Dividend and Interest Income	30,600	3,000
Total Credits	$2,009,600	$1,140,000

Pledge Company purchased 72,000 shares of Stom Company's common stock on January 1, 2009, for $300,000. On that date, Stom Company's stockholders' equity was as follows:

Common Stock, $1 par value	$100,000
Other Contributed Capital	80,000
Retained Earnings	160,000
Treasury Stock (10,000 shares at cost)	(20,000)
Total	$320,000

Additional information:

1. Receivables of Pledge Company include a $55,000, 12% note receivable from Stom Company.
2. Interest amounting to $6,600 has been accrued by each company on the note payable from Stom to Pledge. Stom Company has not yet paid this interest.
3. The difference between book value and the value implied by the purchase price relates to subsidiary land.

Required:

Prepare a consolidated statements workpaper for the year ended December 31, 2012.

PROBLEM 4-10 **Consolidated Workpaper, Equity Method** LO5

Poco Company purchased 80% of Solo Company's common stock on January 1, 2010, for $250,000. On December 31, 2010, the companies prepared the following trial balances:

	Poco	*Solo*
Cash	$ 161,500	$125,000
Inventory	210,000	195,000
Investment in Solo Company	402,000	—0—
Land	75,000	150,000
Cost of Goods Sold	410,000	125,000
Other Expense	100,000	80,000
Dividends Declared	30,000	15,000
Total Debits	$1,388,500	$690,000

	Poco	Solo
Accounts Payable	$ 154,500	$ 35,000
Common Stock	200,000	150,000
Other Contributed Capital	60,000	35,000
Retained Earnings, 1/1	50,000	60,000
Sales	760,000	410,000
Equity in Subsidiary Income	164,000	—0—
Total Credits	$1,388,500	$690,000

Required:

Prepare a consolidated statements workpaper on December 31, 2010. Any difference between book value and the value implied by the purchase price relates to goodwill.

PROBLEM 4-11 **Consolidated Workpaper, Equity Method** LO5

(Note that this is the same problem as Problem 4-7, but assuming the use of the partial equity method.)

Price Company purchased 90% of the outstanding common stock of Score Company on January 1, 2009, for $450,000. At that time, Score Company had stockholders' equity consisting of common stock, $200,000; other contributed capital, $160,000; and retained earnings, $90,000. On December 31, 2013, trial balances for Price Company and Score Company were as follows:

	Price	Score
Cash	$ 109,000	$ 78,000
Accounts Receivable	166,000	94,000
Note Receivable	75,000	—0—
Inventory	309,000	158,000
Investment in Score Company	633,600	—0—
Plant and Equipment	940,000	420,000
Land	160,000	70,000
Dividends Declared	70,000	50,000
Cost of Goods Sold	822,000	242,000
Operating Expenses	250,500	124,000
Total Debits	$3,535,100	$1,236,000
Accounts Payable	$ 132,000	$ 46,000
Notes Payable	300,000	120,000
Common Stock	500,000	200,000
Other Contributed Capital	260,000	160,000
Retained Earnings, 1/1	795,000	210,000
Sales	1,420,000	500,000
Equity in Subsidiary Income	120,600	—0—
Interest Income	7,500	—0—
Total Credits	$3,535,100	$1,236,000

Price Company's note receivable is receivable from Score Company. Interest of $7,500 was paid by Score to Price during 2013. Any difference between book value and the value implied by the purchase price relates to goodwill.

Required:

Prepare a consolidated statements workpaper on December 31, 2013.

PROBLEM 4-12 **Equity Method, Two Consecutive Years** LO5

On January 1, 2010, Parker Company purchased 90% of the outstanding common stock of Sid Company for $180,000. At that time, Sid's stockholders' equity consisted of common stock, $120,000; other contributed capital, $20,000; and retained earnings, $25,000. Assume that any difference between book value of equity and the value implied by the purchase price is attributable to land. On December 31, 2010, the two companies' trial balances were as follows:

	Parker	*Sid*
Cash	$ 65,000	$ 35,000
Accounts Receivable	40,000	30,000
Inventory	25,000	15,000
Investment in Sid Company	184,500	—0—
Plant and Equipment	110,000	85,000
Land	48,500	45,000
Dividends Declared	20,000	15,000
Cost of Goods Sold	150,000	60,000
Operating Expenses	35,000	15,000
Total Debits	$678,000	$300,000
Accounts Payable	$ 20,000	$ 15,000
Other Liabilities	15,000	25,000
Common Stock, par value $10	200,000	120,000
Other Contributed Capital	70,000	20,000
Retained Earnings, 1/1	55,000	25,000
Sales	300,000	95,000
Equity in Subsidiary Income	18,000	—0—
Total Credits	$678,000	$300,000

Required:

A. Prepare a consolidated statements workpaper on December 31, 2010.

B. Prepare a consolidated statements workpaper on December 31, 2011, assuming trial balances for Parker and Sid on that date were:

	Parker	*Sid*
Cash	$ 70,000	$ 20,000
Accounts Receivable	60,000	35,000
Inventory	40,000	30,000
Investment in Sid Company	193,500	—0—
Plant and Equipment	125,000	90,000
Land	48,500	45,000
Dividends Declared	20,000	15,000
Cost of Goods Sold	160,000	65,000
Operating Expenses	35,000	20,000
Total Debits	$752,000	$320,000
Accounts Payable	$ 16,500	$ 16,000
Other Liabilities	15,000	24,000
Common Stock, par value $10	200,000	120,000
Other Contributed Capital	70,000	20,000
Retained Earnings, 1/1	168,000	30,000
Sales	260,000	110,000
Equity in Subsidiary Income	22,500	—0—
Total Credits	$752,000	$320,000

PROBLEM 4-13 **Consolidated Workpaper, Treasury Stock, Equity Method** LO5

(Note that this problem is the same as Problem 4-9, but assuming the use of the partial equity method.)

December 31, 2012, trial balances for Pledge Company and its subsidiary Stom Company on the next page.

	Pledge	*Stom*
Cash and Marketable Securities	$ 184,600	$ 72,000
Receivables (net)	182,000	180,000
Inventory	214,000	212,000
Investment in Stom Company	478,400	—0—
Plant and Equipment (net)	309,000	301,000
Land	85,000	75,000
Cost of Goods Sold	460,000	185,000
Operating Expenses	225,000	65,000
Dividends Declared	50,000	30,000
Treasury Stock (10,000 shares at cost)	—0—	20,000
Total Debits	$2,188,000	$1,140,000
Accounts Payable	$ 96,000	$ 79,000
Accrued Expenses	31,000	18,000
Notes Payable	100,000	200,000
Common Stock, $1 par value	300,000	100,000
Other Contributed Capital	150,000	80,000
Retained Earnings, 1/1	550,000	320,000
Sales	880,000	340,000
Equity in Subsidiary Income	74,400	—0—
Interest Income	6,600	3,000
Total Credits	$2,188,000	$1,140,000

Pledge Company purchased 72,000 shares of Stom Company's common stock on January 1, 2009, for $300,000. On that date, Stom Company's stockholders' equity was as follows:

Common Stock, $1 par value	$100,000
Other Contributed Capital	80,000
Retained Earnings	160,000
Treasury Stock (10,000 shares at cost)	(20,000)
Total	$320,000

Other information:

1. Receivables of Pledge Company include a $55,000, 12% note receivable from Stom Company.
2. Interest amounting to $6,600 has been accrued by each company on the note payable from Stom to Pledge. Stom Company has not yet paid this interest.
3. The difference between book value and the value implied by the purchase price relates to subsidiary land.

Required:

Prepare a consolidated statements workpaper for the year ended December 31, 2012. Note that the percentage purchased is based on outstanding shares of Stom and not issued shares.

PROBLEM 4-14 Interim Purchase, Full Year Reporting Alternative, Cost Method LO6

Punca Company purchased 85% of the common stock of Surrano Company on July 1, 2010, for a cash payment of $590,000. December 31, 2010, trial balances for Punca and Surrano were:

	Punca	*Surrano*
Current Assets	$ 150,000	$ 180,000
Treasury Stock at Cost, 500 shares	—0—	48,000
Investment in Surrano Company	590,000	—0—
Property and Equipment	1,250,000	750,000
Cost of Goods Sold	1,540,000	759,000
Other Expenses	415,000	250,000
Dividends Declared	—0—	50,000
Total	$3,945,000	$2,037,000

Accounts and Notes Payable	$ 277,500	$ 150,000
Dividends Payable	—0—	50,000
Capital Stock, $5 par value	270,000	40,000
Other Contributed Capital	900,000	250,000
Retained Earnings, 1/1	355,000	241,000
Sales	2,100,000	1,300,000
Dividend Income	42,500	6,000
Total	$3,945,000	$2,037,000

Surrano Company declared a $50,000 cash dividend on December 20, 2010, payable on January 10, 2011, to stockholders of record on December 31, 2010. Punca Company recognized the dividend on its declaration date. Any difference between book value and the value implied by the purchase price relates to subsidiary land, included in property and equipment.

Required:

Prepare a consolidated statements workpaper at December 31, 2010, assuming that revenue and expense accounts of Surrano Company for the entire year are included with those of Punca Company. (Full-year reporting alternative.)

PROBLEM 4-15 **Interim Purchase, Partial-Year Reporting Alternative, Cost Method** LO6

Using the data given in Problem 4-14, prepare a workpaper for the preparation of consolidated financial statements at December 31, 2010, assuming that Surrano Company's revenue and expense accounts are included in the consolidated income statement from the date of acquisition only. (Partial-year reporting alternative.) (Round to the nearest dollar.)

PROBLEM 4-16 **Interim Purchase, Full-Year Reporting Alternative, Equity Method** LO6

Pillow Company purchased 90% of the common stock of Satin Company on May 1, 2009, for a cash payment of $474,000. December 31, 2009, trial balances for Pillow and Satin were:

	Pillow	*Satin*
Current Assets	$ 390,600	$ 179,200
Treasury Stock at Cost, 500 shares		32,000
Investment in Satin Company	510,000	—0—
Property and Equipment	1,334,000	562,000
Cost of Goods Sold	1,261,000	584,000
Other Expenses	484,000	242,000
Dividends Declared	—0—	60,000
Total	$3,979,600	$1,659,200
Accounts and Notes Payable	$ 270,240	$ 124,000
Dividends Payable		60,000
Capital Stock, $10 par value	1,000,000	200,000
Other Contributed Capital	364,000	90,000
Retained Earnings	315,360	209,200
Sales	1,940,000	976,000
Equity in Subsidiary Income	90,000	—0—
Total	$3,979,600	$1,659,200

Satin Company declared a $60,000 cash dividend on December 20, 2009, payable on January 10, 2010, to stockholders of record on December 31, 2009. Pillow Company recognized the dividend on its declaration date. Any difference between book value and the value implied by the purchase price relates to subsidiary land, included in property and equipment.

Required:

Prepare a consolidated statements workpaper at December 31, 2009, assuming that revenue and expense accounts of Satin Company for the entire year are included with those of Pillow Company. (Assume the full-year reporting alternative.)

PROBLEM 4-17 **Interim Purchase, Partial-Year Reporting Alternative, Equity Method** LO6

Using the data given in Problem 4-16, prepare a workpaper for the preparation of consolidated financial statements at December 31, 2009, assuming that Satin Company's revenue and expense accounts are included in the consolidated income statement from the date of acquisition only. (Assume the partial-year reporting alternative.) (Round to the nearest dollar.)

PROBLEM 4-18 **Consolidated Statement of Cash Flows, Indirect Method** LO8

A consolidated income statement for 2011 and comparative consolidated balance sheets for 2010 and 2011 for P Company and its 80% owned subsidiary follow:

P COMPANY AND SUBSIDIARY
Consolidated Income Statement
for the Year Ended December 31, 2011

Sales	$1,900,000
Cost of goods sold	1,000,000
Gross margin	900,000
Expenses	300,000
Operating income before tax	600,000
Dividend income	50,000
Income before tax	550,000
Income taxes	220,000
Consolidated net income	330,000
Less: Noncontrolling interest in consolidated net income	66,000
Controlling interest in consolidated net income	$ 264,000

P COMPANY
Consolidated Balance Sheets
December 31, 2010 and 2011

Assets	*2011*	*2010*
Cash	$ 250,000	$ 300,000
Accounts receivable	360,000	250,000
Inventories	210,000	190,000
Equipment (net)	950,000	500,000
Long-term investments	800,000	800,000
Goodwill	175,000	175,000
Total assets	$2,745,000	$2,215,000

P COMPANY
Consolidated Balance Sheets
December 31, 2010 and 2011

Liabilities and Equity	*2011*	*2010*
Accounts payable	$ 268,000	$ 500,000
Accrued payable	260,000	200,000
Bonds payable	200,000	—0—
Premium on bonds payable	40,000	—0—
Noncontrolling interest	148,000	90,000
Common stock, $1 par value	600,000	450,000
Other contributed capital	275,000	225,000
Retained earnings	954,000	750,000
Total equities	$2,745,000	$2,215,000

Other information:

1. Equipment depreciation was $95,000.
2. Equipment was purchased during the year for cash, $545,000.
3. Dividends paid during 2011:
   a. Declared and paid by S Company, $40,000.
   b. Declared and paid by P Company, $60,000.
4. The bonds payable were issued on December 30, 2011, for $240,000.
5. Common stock issued during 2011, 150,000 shares.

Required:

Prepare a consolidated statement of cash flows for the year ended December 31, 2011, using the indirect method.

PROBLEM 4-19 **Consolidated Statement of Cash Flows: Direct Method** LO7

The consolidated income statement for the year December 31, 2012, and comparative balance sheets for 2011 and 2012 for Parks Company and its 90% owned subsidiary SCR, Inc. are as follows:

PARKS COMPANY AND SUBSIDIARY
Consolidated Income Statement
for the Year Ended December 31, 2012

Sales		$239,000
Cost of goods sold		104,000
Gross margin		135,000
Depreciation expense	$27,000	
Other operating expenses	72,000	99,000
Income from operations		36,000
Investment income		4,500
Consolidated net income		40,500
Noncontrolling interest in consolidated net income		3,000
Controlling interest in consolidated net income		$37,500

PARKS COMPANY AND SUBSIDIARY
Consolidated Balance Sheets
December 31, 2011 and 2012

	2012	*2011*
Cash	$ 36,700	$ 16,000
Receivables	55,000	90,000
Inventory	126,000	92,000
Property, plant, and equipment (net of depreciation)	231,000	225,000
Long-term investment	39,000	39,000
Goodwill	60,000	60,000
Total assets	$547,700	$522,000

	2012	2011
Accounts payable	$ 67,500	$ 88,500
Accrued expenses	30,000	41,000
Bonds payable, due July 1, 2020	100,000	150,000
Total liabilities	197,500	279,500
Noncontrolling interest	32,200	30,000
Common stock	187,500	100,000
Retained earnings	130,500	112,500
Total stockholders' equity	318,000	212,500
Total equities	$547,700	$522,000

SCR, Inc. declared and paid an $8,000 dividend during 2012.

Required:

Prepare a consolidated statement of cash flows using the direct method.

5

ALLOCATION AND DEPRECIATION OF DIFFERENCES BETWEEN IMPLIED AND BOOK VALUES

LEARNING OBJECTIVES

1. Calculate the difference between implied and book values and allocate to the subsidiary's assets and liabilities.
2. Describe FASB's position on accounting for bargain acquisitions.
3. Explain how goodwill is measured at the time of the acquisition.
4. Describe how the allocation process differs if less than 100% of the subsidiary is acquired.
5. Record the entries needed on the parent's books to account for the investment under the three methods: the cost, the partial equity, and the complete equity methods.
6. Prepare workpapers for the year of acquisition and the year(s) subsequent to the acquisition, assuming that the parent accounts for the investment alternatively using the cost, the partial equity, and the complete equity methods.
7. Understand the allocation of the difference between implied and book values to long-term debt components.
8. Explain how to allocate the difference between implied and book values when some assets have fair values below book values.
9. Distinguish between recording the subsidiary depreciable assets at net versus gross fair values.
10. Understand the concept of push down accounting.

Investors in eBay are still trying to fully comprehend the company's decision to pay such a large premium to purchase Skype, the voice over internet protocol (VOIP) company which allows customers to make phone calls over the Internet. However, eBay executives only need to remind investors of its decision five years ago to purchase PayPal, a small online payments company, at a high premium as well. Adding this online payment capability to eBay's market proved to be a game-changing decision as PayPal has become a significant new source of revenue beyond eBay's traditional markets. Using this line of reasoning, executives at eBay say that Skype will give a buyer the ability to click on a link in an auction listing and instantly start a conversation over the phone with the seller, smoothing the transaction for everyone involved.[1]

For what reasons might a company need to pay a high premium to acquire a target?

When a company pays a large premium to consummate an acquisition, the allocation of that premium to the accounts in the balance sheet becomes a crucial issue under acquisition accounting rules. As they mature, the balance sheet accounts will impact the income statement via depreciation, cost of goods sold, impairment charges, and so on, affecting the patterns and trends in reported earnings for years to come. These effects on earnings provide incentives for firms to use creative means to avoid depressing future earnings. A popular technique used in past years was to charge large amounts to *in-process research and development* expense.

SFAS No. 142 [ASC 350] fundamentally changed the accounting for one particularly important balance sheet account—goodwill. As a result of this pronouncement by the FASB, goodwill is no longer amortized over a finite life. Instead, goodwill is carried indefinitely on the balance sheet, and the account is not adjusted unless an impairment exists. Reviews for potential impairment must be conducted at least once a year.

As a result, the common complaint from past years that acquisition or purchase accounting "drained" future earnings via the amortization of goodwill was replaced with other concerns. Instead of being expensed through the income statement via the amortization process, goodwill now remains on the balance sheet at the value determined as of the acquisition date, except when impairment is deemed to have occurred.

Further, the current standards of the FASB require that *in-process research and development (R&D)* acquired as part of a business combination must be capitalized, rather than expensed. Thus, the dynamics of the games companies are often accused of playing have shifted, and are continuing to shift, dramatically.

Europe's biggest defense contractor, BAE Systems PLC, said it reported a loss of 467 million pounds ($890 million) in 2004, largely due to a one-time charge reflecting its reduced appraisal of the value of companies it acquired as long as five years ago. BAE said the impairment charges, which totaled 1.04 billion pounds ($1.98 billion), were related to avionics and defense communications businesses that were acquired in 1999 as part of the Marconi Electronic Systems purchase and in its deal with Italy's Finmeccanica SpA to create Eurosystems, a defense electronic group. Other goodwill charges related to the Integrated Defense Solutions business in North America and BAE Systems' naval ships business.[2]

1. What might cause such a large decrease in the valuation of businesses purchased by BAE Systems?
2. What can BAE do in the future to avoid such large impairment charges?

---

[1] *Financial Times*, "eBay Looks to Skype Deal to Mirror PayPal's Success," by Kate MacKenzie, Paul Taylor, and Richard Waters, 9/13/05, p. 29.

[2] *Associated Press*, "BAE Systems Swings to Loss on Back of Large Goodwill Charges," by Jane Wardell, 2/24/05.

Opinions are mixed, however, as to how informative the goodwill impairment disclosures really are. One critic writes: "Even newly revised accounting standards don't adequately address the nature of knowledge-intensive enterprises . . . Analysts and management will discount the charge as an accounting rules change and largely ignore it."[3]

The ultimate impact of the changes in the accounting for R&D, goodwill, and other creative maneuvers has yet to be determined.

The sale of BlackRock, Inc. by PNC Financial Services Group could generate $3.2 billion in unrealized pretax gains resulting from the sale to Merrill Lynch & Co. PNC, which will own roughly 34% of BlackRock after the deal, must account for the holding based on BlackRock's book value, not its market value. This rule applies regardless of whether PNC consolidates the holding on its balance sheet, which it does now as a 70% owner, or uses the equity method of accounting, which will be the case after the deal closes. A new rule by FASB, however, allows PNC to choose to value its holding based on market value when using the equity method. If PNC chooses this valuation method, it will see a pretax gain of $3.2 billion based on BlackRock's current share price. However, using this method presents bookkeeping headaches as the value of the holding would have to be adjusted regularly.[4]

1. What consequences could PNC face by adjusting the value of its holding in BlackRock on a quarterly basis?
2. How would you recommend PNC account for its holding? Discuss advantages and disadvantages of consolidating the financial statements versus reporting the investment using the equity method.

In the preceding chapter, it was often assumed that any difference between implied and book values of the subsidiary's equity was entirely attributable to the under or overvaluation of land, a nonamortizable asset, on the books of the subsidiary. This chapter focuses on a more complex and realistic allocation of the difference to various assets and liabilities in the consolidated balance sheet, and the depreciation or amortization of the difference in the consolidated income statement. In the following pages, we first provide examples of the allocation of the difference between implied and book values ***on the acquisition date.*** We next extend the examples to deal with the ***subsequent*** effects on the consolidated financial statements under the three methods of accounting for investments that we reviewed in Chapter 4.

ALLOCATION OF THE DIFFERENCE BETWEEN IMPLIED AND BOOK VALUES TO ASSETS AND LIABILITIES OF SUBSIDIARY: ACQUISITION DATE

LO1 Computation and Allocation of Difference (CAD).

When consolidated financial statements are prepared, asset and liability values must be adjusted by allocating the difference between implied and book values to specific

[3] "AOL's Charge Shows Accounting Standards Have Dubious Value," by Nigel Rayner, *www.gartner.com,* 1/14/02.

[4] *WSJ,* "PNC's Gain in Merrill-BlackRock Deal May Grow," David Reilly, 2/22/06, p. C3.

recorded or unrecorded tangible and intangible assets and liabilities. In the case of a **wholly owned** subsidiary, the implied value of the subsidiary equals the acquisition price. The following two steps are taken.

LO3 Measurement of goodwill.

a. *Step One*: The difference between the implied value and book value is used first to adjust the individual assets and liabilities to their fair values on the date of acquisition.

b. *Step Two*: If, after adjusting identifiable assets and liabilities to fair values, a residual amount of difference remains, it is treated as follows:

 1. When the implied value exceeds the aggregate fair values of *identifiable** assets less liabilities, the residual amount will be *positive* (a debit balance). A positive residual difference is evidence of an unspecified intangible and is accounted for as goodwill.
 2. When the implied value is below the aggregate fair value of identifiable assets less liabilities, the residual amount will be negative (a credit balance). A negative residual difference is evidence of a bargain purchase, with the difference between acquisition cost and fair value designating the amount of the bargain.** When a bargain acquisition occurs, some of the acquired assets have, in the past, been reduced below their fair values (as reflected after step 1). However, under *FASB Statement No. 141R*,"Business Combinations," [ASC 805–30–25–2], the negative (or credit) balance should be recognized as an ordinary gain in the year of acquisition. Under this standard, no assets should be recorded below their fair values.

* The term identifiable refers to all assets and liabilities (that are recorded under GAAP) except goodwill.

** Note that the following situation is possible and, technically, would be a bargain purchase: FV (of identifiable Net Assets) > Implied Value > BV. Because the fair value is higher than the value implied by the purchase price, the bargain acquisition rules apply, even though the implied value is higher than the book value of the underlying equity. In practice, this situation is less likely to be referred to as a "bargain" than the situation where BV > FV > Implied Value. Nonetheless it is the comparison between FV and Implied Value that determines a bargain, regardless of the level of BV (book value).

LO2 Current and proposed treatment of bargain acquisitions.

A true bargain is not likely to occur except in situations where nonquantitative factors play a role; for example, a closely held company wishes to sell quickly because of the health of a family member.

For *historical* acquisitions only, we next present the **Bargain Rules** under ***prior GAAP*** (before the 2007 standard): (1) Current assets, long-term investments in marketable securities (other than those accounted for by the equity method), assets to be disposed of by sale, deferred tax assets, prepaid assets relating to pension or other postretirement benefit plans, and assumed liabilities were always recorded at fair market value. (2) Any previously recorded goodwill on the seller's books was eliminated (and no new goodwill was recorded). (3) Long-lived assets (including in-process research and development and excluding those specified in (1) above) were recorded at fair market value minus an adjustment for the bargain. (4) An extraordinary gain was recorded only in the event that all long-lived assets (other than those specified in (1) above) were reduced to zero (or to the noncontrolling portion, rather than zero, if the subsidiary was not wholly owned).

When needed, the reduction of noncurrent assets (with the exceptions noted above) was made in proportion to their fair values in determining their assigned values. **However, to reiterate, current GAAP eliminates the above rules and requires an ordinary gain to be recognized instead.**

Acquisitions leading to the recording of goodwill have been far more common in recent years than bargain acquisitions. The impact of goodwill on future earnings has drawn a great deal of attention, with standard setters ultimately lightening the burden by no longer requiring the amortization of goodwill. Other acquired intangibles with ***finite*** useful lives, such as franchises, patents, and software, must still be amortized over their estimated useful lives. The examples presented in this chapter focus primarily on depreciable assets and goodwill. Note, however, that other identified intangibles with finite lives would be accounted for in the same manner as depreciable assets, with the term **amortization expense** replacing the term **depreciation expense**.

Two decades ago the FASB required that R&D incurred in the regular course of business be expensed, and the Board subsequently interpreted the standard to allow the expensing of certain types of R&D transferred in corporate acquisitions. The Board went on to state that the R&D expense, or write-off, amount would be based on the amount paid by the acquiring firm rather than its historical cost to the acquired firm. By allocating large amounts to R&D in the period of the acquisition, firms have sometimes taken a large one-time hit to earnings but avoid an increased asset base (e.g., for return on asset calculations). This practice became increasingly popular in the late 1990s among high-technology firms, drawing the attention of the SEC and causing the firms to complain that they were being singled out for scrutiny. As stated previously, the current *FASB* position on business combinations requires that in-process R&D acquired should be recorded as an asset and amortized over the period of expected benefit.

The SEC was not inclined to sympathize. Agency officials said they were more aggressively enforcing rules that have been in place since 1975. "As the number of companies claiming larger [in-process R&D] write-offs increased in early 1998, we began to dig deeper into the company's appraisal assumptions," said SEC Chief Accountant Lynn Turner. At issue is the size of write-offs that companies take for the premiums they pay when acquiring other companies, particularly high-tech companies. Buyers of technology have capitalized on a rule that lets them take a large one-time write-off for the value of as-yet-undeveloped products they pick up. In addition to reducing the asset base, the buyers could also avoid incurring repeated small charges (depreciation, amortization, or potential impairment losses) that can depress earnings for years.[5]

Case 1: Implied Value "in Excess of" Fair Value of Identifiable Net Assets of a Subsidiary

To illustrate the allocation of the difference between implied and book values to individual assets and liabilities of a subsidiary, assume that on January 1, 2011, S Company has capital stock and retained earnings of $1,500,000 and $500,000, respectively, and identifiable assets and liabilities as presented in Illustration 5-1.

[5] *WSJ*, "High-Tech Firms Upset over SEC Crackdown," by Michael Schroeder, 2/1/99, p. B4.

ILLUSTRATION 5-1

Identifiable Assets and Liabilities of S Company—January 1, 2011

	Fair Value	*Book Value*	*Difference between Fair Value and Book Value*
Inventory	$ 350,000	$ 300,000	$ 50,000
Other Current Assets	450,000	450,000	—0—
Equipment (net)	600,000	300,000	300,000
Land	400,000	250,000	150,000
Other Noncurrent Assets	1,000,000	1,000,000	—0—
Liabilities	(300,000)	(300,000)	—0—
Identifiable Net Assets	$2,500,000	$2,000,000	$500,000

Adjustment of Assets and Liabilities: Wholly Owned Subsidiaries Assume further that P Company acquires a 100% interest in S Company on January 1, 2011, for $2,750,000. The Computation and Allocation Schedule would appear as follows:

Computation and Allocation of Difference between Implied and Book Values

Cost (purchase price)/100% = Implied Value	$2,750,000
Book value of equity	2,000,000
Difference between implied and book value	750,000
Adjust to fair value	
Inventory (assume FIFO)	(50,000)
Equipment (with remaining life of 10 years)	(300,000)
Land	(150,000)
Balance	250,000
Record goodwill	250,000
Balance	$ 0

The consolidated statements workpaper entry to eliminate the investment balance on January 1, 2011, will result in a debit to Difference between Implied and Book Value in the amount of $750,000 as follows:

Capital Stock—S Company	1,500,000	
Retained Earnings—S Company	500,000	
Difference between Implied and Book Value	750,000	
Investment in S Company		2,750,000

Referring to the Computation and Allocation (CAD) Schedule, the workpaper entry to allocate the difference between implied and book value to specific consolidated assets takes the following form:

Inventory	50,000	
Equipment (net)	300,000	
Land	150,000	
Goodwill	250,000	
Difference between Implied and Book Value		750,000

The amount of the difference between implied and book values that is not allocated to specific identifiable assets and liabilities of the subsidiary is recognized as goodwill. As defined earlier, goodwill is the excess of implied value over the ***fair value*** of the identifiable net assets of the subsidiary on the acquisition date [$2,750,000 − $2,500,000 = $250,000].

LO4 Allocation of difference in a partially owned subsidiary.

Adjustment of Assets and Liabilities: Less than Wholly Owned Subsidiaries When P Company exchanges $2,750,000 for a 100% interest in S Company, the implication is that the fair value of the net assets, ***including unspecified intangible assets***, of S Company is $2,750,000. As illustrated earlier, if the recorded book value of those net assets is $2,000,000, adjustments totaling $750,000 are made to specific assets and liabilities, including goodwill, in the consolidated financial statements, serving to recognize the total implied fair value of the subsidiary assets and liabilities.

Assume now that rather than acquiring a 100% interest for $2,750,000, P Company pays $2,200,000 for an 80% interest in S Company. The fair value of the net assets, including unspecified intangible assets, of S Company implied by this transaction is still $2,750,000 ($2,200,000/.80), and the implication remains that the net assets, including unspecified intangible assets, of S Company are understated by $750,000. In the case of a less than wholly owned subsidiary, prior GAAP and practice have restricted the write-up of the net assets of S Company in the consolidated financial statements to the extent of P's acquisition percentage. Current GAAP (***FASB Statement No. 141R and No. 160*** **[ASC 805 and 810]**), however, differ markedly, and require that here too the consolidated net assets should be reflected at their entire fair value.

To illustrate the existence of a noncontrolling interest in the context of, first, a ***positive*** difference between implied and book value and, later, a **negative** difference, refer again to Illustration 5-1.

Assume first that P Company acquires an 80% interest in S Company for $2,200,000. The Computation and Allocation (CAD) Schedule is prepared in Illustration 5-2. The implied value is $2,200,000/80% = $2,750,000.

ILLUSTRATION 5-2

Computation and Allocation of the Difference between Implied and Book Value
Excess of Implied over Fair Value

	Parent Share	*Noncontrolling Share*	*Entire Value*
Purchase Price and Implied Value	**$2,200,000**	**$550,000**	$2,750,000
Book Value of Equity Acquired	1,600,000	400,000	**2,000,000**
Difference between Implied and Book Value	$ 600,000	150,000	**750,000**
Adjust to Fair Value			
Inventory, FIFO Method	$ (40,000)	$(10,000)	**$ (50,000)**
Equipment—net, 10-year life	(240,000)	(60,000)	**(300,000)**
Land	(120,000)	(30,000)	**(150,000)**
Balance (Excess of Implied over Fair Value)	$ 200,000	$ 50,000	$ 250,000
Goodwill	(200,000)	(50,000)	**(250,000)**
Balance	$ —0—	$ —0—	$ —0—

RELATED CONCEPTS

The characteristic of *consistency* suggests that the inventory be written up for the entire difference of $50,000 (see Illustrations 5-1 and 5-2), even if the percentage acquired is less than 100%. *Otherwise* the NCI remains at book value while the controlling share is adjusted to fair value.

In this case, goodwill is equal to the excess of implied value over the fair value of the identifiable net assets of the subsidiary [$2,750,000−$2,500,000 = $250,000]. The following entries have made to eliminate the investment, to recognize the noncontrolling interest (NCI) in equity, and to allocate the difference between implied and book values are worksheet-only entries:

Retained Earnings—S Company	500,000	
Capital Stock—S Company	1,500,000	
Difference between Implied and Book Value	750,000	
Investment in S Company		2,200,000
Noncontrolling Interest in Equity		550,000

Referring to the Computation and Allocation Schedule, the workpaper entry to allocate the difference between implied and book value is:

Inventory	50,000	
Equipment (net)	300,000	
Land	150,000	
Goodwill	250,000	
Difference between Implied and Book Value		750,000

These amounts are all found in the right-hand column of the CAD Schedule.

Case 2: Acquisition Cost "Less Than" Fair Value of Identifiable Net Assets of a Subsidiary

Less than Wholly Owned Subsidiaries Refer to Illustration 5-1 and assume that P Company acquires an 80% interest in S Company for $1,900,000. The implied value of S is $1,900,000/80% = $2,375,000. The difference between *implied* and *book value* is $375,000 [$2,375,000−$2,000,000]. However, the ***fair value*** of the identifiable net assets of the subsidiary ($2,500,000) exceeds the implied value of $2,375,000 by $125,000. The Computation and Allocation Schedule is started as usual, but a negative balance requires the recording of a gain after adjusting the identifiable assets and liabilities to their fair values. The gain represents the initial difference between implied and book values of $375,000 minus the adjustments to net assets of $500,000, or $125,000. The gain is allocated between the noncontrolling and controlling interests in the consolidated entity. As in all CAD schedules in the text, the items in bold represent workpaper entry amounts.

LO4 CAD Schedule for less than wholly owned subsidiary.

Computation and Allocation of Difference Schedule

	Parent Share	*Noncontrolling Share*	*Entire Value*
Purchase price and implied value	**$1,900,000**	**475,000**	2,375,000
Less: Book value of equity acquired	1,600,000	400,000	**2,000,000***
Difference between implied and book value	300,000	75,000	**375,000**
Inventory	(40,000)	(10,000)	**(50,000)**
Equipment	(240,000)	(60,000)	**(300,000)**
Land	(120,000)	(30,000)	**(150,000)**
Balance (excess of FV over implied value)	(100,000)	(25,000)	(125,000)
P's gain	**100,000**		
Increase noncontrolling interest to fair value of assets		**25,000**	
Total allocated bargain			125,000
Balance	—0—	—0—	—0—

*In the workpaper, this is decomposed into Capital Stock and Retained Earnings.

Note that the amounts in bold in parentheses in the Computation and Allocation Schedule require debits in the workpaper entry (to increase assets/decrease liabilities).

The workpaper entries to eliminate the investment account and to allocate the difference between implied and book values may be summarized in general journal form as follows:

Retained Earnings—S Company	500,000	
Capital Stock—S Company	1,500,000	
Difference between Implied and Book Value	375,000	
Investment in S Company		1,900,000
Noncontrolling Interest in Equity (NCI)		475,000
Inventory	50,000	
Equipment (net)	300,000	
Land	150,000	
Gain on Acquisition (income statement account)		100,000
Noncontrolling Interest in Equity		25,000
Difference between Implied and Book Value		375,000

Implied Value Less than Book Value Less than Fair Value of Identifiable Net Assets
It is possible for the value implied by the parent's acquisition cost to be less than the book value as well as the fair value of the net assets of the subsidiary. In that case, the difference between implied and book value initially will be credited in the investment elimination workpaper entry. The analysis of the allocation of this credit balance, however, takes the same form as that just illustrated; that is, we begin by adjusting assets upward first and then determine the necessary gain recognition. For example, refer to Illustration 5-1 and assume that P Company acquired an 80% interest in S Company on January 1, 2011, for $1,500,000. See Illustration 5-3.

ILLUSTRATION 5-3

Computation & Allocation of the Difference between Implied and Book Value (Book Value of Interest Acquired Exceeds Implied Value)

	Parent Share	*Noncontrolling Share*	*Entire Value*
Purchase Price and Implied Value	**$1,500,000**	**375,000**	1,875,000
Book Value of Equity	1,600,000	400,000	**2,000,000**
Difference between Implied and Book Value	$ (100,000)	$ (25,000)	$(125,000)
Inventory	$ (40,000)	$ (10,000)	**$ (50,000)**
Equipment (net)	(240,000)	(60,000)	**(300,000)**
Land	(120,000)	(30,000)	**(150,000)**
Balance (Excess of FV over implied value)	$ (500,000)	$(125,000)	$(625,000)
Gain on Acquisition	**500,000**		
Increase Noncontrolling Interest to FV		**$ 125,000**	
Total Allocated Bargain			$ 625,000
	$ —0—	$ —0—	$ —0—

The workpaper entries to eliminate the investment account and to allocate the difference between implied and book values are presented next in general journal form.

Capital Stock—S Company	1,500,000	
Retained Earnings—S Company	500,000	
Difference between Implied and Book Value		125,000
Investment in S Company		1,500,000
Noncontrolling Interest in Equity (NCI) (.2) ($1,875,000)		375,000

Difference between Implied and Book Value	125,000	
Inventory	50,000	
Equipment (net)	300,000	
Land	150,000	
Gain on Acquisition (income statement account)		500,000
Noncontrolling Interest in Equity		125,000

EFFECT OF ALLOCATION AND DEPRECIATION OF DIFFERENCES BETWEEN IMPLIED AND BOOK VALUES ON CONSOLIDATED NET INCOME: YEAR SUBSEQUENT TO ACQUISITION

Depreciation and amortization in the consolidated income statement should be based on the values allocated to depreciable and amortizable assets in the consolidated balance sheet. When any portion of the difference between implied and book values is allocated to such assets, recorded income must be adjusted in determining consolidated net income in current and future periods. ***This adjustment is needed to reflect the difference between the amount of amortization and/or depreciation recorded by the subsidiary and the appropriate amount based on consolidated carrying values.***

To illustrate, assume that on January 1, 2011, P Company acquires an 80% interest in S Company for $2,200,000, at which time S Company has net assets of $2,000,000 as presented in Illustration 5-1. As previously shown in Illustration 5-2, the implied value of S is $2,200,000/80%, or $2,750,000. The difference between implied and book values in the amount of $750,000 is allocated as follows:

Inventory	$ 50,000
Equipment (net)	300,000
Land	150,000
Goodwill	250,000
Difference between Implied and Book Value	$750,000

A comparison of the recorded and consolidated carrying values of the assets and liabilities of S Company on January 1, 2011, is presented in Illustration 5-4.

ILLUSTRATION 5-4

Comparison of Consolidated and Recorded Carrying Values of Net Assets of S Company, January 1, 2011

	Carrying Value in S Company's Books (Illustration 5-1)	*Allocation of Difference between Implied and Book Value*	*Consolidated Carrying Value*
Inventory	$ 300,000	$ 50,000	$ 350,000
Equipment (net)	300,000	300,000	600,000
Land	250,000	150,000	400,000
Goodwill (excess of implied over fair values)	—0—	250,000	250,000
Other Assets and Liabilities (net)	1,150,000	—0—	1,150,000
Net Assets	$2,000,000	$750,000	$2,750,000

Assume now that all the inventory is sold during 2011 and that the equipment has a remaining life of 10 years from January 1, 2011. Adjustments in the computation of consolidated net income that result from the allocation, amortization, and depreciation of the differences between implied and book values are summarized in Illustration 5-5.

ILLUSTRATION 5-5

Adjustments in Determination of Consolidated Net Income Resulting from Allocation, Amortization, and Depreciation of the Difference between Implied and Book Value

		Annual Adjustment in Determining Consolidated Net Income		
	Difference between Implied and Book Value	*2011*	*2012–2020*	*2021–2030*
Inventory	$ 50,000	$50,000	$ —0—	$ —0—
Equipment (net)	300,000	30,000	30,000	—0—
Land	150,000	—0—	—0—	—0—
Goodwill	250,000	—0—	—0—	—0—
Total	$750,000	$80,000	$30,000	$ —

Note: Inventory is expensed in 2011 assuming the FIFO method and equipment are depreciated over 10 years.

As a result of the sale of the inventory in 2011, S Company will include $300,000 in cost of goods sold, whereas from a consolidated point of view the cost of goods sold should be $350,000 (inventory from Illustration 5-4). Hence, the recorded cost of goods sold must be increased by $50,000 in determining consolidated net income in 2011. This adjustment to cost of goods sold is necessary only in the year(s) the inventory is sold.

S Company will record on its books $30,000 ($300,000/10 years) in depreciation of the equipment each year. Consolidated annual depreciation, however, should be $60,000 ($600,000/10 years). Accordingly, depreciation expense must be increased each year by $30,000 in determining consolidated net income. Note that this amount may be computed directly from the Calculation and Allocation Schedule simply by dividing the adjustment to Equipment ($300,000) by the remaining life (10 years).

Goodwill arising in the acquisition is not recorded by S Company. ***It remains in the consolidated balance sheet indefinitely, and it is adjusted only in the event of impairment.*** In the event of impairment, an adjustment to recorded income would be needed to determine consolidated net income. The allocation of a portion of the difference between implied and book values to land does not require an adjustment to recorded income in determining consolidated net income until it is sold, since land is not a depreciable (or amortizable) asset.

The worksheet entries needed to ensure that all balance sheet and income statement accounts reflect the correct consolidated balances differ depending on which method the parent company uses to account for its investment: complete equity, partial equity, or cost. The correct consolidated balances will not differ, but the means of arriving at them will. Thus, after the worksheet entries are made, the resulting balances should be identical under the three methods.

Much of the consolidating process is the same for all three methods, but important differences exist. Each of the following stand-alone sections presents the entire process, including an impairment loss on goodwill in one year. For those who are interested in focusing on only one or two of the three methods, the other sections may be omitted without loss of continuity. To facilitate this choice, icons in the margin of the pages are used to distinguish between the cost and equity methods when needed. To distinguish between partial and complete equity, separate icons are used. First, however, it is worth noting that ***only three basic accounts are reported differently in the books of the parent.*** A brief review of the entries made by the parent under the three methods (see opening of Chapter 4) reveals two of these accounts: the ***investment account*** itself and the ***income recognized from the subsidiary*** (dividend income or equity in subsidiary income). Since the amount of income recognized from the subsidiary is added into the retained earnings of the parent each year, it follows that the third important account that differs among these methods is the ***retained earnings of the parent.*** To further facilitate an understanding of the differences among the methods, or to aid in skipping redundant sections, we present the cost method first and then we present the sections of the text that *differ* depending on the method choice in blue for the equity methods.

Under all three methods, the worksheet entries will separate current year effects from the effects of the previous years because the current year income statement accounts are open and need to be reported separately and correctly. Hence, worksheet entries to retained earnings (and to the noncontrolling interest in net assets) will always adjust the balance at the ***beginning*** of the current year (or the date of acquisition, if it is the first year) under the cost and partial equity methods. Under the complete equity method, beginning retained earnings of the parent is the same as beginning consolidated retained earnings and therefore needs no adjustment (the noncontrolling interest in equity still requires adjustment). Figures 5-1 through 5-3 present three years of entries for a parent company and for a consolidating worksheet under all three methods. In the following sections, we explain these entries in detail.

FIGURE 5-1
Cost Method
Three Year Summary

Entries on P's Books

	Year 2011		*Year 2012*		*Year 2013*	
Investment in S	2,200,000					
Cash		2,200,000				
Cash	16,000		48,000		60,000	
Dividend Income		16,000		48,000		60,000

Entries on the Worksheet

	Year 2011		*Year 2012*		*Year 2013*	
Dividend Income	16,000		48,000		60,000	
Dividends Declared		16,000		48,000		60,000
Investment in S			84,000		148,000	
Beginning Retained Earnings—P				84,000		148,000
Beginning Retained Earnings—S	500,000		605,000		685,000	
Common Stock—S	1,500,000		1,500,000		1,500,000	
Difference between Implied and Book Value	750,000		750,000		750,000	
Investment in S		2,200,000		2,284,000		2,348,000
Noncontrolling Interest		550,000		571,000		587,000
Cost of Goods Sold	50,000					
Beginning Retained Earnings—P			40,000		40,000	
Noncontrolling Interest			10,000		10,000	
Equipment	300,000		300,000		300,000	
Land	150,000		150,000		150,000	
Goodwill	250,000		250,000		250,000	
Difference between Implied and Book value		750,000		750,000		750,000
Beginning Retained Earnings—P	—		24,000		48,000	
Depreciation Expense	30,000		30,000		30,000	
Noncontrolling Interest	—		6,000		12,000	
Equipment (net)		30,000		60,000		90,000
Beginning Retained Earnings—P	—				16,000	
Loss on Impairment—Goodwill	—		20,000			
Noncontrolling Interest	—				4,000	
Goodwill		—		20,000		20,000

FIGURE 5-2
Partial Equity Method
Three Year Summary

Entries on P's Books

	Year 2011		*Year 2012*		*Year 2013*	
Investment in S	2,200,000					
Cash		2,200,000				
Cash	16,000		48,000		60,000	
Investment in S		16,000		48,000		60,000
Investment in S	100,000		112,000		160,000	
Equity in S Income		100,000		112,000		160,000

Entries on the Worksheet

	Year 2011		*Year 2012*		*Year 2013*	
Investment in S	16,000		48,000		60,000	
Dividends Declared		16,000		48,000		60,000
Equity in S Income	100,000		112,000		160,000	
Investment in S		100,000		112,000		160,000
Beginning Retained Earnings—S	500,000		605,000		685,000	
Common stock—S	1,500,000		1,500,000		1,500,000	
Difference between Implied and Book Value	750,000		750,000		750,000	
Investment in S		2,200,000		2,284,000		2,348,000
Noncontrolling Interest		550,000		571,000		587,000
Cost of Goods Sold	50,000					
Beginning Retained Earnings			40,000		40,000	
Noncontrolling Interest			10,000		10,000	
Equipment	300,000		300,000		300,000	
Land	150,000		150,000		150,000	
Goodwill	250,000		250,000		250,000	
Difference between Implied and Book Value		750,000		750,000		750,000
Beginning Retained Earnings—P	—		24,000		48,000	
Depreciation Expense	30,000		30,000		30,000	
Noncontrolling Interest	—		6,000		12,000	
Equipment (net)		30,000		60,000		90,000
Beginning retained Earnings—P	—				16,000	
Loss on impairment—Goodwill	—		20,000			
Noncontrolling Interest	—				4,000	
Goodwill		—		20,000		20,000

TEST YOUR KNOWLEDGE

NOTE: Solutions to ***Test Your Knowledge*** questions are found at the end of each chapter before the end-of-chapter questions.

Multiple Choice

1. In the event of a bargain acquisition (after carefully considering the fair valuation of all subsidiary assets and liabilities), FASB requires the following accounting:
   a. an ordinary gain is reported in the financial statements of the consolidated entity.
   b. an ordinary loss is reported in the financial statements of the consolidated entity.
   c. negative goodwill is reported on the balance sheet.
   d. assets are written down to zero value, if needed.

FIGURE 5-3

Complete Equity Method
Three Year Summary

Entries on P's Books

	Year 2011		*Year 2012*		*Year 2013*	
Investment in S	2,200,000					
Cash		2,200,000				
Cash	16,000		48,000		60,000	
Investment in S		16,000		48,000		60,000
Investment in S	100,000		112,000		160,000	
Equity in S Income		100,000		112,000		160,000
Equity in S Income	64,000		40,000		24,000	
Investment in S		64,000		40,000		24,000

Entries on the Worksheet

	Year 2011		*Year 2012*		*Year 2013*	
Investment in S	16,000		48,000		60,000	
Dividends declared		16,000		48,000		60,000
Equity in S income	36,000		72,000		136,000	
Investment in S		36,000		72,000		136,000
Beginning retained earnings—S	500,000		605,000		685,000	
Common stock—S	1,500,000		1,500,000		1,500,000	
Difference between implied and book value	750,000		750,000		750,000	
Investment in S		2,200,000		2,284,000		2,348,000
Noncontrolling interest		550,000		571,000		587,000
Cost of goods sold	50,000					
Investment in S			40,000		40,000	
Noncontrolling interest			10,000		10,000	
Equipment	300,000		300,000		300,000	
Land	150,000		150,000		150,000	
Goodwill	250,000		250,000		250,000	
Difference between implied and book value		750,000		750,000		750,000
Investment in S	—		24,000		48,000	
Depreciation expense	30,000		30,000		30,000	
Noncontrolling interest	—		6,000		12,000	
Equipment (net)		30,000		60,000		90,000
Investment in S	—				16,000	
Loss on impairment—goodwill	—		20,000			
Noncontrolling interest	—				4,000	
Goodwill		—		20,000		20,000

CONSOLIDATED STATEMENTS WORKPAPER—INVESTMENT RECORDED USING THE COST METHOD

In the preparation of consolidated financial statements, the recorded balances of individual assets, liabilities, and expense accounts must be adjusted to reflect the allocation, amortization, and depreciation of the differences between implied and book values, as well as any impairment of goodwill. These adjustments are accomplished through the use of ***workpaper entries*** in the preparation of the consolidated statements workpaper.

To illustrate, assume the following:

1. P Company acquires an 80% interest in S Company on January 1, 2011, for $2,200,000, at which time S Company has capital stock of $1,500,000 and retained earnings of $500,000. P Company uses the cost method to record its investment in S Company.
2. The allocation of the difference between implied and book values in the amount of $750,000 [($2,200,000/80%) − $2,000,000], as previously presented in Illustration 5-5, includes $50,000 to Inventory, $300,000 to Equipment (10-year life), $150,000 to Land, and $250,000 to Goodwill.
3. In 2011, S Company reported net income of $125,000 and declared and paid dividends of $20,000. During the annual review of its goodwill, the determination is made that the goodwill is currently worth $255,000.
4. In 2012, S Company reported net income of $140,000 and declared and paid dividends of $60,000. During the annual review of its goodwill, the determination is made that the goodwill is currently worth $230,000 (after performing the two step process described in Chapter 2).
5. In 2013, S Company reported net income of $200,000 and declared and paid dividends of $75,000. During the annual review of its goodwill, the determination is made that the goodwill is currently worth $250,000.

COST

Year of Acquisition

LO5 Recording investment on books of Parent.

Entries on Books of P Company—2011 (Year of Acquisition) Entries recorded on the books of the P Company under the cost method to reflect the acquisition of its interest in S Company and the receipt of dividends in 2011 are as follows:

Investment in S Company	2,200,000	
Cash		2,200,000
To record purchase of an 80% interest in S Company.		
Cash	16,000	
Dividend Income		16,000
To record receipt of dividends from S Company (.80 × $20,000).		

Workpaper Entries—2011—Year of Acquisition The consolidated statements workpaper for the year ended December 31, 2011, is presented in Illustration 5-6. An analysis of the workpaper elimination entries in Illustration 5-6 is presented here:

(1) Dividend Income	16,000	
Dividends Declared		16,000
To eliminate intercompany dividends.		

Cost Method
80% Owned Subsidiary
Year of Acquisition

ILLUSTRATION 5-6
Consolidated Statements Workpaper
P Company and Subsidiary
for Year Ended December 31, 2011

Income Statement	*P Company*	*S Company*	*Eliminations Dr.*	*Eliminations Cr.*	*Noncontrolling Interest*	*Consolidated Balances*
Sales	3,100,000	2,200,000				5,300,000
Dividend Income	16,000		(1) 16,000			
Total Revenue	3,116,000	2,200,000				5,300,000
Cost of Goods Sold	1,700,000	1,360,000	(3a) 50,000			3,110,000
Depreciation—Equipment	120,000	30,000	(3b) 30,000			180,000
Other Expenses	998,000	685,000				1,683,000
Total Cost and Expense	2,818,000	2,075,000				4,973,000
Net/Consolidated Income	298,000	125,000				327,000
Noncontrolling Interest in Income					9,000*	9,000
Net Income to Retained Earnings	298,000	125,000	96,000	—0—	9,000	318,000
Retained Earnings Statement						
1/1 Retained Earnings						
P Company	1,650,000					1,650,000
S Company		500,000	(2) 500,000			
Net Income from above	298,000	125,000	96,000	—0—	9,000	318,000
Dividends Declared						
P Company	(150,000)					(150,000)
S Company		(20,000)		(1) 16,000	(4,000)	
12/31 Retained Earnings to Balance Sheet	1,798,000	605,000	596,000	16,000	5,000	1,818,000
Balance Sheet						
Investment in S Company	2,200,000			(2) 2,200,000		
Difference between Implied and Book Value			(2) 750,000	(3a) 750,000		
Land	1,250,000	250,000	(3a) 150,000			1,650,000
Equipment (net)	1,080,000	270,000	(3a) 300,000	(3b) 30,000		1,620,000
Other Assets (net)	2,402,000	1,885,000				4,287,000
Goodwill (excess of implied over fair value)			(3a) 250,000			250,000
Total Assets	6,932,000	2,405,000				7,807,000
Liabilities	2,134,000	300,000				2,434,000
Capital Stock						
P Company	3,000,000					3,000,000
S Company		1,500,000	(2) 1,500,000			
Retained Earnings from above	1,798,000	605,000	596,000	16,000	5,000	1,818,000
1/1 Noncontrolling Interest in Net Assets				(2) 550,000	550,000	
12/31 Noncontrolling Interest in Net Assets					555,000	555,000
Total Liabilities and Equity	6,932,000	2,405,000	3,546,000	3,546,000		7,807,000

(*) 20% × [$125,000 − $50,000 COGS − $30,000 Depreciation] = $9,000.
(1) To eliminate intercompany dividends.
(2) To eliminate investment account and create noncontrolling interest account.
(3a) To allocate differences between implied and book value.
(3b) To depreciate the difference between implied and book value assigned to equipment (300,000/10).

LO6 Workpaper entries (cost method).

		Debit	Credit
(2)	Beginning Retained Earnings—S Company	500,000	
	Capital Stock—S Company	1,500,000	
	Difference between Implied and Book Value	750,000	
	Investment in S Company		2,200,000
	Noncontrolling Interest in Equity		550,000
	To eliminate the investment account against the equity accounts of S Company using equity balances at the ***beginning of the current year***, and recognize the Noncontrolling Interest in Equity.		

		Debit	Credit
(3a)	Cost of Goods Sold (beginning inventory)	50,000	
	Equipment (net) (10-year remaining life)	300,000	
	Land	150,000	
	Goodwill	250,000	
	Difference between Implied and Book Value		750,000
	To allocate the amount of difference between implied and book value at date of acquisition to specific assets and liabilities, see Illustration 5-2.		

COST

By the end of the first year, under a *FIFO* (*first-in, first-out*) cost flow assumption, the inventory that necessitated the $50,000 adjustment would have been sold. Recall that at the date of acquisition, this adjustment was to Inventory. At the end of the first year, however, the entry is to Cost of Goods Sold (or to Beginning Inventory, as a subcomponent of the Cost of Goods Sold). Since S Company will not have included the additional $50,000 allocated to inventory in its reported *Cost of Goods Sold* (*COGS*), consolidated Cost of Goods Sold must be increased by this workpaper entry. If the inventory were still on hand on December 31, 2011 (for example, if a LIFO flow were assumed), the $50,000 would be allocated to ending inventory in the balance sheet rather than to Cost of Goods Sold.

This entry to Cost of Goods Sold is appropriate only in the year of acquisition. In subsequent years, consolidated Cost of Goods Sold will have been reflected in the 2011 consolidated net income and hence consolidated retained earnings at the end of 2011. Thus, the adjustment ($50,000 debit) in future years will be to Beginning Retained Earnings-P Company (80%) and to the Noncontrolling Interest in Equity (20%).

		Debit	Credit
(3b)	Depreciation Expense ($300,000/10 years)	30,000	
	Equipment (net)[6]		30,000
	To depreciate the amount of difference between implied and book value allocated to equipment, see Illustration 5-5.		

As previously noted, depreciation in the consolidated income statement should be based on the value assigned to the equipment in the consolidated balance sheet. Since the depreciation recorded by S Company is based on the book value of the equipment in its records, consolidated depreciation must be increased by a workpaper entry.

[6] The credit to this entry could alternatively be accumulated depreciation.

The amount of the difference between implied and book values not allocated to specific identifiable assets or liabilities is treated in the consolidated financial statements as goodwill. Companies are not currently required to amortize goodwill. Instead it is adjusted only when impaired. In the year 2011, goodwill is assessed to be worth $255,000, which is more than its carrying value of $250,000. Thus, no impairment entry is needed.

It is possible, of course, to combine the workpaper entries relating to the allocation and depreciation of the differences between implied and book values into one entry. In Illustration 5-6, for example, workpaper entries (3a) and (3b) could be presented in one combined entry as follows:

		Debit	Credit
(3)	Cost of Goods Sold (Beginning Inventory)	50,000	
	Depreciation Expense	30,000	
	Equipment (net) ($300,000−$30,000)	270,000	
	Land	150,000	
	Goodwill	250,000	
	Difference between Implied and Book Value		750,000

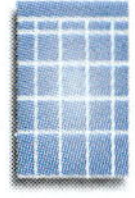
COST

In Illustration 5-6, the calculation of Noncontrolling Interest is also affected by the depreciation of the differences between implied and book values. Since the difference between implied and book values is distributed between the controlling and noncontrolling interests, 20% of the charges to COGS and depreciation expense reduce the noncontrolling interest (NCI) in consolidated earnings. Thus, the noncontrolling interest in earnings is computed as 20% of: [S earnings of $125,000 − $50,000 additional COGS − $30,000 excess depreciation], or $9,000. The other 80% reduces the controlling interest in consolidated net income.

Year Subsequent to Acquisition

LO5 P company entries after acquisition.

Entries on Books of P Company—2012 (Year Subsequent to Acquisition) In 2012, P Company will record dividend income as follows:

	Debit	Credit
Cash	48,000	
Dividend Income		48,000
To record receipt of dividends from S Company (.8 × $60,000).		

Under the Cost Method, the parent company makes no entry for the reported income of the subsidiary.

Workpaper Entries—2012 (Year Subsequent to Acquisition) The consolidated statements workpaper for the year ended December 31, 2012, is presented in Illustration 5-7.

Cost Method
80% Owned Subsidiary
Subsequent to
Year of Acquisition

ILLUSTRATION 5-7
Consolidated Statements Workpaper
P Company and Subsidiary
for Year Ended December 31, 2012

	P	S	Eliminations		Noncontrolling	Consolidated
Income Statement	*Company*	*Company*	*Dr.*	*Cr.*	*Interest*	*Balances*
Sales	3,534,000	2,020,000				5,554,000
Dividend Income	48,000		(2) 48,000			
Total Revenue	3,582,000	2,020,000				5,554,000
Cost of Goods Sold	2,040,000	1,200,000				3,240,000
Depreciation—Equipment	120,000	30,000	(4b) 30,000			180,000
Other Expenses	993,000	650,000	(4c) 20,000			1,663,000
Total Cost and Expense	3,153,000	1,880,000				5,083,000
Net/Consolidated Income	429,000	140,000				471,000
Noncontrolling Interest in Income					18,000*	18,000
Net Income to Retained Earnings	429,000	140,000	98,000	—0—	18,000	453,000
Retained Earnings Statement						
1/1 Retained Earnings						
P Company	1,798,000		(4a) 40,000 (4b) 24,000	(1) 84,000		1,818,000
S Company		605,000	(3) 605,000			
Net Income from above	429,000	140,000	(4c) 98,000	—0—	18,000	453,000
Dividends Declared						
P Company	(150,000)					(150,000)
S Company		(60,000)		(2) 48,000	(12,000)	
12/31 Retained Earnings to Balance Sheet	2,077,000	685,000	767,000	132,000	6,000	2,121,000
Balance Sheet						
Investment in S Company	2,200,000		(1) 84,000	(3) 2,284,000		
Difference between Implied and Book Value			(3) 750,000	(4a) 750,000		
Land	2,000,000	250,000	(4a) 150,000			2,400,000
Equipment (net)	960,000	240,000	(4a) 300,000	(4b) 60,000		1,440,000
Other Assets (net)	2,137,000	2,200,000				4,337,000
Goodwill			(4a) 250,000	(4c) 20,000		230,000
Total Assets	7,297,000	2,690,000				8,407,000
Liabilities	2,220,000	505,000				2,725,000
Capital Stock						
P Company	3,000,000					3,000,000
S Company		1,500,000	(3) 1,500,000			
Retained Earnings from above	2,077,000	685,000	767,000	132,000	6,000	2,121,000
1/1 Noncontrolling Interest in Net Assets			(4a) 10,000 (4b) 6,000	(3) 571,000**	555,000	
12/31 Noncontrolling Interest in Net Assets					561,000	561,000
Total Liabilities and Equity	7,297,000	2,690,000	3,817,000	3,817,000		8,407,000

(*) 20% × (140,000 − 30,000 − 20,000) = 18,000.
(**) $550,000 + [20% × ($605,000 − $500,000)] = $571,000.
(1) To establish reciprocity/convert to equity as of 1/1/12 [.80 × ($605,000−$500,000)].
(2) To eliminate intercompany dividends.
(3) To eliminate investment account and create Noncontrolling Interest account.
(4a) To assign the difference between implied and book value at the date of acquisition to specific assets and liabilities.
(4b) To depreciate the amount of the difference between implied and book value assigned to equipment.
(4c) To record goodwill impairment.

Workpaper elimination entries in Illustration 5-7 are presented in general journal form as follows:

LO6 Workpaper entries after acquisition, subsequent years (cost method).

	Account	Debit	Credit
(1)	Investment in S Company	84,000	
	Beginning Retained Earnings—P Company		84,000
	To convert to equity/establish reciprocity as of 1/1/12 [($605,000 − $500,000) × .80].		

This entry represents the change in retained earnings of S Company from the date of acquisition to the beginning of the current year. This also converts retained earnings to the value that would be recorded if the partial equity method had been used.

COST

	Account	Debit	Credit
(2)	Dividend Income	48,000	
	Dividends Declared		48,000
	To eliminate the intercompany dividends. ($60,000 × 80%).		

In the investment elimination entry, the amount debited or credited to the Difference between Implied and Book Values is equal to the amount of the difference between implied and book values on the date of acquisition. The amount does not change subsequent to acquisition and may be obtained from the Computation and Allocation Schedule (Illustration 5-2). Both the entry to Investment in S and Noncontrolling Interest reflect one year of change since acquisition. For example, the Noncontrolling Interest was valued at $550,000 at acquisition and increased in the first year by 20% × [$125,000−$20,000 (Dividends Declared)] = $21,000. The noncontrolling interest must also be adjusted for the noncontrolling share in depreciation expense and Cost of Goods Sold from 2011, but those adjustments will be shown in separate entries below.

	Account	Debit	Credit
(3)	Beginning Retained Earnings—S Company	605,000	
	Capital Stock—S Company	1,500,000	
	Difference between Implied and Book Value	750,000	
	Investment in S Company ($2,200,000 + $84,000)		2,284,000
	Noncontrolling Interest [$550,000 + 20% ($125,000 − $20,000)]		571,000

Workpaper entry (4) is presented next, first in a combined single entry and then (alternatively) in its components. The authors find the second approach (components) easier to understand, though less space efficient.

	Account	Debit	Credit
(4)	Beginning Retained Earnings—P Company (beginning consolidated retained earnings) (40,000+24,000)	64,000	
	Noncontrolling Interest	16,000	
	Depreciation Expense ($300,000/10)	30,000	
	Impairment Loss on Goodwill ($250,000−$230,000)	20,000	
	Equipment (net) ($300,000−$30,000−$30,000)	240,000	
	Land	150,000	
	Goodwill	230,000	
	Difference between Implied and Book Value		750,000
	To allocate and depreciate the difference between implied and book values.		

COST

Beginning consolidated retained earnings and the noncontrolling interest must be adjusted each year for the cumulative amount of depreciation and other deductions that have been made from consolidated net income because of the depreciation of the difference between implied and book values in the consolidated statements workpapers of prior years. By reducing previously reported consolidated net income, these workpaper adjustments also reduce previously reported consolidated retained earnings and noncontrolling interest. The reduction of beginning consolidated retained earnings and noncontrolling interest is accomplished by debits to the beginning retained earnings of the parent company and to Noncontrolling Interest in Equity in the consolidated statements workpaper. The \$64,000 debit to beginning retained earnings is equal to the 80% × (\$50,000 charged to cost of goods sold plus \$30,000 charged to depreciation expense). The \$16,000 debit to Noncontrolling Interest in Equity is equal to the 20% × (\$50,000 charged to cost of goods sold plus \$30,000 charged to depreciation expense). Where part of the difference between implied and book values is allocated to depreciable assets, the workpaper adjustments to the beginning retained earnings of the parent company and to noncontrolling interest will become progressively larger each year.

To separate the preceding entry into its more digestible components, begin with the allocation of the difference between implied and book values and then proceed to record excess depreciation and goodwill impairment as follows:

(4a)	Beginning Retained Earnings—P Company (previous year's cost of goods sold × 80%)	40,000	
	Noncontrolling Interest (20% of previous year's cost of goods sold)	10,000	
	Equipment	300,000	
	Land	150,000	
	Goodwill	250,000	
	Difference between Implied and Book Value		750,000
	To allocate the amount of difference between implied and book values at date of acquisition to specific assets and liabilities (see Illustration 5-2).		

Entry (4a) is identical to that recorded in the preceding year, with the exception that the entry to Cost of Goods Sold is appropriate only in the year of acquisition. Thus, the adjustment in year 2 (and future years) is split between the controlling and noncontrolling interests in equity (80% to Beginning Retained Earnings of P and 20% to Noncontrolling Interest).

(4b)	Depreciation Expense (current year)	30,000	
	Beginning Retained Earnings—P Company (80% of previous year's depreciation expense)	24,000	
	Noncontrolling Interest (20% of previous year's depreciation expense)	6,000	
	Equipment (net) or Accumulated Depreciation		60,000
	To depreciate the amount of difference between implied and book values allocated to equipment.		

This entry differs from the first-year entry in that the excess depreciation from the year 2011 is now reflected in Beginning Retained Earnings—P Company. Although the adjustment to Equipment (net) was already made in the prior-year workpaper for one year's depreciation adjustment, it was not posted to the books of S Company and hence must be made again. If the following year (2013) were being presented, the debit to Depreciation Expense would remain at 30,000, but the debit to Beginning Retained Earnings would be $48,000 to reflect two prior years of excess depreciation, Noncontrolling Interest in Equity would be debited for $12,000, and the credit to Net Equipment would total $90,000.

COST

Entry (4c) is a new entry that is needed in 2012 because goodwill is assessed to have been impaired. Goodwill is still carried in the workpaper for the consolidated entity at its acquisition value of $250,000, and this amount exceeds its current estimated value of $230,000 in 2012. Therefore, a workpaper entry is needed to reduce the carrying value to $230,000, which entails the recording of an impairment loss of $20,000. This charge, like the excess depreciation, is distributed to the controlling and noncontrolling interests in the income statement for 2012. The impairment loss may be combined with "other expenses" in the consolidating workpaper. In subsequent years, the charge to earnings (like excess depreciation) will flow 80% to the Beginning Retained Earnings of P and 20% to Noncontrolling Interest in Equity.

		Debit	Credit
(4c)	Impairment loss (current year)	20,000	
	Goodwill		20,000
	To reflect the impairment of goodwill recorded in the acquisition of 2011 due to a decline in value as of 2012.		

Clearly, if entries (4a), (4b), and (4c) are recorded separately, the combined entry (4) is not needed.

The amounts charged to expense each year were calculated in Illustration 5-5. Since inventory was sold in 2011, no part of the difference between implied and book value is allocated to inventory in the years after its sale. The amounts allocated to assets (and liabilities) are the unamortized amounts at the end of the year. Thus, the amounts allocated to depreciable assets in the balance sheet will become progressively smaller each year.

In the consolidated statements workpaper for the third year after acquisition (December 31, 2013), for example, the workpaper elimination entry will be as follows (if combined into one entry):

At December 31, 2013:

		Debit	Credit
(4)	Beginning Retained Earnings—P Company (beginning consolidated retained earnings [80%($50,000 + $30,000) from 2011 + 80%($30,000 + $20,000) from 2009]	104,000	
	Beginning Noncontrolling Interest in Equity [20%($50,000 + $30,000) from 2011 + 20%($30,000 + $20,000) from 2009]	26,000	
	Depreciation Expense ($300,000/10)	30,000	
	Equipment (net) ($300,000 − $30,000 − $30,000 − $30,000)	210,000	
	Land	150,000	
	Goodwill	230,000	
	Difference between Implied and Book Value		750,000

Note in the entry for 2013 that the goodwill remains at the $230,000 carrying value, even though it is currently valued at $250,000. Once impairment has been

COST

recorded, no recovery is permitted to be recorded in subsequent years under GAAP.

The debit to the beginning retained earnings of the parent company in 2013 ($64,000 + $40,000) is equal to the amount by which the controlling interest in consolidated net income and consolidated retained earnings had been reduced because of the depreciation and impairment of the difference between implied and book values. These charges amounted to $64,000 for the parent's share in the year 2011 (COGS $40,000 + Depreciation $24,000) and to $40,000 for the parent's share in the year 2012 (Goodwill Impairment $16,000 + Depreciation $24,000), and were reflected in the consolidated statements workpapers for those years. ***However, recall that they were not posted to the ledgers of either P or S Company, thus necessitating the adjustments to Beginning Retained Earnings and Noncontrolling Interest in Equity in subsequent years.*** [See Illustration 5-5; also see entries (3a and 3b) in Illustration 5-6 and entries (4b and 4c) in Illustration 5-7]. The calculation of the debit to Noncontrolling Interest is analogous, reflecting the remaining 20% of the charges to consolidated net income. This entry [(4) for 2013] can also be simplified by breaking it into its components.

Figure 5-1(on page 229) presents the entries in their separate components for all three years side by side for the cost method.

COST METHOD ANALYSIS OF CONTROLLING AND NONCONTROLLING INTERESTS IN CONSOLIDATED NET INCOME AND RETAINED EARNINGS

In the preceding chapter, a t-account approach to the calculation of the controlling and noncontrolling interests in consolidated net income was presented. This approach must now be refined to accommodate the effect of the allocation and depreciation of the difference between implied and book values.

COST

Consolidated net income is the parent company's income from its independent operations plus (minus) the reported subsidiary income (loss) plus or minus adjustments for the period relating to the depreciation/amortization/impairment of the difference between implied and book values.

The calculation of ***controlling and noncontrolling interests in consolidated net income*** for the year ended December 31, 2012, presented in Illustration 5-8, is based on Illustration 5-7. These amounts are, of course, the same as the controlling and noncontrolling interests in consolidated net income shown in the consolidated financial statements workpaper.

Consolidated retained earnings is the parent company's cost basis retained earnings plus (minus) the parent company's share of the increase (decrease) in reported subsidiary retained earnings from the date of acquisition to the current date plus or minus the cumulative effect of adjustments to date relating to the depreciation/amortization of the difference between implied and book values.

The calculation of **consolidated retained earnings** on December 31, 2012, presented in Illustration 5-9, is based on Illustration 5-7. This is the same amount of consolidated retained earnings as that shown in the consolidated statements workpaper presented in Illustration 5-7 and may be used as a means of checking the balance.

ILLUSTRATION 5-8

Calculation of the Noncontrolling Interest in Consolidated Income—Cost Method for Year Ended December 31, 2012

Noncontrolling Interest in Consolidated Income

Additional depreciation and amortization of the difference between implied and book value related to:			
Depreciation Expense ($300,000/10)	30,000	Net income reported by S Company	140,000
Impairment of Goodwill ($250,000 − $230,000)	20,000		
		Adjusted Net Income	90,000
		Noncontrolling Ownership Percentage Interest	20%
		Noncontrolling Interest in Consolidated Income	18,000

80% ($90,000)

Controlling Interest in Consolidated Income

		P Company's net income from its independent operations ($429,000 reported net income less $48,000 dividend income from S Company included therein)	$381,000
		P Company's share of the reported income of S Company (.8 × $90,000)	72,000
		Controlling Interest in Consolidated Net Income	$453,000

ILLUSTRATION 5-9

Analytical Calculation of Consolidated Retained Earnings: Cost Method December 31, 2012

P Company's retained earnings on December 31, 2012		$2,077,000
P Company's share of the increase in S Company's retained from date of acquisition to December 31, 2012 [.8($685,000 − $500,000)]		148,000

Less cumulative effect to December 31, 2012, of the amortization of the difference between implied and book value (parent's share):

	2011	2012	
Inventory (to cost of goods sold)	$40,000	$—0—	
Depreciation from Equipment	24,000	24,000	
Impairment of Goodwill	—0—	16,000	
	64,000	40,000	(104,000)
Consolidated Retained Earnings on December 31, 2012			$2,121,000

(continued)

Alternatively, consolidated retained earnings can be computed by adding beginning consolidated retained earnings to the controlling interest in net income and subtracting dividends declared by P Company.

Beginning Consolidated Retained Earnings	$1,818,000
Plus: Controlling Interest in Consolidated Net Income	453,000
Less: Dividends Declared by P Company	(150,000)
Ending Consolidated Retained Earnings	$2,121,000

Similarly, the noncontrolling interest in equity can be computed as follows:

Beginning Noncontrolling Interest in Equity	$555,000
Plus: Noncontrolling Interest in Consolidated Net Income	18,000
Less: Dividends Declared by S Company to Outsiders	(12,000)
Ending Noncontrolling Interest in Equity	$561,000

TEST YOUR KNOWLEDGE

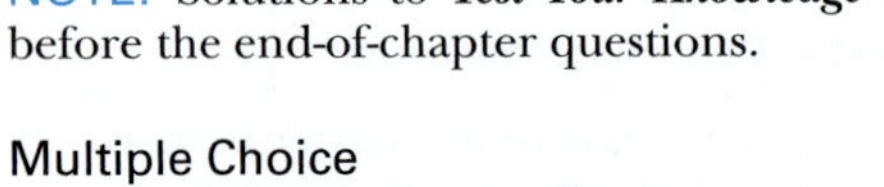

NOTE: Solutions to ***Test Your Knowledge*** questions are found at the end of each chapter before the end-of-chapter questions.

5.2

Multiple Choice

1. The difference between implied and book values that is not allocated to specific identifiable assets or liabilities is treated as goodwill, which is:
   (A) Expensed completely
   (B) Capitalized and amortized over 20 years
   (C) Capitalized and amortized over the expected useful life, not to exceed 40 years
   (D) Capitalized and checked periodically for impairment.

CONSOLIDATED STATEMENTS WORKPAPER—INVESTMENT RECORDED USING PARTIAL EQUITY METHOD

In the preparation of consolidated financial statements, the recorded balances of individual assets, liabilities, and expense accounts must be adjusted to reflect the allocation, depreciation, amortization, and potential impairment of the difference between implied and book values.

Although the equity methods (partial and complete) reflect the effects of certain transactions more fully than the cost method on the books of the parent, the adjustments have not been made to individual underlying asset or income statement accounts. For example, under the partial equity method, the parent records its equity in subsidiary income in its books, but it does not record the underlying revenue and expense accounts that combine to form that total. Also, under this method, the parent does not record excess depreciation, amortization, or impairment of identifiable intangibles arising in the acquisition in its investment account. These adjustments must be accomplished through the use of workpaper entries in the preparation of the consolidated statements workpaper. To illustrate, assume the following:

PARTIAL

1. P Company acquires an 80% interest in S Company on January 1, 2011, for $2,200,000, at which time S Company has capital stock of $1,500,000 and

retained earnings of $500,000. P Company uses the partial equity method to record its investment in S Company.

2. The allocation of the difference between implied and book values in the amount of $750,000 [($2,200,000/80%)−$2,000,000], as previously presented in Illustration 5-5, includes $50,000 to Inventory, $300,000 to Equipment (10-year life), $150,000 to Land, and $250,000 to Goodwill.
3. In 2011, S Company reported net income of $125,000 and declared and paid dividends of $20,000. During the annual review of its goodwill, the determination is made that the goodwill is currently worth $255,000.
4. In 2012, S Company reported net income of $140,000 and declared and paid dividends of $60,000. During the annual review of its goodwill, the determination is made that the goodwill is currently worth $230,000 (after performing the two-step process described in Chapter 2).
5. In 2013, S Company reported net income of $200,000 and declared and paid dividends of $75,000. During the annual review of its goodwill, the determination is made that the goodwill is currently worth $250,000.

LO5 Recording investment by Parent, partial equity method.

Entries on the Books of P Company—2011 (Year of Acquisition) Entries recorded on the books of P Company under the partial equity method are as follows:

PARTIAL

		Debit	Credit
(1)	Investment in S Company	2,200,000	
	Cash		2,200,000
	To record purchase of 80% interest in S Company.		
(2)	Cash	16,000	
	Investment in S Company		16,000
	To record dividends received (.80 × $20,000).		
(3)	Investment in S Company	100,000	
	Equity in Subsidiary Income		100,000
	To record equity in subsidiary income (.80 × $125,000).		

Entries on the Books of P Company—2012 (Year Subsequent to Acquisition)

		Debit	Credit
(4)	Cash	48,000	
	Investment in S Company		48,000
	To record dividends received (.80 × $60,000).		
(5)	Investment in S Company	112,000	
	Equity in Subsidiary Income		112,000
	To record equity in subsidiary income (.80 × $140,000).		

After these entries are posted, the Investment account will appear as follows:

Investment in S Company

(1) Cost	2,200,000		
(3) Subsidiary Income	100,000	(2) Dividends	16,000
12/31/11 Balance	2,284,000		
(5) Subsidiary Income	112,000	(4) Dividends	48,000
12/31/12 Balance	2,348,000		

LO6 Workpaper entries, year of acquisition, partial equity method.

Workpaper Entries—2011 (Year of Acquisition) A consolidated statements workpaper under the partial equity method for the year ended December 31, 2011, is presented in Illustration 5-10. Workpaper entries in Illustration 5-10 are presented in general journal form as follows:

PARTIAL

(1)	Beginning Retained Earnings—S Company	500,000	
	Capital Stock—S Company	1,500,000	
	Difference between Implied and Book Value	750,000	
	Investment in S Company		2,200,000
	Noncontrolling Interest in Equity		550,000
	To eliminate the investment account against the equity accounts of S Company using equity balances at the ***beginning of the current year*** and recognize the noncontrolling interest in equity.		

(2a)	Cost of Goods Sold (beginning inventory)	50,000	
	Equipment (net) (10 year remaining life)	300,000	
	Land	150,000	
	Goodwill	250,000	
	Difference between Implied and Book Value		750,000
	To allocate the amount of difference between implied and book values at date of acquisition to specific assets and liabilities (see Illustration 5-2).		

By the end of the first year, under a FIFO cost flow assumption, the inventory that necessitated the $50,000 adjustment would have been sold. Recall that at the date of acquisition, this adjustment was to Inventory. At the end of the first year, however, the entry is to Cost of Goods Sold (or to Beginning Inventory, as a subcomponent of the Cost of Goods Sold). Since S Company will not have included the additional $50,000 allocated to inventory in its reported Cost of Goods Sold (COGS), consolidated Cost of Goods Sold must be increased by this workpaper entry. If the inventory were still on hand on December 31, 2011 (for example, if a LIFO flow were assumed), the $50,000 would be allocated to ending inventory in the balance sheet rather than to Cost of Goods Sold.

This entry to Cost of Goods Sold is appropriate only in the year of acquisition. In subsequent years, consolidated Cost of Goods Sold will have been reflected in the 2011 consolidated net income. Thus, the adjustment ($50,000 debit) in future years will be split between Beginning Retained Earnings—P Company (80%, or $40,000) and Noncontrolling Interest in Equity (20%, or $10,000).

(2b)	Depreciation Expense ($300,000/10 years)	30,000	
	Equipment (net)		30,000

To depreciate the amount of difference between implied and book value allocated to equipment (see Illustration 5-5).

As previously noted, depreciation in the consolidated income statement should be based on the value assigned to the equipment in the consolidated balance sheet. Since the depreciation recorded by S Company is based on the book value of the equipment in its records, consolidated depreciation must be increased by a workpaper entry.

Partial Equity Method
80% Owned Subsidiary
Year of Acquisition

ILLUSTRATION 5-10
Consolidated Statements Workpaper
P Company and Subsidiary
for Year Ended December 31, 2011

Income Statement	*P Company*	*S Company*	*Eliminations Dr.*	*Eliminations Cr.*	*Noncontrolling Interest*	*Consolidated Balances*
Sales	3,100,000	2,200,000				5,300,000
Equity in Subsidiary Income	100,000		(3a) 100,000			
Total Revenue	3,200,000	2,200,000				5,300,000
Cost of Goods Sold	1,700,000	1,360,000	(2a) 50,000			3,110,000
Depreciation—Equipment	120,000	30,000	(2b) 30,000			180,000
Other Expenses	998,000	685,000				1,683,000
Total Cost and Expense	2,818,000	2,075,000				4,973,000
Net/Consolidated Income	382,000	125,000				327,000
Noncontrolling Interest in Income					9,000*	9,000
Net Income to Retained Earnings	382,000	125,000	180,000	—0—	9,000	318,000
Retained Earnings Statement						
1/1 Retained Earnings						
P Company	1,650,000					1,650,000
S Company		500,000	(1) 500,000			
Net Income from above	382,000	125,000	180,000	—0—	9,000	318,000
Dividends Declared						
P Company	(150,000)					(150,000)
S Company		(20,000)		(3b) 16,000	(4,000)	
12/31 Retained Earnings to Balance Sheet	1,882,000	605,000	680,000	16,000	5,000	1,818,000
Balance Sheet						
Investment in S Company	2,284,000		(3b) 16,000	(1) 2,200,000 (3a) 100,000		
Difference between Implied and Book Value			(1) 750,000	(2a) 750,000		
Land	1,250,000	250,000	(2a) 150,000			1,650,000
Equipment (net)	1,080,000	270,000	(2a) 300,000	(2b) 30,000		1,620,000
Other Assets (net)	2,402,000	1,885,000				4,287,000
Goodwill (Excess of Implied over Fair Value)			(2a) 250,000			250,000
Total Assets	7,016,000	2,405,000				7,807,000
Liabilities	2,134,000	300,000				2,434,000
Capital Stock						
P Company	3,000,000					3,000,000
S Company		1,500,000	(1) 1,500,000			
Retained Earnings from above	1,882,000	605,000	680,000	16,000	5,000	1,818,000
1/1 Noncontrolling Interest in Net Assets				(1) 550,000	550,000	
12/31 Noncontrolling Interest in Net Assets					555,000	555,000
Total Liabilities and Equity	7,016,000	2,405,000	3,646,000	3,646,000		7,807,000

*20% × ($125,000 − $30,000 − $50,000) = $9,000.
(1) To eliminate the investment account against the equity accounts of S Company at the date of acquisition and create noncontrolling interest account.
(2a) To allocate the difference between implied and book value at the date of acquisition to specific assets and liabilities.
(2b) To depreciate the amount of the difference between implied and book value assigned to equipment ($300,000/10 years).
(3a) To reverse the effect of subsidiary income recognized on the books of the parent.
(3b) To reverse the effects of dividends declared by the subsidiary and received by the parents.

It is possible, of course, to combine the workpaper entries relating to the allocation, amortization, and depreciation of the difference between implied and book value into one entry. In Illustration 5-10, for example, workpaper entries (2a) and (2b) could be presented in one combined entry as follows:

(2)	Cost of Goods Sold (beginning inventory)	50,000	
	Depreciation Expense	30,000	
	Equipment (net) ($300,000−$30,000)	270,000	
	Land	150,000	
	Goodwill	250,000	
	Difference between Implied and Book Value		750,000

Next, the workpaper entries to reverse the effect of the parent company entries during the year for subsidiary dividends and income may be separated to record the reversal of dividends in one entry and the reversal of income in another, as follows (and as shown in Illustration 5-10):

(3a)	Equity in Subsidiary Income	100,000	
	Investment in S Company		100,000
	To reverse the effect of subsidiary income recognized in the books of the parent.		

Alternatively, the effects of entries (3a) and (3b) may be combined into one entry, as follows:

(3b)	Investment in S Company	16,000	
	Dividends Declared		16,000
	To reverse the effect of dividends declared by the subsidiary and received by the parent.		

The calculation of noncontrolling interest in Illustration 5-10 is affected by the amortization/depreciation of the differences between implied and book value (20% accrues to the noncontrolling interest).

LO6 Workpaper entries, subsequent year, partial equity.

Workpaper Entries—2012 (Year Subsequent to Acquisition)—Partial Equity Method
Next, a consolidated statements workpaper under the partial equity method for the year ended December 31, 2012, is presented in Illustration 5-11. Workpaper entries in Illustration 5-11 are presented in general journal form below.

PARTIAL

(1)	Beginning Retained Earnings—S Company	605,000	
	Capital Stock—S Company	1,500,000	
	Difference between Implied and Book Value	750,000	
	Investment in S Company ($2,200,000 + $84,000)		2,284,000
	Noncontrolling Interest in Equity [$550,000 + 20%($125,000 − $20,000)]		571,000

For those who have read the cost method discussion, note that ***under the partial equity method, there is no need to establish reciprocity.*** That feature was unique to the cost method and, in fact, may be viewed as a sort of conversion to the equity method.

Partial Equity Method
80% Owned Subsidiary
Subsequent to
Year of Acquisition

ILLUSTRATION 5-11
Consolidated Statements Workpaper
P Company and Subsidiary
for Year Ended December 31, 2012

	P	S	Eliminations		Noncontrolling	Consolidated
Income Statement	*Company*	*Company*	*Dr.*	*Cr.*	*Interest*	*Balances*
Sales	3,534,000	2,020,000				5,554,000
Equity in Subsidiary Income	112,000		(3) 112,000			
Total Revenue	3,646,000	2,020,000				5,554,000
Cost of Goods Sold	2,040,000	1,200,000				3,240,000
Depreciation—Equipment	120,000	30,000	(2b) 30,000			180,000
Other Expenses	993,000	650,000	(2c) 20,000			1,663,000
Total Cost and Expense	3,153,000	1,880,000				5,083,000
Net/Consolidated Income	493,000	140,000				471,000
Noncontrolling Interest in Income					18,000*	18,000
Net Income to Retained Earnings	493,000	140,000	162,000	—0—	18,000	453,000
Retained Earnings Statement						
1/1 Retained Earnings						
P Company	1,882,000		(2a) 40,000			1,818,000
			(2b) 24,000			
S Company		605,000	(1) 605,000			
Net Income from above	493,000	140,000	162,000	—0—	18,000	453,000
Dividends Declared						
P Company	(150,000)					(150,000)
S Company		(60,000)		(3) 48,000	(12,000)	
12/31 Retained Earnings to Balance Sheet	2,225,000	685,000	831,000	48,000	6,000	2,121,000
Balance Sheet						
Investment in S Company	2,348,000			(3) 64,000		
				(1) 2,284,000		
Difference between Implied and Book Value			(1) 750,000	(2a) 750,000		
Land	2,000,000	250,000	(2a) 150,000			2,400,000
Equipment (net)	960,000	240,000	(2a) 300,000	(2b) 60,000		1,440,000
Other Assets (net)	2,137,000	2,200,000				4,337,000
Goodwill (Excess of Implied over Fair Value)			(2a) 250,000	(2c) 20,000		230,000
Total Assets	7,445,000	2,690,000				8,407,000
Liabilities	2,220,000	505,000				2,725,000
Capital Stock						
P Company	3,000,000					3,000,000
S Company		1,500,000	(1) 1,500,000			
Retained Earnings from above	2,225,000	685,000	831,000	48,000	6,000	2,121,000
1/1 Noncontrolling Interest in Net Assets			(2a) 10,000			
			(2b) 6,000	(1) 571,000**	555,000	
12/31 Noncontrolling Interest in Net Assets					561,000	561,000
Total Liabilities and Equity	7,445,000	2,690,000	3,797,000	3,797,000		8,407,000

*20% × ($140,000 − $30,000 − $20,000) = $18,000.
** $550,000 + [20% × ($605,000 − $500,000)] = $571,000.
(1) To eliminate the investment account and create noncontrolling interest account.
(2a) To allocate the difference between implied and book value at the date of acquisition to specific assets and liabilities.
(2b) To depreciate the amount of the difference between implied and book value assigned to equipment ($300,000/10 years).
(3) To reverse the effect of parent company entries during the year for subsidiary dividends and income.
(2c) To record goodwill impairment.

In the investment elimination entry, the amount debited or credited to the Difference between Implied and Book Value is equal to the amount of the Difference between Implied and Book Value on the date of acquisition. The amount does not change subsequent to acquisition and may be obtained from the Computation and Allocation Schedule (Illustration 5-2).

Workpaper entry (2) is presented next, first in a combined single entry and then (alternatively) in its components. The authors find the second approach (components) easier to understand, though less compact.

		Debit	Credit
2)	Beginning Retained Earnings—P Company (Beginning Consolidated Retained Earnings) (40,000 + 24,000)	64,000	
	Noncontrolling Interest	16,000	
	Depreciation Expense ($300,000/10)	30,000	
	Impairment Loss on Goodwill ($250,000 − $230,000)	20,000	
	Equipment (net) ($300,000 − $30,000 − $30,000)	240,000	
	Land	150,000	
	Goodwill	230,000	
	Difference between Implied and Book Value		750,000
	To allocate and depreciate the difference between implied and book values.		

To separate the preceding entry into its more digestible components, begin with the allocation of the difference between implied and book value and then proceed to record excess depreciation as follows:

		Debit	Credit
(2a)	Beginning Retained Earnings—P Company (80% of previous year's cost of goods sold)	40,000	
	Noncontrolling Interest (20% of previous year's cost of goods sold)	10,000	
	Equipment	300,000	
	Land	150,000	
	Goodwill	250,000	
	Difference between Implied and Book Value		750,000
	To allocate the amount of difference between implied and book values at date of acquisition to specific assets and liabilities (see Illustration 5-2).		

PARTIAL

Entry (2a) is identical to that recorded in the preceding year, with the exception that the entry to Cost of Goods Sold is appropriate only in the year of acquisition. Thus, the adjustment in year 2 (and future years) is split between the controlling and noncontrolling interests in equity (80% to Beginning Retained Earnings of P Company and 20% to Noncontrolling Interest).

		Debit	Credit
(2b)	Depreciation Expense (current year)	30,000	
	Beginning Retained Earnings—P Company (previous year's depreciation expense × 80%)	24,000	
	Noncontrolling Interest (previous year's depreciation expense × 20%)	6,000	
	Equipment (net) or Accumulated Depreciation		60,000
	To depreciate the amount of difference between implied and book values allocated to equipment.		

This entry differs from the first-year entry in that the excess depreciation from the year 2011 is now reflected in Beginning Retained Earnings—P Company and Noncontrolling Interest. Although the adjustment to Equipment was already made in the prior year workpaper for one year's depreciation adjustment, it was not posted to the books of S Company and hence must be made again. If the following year (2013) were being presented, the debit to Depreciation Expense would remain at $30,000, but the debit to Beginning Retained Earnings would be $48,000 to reflect two prior years of excess depreciation (with a $12,000 debit to Noncontrolling Interest and a credit to Equipment of $90,000 for all three years).

Entry (2c) is a new entry that is needed in 2012 because goodwill is assessed to have been impaired. Goodwill is still carried in the workpaper for the consolidated entity at its acquisition value of $250,000, and this amount exceeds its current estimated value of $230,000 in 2012. Therefore, a workpaper entry is needed to reduce the carrying value to $230,000, which entails the recording of an impairment loss of $20,000. This charge, like the excess depreciation, is distributed to the controlling and noncontrolling interests in the income statement for 2012. The impairment loss may be combined with "other expenses" in the consolidating workpaper. In subsequent years, the charge to earnings (like excess depreciation) will flow 80% to the Beginning Retained Earnings of P and 20% to Noncontrolling Interest.

RELATED CONCEPTS

FASB Concept No. 5 suggests that losses be recognized when previously recognized economic benefits are reduced, as is the case with goodwill impairment. This *loss of benefit* approach attempts to *match* or *time* the recording of expenses or losses in the Income Statement.

		Debit	Credit
(2c)	Impairment loss (current year)	20,000	
	Goodwill		20,000
	To reflect the impairment of goodwill recorded in the acquisition of 2008 due to a decline in estimated value in 2012.		

Clearly, if entries (2a), (2b), and (2c) are recorded separately, the combined entry (2) is not needed.

		Debit	Credit
(3)	Equity in Subsidiary Income	112,000	
	Dividends Declared		48,000
	Investment in S Company		64,000
	To reverse the effect of parent company entries during the year 2012 for subsidiary dividends and income.		

PARTIAL

Observe that the consolidated balances in Illustration 5-11 are the same as those in Illustration 5-7 (cost method workpaper). The workpaper entries to eliminate the investment account and to allocate and depreciate the difference between implied and book values are the same regardless of whether the investment is recorded using the cost method or the partial equity method. Only the entries for intercompany dividends and income and for reciprocity differ.

Figure 5-2(on page 230) presents the entries in their separate components for all three years (2011 through 2013) side by side for the partial equity method.

TEST YOUR KNOWLEDGE

NOTE: Solutions to ***Test Your Knowledge*** questions are found at the end of each chapter before the end-of-chapter questions.

Multiple Choice

1. Assuming a FIFO cost flow, which account should normally be debited for the inventory adjustment (assuming market value of subsidiary's inventory to be higher than its book value) when allocating the difference between implied and book values at the end of the year of acquisition?
   (A) Inventory
   (B) Beginning Retained Earnings—Parent
   (C) Cost of Goods Sold
   (D) Depreciation Expense

PARTIAL EQUITY METHOD ANALYSIS OF CONTROLLING AND NONCONTROLLING INTERESTS IN CONSOLIDATED NET INCOME AND RETAINED EARNINGS

The t-account calculation of consolidated net income (as well as the controlling and noncontrolling interests therein) does not differ between the cost and partial equity methods. As stated earlier, ***consolidated net income is the parent company's income from its independent operations plus (minus) the reported subsidiary income (loss) plus or minus adjustments for the period relating to the depreciation/amortization of the difference between implied and book value.***

PARTIAL

The calculation of consolidated net income for the year ended December 31, 2012, presented in Illustration 5-12, is based on Illustration 5-11. This, of course, is the same amount of consolidated net income as that calculated in the consolidated statements workpaper presented in Illustration 5-11.

When the parent company uses the partial equity method to account for its investment, the parent company's share of subsidiary income since acquisition is already included in the parent company's reported retained earnings. Consequently, ***consolidated retained earnings are calculated as the parent company's recorded partial equity basis retained earnings plus or minus the cumulative effect of the adjustments to date relating to the depreciation/amortization of the difference between implied and book value.***

The analytical calculation of consolidated retained earnings on December 31, 2012, presented in Illustration 5-13, is based on Illustration 5-11. This, too, is the same amount of consolidated retained earnings as that shown in the consolidated statements workpaper presented in Illustration 5-11.

Alternatively, consolidated retained earnings can be computed by adding beginning consolidated retained earnings to the controlling interest in consolidated net income and subtracting dividends declared by Company P.

Beginning consolidated retained earnings	$1,818,000
Plus: controlling interest in consolidated net income	453,000
Less: dividends declared by P Company	(150,000)
Ending consolidated retained earnings	$2,121,000

ILLUSTRATION 5-12

T-account Calculation of Controlling and Noncontrolling Interest in Consolidated Income for Year Ended December 31, 2012

Noncontrolling Interest in Consolidated Income

Debit		Credit	
Additional depreciation and amortization of the difference between implied and book value related to: Depreciation Expense ($ 300,000/10)	30,000	Net income reported by S Company	140,000
Impairment of goodwill ($250,000 − $230,000)	20,000		
		Adjusted Net Income	90,000
		Noncontrolling Ownership percentage interest	20%
		Noncontrolling Interest Consolidated Income	18,000

.8($90,000)

Controlling Interest in Consolidated Income

Debit	Credit	
	P Company's net income from its independent operations ($493,000 reported net income less $112,000 equity in subsidiary income included therein)	$381,000
	P Company's share of the reported income of S company (.8 × $90,000)	72,000
	Controlling interest in Consolidated Net Income	$453,000

ILLUSTRATION 5-13

Analytical Calculation of Consolidated Retained Earnings December 31, 2012

P Company's retained earnings on December 31, 2012			$2,225,000
Less cumulative effect to December 31, 2012, of the amortization of the difference between implied and book value (parent's share):			
	2011	**2012**	
Inventory (to cost of goods sold)	$40,000	$ —0—	
Depreciation from Equipment	24,000	24,000	
Impairment of Goodwill	—0—	16,000	
	64,000	40,000	(104,000)
Consolidated Retained Earnings on December 31, 2012			$2,121,000

Similarly, the Noncontrolling Interest in Equity can be computed as follows:

Beginning Noncontrolling Interest in Equity	$555,000
Plus: Noncontrolling Interest in Consolidated Net Income	18,000
Less: Dividends Declared by S Company to Outsiders	(12,000)
Ending Noncontrolling Interest in Equity	$561,000

CONSOLIDATED STATEMENTS WORKPAPER—INVESTMENT RECORDED USING COMPLETE EQUITY METHOD

In the preparation of consolidated financial statements, the recorded balances of individual assets, liabilities, and expense accounts must be adjusted to reflect the allocation and depreciation of the differences between implied and book values.

When the parent accounts for its investment using the complete equity method, the parent records excess depreciation, amortization, and impairment arising in the acquisition in its investment account. The income statement effects are recorded as adjustments to the amount recognized as "equity in subsidiary income" each year. Even under this method, however, adjustments are needed to record the effects in the proper accounts for the consolidated entity. For example, the account "equity in subsidiary income" will be eliminated in the consolidated financial statements, and the effects need to be shown directly in "depreciation expense." Similarly, the investment account will be eliminated, and the adjustments for any differences between implied and book values need to be shown directly in the appropriate asset (inventory, land, equipment, goodwill, etc.) and/or liability accounts. These adjustments must be accomplished through the use of ***workpaper entries*** in the preparation of the consolidated statements workpaper.

COMPLETE

To illustrate, assume the following:

1. P Company acquires an 80% interest in S Company on January 1, 2011, for $2,200,000, at which time S Company has capital stock of $1,500,000 and retained earnings of $500,000. P Company uses the complete equity method to record its investment in S Company.
2. The allocation of the difference between implied and book values in the amount of $750,000 [($2,200,000/80%) − $2,000,000], as previously presented in Illustration 5-5, includes $50,000 to Inventory, $300,000 to Equipment (10-year life), $150,000 to Land, and $250,000 to Goodwill.
3. In 2011, S Company reported net income of $125,000 and declared and paid dividends of $20,000. During the annual review of its goodwill, the determination is made that the goodwill is currently worth $255,000.
4. In 2012, S Company reported net income of $140,000 and declared and paid dividends of $60,000. During the annual review of its goodwill, the determination is made that the goodwill is currently worth $230,000 (after performing the two-step process described in Chapter 2).
5. In 2013, S Company reported net income of $200,000 and declared and paid dividends of $75,000. During the annual review of its goodwill, the determination is made that the goodwill is currently worth $250,000.

LO5 Recording investment by Parent, complete equity method.

Entries on Books of P Company—2011 (year of acquisition) and 2012 (subsequent year)
Entries recorded on the books of P Company under the complete equity method are as follows:

2011—Year of Acquisition

		Debit	Credit
(1)	Investment in S Company	2,200,000	
	Cash		2,200,000
	To record purchase of 80% interest in S Company.		
(2)	Cash	16,000	
	Investment in S Company		16,000
	To record dividends received (.80 × \$20,000).		
(3)	Investment in S Company	100,000	
	Equity in Subsidiary Income		100,000
	To record equity in subsidiary income (.80 × \$125,000).		
(4)	Equity in Subsidiary Income	64,000	
	Investment in S Company		64,000
	To adjust equity in subsidiary income for excess depreciation (80% × \$30,000, or \$24,000) and the higher value placed on inventory and thus on cost of goods sold (80% × \$50,000, or \$40,000). No impairment of goodwill in 2008 since its estimated value > carrying value. See Illustration 5-5.		

Entries (3) and (4) could be collapsed into one combined entry of \$36,000 (\$100,000 minus \$64,000).

2012—Year Subsequent to Acquisition

		Debit	Credit
(1)	Cash	48,000	
	Investment in S Company		48,000
	To record dividends received (.80 × \$60,000).		
(2)	Investment in S Company	112,000	
	Equity in Subsidiary Income		112,000
	To record equity in subsidiary income (.80 × \$140,000).		
(3)	Equity in Subsidiary Income	40,000	
	Investment in S Company		40,000
	To reduce equity in subsidiary income for excess depreciation (\$30,000 × 80%) plus impairment of goodwill (\$20,000 × 80%).		

COMPLETE

Again, entries (2) and (3) could be collapsed into one combined entry of \$72,000 (\$112,000 minus \$40,000).

Note also that the inventory adjustment was needed only in the first year under a first-in, first-out (FIFO) cost flow assumption.

After these entries are posted, the Investment account will appear as follows:

Investment in S Company

(1) Cost	2,200,000	(2) Dividends	16,000
(3) Subsidiary Income	100,000	(4) Excess depreciation, and Cost of Goods Sold	64,000
12/31/11 Balance	*2,220,000*		
(2) Subsidiary Income	112,000	(1) Dividends	48,000
		(3) Excess depreciation and goodwill impairment	40,000
12/31/12 Balance	*2,244,000*		

LO6 Workpaper entries, year of acquisition, complete equity.

Workpaper Entries—2011 (Year of Acquisition) A consolidated statements workpaper under the complete equity method for the year ended December 31, 2011, is presented in Illustration 5-14. Workpaper entries in Illustration 5-14 are presented in general journal form as follows:

(1)	Beginning Retained Earnings—S Company	500,000	
	Capital Stock—S Company	1,500,000	
	Difference between Implied and Book Value	750,000	
	Investment in S Company		2,200,000
	Noncontrolling Interest in Equity		550,000

To eliminate the investment account against the equity accounts of S Company using equity balances at the ***beginning of the current year***, and recognize the noncontrolling interest in equity.

(2a)	Cost of Goods Sold (beginning inventory)	50,000	
	Equipment (net) (10-year remaining life)	300,000	
	Land	150,000	
	Goodwill	250,000	
	Difference between Implied and Book Value		750,000

COMPLETE

By the end of the first year, under a FIFO cost flow assumption, the inventory that necessitated the $50,000 adjustment would have been sold. Recall that at the date of acquisition, this adjustment was to Inventory. At the end of the first year, however, the entry is to Cost of Goods Sold (or to Beginning Inventory, as a subcomponent of the Cost of Goods Sold). Since S Company will not have included the additional $50,000 allocated to inventory in its reported Cost of Goods Sold (COGS), consolidated Cost of Goods Sold must be increased by this workpaper entry. If the inventory were still on hand on December 31, 2011 (for example, if a LIFO flow were assumed), the $50,000 would be allocated to ending inventory in the balance sheet rather than to Cost of Goods Sold.

This entry to Cost of Goods Sold is appropriate only in the year of acquisition. In subsequent years, consolidated COGS will have been reflected in the 2011 consolidated net income and hence consolidated retained earnings at the end of 2011. On the books of P Company, the adjustment is reflected in equity in subsidiary income (and thus in ending retained earnings) and in the investment account. Because the investment account must be eliminated in the consolidating process, the entry to COGS is replaced in future years by entries to Investment in S Company ($40,000 debit) and to Noncontrolling Interest ($10,000 debit). These workpaper entries serve to facilitate the elimination of the investment account by reversing an adjustment made by the parent, and to adjust Beginning Noncontrolling Interest in Equity downward for its share (20%) of the charge.

(2b)	Depreciation Expense ($300,000/10 years)	30,000	
	Equipment (net)[7]		30,000
	To depreciate the amount of difference between implied and book value allocated to equipment (see Illustration 5-5).		

[7] The credit to this entry could also be accumulated depreciation.

Complete Equity Method
80% Owned Subsidiary
Year of Acquisition

ILLUSTRATION 5-14
Consolidated Statements Workpaper
P Company and Subsidiary
for Year Ended December 31, 2011

Income Statement	*P Company*	*S Company*	*Eliminations Dr.*	*Eliminations Cr.*	*Noncontrolling Interest*	*Consolidated Balances*
Sales	3,100,000	2,200,000				5,300,000
Equity in Subsidiary Income	36,000		(3b) 100,000	(3c) 64,000		
Total Revenue	3,136,000	2,200,000				5,300,000
Cost of Goods Sold	1,700,000	1,360,000	(2a) 50,000			3,110,000
Depreciation—Equipment	120,000	30,000	(2b) 30,000			180,000
Other Expenses	998,000	685,000				1,683,000
Total Cost and Expense	2,818,000	2,075,000				4,973,000
Net/Consolidated Income	318,000	125,000				327,000
Noncontrolling Interest in Income					9,000*	9,000
Net Income to Retained Earnings	318,000	125,000	180,000	64,000	9,000	318,000
Retained Earnings Statement						
1/1 Retained Earnings						
P Company	1,650,000					1,650,000
S Company		500,000	(1) 500,000			
Net Income from above	318,000	125,000	180,000	64,000	9,000	318,000
Dividends Declared						
P Company	(150,000)					(150,000)
S Company		(20,000)		(3a) 16,000	(4,000)	
12/31 Retained Earnings to Balance Sheet	1,818,000	605,000	680,000	80,000	5,000	1,818,000
Balance Sheet						
Investment in S Company	2,220,000		(3a) 16,000 (3c) 64,000	(1) 2,200,000 (3b) 100,000		
Difference between Implied and Book Value			(1) 750,000	(2a) 750,000		
Land	1,250,000	250,000	(2a) 150,000			1,650,000
Equipment (net)	1,080,000	270,000	(2a) 300,000	(2b) 30,000		1,620,000
Other Assets (net)	2,402,000	1,885,000				4,287,000
Goodwill (Excess of Implied over Fair Value)			(2a) 250,000			250,000
Total Assets	6,952,000	2,405,000				7,807,000
Liabilities	2,134,000	300,000				2,434,000
Capital Stock						
P Company	3,000,000					3,000,000
S Company		1,500,000	(1) 1,500,000			
Retained Earnings from above	1,818,000	605,000	680,000	80,000	5,000	1,818,000
1/1 Noncontrolling Interest in Net Assets				(1) 550,000	550,000	
12/31 Noncontrolling Interest in Net Assets					555,000	555,000
Total Liabilities and Equity	6,952,000	2,405,000	3,710,000	3,710,000		7,807,000

*20% × ($125,000 − $30,000 − $50,000) = $9,000.
(1) To eliminate the investment account and create noncontrolling interest account.
(2a) To allocate differences between implied and book value.
(2b) To depreciate the difference between implied and book value assigned to equipment (300,000/10).
(3a) To eliminate equity in subsidiary income.
(3b) To eliminate intercompany dividends.
(3c) To reverse the adjustments to subsidiary income recognized by the parent.

COMPLETE

As previously noted, depreciation in the consolidated income statement should be based on the value assigned to the equipment in the consolidated balance sheet. Since the depreciation recorded by S Company is based on the book value of the equipment in its records, consolidated depreciation must be increased by a workpaper entry.

The amount of the difference between implied and book values not allocated to specific identifiable assets or liabilities is treated in the consolidated financial statements as goodwill. Companies are not currently required to amortize goodwill. Instead it is adjusted only when impaired. In the year 2011, goodwill is assessed to be worth $255,000, which is more than its carrying value of $250,000. Thus, no impairment entry is needed.

It is possible, of course, to combine the workpaper entries relating to the allocation and depreciation of the differences between implied and book values into one entry. In Illustration 5-14, for example, workpaper entries (2a) and (2b) could be presented in one combined entry as follows:

(2)	Cost of Goods Sold (Beginning Inventory)	50,000	
	Depreciation Expense	30,000	
	Equipment (net) ($300,000−$30,000)	270,000	
	Land	150,000	
	Goodwill	250,000	
	Difference between Implied and Book Value		750,000

Next we reverse the effect of parent company entries during the year for subsidiary dividends and income. Here entries may also be combined or separated to record the reversal of dividends in one entry, the reversal of reported income in a second entry, and the reversal of adjustments to subsidiary income in a third.

(3a)	Investment in S Company	16,000	
	Dividends Declared		16,000

To reverse the effect of dividends declared by the subsidiary and received by the parent.

(3b)	Equity in Subsidiary Income	100,000	
	Investment in S Company		100,000

To reverse the effect of subsidiary reported income recognized in the books of the parent.

(3c)	Investment in S Company	64,000	
	Equity in Subsidiary Income		64,000

To reverse the adjustments to subsidiary income recognized by the parent 80% × ($50,000 cost of goods sold and $30,000 depreciation).

Alternatively, the effects of entries (3a) through (3c) may be combined into one entry, as follows:

(3) Equity in Subsidiary Income	36,000	
Dividends Declared		16,000
Investment in S Company		20,000
To reverse the effect of parent company entries during the year for subsidiary dividends and income.		

The calculation of noncontrolling interest in Illustration 5-14 is affected by the amortization/depreciation of the differences between implied and book value.

Entries on Workpapers—2012 (Year Subsequent to Acquisition) Next, a consolidated statements workpaper under the complete equity method for the year ended December 31, 2012, is presented in Illustration 5-15. Workpaper entries in Illustration 5-15 are presented in general journal form as follows:

COMPLETE

(1) Beginning Retained Earnings—S Company	605,000	
Capital Stock—S Company	1,500,000	
Difference between Implied and Book Value	750,000	
Investment in S Company ($2,200,000 + $84,000)		2,284,000
Noncontrolling Interest [$550,000 + 20% ($125,000 − $20,000)]		571,000

(2) Investment in S Company (adjustments from prior year for 80% depreciation and for 80% COGS: 40,000 + 24,000)	64,000	
Noncontrolling Interest (adjustments from prior year for 20% depreciation & COGS)	16,000	
Depreciation Expense ($300,000/10)	30,000	
Impairment Loss on Goodwill ($250,000 − $230,000)	20,000	
Equipment (net) ($300,000 − $30,000 − $30,000)	240,000	
Land	150,000	
Goodwill	230,000	
Difference between Implied and Book Value		750,000
To allocate and depreciate the difference between implied and book values.		

To separate the preceding entry into its more digestible components, begin with the allocation of the difference between implied and book values and then proceed to record excess depreciation and goodwill impairment as follows:

(2a) Investment in S Company (80% of previous year's cost of goods sold)	40,000	
Noncontrolling Interest (20% of previous year's cost of goods sold)	10,000	
Equipment	300,000	
Land	150,000	
Goodwill	250,000	
Difference between Implied and Book Value		750,000
To allocate the amount of difference between implied and book values at date of acquisition to specific assets and liabilities (see Illustration 5-2).		

Complete Equity Method
80% Owned Subsidiary
Subsequent to Year of Acquisition

ILLUSTRATION 5-15
Consolidated Statements Workpaper
P Company and Subsidiary
for Year Ended December 31, 2011

Income Statement	*P Company*	*S Company*	*Eliminations Dr.*	*Eliminations Cr.*	*Noncontrolling Interest*	*Consolidated Balances*
Sales	3,534,000	2,020,000				5,554,000
Equity in Subsidiary Income	72,000		(3) 72,000			
Total Revenue	3,606,000	2,020,000				5,554,000
Cost of Goods Sold	2,040,000	1,200,000				3,240,000
Depreciation—Equipment	120,000	30,000	(2b) 30,000			180,000
Other Expenses	993,000	650,000	(2c) 20,000			1,663,000
Total Cost and Expense	3,153,000	1,880,000				5,083,000
Net/Consolidated Income	453,000	140,000				471,000
Noncontrolling Interest in Income					18,000*	18,000
Net Income to Retained Earnings	453,000	140,000	122,000	—0—	18,000	453,000
Retained Earnings Statement						
1/1 Retained Earnings						
P Company	1,818,000					1,818,000
S Company		605,000	(1) 605,000			
Net Income from above	453,000	140,000	122,000	—0—	18,000	453,000
Dividends Declared						
P Company	(150,000)					(150,000)
S Company		(60,000)		(3) 48,000	(12,000)	
12/31 Retained Earnings to Balance Sheet	2,121,000	685,000	727,000	48,000	6,000	2,121,000
Balance Sheet						
Investment in S Company	2,244,000		(2a) 40,000	(3) 24,000		
			(2b) 24,000	(1) 2,284,000		
Difference between Implied and Book Value			(1) 750,000	(2a) 750,000		
Land	2,000,000	250,000	(2a) 150,000			2,400,000
Equipment (net)	960,000	240,000	(2a) 300,000	(2b) 60,000		1,440,000
Other Assets (net)	2,137,000	2,200,000				4,337,000
Goodwill (Excess of Implied over Fair Value)			(2a) 250,000	(2c) 20,000		230,000
Total Assets	7,341,000	2,690,000				8,407,000
Liabilities	2,220,000	505,000				2,725,000
Capital Stock						
P Company	3,000,000					3,000,000
S Company		1,500,000	(1) 1,500,000			
Retained Earnings from above	2,121,000	685,000	727,000	48,000	6,000	2,121,000
1/1 Noncontrolling Interest in Net Assets			(2a) 10,000			
			(2b) 6,000	(1) 571,000**	555,000	
12/31 Noncontrolling Interest in Net Assets					561,000	561,000
Total Liabilities and Equity	7,341,000	2,690,000	3,757,000	3,757,000		8,407,000

* 20% × ($140,000 − $30,000 − $20,000) = $18,000.
** $550,000 + [20% × ($605,000 − $500,000)] = $571,000.
(1) To eliminate investment account and create noncontrolling interest account.
(2a) To allocate the amount of difference between implied and book value at date of acquisition to specific assets and liabilities.
(2b) To depreciate the amount of difference between implied and book value allocated to equipment.
(3) To reverse the effect of parent company entries during the year for subsidiary dividends and income.
(2c) To record goodwill impairment.

COMPLETE

Entry(2a) is identical to that recorded in the preceding year, with the exception that the entry to Cost of Goods Sold is appropriate only in the year of acquisition. Consolidated COGS will have been reflected in the 2011 consolidated net income and hence consolidated retained earnings (80%) and Noncontrolling Interest (20%) at the end of 2011. On the books of P Company, the adjustment was reflected in equity in subsidiary income in 2011 (and thus in ending retained earnings) and in the investment account. Because the investment account must be eliminated in the consolidating process, the entry to COGS is replaced here and in future years by an entry ($40,000 debit) to Investment in S Company, and a $10,000 debit to Beginning Noncontrolling Interest in Equity.

This component of the entry captures one of the basic differences between the Complete Equity method and the other two methods. Only under the Complete Equity method does the parent's beginning retained earnings exactly match the amount reported as consolidated retained earnings at the end of the previous year. Hence fewer workpaper adjustments to Beginning Retained Earnings—P Company are needed under the Complete Equity method. The $40,000 adjustment in year 2 (and future years) related to inventory valuation is made to Investment in S Company, serving to facilitate the elimination of the investment account (by reversing an adjustment made by the parent).

(2b)	Depreciation Expense (current year)	30,000	
	Investment in S (80% of previous year's depreciation expense)	24,000	
	Noncontrolling Interest (20% of previous year's depreciation expense)	6,000	
	Equipment (net) or Accumulated Depreciation		60,000
	To depreciate the amount of difference between implied and book values allocated to equipment.		

This entry differs from the first-year entry in that the excess depreciation from the year 2011 is now reflected in a lowered balance in the Investment account, and this entry serves to reverse that adjustment (again to facilitate eliminating the Investment account). Although the adjustment to Equipment (net) was already made in the prior-year workpaper for one year's depreciation adjustment, it was not posted to the books of S Company and hence must be made again. If the following year (2013) were being presented, the debit to Depreciation Expense would remain at 30,000, but the debit to Investment in S Company would be $48,000 to reflect two prior years of excess depreciation, Noncontrolling Interest would be debited for $12,000, and the credit to Net Equipment would total 90,000.

Entry (2c) is a new entry that is needed in 2012 because goodwill is assessed to have been impaired. Goodwill is still carried in the workpaper for the consolidated entity at its acquisition value of $250,000, and this amount exceeds its current estimated value of $230,000 in 2012. Therefore, a workpaper entry is needed to reduce the carrying value to $230,000, which entails the recording of an impairment loss of $20,000. This charge, like the excess depreciation, is distributed to the controlling and noncontrolling interests in the income statement for 2012. The impairment loss may be combined with "other expenses" in the consolidating workpaper.

In subsequent years, the charge to earnings (like excess depreciation) will flow 80% to the Investment in S Company and 20% to Noncontrolling Interest.

(2c) Impairment loss (current year)	20,000	
Goodwill		20,000
To reflect the impairment of goodwill recorded in the acquisition of 2008 due to a decline in value as of 2009.		

Clearly, if entries (2a) through (2c) are recorded separately, the combined entry (2) is not needed.

(3) Equity in Subsidiary Income (after depreciation and goodwill impairment adjustments)	72,000	
Dividends Declared		48,000
Investment in S Company		24,000
To reverse the effect of parent company entries during the year 2009 for subsidiary dividends and income.		

Observe that the consolidated balances in Illustration 5-15 are the same as those in Illustration 5-7 (cost method workpaper) and in Illustration 5-11 (partial equity workpaper). Figure 5-3 (on page 231) presents the entries in their separate components for all three years side by side for the complete equity method.

COMPLETE EQUITY METHOD ANALYSIS OF CONTROLLING INTEREST IN CONSOLIDATED NET INCOME AND RETAINED EARNINGS

When the parent uses the complete equity method, its reported income equals the controlling interest in consolidated net income. As with the other methods, the amount of consolidated income is ***the parent company's income from its independent operations plus (minus) the subsidiary income (loss) plus or minus adjustments for the period relating to the depreciation/amortization and impairment of the difference between implied and book values of depreciable or amortizable assets (and liabilities).*** Note that ***consolidated income,*** as opposed to the ***controlling interest in consolidated income,*** includes both the parent's share and the noncontrolling interest in subsidiary income (loss).

COMPLETE

The amount of consolidated net income for the year ended December 31, 2012, is $471,000, with $18,000 allocated to the noncontrolling interest and the remaining $453,000 to the controlling interest. Observe that the $453,000 is reported both in the farthest left-hand column of Illustration 5-15 (P Company income) and again in the farthest right-hand column, labeled as "Net Income to Retained Earnings" (controlling interest in consolidated net income).

Similarly, the amount of consolidated retained earnings ($2,121,000) at the end of 2012 is the same as the ending retained earnings reported by P Company. Again compare the amount in the retained earnings section in the farthest left-hand column of Illustration 5-15 (P Company) to the amount in the farthest right-hand column (consolidated retained earnings). The amounts agree because P Company recognizes all adjustments in the income statement account "equity in subsidiary income" and thus in retained earnings.

LukOil and ConocoPhillips announced an agreement to form "a broad-based strategic alliance." According to the agreement, ConocoPhillips will become a strategic investor in LukOil after winning an auction to purchase 7.59% of LukOil's shares, which are held by the Russian government. ConocoPhillips will pay $1.99 billion for the stake and intends to tender on the open market non-U.S. LukOil shareholders for an additional 2.4% of the company's equity. The agreement further states that ConocoPhillips may increase its ownership to an aggregate amount of 20%. ConocoPhillips stated that it will report the investment in its financial statements using the equity method of accounting.[8]

ADDITIONAL CONSIDERATIONS RELATING TO TREATMENT OF DIFFERENCE BETWEEN IMPLIED AND BOOK VALUES

We present additional considerations relating to the treatment of the difference between implied and book value in the following sections. These considerations include allocation of the difference between implied and book values to liabilities and to assets with fair values less than book values; the separate disclosure of accumulated depreciation; premature disposals of long-lived assets by the subsidiary; and depreciable assets used in manufacturing.

Allocation of Difference between Implied and Book Values to Debt

Adjustment of Contingent Liabilities and Reserves Often an acquiring firm reassesses the adequacy of the acquired firm's accounting for contingent liabilities, purchase commitments, reserves, and so on, prior to its allocation of any difference between implied and book values. If the accounting for these items falls into a gray area of GAAP, the purchaser may decide to allocate some of the difference between implied and book values to adjust or create liability accounts. For example, suppose that the purchaser assesses a contingent liability of the acquired firm to be both probable and reasonably estimable, whereas the acquired firm had previously disclosed it only in a note because it was deemed reasonably possible (but not probable). By adjusting liabilities upward, the difference to be allocated to assets (and potentially to goodwill) is increased.

Interestingly, although many firms have been criticized for manipulating earnings to avoid recording goodwill, the Walt Disney Company, in its acquisition of Capital/ABC, was accused by some sources of managing earnings via liabilities to record ***excessive*** goodwill. The ***increase in recorded liabilities*** in such a case could be viewed as providing a sort of cushion or management tool for future earnings manipulation.

Disney's accountants created $2.5 billion in liabilities by asserting that Capital Cities/ABC ignored the timing of anticipated cash flows from future programming that the network agreed to finance (at least in part). This implies that after the merger, if programming costs increased, Disney would have an option of writing these amounts off against these liabilities instead of running them through the income statement.[9]

[8] *Dow Jones Newswires,* "LukOil: ConocoPhillips to Become Equity Investor," 9/29/04.

[9] *Barron's,* "Disney's Real Magic," by Abraham Briloff, 3/23/98, pp. 17–20.

Allocation of Difference between Implied and Book Values to Long-Term Debt

LO7 Allocating difference to long-term debt.

Notes payable, long-term debt, and other obligations of an acquired company should be valued for consolidation purposes at their fair values. The fair value of liabilities, as defined by *SFAS No. 157* **[ASC 820]**, is the price that would be paid to transfer a liability in an orderly transaction between market participants at the measurement date. A fair value measurement assumes both, that the liability is transferred to a market participant at the measurement date and that the nonperformance risk relating to that liability is the same before and after its transfer. The fair value of the liability should reflect the nonperformance risk relating to that liability.[10]

The reporting entity should consider the effect of its credit risk (credit standing) on the fair value of the liability. Valuation techniques used to measure fair value should be consistently applied. Valuation techniques consistent with the market approach or income approach should be used to measure fair value. The market approach is defined as a valuation technique that uses prices and other relevant information generated by market transactions involving identical or comparable liabilities. The income approach is defined as an approach that uses valuation techniques to convert future amounts (for example, cash flows or earnings) to a single present amount (discounted). This is the present value technique.

To increase consistency and comparability in fair value measurements and related disclosures, the fair value hierarchy prioritizes the inputs to valuation techniques used to measure fair value into three broad levels. The fair value hierarchy gives the highest priority to quoted prices (unadjusted) in active markets for identical liabilities (Level 1) and the lowest priority to unobservable inputs (Level 3). In some cases, the inputs used to measure fair value might fall in different levels of the fair value hierarchy. The level in the fair value hierarchy within which the fair value measurement in its entirety falls should be determined based on the lowest level input that is significant to the entire fair value measurement. Assessing the significance of a particular input to the fair value measurement in its entirety requires judgment, and consideration of factors specific to the asset or liability.

Assume that S Company has outstanding $500,000 in 6%, 30-year bonds that were issued at par on January 1, 1986, and that interest on the bonds is paid annually. Assume further that on January 1, 2011, when P Company acquires a 100% interest in S Company, the yield rate on bonds with similar risk is 10%. The present value of S Company's bonds payable determined at the effective yield rate on the acquisition date for five periods (the time until maturity) is calculated as follows:

(1) Interest Payments $30,000 × 3.79079 =	$113,724
(2) Principal Payment $500,000 × .62092 =	310,460
Present Value of Future Cash Payments Discounted at 10%	$424,184

(1) The present value of an annuity of one for five periods discounted at 10% is 3.79079.
(2) The present value of an amount of one received five periods hence discounted at 10% is 0.62092.

From the point of view of the consolidated entity, bonds payable are overstated on January 1, 2011, by $75,816 ($500,000 − $424,184) and a corresponding amount

[10] *SFAS No. 157*, "Fair Value Measurement" [Topic 820: "Fair Value Measurement and Disclosure"] states, "If a present value technique is used, the estimated future cash flows should not ignore relevant provisions of the debt agreement (for example, the right of the issuer to prepay)."

of the total difference between implied and book values on the date of acquisition must be allocated to "unamortized discount on bonds payable." In years after acquisition, interest expense reported by the subsidiary will be understated for consolidation purposes. Thus, workpaper entries must be made to amortize the discount in a manner that will reflect consolidated interest expense as a constant rate on the carrying value of the liability to the consolidated entity. An amortization schedule for this purpose is presented in Illustration 5-16. Consolidated statements workpaper entries necessary in the first five years subsequent to P Company's acquisition of S Company are summarized in the following table.

At maturity the bonds will be redeemed at par value ($500,000), which also will be the carrying value to the consolidated entity. In all subsequent years after redemption, $75,816 of the difference between implied and book value will be debited to the beginning retained earnings of the parent company in the consolidated statements workpaper in order to reduce beginning consolidated retained earnings for the cumulative amount of additional interest expense recognized in the consolidated financial statements in prior years. If the complete equity method is used, the debit will be to the Investment account, as the parent should have already reflected the adjustment to earnings in its equity in subsidiary income and hence in its retained earnings.

ILLUSTRATION 5-16

Bond Discount Amortization Schedule

Date	*Interest Expense Recorded by S*	*Consolidated Interest Expense*	*Discount Amortization*	*Consolidated Carrying Value*
1/1/2011	$ —0—	$ —0—	$ —0—	$424,184
12/31/2011	30,000	42,418(1)	12,418(2)	436,602(3)
12/31/2012	30,000	43,660(4)	13,660	450,262
12/31/2013	30,000	45,026	15,026	465,288
12/31/2014	30,000	46,529	16,529	481,817
12/31/2015	30,000	48,183	18,183	500,000
	150,000	225,816	75,816	

(1) .10 × $424,184 = $42,418.
(2) $42,418 − $30,000 = $12,418.
(3) $424,184 + $12,418 = $436,602.
(4) .10 × $436,602 = $43,660.

Cost and Partial Equity Methods

December 31	*2011*		*2012*		*2013*		*2014*		*2015*	
	Debit	*Credit*	*Debit*	*Credit*	*Debit*	*Credit*	*Debit*	*Credit*	*Debit*	*Credit*
Unamortized Discount on Bonds Payable	75,816		75,816		75,816		75,816		75,816	
Difference between Implied and Book Value		75,816		75,816		75,816		75,816		75,816
Beginning Retained Earnings—P Company (Consolidated Retained Earnings)	—0—		12,418		26,078		41,104		57,633	
Interest Expense	12,418		13,660		15,026		16,529		18,183	
Unamortized Discount on Bonds Payable		12,418		26,078		41,104		57,633		75,816

Complete Equity Method

December 31	*2011*		*2012*		*2013*		*2014*		*2015*	
	Debit	*Credit*	*Debit*	*Credit*	*Debit*	*Credit*	*Debit*	*Credit*	*Debit*	*Credit*
Unamortized Discount on Bonds Payable	75,816		75,816		75,816		75,816		75,816	
Difference between Implied and Book Value		75,816		75,816		75,816		75,816		75,816
Investment in S Company	—0—		12,418		26,078		41,104		57,633	
Interest Expense	12,418		13,660		15,026		16,529		18,183	
Unamortized Discount on Bonds Payable		12,418		26,078		41,104		57,633		75,816

The preceding example was based on the assumption that P Company owned a 100% interest in S Company. If P Company owned an 80% interest rather than a 100% interest in S Company, the amount of the difference between implied and book value allocated to unamortized discount on bonds payable on the date of acquisition is still $75,816. However, the subsequent year debits would be split between beginning retained earnings of the parent company (80%) and Noncontrolling Interest (20%) under the cost and partial equity methods. Under the complete equity method, the subsequent year debits would be split between the Investment account (80%) and Noncontrolling Interest (20%).

Allocating the Difference to Assets (Liabilities) with Fair Values Less (Greater) than Book Values

LO8 Allocation when the fair value is below book value.

Sometimes the fair value of an asset on the date of acquisition is less than the amount recorded on the books of the subsidiary. In this case, the allocation of the difference between the fair value and the book value of the asset will result in a reduction of the asset. If the asset is depreciable, this difference will be amortized over the life of the asset as a reduction of depreciation expense. Likewise, the fair value of the long-term debt may be greater rather than less than its recorded value on the date of acquisition. In this case, entries are necessary to allocate the difference between the fair value and book value of the debt to unamortized bond premium and to amortize it over the remaining life of the debt as a reduction of interest expense.

To illustrate, assume that P Company paid $2,240,000 for 80% of the outstanding stock of S Company when S Company had identifiable net assets with a fair value of $2,600,000 and a book value of $2,150,000. The fair values and book values of identifiable assets and liabilities are presented in Illustration 5-17. The Computation and Allocation (CAD) Schedule is presented next.

Assume that the $125,000 allocated to bond premium is amortized over five years using the straight-line method[11] and that the equipment has a remaining life of four years.

[11] The straight-line method is illustrated here as a matter of expediency. Where differences between the straight-line method and the effective interest rate method of amortization are material, the effective interest rate method as shown in Illustration 5-16 should be used.

ILLUSTRATION 5-17

Allocation of Difference between Implied and Book Value

	Fair Value	*Book Value*	*Difference between Fair Value and Book Value*
Securities	550,000	400,000	150,000
Equipment (net)	1,250,000	1,500,000	(250,000)
Land	1,225,000	550,000	675,000
Bonds payable	(725,000)	(600,000)	(125,000)
Other assets and liabilities	300,000	300,000	—0—
Total	2,600,000	2,150,000	450,000

Computation and Allocation of Difference Schedule

	Parent Share	*Noncontrolling Share*	*Entire Value*
Purchase price and implied value	**$2,240,000**	**560,000**	2,800,000
Less: Book value of equity acquired	1,720,000	430,000	**2,150,000**
Difference between implied and book value	520,000	130,000	**650,000**
Increase Securities	(120,000)	(30,000)	**(150,000)**
Decrease Equipment	200,000	50,000	**250,000**
Increase Land	(540,000)	(135,000)	**(675,000)**
Increase Bonds Payable	100,000	25,000	**125,000**
Balance	160,000	40,000	200,000
Record Goodwill	(160,000)	(40,000)	**(200,000)**
Balance	—0—	—0—	—0—

End of First Year after Acquisition (Worksheet Entries) At the end of the first year, the workpaper entries are:

	Debit	Credit
(1) Securities	150,000	
Land	675,000	
Goodwill	200,000	
Equipment (net)		250,000
Unamortized Premium on Bonds Payable		125,000
Difference between Implied and Book Values		650,000

To allocate the difference between implied and book value on the date of acquisition.

Note that the assets accounts increased are recorded by debits and those decreased by credits (Equipment), while a credit records an increase in a liability (increase in Unamortized Premium on Bonds Payable).

	Debit	Credit
(2) Equipment (net)	62,500	
Depreciation expense		62,500

To adjust depreciation expense downward ($250,000/4 years).

	Debit	Credit
(3) Unamortized premium on bonds payable	25,000	
Interest expense		25,000

To amortize premium on bonds payable ($125,000/5 years).

End of Second Year after Acquisition (Worksheet Entries) At the end of the second year the workpaper entries are:

	Debit	Credit
(1) Securities	150,000	
Land	675,000	
Goodwill	200,000	
Equipment (net)		250,000
Unamortized Premium on Bonds Payable		125,000
Difference between Implied and Book Value		650,000

To allocate the difference between implied and book value on the date of acquisition (this entry is repeated in subsequent years because the year of acquisition entry was recorded only on a workpaper).

Cost and Partial Equity Methods			*Complete Equity Method*		
(2) Equipment (net)	125,000		Equipment (net)	125,000	
Beginning Retained Earnings—Company P		50,000	Investment in S Company		50,000
Noncontrolling Interest in Equity		12,500	Noncontrolling Interest in Equity		12,500
Depreciation expense		62,500	Depreciation expense		62,500

To adjust depreciation downward for the current and prior year ($250,000/4 years)

Cost and Partial Equity Methods			*Complete Equity Method*		
(3) Unamortized premium on bond payable	50,000		Unamortized premium on bond payable	50,000	
Beginning Retained Earnings—Company P		20,000	Investment in S Company		20,000
Noncontrolling Interest in Equity (20%)		5,000	Noncontrolling Interest in Equity (20%)		5,000
Interest expense		25,000	Interest expense		25,000

To amortize premium on bond payable for current and prior year($125,000/5 years)

In the second year, under the cost or partial equity method, adjustments to the beginning retained earnings of the parent company and Noncontrolling Interest are necessary so that consolidated retained earnings and Noncontrolling Interest at the beginning of the second year will be equal to the consolidated equity balances reported at the end of the first year. The debits and credits are equal to the adjustments to consolidated net income that resulted from the reduction of depreciation expense ($62,500) and the reduction in interest expense ($25,000) in the prior year's workpaper. Under the complete equity method, no such adjustment to retained earnings is needed since the parent's retained earnings reflect accurately the consolidated retained earnings each year. Instead, entries are needed to the Investment account to facilitate the elimination of that account (by reversing the adjustments reflected therein), as well as to Noncontrolling Interest in Equity.

Reporting Accumulated Depreciation in Consolidated Financial Statements as a Separate Balance

LO9 Depreciable assets at net and gross values.

In previous illustrations, we have assumed that any particular classification of depreciable assets will be presented in the consolidated financial statements as a single balance net of accumulated depreciation. When accumulated depreciation is reported as a separate balance in the consolidated financial statements, the workpaper entry to allocate and depreciate the difference between implied and book value must be slightly modified. To illustrate, assume that P Company acquires a 90% interest in S Company on January 1, 2011, and that the difference between implied and book value in the amount of $200,000 is entirely attributable to equipment with an original life of nine years and a remaining life on January 1, 2011, of five years. Pertinent information regarding the equipment is presented in Illustration 5-18.

ILLUSTRATION 5-18

Determination of Amount of Difference between Implied and Book Value Allocated to Equipment and to Accumulated Depreciation
January 1, 2011

	Fair Value	*Book Value*	*Difference Between Fair Value and Book Value*
Equipment (gross)	$1,200,000	$900,000	$300,000
Accumulated depreciation	400,000	300,000	100,000
Equipment (net)	$ 800,000	$600,000	$200,000
Annual Depreciation (original life nine years, remaining life five years)		$100,000	$ 40,000

In Illustration 5-18, the $1,200,000 fair value of the equipment (gross) is the replacement cost of the equipment if purchased ***new*** and is referred to as **replacement cost new**. The $400,000 in accumulated depreciation in the fair value column is the proportional amount of replacement cost now necessary to bring the net fair market value to $800,000, which is the fair market value of the subsidiary's ***used*** equipment. The $800,000 fair value of the used equipment is sometimes referred to in appraisal reports as the equipment's **sound value**.

If the equipment is to be presented in the consolidated financial statements as one balance net of accumulated depreciation, workpaper elimination entries to allocate and depreciate the difference between implied and book value are similar to those presented in Illustration 5-6 and Illustration 5-7, and are summarized in Illustration 5-19 for three years. However, when equipment and accumulated depreciation are reported as separate balances in the consolidated financial statements, the workpaper elimination entries must be modified as presented in Illustration 5-20. The amount debited to Equipment (gross) minus the amount credited to Accumulated Depreciation in each of the workpaper entries in Illustration 5-20 is the same as the amount debited to Equipment (net) in the workpaper entries in Illustration 5-19, where equipment is presented in the consolidated financial statements net of accumulated depreciation.

To allocate the $200,000 difference assigned to Net Equipment between Equipment (gross) and Accumulated Depreciation, we need to know the replacement cost new and the sound (used) value of the equipment as shown in the appraisal report. Alternatively, these amounts may be inferred. If, for example, the

ILLUSTRATION 5-19

Summary of Workpaper Entries
Equipment Presented Net of Accumulated Depreciation

	1/1/2011		12/31/2011		12/31/2012		12/31/2013	
Cost or Partial Equity Method	*Debit*	*Credit*	*Debit*	*Credit*	*Debit*	*Credit*	*Debit*	*Credit*
Equipment (net)	200,000		200,000		200,000		200,000	
Difference between Implied and Book Value		200,000		200,000		200,000		200,000
Depreciation Expense	—0—		40,000		40,000		40,000	
Beginning Retained Earnings—Parent Company (Beginning Consolidated Retained Earnings)	—0—		—0—		36,000		72,000	
Noncontrolling Interest	—0—		—0—		4,000		80,000	
Equipment (net)		—0—		40,000		80,000		120,000
Complete Equity Method								
Equipment (net)	200,000		200,000		200,000		200,000	
Difference between Implied and Book Value		200,000		200,000		200,000		200,000
Depreciation Expense	—0—		40,000		40,000		40,000	
Investment in S Company	—0—		—0—		36,000		72,000	
Noncontrolling Interest	—0—		—0—		4,000		8,000	
Equipment (net)		—0—		40,000		80,000		120,000

ILLUSTRATION 5-20

Summary of Workpaper Entries
Accumulated Depreciation Presented as Separate Balance

	1/1/2011		12/31/2011		12/31/2012		12/31/2013	
Cost or Partial Equity Method	*Debit*	*Credit*	*Debit*	*Credit*	*Debit*	*Credit*	*Debit*	*Credit*
Equipment (net)	300,000		300,000		300,000		300,000	
Accumulated Depreciation		100,000		100,000		100,000		100,000
Difference between Implied and Book Value		200,000		200,000		200,000		200,000
Depreciation Expense	—0—		40,000		40,000		40,000	
Beginning Retained Earnings—Parent Company (Beginning Consolidated Retained Earnings)	—0—		—0—		36,000		72,000	
Noncontrolling Interest	—0—		—0—		4,000		8,000	
Accumulated Depreciation		—0—		40,000		80,000		120,000
Complete Equity Method								
Equipment (net)	300,000		300,000		300,000		300,000	
Accumulated Depreciation		100,000		100,000		100,000		100,000
Difference between Implied and Book Value		200,000		200,000		200,000		200,000
Depreciation Expense	—0—		40,000		40,000		40,000	
Investment in S Company	—0—		—0—		36,000		72,000	
Noncontrolling Interest	—0—		—0—		4,000		8,000	
Accumulated Depreciation		—0—		40,000		80,000		120,000

equipment is one-third depreciated on January 1, 2011, the $200,000 difference between P Company's interest in the sound value and the book value of the equipment implies that the difference can be "grossed up" by dividing by 2/3 as follows:

Let

Amount of Difference Allocated to Equipment (Gross) = X

Amount of Difference Allocated to Accumulated Depreciation = (1/3)X

Total Difference Allocated to Equipment (Net) = (2/3)X

$$X - (1/3)X = 200{,}000$$
$$(2/3)X = 200{,}000$$
$$X = 200{,}000 \div (2/3) = \$300{,}000 \text{ allocated to Equipment}$$
$$(1/3)X = (1/3)(300{,}000) = \$100{,}000 \text{ allocated to Accumulated Depreciation}$$

Disposal of Depreciable Assets by Subsidiary

Assume that on January 1, 2013, two years after its acquisition by P Company, S Company sells all the equipment referred to in Illustration 5-18 for $480,000. On January 1, 2013 (the date of the sale), the carrying value of the equipment on the books of the subsidiary is $400,000 but $520,000 from the consolidated point of view. These values are presented in Illustration 5-21. S Company reports a gain of $80,000 on the disposal of the equipment in its books.

ILLUSTRATION 5-21

Calculation of Recorded and Consolidated Gain or Loss
Disposal of Equipment

	S Company	*Unamortized Difference*	*Consolidated*
Cost	$ 900,000	$ 300,000	$1,200,000
Accumulated depreciation	500,000	180,000*	680,000
Undepreciated base	400,000	120,000	520,000
Proceeds	(480,000)		(480,000)
(Gain) loss on sale	$ 80,000	$ 120,000	$ 40,000

* $180,000 equals $100,000 allocated at acquisition plus $40,000 from year 2011, plus $40,000 from year 2009.

S Company's Books

Cash	480,000	
Accumulated depreciation	500,000	
Gain on sale		80,000
Equipment		900,000

From the point of view of the consolidated entity, however, there is a loss of $40,000. Recall that the usual workpaper entry to allocate the difference between implied and book value includes:

Equipment	300,000	
Difference between implied and book value		200,000
Accumulated depreciation		100,000

The workpaper entry necessary to adjust the amounts in the December 31, 2013, consolidated financial statements is as follows (shown first for the cost or partial equity methods and second for the complete equity method):

Cost or Partial Equity Method		
Beginning Retained Earnings—Parent Company (80% × $80,000) (depreciation expense adjustment for years 2011 and 2012)	64,000	
Noncontrolling Interest in Equity (20% × $80,000)	16,000	
Gain on Disposal of Equipment (eliminates gain already recorded)	80,000	
Loss on Disposal of Equipment (creates loss account)	40,000	
Difference between Implied and Book Value		200,000

Complete Equity Method		
Investment in S Company (80% × $80,000) (depreciation expense adjustment for years 2011 and 2012)	64,000	
Noncontrolling Interest in Equity (20% × $80,000)	16,000	
Gain on Disposal of Equipment (eliminates gain already recorded)	80,000	
Loss on Disposal of Equipment (creates loss account)	40,000	
Difference between Implied and Book Value		200,000

In the year of sale, any gain or loss recognized by the subsidiary on the disposal of an asset to which any of the difference between implied and book value has been allocated must be adjusted in the consolidated statements workpaper. The preceding entry serves to eliminate the gain recorded by the subsidiary and record the correct loss (or gain) to the consolidated entity. It also debits beginning retained earnings—P Company (or Investment in S Company if the complete equity method is used) and Noncontrolling Interest to "catch up" the effects to the equity accounts of the consolidated entity of two prior years of depreciation expense.

Depreciable Assets Used in Manufacturing

When the difference between implied and book values is allocated to depreciable assets used in manufacturing, workpaper entries necessary to reflect additional depreciation may be more complex because the current and previous years'additional depreciation may need to be allocated among work in process, finished goods on hand at the end of the year, and cost of goods sold. In practice, such refinements are often ignored on the basis of materiality, and all the current year's additional depreciation is charged to cost of goods sold.

PUSH DOWN ACCOUNTING

LO 10 Push down of accounting to the subsidiary's books.

Push down accounting is *the establishment of a new accounting and reporting basis for a subsidiary company in its separate financial statements based on the purchase price paid by the parent company to acquire a controlling interest in the outstanding voting stock of the subsidiary company.* This accounting method is required for the subsidiary in some instances such as in the banking industry, an industry that has been overwhelmed by the frequency and extent of merger activity in recent years.

The valuation implied by the price of the stock to the parent company is "pushed down" to the subsidiary and used to restate its assets (including goodwill) and liabilities in its separate financial statements. If *all* the voting stock is purchased, the assets and liabilities of the subsidiary company are restated so that the excess of the restated amounts of the assets (including goodwill) over the restated amounts of the liabilities equals the purchase price of the stock. Push down accounting is based on the notion that the basis of accounting for purchased assets and liabilities should be the same regardless of whether the acquired company continues to exist as a separate subsidiary or is merged into the parent company's operations. Thus, under push down accounting, the parent company's cost of acquiring a subsidiary is used to establish a new accounting basis for the assets and liabilities of the subsidiary in the subsidiary's separate financial statements. Because push down accounting has not been addressed in authoritative pronouncements of the FASB or its predecessors, practice has been inconsistent. Some acquired companies have used a new push down basis, and others, in essentially the same circumstances, have used preacquisition book values.

Arguments for and against Push Down Accounting

Proponents of push down accounting believe that a new basis of accounting should be required following an acquisition transaction that results in a significant change in the ownership of a company's outstanding voting stock. In essence, they view the transaction as if the new owners had purchased an existing business and established a new company to continue that business. Consequently, they believe that the parent company's basis should be imputed to the subsidiary because the new basis provides more relevant information for users of the subsidiary's separate financial statements. In addition, *SFAS No. 141R* [ASC 805] requires that assets acquired, liabilities assumed, and any noncontrolling interest in the acquiree at the acquisition date be measured at fair value. To provide symmetry, the separate financial statements of the subsidiary should be presented in the same manner.

Those who oppose push down accounting believe that, under the historical cost concept, a change in ownership of an entity does not justify a new accounting basis in its financial statements. Because the subsidiary did not purchase assets or assume liabilities as a result of the transaction, the recognition of a new accounting basis based on a change in ownership, rather than on a transaction on the part of the subsidiary, represents a breach in the historical cost concept in accounting. They argue further that implementation problems might arise. For example, noncontrolling stockholders may not have meaningful comparative financial statements. In addition, restatement of the financial statements may create problems in determining or maintaining compliance with various financial restrictions under debt agreements.

Push down accounting is an issue only if the subsidiary is required to issue separate financial statements for any reason, for example, because of the existence of noncontrolling interests or financial arrangements with nonaffiliates. Three important factors that should be considered in determining the appropriateness of push down accounting are:

1. Whether the subsidiary has outstanding debt held by the public.
2. Whether the subsidiary has outstanding a senior class of capital stock not acquired by the parent company.
3. The level at which a major change in ownership of an entity should be deemed to have occurred, for example, 100%, 90%, 51%.

Public holders of the acquired company's debt need comparative data to assess the value and risk of their investments. These public holders generally have some expressed (or implied) rights in the subsidiary that may be adversely affected by a new basis of accounting. Similarly, holders of preferred stock, particularly if the stock includes a participation feature, may have their rights altered significantly by a new basis of accounting.

Views on the percentage level of ownership change needed to apply a new basis of accounting vary. Some believe that the purchase of substantially all the voting stock (90% or more) should be the threshold level; others believe that the percentage level of ownership change should be that needed for control; for example, more than 50%. A related problem involves the amounts to be allocated to the individual assets and liabilities, noncontrolling interest, and goodwill in the separate statements of the subsidiary. Some believe that values should be allocated on the basis of the fair value of the subsidiary as a whole imputed from the transaction. Thus, if 80% of the voting stock is acquired for $32 million, the fair value of the net assets would be imputed to be $40 million ($32 million/.80), and values would be allocated on that basis. This approach will result in the assignment of the same values to assets and liabilities on the books of the subsidiary as that previously illustrated in the workpaper entry to allocate the difference between implied and book value in the consolidated statements workpaper. Others believe that values should be allocated on the basis of the proportional interest acquired. They believe that new values should be reflected on the books of the subsidiary only to the extent of the price paid in the transaction. Thus, if 80% of a company is acquired for $32 million, the basis of the subsidiary's net assets would be adjusted by the difference between the price paid and the book value of an 80% interest.

Status of Push Down Accounting

The Task Force on Consolidation Problems, Accounting Standards Division of the AICPA, released an issues paper entitled "Push Down Accounting" in 1979. The paper discussed the issues related to push down accounting and cited related literature. The paper also presented the conclusions of the Accounting Standards Executive Committee on the issues discussed in the paper. The majority of the Committee recommended the use of push down accounting where there had been at least a 90% change in ownership.

In 1983, the SEC released *Staff Accounting Bulletin (SAB) No. 54,* **[SEC topic 5; and ASC 805–10–599–4]** which discusses the staff's position on the appropriateness of applying push down accounting in the separate financial statements of subsidiaries acquired in purchase transactions. The SEC believes that purchase transactions that result in an entity becoming substantially wholly owned (as defined in Regulation S-X) should establish a new basis of accounting for the purchased assets and liabilities. When the form of ownership is within the control of the parent company, the basis of accounting for purchased assets and liabilities should be the same regardless of whether the entity continues to exist or is merged into the parent company's operations. ***As a general rule, the SEC requires push down accounting when the ownership change is greater than 95% and objects to push down accounting when the ownership change is less than 80%.*** In addition, the SEC staff expresses the view that the existence of outstanding public debt, preferred stock, or a significant noncontrolling interest in a subsidiary might impact the parent company's ability to control the form of ownership. In these circumstances, push down accounting, though not required, is an acceptable accounting method.

In December 1991, the FASB issued a Discussion Memorandum entitled "*An Analysis of Issues Related to New Basis Accounting*." The discussion memorandum was published to solicit views on which, if any, transactions or events should result in changing the carrying amount of an entity's individual assets, including goodwill, and liabilities to amounts representing their current fair values. Transactions and events discussed include stock purchases, as well as significant borrowing transactions, reorganizations and restructurings, and formations and sales of interests in joint ventures.

In September 2000, a joint project of the IASB/FASB was approved to develop a proposal for a project that would identify those situations in which fresh-start (new basis at fair value) recognition and measurement of all of an entity's assets and liabilities would be appropriate. One commonly identified candidate for application of this approach would be a multiparty business combination or other new entity formation in which no single preexisting entity obtains majority ownership and control of the resulting new entity. Similarly, joint venture formations also are candidates for this accounting treatment. No tentative decision has been reached at the time of this writing.

Push Down Accounting Illustration

To illustrate the application of push down accounting, we use data presented earlier in this chapter, with some modifications, as follows:

1. P Company acquired an 80% interest in S Company on January 1, 2011, for \$2,200,000, at which time S Company had capital stock of \$1,500,000 and retained earnings of \$500,000. The implied value of S Company is \$2,200,000/80% = \$2,750,000.
2. The difference between implied and book value (\$750,000) is allocated as presented in Illustration 5-22.

In this example, we assume that values are allocated on the basis of the fair value of the subsidiary as a whole, imputed from the transaction.

ILLUSTRATION 5-22

Allocation of Difference between Implied and Book Value

	Cost Basis	*Implied (100%) Push Down Base*
Inventory (FIFO basis)	$ 40,000	$ 50,000
Equipment (10-year life)	240,000	300,000
Land	120,000	150,000
Goodwill	200,000	250,000
Total	$600,000	$750,000

3. In 2011, S Company reported net income of \$32,500.

   Note that the net income of S Company (\$32,500) is \$80,000 less than the amount of income reported in Illustration 5-6 because the effect of the depreciation of the difference between implied and book value is recorded on the books of S Company under push down accounting. This difference of $80,000 consists of:

Increase in cost of goods sold	$50,000
Increase in depreciation expense ($300,000/10 years)	30,000
	$80,000

4. S Company declared a dividend of $20,000 on November 15, payable on December 1, 2011.
5. P Company uses the cost method to record its investment in S Company.

S Company Book Entries—2011

On January 1, 2011, the date of acquisition, S Company would make the following entry to record the effect of the pushed down values implied by the purchase of 80% of its stock by P Company:

Inventory, 1/1	50,000	
Equipment	300,000	
Land	150,000	
Goodwill	250,000	
Revaluation Capital		750,000

Assume the following: (1) all beginning inventory was sold during the year; and (2) equipment has a remaining useful life of 10 years from 1/1/2011. Given these assumptions, the $50,000 excess cost allocated to beginning inventory would be included in cost of goods sold when the goods were sold. Similarly, depreciation expense recorded on S Company's books would be $30,000 greater than if the increase in equipment value had not been recorded.

A workpaper for the preparation of consolidated financial statements on December 31, 2011, under push down accounting is presented in Illustration 5-23. Workpaper elimination entries in general journal form are:

(1)	Dividend Income	16,000	
	Dividends Declared—S Company		16,000
(2)	Capital Stock—S Company	1,500,000	
	Retained Earnings 1/1—S Company	500,000	
	Revaluation Capital—S Company	750,000	
	Noncontrolling Interest in Equity		550,000
	Investment in S Company		2,200,000

A comparison of Illustration 5-23 with Illustration 5-6 shows that consolidated net income as well as the controlling interest in consolidated net income and consolidated retained earnings are the same. Thus, when values are assigned on the basis of fair values of the subsidiary as a whole imputed from the transaction, the use of push down accounting has no effect on the consolidated balances.

Note also that no workpaper entries were necessary in Illustration 5-23 to allocate or depreciate the difference between implied and book value since these adjustments have already been made on S Company's books.

Cost Method
80% Owned Subsidiary
Push Down Basis

ILLUSTRATION 5-23
Consolidated Statements Workpaper
P Company and Subsidiary
for Year Ended December 31, 2011

Income Statement	*P Company*	*S Company*	*Eliminations Dr.*	*Eliminations Cr.*	*Noncontrolling Interest*	*Consolidated Balances*
Sales	3,100,000	2,200,000				5,300,000
Dividend Income	16,000		(1) 16,000			
Total Revenue	3,116,000	2,200,000				5,300,000
Cost of Goods Sold	1,700,000	1,410,000				3,110,000
Depreciation—Equipment	120,000	60,000				180,000
Other Expenses	998,000	685,000				1,683,000
Total Cost and Expense	2,818,000	2,155,000				4,973,000
Net/Combined Income	298,000	45,000				327,000
Noncontrolling Interest in Income					9,000*	9,000
Net Income to Retained Earnings	298,000	45,000	16,000	—0—	9,000	318,000
Retained Earnings Statement						
1/1 Retained Earnings						
P Company	1,650,000					1,650,000
S Company		500,000	(2) 500,000			
Net Income from above	298,000	45,000	16,000	—0—	9,000	318,000
Dividends Declared						
P Company	(150,000)					(150,000)
S Company		(20,000)		(1) 16,000	(4,000)	
12/31 Retained Earnings to Balance Sheet	1,798,000	525,000	516,000	16,000	5,000	1,818,000
Balance Sheet						
Investment in S Company	2,200,000			(2) 2,200,000		
Land	1,250,000	400,000				1,650,000
Equipment (net)	1,080,000	540,000				1,620,000
Other Assets (net)	2,402,000	1,885,000				4,287,000
Goodwill		250,000				250,000
Total	6,932,000	3,075,000				7,807,000
Liabilities	2,134,000	300,000				2,434,000
Capital Stock						
P Company	3,000,000					3,000,000
S Company		1,500,000	(2) 1,500,000			
Revaluation Capital		750,000	(2) 750,000			
Retained Earnings from above	1,798,000	525,000	516,000	16,000	5,000	1,818,000
1/1 Noncontrolling Interest in Net Assets				(2) 550,000	550,000	
12/31 Noncontrolling Interest in Net Assets					555,000	555,000
Total	6,932,000	3,075,000	2,766,000	2,766,000		7,807,000

(*) 20% × $45,000 = $9,000.
(1) To eliminate intercompany dividends.
(2) To eliminate investment account and create noncontrolling interest account.

IFRS VS. U.S. GAAP ON RESEARCH & DEVELOPMENT COSTS

As mentioned previously, Research & Development costs that are in process at the time of an acquisition are capitalized at their estimated fair value and expensed over their expected useful life. U.S. GAAP and IFRS are similar in this regard. However, for Research & Development projects undertaken ***apart from an acquisition*** or

subsequent to the acquisition, IFRS distinguish between research costs and development costs while U.S. GAAP generally expense both as incurred.

Under U.S. GAAP, development costs are generally expensed as incurred (as part of R&D expense) unless the costs relate to activities for which there is an alternative future use.

Under IFRS, development costs are capitalized if ***all*** of the following criteria are demonstrated (research costs are expensed):

1. The technical feasibility of completing the intangible asset,
2. The intention to complete the intangible asset,
3. The ability to use or sell the intangible asset,
4. How the intangible asset will generate future economic benefits (the entity should demonstrate the existence of a market or, if for internal use, the usefulness of the intangible asset),
5. The availability of adequate resources to complete the development,
6. The ability to measure reliably the expenditure attributable to the intangible asset during its development.

SUMMARY

1. *Calculate and allocate the difference between implied and book value to the subsidiary's assets and liabilities.* The difference between the value implied by the acquisition price and book value is used first to adjust the individual assets and liabilities to their fair values on the date of acquisition. If implied value exceeds the aggregate fair values of identifiable assets less liabilities, the residual amount will be *positive* (a debit balance). A positive residual difference is evidence of an unspecified intangible and is accounted for as goodwill.
2. *Describe FASB's position on accounting for bargain acquisitions.* When the value implied by the acquisition price is below the aggregate fair value of identifiable assets less liabilities, the residual amount will be negative (a credit balance). A negative residual difference is evidence of a bargain purchase, with the difference between implied value and fair value designating the amount of the bargain. When a bargain acquisition occurs, some of the acquired assets were reduced below their fair values under past GAAP. However, FASB's current position is that no assets are reduced below fair value; instead the credit balance should be shown as an ordinary gain in the year of acquisition.
3. *Explain how goodwill is measured.* Goodwill is measured as the excess of the value implied by the acquisition price over the fair value of the subsidiary's net assets.
4. *Describe how the allocation process differs if less than 100% of the subsidiary is acquired.* Under the economic entity concept adopted by FASB, the consolidated net assets are still written up by the entire difference (on the date of acquisition) between the implied fair value and the book value of the subsidiary company's net assets. The increase in the portion owned by the noncontrolling interest is reflected in an increase in the equity of the noncontrolling interest.
5. *Record the entries needed on the parent's books to account for the investment under the three methods: the cost, the partial equity, and the complete equity methods.* The most important difference between the cost and equity methods pertains to the period in which the parent recognizes subsidiary income on its books. If the cost method is in use, the parent recognizes its share of subsidiary income only when dividends are declared by the subsidiary. If the partial equity method is in use, the investor recognizes its share of the subsidiary's income when reported by the subsidiary. A debit to cash and a credit to the investment account record the receipt of dividends under the partial equity method. The complete equity method differs from the partial equity method in that the share of subsidiary income recognized by the parent is adjusted from the amount reported by the subsidiary. Such adjustments include the amount of excess depreciation implied by the difference between market values and book values of the underlying assets acquired.
6. *Prepare workpapers for the year of acquisition and the year(s) subsequent to the acquisition, assuming that the parent accounts for the investment using the cost, the partial equity, and the complete equity methods.* Under

the cost method, dividends declared by the subsidiary are eliminated against dividend income recorded by the parent. The investment account is eliminated against the equity accounts of the subsidiary, with the difference between implied and book value recorded in a separate account by that name. The difference is then allocated to adjust underlying assets and/or liabilities, and to record goodwill in some cases. Additional entries are made to record excess depreciation on assets written up (or to decrease depreciation if written down). Under the equity method, the dividends declared by the subsidiary are eliminated against the investment account, as is the equity in subsidiary income. The investment account is eliminated in the same way as under the cost method. In subsequent years, the cost method requires an initial entry to establish reciprocity or convert to equity. This entry, which is not needed under the equity method, debits the investment account and credits retained earnings of the parent (for the change in retained earnings of the subsidiary from the date of acquisition to the beginning of the current year multiplied by the parent's percentage). Only under the complete equity method does the parent's beginning retained earnings exactly match the amount reported as consolidated retained earnings at the end of the previous year. Hence, fewer workpaper adjustments to beginning retained earnings of the parent are needed under the complete equity method than under the two other methods. See Figures 5-1 through 5-3 for a complete summary of the three methods.

7. *Understand the allocation of the difference between implied and book value to long-term debt components.* Notes payable, long-term debt, and other obligations of an acquired company should be valued for consolidation purposes at their fair values. Quoted market prices, if available, are the best evidence of the fair value of the debt. If quoted market prices are unavailable, then management's best estimate of the fair value may be based on fair values of debt with similar characteristics or on valuation techniques such as the present value of estimated future cash flows. The present value should be determined using appropriate market rates of interest at the date of acquisition.

8. *Explain how to allocate the difference between implied and book value when some assets have fair values below book values.* In this case, the allocation of the parent company's share of the difference between the fair value and the book value of the asset will result in a reduction of the asset. If the asset is depreciable, this difference will be amortized over the life of the asset as a reduction of depreciation expense.

9. *Distinguish between recording the subsidiary depreciable assets at net versus gross fair values.* When the assets are recorded net, no accumulated depreciation account is used initially. When they are recorded gross, an accumulated depreciation account is needed. To allocate the difference assigned to depreciable assets between the asset account (gross) and the accumulated depreciation account, we must know the replacement cost new and the sound (used) value of the asset as shown in the appraisal report. Alternatively, these amounts may be inferred.

10. *Understand the concept of push down accounting.* Push down accounting is the establishment of a new accounting and reporting basis for a subsidiary company in its separate financial statements based on the purchase price paid by the parent company to acquire a controlling interest in the outstanding voting stock of the subsidiary company. This accounting method is required for the subsidiary in some instances, usually when the ownership level is over 95% for publicly held companies.

TEST YOUR KNOWLEDGE SOLUTIONS

5-1. 1. a

5-2. 1. d

5-3. 1. c

QUESTIONS

LO1 **1.** Distinguish among the following concepts:

- **(a)** Difference between book value and the value implied by the purchase price.
- **(b)** Excess of implied value over fair value.
- **(c)** Excess of fair value over implied value.
- **(d)** Excess of book value over fair value.

LO1 **2.** In what account is the difference between book value and the value implied by the purchase price recorded on the books of the investor? In what account is the "excess of implied over fair value" recorded?

LO4 3. How do you determine the amount of "the difference between book value and the value implied by the purchase price" to be allocated to a specific asset of a less than wholly owned subsidiary?

LO1 4. The parent company's share of the fair value of the net assets of a subsidiary may exceed acquisition cost. How must this excess be treated in the preparation of consolidated financial statements?

LO2 5. What are the arguments for and against the alternatives for the handling of bargain acquisitions? Why are such acquisitions unlikely to occur with great frequency?

LO1 6. P Company acquired a 100% interest in S Company. On the date of acquisition the fair value of the assets and liabilities of S Company was equal to their book value except for land that had a fair value of $1,500,000 and a book value of $300,000. At what amount should the land of S Company be included in the consolidated balance sheet? At what amount should the land of S Company be included in the consolidated balance sheet if P Company acquired an 80% interest in S Company rather than a 100% interest?

LO2 7. Corporation A purchased the net assets of Corporation B for $80,000. On the date of A's purchase, Corporation B had no long-term investments in marketable securities and $10,000 (book and fair value) of liabilities. The fair values of Corporation B's assets, when acquired, were

Current assets	$ 40,000
Noncurrent assets	60,000
Total	$ 100,000

Under *FASB Statement No. 141R* and *No.160* [Topics 805 and 810], how should the $10,000 difference between the fair value of the net assets acquired ($90,000) and the value implied by the purchase price ($80,000) be accounted for by Corporation A?

(a) The $10,000 difference should be credited to retained earnings.

(b) The noncurrent assets should be recorded at $50,000.

(c) The current assets should be recorded at $36,000, and the noncurrent assets should be recorded at $54,000.

(d) A current gain of $10,000 should be recognized.

LO2 8. Meredith Company and Kyle Company were combined in a purchase transaction. Meredith was able to acquire Kyle at a bargain price. The sum of the market or appraised values of identifiable assets acquired less the fair value of liabilities assumed exceeded the cost to Meredith. A determination was made that some of the appraised values were overstated and those assets were adjusted accordingly. After reducing the overstated assets downward, there was still a "negative balance." Proper accounting treatment by Meredith is to report the amount as

(a) An extraordinary item.

(b) Part of current income in the year of combination.

(c) A deferred credit.

(d) Paid in capital.

LO4 9. What is the effect on the noncontrolling share of consolidated income that results from the recording in the consolidated statements workpaper of differences between book value and the value implied by the purchase price (and their allocation to depreciable property, goodwill, etc.)?

Business Ethics

What is insider trading anyway?

Consider the following:

Many years ago, a student in a consolidated financial statements class came to me and said that Grand Central (a multistore grocery and variety chain in Salt Lake City and surrounding towns and cities) was going to be acquired and that I should try to buy the stock and make lots of money. I asked him how he knew and he told me that he worked part-time for Grand Central and heard that Fred Meyer was going to acquire it. I did not know whether the student worked in the accounting department at Grand Central or was a custodian at one of the stores. I thanked him for the information but did not buy the stock. Within a few weeks, the announcement was made that Fred Meyer was acquiring Grand Central and the stock price shot up, almost doubling. It was clear that I had missed an opportunity to make a lot of money . . . I don't know to this day whether or not that would have been insider trading. However, I have never gone home at night and asked my wife if the SEC called. From "Don't go to jail and other good advice for accountants," by Ron Mano, *Accounting Today*, October 25, 1999.

Question: Do you think this individual would have been guilty of insider trading if he had purchased the stock in Grand Central based on this advice? Why or why not? Are there ever instances where you think it would be wise to miss out on an opportunity to reap benefits simply because the behavior necessitated would have been in a gray ethical area, though not strictly illegal? Defend your position.

EXERCISES

EXERCISE 5-1 **Allocation of Cost** LO1

On January 1, 2010, Pam Company purchased an 85% interest in Shaw Company for $540,000. On this date, Shaw Company had common stock of $400,000 and retained earnings of $140,000.

An examination of Shaw Company's assets and liabilities revealed that their book value was equal to their fair value except for marketable securities and equipment:

	Book Value	*Fair Value*
Marketable securities	$ 20,000	$ 45,000
Equipment (net)	120,000	140,000

Required:

A. Prepare a Computation and Allocation Schedule for the difference between book value of equity acquired and the value implied by the purchase price.

B. Determine the amounts at which the above assets (plus goodwill, if any) will appear on the consolidated balance sheet on January 1, 2010.

EXERCISE 5-2 **End of the Year of Acquisition Workpaper Entries** LO1

On January 1, 2012, Payne Corporation purchased a 75% interest in Salmon Company for $585,000. A summary of Salmon Company's balance sheet on that date revealed the following:

	Book Value	*Fair Value*
Equipment	$525,000	$705,000
Other assets	150,000	150,000
	$675,000	$855,000
Liabilities	$ 75,000	$ 75,000
Common stock	225,000	
Retained earnings	375,000	
	$675,000	

The equipment had an original life of 15 years and has a remaining useful life of 10 years.

Required:

For the December 31, 2012, consolidated financial statements workpaper, prepare the workpaper entry to allocate and depreciate the difference between book value and the value implied by the purchase price assuming:

A. Equipment is presented net of accumulated depreciation.

B. Accumulated depreciation is presented on a separate row in the workpaper and in the consolidated statement of financial position.

EXERCISE 5-3 **Allocation of Cost** LO2

Pace Company purchased 20,000 of the 25,000 shares of Saddler Corporation for $525,000. On January 3, 2011, the acquisition date, Saddler Corporation's capital stock and retained earnings account balances were $500,000 and $100,000, respectively.

The following values were determined for Saddler Corporation on the date of purchase:

	Book Value	*Fair Value*
Inventory	$ 50,000	$ 70,000
Other current assets	200,000	200,000
Marketable securities	100,000	125,000
Plant and equipment	300,000	330,000

Required:

A. Prepare the entry on the books of Pace Company to record its investment in Saddler Corporation.

B. Prepare a Computation and Allocation Schedule for the difference between book value and the value implied by the purchase price in the consolidated statements workpaper.

EXERCISE 5-4 **Allocation of Cost and Workpaper Entries at Date of Acquisition** LO2

On January 1, 2012, Porter Company purchased an 80% interest in Salem Company for $260,000. On this date, Salem Company had common stock of $207,000 and retained earnings of $130,500.

An examination of Salem Company's balance sheet revealed the following comparisons between book and fair values:

	Book Value	*Fair Value*
Inventory	$ 30,000	$ 35,000
Other current assets	50,000	55,000
Equipment	300,000	350,000
Land	200,000	200,000

Required:

A. Determine the amounts that should be allocated to Salem Company's assets on the consolidated financial statements workpaper on January 1, 2012.

B. Prepare the January 1, 2012, consolidated financial statements workpaper entries to eliminate the investment account and to allocate the difference between book value and the value implied by the purchase price.

EXERCISE 5-5 **T-Account Calculation of Controlling and Noncontrolling Interest in Consolidated Net Income** LO4

On January 1, 2011, P Company purchased an 80% interest in S Company for $600,000, at which time S Company had retained earnings of $300,000 and capital stock of $350,000. Any difference between book value and the value implied by the purchase price was entirely attributable to a patent with a remaining useful life of 10 years.

Assume that P and S Companies reported net incomes from their independent operations of $200,000 and $100,000, respectively.

Required:

Prepare a t-account calculation of the controlling interest and noncontrolling interest in consolidated net income for the year ended December 31, 2011.

EXERCISE 5-6 **Workpaper Entries** LO1

Park Company acquires an 85%interest in Sunland Company on January 2, 2012. The resulting difference between book value and the value implied by the purchase price in the amount of $120,000 is entirely attributable to equipment with an original life of 15 years and a remaining useful life, on January 2, 2012, of 10 years.

Required:

Prepare the December 31 consolidated financial statements workpaper entries for 2012 and 2013 to allocate and depreciate the difference between book value and the value implied by the purchase price, recording accumulated depreciation as a separate balance.

EXERCISE 5-7 **Workpaper Entries** LO1

On January 1, 2011, Packard Company purchased an 80% interest in Sage Company for $600,000. On this date Sage Company had common stock of $150,000 and retained earnings of $400,000.

Sage Company's equipment on the date of Packard Company's purchase had a book value of $400,000 and a fair value of $600,000. All equipment had an estimated useful life of 10 years on January 2, 2006.

Required:

Prepare the December 31 consolidated financial statements workpaper entries for 2011 and 2012 to allocate and depreciate the difference between book value and the value implied by the purchase price, recording accumulated depreciation as a separate balance.

EXERCISE 5-8 **Workpaper Entries and Gain on Sale of Land** LO1

Padilla Company purchased 80% of the common stock of Sanoma Company in the open market on January 1, 2010, paying $31,000 more than the book value of the interest acquired. The difference between book value and the value implied by the purchase price is attributable to land.

Required:

A. What workpaper entry is required each year until the land is disposed of?

B. Assume that the land is sold on 1/1/13 and that Sanoma Company recognizes a $50,000 gain on its books. What amount of gain will be reflected in consolidated income on the 2013 consolidated income statement?

C. In all years subsequent to the disposal of the land, what workpaper entry will be necessary?

EXERCISE 5-9 **Allocation of Cost and Workpaper Entries** LO1

On January 1, 2010, Point Corporation acquired an 80% interest in Sharp Company for $2,000,000. At that time Sharp Company had capital stock of $1,500,000 and retained earnings of $700,000. The book values of Sharp Company's assets and liabilities were equal to their fair values except for land and bonds payable. The land had a fair value of $100,000 and a book value of $80,000. The outstanding bonds were issued at par value on January 1, 2005, pay 10% annually, and mature on January 1, 2015. The bond principal is $500,000 and the current yield rate on similar bonds is 8%.

Required:

A. Prepare a Computation and Allocation Schedule for the difference between book value and the value implied by the purchase price in the consolidated statements workpaper on the acquisition date.

B. Prepare the workpaper entries necessary on December 31, 2010, to allocate and depreciate the difference between book value and the value implied by the purchase price.

EXERCISE 5-10 **Allocation of Cost and Workpaper Entries** LO1

On January 2, 2010, Page Corporation acquired a 90% interest in Salcedo Company for $3,500,000. At that time Salcedo Company had capital stock of $2,250,000 and retained earnings of $1,250,000. The book values of Salcedo Company's assets and liabilities were equal to their fair values except for land and bonds payable. The land had a fair value of $200,000 and a book value of $120,000. The outstanding bonds were issued on January 1, 2005, at 9% and mature on January 1, 2015. The bonds' principal is $500,000 and the current yield rate on similar bonds is 6%.

Required:

A. Assuming interest is paid annually, prepare a Computation and Allocation Schedule for the difference between book value and the value implied by the purchase price in the consolidated statements workpaper on the acquisition date.

B. Prepare the workpaper entries necessary on December 31, 2010, to allocate and depreciate the difference between book value and the value implied by the purchase price.

EXERCISE 5-11 **Workpaper Entries for Three Years** LO6

On January 1, 2010, Piper Company acquired an 80% interest in Sand Company for $2,276,000. At that time the capital stock and retained earnings of Sand Company were $1,800,000 and $700,000, respectively. Differences between the fair value and the book value of the identifiable assets of Sand Company were as follows:

	Fair Value in Excess of Book Value
Inventory	$45,000
Equipment (net)	50,000

The book values of all other assets and liabilities of Sand Company were equal to their fair values on January 1, 2010. The equipment had a remaining useful life of eight years. Inventory is accounted for on a FIFO basis. Sand Company's reported net income and declared dividends for 2010 through 2012 are shown here:

	2010	*2011*	*2012*
Net Income	$100,000	$150,000	$80,000
Dividends	20,000	30,000	15,000

Required:

Prepare the eliminating/adjusting entries needed on the consolidated worksheet for the years ended 2010, 2011, and 2012. (It is not necessary to prepare the worksheet.)

1. Assume the use of the cost method.

2. Assume the use of the partial equity method.

3. Assume the use of the complete equity method.

EXERCISE 5-12 **Workpaper Entries and Consolidated Retained Earnings, Cost Method** LO6

A 90% interest in Saxton Corporation was purchased by Palm Incorporated on January 2, 2011. The capital stock balance of Saxton Corporation was $3,000,000 on this date, and the balance in retained earnings was $1,000,000. The cost of the investment to Palm Incorporated was $3,750,000.

The balance sheet information available for Saxton Corporation on the acquisition date revealed these values:

	Book Value	*Fair Value*
Inventory (FIFO)	$ 700,000	$ 800,000
Equipment (net)	2,000,000	2,000,000
Land	1,600,000	2,000,000

The equipment was determined to have a 15-year useful life when purchased at the beginning of 2006. Saxton Corporation reported net income in 2011 of $250,000 and $300,000 in 2012. No dividends were declared in either of those years.

Required:

A. Prepare the workpaper entries, assuming that the cost method is used to account for the investment, to establish reciprocity, to eliminate the investment account, and to allocate and depreciate the difference between book value and the value implied by the purchase price in the 2012 consolidated statements workpaper.

B. Calculate the consolidated retained earnings for the year ended December 31, 2012, assuming that the balance in Palm Incorporated's ending retained earnings on that date was $2,000,000.

EXERCISE 5-13 **Push Down Accounting** LO10

Pascal Corporation purchased 90% of the stock of Salzer Company for $2,070,000 on January 1, 2012. On this date, the fair value of the assets and liabilities of Salzer Company was equal to their book value except for the inventory and equipment accounts. The inventory had a fair value of $725,000 and a book value of $600,000. The equipment had a book value of $900,000 and a fair value of $1,075,000.

The balances in Salzer Company's capital stock and retained earnings accounts on the date of acquisition were $1,200,000 and $600,000, respectively.

Required:

In general journal form, prepare the entries on Salzer Company's books to record the effect of the pushed down values implied by the purchase of its stock by Pascal Company assuming that values are allocated on the basis of the fair value of Salzer Company as a whole imputed from the transaction.

EXERCISE 5-14 Workpaper Entries and Consolidated Retained Earnings, Partial Equity LO6

A 90% interest in Saxton Corporation was purchased by Palm Incorporated on January 2, 2011. The capital stock balance of Saxton Corporation was $3,000,000 on this date, and the balance in retained earnings was $1,000,000. The cost of the investment to Palm Incorporated was $3,750,000.

The balance sheet information available for Saxton Corporation on the acquisition date revealed these values:

	Book Value	*Fair Value*
Inventory (FIFO)	$ 700,000	$ 800,000
Equipment (net)	2,000,000	2,000,000
Land	1,600,000	2,000,000

The equipment was determined to have a 15-year useful life when purchased at the beginning of 2006. Saxton Corporation reported net income in 2011 of $250,000 and $300,000 in 2012. No dividends were declared in either of those years.

a. Prepare the worksheet entries, assuming that the partial equity method is used to account for the investment, to eliminate the investment account, and to allocate and depreciate the difference between book value and the value implied by the purchase price in the 2012 consolidated statements workpaper.

b. Calculate the consolidated retained earnings for the year ended December 31, 2012, assuming that the balance in Palm Incorporated's ending retained earnings on that date was $2,495,000.

EXERCISE 5-15 Workpaper Entries and Consolidated Retained Earnings, Complete Equity LO6

A 90% interest in Saxton Corporation was purchased by Palm Incorporated on January 2, 2011. The capital stock balance of Saxton Corporation was $3,000,000 on this date, and the balance in retained earnings was $1,000,000. The cost of the investment to Palm Incorporated was $3,750,000.

The balance sheet information available for Saxton Corporation on the acquisition date revealed these values:

	Book Value	*Fair Value*
Inventory (FIFO)	$ 700,000	$ 800,000
Equipment (net)	2,000,000	2,000,000
Land	1,600,000	2,000,000

The equipment was determined to have a 15-year useful life when purchased at the beginning of 2006. Saxton Corporation reported net income in 2011 of $250,000 and $300,000 in 2012. No dividends were declared in either of those years.

Required:

A. Prepare the worksheet entries, assuming that the complete equity method is used to account for the investment, to eliminate the investment account, and to allocate and depreciate the difference between book value and the value implied by the purchase price in the 2012 consolidated statements workpaper.

B. Calculate the consolidated retained earnings for the year ended December 31, 2012, assuming that the balance in Palm Incorporated's ending retained earnings on that date was $2,705,000.

EXERCISE 5-16 **Goodwill Impairment** LO3

On January 1, 2010, Porsche Company acquired 100% of Saab Company's stock for $450,000 cash. The fair value of Saab's identifiable net assets was $375,000 on this date. Porsche Company decided to measure goodwill impairment using comparable prices of similar businesses to estimate the fair value of the reporting unit (Saab). The information for these subsequent years is as follows:

Year	*Present Value of Future Cash Flows*	*Carrying Value of Saab's Identifiable Net Assets**	*Fair Value of Saab's Identifiable Net Assets*
2011	$400,000	$330,000	$340,000
2012	$400,000	$320,000	$345,000
2013	$350,000	$300,000	$325,000

*Identifiable net assets do not include goodwill.

Required:

Part A: For each year determine the amount of goodwill impairment, if any. Hint: You may wish to refer back to the section entitled Goodwill Impairment Test in Chapter 2.

Part B: Prepare the workpaper entries needed *each year* (2011 through 2013) on the consolidating worksheet to record any goodwill impairment assuming:

1. The cost or partial equity method is used.
2. The complete equity method is used.

PROBLEMS

PROBLEM 5-1 **Workpaper Entries and Consolidated Net Income for Two Years, Cost Method** LO6

On January 1, 2011, Palmero Company purchased an 80% interest in Santos Company for $2,800,000, at which time Santos Company had retained earnings of $1,000,000 and capital stock of $500,000. On the date of acquisition, the fair value of the assets and liabilities of Santos Company was equal to their book value, except for property and equipment (net), which had a fair value of $1,500,000 and a book value of $600,000. The property and equipment had an estimated remaining life of 10 years. Palmero Company reported net income from independent operations of $400,000 in 2011 and $425,000 in 2012. Santos Company reported net income of $300,000 in 2011 and $400,000 in 2012. Neither company declared dividends in 2011 or 2012. Palmero uses the cost method to account for its investment in Santos.

Required:

A. Prepare in general journal form the entries necessary in the consolidated statements workpapers for the years ended December 31, 2011 and 2012.

B. Prepare a schedule or t-account showing the calculation of the controlling and noncontrolling interest in consolidated net income for the years ended December 31, 2011 and December 31, 2012.

PROBLEM 5-2 **Workpaper Entries (including Goodwill Impairment), Consolidated Net Income for Two Years, Partial Equity Method** LO6

On January 1, 2011, Paxton Company purchased a 70% interest in Sagon Company for $1,300,000, at which time Sagon Company had retained earnings of $500,000 and capital stock of $1,000,000. On January 1, 2011, the fair value of the assets and liabilities of Sagon Company was equal to their book value except for bonds payable. Sagon Company had outstanding a $1,000,000 issue of 6% bonds that were issued at par and that mature on January 1, 2016. Interest on the bonds is payable annually, and the yield rate on similar bonds on January 1, 2011, is 10%. Paxton Company reported net income from independent operations of $300,000 in 2011 and $250,000 in 2012. Sagon Company reported net income of $100,000 in 2011 and $120,000 in 2012. Neither company paid or declared dividends in 2011 or 2012. Paxton uses the partial equity method to account for its investment in Santos.

Despite two profitable years, changes in the market during 2012 for Sagon's product line have caused Paxton to be concerned about the future profitability of the unit. The following data are collected to test for goodwill impairment at 12-31-12. (No goodwill impairment has been recorded on the parent's books.)

Paxton chose to measure goodwill impairment using the present value of future cash flows to estimate the fair value of the reporting unit (Sagon).

Year	*Present Value of Future Cash Flows*	*Carrying Value of Sagon's Identifiable Net Assets**	*Fair Value of Sagon's Identifiable Net Assets*
2012	$1,500,000	$1,409,000	$1,320,000

* Identifiable Net Assets do not include goodwill.

Required:

A. Prepare in general journal form the entries necessary in the consolidated statements workpapers for the years ended December 31, 2011, and December 31, 2012. Hint: You may wish to refer back to the section entitled Goodwill Impairment Test in Chapter 2.

B. Prepare in good form a schedule or t-account showing the calculation of the controlling and noncontrolling interest in consolidated net income for the years ended December 31, 2011, and December 31, 2012.

PROBLEM 5-3

Workpaper Entries and Consolidated Net Income, Complete Equity Method LO5 LO6

Perke Corporation purchased 80% of the stock of Superstition Company for $1,970,000 on January 1, 2012. On this date, the fair value of the assets and liabilities of Superstition Company was equal to their book value except for the inventory and equipment accounts. The inventory had a fair value of $725,000 and a book value of $600,000. Sixty percent of Superstition Company's inventory was sold in 2012; the remainder was sold in 2013. The equipment had a book value of $900,000 and a fair value of $1,075,000. The remaining useful life of the equipment is seven years.

The balances in Superstition Company's capital stock and retained earnings accounts on the date of acquisition were $1,200,000 and $600,000, respectively. Perke uses the complete equity method to account for its investment in Superstition. The following financial data are from Superstition Company's records.

	2012	*2013*
Net income	$750,000	$900,000
Dividends declared	150,000	225,000

Required:

A. In general journal form, prepare the entries on Perke Company's books to account for its investment in Superstition Company for 2012 and 2013.

B. Prepare the eliminating entries necessary for the consolidated statements workpapers in 2012 and 2013.

C. Assuming Perke Corporation's net income for 2012 was $1,000,000, calculate the controlling interest in consolidated net income for 2013.

PROBLEM 5-4

Eliminating Entries (including Goodwill Impairment) and Worksheets for Various Years LO1 LO6

On January 1, 2010, Porter Company purchased an 80% interest in the capital stock of Salem Company for $850,000. At that time, Salem Company had capital stock of $550,000 and retained earnings of $80,000.

COMPREHENSIVE

Differences between the fair value and the book value of the identifiable assets of Salem Company were as follows:

	Fair Value in Excess of Book Value
Equipment	$130,000
Land	65,000
Inventory	40,000

The book values of all other assets and liabilities of Salem Company were equal to their fair values on January 1, 2010. The equipment had a remaining life of five years on January 1, 2010. The inventory was sold in 2010.

Salem Company's net income and dividends declared in 2010 and 2011 were as follows:

Year 2010 Net Income of $100,000; Dividends Declared of $25,000

Year 2011 Net Income of $110,000; Dividends Declared of $35,000

Required:

A. Prepare a Computation and Allocation Schedule for the difference between book value of equity acquired and the value implied by the purchase price.

B. Present the eliminating/adjusting entries needed on the consolidated worksheet for the year ended December 31, 2010. (It is not necessary to prepare the worksheet.)

1. Assume the use of the cost method.
2. Assume the use of the partial equity method.
3. Assume the use of the complete equity method.

C. Present the eliminating/adjusting entries needed on the consolidated worksheet for the year ended December 31, 2011. (It is not necessary to prepare the worksheet.)

1. Assume the use of the cost method.
2. Assume the use of the partial equity method.
3. Assume the use of the complete equity method.

Use the following financial data for 2012 for requirements D through G.

	Porter Company	*Salem Company*
Sales	$1,100,000	$ 450,000
Dividend income	48,000	—
Total revenue	1,148,000	450,000
Cost of goods sold	900,000	200,000
Depreciation expense	40,000	30,000
Other expenses	60,000	50,000
Total cost and expense	1,000,000	280,000
Net income	$ 148,000	$ 170,000
1/1 Retained earnings	$ 500,000	$ 230,000
Net income	148,000	170,000
Dividends declared	(90,000)	(60,000)
12/31 Retained earnings	$ 558,000	$ 340,000
Cash	$ 70,000	$ 65,000
Accounts receivable	260,000	190,000
Inventory	240,000	175,000
Investment in Salem Company	850,000	
Land	—0—	320,000
Plant and equipment	360,000	280,000
Total assets	$1,780,000	$1,030,000
Accounts payable	$ 132,000	$ 110,000
Notes payable	90,000	30,000
Capital stock	1,000,000	550,000
Retained earnings	558,000	340,000
Total liabilities and equity	$1,780,000	$1,030,000

Required:

D. Prepare a consolidated financial statements workpaper for the year ended December 31, 2012. Although no goodwill impairment was reflected at the end of 2010 or 2011, the goodwill impairment test conducted at December 31, 2012 revealed implied goodwill from Salem to be only $150,000. The impairment has not been recorded in the books of the parent. (Hint: You can infer the method being used by the parent from the information in its trial balance.)

E. Prepare a consolidated statement of financial position and a consolidated income statement for the year ended December 31, 2012.

F. Describe the effect on the consolidated balances if Salem Company uses the LIFO cost flow assumption in pricing its inventory and there has been no decrease in ending inventory quantities since 2010.

G. Prepare an analytical calculation of consolidated retained earnings for the year ended December 31, 2012.

PROBLEM 5-5 Workpaper Entries and Consolidated Financial Statements LO1 LO6

On January 1, 2011, Palmer Company acquired a 90% interest in Stevens Company at a cost of $1,000,000. At the purchase date, Stevens Company's stockholders' equity consisted of the following:

Common stock	$500,000
Retained earnings	190,000

An examination of Stevens Company's assets and liabilities revealed the following at the date of acquisition:

	Book Value	*Fair Value*
Cash	$ 90,726	$ 90,726
Accounts receivable	200,000	200,000
Inventories	160,000	210,000
Equipment	300,000	390,000
Accumulated depreciation—equipment	(100,000)	(130,000)
Land	190,000	290,000
Bonds payable	(205,556)	(150,000)
Other	54,830	54,830
Total	$690,000	$955,556

Additional Information—Date of Acquisition

Stevens Company's equipment had an original life of 15 years and a remaining useful life of 10 years. All the inventory was sold in 2011. Stevens Company purchased its bonds payable on the open market on January 10, 2011, for $150,000 and recognized a gain of $55,556.

Financial statement data for 2013 are presented here:

	Palmer Company	*Stevens Company*
Sales	$620,000	$340,000
Cost of sales	430,000	240,000
Gross margin	190,000	100,000
Depreciation expense	30,000	20,000
Other expenses	60,000	35,000
Income from operations	100,000	45,000
Dividend income	31,500	0
Net income	$131,500	$ 45,000

	Palmer Company	*Stevens Company*
1/1 Retained earnings	$ 297,600	$210,000
Net income	131,500	45,000
	429,100	255,000
Dividends	(120,000)	(35,000)
12/31 Retained earnings	$ 309,100	$220,000
Cash	$ 201,200	$151,000
Accounts receivable	221,000	173,000
Inventories	100,400	81,000
Investment in Stevens Company	1,000,000	
Equipment	450,000	300,000
Accumulated depreciation—equipment	(300,000)	(140,000)
Land	360,000	290,000
Total assets	$2,032,600	$855,000
Accounts payable	$ 323,500	$135,000
Bonds payable	400,000	
Common stock	1,000,000	500,000
Retained earnings	309,100	220,000
Total liabilities and equity	$2,032,600	$855,000

Required:

A. What method is Palmer using to account for its investment in Stevens? How can you tell?

B. Prepare in general journal form the workpaper entry to allocate and depreciate the difference between book value and the value implied by the purchase price in the December 31, 2011, consolidated statements workpaper.

C. Prepare a consolidated financial statements workpaper for the year ended December 31, 2013.

D. Prepare in good form a schedule or t-account showing the calculation of the controlling and noncontrolling interest in consolidated net income for the year ended December 31, 2013.

PROBLEM 5-6 **Workpaper Entries for Two Years and Sale of Equipment in Year Two** LO6

On January 1, 2011, Perini Company purchased an 85% interest in Silvas Company for $400,000. On this date, Silvas Company had common stock of $90,000 and retained earnings of $210,000. An examination of Silvas Company's assets and liabilities revealed that their book value was equal to their fair value except for the equipment.

	Book Value	*Fair Value*
Equipment	$360,000	
Accumulated depreciation	(120,000)	
	$240,000	$300,000

The equipment had an expected remaining life of six years and no salvage value. Straightline depreciation is used.

During 2011 and 2012, Perini Company reported net income from its own operations of $80,000 and paid dividends of $50,000 in each year. Silvas Company had income of $40,000 each year and paid dividends of $30,000 on each December 31.

Accumulated depreciation is presented on a separate row in the workpaper and in the consolidated financial statements.

Required:

A. Prepare eliminating entries for consolidated financial statements workpaper for the year ended December 31, 2011, assuming:

1. The cost method is used to account for the investment.
2. The partial equity method is used to account for the investment.

B. On January 1, 2012, Silvas Company sold all its equipment for $220,000. Prepare the eliminating entries for the consolidated financial statements workpaper for the year ended December 31, 2012, assuming:

1. The cost method is used to account for the investment.
2. The partial equity method is used to account for the investment.

PROBLEM 5-7 **Workpaper Entries and Sale of Equipment in Year Three, Complete Equity** LO6

On January 1, 2011, Pueblo Corporation purchased a 75% interest in Sanchez Company for $900,000. A summary of Sanchez Company's balance sheet at date of purchase follows:

	Book Value	*Fair Value*
Equipment	$720,000	
Accumulated depreciation	(240,000)	
Equipment (net)	480,000	$660,000
Other assets	450,000	450,000
	$930,000	
Liabilities	$255,000	$255,000
Common stock	300,000	
Retained earnings	375,000	
	$930,000	

The equipment had an original life of 15 years and remaining useful life of 10 years.

During 2011 Pueblo Corporation reported income of $237,000 and paid dividends of $150,000. Sanchez Company reported net income of $123,000 and paid dividends of $120,000. Pueblo uses the complete equity method to account for its investment in Sanchez.

Required:

A. Prepare the elimination entries for the consolidated financial statements workpaper on December 31, 2011. Accumulated depreciation is presented on a separate row in the workpaper and in the consolidated financial statements.

B. Assume that Sanchez Company disposed of all its equipment on January 1, 2013, for $450,000.

1. What amount of gain (loss) will Sanchez Company report?
2. What is the consolidated gain (loss)?
3. Prepare the workpaper entry necessary to allocate the amount of the difference between book value and the value implied by the purchase price that was originally allocated to the equipment that has now been sold to outsiders.
4. What workpaper entry will be necessary to allocate this difference between book value and the value implied by the purchase price in future years?

PROBLEM 5-8 **Eliminating Entries and Consolidated Net Income** 

Patten Corporation acquired an 85% interest in Savage Company for $3,100,000 on January 1, 2011. On this date, the balances in Savage Company's capital stock and retained earnings accounts were $2,000,000 and $700,000, respectively.

An examination of Savage Company's books on this date revealed the following:

	Book Value	*Fair Value*
Current assets	$ 650,000	$ 650,000
Inventory	560,000	610,000
Marketable securities	430,000	430,000
Plant and equipment	1,200,000	1,600,000
Land	400,000	900,000
Liabilities	540,000	540,000

The remaining useful life of the plant and equipment is 10 years, and all the inventory was sold in 2011. The net income from Patten Corporation's own operations was $950,000 in 2011 and $675,000 in 2012. Savage Company's net income for the respective years was $110,000 and $180,000. No dividends were declared.

Required:

A. Prepare a Computation and Allocation Schedule for the difference between book value of equity and the value implied by the purchase price.

B. Prepare the consolidated statements workpaper eliminating entries for 2011 and 2012 in general journal form, under each of the following assumptions:

1. The cost method is used to account for the investment.
2. The partial equity method is used to account for the investment.
3. The complete equity method is used to account for the investment.

C. Calculate the controlling interest in consolidated net income for 2011 and 2012.

PROBLEM 5-9 **Workpaper Entries and Consolidated Net Income for Year of Acquisition** LO6

On January 1, 2011, Pump Company acquired all the outstanding common stock of Sound Company for $556,000 in cash. Financial data relating to Sound Company on January 1, 2011, are presented here:

	Balance Sheet	
	Book Value	*Fair Value*
Cash	$ 104,550	$ 104,550
Receivables	123,000	112,310
Inventories	220,000	268,000
Buildings	331,000	375,000
Accumulated depreciation—buildings	(264,800)	(300,000)
Equipment	145,000	130,000
Accumulated depreciation—equipment	(108,750)	(97,500)
Land	150,000	420,000
Total assets	$ 700,000	$1,012,360

	Book Value	*Fair Value*
Current liabilities	$106,000	$ 106,000
Bonds payable, 8% due 1/1/2025		
Interest payable on 6/30 and 12/31	300,000	
Common stock	200,000	
Premium on common stock	80,000	
Retained earnings	14,000	
Total liabilities and equities	$700,000	

Sound Company would expect to pay 10% interest to borrow long-term funds on the date of acquisition. During 2011, Sound Company wrote its receivables down by $10,690 and recorded a corresponding loss. Sound Company accounts for its inventories at lower of FIFO cost or market. Its buildings and equipment had a remaining estimated useful life on January 1, 2011, of 10 years and $2\frac{1}{2}$ years, respectively. Sound Company reported net income of $80,000 and declared no dividends in 2011.

Required:

A. Prepare in general journal form the December 31, 2011, workpaper entries necessary to eliminate the investment account and to allocate and depreciate the difference between book value and the value implied by the purchase price.

B. Assume that Pump Company's net income from independent operations in 2011 amounts to $500,000. Calculate the controlling interest in consolidated net income for 2011.

PROBLEM 5-10 **Workpaper Entries for Year of Acquisition** LO5 LO6

Pearson Company purchased a 100% interest in Sanders Company and a 90% interest in Taylor Company on January 2, 2011, for $800,000 and $1,300,000, respectively. The account balances and fair values of the acquired companies on the acquisition date were as follows:

	Sanders		Taylor	
	Book Value	*Fair Value*	*Book Value*	*Fair Value*
Current assets	$ 200,000	$200,000	$ 350,000	$350,000
Inventory	400,000	400,000	500,000	575,000
Plant and equipment (net)	300,000	350,000	600,000	600,000
Land	600,000	600,000	550,000	625,000
Total	$1,500,000		$2,000,000	
Current liabilities	$ 500,000	$500,000	$ 300,000	$300,000
Bonds payable	300,000	300,000	600,000	600,000
Capital stock	500,000		800,000	
Retained earnings	200,000		300,000	
Total	$1,500,000		$2,000,000	

Sanders Company's equipment has a remaining useful life of 10 years. Two-thirds of Taylor Company's inventory was sold in 2011, and the rest was sold in the following year. In 2011, Sanders Company reported net income of $500,000 and declared dividends of $100,000. Taylor Company's net income and declared dividends for 2011 were $800,000 and $200,000, respectively.

Required:

A. Prepare in general journal form the entries on the books of Pearson Corporation to account for its investments in 2011.

B. Prepare the elimination entries necessary in the consolidated statements workpaper for the year ended December 31, 2011.

PROBLEM 5-11 **Eliminating Entries (including Goodwill Impairment) and Worksheets for Various Years, Partial Equity Method** LO6

(Note that this is the same problem as Problem 5-4, but assuming the use of the partial equity method.)

On January 1, 2010, Porter Company purchased an 80% interest in the capital stock of Salem Company for $850,000. At that time, Salem Company had capital stock of $550,000 and retained earnings of $80,000. Porter Company uses the partial equity method to record its investment in Salem Company. Differences between the fair value and the book value of the identifiable assets of Salem Company were as follows:

	Fair Value in Excess of Book Value
Equipment	$130,000
Land	65,000
Inventory	40,000

The book values of all other assets and liabilities of Salem Company were equal to their fair values on January 1, 2010. The equipment had a remaining life of five years on January 1, 2010. The inventory was sold in 2010.

Salem Company's net income and dividends declared in 2010 and 2011 were as follows:

Year 2010 Net Income of $100,000; Dividends Declared of $25,000
Year 2011 Net Income of $110,000; Dividends Declared of $35,000

Required:

A. Present the eliminating/adjusting entries needed on the consolidated worksheet for the year ended December 31, 2010. (It is not necessary to prepare the worksheet.)

B. Present the eliminating/adjusting entries needed on the consolidated worksheet for the year ended December 31, 2011. (It is not necessary to prepare the worksheet.)

Use the following financial data for 2012 for requirements C through G.

	Porter Company	*Salem Company*
Sales	$1,100,000	$ 450,000
Equity in subsidiary income	136,000	—0—
Total revenue	1,236,000	450,000
Cost of goods sold	900,000	200,000
Depreciation expense	40,000	30,000
Other expenses	60,000	50,000
Total cost and expense	1,000,000	280,000
Net income	$ 236,000	$ 170,000
1/1 Retained earnings	$ 620,000	$ 230,000
Net income	236,000	170,000
Dividends declared	(90,000)	(60,000)
12/31 Retained earnings	$ 766,000	$ 340,000
Cash	$ 70,000	$ 65,000
Accounts receivable	260,000	190,000
Inventory	240,000	175,000
Investment in Salem Company	1,058,000	
Land	—0—	320,000
Plant and equipment	360,000	280,000
Total assets	$1,988,000	$1,030,000
Accounts payable	$ 132,000	$ 110,000
Notes payable	90,000	30,000
Capital stock	1,000,000	550,000
Retained earnings	766,000	340,000
Total liabilities and equity	$1,988,000	$1,030,000

Required:

C. Although no goodwill impairment was reflected at the end of 2010 or 2011, the goodwill impairment test conducted at December 31, 2012 revealed implied goodwill from Salem to be only $150,000. The impairment has not been recorded in the books of the parent. Prepare a t-account calculation of the controlling and noncontrolling interests in consolidated income for the year ended December 31, 2012.

D. Prepare a consolidated financial statements workpaper for the year ended December 31, 2012.

E. Prepare a consolidated statement of financial position and a consolidated income statement for the year ended December 31, 2012.

F. Describe the effect on the consolidated balances if Salem Company uses the LIFO cost flow assumption in pricing its inventory and there has been no decrease in ending inventory quantities since 2010.

G. Prepare an analytical calculation of consolidated retained earnings for the year ended December 31, 2012.

Note: If you completed Problem 5-4, a comparison of the consolidated balances in this problem with those you obtained in Problem 5-4 will demonstrate that the method (cost or partial equity) used by the parent company to record its investment in a consolidated subsidiary has no effect on the consolidated balances.

PROBLEM 5-12 **Workpaper Entries and Consolidated Financial Statements, Partial Equity Method** LO1 LO6

(Note that this is the same problem as Problem 5-5, but assuming the use of the partial equity method.)

On January 1, 2011, Palmer Company acquired a 90% interest in Stevens Company at a cost of $1,000,000. At the purchase date, Stevens Company's stockholders' equity consisted of the following:

Common stock	$500,000
Retained earnings	190,000

An examination of Stevens Company's assets and liabilities revealed the following at the date of acquisition:

	Book Value	*Fair Value*
Cash	$ 90,726	$ 90,726
Accounts receivable	200,000	200,000
Inventories	160,000	210,000
Equipment	300,000	390,000
Accumulated depreciation—equipment	(100,000)	(130,000)
Land	190,000	290,000
Bonds payable	(205,556)	(150,000)
Other	54,830	54,830
Total	$690,000	$955,556

Additional Information—Date of Acquisition

Stevens Company's equipment had an original life of 15 years and a remaining useful life of 10 years. All the inventory was sold in 2011. Stevens Company purchased its bonds payable on the open market on January 10, 2011, for $150,000 and recognized a gain of $55,556. Palmer Company uses the partial equity method to record its investment in Stevens Company. Financial statement data for 2013 are presented here:

	Palmer Company	*Stevens Company*
Sales	$ 620,000	$340,000
Cost of sales	430,000	240,000
Gross margin	190,000	100,000
Depreciation expense	30,000	20,000
Other expenses	60,000	35,000
Income from operations	100,000	45,000
Equity in subsidiary income	40,500	0
Net income	$ 140,500	$ 45,000
1/1 Retained earnings	$ 315,600	$210,000
Net income	140,500	45,000
	456,100	255,000
Dividends	(120,000)	(35,000)
12/31 Retained earnings	$ 336,100	$220,000

	Palmer Company	*Stevens Company*
Cash	$ 201,200	$151,000
Accounts receivable	221,000	173,000
Inventories	100,400	81,000
Investment in Stevens Company	1,027,000	
Equipment	450,000	300,000
Accumulated depreciation—equipment	(300,000)	(140,000)
Land	360,000	290,000
Total assets	$2,059,600	$855,000
Accounts payable	$ 323,500	$135,000
Bonds payable	400,000	
Common stock	1,000,000	500,000
Retained earnings	336,100	220,000
Total liabilities and equity	$2,059,600	$855,000

Required:

A. Prepare in general journal form the workpaper entry to allocate and depreciate the difference between book value and the value implied by the purchase price in the December 31, 2011, consolidated statements workpaper.

B. Prepare a consolidated financial statements workpaper for the year ended December 31, 2013.

C. Prepare in good form a schedule or t-account showing the calculation of the controlling interest in consolidated net income for the year ended December 31, 2013.

If you completed Problem 5-5, a comparison of the consolidated balances in this problem with those you obtained in Problem 5-5 will demonstrate that the method (cost or partial equity) used by the parent company to record its investment in a consolidated subsidiary has no effect on the consolidated balances.

PROBLEM 5-13 **Push Down Accounting** LO10

On January 2, 2011, Press Company purchased on the open market 90% of the outstanding common stock of Sensor Company for $800,000 cash. Balance sheets for Press Company and Sensor Company on January 1, 2011, just before the stock acquisition by Press Company, were:

	Press Company	*Sensor Company*
Cash	$1,065,000	$ 38,000
Receivables	422,500	76,000
Inventory	216,500	124,000
Building (net)	465,000	322,000
Equipment (net)	229,000	185,000
Land	188,000	100,000
Patents	167,500	88,000
Total assets	$2,753,500	$933,000
Liabilities	$ 667,000	$249,000
Common stock	700,000	300,000
Other contributed capital	846,000	164,000
Retained earnings	540,500	220,000
Total equities	$2,753,500	$933,000

The full implied value of Sensor Company is to be "pushed down" and recorded in Sensor Company's books. The excess of the implied fair value over the book value of net assets acquired is allocated as follows: To equipment, 30%; to land, 20%; to patents, 50%.

Required:

A. Prepare the entry on Sensor Company's books on January 2, 2011, to record the values implied by the 90% stock purchase by Press Company.

B. Prepare a consolidated balance sheet workpaper on January 1, 2011.

PROBLEM 5-14 **Push Down Accounting** LO10

On January 1, 2009, Push Company purchased an 80% interest in the capital stock of WayDown Company for $820,000. At that time, WayDown Company had capital stock of $500,000 and retained earnings of $100,000. Differences between the fair value and the book value of identifiable assets of WayDown Company were as follows:

	Fair Value in Excess of Book Value
Equipment	$125,000
Land	62,500
Inventory	37,500

The book values of all other assets and liabilities of WayDown Company were equal to their fair values on January 1, 2009. The equipment had a remaining life of five years on January 1, 2009. The inventory was sold in 2009. WayDown Company revalued its assets on January 2, 2009. New values were allocated on the basis of the fair value onWayDown Company as a whole imputed from the transaction.

Financial data for 2009 are presented here:

	Push Company	*WayDown Company*
Sales	$1,050,000	$ 400,000
Dividend income	40,000	—0—
Total revenue	1,090,000	400,000
Cost of goods sold	850,000	180,000
Depreciation expense	35,000	50,000
Other expenses	65,000	50,000
Total cost and expense	950,000	280,000
Net income	$ 140,000	$ 120,000
1/1 Retained earnings	$ 480,000	$ 102,500
Net income	140,000	120,000
Dividends declared	(100,000)	(50,000)
12/31 Retained earnings	$ 520,000	$ 172,500
Cash	$ 80,000	$ 35,000
Accounts receivable	250,000	170,000
Inventory	230,000	150,000
Investment in WayDown	820,000	
Goodwill	—0—	200,000
Land	—0—	362,500
Plant and equipment	350,000	300,000
Total assets	$1,730,000	$1,217,500
Accounts payable	$ 160,000	$ 100,000
Notes payable	50,000	20,000
Capital stock	1,000,000	500,000
Revaluation capital		425,000
Retained earnings	520,000	172,500
Total liabilities and equity	$1,730,000	$1,217,500

Required:

A. In general journal form, prepare the entry made by WayDown Company on January 2, 2009, to record the effect of the pushed down values implied by the purchase of its stock by Push Company assuming that values were allocated on the basis of the fair value of WayDown Company as a whole imputed from the transaction.

B. Prepare a consolidated financial statements workpaper for the year ended December 31, 2009.

C. What effect does the decision to apply the full push down approach have on the following items (compared to the case where push down accounting is not used):

1. Consolidated net income?
2. Consolidated retained earnings?
3. Consolidated net assets?
4. Noncontrolling interest in consolidated net assets?

PROBLEM 5-15 **Eliminating Entries and Worksheets for Various Years (including Goodwill Impairment), Complete Equity Method** LO6

(Note that this is the same problem as Problem 5-4 and Problem 5-11, but assuming the use of the complete equity method.)

On January 1, 2010, Porter Company purchased an 80% interest in the capital stock of Salem Company for $850,000. At that time, Salem Company had capital stock of $550,000 and retained earnings of $80,000. Porter Company uses the partial equity method to record its investment in Salem Company. Differences between the fair value and the book value of the identifiable assets of Salem Company were as follows:

	Fair Value in Excess of Book Value
Equipment	$130,000
Land	65,000
Inventory	40,000

The book values of all other assets and liabilities of Salem Company were equal to their fair values on January 1, 2010. The equipment had a remaining life of five years on January 1, 2010. The inventory was sold in 2010.

Salem Company's net income and dividends declared in 2010 and 2011 were as follows:

Year 2010 Net Income of $100,000; Dividends Declared of $25,000

Year 2011 Net Income of $110,000; Dividends Declared of $35,000

Required:

A. Present the eliminating/adjusting entries needed on the consolidated worksheet for the year ended December 31, 2010. (It is not necessary to prepare the worksheet.)

B. Present the eliminating/adjusting entries needed on the consolidated worksheet for the year ended December 31, 2011. (It is not necessary to prepare the worksheet.)

Use the following financial data for 2012 for requirements C through G.

	Porter Company	*Salem Company*
Sales	$1,100,000	$ 450,000
Equity in subsidiary income	77,200	—
Total revenue	1,177,200	450,000
Cost of goods sold	900,000	200,000
Depreciation expense	40,000	30,000
Other expenses	60,000	50,000
Total cost and expense	1,000,000	280,000
Net income	$ 177,200	$ 170,000
1/1 Retained earnings	$ 546,400	$ 230,000
Net income	177,200	170,000
Dividends declared	(90,000)	(60,000)
12/31 Retained earnings	$ 633,600	$ 340,000
Cash	$ 70,000	$ 65,000
Accounts receivable	260,000	190,000
Inventory	240,000	175,000
Investment in Salem Company	925,600	
Land	—0—	320,000
Plant and equipment	360,000	280,000
Total assets	$1,855,600	$1,030,000
Accounts payable	$ 132,000	$ 110,000
Notes payable	90,000	30,000
Capital stock	1,000,000	550,000
Retained earnings	633,600	340,000
Total liabilities and equity	$1,855,600	$1,030,000

Required:

C. Although no goodwill impairment was reflected at the end of 2010 or 2011, the goodwill impairment test conducted at December 31, 2012 revealed implied goodwill from Salem to be only $150,000. The impairment was reflected in the books of the parent. Prepare a t-account calculation of the controlling and noncontrolling interests in consolidated income for the year ended December 31, 2012.

D. Prepare a consolidated financial statements workpaper for the year ended December 31, 2012.

E. Prepare a consolidated statement of financial position and a consolidated income statement for the year ended December 31, 2012.

F. Describe the effect on the consolidated balances if Salem Company uses the LIFO cost flow assumption in pricing its inventory and there has been no decrease in ending inventory quantities since 2010.

G. Prepare an analytical calculation of consolidated retained earnings for the year ended December 31, 2012.

Note: If you completed Problem 5-4 and Problem 5-11, a comparison of the consolidated balances in this problem with those you obtained in Problem 5-4 and Problem 5-11 will demonstrate that the method (cost or partial equity) used by the parent company to record its investment in a consolidated subsidiary has no effect on the consolidated balances.

PROBLEM 5-16 Workpaper Entries and Consolidated Financial Statements, Complete Equity Method LO1 LO6

(Note that this is the same problem as Problem 5-5 or Problem 5-12, but assuming the use of the complete equity method.)

On January 1, 2011, Palmer Company acquired a 90% interest in Stevens Company at a cost of $1,000,000. At the purchase date, Stevens Company's stockholders' equity consisted of the following:

Common stock	$500,000
Retained earnings	190,000

COMPREHENSIVE

An examination of Stevens Company's assets and liabilities revealed the following at the date of acquisition:

	Book Value	*Fair Value*
Cash	$ 90,726	$ 90,726
Accounts receivable	200,000	200,000
Inventories	160,000	210,000
Equipment	300,000	390,000
Accumulated depreciation—equipment	(100,000)	(130,000)
Land	190,000	290,000
Bonds payable	(205,556)	(150,000)
Other	54,830	54,830
Total	$690,000	$955,556

Additional Information—Date of Acquisition

Stevens Company's equipment had an original life of 15 years and a remaining useful life of 10 years. All the inventory was sold in 2011. Stevens Company purchased its bonds payable on the open market on January 10, 2011, for $150,000 and recognized a gain of $55,556. Palmer Company uses the complete equity method to record its investment in Stevens Company. Financial statement data for 2013 are presented on the next page.

	Palmer Company	*Stevens Company*
Sales	$ 620,000	$340,000
Cost of sales	430,000	240,000
Gross margin	190,000	100,000
Depreciation expense	30,000	20,000
Other expenses	60,000	35,000
Income from operations	100,000	45,000
Equity in subsidiary income	35,100	0
Net income	135,100	$ 45,000
1/1 Retained earnings	$ 209,800	$210,000
Net income	135,100	45,000
	344,900	255,000
Dividends	(120,000)	(35,000)
12/31 Retained earnings	$ 224,900	$220,000

	Palmer Company	*Stevens Company*
Cash	$ 201,200	$151,000
Accounts receivable	221,000	173,000
Inventories	100,400	81,000
Investment in Stevens Company	915,800	
Equipment	450,000	300,000
Accumulated depreciation—equipment	(300,000)	(140,000)
Land	360,000	290,000
Total assets	$1,948,400	$855,000
Accounts payable	$ 323,500	$135,000
Bonds payable	400,000	
Common stock	1,000,000	500,000
Retained earnings	224,900	220,000
Total liabilities and equity	$1,948,400	$855,000

Required:

A. Prepare in general journal form the workpaper entry to allocate and depreciate the difference between book value and the value implied by the purchase price in the December 31, 2011, consolidated statements workpaper.

B. Prepare a consolidated financial statements workpaper for the year ended December 31, 2013.

C. Prepare in good form a schedule or t-account showing the calculation of the controlling interest in consolidated net income for the year ended December 31, 2013.

If you completed Problem 5-5 and Problem 5-12, a comparison of the consolidated balances in this problem with those you obtained in Problem 5-5 and Problem 5-12 will demonstrate that the method (cost, partial equity, or complete equity) used by the parent company to record its investment in a consolidated subsidiary has no effect on the consolidated balances.

PROBLEM 5-17 Impact on Future Profits and In-process R&D LO1

The Mcquire Company is considering acquiring 100% of the Sosa Company. The management of Mcquire fears that the acquisition price may be too high. Condensed financial statements for Sosa Company for the current year are as follows:

Income Statement	*2012*
Revenues	$100,000
Cost of Goods Sold	40,000
Gross Margin	60,000
Operating Expenses	35,000
Pretax Income	25,000
Income Tax Expense	10,000
Net Income	15,000

Balance Sheet	*Year Ended 12/31/11*	*Year Ended 12/31/12*
Cash	$ 4,000	$ 4,000
Receivables	10,000	14,000
Inventory	31,000	27,000
Fixed Assets (net)	50,000	55,000
Total Assets	$95,000	$100,000
Current Liabilities	$15,000	$ 17,000
Long-term Liabilities	25,000	18,000
Common Stock	20,000	20,000
Retained Earnings	35,000	45,000
Total Liabilities and Equity	$95,000	$100,000

You believe that Sosa might be currently acquired at a price resulting in a price to earnings (P/E) ratio of 8 to 12 times. Also, the fair market value of Sosa's net assets is approximately $105,000, and the difference between book value and the value implied by the purchase price is due solely to depreciable assets with a remaining useful life of 10 years. Sosa Company is heavily involved in research and development of new baseball bats that enable the batter to hit the ball further. You estimate that $30,000 of the acquisition price might be classified as in-process R&D. Sosa's net income is expected to grow an average of 10% per year for the next 10 years and remain constant thereafter.

Required:

A. If the acquisition occurs on January 1, 2013, determine the amount of income from Sosa Company that would be included in consolidated income assuming the following P/E ratios are used to determine the acquisition price, based on earnings for the year 2012. Suppose that the FASB revoked its requirement that in-process R&D be capitalized and amortized, as the result of extensive lobbying. Instead, in-process R&D will be expensed in the year of acquisition.

1. P/E ratio = 10
2. P/E ratio = 12

B. Now assume that FASB does require (as is currently the case at this writing) that in-process R&D be capitalized (assume an amortization period of 20 years). How would your answer to part A change?

PROBLEM 5-18 Deferred Tax Effects

On January 1, 2012, Pruitt Company issued 25,500 shares of its common stock ($2 par) in exchange for 85% of the outstanding common stock of Shah Company. Pruitt's common stock had a fair value of $28 per share at that time. Pruitt Company uses the cost method to account for its investment in Shah Company and files a consolidated income tax return. A schedule of the Shah Company assets acquired and liabilities assumed at book values (which are equal to their tax bases) and fair values follows.

Item	*Book Value/Tax Basis*	*Fair Value*	*Excess*
Receivables (net)	$125,000	$ 125,000	$ —0—
Inventory	167,000	195,000	28,000
Land	86,500	120,000	33,500
Plant assets (net)	467,000	567,000	100,000
Patents	95,000	200,000	105,000
Total	$940,500	$1,207,000	$266,500
Current liabilities	$ 89,500	$ 89,500	$ —0—
Bonds payable	300,000	360,000	60,000
Common stock	120,000		
Other contributed capital	164,000		
Retained earnings	267,000		
Total	$940,000		

Additional Information:

1. Pruitt's income tax rate is 35%.
2. Shah's beginning inventory was all sold during 2012.
3. Useful lives for depreciation and amortization purposes are:

Plant assets	10 years
Patents	8 years
Bond premium	10 years

4. Pruitt uses the straight-line method for all depreciation and amortization purposes.

Required:

A. Prepare the stock acquisition entry on Pruitt Company's books.

B. Assuming Shah Company earned $216,000 and declared a $90,000 dividend during 2012, prepare the eliminating entries for a consolidated statements workpaper on December 31, 2012.

C. Assuming Shah Company earned $240,000 and declared a $100,000 dividend during 2013, prepare the eliminating entries for a consolidated statements workpaper on December 31, 2013.

6

ELIMINATION OF UNREALIZED PROFIT ON INTERCOMPANY SALES OF INVENTORY

LEARNING OBJECTIVES

1. Describe the financial reporting objectives for intercompany sales of inventory.
2. Determine the amount of intercompany profit, if any, to be eliminated from the consolidated statements.
3. Understand the concept of eliminating 100% of intercompany profit not realized in transactions with outsiders, and know the authoritative position.
4. Distinguish between upstream and downstream sales of inventory.
5. Compute the noncontrolling interest in consolidated net income for upstream and downstream sales, when not all the inventory has been sold to outsiders.
6. Prepare consolidated workpapers for firms with upstream and downstream sales using the cost, partial equity, and complete equity methods.
7. Discuss the treatment of intercompany profit earned prior to the parent-subsidiary affiliation.

"What separates a good year in mergers-and-acquisitions from a bad one? By the Pavlovian measure of Wall Street, it is simple: The more deals, the better the year. But 2007 revealed the fallacy of this approach. Buyers gorged on cheap credit, overpaying along the way. Some raced to rip up transactions signed months earlier. More deals, more problems."[1]

LO4 Upstream and downstream sales.

Affiliated companies may make intercompany sales of inventory or other assets. The term "affiliated group" is used to refer to a parent and all subsidiaries for which consolidated financial statements are prepared; alternatively, this group may be referred to as the economic entity or as the consolidated entity.[2] Sales from a parent company to one or more of its subsidiaries are referred to as ***downstream sales.*** Sales from subsidiaries to the parent company are referred to as ***upstream sales.*** Sales from one subsidiary to another subsidiary are referred to as ***horizontal sales.***

---

[1] *Wall Street Journal,* "What to Look for as Deal Makers Revise Strategies," by Dennis Berman, p. C1, January 15, 2008.

[2] Note that this definition of an affiliated group is broader than the definition imposed by the Tax Code (Section 1504(a)). A parent must own at least 80% of the voting power of all stock classes and 80% of the fair value of its subsidiaries' outstanding stock to qualify as an affiliated group for tax purposes.

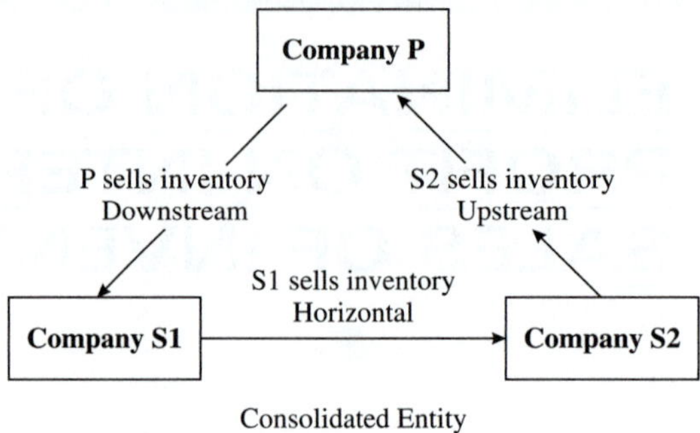

Ordinarily, the selling affiliate will record a profit or loss on such sales. From the point of view of the consolidated entity, however, such profit or loss should not be reported until the inventory or other assets acquired by the purchasing affiliate have been used during the course of operations or sold to parties outside the affiliated group (third parties). Profit (loss) that has not been realized from the point of view of the consolidated entity through subsequent sales to third parties is defined as ***unrealized intercompany profit (loss)*** and must be eliminated in the preparation of consolidated financial statements. The elimination of unrealized profit resulting from intercompany sales of inventory is examined in this chapter. The elimination of unrealized profit resulting from intercompany sales of property and equipment will be examined in the next chapter.

AOL Time Warner reported that intercompany advertising revenue increased to $97 million in the third quarter of 2001 (which represented 5% of the advertising revenue). The networks segment reported that advertising and commerce revenue fell by 6%. Later, a spokesperson for the company stated that these numbers included intercompany sales (a number that would be eliminated for consolidated statements).[3]

EFFECTS OF INTERCOMPANY SALES OF MERCHANDISE ON THE DETERMINATION OF CONSOLIDATED BALANCES

LO1 Financial reporting objectives for intercompany sales.

The workpaper procedures illustrated in this chapter are designed to accomplish the following financial reporting objectives in the consolidated financial statements:

- Consolidated sales include only ***sales to parties outside the affiliated group***.
- Consolidated cost of sales includes only ***the cost to the affiliated group*** of goods that have been sold to parties outside the affiliated group.
- Consolidated inventory on the balance sheet is recorded at its ***cost to the affiliated group***.

Stated another way, the objective of eliminating the effects of intercompany sales of merchandise is to present consolidated balances for sales, cost of sales, and inventory as if the intercompany sale had ***never*** occurred. As a result, the recognition of income or loss on the intercompany transaction, including its allocation between

[3] *The Street.com*, "Why You Can't Avoid Those AOL Ads," by George Mannes, 11/15/2001.

the noncontrolling and controlling interests, is deferred until the profit or loss is confirmed by sales of the merchandise to nonaffiliates.

Thoughtful consideration of these financial reporting objectives will indicate that they are logical and noncontroversial. However, the workpaper procedures for accomplishing these objectives are not self-evident. Thus the workpaper procedures for accomplishing these objectives are the central topic of this chapter. These procedures include workpaper entries to adjust the recorded amounts of sales, cost of sales (or components thereof), and ending inventory to amounts based on the objectives stated above. In addition, the procedures are designed to equate beginning consolidated retained earnings and noncontrolling interest (NCI) in equity with the amounts reported as ending consolidated retained earnings and ending NCI, respectively, in the previous reporting period for firms using the cost or partial equity methods. These procedures also serve to allocate consolidated income properly between the noncontrolling and controlling interests.

In order to concentrate on intercompany profit eliminations and adjustments, reporting complications relating to accounting for the difference between implied and book values are avoided in the initial illustrations by assuming that all acquisitions are made at the book value of the acquired interest in net assets and that the book value of the subsidiary company's net assets equals their fair value on the date the parent company's interest is acquired. (This assumption is later relaxed.) It is also assumed that the affiliates file consolidated income tax returns. If the affiliates file separate tax returns, deferred tax issues arise. These are addressed in the appendix to this chapter.

Determination of Consolidated Sales, Cost of Sales, and Inventory Balances Assuming Downstream Sales

The basic workpaper eliminating entries required because of intercompany sales of merchandise are illustrated using the following simplifying assumptions:

1. P Company sells all goods it buys or manufactures to its wholly owned subsidiary, S Company, at 125% of cost.
2. During the first year of this arrangement, goods that cost P Company $200,000 are sold to S Company for $250,000 (***downstream sale***).
3. During the same year, S Company sold all the goods purchased by it from P Company to third parties for $270,000.

Sales, cost of sales, and inventory balances reported by the affiliated companies are presented in Illustration 6-1. Recall that the cost of sales is computed as:

Beginning inventory
+ Net purchases[4]
Total available for sale
− Ending inventory
Cost of sales

[4] For a manufacturing concern, "purchases" is replaced by the total cost of goods manufactured, which includes labor and overhead in addition to the raw materials used. Nonetheless, when a company purchases manufactured items from an affiliate, the purchasing affiliate would record those items as "purchases" at the amount charged by the selling affiliate.

ILLUSTRATION 6-1

Partial Consolidated Statements Workpaper, Elimination of Intercompany Sale of Inventory, No Unrealized Profit (All Inventory Sold to Third Parties)

	P	S	Eliminations		Consolidated	
Income Statement	*Company*	*Company*	*Dr.*	*Cr.*	*Balances*	*%*
Sales	250,000	270,000	(1) 250,000		270,000	100.0%
Cost of Sales	200,000	250,000		(1) 250,000	200,000	74.1%
Gross Profit	50,000	20,000			70,000	25.9%
Balance Sheet						
Inventory	—0—	—0—			—0—	

(1) To eliminate intercompany sales.

Depending upon the accounting system used, a given company may have a single account in its general ledger entitled "cost of sales" or "cost of goods sold" and a single line on its workpaper or, alternatively, separate accounts for the various components. In this chapter, we assume that the trial balance lists each component separately, and we present the workpaper entries accordingly. Using this approach, the cost of sales line on the income statement is replaced with lines for Beginning Inventory—Income Statement; Purchases; Ending Inventory—Income Statement; and Cost of Sales. Note that under this assumption, Ending Inventory—Income Statement requires an entry distinct from that to the balance sheet account Inventory. The account "Ending Inventory—Income Statement" has a normal credit balance because it is subtracted in computing Cost of Sales. We indicate in parentheses those entries that might be replaced by the use of the single account "cost of sales."

The workpaper entry in the year of the sale to eliminate intercompany sales of merchandise takes the following form:

LO6 Consolidated workpapers for downstream sales.

(1)	Sales	250,000	
	Purchases (Cost of Sales)		250,000
	To eliminate intercompany sales.		

No unrealized intercompany profit exists, since all goods sold by P Company to S Company have been resold to third parties. After the elimination of intercompany sales, consolidated sales of $270,000 equals the amount of sales by the affiliated group (S Company) to third parties, and consolidated cost of sales of $200,000 equals the cost to the affiliated group (P Company) of manufacturing the goods sold.

Failure to eliminate intercompany sales would result in an overstatement of sales and of cost of sales in the consolidated financial statements. If the intercompany sales were not eliminated, the gross profit would be calculated as shown in Illustration 6-2.

ILLUSTRATION 6-2

The Impact on Gross Profit Percentages if Intercompany Sales Are Not Eliminated

	Without Eliminating Intercompany Sales			
Account	*Company P*	*Company S*	*Total*	*%*
Sales	$250,000	$270,000	$520,000	100.0%
Cost of Sales	200,000	250,000	450,000	86.5%
Gross Profit	50,000	20,000	70,000	13.5%

ILLUSTRATION 6-3

Partial Consolidated Statements Workpaper*, Elimination of Downstream Intercompany Sale of Inventory, Unrealized Profit in Ending Inventory (First Year of Intercompany Sales)

Income Statement	*P Company*	*S Company*	*Eliminations Dr.*	*Eliminations Cr.*	*Consolidated Balances*
Sales	250,000	162,000	(1) 250,000		162,000
Beginning Inventory	0	0			0
Purchases	200,000	250,000		(1) 250,000	200,000
	200,000	250,000			200,000
Ending Inventory	0	100,000	(2) 20,000		80,000
Cost of Sales	200,000	150,000			120,000
Gross Profit	50,000	12,000			42,000
Balance Sheet					
Inventory (40% remains)	—0—	100,000		(2) 20,000	80,000

* These entries are the same for firms using the cost, partial equity, and complete equity methods.
(1) To eliminate intercompany sales.
(2) To eliminate unrealized intercompany profit in ending inventory.

RELATED CONCEPTS

The *historical cost* principle suggests that inventory and other assets should not be reported above their cost to the consolidated entity ($80,000).

Compare this to the gross profit computed in Illustration 6-1, with the proper eliminating entry. If the intercompany sales were not eliminated, the consolidated gross profit would be correct but the gross profit percentage would not. Whereas the gross profit percentage should be 25.9% ($70,000/$270,000), failure to eliminate the intercompany sales would show the gross percentage as only 13.5% ($70,000/$520,000). Since both sales and cost of sales would be overstated by the same amounts, consolidated net income is not affected by the failure to eliminate intercompany sales. However, a number of financial ratios based on sales revenues would be distorted if the elimination were not made.

Assume now that S Company sells 60% of the goods purchased from P Company to third parties prior to the end of the current year. Sales, cost of sales, and inventory balances reported by each of the affiliated companies are presented in Illustration 6-3. Entry (1) to eliminate sales and purchases is the same as explained before. However, intercompany profit in the amount of $20,000 [$50,000 × 40%] resides in the ending inventory balance of S Company. This profit has not yet been realized by the consolidated entity through sales to outsiders (third parties). When, at the end of the accounting period, some of the merchandise remains in the inventory of the purchasing affiliate, the intercompany profit recognized thereon must be excluded from consolidated net income and from the inventory balance in the consolidated balance sheet. The workpaper entry to accomplish this elimination and to reduce Inventory on both the Income Statement and the Balance Sheet is as follows:

		Dr.	Cr.
(2)	Ending Inventory—Income Statement (Cost of Sales)	20,000	
	Inventory—Balance Sheet		20,000
	To defer the unrealized gross profit in ending inventory until it is sold to outsiders.		

The form of the entry eliminating intercompany sales, entry (1), implicitly assumes that there is no unrealized intercompany profit. Accordingly, either that entry must be adjusted, or this second entry must be made to remove the unrealized intercompany profit from the ending inventory and to reduce the excessive credit to cost of sales.

The first and second eliminating entries could be combined and one entry prepared as follows, if a single account is used for "cost of sales":

Sales	250,000	
Cost of Sales		230,000
Inventory—Balance Sheet		20,000

As a practical matter, two entries are conventionally prepared as shown in Illustration 6-3. In either case, after adjustment, consolidated sales of $162,000 equals the amount of sales of the affiliated group to third parties. Consolidated cost of sales of $120,000 equals the cost to the affiliated group of the goods sold (60% × $200,000), and the consolidated inventory balance of $80,000 equals the cost to the affiliated group of the goods held by S Company at the end of the year (40% × $200,000).

The above entries for intercompany sales and unrealized profit in ending inventory are the same regardless of whether the parent uses the cost, partial equity, or complete equity method. However, as shown next, the entries for intercompany profit in beginning inventory differ slightly.

Year Two Eliminating Entries—Downstream Sales

Assume now that in the next period P Company sells merchandise to S Company in the amount of $500,000 (cost $400,000) and that S Company sells all its beginning inventory ($100,000 cost to S; $80,000 cost to consolidated entity) and one-half its current purchases from P Company ($250,000 cost to S; $200,000 cost to consolidated entity) to third parties for $378,000. Sales, cost of sales, and inventory balances reported by the affiliated companies are presented in Illustration 6-4. This illustration assumes that either the cost or the partial equity method is used.

ILLUSTRATION 6-4

Partial Consolidated Statements Workpaper—Cost or Partial Equity Method, Elimination of Downstream Intercompany Sale of Inventory, Unrealized Profit in Ending Inventory (Second Year of Intercompany Sales)

	P	*S*	*Eliminations*		*Consolidated*
Income Statement	*Company*	*Company*	*Dr.*	*Cr.*	*Balances*
Sales	500,000	378,000	(1) 500,000		378,000
Beginning Inventory	0	100,000		**(3) 20,000**	80,000
Purchases	400,000	500,000		(1) 500,000	400,000
	400,000	600,000			480,000
Ending Inventory	0	250,000	(2) 50,000		200,000
Cost of Sales	400,000	350,000			280,000
Gross Profit	100,000	28,000	550,000	520,000	98,000
Retained Earnings					
Beginning Retained Earnings					
P Company	XXXX (a)		**(3) 20,000**		XXXX
Balance Sheet					
Inventory	—0—	250,000		(2) 50,000	200,000

(a) Includes $20,000 of gross profit on intercompany sales from the previous year (not yet sold to third parties).
(1) To eliminate intercompany sales.
(2) To eliminate unrealized intercompany profit in ending inventory.
(3) To recognize intercompany profit in beginning inventory realized during the period.

Unrealized intercompany profit in the amount of $50,000 [$250,000 − $200,000] or [$250,000 − ($250,000/1.25)] resides in the ending inventory of S Company. Workpaper eliminating entries (1) and (2) are similar to those discussed in the preceding example. Assuming a first-in, first-out (FIFO) inventory cost flow, intercompany profit in inventories excluded from consolidated net income in one period will be realized by sales to third parties in the next period. The form of the workpaper entry to recognize profit in the buying affiliate's beginning inventory that is realized during the current period depends on the method of accounting for the investment on the books of the parent.

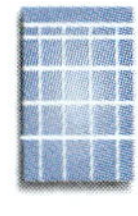

COST

If the parent uses the ***cost*** or ***partial equity*** method of recording its investment in the subsidiary, the entry takes the following form (as shown in Illustration 6-4):

Cost or Partial Equity Method

(3) Beginning Retained Earnings—P Company[5]	20,000	
Beginning Inventory—Income Statement (Cost of Sales)		20,000
To realize the gross profit in beginning inventory deferred in the prior period.		

PARTIAL

The credit to beginning inventory (*Cost of Sales*) in entry (3) is necessary in order to recognize in consolidated income the amount of profit in the beginning inventory that has been confirmed by sales to third parties during the current period. S Company charged cost of sales for its cost of $100,000, whereas the cost to the affiliated group of the beginning inventory of S Company is only $80,000. Accordingly, cost of sales must be decreased by $20,000, which increases consolidated net income by $20,000. The adjustment to Beginning Inventory this period is in the same amount as that to Ending Inventory last period.

For firms using the cost or partial equity method to account for its investment in the subsidiary, the rationale for the debit of $20,000 to beginning retained earnings of P Company is as follows. In the previous year, P Company recorded $50,000 in profit on intercompany sales and transferred it to its Retained Earnings account as part of the normal accounting process. Since, at the beginning of the year, 40% of that amount has not been realized by sales to third parties, it must be eliminated from the beginning retained earnings of P Company to correctly reflect the beginning consolidated retained earnings.

The debit to beginning retained earnings may also be viewed in the following manner. In determining consolidated net income in the prior year, $20,000 was deducted from the reported income and thus from the retained earnings of the affiliated group by a workpaper entry (which, like all workpaper entries, was not posted to the ledger accounts). In order for beginning retained earnings to match the prior year's ending retained earnings (to the consolidated entity), this $20,000 adjustment must be made to beginning retained earnings.

For firms using the ***complete equity*** method, the debit to beginning retained earnings is not needed, assuming the parent correctly adjusted for all intercompany profits/losses in its "revenue from subsidiary" account in the preceding year. Under the complete equity method, consolidated retained earnings is identical to the parent's reported retained earnings and thus no adjustment is needed. The debit to

[5] If the parent firm uses the complete equity method, this debit is replaced by a debit to the Investment in Subsidiary account (see below).

ILLUSTRATION 6-5

Partial Consolidated Statements Workpaper—Complete Equity Method, Elimination of Downstream Intercompany Sale of Inventory, Unrealized Profit in Ending Inventory (Second Year of Intercompany Sales)

Income Statement	*P Company*	*S Company*	*Eliminations Dr.*	*Eliminations Cr.*	*Consolidated Balances*
Sales	500,000	378,000	(1) 500,000		378,000
Beginning Inventory	0	100,000		**(3) 20,000**	80,000
Purchases	400,000	500,000		(1) 500,000	400,000
	400,000	600,000			480,000
Ending Inventory	0	250,000	(2) 50,000		200,000
Cost of Sales	400,000	350,000			280,000
Gross Profit	100,000	28,000	550,000	520,000	98,000
Balance Sheet					
Inventory	—0—	250,000		(2) 50,000	200,000
Investment in Subsidiary	XXX		**(3) 20,000**	XXX	—0—

(1) To eliminate intercompany sales.
(2) To eliminate unrealized intercompany profit in ending inventory.
(3) To recognize intercompany profit in beginning inventory realized during the period.

retained earnings is replaced by a debit to Investment in Subsidiary, which serves simply to facilitate the elimination of this account on the workpaper (as shown in Illustration 6-5):

COMPLETE

Complete Equity Method

(3)	Investment in Subsidiary	$20,000	
	Beginning Inventory—Income Statement (Cost of Sales)		$20,000
	To realize the gross profit in beginning inventory deferred in the prior period.		

Consolidated sales of $378,000 are equal to the amount of sales of the affiliated group to third parties. Consolidated cost of sales of $280,000 equals the cost to the affiliated group of the goods sold and is calculated as follows:

Cost of goods transferred to S Company in prior year and sold this year (40% × $200,000)	$80,000
Cost of goods transferred to S Company in current year and sold this year (50% × $400,000)	200,000
Cost of sales to third parties during current year	$280,000

Consolidated inventory of $200,000 equals the cost to the affiliated group (P Company) of the goods on hand at the end of the year (50% × $400,000).

Over two consecutive periods, assuming a FIFO flow of inventory costs and no new deferrals, differences between the summed net income recorded on the books of the individual affiliates and consolidated net income offset each other, as do the effects of the differences on beginning retained earnings.

If an inventory cost flow assumption other than FIFO is used, unrealized intercompany profit in beginning inventory balances may continue to be included in the ending inventory. In that case, to the extent that unrealized intercompany profit from the beginning of the year remains unrealized, the effects on consolidated net income from the credit to Beginning Inventory—Income Statement (Cost of Sales) in entry (3) and the debit to Ending Inventory—Income Statement (Cost of Sales) in entry (2) offset each other. Thus, as a matter of workpaper procedure, there is no need to be concerned in formulating entry (3) as to whether FIFO or LIFO is used, as long as any unrealized gross profit in ending inventory is appropriately deferred.

Determination of Amount of Intercompany Profit

In the past, regulators have been reluctant to allow banks to develop real estate because of the fear that the banks could obtain cheaper capital and control the rent (and earn larger profits). The Bank of America recently received approval by the OCC to build a 150-room Ritz-Carlton hotel as part of its headquarters. The bank plans to account for over 50% of the occupancy of the hotel.[6]

LO2 Determining the amount of intercompany profit.

In the preceding examples, the amount of intercompany profit subject to elimination was calculated on the basis of the selling affiliate's ***gross profit rate*** stated as a percentage of cost. Recall that gross profit may be stated either as a percentage of sales or as a percentage of cost. When it is stated as a percentage of cost, it is often referred to as "markup." To calculate the amount of intercompany gross profit to be eliminated from ending inventory, be careful to distinguish between percentages stated in terms of sales versus cost of sales. For example, if ending inventory (obtained from an affiliate) of $12,000 reflects a markup of 20% of cost of sales, the gross profit to be eliminated would be calculated as:

Sales	$12,000
Cost of Sales ($12,000/120%)	10,000
Gross Profit (20% × $10,000)	$ 2,000

In contrast, if ending inventory of $12,000 reflects a gross profit of 20% of sales, the gross profit to be eliminated would be $2,400, or 20% of $12,000.

Inventory Pricing Adjustments

When inventory adjustments (write-downs) have been made on the books of one of the affiliated firms due to market fluctuations, the workpaper entries are modified accordingly. To illustrate, assume the following:

1. P Company sells S Company goods costing $200,000 for $250,000 (*downstream sale*);
2. At the end of the year, all these goods remain in the ending inventory of S Company and are written down from $250,000 to $215,000 on that company's books;
3. The write-down on the books of S Company results from the application of the lower-of-cost-or-market rule in pricing its ending inventory; and
4. The related loss is included in the cost of sales of S Company, or may be disclosed separately if considered material.

[6] *WSJ*, "Banks Might Widen Real-Estate Role," by Michael Schroeder, 1/9/06, p. A3.

What amount of intercompany profit is subject to elimination in the preparation of consolidated financial statements? Since the gross profit of $50,000 recognized by P Company is offset by the reduction of gross profit of $35,000 recognized by S Company, only the remaining $15,000 is still subject to elimination in the preparation of consolidated financial statements. The deduction of the amount of the current year's write-down of intercompany inventory from the amount of intercompany profit otherwise subject to elimination also results in the presentation of intercompany inventory at cost to the affiliated group ($215,000 − $15,000 = $200,000). In summary, the amount of intercompany profit subject to elimination should be reduced to the extent that the related goods have been written down by the purchasing affiliate.

Determination of Proportion of Intercompany Profit To Be Eliminated

LO3 Eliminating 100% of intercompany profit.

It is clear that unrealized intercompany profit should not be included in consolidated net income or assets. However, two alternative views of the amount of intercompany profit that should be considered as "unrealized" exist. The elimination methods associated with these two points of view are generally referred to as ***100% (total) elimination*** and ***partial elimination.*** Both current and past GAAP ***require*** 100% elimination of intercompany profit ***in the preparation of consolidated financial statements.*** Because past and current GAAP agree in this regard, and because IFRS are silent in this regard we do not elaborate on the alternative of partial elimination. Under 100% elimination, the entire amount of unconfirmed intercompany profit is eliminated from consolidated net income and the related asset balance. This approach is particularly logical under the proposed view of consolidated financial statements, based on the "entity" rather than "parent" concept, and may be summarized as follows:

> The amount of intercompany profit or loss to be eliminated . . . is not affected by the existence of a minority [noncontrolling] interest. The complete elimination of the intercompany profit or loss is consistent with the underlying assumption that consolidated statements represent the financial position and operating results of a single business enterprise. [*Accounting Research Bulletin (ARB) No. 51*, paragraph 14] [ASC 810-10-45-6]

Determination of the Noncontrolling Interest in Consolidated Income—Upstream or Horizontal Sales

LO5 Noncontrolling interest (NCI) for upstream sales.

Subsidiary as Intercompany Seller In the preceding examples, the selling affiliate was the parent company (downstream sale). Accordingly, even though 100% of the unrealized intercompany profit was eliminated, no modification in the calculation of the noncontrolling interest in consolidated net income or consolidated net assets was necessary. Had the selling affiliate been a less than wholly owned subsidiary (upstream sale), however, the controlling and the noncontrolling interests would have needed to be adjusted to reflect their interest in the amount of unrealized intercompany profit eliminated.

ILLUSTRATION 6-6

Calculation of Noncontrolling Interest in Consolidated Income—Upstream Sales

General Format:

Noncontrolling Interest in Consolidated Income with Upstream Sales

Amortization of the difference between implied and book value	XXXX	Net income reported by subsidiary	$XXXXX
Unrealized intercompany profit recorded by the subsidiary in the current period	XXXX	Intercompany profit recognized by the subsidiary in the prior period(s) that is realized by sales to third parties during the current period	XXXX
		Subsidiary income included in consolidated income	$ XXXX
		Noncontrolling ownership percentage interest	%
		Noncontrolling interest in consolidated income	$ XXXX

Succinct Format:

Noncontrolling Interest in Consolidated Income with Upstream Sales

Amortization of the difference between implied and book value	XXX	Net income reported by subsidiary	$XXXXX
Unrealized profit in ending inventory	XXXX	Realized profit from beginning inventory	XXXX
		Subsidiary income included in consolidated income	$ XXXX
		NCI %	%
		NCI in consolidated income	$ XXXX

Intercompany sales of inventory necessitate adjustments to the calculation of the distribution of income to the controlling and noncontrolling interests. Whether the adjustments directly affect the noncontrolling interest (or only the controlling interest) depends on ***who is the intercompany seller (selling affiliate)***. If the intercompany seller is the subsidiary, it is the subsidiary's income that needs adjustment, therefore directly affecting the noncontrolling interest, as shown in Illustration 6-6.

In essence, the amount of the noncontrolling interest in consolidated net income that is deducted to arrive at the controlling interest is based on the amount of subsidiary income (loss) that has been realized in transactions with third parties. This deduction is, as usual, made on the consolidated statements workpaper (final column) to be presented later in this chapter.

The general and succinct formats for the calculation of the noncontrolling interest in consolidated net income in the case of an *upstream sale* are presented in Illustration 6-6.

The reader is reminded, however, that this modification of the calculation of the noncontrolling interest is applicable only when the subsidiary is the ***selling affiliate*** (upstream or horizontal sales). Where the parent company is the selling affiliate (*downstream sale*), the amount of subsidiary income included in consolidated net income is not affected by the elimination of unrealized intercompany profit and no adjustment is necessary in the calculation of the noncontrolling interest in consolidated net income. (See Illustration 6-11 for the effects of both upstream and downstream sales on income distribution.)

TEST
YOUR KNOWLEDGE

NOTE: Solutions to ***Test Your Knowledge*** questions are found at the end of each chapter before the end-of-chapter questions.

Multiple Choice

1. Pristine Corporation owns 80% of Serendipity Inc.'s common stock. During 2008, Pristine sold Serendipity $250,000 of inventory on the same terms as sales made to third parties. Serendipity sold all the inventory purchased from Pristine in 2008. The following data pertain to sales by each company for the year:

	Pristine	*Serendipity*
Sales	$1,000,000	$700,000
Cost of goods sold	400,000	350,000

How much should be reported as cost of goods sold in the consolidated income statement for 2008?

a. $400,000 b. $500,000 c. $680,000 d. $750,000

2. Polychromasia Company sold inventory costing $30,000 to its subsidiary, Simply Colorful, for double its cost in 2009. Polychromasia owns 80% of Simply Colorful. Simply resold $50,000 of this inventory for $60,000 to outsiders in 2009. How much unrealized profit exists at the end of the year?

   a. $10,000 b. $8,000 c. $5,000 d. $20,000

3. Skipper Company owns all the outstanding common stock of Anchorage Inc. During 2010, Skipper sells merchandise to Anchorage that is in turn sold to outsiders. None of the intercompany merchandise remains in Anchorage's year-end inventory, but some of the intercompany purchases from Skipper have not yet been paid. Identify the accounts that will reflect incorrect balances in the consolidated financial statements if no adjustments are made:

   a. Accounts Receivable and Accounts Payable
   b. Sales, Cost of Goods Sold, Inventory, Accounts Receivable
   c. Sales, Cost of Goods Sold, Accounts Receivable, and Accounts Payable
   d. Accounts Payable, Inventory, and Net Income

COST METHOD: CONSOLIDATED STATEMENTS WORKPAPER—UPSTREAM SALES

Dell Inc. warned investors on March 8, 2006, that it would not achieve its sales and earnings goals for the fiscal period ending May 5. Eleven days later, Dell announced that it intended to start using AMD chips in some high-end servers. Analysts speculated that the move was in response to competitors.[7]

COST

LO6 Consolidated workpapers for upstream Sales-Cost Method.

To illustrate consolidation procedures when the parent company records its investment using the cost method, assume the following:

1. P Company acquired an 80% interest in S Company on January 1, 2011, for $1,360,000, at which time S Company had capital stock of $1,000,000 and retained earnings of $700,000.
2. In 2011, S Company reported net income of $125,000 and declared dividends of $20,000.

[7] *WSJ*, "Dell to Use AMD Chips in Some Servers," by Don Clark and Christopher Lawton, 5/19/06, p. A3.

3. In 2012, S Company reported net income of $140,000 and declared dividends of $60,000.
4. P Company uses the cost method to account for its investment in S Company.
5. The purchase price equals 80% of both the book values and fair values of S Company's net assets on the date of acquisition. Thus, the implied value equals the total book value equals fair value.
6. S Company sells merchandise to P Company as follows (upstream sales):

Year	*Total Sales of S Company to P Company*	*Intercompany Merchandise in 12/31 Inventory of P Company*	*Unrealized Intercompany Profit (25% of Selling Price)*
2011	$ 700,000	$400,000	$100,000
2012	1,000,000	500,000	125,000

COST

Consolidated statements workpapers for the years ended December 31, 2011, and December 31, 2012, are presented in Illustrations 6-7 and 6-8, respectively. Entries ***on the books*** of P Company as well as ***workpaper entries*** necessary in the consolidated statements workpapers for the years ended December 31, 2011, and December 31, 2012, are summarized in general journal form below. The workpaper entries and the determination of the noncontrolling interest are explained in more detail as needed.

Entries on Books of P Company—Cost Method 2011—Year of Acquisition

(1) Investment in S Company	1,360,000	
Cash		1,360,000
To record purchase of S Company stock.		
(2) Cash	16,000	
Dividend Income		16,000
To record receipt of dividends from S Company (.8 × $20,000).		

Consolidated Statements Workpaper Entries—December 31, 2011 (Year of Acquisition)

(1) Sales	700,000	
Purchases		700,000
To eliminate intercompany sales.		

(2) 12/31 Inventory—Income Statement (Cost of Sales)	100,000	
Inventory—Balance Sheet		100,000
To defer (eliminate) unrealized intercompany profit in ending inventory.		

(3) Dividend Income	16,000	
Dividends Declared		16,000
To eliminate intercompany dividends.		

(4) Beginning Retained Earnings—S Company	700,000	
Capital Stock—S Company	1,000,000	
Investment in S Company		1,360,000
NCI in Equity		340,000
To eliminate investment account and create NCI account.		

Cost Method
80% Owned Subsidiary
Upstream Sale of Inventory
Year of Acquisition

ILLUSTRATION 6-7
Consolidated Statements Workpaper
P Company and Subsidiary
for the Year Ended December 31, 2011

Income Statement	*P Company*	*S Company*	*Eliminations Dr.*	*Eliminations Cr.*	*Noncontrolling Interest*	*Consolidated Balances*
Sales	3,104,000	2,200,000	(1) 700,000			4,604,000
Dividend Income	16,000		(3) 16,000			
Total Revenue	3,120,000	2,200,000				4,604,000
Inventory 1/1	500,000	300,000				800,000
Purchases	1,680,000	1,370,000		(1) 700,000		2,350,000
	2,180,000	1,670,000				3,150,000
Inventory 12/31	480,000	310,000	(2) 100,000			690,000
Cost of Goods Sold	1,700,000	1,360,000				2,460,000
Other Expenses	1,124,000	715,000				1,839,000
Total Expense	2,824,000	2,075,000				4,299,000
Net/Consolidated Income	296,000	125,000				305,000
Noncontrolling Interest in Income					5,000*	5,000
Net Income to Retained Earnings	296,000	125,000	816,000	700,000	5,000	300,000
Retained Earnings Statement						
1/1 Retained Earnings						
P Company	1,650,000					1,650,000
S Company		700,000	(4) 700,000			
Net Income from above	296,000	125,000	816,000	700,000	5,000	300,000
Dividends Declared						
P Company	(150,000)					(150,000)
S Company		(20,000)		(3) 16,000	(4,000)	
12/31 Retained Earnings to Balance Sheet	1,796,000	805,000	1,516,000	716,000	1,000	1,800,000
Balance Sheet						
Inventory	480,000	310,000		(2) 100,000		690,000
Investment in S Company	1,360,000			(4) 1,360,000		
Other Assets (net)	5,090,000	2,310,000				7,400,000
Total	6,930,000	2,620,000				8,090,000
Liabilities	2,134,000	815,000				2,949,000
Capital Stock						
P Company	3,000,000					3,000,000
S Company		1,000,000	(4) 1,000,000			
Retained Earnings from above	1,796,000	805,000	1,516,000	716,000	1,000	1,800,000
1/1 Noncontrolling Interest in Net Assets				(4) 340,000	340,000	
12/31 Noncontrolling Interest in Net Assets					341,000	341,000
Total Liabilities and Equity	6,930,000	2,620,000	2,516,000	2,516,000		8,090,000

* .2($125,000 − $100,000) = $5,000.
(1) To eliminate intercompany sales.
(2) To eliminate unrealized intercompany profit in ending inventory.
(3) To eliminate intercompany dividends.
(4) To eliminate the investment account and create noncontrolling interest account.

Cost Method
80% Owned Subsidiary
Upstream Sale of Inventory
Year Subsequent to Acquisition

ILLUSTRATION 6-8
Consolidated Statements Workpaper
P Company and Subsidiary
for the Year Ended December 31, 2012

	P Company	S Company	Eliminations Dr.	Eliminations Cr.	Noncontrolling Interest	Consolidated Balances
Income Statement						
Sales	3,546,000	2,020,000	(2) 1,000,000			4,566,000
Dividend Income	48,000		(5) 48,000			
Total Revenue	3,594,000	2,020,000				4,566,000
Inventory 1/1	480,000	310,000		(4) 100,000		690,000
Purchases	2,070,000	1,250,000		(2) 1,000,000		2,320,000
	2,550,000	1,560,000				3,010,000
Inventory 12/31	510,000	360,000	(3) 125,000			745,000
Cost of Goods Sold	2,040,000	1,200,000				2,265,000
Other Expenses	1,100,000	680,000				1,780,000
Total Expense	3,140,000	1,880,000				4,045,000
Net/Consolidated Income	454,000	140,000				521,000
Noncontrolling Interest in Income					23,000*	23,000
Net Income to Retained Earnings	454,000	140,000	1,173,000	1,100,000	23,000	498,000
Retained Earnings Statement						
1/1 Retained Earnings						
P Company	1,796,000		(4) 80,000	(1) 84,000		1,800,000
S Company		805,000	(6) 805,000			
Net Income from above	454,000	140,000	1,173,000	1,100,000	23,000	498,000
Dividends Declared						
P Company	(150,000)					(150,000)
S Company		(60,000)		(5) 48,000	(12,000)	
12/31 Retained Earnings to Balance Sheet	2,100,000	885,000	2,058,000	1,232,000	11,000	2,148,000
Balance Sheet						
Inventory	510,000	360,000		(3) 125,000		745,000
Investment in S Company	1,360,000		(1) 84,000	(6) 1,444,000		
Other Assets (net)	5,450,000	2,330,000				7,780,000
Total	7,320,000	2,690,000				8,525,000
Liabilities	2,220,000	805,000				3,025,000
Capital Stock						
P Company	3,000,000					3,000,000
S Company		1,000,000	(6) 1,000,000			
Retained Earnings from above	2,100,000	885,000	2,058,000	1,232,000	11,000	2,148,000
1/1 Noncontrolling Interest in Net Assets			(4) 20,000	(6) 361,000**	341,000	
12/31 Noncontrolling Interest in Net Assets					352,000	352,000
Total Liabilities and Equity	7,320,000	2,690,000	3,162,000	3,162,000		8,525,000

* .2($140,000 − $125,000 + $100,000) = $23,000.
** $340,000 + .2($805,000 − $700,000) = $361,000
(1) To convert to equity/establish reciprocity as of 1/1/12 [.8 × ($805,000 − $700,000)].
(2) To eliminate intercompany sales.
(3) To eliminate unrealized intercompany profit in ending inventory.
(4) To recognize profit realized during year and to reduce the controlling and noncontrolling interests for their shares of unrealized intercompany profit at beginning of year.
(5) To eliminate intercompany dividends.
(6) To eliminate investment account and create noncontrolling interest account.

Since the selling affiliate is a partially owned subsidiary, unrealized intercompany profit is subtracted from reported subsidiary income when calculating the noncontrolling interest in consolidated net income as follows:

$$.20 \times (\$125{,}000 - \$100{,}000) = \$5{,}000$$

If the sale of merchandise had been *downstream* rather than *upstream*, the amount of subsidiary income included in consolidated income would not be affected by the elimination of unrealized intercompany profit and no adjustment would be necessary in the calculation of the noncontrolling interest in consolidated income.

Entry on Books of P Company—Cost Method 2012—Year Subsequent to Acquisition

	Debit	Credit
Cash	48,000	
Dividend Income		48,000
To record receipt of dividends from S Company (.80 × $60,000).		

Consolidated Statements Workpaper Entries—December 31, 2012 (Year Subsequent to Acquisition)—Cost Method

		Debit	Credit
(1)	Investment in S Company	84,000	
	Beginning Retained Earnings—P Company		84,000
	To convert to the equity method or to establish reciprocity [.80 × ($805,000 − $700,000)]		

		Debit	Credit
(2)	Sales	1,000,000	
	Purchases (Cost of Sales)		1,000,000
	To eliminate intercompany sales.		

		Debit	Credit
(3)	12/31 Inventory—Income Statement (Cost of Sales)	125,000	
	Inventory—Balance Sheet		125,000
	To eliminate unrealized intercompany profit in ending inventory.		

		Debit	Credit
(4)	Beginning Retained Earnings—P Company (.80 × $100,000)	80,000	
	NCI (.20 × $100,000)	20,000	
	1/1 Inventory—Income Statement (Cost of Sales)		100,000
	To recognize intercompany profit in beginning inventory realized during the year and to reduce the controlling and noncontrolling interests for their shares of unrealized intercompany profit at beginning of year.		

COST

		Debit	Credit
(5)	Dividend Income	48,000	
	Dividends Declared—S Company		48,000
	To eliminate intercompany dividends (.80 × $60,000).		

		Debit	Credit
(6)	Beginning Retained Earnings—S Company	805,000	
	Capital Stock—S Company	1,000,000	
	Investment in S Company ($1,360,000 + $84,000)		1,444,000
	NCI ($340,000 + .2($805,000 − $700,000))		361,000
	To eliminate investment account, and create NCI.		

The unrealized profit in the current year's beginning inventory is the same as the unrealized profit in the prior year's ending inventory. Since the sale is *upstream*, the unrealized profit at the end of the prior year was apportioned between the controlling and noncontrolling interests by reducing the noncontrolling interest in consolidated income in the consolidated statements workpaper in the previous year. Thus, the retained earnings effects in entry (4) are split between P Company's (80%) beginning retained earnings accounts and the NCI (20%).

As a matter of workpaper procedure, adjustments to the controlling interest (consolidated retained earnings) are made by debiting (decreasing) or crediting (increasing) the *beginning* retained earnings row of the parent company. Adjustments to the noncontrolling interest are made by debiting (decreasing) or crediting (increasing) the *beginning* NCI in Net Assets (or Equity).

The net effect of the adjustments to the noncontrolling interest in the income statement and retained earnings statement sections of the consolidated statements workpaper that are necessary in the case of ***upstream sales*** is to adjust the amount of the noncontrolling interest in consolidated net assets. The amount of the noncontrolling interest reported in the consolidated balance sheet is based on the net assets of the subsidiary that have been realized in transactions with third parties. Workpaper entry (6) creates the beginning balance in the noncontrolling interest account reflective of the sum of the 20% interest at acquisition plus the noncontrolling share of changes in Retained Earnings of S since acquisition to the beginning of the current year. This entry could just as easily be numbered as entry (1) or (2), as there is no particular sequence for workpaper entries. Workpaper entry (4) debits the noncontrolling interest, thus adjusting the balance as needed for prior year unrealized profit in inventory (that is to be realized through the current share of consolidated income).

In Illustration 6-8, for example, the noncontrolling interest in consolidated net assets on December 31, 2012, may be calculated as follows. First, as shown in Illustration 6-9, the reported assets are adjusted for the unrealized intercompany profit at the end of the year on upstream sales. Then the noncontrolling interest in realized net assets can be computed either of two ways as shown in Illustration 6-10.

ILLUSTRATION 6-9

Calculation of Realized Assets of Company S
December 31, 2012

	12/31/12	*Unrealized Intercompany Profits in Ending Inventory*	*Realized 12/31/12*
Total Assets—S Company	$2,690,000	125,000	$2,565,000
Total Liabilities—S Company	805,000		805,000
Capital Stock—S Company	1,000,000		1,000,000
Retained Earnings	885,000	125,000	760,000
Total Liabilities and Equity	$2,690,000		$2,565,000

ILLUSTRATION 6-10

Calculation of the Noncontrolling Interest in Consolidated Net Assets
December 31, 2012

Method One:	
Total Realized Assets—S Company (see Illustration 6-9)	$2,565,000
Less: Total Liabilities—S Company	(805,000)
Realized Net Assets—S Company	1,760,000
Noncontrolling percentage	20%
Noncontrolling interest in consolidated net assets	$ 352,000
Method Two:	
Capital Stock—S Company	$1,000,000
Realized Retained Earnings—S Company (see Illustration 6-9)	760,000
Realized Net Assets—S Company	$1,760,000
Noncontrolling percentage	20%
Noncontrolling interest in consolidated net assets	$ 352,000

COST METHOD—ANALYSIS OF CONSOLIDATED NET INCOME AND CONSOLIDATED RETAINED EARNINGS

In Chapter 5, the calculations of consolidated net income and consolidated retained earnings were refined to accommodate the effect of the amortization, depreciation, and impairment of differences between implied and book values. These analyses must now be further refined to accommodate the effect of unrealized intercompany profit.

The noncontrolling interest in consolidated net income is calculated after subtracting end-of-year unrealized intercompany profit and adding intercompany profit realized during the current year to the net income reported by the subsidiary, as presented in Illustration 6-11. If the sale of merchandise had been downstream rather than upstream, the amount of subsidiary income included in consolidated net income would not be affected by the workpaper entries related to unrealized intercompany profit, and no adjustment would be necessary in the calculation of the noncontrolling interest in consolidated income.

Consolidated Net Income

Consolidated net income is the parent company's income from its independent operations that has been realized in transactions with third parties plus (minus) subsidiary income (loss) that has been realized in transactions with third parties plus or minus adjustments for the period relating to the depreciation, amortization, and impairment of differences between implied and book values.

Using the data from Illustration 6-8, the calculation of the controlling and noncontrolling interests in consolidated net income for the year ended December 31, 2012, is presented in t-account form in Illustration 6-11.

ILLUSTRATION 6-11

Calculation of the Controlling and Noncontrolling Interest in Consolidated Income—Cost Method for the Year Ended December 31, 2012

Noncontrolling Interest in Consolidated Income			
Unrealized profit on upstream sales in ending inventory	125,000	Net income reported by S Company	$140,000
Amortization of the difference between implied and book value	0	Realized profit (upstream sales) from beginning inventory	100,000
		Subsidiary income included in consolidated income	$115,000
		Noncontrolling ownership percentage interest	20%
		Noncontrolling interest in consolidated income	$ 23,000
Controlling Interest in Consolidated Income			80%
		Net income internally generated by P Company ($454,000 less $48,000 dividend income)	$406,000
Unrealized profit on downstream sales to S Company (ending inventory)	0	Realized profit (downstream sales) from begin. inventory	0
		P Company's percentage of S Company's income realized from third parties, .80($115,000)	92,000
		Controlling Interest in Consolidated Income	$498,000

Consolidated Retained Earnings

Consolidated retained earnings is the parent company's cost basis retained earnings that has been realized in transactions with third parties plus (minus) the parent company's share of the increase (decrease) in subsidiary retained earnings that has been realized in transactions with third parties from the date of acquisition to the current date plus or minus the cumulative effect of adjustments to date relating to the amortization, depreciation, and impairment of differences between implied and book values.

On the basis of Illustration 6-8, a t-account calculation of consolidated retained earnings on December 31, 2012, is shown in Illustration 6-12. Notice that the retained earnings calculation reflects cumulative rather than only current-year data, in contrast to the distribution of current income (Illustration 6-11). There is no need, however, to include the realized profit in beginning inventory from January 1, 2012, or the unrealized profit in ending inventory at December 31, 2011, in the retained earnings calculation as they would cancel out.

ILLUSTRATION 6-12

Calculation of Consolidated Retained Earnings for the Year Ended December 31, 2012

Consolidated Retained Earnings

P Company's share of unrealized profit on upstream sales from S Company (in P's ending inventory), .8($125,000)	100,000	P Company's Retained Earnings on 12/31/12		$2,100,000
Unrealized profit on downstream sales to S Company (in S's ending Inventory)	0	Increase in S Company's Retained Earnings since acquisition ($885,000 − $700,000)	185,000	
		Less: Cumulative amount of depreciation of the differences between implied and book values	0	
		Adjusted increase	185,000	
		P Company's share thereof	0.80	148,000
		Consolidated Retained Earnings		$2,148,000

Comprehensive Example: Upstream and Downstream Sales—Cost Method

COST

To illustrate all aspects of the t-account calculations of consolidated net income and consolidated retained earnings, assume that:

1. Pepper Company acquired 80% of the voting stock of Salt Company on January 1, 2011, when Salt Company's retained earnings amounted to $150,000.
2. The difference between implied and book value on the date of acquisition was allocated as follows:

Land	$50,000
Equipment (10-year life)	20,000
Goodwill	40,000

3. Salt Company reported retained earnings of $260,000 on January 1, 2014, and $320,000 on December 31, 2014.
4. Salt Company reported net income of $90,000 and declared dividends of $30,000 in 2014.
5. Pepper Company reported net income in 2014 in the amount of $724,000 and retained earnings on December 31, 2014, of $3,500,000.

6. There were no intercompany sales prior to 2013, and unrealized profits on January 1 and on December 31, 2014, resulting from intercompany sales, are as summarized below:

	Unrealized Intercompany Profit on	
Resulting From	*1/1/14*	*12/31/13*
Sales by Salt Company to Pepper Company	$10,000	$ 5,000
Sales by Pepper Company to Salt Company	15,000	20,000

T-account calculations of the controlling and noncontrolling interests in consolidated net income for the year ended December 31, 2014, and consolidated retained earnings on December 31, 2014, are presented in Illustrations 6-13 and 6-14 respectively.

ILLUSTRATION 6-13

Calculation of the Controlling and Noncontrolling Interest in Consolidated Income for the Year Ended December 31, 2014

Noncontrolling Interest in Combined Income

Unrealized profit on *upstream* sales in ending inventory	5,000	Net income reported by Salt Company	$ 90,000
Depreciation ($20,000/10)	2,000	Realized profit (*upstream* sales) from beginning inventory	10,000
		Subsidiary income included in consolidated income	$ 93,000
		Noncontrolling ownership percentage interest	20%
		Noncontrolling interest in consolidated income	$ 18,600

80%

Controlling Interest in Income

Unrealized profit on *downstream* sales to Salt Company (ending inventory)	20,000	Net income internally generated by Pepper Company ($724,000 less $24,000 dividends from Salt)	$ 700,000
		Realized profit (*downstream* sales) from begin. inventory	15,000
		Pepper Company's percentage of Salt Company's income realized from third parties, .80($93,000)	$ 74,400
		Controlling Interest in Consolidated Income	$769,400

ILLUSTRATION 6-14

Calculation of Consolidated Retained Earnings—Cost Method for the Year Ended December 31, 2014

Consolidated Retained Earnings

P Company's share of unrealized profit on *upstream* sales from S Company (in P's ending inventory), .8($5,000)	4,000	P Company's Retained Earnings on 12/31/14		$3,500,000
Unrealized profit on *downstream* sales to S Company (in S's ending inventory)	20,000	Increase in S Company's Retained Earnings since acquisition ($320,000 − $150,000)	170,000	
		Less: Cumulative amount of depreciation of the differences between implied and book values	(10,000)	
		Adjusted increase	160,000	
		P Company's share thereof	80%	128,000
		Consolidated Retained Earnings		$3,604,000

CONSOLIDATED STATEMENTS WORKPAPER—PARTIAL EQUITY METHOD

LO6 Consolidated workpapers—partial equity method.

The balances reported by the parent company in income, retained earnings, and the investment account differ depending on the method used by the parent company to record its investment. As demonstrated in Chapters 4 and 5, however, the method used by the parent company to record its investment has no effect on the consolidated balances. To illustrate consolidation procedures when the parent company records its investment using the partial equity method, assume the following:

PARTIAL

1. P Company acquired an 80% interest in S Company on January 1, 2011, for \$1,360,000, at which time S Company had capital stock of \$1,000,000 and retained earnings of \$700,000.
2. In 2011, S Company reported net income of \$125,000 and declared dividends of \$20,000.
3. In 2012, S Company reported net income of \$140,000 and declared dividends of \$60,000.
4. P Company uses the partial equity method to account for its investment in S Company.
5. The purchase price equals 80% of both the book values and fair values of S Company's net assets on the date of acquisition. Thus, implied value equals total book value equals fair value of S net assets.
6. S Company sells merchandise to P Company as follows (upstream sales):

	Total Sales of S Company to P Company	*Intercompany Merchandise in 12/31 Inventory of P Company*	*Unrealized Intercompany Profit (25% of Selling Price)*
2011	\$ 700,000	\$400,000	\$100,000
2012	1,000,000	500,000	125,000

Entries on Books of P Company—Partial Equity Method

Entries recorded on the books of P Company under the partial equity method are as follows:

2011—Year of Acquisition—Partial Equity

		Debit	Credit
(1)	Investment in S Company	1,360,000	
	Cash		1,360,000
	To record purchase of 80% interest in S Company.		
(2)	Cash	16,000	
	Investment in S Company		16,000
	To record dividends received (.80 × \$20,000).		
(3)	Investment in S Company	100,000	
	Equity in Subsidiary Income		100,000
	To record equity in subsidiary income (.80 × \$125,000).		

2012—Year Subsequent to Acquisition—Partial Equity

		Debit	Credit
(4)	Cash	48,000	
	Investment in S Company		48,000
	To record dividends received (.80 × \$60,000).		
(5)	Investment in S Company	112,000	
	Equity in Subsidiary Income		112,000
	To record equity in subsidiary income (.80 × \$140,000).		

After these entries are posted, the investment account will appear as follows:

Investment in S Company

(1) Cost	1,360,000	(2) Dividends	16,000
(3) Subsidiary Income	100,000		
12/31/11 Balance	***1,444,000***		
(5) Subsidiary Income	112,000	(4) Dividends	48,000
12/31/12 Balance	***1,508,000***		

Workpaper Entries—2012—Partial Equity Consolidated workpapers under the partial equity method for the years ended December 31, 2011 and 2012, are presented in Illustrations 6-15 and 6-16. Workpaper entries in Illustration 6-16 (the year subsequent to acquisition) are presented in general journal form as follows:

PARTIAL

(1)	Equity in Subsidiary Income	112,000	
	Dividends Declared		48,000
	Investment in S Company		64,000
	To reverse the effect of parent company entries during the year for subsidiary dividends and income.		

(2)	Sales	1,000,000	
	Purchases (Cost of Sales)		1,000,000
	To eliminate intercompany sales.		

(3)	12/31 Inventory—Income Statement (Cost of Sales)	125,000	
	Inventory—Balance Sheet		125,000
	To eliminate unrealized intercompany profit in ending inventory.		

(4)	Beginning Retained Earnings—P Company (.80 × $100,000)	80,000	
	NCI in Equity (.20 × $100,000)	20,000	
	1/1 Inventory—Income Statement (Cost of Sales)		100,000
	To recognize intercompany profit in beginning inventory realized during the year and to reduce controlling and noncontrolling interest for their share of unrealized intercompany profit at beginning of year.		

Entries (2), (3), and (4) are the same as the corresponding entries in Illustration 6-8 (investment recorded using cost method).

(5)	Beginning Retained Earnings—S Company	805,000	
	Capital Stock—S Company	1,000,000	
	Investment in S Company ($1,508,000 − $64,000)		1,444,000
	NCI in Equity ($340,000 + .20($805,000 − $700,000))		361,000
	To eliminate investment account.		

This entry is the same as entry (6) in Illustration 6-8 (investment recorded using cost method). Workpaper entry (5) creates the balance in the noncontrolling interest account reflective of the sum of the 20% interest at acquisition plus the noncontrolling share of changes in Retained Earnings of S since acquisition. This entry could just as easily be numbered as entry (1) or (2), as there is no particular sequence for workpaper entries. Workpaper entry (4) debits the noncontrolling interest, thus adjusting the balance as needed for prior year unrealized profit in inventory.

Partial Equity Method
80% Owned Subsidiary
Upstream Sale of Inventory
Year of Acquisition

ILLUSTRATION 6-15
Consolidated Statements Workpaper
P Company and Subsidiary
for the Year Ended December 31, 2011

	P Company	S Company	Eliminations Dr.	Eliminations Cr.	Noncontrolling Interest	Consolidated Balances
Income Statement						
Sales	3,104,000	2,200,000	(2) 700,000			4,604,000
Equity in Subsidiary Income	100,000		(1) 100,000			
Total Revenue	3,204,000	2,200,000				4,604,000
Inventory 1/1	500,000	300,000				800,000
Purchases	1,680,000	1,370,000		(2) 700,000		2,350,000
	2,180,000	1,670,000				3,150,000
Inventory 12/31	480,000	310,000	(3) 100,000			690,000
Cost of Goods Sold	1,700,000	1,360,000				2,460,000
Other Expenses	1,124,000	715,000				1,839,000
Total Cost and Expense	2,824,000	2,075,000				4,299,000
Net/Combined Income	380,000	125,000				305,000
Noncontrolling Interest in Income					5,000*	5,000
Net Income to Retained Earnings	380,000	125,000	900,000	700,000	5,000	300,000
Retained Earnings Statement						
1/1 Retained Earnings						
P Company	1,650,000					1,650,000
S Company		700,000	(4) 700,000			
Net Income from above	380,000	125,000	900,000	700,000	5,000	300,000
Dividends Declared						
P Company	(150,000)					(150,000)
S Company		(20,000)		(1) 16,000	(4,000)	
12/31 Retained Earnings to Balance Sheet	1,880,000	805,000	1,600,000	716,000	1,000	1,800,000
Balance Sheet						
Inventory	480,000	310,000		(3) 100,000		690,000
Investment in S Company	1,444,000			(1) 84,000 (4) 1,360,000		
Other Assets (net)	5,090,000	2,310,000				7,400,000
Total	7,014,000	2,620,000				8,090,000
Liabilities	2,134,000	815,000				2,949,000
Capital Stock						
P Company	3,000,000					3,000,000
S Company		1,000,000	(4) 1,000,000			
Retained Earnings from above	1,880,000	805,000	1,600,000	716,000	1,000	1,800,000
1/1 Noncontrolling Interest in Net Assets				(4) 340,000	340,000	
12/31 Noncontrolling Interest in Net Assets					341,000	341,000
Total Liabilities and Equity	7,014,000	2,620,000	2,600,000	2,600,000		8,090,000

*.20($125,000 − $100,000) = $5,000.
(1) To reverse the effect of parent company entries during the year for subsidiary dividends and income.
(2) To eliminate intercompany sales.
(3) To eliminate unrealized intercompany profit in ending inventory.
(4) To recognize profit realized during year and to reduce the controlling and noncontrolling interests for their shares of unrealized intercompany profit at beginning of year.
(5) To eliminate investment account and create noncontrolling interest account.

Partial Equity Method
80% Owned Subsidiary
Upstream Sale of Inventory
Year Subsequent to Acquisition

ILLUSTRATION 6-16
Consolidated Statements Workpaper
P Company and Subsidiary
for the Year Ended December 31, 2012

	P Company	*S Company*	*Eliminations Dr.*	*Eliminations Cr.*	*Noncontrolling Interest*	*Consolidated Balances*
Income Statement						
Sales	3,546,000	2,020,000	(2) 1,000,000			4,566,000
Equity in Subsidiary Income	112,000		(1) 112,000			
Total Revenue	3,658,000	2,020,000				4,566,000
Inventory 1/1	480,000	310,000		(4) 100,000		690,000
Purchases	2,070,000	1,250,000		(2) 1,000,000		2,320,000
	2,550,000	1,560,000				3,010,000
Inventory 12/31	510,000	360,000	(3) 125,000			745,000
Cost of Goods Sold	2,040,000	1,200,000				2,265,000
Other Expenses	1,100,000	680,000				1,780,000
Total Cost and Expense	3,140,000	1,880,000				4,045,000
Net/Consolidated Income	518,000	140,000				521,000
Noncontrolling Interest in Income					23,000*	23,000
Net Income to Retained Earnings	518,000	140,000	1,237,000	1,100,000	23,000	498,000
Retained Earnings Statement						
1/1 Retained Earnings						
P Company	1,880,000		(4) 80,000			1,800,000
S Company		805,000	(5) 805,000			
Net Income from above	518,000	140,000	1,237,000	1,100,000	23,000	498,000
Dividends Declared						
P Company	(150,000)					(150,000)
S Company		(60,000)		(1) 48,000	(12,000)	
12/31 Retained Earnings to Balance Sheet	2,248,000	885,000	2,122,000	1,148,000	11,000	2,148,000
Balance Sheet						
Inventory	510,000	360,000		(3) 125,000		745,000
Investment in S Company	1,508,000			(1) 64,000 (5) 1,444,000		
Other Assets (net)	5,450,000	2,330,000				7,780,000
Total	7,468,000	2,690,000				8,525,000
Liabilities	2,220,000	805,000				3,025,000
Capital Stock						
P Company	3,000,000					3,000,000
S Company		1,000,000	(5) 1,000,000			
Retained Earnings from above	2,248,000	885,000	2,122,000	1,148,000	11,000	2,148,000
1/1 Noncontrolling Interest in Net Assets			(4) 20,000	(5) 361,000	341,000	
12/31 Noncontrolling Interest in Net Assets					352,000	352,000
Total Liabilities and Equity	7,468,000	2,690,000	3,142,000	3,142,000		8,525,000

* .20($140,000 − $125,000 + $100,000) = $23,000.
** $340,000 + .2($805,000 − $700,000) = $361,000.
(1) To reverse the effect of parent company entries during the year for subsidiary dividends and income.
(2) To eliminate intercompany sales.
(3) To eliminate unrealized intercompany profit in ending inventory.
(4) To recognize profit realized during year and to reduce the controlling and noncontrolling interests for their shares of unrealized intercompany profit at beginning of year.
(5) To eliminate investment account and create noncontrolling interest account.

Observe that the consolidated balances in Illustration 6-16 are the same as those in Illustration 6-8 (cost method workpaper). However, when the parent company records its investment using the partial equity method, entry (1) in Illustration 6-16 replaces the cost method entries to establish reciprocity and to eliminate dividend income [entries (1) and (5) in Illustration 6-8]. Most importantly, a comparison of entries (2), (3), and (4) in Illustration 6-16 with entries (2), (3), and (4) in Illustration 6-8 demonstrates that the workpaper entries to eliminate intercompany sales and unrealized intercompany profit are the same regardless of whether the investment is recorded using the cost method or the partial equity method.

PARTIAL EQUITY METHOD—ANALYSIS OF CONSOLIDATED NET INCOME AND CONSOLIDATED RETAINED EARNINGS

The t-account calculation of the controlling and noncontrolling interests in consolidated net income is independent of the method used by the parent company to record its investment. As stated earlier, ***consolidated net income is the parent company's income from its independent operations that has been realized in transactions with third parties plus (minus) reported subsidiary income (loss) that has been realized in transactions with third parties plus or minus adjustments for the period relating to the depreciation, amortization, and impairment differences between implied and book values.***

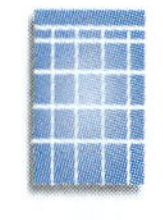

PARTIAL

On the basis of Illustration 6-16, the t-account calculation of consolidated net income for the year ended December 31, 2012, is demonstrated in Illustration 6-17.

When the parent company uses the partial equity method to record its investment, the parent company's share of subsidiary income since acquisition is already included in the parent company's reported retained earnings. Consequently, ***consolidated retained earnings is calculated as the parent company's recorded partial equity basis retained earnings that has been realized in transactions with third parties plus or minus the cumulative effect of the adjustments to date relating to the depreciation, amortization, and impairment of differences between implied and book values.***

ILLUSTRATION 6-17

Calculation of the Controlling and Noncontrolling Interest in Consolidated Income—Partial Equity Method for the Year Ended December 31, 2012

Noncontrolling Interest in Consolidated Income			
Unrealized profit on *upstream* sales in ending inventory	125,000	Net income reported by S Company	$140,000
Depreciation of differences between implied and book values	0	Realized profit (*upstream* sales) from beginning inventory	100,000
		Subsidiary income included in consolidated income	$115,000
		Noncontrolling ownership percentage interest	20%
		Noncontrolling interest in consolidated income	$ 23,000
Controlling Interest in Income			
		Net income internally generated by P Company ($518,000 less $112,000 equity income)	$406,000
Unrealized profit on *downstream* sales to S Company (ending inventory)	0	Realized profit (*downstream* sales) from begin. inventory	0
		P Company's percentage of S Company's income realized from third parties, .80($115,000)	92,000
		Controlling Interest in Consolidated Income	$498,000

80% ($115,000 subsidiary income → 92,000)

ILLUSTRATION 6-18

Calculation of Consolidated Retained Earnings—Partial Equity Method for the Year Ended December 31, 2012

Consolidated Retained Earnings

P Company's share of unrealized profit on *upstream* sales from S Company (in P's ending inventory), .8($125,000)	100,000	P Company's Retained Earnings on 12/31/12	$2,248,000
Unrealized profit on *downstream* sales to S Company (in S's ending inventory)	0		
		Consolidated Retained Earnings	$2,148,000

On the basis of Illustration 6-16, the t-account calculation of consolidated retained earnings on December 31, 2012, is shown in Illustration 6-18. There is no need to include adjustments for 12/31/11 ending inventory or 1/1/12 beginning inventory as they cancel out.

TEST YOUR KNOWLEDGE

NOTE: Solutions to ***Test Your Knowledge*** questions are found at the end of each chapter before the end-of-chapter questions.

Multiple Choice

1. Peller owns 80% of Sando Company common stock. During the fourth quarter of 2009, Sando sold inventory to Peller for $200,000. At the end of December 2009, half this inventory remained in Peller's ending inventory. For the year 2009, Peller's gross profit percentage was 30% while Sando's was 40%. How much unrealized profit should be eliminated from ending inventory on December 31, 2009?
   a. $80,000
   b. $40,000
   c. $32,000
   d. $30,000
2. Pony owns 80% of Shetland. During 2010, Shetland sold $100,000 of merchandise at a 25% gross profit to its parent. One-tenth of the goods remain unsold by Pony at the end of 2010. How much gross profit will the noncontrolling interest receive as a result of these sales?
   a. $22,500
   b. $4,500
   c. $5,000
   d. $25,000

CONSOLIDATED STATEMENTS WORKPAPER—COMPLETE EQUITY METHOD

LO6 Consolidated workpapers—complete equity method.

The balances reported by the parent company in income, in retained earnings, and in the investment account differ depending on the method used by the parent company to record its investment. As illustrated in Chapters 4 and 5, however, the method used by the parent company to record its investment has no effect on the consolidated balances. To illustrate consolidation procedures when the parent company records its investment using the complete equity method, assume the following:

COMPLETE

1. P Company acquired an 80% interest in S Company on January 1, 2011, for $1,360,000, at which time S Company had capital stock of $1,000,000 and retained earnings of $700,000.

2. In 2011, S Company reported net income of $125,000 and declared dividends of $20,000.
3. In 2012, S Company reported net income of $140,000 and declared dividends of $60,000.
4. P Company uses the complete equity method to account for its investment in S Company.
5. The purchase price equals 80% of both the book values and fair values of S Company's net assets on the date of acquisition. Thus, implied value of S equals the book value and the fair value of S net assets.
6. S Company sells merchandise to P Company as follows (upstream sales):

COMPLETE

	Total Sales of S Company to P Company	*Intercompany Merchandise in 12/31 Inventory of P Company*	*Unrealized Intercompany Profit (25% of Selling Price)*
2011	$ 700,000	$400,000	$100,000
2012	1,000,000	500,000	125,000

Entries on Books of P Company—Complete Equity Method

Entries recorded on the books of P Company under the complete equity method are as follows:

2011—Year of Acquisition—Complete Equity Method

		Debit	Credit
(1)	Investment in S Company	1,360,000	
	Cash		1,360,000
	To record purchase of 80% interest in S Company.		
(2)	Cash	16,000	
	Investment in S Company		16,000
	To record dividends received (.80 × $20,000).		
(3)	Investment in S Company	100,000	
	Equity in Subsidiary Income		100,000
	To record equity in subsidiary income (.80 × $125,000).		
(4)	Equity in Subsidiary Income	80,000	
	Investment in S Company		80,000
	To adjust equity in subsidiary income for P Company's share of unrealized intercompany profit (.80 × $100,000) in ending inventory.		

Entries (3) and (4) can be collapsed into one entry.

2012—Year Subsequent to Acquisition—Complete Equity Method

		Debit	Credit
(5)	Cash	48,000	
	Investment in S Company		48,000
	To record dividends received (.80 × $60,000).		
(6)	Investment in S Company	112,000	
	Equity in Subsidiary Income		112,000
	To record equity in subsidiary income (.80 × $140,000).		
(7)	Investment in S Company	80,000	
	Equity in Subsidiary Income		80,000
	To adjust equity in subsidiary income for realized intercompany profit in beginning inventory (.80 × $100,000).		
(8)	Equity in Subsidiary Income	100,000	
	Investment in S Company		100,000
	To adjust equity in subsidiary income for unrealized intercompany profit in ending inventory (.80 × $125,000).		

After these entries are posted, the investment account will appear as follows:

COMPLETE

Investment in S Company

(1) Cost	1,360,000	(2) Dividends	16,000
(3) Subsidiary Income	100,000	(4) Profit in Ending Inventory (80%)	80,000
12/31/11 Balance	***1,364,000***		
(6) Subsidiary Income	112,000	(5) Dividends	48,000
(7) Profit in Beginning Inventory (80%)	80,000	(8) Profit in Ending Inventory (80%)(125,000) =	100,000
12/31/12 Balance	***1,408,000***		

Workpaper Entries—2012—Complete Equity Method Consolidated workpapers under the complete equity method for the years ended December 31, 2011 and 2012, are presented in Illustrations 6-19 and 6-20. Workpaper entries in Illustration 6-20 (the year subsequent to acquisition) are presented in general journal form as follows:

		Debit	Credit
(1)	Equity in Subsidiary Income ($112,000 + $80,000 − $100,000)	92,000	
	Dividends Declared		48,000
	Investment in S Company		44,000
	To reverse the effect of parent company entries during the year for subsidiary dividends and income (adjusted for parent's share of gross profit realized/unrealized as needed).		

		Debit	Credit
(2)	Sales	1,000,000	
	Purchases (Cost of Sales)		1,000,000
	To eliminate intercompany sales.		

		Debit	Credit
(3)	12/31 Inventory—Income Statement (Cost of Sales)	125,000	
	Inventory—Balance Sheet		125,000
	To eliminate unrealized intercompany profit in ending inventory.		

		Debit	Credit
(4)	***Investment in S Company** (.80 × $100,000)*	80,000	
	NCI in Equity (.20 × $100,000)	20,000	
	1/1 Inventory—Income Statement (Cost of Sales)		100,000
	To recognize intercompany profit in beginning inventory realized during the year in the proper accounts for presentation on the consolidated financial statements; that is, even though the parent has adjusted its equity in subsidiary income, the effect must be shown in the cost of sales account (as the equity in subsidiary income is eliminated).		

Entries (2), (3), and (4) are the same as the corresponding entries in Illustration 6-8 (investment recorded using cost method) with one exception, shown in bold in entry (4). The exception is that the debit to Investment in S Company in entry (4) above replaces the debit to Beginning Retained Earnings—P Company under the cost or partial equity methods. The difference is that under the complete equity method, P Company had appropriately adjusted the investment account for its share of unrealized gross profit in inventory at the end of 2011. But now the entire investment account must be eliminated.

Complete Equity Method
80% Owned Subsidiary
Upstream Sale of Inventory
Year of Acquisition

ILLUSTRATION 6-19
Consolidated Statements Workpaper
P Company and Subsidiary
for the Year Ended December 31, 2011

Income Statement	*P Company*	*S Company*	*Eliminations Dr.*	*Eliminations Cr.*	*Noncontrolling Interest*	*Consolidated Balances*
Sales	3,104,000	2,200,000	(2) 700,000			4,604,000
Equity in Subsidiary Income	20,000		(1) 20,000			
Total Revenue	3,124,000	2,200,000				4,604,000
Inventory 1/1	500,000	300,000				800,000
Purchases	1,680,000	1,370,000		(2) 700,000		2,350,000
	2,180,000	1,670,000				3,150,000
Inventory 12/31	480,000	310,000	(3) 100,000			690,000
Cost of Goods Sold	1,700,000	1,360,000				2,460,000
Other Expenses	1,124,000	715,000				1,839,000
Total Cost and Expense	2,824,000	2,075,000				4,299,000
Net/Consolidated Income	300,000	125,000				305,000
Noncontrolling Interest in Income					5,000*	5,000
Net Income to Retained Earnings	300,000	125,000	820,000	700,000	5,000	300,000
Retained Earnings Statement						
1/1 Retained Earnings						
P Company	1,650,000					1,650,000
S Company		700,000	(4) 700,000			
Net Income from above	300,000	125,000	820,000	700,000	5,000	300,000
Dividends Declared						
P Company	(150,000)					(150,000)
S Company		(20,000)		(1) 16,000	(4,000)	
12/31 Retained Earnings to Balance Sheet	1,800,000	805,000	1,520,000	716,000	1,000	1,800,000
Balance Sheet						
Inventory	480,000	310,000		(3) 100,000		690,000
Investment in S Company	1,364,000			(1) 4,000 (4) 1,360,000		
Other Assets (net)	5,090,000	2,310,000				7,400,000
Total	6,934,000	2,620,000				8,090,000
Liabilities	2,134,000	815,000				2,949,000
Capital Stock						
P Company	3,000,000					3,000,000
S Company		1,000,000	(4) 1,000,000			
Retained Earnings from above	1,800,000	805,000	1,520,000	716,000	1,000	1,800,000
1/1 Noncontrolling Interest in Net Assets				(4) 340,000	340,000	
12/31 Noncontrolling Interest in Net Assets					341,000	341,000
Total Liabilities and Equity	6,934,000	2,620,000	2,520,000	2,520,000		8,090,000

* .20($125,000 − $100,000) = $5,000.
(1) To reverse the effect of parent company entries during the year for subsidiary dividends and income.
(2) To eliminate intercompany sales.
(3) To eliminate unrealized intercompany profit in ending inventory.
(4) To recognize profit realized during year and to reduce the controlling and noncontrolling interests for their shares of unrealized intercompany profit at beginning of year.
(5) To eliminate investment account and create noncontrolling interest account.

Complete Equity Method
80% Owned Subsidiary
Upstream Sale of Inventory
Year Subsequent to Acquisition

ILLUSTRATION 6-20
Consolidated Statements Workpaper
P Company and Subsidiary
for the Year Ended December 31, 2012

	P Company	S Company	Eliminations Dr.	Eliminations Cr.	Noncontrolling Interest	Consolidated Balances
Income Statement						
Sales	3,546,000	2,020,000	(2) 1,000,000			4,566,000
Equity in Subsidiary Income	92,000		(1) 92,000			
Total Revenue	3,638,000	2,020,000				4,566,000
Inventory 1/1	480,000	310,000		(4) 100,000		690,000
Purchases	2,070,000	1,250,000		(2) 1,000,000		2,320,000
	2,550,000	1,560,000				3,010,000
Inventory 12/31	510,000	360,000	(3) 125,000			745,000
Cost of Goods Sold	2,040,000	1,200,000				2,265,000
Other Expenses	1,100,000	680,000				1,780,000
Total Cost and Expense	3,140,000	1,880,000				4,045,000
Net/Consolidated Income	498,000	140,000				521,000
Noncontrolling Interest in Income					23,000*	23,000
Net Income to Retained Earnings	498,000	140,000	1,217,000	1,100,000	23,000	498,000
Retained Earnings Statement						
1/1 Retained Earnings						
P Company	1,800,000					1,800,000
S Company		805,000	(5) 805,000			
Net Income from above	498,000	140,000	1,217,000	1,100,000	23,000	498,000
Dividends Declared						
P Company	(150,000)					(150,000)
S Company		(60,000)		(1) 48,000	(12,000)	
12/31 Retained Earnings to Balance Sheet	2,148,000	885,000	2,022,000	1,148,000	11,000	2,148,000
Balance Sheet						
Inventory	510,000	360,000		(3) 125,000		745,000
Investment in S Company	1,408,000		(4) 80,000	(1) 44,000 (5) 1,444,000		
Other Assets (net)	5,450,000	2,330,000				7,780,000
Total	7,368,000	2,690,000				8,525,000
Liabilities	2,220,000	805,000				3,025,000
Capital Stock						
P Company	3,000,000					3,000,000
S Company		1,000,000	(5) 1,000,000			
Retained Earnings from above	2,148,000	885,000	2,022,000	1,148,000	11,000	2,148,000
1/1 Noncontrolling Interest in Net Assets**			(4) 20,000	(5) 361,000	341,000	
12/31 Noncontrolling Interest in Net Assets					352,000	352,000
Total Liabilities and Equity	7,368,000	2,690,000	3,122,000	3,122,000		8,525,000

* .20($140,000 − $125,000 + $100,000) = $23,000.
** $340,000 + .2($805,000 − $700,000) = $361,000.
(1) To reverse the effect of parent company entries during the year for subsidiary dividends and income.
(2) To eliminate intercompany sales.
(3) To eliminate unrealized intercompany profit in ending inventory.
(4) To recognize profit realized during year and to reduce the controlling and noncontrolling interests for their shares of unrealized intercompany profit at beginning of year.
(5) To eliminate investment account and create noncontrolling interest account.

COMPLETE

(5) Beginning Retained Earnings—S Company	805,000	
Capital Stock—S Company	1,000,000	
Investment in S Company		1,444,000
NCI in Equity ($340,000 + .2($805,000 − $700,000))		361,000
To eliminate the investment account.		

This entry is the same as entry (5) in Illustration 6-16 (partial equity method) or entry (6) in Illustration 6-8 (cost method). Workpaper entry (5) creates the balance in the noncontrolling interest account reflective of the sum of the 20% interest at acquisition plus the noncontrolling share of changes in Retained Earnings of S since acquisition. This entry could just as easily be numbered as entry (1) or (2), as there is no particular sequence for workpaper entries. Workpaper entry (4) debits the noncontrolling interest, thus adjusting the balance as needed for prior year unrealized profit in inventory.

Observe that the consolidated balances in Illustration 6-20 are also the same as those in Illustration 6-8 (cost method workpaper) or in Illustration 6-16 (partial equity workpaper). However, when the parent company records its investment using the complete equity method, entry (1) in Illustration 6-20 replaces the cost method entries to establish reciprocity and to eliminate dividend income [entries (1) and (5) in Illustration 6-8]. Most importantly, a comparison of entries (2), (3), and (4) in Illustration 6-20 with entries (2), (3), and (4) in Illustration 6-8 or in Illustration 6-16 demonstrates that the workpaper entries to eliminate intercompany sales and unrealized intercompany profit differ in only one respect. That is, the parent company's retained earnings account needs no adjustment under the complete equity method. Any adjusting/eliminating entries made to that account under the other two methods are replaced by an entry to the Investment account under the complete equity method.

COMPLETE EQUITY METHOD—ANALYSIS OF CONSOLIDATED NET INCOME AND CONSOLIDATED RETAINED EARNINGS

Consolidated net income is the sum of the following components: ***the parent company's net income from its independent operations that has been realized in transactions with third parties plus (minus) reported subsidiary income (loss) that has been realized in transactions with third parties plus or minus adjustments for the period relating to the depreciation, amortization, and impairment of differences between implied and book values.*** See Illustration 6-17.

Under the complete equity method, no formal calculation of the controlling interest in consolidated net income is needed. The parent company has already made adjustments for realized/unrealized gross profit depending upon whether or not such profit has been confirmed through transactions with outsiders. Thus, the controlling interest in ***consolidated net income equals the parent company's recorded income.***

When the parent company uses the complete equity method to record its investment, the parent company's share of subsidiary income (including any needed adjustments for intercompany profits) since acquisition is already included in the parent company's reported retained earnings. Consequently, ***consolidated retained earnings is equal to the parent company's recorded complete equity basis retained earnings.***

SUMMARY OF WORKPAPER ENTRIES RELATING TO INTERCOMPANY SALES OF INVENTORY

Consolidated statement workpaper eliminating entries for intercompany sales of inventory are summarized in Illustration 6-21. The entries are the same whether the parent company uses the cost method or the partial equity method to record its

ILLUSTRATION 6-21
Intercompany Profit—Inventories
Summary of Workpaper Elimination Entries

	Selling Affiliate Is the Parent (Downstream Sales)			*Selling Affiliate Is a Subsidiary (Upstream Sales)*		
To eliminate intercompany sales:						
All Methods	Sales	X		Sales	X	
	Purchases (Cost of Sales)		X	Purchases (Cost of Sales)		X
To eliminate intercompany profit in ending inventory:						
All Methods	Ending Inventory (Cost of Sales)	X		Ending Inventory (Cost of Sales)	X	
	Inventory (*Balance Sheet*)		X	Inventory (*Balance Sheet*)		X
To recognize intercompany profit in beginning inventory realized during the year:						
Cost or Partial Equity Methods	Beginning Retained Earnings—P	X		Beginning Retained Earnings—P	X	
				NCI in Equity	X	
	Beginning Inventory—*Income Statement (Cost of Sales)*		X	Beginning Inventory—*Income Statement (Cost of Sales)*		X
Complete Equity Method	Investment in S Company	X		Investment in S Company	X	
				NCI in Equity	X	
	Beginning Inventory—*Income Statement (Cost of Sales)*		X	Beginning Inventory—*Income Statement (Cost of Sales)*		X

investment. However, the form of the workpaper entry for unrealized profit in beginning inventories differs between upstream and downstream sales and between the complete equity method and the other two.

INTERCOMPANY PROFIT PRIOR TO PARENT–SUBSIDIARY AFFILIATION

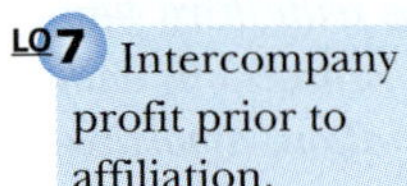
LO7 Intercompany profit prior to affiliation.

Generally accepted accounting standards are silent as to the appropriate treatment of unrealized profit on assets that result from sales between companies prior to affiliation (preaffiliation profit). The question is whether preaffiliation profit should be eliminated in consolidation. In our opinion, workpaper entries eliminating preaffiliation profit are inappropriate.

If the selling company is the new subsidiary, the profit recognized by it prior to its acquisition is implicitly considered in determining the book value of the interest acquired by the parent company. Accordingly, such profit is automatically eliminated from consolidated retained earnings in the investment elimination entry. A second elimination would therefore result in a double reduction of the amount of preaffiliation profit from consolidated retained earnings on the date of acquisition. When the assets are sold to third parties in subsequent years, consolidated net income would be increased by a corresponding amount, thus restoring the amount of the second reduction to consolidated retained earnings. The net result is to make an unwarranted reduction of consolidated retained earnings on the date of acquisition in order to report preacquisition profit in consolidated net income in years subsequent to affiliation that has already been reported by the subsidiary prior to affiliation. In our opinion such effects lack both conceptual and practical merit.

If the selling company is the parent, the preaffiliation profit will ultimately be included in consolidated retained earnings in any case. However, a reduction of such profit from consolidated retained earnings on the date of affiliation simply results in the inclusion of the profit in the consolidated net income of subsequent years. Again, the effect of the elimination would be to report the profit twice, once before affiliation and once after affiliation. Support for the elimination of preaffiliation profit is based primarily on the application of conservatism to the valuation of consolidated assets on the date of acquisition.

SUMMARY

1. *Describe the financial reporting objectives for intercompany sales of inventory.* Intercompany sales of inventory are eliminated, and adjustments made, to report sales revenue, cost of sales, and inventory balances as if the intercompany sale had not occurred. Thus, consolidated sales reflects only sales with "outsiders," consolidated cost of sales reflects the cost to the consolidated entity, and consolidated inventory is reported at its cost to the consolidated entity (affiliated group).
2. *Determine the amount of intercompany profit, if any, to be eliminated from the consolidated statements.* Intercompany sales (and selling prices) do affect the allocation of profits to the controlling and noncontrolling interests, once the profit is realized through sales to outsiders. Thus, intercompany profit needs to be eliminated *only if* assets are still on the books of the consolidated entity (one of the members of the affiliated group). In such cases, the amount of profit to be eliminated may be calculated using the selling affiliate's gross profit rate, which may be stated as a percentage of either sales or costs. (The amount of profit to be eliminated is the same, regardless of how the percentage is stated.)
3. *Understand the concept of eliminating 100% of intercompany profit not realized in transactions with outsiders, and know the authoritative position.* Proponents of 100% elimination regard *all* the intercompany profit associated with assets remaining in the affiliated group to be unrealized. Proponents of partial elimination regard only the parent company's share of the profit recognized by the selling affiliate to be unrealized. Both current and past GAAP require 100% elimination of intercompany profit in the preparation of consolidated financial statements.
4. *Distinguish between upstream and downstream sales of inventory.* Sales from a parent company to one or more of its subsidiaries are referred to as ***downstream sales.*** Sales from subsidiaries to the parent company are referred to as ***upstream sales.***
5. *Compute the noncontrolling interest in consolidated net income for upstream and downstream sales, when not all the inventory has been sold to outsiders.* For downstream sales, no modification to the calculation of the noncontrolling interest in consolidated income is needed. For upstream or horizontal sales, however, the noncontrolling interest in income must be adjusted. The reported income of the subsidiary (the selling affiliate) is *reduced* by the amount of gross profit remaining in ending inventory of the purchasing affiliate before multiplying by the noncontrolling percentage interest; *it is increased for gross profit realized from beginning inventory.*
6. *Prepare consolidated workpapers for firms with upstream and downstream sales using the cost, partial equity, and complete equity methods.* In the consolidated workpapers, eliminating and adjusting entries serve to eliminate intercompany sales and adjust both beginning and ending inventories for the effects of any gross profit included from intercompany sales. The noncontrolling interest in consolidated income reflects the adjustment described in the preceding learning objective for upstream (or horizontal) sales. The final column of the workpapers is identical, regardless of whether the parent uses the cost, partial equity, or complete equity method for consolidated investments.
7. *Discuss the treatment of intercompany profit earned prior to the parent-subsidiary affiliation.* Generally accepted accounting standards are silent as to the appropriate treatment of unrealized profit on assets that result from sales between companies prior to affiliation (preaffiliation profit). The question is whether preaffiliation profit should be eliminated in consolidation. In our opinion, workpaper entries eliminating preaffiliation profit are inappropriate.

APPENDIX

Deferred Taxes and Intercompany Sales of Inventory

DEFERRED TAX CONSEQUENCES ARISING BECAUSE OF UNREALIZED INTERCOMPANY PROFIT

If the affiliated companies file consolidated income tax returns, profits from intercompany transactions are included in taxable income in the same years that they are included in the consolidated income statement. In that case, the amount at which the asset is reported in the consolidated financial statements and its tax basis are the same, and it is not necessary to consider deferred tax consequences.

However, when the affiliates file separate income tax returns, the tax basis for an asset sold between affiliates is based on the price paid by the purchasing affiliate. Thus, the tax basis of the asset will differ from the amount reported for that asset in the consolidated financial statements. Assuming that the selling affiliate recognized a profit on the intercompany sale, the amount of this difference is equal to the ***unrealized*** profit associated with that asset on the balance sheet date. This difference is a temporary difference that will result in deductible amounts on the tax return of the ***purchasing affiliate*** in a future year(s) when the profit is considered realized in the consolidated financial statements through the sale or depreciation of the asset.

However, under *SFAS No. 109,* "Accounting for Income Taxes," [ASC 740] the measure-ment of the tax benefit for temporary differences related to unrealized profit on intercompany sales is not subject to the basic principles that apply to other temporary differences that will result in deductible amounts in future years. Rather, the provisions of *ARB No. 51,* "Consolidated Financial Statements," [ASC 810] relating to income taxes paid on intercompany profit, are applied.

This standard requires deferral of income taxes ***paid by the seller*** on intercompany profits on assets remaining within the consolidated group. In effect, the taxes paid by the selling affiliate on these profits are treated as prepaid taxes in the consolidated financial statements, and the tax expense is reported in the consolidated financial statements in the same period that the profit is reported as realized. By adopting these provisions, deferred tax effects are based on the income taxes paid by the selling affiliate rather than on the future tax benefit to the purchasing affiliate. The amounts calculated under these two approaches would be different, for example, if the affiliates had different marginal tax rates or were in different tax jurisdictions, or when expected future tax rates differ from the tax rate used to determine the tax paid or accrued by the selling affiliate.

The balances reported by the parent company in income, retained earnings, and the investment account differ depending on the method used by the parent company to record its investment. As illustrated in previous chapters, however, the method used by the parent company to record its investment has no effect on the consolidated balances. Workpaper entries to record deferred tax consequences of unrealized intercompany profit and undistributed subsidiary income are also the same when the parent company records its investment using the partial equity method or the cost method to record its investment. Hence, these methods are illustrated jointly in the following section. The complete equity method differs slightly, however, as illustrated in the final section of this appendix.

INTERCOMPANY SALES OF INVENTORY—COST AND PARTIAL EQUITY METHOD

To illustrate the treatment in the consolidated financial statements of deferred income taxes relating to intercompany sales of inventory assume that:

1. S Company is a 70% owned subsidiary of P Company.
2. The companies file separate income tax returns and the marginal income tax rates for both companies are 40%.
3. On December 31, 2008, there is $500,000 of unrealized intercompany profit in the ending inventory of the purchasing affiliate.
4. S Company reports net income of $900,000 in 2008 and $600,000 in 2009.

Workpaper eliminating entries relating to the unrealized profit included in inventory of the purchasing affiliate differ depending on whether the selling affiliate is the parent company (downstream sale) or the subsidiary (upstream or horizontal sale). Entries in the December 31, 2008, and December 31, 2009, consolidated statements workpapers under each of these conditions are illustrated below:

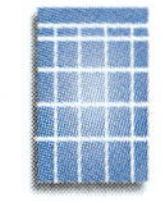
PARTIAL

COST

Consolidated Statements Workpaper Entries—Cost and Partial Equity Methods—December 31, 2008

Downstream Sales			*Upstream Sales*		
12/31 Inventory—			12/31 Inventory—		
(Income Statement)	500,000		(Income Statement)	500,000	
Inventory		500,000	Inventory		500,000
To eliminate unrealized profit in ending inventory.					
Deferred Tax Asset	200,000		Deferred Tax Asset	200,000	
Tax Expense		200,000	Tax Expense		200,000
To defer income tax paid or accrued by the selling affiliate on unrealized intercompany profit (.4 × $500,000 = $200,000).					

Although the workpaper entries are the same, the computation of noncontrolling interest in consolidated net income is affected by upstream sales. The ***after-tax*** unrealized intercompany profit of $300,000 [($500,000 − $200,000) or (.60 × $500,000)] must be subtracted from reported subsidiary income in computing subsidiary income included in consolidated net income. For example, if the sale is upstream and S Company reports net income of $900,000 in 2008, the noncontrolling interest in consolidated net income is $180,000 [.30 × ($900,000 − (.60 × $500,000))]. Alternatively, the following schedule illustrates the previous points.

Upstream Sales

	S Company (000s)	
	With Intercompany Profit	*Without Intercompany Profit*
Income from Independent Operations	$1,000	$1,000
Unrealized Profit in Ending Inventory	500	
Pretax Income	$1,500	$1,000
Tax Expense (40%)	600	400
Net Income	900	600

		S Company (000s)	
		With Intercompany Profit	*Without Intercompany Profit*
Less: After-tax unrealized profit in inventory			
Unrealized profit	500		
Tax on unrealized profit (40%)	200	(300)	
Subsidiary Income in Consolidated Net Income		$600	$600
Noncontrolling Interest percentage		30%	30%
Noncontrolling Interest in Consolidated Net Income		$180	$180

PARTIAL

If the sale is downstream, the amount of subsidiary income included in consolidated net income is not affected by the elimination of unrealized intercompany profit and no adjustment is necessary in the calculation of the noncontrolling interest in consolidated net income.

Assume that in the next year, the inventory is sold.

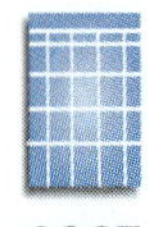
COST

Consolidated Statements Workpaper Entries—Cost and Partial Equity Methods—December 31, 2009

Downstream Sales			*Upstream Sales*		
1/1 Retained Earnings—P Company	500,000		1/1 Retained Earnings—P Company (.7 × $500,000)	350,000	
			1/1 NCI—(.3 × $500,000)	150,000	
1/1 Inventory (Income Statement)		500,000	1/1 Inventory (Income Statement)		500,000

To recognize intercompany profit realized during the year and to reduce the controlling and the noncontrolling interests for their share of unrealized intercompany profit at the beginning of the year.

Downstream Sales			*Upstream Sales*		
Tax Expense	200,000		Tax Expense	200,000	
1/1 Retained Earnings—+P Company		200,000	1/1 Retained Earnings—P Company (.7 × $200,000)		140,000
			1/1 NCI—(.3 × $200,000)		60,000

To recognize income tax expense on intercompany profit considered realized during the year and to adjust the controlling and noncontrolling interests for the tax consequence of unrealized intercompany profit eliminated in the previous entry.

Note that since the inventory is now sold to outsiders, there are no longer any deferred tax items recorded on the consolidated balance sheet.

In the case of upstream sales, the net after-tax adjustment to the noncontrolling interest at the ***beginning of the year*** is $90,000 ($150,000 − $60,000), which is the same amount by which the noncontrolling interest in consolidated net income was reduced for after-tax unrealized intercompany profit at the end of the prior year. [.3 × ($500,000 − $200,000) = $90,000].

PARTIAL

If the sale is upstream, the noncontrolling interest in consolidated net income for 2009 is calculated after adding the after-tax amount of intercompany profit that is included in consolidated net income in the current year (.60 × $500,000 = $300,000). For example, if the sale is upstream and S Company reports net income of $600,000 in 2009, the noncontrolling interest in consolidated net income is

COST

$270,000 [.30 × ($600,000 + $300,000)]. If the sale is downstream, no adjustment is necessary in the calculation of the noncontrolling interest in consolidated net income. These concepts are illustrated fully in the next section.

UNDISTRIBUTED SUBSIDIARY INCOME—THE IMPACT OF UNREALIZED INTERCOMPANY PROFIT ON THE CALCULATION OF DEFERRED TAXES

Cost and Partial Equity Methods

The workpaper entries needed to report the tax consequences of past and current undistributed earnings of a subsidiary were described in Appendix B in Chapter 4. Workpaper entries are necessary under the cost method when there is undistributed subsidiary income and the affiliates file separate income tax returns. Now that we have discussed the effects of unrealized intercompany profits, it is important to note that the calculation of the tax consequences of undistributed income is based on the undistributed income of the subsidiary that has been ***included in consolidated net income.*** Thus, before calculating the deferred tax consequences relating to undistributed subsidiary income, the amount of undistributed income of the subsidiary must be adjusted for the ***after-tax amount of*** unrealized intercompany profit ***recorded by the subsidiary*** that has been recognized in the determination of consolidated net income.

To illustrate, assume that:

PARTIAL

1. P Company acquired 75% of the voting stock of S Company when S Company's retained earnings amounted to $150,000.
2. S Company reported retained earnings of $260,000 on January 1, 2009, and $320,000 on December 31, 2009.
3. S Company reported net income of $90,000 and declared dividends of $30,000 in 2009.
4. P Company reported net income from independent operations in 2009 in the amount of $700,000 and retained earnings on December 31, 2009, of $3,500,000.
5. The affiliates file separate income tax returns.
6. Undistributed income is expected to be received in the form of future dividends.
7. The dividends received deduction is 80%, and past, current, and future expected marginal income tax rates are 40%.

COST

8. There were no intercompany sales prior to 2008, and unrealized profits on January 1 and on December 31, 2009, resulting from intercompany sales are as summarized below:

	Unrealized Intercompany Profit on	
Resulting From	*1/1/09*	*12/31/09*
Sales by S Company to P Company	$10,000	$ 5,000
Sales by P Company to S Company	15,000	20,000

ILLUSTRATION 6-22

Undistributed Income of S Company That Has Been Included in Consolidated Income

S Company	*From Acquisition to 1/1/2009*	*For Calendar Year 2009*	*From Acquisition to 12/31/2009*
Retained earnings 1/1/2009	$260,000		
Retained earnings 12/31/2009			$320,000
Retained earnings date of acquisition	(150,000)		(150,000)
Increase in retained earnings	110,000		170,000
Net income 2009		$90,000	
Dividends 2009		(30,000)	
After-tax unrealized profit on 1/1/2009 (.6 × $10,000)	(6,000)	6,000	
After-tax unrealized profit on 12/31/2009 (.6 × $5,000)		(3,000)	(3,000)
Undistributed income that has been included in consolidated income	$104,000	$63,000	$167,000

ILLUSTRATION 6-23

Calculation of the Noncontrolling Interest and Controlling Interest in Consolidated Income for the Year Ended December 31, 2009

Noncontrolling Interest in Consolidated Income

After-tax unrealized profit on upstream sales in ending inventory (.6 × $5,000)	3,000	Net income reported by S Company	$ 90,000
Amortization of the difference between implied and book value	0	After-tax realized profit (upstream sales) from beginning inventory (.6 × $10,000)	6,000
		Subsidiary income included in consolidated income	$ 93,000
		Noncontrolling ownership percentage interest	25%
		Noncontrolling interest in consolidated income	$ 23,250

Controlling Interest in Income

		Net income internally generated by P Company	$700,000
After-tax unrealized profit on downstream sales to S Company (ending inventory) (.6 × $20,000)	12,000	After-tax realized profit (downstream sales) from begin. Inventory (.6 × $15,000)	9,000
Deferred taxes on undistributed income of S Company ($93,000 − $30,000) (.75) (.20) (.40)	3,780	P Company's percentage of S Company's income realized from third parties, .75 ($93,000)	69,750
		Controlling Interest in Income	$762,970

75%

The calculation of the amounts of the undistributed income of S Company that is included in consolidated net income is presented in Illustration 6-22. Illustration 6-23 shows the calculation of the noncontrolling and controlling interests in consolidated net income for 2009.

Complete Equity Method—Intercompany Sales of Inventory

When the parent uses the complete equity method to account for the investment, the parent accounts for deferred taxes related to undistributed *adjusted* subsidiary

COMPLETE

income on its own books. This occurs because there is a difference between taxable income (dividends received from the subsidiary) and equity income (reported on the income statement) on the books of the parent, necessitating parent company entries for deferred taxes.

To illustrate the treatment in the consolidated financial statements of deferred income taxes relating to intercompany sales of inventory, assume that:

1. S Company is a 70% owned subsidiary of P Company.
2. The companies file separate income tax returns and the marginal income tax rates for both companies are 40%.
3. On December 31, 2008, there is $500,000 of unrealized intercompany profit in the ending inventory of the purchasing affiliate.
4. S Company reports net income of $900,000 in 2008 and $600,000 in 2009.

On the books of the parent, the following entries are made to account for the effects of intercompany sales of inventory.

Equity in Subsidiary Income	500,000	
Investment in S Company		500,000
To adjust equity in subsidiary income for unrealized intercompany profit in ending inventory.		

Deferred Tax Asset	200,000	
Tax Expense		200,000

Workpaper eliminating entries relating to the unrealized profit included in inventory of the purchasing affiliate differ in subsequent years, depending on whether the selling affiliate is the parent company (downstream sale) or the subsidiary (upstream or horizontal sale). Entries in the December 31, 2008, and December 31, 2009, consolidated statements workpapers under each of these conditions are illustrated below:

Consolidated Statements Workpaper Entries—Complete Equity Method December 31, 2008

Downstream Sales			*Upstream Sales*		
Ending Inventory—(Income Statement)	500,000		Ending Inventory—(Income Statement)	500,000	
Inventory (Balance Sheet)		500,000	Inventory (Balance Sheet)		500,000
To eliminate unrealized profit in ending inventory.					

In the year 2009, the inventory is sold. The entry on the books of the parent to reflect the reversal of the deferred tax asset is as follows:

Tax Expense	200,000	
Deferred Tax Asset		200,000

Then the following entry is made on the workpaper:

Consolidated Statements Workpaper Entries—Complete Equity Method December 31, 2009

Downstream Sales			*Upstream Sales*		
Investment in S	500,000		Investment in S (.7 × $500,000)	350,000	
			NCI— (.3 × $500,000)	150,000	
1/1 Inventory (Income Statement)		500,000	1/1 Inventory (Income Statement)		500,000

To recognize intercompany profit realized during the year and to reduce the controlling and the noncontrolling interests for their share of unrealized intercompany profit at the beginning of the year.

COMPLETE

Note that since the inventory is now sold to outsiders, there are no longer any deferred tax items recorded on the consolidated balance sheet.

In the case of upstream sales, the net after-tax adjustment to the noncontrolling interest at the ***beginning of the year*** is $90,000 ($150,000 − $60,000), the same amount by which the noncontrolling interest in consolidated net income was reduced for after-tax unrealized intercompany profit at the end of the prior year (2008) [.3 × ($500,000 − $200,000) = $90,000].

If the sale is upstream, the noncontrolling interest in consolidated income is calculated after adding the after-tax amount of intercompany profit that is included in consolidated net income in the current year (.60 × $500,000 = $300,000). For example, if the sale is upstream and S Company reports net income of $600,000 in 2009, the noncontrolling interest in consolidated net income is $270,000 [.30 × ($600,000 + $300,000)]. If the sale is downstream, no adjustment is necessary in the calculation of the noncontrolling interest in consolidated net income.

TEST YOUR KNOWLEDGE SOLUTIONS

6-1	1. b	2. c	3. c
6-2	1. b	2. b	

QUESTIONS

(The letter A indicated for a question, exercise, or problem refers to the appendix.)

LO2 **1.** Does the elimination of the effects of intercompany sales of merchandise always affect the amount of reported consolidated net income? Explain.

LO2 **2.** Why is the gross profit on intercompany sales, rather than profit after deducting selling and administrative expenses, ordinarily eliminated from consolidated inventory balances?

LO2 **3.** P Company sells inventory costing $100,000 to its subsidiary, S Company, for $150,000. At the end of the current year, one-half of the goods remains in S Company's inventory. Applying the lower of cost or market rule, S Company writes down this inventory to $60,000. What amount of intercompany profit should be eliminated on the consolidated statements workpaper?

LO5 **4.** Are the adjustments to the noncontrolling interest for the effects of intercompany profit eliminations illustrated in this text necessary for fair presentation in accordance with generally accepted accounting principles? Explain.

LO5 5. Why are adjustments made to the calculation of the noncontrolling interest for the effects of intercompany profit in upstream but not in downstream sales?

LO5 6. What procedure is used in the consolidated statements workpaper to adjust the noncontrolling interest in consolidated net assets at the beginning of the year for the effects of intercompany profits?

LO5 7. What is the essential procedural difference between workpaper eliminating entries for unrealized intercompany profit made when the selling affiliate is a less than wholly owned subsidiary and those made when the selling affiliate is the parent company or a wholly owned subsidiary?

LO1 8. Define the controlling interest in consolidated net income using the t-account or analytical approach.

LO4 9. Why is it important to distinguish between upstream and downstream sales in the analysis of intercompany profit eliminations?

LO1 10. In what period and in what manner should profits relating to the intercompany sale of merchandise be recognized in the consolidated financial statements?

Business Ethics

One issue concerning Enron's collapse centered on the amount of non-audit fees paid by Enron to its external auditor, Arthur Andersen. For each of the following items, discuss the potential ethical issues between the firm and its auditor. For each item, list at least one reason why the statement might be viewed as a threat to the auditor's independence, and at least one reason why it might not be viewed as such a threat.

1. The firm's auditor is heavily involved in non-audit services.
2. The audit partner's compensation depends on both audit and non-audit fees from the same client.
3. In 1995, Congress passed the Private Securities Litigation Reform Act. This act reduced plaintiffs' ability to sue auditors.

EXERCISES

EXERCISE 6-1 **Downstream Sales** LO2

P Company owns 80% of the outstanding stock of S Company. During 2011, S Company reported net income of $525,000 and declared no dividends. At the end of the year, S Company's inventory included $487,500 in unrealized profit on purchases from P Company. Intercompany sales for 2011 totaled $2,700,000.

Required:

Prepare in general journal form all consolidated financial statement workpaper entries necessary at the end of the year to eliminate the effects of the 2011 intercompany sales.

EXERCISE 6-2 **Noncontrolling Interest, Downstream Sales** LO5

Refer to Exercise 6-1. Calculate the amount of the noncontrolling interest to be deducted from consolidated income in arriving at 2011 controlling interest in consolidated net income.

EXERCISE 6-3 **Noncontrolling Interest, Upstream Sales** LO5

Peabody Company owns 90% of the outstanding capital stock of Sloane Company. During 2011 and 2012 Sloane Company sold merchandise to Peabody Company at a markup of 25% of selling price. The selling price of the merchandise sold during the two years was $20,800 and $25,000, respectively. At the end of each year, Peabody Company had in its inventory one-fourth of the goods purchased that year from Sloane Company. Sloane Company reported net income of $30,000 in 2011 and $35,000 in 2012.

Required:

Determine the amount of the noncontrolling interest in consolidated income to be reported for 2011 and 2012.

EXERCISE 6-4 **Controlling Interest, Downstream Sales** LO2

On January 1, 2011, Pearce Company purchased an 80% interest in the capital stock of Searl Company for $2,460,000. At that time, Searl Company had capital stock of $1,500,000 and retained earnings of $300,000. The difference between book of value Searl equity and the value implied by the purchase price was attributed to specific assets of Searl Company as follows:

375,000	to equipment of Searl Company with a five-year remaining life.
187,500	to land held by Searl Company.
112,500	to inventory of Searl Company. Searl uses the FIFO assumption in pricing its inventory, and
600,000	that could not be assigned to specific assets or liabilities of Searl Company.
$1,275,000	Total

At year-end 2011 and 2012, Searl had in its inventory merchandise that it had purchased from Pearce at a 25% markup on cost during each year in the following amounts:

2011	$ 90,000
2012	$105,000

During 2011, Pearce reported net income from independent operations (including sales to affiliates) of $1,500,000, while Searle reported net income of $600,000. In 2012, Pearce's net income from independent operations (including sales to affiliates) was $1,800,000 and Searl's was $750,000.

Required:

Calculate the controlling interest in consolidated net income for 2011 and 2012.

EXERCISE 6-5 **Controlling Interest, Upstream Sales** LO2

Refer to Exercise 6-4. Using the same figures, assume that the merchandise mentioned was included in Pearce's inventory, having been purchased from Searl.

Required:

Calculate the controlling interest in consolidated net income for 2011 and 2012.

EXERCISE 6-6 **Controlling Interest, Upstream Sales** LO2

Payne Company owns all the outstanding common stock of Sierra Company and 80% of the outstanding common stock of Santa Fe Company. The amount of intercompany profit included in the inventories of Payne Company on December 31, 2011, and December 31, 2012, is indicated here:

	Intercompany Profit on Goods Purchased From		
	Sierra Company	*Santa Fe Company*	*Total*
Inventory, 12/31/11	$3,800	$4,600	$8,400
Inventory, 12/31/12	4,800	2,300	7,100

The three companies reported net income from their independent operations (including sales to affiliates) for the year ended December 31, 2012, as follows:

Payne Company	$280,000
Sierra Company	172,000
Santa Fe Company	120,000

Required:

Calculate the controlling interest in consolidated net income for the year ended December 31, 2012.

EXERCISE 6-7 **Workpaper Entries, Downstream Sales** LO2

Perkins Company owns 85% of Sheraton Company. Perkins Company sells merchandise to Sheraton Company at 20% above cost. During 2011 and 2012, such sales amounted to $450,000 and $486,000, respectively. At the end of each year, Sheraton Company had in its inventory one-third of the amount of goods purchased from Perkins during that year.

Required:

Prepare the workpaper entries necessary to eliminate the effects of the intercompany sales for 2011 and 2012.

EXERCISE 6-8 **Workpaper Entries, Upstream Sales** LO2

Refer to Exercise 6-7. Using the same figures, assume that the sales were upstream instead of downstream.

Required:

Prepare the workpaper entries necessary to eliminate the effects of the intercompany sales for 2011 and 2012.

EXERCISE 6-9 **Upstream and Downstream Sales** LO2

Peat Company owns a 90% interest in Seaton Company. The consolidated income statement drafted by the controller of Peat Company appeared as follows:

Peat Company and Subsidiary
Consolidated Income Statement
for Year Ended December 31, 2012

Sales		$14,000,000
Cost of Sales	$9,200,000	
Operating Expense	1,800,000	11,000,000
Consolidated Income		3,000,000
Less Noncontrolling Interest in Consolidated Income		200,000
Controlling Interest in Consolidated Net Income		$ 2,800,000

During your audit you discover that intercompany sales transactions were not reflected in the controller's draft of the consolidated income statement. Information relating to intercompany sales and unrealized intercompany profit is as follows:

	Cost	*Selling Price*	*Unsold at Year-End*
2011 Sales—Seaton to Peat	$1,500,000	$1,800,000	1/3
2012 Sales—Peat to Seaton	900,000	1,400,000	2/5

Required:

Prepare a corrected consolidated income statement for Peat Company and Seaton Company for the year ended December 31, 2012.

PROBLEMS

PROBLEM 6-1 **Upstream Sales** LO2 LO5

Peel Company owns 90% of the common stock of Seacore Company. Seacore Company sells merchandise to Peel Company at 20% above cost. During 2011 and 2012, such sales amounted to $436,000 and $532,000, respectively. At the end of each year, Peel Company had in its inventory one-fourth of the goods purchased from Seacore Company during that year.

Peel Company reported $300,000 in net income from its independent operations in 2011 and 2012. Seacore Company reported net income of $130,000 in each year and did not declare any dividends in any year. There were no intercompany sales prior to 2011.

Required:

A. Prepare in general journal form all entries necessary on the consolidated financial statements workpaper to eliminate the effects of the intercompany sales for each of the years 2011 and 2012.

B. Calculate the amount of noncontrolling interest to be deducted from consolidated income in the consolidated income statement for 2012.

C. Calculate controlling interest in consolidated income for 2012.

PROBLEM 6-2 **Upstream Sales** LO2 LO5

Shell Company, an 85% owned subsidiary of Plaster Company, sells merchandise to Plaster Company at a markup of 20% of selling price. During 2011 and 2012, intercompany sales amounted to $442,500 and $386,250, respectively. At the end of 2011, Plaster had one-half of the goods that it purchased that year from Shell in its ending inventory. Plaster's 2012 ending inventory contained one-fifth of that year's purchases from Shell. There were no intercompany sales prior to 2011.

Plaster had net income in 2011 of $750,000 from its own operations and in 2012 its independent income was $780,000. Shell reported net income of $322,500 and $335,400 for 2011 and 2012, respectively.

Required:

A. Prepare in general journal form all entries necessary on the consolidated financial statement workpapers to eliminate the effects of the intercompany sales for each of the years 2011 and 2012.

B. Calculate the amount of noncontrolling interest to be deducted from consolidated income in the consolidated income statement for 2012.

C. Calculate controlling interest in consolidated income for 2012.

PROBLEM 6-3 **Downstream Sales** LO2 LO5

Peer Company owns 80% of the common stock of Seacrest Company. Peer Company sells merchandise to Seacrest Company at 25% above its cost. During 2011 and 2012 such sales amounted to $265,000 and $475,000, respectively. The 2011 and 2012 ending inventories of Seacrest Company included goods purchased from Peer Company for $125,000 and $170,000, respectively.

Peer Company reported net income from its independent operations (including intercompany profit on inventory sales to affiliates) of $450,000 in 2011 and $480,000 in 2012. Seacrest reported net income of $225,000 in 2011 and $275,000 in 2012 and did not declare dividends in either year. There were no intercompany sales prior to 2011.

Required:

A. Prepare in general journal form all entries necessary in the consolidated financial statements workpapers to eliminate the effects of the intercompany sales for each of the years 2011 and 2012.

B. Calculate the amount of noncontrolling interest to be deducted from consolidated income in the consolidated income statements for 2011 and 2012.

C. Calculate controlling interest in consolidated income for 2012.

PROBLEM 6-4 **Upstream and Downstream Sales** LO2 LO5

Pace Company owns 85% of the outstanding common stock of Sand Company and all the outstanding common stock of Star Company. During 2012, the affiliates engaged in intercompany sales as follows:

Sales of Merchandise	
Pace to Sand	$ 40,000
Sand to Pace	60,000
Sand to Star	75,000
Star to Pace	50,000
	$225,000

The following amounts of intercompany profits were included in the December 31, 2011, and December 31, 2012, inventories of the individual companies:

	Intercompany Profit in December 31, 2011, Inventory of			
Selling Company	*Pace*	*Sand*	*Star*	*Total*
Pace Company		$7,000		$ 7,000
Sand Company	$ 5,000		$3,000	8,000
Star Company	8,000			8,000
Total	$13,000	$7,000	$3,000	$23,000

	Intercompany Profit in December 31, 2012, Inventory of			
Selling Company	*Pace*	*Sand*	*Star*	*Total*
Pace Company		$2,000		$ 2,000
Sand Company	$ 6,000		$9,000	15,000
Star Company	4,000			4,000
Total	$10,000	$2,000	$9,000	$21,000

Income from each company's independent operations (including sales to affiliates) for the year ended December 31, 2012, is presented here:

Pace Company	$200,000
Sand Company	150,000
Star Company	125,000

Required:

A. Prepare in general journal form the workpaper entries necessary to eliminate intercompany sales and intercompany profit in the December 31, 2012, consolidated financial statements workpaper.

B. Calculate the balance to be reported in the consolidated income statement for the following line items:

Consolidated income

Noncontrolling interest in consolidated income

Controlling interest in consolidated income

PROBLEM 6-5 **Intercompany Downstream Sales, Cost Method LO6**

Pruitt Corporation owns 90% of the common stock of Sedbrook Company. The stock was purchased for $625,500 on January 1, 2009, when Sedbrook Company's retained earnings were $95,000. Preclosing trial balances for the two companies at December 31, 2013, are presented here:

	Pruitt Corporation	*Sedbrook Company*
Cash	$ 90,800	$ 96,000
Accounts Receivable (net)	243,300	135,000
Inventory 1/1	165,000	132,000
Investment in Sedbrook Co.	625,500	
Other Assets	550,000	480,000
Dividends Declared	110,000	35,000
Purchases	935,000	420,000
Other Expenses	198,000	165,000
Total	$2,917,600	$1,463,000
Accounts Payable	$ 77,000	$ 36,000
Other Liabilities	120,700	47,000
Common Stock	880,000	600,000
Retained Earnings (1/1)	598,400	144,000
Sales	1,210,000	636,000
Dividend Income	31,500	—
Total	$2,917,600	$1,463,000
Ending Inventory	$ 220,000	$ 144,000

The January 1, 2013, inventory of Sedbrook Company includes $25,000 of profit recorded by Pruitt Corporation on 2012 sales. During 2013, Pruitt Corporation made intercompany sales of $250,000 with a markup of 20% on cost. The ending inventory of Sedbrook Company includes goods purchased in 2013 from Pruitt for $60,000.

Required:

A. Prepare the consolidated statements workpaper for the year ended December 31, 2013.

B. Calculate consolidated retained earnings on December 31, 2013, using the analytical or t-account approach.

PROBLEM 6-6 **Trial Balance Workpaper—Cost Method LO6**

Using the information in Problem 6-5, prepare a consolidated statements workpaper using the trial balance format.

PROBLEM 6-7 **Upstream Workpaper—Cost Method LO6**

Paque Corporation owns 90% of the common stock of Segal Company. The stock was purchased for $810,000 on January 1, 2009, when Segal Company's retained earnings were $150,000.

Financial data for 2013 are presented here:

	Paque Corporation	*Segal Company*
Sales	$1,650,000	$795,000
Dividend Income	54,000	
Total Revenue	1,704,000	795,000
Cost of Goods Sold:		
Beginning Inventory	225,000	165,000
Purchases	1,275,000	525,000

	Paque Corporation	Segal Company
Cost of Goods Available	1,500,000	690,000
Less: Ending Inventory	210,000	172,500
Cost of Goods Sold	1,290,000	517,500
Other Expenses	310,500	206,250
Total Cost and Expense	1,600,500	723,750
Net Income	$ 103,500	$ 71,250
1/1 Retained Earnings	811,500	180,000
Net Income	103,500	71,250
Dividends Declared	(150,000)	(60,000)
12/31 Retained Earnings	$ 765,000	$ 191,250
Cash	$ 93,000	$ 75,000
Accounts Receivable	319,500	168,750
Inventory	210,000	172,500
Investment in Segal Company	810,000	
Other Assets	750,000	630,000
Total Assets	$2,182,500	$1,046,250
Accounts Payable	$ 105,000	$ 45,000
Other Current Liabilities	112,500	60,000
Capital Stock	1,200,000	750,000
Retained Earnings	765,000	191,250
Total Liabilities and Equity	$2,182,500	$1,046,250

The January 1, 2013, inventory of Paque Corporation includes $45,000 of profit recorded by Segal Company on 2012 sales. During 2013, Segal Company made intercompany sales of $300,000 with a markup of 20% of selling price. The ending inventory of Paque Corporation includes goods purchased in 2013 from Segal Company for $75,000.

Required:

A. Prepare the consolidated statements workpaper for the year ended December 31, 2013.

B. Prepare a t-account calculation of controlling interest in consolidated net income for the year ended December 31, 2013.

PROBLEM 6-8

COMPREHENSIVE

Upstream Eliminating Entries and Consolidated Net Income, Comprehensive Problem LO6

On January 2, 2011, Patten Company purchased a 90% interest in Sterling Company for $1,400,000. At that time Sterling Company had capital stock outstanding of $800,000 and retained earnings of $425,000. The difference between book value of equity acquired and the value implied by the purchase price was allocated to the following assets:

Inventory	$ 41,667
Plant and Equipment (net)	200,000
Goodwill	88,889

The inventory was sold in 2011. The plant and equipment had a remaining useful life of 10 years on January 2, 2011.

During 2011 Sterling sold merchandise with a cost of $950,000 to Patten at a 20% markup above cost. At December 31, 2011, Patten still had merchandise in its inventory that it purchased from Sterling for $576,000.

In 2011, Sterling Company reported net income of $410,000 and declared no dividends.

Required:

A. Prepare in general journal form all entries necessary on the consolidated financial statements workpaper to eliminate the effects of the intercompany sales, to eliminate the investment account, and allocate the difference between book value of equity acquired and the value implied by the purchase price.

B. Assume that Patten Company reports net income of $2,000,000 from its independent operations. Calculate controlling interest in consolidated net income.

C. Calculate noncontrolling interest in consolidated income.

PROBLEM 6-9

COMPREHENSIVE

Upstream and Downstream Workpaper, Comprehensive Problem, Cost Method LO6

On January 1, 2009, Perry Company purchased 80% of Selby Company for $990,000. At that time Selby had capital stock outstanding of $350,000 and retained earnings of $375,000.

The fair value of Selby Company's assets and liabilities is equal to their book value except for the following:

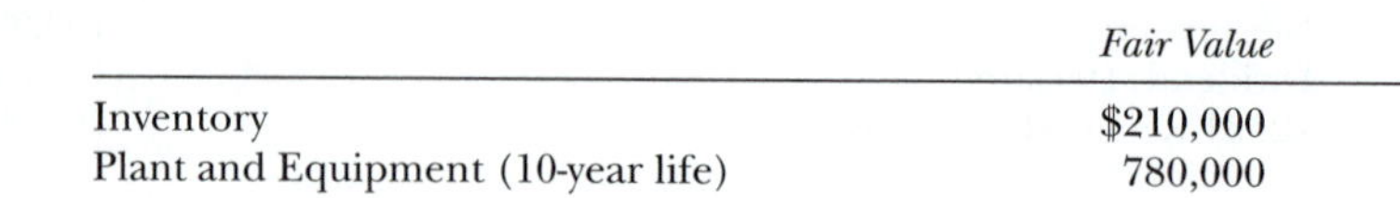

	Fair Value	*Book Value*
Inventory	$210,000	$160,000
Plant and Equipment (10-year life)	780,000	630,000

One-half of the inventory was sold in 2009, the remainder was sold in 2010.

At the end of 2009, Perry Company had in its ending inventory $60,000 of merchandise it had purchased from Selby Company during the year. Selby Company sold the merchandise at 25% above cost. During 2010, Perry Company sold merchandise to Selby Company for $310,000 at a markup of 20% of the selling price. At December 31, 2010, Selby still had merchandise that it purchased from Perry Company for $82,000 in its inventory.

Financial data for 2010 are presented here:

	Perry Company	*Selby Company*
Sales	$1,400,000	$ 800,000
Dividend Income	20,000	—
Total Revenue	1,420,000	800,000
Cost of Goods Sold:		
Beginning Inventory	230,000	145,000
Purchases	900,000	380,000
Cost of Goods Available	1,130,000	525,000
Less: Ending Inventory	450,000	200,000
Cost of Goods Sold	680,000	325,000
Other Expenses	250,000	195,000
Total Cost and Expense	930,000	520,000
Net Income	$ 490,000	$ 280,000
1/1 Retained Earnings	$1,500,000	$ 480,000
Net Income	490,000	280,000
Dividends Declared	(50,000)	(25,000)
12/31 Retained Earnings	$1,940,000	$ 735,000
Cash	$ 95,000	$ 70,000
Accounts Receivable (net)	302,000	90,000
Inventory	450,000	200,000
Investment in Selby Company	990,000	
Plant and Equipment (net)	850,000	585,000
Other Assets (net)	390,000	230,000
Total Assets	$3,077,000	$1,175,000
Accounts Payable	$ 75,000	$ 30,000
Other Liabilities	102,000	60,000
Common Stock	960,000	350,000
Retained Earnings	1,940,000	735,000
Total Liabilities and Equity	$3,077,000	$1,175,000

Required:

A. Prepare the consolidated statements workpaper for the year ended December 31, 2010.

B. Calculate consolidated retained earnings on December 31, 2010, using the analytical or t-account approach.

PROBLEM 6-10 **Controlling and Noncontrolling Interest** LO2 LO5

Penn Company owns a 90% interest in Salvador Company and an 80% interest in Sencal Company. Profit remaining in ending inventories from intercompany sales for 2011 and 2012 is indicated below.

	Intercompany Profit in Ending Inventory of			
	2011		*2012*	
Selling Company	*Salvador*	*Sencal*	*Salvador*	*Sencal*
Penn	$8,000	$4,000	$5,000	$ 9,000
Salvador		6,000		10,000
Sencal	5,000		2,000	

Salvador Company reported net income of $50,000 in 2011 and $45,000 in 2012, whereas Sencal Company's net income was $60,000 and $75,000 in 2011 and 2012, respectively.

Penn Company's net income from its own operations (including sales to affiliates) for 2011 and 2012 was $600,000 and $400,000, respectively.

Required:

A. Determine noncontrolling interest in consolidated income for 2011 and 2012.

B. Calculate the controlling interest in consolidated income for 2011 and 2012.

PROBLEM 6-11 **Downstream Workpaper—Partial Equity Method** LO6

Pruitt Corporation owns 90% of the common stock of Sedbrook Company. The stock was purchased for $540,000 on January 1, 2009, when Sedbrook Company's retained earnings were $100,000. Preclosing trial balances for the two companies at December 31, 2013, are presented here:

	Pruitt Corporation	*Sedbrook Company*
Cash	$ 83,000	$ 80,000
Accounts Receivable (net)	213,000	112,500
Inventory 1/1	150,000	110,000
Investment in Sedbrook Co.	578,250	
Other Assets	500,000	400,000
Dividends Declared	100,000	30,000
Purchases	850,000	350,000
Other Expenses	180,000	137,500
	$2,654,250	$1,220,000
Accounts Payable	$ 70,000	$ 30,000
Other Liabilities	75,000	40,000
Common Stock	800,000	500,000
Retained Earnings	562,000	120,000
Sales	1,100,000	530,000
Equity in Subsidiary Income	47,250	
	$2,654,250	$1,220,000
Ending Inventory	$ 200,000	$ 120,000

The January 1, 2013, inventory of Sedbrook Company includes $30,000 of profit recorded by Pruitt Corporation on 2012 sales. During 2013, Pruitt Corporation made intercompany sales of $200,000 with a markup of 25% on cost. The ending inventory of Sedbrook Company includes goods purchased in 2013 from Pruitt for $50,000. Pruitt Corporation uses the partial equity method to record its investment in Sedbrook Company.

Required:

A. Prepare the consolidated statements workpaper for the year ended December 31, 2013.

B. Calculate consolidated retained earnings on December 31, 2013, using the analytical or t-account approach.

PROBLEM 6-12 **Downstream Trial Balance Workpaper** LO6

Using the information in Problem 6-11, prepare a consolidated statements workpaper using the trial balance format.

PROBLEM 6-13 **Upstream Workpaper—Partial Equity Method** LO6

(*Note*: This is the same problem as Problem 6-7, but assuming the use of the partial equity method.)

Paque Corporation owns 90% of the common stock of Segal Company. The stock was purchased for $810,000 on January 1, 2009, when Segal Company's retained earnings were $150,000.

Financial data for 2013 are presented here:

	Paque Corporation	*Segal Company*
Sales	$1,650,000	$ 795,000
Equity in Subsidiary Income	64,125	
Total Revenue	1,714,125	795,000
Cost of Goods Sold:		
Beginning Inventory	225,000	165,000
Purchases	1,275,000	525,000
Cost of Goods Available	1,500,000	690,000
Less: Ending Inventory	210,000	172,500
Cost of Goods Sold	1,290,000	517,500
Other Expenses	310,500	206,250
Total Cost and Expense	1,600,500	723,750
Net Income	$ 113,625	$ 71,250
1/1 Retained Earnings	838,500	180,000
Net Income	113,625	71,250
Dividends Declared	(150,000)	(60,000)
12/31 Retained Earnings	$ 802,125	$ 191,250
Cash	$ 93,000	$ 75,000
Accounts Receivable	319,500	168,750
Inventory	210,000	172,500
Investment in Segal Company	847,125	
Other Assets	750,000	630,000
Total Assets	$2,219,625	$1,046,250
Accounts Payable	$ 105,000	$ 45,000
Other Current Liabilities	112,500	60,000
Capital Stock	1,200,000	750,000
Retained Earnings	802,125	191,250
Total Liabilities and Equity	$2,219,625	$1,046,250

The January 1, 2013, inventory of Paque Corporation includes $45,000 of profit recorded by Segal Company on 2012 sales. During 2013, Segal Company made intercompany sales of $300,000 with a markup of 20% of selling price. The ending inventory of Paque Corporation includes goods purchased in 2013 from Segal Company for $75,000. Paque Corporation uses the partial equity method to record its investment in Segal Company.

Required:

A. Prepare the consolidated statements workpaper for the year ended December 31, 2013.

B. Calculate consolidated retained earnings on December 31, 2013, using the analytical or t-account approach.

C. If you completed Problem 6-7, compare the consolidated balances obtained in requirement A with those obtained in Problem 6-7.

PROBLEM 6-14 **Upstream and Downstream Workpaper—Partial Equity Method** LO6

On January 1, 2010, Perry Company purchased 80% of Selby Company for $960,000. At that time Selby had capital stock outstanding of $400,000 and retained earnings of $400,000.

The fair value of Selby Company's assets and liabilities is equal to their book value except for the following:

	Fair Value	*Book Value*
Inventory	$230,000	$155,000
Plant and Equipment (10-year life)	800,000	600,000

One-half of the inventory was sold in 2010; the remainder was sold in 2011.

COMPREHENSIVE

At the end of 2010, Perry Company had in its ending inventory $54,000 of merchandise it had purchased from Selby Company during the year. Selby Company sold the merchandise at 20% above cost. During 2011, Perry Company sold merchandise to Selby Company for $300,000 at a markup of 20% of the selling price. At December 31, 2011, Selby still had merchandise that it purchased from Perry Company for $78,000 in its inventory.

Financial data for 2011 are presented here:

	Perry Company	*Selby Company*
Sales	$1,385,000	$ 720,000
Equity in Subsidiary Income	208,000	
Total Revenue	1,593,000	720,000
Cost of Goods Sold:		
Beginning Inventory	210,000	155,000
Purchases	875,000	360,000
Cost of Goods Available	1,085,000	515,000
Less: Ending Inventory	400,000	225,000
Cost of Goods Sold	685,000	290,000
Other Expenses	225,000	170,000
Total Cost and Expense	910,000	460,000
Net Income	$ 683,000	$ 260,000
1/1 Retained Earnings	$1,472,700	$ 450,000
Net Income	683,000	260,000
Dividends Declared	(40,000)	(30,000)
12/31 Retained Earnings	$2,115,700	$ 680,000
Cash	$ 90,000	$ 65,000
Accounts Receivable (net)	297,000	85,000
Inventory	400,000	225,000
Investment in Selby Company	1,184,000	
Plant and Equipment (net)	880,000	540,000
Other Assets (net)	384,000	230,000
Total Assets	$3,235,000	$1,145,000
Accounts Payable	$ 24,300	$ 25,000
Other Liabilities	95,000	40,000
Common Stock	1,000,000	400,000
Retained Earnings	2,115,700	680,000
Total Liabilities and Equity	$3,235,000	$1,145,000

Required:

A. Prepare the consolidated statements workpaper for the year ended December 31, 2011.

B. Calculate consolidated retained earnings on December 31, 2011, using the analytical or t-account approach.

PROBLEM 6-15 **Upstream and Downstream Sales, Journal Entries, and Controlling and Noncontrolling Interests** LO2 LO5

On January 1, 2009, Paul Company purchased 80% of the voting stock of Simon Company for $1,360,000 when Simon Company had retained earnings and capital stock in the amounts of $450,000 and $1,000,000, respectively. The difference between implied and book value is allocated to a franchise and is amortized over 25 years. Simon Company's retained earnings amount to $780,000 on January 1, 2012, and $960,000 on December 31, 2012. In 2012, Simon Company reported net income of $270,000 and declared dividends of $90,000. Paul Company reported net income from independent operations in 2012 in the amount of $700,000 and retained earnings on December 31, 2012, of $1,500,000. During 2012, intercompany sales of merchandise from Paul to Simon amounted to $70,000 and from Simon to Paul were $50,000. Unrealized profits on January 1 and on December 31, 2012, resulting from intercompany sales are as summarized here:

	Unrealized Intercompany Profit on	
Resulting From	*1/1/12*	*12/31/12*
Sales by Simon Company to Paul Company	$20,000	$10,000
Sales by Paul Company to Simon Company	30,000	5,000

There were no intercompany sales prior to 2011.

Required:

A. Prepare in general journal form the entries necessary in the December 31, 2012, consolidated statements workpaper to eliminate the effects of the intercompany sales.

B. Calculate controlling interest in consolidated net income for the year ended December 31, 2012.

C. Calculate consolidated retained earnings on December 31, 2012.

D. Calculate noncontrolling interest in consolidated income for the year ended December 31, 2012.

PROBLEM 6-16 **Complete Equity with Downstream Sales** LO6

(*Note*: This is the same problem as Problem 6-11, but assuming the use of the complete equity method.)

Pruitt Corporation owns 90% of the common stock of Sedbrook Company. The stock was purchased for $540,000 on January 1, 2009, when Sedbrook Company's retained earnings were $100,000. Preclosing trial balances for the two companies at December 31, 2013, are presented here:

	Pruitt Corporation	*Sedbrook Company*
Cash	$ 83,000	$ 80,000
Accounts Receivable (net)	213,000	112,500
Inventory 1/1	150,000	110,000
Investment in Sedbrook Co.	568,250	
Other Assets	500,000	400,000
Dividends Declared	100,000	30,000
Purchases	850,000	350,000
Other Expenses	180,000	137,500
	$2,644,250	$1,220,000
Accounts Payable	$ 70,000	$ 30,000
Other Liabilities	75,000	40,000
Common Stock	800,000	500,000
Retained Earnings, 1/1	532,000	120,000
Sales	1,100,000	530,000
Equity in Subsidiary Income	67,250	
	$2,644,250	$1,220,000
Ending Inventory	$ 200,000	$ 120,000

The January 1, 2013, inventory of Sedbrook Company includes $30,000 of profit recorded by Pruitt Corporation on 2012 sales. During 2013, Pruitt Corporation made intercompany sales of $200,000 with a markup of 25% on cost. The ending inventory of Sedbrook Company includes goods purchased in 2013 from Pruitt for $50,000. Pruitt Corporation uses the complete equity method to record its investment in Sedbrook Company.

Required:

A. Prepare the consolidated statements workpaper for the year ended December 31, 2013.

B. Calculate consolidated retained earnings on December 31, 2013, using the analytical or t-account approach.

C. If you completed Problem 6-11, compare the consolidated balances obtained in requirement A with those obtained in that problem.

PROBLEM 6-17 **Complete Equity with Upstream Sales**  LO6

(*Note*: This is the same problem as Problem 6-7 and Problem 6-13, but assuming the use of the complete equity method.)

Paque Corporation owns 90% of the common stock of Segal Company. The stock was purchased for $810,000 on January 1, 2009, when Segal Company's retained earnings were $150,000.

Financial data for 2013 are presented here:

	Paque Corporation	*Segal Company*
Sales	$1,650,000	$ 795,000
Equity in Subsidiary Income	91,125	
Total Revenue	1,741,125	795,000
Cost of Goods Sold:		
Beginning Inventory	225,000	165,000
Purchases	1,275,000	525,000
Cost of Goods Available	1,500,000	690,000
Less: Ending Inventory	210,000	172,500
Cost of Goods Sold	1,290,000	517,500
Other Expenses	310,500	206,250
Total Cost and Expense	1,600,500	723,750
Net Income	$ 140,625	$ 71,250
1/1 Retained Earnings	798,000	180,000
Net Income	140,625	71,250
Dividends Declared	(150,000)	(60,000)
12/31 Retained Earnings	$ 788,625	$ 191,250
Cash	$ 93,000	$ 75,000
Accounts Receivable	319,500	168,750
Inventory	210,000	172,500
Investment in Segal Company	833,625	
Other Assets	750,000	630,000
Total Assets	$2,206,125	$1,046,250
Accounts Payable	105,000	45,000
Other Current Liabilities	112,500	60,000
Capital Stock	1,200,000	750,000
Retained Earnings	788,625	191,250
Total Liabilities and Equity	$2,206,125	$1,046,250

The January 1, 2013, inventory of Paque Corporation includes $45,000 of profit recorded by Segal Company on 2012 sales. During 2013, Segal Company made intercompany sales of $300,000 with a markup of 20% of selling price. The ending inventory of Paque Corporation includes goods purchased in 2013 from Segal Company for $75,000. Paque Corporation uses the complete equity method to record its investment in Segal Company.

Required:

A. Prepare the consolidated statements workpaper for the year ended December 31, 2013.

B. Calculate consolidated retained earnings on December 31, 2013, using the analytical or t-account approach.

C. If you completed Problem 6-7 or Problem 6-13, compare the consolidated balances obtained in requirement A with those obtained in those problems.

PROBLEM 6-18 **Comprehensive Complete Equity Problem, Cost Greater Than Fair Value with Intercompany Sales of Inventory**

(*Note*: This is the same problem as Problem 6-14, but assuming the use of the complete equity method.)

On January 1, 2010, Perry Company purchased 80% of Selby Company for $960,000. At that time Selby had capital stock outstanding of $400,000 and retained earnings of $400,000.

The fair value of Selby Company's assets and liabilities is equal to their book value except for the following:

	Fair Value	*Book Value*
Inventory	$230,000	$155,000
Plant and Equipment (10-year life)	800,000	600,000

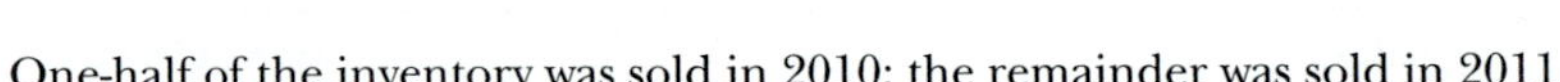

One-half of the inventory was sold in 2010; the remainder was sold in 2011.

COMPREHENSIVE

At the end of 2010, Perry Company had in its ending inventory $54,000 of merchandise it had purchased from Selby Company during the year. Selby Company sold the merchandise at 20% above cost. During 2011, Perry Company sold merchandise to Selby Company for $300,000 at a markup of 20% of the selling price. At December 31, 2011, Selby still had merchandise that it purchased from Perry Company for $78,000 in its inventory.

Financial data for 2011 are presented here:

	Perry Company	*Selby Company*
Sales	$1,385,000	$ 720,000
Equity in Subsidiary Income	153,600	
Total Revenue	1,538,600	720,000
Cost of Goods Sold:		
Beginning Inventory	210,000	155,000
Purchases	875,000	360,000
Cost of Goods Available	1,085,000	515,000
Less: Ending Inventory	400,000	225,000
Cost of Goods Sold	685,000	290,000
Other Expenses	225,000	170,000
Total Cost and Expense	910,000	460,000
Net Income	$ 628,600	$ 260,000
1/1 Retained Earnings	1,419,500	450,000
Net Income	628,600	260,000
Dividends Declared	(40,000)	(30,000)
12/31 Retained Earnings	$2,008,100	$ 680,000
Cash	$ 90,000	$ 65,000
Accounts Receivable	297,000	85,000
Inventory	400,000	225,000

	Perry Company	*Selby Company*
Investment in Selby Company	1,076,400	
Plant and Equipment (net)	880,000	540,000
Other Assets	384,000	230,000
Total Assets	$3,127,400	$1,145,000
Accounts Payable	24,300	25,000
Other Current Liabilities	95,000	40,000
Common Stock	1,000,000	400,000
Retained Earnings	2,008,100	680,000
Total Liabilities and Equity	$3,127,400	$1,145,000

Required:

A. Prepare the consolidated statements workpaper for the year ended December 31, 2011.

B. Calculate consolidated retained earnings on December 31, 2011, using the analytical or t-account approach.

C. If you completed Problem 6-14, compare the consolidated balances obtained in requirement A with those obtained in those problems.

PROBLEM 6-19A **Deferred Taxes and Intercompany Sales of Inventory**

Pearson Company owns 80% of the common stock of Sedbrook Company. Pearson Company sells merchandise to Sedbrook Company at 25% above its cost. During 2011 and 2012, such sales amounted to $265,000 and $475,000, respectively. The 2011 and 2012 ending inventories of Sedbrook Company included goods purchased from Pearson Company for $150,000 and $195,000, respectively.

Pearson Company reported net income from its independent operations (including sales to affiliates) of $450,000 in 2011 and $480,000 in 2012. Sedbrook reported net income of $225,000 in 2011 and $275,000 in 2012 and did not declare dividends in either year. There were no intercompany sales prior to 2011. The affiliated companies file separate income tax returns and have marginal income tax rates of 30%. Ignore the income tax consequences of undistributed subsidiary income.

Required:

A. Prepare in general journal form all entries necessary in the consolidated financial statements workpapers to eliminate the effects of the intercompany sales for each of the years 2011 and 2012.

B. Calculate the amount of noncontrolling interest to be reported in the consolidated income statements for 2011 and 2012.

C. Calculate the controlling interest in consolidated net income for 2012.

PROBLEM 6-20A **Deferred Taxes, Intercompany Sales of Inventory, Cost Method**

Peek Corporation owns 70% of the common stock of Seacrest Company. The stock was purchased for $420,000 on January 1, 2007, when Seacrest Company's retained earnings were $100,000. Preclosing trial balances for the two companies at December 31, 2011, are presented here:

	Peck Corporation	*Seacrest Company*
Cash	$ 35,000	$ 100,000
Accounts Receivable (net)	211,000	107,750
Inventory—1/1	150,000	110,000
Investment in Seacrest Company	420,000	

	Peck Corporation	*Seacrest Company*
Other Assets	500,000	400,000
Dividends Declared	100,000	10,000
Purchases	850,000	350,000
Other Expenses	180,000	114,000
Income Tax Expense	27,000	28,250
Total	$2,473,000	$1,220,000
Accounts Payable	$ 70,000	$ 30,000
Other Liabilities	55,000	35,000
Deferred Tax Liability	20,000	5,000
Common Stock	680,000	500,000
Retained Earnings	541,000	120,000
Sales	1,100,000	530,000
Dividend Income	7,000	
Total	$2,473,000	$1,220,000
Inventory—12/31	$ 140,000	$ 115,000

The January 1, 2011, inventory of Peck Corporation includes $10,000 of profit recorded by Seacrest Company on 2010 sales. During 2011, Seacrest Company made intercompany sales of $100,000 with a markup of 25% on cost. The ending inventory of Peck Corporation includes goods purchased in 2011 from Seacrest Company for $40,000.

The affiliates file separate tax returns, and the prior, current, and expected future marginal income tax rates for both companies are 40%. Dividends received from Seacrest Company are subject to an 80% dividends received exclusion.

Required:

A. Prepare a consolidated statements workpaper for the year ended December 31, 2011.

B. Calculate the controlling interest in consolidated net income for the year ended December 31, 2011, and consolidated retained earnings on December 31, 2011, using the analytical or t-account approach.

PROBLEM 6-21A **Deferred Taxes, Intercompany Sales of Inventory, Partial Equity Method**

Petra Corporation owns 70% of the common stock of Swain Company. The stock was purchased for $420,000 on January 1, 2007, when Swain Company's retained earnings were $100,000. Preclosing trial balances for the two companies at December 31, 2011, are presented here:

	Petra Corporation	*Swain Company*
Cash	$ 35,000	$ 100,000
Accounts Receivable (net)	211,000	107,750
Inventory—1/1	150,000	110,000
Investment in Swain Company	456,925	
Other Assets	500,000	400,000
Dividends Declared	100,000	10,000
Purchases	850,000	350,000
Other Expenses	180,000	114,000
Income Tax Expense	27,000	28,250
	$2,509,925	$1,220,000
Accounts Payable	$ 70,000	$ 30,000
Other Liabilities	55,000	35,000
Deferred Tax Liability	20,000	5,000

	Petra Corporation	*Swain Company*
Common Stock	680,000	500,000
Retained Earnings	555,000	120,000
Sales	1,100,000	530,000
Equity in Subsidiary Income	29,925	
	$2,509,925	$1,220,000
Inventory—12/31	$ 140,000	$ 115,000

The January 1, 2011, inventory of Petra Corporation includes $10,000 of profit recorded by Swain Company on 2010 sales. During 2011, Swain Company made intercompany sales of $100,000 with a markup of 25% on cost. The ending inventory of Petra Corporation includes goods purchased in 2011 from Swain Company for $40,000.

The affiliates file separate tax returns, and the marginal income tax rate for both companies is 40%. Dividends received from Swain Company are subject to an 80% dividends received exclusion.

Required:

A. Prepare a consolidated statements workpaper for the year ended December 31, 2011.

B. Calculate the controlling interest in consolidated net income for the year ended December 31, 2011, and consolidated retained earnings on December 31, 2011, using the analytical or t-account approach.

7

ELIMINATION OF UNREALIZED GAINS OR LOSSES ON INTERCOMPANY SALES OF PROPERTY AND EQUIPMENT

LEARNING OBJECTIVES

1. Understand the financial reporting objectives in accounting for intercompany sales of *nondepreciable* assets on the consolidated financial statements.
2. State the additional financial reporting objectives in accounting for intercompany sales of *depreciable* assets on the consolidated financial statements.
3. Explain when gains or losses on intercompany sales of depreciable assets should be recognized on a consolidated basis.
4. Explain the term "realized through usage."
5. Describe the differences between upstream and downstream sales in determining consolidated net income and the controlling and noncontrolling interests in consolidated income.
6. Compare the eliminating entries when the selling affiliate is a subsidiary (less than wholly owned) versus when the selling affiliate is the parent company.
7. Compute the noncontrolling interest in consolidated net income when the selling affiliate is a subsidiary.
8. Compute consolidated net income considering the effects of intercompany sales of depreciable assets.
9. Describe the eliminating entry needed to adjust the consolidated financial statements when the purchasing affiliate sells a depreciable asset that was acquired from another affiliate.
10. Explain the basic principles used to record or eliminate intercompany interest, rent, and service fees.

"Some corporate mergers have little effect on customers. But when big airlines merge, it changes life for travelers . . . For the fractured airline industry, where nine big airlines fight coast-to-coast, removing large competitors and building up flight schedules could be a way to better survive high oil prices and recession instead of the bankruptcies and turmoil of past downturns . . . But for travelers, big-airline couplings historically have meant headaches . . . Some communities could see reduced service if mergers allow the combined airlines to close hub operations."[1]

[1] *Wall Street Journal,* "Mergers Benefit Airlines; Shame About the Fliers," by Scott McCartney, p. D1, January 15, 2008.

Affiliated companies often recognize gains or losses on intercompany sales of property or equipment. They also may recognize revenue or expense in connection with intercompany loans, intercompany service fees, or intercompany operating leases. As with intercompany sales of inventory discussed in Chapter 6, workpaper entries are also necessary in these situations in order to present related balances in the consolidated financial statements as if the intercompany transactions had never occurred.

In this chapter, the effects on the preparation of consolidated financial statements of intercompany transactions involving property and equipment, loans, services, and operating leases are described and illustrated.

Certain complications (specifically, those related to accounting for the difference between the value implied by the acquisition cost and book value) are avoided in all illustrations by assuming: (1) all acquisitions are made at the book value of the acquired interest in net assets, and (2) the book value of the subsidiary net assets equals their fair value on the date the parent company's interest is acquired. It is further assumed that the affiliates file consolidated income tax returns.

INTERCOMPANY SALES OF LAND (NONDEPRECIABLE PROPERTY)

RELATED CONCEPTS

To recognize gains or losses on PPE sales before the assets are sold to outside parties would violate the *revenue recognition* principle from the perspective of the consolidated economic entity.

LO1 Financial reporting objectives—nondepreciable property.

When there have been intercompany sales of *nondepreciable* property, workpaper entries are necessary to accomplish the following financial reporting objectives in the consolidated financial statements.

- To include gains or losses on the sale of nondepreciable property in consolidated net income only at the time such property is ***sold to parties outside the affiliated group*** and in an amount equal to the difference between the cost of the property to the affiliated group and the proceeds received from outsiders.
- To present nondepreciable property in the consolidated balance sheet at ***its cost to the affiliated group***.

Workpaper procedures to accomplish these objectives are presented here. In addition, for firms using the cost or partial equity methods to account for the investments in subsidiaries, the workpaper entries serve to equate beginning consolidated retained earnings with the amount of consolidated retained earnings reported at the end of the prior reporting period. For all firms, the entries (in the case of upstream sales) also serve to equate beginning NCI (in equity) with ending NCI (in equity) at the end of the prior period.

Assume that S Company (an 80% owned subsidiary) sells land to P Company for $500,000 that cost S Company $300,000 (an upstream sale of land). Entries made on the books of each affiliate to record this intercompany sale are presented below.

Entry on Books of S Company

Cash	500,000	
Land		300,000
Gain on Sale of Land		200,000

Entry on Books of P Company

Land	500,000	
Cash		500,000

Additional Entry for Complete Equity Method Only: P Company Books

Equity in Subsidiary Income	160,000	
Investment in S Company		160,000

If P Company uses the complete equity method to account for its investment in S Company, the additional entry shown above is needed on the books of P Company to reduce its income from subsidiary by its share (80%) of the intercompany gain. Under this method, the amount of income reported on the books of the parent is its share of the subsidiary's reported income that has been realized in transactions with third parties.

In the year of the intercompany sale, a workpaper entry is necessary to eliminate the $200,000 gain reported by S Company and to reduce the land balance from the $500,000 recorded on the books of P Company to its $300,000 cost to the affiliated group. Both objectives are accomplished in one workpaper entry as follows:

Workpaper Entry in Year of Intercompany Sale

Gain on Sale of Land	200,000	
Land		200,000

If S Company reported $900,000 in income, the noncontrolling interest in consolidated net income is $140,000 [.20 × ($900,000 − $200,000) = $140,000]. The noncontrolling interest in consolidated income is based on the amount of income of S Company that was realized in transactions with third parties ($900,000 in reported income less $200,000 unrealized gain on sale of land). Stated another way, the noncontrolling interest in consolidated income is based on the amount of income from the subsidiary included in consolidated net income (after all workpaper adjustments). Since $200,000 of subsidiary income is excluded from consolidated net income, the noncontrolling interest in consolidated income is reduced by $40,000 (.2 × $200,000).

In subsequent years, so long as P Company owns the land, it will be reported in the ***statements of P Company*** at the intercompany selling price of $500,000. However, in the ***consolidated balance sheet***, the land should continue to be reported at its cost to the affiliated group of $300,000. Since in the year of the sale consolidated income was reduced by $200,000, the controlling interest in net income and consolidated retained earnings were reduced by $160,000 (.8 × $200,000) in that year. The workpaper entry necessary in all subsequent years, until the land is disposed of by P Company, is as follows:

Workpaper Entry in Subsequent Years

Cost or Partial Equity			Complete Equity		
Beginning Retained Earnings—P Company	160,000		Investment in S Company	160,000	
Beginning NCI	40,000		Beginning NCI	40,000	
Land		200,000	Land		200,000

Because the subsidiary is the intercompany seller, the $200,000 of unrealized profit is allocated between the controlling interest ($160,000 = .8 × $200,000) and the noncontrolling interest ($40,000 = .2 × $200,000) based on their percentage interests in the selling affiliate. As in Chapter 6, the workpaper procedure to adjust the controlling interest (consolidated retained earnings) is to debit the beginning retained earnings of the parent company (or investment account, if P Company uses the complete equity method). The workpaper procedure to adjust the noncontrolling interest is to debit the beginning NCI in equity. *If the intercompany seller had been the parent (downstream sale), the entire $200,000 would go to the controlling interest,* resulting in a $200,000 debit to the beginning retained earnings of the parent company under the cost or partial equity method.

If and when the land is sold by P Company to a nonaffiliate, P company will use the $500,000 carrying value of the land on its books to calculate any gain or loss. For example, if P Company sells the land it purchased for $500,000 from S Company to an outside party for $550,000, P company will record a gain on the sale of $50,000 ($550,000 – $500,000). However, the cost of the land to the affiliated group is $300,000, and the gain to the affiliated group confirmed by its sale for $550,000 to a nonaffiliate is $250,000 ($550,000 – $300,000). The workpaper entry to adjust the $50,000 gain reported by P Company to the $250,000 gain realized on the sale by the affiliated group is as follows:

Cost or Partial Equity			Complete Equity		
Beginning Retained Earnings—P Company	160,000		Investment in S Company	160,000	
Beginning NCI	40,000		Beginning NCI	40,000	
Gain on Sale of Land		200,000	Gain on Sale of Land		200,000

The debits are the same as if the sale to outsiders had not occurred. In the year of the sale of the land to outsiders, it is still necessary to adjust ***beginning*** consolidated retained earnings (or the investment account, under the complete equity method) and beginning NCI. This entry under the cost and partial equity methods serves to equate ***beginning*** consolidated retained earnings in the year of sale with the consolidated retained earnings reported at the end of the prior year. Under the complete equity method, as previously stated, the retained earnings of the parent company always equals the correct consolidated retained earnings; thus no adjustment is needed. Instead a debit to the investment account facilitates the elimination of the investment account.[2]

In the year of the sale of the land to outsiders, consolidated net income is increased by $200,000, and consolidated net income, consolidated retained earnings, and noncontrolling interest in consolidated income are increased accordingly.

To the consolidated entity, the sales price (to third parties) of $550,000 exceeds the cost (to the consolidated entity) of $300,000, resulting in a gain of $250,000 to be included in consolidated income in the year of the sale to a third party.

At the end of the year of the sale to outsiders, the amount of *cumulative* profit on the sale of the land recorded on the books of the affiliates and the amount of profit on the sale of the land recognized in the consolidated financial statements are equal, as shown on the next page.

---

[2] The investment account is reduced on the parent's books at the same time that the unrealized income is deducted from the parent's income under the complete equity method. Thus, the usual workpaper entry to eliminate the investment account against the underlying subsidiary equity accounts eliminates an amount greater than the actual beginning investment account balance. That entry, combined with the entry above, however, will eliminate the investment to exactly zero.

Cumulative Profit Recorded on the Individual Books of Affiliates		
S Company on sale to P Company	$200,000	(year sold to affiliate)
P Company on sale to nonaffiliate	50,000	(year sold to third party)
Total	$250,000	

Profit Reported in Consolidated Income Statement in Year of Sale		
Reported by P Company	$ 50,000	(year sold to third party)
Workpaper adjustment	200,000	(year sold to third party)
Reported in consolidated net income	$250,000	

Retained earnings is thus correct in future years without adjustment, and no further workpaper entries relating to the intercompany sale of land are necessary in subsequent periods.

INTERCOMPANY SALES OF DEPRECIABLE PROPERTY (MACHINERY, EQUIPMENT, AND BUILDINGS)

Realization through Usage

LO4 Intercompany gain realized through usage.

A firm may sell property or equipment to an affiliate for a price that differs from its book value. In the year of the sale, the amount of intercompany gain (loss) recorded by the selling affiliate must be eliminated in consolidation. After the sale, the purchasing affiliate will calculate depreciation on the basis of its cost, which is the intercompany selling price. The depreciation recorded by the purchasing affiliate will, therefore, be excessive (deficient) from a consolidated point of view and will also require adjustment.

From the view of the consolidated entity, the intercompany gain (loss) is considered to be realized from the use of the property or equipment in the generation of revenue. Because such use is measured by depreciation, the recognition of the realization of intercompany profit (loss) is accomplished through depreciation adjustments.

LO3 Recognition of gains (losses) through depreciation adjustments.

To contrast the intercompany sale of a depreciable asset to the intercompany sale of land, consider the following. Parental Guidance Company sells property with a book value of $2,000 to its fully owned subsidiary, Subservient Recipient Company, for $5,000. Assume first that the property is nondepreciable land. When will the $3,000 gain be recognized in the consolidated financial statements?

The answer is: not until it is sold to outsiders. If the property is sold immediately by Subservient Recipient Company for $5,000, the $3,000 gain will be recognized immediately by the consolidated entity. If, on the other hand, it isn't sold until year 4, the gain will not be realized to the consolidated entity until year 4. Now suppose instead that the property (with a book value of $2,000) is depreciable equipment, with a remaining life of three years. Again it is sold to Subservient Recipient Company for $5,000. When will the $3,000 gain be recognized in the consolidated financial statements?

The answer might at first seem to be: not until it is sold to outsiders. But consider the combined effect on consolidated income of the intercompany sale and the depreciation adjustments needed on the consolidated workpaper. On the books of Subservient Recipient Company, depreciation expense is based on a purchase price of $5,000 (straight-line depreciation over three years). But to the consolidated entity, depreciation expense should be based on the book value of $2,000 (also over three years). The difference is $1,000 per year (equal to the $3,000 gain on the intercompany sale spread over three years). Thus, as the depreciation expense is adjusted downward, consolidated income is increased to realize a portion of the gain each year. The depreciation adjustment in such a case is often referred to as gain or revenue ***realization through usage.***

When there have been intercompany sales of depreciable property, workpaper entries are necessary to accomplish the following financial reporting objectives in the consolidated financial statements.

LO2 Financial reporting objectives—depreciable property.

- To report as gains or losses in the consolidated income statement only those that result from the sale of depreciable property ***to parties outside the affiliated group.***
- To present property in the consolidated balance sheet at ***its cost to the affiliated group.***
- To present accumulated depreciation in the consolidated balance sheet based on the ***cost to the affiliated group*** of the related assets.
- To present depreciation expense in the consolidated income statement based on the ***cost to the affiliated group*** of the related assets.

Workpaper procedures to accomplish these objectives are presented next. For firms using the cost or partial equity method, an additional objective is to equate beginning consolidated retained earnings with the amount of consolidated retained earnings reported at the end of the prior reporting. For firms using the complete equity method, this final objective is not necessary because the parent's retained earnings already reflects all adjustments accurately. For upstream sales, the entries also serve to equate current period beginning NCI and prior period ending NCI.

Illustration of Basic Workpaper Elimination Entries—Downstream Sales

The basic workpaper eliminating entries required because of intercompany sales of depreciable property are illustrated using the following simplifying assumptions. We first illustrate a downstream sale of depreciable property; the parent is the intercompany seller. Upstream sales are illustrated later in the chapter.

1. On January 1, 2009, P Company sells to S Company, a 90% owned subsidiary, equipment with a book value of $750,000 (original cost $1,350,000 and accumulated depreciation of $600,000) for $900,000.
2. On the date of the sale, the equipment has an estimated remaining useful life of three years, has no residual value, and is depreciated using the straight-line method.
3. No other equipment is owned by S Company or P Company.

The entries on the books of P Company and S Company to record the intercompany sale are summarized in general journal form below.

P Company Books		
Cash	900,000	
Accumulated Depreciation	600,000	
Equipment		1,350,000
Gain on Sale of Equipment		150,000

S COMPANY BOOKS

Equipment	900,000	
Cash		900,000
Depreciation Expense	300,000	
Accumulated Depreciation		300,000

Workpaper Entries—Year of the Intercompany Sale

Balances on December 31, 2009, of the accounts of the affiliated companies affected by these transactions are presented in Illustration 7-1. Workpaper entries in the year of the sale are presented below in general journal form.

(1) Equipment ($1,350,000 − $900,000)	450,000	
Gain on Sale of Equipment	150,000	
Accumulated Depreciation		600,000
To eliminate the intercompany gain and restore equipment to its original cost to the consolidated entity (along with its accumulated depreciation at the point of the intercompany sale).		

P Company recorded a gain of $150,000 on the intercompany sale and S Company recorded the equipment at $900,000. From the point of view of the consolidated entity, however, no gain should be reported on the intercompany sale, and equipment should be reported at cost to the affiliated group. The effect of this entry is to decrease consolidated net income by $150,000. It also restores equipment and accumulated depreciation to their amounts prior to the intercompany sale. Without this entry, equipment would be reported in the consolidated balance sheet at its intercompany selling price of $900,000 instead of its historical cost of $1,350,000. Further, without the entry, accumulated depreciation on the equipment would commence from the point of the intercompany sale instead of from the original acquisition by the consolidated entity.

ILLUSTRATION 7-1

Partial Consolidated Statements Workpaper, Elimination of Intercompany Sale of Equipment, Year of Intercompany Sale, December 31, 2009

			Eliminations		
Income Statement	*P Company*	*S Company*	*Dr.*	*Cr.*	*Consolidated Balances*
Gain on Sale of Equipment	(150,000)		(1) 150,000		
Depreciation Expense		300,000		(2) 50,000	250,000
Balance Sheet					
Equipment		900,000	(1) 450,000		1,350,000
Accumulated Depreciation		(300,000)	(2) 50,000	(1) 600,000	(850,000)

(1) To eliminate the intercompany gain and restore equipment to its original cost to the consolidated entity.
(2) To adjust depreciation expense to the correct amount to the consolidated entity.

(2) Accumulated Depreciation	50,000	
Depreciation Expense		50,000
To adjust depreciation expense to the correct amount to the consolidated entity, thus realizing a portion of the gain through usage.		

The purchasing affiliate (S Company) will record depreciation in the amount of $300,000 ($900,000/3 years) each year. From the point of view of the consolidated entity, only $250,000 ($750,000/3 years) in depreciation on the equipment should be recognized. The effect of entry (2) is to increase consolidated net income by $50,000 and thus treat an equivalent amount of intercompany profit as realized through the use of the equipment.

The net effect of entries (1) and (2) is to reduce consolidated income by $100,000 (the original $150,000 of intercompany gain recorded by P Company for the sale less the $50,000 of intercompany gain that is considered realized during the year through the utilization of the equipment by S Company).

Workpaper Entries—Years Subsequent to the Year of the Intercompany Sale

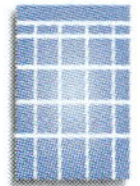
COST

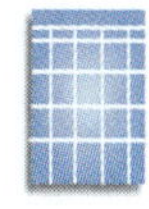
PARTIAL

Balances of the affected accounts of the affiliated companies on December 31, 2010, are presented in Illustration 7-2. In years subsequent to the year of the intercompany sale, the basic workpaper elimination entries related to the intercompany sale are presented below. As indicated, some entries differ slightly depending on whether the firm accounts for its investment using the cost, partial equity, or complete equity method. In the context of this chapter, the cost and partial equity entries are the same, while the complete equity entries differ with one respect; that is, entries to Beginning Retained Earnings—P Company are replaced by entries to Investment in S Company under the complete equity method.

ILLUSTRATION 7-2

Partial Consolidated Statements Workpaper, Elimination of Unrealized Profit on Intercompany Sale of Equipment, Year Subsequent to Intercompany Sale, December 31, 2010

Income Statement	*P Company*	*S Company*	*Eliminations Dr.*	*Eliminations Cr.*	*Consolidated Balances*
Depreciation Expense		300,000		(2) 50,000	250,000
Retained Earnings Statement					
1/1 Retained Earnings—P Company (Consolidated)	2,000,000		(1) 150,000	(2) 50,000	1,900,000
Balance Sheet					
Equipment		900,000	(1) 450,000		1,350,000
Accumulated Depreciation		(600,000)	(2) 100,000	(1) 600,000	(1,100,000)

(1) To eliminate the intercompany gain and restore equipment to its original cost to the consolidated entity.
(2) To adjust depreciation expense to the correct amount to the consolidated entity.

2010 Workpaper Entries

	Cost or Partial Equity			Complete Equity		
(1)	Equipment	450,000		Equipment	450,000	
	Beginning Retained Earnings—P Company	150,000		Investment in S	150,000	
	Accumulated Depreciation		600,000	Accumulated Depreciation		600,000

To eliminate the prior period intercompany gain and restore equipment to its original cost to the consolidated entity (along with its accumulated depreciation at the point of the intercompany sale).

In entry (1), the first entry from the prior year (2009) is repeated, with the debit to gain now replaced by a debit to the beginning retained earnings of the parent under the cost or partial equity methods. The debit to the equipment account and the credit to the accumulated depreciation account are for the same amount each year. This entry is necessary again (with any income statement accounts, e.g., gain, replaced by beginning retained earnings in subsequent years) because workpaper entries are not posted. If P Company uses the complete equity method, the debit to Beginning Retained Earnings—P Company is not needed, as the prior year income was adjusted for all unrealized amounts. The debit in this workpaper entry is replaced by a debit to the investment account to facilitate its elimination. Later in this chapter, both methods are illustrated in their entirety.

2010 Workpaper Entries

	Cost or Partial Equity			Complete Equity		
(2)	Accumulated Depreciation	100,000		Accumulated Depreciation	100,000	
	Depreciation Expense (current year)		50,000	Depreciation Expense (current year)		50,000
	Beginning Retained Earnings—P Company (prior year)		50,000	Investment in S		50,000

To adjust depreciation for the current and prior year on equipment sold to affiliate.

The explanation for entry (2) is the same as the preceding year with two modifications. Accumulated depreciation is adjusted for two years now, and the income statement account "depreciation expense" from the first year is now replaced by a credit to beginning retained earnings of P Company (or by a credit to Investment, for firms using the complete equity method).

As a result of these entries, consolidated depreciation expense ($250,000), consolidated equipment ($1,350,000), and consolidated accumulated depreciation ($1,100,000) are all based on the cost of the equipment to the affiliated companies. The net effect of these workpaper entries is to increase consolidated income by $50,000, which is the amount of gain recorded on the intercompany sale that is considered realized from a consolidated point of view through the utilization of the equipment during the current year.

The entries in the December 31, 2011, consolidated statements workpaper to eliminate the effects of the intercompany sale are as follows:

2010 Workpaper Entries

	Cost or Partial Equity			Complete Equity		
(1)	Equipment	450,000		Equipment	450,000	
	Beginning Retained Earnings—P Company	150,000		Investment in S	150,000	
	Accumulated Depreciation		600,000	Accumulated Depreciation		600,000
	To reduce consolidated retained earnings for gain on intercompany sale and to restore equipment to its original cost to the consolidated entity (along with its accumulated depreciation at the point of the intercompany sale).					
(2)	Accumulated Depreciation ($50,000 × 3 year)	150,000		Accumulated Depreciation	150,000	
	Depreciation Expense (current year)		50,000	Depreciation Expense (current year)		50,000
	Beginning Retained Earnings—P Company (prior years)		100,000	Investment in S (prior years)		100,000
	To reverse amount of excess depreciation recorded during current year and to recognize amounts of intercompany gain realized in current and prior periods through usage (two prior years of depreciation expense since sale).					

Over the life of the equipment, the amount of gain recognized in the consolidated income statement will be the same as the amount of gain recorded by the selling affiliate, and no further adjustments will be necessary in the consolidated statements workpaper. The recognition of the gain on the sale of the equipment on the books of the selling affiliate and in the consolidated income statement may be compared as follows:

	On Books of Selling Affiliate	*In Consolidated Income Statement*
Gain on Sale of Equipment—2009	$150,000	
Reduction of Depreciation Expense:		
2009		$ 50,000
2010		50,000
2011		50,000
	$150,000	$150,000

Determination of Noncontrolling Interest

LO6 Subsidiary vs. parent as the seller.

Subsidiary as Intercompany Seller (Upstream Sale) In the preceding example, the selling affiliate was the parent company (downstream sale). Accordingly, even though 100% of the unrealized intercompany gain was eliminated, no modification in the calculation of the noncontrolling interest in consolidated income or consolidated net assets was necessary. Had the selling affiliate been a less than wholly owned subsidiary (upstream sale), however, workpaper modifications in the determination of the noncontrolling interest would have been necessary if the controlling and noncontrolling interests were to be adjusted in proportion to their interest in the amount of unrealized intercompany profit eliminated.

Intercompany sales of property, plant, and equipment, as in the case of intercompany inventory sales, necessitate adjustments to the calculation of the distribution of income to the controlling and noncontrolling interests. Whether the adjustments

LO7 Computing the noncontrolling interest.

directly affect the noncontrolling interest (or only the controlling interest) depends on ***who is the intercompany seller***. If the intercompany seller is the subsidiary, it is the subsidiary's income that needs adjustment, hence directly affecting the noncontrolling interest, as shown in Illustration 7-3.

Procedurally, the steps needed differ slightly between the year of the intercompany sale and subsequent years. To calculate the noncontrolling interest in consolidated income, begin as always with the subsidiary's reported income. As always, subtract any excess depreciation, amortization, or impairment charges related to differences between implied and book values. In the year of the intercompany upstream sale (subsidiary is the intercompany seller), adjust the subsidiary's reported income by subtracting the unrealized gain on the intercompany sale (or adding an unrealized loss, as appropriate). Next, add the portion of the intercompany gain (loss) that is considered *realized through usage* (i.e., the depreciation adjustment for the year of the sale). This is shown in Illustration 7-3 for the year 2009 in t-account form.

ILLUSTRATION 7-3

Calculation of the Noncontrolling Interest in Consolidated Income, Upstream Sales of Equipment

Noncontrolling Interest in Consolidated Income—Year of Sale—2009

Unrealized gain on upstream sales of equipment	150,000	Net income reported by S Company	$300,000
Amortization and depreciation of difference between implied and book value	0	Depreciation adjustment (gain realized through usage)	50,000
		Subsidiary Income included in Consolidated Income	$200,000
		Noncontrolling Ownership percentage interest	10%
		Noncontrolling Interest in Consolidated Income	$ 20,000

Noncontrolling Interest in Consolidated Income—Year Subsequent to Sale—2010

Amortization and depreciation of difference between implied and book value	0	Net income reported by S Company	$175,000
		Depreciation adjustment (gain realized through usage)	50,000
		Subsidiary Income included in Consolidated Income	$225,000
		Noncontrolling Ownership percentage interest	10%
		Noncontrolling Interest in Consolidated Income	$ 22,500

Noncontrolling Interest in Consolidated Income—Year Subsequent to Sale—2011

Amortization and depreciation of difference between implied and book value	0	Net income reported by S Company	$200,000
		Depreciation adjustment (gain realized through usage)	50,000
		Subsidiary Income included in Consolidated Income	$250,000
		Noncontrolling Ownership percentage interest	10%
		Noncontrolling Interest in Consolidated Income	$ 25,000

The calculations are the same in subsequent years except that the intercompany gain (or loss) does not need to be subtracted (or added) since it is not included in the subsidiary's reported income in those years. Realization through usage, however, occurs as long as the property is being used by the intercompany buyer (the parent, in the case of an upstream sale). Note, however, that the *adjustment for realization through usage* appears on the t-account to compute the *noncontrolling interest* in the case of upstream sales.

For example, assume that S Company is 90% owned, was the selling affiliate in the previous illustration, and reports $300,000 in income (including the $150,000 intercompany gain) in the year 2009, $175,000 of income in 2010, and $200,000 in 2011. The calculation of the noncontrolling interest in consolidated income in each of the respective years is presented in Illustration 7-3.

The adjustments shown in Illustration 7-3 are needed only if we assume the subsidiary is the intercompany seller. With this assumption, adjustments are also needed to the workpaper eliminating/adjusting entries presented in the previous section of this chapter. Specifically, the workpaper entries to Beginning Retained Earnings—P Company in the preceding example for firms using the cost or partial equity method are replaced by entries to *both* Beginning Retained Earnings—P Company (controlling interest percentage) and Beginning NCI in equity (noncontrolling interest percentage). No other changes are needed. If P Company uses the complete equity method, any debits or credits to Beginning Retained Earnings—P Company are not needed, as prior years' income is adjusted on the books of the parent for unrealized gains and for any amount realized through usage. Thus any debits or credits to beginning retained earnings of the parent in workpaper entries are replaced by debits or credits to the investment account, once more facilitating its elimination.

If S Company were the selling affiliate, entry (1) in Illustration 7-2 for 2010 would be modified as follows in order to adjust the controlling and the noncontrolling interests in net assets at the beginning of the year:

Upstream Sale

	Cost or Partial Equity			Complete Equity		
(1)	Equipment	450,000		Equipment	450,000	
	Beginning Retained Earnings—P Company	135,000		Investment in S Company	135,000	
	Beginning NCI (.10 × $150,000)	15,000		Beginning NCI (.10 × $150,000)	15,000	
	Accumulated Depreciation		600,000	Accumulated Depreciation		600,000

To reduce the controlling and noncontrolling interests for their respective shares of the unrealized intercompany gain at the date of the intercompany sale, and restore equipment and accumulated depreciation to original amounts to the consolidated entity.

As explained in the discussion of unrealized intercompany profit in inventory, as a matter of workpaper procedure, the noncontrolling interest in net assets (or equity) is adjusted for intercompany gains (losses) by debiting (decrease in noncontrolling interest) or crediting (increase in noncontrolling interest) the beginning NCI balance.

To reduce repetition and conserve space, we do not present the three methods (cost, partial equity, and complete equity) in standalone sections in Chapters 7 through 10 to the same extent as in earlier chapters. In Chapters 7 and 10, the cost and partial equity methods are quite similar (under the assumptions in our presentation), while the complete equity method is different. In Chapters 8 and 9, in contrast, the partial and complete equity methods are similar, while the cost method is different. Thus, in the following section, we combine the presentation of the cost and partial equity methods. Worksheets are presented separately.

For the fiscal year 2005, Fleetwood Enterprises, Inc. eliminated $128 million of intercompany sales from consolidated revenues. Moreover, it was difficult to compare the performance of the Housing Group because the company made $27 million of sales to its own retail stores in the fourth quarter last year in which a majority of these stores were closed.[3]

CONSOLIDATED STATEMENTS WORKPAPER—COST AND PARTIAL EQUITY METHODS

Subsidiary Is Intercompany Seller (Upstream Sale)

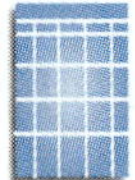
COST

PARTIAL

Assume that P Company acquires an 85% interest in S Company for $1,190,000 in 2007, when the retained earnings and capital stock of S Company amount to $400,000 and $1,000,000, respectively. The retained earnings of S Company on January 1, 2009, are $666,000. On January 1, 2009, S Company sells P Company equipment with a book value of $500,000 (original cost of $800,000 and accumulated depreciation of $300,000) for $600,000. On January 1, 2009, the equipment has an estimated remaining useful life of five years and is depreciated using the straight-line method. S Company will record a gain of $100,000 on the sale of the equipment, and each year P Company will record depreciation that is $20,000 [($600,000 − $500,000)/5 years] greater than depreciation based on the cost of the equipment to the consolidated group. Consolidated statements workpapers for the years ended December 31, 2009, and December 31, 2010, are presented in Illustrations 7-4A and 7-5A, respectively, assuming the use of the *cost* method by P Company to account for its investment in S Company. Consolidated statements workpapers for the years ended December 31, 2009, and December 31, 2010, are presented in Illustrations 7-4B and 7-5B, respectively, assuming the use of the *partial equity* method by P Company to account for its investment in S Company.

LO6 Workpaper entries—upstream sales.

The balances reported by the parent company in income, in retained earnings, and in the investment account differ depending on the method used by the parent company to record its investment. As illustrated in prior chapters, however, the method used by the parent company to record its investment has no effect on the *consolidated* balances.

Also as illustrated in earlier chapters, when the parent company records its investment using the partial equity method, a workpaper entry to reverse the effect of parent company entries during the year for subsidiary dividends and income replaces the cost method entries to establish reciprocity (convert to equity) and to

[3] PRNewswire—FirstCall via COMTEX News Network, Riverside, California, 5/4/06.

eliminate dividend income. However, as demonstrated in Chapters 5 and 6, the workpaper entries to allocate the difference between implied and book value, to record additional amortization, depreciation, and/or impairment on differences between market and book values, to eliminate intercompany sales, and to eliminate unrealized intercompany profit are the same regardless of whether the investment is recorded using the cost method or the partial equity method. The workpapers entries to eliminate the effects of intercompany sales of equipment are also the same when the parent uses the partial equity or the cost method. Therefore, to conserve space and avoid excessive repetition, we discuss the workpaper entries for the cost and partial equity methods together in the following section. When the investment is recorded using the complete equity method, however, the workpaper entries differ slightly, as illustrated in the next section.

Consolidated Statements Workpaper Entries—December 31, 2009 (Year of Intercompany Sale)

Workpaper entries in Illustrations 7-4A and 7-4B are presented in general journal form as follows:

(1)	Investment in S Company	226,100	
	Beginning Retained Earnings—P Company		226,100
	To convert to equity/establish reciprocity [.85 × ($666,000 − $400,000) = $226,100].		

Entry (1) above is needed only for firms using the cost method to account for their investments in the subsidiary. This distinction is particularly easy to remember if the entry is thought of as the entry to convert to equity. If the parent is already using the equity method, there is no need to convert to equity. Thus, in Illustration 7-4B, entry (1) above is replaced with an entry eliminating the equity in subsidiary income of $122,400 (85% × $144,000) against the investment account. Unless noted, the following workpaper entries are the same whether the parent uses the cost method or the partial equity method.

(2)	Gain on Sale of Equipment	100,000	
	Property and Equipment ($800,000 − 600,000)	200,000	
	Accumulated Depreciation		300,000
	To eliminate the unrealized gain recorded on intercompany sale of equipment ($100,000) and restore equipment to its original cost (and accumulated depreciation to its balance at the date of the intercompany sale).		

(3)	Accumulated Depreciation	20,000	
	Depreciation Expense		20,000
	To adjust depreciation on equipment sold to affiliate, thus realizing a portion of the gain through usage ($100,000/5 years = $20,000).		

(4)	Beginning Retained Earnings—S Company	666,000	
	Capital Stock—S Company	1,000,000	
	Investment in S Company ($1,190,000 + $226,100)		1,416,100
	NCI in Equity [$210,000 + .15 ($666,000 − $400,000)]		249,000
	To eliminate investment account against underlying equity accounts of S Company, and recognize NCI.		

Since the selling affiliate is a partially owned subsidiary (upstream sale), the calculation of the noncontrolling interest in consolidated net income is modified by subtracting the amount of the gain recognized by the subsidiary and adding the amount of the gain considered to be realized (through depreciation) to the reported net income of the subsidiary [.15 × ($144,000 − $100,000 + $20,000) = $9,600].

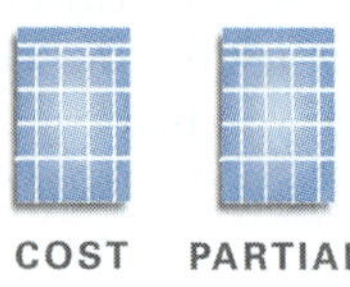

Noncontrolling Interest in Consolidated Net Income

		Internally generated income of S Company	$144,000
Unrealized gain on intercompany (upstream) sale	100,000	Gain realized through usage (depreciation adjustment)	20,000
		Adjusted income of subsidiary	$ 64,000
		Noncontrolling percentage	× 15%
		Noncontrolling interest in income	$ 9,600

(85%)
(64,000)

Note that the $9,600 appears in Illustration 7-4A as the noncontrolling interest in income.

If the sale of the equipment had been *downstream* rather than *upstream*, the amount of subsidiary income included in consolidated net income would not be affected by the workpaper entries related to unrealized intercompany gain and no adjustment would be necessary in the calculation of the noncontrolling interest in consolidated net income. Instead the *controlling* interest would be affected as indicated in bold type in the following t-account:

Controlling Interest in Consolidated Net Income

		Internally generated income of P Company	$300,000
Unrealized gain on intercompany (downstream) sale	**XX**	**Realization of gain through usage (depreciation adjustment)**	**XX**
		Other needed adjustments (see Chapters 5–6)	XX
		Percentage of subsidiary adjusted income, or (ownership percentage) (subsidiary income) .85($64,000)	$ 54,400
		Controlling interest in income	$354,400

Consolidated Statements Workpaper Entries—December 31, 2010 (Year Subsequent to Intercompany Sale)

Workpaper entries in Illustrations 7-5A and 7-5B are presented in general journal form for the year subsequent to the intercompany sale as follows:

(1) Investment in S Company	348,500	
Beginning Retained Earnings—P Company		348,500
To convert to equity/establish reciprocity [.85 × ($810,000 − $400,000)].		

As in the previous year, entry (1) above is needed only for firms using the cost method to account for their investments in the subsidiary. If the parent is already using the equity method, there is no need to convert to equity. In Illustration 7-5B, entry (1) is replaced by an entry once again eliminating equity in subsidiary income against the investment account.

Cost Method

85% Owned Subsidiary

Upstream Sale of Equipment

ILLUSTRATION 7-4A

Consolidated Statements Workpaper

P Company and Subsidiary

for the Year Ended December 31, 2009

	P	S	Eliminations		Noncontrolling	Consolidated
Income Statement	*Company*	*Company*	*Dr.*	*Cr.*	*Interest*	*Balances*
Sales	3,500,000	2,000,000				5,500,000
Gain on Sale of Equipment		100,000	(2) 100,000			
Total Revenue	3,500,000	2,100,000				5,500,000
Cost of Sales	1,800,000	1,130,000				2,930,000
Depreciation Expense	380,000	330,000		(3) 20,000		690,000
Income Tax Expense	200,000	96,000				296,000
Other Expense	820,000	400,000				1,220,000
Total Cost and Expense	3,200,000	1,956,000				5,136,000
Consolidated Net Income	300,000	144,000				364,000
Noncontrolling Interest in Income					9,600*	9,600
Net Income to Retained Earnings	300,000	144,000	100,000	20,000	9,600	354,400
Retained Earnings Statement						
1/1 Retained Earnings						
P Company	1,500,000			(1) 226,100		1,726,100
S Company		666,000	(4) 666,000			
Net Income from above	300,000	144,000	100,000	20,000	9,600	354,400
12/31 Retained Earnings to Balance Sheet	1,800,000	810,000	766,000	246,100	9.600	2,080,500
Balance Sheet						
Current Assets	1,000,000	570,000				1,570,000
Investment in S Company	1,190,000		(1) 226,100	(4) 1,416,100		
Land	1,000,000	200,000				1,200,000
Property and Equipment	3,800,000	2,700,000	(2) 200,000			6,700,000
(Accumulated Depreciation)	(1,520,000)	(960,000)	(3) 20,000	(2) 300,000		(2,760,000)
Total Assets	5,470,000	2,510,000				6,710,000
Liabilities	670,000	700,000				1,370,000
Capital Stock						
P Company	3,000,000					3,000,000
S Company		1,000,000	(4) 1,000,000			
Retained Earnings from above	1,800,000	810,000	766,000	246,100	9,600	2,080,500
1/1 Noncontrolling Interest in Net Assets**				(4) 249,900	249,900	
12/31 Noncontrolling Interest					259,500	259,500
Total Liabilities and Equity	5,470,000	2,510,000	2,212,100	2,212,100		6,710,000

* .15 × ($144,000 − $100,000 + $20,000) = $9,600.

** $210,000 + .15 × ($666,000 − $400,000) = $249,900.

(1) To convert to equity/establish reciprocity [.85 × ($666,000 − $400,000) = $226,100].

(2) To eliminate the unrealized gain recorded on intercompany sale of equipment ($100,000) and restore equipment to its original cost (and accumulated depreciation to its balance at the date of the intercompany sale).

(3) To adjust depreciation on equipment sold to affiliate, thus realizing a portion of the gain through usage ($100,000/5 years = $20,000).

(4) To eliminate investment account against underlying equity accounts of S Company and create noncontrolling interest account.

Partial Equity Method
85% Owned Subsidiary
Upstream Sale of Equipment
Year of Sale

ILLUSTRATION 7-4B
Consolidated Statements Workpaper
P Company and Subsidiary
for Year Ended December 31, 2009

	P Company	S Company	Eliminations Dr.	Eliminations Cr.	Noncontrolling Interest	Consolidated Balances
Income Statement						
Sales	3,500,000	2,000,000				5,500,000
Equity in Subsidiary Income	122,400		(1) 122,400			
Gain on Sale of Equipment		100,000	(2) 100,000			
Total Revenue	3,622,400	2,100,000				5,500,000
Cost of Sales	1,800,000	1,130,000				2,930,000
Depreciation Expense	380,000	330,000		(3) 20,000		690,000
Income Tax Expense	200,000	96,000				296,000
Other Expense	820,000	400,000				1,220,000
Total Cost and Expense	3,200,000	1,956,000				5,136,000
Net/Consolidated Income	422,400	144,000				364,000
Noncontrolling Interest in Income					9,600*	9,600
Net Income to Retained Earnings	422,400	144,000	222,400	20,000	9,600	354,400
Retained Earnings Statement						
1/1 Retained Earnings						
P Company	1,726,100					1,726,100
S Company		666,000	(4) 666,000			
Net Income from above	422,400	144,000	222,400	20,000	9,600	354,400
12/31 Retained Earnings to Balance Sheet	2,148,500	810,000	888,400	20,000	9,600	2,080,500
Balance Sheet						
Current Assets	1,000,000	570,000				1,570,000
Investment in S Company**	1,538,500			(1) 122,400 (4) 1,416,100		
Land	1,000,000	200,000				1,200,000
Property and Equipment	3,800,000	2,700,000	(2) 200,000			6,700,000
(Accumulated Depreciation)	(1,520,000)	(960,000)	(3) 20,000	(2) 300,000		(2,760,000)
Total Assets	5,818,500	2,510,000				6,710,000
Liabilities	670,000	700,000				1,370,000
Capital Stock						
P Company	3,000,000					3,000,000
S Company		1,000,000	(4) 1,000,000			
Retained Earnings from above	2,148,500	810,000	888,400	20,000	9,600	2,080,500
1/1 Noncontrolling Interest in Net Assets**				(4) 249,900	249,900	
12/31 Noncontrolling Interest					259,500	259,500
Total Liabilities and Equity	5,818,500	2,510,000	2,108,400	2,108,400		6,710,000

* .15 × ($144,000 − $100,000 + $20,000) = $9,600.
** The investment account equals $1,190,000 + 85% of the increase in S Company's Retained Earnings from the date of acquisition to the beginning of the year ($666,000 − 400,000) plus the current period's equity in subsidiary income ($122,400).
*** $210,000 + .15 × ($666,000 − $400,000) = $249,900.
(1) To eliminate equity in subsidiary income and intercompany dividends, if any.
(2) To eliminate the unrealized gain recorded on intercompany sale of equipment and restore equipment to its original cost (and accumulated depreciation to its balance at the date of the intercompany sale).
(3) To adjust depreciation on equipment sold to affiliate, thus realizing a portion of gain through usage ($100,000/5 years = $20,000).
(4) To eliminate investment account against the underlying equity accounts of S Company and create noncontrolling interest account.

(2) Beginning Retained Earnings—P Company (100,000 × .85)	85,000	
Beginning NCI (100,000 × .15)	15,000	
Property and Equipment (800,000 − 600,000)	200,000	
Accumulated Depreciation		300,000
To reduce the controlling and noncontrolling interests for their shares of unrealized intercompany gain ($100,000), and to restore equipment and accumulated depreciation to their original balances at the date of the intercompany sale.		

COST PARTIAL

(3) Accumulated Depreciation	40,000	
Depreciation Expense (current year)		20,000
Beginning Retained Earnings—P Company (20,000 × .85)		17,000
Beginning NCI (20,000 × .15)		3,000
To reverse amount of excess depreciation recorded during current year and prior year and to recognize intercompany gain realized through usage.		

(4) Beginning Retained Earnings—S Company	810,000	
Capital Stock—S Company	1,000,000	
Investment in S Company ($1,190,000 + $348,500)		1,538,500
NCI (210,000 + .15 (810,000 − 400,000))		271,500
To eliminate investment account against the underlying equity accounts of S Company.		

The noncontrolling interest recognized in entry (4) above is calculated as the sum of the NCI at acquisition plus 15% of the increase in subsidiary retained earnings from acquisition to the beginning of the current year. The noncontrolling interest in consolidated income is calculated after adding the portion of the gain considered realized during the year to the net income reported by the subsidiary [.15 × ($162,000 + $20,000) = $27,300].

Noncontrolling Interest in Income (year subsequent to sale)

Internally generated income of S Company	$162,000
Gain realized through usage (depreciation adjustment)	20,000
Adjusted income of subsidiary	$182,000
Noncontrolling percentage	× 15%
Noncontrolling interest in income	$ 27,300

The net effect of the adjustments to the noncontrolling interest in the income statement and retained earnings sections of the consolidated statements workpaper for upstream sales also serves to adjust the noncontrolling interest in consolidated net assets. The amount of the noncontrolling interest reported in the consolidated balance sheet is based on the net assets of the subsidiary that have been realized in transactions with third parties. For example, the amount of the noncontrolling interest in consolidated net assets shown in Illustrations 7-5A and 7-5B is calculated in Illustration 7-6.

Cost Method
85% Owned Subsidiary
Upstream Sale of Equipment
Year Subsequent to Sale

ILLUSTRATION 7-5A
Consolidated Statements Workpaper
P Company and Subsidiary
for the Year Ended December 31, 2010

Income Statement	*P Company*	*S Company*	*Eliminations Dr.*	*Eliminations Cr.*	*Noncontrolling Interest*	*Consolidated Balances*
Sales	4,000,000	2,200,000				6,200,000
Cost of Sales	2,100,000	1,180,000				3,280,000
Depreciation Expense	380,000	330,000		(3) 20,000		690,000
Income Tax Expense	272,000	108,000				380,000
Other Expense	840,000	420,000				1,260,000
Total Cost and Expense	3,592,000	2,038,000				5,610,000
Net/Consolidated Income	408,000	162,000				590,000
Noncontrolling Interest in Income					27,300*	27,300
Net Income to Retained Earnings	408,000	162,000	—0—	20,000	27,300	562,700
Retained Earnings Statement						
1/1 Retained Earnings						
P Company	1,800,000		(2) 85,000	(1) 348,500 (3) 17,000		2,080,500
S Company		810,000	(4) 810,000			
Net Income from above	408,000	162,000	—0—	20,000	27,300	562,700
12/31 Retained Earnings to Balance Sheet	2,208,000	972,000	895,000	385,500	27,300	2,643,200
Balance Sheet						
Current Assets	1,190,000	790,000				1,980,000
Investment in S Company	1,190,000		(1) 348,500	(4) 1,538,500		
Land	1,600,000	200,000				1,800,000
Property and Equipment	3,800,000	2,700,000	(2) 200,000			6,700,000
(Accumulated Depreciation)	(1,900,000)	(1,290,000)	(3) 40,000	(2) 300,000		(3,450,000)
Total Assets	5,880,000	2,400,000				7,030,000
Liabilities	672,000	428,000				1,100,000
Capital Stock						
P Company	3,000,000					3,000,000
S Company		1,000,000	(4) 1,000,000			
Retained Earnings from above	2,208,000	972,000	895,000	385,500	27,300	2,643,200
1/1 Noncontrolling Interest in Net Assets**			(2) 15,000	(4) 271,500 (3) 3,000	259,500	
12/31 Noncontrolling Interest in Net Assets					286,800	286,800
Total Liabilities and Equity	5,880,000	2,400,000	2,498,500	2,498,500		7,030,000

* .15 × ($162,000 + $20,000) = $27,300.
** $210,000 + .15 × ($810,000 − $400,000) = $271,500.
(1) To convert to equity/establish reciprocity as of 1/1/10 [.85 × ($810,000 − $400,000)].
(2) To reduce controlling and noncontrolling interests for their shares of unrealized intercompany gain and to restore equipment and accumulated depreciation to their original balances.
(3) To reverse amount of excess depreciation recorded during current year and prior year and to recognize intercompany gain realized through usage.
(4) To eliminate investment account and create noncontrolling interest account.

Partial Equity Method
85% Owned Subsidiary
Upstream Sale of Equipment
Year Subsequent to Sale

ILLUSTRATION 7-5B
Consolidated Statements Workpaper
P Company and Subsidiary
for the Year Ended December 31, 2010

			Eliminations			
Income Statement	*P Company*	*S Company*	*Dr.*	*Cr.*	*Noncontrolling Interest*	*Consolidated Balances*
Sales	4,000,000	2,200,000				6,200,000
Equity Income	137,000		(1) 137,700			
Total Revenue	4,137,700	2,200,000				6,200,000
Cost of Sales	2,100,000	1,180,000				3,280,000
Depreciation Expense	380,000	330,000		(3) 20,000		690,000
Income Tax Expense	272,000	108,000				380,000
Other Expense	840,000	420,000				1,260,000
Total Cost and Expense	3,592,000	2,038,000				5,610,000
Net/Consolidated Income	545,700	162,000				590,000
Noncontrolling Interest in Income					27,300*	27,300
Net Income to Retained Earnings	545,700	162,000	137,700	20,000	27,300	562,700
Retained Earnings Statement						
1/1 Retained Earnings						
P Company	2,148,500		(2) 85,000	(3) 17,000		2,080,500
S Company		810,000	(4) 810,000			
Net Income from above	545,700	162,000	137,700	20,000	27,300	562,700
12/31 Retained Earnings to Balance Sheet	2,694,200	972,000	1,032,700	37,000	27,300	2,643,200
Balance Sheet						
Current Assets	1,190,000	790,000				1,980,000
Investment in S Company	1,676,200			(1) 137,700		
				(4) 1,538,500		
Land	1,600,000	200,000				1,800,000
Property and Equipment	3,800,000	2,700,000	(2) 200,000			6,700,000
(Accumulated Depreciation)	(1,900,000)	(1,290,000)	(3) 40,000	(2) 300,000		(3,450,000)
Total Assets	6,366,200	2,400,000				7,030,000
Liabilities	672,000	428,000				1,100,000
Capital Stock						
P Company	3,000,000					3,000,000
S Company		1,000,000	(4) 1,000,000			
Retained Earnings from above	2,694,200	972,000	1,032,700	37,000	27,300	2,643,200
1/1 Noncontrolling Interest in Net Assets**			(2) 15,000	(4) 271,500		
				(3) 3,000	259,500	
12/31 Noncontrolling Interest in Net Assets					286,800	286,800
Total Liabilities and Equity	6,366,200	2,400,000	2,287,700	2,287,700		7,030,000

* .15 × ($162,000 + $20,000) = $27,300.
** $210,000 + .15 × ($810,000 − $400,000) = $271,500.
(1) To eliminate equity in subsidiary income and intercompany dividends, if any.
(2) To reduce controlling and noncontrolling interests for their shares of unrealized intercompany gain and to restore equipment and accumulated depreciation to their original balances.
(3) To reverse amount of excess depreciation recorded during current and prior year and to recognize intercompany gain realized through usage.
(4) To eliminate investment account and create noncontrolling interest account.

ILLUSTRATION 7-6

Calculation of the Noncontrolling Interest in Consolidated Net Assets

Capital Stock—S Company		$1,000,000
Realized Retained Earnings—S Company		
Reported Retained Earnings	$972,000	
Unrealized Intercompany Profit on 12/31/10 ($100,000 − $20,000 − $20,000)	(60,000)	912,000
Realized Net Assets—S Company		$1,912,000
Noncontrolling Ownership Percentage		15%
Noncontrolling Interest in Consolidated Net Assets (.15 × $1,912,000)		$ 286,800

Disposal of Property and Equipment by Purchasing Affiliate

LO9 Disposal of Property and Equipment by purchaser.

Assume that on January 1, 2011, P Company sells the equipment it purchased from S Company to a party outside the affiliated group for $400,000. The recorded and consolidated book values of the equipment on January 1, 2011, are calculated in Illustration 7-7. P Company will record a $40,000 gain on the sale of the equipment to the party outside the affiliated group, calculated as:

Selling price	$400,000
Book value (on P Company's books)	360,000
Gain on sale (recorded by P Company)	40,000

The following entry is made on the books of P Company to record the sale:

P Company Books (Cost or Partial Equity Method)		
Cash	400,000	
Accumulated Depreciation	240,000	
Property and Equipment		600,000
Gain on Sale of Equipment		40,000

However, the consolidated book value of the equipment on the date of the sale by P Company is only $300,000, and from the point of view of the consolidated entity a $100,000 gain on the sale (selling price of $400,000 minus book value to consolidated entity of $300,000) should be recognized. The entry on the December 31, 2011, consolidated statements workpaper necessary to achieve this result follows:

ILLUSTRATION 7-7

Calculation of Book Value of Equipment on January 1, 2011

On Books of P Company	
Cost (to P Company)	$600,000
Accumulated Depreciation [($600,000/5) × 2]	240,000
Recorded Book Value—January 1, 2011	$360,000
Consolidated	
Cost (original cost to S Company)	$800,000
Accumulated Depreciation [$300,000 + ([($800,000 − $300,000)/5] × 2)]	500,000
Consolidated Book Value—January 1, 2011	$300,000

COST PARTIAL

Beginning Retained Earnings—P Company (.85 × \$60,000)	51,000	
Beginning NCI (.15 × \$60,000)	9,000	
Gain on Sale of Equipment		60,000

To adjust reported gain on the sale of equipment by P Company to third party from \$40,000 recorded by P Company to \$100,000 to be reported on the consolidated statement.

ILLUSTRATION 7-8

Reconciliation of Income Recorded on Books with Income Reported on Consolidated Financial Statements

Amount of profit recorded by affiliates	
2009—Gain on sale from S Company to P Company	\$100,000
2011—Gain on sale by P Company to nonaffiliate	40,000
Additional depreciation expense recorded by affiliates:	
2009	(20,000)
2010	(20,000)
Net amount of profit recorded by affiliates	\$100,000
Amount of profit realized in the consolidated income statement	
Selling price to the consolidated entity	\$400,000
Book value to the consolidated entity	300,000
Net amount of profit to the consolidated entity	\$100,000

The above entry also serves to adjust the controlling and noncontrolling interests for their share of unrealized intercompany gain at beginning of year (\$100,000 original gain minus \$40,000 realized through usage [\$20,000 in 2009 and \$20,000 in 2010] = \$60,000).

Note that the entry does not include any adjustment to equipment or accumulated depreciation after the disposal, as these accounts are accurately reflected at zero. Also, it is not necessary to calculate the \$60,000 adjustment to the controlling and noncontrolling interests directly in the above entry as it will always equal the gain adjustment. From a consolidated point of view, the amount of gain recorded by the selling affiliate will always be understated (or the amount of loss recorded will always be overstated) by an amount that is equal to the unrealized intercompany gain associated with the equipment on the date of its premature disposal.

After December 31, 2011, no more book or workpaper entries relating to this equipment will be required, because by that date the amount of gain recorded by the affiliates is equal to the amount of gain considered realized in the consolidated financial statements. The equality of the recorded and consolidated amounts is confirmed in Illustration 7-8.

CALCULATION OF CONSOLIDATED NET INCOME AND CONSOLIDATED RETAINED EARNINGS

In Chapter 6, the t-account calculation of the controlling and noncontrolling interests in consolidated net income was refined to accommodate the effect of unrealized intercompany profit in inventory. We now refine it further to include unrealized gain or loss on intercompany sales of equipment.

Consolidated Net Income

LO8 Consolidated net income—computation and allocation.

After modification for the effects of unrealized intercompany profit, consolidated net income was calculated in Chapter 6 as the parent company's income from its independent operations that has been realized in transactions with third parties plus (minus) subsidiary income (loss) that has been realized in transactions with third parties plus or minus adjustments for the period relating to the depreciation, amortization, or impairment of differences between implied and book values.

On the basis of Illustration 7-4A, the t-account calculations of the noncontrolling and controlling interests in consolidated net income for the year ended December 31, 2009, are demonstrated in Illustration 7-9. The amount of controlling interest in consolidated net income calculated in Illustration 7-9 is the same as that shown in the consolidated statements workpaper in Illustration 7-4A.

On the basis of Illustration 7-5A, the t-account allocation of consolidated net income for the year ended December 31, 2010, is presented in Illustration 7-10. The sum of the controlling and noncontrolling interests in consolidated net income calculated in Illustration 7-10 is, of course, the same as that shown as consolidated net income in the consolidated statements workpaper in Illustration 7-5A.

Consolidated Retained Earnings

Consolidated retained earnings were calculated in Chapter 6 as the parent company's cost method retained earnings that have been realized in transactions with third parties plus (minus) the parent company's share of the increase (decrease) in subsidiary retained earnings that has been realized in transactions with third parties

ILLUSTRATION 7-9

Calculation of Controlling and Noncontrolling Interests in Net Income for Year Ended December 31, 2009 Year of Intercompany Sale of Equipment

Noncontrolling Interest in Consolidated Income—Year 2009

		Internally generated income of S Company	$144,000
Unrealized profit on upstream sales in ending inventory	0	Gain realized through usage (depreciation adjustment)	20,000
Unrealized gain on 2009 intercompany sale of equipment (upstream sales)	100,000	Realized profit (upstream sales) from beginning inventory	0
Amortization of excess depreciation	0		
		Subsidiary Income included in Consolidated Income	$ 64,000
		Noncontrolling Ownership percentage interest	15%
		Noncontrolling Interest in Consolidated Income	$ 9,600

(85%) (64,000)

Controlling Interest in Consolidated Income—Year 2009

Unrealized gain on intercompany sale (downstream sales)	0	Net income internally generated by P Company	$300,000
		Gain realized through usage (depreciation adjustment)	0
Unrealized profit on downstream sales to S Company (ending inventory)	0	Realized profit (downstream sales) from beginning inventory	0
		P Company's percentage of S Company's income realized from third parties, .85($64,000)	54,400
		Controlling Interest in Consolidated Income	$354,400

ILLUSTRATION 7-10

Calculation of Controlling and Noncontrolling Interests in Net Income for Year Ended December 31, 2010 Year Subsequent to the Year of Intercompany Sale of Equipment

Noncontrolling Interest in Consolidated Income—Year 2010

		Internally generated income of S Company	$162,000
Unrealized profit on upstream sales in ending inventory	0	Gain realized through usage (depreciation adjustment)	20,000
Unrealized gain on 2006 intercompany sale of equipment (upstream sales)	0	Realized profit (upstream sales) from beginning inventory	0
Amortization of excess depreciation	0		
		Subsidiary Income included in Consolidated Income	$182,000
		Noncontrolling Ownership percentage interest	15%
		Noncontrolling Interest in Consolidated Income	$ 27,300

(85%)
($182,000)

Controlling Interest in Consolidated Income—Year 2010

Unrealized gain on 2010 intercompany sales of equipment (downstream sales)	0	Net income internally generated by P Company	$408,000
		Gain realized through usage (depreciation adjustment)	0
Unrealized profit on downstream sales to S Company (ending inventory)	0	Realized profit (downstream sales) from beginning inventory	0
		P Company's percentage of S Company's income realized from third parties, .85($182,000)	154,700
		Controlling Interest in Consolidated Income	$562,700

from the date of acquisition to the current date plus or minus the cumulative effect of adjustments to date relating to the depreciation, amortization, and impairment of differences between implied and book values.

On the basis of Illustration 7-5A, the t-account calculation of consolidated retained earnings on December 31, 2010, is demonstrated in Illustration 7-11.

ILLUSTRATION 7-11

Calculation of Consolidated Retained Earnings, December 31, 2010

Consolidated Retained Earnings

			P Company's Retained Earnings on 12/31/10	$2,208,000
Inventory	P Company's Share of unrealized profit on upstream sales from S Company (in P's ending inventory)	0		
	Unrealized profit on downstream sales to S Company (in S's ending inventory)	0	Increase in S Company's Retained Earnings since acquisition ($972,000 − $400,000)	572,000
	P Company's share of unrealized gain on upstream sales of equipment from S Company		Less: cumulative amount of depreciation of the differences between implied and book values	0
Equipment	(100,000 − 20,000 − 20,000).85	51,000	Adjusted Increase	572,000
	Unrealized gain on downstream sales of equipment to S Company	0	P Company's share thereof	0,85
				486,200
			Consolidated Retained Earnings	$2,643,200

As mentioned earlier, the workpaper entries to eliminate the effects of intercompany sales of equipment are the same when the parent uses the partial equity or the cost method, but differ slightly when the investment is recorded using the complete equity method. Therefore, we illustrate the complete equity method next.

TEST YOUR KNOWLEDGE

NOTE: Solutions to ***Test Your Knowledge*** questions are found at the end of each chapter before the end-of-chapter questions.

Multiple Choice

1. Parting Ways owns all of the common stock of Smarts Inc. On January 1, 2009, Parting sold to Smarts for a $5,000 gain a fixed asset that Smarts will use over the next five years. How should this gain be reflected in the consolidated financial statements?
   a. Not be recorded
   b. Be recognized over five years
   c. Be recognized in its entirety in the year of sale
   d. Be recognized only when the fixed asset is resold to outsiders after Smarts has finished using it
2. Punn Corporation owns all the common stock of Prey Inc. On January 2, 2010, Punn sells a machine with a book value of $30,000 to Prey for $40,000. Prey uses straight-line depreciation and intends to use the machine for five years. The adjustments (net) needed to compute the consolidated net income (before tax) for the years 2010 and 2011 are:
   a. $(10,000), 2010; $0, 2011
   b. $(10,000), 2010; $2,000, 2011
   c. $(8,000), 2010; $0, 2011
   d. $(8,000), 2010; $2,000, 2011
3. Price Corp. owns 80% of the common stock of Stairways to Heaven. Stairways sold an asset with a carrying value of $10,000 to its parent for $15,000 on January 1, 2006. Price intended to use the asset for five years but actually sold it on December 31, 2007, to a third party for $17,000. If no adjustments were made for this intercompany transaction in the consolidating process, identify the amounts (and direction) of balance sheet misstatements at the end of 2007.
   a. No misstatements occur.
   b. The noncontrolling interest is overstated by $600.
   c. The noncontrolling interest is overstated by $2,000.
   d. Retained earnings and controlling interest are both overstated by $2,400.

CONSOLIDATED STATEMENTS WORKPAPER—COMPLETE EQUITY METHOD

Subsidiary Is Intercompany Seller (Upstream Sale)

Assume that P Company acquires an 85% interest in S Company for $1,190,000 in 2007, when the retained earnings and capital stock of S Company amount to $400,000 and $1,000,000, respectively. The retained earnings of S Company on January 1, 2009, are $666,000. On January 1, 2009, S Company sells P Company

LO6 Upstream sales—complete equity method

equipment with a book value of $500,000 (original cost of $800,000 and accumulated depreciation of $300,000) for $600,000. On January 1, 2009, the equipment has an estimated remaining useful life of five years and is depreciated using the straight-line method. S Company will record a gain of $100,000 on the sale of the equipment, and each year P Company will record depreciation that is $20,000 [($600,000 − $500,000)/5 years] greater than depreciation based on the cost of the equipment to the consolidated group.

COMPLETE

Under the complete equity method, P Company makes additional entries to adjust its equity in subsidiary income for amounts unrealized (and subsequently realized) in intercompany transactions. In this example, in 2009, P Company would make the following entries:

P Company Books (Complete Equity)

Investment in S Company	122,400	
Equity in Subsidiary Income		122,400
To record the parent's 85% share of subsidiary reported net income in 2009.		

Equity in Subsidiary Income	85,000	
Investment in S Company		85,000
To adjust subsidiary income downward for the unrealized gain on the intercompany sale of equipment (100,000 × 85%).		
Investment in S Company	17,000	
Equity in Subsidiary Income		17,000
To adjust subsidiary income upward for the portion of the gain realized through usage (20,000 × 85%, or 85,000/5 years).		

Consolidated statements workpapers for the years ended December 31, 2009, and December 31, 2010, are presented in Illustrations 7-12 and 7-13, respectively.

Consolidated Statements Workpaper Entries—December 31, 2009

Workpaper entries in Illustration 7-12 are presented in general journal form as follows:

(1) Equity in Subsidiary Income ($122,400 − $85,000 + $17,000)	54,400	
Dividends Declared—S Company		0
Investment in S Company		54,400
To eliminate equity in subsidiary income and intercompany dividends, if any.		

(2) Gain on Sale of Equipment	100,000	
Property and Equipment	200,000	
Accumulated Depreciation		300,000
To eliminate the unrealized gain recorded on intercompany sale of equipment and restore equipment to its original cost (and accumulated depreciation to its balance at the date of the intercompany sale).		

(3) Accumulated Depreciation	20,000	
Depreciation Expense		20,000
To adjust depreciation on equipment sold to affiliate, thus realizing a portion of gain through usage ($100,000/5 years = $20,000).		

Complete Equity Method
85% Owned Subsidiary
Upstream Sale of Equipment
Year of Sale

ILLUSTRATION 7-12
Consolidated Statements Workpaper
P Company and Subsidiary
for the Year Ended December 31, 2009

Income Statement	*P Company*	*S Company*	*Eliminations Dr.*	*Eliminations Cr.*	*Noncontrolling Interest*	*Consolidated Balances*
Sales	3,500,000	2,000,000				5,500,000
Equity in Subsidiary Income	54,400		(1) 54,400			
Gain on Sale of Equipment		100,000	(2) 100,000			
Total Revenue	3,554,400	2,100,000				5,500,000
Cost of Sales	1,800,000	1,130,000				2,930,000
Depreciation Expense	380,000	330,000		(3) 20,000		690,000
Income Tax Expense	200,000	96,000				296,000
Other Expense	820,000	400,000				1,220,000
Total Cost and Expense	3,200,000	1,956,000				5,136,000
Net/Consolidated Income	354,400	144,000				364,000
Noncontrolling Interest in Income					9,600*	9,600
Net Income to Retained Earnings	354,400	144,000	154,400	20,000	9,600	354,400
Retained Earnings Statement						
1/1 Retained Earnings						
P Company	1,726,100					1,726,100
S Company		666,000	(4) 666,000			
Net Income from above	354,400	144,000	154,400	20,000	9,600	354,400
12/31 Retained Earnings to Balance Sheet	2,080,500	810,000	820,400	20,000	9,600	2,080,500
Balance Sheet						
Current Assets	1,000,000	570,000				1,570,000
Investment in S Company**	1,470,500			(1) 54,400 (4) 1,416,100		
Land	1,000,000	200,000				1,200,000
Property and Equipment	3,800,000	2,700,000	(2) 200,000			6,700,000
(Accumulated Depreciation)	(1,520,000)	(960,000)	(3) 20,000	(2) 300,000		(2,760,000)
Total Assets	5,750,500	2,510,000				6,710,000
Liabilities	670,000	700,000				1,370,000
Capital Stock						
P Company	3,000,000					3,000,000
S Company		1,000,000	(4) 1,000,000			
Retained Earnings from above	2,080,500	810,000	820,400	20,000	9,600	2,080,500
1/1 Noncontrolling Interest in Net Assets				(4) 249,900	249,900	
12/31 Noncontrolling Interest					259,500	259,500
Total Liabilities and Equity	5,750,500	2,510,000	2,040,400	2,040,400		6,710,000

* .15 × ($144,000 − $100,000 + $20,000) = $9,600.

** The investment account equals $1,190,000 + 85% of the increase in S Company's Retained Earnings from the date of acquisition to the beginning of the year ($666,000 − 400,000) plus the current period's equity in subsidiary income ($54,400).

(1) To eliminate equity in subsidiary income and intercompany dividends, if any.

(2) To eliminate the unrealized gain recorded on intercompany sale of equipment and restore equipment to its original cost (and accumulated depreciation to its balance at the date of the intercompany sale).

(3) To adjust depreciation on equipment sold to affiliate, thus realizing a portion of the gain through usage ($100,000/5 years = $20,000).

(4) To eliminate investment account against the underlying equity accounts of S Company and create noncontrolling interest account.

(4) Beginning Retained Earnings—S Company	666,000	
Capital Stock—S Company	1,000,000	
Investment in S Company ($1,190,000 + $226,100)		1,416,100
NCI in Equity ($210,000 + .15 ($666,000 − $400,000))		249,900
To eliminate investment account against underlying equity accounts of S Company, and recognize NCI.		

Since the selling affiliate is a partially owned subsidiary (upstream sale), the calculation of the noncontrolling interest in consolidated net income is modified by subtracting the amount of the gain recognized by the subsidiary and adding the amount of the gain considered to be realized (through depreciation) to the reported net income of the subsidiary [.15 × ($144,000 − $100,000 + $20,000) = $9,600].

Noncontrolling Interest in Income

		Internally generated income of S Company	$144,000
Unrealized gain on intercompany sale	$100,000	Gain realized through usage (depreciation adjustment)	20,000
		Adjusted income of subsidiary	$ 64,000
		Noncontrolling percentage	× 15%
		Noncontrolling interest in income	$ 9,600

COMPLETE

If the sale of the equipment had been downstream rather than upstream, the amount of subsidiary income included in consolidated income would not be affected by the workpaper entries related to unrealized intercompany gain and no adjustment would be necessary in calculating the ***noncontrolling interest*** in consolidated income.

Consolidated Statements Workpaper Entries—December 31, 2010

In the year 2010, P Company would again make an entry to adjust its equity in subsidiary income for the portion of the gain on the intercompany sale that is realized through usage. This entry may be recorded separately from the one to record P's share of subsidiary *reported* income, as shown below, or the two could be collapsed into one entry for $154,700 ($137,700 + $17,000).

P Company Books (Complete Equity Method)

Investment in S Company	137,700	
Equity in Subsidiary Income		137,700
To record the parent's 85% share of subsidiary reported net income in 2010.		
Investment in S Company	17,000	
Equity in Subsidiary Income		17,000
To adjust subsidiary income upward for the portion of the gain realized through usage (20,000 × 85%, or 85,000/5 years).		

Workpaper entries in Illustration 7-13 are presented in general journal form as follows:

(1) Equity in Subsidiary Income	154,700	
Dividends Declared—S Company		0
Investment in S Company		154,700
To eliminate equity in subsidiary income and intercompany dividends, if any.		

Complete Equity Method
85% Owned Subsidiary
Upstream Sale of Equipment
Year Subsequent of Sale

ILLUSTRATION 7-13
Consolidated Statements Workpaper
P Company and Subsidiary
for the Year Ended December 31, 2010

Income Statement	*P Company*	*S Company*	*Eliminations Dr.*	*Eliminations Cr.*	*Noncontrolling Interest*	*Consolidated Balances*
Sales	4,000,000	2,200,000				6,200,000
Equity Income	154,700		(1) 154,700			
Total Revenue	4,154,700	2,200,000				6,200,000
Cost of Sales	2,100,000	1,180,000				3,280,000
Depreciation Expense	380,000	330,000		(3) 20,000		690,000
Income Tax Expense	272,000	108,000				380,000
Other Expense	840,000	420,000				1,260,000
Total Cost and Expense	3,592,000	2,038,000				5,610,000
Net/Consolidated Income	562,700	162,000				590,000
Noncontrolling Interest in Income					27,300*	27,300
Net Income to Retained Earnings	562,700	162,000	154,700	20,000	27,300	562,700
Retained Earnings Statement						
1/1 Retained Earnings						
P Company	2,080,500					2,080,500
S Company		810,000	(4) 810,000			
Net Income from above	562,700	162,000	154,700	20,000	27,300	562,700
12/31 Retained Earnings to Balance Sheet	2,643,200	972,000	964,700	20,000	27,300	2,643,200
Balance Sheet						
Current Assets	1,190,000	790,000				1,980,000
Investment in S Company	1,625,200		(2) 85,000	(1) 154,700 (3) 17,000 (4) 1,538,500		
Land	1,600,000	200,000				1,800,000
Property and Equipment	3,800,000	2,700,000	(2) 200,000			6,700,000
(Accumulated Depreciation)	(1,900,000)	(1,290,000)	(3) 40,000	(2) 300,000		(3,450,000)
Total Assets	6,315,200	2,400,000				7,030,000
Liabilities	672,000	428,000				1,100,000
Capital Stock						
P Company	3,000,000					3,000,000
S Company		1,000,000	(4) 1,000,000			
Retained Earnings from above	2,643,200	972,000	964,700	20,000	27,300	2,643,200
1/1 Noncontrolling Interest in Net Assets			(2) 15,000	(4) 271,500 (3) 3,000	259,500	
12/31 Noncontrolling Interest in Net Assets**					286,800	286,800
Total Liabilities and Equity	6,315,200	2,400,000	2,304,700	2,304,700		7,030,000

* .15 × ($162,000 + $20,000) = $27,300.
** $210,000 + .15 × ($810,000 − $400,000) = $271,500.
(1) To eliminate equity in subsidiary income and intercompany dividends, if any.
(2) To reduce controlling and noncontrolling interests for their shares of unrealized intercompany gain and to restore equipment and accumulated depreciation to their original balances.
(3) To reverse amount of excess depreciation recorded during current and prior year and to recognize intercompany gain realized through usage.
(4) To eliminate investment account and create noncontrolling interest account.

	Dr.	Cr.
(2) Investment in S Company (100,000 × .85)	85,000	
Beginning NCI (100,000 × .15)	15,000	
Property and Equipment	200,000	
Accumulated Depreciation		300,000
To reduce the noncontrolling interest for its share of unrealized intercompany gain, to restore equipment and accumulated depreciation to their original balances at the date of the intercompany sale, and to facilitate the elimination of the investment account.		

COMPLETE

Consider the debit to the investment account in entry (2), recalling that the investment account is reduced on the parent's books when the unrealized income is deducted from the parent's equity in subsidiary income under the complete equity method. Thus, the usual workpaper entry to eliminate the investment account against the underlying subsidiary equity accounts [entry (4) below] eliminates an amount greater than the actual beginning investment account balance. That entry, combined with entries (2) and (3), however, will eliminate the investment to exactly zero.

	Dr.	Cr.
(3) Accumulated Depreciation	40,000	
Depreciation Expense		20,000
Investment in S Company (20,000 × .85)		17,000
Beginning Retained Earnings—S Company (20,000 × .15)		3,000
To adjust depreciation recorded in current year and prior year, thus recognizing intercompany gain realized through usage (prior year adjustment for controlling interest to Investment account).		

	Dr.	Cr.
(4) Beginning Retained Earnings—S Company	810,000	
Capital Stock—S Company	1,000,000	
Investment in S Company		1,538,500
NCI (210,000 + .15 (810,000 − 400,000))		271,500
To eliminate investment account against underlying equity accounts of S Company and recognize NCI.		

The noncontrolling interest in consolidated net income is calculated after adding the portion of the gain considered realized during the year to the net income reported by the subsidiary [.15 × ($162,000 + $20,000) = $27,300].

Noncontrolling Interest in Income

	Internally generated income of S Company	$162,000
	Gain realized through usage (depreciation adjustment)	20,000
	Adjusted income of subsidiary	$182,000
	Noncontrolling percentage	× 15%
	Noncontrolling interest in income	$ 27,300

Disposal of Property and Equipment by Purchasing Affiliate

LO9 Disposal of property by purchaser—complete equity.

Assume that on January 1, 2011, P Company sells the equipment it purchased from S Company to a party outside the affiliated group for $400,000. The recorded and consolidated book values of the equipment on January 1, 2011, are calculated in Illustration 7–14. P Company will record a $40,000 gain on the sale of the equipment to the party outside the affiliated group, calculated as:

Selling price	$400,000
Book value (on P Company's books)	360,000
Gain on sale (recorded by P Company)	40,000

The following entry is made on the books of P Company to record the sale:

COMPLETE

P Company Books—Complete Equity Method		
Cash	400,000	
Accumulated Depreciation	240,000	
Property and Equipment		600,000
Gain on Sale of Equipment		40,000

ILLUSTRATION 7-14

Calculation of Book Value of Equipment on January 1, 2011

On Books of P Company	
Cost (to P Company)	$600,000
Accumulated Depreciation [($600,000/5) × 2]	240,000
Recorded Book Value—January 1, 2011	$360,000
Consolidated	
Cost (original cost to S Company)	$800,000
Accumulated Depreciation [$300,000 + ([$800,000 − $300,000)/5] × 2)]	500,000
Consolidated Book Value—January 1, 2011	$300,000

In addition, P Company would make an entry to adjust its equity in subsidiary income for the amount of the intercompany gain realized in the current period (85% of: the original $100,000 gain minus the depreciation adjustments of $40,000 for 2009–2010; or $51,000). This entry is made for 85% of the realized gain as the original intercompany transaction was an upstream sale, and thus the controlling interest in the realized gain is 85% of $60,000, or $51.000.

Investment in S Company	51,000	
Equity in Subsidiary Income		51,000

However, the consolidated book value of the equipment on the date of the sale by P Company is only $300,000, and from the point of view of the consolidated entity a $100,000 gain on the sale (selling price of $400,000 minus book value to consolidated entity of $300,000) should be recognized. The entry on the December 31, 2011, consolidated statements workpaper necessary to achieve this result follows:

Investment in S Company (.85 × $60,000)	51,000	
Beginning NCI (.15 × $60,000)	9,000	
Gain on Sale of Equipment		60,000
To adjust reported gain on the sale of equipment by P Company to third party from $40,000 gain recorded by P Company to $100,000 gain to the consolidated equity.		

The above entry also serves to adjust the noncontrolling interest for its share of unrealized intercompany gain at the beginning of year ($100,000 original gain minus $40,000 realized through usage [$20,000 in 2009 and $20,000 in 2010] = $60,000 × 15%), and to facilitate the elimination of the investment account (by debiting it for the controlling share $60,000 × 85%).

COMPLETE

Note that the entry does not include any adjustment to equipment or accumulated depreciation after the disposal, as these accounts are accurately reflected at zero. Also, it is not necessary to calculate the $60,000 adjustment to the controlling and noncontrolling interests directly in the above entry as it will always equal the gain adjustment. From a consolidated point of view, the amount of gain recorded by the selling affiliate will always be understated (or the amount of loss recorded will always be overstated) by an amount that is equal to the unrealized intercompany profit associated with the equipment on the date of its premature disposal.

After December 31, 2011, no more book or workpaper entries relating to this equipment will be required. Under the complete equity method, entries are needed up through December 31, 2011, even though profit is accurately reflected in the books of P Company. Because the adjustments are reflected in P's books in the account Equity in Subsidiary Income and that account is eliminated in the consolidating process, it is still necessary to adjust the underlying accounts (gain, depreciation expense, etc.) until the asset is sold to outsiders and appropriately removed from the books entirely.

CALCULATION AND ALLOCATION OF CONSOLIDATED NET INCOME; CONSOLIDATED RETAINED EARNINGS: COMPLETE EQUITY METHOD

LO8 Consolidated net income—complete equity method.

For firms using the complete equity method, the controlling interest in consolidated net income will always equal the net income reported by the parent. Thus it is not necessary to reconcile the two. It is, nonetheless, useful to know how to check the amount of the controlling and noncontrolling interests in consolidated income using the t-account approach presented in Illustrations 7-9 and 7-10. Similarly, consolidated retained earnings will equal the retained earnings reported by the parent at any point, assuming the parent has correctly adjusted for any and all unrealized (and subsequently realized) intercompany profit. This amount may be verified using the t-account approach presented in Illustration 7-11.

SUMMARY OF WORKPAPER ENTRIES RELATING TO INTERCOMPANY SALES OF EQUIPMENT

Consolidated statements workpaper eliminating entries for intercompany sales of equipment are summarized in Illustration 7-15. The entries are the same whether the parent company uses the cost method or the partial equity method to record its investment. However, the form of the workpaper entry to adjust for unrealized intercompany profit at the beginning of the year differs as between upstream and downstream sales and between the complete equity method and the other two.

INTERCOMPANY INTEREST, RENTS, AND SERVICE FEES

LO10 Intercompany interest, rents, service fees.

Income and expenses relating to interest, fees, and rents should be reported in the consolidated income statement only when they arise from transactions with parties outside the affiliated group. In addition, as discussed in Chapter 3, only receivables and payables that are receivable from or payable to parties outside the affiliated group should be reported in the consolidated balance sheet.

ILLUSTRATION 7-15

Intercompany Gain on Sale of Equipment
Summary of Workpaper Elimination Entries

Selling Affiliate Is the Parent (or Wholly Owned Subsidiary) **(Downstream Sales)**

Entries in Year of Intercompany Sale (Cost, Partial Equity, and Complete Equity):

Account	Debit	Credit
Gain on Sale	xx	
Equipment	xx	
Accumulated Depreciation		xx

To eliminate unrealized gain on intercompany sale in year of sale and to restore equipment to its original cost and accumulated depreciation to its balance at the date of the intercompany sale.

Account	Debit	Credit
Accumulated Depreciation	xx	
Depreciation Expense		xx

To reverse amount (if any) of excess depreciation recorded during current year, thus recognizing an equivalent amount of intercompany profit as realized.

Entries in Years Subsequent to the Year of Intercompany Sale (Downstream):

Cost and Partial Equity

Account	Debit	Credit
Beginning Retained Earnings—P Company	xx	
Equipment	xx	
Accumulated Depreciation		xx

To reduce consolidated retained earnings for the intercompany gain, to restore accumulated depreciation and equipment to their original balances at the date of intercompany sale.

Account	Debit	Credit
Accumulated Depreciation	xx	
Depreciation Expense		xx
Beginning Retained Earnings—P Company		xx

Complete Equity

Account	Debit	Credit
Investment in S Company	xx	
Equipment	xx	
Accumulated Depreciation		xx

To facilitate elimination of the investment account and to restore accumulated depreciation and equipment to their original balances at the date of the intercompany sale.

Account	Debit	Credit
Accumulated Depreciation	xx	
Depreciation Expense		xx
Investment in S Company		xx

To reverse amount of excess depreciation recorded during current year and prior year, thus recognizing intercompany gain realized through usage.

Selling Affiliate Is a Subsidiary (Less than Wholly Owned Subsidiary) **(Upstream Sales)**

Account	Debit	Credit
Gain on Sale	xx	
Equipment	xx	
Accumulated Depreciation		xx

To eliminate unrealized gain on intercompany sale in year of sale and to restore equipment to its original cost and accumulated depreciation to its balance at the date of the intercompany sale.

Account	Debit	Credit
Accumulated Depreciation	xx	
Depreciation Expense		xx

To reverse amount (if any) of excess depreciation recorded during current year, thus recognizing an equivalent amount of intercompany profit as realized.

(Upstream):

Cost and Partial Equity

Account	Debit	Credit
Beginning Retained Earnings—P	xx	
NCI in Equity	xx	
Equipment	xx	
Accumulated Depreciation		xx

To reduce the controlling and noncontrolling interests for their respective shares of the intercompany gain, to restore accumulated depreciation and equipment to their original balances at the date of the intercompany sale.

Account	Debit	Credit
Accumulated Depreciation	xx	
Depreciation Expense		xx
Beginning Retained Earnings—P Company		xx
NCI in Equity		xx

Complete Equity

Account	Debit	Credit
Investment in S Company	xx	
NCI in Equity	xx	
Equipment	xx	
Accumulated Depreciation		xx

To reduce the noncontrolling interest for its share of the intercompany gain, to facilitate the elimination of the investment account and restore accumulated depreciation and equipment to their original balances at the date of the intercompany sale.

Account	Debit	Credit
Accumulated Depreciation	xx	
Depreciation Expense		xx
Investment in S Company		xx
NCI in Equity		xx

To reverse amount of excess depreciation recorded during current year and prior year, thus recognizing intercompany gain realized through usage.

Intercompany Interest

When interest is charged on intercompany loans, the intercompany interest income on the lending affiliate's books is equal to the intercompany interest expense on the borrowing affiliate's books. The workpaper entry to eliminate intercompany interest is:

Interest Income	XXX	
Interest Expense		XXX

Since equal amounts of revenue and expense are removed from combined income, the net amount of consolidated net income is not affected by this entry. When intercompany loans or interest remain unpaid on the balance sheet date, additional entries are necessary to eliminate related intercompany payables and receivables as follows:

Notes Payable	XXX	
Notes Receivable		XXX
Interest Payable	XXX	
Interest Receivable		XXX

Intercompany Rents

When there is an intercompany operating lease, intercompany rent income on the books of the lessor will equal intercompany rent expense on the books of the lessee. The workpaper entry to eliminate intercompany rent is:

Rent Income	XXX	
Rent Expense		XXX

Since equal amounts of revenue and expense are removed from consolidated income, the net amount of consolidated net income is not affected by this entry.

Intercompany Service Fees

When one affiliate charges fees to another, the form of the eliminating entry is determined by how the transaction is recorded by the affiliates. If the affiliate that provides the service treats the fee as revenue and the affiliate that receives the service treats the fee as an expense, the necessary workpaper entry is simply a debit to service fee revenue and a credit to service fee expense. On the other hand, the affiliate that receives the service may treat the amount it is charged for the service as a capital addition. For example, fees for architectural services to an affiliate may be treated by the purchasing affiliate as part of the cost of a building. In this case, architectural fees should be debited for the amount recorded as revenue on the intercompany transaction, appropriate expense accounts (as recorded on the selling affiliates books) should be credited for the cost to the selling affiliate of providing the services, and the building should be credited for the difference between the revenue recorded and the cost of providing the service. Additional workpaper entries will also be necessary in subsequent years to report balances for the building, accumulated depreciation, and depreciation expense at amounts based on the cost of the building to the affiliated group.

For example, assume that P Company bills its subsidiary, S Company, $400,000 for architectural services. The cost to P Company of providing the services is $250,000. S Company charges the services to the cost of a building that it opens at the beginning of the next year with an estimated useful life of 15 years. Workpaper entries to eliminate the effects of the intercompany service fee are as follows:

In the Year the Services Are Rendered

Cost and Partial Equity			Complete Equity		
Architectural Fees	400,000		Architectural Fees	400,000	
Salary Expense		200,000	Salary Expense		200,000
Travel Expense		15,000	Travel Expense		15,000
Other Expense		35,000	Other Expense		35,000
Building		150,000	Building		150,000

In the Year the Building Is Opened

Cost and Partial Equity			Complete Equity		
Beginning Retained Earnings—P Company	150,000		Investment in S Company	150,000	
Building		150,000	Building		150,000
Accumulated Depreciation	10,000		Accumulated Depreciation	10,000	
Depreciation Expense		10,000	Depreciation Expense		10,000

In the Fifth Year After the Building Is Opened

Cost and Partial Equity			Complete Equity		
Beginning Retained Earnings—P Company	110,000		Investment in S Company	110,000	
Accumulated Depreciation	40,000		Accumulated Depreciation	40,000	
Building		150,000	Building		150,000
Accumulated Depreciation	10,000		Accumulated Depreciation	10,000	
Depreciation Expense		10,000	Depreciation Expense		10,000

Thus eliminating entries relating to intercompany transactions depend on how these transactions are recorded on the books of the affiliates. In all cases, however, the financial reporting objectives identified in previous sections of this chapter and in Chapter 6 apply. In the preceding example, the reporting objectives were:

- To include in revenue only the amounts that result from ***transactions with parties outside the affiliated group***.
- To present property in the consolidated balance sheet at ***its cost to the affiliated group***.
- To present accumulated depreciation in the consolidated balance sheet based on the ***cost to the affiliated group*** of the related assets.
- To present depreciation expense in the consolidated income statement based on the ***cost to the affiliated group*** of the related assets.

In order to apply the objectives identified in this chapter and in Chapter 6 to a situation that is not illustrated in this text, the student may wish to work out the workpaper entries necessary in a situation like the following. S Company is in the business of selling equipment that it manufactures. S Company treats equipment manufactured as finished goods inventory. S Company sells some equipment that it manufactured to its parent company at a profit. The equipment is capitalized and depreciated on the books of the parent company.

SUMMARY

1. *Understand the financial reporting objectives in accounting for intercompany sales of* ***nondepreciable*** *assets on the consolidated financial statements.* The consolidated financial statements should include gains or losses only when the property is sold to outsiders (parties outside the affiliated group) for the difference between the cost to the consolidated entity and the proceeds from outsiders. Until it is sold to outsiders, the property should be presented in the consolidated balance sheet at its cost to the affiliated group.
2. *State the additional financial reporting objectives in accounting for intercompany sales of* ***depreciable*** *assets on the consolidated financial statements.* Accumulated depreciation should be presented in the consolidated balance sheet based on the cost of the asset to the affiliated group, and depreciation expense should be presented in the consolidated income statement also based on the cost to the affiliated group.
3. *Explain when gains or losses on intercompany sales of depreciable assets should be recognized on a consolidated basis.* Gains or losses on intercompany sales of depreciable assets are recognized either when the asset is sold to outsiders, or gradually over time as it is depreciated.
4. *Explain the term "realized through usage."* After an intercompany sale, the purchasing affiliate will calculate depreciation on the basis of its cost, which is the intercompany selling price. The depreciation recorded by the purchasing affiliate will, therefore, be excessive (deficient) from a consolidated point of view and will also require adjustment. From the view of the consolidated entity, the intercompany gain (loss) is considered to be realized from the use of the property or equipment in the generation of revenue.
5. *Describe the differences between upstream and downstream sales in determining consolidated net income and the controlling and noncontrolling interests in consolidated income.* There is no difference between upstream and downstream sales in determining consolidated income. However, the controlling and noncontrolling interests are affected differently. For downstream sales, the elimination of intercompany gains as well as the subsequent depreciation adjustments affect only the controlling interest. For upstream sales, the adjustments are made to the subsidiary income, and thus affect both the noncontrolling and controlling interests in the proportion of subsidiary ownership.
6. *Compare the eliminating entries when the selling affiliate is a subsidiary (less than wholly owned) versus when the selling affiliate is the parent company.* Because of the differences explained in the preceding item (#5), the eliminating entries are similarly affected. Specifically, the entries in subsequent years for downstream sales that reflect prior years' income or expense adjustments [entries to Retained Earnings—Parent (under the cost or partial equity method) or Investment in Subsidiary (under the complete equity method)] are replaced by eliminating entries for upstream sales to both Retained Earnings—Parent and to NCI in Equity under the cost or partial equity method or to both Investment in Subsidiary and NCI under the complete equity method.
7. *Compute the noncontrolling interest in consolidated net income when the selling affiliate is a subsidiary.* The noncontrolling interest in consolidated income is computed as the noncontrolling interest percentage of the internally generated income of the subsidiary minus the unrealized gain on upstream sales (year of sale only) plus the amount of the gain realized through usage (depreciation adjustment).
8. *Compute consolidated net income considering the effects of intercompany sales of depreciable assets.* Consolidated net income is computed as the internally generated income of the parent minus the unrealized gain on downstream sales (year of sale only) plus the amount of the gain realized through usage (depreciation adjustment) plus the subsidiary income adjusted for upstream sales minus any other adjustments needed (such as excess depreciation, described in earlier chapters).
9. *Describe the eliminating entry needed to adjust the consolidated financial statements when the purchasing affiliate sells a depreciable asset that was acquired from another affiliate.* The entry does not include any adjustment to equipment or accumulated depreciation after the disposal, as these accounts are accurately reflected at zero. The entry merely adjusts the gain or loss reported by the purchasing affiliate from the amount it recorded to the correct amount from the perspective of the consolidated entity (based on original cost and depreciation), and adjusts the controlling and noncontrolling interests for the unrealized intercompany profit associated with the equipment on the date of its premature disposal (which equals the over- or understatement of the gain or loss).

10. *Explain the basic principles used to record or eliminate intercompany interest, rent, and service fees.* Income and expenses relating to interest, fees, and rents should be reported in the consolidated income statement only when they arise from transactions with parties outside the affiliated group. In addition, only receivables and payables that are receivable from or payable to parties outside the affiliated group should be reported in the consolidated balance sheet.

APPENDIX

Deferred Tax Consequences Related to Intercompany Sales of Equipment

To keep the focus of this appendix on deferred tax consequences rather than alternative methods of accounting for investments, we present the discussion only once. The balances reported by the parent company in income, retained earnings, and the investment account differ depending on the method used by the parent company to record its investment. As illustrated in previous chapters, however, the method used by the parent company to record its investment has no effect on the consolidated balances.

As has also been illustrated in previous chapters, when the parent company records its investment using the equity method, a workpaper entry to reverse the effect of parent company entries during the year for subsidiary dividends and income replaces the cost method entries to establish reciprocity and to eliminate dividend income. However, workpaper entries to allocate the difference between implied and book values, to amortize, depreciate, or record impairment of differences between implied and book values of depreciable or amortizable assets, to eliminate intercompany sales, and to eliminate unrealized intercompany profit are the same regardless of whether the investment is recorded using the cost method or the partial equity method. Workpaper entries to record deferred tax consequences of unrealized intercompany profit and undistributed subsidiary income are also the same when the parent company records its investment using the partial equity method or the cost method. The principal difference between the workpaper entries for these methods and for the complete equity method is that entries to Retained Earnings—P Company are generally replaced by entries to the Investment in S Company, as indicated by an asterisk in the following analysis.

To illustrate the treatment in the consolidated financial statements of deferred income taxes relating to intercompany sales of equipment, assume that P Company owns a 70% interest in S Company and that on January 1, 2008, S Company sells P Company equipment with a book value of $500,000 (original cost of $800,000 and accumulated depreciation of $300,000) for $600,000. On January 1, 2008, the equipment has a remaining useful life of five years and is depreciated using the straight-line method. The marginal income tax rates for both companies are 40% and separate income tax returns are filed.

S Company will record a gain of $100,000 on the sale of the equipment and each year P Company will record depreciation that is $20,000 greater than depreciation based on the cost of the equipment to the selling affiliate. Workpaper eliminating entries in the December 31, 2008, and December 31, 2009, consolidated statements workpapers relating to the unrealized profit on the intercompany sale of the equipment are illustrated below:

Consolidated Statements Workpaper Entries—December 31, 2008

		Debit	Credit
(1)	Gain on Sale of Equipment	100,000	
	Property and Equipment		100,000
	To eliminate unrealized profit recorded on intercompany sale of equipment.		
(2)	Accumulated Depreciation	20,000	
	Depreciation Expense		20,000
	To reverse the amount of excess depreciation recorded during the current year.		
(3)	Deferred Tax Asset	32,000	
	Income Tax Expense		32,000
	To defer the net amount of income tax paid or accrued by the affiliates on the amount of unrealized intercompany profit in equipment at the end of the year [.4 × ($100,000 − $20,000)].		
(4)	Property and Equipment	300,000	
	Accumulated Depreciation		300,000
	To restate property and equipment at original cost to the selling affiliate.		

Since the selling affiliate is a partially owned subsidiary (upstream sale), the calculation of the noncontrolling interest in consolidated income requires that the ***after-tax*** amount of gain recorded by the subsidiary (.60 × $100,000 = $60,000) be subtracted from the reported net income of the subsidiary and that the ***after-tax*** amount of the gain realized through depreciation (.6 × $20,000 = $12,000) be added to the reported net income of the subsidiary *before* multiplying by the noncontrolling interest percentage. Assuming that S Company reported net income of $144,000 in 2008, the noncontrolling interest in consolidated income is $28,800 [.30 × ($144,000 − $60,000 + $12,000)].

If the sale of equipment is downstream, no adjustments to the reported net income of the subsidiary are necessary in the calculation of the noncontrolling interest in consolidated income.

Consolidated Statements Workpaper Entries—December 31, 2009

		Debit	Credit
(1)	1/1 Retained Earnings—P Company* [.70 × ($100,000 − $20,000)]	56,000	
	1/1 NCI [.30 × ($100,000 − $20,000)]	24,000	
	Accumulated Depreciation	20,000	
	Equipment		100,000
	To reduce the controlling and the noncontrolling interests for their respective shares of unrealized intercompany profit at the beginning of the year, to reduce accumulated depreciation by the amount of excess depreciation accumulated to the beginning of the year, and to reduce the carrying value of equipment to its book value on the date of the intercompany sale.		
(2)	Accumulated Depreciation	20,000	
	Depreciation Expense		20,000
	To reverse the amount of excess depreciation recorded (during the current year.		
(3)	Deferred Tax Asset	24,000	
	Income Tax Expense	8,000	
	1/1 Retained Earnings—P Company*		22,400
	1/1 NCI		9,600
	To recognize deferred taxes for taxes paid in prior years on the amount of intercompany profit still considered unrealized at. the ***end of the year***		

(continued)

[.40 × ($100,000 − $20,000 − $20,000) = $24,000], to recognize income tax expense on intercompany profit considered to be realized during the current year (.40 × $20,000 = $8,000), to adjust consolidated retained earnings for the controlling interest's share of the tax consequence of unrealized profit at the beginning of the year (.70 × $32,000 = $22,400), and to adjust the noncontrolling interest for its share of the tax consequence of unrealized profit at the beginning of the year (.30 × $32,000 = $9,600).

* Entry to R/E—P Company is replaced by an entry to Investment in S Company under the complete equity method.

(4)	Property and Equipment	300,000	
	Accumulated Depreciation		300,000
	To restate property and equipment to original cost to the selling affiliate.		

The noncontrolling interest in consolidated income is calculated after adding the ***after-tax*** profit considered realized during the year (.6 × $20,000 = $12,000) to the reported net income of the subsidiary. If S Company reported net income of $162,000 in 2009, the noncontrolling interest in consolidated income is $52,200 [.30 × ($162,000 + $12,000)].

IMPACT OF UNREALIZED INTERCOMPANY PROFIT ON THE CALCULATION OF DEFERRED TAX CONSEQUENCES RELATED TO UNDISTRIBUTED SUBSIDIARY INCOME

Earlier we emphasized that the calculation of the tax consequences of undistributed income is based on the undistributed income of the subsidiary that has been ***included in consolidated income.*** Thus, before calculating the deferred tax consequences relating lo undistributed subsidiary income, the amount of undistributed income must be adjusted for the ***after-tax*** amount of unrealized intercompany profit ***recorded by the subsidiary*** that has been recognized in the determination of consolidated income.

To illustrate, assume that:

1. P Company acquired 70% of the voting stock of S Company when S Company's retained earnings amounted to $150,000.
2. On January 1, 2008, S Company recorded a $100,000 gain on the sale to P Company of equipment with a remaining life of five years.
3. On January 1, 2009, P Company recorded a $60,000 gain on the sale to S Company of equipment with a remaining life of six years.
4. S Company reported retained earnings of $260,000 on January 1, 2009, and $320,000 on December 31, 2009.
5. S Company reported net income of $90,000 and declared dividends of $30,000 in 2009.
6. P Company reported net income from independent operations in 2009 in the amount of $700,000 and retained earnings on December 31, 2009, of $3,500,000.
7. The affiliates file separate income tax returns.
8. Undistributed income is expected to be received in the form of future dividends.
9. The dividends received deduction is 80%, and the past, current, and expected future marginal income tax rates are 40%.

The calculation of the amounts of the undistributed income of S Company that have been included in consolidated income is presented in Illustration 7-16.

ILLUSTRATION 7-16

Undistributed Income of S Company That Has Been Included in Consolidated Income

S Company	*From Acquisition to 1/1/09*	*For Calendar Year 2009*	*From Acquisition to 12/31/09*
Retained earnings 1/1/09	$ 260,000		
Retained earnings 12/31/09			$ 320,000
Retained earnings date of acquisition	(150,000)		(150,000)
Increase in retained earnings	110,000		170,000
Net income 2009		$ 90,000	
Dividends 2009		(30,000)	
After-tax unrealized profit on 1/1/09 [.6 × ($100,000 − $20,000)]	(48,000)		
After-tax profit realized in 2009 (.6 × $20,000)		12,000	
After-tax unrealized profit on 12/31/09 [.6 × ($100,000 − $20,000 − $20,000)]			(36,000)
Undistributed income that has been included in consolidated income	$ 62,000	$ 72,000	$ 134,000

The following entry is needed in the December 31, 2009, consolidated statements workpaper to report the income tax consequences of past and current undistributed subsidiary income:

1/1 Retained Earnings—P Company (1)*	3,472	
Income Tax Expense (balancing amount) (2)	4,032	
Deferred Income Tax Liability (3)		7,504

(1)$62,000 × 70% × 20% × 40% = $3,472
(2)$7,504 − $3,472 = $4,032
(3)$134,000 × 70% × 20% × 40% = $7,504
* Entry to Retained Earnings—P Company is replaced by an entry in the same amount to the Investment in S Company account tinder the complete equity method.

Note that the calculation of the deferred income tax liability on undistributed subsidiary income is not affected by unrealized intercompany profit recorded by the parent company on sales to the subsidiary (downstream sales). The calculation is also not affected by the allocation, depreciation, or amortization of any differences between market and book values.

CALCULATIONS (AND ALLOCATION) OF CONSOLIDATED NET INCOME AND CONSOLIDATED RETAINED EARNINGS

When the affiliated companies file separate income tax returns, the calculations of consolidated net income and consolidated retained earnings must be modified to incorporate income tax consequences. When calculating the amounts of net income or retained earnings that have been realized in transactions with third parties, adjustments must now be made for the ***after-tax amounts*** of unrealized intercompany profit. In addition, consolidated net income is reduced by the income tax consequence of undistributed income for the current year and consolidated retained earnings is reduced by the income tax consequence of undistributed income from the date of acquisition to the date of the calculation.

The calculation of consolidated net income in Illustration 7-17 and the calculation of consolidated retained earnings in Illustration 7-18 are based on the same assumptions as those used in the preparation of Illustration 7-16.

ILLUSTRATION 7-17

Calculation of Controlling and Noncontrolling Interests in Income for Year Ended December 31, 2009

Deferred Tax Considerations

Noncontrolling Interest in Consolidated Net Income—Year 2009

Unrealized profit on upstream sales in ending inventory (after-tax)	0	Internally generated income of S Company	$ 90,000
Unrealized gain on 2009 intercompany sale of equipment—upstream sales (after-tax)	0	After-tax gain realized through usage (depreciation adjustment) .60($20,000)	12,000
Amortization of excess depreciation	0	Realized profit (upstream sales) from beginning inventory (after-tax)	0
		Subsidiary Income included in Consolidated Income	$ 102,000
		Noncontrolling Ownership percentage interest	30%
		Noncontrolling Interest in Consolidated Income	$ 30,600

(70%)

Controlling Interest in Income—Year 2009

After-tax unrealized gain on 2009 intercompany sales of equipment (downstream sales) .6($60,000)	36,000	Net income internally generated by P Company	$ 700,000
		After-tax gain realized through usage (depreciation adjustment) .6($10,000)	6,000
Unrealized profit on downstream sales to S Company (ending inventory) (after-tax)	0	Realized profit (downstream sales) from beginning inventory (after-tax)	0
		P Company's percentage of S Company's income realized from third parties, .70($102,000)	71,400
Deferred taxes on S Company's undistributed income for 2009 [($102,000 – 30,000) (.7)(.2)(.4)]	4,032		
		Controlling interest in consolidated income	$ 737,368

ILLUSTRATION 7-18

Calculation of Consolidated Retained Earnings December 31, 2009

P Company's retained earnings on 12/31/09		$ 3,500,000
Less the after-tax amount of P Company's retained earnings that have not been realized in transactions with third parties [.6 × ($60,000 – $10,000)]		(30,000)
P Company's retained earnings that have been realized in transactions with third parties		3,470,000
Increase in retained earnings of S Company from date of acquisition to 12/31/09 ($320,000 – $150,000)	$ 170,000	
Less cumulative amortization of differences between implied and book values		—0—
Less after-tax unrealized profit, included in S Company's retained earnings on 12/31/09 [.6 × ($100,000 – $20,000 – $20,000)]	(36,000)	
Increase in reported retained earnings of S Company since acquisition that has been realized in transactions with third parties	$ 134,000	
P Company's share thereof (.70 × $134,000)		93,800
Less income tax consequence of undistributed income of S Company that has been included in consolidated income from date of acquisition to 12/31/09 ($134,000 × .70 × .20 × .40)		(7,504)
Consolidated retained earnings 12/31/09		$ 3,556,296

TEST YOUR KNOWLEDGE SOLUTIONS

7-1 b
7-2 d
7-3 a

QUESTIONS

(The letter A or B indicated for a question, exercise, or problem refers to a related appendix.)

LO1 LO3 **1.** From a consolidated point of view, when should profit be recognized on intercompany sales of depreciable assets? Nondepreciable assets?

LO3 **2.** In what circumstances might a consolidated gain be recognized on the sale of assets to a nonaffiliate when the selling affiliate recognizes a loss?

LO6 **3.** What is the essential procedural difference between workpaper eliminating entries for unrealized intercompany profit when the selling affiliate is a less than wholly owned subsidiary and such entries when the selling affiliate is the parent company or a wholly owned subsidiary?

LO8 **4.** Define the controlling interest in consolidated net income using the t-account approach.

LO5 **5.** Why is it important to distinguish between upstream and downstream sales in the analysis of intercompany profit eliminations?

LO3 **6.** In what period and in what manner should profits relating to the intercompany sale of depreciable property and equipment be recognized in the consolidated financial statements?

LO8 **7.** Define consolidated retained earnings using the analytical approach.

Business Ethics

Some people believe that the use of executive stock options is directly related to the increased number of earnings restatements. For each of the following items, discuss the potential ethical issues that might be related to earnings management within the firm.

1. Should stock options be expensed on the Income Statement?

2. Should the CEO or CFO be a past employee of the firm's audit firm?

3. Should the firm's audit committee be composed entirely of outside members and be solely responsible for hiring the firm's auditors?[4]

EXERCISES

EXERCISE 7-1 **Controlling Interest in Income** LO8

On January 1, 2011, Sherwood Company, an 80% owned subsidiary of Paradise Company, sold to Paradise Company equipment with a book value of $600,000 for $840,000. The equipment had an estimated remaining useful life of eight years on the date of the intercompany sale.

Paradise Company reported net income from its independent operations of $550,000, and Sherwood Company reported net income of $300,000 in the years of 2011 and 2012.

Required:

Calculate the controlling interest in combined net income for the years ended December 31, 2011, and December 31, 2012.

[4] *The CPA Journal*, "Proposals to Improve the Image of the Public Accounting Profession," by Franklin Strier, 3/06, p. 67.

EXERCISE 7-2 **Controlling Interest in Income** LO8

On January 1, 2011, Polar Company, which owns an 80% interest in Superior Company, sold Superior Company equipment with a book value of $400,000 for $560,000. The equipment had an estimated remaining useful life of eight years on the date of the intercompany sale.

Polar Company reported net income from its independent operations (including sales to affiliates) of $400,000, and Superior Company reported net income of $200,000 from its independent operations in 2011 and 2012.

Required:

Calculate the controlling interest in consolidated net income for the years ended December 31, 2011, and December 31, 2012.

EXERCISE 7-3 **Workpaper Entries—Intercompany Sale of Equipment** LO6 LO8

Pearson Company owns 90% of the outstanding common stock of Spring Company. On January 1, 2011, Spring Company sold equipment to Pearson Company for $200,000. Spring Company had purchased the equipment for $300,000 on January 1, 2006, and had depreciated it using a 10% straight-line rate. The management of Pearson Company estimated that the equipment had a remaining useful life of five years on January 1, 2011. In 2012, Pearson Company reported $150,000 and Spring Company reported $100,000 in net income from their independent operations (including sales to affiliates).

Required:

A. Prepare in general journal form the workpaper entries relating to the intercompany sale of equipment that are necessary in the December 31, 2011, and December 31, 2012, consolidated financial statements workpapers.

B. Calculate controlling interest in consolidated income for 2012.

EXERCISE 7-4 **Entries—Intercompany Sale of Land** LO6

Procter Company owns 90% of the outstanding stock of Silex Company. On January 1, 2011, Silex Company sold land to Procter Company for $350,000. Silex had originally purchased the land on June 30, 2007, for $200,000.

Procter Company plans to construct a building on the land bought from Silex in which it will house new production machinery. The estimated useful life of the building and the new machinery is 15 years.

Required:

A. Prepare the entries on the books of Procter related to the intercompany sale of land for the years ended December 31, 2011, and December 31, 2012.

B. Prepare in general journal form the workpaper entries necessary because of the intercompany sale of land in:

(1) The consolidated financial statements workpaper for the year ended December 31, 2011.

(2) The consolidated financial statements workpaper for the year ended December 31, 2012.

EXERCISE 7-5 **Upstream and Downstream Sale** LO6

Patterson Company owns 80% of the outstanding common stock of Stevens Company. On June 30, 2010, land costing $500,000 is sold by one affiliate to the other for $800,000.

Required:

Prepare in general journal form the workpaper entries necessary because of the intercompany sale of land in the consolidated financial statements workpaper for the year ended December 31, 2011, assuming that:

A. Patterson Company purchased the land from Stevens Company.

B. Stevens Company purchased the land from Patterson Company.

EXERCISE 7-6 **Calculating Gain on Sale** LO9

P Company owns 90% of the outstanding common stock of S Company. On January 1, 2011, S Company sold land to P Company for $600,000. S Company originally purchased the land for $400,000.

On January 1, 2012, P Company sold the land purchased from S Company to a company outside the affiliated group for $700,000.

Required:

A. Calculate the amount of gain on the sale of the land that is recognized on the books of P Company in 2012.

B. Calculate the amount of gain on the sale of the land that should be recognized in the consolidated financial statements in 2012.

C. Prepare in general journal form the workpaper entries necessary because of the intercompany sale of land in the consolidated financial statements workpaper for the year ended December 31, 2012.

EXERCISE 7-7 **Entries—Intercompany Sale of Inventory and Equipment** LO7 LO9

On January 1, 2010, Price Company acquired an 80% interest in the common stock of Smith Company on the open market for $750,000, the book value at that date.

On January 1, 2011, Price Company purchased new equipment for $14,500 from Smith Company. The equipment cost $9,000 and had an estimated life of five years as of January 1, 2011.

During 2012, Price Company had merchandise sales to Smith Company of $100,000; the merchandise was priced at 25% above Price Company's cost. Smith Company still owes Price Company $17,500 on open account and has 20% of this merchandise in inventory at December 31, 2012. At the beginning of 2012, Smith Company had in inventory $25,000 of merchandise purchased in the previous period from Price Company.

Required:

A. Prepare all workpaper entries necessary to eliminate the effects of the intercompany sales on the consolidated financial statements for the year ended December 31, 2012.

B. Assume that Smith Company reports net income of $40,000 for the year ended December 31, 2012. Calculate the amount of noncontrolling interest to be deducted from consolidated income in the consolidated income statement for the year ended December 31, 2012.

EXERCISE 7-8 **Controlling Interest in Income** LO8

On January 1, 2011, P Company acquired a 90% interest in S Company. During 2012, S Company sold merchandise to P Company at 25% above cost in the amount (selling price) of $225,000. At the end of the year, P Company had in its inventory one-third of the amount of goods purchased from S Company.

On January 1, 2012, P Company sold equipment that had a book value of $80,000 to S Company for $120,000. The equipment had an estimated remaining life of four years.

S Company reported net income of $120,000, and P Company reported net income of $300,000 from their independent operations (including sales to affiliates) for the year ended December 31, 2012.

Required:

Calculate controlling interest in consolidated net income for the year ended December 31, 2012.

EXERCISE 7-9 **Workpaper Entries—Sales of Services** LO10

P Company owns 80% of the outstanding stock of S Company. The 2011 sales of S Company included revenue of $390,000 consisting of consulting services billed to P Company at cost plus 30%. P Company was billed the full $390,000; of this amount, $260,000 was charged to selling expenses and $130,000 was charged to administrative expense.

Required:

Prepare in general journal form the workpaper entry necessary to eliminate the effects of intercompany sales of services in the consolidated financial statements workpaper for the year ended December 31, 2011.

EXERCISE 7-10 **Workpaper Entries—Intercompany Fees** LO10

During 2010, Pier One Company billed its 80% owned subsidiary, Scale Company, $700,000 for architectural services. The cost to Pier One Company of providing the services was $400,000 for salaries and $150,000 for other operating expenses. Scale Company charged the architecture fees to the cost of a building that it opened on January 1, 2011. The building had an estimated useful life of 30 years.

Required:

Prepare in general journal form the workpaper entries relating to the intercompany fees that are necessary in the consolidated statements workpapers for the years ended December 31, 2010, 2011, and 2012.

EXERCISE 7-11 **Workpaper Entries—Upstream and Downstream Sales** LO6 LO8

Pinta Company, a forklift manufacturer, owns 80% of the voting stock of Standard Company. On January 1, 2011, Pinta Company sold forklifts to Standard Company for $400,000. The forklifts, which represented inventory to Pinta Company, had a cost to Pinta Company of $310,000. The management of Standard Company estimated that the forklifts had a useful life of nine years from the date of purchase. Standard Company uses the straight-line method to depreciate its capital assets.

In 2011, Pinta Company reported $700,000 in net income from its independent operations (including sales to affiliates), and Standard Company reported $250,000 in net income from its operations.

Required:

A. Prepare in general journal form the workpaper entries necessary because of the intercompany sales in:

(1) The consolidated financial statements workpaper for the year ended December 31, 2011.

(2) The consolidated financial statements workpaper for the year ended December 31, 2012.

B. Calculate controlling interest in consolidated net income for the year ended December 31, 2011.

EXERCISE 7-12 **Workpaper Entries—Sale of Equipment** LO6

Pomeroy Corporation owns an 80% interest in Sherer Company and a 90% interest in Tampa Company. On January 2, 2011, Tampa Company sold equipment with a book value of $600,000 to Sherer Company for $780,000. This equipment has a remaining useful life of three years. Sherer Company reported $100,000 and Tampa Company reported $150,000 in net income (including sales to affiliates) in 2011.

Required:

Prepare the 2011 and 2012 consolidated statements workpaper entries to eliminate the effects of this sale of equipment.

PROBLEMS

PROBLEM 7-1 **Workpaper Journal Entries and Income Statement Balances** LO6 LO7 LO8

Powell Company owns 80% of the outstanding common stock of Sullivan Company. On June 30, 2011, Sullivan Company sold equipment to Powell Company for $500,000. The equipment cost Sullivan Company $780,000 and had accumulated depreciation of $400,000 on the date of the sale. The management of Powell Company estimated that the equipment had a remaining useful life of four years from June 30, 2011. In 2012, Powell Company reported $300,000 and Sullivan Company reported $200,000 in net income from their independent operations (including sales to affiliates but excluding dividend or equity income from subsidiary).

Required:

A. Prepare in general journal form the workpaper entries necessary because of the intercompany sale of equipment in:

(1) The consolidated financial statements workpaper for the year ended December 31, 2011.

(2) The consolidated financial statements workpaper for the year ended December 31, 2012.

B. Calculate the balances to be reported in the consolidated income statement for the year ended December 31, 2012, for the following items:

(1) Consolidated income.

(2) Noncontrolling interest in consolidated income.

(3) Controlling interest in consolidated income.

PROBLEM 7-2 **Workpaper Journal Entries** LO6 LO8

Pico Company, a truck manufacturer, owns 90% of the voting stock of Seward Company. On January 1, 2011, Pico Company sold trucks to Seward Company for $350,000. The trucks, which represented inventory to Pico Company, had a cost to Pico Company of $260,000. The management of Seward Company estimated that the trucks had a useful life of six years from the date of purchase. Seward Company uses the straight-line method to depreciate its capital assets.

In 2011, Pico Company reported $600,000 in net income from its independent operations (including sales to affiliates but excluding dividend or equity income from subsidiary), and Seward Company reported $200,000 in net income from its operations.

Required:

A. Prepare in general journal form the workpaper entries necessary because of the intercompany sales in:

(1) The consolidated financial statements workpaper for the year ended December 31, 2011.

(2) The consolidated financial statements workpaper for the year ended December 31, 2012.

B. Calculate controlling interest in consolidated net income for the year ended December 31, 2011.

PROBLEM 7-3 **P Company Entries and Determining Gain or Loss on Sale** LO6 LO9

On January 1, 2011, P Company purchased equipment from its 80% owned subsidiary for $600,000. The carrying value of the equipment on the books of S Company was $450,000. The equipment had a remaining useful life of six years on January 1, 2011. On January 1, 2012, P Company sold the equipment to an outside party for $550,000.

Required:

A. Prepare in general journal form the entries necessary in 2011 and 2012 on the books of P Company to account for the purchase and sale of the equipment.

B. Determine the consolidated gain or loss on the sale of the equipment and prepare in general journal form the entry necessary on the December 31, 2012, consolidated statements workpaper to properly reflect this gain or loss.

PROBLEM 7-4

Workpaper—Cost Method LO6 LO9

Prout Company owns 80% of the common stock of Sexton Company. The stock was purchased for $1,600,000 on January 1, 2009, when Sexton Company's retained earnings were $800,000. On January 1, 2011, Prout Company sold fixed assets to Sexton Company for $360,000. These assets were originally purchased by Prout Company for $400,000 on January 1, 2001, at which time their estimated depreciable life was 25 years. The straight-line method of depreciation is used.

On December 31, 2012, the trial balances of the two companies were as shown here:

	Prout Company	*Sexton Company*
Current Assets	$ 568,000	$ 271,000
Fixed Assets	1,972,000	830,000
Other Assets	1,000,800	1,600,000
Investment in Sexton Company	1,600,000	
Dividends Declared	120,000	100,000
Cost of Goods Sold	942,000	795,000
Other Expenses (including depreciation)	145,000	90,000
Income Tax Expense	187,200	90,000
Total	$6,535,000	$3,776,000
Liabilities	$ 305,000	$ 136,000
Accumulated Depreciation	375,000	290,000
Sales	1,475,000	1,110,000
Dividend Income	80,000	
Common Stock	3,000,000	1,200,000
Retained Earnings 1/1	1,300,000	1,040,000
Total	$6,535,000	$3,776,000

Required:

A. Prepare a consolidated statements workpaper for the year ended December 31, 2012.

B. Assuming that on January 1, 2013, Sexton Company sells the fixed assets purchased from Prout Company to a party outside the affiliated group for $300,000:

(1) Prepare the entry that would have been entered on the books of Sexton Company to record the sale.

(2) Prepare entries for the December 31, 2013, consolidated statements workpaper necessitated by the sale of the assets.

(3) Prepare any workpaper entries that will be needed in the December 31, 2014, consolidated statements workpaper in regard to these fixed assets.

PROBLEM 7-5

Trial Balance Workpaper—Cost Method LO6 LO9

Using the information presented in Problem 7-4, prepare a consolidated financial statements workpaper for the year ended December 31, 2012, using the trial balance format.

PROBLEM 7-6

Workpaper—Cost Method LO6 LO8

Pitts Company owns 80% of the common stock of Shannon Company. The stock was purchased for $960,000 on January 1, 2009, when Shannon Company's retained earnings were $675,000. On January 1, 2011, Shannon Company sold fixed assets to Pitts Company for $960,000; Shannon Company had purchased these assets for $1,350,000 on January 1, 2001, at which time their estimated useful life was 25 years. The estimated remaining useful life to Pitts Company on 1/1/11 is 10 years. Both companies employ the straight-line method of depreciation.

The financial data for 2012 are presented here:

	Pitts Company	Shannon Company
Sales	$1,950,000	$1,350,000
Dividend Income	60,000	
Total Revenue	2,010,000	1,350,000
Cost of Goods Sold	1,350,000	900,000
Other Expenses	225,000	150,000
Total Cost and Expense	1,575,000	1,050,000
Net Income	$ 435,000	$ 300,000
1/1 Retained Earnings	$1,215,000	$1,038,000
Net Income	435,000	300,000
Dividends Declared	(150,000)	(75,000)
12/31 Retained Earnings	$1,500,000	$1,263,000
Inventory	$ 498,000	$ 225,000
Investment in Shannon Company	960,000	
Fixed Assets	2,168,100	2,625,000
Accumulated Depreciation—Fixed Assets	(900,000)	(612,000)
Total Assets	$2,726,100	$2,238,000
Liabilities	$ 465,600	$ 450,000
Common Stock	760,500	525,000
Retained Earnings	1,500,000	1,263,000
Total Liabilities and Equity	$2,726,100	$2,238,000

Required:

A. Prepare a consolidated statements workpaper for the year ended December 31, 2012.

B. Calculate consolidated retained earnings on December 31, 2012, using an analytical or t-account approach.

PROBLEM 7-7 **Workpaper, Cost Method, Comprehensive Problem** LO6 LO8

Parsons Company acquired 90% of the outstanding common stock of Shea Company on June 30, 2011, for $426,000. On that date, Shea Company had retained earnings in the amount of $60,000, and the fair value of its recorded assets and liabilities was equal to their book value. The excess of implied over the fair value of the recorded net assets was attributed to an unrecorded manufacturing formula held by Shea Company, which had an expected remaining useful life of five years from June 30, 2011.

COMPREHENSIVE

Financial data for 2013 are presented here:

	Parsons Company	Shea Company
Sales	$2,555,500	$1,120,000
Dividend Income	54,000	
Total Revenue	2,609,500	1,120,000
Cost of Goods Sold	1,730,000	690,500
Expenses	654,500	251,000
Total Cost and Expense	2,384,500	941,500
Net Income	$ 225,000	$ 178,500
1/1 Retained Earnings	$ 595,000	$ 139,500
Net Income	225,000	178,500
Dividends Declared	(100,000)	(60,000)
12/31 Retained Earnings	$ 720,000	$ 258,000
Cash	$ 119,500	$ 132,500
Accounts Receivable	342,000	125,000
Inventory	362,000	201,000
Other Current Assets	40,500	13,000
Land	150,000	
Investment in Shea Company	426,000	
Property and Equipment	825,000	241,000
Accumulated Depreciation	(207,000)	(53,500)
Total Assets	$2,058,000	$ 659,000

Accounts Payable	$ 295,000	$ 32,000
Other Liabilities	43,000	19,000
Capital Stock	1,000,000	300,000
Additional Paid-in Capital		50,000
Retained Earnings	720,000	258,000
Total Liabilities and Equity	$2,058,000	$ 659,000

On December 31, 2011, Parsons Company sold equipment (with an original cost of $100,000 and accumulated depreciation of $50,000) to Shea Company for $97,500. This equipment has since been depreciated at an annual rate of 20% of the purchase price. During 2012 Shea Company sold land to Parsons Company at a profit of $15,000.

The inventory of Parsons Company on December 31, 2012, included goods purchased from Shea Company on which Shea Company recognized a profit of $7,500. During 2013, Shea Company sold goods to Parsons Company for $375,000, of which $60,000 was unpaid on December 31, 2013. The December 31, 2013, inventory of Parsons Company included goods acquired from Shea Company on which Shea Company recognized a profit of $10,500.

Required:

A. Prepare a consolidated financial statements workpaper for the year ended December 31, 2013.

B. Prepare a schedule to calculate consolidated retained earnings on December 31, 2013, using an analytical or t-account approach. (Hint: Due to rounding, you may be out of balance by $1. To avoid this, you should carry decimals until the final calculation.)

PROBLEM 7-8

Workpaper—Cost Method, Comprehensive Problem LO6

On January 1, 2010, Phelps Company purchased an 85% interest in Sloane Company for $955,000 when the retained earnings of Sloane Company were $150,000. The difference between implied and book value was assigned as follows:

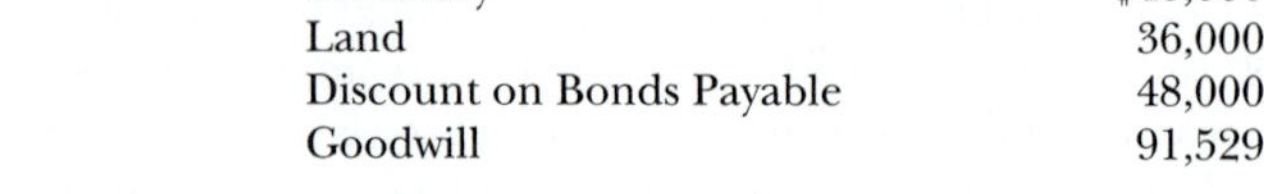

Inventory	$48,000
Land	36,000
Discount on Bonds Payable	48,000
Goodwill	91,529

COMPREHENSIVE

One-half of the inventory was sold in 2010 and the remaining inventory was sold in 2011. The bonds mature in eight years.

On December 31, 2010, Phelps Company's inventory contained $10,000 in unrealized intercompany profit. During 2011 Phelps Company sold merchandise with a cost of $200,000 to Sloane Company at a 30% markup on cost. Only $65,000 (selling price) of this merchandise remains in Sloane Company's 2011 ending inventory. As of December 31, 2011, Sloane Company owes Phelps Company $40,000 for merchandise purchased during 2011.

Equipment with a book value of $500,000 was sold by Sloane Company on January 2, 2011, to Phelps Company for $640,000. This equipment had an estimated useful life when purchased by Sloane Company on July 1, 2008, of 10 years.

Financial data for 2011 are presented here:

	Phelps Company	*Sloane Company*
Sales	$1,291,500	$ 560,000
Other Income		140,000
Dividend Income	42,500	
Total Revenue	1,334,000	700,000
Cost of Goods Sold	660,000	300,000
Depreciation Expense	138,000	20,000
Interest Expense	8,000	10,000
Other Expenses	174,000	140,000
Total Cost and Expense	980,000	470,000
Net Income	$ 354,000	$ 230,000

1/1 Retained Earnings	$ 350,500	$ 250,000
Net Income	354,000	230,000
Dividends Declared	(100,000)	(50,000)
12/31 Retained Earnings	$ 604,500	$ 430,000
Cash	$ 127,000	$ 70,000
Accounts Receivable	300,000	210,000
Inventory	270,000	175,000
Investment in Sloane Company	955,000	
Land	100,000	290,000
Plant and Equipment	800,000	800,000
Accumulated Depreciation	(200,000)	(200,000)
Total Assets	$ 2,352,000	$ 1,345,000
Accounts Payable	$ 167,500	$ 65,000
Bonds Payable	80,000	100,000
Capital Stock	1,500,000	750,000
Retained Earnings	604,500	430,000
Total Liabilities and Equity	$ 2,352,000	$ 1,345,000

Required:

Prepare a consolidated financial statements workpaper for the year ended December 31, 2011.

PROBLEM 7-9 **Workpaper with Intercompany Sales of Inventory and Land, Cost Method** LO6

Pierce Company acquired a 90% interest in Sanders Company on January 1, 2011, for $1,480,000. At this time, Sanders Company's common stock and retained earnings balances were $1,000,000 and $500,000, respectively. An examination of the books of Sanders on the date of purchase revealed the following:

	Book Value	*Fair Value*
Current Assets	$300,000	$300,000
Marketable Securities	200,000	200,000
Inventory	175,000	225,000
Plant and Equipment (net)	650,000	800,000
Land	500,000	600,000

COMPREHENSIVE

Sanders Company's equipment has a remaining life of 10 years. Eighty percent of the inventory was sold in 2011, the remainder in 2012.

During 2011, Pierce Company sold merchandise costing $400,000 to Sanders at a 25% markup on cost, and Sanders sold merchandise to Pierce Company for $100,000 (this price included $25,000 in profit). In 2012, Pierce Company sold merchandise to Sanders Company for $350,000, while Sanders Company sold merchandise to Pierce Company for $80,000. The 2011 markup percentages were also used on the 2012 sales.

The selling price of intercompany merchandise remaining in ending inventories for both years is summarized here:

Merchandise from Intercompany Sales in Ending Inventory of	*2011*	*2012*
Pierce Company	$40,000	$20,000
Sanders Company	50,000	30,000

In 2012, Sanders Company also sold a piece of land that had a book value of $250,000 to Pierce Company for $300,000. On December 31, 2012, Pierce Company holds a $60,000 receivable on the merchandise it sold to Sanders Company.

Adjusted trial balances for the year ended December 31, 2012 are shown here:

	Pierce	*Sanders*
Cash	$ 200,000	$ 150,000
Accounts Receivable	300,000	250,000
Marketable Securities	100,000	200,000
Inventory 12/31	300,000	250,000
Investment in Sanders Company	1,480,000	
Land	400,000	350,000
Plant and Equipment (net)	1,000,000	800,000
Cost of Goods Sold	600,000	400,000
Depreciation Expense	60,000	40,000
Other Expenses	400,000	260,000
Dividends Declared	120,000	70,000
Total	$4,960,000	$2,770,000
Accounts Payable	$ 241,000	$ 140,000
Notes Payable	350,000	100,000
Common Stock	1,900,000	1,000,000
1/1 Retained Earnings	706,000	580,000
Sales	1,700,000	900,000
Gain on Sale of Land		50,000
Dividend Income	63,000	
Total	$4,960,000	$2,770,000

Required:

Prepare a consolidated statements workpaper for the year ended December 31, 2012.

PROBLEM 7-10 **Workpaper—Partial Equity Method** LO6 LO9

(*Note*: This is the same Problem as Problem 7-4, but assuming the use of the partial equity method.)

Prout Company owns 80% of the common stock of Sexton Company. The stock was purchased for $1,600,000 on January 1, 2009, when Sexton Company's retained earnings were $800,000. On January 1, 2011, Prout Company sold fixed assets to Sexton Company for $360,000. These assets were originally purchased by Prout Company for $400,000 on January 1, 2001, at which time their estimated depreciable life was 25 years. The straight-line method of depreciation is used.

On December 31, 2012, the trial balances of the two companies were as shown here:

	Prout Company	*Sexton Company*
Current Assets	$ 568,000	$ 271,000
Fixed Assets	1,972,000	830,000
Other Assets	1,000,800	1,600,000
Investment in Sexton Company	1,820,000	
Dividends Declared	120,000	100,000
Cost of Goods Sold	942,000	795,000
Other Expenses (including depreciation)	145,000	90,000
Income Tax Expense	187,200	90,000
Total	$6,755,000	$3,776,000
Liabilities	$ 305,000	$ 136,000
Accumulated Depreciation	375,000	290,000
Sales	1,475,000	1,110,000
Equity in Subsidiary Income	108,000	
Common Stock	3,000,000	1,200,000
Retained Earnings 1/1	1,492,000	1,040,000
Total	$6,755,000	$3,776,000

Required:

A. Prepare a consolidated statements workpaper for the year ended December 31, 2012.

B. Assuming that on January 1, 2013, Sexton Company sells the fixed assets purchased from Prout Company to a party outside the affiliated group for $300,000:

(1) Prepare the entry that would have been entered on the books of Sexton Company to record the sale.

(2) Prepare entries for the December 31, 2013, consolidated statements workpaper necessitated by the sale of the assets.

(3) Prepare any workpaper entries that will be needed in the December 31, 2014, consolidated statements workpaper in regard to these fixed assets.

PROBLEM 7-11 **Trial Balance format—Workpaper—Partial Equity Method** LO6 LO9

Using the information presented in Problem 7-10 prepare a consolidated financial statements workpaper for the year ended December 31, 2012, using the trial balance format.

PROBLEM 7-12 **Workpaper—Partial Equity Method** LO6 LO8

Prather Company owns 80% of the common stock of Stone Company. The stock was purchased for $960,000 on January 1, 2009, when Stone Company's retained earnings were $675,000. On January 1, 2011, Stone Company sold fixed assets to Prather Company for $960,000; Stone Company had purchased these assets for $1,350,000 on January 1, 2001, at which time their estimated useful life was 25 years. The estimated remaining useful life to Prather Company on 1/1/11 is 10 years. Both companies employ the straight-line method of depreciation.

The financial data for 2012 are presented here:

	Prather Company	*Stone Company*
Sales	$1,950,000	$1,350,000
Equity in Subsidiary Income	240,000	
Total Revenue	2,190,000	1,350,000
Cost of Goods Sold	1,350,000	900,000
Other Expenses	225,000	150,000
Total Cost and Expense	1,575,000	1,050,000
Net Income	$ 615,000	$ 300,000
1/1 Retained Earnings	$1,505,400	$1,038,000
Net Income	615,000	300,000
Dividends Declared	(150,000)	(75,000)
12/31 Retained Earnings	$1,970,400	$1,263,000
Inventory	$ 498,000	$ 225,000
Investment in Stone Company	1,430,400	
Fixed Assets	2,168,100	2,625,000
Accumulated Depreciation—Fixed Assets	(900,000)	(612,000)
Total Assets	$3,196,500	$2,238,000
Liabilities	$ 465,600	$ 450,000
Common Stock	760,500	525,000
Retained Earnings	1,970,400	1,263,000
Total Liabilities and Equity	$3,196,500	$2,238,000

Required:

A. Prepare a consolidated statements workpaper for the year ended December 31, 2012.

B. Calculate consolidated retained earnings on December 31, 2012, using an analytical or t-account approach.

PROBLEM 7-13 **Workpaper—Partial Equity Method, Comprehensive Problem** LO6 LO8

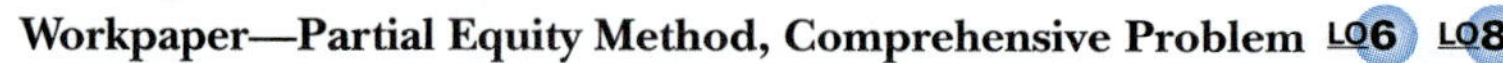

COMPREHENSIVE

Padilla Company acquired 90% of the outstanding common stock of Sanchez Company on June 30, 2011, for $426,000. On that date, Sanchez Company had retained earnings in the amount of $60,000, and the fair value of its recorded assets and liabilities was equal to their book value. The excess of implied over fair value of the recorded net assets was attributed to an unrecorded manufacturing formula held by Sanchez Company, which had an expected remaining useful life of five years from June 30, 2011.

Financial data for 2013 are presented here:

	Padilla Company	*Sanchez Company*
Sales	$2,555,500	$1,120,000
Equity in Subsidiary Income	160,650	
Total Revenue	2,716,150	1,120,000
Cost of Goods Sold	1,730,000	690,500
Expenses	654,500	251,000
Total Cost and Expense	2,384,500	941,500
Net Income	$ 331,650	$ 178,500
1/1 Retained Earnings	666,550	139,500
Net Income	331,650	178,500
Dividends Declared	(100,000)	(60,000)
12/31 Retained Earnings	$ 898,200	$ 258,000
Cash	$ 119,500	$ 132,500
Accounts Receivable	342,000	125,000
Inventory	362,000	201,000
Other Current Assets	40,500	13,000
Land	150,000	
Investment in Sanchez Company	604,200	
Property and Equipment	825,000	241,000
Accumulated Depreciation	(207,000)	(53,500)
Total Assets	$2,236,200	$ 659,000
Accounts Payable	$ 295,000	$ 32,000
Other Liabilities	43,000	19,000
Capital Stock	1,000,000	300,000
Additional Paid-in Capital		50,000
Retained Earnings	898,200	258,000
Total Liabilities and Equity	$2,236,200	$ 659,000

On December 31, 2011, Padilla Company sold equipment (with an original cost of $100,000 and accumulated depreciation of $50,000) to Sanchez Company for $97,500. This equipment had been depreciated at an annual rate of 20% of the purchase price. During 2012, Sanchez Company sold land to Padilla Company at a profit of $15,000.

The inventory of Padilla Company on December 31, 2012, included goods purchased from Sanchez Company on which Sanchez Company recognized a profit of $7,500. During 2013, Sanchez Company sold goods to Padilla Company for $375,000, of which $60,000 was unpaid on December 31, 2013. The December 31, 2013, inventory of Padilla Company included goods acquired from Sanchez Company on which Sanchez Company recognized a profit of $10,500.

Required:

A. Prepare a consolidated financial statements workpaper for the year ended December 31, 2013.

B. Prepare a schedule to calculate consolidated retained earnings on December 31, 2013, using an analytical or t-account approach.

PROBLEM 7-14 **Entries and Computation of Income and Retained Earnings** LO6 LO7 LO8

Platt Company acquired an 80% interest in Sloane Company when the retained earnings of Sloane Company were $300,000. On January 1, 2011, Sloane Company recorded a $250,000 gain on the sale to Platt Company of equipment with a remaining life of five years. On January 1, 2012, Platt Company recorded a $180,000 gain on the sale to Sloane Company of equipment with a remaining life of six years. Sloane Company reported net income of $180,000 and declared dividends of 60,000 in 2012. It reported retained earnings of $520,000 on January 1, 2012, and $640,000 on December 31, 2012. Platt Company reported net income from independent operations of $400,000 in 2012 and retained earnings of $1,800,000 on December 31, 2012.

Required:

A. Prepare in general journal form the entries necessary in the December 31, 2012, consolidated statements workpaper to eliminate the effects of the intercompany sales.

B. Calculate controlling interest in consolidated net income for the year ended December 31, 2012.

C. Calculate consolidated retained earnings on December 31, 2012.

D. Calculate noncontrolling interest in consolidated income for the year ended December 31, 2012.

PROBLEM 7-15 **Workpaper—Complete Equity Method** LO6 LO9

(*Note*: This is the same Problem as Problems 7-4 and 7-10, but assuming the use of the complete equity method.)

Prout Company owns 80% of the common stock of Sexton Company. The stock was purchased for $1,600,000 on January 1, 2009, when Sexton Company's retained earnings were $800,000. On January 1, 2011, Prout Company sold fixed assets to Sexton Company for $360,000. These assets were originally purchased by Prout Company for $400,000 on January 1, 2001, at which time their estimated depreciable life was 25 years. The straight-line method of depreciation is used.

On December 31, 2012, the trial balances of the two companies were as shown here:

	Prout Company	*Sexton Company*
Current Assets	$ 568,000	$ 271,000
Fixed Assets	1,972,000	830,000
Other Assets	1,000,800	1,600,000
Investment in Sexton Company	1,716,000	
Dividends Declared	120,000	100,000
Cost of Goods Sold	942,000	795,000
Other Expenses (including depreciation)	145,000	90,000
Income Tax Expense	187,200	90,000
Total	$6,651,000	$3,776,000
Liabilities	$ 305,000	$ 136,000
Accumulated Depreciation	375,000	290,000
Sales	1,475,000	1,110,000
Equity in Subsidiary Income	116,000	
Common Stock	3,000,000	1,200,000
Retained Earnings 1/1	1,380,000	1,040,000
Total	$6,651,000	$3,776,000

Required:

A. Prepare a consolidated statements workpaper for the year ended December 31, 2012.

B. Assuming that on January 1, 2013, Sexton Company sells the fixed assets purchased from Prout Company to a party outside the affiliated group for $300,000:

(1) Prepare the entry that would have been entered on the books of Sexton Company to record the sale.

(2) Prepare entries for the December 31, 2013, consolidated statements workpaper necessitated by the sale of the assets.

(3) Prepare any workpaper entries that will be needed in the December 31, 2014, consolidated statements workpaper in regard to these fixed assets.

C. If you completed Problem 7-4, compare the consolidated balance obtained in requirement A to those obtained in Problem 7-4.

PROBLEM 7-16 **Workpaper—Complete Equity Method** LO6 LO8

Prather Company owns 80% of the common stock of Stone Company. The stock was purchased for $960,000 on January 1, 2009, when Stone Company's retained earnings were $675,000. On January 1, 2011, Stone Company sold fixed assets to Prather Company for $960,000; Stone Company had purchased these assets for $1,350,000 on January 1, 2001, at which time their estimated useful life was 25 years. The estimated remaining useful life to Prather Company on 1/1/11 is 10 years. Both companies employ the straight-line method of depreciation.

The financial data for 2012 are presented here:

	Prather Company	*Stone Company*
Sales	$1,950,000	$1,350,000
Equity in Subsidiary Income	252,000	
Total Revenue	2,202,000	1,350,000
Cost of Goods Sold	1,350,000	900,000
Other Expenses	225,000	150,000
Total Cost and Expense	1,575,000	1,050,000
Net Income	$ 627,000	$ 300,000
1/1 Retained Earnings	$1,397,400	$1,038,000
Net Income	627,000	300,000
Dividends Declared	(150,000)	(75,000)
12/31 Retained Earnings	$1,874,400	$1,263,000
Inventory	$ 498,000	$ 225,000
Investment in Stone Company	1,334,400	
Fixed Assets	2,168,100	2,625,000
Accumulated Depreciation—Fixed Assets	(900,000)	(612,000)
Total Assets	$3,100,500	$2,238,000
Liabilities	$ 465,600	$ 450,000
Common Stock	760,500	525,000
Retained Earnings	1,874,400	1,263,000
Total Liabilities and Equity	$3,100,500	$2,238,000

Required:

A. Prepare a consolidated statements workpaper for the year ended December 31, 2012.

B. Calculate consolidated retained earnings on December 31, 2012, using a t-account or analytical approach.

PROBLEM 7-17 **Workpaper—Complete Equity Method, Comprehensive Problem** LO6 LO8

COMPREHENSIVE

Padilla Company acquired 90% of the outstanding common stock of Sanchez Company on June 30, 2011, for $426,000. On that date, Sanchez Company had retained earnings in the amount of $60,000, and the fair value of its recorded assets and liabilities was equal to their book value. The excess of implied over fair value of the recorded net assets was attributed to an unrecorded manufacturing formula held by Sanchez Company, which had an expected remaining useful life of five years from June 30, 2011.

Financial data for 2013 are presented here:

	Padilla Company	*Sanchez Company*
Sales	$2,555,500	$1,120,000
Equity in Subsidiary Income	156,050	
Total Revenue	2,711,550	1,120,000
Cost of Goods Sold	1,730,000	690,500
Expenses	654,500	251,000
Total Cost and Expense	2,384,500	941,500
Net Income	$ 327,050	$ 178,500

	Padilla Company	Sanchez Company
1/1 Retained Earnings	591,200	139,500
Net Income	327,050	178,500
Dividends Declared	(100,000)	(60,000)
12/31 Retained Earnings	$ 818,250	$ 258,000
Cash	$ 119,500	$ 132,500
Accounts Receivable	342,000	125,000
Inventory	362,000	201,000
Other Current Assets	40,500	13,000
Land	150,000	
Investment in Sanchez Company	524,250	
Property and Equipment	825,000	241,000
Accumulated Depreciation	(207,000)	(53,500)
Total Assets	$2,156,250	$ 659,000
Accounts Payable	$ 295,000	$ 32,000
Other Liabilities	43,000	19,000
Capital Stock	1,000,000	300,000
Additional Paid-in Capital		50,000
Retained Earnings	818,250	258,000
Total Liabilities and Equity	$2,156,250	$ 659,000

On December 31, 2011, Padilla Company sold equipment (with an original cost of $100,000 and accumulated depreciation of $50,000) to Sanchez Company for $97,500. This equipment has since been depreciated at an annual rate of 20% of the purchase price. During 2012, Sanchez Company sold land to Padilla Company at a profit of $15,000.

The inventory of Padilla Company on December 31, 2012, included goods purchased from Sanchez Company on which Sanchez Company recognized a profit of $7,500. During 2013, Sanchez Company sold goods to Padilla Company for $375,000, of which $60,000 was unpaid on December 31, 2013. The December 31, 2013, inventory of Padilla Company included goods acquired from Sanchez Company on which Sanchez Company recognized a profit of $10,500.

Required:

A. Prepare a consolidated financial statements workpaper for the year ended December 31, 2013.

B. Prepare a schedule to calculate consolidated retained earnings on December 31, 2013, using a t-account or analytical approach.

PROBLEM 7-18A Deferred Tax Consequences of Intercompany Inventory and Equipment

Peer Company acquired an 80% interest in Sells Company on January 1, 2011, for $1,600,000. On this date, the common stock and retained earnings balances were $1,500,000 and $500,000, respectively. During the year, Peer Company sold merchandise to Sells Company for $200,000. Only one-fourth of this merchandise was in Sells Company's 2011 ending inventory, and $10,000 of this amount is unrealized profit.

On January 2, 2011, Sells Company sold equipment with a book value of $300,000 to Peer Company for $400,000. The equipment has a remaining useful life of four years. Sells Company's net income for 2011 was $300,000, while Peer Company's was $800,000. Neither company declared dividends in 2011. The affiliated companies file separate income tax returns, the dividends received exclusion is 80%, and the prior, current, and expected future marginal income tax rates for both companies are 40%.

Required:

A. Prepare in general journal form all consolidated statements workpaper entries necessary for 2011.

B. Calculate the controlling interest in consolidated net income for the year ended December 31, 2011.

C. Calculate the noncontrolling interest in consolidated income for the year ended December 31, 2011.

8

CHANGES IN OWNERSHIP INTEREST

LEARNING OBJECTIVES

1 Identify the types of transactions that change the parent company's ownership interest in a subsidiary.

2 Describe the process needed when the parent acquires subsidiary shares through multiple open market purchases.

3 Explain how the parent reports the difference between selling price and book value when shares are sold subsequent to acquisition.

4 Compute the controlling interest in income after the parent sells some shares of the subsidiary company.

5 Describe the effect on the eliminating process when the subsidiary issues new shares entirely to the parent, and the parent pays either more or less than the book value of the subsidiary shares.

6 Describe the impact on the parent's investment account when the subsidiary issues new shares and either the new shares are purchased ratably by the parent and noncontrolling shareholders or entirely by the noncontrolling shareholders.

The U.S. Federal Communications Commission will review a rule that bans companies from owning a television station or a radio station in the same market as a newspaper. In addition, the FCC is considering allowing companies to own two of the top four television stations in the same market. If allowed, these changes are expected to increase consolidation in the market.[1]

Two assumptions regarding the equity interest acquired have been followed in previous chapters dealing with consolidated financial statements. Although not expressly stated, those assumptions were:

1. The interest in the subsidiary was obtained through a single open-market transaction.
2. The percentage of ownership remained constant.

[1] Reuters, "FCC Launches Battle over Media Ownership Limits," 6/21/06.

LO 1 Changes in ownership and differences between current and proposed GAAP.

These assumptions are not always valid. For example, control of a purchased subsidiary might not be obtained until two or more stock purchases have been made. Similarly, the percentage of ownership may change for several reasons, such as (1) additional shares of the subsidiary may be purchased on the open market; (2) some of the shares held by the parent company may be sold; (3) the subsidiary may engage in capital transactions with the parent company and/or outside parties that change the parent company's percentage of ownership. In this chapter, we focus on changes in the ownership interest with only two principal companies involved, one parent and one subsidiary.

A summary of transactions and the accounting treatment for each follows:

Topic	*Previous GAAP*	*GAAP (SFAS No. 141R and No. 160) [ASC 805 and 810]*	*Related Exercises and Problems*
		Parent Transactions with Third Parties	
Parent acquires in stages			
Control not achieved upon the first purchase.	Difference between cost and fair value measured in steps.	Revalue initial investment to fair value when control is achieved. Adjustment to Income Statement.	Exs. 8-1, 8-4 p 8-1, 8-7, 8-12, 8-13, 8-14, 8-15
Control achieved in the first purchase.	Same as above.	In the second purchase, adjustment to contributed capital of controlling interest.	Exs. 8-2, 8-3, 8-5 p 8-3, 8-4, 8-5, 8-6
Parent sells shares to third parties			
Completely.	Gain/loss on difference between selling price and book value.	Gain/loss on difference between selling price and book value (no change from prior GAAP).	
Loss of control, but maintains some ownership.	Gain/loss on difference between selling price and book value of shares sold.	The entire interest must be adjusted to fair value, and a gain or loss recorded on all shares owned prior to sale.	p 8-2, 8-11
Sold some shares, but maintains control.	Gain/loss recognized (same as above).	Adjustment to contributed capital of controlling interest, no gain or loss in Income Statement.	Exs. 8-2, 8-3, 8-5 p 8-3, 8-4, 8-5, 8-6, 8-7
		Subsidiary Transactions with and without the Parent	
Issues additional shares			
Parent's ownership decreases (no participation by the controlling interest).	Sale of investment with gain/loss to Income Statement.	Adjustment to contributed capital of controlling interest.	Ex. 8-8 p 8-9
Parent's ownership increases (no participation by the noncontrolling interest).	Compute and allocate difference between implied and book value of additional investment.	Assuming the Parent already has control, no new adjustments are made for changes in fair value. Otherwise, see above ("Parent acquires in stages").	Exs. 8-6, 8-7 p 8-8

Justification for these recommended accounting treatments is based on the concept of economic substance over form. That is, a parent company can effectively increase its ownership interest in a subsidiary by either (1) buying additional subsidiary shares directly from third parties or (2) having a subsidiary purchase its (subsidiary's) shares from third parties. Similarly, the parent can effectively decrease its ownership interest by either (1) selling some of its subsidiary shares directly to third parties or (2) having a subsidiary sell additional shares (including treasury shares) to third parties. Since the economic substance is essentially the same from the parent company's point of view, the transactions should be accounted for in a consistent manner. Accounting for these changes in the parent company's percentage of ownership is discussed and illustrated in this chapter.

RELATED CONCEPTS

The date when control is achieved is treated as the acquisition date because it reflects the point at which the two firms become one *economic entity*.

Recall that the recent changes by FASB, however, focus on the entity rather than on the parent's perspective. Thus, this is a significant change from previous standards. Under past GAAP, acquisitions of additional shares in an investee were handled in a step-by-step manner, with Computation and Allocation Schedules prepared for each portion purchased. Sales of shares were handled in much the same manner as any sale of an asset: the difference between the selling price and the basis of the shares sold is shown as a gain or loss in income. Shares retained are not adjusted. In contrast, current GAAP requires the following for acquisitions that take place in stages and for partial sales:

a. Measure and recognize the acquiree's identifiable assets and liabilities at 100% of their fair values on the date the acquirer obtains *control*, and

b. Recognize all the acquiree's goodwill (not just the parent's share), measured as the difference between the fair value of the acquiree on the acquisition date and the fair value of the identifiable net assets.

c. Any previously held noncontrolling equity interests should be remeasured to fair value, with the resulting adjustment recognized in income.

d. After control is achieved, subsequent adjustments due to increased ownership are shown as Additional Contributed Capital, not as income.

e. If a parent loses control, the retained investment should be remeasured to fair value and the adjustments recognized in net income.

PARENT ACQUIRES SUBSIDIARY STOCK THROUGH SEVERAL OPEN-MARKET PURCHASES—COST METHOD

COST

Sometimes the controlling interest in a subsidiary is acquired through the initial stock purchase; at other times control is not achieved until two or more stock purchases have been made. When control is achieved on the first purchase, the date of acquisition is the purchase date. However, when more than one purchase is made before control is obtained, the acquisition date is the date when control is achieved. Determination of the date of acquisition is important because previously purchased shares must be revalued and the gain or loss included in income. Under prior GAAP, the previously held interests were not revalued at the date of subsequent purchases. Under current GAAP, subsidiary retained earnings accumulated before control is achieved constitutes a portion of the equity acquired by the parent company, whereas the parent's share of subsidiary retained earnings accumulated after acquisition is properly included in consolidated retained earnings.

Under *SFAS No. 141R, Business Combinations* [ASC 805-10-25-9], the previously held noncontrolling equity interest should be remeasured to fair value *when control is achieved*, and the resulting adjustment should be recognized in net income. Similarly, if a parent loses control but retains a noncontrolling interest, the portion retained should be remeasured to fair value on the date control is surrendered and the adjustment reflected in the income statement.

The fair values of the acquirer's interest in the acquiree and the noncontrolling interest on a per-share basis might differ. The main difference is likely to be the inclusion of a control premium in the per-share fair value of the acquirer's interest in the acquiree or, conversely, the inclusion of a discount for lack of control (also referred to as a minority interest discount) in the per-share fair value of the noncontrolling interest. In this textbook, for practical considerations, we assume that the per-share fair value for pricing the controlling and noncontrolling shares are the same.

To illustrate the consolidation of an investment acquired in stages, assume that S Company had 10,000 shares of $10 par value common stock outstanding during 2007–2010 and retained earnings as follows:

	S Company Retained Earnings
January 1, 2007 (1st stock purchase)	$ 40,000
January 1, 2009(control achieved)	120,000
January 1, 2010	185,000
December 31, 2010	265,000

P Company purchased S Company common stock on the open market for cash as follows:

Date	*Shares Acquired*	*Cost*	*Cost/share*
January 1, 2007	1,500 (15% of 10,000 shares)	$ 24,000	$16/share
January 1, 2009	7,500 (75% of 10,000 shares)	187,500	$25/share
Total	9,000 (90% of 10,000 shares)	$211,500	

Thus on P's books, the following entries are made:

January 1, 2007		
Investment in S Company	24,000	
Cash		24,000
January 1, 2009		
Investment in S Company	187,500	
Cash		187,500

Some additional simplifying assumptions are made to concentrate attention on the new issues introduced and because the complexities avoided by the assumptions have been discussed in detail in previous chapters. The assumptions are:

1. Any difference between implied and book values of the purchases relates solely to goodwill and is, therefore, not subject to amortization or depreciation but is reviewed periodically for impairment.
2. S Company distributes no dividends during the periods under consideration.

The initial purchase of the 15% interest in S Company is recorded at its cost of $24,000 and reported as an investment on P Company's balance sheets on December 31, 2007 and 2008. No income on the investment is recognized for either 2007 or 2008 because no dividends were distributed by S Company. The second purchase on January 1, 2009, is also recorded in the investment account at its cost of

\$187,500. Again, no income is recognized on the investment during 2009 because S Company declared no dividends.

Since P Company now has controlling ownership of S Company, the investment must be consolidated. In the preparation of a consolidated workpaper on December 31, 2009, it is necessary to determine the amount of S Company equity to eliminate, as well as the difference between implied and book value. Note that P Company owns 90% of S Company after the second purchase, which constitutes control.

The payment by P Company of \$187,500 for 75% of S implies a total value at this date, which is the acquisition date, or \$250,000, \$188,000 divided by 75%. P now owns a total of 90% of S Company, or a total value of \$225,000, while the noncontrolling share is 10%, or \$25,000. The Computation and Allocation Schedule implied by this second purchase is as follows:

Computation and Allocation of Difference Schedule

	Parent Share	*Noncontrolling Share*	*Entire Value*
Value implied by purchase price	**\$225,000**	**25,000**	250,000
Less: Book value of equity acquired	198,000	22,000	**220,000**
Difference between implied and book value	27,000	3,000	**30,000**
Record goodwill	(27,000)	(3,000)	**(30,000)**
Balance	0	0	0

Cost Method

Because P Company has owned a percentage of S Company (15%) since January 1, 2007, an entry is needed on P's books to revalue the 1,500 shares purchased in 2009 to their fair value as of the date of control (January 1, 2009). Initially, these 1,500 shares were purchased for \$16 per share, but now the shares are worth \$25 per share (or a \$9 per share increase). Thus the investment in S must be increased to \$13,500 (or \$9 × 1,500 shares) for consolidation. Before this entry can be made, the carrying value of the initial investment (1,500 shares) must be determined. Recall that S Company retained earnings increased from \$40,000 on January 1, 2007, to \$120,000 on January 1, 2009. During that time, P Company owned 15% of S Company; thus, since the consolidation is being retroactively applied to cover this time period, this is equivalent to the entry for reciprocity in previous chapters. Therefore, the carrying value of the initial investment for consolidated purposes is computed as:

Initial purchase price (1,500 shares at \$16/share)	\$24,000
Change in retained earnings of S since acquisition × 15%:	
[.15 × (\$120,000 − \$40,000)]	12,000
Carrying value (implied) of initial investment	36,000

Thus the gain on revaluation of the initial shares is computed as:

Implied value (\$25/share × 1,500)	\$37,500
Implied carrying value of initial shares	36,000
Revaluation gain	1,500

Thus the following entry is made on P company books.

Investment in S Company	\$1,500	
Gain on revaluation		\$1,500

To adjust from the implied carrying value of \$36,000 to fair value of \$37,500 (or \$25/share × 1,500 shares).

Note that the implied carrying value of $36,000, as shown above and used in the calculation of the $1,500 gain does not match the actual carrying value on the books of the parent under the cost method. The reason for the difference is that the $12,000 change in retained earnings of S (on the 15% original purchase) is not applied retroactively to the investment in S and the retained earnings accounting of P (as it is under the equity method, illustrated subsequently). Thus, a workpaper entry is needed on December 31, 2009, to convert to equity (establish reciprocity) from 2007 to the beginning of 2009 if P Company uses the cost method to account for its investment in S. This entry must be repeated in every future worksheet.

Investment in S Company	12,000	
1/1 Retained Earnings—P Company		12,000
[.15 × ($120,000 − $40,000) change in retained earnings from 1/1/07 to 1/1/09].		

Note that the FASB standards are not explicit with respect to the recording on the books of the parent company in a situation like the one illustrated here. Instead the standards focus on the correct reporting for the consolidated entity. A case could be made for recording (as a gain on the books of P under the cost method) the entire difference between the implied value of $37,500 and the actual carrying value of $24,000, or $13,500. So long as the correct eliminating entries are made on the consolidating worksheet, this approach would not be inconsistent with GAAP. However, we believe the alternative of recording only the gain of $1,500 to be preferable for the following reason: Since the $12,000 is treated retroactively under the equity method, it never flows through the income statement of the parent. If we show it as a gain to the parent under the cost method, this introduces a permanent rather than temporary difference in the revenue reported by the parent company between the cost and equity methods. Thus, we believe the approach illustrated here to be the better alternative.

Workpaper Elimination Entries

On the workpaper, the investment is eliminated by the following entry (per CAD Schedule):

Common Stock—S Company	100,000	
1/1 Retained Earnings—S Company	120,000	
Difference between Implied and Book Value	30,000	
Investment in S Company ($187,500 + $37,500)		225,000
Noncontrolling Interest in Equity		25,000

The workpaper is then completed as illustrated in previous chapters.

If the cost method is used, in subsequent periods reciprocity (equity conversion) is established by taking 90% of the increase (decrease) in S Company's retained earnings from January 1, 2009, to the beginning of the current year, and then adding the $12,000 initial adjustment (from 1/1/07 to 1/1/09, at 15%). For example, for the preparation of a consolidated statements workpaper on December 31, 2010, reciprocity (equity conversion) would be established as follows:

Amount from the December 31, 2009, workpaper	$12,000
Add: Change in Retained Earnings	
[.90 × ($185,000 − $120,000)]	58,500
Total	$70,500

The reciprocity entry is not needed if P Company uses the equity method. The computation of the noncontrolling interest in consolidated net income is made by multiplying the *end-of-year* noncontrolling interest percentage times realized subsidiary income.

In the preceding example, the difference between implied and book values was assumed to relate to goodwill. If the differences were allocable to depreciable or amortizable assets (and liabilities), the difference would be assigned to the appropriate assets and/or liabilities as usual.

Comparison to IFRS

IFRS 3, *Business Combinations,* provides the guidance for step acquisitions under international standards. Under IFRS 3, all previous ownership interests are adjusted to fair value, with any gain or loss recorded in earnings. This is similar to the rules issued by the FASB.

PARENT SELLS SUBSIDIARY STOCK INVESTMENT ON THE OPEN MARKET—COST METHOD

Control Maintained

COST

Under *SFAS No. 160* [**ASC 810–10–45–22, 24**] the treatment of the sale of a portion (but not all) of its investment by a parent company depends on whether or not the sale results in the loss of effective control of the subsidiary. If control is maintained, no gain or loss is recognized in the income statement. Instead, an adjustment is made to additional contributed capital of the controlling interest. However, if control is lost, the entire interest is adjusted to fair value, and a gain or loss recorded in income on all shares owned prior to sale. This treatment is discussed in the next section. It should be noted that under past GAAP, the treatment of the sale of a portion of an investment by the parent company was the same, regardless of whether or not control was surrendered.

The following illustration is based on current GAAP.

Recall the information from the previous example. P Company owns 9,000 shares of S Company that were revalued to $25 a share on the date of acquisition, or $225,000. Assume that P Company sold 1,800 shares of the 9,000 shares of S Company stock on July 1, 2010, for $84,600 ($47/share). The cost of the 1,800 shares sold equals $45,000 (or 20% of $225,000). The percentage of P Company shares sold is calculated by dividing the shares sold by the total owned by P (1,800/9,000 = 20%). After the sale, P Company retains control with a 72% ((9,000 × 80%)/10,000) interest. It should be noted that the 1,800 shares sold represent 18% of total S Company shares.

To record the sale of the shares, P Company makes the following entry in its books on July 1, 2010.

P Company's Books		
Cash	84,600	
Investment in S Company (20% × $225,000)		45,000
Additional Contributed Capital—P Company		39,600

After this entry, the balance in the investment in S Company account on P Company books will be $168,000 (or $24,000 + $187,500 + $1,500 − $45,000).

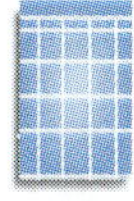

COST

From a consolidated standpoint, the cost of the shares sold ($45,000) needs to be adjusted for 18% of the undistributed earnings since the date of acquisition. This is computed as follows:

Cost of Shares (1,800 × $25/share)		$45,000
Plus: Undistributed Income:		
(A) Change in Retained Earnings from the date of acquisition (1/1/09) to the beginning of the year (1/1/10)		
($185,000 − $120,000)	$65,000	
Ownership percentage sold	18%	11,700
(B) Earnings from beginning of current year to the date of sale (1/1/10 to 7/1/10)		
($80,000/2)	40,000	
Ownership percentage sold	18%	7,200
Adjusted cost of shares sold		$63,900

Therefore, the correct consolidated amount of additional contributed capital on the sale is $20,700, computed by subtracting the adjusted cost of $63,900 from the selling price of $84,600, or:

Selling price of shares (1,800 × $47/share)	$84,600
Adjusted cost of shares sold	63,900
Additional paid in capital—P Company	$20,700

Since additional contributed capital of $39,600 is already recorded on the parent's books (see entry above), an adjustment is needed on the workpapers to reduce it to $20,700. The adjustments, totaling $18,900, needed on the consolidated workpaper are as follows (these amounts are already computed above, 11,700 + 7,200 = 18,900):

(1) Additional Contributed Capital—P Company	11,700	
1/1 Retained Earnings—P Company (Consolidated Retained Earnings)		11,700
(2) Additional Contributed Capital—P Company	7,200	
Subsidiary Income Sold		7,200

The first entry represents undistributed income to the beginning of the year of sale on the shares sold accruing to the 18% of shares sold [($185,000 − $120,000) × 18%]. This amount reduces the additional contributed capital and increases retained earnings for the prior year's unrecorded earnings in P's retained earnings.

The second entry adjusts for the subsidiary income earned during the first six months of 2010 that was sold to the noncontrolling stockholders. From January 1, 2010, to July 1, 2010, S Company earned $40,000. Because 18% of Company S is sold, $7,200 (18% × $40,000) represents net income purchased by the noncontrolling stockholders. The $7,200 should be excluded from noncontrolling interest in consolidated income, since it was purchased by the noncontrolling stockholders rather than being earned by them.

COST

A workpaper for the preparation of consolidated financial statements on December 31, 2010, is presented in Illustration 8-1. Data necessary to complete the workpaper, other than those previously provided, are assumed. Workpaper entries, in addition to those made to adjust the additional contributed capital, are:

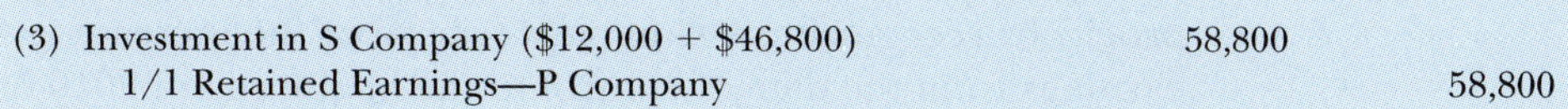

(3) Investment in S Company ($12,000 + $46,800)	58,800	
1/1 Retained Earnings—P Company		58,800

Cost Method

Sale of Part of Investment

72% Owned Subsidiary

ILLUSTRATION 8-1
Consolidated Statements Workpaper
P Company and Subsidiary
for the Year Ended December 31, 2010

	P Company	S Company	Eliminations Dr.	Eliminations Cr.	Noncontrolling Interest	Consolidated Balances
Income Statement						
Net Income Before Gain on Sale of Investment	120,000	80,000				200,000
Net/Consolidated Income	120,000	80,000				200,000
Subsidiary Income Sold				(2) 7,200		7,200
Noncontrolling Interest in Income .28($80,000)					22,400	(22,400)
Net Income to Retained Earnings	120,000	80,000	—	7,200	22,400	184,800
Retained Earnings Statement						
1/1 Retained Earnings						
P Company	283,500			(1) 11,700 (3) 58,800		354,000
S Company		185,000	(4) 185,000			
Net Income from above	120,000	80,000	—	7,200	22,400	184,800
Dividends Declared 10/30						
P Company	(40,000)					(40,000)
12/31 Retained Earnings to Balance Sheet	363,500	265,000	185,000	77,700	22,400	498,800
Balance Sheet						
Current Assets	235,100	100,000				335,100
Investment in S Company	168,000		(3) 58,800	(4) 226,800		
Difference Between Implied and Book Value			(4) 30,000	(5) 30,000		
Other Assets (Goodwill)	512,600	300,000	(5) 30,000			842,600
Land	90,000	40,000				130,000
Total Assets	1,005,700	440,000				1,307,700
Liabilities	102,600	75,000				177,600
Common Stock						
P Company	500,000					500,000
S Company		100,000	(4) 100,000			
Additional Contributed Capital— P Company	39,600		(1) 11,700 (2) 7,200			20,700
Retained Earnings from above	363,500	265,000	185,000	77,700	22,400	498,800
Noncontrolling Interest in Net Assets				(4) 88,200	88,200	
					110,600	110,600
Total Liabilities and Equity	1,005,700	440,000	422,700	422,700		1,307,700

(1) To adjust contributed capital for undistributed income on shares sold.
(2) To adjust for current year's income sold to noncontrolling stockholders.
(3) To establish reciprocity for remaining 72%.
(4) To eliminate investment in S Company and create noncontrolling interest account.
(5) To allocate the difference between implied and book value.

Entry (3) contains two components. The first component is the $12,000 adjustment for the 1,500 shares purchased before control was obtained and retroactively adjusting the books for retained earnings. The second component establishes reciprocity by recognizing P Company's share of the increase in S Company's retained earnings from the date of control to the beginning of 2010 on the *shares still held at the end of 2010* (i.e., 72% of the change in retained earnings). The total adjustment is computed as follows:

From January 1, 2007, to January 1, 2009 15% × ($120,000 – $40,000)	$12,000
From January 1, 2009, to January 1, 2010 72% × ($185,000 – $120,000)	46,800
Total	$58,800

After conversion/reciprocity is established, the workpaper investment elimination entry is:

(4) Common Stock—S Company	100,000	
1/1 Retained Earnings—S Company	185,000	
Difference between Implied and Book Value	30,000	
Investment in S Company (72%)		
($225,000 – $45,000 + $46,800)		226,800
Noncontrolling Interest		
[25,000 + 28% (185,000 – 120,000) + 45,000]		88,200

The workpaper entry to allocate the difference between implied and book value is:

(5) Goodwill	30,000	
Difference between Implied and Book Value		30,000

1. The additional contributed capital recognized for consolidation purposes is adjusted to $20,700, consisting of the $39,600 recorded capital less the portion of the additional contributed capital recognized in consolidated income in prior years ($11,700) and the portion of the current year's income to the date of sale associated with the shares sold ($7,200).

COST

2. Noncontrolling interest in consolidated income is represented by the December 31, 2010, noncontrolling interest percentage times reported subsidiary income (28% × $80,000), or $22,400. Note, however, in Illustration 8-1 that $7,200 of subsidiary income appears in the consolidated income statement columns of the workpaper as "subsidiary income sold." The $7,200 represents the amount that was purchased by the noncontrolling stockholders from the parent. Thus, the noncontrolling interest in consolidated income reported in the formal consolidated income statement reflects a net amount of $13,800 ($20,000 – $7,200). Note, however, that the full $20,000 is included as a part of the noncontrolling interest on the balance sheet (the $13,800 noncontrolling interest share of consolidated income plus the $7,200 purchased by the noncontrolling stockholders). That is, the full $20,000 represents an appropriate claim by the noncontrolling stockholders against the consolidated net assets, although $14,000 represents assets earned during the period and $6,000 reflects assets purchased.

In subsequent periods, the amount needed to convert to equity/establish reciprocity is the total of 15% of the increase in S Company's retained earnings from

January 1, 2007 to January 1, 2009 (always $12,000), plus 72% of the change in S Company's retained earnings thereafter. Thus, the entry needed to establish reciprocity for a workpaper on December 31, 2011, would be:

Investment in S Company	116,400	
1/1 Retained Earnings—P Company		116,400
[15% × ($120,000 − $40,000)] + [72% × ($265,000 − $120,000)]		

TEST YOUR KNOWLEDGE

NOTE: Solutions to ***Test Your Knowledge*** questions are found at the end of each chapter before the end-of-chapter questions.

Multiple Choice

1. Proper Company purchased the outstanding common stock of Silly Company in increments as follows:
   January 1, 2008, Purchased 15%
   June 1, 2008, Additional 20%
   August 1, 2008, Additional 30%
   September 30, 2008, Remaining 35%
   Both Proper and Silly have fiscal years ending on September 30. Silly's stock was acquired at book value. The controlling interest in net income for the consolidated entity for the fiscal year ending September 30, 2008, should include which of the following percentages of subsidiary earnings?
   a. 100%, January–September 2008.
   b. 65%, January–September 2008.
   c. 15%, January–May 2008; 20%, June–July 2008; and 30%, August–September 2008.
   d. None of the above.

2. Suppose a parent company owns 90% of a particular subsidiary at the beginning of its fiscal year, but during the year the parent sells 10% of its interest, thus reducing its ownership percentage to 80%. The most popular view of this transaction under proposed consolidations theory is:
   a. Any increase or decrease in equity as a result of the sale should be adjusted to donated capital.
   b. The transaction occurs between the controlling and noncontrolling owner groups and has no effect on consolidated income.
   c. The transaction is a sale of an investment at either a gain or loss, depending upon the selling price.
   d. The transaction results in an adjustment to additional contributed capital of the controlling interest, with no gain or loss in the income statement.

EQUITY METHOD—PURCHASES AND SALES OF SUBSIDIARY STOCK BY THE PARENT

EQUITY

As stated in the previous section (cost method), sometimes the controlling interest in a subsidiary is acquired through the initial stock purchase; at other times control is not achieved until two or more stock purchases are made. When control is achieved on the first purchase, the date of acquisition is the purchase date. However, when more than one purchase is made before control is obtained, the acquisition date is defined as the date at which control is achieved.

Determination of the date of acquisition is important under purchase accounting because subsidiary retained earnings accumulated before that date constitute a portion of the equity acquired by the parent company, whereas the parent's share of subsidiary retained earnings accumulated after acquisition is properly included in consolidated retained earnings.

Recall that under the equity method, the parent company adjusts its investment in subsidiary account for its share of subsidiary income or loss and dividends distributed. Under the complete equity method (as compared to the partial equity method), additional adjustments are made on the books of the parent company to adjust for excess depreciation, amortization, elimination of unrealized intercompany profit, and so forth.

However, under the assumptions presented at the beginning of this chapter (no intercompany sales and the difference between implied and book value attributed to goodwill), the complete and partial equity methods require the same procedures (and, as always, yield the same consolidated results). To illustrate the procedures followed for open-market purchases and sales of subsidiary stock under the equity method, the previous cost method example will be used. For convenience, the facts are repeated here:

1. S Company had 10,000 shares of $10 par value common stock outstanding during 2007–2010 and retained earnings as follows:

	S Company Retained Earnings
January 1, 2007	$ 40,000
January 1, 2009	120,000
January 1, 2010	185,000
December 31, 2010	265,000

2. P Company purchased S Company common stock on the open market as follows:

Date	*Shares Acquired*	*Cost*	*Cost/share*
January 1, 2007	1,500 (15% of 10,000 shares)	$ 24,000	$16/share
January 1, 2009	7,500 (75% of 10,000 shares)	187,500	$25/share
Total	9,000 (90% of 10,000 shares)	$211,500	

EQUITY

3. Any difference between implied and book value of net assets acquired relates to goodwill.
4. S Company distributed no dividends during the periods under consideration. Since no dividends were declared, the change in retained earnings represents the net income for that year.
5. P Company sold 1,800 shares of S Company stock on July 1, 2010, for $84,600.

As with the cost method, the initial purchase of the 15% interest is recorded at its cost of $24,000 and reported as an investment on P Company's balance sheets on December 31, 2007 and 2008. The second purchase on January 1, 2009, is also recorded in the investment account at its cost of $187,500. Since P Company now has a 90% interest in S Company and intends to apply the equity method, the investment account must be restated to recognize P Company's share (15%) of the increase in S Company's retained earnings from January 1, 2007, to January 1, 2009. In essence, consolidation is being retroactively applied to the time period when the parent owned only 15% of the subsidiary. This results in the following entry on P Company books:

Investment in S Company	12,000	
1/1 Retained Earnings—P Company		12,000
[.15 × ($120,000 × $40,000) or the change in retained earnings from 1/1/07 to 1/1/09].		

Then, to adjust the investment to fair value as of the date of acquisition, the gain on revaluation of the initial shares is computed as:

Implied value ($25/share × 1,500)	$37,500
Carrying value of initial shares	36,000
Revaluation gain	1,500

Thus the following entry is made on P company books.

P Company's Books

Investment in S Company	$1,500	
Gain on revaluation		$1,500
To adjust from the carrying value of $36,000 to fair value of $37,500 (or $25/share × 1,500 share).		

P Company will recognize its share of S Company income for 2009 with the following entry:

P Company's Books

Investment in S Company	58,500	
Equity in Subsidiary Income		58,500
[90% × ($185,000 − $120,000)]		

EQUITY

Recall (from item 4) that because there were no dividends declared by S Company, the change in retained earnings equals the amount of net income.

When a sale of subsidiary shares is made during a fiscal period, the parent's share of the subsidiary's income to the date of sale is normally recorded by a book entry if the information is available. Thus, assuming P Company received a six-month interim income statement from S Company reporting $40,000 of net income, the following entry will be made by P Company on June 30, 2010.

P Company's Books		
Investment in S Company	36,000	
Equity in Subsidiary Income (90% × $40,000)		36,000

After this entry, the Investment in S Company account will appear as follows:

Investment in S Company	
1/1/07 Purchase (15%)	24,000
1/1/09 Adjustment of 15% to fair value	1,500
1/1/09 Purchase (75%)	187,500
1/1/09 Adjustment	12,000
12/31/09 Subsidiary Income	58,500
6/30/10 Subsidiary Income	36,000
Balance	319,500

To record the sale of the S Company shares on July 1, 2010, P Company will make the following entry (recall that P Company is selling 20% of its shares):

P Company's Books		
Cash	84,600	
Investment in S Company*		63,900
Additional contributed capital		20,700

* $63,900 = 20% of $319,500, the carrying value of the investment.

The $20,700 difference between selling price and carrying value is appropriately reported as an adjustment to the parent's additional contributed capital for consolidated purposes and, as always, agrees with the amount reported for consolidated purposes under the cost method (Illustration 8-1). Since the investment account was brought up to date as of the date of sale under the equity method on P Company books, no *workpaper* adjustments to the gain are necessary.

After the sale of the 1,800 shares, P Company holds a 72% interest in S Company. Thus, for the second six months of 2010 (and for subsequent periods), P Company will recognize 72% of the reported income and dividends received from S Company. The December 31, 2010, book entry by P Company is:

P Company's Books		
Investment is S Company	28,800	
Equity in Subsidiary Income 72% × $40,000		28,800
To record equity income for the second 6 months of 2010.		

A December 31, 2010, workpaper, using the same basic information as under the cost basis (Illustration 8-1), is presented in Illustration 8-2. Notice, again, that consolidated net income, consolidated retained earnings, and consolidated balance sheet totals are identical in Illustrations 8-1 and 8-2.

Equity Method

Sale of Part of Investment

72% Owned Subsidiary

ILLUSTRATION 8-2
Consolidated Statements Workpaper
P Company and Subsidiary
for the Year Ended December 31, 2010

Income Statement	*P Company*	*S Company*	*Eliminations Dr.*	*Eliminations Cr.*	*Noncontrolling Interest*	*Consolidated Balances*
Net Income Before Gain on Sale and Equity in Subsidiary Income	120,000	80,000				200,000
Equity in Subsidiary Income	64,800		(1) 64,800			
Net/Combined Income	184,800	80,000				2,00,000
Subsidiary Income Sold				(1) 7,200		7,200
Noncontrolling Interest in Income					22,400	(22,400)
Net Income to Retained Earnings	184,800	80,000	64,800	7,200	22,400	184,800
Retained Earnings Statement						
1/1 Retained Earnings						
P Company	354,000					354,000
S Company		185,000	(2) 185,000			
Net Income from above	184,800	80,000	64,800	7,200	22,400	184,800
Dividends Declared 10/30 P Company	(40,000)					(40,000)
12/31 Retained Earnings to Balance Sheet	498,800	265,000	249,800	7,200	22,400	498,800
Balance Sheet						
Current Assets	235,100	100,000				335,100
Investment in S Company	284,400			(1) 57,600 (2) 226,800		
Goodwill			(3) 30,000			30,000
Difference Between Implied and Book Value			(2) 30,000	(3) 30,000		
Other Assets	512,600	300,000				812,600
Land	90,000	40,000				130,000
Total Assets	1,122,100	440,000				1,307,700
Liabilities	102,600	75,000				177,600
Common Stock						
P Company	500,000					500,000
S Company		100,000	(2) 100,000			
Additional Contributed Capital—P Company	20,700					20,700
Retained Earnings from above	498,800	265,000	249,800	7,200	22,400	498,800
1/1 Noncontrolling interest in Net Assets				(2) 88,200	88,200	
12/31 Noncontrolling Interest in Net Asset					110,600	110,600
Total Liabilities and Equity	1,122,100	440,000	409,800	409,800		1,307,700

(1) To reverse the effect of subsidiary income for the year.
(2) To eliminate investment in S Company.
(3) To allocate the difference between implied and book value.

PARENT SELLS SUBSIDIARY STOCK INVESTMENT ON THE OPEN MARKET—COST METHOD

Loss of Control

Under *SFAS No. 160* [**paragraphs 810–10–45–22, 24**] the treatment of the sale of a portion (but not all) of its investment by a parent company depends on

COST

whether or not the sale results in the loss of effective control of the subsidiary. If control is maintained, no gain or loss is recognized in the income statement. Instead, an adjustment is made to additional contributed capital of the controlling interest. However, if control is lost, the entire interest is adjusted to fair value, and a gain or loss recorded in income on all shares owned prior to sale. It should be noted that under past GAAP, the treatment of the sale of a portion of an investment by the parent company was the same, regardless of whether or not control was surrendered.

The parent accounts for the deconsolidation by recognizing a gain or loss in net income attributable to the parent, measured as the difference between:

1. The carrying value of S Company
2. The sum of the following:
   a. The fair value of the consideration received
   b. The fair value of the retained noncontrolling interest (at the date of deconsolidation)
   c. The carrying value of the former noncontrolling interest (at the date of deconsolidation).[2]

Consider the following. Suppose P Company owns 9,000 shares of S Company (90% of S Company) that were acquired at $25 a share (or $225,000) on January 1, 2009. During 2009, S Company reported $60,000 of income and did not pay any dividends.

P Company's Books		
Investment (9,000 shares × $25/share)	225,000	
Cash		225,000

On January 1, 2010, P Company sold two-thirds of its investment (6,000 shares of the 9,000 shares) of S Company stock, for $180,000 ($30/share). After the sale, P Company has lost control and now only maintains a 30% ((9,000 − 6,000)/10,000) interest.

The carrying value of S company, on January 1, 2010, is computed as follows:

Carrying value of S Company		
Carrying value of S Company (on 1/1/2010)		
P Company's carrying value of Company S		
Initial cost (9,000 shares × $25/share)	$225,000	
Increase in retained earnings ($60,000 × 0.90)	54,000	
Carrying value of Investment in S Company 1/1/2010		279,000
Noncontrolling carrying value in Company S		
Initial value (1,000 shares × $25/share)	$25,000	
Increase in retained earnings ($60,000 × 0.10)	6,000	
Carrying value of Investment in S Company 1/1/2010		31,000
Total carrying value of S Company (1/1/2010)		310,000

COST

[2] This amount also includes any accumulated other comprehensive income attributable to the noncontrolling interest.

The gain or loss in net income attributable to P Company is computed as follows:

Gain or loss is the difference in:		
(1) Total carrying value of S Company		310,000
(2) Sum of:		
Fair value of consideration received (6,000 shares)	$180,000	
Fair value of retained NCI (3,000 × $30)	90,000	
Carrying value of the NCI (1,000 shares)	31,000	
Total		301,000
Loss attributable to P Company		$ 9,000

The loss is split between the 6,000 shares that are sold and the 3,000 shares that are still held as an investment. To record the sale of the shares, P Company makes the following entry in its books on January 1, 2010.

P Company's Books

(1) Cash (6,000 × $30/share)	180,000	
Realized loss on sale (on 6,000 shares sold)	6,000	
Investment in S Company (2/3 × $279,000)		186,000
(2) Unrealized loss (on 3,000 shares retained)	3,000	
Investment in S Company (remaining 3,000 shares)		3,000
To reduce the remaining shares to market value.		

Because P Company now holds a 30% (not controlling) interest in S Company, the investment must be carried on the books using the equity method, even if P Company uses the cost method for its controlled subsidiaries. Thus the investment account must be adjusted for previous earnings of S Company (i.e., the reciprocity entry usually made on the consolidated workpaper).

(3) Investment in S Company ($60,000 × 0.90)	54,000	
1/1 Retained Earnings—P Company		54,000

After this entry, the balance in the investment in S Company account on P Company books will be equal to its fair value of $90,000 (or $225,000 + $54,000 − $186,000 − $3,000). Consolidated financial statements will no longer be required because P Company has lost control.

SUBSIDIARY ISSUES STOCK

COST

A parent company's equity interest in a subsidiary also may change as the result of the issuance of additional shares of stock by the subsidiary. The effect of these subsidiary stock transactions on the parent company depends on whether the parent is a party to the transactions, as well as on the price at which the subsidiary shares are sold. Throughout this section, most adjustments, will affect only the additional contributed capital (controlling interest) or the noncontrolling interest in equity. This approach is consistent with the FASB's position that transactions in the shares of a subsidiary by any of the affiliates are transactions in the equity of the consolidated group. Subsidiary shares are part of the residual interest remaining after subtracting consolidated liabilities from net assets; thus, no gains or losses should be recognized.

Issuance of Additional Shares by a Subsidiary

Assume that the parent company already has a controlling interest in a subsidiary, and the subsidiary issues additional shares of its common stock. The newly issued shares may be purchased (1) entirely by the parent company, (2) partly by the parent company and partly by the noncontrolling stockholders, or (3) entirely by the noncontrolling stockholders.

When shares are purchased by the noncontrolling stockholders, the situation is analogous to a sale of shares by P Company while maintaining control. If the shares are purchased by the noncontrolling stockholders for more than book value, the effect is equivalent to a sale of a portion of its interest by P Company with an increase in the parent's additional contributed capital. Conversely, if the shares are purchased by the noncontrolling stockholders for less than book value, the effect is equivalent to a sale of a portion of its interest with a decrease in the parent's additional contributed capital. To keep the focus on the relevant issues in the next section as we illustrate these possibilities and to conserve space, we combine the presentation of cost and equity methods. Adjustments to the parent's additional contributed capital resulting from subsidiary stock issuance transactions that decrease the parent company's percentage of ownership are recorded on the parent's books the same way under both methods. The effects of subsidiary stock issuance transactions that change the parent's percentage of ownership are adjusted to the additional contributed capital when the investment is eliminated on the consolidated workpaper, as illustrated in the following section. In either case, subsequent recognition of the parent's share of subsidiary income and dividends is based on the new percentage of ownership. Of course, no entries are needed to establish reciprocity/convert to equity when the equity method is being used. Otherwise the entries are the same as those presented for the cost method.

One Hundred Percent of New Shares Purchased by the Parent Company When shares are purchased by the parent company directly from the subsidiary, care must be exercised in the determination of equity acquired. This occurs because the number of subsidiary shares outstanding is increased and the proceeds from the stock issue flow increase the subsidiary's total stockholders' equity.

If the parent company holds less than a 100% interest and purchases the entire new issue of stock directly from the subsidiary, one of two situations must exist. Either (1) the preemptive right has previously been waived or (2) the noncontrolling stockholders have elected not to exercise their rights. The purchase of the entire new issue by the parent company will increase the parent company's percentage of ownership with an equal reduction in the noncontrolling interest's percentage of ownership. Since a subsidiary's stock transactions affect the balances in the subsidiary's stockholders' equity accounts, a special computational method is needed to determine the change in the parent's share of the subsidiary's equity. The change is determined by comparing the parent's share of the subsidiary's equity immediately before and immediately after the new purchase.

COST

New Shares Issued above Existing Carrying Value per Share

LO5 Issue of new shares entirely to the parent.

To illustrate, assume that P Company purchased 14,000 shares (70%) of S Company's $10 par value common stock on January 1, 2003, for $210,000, which included a $20,000 excess of implied over book value; the excess cost was assigned to land. S Company's retained earnings on January 1, 2003, were $50,000. See Computation and Allocation Schedule below.

Computation and Allocation of Difference between Implied and Book Value

January 1, 2003	*Parent Share*	*Noncontrolling Share*	*Implied Value*
Cost	$210,000	$90,000	$300,000
Equity Acquired:			
Common Stock (1)	140,000	60,000	200,000
Other Contributed Capital (2)	21,000	9,000	30,000
Retained Earnings (3)	35,000	15,000	50,000
Total	196,000	84,000	280,000
Difference Between Implied and Book Value	$ 14,000	$ 6,000	$ 20,000
Adjust Land to fair value	(14,000)	(6,000)	(20,000)
Balance	—0—	—0—	—0—

(1) 70% × $200,000.
(2) 70% × $30,000.
(3) 70% × $50,000.

On January 1, 2011, P Company purchased 4,000 additional shares of S Company stock directly from S Company at its current market price of $22 per share ($88,000). This price is ***greater*** than the existing book value per share of S Company. Noncontrolling stockholders elected not to participate in the new issue. S Company's stockholders equity on January 1, 2008, was:

COST

S Company's Stockholders' Equity and Book Value per Share

January 1, 2011	*Immediately before the New Issue*	*New Issue*	*Immediately after the New Issue*
Common Stock, $10 Par Value	$200,000	$40,000	$240,000
Other Contributed Capital	30,000	48,000	78,000
Retained Earnings	120,000	—0—	120,000
Total Stockholders' Equity	$350,000	$88,000	$438,000
Common Shares	20,000	4,000	24,000
Book Value per Share	$ 17.50	$ 22.00	$ 18.25

Note that after P Company buys the new shares, the book value per share of S Company goes from $17.50 to $18.25. There are 24,000 shares of S Company stock outstanding after the new issue, 18,000 of which are owned by P Company. Thus, P Company's percentage of ownership has increased to 75% (18,000 shares/24,000 shares). The computation of the book value of the equity interest acquired in the purchase of the new shares is as follows:

P Company's Carrying Value of the Investment in S Company

	Before New Purchase (70%)	*After New Purchase (75%)*	*Book Value of Interest Acquired*
Common Stock	(1) $140,000	(4) $180,000	$40,000
Other Contributed Capital	(2) 21,000	(5) 58,500	37,500
Retained Earnings	(3) 84,000	(6) 90,000	6,000
Total Stockholders' Equity	$245,000	$328,500	$83,500
Land to fair value	(7) 14,000	(8) 15,000	1,000
Carrying Value in S Company	259,000	343,500	$84,500

(1) .7 × $200,000.
(2) .7 × $30,000.
(3) .7 × $120,000.
(4) .75 × $240,000.
(5) .75 × $78,000.
(6) .75 × $120,000.
(7) .7 × $20,000.
(8) .75 × $20,000.

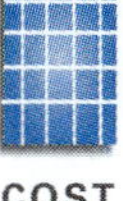
COST

The cost of the new shares was $88,000 and the book value of the interest acquired was $84,500, as determined above. The difference is debited to the parent's additional contributed capital. It should be noted that the $4,500 excess cost resulted because P Company purchased the additional shares from S Company at a price of $22 per share, which exceeded the $17.50 book value of S Company's shares ($350,000/20,000 shares). The noncontrolling shareholders' book value per share increased from $17.50 to $18.25, or 0.75 per share. Since they own 6,000 shares, the book value of their shares increased by $4,500 (or .75 × 6,000) and decreased by the difference between implied and book value (assigned to land) considered transferred to P Company of $1,000, yielding a net increase of $3,500.

Although the noncontrolling stockholders did not participate in the new issue and their percentage of ownership decreased (30% to 25%), the amount of their total book value interest in S Company's net assets increased by $3,500. It is not a coincidence that the increase in the noncontrolling interest equals the amount debited to the parent's additional contributed capital. The noncontrolling interest will increase if the cost of the new shares is greater than the carrying value of the interest acquired. Because the shares were purchased directly from the subsidiary, the $3,500 represents a transfer of interest from the controlling interest to the noncontrolling stockholders. This can be verified as follows:

Noncontrolling Interest in S Company

Before the new issue	.30 × $350,000 =	$105,000
After the new issue	.25 × $438,000 =	109,500
Increase in noncontrolling interest		$ 4,500
Less: land value transferred to P (5% of $20,000)		(1,000)
Net increase		$ 3,500

Essentially, because the controlling stockholders paid more than the existing carrying value per share, the noncontrolling stockholders' carrying value must increase.

To record the purchase of the new shares, P Company will make the following entry:

P Company's Books		
Investment in S Company	88,000	
Cash		88,000

If a workpaper were prepared immediately after the purchase of the new shares, the workpaper entries to establish reciprocity (convert to equity) and eliminate the investment account would be:

Investment in S Company	49,000	
1/1 Retained Earnings—P Company [70% × ($120,000 − 50,000)]		49,000
To establish reciprocity (convert to equity).*		
*Conversion entry not needed if equity method is used.		

COST

Common Stock—S Company	240,000	
Other Contributed Capital—S Company	78,000	
Retained Earnings—S Company	120,000	
Difference between Implied and Book Value	20,000	
Additional Contributed Capital—P	3,500	
Investment in S ($210,000 + $88,000 + $49,000)		347,000
Noncontrolling interest in S Company ($90,000 + $21,000 + $3,500)		114,500
To eliminate the investment and create the NCI.		

Because this entry only reflects the change in Retained Earnings—S Company up to the *beginning of the year*, we use the percentage of ownership as of the beginning of the year (70%). In later years, reciprocity is established on the basis of a 70% interest to the date of purchase of the new shares plus a 75% interest thereafter. The elimination of S Company's stockholders' equity, however, is based on the level of ownership held after the purchase of the new shares (75%).

New Shares Issued at or below the Existing Book Value per Share

In the previous example, the parent paid more than the existing book value per share of S Company. If the new shares are issued at a price ***equal*** to their book value, the parent's additional contributed capital will change only by difference between implied and purchase price considered transferred. For example, if the shares are issued at their book value of $17.50 per share (or $70,000), the computation is as follows:

P Company's Share of S Company's Net Assets

Before the new issue	.70 × $350,000 =	$245,000
After the new issue	.75[$350,000 + (4,000 × $17.50)] =	$315,000
Increase in P Company's share		70,000
Land value transferred to P ((75% − 70%) × $20,000)		1,000
Total		71,000
Cost of investment (4,000 × $17.50)		70,000
Difference		$ 1,000

Although the noncontrolling stockholders' percentage of ownership decreases from 30% to 25%, their share of the net assets of S Company decreased only by the land value transferred, as shown here:

Noncontrolling Interest in S Company

Before the new issue	.30 × $350,000 =	$ 105,000
After the new issue	.25 × ($350,000 + $70,000) =	105,000
Decrease in noncontrolling share		$ —0—
Land value transferred to P ((75% − 70%) × $20,000)		1,000
Difference		$ 1,000

COST

If the new shares are issued at a price ***less*** than their book value, total noncontrolling book value interest decreases, and the controlling book value interest increases by more than the amount of the land value transferred. In this case, an excess of book value over implied value results. For example, assume the new shares were issued at $14 per share (or $56,000). The excess of book value over cost is computed as follows:

Before the new issue	.70 × $350,000 =	$ 245,000
After the new issue	.75[$350,000 + (4,000 × $14)] =	$ 304,500
Increase in P Company's share (book value acquired)		59,500
Plus land value transferred to P ((75% − 70%) × $20,000)		1,000
Total		60,500
Cost of the investment (4,000 × $14)		56,000
Increase in additional contributed capital		$ 4,500

The resulting decrease in the noncontrolling interest is verified as:

Noncontrolling Interest in S Company

Before the new issue	.30 × $350,000 =	$ 105,000
After the new issue	.25[$350,000 + (4,000 × $14)] =	$ 101,500
Decrease in noncontrolling interest		$ 3,500
Less: land value transferred to P (0.30 − 0.25) × $20,000)		1,000
Total decrease in NCI		$ 4,500

In this case, the journal entry by P Company to record the purchase of the new shares is:

P Company's Books		
Investment in S Company	56,000	
Cash		56,000

In this case, the $4,500 excess of book value over cost is treated as an increase in the additional contributed capital of the parent. Thus, the workpaper entries to establish reciprocity and eliminate the investment account in the preparation of a consolidated workpaper immediately after the purchase are:

Investment in S Company	49,000	
1/1 Retained Earnings—P Company [70% × ($120,000 − $50,000)]		49,000
To establish reciprocity/convert to equity*		

COST

Common Stock—S Company	240,000	
Other Contributed Capital—S Company	46,000	
Retained Earnings—S Company	120,000	
Difference between Implied and Book Value	20,000	
Investment in S Company ($210,000 + $56,000 + $49,000)		315,000
Additional contributed capital—P		4,500
Noncontrolling interest in S Company [$90,000 + ($120,000 − 50,000) × 30% − $4,500]		106,500
To eliminate the investment account and create NCI 108,642		

*Entry not needed if equity method is used.

New Shares Purchased Ratably by Parent and Noncontrolling Stockholders In the previous example, noncontrolling stockholders elected not to exercise their right to purchase a ratable number of the new shares. If the noncontrolling stockholders had elected to exercise their rights, the percentage of stock owned by the parent and noncontrolling stockholders after the new issue would be the same as their respective interests prior to the new issue. Assume, for example, that the shares are issued at $22 each, that P Company is permitted to purchase only its ratable share of the new issue, and that the remaining shares are purchased by the noncontrolling stockholders. Thus, P Company would purchase 2,800 of the 4,000 new shares and retain its 70% (16,800 shares/24,000 shares) interest in S Company. Comparison of cost with the book value of the interest acquired by P Company is as follows:

Cost of investment (2,800 × $22)		$ 61,600
Book value of equity interest acquired:		
P Company's share of S Company's net assets:		
Before the new purchase .7($350,000)	$245,000	
After the new purchase .7[$350,000 + (4,000 × $22)]	306,600	
Increase in P Company's share of S Company		61,600
Land value transferred (0.70 − 0.70) ($20,000)		—0—
Difference		$ —0—

Note that the book value of the interest acquired is equal to the cost of the shares to P Company; thus, there is no need to adjust the parent's additional contributed capital. This condition will always result if the shares are purchased ratably by the existing stockholders, regardless of whether the new shares are issued at a price below, equal to, or above their book value.

New Shares Purchased Entirely by Noncontrolling Stockholders Occasionally, in order to obtain an additional capital increment for the consolidated entity or to meet the requirements of employee stock options or stock purchase plans, the subsidiary may issue new shares entirely to noncontrolling stockholders. Since any shares purchased by the parent represent a transfer of funds within the affiliated group, purchases by the parent do not provide any additional capital to the group as a whole. As long as the number of new shares issued is not so large that it reduces the parent's percentage of ownership below that needed for control, new financing can be made available and control retained. The issuance of all the new shares to noncontrolling stockholders does, of course, reduce the parent's percentage of ownership. Thus, the economic substance of the transaction is a sale of interest by P Company. However, the book value of the parent's interest in the subsidiary may

COST

increase, decrease, or remain unchanged depending on the relationship of the issue price to book value per share of stock. To illustrate, assume the previous example except that the 4,000 new shares were issued entirely to noncontrolling stockholders at the current market price of $22 per share. The new issue results in a decrease in P Company's percentage of ownership from 70% to 58.33% (14,000 shares/24,000 shares). The change in the book value of P Company's interest in S Company is determined as before by an immediately "before" and "after" computation as follows:

P Company's Share of S Company's Net Assets

Before the new issue	70% × $350,000 =	$245,000
After the new issue	58.33% × [$350,000 + (4,000 × $22)] =	255,500
Increase		$ 10,500
Less: land value transferred to NCI (0.70 − 0.5833) ($20,000)		(2,333)
Net increase		$ 8,167

Although P Company's ownership interest decreased from 70% to 58.33%, the book value of its interest in S Company after the new issue increased by $8,166. The $8,166 increase in P Company's book value interest is accompanied by a decline in the noncontrolling book value interest relative to the cost of the new shares. The total $88,000 cost of the new shares is allocated between the controlling and noncontrolling interests in essence, even though the noncontrolling interest paid the entire amount as follows:

Cost of new shares to noncontrolling interest (4,000 × $22)			$88,000
Less equity in net assets acquired:			
Noncontrolling interest's share of net assets:			
Before the purchase .3($350,000)	$105,000		
After the purchase 41.667% × ($350,000 + $88,000)	182,500	77,500	
Plus land value transferred to NCI (41.67% − 30%) ($20,000)		2,333	
Increase in noncontrolling interest			79,833
Increase in controlling interest			8,167

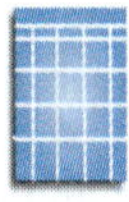
COST

Since the purchase of the shares by the noncontrolling stockholders decreased P Company's ownership percentage, the situation is analogous to a sale of shares by P Company, while retaining control. The transfer of the $8,167 interest in consolidated net assets from the noncontrolling stockholders to the controlling stockholders is recorded on the books of P Company as follows:

P Company's Books

Investment in S Company	8,167	
Additional Contributed Capital		8,167

Because the shares were purchased by the noncontrolling stockholders for more than book value, P Company's percentage interest decreased, and P Company's interest in the consolidated net assets increased, the effect is the equivalent of a sale of a portion of its interest by P Company, while retaining control. Note that, in this example, the new shares are purchased by the noncontrolling stockholders at a price in excess of book value, which results in an increase in P Company's share of consolidated net assets. If the new shares are issued at book value, the parent's additional contributed capital will change only by the amount of land value transferred:

P Company's Share of S Company's Net Assets

Before the new issue	70% × 350,000 =	245,000
After the new issue	58.33% × [350,000 + (4,000 × $17.5)] =	245,000
		—0—
Land value transferred to NCI ((70% − 58.33%) × $20,000)		2,333
Difference		($ 2,333)

If the shares are issued below book value, P Company's book value interest decreases and a book entry debiting Additional Contributed Capital and crediting Investment in S Company is made. For example, assuming the issue of the entire 4,000 shares to noncontrolling stockholders at $14 per share (or $56,000), the computation and journal entry are:

P Company's Share of S Company's Net Assets

Before the new issue	70% × $350,000 =	245,000
After the new issue	58.33% × [$350,000 + (4,000 × $14)] =	236,833
Decrease		8,167
Less land value transferred to NCI ((70% − 58.33%) × $20,000)		2,333
Total decrease in book value interest		$ 10,500

P Company's Books

Additional Contributed Capital	10,500	
Investment in S Company		10,500

SUMMARY

1. *Identify the types of transactions that change the parent company's ownership interest in a subsidiary and summarize the differences between current and proposed GAAP.* The parent may buy additional shares of the subsidiary from third parties; the parent may sell subsidiary shares to third parties; the subsidiary may issue additional shares, either to the parent or to others, or both; the subsidiary may buy its own shares either from its parent or from others.
A computation and allocation schedule should be prepared when effective control is achieved. FASB requires the following for acquisitions that take place in stages and for partial sales:
    a. Measure and recognize the acquirer's identifiable assets and liabilities at 100% of their fair values on the date acquirer obtains control, and
    b. Recognize all the acquirer's goodwill (not just the parent's share), measured as the difference between the fair value of the acquiree on the acquisition date and the fair value of the identifiable net assets.
    c. Any previously held noncontrolling equity interests should be remeasured to fair value, with the resulting adjustment recognized in income.
    d. After control is achieved, subsequent adjustments due to increased ownership are shown as Additional Contributed Capital, not as income.
    e. If a parent loses control, the retained investment should be remeasured to fair value and the adjustments recognized in net income.
2. *Describe the process needed when the parent acquires subsidiary shares through multiple open market purchases.* The initial investment(s) is revalued to fair value when control is achieved, and adjustments are recorded in the income statement. Subsequent purchases result in adjustments to additional contributed capital.
3. *Explain how the parent reports the difference between selling price and book value when shares are sold subsequent to acquisition.* If the parents maintains control, the difference is an adjustment to additional contributed capital. If not, the difference after

adjusting any remaining ownership to fair value, is treated as a gain or loss.

4. *Compute the controlling interest in income after the parent sells some shares of the subsidiary company.* The controlling interest in income is computed as the internally generated income of the parent plus or minus the usual adjustments for excess depreciation, and so on, plus the controlling percentage of the subsidiary adjusted income. The controlling percentage of the subsidiary adjusted income is layered in the year of sale so that the portion of the year's income prior to the sale reflects the initial percentage ownership and the portion subsequent to the sale reflects the new lower percentage ownership.

5. *Describe the effect on the eliminating process when the subsidiary issues new shares entirely to the parent, and the parent pays either more or less than the book value of the subsidiary shares.* The number of subsidiary shares outstanding is increased, and the proceeds from the stock issue flow increase the subsidiary's total stockholders' equity. This affects the additional contributed capital of the parent and the noncontrolling interest. The change in the parent's share of the subsidiary's equity is determined by comparing the parent's share of the subsidiary's equity immediately before and immediately after the new purchase. The noncontrolling interest will increase if the cost of the new shares is greater than the book value of the interest acquired and decrease if the cost is less than the book value. This change must be decreased (increased) for the value of goodwill transferred between the controlling and noncontrolling interests.

6. *Describe the impact on the parent's investment account when the subsidiary issues new shares and other the new shares are purchased ratably by the parent and noncontrolling shareholders or entirely by the noncontrolling shareholders.* If the shares are purchased ratably by both, the percentage of stock owned by the parent and noncontrolling stockholders after the new issue would be the same as their respective interests prior to the new issue. If the shares are purchased entirely by the noncontrolling shareholders, the parent's percentage of ownership is reduced. Thus, the economic substance of the transaction is a sale of interest by P Company. However, the book value of the parent's interest in the subsidiary may increase, decrease, or remain unchanged depending on the relationship of the issue price to book value per share of stock. If the price is higher than book value, the parent's interest increases. If the price is lower than book value, the parent's interest decreases.

TEST YOUR KNOWLEDGE SOLUTIONS

8-1 d 8-2 d

QUESTIONS

LO1 1. Identify three types of transactions that result in a change in a parent company's ownership interest in its subsidiary.

LO2 2. Why is the date of acquisition of subsidiary stock important under the purchase method?

LO3 3. When a parent company has obtained control of a subsidiary through several purchases and subsequently sells a portion of its shares in the subsidiary, how is the carrying value of the shares sold determined?

LO3 4. When a parent company that records its investment using the cost method during a fiscal year sells a portion of its investment, explain the correct accounting for any differences between selling price and recorded values.

LO3 5. ABC Corporation purchased 10,000 shares (80%) of EZ Company at $35 per share and sold them several years later for $35 per share. The consolidated income statement reports a loss on the sale of this investment. Explain.

LO5 6. Explain how a parent company that owns less than 100% of a subsidiary can purchase an entire new issue of common stock directly from the subsidiary.

LO6 7. When a subsidiary issues additional shares of stock to noncontrolling stockholders and such issuance results in an increase in the book value of the parent's share of the subsidiary's equity, how should the increase be reflected in the financial statements? What if it results in a decrease?

LO5 LO6 8. P Company holds an 80% interest in S Company. Determine the effect (that is, increase, decrease, no change, not determinable) on both the total book value of the noncontrolling interest and the noncontrolling interest's percentage of ownership in the net assets of S Company for each of the following situations:

a. P Company acquires additional shares directly from S Company at a price equal to the book value per share of the S Company stock immediately prior to the issuance.

b. S Company acquires its own shares on the open market. The cost of these shares is less than their book value.

c. Assume the same situation as in (b) except that the cost of the shares is greater than their book value.

d. P Company and a noncontrolling stockholder each acquire 100 shares directly from S Company at a price below the book value per share.

Business Ethics

During a recent review of the quarterly financial statements and supporting ledgers, you noticed several unusual journal entries. While the dollar amounts of the journal entries were not large, there did not appear to be supporting documentation. You decide to bring the matter to the attention of your immediate supervisor. After you mentioned the issue, the supervisor calmly stated that the matter would be looked into and that you should not worry about it.

1. You feel a bit uncomfortable about the situation. What is your responsibility and what action, if any, should you take?

EXERCISES

EXERCISE 8-1 **Multiple Stock Purchases—Journal Entries** LO2

Peck Company purchased Sanno Company common stock in a series of open-market cash purchases from 2009 through 2011 as follows:

Date	*Shares Acquired*	*Cost*
January 1, 2009	1,800	$ 46,000
January 1, 2010	4,500	95,000
January 1, 2011	9,900	262,350

Sanno Company had 18,000 shares of $20 par value common stock outstanding during the entire period. Retained earnings balances for Sanno Company on relevant dates were

January 1, 2009	$ 20,000
January 1, 2010	(30,000)
January 1, 2011	85,000
December 31, 2011	170,000

Dividends in the amount of $50,000 were distributed by Sanno Company only in 2011. Any difference between implied and book values is assigned to goodwill. Peck Company uses the cost method to account for its investment in Sanno Company.

Required:

A. Prepare the journal entries that Peck Company would record on its books during 2011 to account for its investment in Sanno Company.

B. Prepare the workpaper eliminating entries necessary to prepare a consolidated statements workpaper on December 31, 2011.

EXERCISE 8-2 **Parent Company Entries—Multiple Stock Purchase and Sale of Stock, Cost Method** LO2 LO3

Papke Company acquired 85% of the common stock of Serbin Company in two separate cash transactions. The first purchase of 72,000 shares (60%) on January 1, 2010, cost $490,000. The second purchase, on January 1, 2011, of 30,000 shares (25%) cost $220,000. Serbin Company's stockholders' equity was as follows:

	2010	*2011*
Common Stock, $5 par	$600,000	$600,000
Retained Earnings, 1/1	175,000	201,000
Net Income	46,000	60,000
Dividends Declared, 9/30	(20,000)	(25,000)
Retained Earnings, 12/31	201,000	236,000
Total Stockholders' Equity, 12/31	$801,000	$836,000

On April 1, 2011, after a significant rise in the market price of Serbin Company's stock, Papke Company sold 21,600 of its Serbin Company shares for $260,000. Serbin Company notified Papke Company that its net income for the first three months was $15,000. The shares sold were identified as those obtained in the first purchase. Any difference between implied and book values relates to goodwill. Papke uses the cost method to account for its investment in Serbin Company.

Required:

Prepare the journal entries Papke Company would record on its books during 2011 to account for its investment in Serbin Company.

EXERCISE 8-3 **Workpaper Entries—Multiple Stock Purchases** LO4

Use the data provided in Exercise 8-2.

Required:

A. Prepare the workpaper eliminating entries needed for a consolidated statements workpaper on December 31, 2011.

B. Determine the amount of noncontrolling interest that would be reported on the consolidated balance sheet on December 31, 2011.

EXERCISE 8-4 **Parent Company Entries—Multiple Stock Purchases, Equity Method** LO2 LO3 LO4

Use the data from Exercise 8-1, but assume use of either the complete or the partial equity method rather than the cost method.

Required:

A. Prepare the journal entries Peck Company will make on its books during 2010 and 2011 to account for its investment in Sanno Company.

B. Prepare workpaper eliminating entries necessary to prepare a consolidated statements workpaper on December 31, 2011.

EXERCISE 8-5 **Parent Company and Workpaper Entries—Equity Method** LO2 LO4

Use the data presented in Exercise 8-2, but assume use of the complete or the partial equity method rather than the cost method.

Required:

A. Prepare the journal entries Papke Company will make on its books during 2010 and 2011 to account for its investment in Serbin Company.

B. Prepare the workpaper eliminating entries needed for a consolidated statements workpaper on December 31, 2011.

EXERCISE 8-6 **Parent Company and Workpaper Entries—New Shares Issued by Subsidiary** LO5

On January 1, 2011, Pace Company purchased 250,000 shares of common stock directly from its subsidiary, Sime Company, for $1.50 per share. Noncontrolling stockholders elected not to participate in the new issue.

Pace Company acquired its initial 92.5% interest in Sime Company by purchasing on the open market 462,500 shares of Sime's common stock for $578,125 on January 1, 2007. Sime Company's stockholders' equity just before each of the two purchases was as follows:

	December 31 2006	*December 31 2010*
Common Stock $1 par	$500,000	$500,000
Other Contributed Capital	40,000	40,000
Retained Earnings	60,000	150,000
Total	$600,000	$690,000

During 2011 Sime Company reported $90,000 net income and declared a dividend in the amount of $30,000. Any difference between implied and book values relates to subsidiary land. Pace uses the cost method to account for its investment.

Required:

A. Prepare the journal entry on Pace Company's books to record the purchase of the additional shares on January 1, 2011.

B. Prepare the eliminating entries needed for the preparation of a consolidated statements workpaper on December 31, 2011.

EXERCISE 8-7 **Parent Company and Workpaper Entries—New Shares Issued by Subsidiary** LO5

Use the same data provided in Exercise 8-6, with the exception that Pace Company purchased the additional shares from Sime Company on January 1, 2011, at a price of $1.30 per share rather than $1.50.

Required:

A. Prepare the journal entry on Pace Company's books to record the purchase of the additional shares on January 1, 2011.

B. Prepare the eliminating entries needed for the preparation of a consolidated statements workpaper on December 31, 2011.

EXERCISE 8-8 **Parent Company and Workpaper Entries—New Shares Issued by Subsidiary** LO6

Padilla Company acquired 80% of the outstanding common stock of Skon Company on January 1, 2009, for $132,000. At the date of purchase, Skon Company had a balance in its $2 par value common stock account of $120,000 and retained earnings of $30,000.

On January 1, 2011, Skon Company issued 15,000 shares of its previously unissued stock to noncontrolling stockholders for $3.00 per share. On this date, Skon Company had a retained earnings balance of $50,500. The difference between implied and book values relates to subsidiary land. No dividends were paid in 2011.

Skon Company reported income of $10,000 in 2011.

Required:

A. Prepare the journal entry on Padilla's books to record the effect of the issuance assuming

(1) Cost method

(2) Complete or partial equity method

B. Prepare the eliminating entries needed for the preparation of a consolidated statements workpaper on December 31, 2011 assuming

(1) Cost method

(2) Complete or partial equity method

PROBLEMS

PROBLEM 8-1 **Multiple Stock Purchases** LO2

Sarko Company had 300,000 shares of $10 par value common stock outstanding at all times, and retained earnings balances as indicated here:

	Retained Earnings
January 1, 2010	$260,000
January 1, 2011	540,000
January 1, 2012	630,000
January 1, 2013	820,000

Pelzer Company acquired Sarko Company stock through open-market purchases as follows:

Date	*% Acquired*	*Shares*	*Cost*
1/1/10	10%	30,000	$ 365,000
1/1/11	25%	75,000	960,000
1/1/12	45%	135,000	1,890,000
	80%		

Sarko Company declared no dividends during this period. The fair values of Sarko Company's assets and liabilities were approximately equal to their book values throughout this period (2010 through 2012). Pelzer Company uses the cost method.

Required:

A. Prepare a schedule to compare investment cost with the book value of equity acquired.

B. Prepare elimination entries for the preparation of a consolidated statements workpaper on December 31, 2012.

PROBLEM 8-2 **Workpaper—Sale of Shares by Parent, Cost Method—Loss of Control**

The accounts of Pyle Company and its subsidiary, Stern Company, are summarized below as of December 31, 2011:

Debits	*Pyle*	*Stern*
Current Assets	$ 600,000	$ 320,000
Investment in Stern Company	480,000	
Other Assets	1,180,000	668,000
Dividends Declared, 11/1	80,000	60,000
	$2,340,000	$1,048,000
Credits		
Liabilities	$ 190,000	$ 90,000
Common Stock, $5 par	500,000	300,000
Other Contributed Capital	230,000	180,000
1/1 Retained Earnings	1,200,000	292,000
Net Income	220,000	186,000
	$2,340,000	$1,048,000

Pyle Company made the following open-market purchase and sale of Stern Company common stock:

January 2, 2009, purchased 51,000 shares (85% of Stern), cost $510,000, $10/share;
January 1, 2011, sold 40,000 shares (two-thirds of Stern), proceeds, $480,000, $12/share.

The book value of Stern Company's net assets on January 2, 2009, $600,000, approximated the fair value of those net assets, including retained earnings of $120,000. Subsequent changes in book value of the net assets are entirely attributable to earnings of Stern Company. Stern Company earns its income evenly throughout the year.

Required:

Prepare the journal entries needed on Pyle Company's books to record the transactions regarding the investment in Stern Company account assuming that the cost method is used to account for the investment.

PROBLEM 8-3 **Workpaper—Sale of Shares by Parent, Cost Method** LO2 LO3 LO4

The accounts of Pyle Company and its subsidiary, Stern Company, are summarized below as of December 31, 2011:

Debits	*Pyle*	*Stern*
Current Assets	$ 600,000	$ 320,000
Investment in Stern Company	480,000	
Other Assets	1,180,000	668,000
Dividends Declared, 11/1	80,000	60,000
	$2,340,000	$1,048,000

Credits		
Liabilities	$ 190,000	$ 90,000
Common Stock, $5 par	500,000	300,000
Other Contributed Capital	230,000	180,000
1/1 Retained Earnings	1,200,000	292,000
Net Income	220,000	186,000
	$2,340,000	$1,048,000

Pyle Company made the following open-market purchase and sale of Stern Company common stock: January 2, 2009, purchased 51,000 shares, cost $510,000; April 1, 2011, sold 3,000 shares, proceeds, $100,000.

The book value of Stern Company's net assets on January 2, 2009, $600,000, (including retained earnings of $120,000) approximated the fair value of those net assets. Subsequent changes in book value of the net assets are entirely attributable to earnings of Stern Company. Stern Company earns its income evenly throughout the year.

Required:

Prepare a consolidated financial statements workpaper as of December 31, 2011. Begin the income statement section of the workpaper with "Net Income Before Dividend Income" which is $172,000 and $186,000 for Pyle Company and Stern Company, respectively.

PROBLEM 8-4 **Workpaper—Purchase and Sale of Shares, Cost Method** LO3 LO4

Trial balances for Porter Company and its subsidiary, Spitz Company, as of December 31, 2011, follow:

Debits	*Porter*	*Spitz*
Cash	$ 90,000	$ 40,000
Accounts Receivable (net)	62,000	38,000
Inventory	106,000	64,000
Investment in Spitz Company	121,500	
Plant Assets	320,000	149,000
Land	69,000	46,000
Dividends Declared, 10/1	50,000	30,000
Total	$818,500	$367,000

Credits	Porter	Spitz
Liabilities	$102,000	$ 61,000
Common Stock, $2 per value	250,000	100,000
Other Contributed Capital	172,500	20,000
1/1 Retained Earnings	206,500	126,000
Income Summary	87,500	60,000
Total	$818,500	$367,000

Porter Company made the following open-market purchase and sate of Spitz Company common stock: January 1, 2007, purchased 45,000 shares for $135,000; May 1, 2011, sold 4,500 shares for $28,000.

The book value of Spitz Company's net assets on January 1, 2007, was $140,000; the excess of cost over net assets acquired relates to land. Subsequent changes in the book value of Spitz Company's net assets are entirely attributable to earnings retained in the business. Spitz Company earns its income evenly throughout the year. Porter Company uses the cost method to account for its investment.

Required:

Prepare a consolidated financial statements workpaper as of December 31, 2011. Begin the income statement section of the workpaper with "Net Income Before Dividend Income" which is $63,200 for Porter Company and $60,000 for Spitz Company.

PROBLEM 8-5 **Workpaper—Sale of Shares by Parent, Equity Method** LO3 LO4

(*Note:* This is the same problem as Problem 8-3, but assuming use of the complete or the partial equity method.)

The accounts of Pyle Company and its subsidiary, Stern Company, are summarized below as of December 31, 2011:

Debits	Pyle	Stern
Current Assets	$ 600,000	$ 320,000
Investment in Stern Company	718,400	
Other Assets	1,180,000	668,000
Dividends Declared, 11/1	80,000	60,000
Total	$2,578,400	$1,048,000

Credits	Pyle	Stern
Liabilities	$ 190,000	90,000
Common Stock, $5 par value	500,000	300,000
Other Contributed Capital	219,075	180,000
1/1 Retained Earnings	1,346,200	292,000
Net Income	323,125	186,000
Total	$2,578,400	$1,048,000

Pyle Company made the following open-market purchase and sale of Stern Company common stock: January 2, 2009, purchased 51,000 shares, cost $510,000; April 1, 2011, sold 3,000 shares, proceeds, $100,000.

The book value of Stern Company's net assets on January 2, 2009, $600,000 (including retained earnings of $120,000), approximated the fair value of those net assets. Subsequent changes in book value of the net assets are attributable to earnings of Stern Company. Stern Company earns its income evenly throughout the year.

Required:

Prepare a consolidated financial statements workpaper as of December 31, 2011. Begin the income statement section of the workpaper with "Income before Equity in Subsidiary Income and Gain on Sale of Investment," which is $172,000 and $186,000 for Pyle Company and Stern Company, respectively.

PROBLEM 8-6 **Workpaper—Purchase and Sale of Shares, Equity Method** LO3 LO4

(*Note:* This is the same problem as Problem 8-4, but assuming use of the complete or the partial equity method.)

Trial balances for Porter Company and its subsidiary, Spitz Company, as of December 31, 2011, follow:

Debits	*Porter*	*Spitz*
Cash	$ 90,000	$ 40,000
Accounts Receivable (net)	62,000	38,000
Inventory	106,000	64,000
Investment in Spitz Company	231,660	
Plant Assets	320,000	149,000
Land	69,000	46,000
Dividends Declared, 10/1	50,000	30,000
Total	$928,660	$367,000

Credits		
Liabilities	$102,000	$ 61,000
Common Stock, $2 par value	250,000	100,000
Other Contributed Capital	161,160	20,000
1/1 Retained Earnings	301,900	126,000
Income Summary	113,600	60,000
Total	$928,660	$367,000

Porter Company made the following open-market purchase and sale of Spitz Company common stock: January 1, 2007, purchased 45,000 shares for $135,000; May 1, 2011, sold 4,500 shares for $28,000.

The book value of Spitz Company's net assets on January 1, 2007 was $140,000; the excess of cost over net assets acquired relates to land. Subsequent changes in the book value of Spitz Company's net assets are entirely attributable to earnings retained in the business. Spitz Company earns its income evenly throughout the year.

Required:

Prepare a consolidated financial statements workpaper as of December 31, 2011. Begin the income statement section of the workpaper with "Net Income before Equity in Subsidiary Income and Gain on Sale of Investment," which is $63,200 for Porter Company and $60,000 for Spitz Company.

PROBLEM 8-7 **Multiple Stock Purchases and Sale of Shares** LO3 LO4

On January 1, 2011, Plum Company made an open-market purchase of 30,000 shares of Spivey Company common stock for $122,000. At that time, Spivey Company had common stock ($2 par) of $600,000 and retained earnings of $240,000. On July 1, 2011, an additional 210,000 shares were purchased on the open market by Plum Company at a cost of $789,600 or $3,76 a share. On November 1, 2011, 3,000 of the shares purchased on January 1, 2011, were sold on the open market for $21,000. Assume that any excess of implied value over book value acquired relates to subsidiary goodwill.

During 2011, Plum Company earned $22,000 (excluding any gain or loss on the sale of the shares). Plum Company received income statements from Spivey Company reporting the following results.

	Spivey Company Income
January 1, 2011 to June 30, 2011	$ 60,000
January 1, 2011 to October 31, 2011	96,000
For the year ended December 31, 2011	130,000

Neither company declared dividends during the year. Plum Company's retained earnings were $460,000 on January 1, 2011.

Required:

A. Prepare the book entries Plum Company would make during 2011 to account for its investment in Spivey Company, assuming

(1) The use of the cost method.

(2) The use of either the complete or the partial equity method.

B. Prepare in general journal form the eliminating entries for a consolidated statements workpaper on December 31, 2011, assuming

(1) The use of the cost method.

(2) The use of either the complete or the partial equity method.

C. Compute controlling interest in consolidated net income for 2011.

PROBLEM 8-8 **New Shares Purchased by Parent** LO6

Pryor Company acquired 51,000 shares of Spero Company's common stock on January 1, 2010, for $400,000 when Spero Company had common stock ($5 par) of $300,000 and retained earnings of $200,000.

On January 1, 2012, Spero Company issued 7,500 additional shares of its common stock for $8.50 per share. The new shares were purchased entirely by Pryor Company. Spero Company's retained earnings had increased to $360,000 by that date.

During 2012, Spero Company declared dividends of $40,000 and reported net income at year-end of $90,000. Pryor Company uses the cost method. Assume that any difference between implied and book values relates to subsidiary land.

Required:

A. Prepare the journal entry on Pryor's books to record the purchase of the new shares.

B. Prepare in general journal form the workpaper entries needed for the preparation of a consolidated statements workpaper on December 31, 2012.

PROBLEM 8-9 **New Subsidiary Shares Issued to Outsider** LO6

On January 1, 2010, Purdy Company acquired 84% of the capital stock of Sally Company for $840,000. On that date, Sally Company's stockholders' equity was:

Capital Stock, $20 par	$600,000
Other Contributed Capital	200,000
Retained Earnings	160,000
Total	$960,000

The difference between implied and book values relates to land owned by Sally Company.

On January 2, 2012, Sally Company issued 6,000 shares of its authorized capital stock, with a market value of $55 per share, to Marcy Smith in exchange for a patent. Sally Company's retained earnings balance on this date was $400,000, capital stock and other contributed capital balances had not changed during 2010 and 2011.

Required:

A. Prepare (1) the entry on Purdy's books to record the effect of the issuance, and (2) the elimination entries for the preparation of a consolidated balance sheet workpaper immediately after the new issue of shares assuming use of the cost method.

B. Assuming that the market value of the new shares issued was $34 per share, repeat requirement A above.

PROBLEM 8-10 **Open Market Purchases and Sales of Stock—Cost Method** LO3 LO4

On January 2, 2010, Pullen Company purchased, on the open market, 135,000 shares of Souza Company common stock for $665,000. At that time, Souza Company had common stock ($2 par value) of $300,000 and retained earnings of $400,000. On May 1, 2011, Pullen

Company sold 13,500 of its Souza Company shares on the open market for $91,000. Changes in Souza Company retained earnings during 2011 follow:

Retained Earnings 1/1/11	$500,000
Net Income for 2011 (earned evenly throughout the year)	270,000
Dividends Declared on 11/1/11 and paid on 12/16/11	(70,000)
Retained Earnings, 12/31/11	$700,000

Pullen Company, which uses the cost method to record its investment in Souza Company, reported net income for 2011 amounting to $352,500. Any difference between implied and book values relates to subsidiary land.

Required:

A. Prepare the book entries Pullen Company will make during 2011 to account for its investment in Souza Company.

B. Prepare, in general journal form, the eliminating entries needed to prepare a consolidated statements workpaper on December 31, 2011.

C. Compute controlling interest in consolidated net income for 2011.

D. Prepare the workpaper entry to establish reciprocity for the 2012 consolidated statements workpaper.

PROBLEM 8-11 **Workpaper—Sale of Shares by Parent, Equity Method—Loss of Control** LO3 LO4

The accounts of Pyle Company and its subsidiary, Stern Company, are summarized below as of December 31, 2011:

Debits	*Pyle*	*Stern*
Current Assets	$ 600,000	$ 320,000
Investment in Stern Company	480,000	
Other Assets	1,180,000	668,000
Dividends Declared, 11/1	80,000	60,000
	$2,340,000	$1,048,000
Credits		
Liabilities	$ 190,000	$ 90,000
Common Stock, $5 par	500,000	300,000
Other Contributed Capital	230,000	180,000
1/1 Retained Earnings	1,200,000	292,000
Net Income	220,000	186,000
	$2,340,000	$1,048,000

Pyle Company made the following open-market purchase and sale of Stern Company common stock:

January 2, 2009, purchased 51,000 shares (85% of Stern), cost $510,000, $10/share;

January 1, 2011, sold 40,000 shares (two-thirds of Stern), proceeds, $480,000, $12/share.

The book value of Stern Company's net assets on January 2, 2009, $600,000, approximated the fair value of those net assets, including retained earnings of $120,000. Subsequent changes in book value of the net assets are entirely attributable to earnings of Stern Company. Stern Company earns its income evenly throughout the year.

Required:

Prepare the journal entries needed on Pyle Company's books to record the transactions regarding the investment in Stern Company account assuming the equity method is used to account for the investment.

PROBLEM 8-12 **Worksheet, Multiple Stock Purchases, Cost Method** LO2

Trial balances for Phan Company and its subsidiary Sato Company on December 31, 2010, are as follows:

	Phan	*Sato*
Current Assets	$ 165,500	$ 138,000
Investment in Sato Company	334,425	
Other Assets	920,000	672,000
Dividends Declared	150,000	70,000
Cost of Goods Sold	1,100,000	320,000
Other Expenses	350,000	130,000
	$3,019,925	$1,330,000
Liabilities	$ 142,050	$ 160,000
Capital Stock, $10 par	600,000	400,000
Paid in Capital	100,000	
1/1 Retained Earnings	326,325	165,000
Sales	1,800,000	605,000
Gain on revaluation	13,925	
Dividend Income	37,625	
	$3,019,925	$1,330,000

Phan Company acquired its investment in Sato Company through open-market purchases of stock as follows:

Date	*Shares Purchased*	*Cost*	*Sato Company Retained Earnings Balance*
1/1/09	9,000	$110,500	$ 46,000
1/1/10	12,500	210,000	165,000
1/1/11	14,500	280,000	250,000
Total	36,000	$600,500	

Any difference between implied and book values of the interest acquired relates to Sato Company land, which is included in Other Assets.

Sato Company issued 40,000 shares of stock on July 1, 2006, its date of incorporation. No other capital stock transactions were undertaken by Sato Company after that time.

Required:

Prepare a consolidated financial statements workpaper for Phan Company and its subsidiary Sato Company on December 31, 2010.

PROBLEM 8-13 **Worksheet, Multiple Stock Purchases, Cost Method** LO2

This is a continuation of problem 8-12.

Trial balances for Phan Company and its subsidiary Sato Company on December 31, 2011, are as follows:

	Phan	*Sato*
Current Assets	$ 165,500	$ 218,000
Investment in Sato Company	614,425	
Other Assets	920,000	672,000
Dividends Declared	150,000	70,000
Cost of Goods Sold	1,100,000	325,000
Other Expenses	350,000	125,000
	$3,299,925	$1,410,000
Liabilities	$ 159,050	$ 160,000
Capital Stock, $10 par	600,000	400,000
Paid in Capital	100,000	
1/1 Retained Earnings	577,875	250,000
Sales	1,800,000	600,000
Dividend Income	63,000	
	$3,299,925	$1,410,000

Phan Company acquired its investment in Sato Company through open-market purchases of stock as follows:

Date	*Shares Purchased*	*Cost*	*Sato Company Retained Earnings Balance*
1/1/09	9,000	$110,500	$ 46,000
1/1/10	12,500	210,000	165,000
1/1/11	14,500	280,000	250,000
Total	36,000	$600,500	

Required:

Refer to problem 8-12. Prepare the consolidated financial statement workpaper for Phan Company and its subsidiary Sato Company on December 31, 2011. Use the cost method.

PROBLEM 8-14 **Worksheet, Multiple Stock Purchases, Equity Method** LO2 **(record gain on revaluation as difference in cost)**

Trial balances for Phan Company and its subsidiary Sato Company on December 31, 2010, are as follows:

	Phan	*Sato*
Current Assets	$ 165,500	$ 138,000
Investment in Sato Company	406,888	
Other Assets	920,000	672,000
Dividends Declared	150,000	70,000
Cost of Goods Sold	1,100,000	320,000
Other Expenses	350,000	130,000
	$3,092,388	$1,330,000
Liabilities	$ 142,050	$ 160,000
Capital Stock, $10 par	600,000	400,000
Paid in Capital	100,000	
1/1 Retained Earnings	353,100	165,000
Sales	1,800,000	605,000
Gain on revaluation	13,925	
Equity Income	83,313	
	$3,092,388	$1,330,000

Phan Company acquired its investment in Sato Company through open-market purchases of stock as follows:

Date	*Shares Purchased*	*Cost*	*Sato Company Retained Earnings Balance*
1/1/09	9,000	$110,500	$ 46,000
1/1/10	12,500	210,000	165,000
1/1/11	14,500	280,000	250,000
Total	36,000	$600,500	

Any difference between implied and book values of the interest acquired relates to Sato Company land, which is included in Other Assets.

Sato Company issued 40,000 shares of stock on July 1, 2006, its date of incorporation. No other capital stock transactions were undertaken by Sato Company after that time.

Required:

Prepare a consolidated financial statements workpaper for Phan Company and its subsidiary Sato Company on December 31, 2010.

PROBLEM 8-15 **Worksheet, Multiple Stock Purchases, Equity Method** LO2

This is a continuation of problem 8-14.

Trial balances for Phan Company and its subsidiary Sato Company on December 31, 2011, are as follows:

	Phan	*Sato*
Current Assets	$ 165,500	$ 218,000
Investment in Sato Company	758,888	
Other Assets	920,000	672,000
Dividends Declared	150,000	70,000
Cost of Goods Sold	1,100,000	325,000
Other Expenses	350,000	125,000
	$3,444,388	$1,410,000
Liabilities	$ 159,050	$ 160,000
Capital Stock, $10 par	600,000	400,000
Paid in Capital	100,000	
1/1 Retained Earnings	650,338	250,000
Sales	1,800,000	600,000
Equity Income	135,000	
	$3,444,388	$1,410,000

Phan Company acquired its investment in Sato Company through open-market purchases of stock as follows:

Date	*Shares Purchased*	*Cost*	*Sato Company Retained Earnings Balance*
1/1/09	9,000	$110,500	$ 46,000
1/1/10	12,500	210,000	165,000
1/1/11	14,500	280,000	250,000
Total	36,000	$600,500	

Required:

Refer to problem 8-14. Prepare the consolidated financial statement workpaper for Phan Company and its subsidiary Sato Company on December 31, 2011. Use the equity method.

9

INTERCOMPANY BOND HOLDINGS AND MISCELLANEOUS TOPICS—CONSOLIDATED FINANCIAL STATEMENTS

LEARNING OBJECTIVES

1. Describe the term "constructive retirement of debt."
2. Describe how the gain or loss on constructive retirement of intercompany bond holdings is allocated between the purchasing and issuing companies.
3. Explain the impact on the consolidated financial statements when a company issues a note to an affiliated company, which then discounts the note with an outside company.
4. Determine the effect on the consolidated financial statements when a subsidiary issues a stock dividend.
5. Understand the difference in how stock dividends and cash dividends issued by a subsidiary company affect the consolidated financial statements.
6. Determine the impact on the investment account when a subsidiary issues a stock dividend from preacquisition earnings and from postacquisition earnings.
7. Explain how the purchase price is allocated when the subsidiary has both common and preferred stock outstanding.
8. Determine the controlling interest in income when the parent company owns both common and preferred stock of the subsidiary.

"For the first time in four years, investors would have been better to ignore the asset-allocation advice of Wall Street's brightest minds and just buy bonds in the final months of 1997. As stock indexes swung wildly throughout the fourth quarter, bond prices marched higher, sending interest rates to their lowest levels since the 1960s. . . . Investors began to view fixed-income investments as a source of profits as well as a haven from the turbulence that dominated most other financial markets."[1]

[1] *WSJ*, "Most of Wall Street's Firms Missed Boat on Bond Move," by Suzanne McGee, 2/4/98, p. C1.

In this chapter, we discuss several areas related to the preparation of consolidated financial statements, including:

1. Intercompany bond holdings.
2. Intercompany notes receivable discounted.
3. Stock dividends issued by a subsidiary company.
4. Cash dividends from preacquisition earnings.
5. Preferred stock of a subsidiary.

All new aspects of consolidations introduced in this chapter are the same whether the parent uses the cost or partial equity method. As in prior chapters, the complete equity method differs from the other two in that the beginning retained earnings of the parent always equals the beginning consolidated retained earnings under the complete equity method.[2] Hence no entries are needed to the beginning retained earnings of the parent in the consolidating workpaper. There is, of course, no entry under this method (nor under the partial equity method) to establish reciprocity/convert to equity.

Reporting complications relating to accounting for the difference between the implied value of a subsidiary (based on acquisition cost) and the book value are avoided by assuming that all acquisitions of common stock are made at the book value of the acquired interest in net assets, and that the book values of the subsidiary's assets and liabilities are equal to their fair values on the date of acquisition. Also, deferred tax consequences are avoided by assuming the affiliates file consolidated tax returns. To conserve space, we present the entries for the cost and the complete equity methods only. The workpaper entries for the partial equity method would be identical to those for the cost method with one exception. As in previous chapters, a workpaper entry to reverse the effect of the parent company entries during the year for subsidiary income and dividends replaces the cost method entries to establish reciprocity/convert to equity and eliminate dividend income, if any.

INTERCOMPANY BOND HOLDINGS

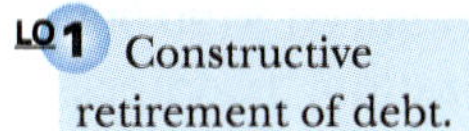
LO1 Constructive retirement of debt.

An affiliate company may purchase bonds issued by another affiliate directly from the issuing company or from outsiders after the original issue. In either case, because the bonds are held within the affiliated group, the intercompany bond investment (a receivable) and the bonds payable (a liability), along with any related intercompany interest expense and interest revenue, must be eliminated. In other words, because the bonds are not held by external parties, they are viewed as being ***constructively retired*** in the consolidated financial statements. Constructively retired means that the bonds are considered retired from a consolidated entity point of view, but legally the bonds are still outstanding as far as the issuing company is concerned. Since this is viewed as an early retirement of debt, a gain or loss on the constructive retirement is computed and allocated to the affiliated companies. A brief review of accounting for bond transactions is presented in the next section before the preparation of a consolidated statements workpaper involving intercompany bond holdings is illustrated.

[2] An exception occurs under the complete equity method when the treasury stock method is used for reciprocal holdings.

ACCOUNTING FOR BONDS—A REVIEW

To review accounting for bonds, assume that a company issued $100,000 par value bonds on January 2, 2010, for $90,000. The bonds mature 10 years later and pay 12% interest each December 31. The bonds were all acquired by one investor, and the fiscal year-end of both entities is December 31. The journal entries for the first year of operations, assuming straight-line amortization of the discount, are:[3]

Issuing Company

	2010		
Jan. 2	Cash	90,000	
	Discount on Bonds Payable	10,000	
	Bonds Payable		100,000
Dec. 31	Interest Expense	12,000	
	Cash		12,000
31	Interest Expense	1,000	
	Discount on Bonds Payable		1,000

Investor Company

	2010		
Jan. 2	Investment in Bonds	90,000	
	Cash		90,000
Dec. 31	Cash	12,000	
	Interest Revenue		12,000
31	Investment in Bonds	1,000	
	Interest Revenue		1,000

RELATED CONCEPTS

When using *present value* techniques to estimate the fair value of a bond payable, the objective is to estimate the price at which other entities are willing to hold the entity's liabilities as an asset.

From the point of view of the issuing company, $90,000 was received, but the company must pay $100,000 to the bondholders when the bonds mature 10 years later. Instead of deferring the $10,000 discount to be reported as a reduction in income in the year that the bonds mature, one-tenth of the discount ($1,000) is amortized each year as an increase in interest expense. The increase in expense results in a reduction of $1,000 in net income each year, which also reduces the retained earnings balance. At the end of 10 years, the issuing company's retained earnings is reduced $120,000 for the cash interest paid and $10,000 for the discount amortization. In effect, the $10,000 discount is recognized as additional interest expense over the life of the bonds. From the investor's point of view, $90,000 is paid for the bonds, but if the bonds are held to maturity, $100,000 will be received. One-tenth of this $10,000 is added to interest revenue each period, which results in an increase in reported income. As a result of acquiring the bond investment at a discount, retained earnings is increased $1,000 each year for a cumulative total of $10,000 over the life of the bonds.

If, in the foregoing example, the bonds had been issued for $110,000, the issuing company receives $10,000 more on the date of issue than must be paid when the bonds mature, while the investor will receive $10,000 less than the purchase price when the bonds mature. The investor (issuing) company, rather than reporting a reduction (increase) in income when the bonds mature, records one-tenth of the reduction (increase) each year as the premium on the bonds is amortized to interest

[3] For simplicity, it is assumed in this chapter that straight-line amortization is used. However, the reader is reminded that the interest method is required unless the straight-line method does not result in a material difference. *Opinion of the Accounting Principles Board No. 21*, "Interest on Receivables and Payables" (New York: AICPA, 1971), par. 15, [ASC 835-30-35-4].

revenue (expense) over the remaining life of the bonds. The effect is that the net income of the investor (issuing) company is $1,000 less (greater) each year as a result of amortizing the premium. The effect on income is, of course, also reflected in the reported retained earnings balance. Another way of viewing the amortization is that both parties are adjusting interest on the income statement from the coupon rate toward the market rate at date of issue.

CONSTRUCTIVE GAIN OR LOSS ON INTERCOMPANY BOND HOLDINGS

The purchase of an affiliate's bonds does not alter the accounting in the books of the individual companies. As noted in the preceding section, the issuing company and the purchasing company recognize a gain or loss on the bond transaction indirectly as the related premium or discount is amortized to interest expense and interest revenue over the remaining life of the bonds. Thus, on the books of the individual companies, the bonds are accounted for as if the transactions were with independent parties. In the preparation of consolidated statements, however, the acquisition of an affiliate's outstanding bonds from outsiders is considered a ***constructive retirement*** of the bond obligation by the consolidated entity.[4] The generally accepted practice of accounting for the early extinguishment of debt is to report an ordinary gain (loss) if the carrying value of the bonds is greater than (less than) the purchase price.[5] Thus, as with the intercompany sale of inventory or other assets, the constructive gain or loss is eventually recognized both on the books of the individual companies and the consolidated financial statements but in different periods.

Observe, however, that the constructive gain or loss on the bond retirement ***is recognized in the consolidated income statement prior to the recognition of the gain or loss on the books of the individual companies.*** In contrast (see Chapter 6), a gain or loss on the intercompany sale of inventory or other assets ***is recognized currently on the books of the selling company, but the gain or loss is deferred for consolidation purposes*** until the profit or loss is confirmed by an arm's-length transaction with an independent party. Thus, the objectives of the intercompany bond workpaper entries are essentially opposite the objectives of making workpaper entries for the intercompany sale of inventory or other assets. That is to say, in the period the bonds are purchased, workpaper entries are made to accelerate the recognition of the constructive gain or loss. After the bonds are purchased, workpaper entries are then needed to eliminate the portion of the constructive gain or loss recorded during the period on the books of the individual companies. In the case of the intercompany sale of inventory or other assets, workpaper entries are made in the year of the sale to eliminate or defer the profit or loss recorded on the books of the individual companies. In subsequent periods when the asset is sold to a third party and the profit or loss realized from a consolidated point of view, workpaper entries are made to recognize the profit or loss.

As noted in a preceding paragraph, the gain or loss on the bond retirement is computed as the difference between the carrying value (book value) of the liability

[4] When one affiliate purchases bonds directly from another affiliate, the purchase price of the bond investment will be equal to the issue price of the bonds. Therefore, there is no constructive gain or loss reported in the consolidated income statement. However, under the approach used in this text, if the issue price is greater than or less than par value, one company will be allocated a gain and the other allocated a loss of an equal amount.

[5] A gain or loss on the early extinguishments of debt was once reported as an extraordinary item net of related income tax consequences (*SFAS No. 4*). This treatment is no longer allowed (*SFAS No. 145*), [ASC 470–50–40–2].

and the purchase price of the bonds. There is general agreement on the amount of the gain or loss to be reported, but not on how the gain or loss should be allocated between the affiliated companies involved in the bond transaction for purposes of calculating the controlling and noncontrolling interests in consolidated net income.

Allocation of Constructive Gain or Loss

Four methods for allocating the constructive gain or loss between the parent and subsidiary have been supported in practice in the past and in the accounting literature.

1. The constructive gain or loss is allocated entirely to the issuing company. Support for this method is based on the contention that the purchasing affiliate, as a member of the consolidated group operating under the control of common management, was simply acting as an agent for the issuing company. Thus, any gain or loss on the constructive retirement is allocated entirely to the issuing company.
2. The constructive gain or loss is allocated entirely to the purchasing company. Support for this method rests on the contention that the purchasing company initiated the transaction and should be assigned the full amount of the gain or loss.
3. The constructive gain or loss is allocated entirely to the parent company. Under this approach, it is maintained that the management of the parent company controls the financing decisions of the consolidated affiliates. Since management directed or permitted the purchase of the bonds, any gain or loss is allocated entirely to the parent company.
4. The constructive gain or loss is allocated between the purchasing and issuing companies. This method recognizes that a discount or premium will often be associated with both the issuance and purchase of the bonds on the open market. A gain or loss will be recognized over the remaining life of the bonds as each company amortizes the related discount or premium to interest expense and interest revenue. If the bonds are held to maturity, the full amount of the gain or loss will be recognized by the two entities.

LO2 Allocating the constructive gain or loss.

The authors consider the fourth method to be the soundest conceptually. The method is consistent with the allocation of a gain or loss between the parent and subsidiary on other types of intercompany transactions. It also recognizes that if the purchasing company holds the bonds to maturity, the maturity value is paid by the issuing company. In such cases, each company realizes a gain or loss on the bond issuance or purchase that has been recognized on the books of the individual companies over the life of the bonds. Thus, if one of the companies is a partially owned subsidiary, the noncontrolling shareholders have an interest in the portion of the gain or loss allocated to, and recorded by, the subsidiary.

Computing the Constructive Gain or Loss

On the date that bonds of an affiliate are purchased, a constructive gain or loss is computed and this total gain or loss is allocated between the issuing and purchasing companies. The portion of the gain or loss allocated to the issuing company is the difference between the book value (carrying value) of the bonds issued and their par value; the portion allocated to the purchasing company is the difference between the par value of the bonds and their cost. There is no constructive gain or loss to either the purchasing company or the issuing company if the bonds are issued at par value. If the issue price and the purchase price of the bonds were not equal to par value, there are four possible combinations that can result when a constructive gain or loss to the consolidated entity is allocated between two affiliated companies. The combinations are shown below assuming two different book values of $110,000 and $90,000 and two different purchase prices of $115,000 and $85,000. The bonds have a par value of $100,000 in all situations.

Issuing Company				*Purchasing Company*
1. Book value $110,000	>	Par value $100,000	>	Purchase price $ 85,000
2. Book value $ 90,000	<	Par value $100,000	<	Purchase price $115,000
3. Book value $110,000	>	Par value $100,000	<	Purchase price $115,000
4. Book value $ 90,000	<	Par value $100,000	>	Purchase price $ 85,000

The constructive gain or loss for combination 3 is illustrated below. To compute the gain or loss allocated to each affiliate, the par value is subtracted from the book value and then the purchase price is subtracted from the par value. If the number is positive, it is a gain; if it is negative, it is a loss.

Issuing company	Book value	$110,000	+$10,000	Constructive gain
	Par value	$100,000		
Purchasing company	Purchase price	$115,000	−$15,000	Constructive loss
	Net constructive gain (loss)		($5,000)	

There is a net constructive loss of $5,000 to the consolidated entity because the purchase price of the bonds on the open market exceeded the carrying value of the debt.

To illustrate another situation, assume that $100,000 par value bonds with a book value of $90,000 were purchased by an affiliated company for $85,000 (combination 4 above).

Issuing company	Book value	$ 90,000	−$10,000	Constructive gain
	Par value	$100,000		
Purchasing company	Purchase price	$ 85,000	+$15,000	Constructive loss
	Net constructive gain (loss)		$ 5,000	

In this case there is a favorable settlement of debt (carrying value > purchase price) and a constructive gain of $5,000 is reported in the consolidated income statement, of which a $10,000 loss is allocated to the issuing company and a $15,000 gain is allocated to the purchasing company.

Constructive Gains and Losses

	Originally Issued At	
	Premium	*Discount*
Issuing Company	Constructive Gain	Constructive Loss
	Purchased At	
	Premium	*Discount*
Purchasing Company	Constructive Loss	Constructive Gain

In the year that the bonds are constructively retired, if either the issuing company or the purchasing company is a partially owned subsidiary, the noncontrolling interest in consolidated net income is reduced (increased) by a loss (gain). In subsequent periods, the income of the subsidiary will be decreased or increased as the related discount or premium is amortized. The noncontrolling interest is also affected by this increase or decrease in income.

ACCOUNTING FOR INTERCOMPANY BONDS ILLUSTRATED

To illustrate entries that are necessary on the books of the affiliated companies and in the consolidated statements workpaper when one affiliate holds bonds of another affiliate, the following are assumed:

1. P Company acquired an 80% interest in S Company for $1,200,000 on January 2, 2009, when the retained earnings and common stock accounts of S Company were $500,000 and $1,000,000, respectively.
2. On December 31, 2012, P Company acquired $300,000 of S Company's par value bonds (60% of S Company's bonds) on the open market for $310,000 after the semiannual interest payment had been made. At the time of purchase there were $500,000 par value bonds outstanding with a book value of $480,000. The bonds mature in four years on December 31, 2016, and carry a nominal interest rate of 9%. Interest is paid semiannually on June 30 and December 31.
3. Both companies use the straight-line method to amortize bond discounts and premiums because the results obtained do not materially differ from those that would be obtained if the effective-interest method were used.
4. The fiscal year-end of both companies is December 31.

In this illustration, bonds of the subsidiary are purchased by the parent company. Book entries, as well as consolidated statements workpaper entries and procedures, would be similar if the parent company bonds were purchased by a subsidiary company, except that, the Investment in Bonds account is carried on the books of the subsidiary and the bond liability is carried on the parent company's books.

Also note that, in this example, the parent purchased the bonds at a premium (on investment), while the subsidiary issued the bonds at a discount (on bonds payable). Clearly it is possible that the reverse might occur (purchase at a discount, issue at a premium) or that both the purchase and the issue might occur at a premium, or both at a discount.

BOOK ENTRY RELATED TO BOND INVESTMENT

P Company will prepare the following entry to record the bond investment:

Dec. 31	Investment in S Company Bonds	310,000	
	Cash		310,000

Note that the usual practice of recording a bond investment does not separate the discount or premium. Since the bonds were purchased on the open market, there is no entry made on the issuing company's books. In this illustration, the bonds were purchased on the last day of the fiscal period after the semiannual interest had been paid. Thus, there is no accrued interest to be recorded in the current period.

Consolidated Statements Workpaper—2012

The total gain or loss on the constructive retirement to be reported in the 2012 consolidated income statement, and the constructive gain or loss allocated to each company are computed as follows:

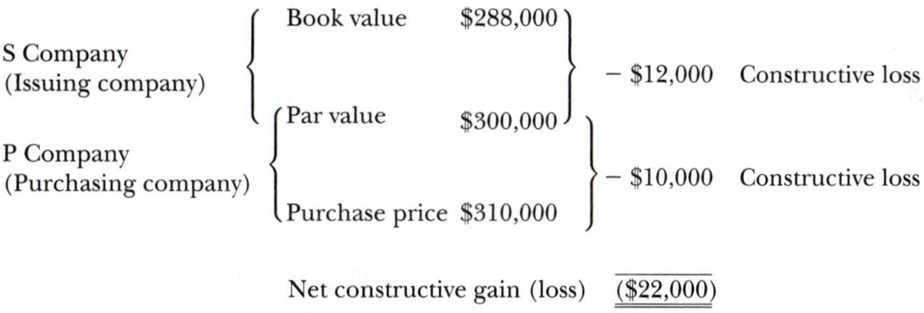

If the purchase price were less than the book value of $288,000, a total constructive gain would result.

On the books of the individual companies, the constructive loss is not recorded in the year that the bonds are purchased on the open market. From a consolidated entity point of view, however, the purchase is a constructive retirement of debt. Thus, the constructive loss is recognized in the determination of combined income in the year of the purchase.

Workpaper entries necessary in the consolidated statements workpaper for the year ended December 31, 2012, are presented in general journal form below. The consolidated statements workpaper for 2012 is presented in Illustration 9-1.

Cost Method
80% Owned Subsidiary
Constructive Retirement of Subsidiary's Bonds—Year of Retirement

ILLUSTRATION 9-1
Consolidated Statements Workpaper
P Company and Subsidiary
for the Year Ended December 31, 2012

Income Statement	*P Company*	*S Company*	*Eliminations Dr.*	*Eliminations Cr.*	*Noncontrolling Interest*	*Consolidated Balances*
Sales	3,104,000	2,200,000				5,304,000
Dividend Income	16,000		(5) 16,000			—0—
Total Revenue	3,120,000	2,200,000				5,304,000
Cost of Goods Sold	1,700,000	1,360,000				3,060,000
Interest Expense		50,000				50,000
Other Expense	1,124,000	665,000				1,789,000
Loss on Constructive Retirement			(2) 10,000			
of Bonds			(3) 12,000			22,000
Total Cost and Expense	2,824,000	2,075,000				4,921,000
Consolidated Net Income	296,000	125,000				383,000
Noncontrolling Interest in Income*					22,600*	22,600
Net Income to Retained Earnings	296,000	125,000	38,000	—	22,600	360,400
Retained Earnings Statement						
1/1 Retained Earnings						
P Company	1,650,000			(1) 160,000		1,810,000
S Company		700,000	(6) 700,000			
Net Income from above	296,000	125,000	38,000		22,600	360,400
Dividends Declared						
P Company	(150,000)					(150,000)
S Company		(20,000)		(5) 16,000	(4,000)	
12/31 Retained Earnings to Balance Sheet	1,796,000	805,000	738,000	176,000	18,600	2,020,400
Balance Sheet						
				(2) 10,000		
Investment in S Company Bonds	310,000			(4) 300,000		—0—
Investment in S Company Stock	1,200,000		(1) 160,000	(6) 1,360,000		—0—
Other Assets	5,420,000	2,620,000				8,040,000
Total Assets	6,930,000	2,620,000				8,040,000
9% Bonds Payable		500,000	(4) 300,000			200,000
Discount on Bonds Payable		(20,000)		(3) 12,000		(8,000)
Other Liabilities	2,134,000	335,000				2,469,000
Capital Stock						
P Company	3,000,000					3,000,000
S Company		1,000,000	(6) 1,000,000			
Retained Earnings from above	1,796,000	805,000	738,000	176,000	18,600	2,020,400
1/1 Noncontrolling Interest in Net Assets**				(6) 340,000	340,000	
12/31 Noncontrolling Interest in Net Assets					358,600	358,600
Total Liabilities and Equity	6,930,000	2,620,000	2,198,000	2,198,000		8,040,000

* Noncontrolling interest in income computation: ($125,000 − $12,000) × .20 = $22,600.
** $300,000 + ($700,000 − $500,000) × .20 = $340,000.
(1) To establish reciprocity (convert to equity) as of 1/1/2012 [($700,000 − $500,000) × .80 = $160,000].
(2) To recognize constructive loss not recorded by P Company and adjust the bond investment to par value.
(3) To recognize the constructive loss not recorded by S Company and adjust the intercompany bonds payable to par value.
(4) To eliminate intercompany bond investment and liability.
(5) To eliminate intercompany dividends.
(6) To eliminate investment account and create noncontrolling interest account.

Consolidated Statements Workpaper Entries—2012

	Debit	Credit
(1) Investment in S Company Stock	160,000	
Beginning Retained Earnings—P Company		160,000
To establish reciprocity, or convert to equity		

The reciprocity (conversion to equity) entry, computed as follows, is not needed if the partial equity method is used:

Retained earnings balance—January 1, 2012	$700,000
Retained earnings balance—date of acquisition	500,000
Increase in retained earnings	200,000
Percentage interest held by P Company	.80
Amount to establish reciprocity	$160,000

	Debit	Credit
(2) Loss on Constructive Retirement of Bonds	10,000	
Investment in S Company Bonds		10,000
To recognize the constructive loss not recorded by P Company and *adjust the bond investment to par value* (i.e., the premium paid by P Company over the par value).		
(3) Loss on Constructive Retirement of Bonds	12,000	
Discount on Bonds Payable		12,000
To recognize the constructive loss not recorded by the subsidiary and *adjust the intercompany bonds to par value* (i.e., the difference between the carrying value to S Company and par value).		

Entries (2) and (3) recognize the constructive loss allocated to each company and adjust the bond investment and carrying value of the intercompany debt to par value in preparation for the elimination of the intercompany receivable and payable.

	Debit	Credit
(4) Bonds Payable	300,000	
Investment in S Company Bonds		300,000
To eliminate intercompany bond investment and liability.		
(5) Dividend Income	16,000	
Dividends Declared—S Company		16,000
To eliminate intercompany dividends.		
(6) Beginning Retained Earnings—S Company	700,000	
Common Stock—S Company	1,000,000	
Investment in S Company Stock		1,360,000
Noncontrolling Interest in Equity		340,000
To eliminate investment account and create noncontrolling interest.		

Entries (2), (3), and (4) could be combined into one entry as follows:

	Debit	Credit
Loss on Constructive Retirement of Bonds	22,000	
Bonds Payable	300,000	
Discount on Bonds Payable		12,000
Investment in S Company Bonds		310,000

Complete Equity Method If the complete equity method is used, entry (1), the reciprocity entry, is not needed and the following entry replaces entry (5) above. The consolidated statements workpaper for 2012, assuming the use of the complete equity method, is presented in Illustration 9-2.

	Debit	Credit
Equity in S Company Income	80,400	
Dividends Declared		16,000
Investment in S Company Stock		64,400
To eliminate the intercompany income and dividends.		

Complete Equity Method
80% Owned Subsidiary
Constructive Retirement of
Subsidiary's Bonds—Year of Retirement

ILLUSTRATION 9-2
Consolidated Statements Workpaper
P Company and Subsidiary
for the Year Ended December 31, 2012

	P	S	Eliminations		Noncontrolling	Consolidated
Income Statement	*Company*	*Company*	*Dr.*	*Cr.*	*Interest*	*Balances*
Sales	3,104,000	2,200,000				5,304,000
Equity Income	80,400		(3) 80,400			—0—
Total Revenue	3,184,400	2,200,000				5,304,000
Cost of Goods Sold	1,700,000	1,360,000				3,060,000
Interest Expense		50,000				50,000
Other Expense	1,124,000	665,000				1,789,000
Loss on Constructive Retirement of Bonds			(1) 22,000			22,000
Total Cost and Expense	2,824,000	2,075,000				4,921,000
Consolidated Net Income	360,400	125,000				383,000
Noncontrolling Interest in Income					22,600*	22,600
Net Income to Retained Earnings	360,400	125,000	102,400	—	22,600	360,400
Retained Earnings Statement						
1/1 Retained Earnings						
P Company	1,810,000					1,810,000
S Company		700,000	(4) 700,000			
Net Income from above	360,400	125,000	102,400		22,600	360,400
Dividends Declared						
P Company	(150,000)					(150,000)
S Company		(20,000)		(3) 16,000	(4,000)	
12/31 Retained Earnings to Balance Sheet	2,020,400	805,000	802,400	16,000	18,600	2,020,400
Balance Sheet						
Investment in S Company Bonds	310,000			(1) 10,000 (2) 300,000		—0—
Investment in S Company Stock	1,424,400			(3) 64,400 (4) 1,360,000		—0—
Other Assets	5,420,000	2,620,000				8,040,000
Total Assets	7,154,400	2,620,000				8,040,000
9% Bonds Payable		500,000	(2) 300,000			200,000
Discount on Bonds Payable		(20,000)		(1) 12,000		(8,000)
Other Liabilities	2,134,000	335,000				2,469,000
Capital Stock						
P Company	3,000,000					3,000,000
S Company		1,000,000	(4) 1,000,000			
Retained Earnings from above	2,020,400	805,000	802,400	16,000	18,600	2,020,400
1/1 Noncontrolling Interest in Net Assets**				(4) 340,000	340,000	
12/31 Noncontrolling Interest in Net Assets					358,600	358,600
Total Liabilities and Equity	7,154,400	2,620,000	2,102,400	2,102,400		8,040,000

* Noncontrolling interest in income computation: ($125,000 − $12,000) × .20 = $22,600.
** $300,000 + ($700,000 − $500,000) × .20 = $340,000.
(1) To recognize the constructive loss and adjust the bond investment and the intercompany bond to par value.
(2) To eliminate intercompany bond investment and liability.
(3) To eliminate intercompany income and dividends.
(4) To eliminate investment account and create noncontrolling interest account.

Since the bonds were purchased on the open market on the *last day of the fiscal period,* there is no intercompany interest reported in the 2012 income statement. Accordingly, no elimination of intercompany interest revenue and expense is required in the 2012 consolidated statements workpaper. Since the amount of net income reported by S Company that is included in consolidated net income is reduced by the constructive loss allocated to S Company, noncontrolling interest in consolidated income is 20% of the income reported by S Company reduced by the constructive loss of $12,000 allocated to the subsidiary [.20 × ($125,000 − $12,000) = $22,600].

A careful review of Illustrations 9-1 and 9-2 will reveal these important points concerning the objectives of the bond elimination entries:

1. Since the bonds were purchased this year, the constructive loss is reported in full in the determination of combined income.
2. Interest expense is the amortized interest paid to outside parties during the fiscal period. In this illustration, the intercompany portion was purchased on December 31. Therefore, the bonds were held by outside parties for the full 12 months. Interest expense reported in the consolidated income statement is for the full year, which is equal to the cash interest paid of $45,000 plus discount amortization of $5,000. As shown in the next illustration, if the bonds are held by P Company during the period, interest expense, net of amortization, is eliminated. Thus, for a 12-month period, $30,000 in interest expense is eliminated, resulting in consolidated interest expense of $20,000 ($50,000 times the 40% held by outside parties).
3. The book value of the debt is the amount held by outside parties on the balance sheet date, which is $192,000 [($500,000 − $20,000) × .40]. The 60% held by the parent is eliminated by workpaper entries (2) and (4) in Illustration 9-1 and (1) and (2) in Illustration 9-2.

Consolidated net income and retained earnings for the year ended December 31, 2012, using the t-account approach, are computed as shown in Figure 9-1. If the equity method is used, the reconciliation of retained earnings is not needed.

Year Subsequent to Acquisition of Bonds, Entries on the Books of Affiliated Companies—2013

During 2013, the two companies record on their individual books the following entries related to the bond transaction:

P Company's Books

Entries on June 30 and December 31

Cash	13,500	
Interest Revenue		13,500
To record receipt of interest ($300,000 × .09 × 6/12).		
Interest Revenue	1,250	
Investment in S Company Bonds		1,250
To amortize premium on outstanding bonds ($10,000 ÷ 8 periods).		

For the full year 2013, P Company received total cash of $27,000, recognized total interest revenue of $24,500, and recorded amortization of the premium on the bond of $2,500.

FIGURE 9-1

T-Account Approach to Controlling Interest in Consolidated Net Income and Consolidated Retained Earnings

Controlling Interest in Consolidated Net Income—2012

		Reported net income of P Company		$296,000
		Less: Dividend income		(16,000)
		Net income from independent operations		280,000
		Less: Constructive loss not recorded by P Company in the current year (premium amortization)		(10,000)
		P Company's contribution to consolidated income		270,000
		Reported net income of S Company	$125,000	
		Less: Constructive loss not recorded by S Company	(12,000)	
		S Company's contribution to combined income	113,000	
		Percentage interest in S Company	.80	90,400
		Controlling Interest in Consolidated net income		$360,400

Consolidated Retained Earnings—December 31, 2012

Constructive loss on bond retirement not recorded by P Company	10,000	Ending retained earnings—P Company, December 31, 2012 (Cost Method)		$1,796,000
		Retained earnings adjusted for unrecorded constructive loss		1,786,000
		Ending retained earnings—S Company	$805,000	
		Less: Retained earnings—date of acquisition	(500,000)	
		Increase in recorded retained earnings	305,000	
		Less: Constructive loss on bond retirement not recorded by S Company	(12,000)	
		Adjusted increase in recorded retained earnings	293,000	
		Percentage interest in S Company	.80	234,400
		Consolidated retained earnings on December 31, 2012		$2,020,400

COMPLETE

Complete Equity Method—Additional Entries on the Books of P Company Subsequent to Acquisition of Debt

In the years subsequent to the acquisition of the subsidiary's debt, there are additional entries needed by P Company. The following entries would be made to the Investment in S Company Stock account in the year subsequent to acquisition:

Investment in S Company Stock	112,000	
Equity in S Company Income		112,000
To record equity income (80% of $140,000).		
Cash	48,000	
Investment in S Company Stock		48,000
To record dividends received (80% of $60,000).		
Investment in S Company Stock	4,900	
Equity in S Company Income		4,900
To eliminate the intercompany effect from the amortization of P Company's share of the constructive loss.		

This last entry ensures that P Company's income equals consolidated income. The $4,900 can be computed several ways. First, the total constructive loss is $22,000, of which P Company is allocated $19,600. Since the total loss will be recognized to income over the term of the bond through amortization and because the bond has four years remaining, one-fourth of the loss is amortized in each period ($19,600/4 = $4,900). Because this is an intercompany transaction, under the complete equity method, an additional $4,900 must be added to income to offset the additional expense. Recall that the entire $22,000 is recognized as a loss in the year of purchase. Alternatively, the $4,900 can be computed by comparing the amount of interest expense and interest revenue recognized by each company as follows:

Interest Expense (60% of S Company's $50,000 interest expense reported in 2013)	$30,000
Interest Revenue recognized by P Company (2013)	24,500
Excess Expense	5,500
Controlling interest's share of the total constructive loss ($19,600/$22,000) =	×.8909
	4,900

S Company's Books

Entries on June 30 and December 31

Interest Expense	22,500	
Cash		22,500
To record payment of interest ($500,000 × .09 × 6/12).		
Interest Expense	2,500	
Discount on Bonds Payable		2,500
To amortize discount on outstanding bonds ($20,000 ÷ 8 periods).		

Thus, S Company paid $45,000 in cash interest and amortized $5,000 of the bond discount. Since 60% of the bonds ($300,000) were purchased by P Company, S Company paid $27,000 cash to P Company and amortized $3,000 of the related bond discount.

Recall in the prior year, a constructive loss of $22,000 was reported on the consolidated income statement. This amount is equal to the sum of the premium yet to be amortized by P Company ($10,000) and the discount yet to be amortized by S Company ($12,000). Therefore, as the companies amortize these amounts, they, in essence, recognize a portion of the total constructive loss throughout the term of the bond. For the full year (2013), $2,500 ($1,250 × 2) of the total constructive loss was recognized on the books of P Company as a result of amortizing the premium on the investment. S Company recognized $3,000 [($2,500 × 2) × .60] of its share of the loss through the amortization of the discount. To prevent double counting, these amortization amounts must be eliminated for consolidated purposes.

The account balances related to the intercompany bond holdings at the end of 2013 are:

P Company's Books

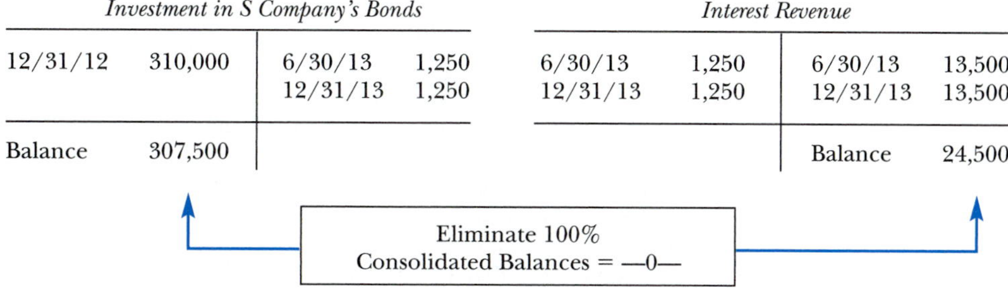

Investment in S Company's Bonds

12/31/12	310,000	6/30/13	1,250
		12/31/13	1,250
Balance	307,500		

Interest Revenue

6/30/13	1,250	6/30/13	13,500
12/31/13	1,250	12/31/13	13,500
		Balance	24,500

S Company's Books

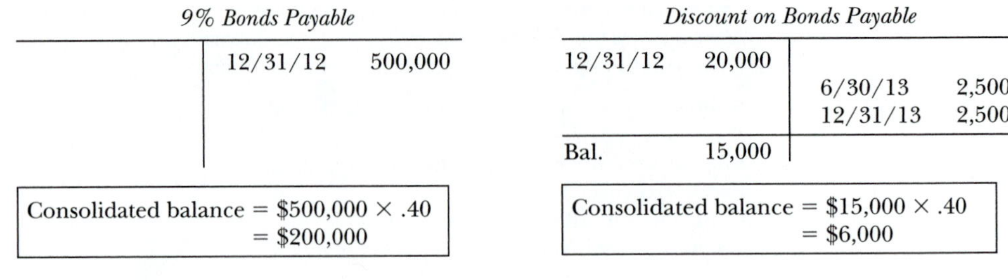

9% Bonds Payable			
		12/31/12	500,000

Consolidated balance = $500,000 × .40
= $200,000

Discount on Bonds Payable			
12/31/12	20,000		
		6/30/13	2,500
		12/31/13	2,500
Bal.	15,000		

Consolidated balance = $15,000 × .40
= $6,000

Interest Expense		
2013		
6/30/13	22,500	
6/30/13	2,500	
12/31/13	22,500	
12/31/13	2,500	
Balance	50,000	

Consolidated balance = $50,000 × .40
= $20,000

Rationale: For consolidated balances, 60% of the bonds held by the affiliated company must be eliminated. The remaining 40%, held by outside parties, is reported in the consolidated financial statement.

Consolidated Statements Workpaper Entries—December 31, 2013

Workpaper entries necessary in the consolidated statements workpaper for the year ended December 31, 2013, are presented in general journal form below. The consolidated statements workpaper for 2013 is presented in Illustration 9-3.

		Debit	Credit
(1)	Investment in S Company Stock	244,000	
	Beginning Retained Earnings—P Company		244,000
	To establish reciprocity/convert to equity [($805,000 − $500,000) × .80 = $244,000].		
(2)	Beginning Retained Earnings—P Company	10,000	
	Investment in S Company Bonds		10,000
	To adjust beginning retained earnings for constructive loss (recorded in prior year as workpaper entry only; see 2012 entry (2) and to adjust investment to par.		
(3)	Beginning Retained Earnings—P Company ($12,000 × .80)	9,600	
	Beginning Noncontrolling Interest ($12,000 × .20)	2,400	
	Discount on Bonds Payable ($15,000 × .60)		12,000
	To adjust beginning retained earnings balances for unrecorded constructive loss at beginning of the year (recorded in 2012 as workpaper entry only; see 2012 entry (3)) and adjust intercompany bonds to par value.		
(4)	Investment in S Company Bonds	2,500	
	Interest Revenue ($1,250 + $1,250)		2,500
	To reverse the amortization of premium on investment recorded by P Company during the current year (and not needed by consolidated entity since the constructive loss was recorded in its entirety in 2012).		

Cost Method
80% Owned Subsidiary
Constructive Retirement of Subsidiary's Bonds—One Year after Retirement

ILLUSTRATION 9-3
Consolidated Statements Workpaper
P Company and Subsidiary
for the Year Ended December 31, 2013

	P Company	*S Company*	*Eliminations Dr.*	*Eliminations Cr.*	*Noncontrolling Interest*	*Consolidated Balances*
Income Statement						
Sales	3,546,000	2,020,000				5,566,000
Dividend Income	48,000		(8) 48,000			—0—
Interest Income	24,500		(6) 27,000	(4) 2,500		—0—
Total Revenue	3,618,500	2,020,000				5,566,000
Cost of Goods Sold	2,040,000	1,200,000				3,240,000
Interest Expense		50,000		(5) 3,000 (6) 27,000		20,000
Other Expense	1,124,500	630,000				1,754,500
Total Cost and Expense	3,164,500	1,880,000				5,014,500
Net/Consolidated Income	454,000	140,000				551,500
Noncontrolling Interest in Income*					28,600*	28,600
Net Income to Retained Earnings	454,000	140,000	75,000	32,500	28,600	522,900
Retained Earnings Statement						
1/1 Retained Earnings						
P Company	1,796,000		(2) 10,000 (3) 9,600	(1) 244,000		2,020,400
S Company		805,000	(9) 805,000			
Net Income from above	454,000	140,000	75,000	32,500	28,600	522,900
Dividends Declared						
P Company	(150,000)					(150,000)
S Company		(60,000)		(8) 48,000	(12,000)	
12/31 Retained Earnings to Balance Sheet	2,100,000	885,000	899,600	324,500	16,600	2,393,300
Balance Sheet						
Investment in S Company Bonds	307,500		(4) 2,500	(2) 10,000 (7) 300,000		—0—
Investment in S Company Stock	1,200,000		(1) 244,000	(9) 1,444,000		—0—
Other Assets	5,812,500	2,690,000				8,502,500
Total Assets	7,320,000	2,690,000				8,502,500
9% Bonds Payable		500,000	(7) 300,000			200,000
Discount on Bonds Payable		(15,000)	(5) 3,000	(3) 12,000		(6,000)
Other Liabilities	2,220,000	320,000				2,540,000
Capital Stock						
P Company	3,000,000					3,000,000
S Company		1,000,000	(9) 1,000,000			
Retained Earnings from above	2,100,000	885,000	899,600	324,500	16,600	2,393,300
1/1 Noncontrolling Interest in Net Assets**			(3) 2,400	(9) 361,000**	358,600	
12/31 Noncontrolling Interest in Net Assets					375,200	375,200
Total Liabilities and Equity	7,320,000	2,690,000	2,451,500	2,451,500		8,502,500

* ($140,000 + $3,000) × .20 = $28,600.
** $300,000 + ($805,000 − $500,000) × .20 = $361,000.
(1) To establish reciprocity (convert to equity) as of 1/1/2013 [($805,000 − $500,000) × .80 = $244,000].
(2) To adjust beginning retained earnings for unrecorded constructive loss recorded in prior years as workpaper entry only and adjust bond investment to par value.
(3) To adjust beginning retained earnings for unrecorded constructive loss at the beginning of year, adjust interest expense for the loss recorded this period, and adjust intercompany bond payable to par value.
(4) To reverse the amortization of premium on investment recorded by P Company during the year.
(5) To reverse the amortization of discount on bonds payable recorded by S Company during the year.
(6) To eliminate intercompany interest.
(7) To eliminate intercompany bond investment and bonds payable.
(8) To eliminate intercompany dividends.
(9) To eliminate the investment account and create noncontrolling interest account.

(5) Discount on Bonds Payable ($5,000 × .60)	3,000	
Interest Expense		3,000
To reverse amortization of discount on bonds payable recorded by S Company during current year (and not needed by consolidated entity since the constructive loss was recorded in its entirety in 2012).		

Recall that the individual companies record a portion of the loss ($5,500 in total) this year as amortization of the discount ($5,000 × .60 = $3,000) and premium ($2,500). Workpaper entries are necessary to add back this portion of the loss reported as a reduction in the current income of the individual companies because the entire loss was reported in the consolidated income statement in the year that the bonds were acquired by P Company. Failure to do so will result in reporting the constructive loss twice, once in the year of acquisition and again in subsequent periods when the companies record the loss. The credit to interest revenue for $2,500 [entry (4)] and the credit to interest expense for $3,000 [entry (5)] increase combined income by $5,500.

(6) Interest Revenue ($45,000 × .60) or ($13,500 + $13,500)	27,000	
Interest Expense		27,000
To eliminate intercompany interest.		
(7) Bonds Payable ($500,000 × .60)	300,000	
Investment in S Company Bonds		300,000
To eliminate intercompany bond investment and bonds payable.		
(8) Dividend Income	48,000	
Dividends Declared		48,000
To eliminate intercompany dividends.		
(9) Beginning Retained Earnings—S Company	805,000	
Common Stock—S Company	1,000,000	
Investment in S Company Stock		1,444,000
Noncontrolling Interest in Net Assets		361,000
To eliminate the investment account and recognize NCI in Net Assets.		

Workpaper entries (2) through (7) could be combined into one entry as follows:

Beginning Retained Earnings—P Company	19,600	
Beginning Noncontrolling Interest	2,400	
Interest Revenue	24,500	
Bonds Payable	300,000	
Interest Expense		30,000
Discount on Bonds Payable		9,000
Investment in S Company Bonds		307,500

Noncontrolling interest in consolidated net income is 20% of the income reported by S Company plus the portion of the loss recorded by S during 2013, but fully reported in the 2012 consolidated income statement, the year the bonds were constructively retired [.20 × ($140,000 + $3,000) = $28,600].

Consolidated Statements Workpaper Entries—2013

The Complete Equity Method

COMPLETE

		Debit	Credit
(1)	Investment in S Company Stock	19,600	
	Beginning NCI ($12,000 × .20)	2,400	
	Investment in S Company Bonds		10,000
	Discount on Bonds Payable ($15,000 × .60)		12,000
	To adjust beginning retained earnings balance and NCI for unrecorded constructive loss at beginning of the year (recorded in 2012 in workpaper entry only; see 2012 entry 3) and adjust intercompany bonds to par value.		
(2)	Investment in S Company Bonds	2,500	
	Interest Revenue ($1,250 + $1,250)		2,500
	To reverse the amortization of premium on investment recorded by P Company during the current year (and not needed by consolidated entity since the constructive loss was recorded in its entirety in 2012).		
(3)	Discount on Bonds Payable ($5,000 × .60)	3,000	
	Interest Expense		3,000
	To reverse amortization of discount on bonds payable recorded by Company during current year (and not needed by consolidated entity since the constructive loss was recorded in its entirety in 2012).		
(4)	Bonds Payable ($500,000 × .60)	300,000	
	Investment in S Company Bonds		300,000
	To eliminate intercompany bond investment and bonds payable.		
(5)	Interest Revenue ($45,000 × .60) or ($13,500 + $13,500)	27,000	
	Interest Expense		27,000
	To eliminate intercompany interest.		
(6)	Equity Income	116,900	
	Investment in P Company Stock		68,900
	Dividends Declared		48,000
	To eliminate intercompany dividends and income.		
(7)	Beginning Retained Earnings—S Company	805,000	
	Common Stock—S Company	1,000,000	
	Investment in S Company Stock		1,444,000
	Beginning NCI		361,000
	To eliminate the investment account and recognize NCI.		

Whether a single entry or a series of entries are made, the eliminating entries must accomplish the following under the cost (or complete equity) method (Illustration 9-4):

1. Under the ***cost*** or ***partial equity method***, the parent company's beginning retained earnings is reduced by:
   a. 100% of the constructive loss allocated to P Company that has not been recorded in prior periods as a decrease in interest revenue via the periodic amortization of premium ($10,000).
   b. 80% of the constructive loss allocated to S Company that has not been recorded in prior periods as an increase in interest expense via the periodic discount amortization ($9,600).

   Under the ***complete equity method***, the parent company's beginning retained earnings does not need to be adjusted for these amounts because each year adjustments are made to the parent company accounts Equity in Subsidiary Income (and hence to retained earnings of P Company) and Investment in S Company.

Complete Equity Method
80% Owned Subsidiary
Constructive Retirement of Subsidiary's Bonds—
One Year after Retirement

ILLUSTRATION 9-4
Consolidated Statements Workpaper
P Company and Subsidiary
for the Year Ended December 31, 2013

Income Statement	*P Company*	*S Company*	*Eliminations Dr.*	*Eliminations Cr.*	*Noncontrolling Interest*	*Consolidated Balances*
Sales	3,546,000	2,020,000				5,566,000
Equity Income	116,900		(6) 116,900			—0—
Interest Income	24,500		(5) 27,000	(2) 2,500		—0—
Total Revenue	3,687,400	2,020,000				5,566,000
Cost of Goods Sold	2,040,000	1,200,000				3,240,000
Interest Expense		50,000		(3) 3,000 (5) 27,000		20,000
Other Expense	1,124,500	630,000				1,754,500
Total Cost and Expense	3,164,500	1,880,000				5,014,500
Net/Consolidated Income	522,900	140,000				551,500
Noncontrolling Interest in Income					28,600*	28,600
Net Income to Retained Earnings	522,900	140,000	143,900	32,500	28,600	522,900
Retained Earnings Statement						
1/1 Retained Earnings						
P Company	2,020,400					2,020,400
S Company		805,000	(7) 805,000			
Net Income from above	522,900	140,000	143,900	32,500	28,600	522,900
Dividends Declared						
P Company	(150,000)					(150,000)
S Company		(60,000)		(6) 48,000	(12,000)	
12/31 Retained Earnings to Balance Sheet	2,393,300	885,000	948,900	80,500	16,600	2,393,300
Balance Sheet						
Investment in S Company Bonds	307,500		(2) 2,500	(1) 10,000 (4) 300,000		—0—
Investment in S Company Stock	1,493,300		(1) 19,600	(6) 68,900 (7) 1,444,000		—0—
Other Assets	5,812,500	2,690,000				8,502,500
Total Assets	7,613,300	2,690,000				8,502,500
9% Bonds Payable		500,000	(4) 300,000			200,000
Discount on Bonds Payable		(15,000)	(3) 3,000	(1) 12,000		(6,000)
Other Liabilities	2,220,000	320,000				2,540,000
Capital Stock						
P Company	3,000,000					3,000,000
S Company		1,000,000	(7) 1,000,000			
Retained Earnings from above	2,393,300	885,000	948,900	80,500	16,600	2,393,300
1/1 Noncontrolling Interest in Net Assets			(1) 2,400	(7) 361,000**	358,600	
12/31 Noncontrolling Interest in Net Assets					375,200	375,200
Total Liabilities and Equity	7,613,300	2,690,000	2,276,400	2,276,400		8,502,500

* ($140,000 + $3,000) × .20 = $28,600.
** $300,000 + ($805,000 − $500,000) × .20 = $361,000.
(1) To adjust the investment in S Company Stock account and beginning retained earnings of S Company for the constructive loss reported in the previous year.
(2) To reverse the amortization of premium on investment recorded by P Company during the current year.
(3) To reverse the amortization of discount on bonds payable recorded by S Company during the current year.
(4) To eliminate intercompany bond investment and bonds payable.
(5) To eliminate intercompany interest.
(6) To eliminate intercompany dividends and income.
(7) To eliminate the investment account and create noncontrolling interest.

Thus, replacing the entries to Beginning Retained Earnings—P Company with entries to the investment account facilitates the elimination of the investment account under the complete equity method.

The sum of these two components is the controlling interest share of the constructive loss not recorded on the books of the affiliated companies as of the beginning of the current period. This sum is also equal to (a) 100% of the unamortized premium on the books of the parent ($10,000) plus (b) the parent's share of the unamortized discount related to the intercompany bonds on the subsidiary's books (.80 × $12,000 = $9,600) at the beginning of the year.

2. The beginning retained earnings balance of the subsidiary is reduced by the noncontrolling interest share of the constructive loss allocated to the subsidiary that has not been recorded in prior periods through periodic amortization of the discount related to the intercompany bonds.
3. The interest expense and interest revenue related to the intercompany bonds and reported by the respective companies are eliminated from the income statement.
4. The bond investment and the carrying value of the intercompany bonds are eliminated from the balance sheet.

Consolidated net income and retained earnings for the year ended December 31, 2013, using the t-account approach, are computed as shown in Figure 9-2.

Second Year Subsequent to the Debt Acquisition—2014

In subsequent years until the bonds mature, the companies will continue to recognize a portion of the loss each year as the discount and premium are amortized on their separate books. The consolidated statements workpaper entries are similar to those illustrated for 2014. Recall that the constructive loss occurred on the last day of 2012. Thus 2013 was the first year necessitating amortization reversals, and 2013 is the second. Workpaper entries in general journal form related to the intercompany bondholdings in the 2014 consolidated statements workpaper are as follows:

Consolidated Statement Workpapers Entries—2014

(1) Beginning Retained Earnings—P Company*	10,000	
Investment in S Company Bonds		10,000
To adjust beginning retained earnings for constructive loss (recorded in 2012 as workpaper entry only; see 2012 entry (2)) and to adjust investment to par.		
(2) Beginning Retained Earnings—P Company ($12,000 × .80)*	9,600	
Beginning NCI ($12,000 × .20)	2,400	
Discount on Bonds Payable ($20,000 × .60)		12,000
To adjust beginning retained earnings balance and NCI for constructive loss (recorded in 2012 as workpaper entry only; see 2012 entry (3) and adjust intercompany bonds to par value.		
(3) Investment in S Company Bonds	5,000	
Retained Earnings—P Company*		2,500
Interest Revenue ($1,250 + $1,250)		2,500
To reverse the amortization of premium on investment recorded by P Company during the current year and prior year (and not needed by consolidated entity since the constructive loss was recorded in its entirety in 2012).		

(4) Discount on Bonds Payable ($10,000 × .60)	6,000	
Retained Earnings—P Company*		3,000
Interest Expense		3,000
To reverse amortization of discount on bonds payable recorded by S Company during current year and prior year (and not needed by consolidated entity since the constructive loss was recorded in its entirety in 2012).		

Under the complete equity method, the amounts in entries (1) through (4) recorded to P Company's beginning retained earnings would be assigned to the Investment in S Company Stock account. These accounts are marked with an asterisk.

(5) Interest Revenue	27,000	
Interest Expense		27,000
To eliminate intercompany interest.		
(6) Bonds Payable	300,000	
Investment in S Company Bonds		300,000
To eliminate intercompany bond investment and bonds payable.		

FIGURE 9-2

T-Account Approach to Consolidated Net Income and Retained Earnings

Consolidated Net Income—2013

Debit		Credit		
		Reported net income of P Company		$454,000
		Less: Dividend income		(48,000)
		Net income from independent operations		406,000
		Add: Constructive loss recorded by P Company in the current year (premium amortization)		2,500
		P Company's contribution to consolidated income		408,500
		Reported net income of S Company	$140,000	
		Add: Constructive loss recorded by S Company in the current year (discount amortization)	3,000	
		S Company's contribution to consolidated income	143,000	
		Percentage interest in S Company	.80	114,400
		Controlling Interest in consolidated net income		$522,900

Consolidated Retained Earnings—December 31, 2013

Debit		Credit		
		Ending retained earnings—P Company, December 31, 2013 (Cost Method)		$2,100,000
Constructive loss on bond retirement not recorded by P Company ($10,000 − $2,500)	7,500			
		Retained earnings adjusted for unrecorded constructive loss		2,092,500
		Ending retained earnings—S Company	$ 885,000	
		Less: Retained earnings—date of acquisition	(500,000)	
		Increase in recorded retained earnings	1,385,000	
		Less: Constructive loss on bond retirement not recorded by S Company ($12,000 − 3,000)	(9,000)	
		Adjusted increase in recorded retained earnings	1,376,000	
		Percentage interest in S Company	.80	1,100,800
		Consolidated retained earnings on December 31, 2013		$3,193,300

Three-Year Comparison

Figures 9-3 and 9-4 show the entries on P Company's books, S Company's books, and the consolidated workpaper entries using both the cost method and the complete equity method. For the year 2014, S Company income is assumed to be $200,000 with $75,000 of dividends declared.

FIGURE 9-3
Cost Method
Three-Year Summary

Entries on P Company's Books

	Year 2012		*Year 2013*		*Year 2014*	
Investment in S Company Bond	310,000					
Cash		310,000				
Cash	16,000		48,000		60,000	
Dividend Income		16,000		48,000		60,000
Cash (on an annual basis)			27,000		27,000	
Investment in S Company Bond				2,500		2,500
Interest Income				24,500		24,500

Entries on S Company's Books

	Year 2012		*Year 2013*		*Year 2014*	
Interest Expense			30,000		30,000	
Discount on Bond Payable				3,000		3,000
Cash				27,000		27,000

Entries on the Workpaper

	Year 2012		*Year 2013*		*Year 2014*	
Investment in S	160,000		244,000		308,000	
Beginning Retained Earnings—P Company		160,000		244,000		308,000
Loss on Constructive Retirement of Bond	22,000					
Beginning Retained Earnings—P Company			19,600		19,600	
Beginning NCI in Equity			2,400		2,400	
Discount on Bond Payable		12,000		12,000		12,000
Investment in S Company Bond		10,000		10,000		10,000
Investment in S Company Bond			2,500		5,000	
Interest Income				2,500		2,500
Beginning Retained Earnings—P Company						2,500
Discount on Bond Payable			3,000		6,000	
Interest Expense				3,000		3,000
Beginning Retained Earnings—P Company						3,000
Interest Income			27,000		27,000	
Interest Expense				27,000		27,000
Bond Payable	300,000		300,000		300,000	
Investment in S Company Bond		300,000		300,000		300,000
Dividend Income	16,000		48,000		60,000	
Dividend Declared		16,000		48,000		60,000
Beginning Retained Earnings—S Company	700,000		805,000		885,000	
Common Stock—S Company	1,000,000		1,000,000		1,000,000	
Difference between Implied and Book Value	0		0		0	
Investment in S Company		1,360,000		1,444,000		1,508,000
Noncontrolling Interest in Equity		340,000		361,000		377,000

FIGURE 9-4

Complete Equity Method, Three-Year Summary

Entries on P Company's Books

	Year 2012		*Year 2013*		*Year 2014*	
Investment in S Company Bond	310,000					
Cash		310,000				
Cash (for Interest)			27,000		27,000	
Investment in S Company Bonds				2,500		2,500
Interest Income				24,500		24,500
Cash (for Dividends)	16,000		48,000		60,000	
Investment in S Company		16,000		48,000		60,000
Investment in S Company	100,000		112,000		160,000	
Equity in S Income		100,000		112,000		160,000
Equity in S Income	19,600					
Investment in S Company Stock		19,600				
Investment in S Company Stock			4,900		4,900	
Equity in S Income ($19,600/4)				4,900		4,900

Entries on S Company's Books

	Year 2012		*Year 2013*		*Year 2014*	
Interest Expense			30,000		30,000	
Discount on Bond Payable				3,000		3,000
Cash				27,000		27,000

Entries on the Workpaper

	Year 2012		*Year 2013*		*Year 2014*	
Equity in S Income	80,400		116,900		164,900	
Dividends Declared		16,000		48,000		60,000
Investment in S Company Stock		64,400		68,900		104,900
Beginning Retained Earnings—S Company	700,000		805,000		885,000	
Common Stock—S Company	1,000,000		1,000,000		1,000,000	
Difference between Implied and Book Value	0		0		0	
Investment in S Company		1,360,000		1,444,000		1,508,000
Noncontrolling Interest in Equity		340,000		361,000		377,000
Loss on Constructive Retirement of Bonds	22,000					
Investment in S Company Stock			19,600		19,600	
Beginning NCI in Equity			2,400		2,400	
Investment in S Company Bond		10,000		10,000		10,000
Discount on Bonds Payable		12,000		12,000		12,000
Interest Income			27,000		27,000	
Interest Expense				27,000		27,000
Bonds Payable	300,000		300,000		300,000	
Investment in S Company Bond		300,000		300,000		300,000
Investment in S Company Bonds			2,500		5,000	
Interest Income				2,500		2,500
Investment in S Company Stock						2,500
Discount on Bonds Payable			3,000		6,000	
Interest Expense				3,000		3,000
Investment in S Company Stock						3,000

TEST YOUR KNOWLEDGE

NOTE: Solutions to ***Test Your Knowledge*** questions are found at the end of each chapter before the end-of-chapter questions.

Multiple Choice

1. Sandler Company is a wholly owned subsidiary of Portnoy Company. On January 1, 2009, Sandler has $100,000 of 8% bonds outstanding. These bonds were issued at face value and had five years to maturity as of January 1, 2009. Both Sandler and Portnoy amortize any premium or discount using the straight-line method. On January 1, 2009, Portnoy bought Sandler's bonds for $98,000. The amount(s) that should appear on the consolidated balance sheet of Portnoy and Sandler relative to these bonds is (are):
   a. Bonds payable $100,000
   b. Bonds payable $100,000, discount $2,000
   c. Bonds payable $100,000, discount $1,600
   d. The bonds do not appear.
2. Company Planets Galore owns 100% of the common stock of Saturn Inc. Saturn carries 10-year 8% bonds, issued to yield 7%, on its balance sheet. On January 1 of the current year, Planets Galore bought all Saturn's outstanding bonds at a price reflecting a current effective interest rate of 9%. How should this transaction be reflected in the consolidated financial statements for the current year?
   a. The bonds remain in the balance sheet and are accounted for at a 9% effective rate.
   b. The bonds remain in the balance sheet and are accounted for at a 7% effective rate.
   c. The bonds are treated as having been retired, with an ordinary loss shown on the consolidated income statement.
   d. The bonds are treated as having been retired, with an ordinary gain shown in the consolidated income statement.
3. Company S is a wholly owned subsidiary of Company P. On January 1, 2009, Company S had $100,000 of 8% bonds outstanding. The bonds had five years remaining to maturity as of January 1, 2009, and an unamortized discount of $3,000. Company P purchased the bonds for $98,000 on January 1, 2009.The adjustment to the Consolidated income of the two companies required in the consolidating process for *2010* is:
   a. Increase $8,600
   b. Decrease $8,600
   c. Increase $200
   d. Decrease $200

INTERIM PURCHASE OF INTERCOMPANY BONDS

In the preceding illustration, the intercompany bonds were initially purchased on December 31, the fiscal year-end of both affiliates. Had the bonds been held during 2012, P Company would have amortized a portion of the premium and S Company would have amortized a part of the discount that was related to the intercompany bonds. Thus, a part of the constructive loss would have been recorded in 2012 by the individual companies. Assuming that P Company amortized $500 and S Company amortized $600 during 2012, the original workpaper entries (2) and (3) for constructive losses are modified as follows:

(2) Loss on Constructive Retirement Bonds	10,000	
Interest Revenue		500
Investment in S Company Bonds		9,500
(3) Loss on Constructive Retirement of Bonds	12,000	
Interest Expense		600
Discount on Bonds Payable		11,400

The consolidated income statement will still show a total loss on the constructive retirement of $22,000. The credits to interest revenue and interest expense add back the portion of the loss that was recorded by the individual companies, but which is reported in total in 2012, the year the bonds were constructively retired. Failure to add back the $1,100 ($500 + $600) to the reported income of the individual companies will result in reporting this portion of the loss twice, as part of the $22,000 and again as a reduction in interest revenue and as an increase in interest expense, both of which have reduced reported income.

NOTES RECEIVABLE DISCOUNTED

LO3 Discounting a note issued to an affiliated company with an outside company.

Occasionally a company may issue a note to an affiliated company that may then discount the note with an outside party, or a company holding a note receivable from an outside party may discount the note with an affiliated company. The affiliate acquiring the note may discount the note again with an outside party. From a consolidation point of view, a receivable held by one of the affiliated companies should be reported in the consolidated balance sheet only if the note is due from an outside party. A contingent liability should be disclosed if a note has been discounted with an outside party and the endorsement was with recourse.

To illustrate the workpaper elimination entries required, assume that P Company issued a $100,000 note to its subsidiary, S Company, for cash. The two companies prepare the usual entries on their own books when the debt is issued, that is, P Company debits cash and establishes a note payable account and S Company credits cash and records a note receivable. Assume further that S Company discounted the note at a nonaffiliated bank before maturity. Ignoring interest for simplicity, one of two methods might be used by Company S to record the discounting of a note. These methods are:

S Company's Books

Method 1:	Cash	100,000	
	Notes Receivable		100,000
Method 2:	Cash	100,000	
	Notes Receivable Discounted		100,000

If consolidated statements are prepared before the note matures, an elimination entry may be required, depending on the method used by S Company to record the discounting of the note. If Method 1 is used to record the discounted note, the credit to notes receivable would cancel the debit made to notes receivable when the note was received. The consolidated balance sheet would appropriately report the $100,000 note held by the bank and still reported on the books of P Company as a liability. If the second method was used, the notes receivable and the notes receivable discounted accounts would have to be eliminated, because the consolidated group is not contingently liable for the note, but is the primary maker of the note held by an outside party.

Now assume that P Company discounts with S Company a note that had originally been received from one of its customers. Now, P Company might record the transfer in one of two ways. Again, if the first method (above) is used, no elimination would be required, for the reasons discussed in the preceding paragraph. However, if the second method was used, both companies would report the same note receivable as an asset, and P Company would show a contingent liability for a note receivable discounted. In the consolidating workpaper, one note receivable must be eliminated, along with the note receivable discounted account, as shown below in the partial balance sheet section of a consolidated statements workpaper:

			Eliminations		
Debits	*P Company*	*S Company*	*Dr.*	*Cr.*	*Consolidated Balances*
Notes Receivable	100,000	100,000		(1) 100,000	100,000
Credits					
Notes Receivable Discounted	100,000		(1) 100,000		—0—

The consolidated balance sheet would report one receivable from an outside party. The note was discounted to an affiliated company and, therefore, there is no contingent liability to an outside party.

Next, assume that S Company discounted the customer's note with an outside firm. If both companies used Method 1 to record the two discounting transactions, no elimination entry would be required. If the second method was used, the accounts would appear as follows in the trial balances of the two companies:

Debits	*P Company*	*S Company*
Notes Receivable	100,000	100,000
Credits		
Notes Receivable Discounted	100,000	100,000

In this case, one of the notes receivable and one of the notes receivable discounted should be eliminated. The consolidated balance sheet would report:

Notes Receivable	$100,000
Less: Notes Receivable Discounted	100,000
	—0—

Alternatively, both notes receivable and both discount accounts could be eliminated and the contingent liability disclosed in a footnote to the consolidated statement.

In the foregoing examples the notes were always transferred from the parent to the subsidiary. The same analysis is appropriate if the notes were transferred from the subsidiary to the parent.

STOCK DIVIDENDS ISSUED BY A SUBSIDIARY COMPANY

LO4 Stock dividends issued by a subsidiary.

LO5 Stock dividends vs. cash dividends.

A subsidiary may issue ***stock dividends*** in the same class of stock that is held by the parent company. The parent company records the receipt of the shares in a memorandum entry only, since a dividend in like stock is not considered income to the recipient. For consolidated purposes, the stock dividend does not alter the investor's proportionate interest in the subsidiary. On the books of the subsidiary, the declaration of a stock dividend is recorded as a transfer from the retained earnings account to one or more paid-in capital accounts. The amount transferred is dependent on whether the dividend is a large or small stock dividend. (Recall that a large stock dividend, one in which the number of shares issued is greater than 20–25% of the outstanding shares, reduces retained earnings by the par value of the stock issued, while a small stock dividend reduces retained earnings by the market value of the stock issued.) Also, stock dividends are assumed to be distributed from the earliest earnings accumulated in the retained earnings balance. Conversely, a cash dividend is considered to be a distribution of the most recent profits (usually current period income).

To illustrate the effects of a stock dividend on the preparation of the consolidated statements workpaper, assume that P Company purchased 4,000 shares of S Company's $100 par value common stock on January 2, 2009, for $560,000. At the time of purchase, S Company reported common stock and retained earnings balances of $500,000 and $200,000, respectively. If consolidated statements were prepared on January 2, 2009, the investment eliminating entry would be:

Capital Stock—S Company	500,000	
1/1 Retained Earnings—S Company	200,000	
Investment in S Company		560,000
Noncontrolling Interest in Equity		140,000

Now assume that S Company reports net income of $50,000 and declares a 30% stock dividend (1,500 shares) on December 31, 2009. S Company would record the dividend as follows, assuming that the company capitalized the par value of the stock issued:

Stock Dividend Declared (or Retained Earnings)	150,000	
Capital Stock (1,500 shares × $100)		150,000

Note that this entry has no effect on the total stockholders' equity. Only the composition of the account balances changes as shown here:

	S Company's Capital Account Balances		
Accounts	*Before the Stock Dividend*	*Stock Dividend*	*After the Stock Dividend*
Capital Stock	$500,000	150,000	$650,000
Retained Earnings	250,000*	(150,000)	100,000
Totals	$750,000	—0—	$750,000

* $200,000 + $50,000

If the dividend had been considered a small stock dividend, the totals in the schedule above would not change. To record a small stock dividend, the retained earnings account is normally reduced by an amount equal to the number of shares to be issued times the fair market value per share; capital stock and other paid-in capital accounts are increased by the same amount.

The only book entry made by P Company in 2009 is the following memorandum entry to record the receipt of the 1,200 shares from S Company, since no cash dividends were declared during the period.

Memorandum entry—Received 1,200 shares (1,500 × .80) of S Company common stock based on the declaration of a 30% stock dividend.

A condensed consolidated statements workpaper for the year ended December 31, 2009, is presented in Illustration 9-5. In the year that the stock dividend is declared, one additional workpaper eliminating entry is made to eliminate the effects of the dividend on the parent's interest in the capital accounts of the subsidiary. This entry is necessary because the capital stock account has been increased by $150,000, but the stock dividend declared account has not been closed to retained earnings. In other words, the balance in the capital stock account is the ending balance and needs to be restored to the beginning of year balance before elimination of the investment account.

The workpaper entries in general journal form are as follows:

Workpaper Entries—Year Stock Dividends Are Declared

		Debit	Credit
(1)	Capital Stock—S Company	120,000	
	Stock Dividends Declared—S Company		120,000
	To reverse effects of stock dividend ($150,000 × .80).		
(2)	1/1 Retained Earnings—S Company	200,000	
	Capital Stock—S Company	500,000	
	Investment in S Company		560,000
	Noncontrolling Interest in Equity		140,000
	To eliminate investment account and recognize noncontrolling interest.		

In the closing process the stock dividends declared account is closed to the retained earnings account. In subsequent periods, the two workpaper entries are combined as follows (this is the entry before the reciprocity entry):

	Debit	Credit
1/1 Retained Earnings—S Company ($200,000 − $150,000)	50,000	
Capital Stock—S Company ($500,000 + $150,000)	650,000	
Investment in S Company		560,000
Noncontrolling Interest		140,000
To eliminate investment account and recognize NCI before reciprocity.		

The result is that the debit to capital stock is increased $150,000, and a corresponding decrease is made in the debit to the retained earnings balance.

In the consolidated workpapers the entry to establish reciprocity is based on the undistributed income earned by the subsidiary since the date of acquisition. A cash dividend declared by the subsidiary is generally considered to be a distribution of the most recent profits, which, of course, reduces undistributed profits of the subsidiary accumulated after the date the parent obtained control of the subsidiary. Conversely, the source of a stock dividend is the earliest earnings accumulated in the retained earnings balance.

Cost Method	ILLUSTRATION 9-5					
80% Owned Subsidiary	Consolidated Statements Workpaper					
Subsidiary Issued	P Company and Subsidiary					
Stock Dividend	for the Year Ended December 31, 2009					
	P	*S*	*Eliminations*		*Noncontrolling*	*Consolidated*
Income Statement	*Company*	*Company*	*Dr.*	*Cr.*	*Interest*	*Balances*
Net/Consolidated Income	240,000	50,000				290,000
Noncontrolling Interest in Income ($50,000 × .20)					10,000	(10,000)
Net Income to Retained Earnings	240,000	50,000			10,000	280,000
Retained Earnings Statement						
1/1 Retained Earnings						
P Company	460,000					460,000
S Company		200,000	(2) 200,000			
Net Income from above	240,000	50,000			10,000	280,000
Dividends Declared S Company—Stock Dividend		(150,000)		(1) 120,000	(30,000)	
12/31 Retained Earnings to Balance Sheet	700,000	100,000	200,000	120,000	(20,000)	740,000
Balance Sheet						
Investment in S Company	560,000			(2) 560,000		—0—
Fixed Assets	1,240,000	800,000				2,040,000
Total Assets	1,800,000	800,000				2,040,000
Total Liabilities	200,000	50,000				250,000
Capital Stock						
P Company	900,000					900,000
S Company		650,000	(1) 120,000 (2) 500,000		30,000	
Retained Earnings from above	700,000	100,000	200,000	120,000	(20,000)	740,000
1/1 Noncontrolling Interest in Net Assets				(2) 140,000	140,000	
12/31 Noncontrolling Interest in Net Assets					150,000	150,000
Total Liabilities and Equity	1,800,000	800,000	820,000	820,000		2,040,000

(1) To reverse effects of the stock dividend.
(2) To eliminate investment account and create noncontrolling interest account.

In this illustration the procedures to compute the amount of the entry to establish reciprocity must be modified to recognize that the retained earnings balance at the date of acquisition has been reduced to $50,000 as a result of the stock dividend. The workpaper entries for the ***second*** year December 31, 2010, are as follows:

			Dr.	Cr.
(1)	Investment in S Company		40,000	
	Beginning Retained Earnings—P Company			40,000
	To establish reciprocity as of 1/1/10 ($50,000 × .80).			
	1/1 Retained earnings balance ($200,000 − $150,000 + $50,000)		$100,000	
	Retained earnings balance—date of acquisition	$200,000		
	Less: Stock dividend	150,000		
	Adjusted retained earnings balance—date of acquisition		50,000	
	Increase in retained earnings since date of acquisition		$ 50,000	
(2)	Beginning Retained Earnings—S Company		100,000	
	Common Stock—S Company		650,000	
	Investment in S Company ($560,000 + $40,000)			600,000
	Noncontrolling Interest in Equity			150,000
	To eliminate investment account and recognize NCI.			

A portion of the retained earnings section of the December 31, 2010 workpaper is presented here:

	P Company	S Company	Eliminations Dr.	Eliminations Cr.	Noncontrolling Interest	Consolidated Balances
1/1 Retained Earnings						
P Company	700,000			(1) 40,000		740,000
S Company		100,000	(2) 80,000		20,000	

Observe that these entries make the beginning retained earnings balances for the second year equal to the first year's ending retained earnings balances reported for the noncontrolling interest and the consolidated retained earnings on the December 31, 2009, workpaper (see Illustration 9-5).

The issuance of a stock dividend does not affect the computation of consolidated retained earnings. As proof, the consolidated retained earnings balance as of December 31, 2009, can be computed as follows:

P Company's retained earnings balance at December 31, 2009	$700,000
P Company's share of the change in the subsidiary's adjusted retained earnings since the date of acquisition ($50,000 × .80)	40,000
Consolidated retained earnings—December 31, 2009	$740,000

Stock Dividends Issued from Postacquisition Earnings

LO6 Subsidiary stock dividends issued from postacquisition earnings.

In the foregoing illustration, the retained earnings transferred to paid-in capital ($150,000) was less than the retained earnings balance ($200,000) at the date of acquisition. If the stock dividend had been more than $200,000, some of the postacquisition earnings of the subsidiary would have been capitalized. For example, assume that S Company made the following entry to record the stock dividend:

Stock Dividends Declared (or Retained Earnings)	220,000	
Capital Stock		220,000

The entry capitalized $200,000 of the retained earnings that existed at the date of acquisition plus $20,000 of the net income reported after the date of acquisition. The capitalization of the current earnings does not affect consolidated retained earnings, which is still $740,000 as determined in Illustration 9-5, but it does result in the inclusion of earnings in the consolidated retained earnings balance that have been capitalized and are not available for the payment of dividends. The amount of the subsidiary's postacquisition earnings that have been capitalized and included in the consolidated retained earnings should be disclosed in the consolidated financial statements. Some may contend that the portion of the retained earnings that has been capitalized should be reported as contributed capital in the consolidated balance sheet. In response to this contention, the Committee on Accounting Procedures of the American Institute of Certified Public Accountants made the following comment:

> Occasionally, subsidiary companies capitalize earned surplus [retained earnings] arising since acquisition, by means of a stock dividend or otherwise. This does not require a transfer to capital surplus on consolidation, inasmuch as the retained

earnings in the consolidated financial statements should reflect the accumulated earnings of the consolidated group not distributed to the shareholders of, or capitalized by, the parent company.[6]

DIVIDENDS FROM PREACQUISITION EARNINGS

LO6 Subsidiary stock dividends issued from preacquisition earnings.

The nature of a liquidating dividend (dividend from preacquisition earnings) and the entries to record a liquidating dividend were discussed in Chapter 3. The objective of this section is to illustrate the effects of a liquidating dividend on the consolidated statements workpaper entries.

To illustrate the workpaper adjustment required when a liquidating dividend is involved, assume that P Company acquired an 80% interest in S Company on January 2, 2009, for $560,000. At the time of purchase, S Company had capital stock and retained earnings in the amounts of $500,000 and $200,000, respectively. During the first year that the investment was held, S Company reported net income of $200,000. On December 31, 2009, the subsidiary declared and paid a cash dividend of $250,000. In this case, $50,000 of the dividend is a distribution of earnings accumulated before the controlling interest was obtained in the subsidiary. As discussed in Chapter 3, there is general agreement that a liquidating dividend should be accounted for as a return of part of the original investment rather than income to the parent company.

Recall that the source of a cash dividend is considered to be the most recent earnings. Under the cost method the following entry is made on the books of P Company to recognize that $200,000 of the dividend is based on the current earnings and $50,000 is a distribution of preacquisition earnings:

P Company's Books

Cash	200,000	
Dividend Income ($200,000 × .80)		160,000
Investment in S Company ($50,000 × .80)		40,000
To record receipt of a cash dividend from S Company		

This entry reduces the investment account balance to $520,000. In the year of the liquidating dividend, one additional workpaper entry must be made to reverse the effects of the liquidating dividend, since the dividend has been adjusted to the investment account, but the dividends declared are still shown as a separate amount in the trial balance of S Company. Although the consolidated statements workpaper is not presented, the December 31, 2009, eliminating entries are as follows:

(1) Dividend Income	160,000	
Dividends Declared—S Company		160,000
To eliminate intercompany dividends		
(2) Investment in S Company	40,000	
Dividends Declared—S Company		40,000
To reverse the liquidating dividend.		

[6] Committee on Accounting Procedure, American Institute of Certified Public Accountants, *Accounting Research and Terminology Bulletin*, Final Edition (New York: AICPA, 1961), *Bulletin No. 51*, par. 18, [**ASC 810–10–45–9**].

(3) Beginning Retained Earnings—S Company	200,000	
Capital Stock—S Company	500,000	
Investment in S Company		560,000
Noncontrolling Interest in Equity		140,000
To eliminate investment account and create noncontrolling interest.		

In the workpapers prepared in subsequent years, the amount of the entry made to establish reciprocity is based on the difference between the current year's beginning retained earnings balance and the retained earnings balance at the date of acquisition reduced by the $50,000 liquidating dividend. The investment elimination entry is a combination of entries (2) and (3) above. The December 31, 2010 (the second year) workpaper entry would be:

(1) Beginning Retained Earnings—S Company ($200,000 − 50,000)	150,000	
Capital Stock—S Company	500,000	
Investment in S Company		520,000
Noncontrolling Interest in Equity		130,000
To eliminate investment account and recognize NCI.		

No entry is needed to establish reciprocity, because all the earnings of the subsidiary since acquisition ($200,000) have been distributed, and the parent's share is reported in the retained earnings balance of P Company.

SUBSIDIARY WITH BOTH PREFERRED AND COMMON STOCK OUTSTANDING

A subsidiary company may have both common and preferred stock outstanding. To justify consolidation, the parent must hold a controlling interest in the outstanding voting stock. At the same time, the parent may or may not hold shares of the preferred stock. In either case, in the preparation of consolidated financial statements, the shares of the preferred stock not held by the parent company are considered part of the noncontrolling interest.

Determining Equity Interest of Each Class of Stockholders

LO7 Allocating the purchase price between common and preferred stockholders.

The existence of preferred stock creates special problems in the preparation of consolidated financial statements because each class of stockholders has an interest in the net assets of the firm. To determine the equity interest of each class of stockholders on a certain date, it is necessary to allocate the subsidiary's stockholders' equity between the preferred and common stock interests. In doing so, the provisions of the preferred stock issue, in particular the ***call price***, sometimes called the ***redemption price***, and dividend provisions, must be analyzed and provided for in making the allocation. After the date of acquiring the controlling interest, the operating results of the subsidiary must also be allocated to determine the interest of the two classes of stockholders in the changes in the retained earnings balance. The dividend preference of the preferred stock issue will determine the amounts allocated to each class of stockholders.

ILLUSTRATION 9-6

Allocation of Retained Earnings Balance and Net Income When Subsidiary Has Both Common and Preferred Stock Outstanding

	Accumulated Retained Earnings Balance		*Allocation of Net Income*	
	*Preferred Stock**	*Common Stock*	*Preferred Stock*	*Common Stock*
Noncumulative/ nonparticipating	1. Zero.	2. Balance in retained earnings account.	1. Current year's dividend if one was declared.	2. Net income in excess of preferred dividend.
Cumulative/ nonparticipating	1. Dividends in arrears.	2. Balance after subtracting dividend in arrears.	1. Current year's dividend whether declared or not.	2. Net income in excess of preferred dividend.
Noncumulative/ fully participating	1. Allocated between preferred and common stock.		1. Current year's dividend if one was declared.	2. Current year's dividend if declared on common, but not to exceed the amount to match the percentage on preferred.
			3. Remaining net income is allocated between preferred and common stock.†	
Cumulative/ fully participating‡	1. Dividends in arrears.		1. Current year's dividend whether declared or not.	2. Current year's dividend if declared on common, but not to exceed the amount to match the percentage on preferred.
	2. Balance after subtracting any dividend in arrears is allocated between preferred and common stock.†		3. Remaining net income is allocated between preferred and common stock.†	

* It is assumed that the call price of the preferred stock is equal to the stock's par value. If the call price is greater, the preferred stock interest in retained earnings is increased by the amount of the call premium and a corresponding reduction is made in the common stock interest.

† It is assumed that the allocation is based on the ratio of the par values of each class of stock.

‡ It is assumed that a common stock dividend is lost if not declared in any one year to match the preference rate on the preferred stock. In other words, before the participation feature is effective, the common stockholders normally receive a dividend equal to the same percentage paid to the preferred stockholders. However, if an equal percentage is not declared on the common stock during the period, it is lost to the common stockholders and will not be paid in subsequent periods. Since the preferred stock is cumulative, a passed dividend on preferred stock is considered in arrears in the determination of dividend payments in future periods. Such a dividend agreement with the preferred stockholders could be detrimental to the interest of the common stockholders. Alternative agreements could be negotiated, and this is only one possibility.

The effects that the various rights and priorities granted to the preferred stockholders have on the determination of the book value interests and the claim to earnings are discussed in other accounting texts. The procedures and the steps (indicated numerically) for determining such allocations for some of the more common alternatives are summarized in Illustration 9-6.

Illustration 9-6 does not include the steps to be taken in the allocation of a deficit balance in the retained earnings account or a subsidiary reporting a net loss during an operating period. If the preferred stock is noncumulative, nonparticipating, and has a call price equal to par value, the full deficit in the retained earnings account or net loss is allocated totally to the common stock interest. If the preferred stock is cumulative and nonparticipating, a deficit balance in retained earnings is assigned to the common stock, unless there are dividends in arrears, in which case the amount of the preferred dividends in arrears increases the book value interest of the preferred stockholders and is added to the deficit assigned to the common equity. In the case of a net loss, the current year's dividends on the preferred stock are added to the preferred interest and added to the net loss (which reduces the common interest) to determine the interest of the common stockholders in current operations. In the case of deficit operations, the participating provision can be ignored.

Allocation of Difference between Cost of Preferred Stock Investment and Book Value Interest Acquired

In the case of a common stock investment, the difference between implied value of the investment and the book value of the interest acquired is allocated to undervalued or overvalued assets and liabilities. However, because holders of cumulative/nonparticipating preferred stock do not have a residual interest in the firm's net assets, the excess paid for a preferred stock interest is generally not related to the market value of the firm's net assets. If the preferred stock is nonconvertible and nonparticipating, the market price is more closely associated with the preferred dividend return related to the market rate of return on investments of similar risk. In essence, the market factors that cause movements in the market value of the preferred stock are similar to the market factors that cause movements in the market value of the firm's bonds. Thus, the difference between the cost of preferred stock and the book value of the interest acquired is similar to a discount or premium on a bond issue. One of the major differences between preferred stock and debt is that a preferred stock issue does not normally have a maturity date.

Because the preferred stock does not normally have a maturity date, the period selected to amortize the difference would be arbitrary. One approach is to recognize the difference as a loss in the consolidated income statement in the year of the purchase. However, in our view, the acquisition of outstanding preferred stock by the consolidated entity reflects a constructive retirement of the stock and should be accounted for as an equity transaction. Thus, the difference between cost and the book value interest acquired (a debit difference) is accounted for as a reduction in consolidated other contributed capital, or if none exists, is recorded as a reduction in consolidated retained earnings. If the book value of the interest acquired is greater than the cost of the preferred stock, the credit difference is carried to other contributed capital.

Most preferred stock agreements contain the cumulative feature and are nonparticipating. For this reason, the preparation of consolidated financial statements when cumulative/nonparticipating preferred stock is outstanding is illustrated in the next section. The reader must recognize, however, that the illustration is only one of many possibilities, since the rights and priorities granted to the preferred stockholders may take numerous forms. When there is preferred stock outstanding, the stock agreement should be carefully reviewed to assess the rights and priorities of each class of stock. Allocations of the stockholders' equity and net income should be made in accordance with the agreement.

CONSOLIDATING A SUBSIDIARY WITH PREFERRED STOCK OUTSTANDING

To illustrate the accounting for a subsidiary and the consolidated statements workpaper procedures to be followed when the subsidiary has both preferred stock and common stock outstanding, the following information concerning the capital accounts of S Company as of January 2, 2009, is assumed:

8%, $100 par value preferred stock, cumulative, nonparticipating, dividends in arrears for 2008, call price is $103 with 5,000 shares outstanding	$ 500,000
Common stock, $10 par value	1,000,000
Other contributed capital—excess on issue of common stock over par	305,000
Retained earnings	200,000
Total stockholders' equity	$2,005,000

On January 2, 2009, P Company acquired 80% of the outstanding common stock for $1,160,000 and 30% of the outstanding preferred stock for $180,000. The entry to record the purchase is:

P Company's Books

Investment in S Company Preferred Stock	180,000	
Investment in S Company Common Stock	1,160,000	
Cash		1,340,000

During the year, S Company reported net income of $200,000 and declared no cash dividends.

The stockholders' equity accounts of S Company must be allocated to determine the book value interest in the net assets of the preferred and common stockholders. The allocation on the date of acquisition would be made as shown in Illustration 9-7.[7]

In this illustration, if the preferred shares were called, a payment of $111 ($103 call price + $8 dividend in arrears) must be made to acquire each share of stock. Accordingly, retained earnings of $55,000 (5,000 shares outstanding × $11 per share) is allocated to the preferred stockholders' interest. Thus, on the date of acquisition the preferred stock interest in the net assets ($555,000) is equal to the call price of $515,000 plus the $40,000 dividends in arrears.

Consolidated Statements Workpaper—2009

Workpaper procedures are similar to those illustrated in earlier sections of this text. The only difference is that an additional workpaper entry must be made to eliminate the preferred stock investment account. The consolidating statements workpaper at

[7] Another approach to determine the allocation of equity interest is:

Book value of net assets		$2,005,000
Less: Allocated to preferred stock		
Par value of preferred stock	$500,000	
Call premium (5,000 shares × $3)	15,000	
Dividends in arrears (5,000 shares × $8)	40,000	
Total allocated to preferred stock		555,000
Residual allocated to common stock		$1,450,000

ILLUSTRATION 9-7

Allocation of Difference between Implied and Book Value—Date of Acquisition—1/2/2009

Computation and Allocation of Difference between Implied and Book Value Acquired—Preferred Stock

	Parent Share	*Noncontrolling Share*	*Entire Value*
Purchase price and implied value	**$180,000**	**420,000***	600,000
Less: Book value of equity acquired:			
$100 par preferred stock −8%	(150,000)	(350,000)	**(500,000)**
Retained Earnings**	(16,500)	(38,500)	**(55,000)**
Difference between implied and book value	13,500	31,500	**45,000**
Reduce Paid-in-Capital—Parent	**(13,500)**		
Reduce Noncontrolling Interest in Equity*		**(31,500)***	
Total allocated			(45,000)
Balance	0	0	0

* Noncontrolling interest after adjustment = $420,000 − $31,500 = $388,500
** ($103 call price + $8 dividends in arrears − $100 par value) × 5,000 shares = $11 × 5,000 = $55,000

Computation and Allocation of Difference between Implied and Book Value Acquired—Common Stock

	Parent Share	*Noncontrolling Share*	*Entire Value*
Purchase price and implied value	**$1,160,000**	**290,000**	1,450,000
Less: Book value of equity acquired:			
$10 par common stock	(800,000)	(200,000)	**(1,000,000)**
Other contributed capital—common stock	(244,000)	(61,000)	**(305,000)**
Retained earnings*	(116,000)	(29,000)	**(145,000)**
Difference between implied and book value	0	0	0

* $200,000 − $55,000 = $145,000

December 31, 2009, is contained in Illustration 9-8. The balances are assumed except for the ones previously given. Note that the beginning retained earnings balance of S Company is allocated between the two classes of stock. Making the allocation in the workpaper is necessary because dividends in arrears are not recorded in the accounts of S Company. If P Company uses the cost method, dividends in arrears are not recorded as dividend income. However, if the complete equity method is used, dividends on cumulative preferred stock are recognized as income regardless of whether they are paid. Therefore, in 2009, under the complete equity method, P Company records equity income from the preferred stock investment of $12,000 (.3 × $40,000).

Consolidated Statements Workpaper Entries—2009

Cost Method or Partial Equity Method

		Debit	Credit
(1a)	Beginning Retained Earnings—S Company	55,000	
	Preferred Stock—S Company	500,000	
	Difference between Implied and Book Value	45,000	
	Investment in S Company Preferred Stock		180,000
	Noncontrolling Interest in Equity		420,000
	To eliminate the preferred stock investment account and recognize the noncontrolling interest in equity.		
(1b)	Other Contributed Capital—P Company	13,500	
	Noncontrolling Interest in Equity	31,500	
	Difference between Implied and Book Value		45,000
	To allocate the difference between implied and book values of preferred stock to equity.		

Cost Method
80% Owned Subsidiary
Subsidiary Has Preferred
Stock Outstanding

ILLUSTRATION 9-8

Condensed Consolidated Statements Workpaper
P Company and Subsidiary
for the Year Ended December 31, 2009

	P	*S*	*Eliminations*		*Noncontrolling*	*Consolidated*
Income Statement	*Company*	*Company*	*Dr.*	*Cr.*	*Interest*	*Balances*
Net/Consolidated Income	800,000	200,000				1,000,000
Noncontrolling Interest						
in Dividend Income						
Preferred Stock (in arrears)						
($40,000 × .70)					28,000	
Common Stock						
[($200,000 − $40,000) × .20]					32,000	(60,000)
Net Income to Retained Earnings	800,000	200,000	—	—	60,000	940,000
Retained Earnings Statement						
1/1 Retained Earnings						
P Company	1,450,000					1,450,000
S Company						
Preferred Stock		55,000	(1a) 55,000			
Common Stock		145,000	(2) 145,000			
Net Income from above	800,000	200,000			60,000	940,000
Dividends Declared P Company	(500,000)					(500,000)
12/31 Retained Earnings						
to Balance Sheet	1,750,000	400,000	200,000	—	60,000	1,890,000
Balance Sheet						
Investment in S Company						
Preferred Stock	180,000			(1a) 180,000		—0—
Investment in S Company						
Common Stock	1,160,000			(2) 1,160,000		—0—
Difference between Implied and						
Book Value—Preferred Stock			(1a) 45,000	(1b) 45,000		
Other Assets	5,410,000	2,805,000				8,215,000
Total Assets	6,750,000	2,805,000				8,215,000
Liabilities	1,600,000	600,000				2,200,000
Preferred Stock						
S Company		500,000	(1a) 500,000			
Common Stock						
P Company	3,000,000					3,000,000
S Company		1,000,000	(2) 1,000,000			
Other Contributed Capital						
P Company	400,000		(1b) 13,500			386,500
S Company		305,000	(2) 305,000			
Retained Earnings from above	1,750,000	400,000	200,000		60,000	1,890,000
1/1 Noncontrolling Interest			(1b) 31,500	(1a) 420,000	678,500	
in Net Assets				(2) 290,000		
12/31 Noncontrolling Interest						
in Net Assets					738,500	738,500
Total Liabilities and Equity	6,750,000	2,805,000	2,095,000	2,095,000		8,215,000

(1a) To eliminate the preferred stock investment account and create noncontrolling interest account.
(1b) To allocate the difference between implied and book value to equity.
(2) To eliminate the common stock investment account and create noncontrolling interest account.

		$	Noncontrolling Percentage	Total
Total stockholders' equity		$2,205,000		
Allocated to the preferred:				
Par value	$500,000			
Call premium	15,000			
Dividends in arrears	80,000			
Book value of preferred stock		595,000	0.70	$416,500
Book value of common stock		$1,610,000	0.20	322,000
Noncontrolling interest—12/31				$738,500

As shown in Illustration 9-7, the cost of the preferred stock acquired at $180,000 implies a total value for preferred stock of $180,000/30%, or $600,000. The difference between the implied value and the book value of $555,000 is $45,000. This amount is not allocated to specific assets or liabilities, as in the case of common stock differences, but is accounted for as an equity transaction. Of the $45,000 difference, 30%, or $13,500, is attributable to Company P and is charged to Other Contributed Capital of P. The remaining 70%, or $31,500, serves to reduce the noncontrolling interest in equity. Thus, the net amount of noncontrolling interest implied by the cost of the preferred stock is $600,000 × 70%, or $420,000, less the $31,500 allocation [from entries (1a) and (1b)], or $388,500.

(2) Beginning Retained Earnings—S Company	145,000	
Common Stock—S Company	1,000,000	
Other Contributed Capital—S Company	305,000	
Investment in S Company Common Stock		1,160,000
NCI in Equity		290,000
To eliminate the common stock investment account and recognize NCI.		

In computing the noncontrolling interest in consolidated net income, S Company's contribution to consolidated income is first allocated between the two classes of stock. Because of the cumulative feature of the preferred stock, $40,000 of S Company's net income is first allocated to the cumulative preferred stock even though no cash dividends were declared in this period. This of course reduces the amount of income available for distribution to the common stockholders. The residual net income of $160,000 is allocated to the common stockholders' interest since the preferred stock is nonparticipating. Noncontrolling interest in the consolidated income for 2009 is computed as follows:

	Contribution to Consolidated Income	*Noncontrolling Percentage*	*Noncontrolling Interest*
Reported net income of S Company	$200,000		
Income allocated to preferred stock	40,000	.70	$28,000
Income allocated to common stock	$160,000	.20	32,000
Noncontrolling interest in consolidated income			$60,000

LO8 Determining controlling interest.

Such an allocation is necessary whether or not P Company holds any of the preferred stock.

Note that the allocation of net income is unaffected by dividends in arrears on preferred stock at the beginning of the year. The allocation of net income reflects the increase in the book value interest of each class of stock due to operations of the current period only. Dividends in arrears at the beginning of the year are recognized as an allocation of the beginning retained earnings balance.

Consolidated net income for 2009 and consolidated retained earnings as of December 31, 2009, can be verified as shown in Illustration 9-9.

ILLUSTRATION 9-9

T-Account Approach to Consolidated Net Income and Retained Earnings

Controlling Interest in Consolidated Net Income—2009		
Net income from independent operations of Company		$ 800,000
P Company's share of S Company's reported income:	$ 12,000	
Allocated to preferred stock interest: $40,000 × .30		
Allocated to common stock interest: $160,000 × .80 =	128,000	$140,000*
Controlling Interest in Consolidated net income		$940,000

Consolidated Retained Earnings—December 31, 2009		
P Company's December 31, 2009, retained earnings balance		1,750,000
Undistributed net income earned since date of acquisition		
Preferred stock ($40,000 × .30) =	$ 12,000	
Common stock ($160,000 × .80) =	128,000	$ 140,000*
Consolidated retained earnings on December 31, 2009		$1,890,000

* Undistributed net income can be computed as follows when income statements of prior years are not available:

	Retained Earnings Allocation		
Retained Earnings Balance	*Preferred Stock*	*Common Stock*	*Total*
End of current year	$95,000	$305,000	$400,000
Date of acquisition	55,000	145,000	200,000
Increase in retained earnings	40,000	160,000	$200,000
Percentage interest	.30	.80	
Share of undistributed income	$12,000	$128,000	$140,000

Complete Equity Method The consolidated workpapers assuming that P Company uses the complete equity method are reported in Illustration 9-10. Recall that the Investment in S Company Common Stock account is increased by equity income ($128,000) and decreased by dividends received (none were received in 2009). However, equity income on the cumulative preferred stock must still be recognized even though no dividends were declared in 2009. In this case, the equity income in preferred stock ($12,000) increases the Investment in S Company Preferred Stock account. Therefore, on the consolidated workpapers, this entry must be reversed (see entry (3) in Illustration 9-10).

Accounting Subsequent to the Year of Acquisition—2010

Now assume that S Company reported net income of $300,000 in 2010 and paid cash dividends of $120,000 to the preferred stockholders ($80,000 for the arrearages of 2008 and 2009 plus $40,000 for the current year) and $50,000 to the common stockholders.

Cost Method: Entries on the Books of P Company—2010 P Company would record receipt of the cash dividends as follows:

Cash	36,000	
Dividend Income		24,000
Investment in S Company Preferred Stock		12,000
To record receipt of dividends on preferred stock investment ($12,000 represents dividends in arrears at the acquisition date). ($120,000 × .30 = $36,000).		

Note that the distribution of $40,000 for preferred dividends in arrears at the date of acquisition is a liquidating dividend, and P Company's 30% thereof is accounted for as a reduction in the investment account.

Cash	40,000	
Dividend Income		40,000
To record the receipt of dividends on the common stock investment ($50,000 × .80 = $40,000).		

Complete Equity Method: Entries on the Books of P Company—2010 P Company would record the receipt of the cash dividends as follows:

Cash	36,000	
Equity Income—S Company Preferred Stock		12,000
Investment in S Company Preferred Stock (dividends in arrears recognized as revenue in 2009)		12,000
Investment in S Company Common Stock (dividends in arrears at date of acquisition, liquidating dividend)		12,000
To record receipt of dividends on preferred stock investment ($120,000 × .30 = $36,000).		

Note that the distribution of $40,000 for preferred dividends in arrears at the date of acquisition is a liquidating dividend, and P Company's 30% (or $12,000) is accounted for as a reduction in the Investment in S Company Common Stock account:

Investment in S Company Common Stock	208,000	
Equity Income in S Company Common Stock		208,000
To record equity in subsidiary income ($300,000 S Company income − $40,000 allocated to preferred stock) × .80.		

Complete Equity Method
80% Owned Subsidiary
Subsidiary Has Preferred
Stock Outstanding

ILLUSTRATION 9-10
Condensed Consolidated Statements Workpaper
P Company and Subsidiary
for the Year Ended December 31, 2009

Income Statement	*P Company*	*S Company*	*Eliminations Dr.*	*Eliminations Cr.*	*Noncontrolling Interest*	*Consolidated Balances*
Income before Equity Income	800,000	200,000				1,000,000
Equity Income in Common Stock	128,000		(4) 128,000			
Equity Income in Preferred Stock	12,000		(3) 12,000			
Net/Consolidated Income	940,000					
Noncontrolling Interest in Income						
Preferred Stock ($40,000 × .70)					28,000	
Common Stock						
[($200,000 − $40,000) × .20]					32,000	(60,000)
Net Income to Retained Earnings	940,000	200,000	140,000	—	60,000	940,000
Retained Earnings Statement						
1/1 Retained Earnings						
P Company	1,450,000					1,450,000
S Company						
Preferred Stock		55,000	(1a) 55,000			
Common Stock		145,000	(2) 145,000			
Net Income from above	940,000	200,000	140,000		60,000	940,000
Dividends Declared P Company	(500,000)					(500,000)
12/31 Retained Earnings						
to Balance Sheet	1,890,000	400,000	340,000	—	60,000	1,890,000
Balance Sheet						
Investment in S Company						
Preferred Stock	192,000			(3) 12,000 (1a) 180,000		—0—
Investment in S Company						
Common Stock	1,288,000			(2) 1,160,000 (4) 128,000		—0—
Difference between Implied and						
Book Value—Preferred Stock			(1a) 45,000	(1b) 45,000		
Other Assets	5,410,000	2,805,000				8,215,000
Total Assets	6,890,000	2,805,000				8,215,000
Liabilities	1,600,000	600,000				2,200,000
Preferred Stock						
S Company		500,000	(1a) 500,000			
Common Stock						
P Company	3,000,000					3,000,000
S Company		1,000,000	(2) 1,000,000			
Other Contributed Capital						
P Company	400,000		(1b) 13,500			386,500
S Company		305,000	(2) 305,000			
Retained Earnings from above	1,890,000	400,000	340,000		60,000	1,890,000
1/1 Noncontrolling Interest in Net Assets			(1b) 31,500	(1a) 420,000 (2) 290,000	678,500	
12/31 Noncontrolling Interest						
in Net Assets					738,500	738,500
Total Liabilities and Equity	6,890,000	2,805,000	2,235,000	2,235,000		8,215,000

(1a) To eliminate the preferred stock investment account and create noncontrolling interest account.
(1b) To allocate the difference between implied and book value to equity.
(2) To eliminate the common stock investment account and create noncontrolling interest account.
(3) To eliminate equity income in preferred stock.
(4) To eliminate equity income in common stock.

Consolidated Statements Workpaper—2010

Consolidated statements workpapers for December 31, 2010 are presented in Illustration 9-11, using the cost method and in Illustration 9-12 assuming the complete equity method. To facilitate making the eliminating entries, the beginning retained earnings balance of $400,000 of S Company is allocated between the two classes of stock as follows:

Retained earnings balance—1/1		$400,000
Allocated to preferred stock:		
Undistributed income assigned to preferred stock interest—2008 and 2009—$40,000 × 2 years =	$80,000	
Call premium ($3/share)	15,000	95,000
Residual assigned to common stock		$305,000

Consolidated Statements Workpaper Entries—2010

Cost Method The December 31, 2010, workpaper elimination entries in journal form (Illustration 9-11) are as follows:

		Debit	Credit
(1)	Investment in S Company Preferred Stock	12,000	
	Investment in S Company Common Stock	128,000	
	Beginning Retained Earnings—P Company		140,000
	To establish reciprocity/convert to equity as of 1/1/10.		
	($95,000 − $55,000) × .3 = $12,000		
	($305,000 − $145,000) × .80 = $128,000		
(2)	Dividend Income	64,000	
	Dividends Declared—S Company (Preferred)		24,000
	Dividends Declared—S Company (Common)		40,000
	To eliminate intercompany dividends.		
(3)	Investment in S Company Preferred Stock	12,000	
	Dividends Declared—S Company ($40,000 × .3)		12,000
	To reverse the liquidating dividend (dividends in arrears at the date of acquisition).		
(4a)	Beginning Retained Earnings—S Company	95,000	
	Preferred Stock—S Company	500,000	
	Difference between Implied and Book Value	45,000	
	Investment in S Company Preferred Stock		192,000
	Noncontrolling Interest in Equity		448,000
	To eliminate the preferred stock investment account and recognize the noncontrolling interest in equity.		
(4b)	Other Contributed Capital—P Company	13,500	
	Noncontrolling Interest in Equity	31,500	
	Difference between Implied and Book Value		45,000
	To allocate the difference between implied and book values of preferred stock to equity.		
(5)	Beginning Retained Earnings—S Company	305,000	
	Common Stock—S Company	1,000,000	
	Other Contributed Capital—S Company	305,000	
	Investment in S Company Common Stock		1,288,000
	NCI in Equity		322,000
	To eliminate common stock investment account and recognize NCI.		

Cost Method
80% Owned Subsidiary
Subsidiary Has Preferred
Stock Outstanding

ILLUSTRATION 9-11
Consolidated Statements Workpaper
P Company and Subsidiary
for the Year Ended December 31, 2010

	P	*S*	*Eliminations*		*Noncontrolling*	*Consolidated*
Income Statement	*Company*	*Company*	*Dr.*	*Cr.*	*Interest*	*Balances*
Net/Income before Dividend Income	636,000	300,000				936,000
Dividend Income ($24,000 preferred + $40,000 common)	64,000		(2) 64,000			—0—
Net/Consolidated Income	700,000	300,000				936,000
Noncontrolling Interest in Income						
Preferred Stock ($40,000 × .70)					28,000	
Common Stock ($260,000 × .20)					52,000	(80,000)
Net Income to Retained Earnings	700,000	300,000	64,000	—	80,000	856,000
Retained Earnings Statement						
1/1 Retained Earnings						
P Company	1,750,000			(1) 140,000		1,890,000
S Company						
Preferred Stock		95,000	(4a) 95,000			
Common Stock		305,000	(5) 305,000			
Net Income from above	700,000	300,000	64,000		80,000	856,000
Dividends Declared						
P Company	(500,000)					(500,000)
S Company				(2) 24,000		
Preferred Stock		(120,000)		(3) 12,000	(84,000)	
Common Stock		(50,000)		(2) 40,000	(10,000)	
12/31 Retained Earnings to Balance Sheet	1,950,000	530,000	464,000	216,000	(14,000)	2,246,000
Balance Sheet						
Investment in S Company Preferred Stock ($180,000 − $12,000)	168,000		(1) 12,000 (3) 12,000	(4a) 192,000		—0—
Difference between Implied and Book Value—Preferred Stock,			(4a) 45,000	(4b) 45,000		
Investment in S Company Common Stock	1,160,000		(1) 128,000	(5) 1,288,000		—0—
Other Assets	5,322,000	2,785,000				8,107,000
Total Assets	6,650,000	2,785,000				8,107,000
Liabilities	1,300,000	450,000				1,750,000
Preferred Stock						
S Company		500,000	(4a) 500,000			
Common Stock						
P Company	3,000,000					3,000,000
S Company		1,000,000	(5) 1,000,000			
Other Contributed Capital						
P Company	400,000		(4b) 13,500			386,500
S Company		305,000	(5) 305,000			
Retained Earnings from above	1,950,000	530,000	464,000	216,000	(14,000)	2,246,000
1/1 Noncontrolling Interest in Net Assets			(4b) 31,500	(4a) 448,000 (5) 322,000	738,500	
12/31 Noncontrolling Interest in Net Assets					724,500	724,500
Total Liabilities and Equity	6,650,000	2,785,000	2,511,000	2,511,000		8,107,000

(1) To establish reciprocity (convert to equity) as of 1/1/10.
(2) To eliminate intercompany dividends.
(3) To reverse liquidating dividend.
(4a) To eliminate preferred stock investment account and create noncontrolling interest account.
(4b) To allocate the difference between implied and book value to equity.
(5) To eliminate common stock investment account and create noncontrolling interest account. ($290,000 + ($305,000 − $145,000) × .20 = $322,000).

Complete Equity Method
80% Owned Subsidiary
Subsidiary Has Preferred
Stock Outstanding

ILLUSTRATION 9-12
Consolidated Statements Workpaper
P Company and Subsidiary
for the Year Ended December 31, 2010

	P	*S*	*Eliminations*		*Noncontrolling*	*Consolidated*
Income Statement	*Company*	*Company*	*Dr.*	*Cr.*	*Interest*	*Balances*
Net/Income before						
Dividend Income	636,000	300,000				936,000
Equity Income in S Company						
Common Stock	208,000		(3) 208,000			
Equity Income in S Company						
Preferred Stock	12,000		(1) 12,000			—0—
Net/Consolidated Income	856,000	300,000				936,000
Noncontrolling Interest in Income						
Preferred Stock ($40,000 × .70)					28,000	
Common Stock ($260,000 × .20)					52,000	(80,000)
Net Income to Retained Earnings	856,000	300,000	220,000	—	80,000	856,000
Retained Earnings Statement						
1/1 Retained Earnings						
P Company	1,890,000					1,890,000
S Company						
Preferred Stock		95,000	(2a) 95,000			
Common Stock		305,000	(4) 305,000			
Net Income from above	856,000	300,000	220,000		80,000	856,000
Dividends Declared						
P Company	(500,000)					(500,000)
S Company						
Preferred Stock		(120,000)		(1) 36,000	(84,000)	
Common Stock		(50,000)		(3) 40,000	(10,000)	
12/31 Retained Earnings						
to Balance Sheet	2,246,000	530,000	620,500	76,000	(14,000)	2,246,000
Balance Sheet						
Investment in S Company						
Preferred Stock						
($192,000 − $12,000)	180,000		(1) 12,000	(2a) 192,000		—0—
Difference between implied and						
book value–Preferred stock			(2a) 45,000	(2b) 45,000		
Investment in S Company				(3) 168,000		
Common Stock	1,444,000		(1) 12,000	(4) 1,228,000		—0—
Other Assets	5,322,000	2,785,000				8,107,000
Total Assets	6,946,000	2,785,000				8,107,000
Liabilities	1,300,000	450,000				1,750,000
Preferred Stock						
S Company		500,000	(2a) 500,000			
Common Stock						
P Company	3,000,000					3,000,000
S Company		1,000,000	(4) 1,000,000			
Other Contributed Capital						
P Company	400,000		(2b) 13,500			386,500
S Company		305,000	(4) 305,000			
Retained Earnings from above	2,246,000	530,000	620,000	76,000	(14,000)	2,246,000
1/1 Noncontrolling Interest			(2b) 31,500	(2a) 448,000	738,500	
in Net Assets				(4) 322,000		
12/31 Noncontrolling Interest						
in Net Assets					724,500	724,500
Total Liabilities and Equity	6,946,000	2,785,000	2,539,000	2,539,000		8,107,000

(1) To eliminate intercompany dividends of $36,000 (30% of $12,000), of which $12,000 represents a liquidating dividend (dividends in arrears on the date of acquisition of the preferred stock), $12,000 a reversal of the prior year's equity income previously recognized, and $12,000 of current year's dividends.
(2a) To eliminate preferred stock investment account and create noncontrolling interest account.
(2b) To eliminate the difference between implied and book value to equity.
(3) To eliminate intercompany income and dividends.
(4) To eliminate common stock investment account and create noncontrolling interest account. ($290,000 + ($305,000 − $145,000) × .20) = $322,000.

At the end of the year, there are no dividends in arrears on the preferred stock. This means that all income allocated to the preferred stock interest since the date of acquisition has been distributed. Thus, at the end of the period, $15,000 of the ending retained earnings balance is allocated to the preferred stock for the call premium. The residual balance of $515,000 is allocated to the common stock interest.

Consolidated net income and retained earnings for the year ended December 31, 2010, using the t-account approach, are computed as follows:

Controlling Interest in Consolidated Net Income

Internally generated income of P Company ($700,000 − $64,000 dividends)	$636,000
Other needed adjustments (see Chapters 5 and 6)	
Percentage of subsidiary adjusted income (%) ($ subsidiary income):	
Assigned to preferred stock $40,000 × .30 =	12,000
Assigned to common stock $260,000 × .80 =	208,000
Controlling interest in income	$856,000

Consolidated Retained Earnings P Company's interest in the undistributed net income at the end of 2010 is computed as follows:

Retained Earnings—S Company	*Preferred Stock*	*Common Stock*	*Total*
End of current year	$15,000	$515,000	$530,000
Date of acquisition	15,000*	145,000	160,000*
Undistributed income	—0—	370,000	$370,000
Percentage interest	.30	.80	
Share of undistributed income	$ —0—	$296,000	$296,000

* Dividends in arrears of $40,000 were paid and accounted for as a liquidating dividend.

Consolidated Retained Earnings

P Company's ending retained earnings balance	$1,950,000
P Company's share of undistributed income of S Company earned since date of acquisition	
Preferred stock	—0—
Common stock	296,000
Consolidated retained earnings, December 31, 2010	$2,246,000

The entry to establish reciprocity/convert to equity in the December 31, 2011, consolidated statements workpaper is:

Investment in S Company Common Stock	296,000	
Beginning Retained Earnings—P Company		296,000

A reciprocity entry is not needed for the preferred stock interest because there is no undistributed income relating to the preferred stock at the end of 2010 (and, as usual, no reciprocity entry is needed under the partial or complete equity methods).

Complete Equity Method The December 31, 2010, workpaper elimination entries in journal form (Illustration 9-12) are as follows:

		Debit	Credit
(1)	Investment in S Company Preferred Stock (dividends in arrears recognized in prior year)	12,000	
	Investment in S Company Common Stock (dividends in arrears on date of acquisition)	12,000	
	Equity Income—S Company Preferred Stock (current period dividends)	12,000	
	Dividends Declared—S Company (Preferred)		36,000
	To eliminate intercompany dividends of \$36,000 (30% of \$120,000), of which \$12,000 represents a liquidating dividend (dividends in arrears on the date of acquisition on the preferred stock), \$12,000 a reversal of the prior year's equity income previously recognized, and \$12,000 current year's dividends.		
(2a)	Beginning Retained Earnings—S Company	95,000	
	Preferred Stock—S Company	500,000	
	Difference between Implied and Book Value	45,000	
	Investment in S Company Preferred Stock		192,000
	Noncontrolling Interest in Equity		448,000
	To eliminate the preferred stock investment account and recognize the noncontrolling interest in equity.		
(2b)	Other Contributed Capital—P Company	13,500	
	Noncontrolling Interest in Equity	31,500	
	Difference between Implied and Book Value		45,000
	To allocate the difference between implied and book values of preferred stock to equity.		
(3)	Equity Income in S Company Common Stock	208,000	
	Dividends Declared—S Company Common Stock		40,000
	Investment in S Company Common Stock		168,000
	To eliminate intercompany income and dividends.		
(4)	Beginning Retained Earnings—S Company	305,000	
	Common Stock—S Company	1,000,000	
	Other Contributed Capital—S Company	305,000	
	Investment in S Company Common Stock		1,288,000
	NCI in Equity		322,000
	To eliminate common stock investment account and recognize NCI.		

SUMMARY

1. *Describe the term "constructive retirement of debt."* An affiliate company may purchase bonds issued by another affiliate directly from the issuing company or from outsiders after the original issue. Because the bonds are held within the affiliated group, they are viewed as being ***constructively retired*** in the consolidated financial statements. The bonds, however, remain outstanding legally from the perspective of the issuing company.
2. *Describe how the gain or loss on constructive retirement of intercompany bond holdings is allocated between the purchasing and issuing companies.* Although the gain or loss may be allocated entirely to the issuing company, entirely to the purchasing company, or entirely to the parent company, the preferred method allocates it between the purchasing and issuing companies, thus allocating it between the controlling and noncontrolling interests. This method recognizes that a discount or premium is often associated with both the issuance and purchase of the bonds on the open market. The gain or loss is recognized over the life of the bonds as each company amortizes the related discount or premium to interest expense and interest revenue.
3. *Explain the impact on the consolidated financial statements when a company issues a note to an affiliated company, which then discounts the note with an outside company.* A receivable held by one of the affiliated companies should be reported in the consolidated balance sheet only if the note is due from an outside party. A contingent liability should be disclosed if a note has been discounted with an outside party and the endorsement was with recourse.

4. *Determine the effect on the consolidated financial statements when a subsidiary issues a stock dividend.* The parent company records the receipt of the shares in a memorandum entry only, since a dividend in like stock is not considered income to the recipient. For consolidated purposes, the stock dividend does not alter the investor's proportionate interest in the subsidiary. Although the composition of the subsidiary's stockholders' equity accounts is changed, neither the total stockholders' equity nor the noncontrolling interest is altered.

5. *Understand the difference in how stock dividends and cash dividends issued by a subsidiary company affect the consolidated financial statements.* A cash dividend declared by the subsidiary is generally considered to be a distribution of the most recent profits, which reduces undistributed profits of the subsidiary accumulated after the date the parent obtained control of the subsidiary. Conversely, the source of a stock dividend is the earliest earnings accumulated in the retained earnings balance. Under the cost method, the amount of the entry to establish reciprocity must be modified to recognize that the retained earnings balance at the date of acquisition has been reduced as a result of the stock dividend.

6. *Determine the impact on the investment account when a subsidiary issues a stock dividend from preacquisition earnings and from postacquisition earnings.* The amount of the subsidiary's postacquisition earnings that have been capitalized and included in the consolidated retained earnings should be disclosed in the consolidated financial statements, but the parent's investment account is not affected. Stock dividends from preacquisition earnings do not affect the investment account or the computation of consolidated retained earnings.

7. *Explain how the purchase price is allocated when the subsidiary has both common and preferred stock outstanding.* In the preparation of consolidated financial statements, the shares of the preferred stock not held by the parent company are considered part of the noncontrolling interest. To determine the equity interest of each class of stockholders on a certain date, it is necessary to allocate the subsidiary's stockholders' equity between the preferred and common stock interests, referring to the provisions of the preferred stock issue and analyzing dividend provisions.

8. *Determine the controlling interest in consolidated income when the parent company owns both common and preferred stock of the subsidiary.* The controlling interest in income includes the internally generated income of the parent plus or minus other needed adjustments discussed in previous chapters plus the parent's share of the subsidiary's adjusted income. The parent's share of the subsidiary's income includes an amount assigned for its ownership of the subsidiary's common stock plus an amount assigned for its ownership of the subsidiary's preferred stock.

TEST YOUR KNOWLEDGE SOLUTIONS

9.1 1 d
2 d
3 c

QUESTIONS

LO1 1. Define "constructive retirement of debt." How is the total constructive gain or loss computed?

LO2 2. The gain or loss on the constructive retirement of debt is recognized subsequently by the individual companies. Explain.

LO2 3. Allocating the gain or loss on constructive bond retirement between the purchasing and issuing companies is preferred conceptually. Describe how this allocation would be made.

LO2 4. Give the primary argument(s) in favor of assigning the *total* gain or loss on constructive bond retirement to the company that issued the bonds.

LO2 5. Under the allocation method followed in this text, how is the noncontrolling interest in consolidated income affected by intercompany bondholdings?

LO2 6. Investor Company purchased 70% of the $500,000 par value outstanding bonds of Investee

Company, a 70% owned subsidiary. The bonds cost $338,000 and had a carrying value of $360,000 on the date of purchase.

a. What portion of the gain or loss resulting from the constructive bond retirement should be allocated to Investor Company?

b. What portion of the constructive gain or loss should be allocated to Investee Company?

LO3 **7.** An outside party issued a note to Affiliate X, who then sold the note to Affiliate Y. Y discounted the note at an unaffiliated bank, endorsing it with recourse. Which party is primarily liable and which party is contingently liable for the note?

LO5 **8.** Cash dividends are viewed as a distribution of the most recent earnings. How are stock dividends viewed?

LO5 **9.** Explain how the reciprocity calculation is modified in periods after the declaration of a stock dividend for firms using the cost method.

LO6 **10.** What journal entry, if any, would the parent company make to record the receipt of a stock dividend?

LO4 **11.** What effect does a stock dividend have on the consolidated statements workpaper in the year of declaration? In subsequent periods?

LO7 **12.** How does the existence of preferred stock affect the calculation of noncontrolling interest?

LO7 **13.** Explain how to account for the difference between implied and book value interest of an investment in preferred stock of a subsidiary.

LO8 **14.** What effect would cumulative preferred stock have on the allocation of a net loss to the common stockholders?

Business Ethics

The company that you work for is a subsidiary of a larger company. At the beginning of each year, the subsidiary prepares a budget for the year that includes a forecast of revenues for the coming year. The subsidiary sells a significant amount of inventory to the parent to be used in the manufacture of another product. The subsidiary's revenues for the current year are short of the budgeted amount. An error in the books has misclassified an intercompany sale as an ordinary sale. The manager of the subsidiary asks you not to fix the error until after the books are closed.

What is your responsibility? What action, if any, should you take? Why?

EXERCISES

EXERCISE 9-1 Computing the Constructive Gain or Loss on Retirement of Debt LO2

Pacelli Company issued 10-year, 10% bonds with a par value of $1,000,000 on January 2, 2010, for $940,000. Interest is paid semiannually on June 30 and December 31. On December 31, 2011, $800,000 of the par value bonds were purchased by Salez Company for $820,000. Salez Company is an 80%-owned subsidiary of Pacelli Company. Both companies use the straight-line method to amortize bond discounts and premiums.

Salez Company declared cash dividends of $60,000 each year during the period 2011–2012.

Required:

A. Compute the total gain or loss on the constructive retirement of debt.

B. Allocate the total gain or loss between Pacelli Company and Salez Company.

C. Prepare the book entries related to the bonds made by the individual companies during 2012.

D. Assume that the two companies reported net income as follows:

	Pacelli Company	*Salez Company*
2011	$260,000	$140,000
2012	280,000	190,000

Compute controlling interest in consolidated net income and the noncontrolling interest in consolidated income for 2011 and 2012.

EXERCISE 9-2 **Intercompany Bond Workpaper Elimination Entries** LO2

Refer to the data provided in Exercise 9-1.

Required:

Prepare in general journal form the intercompany bond elimination entries required in the preparation of the December 31, 2011, December 31, 2012, and December 31, 2013, consolidated statements workpapers.

EXERCISE 9-3 **Computing the Constructive Gain or Loss on Debt Retirement and Book Entries** LO2

Weber Company issued five-year, 10% bonds on January 2, 2011, for 105. Par value is $850,000. Interest is paid semiannually on June 30 and December 31. Weber Company is a 90%-owned subsidiary of Fairfield Company. On December 31, 2011, Fairfield Company purchased $510,000 of Weber Company's par value bonds at 90 after the semiannual interest payment had been made. Weber Company declared dividends of $60,000 in 2011 and $80,000 in 2012. Both companies use the straight-line method to amortize bond discount and premium.

Required:

A. Compute the total gain or loss on the constructive retirement of the debt.

B. Allocate the total gain or loss between Weber Company and Fairfield Company.

C. Prepare the book entries related to the bonds made by the individual companies in 2012.

D. Assume that the two companies reported net income as follows:

	Fairfield Company	*Weber Company*
2011	$275,000	$190,000
2012	350,000	225,000

Compute controlling interest in consolidated net income and the noncontrolling interest in consolidated income for 2011 and 2012.

EXERCISE 9-4 **Intercompany Bond Workpaper Elimination Entries** LO2

Use the information relating to Weber Company and Fairfield Company in Exercise 9-3.

Required:

Prepare in general journal form the intercompany bond elimination entries for the consolidated statements workpapers prepared on December 31, 2011, December 31, 2012, and December 31, 2013.

EXERCISE 9-5 **Computing Carrying Value, Interest Revenue and Expense, Controlling and Noncontrolling Income** LO2

On January 2, 2011, Peoples, Inc. acquired an 80% interest in Schmidt Corporation for $900,000. Schmidt reported total stockholders' equity of $1,000,000 on this date. An examination of Schmidt's books revealed that book value was equal to fair value for all assets and liabilities except for inventory, which was undervalued by $60,000. All of the undervalued inventory was sold during 2011.

Peoples also purchased 30% of the $500,000 par value outstanding bonds of Schmidt Corporation for $140,000 on January 2, 2011. The bonds mature in 10 years, carry an 11% annual interest rate payable on June 30 and December 31, and had a carrying value of $505,000 on the date of purchase. Both companies use the straight-line method to amortize bond discounts and premiums.

Peoples reported net income of $300,000 for 2011 and paid dividends of $130,000 during 2011. Schmidt Corporation reported net income of $320,000 for 2011 and paid dividends of $90,000 during the year.

Required:

Compute the following items at December 31, 2011:

1. Carrying value of the debt.
2. Interest revenue reported by Peoples, Inc.
3. Interest expense reported by Schmidt Corporation
4. Balance in the Investment in Schmidt Bonds account.
5. Controlling interest in consolidated net income for 2011 using the t-account approach.
6. Noncontrolling interest in consolidated income for 2011.

EXERCISE 9-6 **Discounting a Note, Computing Proceeds, and Workpaper Eliminating Entry** LO3

Wyatt Corporation, an 80%-owned subsidiary, accepted a $60,000, 12%, 90-day note from a customer for services performed. On that same date, because Wyatt Corporation was in need of cash for operations, the subsidiary endorsed the note over to its parent company in exchange for $60,000. After holding the note for 30 days, the parent discounted the note with an independent bank. The discount rate was 13%. Both companies record discounted notes in a Discounted Notes Receivable account.

Required:

A. Compute the proceeds received by the parent company from discounting the note.
B. Prepare the workpaper entry, if any, needed to eliminate the note. If none is needed, explain why.

EXERCISE 9-7 **Subsidiary Stock Dividend—Cost Method** LO4

Perez, Inc. owns 7,000 shares (70% interest) of Salata Company's $100 par value common stock. The stock was purchased for $1,250,000 on January 2, 2010, when Salata reported a common stock balance of $1,000,000, a retained earnings balance of $400,000, and other contributed capital balance of $100,000. Any difference between implied and book value interest acquired is attributable to the under- or overvaluation of land. During 2011, Salata reported net income of $80,000. Because the company was short of liquid assets, dividends have not been paid since 2006. During 2011, however, the company declared and issued a 15% stock dividend (market price of common stock on the date of issue, $160 per share). The retained earnings balance at the beginning of 2011 was $500,000.

Required:

A. Prepare the journal entries required in the books of Perez, Inc. during 2011.
B. Prepare in general journal form the workpaper entries necessary in the consolidated statements workpaper for the year ended December 31, 2011.
C. Prepare the workpaper entry to establish reciprocity to be made in the 2012 consolidated statements workpaper.

EXERCISE 9-8 **Liquidating Dividend** LO6

On January 1, 2011, Pacelli Company acquired a 90% interest in Swartz Corporation for $720,000. On this date, Swartz Corporation reported common stock of $500,000 and retained earnings of $200,000. Any difference between implied and book value interest acquired is attributable to the under- or overvaluation of land.

Other information pertaining to Swartz Corporation follows:

2011 Net income	$65,000
2011 Cash dividends	90,000
2012 Net income	80,000
2012 Cash dividends	40,000

Pacelli Company uses the partial equity method to account for its investment in Swartz Corporation.

Required:

A. Prepare the general journal entries for 2011 and 2012 to record the receipt of the cash dividends.

B. Prepare all determinable workpaper entries that would be made in the preparation of 2011 consolidated statements workpaper.

C. Prepare all determinable workpaper entries that would be made in the preparation of consolidated statements for 2012.

D. How would the entry in part A change if the cost method was used to account for the investment?

EXERCISE 9-9 **Purchase Common and Preferred Stock** LO8

On January 2, 2011, Pasqual Corporation purchased 80% of the outstanding common stock and 30% of the outstanding cumulative, nonparticipating, preferred stock of Sung Company for $400,000 and $70,000, respectively. At this date, Sung Company reported account balances of $400,000 in common stock, $200,000 in preferred stock, and $100,000 in retained earnings. No other contributed capital accounts exist. The difference between implied and book value of the common stock is attributable to under- or overvalued land. Dividends on the 12% cumulative preferred stock (par $10) were not paid during 2010.

Other information:

	Pasqual Corporation	*Sung Company*
1/2/2011 Retained Earnings	$45,000	$100,000
2011 Reported Net Income	84,600	90,000
2011 Dividends Declared	25,000	50,000

Required:

A. Prepare the journal entries made by Pasqual Corporation in 2011 to account for the investments assuming (1) the cost method is used, (2) the partial equity method is used, and (3) the complete equity method is used.

B. Compute the noncontrolling interest in Sung Company's net income.

C. Prepare the 2011 workpaper entries related to the foregoing investments assuming (1) the cost method is used to account for the investment, (2) the partial equity method is used to account for the investment, and (3) the complete equity method is used to account for the investment.

EXERCISE 9-10 **Various Preferred Stock Characteristics—Workpaper Entries** LO7

Sam's Company reported the following stockholders' equity account balances on December 31, 2011.

Preferred stock (12%, $100 par value, call price is $105)	$100,000
Common stock, $10 par value	500,000
Other contributed capital—premium on issue of common stock	160,000
Retained earnings	110,000
Total	$870,000

On December 31, 2011, Peterson, Inc. acquired 60% of Sam Company's common stock for $550,000 and 40% of its preferred stock for $55,000.

The difference between the implied value of the common stock (preferred stock) and the book value is allocated entirely to land (other contributed capital and noncontrolling interest).

Required:

Prepare in general journal form the December 31, 2011, workpaper entries to eliminate the investment in common and preferred stock for each of the following independent cases:

Case 1: The preferred stock is noncumulative and nonparticipating.

Case 2: The preferred stock is cumulative and nonparticipating, and dividends were not paid in 2010 and 2011.

Case 3: The preferred stock is noncumulative and fully participating.

EXERCISE 9-11 Various Preferred Stock Characteristics—Compute Consolidated Income LO7 LO8

On January 1, 2011, Perez Company acquired 80% of Serrano Company's $300,000 par value common stock for $200,000 and 40% of Serrano Company's 8%, $100,000 par value preferred stock for $86,000. During 2011, Serrano Company reported net income of $80,000 and declared cash dividends of $45,000. Perez Company reported net income (including dividends from subsidiary) of $200,000 in 2011.

Required:

In each of the following independent cases, compute consolidated net income for 2011.

Case 1: The preferred stock is noncumulative and nonparticipating.

Case 2: The preferred stock is cumulative and nonparticipating. Dividends were in arrears two years as of January 1, 2011.

Case 3: The preferred stock is noncumulative and fully participating.

Case 4: The preferred stock is cumulative and fully participating. Dividends were in arrears one year as of January 1, 2011.

EXERCISE 9-12 Computing the Constructive Gain or Loss on Retirement of Debt (effective interest) LO2

Pacman Company issued 5-year, 8% bonds with a par value of $100,000 on December 31, 2009, for $92,278 (sold to yield 10%). Interest is paid semiannually on June 30th and December 31st. On December 31, 2010, $80,000 of the par value bonds were purchased by Space Invaders Company for $77,362 (a 9% yield). Space Invaders Company is a 70%-owned subsidiary of Pacman Company. Both companies use the effective interest method to amortize bond discounts and premiums. Space Invaders Company declared cash dividends of $60,000 each year during the period 2010–2011.

Required: (round answers to the nearest dollar)

A. Compute the total gain or loss on the constructive retirement of debt.

B. Allocate the total gain or loss between Pacman Company and Space Invaders Company.

C. Prepare the book entries related to the bonds made by the individual companies during 2012. Hint: it will be helpful to prepare bond amortization schedules.

D. Assume that the two companies reported ***net income*** as follows:

		Pacman Company		
	Cost Method	*Partial Equity*	*Complete Equity*	*Space Invaders Company*
2010	$260,000	$316,000	$312,677	$140,000
2011	280,000	371,000	371,708	190,000

Compute controlling interest in consolidated net income and the noncontrolling interest in consolidated income for 2010 and 2011.

EXERCISE 9-13 Intercompany Bond Workpaper Elimination Entries (effective interest) LO2

Refer to the data provided in Exercise 9-12.

Required:

Prepare in general journal form the intercompany bond elimination entries required in the preparation of the December 31, 2010, December 31, 2011, and December 31, 2012, consolidated statements workpapers.

PROBLEMS

PROBLEM 9-1 **Constructive Gain or Loss on Bonds** LO2

On January 1, 2006, Pace Corporation issued $500,000 par value, 10-year, 15% bonds. Interest is payable each June 30 and December 31. On January 1, 2009, Supra Corporation, a 90%-owned subsidiary, purchased on the open market all of the parent company bonds. Both companies have a December 31 year-end. For this problem, assume the following four independent cases.

	Issue Price by Pace Corporation on January 1, 2006	*Purchase Price by Supra Corporation on January 1, 2009*
Case 1	$512,000	$514,000
Case 2	488,000	486,000
Case 3	512,000	486,000
Case 4	488,000	514,000

Required:

A. For cases 1 and 2, compute the total constructive gain or loss and the portion allocated to each company.

B. For cases 1 and 2 prepare the journal entry or entries to be made by Pace Corporation and Supra Corporation on June 30, 2009. Both companies amortize discounts and premiums each interest payment date and use the straight-line method of amortization. Assume that Pace uses the partial equity method to account for its investment in Supra.

C. Complete the following schedules as of December 31, 2009, after the December 31 interest payment (receipt) and amortization of discount or premium have been recorded.

	Issue Price	
Pace Corporation	*$512,000*	*$488,000*
Bond Payable	______	______
Unamortized Premium (discount)	______	______
Carrying Value of Bonds	______	______
2009 Cash Payment for Interest	______	______
(Premium) Discount Amortization	______	______
2009 Bond Interest Expense	______	______
Increase (decrease) in Net Income from Amortization	______	______

	Purchase Price	
Supra Corporation	*$514,000*	*$486,000*
Investment in Pace Corp. Bonds	______	______
2009 Cash Receipts for Interest	______	______
(Premium) Discount Amortization	______	______
2009 Bond Interest Income	______	______
Increase (decrease) in Net Income from Amortization	______	______

	Case			
	1	*2*	*3*	*4*
Amount of constructive gain (loss) recognized by Pace Corporation	______	______	______	______
Amount of constructive gain (loss) recognized by Supra Corporation	______	______	______	______

D. For cases 1 and 2, prepare in general journal form the intercompany bond elimination entries required in the December 31, 2009, consolidated statements workpaper.

PROBLEM 9-2 **Constructive Gain or Loss on Bond Retirement with Workpaper—Cost Method** LO2

Prezo Company purchased 80% of Satz Company's common stock for $880,000 on January 2, 2009. Condensed financial information for Prezo Company and Satz Company is given below.

Balance Sheet
December 31, 2009

	Prezo Co.	*Satz Co.*
Current Assets	$ 920,000	$ 580,000
Investment in Satz Company Common Stock	880,000	
Investment in Satz Company Bonds	227,143	
Other Assets	2,345,457	1,320,000
	$4,372,600	$1,900,000
Bonds Payable (10%)	$ 700,000	$ 400,000
Premium on Bonds Payable	20,000	9,000
Other Liabilities	1,434,600	141,000
Common Stock	1,600,000	800,000
Retained Earnings	618,000	550,000
	$4,372,600	$1,900,000

Retained Earnings Statement
for the Year Ended December 31, 2009

	Prezo Co.	*Satz Co.*
1/1 Balance	$ 480,000	$ 300,000
Net Income	388,000	400,000
Dividends	(250,000)	(150,000)
12/31 Balance	618,000	$ 550,000

Income Statement
for the Year Ended December 31, 2009

	Prezo Co.	*Satz Co.*
Sales	$2,680,000	$1,860,000
Dividend Income	120,000	
Other Income	266,000	120,000
Total Revenue	3,066,000	1,980,000
Expenses	2,678,000	1,580,000
Net Income	$ 388,000	$ 400,000

On July 1, 2009, Prezo Company purchased 60% of Satz Company's bonds for $225,000. The bonds mature on December 31, 2012. Interest of 10% per annum is paid on June 30 and December 31 each year. Both companies use the straight-line method to amortize bond discounts and premiums.

Required:

A. Compute the gain or loss on the constructive retirement of the bonds allocated to each of the affiliated companies.

B. Prepare a consolidated financial statements workpaper on December 31, 2009.

C. Prepare in good form a schedule showing the calculation of consolidated net income for the year ended December 31, 2009.

PROBLEM 9-3 **Workpaper, Cost Method—Constructive Gain or Loss with Stock Dividend** LO2 LO4

On January 1, 2010, Pasta Company purchased an 80% interest in Salsa Company for $152,000. On this date, Salsa Company reported capital stock and retained earnings of $100,000 and $90,000, respectively. During 2010, Salsa Company reported net income of $30,000 and declared a cash dividend of $35,000. At the end of 2011, Salsa Company was facing a cash shortage. Rather than distributing a cash dividend to the common stockholders, the board of directors elected to issue a 30% stock dividend. Salsa Company's accountant recorded the stock dividend as follows:

Stock Dividend Declared	30,000	
Common Stock		30,000

On December 31, 2011, Pasta Company purchased on the open market bonds of Salsa Company with a par value of $100,000 for $94,000. Financial data for the two companies as of December 31, 2011, follows:

Income Statement	*Pasta Company*	*Salsa Company*
Sales	$370,000	$200,000
Other Revenues	15,000	2,000
	385,000	202,000
Cost of Goods Sold	180,000	110,000
Other Expenses	80,000	30,000
Net Income	$125,000	$ 62,000
Retained Earnings	*Pasta Company*	*Salsa Company*
1/1 Retained Earnings	$ 96,000	$ 85,000
Net Income	125,000	62,000
Less: Dividends Declared		
Stock Dividend Declared	(30,000)	(30,000)
12/31 Retained Earnings	$191,000	$117,000
Balance Sheet		
Current Assets	$171,000	$169,000
Investment in Salsa Company Stock	148,000	
Investment in Salsa Company Bonds	94,000	
Other Assets	300,000	315,000
Totals	$713,000	$484,000
Accounts Payable	$ 72,000	$ 40,000
Long-Term Bonds Payable	250,000	200,000*
Discount on Bonds Payable	—	(3,000)
Common Stock ($10 par value)	200,000	130,000
Retained Earnings	191,000	$117,000
Totals	$713,000	$484,000

* 8%, maturity date December 31, 2014.

Required:

A. Prepare a consolidated statements workpaper on December 31, 2011.

B. Prepare in general journal form the entry that would be made in the December 31, 2012, workpaper to establish reciprocity as of January 1, 2012.

PROBLEM 9-4 **Workpaper, Partial Equity Method—Constructive Gain or Loss on Bonds** LO2
Condensed financial information for Prince Company and South Company follows:

Balance Sheet
December 31, 2011

	Prince Company	*South Company*
Current Assets	$ 826,000	$ 700,000
Investment in South Company Stock	1,120,000	
Investment in South Company Bonds	312,000	
Other Assets	1,252,000	1,400,000
Totals	$3,510,000	$2,100,000
Bonds Payable	$ 300,000	$ 500,000
Premium on Bonds Payable	20,000	40,000
Other Liabilities	380,000	160,000
Common Stock	2,000,000	1,000,000
Retained Earnings	810,000	400,000
Totals	$3,510,000	$2,100,000

Separate Statements of Income and Retained Earnings
for the Year Ended December 31, 2011

	Prince Company	*South Company*
Sales	$3,000,000	$2,000,000
Equity in Subsidiary Income	160,000	
Other Income	100,000	200,000
Total Revenues	3,260,000	2,200,000
Expenses	2,800,000	2,000,000
Net Income	460,000	200,000
1/1 Retained Earnings Balance	600,000	300,000
	1,060,000	500,000
Dividends	(250,000)	(100,000)
12/31 Retained Earnings Balance	$ 810,000	$ 400,000

Prince Company purchased 80% of South Company's common stock for $1,000,000 at the beginning of 2010 and uses the partial equity method to account for the investment. At the time of purchase, South Company reported a common stock balance of $1,000,000 and a retained earnings balance of $250,000.

On July 1, 2011, Prince Company purchased 60% of South Company's 10% bonds for $315,000. The bonds mature on December 31, 2013. Interest is paid on June 30 and December 31.

Required:

A. Prepare the entries made on the books of Prince Company during 2011 to record its interest in South Company and account for the bond investment.

B. Prepare a consolidated financial statements workpaper on December 31, 2011.

PROBLEM 9-5 **Workpaper, Cost Method—Preferred Stock** LO7 LO8

On January 1, 2006, Pabst Company acquired 80% of Secor Company's common stock and 30% of Secor Company's 10% preferred stock. Pabst Company paid $680,000 for the common stock and $135,000 for the preferred stock. The preferred stock is cumulative and nonparticipating and has a call price of $104. On the date of acquisition, there were no dividends in arrears. On January 1, 2006, Secor Company reported the following account balances:

10% Preferred Stock ($100 par value)	$ 400,000
Common Stock ($10 par value)	500,000
Other Contributed Capital (Sale of common stock in excess of par value)	100,000
Retained Earnings	230,000
Total	$1,230,000

Condensed preclosing trial balances for the two companies at December 31, 2011 are presented below.

Income Statement	*Pabst Company*	*Secor Company*
Sales	$ 700,000	$ 450,000
Expenses	(580,000)	(350,000)
Net Income	$ 120,000	$ 100,000
Retained Earnings		
1/1 Balance	$ 507,000	$ 430,000
Net Income	120,000	100,000
Less: Dividends Declared	(100,000)	
12/31 Balance	$ 527,000	$ 530,000
Balance Sheet		
Current Assets	$1,618,000	$ 890,000
Investment in Secor Company Common Stock	680,000	
Investment in Secor Company Preferred Stock	135,000	
Other Assets	1,025,000	1,000,000
Totals	$3,458,000	$1,890,000
Liabilities	$ 931,000	$ 360,000
Preferred Stock	400,000	400,000
Common Stock	1,000,000	500,000
Other Contributed Capital	600,000	100,000
Retained Earnings	527,000	530,000
Totals	$3,458,000	$1,890,000

On December 31, 2011, dividends on the preferred stock were in arrears for 2010 and 2011.

Required:

Prepare a consolidated statements workpaper for the year ended December 31, 2011. Assume that any difference between the implied value and book value of Secor is attributable to an undervaluation in the land of Secor Company in the case of common stock, and any difference between the implied value of preferred stock and the book value is assignable to other contributed capital or to the noncontrolling interest.

PROBLEM 9-6 **Workpaper, Cost Method—Preferred Stock** LO7 LO8

PAL Corporation acquired 40% of the outstanding preferred stock of Saltz, Inc. for $60,000 and 90% of that firm's outstanding common stock for $600,000 on January 1, 2010. On the date that the controlling interest was acquired, the stockholders' equity section of Saltz, Inc. was as follows.

Preferred stock—10%, cumulative, fully participating, liquidation value is equal to par value	$100,000
Common stock—$10 par value	400,000
Retained earnings	200,000
Total	$700,000

There were no dividends in arrears on January 1, 2012. For the fiscal year ended December 31, 2010, Saltz, Inc. reported net income of $130,000. No cash or stock dividends were declared by the company during 2010.

The difference between the implied and book value of the equity interest in the common stock relates to the land owned by Saltz, Inc. Condensed financial information for the two companies at December 31, 2010, is presented below.

Income Statement Date	*PAL Corp.*	*Saltz Inc.*
Sales	$890,000	$750,000
Interest, Dividends, and Other Revenues	91,000	50,000
Cost of Goods Sold	(500,000)	(400,000)
Selling, Administrative, and Other Expenses	(330,000)	(280,000)
Net Income	$151,000	$120,000
Retained Earnings		
1/1 Balance	$560,000	$330,000
Net Income	151,000	120,000
Less: Dividends Declared		(90,000)
12/31 Balance	$711,000	$360,000
Balance Sheet		
Current Assets	$ 810,000	$380,000
Investment in Common Stock	600,000	
Investment in Preferred Stock	60,000	
Other Assets	1,276,000	600,000
Totals	$2,746,000	$980,000
Liabilities	$1,335,000	$120,000
Preferred Stock		100,000
Common Stock	700,000	400,000
Retained Earnings	711,000	360,000
Totals	$2,746,000	$980,000

Required:

A. Prepare a schedule to compute the difference between the implied value of the common stock and the book value of Saltz.

B. Prepare consolidated statements workpapers for the year ended December 31, 2011.

PROBLEM 9-7 **Preferred Stock** LO7 LO8

COMPREHENSIVE

P Company owns 80% of S Company's common stock (cost $650,000) and 20% of its preferred stock (cost $50,000). Both interests were acquired on January 1, 2009. On the date of purchase, S Company's stockholders' equity consisted of the following accounts.

Preferred stock	$200,000
Common stock	500,000
Retained earnings	160,000

The preferred stock is $25 par value, 9% cumulative, and nonparticipating. The call price is $27 per share. Dividends have been declared in all years except for 2010.

An examination of S Company's assets and liabilities revealed that their book values were equal to fair values except for the inventory and equipment.

	Book Value	*Fair Value*
Inventory	$120,000	$150,000
Equipment (net)	560,000	640,000

The equipment had a remaining life of five years at the date of the equity purchase, and the FIFO cost flow assumption is used in costing inventory.

S Company sells inventory to P Company at 25% above cost. During 2010 and 2011, such sales amounted to $350,000 and $390,000, respectively. The 2010 and 2011 ending inventories of P Company included goods purchased from S Company for $77,500 and $54,000, respectively.

The companies file consolidated tax returns. Ignore deferred income taxes when assigning the difference between implied and book value.

Selected data for the 2011 December 31 fiscal year-end are given below:

	P Company	*S Company*
Net income (including dividend income and sales to affiliates)	$234,500	$100,000
1/1/11 Retained earnings	430,000	310,000
Dividends declared and paid	80,000	50,000

Required:

A. Prepare a schedule to compute the book value interest acquired for each equity investment.

B. Prepare a schedule to assign the difference between the implied value of the common stock investment and the book value of S.

C. Compute the following items:

(1) Dividends received during 2011 by P Company from S Company for each equity interest held.

(2) Noncontrolling interest in 2011 consolidated net income.

(3) Controlling interest in consolidated net income for 2011.

(4) Consolidated retained earnings on January 1, 2011.

PROBLEM 9-8 **Comprehensive Workpaper—Cost Method**

Parson Industries purchased 80% of the common stock of Succo Company on January 1, 2010, for $300,000 when Succo Company's capital consisted of common stock of $200,000, preferred stock of $100,000, other contributed capital of $50,000, and retained earnings of $62,000.

The $100 par value preferred is 15%, cumulative and nonparticipating, and has a call price of $104 per share. Dividends on the preferred stock were not paid in 2009.

Trial balances for the parent and subsidiary for the December 31, 2011, year-end are presented below.

COMPREHENSIVE

Income Statement	*Parson Industries*	*Succo Company*
Sales	$ 404,000	$300,000
Dividend Income	4,000	
Cost of Goods Sold	(200,000)	(160,000)
Operating Expenses	(36,400)	(50,000)
Income Taxes	(40,200)	(27,000)
Net Income	$ 131,400	$ 63,000

Retained Earnings	*Parson Industries*	*Succo Company*
1/1 Retained Earnings	$ 157,400	$107,000
Net Income	131,400	63,000
Less: Dividends Declared	(65,000)	(50,000)
12/31 Retained Earnings	$ 223,800	$120,000

Balance Sheet		
Cash and Receivables	$ 396,800	$205,000
Inventories	200,000	170,000
Land	300,000	120,000
Buildings and Equipment	697,000	245,000
Accumulated Depreciation	(100,000)	(70,000)
Investment in Succo Company	300,000	
Totals	$1,793,800	$670,000
Current Liabilities	$ 370,000	$100,000
Bonds Payable	400,000	100,000
Preferred Stock		100,000
Common Stock, $10 par value	600,000	200,000
Other Contributed Capital	200,000	50,000
Retained Earnings	223,800	120,000
Totals	$1,793,800	$670,000

Additional Information:

1. At the beginning of 2011, dividends on the preferred stock were in arrears for 2009 and 2010.
2. Succo Company owed Parson Industries $10,000 for purchases of inventory on account.
3. At the date of acquisition, the portion of the difference between the implied value and book value of Succo that was attributed to tangible assets of Succo Company was allocated as follows:

Equipment (net)	$12,500
Inventories	6,250
Land	6,250

   The amount not allocated to tangible assets was allocated to goodwill (excess of implied over fair value). The equipment had a remaining life of 20 years at the date of acquisition. Succo Company uses the FIFO cost flow assumption in pricing inventory.
4. The building and equipment account of Parson Industries includes $50,000 of equipment acquired from Succo Company on July 1, 2010. When sold to Parson Industries, the asset was carried on the books of Succo Company at a cost of $100,000 and accumulated depreciation of $20,000. The asset is being depreciated by Parson Industries over a remaining life of five years. Parson Industries uses the straight-line method of depreciation.
5. The 2010 and 2011 ending inventories of Succo Company included goods purchased from Parson Industries for $15,000 and $25,000, respectively. Parson Industries sells merchandise to Succo Company at 20% above cost. During 2011, such sales amounted to $100,000.
6. The affiliates file consolidated tax returns. Ignore deferred income taxes in the assignment of the difference between implied and book value.

Required:

A. Compute the difference between implied value and book value of Succo Company equity at the date of acquisition and allocate the difference to undervalued assets of Succo Company.

B. Prepare a consolidated statements workpaper for the year ended December 31, 2011.

C. Prepare a schedule showing the calculation of controlling interest in consolidated net income for the year ended December 31, 2011.

PROBLEM 9-9 **Comprehensive Workpaper—Complete Equity Method** LO7 LO8

Parson Industries purchased 80% of the common stock of Succo Company on January 1, 2010, for $300,000 when Succo Company's capital consisted of common stock of $200,000, preferred stock of $100,000, other contributed capital of $50,000, and retained earnings of $62,000.

The $100 par value preferred is 15%, cumulative and nonparticipating, and has a call price of $104 per share. Dividends on the preferred stock were not paid in 2009.

Trial balances for the parent and subsidiary for the December 31, 2011, year-end are presented below.

Income Statement	*Parson Industries*	*Succo Company*
Sales	$ 404,000	$300,000
Equity Income	31,433	
Cost of Goods Sold	(200,000)	(160,000)
Operating Expenses	(36,400)	(50,000)
Income Taxes	(40,200)	(27,000)
Net Income	$ 158,833	$ 63,000
Retained Earnings		
1/1 Retained Earnings	$ 192,000	$107,000
Net Income	158,833	63,000
Less: Dividends Declared	(65,000)	(50,000)
12/31 Retained Earnings	$ 285,833	$120,000
Balance Sheet		
Cash and Receivables	$ 396,800	$205,000
Inventories	200,000	170,000
Land	300,000	120,000
Buildings and Equipment	697,000	245,000
Accumulated Depreciation	(100,000)	(70,000)
Investment in Succo Company	362,033	
Totals	$1,855,833	$670,000
Current Liabilities	$ 370,000	$100,000
Bonds Payable	400,000	100,000
Preferred Stock		100,000
Common Stock, $10 par value	600,000	200,000
Other Contributed Capital	200,000	50,000
Retained Earnings	285,833	120,000
Totals	$1,855,833	$670,000

Additional Information:

1. At the beginning of 2011, dividends on the preferred stock were in arrears for 2009 and 2010.
2. Succo Company owed Parson Industries $10,000 for purchases of inventory on account.
3. At the date of acquisition, the portion of the difference between the implied and book value interest acquired that was attributed to tangible assets of Succo Company was allocated as follows:

Equipment (net)	$12,500
Inventories	6,250
Land	6,250

The amount not allocated to tangible assets was allocated to goodwill (excess of implied over fair value). The equipment had a remaining life of 20 years at the date of acquisition. Succo Company uses the FIFO cost flow assumption in pricing inventory.

4. The building and equipment account of Parson Industries includes $50,000 of equipment acquired from Succo Company on July 1, 2010. When sold to Parson Industries, the asset was carried on the books of Succo Company at a cost of $100,000 and accumulated depreciation of $20,000. The asset is being depreciated by Parson Industries over a remaining life of five years. Parson Industries uses the straight-line method of depreciation.
5. The 2010 and 2011 ending inventories of Succo Company included goods purchased from Parson Industries for $15,000 and $25,000, respectively. Parson Industries sells merchandise to Succo Company at 20% above cost. During 2011, such sales amounted to $100,000.
6. The affiliates file consolidated tax returns. Ignore deferred income taxes in the assignment of the difference between implied and book value.

Required:

A. Compute the difference between implied value and book value of Succo Company equity at the date of acquisition and allocate the difference to undervalued assets of Succo Company.
B. Prepare a consolidated statements workpaper for the year ended December 31, 2011.
C. Prepare a schedule showing the calculation of controlling interest in consolidated net income for the year ended December 31, 2011.

PROBLEM 9-10 Constructive Gain or Loss on Bond Retirement with Workpaper—Cost Method (effective interest method) LO2

Prezo Company purchased 80% of Satz Company's common stock for $880,000 on January 2, 2011. Condensed financial information for Prezo Company and Satz Company is given below.

Balance Sheet
December 31, 2011

	Prezo Co.	*Satz Co.*
Current Assets	$ 920,000	$ 580,000
Investment in Satz Company Common Stock	880,000	
Investment in Satz Company Bonds	246,189	
Other Assets	2,326,411	1,320,000
	$4,372,600	$1,900,000
Bonds Payable (10%)	$ 700,000	$ 400,000
Premium on Bonds Payable		20,968
Other Liabilities	1,454,600	129,032
Common Stock	1,600,000	800,000
Retained Earnings	618,000	550,000
	$4,372,600	$1,900,000

Retained Earnings Statement
for the Year Ended December 31, 2011

	Prezo Co.	*Satz Co.*
1/1 Balance	$ 480,000	$ 300,000
Net Income	388,000	400,000
Dividends	(250,000)	(150,000)
12/31 Balance	$ 618,000	$ 550,000

Income Statement
for the Year Ended December 31, 2011

	Prezo Co.	*Satz Co.*
Sales	$2,680,000	$1,860,000
Dividend Income	120,000	
Other Income	266,000	120,000
Total Revenue	3,066,000	1,980,000
Expenses	2,678,000	1,580,000
Net Income	$ 388,000	$ 400,000

On July 1, 2011, Prezo Company purchased 60% of Satz Company's bonds for $ 247,071 (a 9% yield). The bonds mature on December 31, 2014. Interest of 10% per annum is paid on June 30 and December 31 each year. Both companies use the effective interest method to amortize bond discounts and premiums. The Satz Co. bond was originally issued to yield 8% and Prezo Company's bond was issued at par.

Required:

A. Compute the gain or loss on the constructive retirement of the bonds allocated to each of the affiliated companies.

B. Prepare a consolidated financial statements workpaper on December 31, 2011.

C. Prepare in good form a schedule showing the calculation of consolidated net income for the year ended December 31, 2011.

10

INSOLVENCY—LIQUIDATION AND REORGANIZATION

LEARNING OBJECTIVES

1. Distinguish between a Chapter 7 and a Chapter 11 bankruptcy.
2. Describe the five priority categories of unsecured claims and list the order in which they are settled.
3. Distinguish between a voluntary and involuntary bankruptcy petition.
4. Distinguish among fully secured, partially secured, and unsecured claims of creditors.
5. Describe contractual agreements that the debtor and its creditors may enter into outside of formal bankruptcy proceedings to resolve the debtor's insolvent position.

"It's bankrupt. Its reputation is in tatters. And it has been forced from its plush headquarters building. Yet working for Lehman Brothers Holdings Inc.—what remains of it—has become one of the hottest jobs on Wall Street. That's because Lehman, though a shadow of its former self after selling many of its businesses . . . retains a broad patchwork of assets."[1]

Previous chapters have treated problems relating to the expansion of business activity through mergers and stock acquisitions, as well as the procedures followed in reporting the effects of the expanded operations. But just as some companies expand, others face financial circumstances that cause contraction or cessation of business activities. Every year many businesses, small and large, encounter financial difficulties, and many are forced to seek relief through accommodations with creditors or some form of reorganization in order to survive. Those that are unable to obtain such relief generally terminate operations by liquidating the business unit.

This chapter deals with the various relief procedures available to an insolvent debtor. ***Insolvency*** refers to the inability of a debtor to pay its obligations as they become due. Our discussion includes relief procedures not requiring court actions, as well as the legal procedures available under the Bankruptcy Reform Act of 1978, relevant provisions of which are discussed in later sections of this chapter. Although the Bankruptcy Reform Act provides for relief of all types of insolvent debtors, including individuals, our discussion will concentrate on the provisions of the act dealing with insolvent business entities.

---

[1] *Wall Street Journal*, "Now Hiring: Lehman," by Peter Lattman, p. A1, February 2, 2008.

A new view of insolvency, sometimes referred to as deepening insolvency, focuses on the cases where (a) a company incurs debt that would be beyond its ability to repay in the future—cash flow insolvency, or (b) a company engages in a transaction or business that its capital base cannot support—low capital insolvency.[2]

RELATED CONCEPTS

This view could fuel added scrutiny of the auditor's role in assessing going *concern* likelihood.

When a business becomes insolvent, it generally has three possible courses of action: (1) the debtor and its creditors may enter into a contractual agreement, outside of formal bankruptcy proceedings; (2) the debtor or its creditors may file a bankruptcy petition, after which the debtor is liquidated under Chapter 7 of the Bankruptcy Reform Act; or (3) the debtor or its creditors may file a petition for reorganization under Chapter 11 of the Bankruptcy Reform Act.

CONTRACTUAL AGREEMENTS

A business that is unable to pay its obligations as they mature may attempt to reach an accommodation with its creditors without recourse to legal action. The procedures are relatively simple. The debtor and its creditors meet and develop a voluntary agreement or plan for settlement of obligations. The possibilities generally include (1) an extension of payment periods, (2) composition agreements, (3) formation of a creditors' committee, or (4) a voluntary assignment of assets.

Extension of Payment Periods

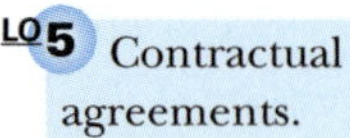
LO 5 Contractual agreements.

When the insolvency results from temporary financial difficulties and the debtor is expected to operate profitably in the future if it receives some minor relief, its creditors may find it advantageous in the long run to extend the period of payment of outstanding debts. In this situation, the debtor continues to manage the business with the expectation of obtaining sufficient profitability and financial strength to settle existing debts in full. Such an agreement is often effective for a business with few creditors. No particular accounting problem is encountered, in that interest on the debt normally continues at the originally contracted rate(s) and is paid or accrued periodically. No accounting entries are needed to reflect the extension of the payment period(s), although the nature of the new agreement should be disclosed in notes to the financial statements. *Statement of Financial Accounting Standards (SFAS) No. 15* **[ASC 470–50–40–6]** provides that where a debt restructuring involves only a modification of terms of payment, the debtor should account for the effects of the restructuring *prospectively* from the time of restructuring and should not change the carrying amount of the payable, unless the carrying amount exceeds the total future cash payments of principal and interest specified by the new terms.[3] Thus, no gain is recognized when the restructuring involves an extension of the payment period only.

Composition Agreements (Creditors Accept Less Than Full Amount)

A composition agreement is an agreement between the debtor and its creditors under which the creditors agree to accept less than the full amount of their claims. In

[2] *"Deepening Insolvency: An Emerging Threat?"* by Kelly Hnatt, *Journal of Accountancy,* February 2008, p. 41.

[3] *Statement of Financial Accounting Standards No.15,* "Accounting by Debtors and Creditors for Troubled Debt Restructurings" (Norwalk, CT.: FASB, 1997), par. 16. [ASC 470–60–35–5]

addition, accrued interest is sometimes canceled or the interest rate lowered. Creditors are often given some immediate cash payment, and the amount of the remaining debts and their interest rates are renegotiated. The benefit to the creditors is that they receive an immediate cash payment and expect to eventually receive more than they would if the debtor were forced to liquidate. The benefit to the debtor, of course, is that it can continue to operate with the expectation of returning to profitable operations and, therefore, survive.

Formation of a Creditors' Committee

The debtor and its creditors may agree to the formation of a creditors' committee that is responsible for managing the debtor's business affairs for the period during which plans are developed to rehabilitate, reorganize, or liquidate the business. Often, an extension of payment periods for debtor obligations is agreed to while the committee deliberates the ultimate disposition of the business. If the decision is to rehabilitate the business, the agreement may include the cancellation or restructuring of existing debts and possible infusion of new capital by the creditors. When the rehabilitation plan is completed, operating control of the business is generally returned to the debtor. If the decision is to reorganize or liquidate the business, the debtor's property may be turned over to a trustee who is responsible for conducting the affairs of the business during the period of reorganization or liquidation.

Voluntary Assignment of Assets

A debtor may elect to place its property under the control of a trustee for the benefit of its creditors. The purpose of the assignment is to permit the trustee to sell the property and distribute the proceeds among the creditors. If the creditors agree, the assignment results in the full discharge of the debtor's obligations to them. If there are proceeds remaining after payment of the creditors, they are returned to the debtor.

Chrysler said the company would likely have to file for Chapter 11 protection if it doesn't get additional loans from the government and concessions from unions, creditors, and dealers. Chrysler said it would need $24 billion in financing if the company were to file for bankruptcy. Company officials, however, did not believe that Chapter 11 filing was necessary for Chrysler's survival.[4]

The number of failed banks in 2008 totaled 25 equaling then cumulative number of bank failures since 2001. In addition, the FDIC included 27 more financial institutions on a "problem list," which totaled 117 by the end of the second quarter of 2008. The FDIC also noted that, in the second quarter of 2008, insured institutions added twice as much in loan-loss provisions than they actually wrote off but that the amount of loss provisions still grew at a smaller rate than noncurrent loan balances.[5]

---

[4] *WSJ*, Wednesday February 18, 2009, 'GM to End Brands, Cut 47,000 More Jobs,' page A1.

[5] *FDIC Quarterly* 2, no. 3, 2008.

BANKRUPTCY

Article I, Section 8 of the U.S. Constitution gives the Congress authority to enact uniform bankruptcy laws. Congress passed the first bankruptcy law in 1800 and has repealed and enacted new laws on several occasions since that time. The most significant revision is the Bankruptcy Reform Act of 1978 (hereafter referred to as the Reform Act), which became effective in October 1979. The Bankruptcy Act was amended in 1984, 1988, 1990, and 1994. The Reform Act consists of eight chapters:

Chapter 1	General Provisions
Chapter 3	Case Administration
Chapter 5	Creditors, the Debtor, and the Estate
Chapter 7	Liquidation
Chapter 9	Adjustment of Debts of a Municipality
Chapter 11	Reorganization
Chapter 12	Adjustment of Debts of Family Farmers with Regular Income
Chapter 13	Adjustment of Debts of an Individual with Regular Income[6]

Chapters 1, 3, and 5 cover general issues, a description of the administrative process, and definitions of various terms that apply to bankruptcy proceedings. The Reform Act provides that a bankruptcy petition may be filed under one of Chapters 7, 9, 11, 12, or 13. Chapter 9, which applies to municipalities seeking voluntary relief, and Chapter 13, which applies to bankruptcy petitions by individuals, will not be discussed here. We will concentrate on petitions by business entities under Chapter 7 (Liquidation) and Chapter 11 (Reorganization).

Provisions of the Reform Act apply to individuals, corporations, and partnerships, all of which are referred to as ***persons***, as well as to municipalities seeking voluntary relief from their creditors (municipalities cannot be forced into bankruptcy proceedings). Insurance companies and most financial institutions are excluded because they are covered by other specific statutes.

As mentioned earlier, when a business is unable to pay its obligations as they mature, it may attempt to negotiate some type of contractual agreement with its creditors without initiating a bankruptcy proceeding. If a satisfactory agreement cannot be reached, a legal petition for bankruptcy will be initiated by either the debtor (a voluntary petition) or its creditors (an involuntary petition). The Reform Act uses the single term ***debtor*** to refer to the subject of a bankruptcy proceeding.

In 2004, approximately 1.6 million debtors—representing 70% of all bankruptcies—filed for Chapter 7 relief. They walked away from literally billions of dollars of debt. A new law passed in 2005 requires debtors to first undergo a "means" test and credit counseling before they are permitted to file under Chapter 7. The result is likely to be a decrease in Chapter 7 filings and an increase in Chapter 13 filings, which require the debt to be repaid over time.[7]

[6] Several revisions to the bankruptcy statute over time have resulted in the elimination of some chapters by their consolidation with others. For example, Chapters VIII, X, XI, and XII (before the Reform Act, Roman numerals were used) were consolidated into Chapter 11 of the Reform Act. Because of these revisions, the act contains only uneven chapter numbers.

[7] *Journal of Accountancy*, "Bankruptcy Reform Is Here," by Lawrence Clark, Randall Hanson, and James Smith. 11/05, p. 51.

In April 2005, the Bankruptcy Abuse Prevention and Consumer Protection Act of 2005 was signed; it became effective in October 2005. The aim of this law is to protect creditors from abuses related to Chapter 7 bankruptcies. Most debts have been discharged completely under Chapter 7 in past years; while attractive to struggling debtors, creditors view this leniency as an invitation to abuse. The alternatives under Chapters 11 and 13 focus instead on helping the debtor to work out realistic payment plans and become financially stable rather than discharging their debts with ease. However, the major changes under the 2005 act relate to individual debtors rather than to businesses.

Voluntary Petitions

LO3 Voluntary vs. involuntary petitions.

A debtor may file a voluntary petition with a bankruptcy court for liquidation under Chapter 7 or for reorganization under Chapter 11. Filing of a voluntary or involuntary petition constitutes an ***order for relief***, which prohibits the start or continuation of legal action against the debtor by its creditors. The bankruptcy judge, however, may refuse a voluntary petition if refusal is considered to be in the best interest of the creditors.

The bankruptcy petition (either voluntary or involuntary) is an official form that initiates bankruptcy proceedings and establishes an ***estate*** consisting of the debtor's assets. The debtor must file a form listing all its property (at current market values) and its debts. This form, called a Statement of Assets and Liabilities, consists of the following separate schedules:

Schedule A. Statement of All Liabilities of Debtor
- Schedule A-1. Creditors Having Priority (with amount of claims)
- A-2. Creditors Holding Security (with market value of security and amount of claims)
- A-3. Creditors Having Unsecured Claims without Priority (with amount of claims)

Schedule B. Statement of All Property of Debtor.
- Schedule B-1. Real Property (with market values)
- B-2. Personal Property (with market values)
- B-3. Property Not Otherwise Scheduled (property discovered later)
- Schedule B-4. Property Claimed as Exempt (pertains to individuals only)

In addition, the debtor must complete a questionnaire, called a Statement of Affairs, containing questions concerning all aspects of its financial condition and operations.

The expected bankruptcy filing, which is believed to be more than 1,000 pages long, will list WorldCom's top 20 creditors, although the list will be subject to revision. Bondholders are the dominant creditors and will have one of the lou dest voices in determining the company's fate. Major bondholders are believed to include pension funds, insurance companies, mutual funds, and distressed-debt investors.[8]

[8] *WSJ*, "WorldCom Plans Bankruptcy Filing," by Shawn Young, Carrick Mollenkamp, Jared Sandberg, and Henny Sender, 7/22/02, p. A3.

Involuntary Petitions

In an involuntary proceeding, creditors initiate the action by filing a petition for liquidation or reorganization with the bankruptcy court. If there are 12 or more creditors, the petition must be signed by 3 or more such creditors whose claims aggregate at least $12,300 more than the value of any liens on the property of the debtor.[9] If there are fewer than 12 creditors, the petition may be filed by one or more such creditors whose claims aggregate at least $10,000 more than the value of any liens on the debtor's property. Involuntary petitions may be filed under either Chapter 7 or Chapter 11 of the Reform Act. The bankruptcy court will generally enter an order for relief against the debtor only if evidence indicates that the debtor, in fact, has not been paying its debts as they become due.

Secured and Unsecured Creditors

LO4 Secured and unsecured creditors.

LO2 Five priority categories for unsecured claims.

Creditors are classified by law as ***secured*** or ***unsecured***. Secured creditors are those whose claims are secured by liens or pledges of specific assets. If the proceeds from the sale of a pledged asset(s) exceed the secured claim, the excess proceeds are available for distribution to unsecured creditors. If the secured claim exceeds the proceeds from the sale of a pledged asset(s), the remaining claim constitutes an unsecured claim. Unsecured creditors do not have claims to proceeds received from the sale of specific assets but are paid from whatever total money remains after secured creditors have been satisfied. That is, secured creditors are paid first with the proceeds from the sale of specific assets upon which they have liens. Thereafter, unsecured creditors, including those having priority, are paid from whatever proceeds remain from the realization process. Thus, it is probably better to classify claims as fully secured, partially secured, or unsecured. Fully secured claims are those with liens against assets whose realizable value is equal to or in excess of the claim. Partially secured claims are those with liens against assets whose realizable value is less than the amount of the claim.

The Reform Act assigns priorities to certain claims, and each rank must be satisfied in full before the next-lower rank is paid. The following order of priority for ***unsecured*** creditors is specified as follows:

1. Administration expenses, fees, and charges incurred in administering the bankrupt's estate.
2. Unsecured claims for wages, salaries, or commissions earned by an employee within 90 days before the date of filing of the petition, but limited to the extent of $4,650 per employee.
3. Unsecured claims for contributions to employee benefit plans from services rendered within 180 days before the date of the filing of the petition, but subject to certain limitations.
4. Unsecured claims of individuals, to the extent of $2,100 for each such individual, arising from the deposit of money in connection with the purchase, lease, or rental of property or services that were not delivered or performed.
5. Unsecured claims of governmental units for unpaid taxes.

After all these priorities have been satisfied, any remaining unsecured creditors participate pro rata in any remaining realization proceeds. The distribution to unsecured creditors is termed a ***dividend*** and is generally expressed in terms of the percentage of the total unsecured claims that will be paid. For example, if $100,000 of proceeds remains

[9] Prior to April 1, 2004, the aggregated claim requirement was $10,000. Section 104 provided for an adjustment every three years. Thus, the next adjustment is expected to be in April 2007.

after all secured claims and claims having priority have been paid, and total unsecured claims amount to $400,000, each unsecured creditor will receive a 25% dividend.

LIQUIDATION (CHAPTER 7)

LO 1 Chapter 1 versus Chapter 11.

RELATED CONCEPTS

A primary underlying concept in accounting is historical cost. This principle only makes sense if the going concern assumption is met. For instance, depreciation allocations do not make sense if the firm is not expected to continue to exist.

In addition to a voluntary assignment of assets, which constitutes a liquidation without bankruptcy proceedings, a voluntary or involuntary petition for liquidation may be filed under Chapter 7 of the Reform Act. Upon filing, the bankruptcy court must decide whether to accept or dismiss the petition. Although dismissals occur infrequently, the debtor may dispute an ***involuntary petition***, in which case a trial will be held to determine whether the petition should be dismissed.

If the petition is accepted, an order for relief is entered and the bankruptcy court will appoint an interim trustee to oversee activities until a permanent trustee is selected. In addition, the court must call a meeting of the debtor's creditors, who will select a trustee and elect a creditors' committee to assist the trustee in the administration of the estate. If the creditors cannot agree on a trustee, the interim trustee becomes the trustee. Only creditors who have filed a claim at or before the meeting are entitled to vote. The interim trustee examines the claims and accepts them or, if improper, disallows them. The debtor must attend the creditors' meeting to answer questions by the creditors and the trustee, to clarify the contents of the Statement of Affairs included with the petition, and to generally assist the trustee in the preparation of an inventory of property and the examination of claims.

VisionAire Corp., the Chesterfield company that has spent millions of dollars to develop a cheaper business jet but hasn't sold a plane, admitted that it's in a cash crunch after creditors filed an involuntary petition last week to force the company into Chapter 7 bankruptcy. The five creditors, who filed the petition at U.S. District Court in St. Louis, have had court judgments against VisionAire, or they are seeking reimbursement on a letter of credit. They are owed nearly $686,000, the filing said. VisionAire has until August 6 to file a response.[10]

Duties of the Trustee

The duties of the trustee in liquidation are specified in the Reform Act. The trustee shall:

1. Collect and reduce to money the property of the estate.
2. Account for all money and property received.
3. Investigate the financial affairs of the debtor.
4. Examine claims and disallow any that are improper.
5. Furnish reasonable requests for information about the estate and its administration to parties of interest.
6. Operate the business of the debtor during the liquidation period if authorized by the court, and file periodic reports and summaries of operations.
7. Pay creditors as promptly as possible, giving due regard to secured claims and priorities.
8. File a final report on the administration of the estate, including a statement of receipts and disbursements.

In addition, the trustee has the authority to hire attorneys, accountants, appraisers, and other professionals to assist in carrying out his or her duties.

[10] *St. Louis Dispatch*, "Five Creditors Seek to Force VisionAire into Bankruptcy," by Chern Yeh Kwok, 7/25/02, p. C.1.

REORGANIZATION UNDER THE REFORM ACT (CHAPTER 11)

LO7 Chapter 1 versus Chapter 11.

Creditors of an insolvent debtor may believe that their long-range interests would be better served by rehabilitating or reorganizing the debtor than by having it liquidated. In such a case, the creditors and debtor may agree to a plan for reorganization without recourse to the judicial process by employing one or more of the contractual agreements discussed earlier in this chapter. Alternatively, the debtor or creditors may prefer to file with the bankruptcy court a petition for reorganization under Chapter 11 of the Reform Act. The company has the exclusive right to develop its reorganization plan within the first 120 days, after which any interested parties may propose a bankruptcy plan. The court can extend the exclusivity period, but the exclusivity period cannot extend beyond 18 months.

The Reform Act provides that, as soon as practicable after the acceptance of a petition for reorganization, the court shall appoint a committee of creditors holding unsecured claims, ordinarily consisting of those holding the seven largest claims against the debtor. The court may appoint additional committees of creditors or of stockholders if necessary to assure adequate representation of creditors and stockholders. If a committee of stockholders is appointed, it will normally consist of the persons who hold the seven largest amounts of equity securities.

The committee appointed by the court has the following powers and duties:

1. Select and authorize the appointment of one or more attorneys, accountants, or other agents, to represent or perform services for the committee.
2. Consult with the trustee or debtor concerning the administration of the case.
3. Investigate the acts, conduct, assets, liabilities, and financial condition of the debtor, the operation of the debtor's business and the desirability of the continuance of such business, and any other matter relevant to the case or to the formulation of a plan.
4. Participate in the formulation of a plan, advise those represented by the committee of the committee's recommendations as to any plan formulated, and collect and file with the court acceptances of a plan.
5. Request the appointment of a trustee if a trustee has not previously been appointed in the case.[11]
6. Perform such other services as are in the interest of those represented.

The court may permit the debtor to maintain possession of its assets and conduct the affairs of the business, or it may appoint a trustee. If a trustee is appointed, his or her primary duties in reorganization are:

1. Be accountable for all property received.
2. Examine claims and object to the allowance of any claim that is improper.
3. Furnish such information concerning the estate and the estate's administration as is requested by a party in interest.
4. If the business of the debtor is authorized to be operated, file with the court and with any governmental unit charged with responsibility for collection of any tax arising out of such operation, periodic reports and summaries of the operation of the business.
5. If the debtor has not done so, file with the court a list of creditors, a schedule of assets and liabilities, and a statement of the debtor's financial affairs.

---

[11] A trustee must be appointed if the debtor's debts (other than debts for goods, services, or taxes) exceed $5,000,000.

6. File a plan of reorganization.
7. After confirmation of a plan, file such reports as are required by the court.

The reorganization plan may propose the alteration of legal, contractual, and equity interests of any class of creditors or equity security holders. Unsecured creditors will generally accept payment of a portion of their claims and cancellation of the remainder of their claims. The plan must be equitable to all parties by providing for the same treatment for each claim or interest of a particular class. The plan must also contain adequate means for its own execution; that is, it must contain specific provisions for such things as (1) the retention of any property by the debtor, (2) the transfer of property to other entities, (3) the merger or consolidation of the debtor with another company, (4) the sale of property or the distribution of property to parties of interest, and (5) the issuance of securities of the debtor for cash, property, or existing securities of the debtor. After the plan is filed with the court, it must be accepted by two-thirds in amount and one-half in number of the allowed claims of each class of creditors, and by two-thirds in amount of the allowed interests of each class of stockholders. In addition, the court must approve of the overall fairness of the plan before it will be accepted.

When a firm files for bankruptcy, one of the first things that it will do is to ask the bankruptcy-court judge to approve a loan in the form of senior secured debtor-in-possession financing. This type of debt provides the banks a 'superiority' status, which means that they will be paid for new loans before anyone else.[12]

TEST YOUR KNOWLEDGE

NOTE: Solutions to ***Test Your Knowledge*** questions are found at the end of each chapter before the end-of-chapter questions.

Multiple Choice

1. The highest priority for payment of unsecured claims in a bankruptcy proceeding is
   a. Wages up to $4,650 earned within three months before the petition
   b. Unpaid federal income taxes
   c. Administrative expenses of the bankruptcy
   d. Wages owed to an insolvent employee

True or False

2. ________ Insolvency means that a debtor has more current liabilities than current assets.
3. ________ If an insolvent debtor has more than 12 creditors, an involuntary petition must be signed by at least 3 of those creditors.
4. ________ Unsecured creditors with priority will receive full satisfaction before secured creditors are paid.
5. ________ Either a debtor or its creditors may file a petition for reorganization under Chapter 11 of the Reform Act.

[12] *WSJ*, "WorldCom Plans Bankruptcy Filing," by Shawn Young, Carrick Mollenkamp, Jared Sandberg, and Henny Sender, 7/22/02, p. A3.

Fresh Start Accounting and Quasi Reorganization

In 1990, the AICPA released *Statement of Position (SOP) 90-7* providing guidance on reporting standards for firms in bankruptcy and emerging from bankruptcy. When firms emerge from bankruptcy (also referred to as confirmation of the plan of reorganization), *SOP 90-7* provides for ***fresh start*** accounting [ASC 852–10–45–19 to 20]. Basically, the implication is that a new firm exists. Because of this, assets and liabilities are reported at fair values and beginning retained earnings is reported at zero (the prior balance, positive or negative, is eliminated). Two conditions must exist before fresh start accounting can be used. The fair value of the assets must be less than the post liabilities and allowed claims, and the original owners must own less than 50% of the voting stock after reorganization.

While fresh start accounting applies only to firms emerging from bankruptcy, a less formal procedure, know as quasi reorganization, is often applied in periods of declining prices. Per *Accounting Research Bulletin No. 43* [ASC 852–20], three steps are required:

1. Authorization from creditors and stockholders is required.
2. All assets are revalued to fair values with losses recorded in retained earnings.
3. The deficit in retained earnings is eliminated by charging to (reducing) paid-in capital.

If paid-in capital is not sufficient to eliminate retained earnings, the capital stock account is reduced, thus causing a reduction in the par value of the stock. No retained earnings can be created in a quasi reorganization, and retained earnings must be "dated" for 10 years. This means that the firms disclose on the balance sheet that the balance in retained earnings has only been accumulated since the date of the quasi reorganization.

Accounting for Reorganizations—Troubled Debt Restructurings

Standards followed in accounting for reorganizations are contained in *SFAS No. 15*, "Accounting by Debtors and Creditors for Troubled Debt Restructurings." The standards deal primarily with valuation problems, the recognition of gain or loss on restructuring, and general disclosure requirements. In general, *SFAS No. 15* does not apply to bankruptcy cases where there is a general restatement of liabilities; it applies only when dealing with individual creditors. In the appropriate section below, we highlight the primary differences between a bankruptcy and a nonbankruptcy. *SFAS No. 114*, as amended by *SFAS No. 118*, dictates the accounting for a creditor in a debt restructuring [ASC 470–60 and 310–40].

Debt may be restructured in any one (or a combination) of the following methods:

1. The debtor may transfer assets in full settlement of the payable.
2. The debtor may give an equity interest in its firm in full settlement of the payable.
3. The creditor may modify terms of the payable.

Transfer of Assets A debtor that transfers assets to a creditor in full settlement of a payable recognizes a gain on the restructuring. The gain is measured by the excess of the carrying value of the payable over the fair value of the assets transferred. The ***carrying value*** of the payable is the face amount increased or decreased by applicable accrued interest and applicable unamortized premium, discount, finance charges, or issue costs. The ***fair value*** of the assets transferred is the amount that the debtor could reasonably expect to receive in a current sale between a willing buyer and a willing seller, that is, other than in a forced sale. The difference between the fair value and the carrying amount of the assets transferred is a gain or loss on the transfer of assets and is reported as a component of net income for the period of transfer. The gain on restructuring is included in net income in the period of restructuring. Assume, for example, that a debtor transferred land with a cost of $20,000 and a fair value of $15,000 to a creditor in full settlement of a $25,000 payable. Ignoring income tax effects, the debtor would report a $5,000 loss ($20,000 − $15,000) from the transfer of assets and a $10,000 ordinary gain ($25,000 − $15,000) from debt restructuring.

Grant of an Equity Interest A debtor that issues an equity interest in its firm to a creditor in full settlement of a payable shall account for the equity interest at its fair value. The difference between the fair value of the equity interest issued and the carrying amount of the payable is reported as a gain on restructuring. The debtor determines its gain based on undiscounted cash flows.

Modification of Terms A debtor, in a troubled debt restructuring involving only modification of terms of a payable, accounts for the effects of the restructuring *prospectively* from the time of restructuring. The carrying value of the payable is not changed at the time of restructuring unless the carrying value exceeds the total future cash payments specified by the new terms. That is, the effects of changes in the amounts or timing (or both) of future cash payments designated as either interest or face amount are reflected in future periods. Interest expense is computed in such a way that a constant effective interest rate is applied to the carrying value of the payable at the beginning of each period between restructuring and maturity. The new effective interest rate is the discount rate that equates the present value of the future cash payments specified by the new terms with the carrying value of the payable. This is the approach that is followed in bankruptcy regardless of whether the total future cash payments exceed the existing carrying value of the debt plus accrued interest.

If, however, in an nonbankruptcy case, the total future cash payments specified by the new terms, including both payments designated as interest and those designated as face amount, are less than the carrying value of the payable, the debtor should reduce the carrying value to an amount equal to the total future cash payments specified by the new terms and recognize a gain on restructuring. Thereafter, all cash payments under the terms of the payable should be accounted for as reductions of the carrying value of the payable, and no interest expense should be recognized on the payable for any period between the restructuring and maturity.

A restructuring may involve a combination of asset transfer, grant of an equity interest, and modification of terms. In those cases, assets transferred or the equity interest given are treated first and measured as described earlier. The carrying value of the payable is reduced by the total fair value of the assets transferred or equity interest given, and a gain or loss on the transfer of assets is recognized for the difference between the fair value and carrying value of the assets transferred. A gain on restructuring is then recognized only if the remaining carrying value of the payable exceeds the total future cash payments specified by the terms of the debt remaining unsettled.[13]

---

[13] *Statement of Financial Accounting Standards No. 15*, Par. 19 [ASC 470-60-35].

A creditor in a modification of the terms computes the loss by discounting all the future cash flows (face value and interest) using the original effective interest rate. If this amount is less than the carrying value of the existing debt (plus accrued interest), the difference is charged to bad debt expense with a credit to a valuation allowance account (less accrued interest). Then, as interest payments are received, the valuation allowance account is amortized and the cash interest receipts are recorded as interest revenue over the remaining life of the debt.

For cash-strapped companies in bankruptcy proceedings caught in the balance between staying open and shutting down, debtor-in-possession loan agreements have become the lifeline that keeps employees paid, vendors delivering, and the doors open.

Such loans, known as DIP financing, have gained more attention as household names in Chapter 11, such as retailer Kmart Corp., with $2 billion in DIP financing, and cable company Adelphia Communications Corp., with a $1.5 billion DIP loan, have secured this type of lending to stay afloat.[14]

Restructuring Illustration

To illustrate the accounting process, assume that Box Company filed a petition for reorganization with the bankruptcy court. The reorganization plan has been approved by the parties of interest and the court. Box Company's balance sheet on April 30, 2009, prior to reorganization, is shown in Illustration 10-1.

ILLUSTRATION 10-1

Box Company Balance Sheet April 30, 2009

Current Assets		
Cash		$ 86,000
Accounts Receivable	$120,000	
Less: Allowance for Uncollectibles	13,000	107,000
Inventories		142,000
Total Current Assets		335,000
Plant and Equipment	680,000	
Less: Accumulated Depreciation	275,000	405,000
Land Held as an Investment		80,000
Total Assets		$820,000
Current Liabilities		
Accounts Payable—Secured by Inventory		$ 60,000
Accounts Payable—Unsecured		134,000
Notes Payable—Unsecured		200,000
Accrued Expenses—with Priority		24,000
Accrued Interest Payable		50,000
Total Current Liabilities		468,000
Bonds Payable—Unsecured		450,000
Total Liabilities		918,000
Stockholders' Equity		
Common Stock, $1 par value	$500,000	
Retained Earnings (deficit)	(598,000)	
Total Stockholders' Deficiency		(98,000)
Excess of Liabilities over Stockholders' Deficiency		$820,000

[14] *WSJ*, "Debtor Loans Help Cash-Poor Firms," by Marc Hopkins, 7/24/02, p. B3G.

Provisions of the reorganization plan and the appropriate journal entries to account for the restructuring follow:

1. Creditors represented by the unsecured accounts payable agree to accept the accounts receivable of Box Company in full settlement of their claims. The fair value of the receivables, which is not guaranteed by Box Company, is $100,000. CV indicates carrying value, while FV indicates fair value.

Allowance for Uncollectibles	13,000	
Loss on Transfer of Assets (CV less FV)	7,000	
Accounts Receivable		20,000
To reduce the receivable to fair value.		
Accounts Payable—Unsecured	134,000	
Accounts Receivable (at fair value)		100,000
Gain on Restructuring of Debt		34,000
To record the settlement of the payable with the receivable.		

Notice that a loss on transfer of assets is recognized for the difference between the book value of the receivables ($107,000) and their fair value ($100,000). A gain on restructuring is then recognized for the difference between the carrying value of the payable ($134,000) and the fair value of the receivables ($100,000).

2. Accrued expenses with priority are paid in full.

Accrued Expenses	24,000	
Cash		24,000

3. A creditor holding a $120,000 note from Box Company agrees to accept the land held as an investment in full settlement of the note plus accrued interest of $8,000. The land has a fair value of $95,000.

Land (increase to fair value)	15,000	
Gain on Transfer of Assets (FV less CV)		15,000
Notes Payable (at carrying value)	120,000	
Accrued Interest Payable	8,000	
Land (at fair value)		95,000
Gain on Restructuring of Debt		33,000

The land is increased to its fair value and a gain on transfer of assets is recognized in the amount of $15,000. The land and payable are then written off and a gain on restructuring is recognized for the difference between the carrying value of the payable ($128,000) and the fair value of the land ($95,000).

4. A creditor holding a 14%, $80,000 note from Box Company (on which $4,000 interest has accrued) agrees to extend the maturity date of the note for two years (until April 30, 2011) and reduce the interest rate to 8%.

Note Payable	80,000	
Accrued Interest Payable	4,000	
Restructured Debt		84,000

Since the total future cash payments of $92,800 (principal of $80,000 and interest of $12,800) exceed the carrying value of the debt ($84,000), no gain on restructuring is recognized. Interest expense is recorded in the future by computing the effective interest rate that, when applied to the carrying amount of the payable at the beginning of the period, will amortize the debt over the period to maturity.

5. Bondholders agree to accept an equity interest in Box Company of 150,000 shares of common stock in exchange for the par value of the bonds. Accrued interest of $38,000 is to be paid in cash by January 1, 2010. The market value of the common stock is $1.25 per share.

Bonds Payable	450,000	
Common Stock (150,000 × $1)		150,000
Other Contributed Capital (150,000 × $.25)		37,500
Gain on Restructuring of Debt		262,500

Since the carrying value of the bonds payable exceeds the fair value of the equity interest given, a gain on restructuring is recognized.

6. Bankruptcy administration expenses totaling $16,000 are paid in cash.

Bankruptcy Administration Expenses	16,000	
Cash		16,000

The net gain on transfer of assets ($15,000 − $7,000) will be reported as a part of operations on the income statement, and the gain on restructuring of debt of $329,500 ($34,000 + $33,000 + $262,500) is reported in net income. If the conditions are met, the gain on restructuring may be reported as an extraordinary item. After giving effect to the reorganization entries, Box Company's balance sheet will be as shown in Illustration 10-2.

Notice that, although the stockholders' deficiency has been eliminated, there is still a retained earnings deficit. If desired by the parties of interest, the reorganization plan could have included a provision to decrease the par value of the common stock and eliminate the accumulated deficit.

ILLUSTRATION 10-2

Box Company Balance Sheet May 1, 2009

Current Assets		
Cash		$ 46,000
Inventories		142,000
Total Current Assets		188,000
Plant and Equipment	$680,000	
Less: Accumulated Depreciation	275,000	405,000
Total Assets		$593,000
Current Liabilities		
Accounts Payable		$ 60,000
Accrued Interest Payable (due 1/1/2010)		38,000
Total Current Liabilities		98,000
Restructured Debt—due 4/30/11		84,000
Total Liabilities		182,000
Stockholders' Equity		
Common Stock, $1 par value	$650,000	
Other Contributed Capital	37,500	
Retained Earnings (deficit) ($598,000 − 8,000 − 329,500)	(276,500)	
Total Stockholders' Equity		411,000
Total Liabilities and Stockholders' Equity		$ 593,000

Midway through 2002, the number of firms converting Chapter 11 bankruptcies into Chapter 7 almost doubled compared to the previous year. Under Chapter 11, debtors have the right to propose a plan of reorganization and this plan can be expensive because of the administration costs and the costs of the professionals needed to help reorganize the firm. Often debtor companies compare the expected cash from Chapter 11 reorganization with the liquidation values expected under Chapter 7. Debtor firms know that once they declare Chapter 7, the prices of the assets decrease as buyers then know that the firm has to sell the assets.[15]

TEST YOUR KNOWLEDGE

NOTE: Solutions to ***Test Your Knowledge*** questions are found at the end of each chapter before the end-of-chapter questions.

Short Answer

Assume that a debtor owes a creditor a $10,000 note payable with $2,000 accrued interest. Determine the amount of the gain or loss included in ordinary income and/or the amount of the gain or loss from restructuring.

1. Land with a book value of $8,000 and a fair value of $9,000 is given in full payment of the amount owed.
2. Instead assume that the creditor will accept a non-interest-bearing note payable of $10,000 due in one year. The present value of this note is $9,500.

The "Accounting" Statement of Affairs[16]

The Reform Act provides that a plan for reorganization will not be approved by the court unless it can be shown that creditors will receive at least as much as they would receive if the debtor were liquidated. Consequently, it is important that the estimated amounts to be received by all parties be determined before filing either a liquidation or reorganization petition with the court. The ***Statement of Affairs*** is a report designed to show the estimated amount that would be received by each class of claim in the event of liquidation. It is essentially a balance sheet prepared on the basis of an assumption of liquidation rather than on the going-concern assumption. The appropriate emphasis is no longer one of reporting residual costs, but one of reporting on the legal status of resources and claims against those resources. Thus, assets are reported at their expected realizable values, rather than at book values.

In addition, the current/noncurrent distinction is set aside, and assets are segregated into those that are pledged with fully secured creditors, those that are pledged with partially secured creditors, and those that are essentially "free" and therefore available to settle unsecured claims. Likewise, the current/noncurrent distinction for liabilities is meaningless; that is, if the company liquidates, all liabilities are current. Thus, liabilities are classified on the basis of their legal status as those having priority, those that are fully secured, those that are partially secured, and those that are unsecured.

In summary, the Statement of Affairs is an accounting report that is designed to permit the user to determine the total expected amounts that could be realized on

[15] Dow Jones Corporate Filings Alert, "Conversions of Chapter 11 Cases to Chapter 7 Liquidations on Rise," by Tom Becker, 7/25/02.

[16] This statement is an accounting report and should not be confused with the Statement of Affairs the Bankruptcy Reform Act requires from the debtor company, which is simply a series of questions concerning the debtor company's financial position.

the disposition of the assets, the priorities in the use of the realization proceeds in satisfying claims, and the potential net deficiency that would result if the assets were realized and claims liquidated. In that respect, stockholders' or owners' equity balances have no significance.

Illustration of a Statement of Affairs As an illustration of a Statement of Affairs, assume that the Preston Company had the following balance sheet on April 30, 2009, at which time the company is contemplating filing a petition for liquidation or reorganization.

Additional information concerning estimated realizable values and other balance sheet relationships follows:

1. The notes receivable are expected to be fully realized, and they have been pledged as collateral on a bank note in the principal amount of $20,000 plus accrued interest of $600.
2. Accounts receivable have an estimated collectible value of $28,000.
3. Inventories have a realizable value of $102,280.

Preston Company
Balance Sheet April 30, 2009

Assets	
Cash	$ 8,200
Notes Receivable	24,000
Accounts Receivable (net)	47,000
Inventories	119,000
Prepaid Expenses	1,200
Investment in Beta Company Stock, 1,000 Shares at Market Value	26,500
Land	42,000
Buildings (net)	198,000
Machinery and Equipment (net)	93,000
Total Assets	$558,900
Liabilities and Stockholders' Equity	
Bank Notes Payable	$ 32,000
Accounts Payable	195,000
Accrued Salaries and Wages	13,500
Accrued Interest	
On bank notes	1,100
On mortgage note	8,500
Mortgage Note Payable	200,000
Capital Stock	250,000
Retained Earnings (deficit)	(141,200)
Total Liabilities and Stockholders' Equity	$558,900

4. The recovery value of prepaid expenses is $600.
5. The Investment in Beta Company stock is pledged as collateral on a bank note payable in the principal amount of $12,000 plus accrued interest of $500.
6. Land and buildings have an appraised value of $140,000 and serve as collateral on the mortgage note payable.
7. The machinery and equipment have an estimated disposal value of $38,000.

The statement of affairs for Preston Company, along with a ***deficiency account*** summarizing estimated gains and losses on the realization of assets, is presented in Illustration 10-3.

ILLUSTRATION 10-3

Preston Company Statement of Affairs April 30, 2009

Book Value	*Assets*			*Realizable Value*	*Deficiency Account*
	Assets Pledged with Fully Secured Creditors				(Loss)/Gain
$ 24,000	Notes Receivable		$ 24,000		
	Bank Note Payable	$20,000			
	Accrued Interest	600	20,600	$ 3,400	
26,500	Investment in Stock of Beta Company		26,500		
	Bank Note Payable	$12,000			
	Accrued Interest	500	12,500	14,000	
	Assets Pledged with Partially Secured Creditors				
240,000	Land and Buildings		140,000		(100,000)
	Mortgage Note Payable	200,000			
	Accrued Interest	8,500	208,500		
	Unsecured amount (see below)		(68,500)		
	Free Assets				
8,200	Cash			8,200	
47,000	Accounts Receivable			28,000	(19,000)
1,200	Prepaid Expenses			600	(600)
119,000	Inventories			102,280	(16,720)
93,000	Machinery and Equipment			38,000	(55,000)
	Total Net Realizable Value			194,480	
	Liabilities having Priority—Salaries and Wages			13,500	
	Net Free Assets			180,980	
	Estimated Deficiency to Unsecured Creditors (balancing amount)			82,520	
$558,900				$263,500	(191,320)

Book Value	*Equities*		*Unsecured Liabilities*	
	Liabilities Having Priority			
$ 13,500	Accrued Salaries and Wages	$ 13,500		
	Fully Secured Creditors			
32,000	Notes Payable	32,000		
1,100	Accrued Interest	1,100		
	Partially Secured Creditors			
200,000	Mortgage Note Payable	200,000		
8,500	Accrued Interest	8,500		
	Total	208,500		
	Land and Buildings	140,000	$ 68,500	
	Unsecured Creditors			
195,000	Accounts Payable		195,000	
	Stockholders' Equity			
250,000	Capital Stock			250,000
(141,200)	Retained Earnings (deficit)			(141,200)
$558,900			$263,500	$108,800
	Estimated deficiency			$(82,520)

Preston Company
Deficiency Account April 30, 2009

Estimated Losses		*Estimated Gains*	
Accounts Receivable	$ 19,000	Capital Stock	$250,000
Inventory	16,720	Retained Earnings	(141,200)
Prepaid Expenses	600	Estimated Deficiency to Unsecured Creditors	82,520
Land and Buildings	100,000		
Machinery and Equipment	55,000		
Total	$191,320	Total	$191,320

Several comments concerning Illustration 10-3 should be noted:

1. Assets pledged with fully secured creditors—notes receivable and the investment in stock of Beta Company—have realizable values in excess of the secured debts in an amount of \$17,400, which becomes available for distribution to unsecured creditors.
2. Assets pledged with partially secured creditors—land and buildings—have a realizable value that is \$68,500 less than the total related debt. Thus, mortgage holders have a \$68,500 remaining claim that ranks as an unsecured one.
3. Free assets are those that have not been pledged with specific liabilities and are, therefore, available to satisfy general unsecured creditors. Note that the "free" assets include the excess of the realizable value of pledged assets over the related debts of fully secured creditors.
4. In the Deficiency Account, the capital stock and retained earnings deficit are included in the estimated gains column only to indicate the extent to which total potential deficiency is covered by stockholders' equity.
5. The final settlement with the unsecured creditors can be computed by dividing the "net free assets" by the total amount owed to unsecured creditors:

$$\frac{\$180{,}980}{\$263{,}500} = 68.7\%$$

Thus, it is estimated that each unsecured creditor will receive approximately 69% of the amount due under the claim.

In rare cases, DIP (debtor-in-possession) lending is provided by the company buying the assets of the firm in **bankruptcy** proceedings, as in AMR Corp.'s purchase, through its American Airlines unit, of Trans World Airlines for \$500 million. "They provided the DIP so they could get the transaction done," said Harvey L. Tepner, an attorney with Loeb Partners Corp., an investment and merchant-banking firm in New York City. "In that case, the exit strategy was [American Airlines] would pay themselves back through the operation of the airline," he said. "**Chapter 11** is a great marketplace for M&A activity."[17]

TRUSTEE ACCOUNTING AND REPORTING

As indicated earlier, a trustee is often appointed to assume the responsibility of managing the debtor's business for the period during which a reorganization plan is developed or the business is liquidated. The trustee takes title to the debtor's assets and is accountable to the court, the creditors, and other parties of interest for the subsequent utilization or realization of the assets. From an accounting standpoint, two main approaches are available to the trustee. He or she may continue to use the debtor's accounting records, which is the approach often used when it is expected that the business will be rehabilitated and returned to the control of the debtor at

[17] *WSJ*, "Debtor Loans Help Cash-Poor Firms," by Marc Hopkins, 7/24/02, p. B3G.

some future date or when the business is expected to be sold as an operating unit. Or the trustee may open a new set of books, the approach frequently used when the assets are to be realized and liabilities liquidated. In either case, the better approach is probably to open a new set of books, because it will make it easier to distinguish between the assets and liabilities of the debtor that existed before the appointment of the trustee and those arising after his or her appointment.

When new books are opened, the trustee records, at their book values, the assets (as well as any related valuation accounts) that have been placed under trustee control. The net credit in the entry is to an account normally titled with the name of the debtor company and the term "in receivership," for example, "Axon Company—In Receivership." No existing liabilities are recorded by the trustee, but liabilities incurred later are recorded. Although liabilities existing at the date the trustee takes control are not recorded, the trustee may pay these liabilities in the course of operating the company or as part of the realization and liquidation process. This payment of preexisting debts, of course, reduces the assets for which the trustee is accountable.

The transfer of the assets to the trustee is recorded on the debtor's books by crediting the various asset accounts (with debits to related valuation accounts) and debiting an account in the name of the trustee. Subsequent activities engaged in by the trustee are recorded on the trustee's books with entries on the debtor's books where appropriate, for example, to record the payment of preexisting debts by the trustee.

As an example of the accounting procedures used where the trustee opens a new set of books, assume that Axon Company has the following account balances on October 1, 2009, at which time Gary Trent was appointed trustee.

Cash	$ 6,400
Receivables	32,000
Inventory	48,600
Property and equipment	120,000
Total	$207,000
Allowance for uncollectibles	$ 2,900
Accumulated depreciation	44,100
Accounts payable	75,000
Capital stock	180,000
Retained earnings (deficit)	(95,000)
Total	$207,000

During the period from October 1, 2009, through December 31, 2009, the following transactions occurred:

(1) All Axon Company's assets were transferred to the trustee.

(2) Additional merchandise inventory was purchased by the trustee on account in amount of $26,000.

(3) Sales for the period were: on account, $52,000; cash, $7,000.

(4) Cash was collected by the trustee on

Accounts receivable (old)	$18,000
Accounts receivable (new)	46,000

(5) Payments were made by the trustee for

Accounts payable (old)	$43,000
Accounts payable (new)	14,000
Operating expenses	10,500
Trustee's expenses	2,000

(6) Adjusting entries recorded by the trustee on December 31, 2009 were:

Estimated uncollectibles on	
Accounts receivable (old)	$ 3,500
Accounts receivable (new)	400
Accounts receivable written off on accounts receivable (old)	4,500
Depreciation expense	7,600

(7) The merchandise inventory balance on December 31 was $42,000.

Entries to record the effect of these transactions on the trustee's and the debtor's books are presented in Illustration 10-4. In order to prepare financial statements for Axon Company on December 31, 2009, the trustee's accounts must be combined with Axon Company's accounts. A combining workpaper for this purpose is presented in Illustration 10-5.

ILLUSTRATION 10-4

Journal Entries

	Trustee's Books			*Axon Company's Books*		
(1)	Cash	6,400		Gary Trent, Trustee	160,000	
	Receivables (old)	32,000		Allowance for Uncollectibles	2,900	
	Inventory	48,600		Accumulated Depreciation	44,100	
	Property and Equipment	120,000		Cash		6,400
	Allowance for Uncollectibles		2,900	Receivables		32,000
	Accumulated Depreciation		44,100	Inventory		48,600
	Axon Company—in Receivership		160,000	Property and Equipment		120,000
(2)	Purchases	26,000		No entry		
	Accounts Payable (new)		26,000			
(3)	Cash	7,000		No entry		
	Accounts Receivable (new)	52,000				
	Sales		59,000			
(4)	Cash	64,000		No entry		
	Accounts Receivable (old)		18,000			
	Accounts Receivable (new)		46,000			
(5)	Axon Company—in Receivership	43,000		Accounts Payable	43,000	
	Accounts Payable (new)	14,000		Gary Trent, Trustee		43,000
	Operating Expenses	10,500				
	Trustee's Expenses	2,000				
	Cash		69,500			
(6)	Bad Debts Expense	3,900		No entry		
	Depreciation Expense	7,600				
	Allowance for Uncollectibles (old)		3,500			
	Allowance for Uncollectibles (new)		400			
	Accumulated Depreciation		7,600			
	Allowance for Uncollectibles (old)	4,500		No entry		
	Accounts Receivable (old)		4,500			
(7)	Sales	59,000		Gary Trent, Trustee	2,400	
	Inventory		6,600	Income Summary		2,400
	Purchases		26,000	Income Summary	2,400	
	Operating Expenses		10,500	Retained Earnings		2,400
	Trustee's Expenses		2,000			
	Bad Debts Expense		3,900			
	Depreciation Expense		7,600			
	Income Summary		2,400			
	Income Summary	2,400				
	Axon Company in Receivership		2,400			

ILLUSTRATION 10-5

Axon Company—in Receivership Combining Workpaper
December 31, 2009

	Trial Balance		Adjustments and Eliminations		Combined	
Debits	Trustee	Axon Company	Dr.	Cr.	Income Statement	Balance Sheet
Cash	7,900					7,900
Accounts Receivable (old)	9,500					9,500
Accounts Receivable (new)	6,000					6,000
Inventory	48,600			(1) 6,600		42,000
Property and Equipment	120,000					120,000
Purchase	26,000			(1) 26,000		
Operating Expenses	10,500				10,500	
Trustee Expenses	2,000				2,000	
Bad Debts Expense	3,900				3,900	
Depreciation Expense	7,600				7,600	
Cost of Goods Sold			(1) 32,600		32,600	
Gary Trent, Trustee		117,000		(2) 117,000		
Total	242,000	117,000			56,600	185,400
Credits						
Allowance for Uncollectibles (old)	1,900					1,900
Allowance for Uncollectibles (new)	400					400
Accumulated Depreciation	51,700					51,700
Accounts Payable (old)		32,000				32,000
Accounts Payable (new)	12,000					12,000
Capital Stock		180,000				180,000
Retained Earnings (deficit)		(95,000)				(95,000)
Sales	59,000				59,000	
Axon Company, in Receivership	117,000		(2) 117,000			
Total	242,000	117,000	149,600	149,600	59,000	
Net Income					2,400	2,400
Total					56,600	185,400

(1) To adjust inventory and set up cost of goods sold.
(2) To eliminate reciprocal accounts.

REALIZATION AND LIQUIDATION ACCOUNT

When a trustee is appointed to handle the affairs of a company in financial difficulty, the court expects to receive periodic reports summarizing the realization and distribution activities of the fiduciary.[18] Although the traditional financial statements may be prepared by the fiduciary, court officials are interested primarily in the changes that have occurred in the monetary items during a period. The legal form used to report these activities is termed a ***realization and liquidation account.*** The report has three main sections—assets, liabilities, and revenues and expenses. The asset section consists of four parts, illustrated as follows:

Assets

Assets to be realized	Assets realized
Assets acquired	Assets not realized

[18] A fiduciary is a person to whom property is entrusted to hold, control, or manage for another.

The ***assets to be realized*** part identifies the individual assets to which the trustee has taken title from the debtor. Cash is not included in the report because it is already realized. Although cash is excluded, the court is given a copy of the cash account of the trustee, which shows the beginning amount received from the debtor, as well as all the individual receipts and disbursements for the period covered. The ***assets acquired*** part itemizes the assets either discovered or received from operating activities during the period. The ***assets realized*** part identifies proceeds received from the conversion of specific assets. The ***assets not realized*** part identifies the assets remaining with the trustee at the end of the reporting period.

In a similar manner, the liabilities section consists of four parts, as indicated below:

Liabilities

Liabilities liquidated	Liabilities to be liquidated
Liabilities not liquidated	Liabilities incurred

The ***liabilities to be liquidated*** part identifies the liabilities that the trustee took responsibility for at the date of appointment. ***Liabilities incurred*** reflect the liabilities incurred by the trustee for operating activities during the period. ***Liabilities liquidated*** identify specific liabilities paid by the trustee, and ***liabilities not liquidated*** reflect those that remain to be paid by the trustee.

The revenues and expenses section of the report lists the supplementary expenses incurred and revenues received by the trustee during the period, as follows:

Revenues and Expenses

Supplementary charges	Supplementary credits

The realization and liquidation account is prepared in the typical account form with debits on the left side and credits on the right side of the account. Any figure needed to balance the account reflects a gain or loss for the reported period.

As an example of a realization and liquidation account, assume Illustration 10-5 concerning the receivership of Gary Trent for Axon Company. The realization and liquidation account is presented in Illustration 10-6.

A copy of the Cash account of the trustee that would be included with the report is presented below:

Cash

Balance, 10/1	6,400	Accounts payable (old)	43,000
Sales	7,000	Accounts payable (new)	14,000
Accounts receivable (old)	18,000	Operating expenses	10,500
Accounts receivable (new)	46,000	Trustee's expenses	2,000
Balance, 12/31	7,900		

Note that the balancing figure (labeled "net gain") in the realization and liquidation account is the same as the $2,400 net income reported for the period October 1 to December 31, 2009, in Illustration 10-5. This is as it should be, since no assets were realized during the period except through normal operating activities. If assets had been realized by other than normal operating activities (for example, the sale of land), any gain or loss would increase or decrease the net gain reported in the Realization and Liquidation account. The transaction could be treated in one

ILLUSTRATION 10-6

Axon Company, Gary Trent, Trustee, Realization and Liquidation Account, October 1, 2009, to December 31, 2009

Assets to Be Realized			**Assets Realized**		
Receivables (old)	$ 32,000		Accounts Receivable (old)		$ 18,000
Less: Allowance for Uncollectibles	2,900	$ 29,100	Accounts Receivable (new)		46,000
Inventory		48,600			
Property and Equipment	120,000		**Assets Not Realized**		
Less: Accumulated Depreciation	44,100	75,900	Accounts Receivable (old)	$ 9,500	
			Less: Allowance for Uncollectibles	1,900	7,600
Assets Acquired			Accounts Receivable (new)	6,000	
Accounts Receivable (new)		52,000	Less: Allowance for Uncollectibles	400	5,600
			Inventory		42,000
Supplementary Charges			Property and Equipment	120,000	
Purchases		26,000	Less: Accumulated Depreciation	51,700	68,300
Operation Expenses		10,500			
Trustee's Expenses		2,000	**Supplementary Credits**		
			Sales		59,000
Liabilities Liquidated					
Accounts Payable (old)		43,000	**Liabilities to Be Liquidated**		
Accounts Payable (new)		14,000	Accounts Payable (old)		75,000
Liabilities Not Liquidated			**Liabilities Incurred**		
Accounts Payable (old)		32,000	Accounts Payable (new)		26,000
Accounts Payable (new)		12,000			
Net Gain		2,400			
Total		$347,500	Total		$347,500

of two ways. Assets realized could be reported at the amount received from the sale of the asset (the traditional approach), or they might be reported at the book value of the asset sold and any gain or loss on the sale reported as a supplemental credit or supplemental charge. For example, assume that the property and equipment account of Axon Company included a parcel of land that cost $25,000 and that the parcel was sold by the trustee for $35,000. The traditional approach would report assets realized at $35,000 with a decrease in assets not realized of $25,000. The $10,000 difference between the two would be reflected as part of a net gain of $12,400, rather than the $2,400 in Illustration 10-6. The items that would be different in Illustration 10-6 are:

Assets Realized

Property and Equipment		$35,000

Assets Not Realized

Property and Equipment ($120,000 − $25,000)	$95,000	
Less: Accumulated Depreciation	51,700	43,300
Net Gain		12,400

The basic weakness in this approach is that the components of the "net gain" or "net loss" are not disclosed.

An alternative is to report the sale of the land as assets realized at book value, $25,000, a decrease in assets not realized of $25,000, and a supplementary credit

"Gain on sale of land" of $10,000. Although the net gain needed to balance the account is still $12,400, the reader of the report is able to identify the components of the net gain. The items that would be different in Illustration 10-6 under this approach are:

Assets Realized		
Property and Equipment		$25,000
Assets Not Realized		
Property and Equipment ($120,000 – $25,000)	$95,000	
Less: Accumulated Depreciation	51,700	43,300
Supplementary Credits		
Gain on Sale of Land		10,000
Net Gain		12,400

Similar alternative treatments could be afforded the favorable or unfavorable liquidation of liabilities.

Other items on the realization and liquidation account deserve comment:

1. Note that we have elected to show sales of merchandise as supplementary credits and purchases of merchandise as supplementary charges. As an alternative, the trustee might report sales of merchandise as ***assets realized*** and purchases of merchandise as ***assets acquired***. We believe our treatment is more informative because it separates operating effects from nonoperating effects, although the latter treatment is more common in practice.
2. Expenses representing cost allocations (such as depreciation) and estimated bad debts expense are not reported separately. These expenses are reflected in the report, however, as increases in accumulated depreciation and allowance for uncollectibles in the ***assets not realized*** part of the report. Thus, because the net gain (loss) for the period is a balancing figure, these expenses are factors in the determination of that net gain (loss).

The auditor has a responsibility to evaluate whether there is substantial doubt about the entity's ability to continue as a going concern for a reasonable period of time. *Reasonable period of time* is defined as a period not to exceed one year beyond the date of the financial statements being audited. Currently, AU Section 341, *The Auditor's Consideration of an Entity's Ability to Continue as a Going Concern,* of the AICPA Codification of Statements on Auditing Standards contains the guidance about the going concern assessment. The Public Company Accounting Oversight Board (PCAOB) adopted AU Section 341 on an initial transitional basis.

Conditions and events that may raise a substantial doubt about an entity's ability to continue as a going concern include negative financial trends such as recurring operating losses, working capital deficiencies, negative cash flows from operations, and/or adverse key financial ratios. Other indications of possible financial difficulties might include such events as defaulting on loans, having not paid dividends, seeking new sources of financing, selling assets, or restructuring debt.

FASB issued an exposure draft in October, 2008 on 'Going Concern.' The Board decided to carry forward the going concern guidance from AU Section 341, subject to several modifications to align the guidance with International Financial Reporting Standards (IFRSs). One modification is to change the time horizon for the going concern assessment. AU Section 341 states that there is "a responsibility to evaluate whether there is substantial doubt about the entity's ability to continue as a going concern for a reasonable period of time, not to exceed one year beyond the date of the financial statements being audited." International Accounting Standard (IAS) 1, *Presentation of Financial Statements*, requires that an entity consider "all available information about the future, which is at least, but is not limited to, twelve months from the end of the reporting period" when assessing whether the going concern assumption is appropriate. The Board decided to use the time horizon in IAS 1 because it avoids a bright-line time horizon that might allow significant events or conditions occurring just beyond the one-year time horizon not to be disclosed. The other modifications to align the going concern guidance with IFRSs include using the wording in IAS 1 with respect to the type of information that should be considered in making the going concern assessment (*all available information about the future*) and requiring an entity to disclose when it does not present financial statements on a going concern basis.

SUMMARY

1. *Distinguish between a Chapter 7 and a Chapter 11 bankruptcy.* In a Chapter 7 bankruptcy, the company ceases operations and the assets are generally sold by a trustee. In a Chapter 11 bankruptcy, the business is reorganized and the creditors agree on a plan for payment of their claims.
2. *Describe the five priority categories of unsecured claims and list the order in which they are settled.* The five categories listed in order of priority are: (a) administration expenses, fees, and charges incurred in administering the bankrupt's estate; (b) unsecured claims for wages, salaries, or commissions earned by an employee within 90 days before the date of filing of the petition; (c) unsecured claims for contributions to employee benefit plans from services rendered within 180 days before the date of the filing of the petition; (d) unsecured claims of individuals arising from the deposit of money in connection with the purchase, lease, or rental of property or services that were not delivered or performed; and (e) unsecured claims of governmental units for unpaid taxes.
3. *Distinguish between a voluntary and involuntary bankruptcy petition.* A debtor may file a voluntary petition with a bankruptcy court for liquidation under Chapter 7 or for reorganization under Chapter 11. In an involuntary proceeding, creditors initiate the action by filing a petition for liquidation or reorganization with the bankruptcy court. Filing of a voluntary or involuntary petition constitutes an ***order for relief***, which prohibits the start or continuation of legal action against the debtor by its creditors.
4. *Distinguish among fully secured, partially secured, and unsecured claims of creditors.* Fully secured claims are those with liens against assets whose realizable value is equal to or in excess of the claim. Partially secured claims are those with liens against assets whose realizable value is less than the amount of the claim. Unsecured creditors, including those having priority, are paid from whatever proceeds remain from the realization process.
5. *Describe contractual agreements that the debtor and its creditors may enter into outside of formal bankruptcy proceedings to resolve the debtor's insolvent position.* These agreements generally include (a) an extension of payment periods; (b) composition agreements where the creditors agree to accept less than the full amount to their claims; (c) formation of a creditors' committee where the parties agree to the formation of a creditors' committee that is responsible for managing the debtor's business affairs for the period during which plans are developed to rehabilitate, reorganize, or liquidate the business; or (d) a voluntary assignment of assets where the debtor may elect to place its property under the control of a trustee for the benefit of its creditors.

TEST YOUR KNOWLEDGE SOLUTIONS

10-1 1. c

2. False

3. True

4. False

5. True

10-2 1. Ordinary gain on revaluation of land is $1,000 and the restructuring gain is $3,000.

2. The restructuring gain is $2,000. (The debtor uses undiscounted cash flows to compute the gain.)

QUESTIONS

LO5 1. List the primary types of contractual agreements between a debtor company and its creditors and briefly explain what is involved in each of them.

LO3 2. Distinguish between a voluntary and involuntary bankruptcy petition.

LO4 3. Distinguish among fully secured, partially secured, and unsecured claims of creditors.

LO2 4. Five priority categories of unsecured claims must be paid before general unsecured creditors are paid. Briefly describe what makes up each category.

LO4 5. What are "dividends" in a bankruptcy proceeding?

LO7 6. For each of the following debt restructurings, indicate whether a gain is recognized and, if so, how the gain is measured and reported.

(a) Transfer of assets by the debtor to the creditor.

(b) Grant of an equity interest by the debtor to the creditor.

(c) Modification of the terms of the payable.

LO1 7. What is the purpose of a Statement of Affairs?

LO4 8. One of the officers of a corporation that had just received a discharge in bankruptcy said, "Good, now we don't owe anyone." Is he correct?

LO1 9. What are the duties of a trustee in a liquidation proceeding?

LO1 10. What is the purpose of a combining workpaper prepared by a trustee?

LO1 11. What is the purpose of a realization and liquidation account?

Business Ethics

From an ethical perspective, some believe that it is never justifiable for an individual or business to declare bankruptcy. Others believe that some actions are appropriate only in extreme circumstances. Without question, as stated in the *Journal of Accountancy*, November 2005, page 51, "the ease with which debtors have been able to walk away from debt has frustrated creditors for years."

1. Describe the differences between Chapter 7 (liquidations) and Chapter 11 (reorganizations) from an ethical standpoint. Who is most likely to be hurt by a Chapter 7 bankruptcy?
2. Discuss the Bankruptcy Abuse Prevention and Consumer Protection Act of 2005. Do you believe the changes wrought by this act will serve to protect creditors?
3. The Protection Act of 2005 requires individuals, but not businesses, to undergo a "means" test before they can seek Chapter 7 relief. Do you believe this change should be applied to businesses as well? Why or why not?
4. Do you think that you would ever resort to filing for bankruptcy relief yourself? Why or why not?

EXERCISES

EXERCISE 10-1 **Multiple Choice** LO1 LO2 LO3 LO5

Select the best answer for each of the following:

1. Johnson joined other creditors of Alpha Company in a composition agreement seeking to avoid the necessity of a bankruptcy proceeding against Alpha. Which statement describes the composition agreement?

(a) It provides that the creditors will receive less than the full amount of their claims.

(b) It provides a temporary delay, not to exceed six months, insofar as the debtor's obligation to repay the debts included in the composition is concerned.

(c) It must be approved by all creditors.

(d) It provides for the appointment of a receiver to take over and operate the debtor's business.

2. Freeman Company ceased doing business and is in bankruptcy. Among the claimants are employees seeking unpaid wages. The following statements describe the possible status of such claims in a bankruptcy proceeding or legal limitations placed upon them. Which one is an ***incorrect*** statement?

(a) The amounts of excess wages not entitled to a priority are mere unsecured claims.

(b) Such claims include wages earned within 180 days before the filing of the bankruptcy petition, but not to exceed $4,650 in amount.

(c) Such claims are entitled to priority.

(d) If a priority is afforded such claims, it cannot exceed $4,650 per wage earner.

3. Which of the entities listed is not subject to an involuntary bankruptcy petition?

(a) A municipality.

(b) A partnership.

(c) A wholesaler company.

(d) A retailing corporation.

4. The highest priority for payment of unsecured claims in a bankruptcy proceeding is:

(a) Wages up to $4,650 earned within three months before the petition.

(b) Unpaid federal income taxes.

(c) Administrative expenses of the bankruptcy.

(d) Wages owed to an insolvent employee.

5. Which of the following situations that arise because of a debtor's financial difficulties and would not otherwise be acceptable to the creditor must be accounted for as a troubled debt restructuring?

(a) As part of a negotiated settlement designed to maintain a relationship with a debtor, a creditor reduces the effective interest rate on debt outstanding to reflect the lower market interest rate currently applicable to debt of that risk class.

(b) Because of a court order, a creditor reduces the stated interest rate for the remaining original life of the debt.

(c) Because of a court order, a creditor accepts as full satisfaction of its receivable a building the fair value of which equals the creditor's recorded investment in the receivable.

(d) As part of a negotiated settlement, a creditor accepts as full satisfaction of its receivable a building the fair value of which equals the debtor's carrying amount of the payable.

EXERCISE 10-2 **True or False** LO1 LO3 LO4

Indicate whether each of the following is true or false. If an answer is false, explain why.

______ 1. Insolvency means that a debtor has more current liabilities than current assets.

______ 2. Voluntary bankruptcy petitions may be filed under either Chapter 7 or Chapter 11 of the Reform Act.

______ 3. If an insolvent debtor has more than 12 creditors, an involuntary petition must be signed by at least three of those creditors.

______ 4. Unsecured creditors with priority will receive full satisfaction before secured creditors are paid.

______ 5. Either a debtor or its creditors may file a petition for reorganization under Chapter 11 of the Reform Act.

______ **6.** In a reorganization involving a transfer of assets, the debtor will recognize a gain on restructuring measured by the excess of the carrying value of the payable settled over the book value of the assets transferred.

______ **7.** Restructuring gains that arise from troubled debt restructurings are reported by the debtor as extraordinary gains.

______ **8.** The statement of affairs is a report designed to estimate the amount expected to be earned by a debtor company during the time period needed to complete a reorganization.

EXERCISE 10-3 **Transfer of Assets** LO1

Bar Company, which is in financial difficulty and in the process of a voluntary reorganization, has agreed to transfer to a creditor a copyright it owns in full settlement of a $150,000 note payable and $15,000 in accrued interest. The copyright, which originally cost $100,000, has an accumulated amortization balance of $55,000 and a current fair value of $95,000.

Required:

A. Prepare the journal entries on Bar Company's books to record the transfer of the copyright.

B. Explain the proper treatment of any gain or loss recognized in (A).

C. Assuming the fair value of the copyright was $30,000, repeat the requirement in (A).

EXERCISE 10-4 **Modification of Terms** LO1

Lake Company, a major creditor of financially troubled Spain Company, has agreed to modify the terms of a debt owed to Lake Company. The debt consists of a $900,000, 12% note that is due currently along with accrued interest of $95,000. Lake Company agreed to extend the due date of the note and accrued interest for three years and to reduce the interest rate to 5% per annum (on both maturity value and accrued interest), with interest to be paid annually.

Required:

A. Should a gain on restructuring be recognized by Spain Company? Explain.

B. Prepare the entry that should be made on Spain Company's books on the date of restructure.

EXERCISE 10-5 **Modification of Terms** LO1

Assume the same situation described in Exercise 10-4 except that the terms of modification of the debt are

1. Accrued interest of $95,000 is to be canceled.
2. The face value of the note is reduced to $600,000, payable at the end of three years. Interest on the new face value at 8% is to be paid annually.

Required:

A. Should a gain on restructuring be recognized? Explain.

B. Prepare entries on the books of Spain Company to record the restructuring.

C. Prepare the entry on Spain Company's books to record the interest payment at the end of the first year after restructuring.

EXERCISE 10-6 **Settlement of Priority Claims** LO4

The following data are taken from the statement of affairs of the Monroe Company. (Assume that the realizable values of assets are accurate.)

Assets pledged with fully secured creditors (realizable value, $190,000)	$240,000
Assets pledged with partially secured creditors (realizable value, $90,000)	110,000

Free assets (realizable value, $102,000)	160,000
Fully secured creditor claims	91,000
Partially secured creditor claims	120,000
Unsecured creditor claims with priority	30,000
General unsecured creditor claims	350,000

Required:

Compute the amount that will be paid to each class of creditor.

EXERCISE 10-7 **Statement of Affairs** LO1

Ball Company is facing bankruptcy proceedings. A balance sheet dated June 30, 2009, and other information are presented below:

Ball Company Balance Sheet
June 30, 2009

Cash	$ 20,400
Accounts Receivable (net)	170,000
Inventory	180,000
Property and Equipment (net)	430,000
Total Assets	$800,400
Accounts Payable	$350,000
Accrued Wages	120,000
Notes Payable	200,000
Common Stock	400,000
Retained Earnings (deficit)	(269,600)
Total Equities	$800,400

Estimated realizable values of the company's assets are:

Accounts Receivable	$ 95,000
Inventory	110,000
Property and Equipment	320,000

Accounts receivable and inventory are each pledged as security on individual notes payable in the amount of $100,000 each.

Required:

Prepare a statement of affairs and determine the estimated settlement per dollar for general unsecured creditors. (Assume that all accrued wages are priority items.)

EXERCISE 10-8 **Reorganization Balance Sheet** LO1

The following balance sheet was prepared for Crane Company on December 31, 2009:

Crane Company Balance Sheet
December 31, 2009

Cash		$ 33,000
Accounts Receivable	$52,500	
Less: Allowance for Uncollectibles	3,800	48,700
Inventory		71,000
Property and Equipment (net)		142,000
Goodwill		20,000
Total Assets		$314,700
Accounts Payable		$ 66,000
10% Bonds Payable, due 6/30/12		130,000
Common Stock, $20 par, 10,000 Shares Outstanding		200,000
Retained Earnings (deficit)		(81,300)
Total Equities		$314,700

Crane Company has had operating difficulties, accumulating a deficit over several years before 2009. During 2009, however, Crane reported a significantly lower operating loss, and prospects for the future are relatively bright. Although management and stockholders are optimistic about the future, it is almost certain that the company will lack the necessary working capital to handle existing obligations and expected future growth. In light of these facts, Crane has filed for reorganization under Chapter 11 of the Bankruptcy Reform Act of 1978. The reorganization plan, the provisions of which are set out below, has received the approval of stockholders, creditors, and the court. Provisions of the reorganization plan are as follows:

1. Accounts receivable are to be written down to $40,000 to reflect their current expected realizable value.
2. Inventory is fairly valued, but goodwill is to be written off, and property and equipment is to be written down to its fair value of $118,000.
3. The $20 par value common stock is to be replaced with $4 par value common stock on a share-for-share basis in order to create some reorganization capital, which will be used to eliminate the deficit.
4. The bondholders agree to exchange their bonds for new 8% bonds in the same maturity amount, but with a due date of June 30, 2016, and 6,000 shares of $4 par value common stock. The stock will be divided ratably among the bondholders. The fair value of the common stock is equal to its par value.
5. Accounts payable are expected to be paid in full, although creditors have agreed to extend due dates by as much as six months.
6. Any accumulated deficit is to be eliminated.

Required:

A. Prepare journal entries to record the effects of the reorganization plan.
B. Prepare a balance sheet as it would appear immediately after the reorganization.

EXERCISE 10-9 **Trustee Accounting** LO1

TRX Company has been forced into receivership, and you have been appointed trustee. You decide to open your own set of books in order to distinguish more clearly between transactions occurring before and after your appointment. The following account balances were reported on September 1, 2009:

Cash	$ 26,700
Accounts Receivable	130,400
Inventory	191,900
Property and Equipment	590,400
Total	$939,400
Allowance for Uncollectibles	$ 16,000
Accumulated Depreciation	211,500
Accounts Payable	308,400
Capital Stock	800,000
Retained Earnings (deficit)	(396,500)
Total	$939,400

In the four months immediately after your appointment, the following transaction occurred:

1. Sales were made in the amount of $296,000, of which $31,500 were cash sales.
2. Receivables were collected in the following amounts:

Old receivables	$ 76,800
New receivables	242,200

3. Additional inventory was purchased on account in the amount of $127,500.
4. Cash payments were made as follows:

On old accounts payable	$206,500
On new accounts payable	61,600
For operating expenses	46,000
For trustee fees	13,000

5. Journal entries were made to record:
   (a) Bad debt expense of $21,600, of which $8,600 related to new accounts receivable.
   (b) Depreciation expense of $32,400.
   (c) Write-off of old accounts receivable of $21,000.

The inventory balance at the end of your first four months as trustee (the end of the fiscal year for TRX Company) was $149,700.

Required:

Prepare journal entries to record the foregoing on your set of books. Include appropriate closing entries.

EXERCISE 10-10 Combining Workpaper LO1

Use the data provided in Exercise 10-9.

Required:

Prepare a combining workpaper for TRX Company as of the end of the first four months of receivership (December 31, 2009).

PROBLEMS

PROBLEM 10-1 Journal Entries for Reorganization LO1

On February 1, 2009, Clover Company filed a petition for reorganization under the bankruptcy statutes. The court approved the plan on September 1, 2009, including the following provisions:

1. Unsecured creditors of open accounts amounting to $71,600 are paid 42 cents on the dollar in full settlement.
2. Clover Company is to exchange accounts receivable in the face amount of $92,000 and an allowance for uncollectible accounts of $19,450 for the full settlement of $132,400 owed on open account to one of its major unsecured creditors. The estimated fair value of the receivables is $69,000.
3. Accrued expenses of $14,620, representing priority items, are to be paid in full.
4. Clover Company's only other major unsecured creditor agreed to a five-year extension of the $300,000 principal owed him on a 10% note payable. Accrued interest on the note on September 1, 2009, amounts to $27,000, one-third of which is to be paid in cash and the remainder canceled. In addition, no interest is to be charged during the remaining five years to maturity of the note.

Required:

Prepare journal entries on the books of Clover Company to give effect to the fore going provisions.

PROBLEM 10-2 **Reorganization Entries and Balance Sheet** LO1

On September 30, 2008, SRP Company filed a petition for reorganization with a bankruptcy court. The plan was approved by the court and all parties of interest on January 2, 2009, when SRP Company's balance sheet was as follows:

SRP Company Balance Sheet
January 2, 2009

Cash		$ 32,200
Accounts Receivable	$ 71,450	
Less: Allowance for Uncollectibles	16,750	54,700
Inventories		126,600
Plant and Equipment	322,000	
Less: Accumulated Depreciation	180,700	141,300
Land		20,800
Patents		92,000
Total Assets		$467,600
Current Liabilities		
Accounts Payable—Unsecured		$142,700
12% Notes Payable—Unsecured		57,000
Accrued Wages—with Priority		11,900
Accrued Interest Payable		38,400
Total Current Liabilities		250,000
10% Note Payable—Unsecured		54,400
9% Mortgage Note Payable—Secured by Equipment		80,000
Stockholders' Equity		
Common Stock, $.50 par value, 2,500,000 Shares Authorized, 480,000 shares issued and Outstanding		240,000
Retained Earnings (deficit)		(156,800)
Total Equities		$467,600

The terms of the reorganization plan are as follows:

1. Creditors represented by $69,000 of the unsecured accounts payable agree to accept the accounts receivable of SRP Company in full settlement of their claims. The fair value of the receivables is $51,000.
2. Creditors represented by $54,000 of the unsecured accounts payable agree to accept a patent with a book value of $42,000 and a fair value of $50,000 in full settlement of their claims.
3. Creditors of the remaining unsecured accounts payable agree to accept $.60 on the dollar. Cash is paid to these creditors and to the creditors with priority.
4. The creditor holding the 12%, $57,000 note (on which there is $6,000 accrued interest) agreed to extend the due date for two years from January 3, 2009, and to reduce the interest rate to 6% on the current carrying value of the debt ($63,000), payable annually.
5. The holder of the 10%, $54,400 unsecured note (on which there is $11,900 accrued interest) agreed to cancel the accrued interest and $14,400 of the principal; interest on the new note at 10% is due annually, with the principal due on January 3, 2012.
6. The holder of the 9%, $80,000 mortgage note (on which there is $20,500 accrued interest) agreed to accept 100,000 shares of common stock in exchange for full satisfaction of the debt. The common stock has a fair value of $.59 per share.
7. The par value of the common stock is reduced to $.10 per share and any remaining accumulated deficit is eliminated.

Required:

A. Prepare journal entries to give effect to the reorganization.

B. Prepare a post-reorganization balance sheet dated January 2, 2009.

C. Prepare journal entries to accrue interest on December 31, 2009, and to record the payment of interest on January 2, 2010.

PROBLEM 10-3 **Statement of Affairs and Deficiency Account** LO1

Prost Company has filed a bankruptcy petition. Its account balances at December 31, 2009, are presented here:

Cash	$ 2,500
Notes Receivable	60,000
Accounts Receivable (net)	76,000
Inventories	
Finished Goods	43,000
Work in Process	60,000
Raw Materials	51,000
Prepaid Expenses	4,000
Investment in Stock	12,000
Land	140,000
Property and Equipment (net)	400,000
Goodwill	10,000
Total	$858,500
Accounts Payable	$220,000
Accrued Wages (all with priority)	45,000
Bank Notes Payable	225,000
Mortgage Payable	350,000
Common Stock	380,000
Retained Earnings (deficit)	(361,500)
Total	$858,500

The following additional information is available:

1. All notes receivable with the exception of one for $2,500 are expected to be collected. The notes receivable are pledged as security on the bank notes payable.
2. Of the total accounts receivable, $55,000 is expected to be collected. The accounts receivable are also pledged as security on the bank notes payable.
3. Finished goods can be sold at 30% above cost. Selling expenses will be approximately 15% of selling price. Work in process is to be completed at an additional cost of $30,000, of which $19,000 represents the cost of raw materials. The expected selling price of the work in process (after completion) is 10% above cost, with selling expenses of 15% of selling price. Unused raw materials can be sold for $18,000.
4. Prepaid expenses are fully recoverable.
5. The investment in stock consists of 100 shares of MBI Company with a current market value of $19,000.
6. Land is appraised at $200,000, and plant and equipment is appraised at $205,000. The land and plant and equipment serve as collateral on the mortgage payable. Accrued but unrecorded interest on the mortgage payable amounts to $3,000.

Required

A. Prepare a statement of affairs, including a deficiency account.

B. Compute the estimated dividend to be paid general unsecured creditors.

PROBLEM 10-4 **Realization and Liquidation Account** LO1

A balance sheet for Bran Company on June 30, 2009, the date Jim Brown was appointed trustee, is presented here:

Bran Company Balance Sheet
June 30, 2009

Cash		$ 15,000
Accounts Receivable	$ 45,000	
Less: Allowance for Uncollectibles	6,000	39,000
Inventory		104,000
Plant and Equipment	215,000	
Less: Accumulated Depreciation	70,000	145,000
Total Assets		$303,000
Accounts Payable		$145,000
Common Stock		225,000
Retained Earnings (deficit)		(67,000)
Total Liabilities and Equities		$303,000

The following information concerning the period from June 30, 2009, to December 31, 2009, is also available:

1. All Bran Company's assets were transferred to the trustee.
2. Sales for the period were $130,000, of which $30,000 were cash sales.
3. Receivables collected by the trustee in cash were:

Old receivables	$38,000
New receivables	85,000

4. Merchandise inventory was purchased on account by the trustee in the amount of $35,000.
5. Cash payments were made by the trustee for:
   (a) Accounts payable (old), $110,000
   (b) Accounts payable (new), $30,000
   (c) Operating expenses, $47,000
   (d) Trustee expense, $2,000
6. Adjusting entries recorded by the trustee on December 31, 2009, were:
   (a) Estimated uncollectibles

Accounts receivable (old)	$ 1,000
Accounts receivable (new)	2,000

   (b) Accounts receivable written off (old), $7,000
   (c) Depreciation expense, $10,000
7. The merchandise inventory balance on December 31 was $75,000.
8. The plant and equipment included a parcel of land and a piece of equipment, both of which were sold by the trustee for cash. The land cost $14,000 and was sold for $25,000. The equipment, which had a book value of $25,000 (cost, $50,000; accumulated depreciation, $25,000), was sold for $13,000.

Required:

Prepare a realization and liquidation account, including a copy of the cash account, for the period June 30, 2009, to December 31, 2009. Use the alternate approach for reporting the components of the net gain or loss on the sale of land and equipment.

PROBLEM 10-5 **Trustee Accounting and Combining Workpaper** LO1

Plum Company has been in receivership for the past five months. At the beginning of this period, the following trial balance was taken from Plum Company's books.

Cash	$ 4,500
Accounts Receivable	15,000
Inventory	142,650
Property and Equipment	90,600
	$252,750
Allowance for Uncollectibles	$ 3,750
Accumulated Depreciation	36,825
Accounts Payable	143,175
Capital Stock	135,000
Retained Earnings (deficit)	(66,000)
	$252,750

The trustee, P. Smith, who was appointed to manage the debtor's business during the period of liquidation, opened a new set of books and took title to Plum Company's assets on June 1, 2009. The activities of the trustee during the five-month period ended October 31, 2009, are as follows:

1. The trustee sold all Plum Company's inventory for $153,000, of which $75,000 represented credit sales.
2. Cash was collected on old receivables, $11,250, and on new receivables, $64,500.
3. Expenses paid during the period were

Operating expenses	$11,850
Trustee expenses	3,000

4. The trustee recorded depreciation expense of $5,250.
5. The trustee paid off all the accounts payable.
6. Estimated uncollectibles on the new accounts receivable were $2,250; the trustee wrote off all the remaining old accounts receivable.
7. The trustee sold all the property and equipment for $43,500.

Required:

A. Prepare journal entries to record the effects of these transactions on the books of both the trustee and Plum Company.
B. Prepare a combining workpaper at the end of the five-month period, October 31, 2009.

PROBLEM 10-6 **Realization and Liquidation Account** LO1

Use the data provided in Problem 10-5.

Required:

Prepare a realization and liquidation account for Plum Company to cover the five-month period of receivership (June 1, 2009, to October 31, 2009). Use the alternate approach to present the components of the net gain or net loss, and include a copy of the trustee's cash account for the period.

PROBLEM 10-7 **Statement of Affairs and Deficiency Account** LO1

Miner Company is being forced into bankruptcy. The company's creditors and stockholders have requested an estimate of the results of a liquidation of the company. Miner's trial balance follows:

Miner Company Trial Balance
May 31, 2009

	Debit	*Credit*
Cash	$ 6,000	
Accounts Receivable	63,000	
Allowance for Bad Debts		$ 2,000
Notes Receivable	50,000	
Accrued Interest on Notes Receivable	1,200	
Inventory	60,000	
Buildings	182,000	
Accumulated Depreciation—Buildings		63,000
Equipment	14,600	
Accumulated Depreciation—Equipment		1,400
Prepaid Insurance	1,100	
Goodwill	8,500	
Accrued Wages—with Priority		6,000
Taxes Payable—with Priority		2,400
Accounts Payable		170,000
Notes Payable		80,000
Accrued Interest Payable		1,600
Common Stock		110,000
Retained Earnings (deficit)	50,000	
	$436,400	$436,400

The assets are expected to bring cash on conversion in the following amounts:

Accounts receivable	$50,000
Notes receivable including $1,000 accrued interest	40,800
Inventory	30,000
Building	75,000
Equipment	4,200
Prepaid insurance	400

The notes receivable are pledged as security on a note payable of $40,000. A note payable of $20,000 is secured by a lien on the building, and the equipment is pledged as security on a note payable of $10,000. One-half of the interest payable relates to the $40,000 note payable; the other half of the interest payable relates to the $20,000 note payable. There is no accrued interest on the other notes payable.

Required:

Prepare a statement of affairs as of May 31, 2009. Include a deficiency account, and determine the estimated dividend rate to the general unsecured creditors.

PROBLEM 10-8 **Statement of Affairs and Deficiency Account** LO1

A receiver was appointed by the court to manage the affairs of Davis Manufacturing Company on March 31, 2009. On this date, the following balance sheet applied:

Davis Manufacturing Company Balance Sheet
March 31, 2009

Cash	$ 22,500
Accounts Receivable	115,500
Notes Receivable	60,000
Accrued Interest on Notes Receivable	1,375
Inventories	
Finished Goods	140,000
Work in Process	97,500
Raw Materials	60,000
Supplies	7,750
Prepaid Expenses	3,000
Investment in Stock	66,250
Land	105,000
Buildings (net)	495,000
Equipment (net)	232,500
Total	$1,406,375
Notes Payable	$ 196,000
Accounts Payable	587,500
Wages Payable (all with priority)	33,750
Payroll Taxes Payable (all with priority)	5,250
Accrued Interest Payable	
On Notes Payable	2,750
On Mortgage Note Payable	21,250
Mortgage Note Payable	440,000
Common Stock	469,000
Retained Earnings (deficit)	(349,125)
Total	$1,406,375

Additional Information:

1. The cash account includes a $500 travel advance that has been spent.
2. Of the total accounts receivable, $75,000 is believed to be collectible. The remaining accounts are doubtful, but it is believed that about one-third of these will be realized eventually. The accounts receivable are pledged as security on a $10,000 note payable.
3. Notes receivable of $50,000 have been pledged as security on a note payable of $45,000. This portion of the notes receivable has an estimated realizable value of $35,000. The remaining notes receivable, including the accrued interest, are expected to be fully collected. The $45,000 note payable has accrued interest due of $1,000.
4. The finished-goods inventory is expected to sell at 20% above its cost, with expenses involved in its disposition approximating 10% of selling price. The work in process inventory can be completed at an additional cost of $55,000, of which $40,000 represents materials used from the present raw materials inventory. The completed work in process should then sell for $145,000; the remaining raw materials should sell for one-half their cost. Supplies are expected to realize $1,300.
5. The investment in stock consists of 2,000 shares of Monelli Vineyards. The stock has a current market value of $50 per share and is pledged as security on a note payable of $41,000. Interest accrued on the note payable amounts to $1,750.
6. The land and buildings have been appraised at $165,000 and $260,000, respectively. They are pledged as collateral on the mortgage note payable.
7. The equipment is expected to realize $100,000.
8. Prepaid expenses are nonrealizable.

Required:

A. Prepare a statement of affairs.
B. Prepare a deficiency account detailing estimated gains and losses.
C. Calculate the dividend rate per dollar of unsecured liabilities.

INTERNATIONAL FINANCIAL REPORTING STANDARDS

LEARNING OBJECTIVES

1. Describe how the changing world environment is leading to an increased focus on international financial reporting standards (IFRS).
2. Explain some of the major differences between IFRS and U.S. GAAP.
3. List the seven milestones that must be achieved before the SEC will require adoption of IFRS.
4. Describe three major joint convergence topics of the IFRS and FASB.
5. List the steps that a non-U.S. company must follow to list its shares on a U.S. stock market.
6. Explain the role of form *20-F* filed with the Securities and Exchange Commission.
7. Indicate the role of American Depository Receipts in the issuing of securities of non-U.S. companies in the United States.

"We're not going to embrace any standard that isn't as good as our own. We're the best capital market in the world."[1]

THE INCREASING IMPORTANCE OF INTERNATIONAL ACCOUNTING STANDARDS

The accounting community in the United States was taken by surprise by the vote of the Securities and Exchange Commission (SEC) in June 2007 to eliminate the need for foreign private investors to reconcile their financial statements to U.S. generally accepted principles (GAAP) if the issuers use International Financial Reporting Standards (IFRS) as issued by the International Accounting Standards Board (IASB). Then in July 2007, in another surprising move, the SEC voted unanimously to publish a concept release for comment on allowing U.S. issuers to prepare their financial statements using IFRS as issued by the IASB. Thus the SEC has opened the door to making one global accounting standard for all countries more than a remote possibility. Investors are left wondering how comparable and consistent the

[1] Arthur Levitt Jr., Chairman, SEC, Speech at New York University, 9/28/98.

financial statements will be, if this occurs, and more importantly how consistently will the auditing standards be applied.

The International Accounting Standards Committee (IASC) was founded in 1973. Since then (and up to its reformation in 2001), it has been the driving force toward global harmonization of accounting practices. Its objective was to formulate and to publish standards to be followed in the preparation of financial statements, to promote worldwide acceptance of these standards, and to work generally for improvements in international accounting. Initially, the IASC made decisions on accounting issues and reported them in the form of **International Accounting Standards (IAS)**. The first international accounting standard was issued in January 1975; 41 standards were issued by January 2001. These international accounting standards (IAS) are listed in Appendix A.

In January 2001, the IASC announced formation of the International Accounting Standards Board (IASB). This board is comprised of members from various countries (including the United States) whose goal is to develop high-quality internationally accepted accounting standards for users of financial statements. The board includes 12 full-time members and two part-time members. This board is responsible for issuing standards known as **International Financial Reporting Standards (IFRS)**. In April 2001, the IASB approved a resolution stating that all IASC Standards and Standing Interpretation Committee (SIC) interpretations in effect as of April 1, 2001 (the date on which the IASB assumed its duties), would remain in effect until amended or withdrawn by the IASB. To date, eight IFRS have been issued. These standards are listed in Appendix A.

The IASB has made significant progress recently toward the harmonization of accounting standards. By 2005, over 90 countries had announced they would be following IFRS. As of January 1, 2009, 113 countries had adopted IFRS and it was expected that the list would grow to over 150 countries in the following three years.

THE ROAD TO CONVERGENCE—U.S. GAAP AND IFRS

LO 1 Increased focus on international accounting standards.

After a joint meeting in September 2002, the FASB and the IASB issued their Norwalk Agreement including a "memorandum of understanding." Each acknowledged its commitment to the development of high quality, compatible accounting standards to be used for both domestic and cross-border financial reporting. At that meeting, the FASB and the IASB pledged their efforts to make their existing financial reporting standards fully compatible as soon as practicable and to coordinate their future work to ensure that once achieved, compatibility would be maintained.

At meetings in April and October 2005, the FASB and the IASB reaffirmed their commitment to the convergence of U.S. generally accepted accounting principles (U.S. GAAP) and International Financial Reporting Standards (IFRSs). A common set of high-quality global standards has been stressed as the long-term strategic priority of both the FASB and the IASB. In September 2008, the IASB and FASB issued a progress report and timetable for completion, recognizing the relevance of a roadmap for the removal of the reconciliation requirement for non-U.S. companies using IFRS. The boards indicated nine major joint projects that over time should serve to improve and converge their respective conceptual frameworks.

On November 14, 2008, the SEC released a roadmap for the adoption of IFRS by U.S. issuers. As capital markets have become increasingly global, U.S. investors have increased opportunities for international investment. In this environment, U.S. investors should benefit from an enhanced ability to compare financial information of

U.S. companies with that of non-U.S. companies. The SEC has long expressed its support for a single set of high-quality global accounting standards as an important means of enhancing this comparability. Whether or not IFRS have the potential to provide the best common platform for global reporting is still being debated, and recent changes in the SEC administration could lead to altered plans. Nonetheless, we present the proposed Roadmap, which addresses the basis for considering the mandatory use of IFRS by U.S. issuers and also sets forth seven milestones for completion. These milestones relate to:

1. Improvements in accounting standards;
2. The accountability and funding of the IASC Foundation;
3. The improvement in the ability to use interactive data for IFRS reporting;
4. Education and training relating to IFRS;
5. Limited early use of IFRS where this would enhance comparability for U.S. investors;
6. The anticipated timing of future rulemaking by the Commission; and
7. The implementation of the mandatory use of IFRS by U.S. issuers.

The first four milestones relate to issues that need to be addressed before mandatory adoption of IFRS by U.S. entities can occur, while the last three milestones describe a transition plan for mandatory adoption.

Obviously, adoption of IFRS has significant implications for the FASB. The SEC roadmap does not address the method used to mandate IFRS for U.S. issuers. One of the options would be for the FASB to continue to be the designated standard setter for purposes of establishing the financial reporting standards. In this option the FASB would incorporate all provisions under IFRS, and all future changes to IFRS, directly into generally accepted accounting principles as used in the United States (i.e., U.S. GAAP). This type of approach has been adopted by a significant number of other countries (such as China) when they adopted IFRS as the basis of financial reporting in their capital markets. An alternative is that the FASB would no longer set U.S. standards.

With a single set of accounting standards, investors can more easily compare information and should be in a better position to make informed investment decisions. In order for the desired objectives to be achieved, a single set of high-quality standards would be applied globally to financial reporting in a consistent fashion across companies, industries, and countries.

Improvements in Accounting Standards

When the SEC considers mandating use of IFRS by U.S. issuers in 2011, it will consider whether those accounting standards are of high quality and sufficiently comprehensive. The SEC anticipates that the two boards will continue to work toward the completion of their joint work plan (estimated to be completed in 2011) and other projects that are expected to improve financial reporting (discussed later in the chapter). In addition, it is important that accounting standards be established under a robust, *independent* process that includes careful consideration of possible alternative approaches and *due process*, which allows for input from and consideration of views expressed by affected parties, including investors. It is also important that accounting standards are *timely* to keep standards current and reflect emerging accounting issues and changing business practices. Further, it is important that the accounting standards produced are capable of improving the accuracy and effectiveness of financial reporting and the protection of investors, and of resulting in high quality financial reporting relative to the standards which may be replaced. Thus, in considering future action as set out in the Roadmap, the Commission would also assess whether it believes that the IASB continues to develop its standards, including converged standards, through a process that reflects these elements.

The Accountability and Funding of the IASC Foundation

LO3 SEC milestones to be achieved for adoption of IFRS.

Based in London, the IASB is an accounting standard setting body established to develop global standards for financial reporting. The board is overseen by the IASC Foundation, a stand-alone, not-for profit organization, also based in London but incorporated in Delaware. The Foundation is responsible for the activities of the IASB and other work that centers on IFRS, such as initiatives related to translation of IFRS from the English language, education about IFRS and the development of interactive data taxonomies for IFRS. The IASC Foundation is governed by 22 trustees ("IASC Foundation Trustees") whose backgrounds are geographically diverse. The IASC Foundation has financed IASB operations principally through voluntary contributions from market participants from across the world's capital markets, ranging from firms in the accounting profession to companies, international organizations, central banks and governments. Funding commitments were made for the period 2001–2005 and then extended for an additional two years. In June 2006, the IASC Foundation Trustees agreed on four elements to govern the establishment of a funding approach with the purpose of enabling the IASC Foundation to remain a private-sector organization with the resources necessary to conduct its work in a timely fashion. The IASC Foundation Trustees determined that characteristics of the new scheme for 2008 would be broad-based, compelling, open-ended and country-specific. These Trustees continue to make progress toward obtaining the necessary funding.

The SEC plans to consider the degree to which the IASC Foundation has a secure, stable funding mechanism in place that permits it to function independently and that enhances the IASB's standard setting process. The Foundation has developed targeted contribution levels from individual jurisdictions. Realizing the IASC Foundation's goal of receiving open-ended funding commitments from a broad base of constituents should encourage the independent functioning of the IASB in its standard-setting process. Otherwise, the IASB is likely to find itself subject to either a perceived or an actual connection between the availability of funding and the outcome of its standard setting process. National accounting standard setters traditionally have been accountable to a national securities regulator or other government authority. In the United States, the Financial Accounting Foundation ("FAF"), the sponsor of the FASB, is overseen by the SEC. The IASC Foundation has not historically had a similar link to any national securities regulators. Recognizing that such a relationship would enhance the public accountability of the IASC Foundation, its Trustees have proposed amendments to its constitution to establish a link between the IASC Foundation and a monitoring group composed of securities authorities charged with standard setting duties in their respective jurisdictions. The securities authorities, including the SEC, envision that the monitoring group will participate in and approve nominations for IASC Foundation Trustees, review the funding arrangements of the IASC Foundation for adequacy and appropriateness, and address matters that the IASC Foundation Trustees are responsible for, such as oversight of the IASB.

Improvement in the Ability to Use Interactive Data for IFRS Reporting

In May 2008 the SEC proposed rules to require companies to provide their financial statements to the Commission as well as on their corporate Web sites in interactive data format using the eXtensible Business Reporting Language ("XBRL"). Under these proposed rules, financial statement information could be submitted by public companies in interactive data format, and financial information could then be downloaded directly into spreadsheets, analyzed in a variety of ways, or used within investment models in any of a number of software formats. The rules proposed, if adopted, would apply both to domestic and foreign public companies that prepare their financial statements in accordance with U.S. GAAP, and foreign private issuers that prepare their financial statements using IFRS. Under the proposal, foreign private issuers that prepare their financial statements using IFRS as issued by the IASB would be required to provide financial statements in interactive data format beginning in periods ending on or after December 15, 2010. To realize the anticipated improvements in the usefulness and comparability of financial data, U.S. issuers would need to be capable of providing IFRS financial statements to the SEC in interactive data format at a greater level of detail than is currently available. Thus, the state of development of an IFRS list of tags for interactive data reporting is likely to enter into the SEC's determination of whether to require the use of IFRS for all U.S. issuers.

The SEC has estimated that the cost to adopt IFRS for the 110 firms that would qualify for early adoption of IFRS would be around $32 million over the first three years of adoption.

Education and Training

A requirement for U.S. issuers to report in accordance with IFRS would increase the need for effective training and education about IFRS for a number of groups, including investors, accountants, auditors and others involved in the preparation and use of financial statements, due to differences between U.S. GAAP and IFRS. Investor education is especially important, as users of financial statements should be able to work with published financial information. The main benefits from a single set of globally accepted accounting standards will be realized only if investors understand the basis for the reported results. Accounting standards and practices differ across geographical regions and cultures. In the segmented business world of the past, where the investors, creditors, and other key constituents to a company were typically confined within the geographical boundaries of the country of operation, such cross-border differences in accounting treatments were not the major issue that they are today.

Limited Early Use of IFRS Where This Would Enhance Comparability for U.S. Investors

As part of the SEC Roadmap, proposed amendments allow a limited number of U.S. issuers to file IFRS financial statements prior to any mandated use of IFRS in Commission filings. These proposed amendments allow the limited early use of IFRS by

U.S. issuers in those instances where it would enhance the comparability of financial reporting to U.S. investors for purposes of comparing the largest U.S. issuers with the largest non-U.S. companies in the same industry. Further, the SEC believed, at the time of this proposal, that providing the alternative to U.S. issuers to file IFRS financial statements would broaden the awareness and attention given to IFRS. It is probably unlikely that firms will make this election so long as there remains any concern that the SEC might not ultimately require mandatory adoption of IFRS.

Anticipated Timing of Future Rulemaking by the Commission

In 2011, the SEC should decide whether or not to proceed with rules requiring some U.S. public companies to file IFRS-based financial statements by 2014. This decision should be based on whether it is viewed at that time as in the best interest of the public and investors. To aid in this decision, the staff of the SEC has already begun a comprehensive review of all Commission rules relating to financial reporting in order to recommend amendments that would fully implement IFRS reporting throughout the regulatory framework for registration and reporting under the Exchange Act and the Securities Act. Currently, U.S. issuers are required to include in their SEC filings three years of audited U.S. GAAP financial statements, and the SEC indicated that it expects that it would most likely require three years of audited financial statements in the first year of IFRS reporting.

Implementation of the Mandatory Use of IFRS

A staged transition, as opposed to all U.S. issuers transitioning at once, is being considered. Provisionally, under the transition, IFRS filings would begin for large accelerated filers for fiscal years ending on or after December 15, 2014. Other accelerated filers would begin IFRS filings for years ending on or after December 15, 2015. Nonaccelerated filers, including smaller reporting companies, would begin IFRS filings for years ending on or after December 15, 2016. In each instance, this would allow the filer to begin its books and records and internal accounting controls with respect to IFRS reporting for all three years of audited financial statements that would be required in its first year of IFRS reporting (e.g., 2012–2014 for large accelerated filers, 2013–2015 for accelerated filers, and 2014–2016 for non-accelerated filers).

SIGNIFICANT SIMILARITIES AND DIFFERENCES BETWEEN U.S. GAAP AND IFRS

In general, U.S. GAAP is considered to be more rules-based, while IFRS is considered to be more principles-based, although this dichotomy is an over-simplification as most U.S. rules are rooted in principles, and the IASB is embracing more interpretative details of its principles over time. Still the fact remains that U.S. GAAP includes far more details at present than IFRS. For example, in the criteria for capital leases, in the U.S. if a lease term is greater than 75% of the asset's useful life, it is a capital lease. Under IASB rules, a lease is classified as capital[2] if it covers a "substantial portion" of the asset's economic life.

[2] International standards typically refer to capital leases as financing leases.

GAAP HIERARCHY—U.S. VERSUS IFRS

RELATED CONCEPTS

In discussions between the FASB and IASB on developing a joint conceptual framework, the first issue debated was whether the objective should be to provide information to a wide range of users or only to existing shareholders. They agreed that information should be provided to all users making risky investments.

GAAP Hierarchy refers to how an entity identifies the sources of accounting principles and the framework for selecting the principles used in preparing financial statements. The objective of the GAAP hierarchy is to provide a consistent framework for selecting accounting principles to be used in preparing financial statements that are presented in conformity with U.S. generally accepted accounting principles. Generally, the hierarchy contains multiple levels with the highest level given the most weight. Most standard setters have a stated hierarchy to guide preparers of the financial statements.

On June 30, 2009, the FASB issued its final statement in the *SFAS* series: *SFAS No. 168, The FASB Accounting Standards Codification*™ *and the Hierarchy of Generally Accepted Accounting Principles—a replacement of FASB Statement No. 162.* As of the effective date of this pronouncement (annual and interim periods ending after September 15, 2009), the FASB *Accounting Standards Codification* (ASC) became the source of authoritative accounting and reporting standards for non-governmental entities in the US. In essence this statement reduced the GAAP hierarchy to two levels: one that is authoritative (included in the FASB ASC) and one that is non-authoritative (not included in the FASB ASC). The exception would be all rules and interpretations issued by the SEC which are also sources of authoritative GAAP for SEC registrants. *FASB Statement No. 168* is the final statement issued by the FASB in that form, and there will no longer be Emerging Issue Task Force (EITF) abstracts, staff bulletins, or AICPA Accounting Statement of Position. Instead FASB will issue Accounting Standards Updates. For example, *FASB Statement No. 168* is referred to as Accounting Standards Update No. 2009-02.

The codification includes approximately 90 topics on all accounting standards from the previous hierarchy, as well as some relevant portions of selected SEC staff interpretations and guidance. (Keep in mind that the FASB ASC is not the authoritative source of SEC guidance.) The new codification should reduce the extent of time and effort needed to solve accounting reporting issues, provide accurate and timely updates as new standards are released, and clearly distinguish between what is and what is not authoritative. Finally, this change, if implemented and used as intended, should aid in the convergence with IFRS.

Historically (prior to May 2008), the GAAP hierarchy was defined in the American Institute of Certified Public Accountants' *Statement on Auditing Standards (SAS) No. 69*, "The Meaning of Present Fairly in Conformity With Generally Accepted Accounting Principles." An unusual feature of this definition was that *SAS No. 69* was directed to the auditor rather than to the client of the auditor. *SFAS No. 162* corrected this issue by establishing that the GAAP hierarchy be directed to entities because it is the entity and not its auditor that is responsible for selecting accounting principles for financial statements that are presented in conformity with GAAP. Thus, in its short tenure before being replaced by the FASB Codification, the GAAP hierarchy was provided in *SFAS No. 162, The Hierarchy of Generally Accepted Accounting Principles.*

The hierarchy in *SAS No. 69* remains the primary GAAP hierarchy for state and local governmental entities and federal governmental entities. GAAP hierarchies are listed below, with the current U.S. GAAP hierarchy presented first, followed by the historical U.S. GAAP hierarchy, and then the IFRS hierarchy.

U.S. GAAP Hierarchy (*SFAS No. 168*)—Effective September 2009

Authoritative: Included in the FASB Accounting Standards Codification

Non-Authoritative: Not-included in the FASB Accounting Standards Codification

Exceptions: SEC registrants must also follow SEC rules and regulations issued under the authority of federal securities laws.

Historical U.S. GAAP Hierarchy (*SFAS No. 162*)—Prior to September 2009

Category (a) consists of FASB Statements (163 statements) and Interpretations (48 interpretations), Accounting Principle Board (APB) Opinions (31 opinions) and AICPA Accounting Research Bulletins (51 bulletins).

Category (b) consists of FASB Technical Bulletins (55 bulletins) and, if cleared by the FASB, AICPA Industry Audit and Accounting Guides and AICPA Statements of Position. The auditor should assume such pronouncements are cleared by the FASB unless the pronouncement indicates otherwise.

Category (c) consists of AICPA Accounting Standards Executive Committee (AcSEC) Practice Bulletins that have been cleared by the FASB and consensus positions of the FASB Emerging Issues Task Force (EITF) (more than 100 since 2000). The auditor should assume such pronouncements are cleared by the FASB unless the pronouncement indicates otherwise.

Category (d) includes AICPA accounting interpretations and implementation guides ("Qs and As") published by the FASB staff (62 not superseded), and practices that are widely recognized and prevalent either generally or in the industry.

If the accounting treatment for a transaction or event is not specified by a pronouncement or established in practice as described in categories (*a*)–(*d*), an entity shall first consider accounting principles for similar transactions or events within categories (*a*)–(*d*) and then other accounting literature. Other accounting literature includes, for example, FASB Concepts Statements, AICPA Issues Papers, International Financial Reporting Standards (IFRSs) of the International Accounting Standards Board (IASB), pronouncements of other professional associations or regulatory agencies.

In *IAS 8* (revised in 2003), the IASB determined the hierarchy to be followed in choosing accounting procedures to be used in preparing financing statements under IFRS. This hierarchy is:

IFRS Hierarchy (issued by the IASB)

1. IFRS/IAS statements (8 IFRS and 41 IAS standards) and IFRIC/SIC Interpretations (32 SIC and 14 IFRIC). SIC stands for the Standards Interpretations Committee.
2. Apply a method that is relevant, reliable, represents faithfully the financial position, the performance, and cash flows of the firm; reflect the economic substance of the firm.
3. Look to recent pronouncements of other standard setters which use a similar conceptual framework (i.e., U.S. GAAP).
4. The conceptual framework.

At present, there are differences between the U.S. and IFRS hierarchies in the status of the conceptual frameworks within the GAAP hierarchy. For an entity preparing financial statements under International Financial Reporting Standards (IFRS), the

IASB's *Framework* provides guidance when there is no standard or interpretation that specifically applies to a transaction or other event or condition, or that deals with a similar and related issue. In those situations, the entity's management is required to consider the definitions, recognition criteria, and measurement concepts for assets, liabilities, income, and expenses in the *Framework*. Under U.S. GAAP, the FASB's Concepts Statements have historically had a lower status—they were ranked after category 'd' under 'other literature.' However, the FASB intends to incorporate the new conceptual framework (resulting from the joint project of the FASB and IASB) into the codification of authoritative standards by its completion, thus raising its status.

Note the third item under the IFRS hierarchy. One concern about U.S. firms adopting IFRS is that there are fewer standards about revenue recognition in IFRS than in U.S. GAAP. However, if a U.S. firm adopts IFRS and has been recognizing revenue according to a specific U.S. rule, this firm might still be required to follow the U.S. rule because of item (3) of the IFRS hierarchy, which refers to pronouncements of other standard setters.

Similarities and Differences between FASB and IASB

LO2 Differences between IFRS and U.S. GAAP.

In Illustrations 11-1, 11-2, and 11-3, a listing of similarities and differences between IFRS and U.S. GAAP is provided.[3] Be aware, however, that the principles and rules are constantly changing under both IFRS and U.S. GAAP, making it important to check continually for recent updates or modifications. In Illustration 11-1, various financial statement presentation issues are addressed. IFRS financial statements include a balance sheet, an income statement and comprehensive income, a cash flow statement, either a statement of changes in equity (SOCE) or a statement of recognized income or expense (SORIE). Two years of reports are required for all financial statements. In the United States, SEC registrants are required to provide three years of financial statement except for the balance sheet, where two years of statements are required.

IFRS does not prescribe a format for presenting balance sheet items, but generally requires a current/non-current format with items being listed in order of *increasing* liquidity. In the United States, items are listed on the balance sheet in order of *decreasing* liquidity.

There are several differences affecting the income statement. In the United States, expense items are usually listed on the income statement by function, such as selling expense, administration expense, cost of goods sold, etc. Under IFRS, expenditures can be listed by nature or by function. Examples of expenses listed by nature would be raw materials used, salary expense, depreciation expense, etc. If the firm reports expenses by function, they are required (under IAS 1) to disclose the expenses by nature in the footnotes. In the United States, firms are allowed to report expenses by nature, but seldom do. In addition, under IFRS, extraordinary items are prohibited, but if the item is unusual and/or infrequent and the amount is significant, firms using IFRS must disclose the information in the footnotes. Reporting such items on the face of the income statement is allowed but not required. Under U.S. GAAP, such material items must be reported on the face of the income statement and/or in the disclosure notes.

---

[3] Additional comparisons of IFRS and U.S. GAAP are provided in Illustrations 2-6 and in Chapter 4.

ILLUSTRATION 11-1

Comparison of Financial Statement Presentation under U.S. GAAP and IFRS, Select Items

Topic	*U.S. GAAP*	*IFRS*
1. Financial periods presented	Generally, comparative financial statements are presented. Public companies are required to present two years for the balance sheet and three years for all other financial statements.	Comparative information must be presented for all amounts reported in the financial statements.
2. Balance sheet presentation	Entities may present either a classified or a non-classified balance sheet. Items on the balance sheet are listed in order of decreasing liquidity. Public companies must follow Reg S-X.	IFRS does not prescribe a format, but generally requires a current/noncurrent format be used and listed in order of increasing liquidity unless a liquidity format is more relevant and reliable.
3. Income statement presentation	Presented either as a single-step or multiple step format. Expenditures are usually listed by function.	IFRS does not prescribe a format, but expenditures are listed either by function or nature.
4. Extraordinary items	These are unusual and infrequent. These items are reported separately, but occur rarely.	Prohibited.
5. Unusual items	Individually significant items are reported on the face of the income statement and disclosed in the notes.	Separate disclosure is required, but may be reported on the income statement.
6. Deferred taxes classified	Deferred taxes are presented as current or noncurrent based on the nature of the related asset or liability.	Deferred taxes are presented as noncurrent (convergence to US GAAP is expected).
7. Statement of cash flows	Standard headings but more guidance on items in each category (cash interest paid is included in operations). Direct or indirect formats allowed for cash from operations.	Standard headings but limited guidance on contents (i.e., cash interest paid may be reported in operating or financing). Direct or indirect format allowed. Allows reconciliation of profit before tax to cash from operations.

Illustration 11-2 provides similarities and differences for certain balance sheet items and some disclosures. One of the largest differences between U.S. GAAP and IFRS is that the use of LIFO inventory is prohibited by IFRS. The primary reason given is that the cost flow and the physical flow do not match. Related to inventory issues are recoveries of previously written down inventory. Under IFRS, firms are allowed to recover costs up to the original amount written off if the conditions that gave rise to the write-off no longer exist. Under U.S. GAAP, the reduced value of the inventory becomes the new cost basis for the inventory and no recovery is allowed.

ILLUSTRATION 11-2

Comparison of Statement of Financial Position (Balance Sheets) and Disclosures under U.S. GAAP and IFRS

Topic	*U.S. GAAP*	*IFRS*
1. Inventory	Carried at the lower of cost or market, where market is current replacement cost (if not greater than selling price less costs to complete or if not less than net realizable value less a normal profit). LIFO permitted.	Carried at lower of cost or realizable value. Realizable value is the best estimate of the amount expected to be realized considering the business purpose (may not always be fair value). LIFO is prohibited.
2. Reversal of inventory write-downs	Write-downs of inventory to lower of cost or market create a new cost basis. Reversals of previously written down amounts are prohibited.	Previously written down amounts can be reversed up to the original impairment loss if the reason for impairment no longer exists.
3. Development costs	Both research and development costs are expenses as incurred unless addressed by a separate standard. (In the case of computer software, development costs are capitalized once technological feasibility is established.	Development costs are capitalized when technical and economic feasibility can be demonstrated with specific criteria.
4. Property, Plant, and Equipment	Historical cost is used. Revaluations are not allowed.	Historical cost or revalued amounts are used. Regular revaluation of assets is required once the revaluation option is chosen.
5. Reviews for impairment of long-lived assets	Performed whenever events or changes in circumstances indicate that the carrying amount of the asset may not be recoverable.	Performed at each reporting date.
6. Method for determining long-lived asset impairment.	A two-step approach is used. If the recoverability test is not met, then the impairment test is performed (the amount that the carrying value exceeds it fair value).	A one-step approach is used, measured as the amount by which the carrying value exceeds its recoverable amount. The recoverable amount is the higher of the fair value less costs to sell or the present value of future cash flows less costs to dispose.
7. Provisions for liabilities	Recorded if probably and can be reasonable estimated. Probable is interpreted as 'likely.'	A present obligation (with uncertain timing or uncertain amount) that is recorded if probably ('more likely than not') and can be reasonable estimated.
8. Contingent liability	If probably and can be estimated, the liability *is recognized* in the financial statements. Otherwise, the obligation is footnoted (unless remote).	A possible obligation that will be confirmed by uncertain future events. *Not recognized* in the financial statements. Disclosed if not remote.
9. Reduced disclosure of contingent liabilities	No reduced disclosure permitted.	Reduced disclosure permitted if it would severely prejudice the entity's position with another party to the obligation.
10. Measurement of provision—range of outcomes	Most likely outcome should be accrued. When no outcome is more likely, accrue the minimum range of outcomes.	Best estimate of obligation (typically the expected value) should be used. If any outcome is as likely, use the midpoint of the estimates.

ILLUSTRATION 11-3

Comparison of Various Topics and Disclosures under U.S. GAAP and IFRS

Topic	*U.S. GAAP*	*IFRS*
1. Stock dividends declared after balance sheet date	SEC requires that the financial statements be adjusted for stock dividends declared after the balance sheet date.	Financial statements are not adjusted for stock dividends occurring after the balance sheet date.
2. Related party	Similar to IFRS.	The nature of the relationship (seven categories), amount of the transactions, outstanding balances, terms and types of the transactions are disclosed.
3. Compensation of key employees	Not required to be disclosed within the financial statements.	Required within the financial statements.
4. Capitalization of interest	Requires interest be capitalized as part of the cost of a qualifying asset.	Interest is capitalized as part of the cost of a qualifying asset.
5. Depreciation	Component depreciation is allowed, but seldom used.	Component depreciation is required.
6. Earnings per share (EPS)	Basic and diluted earnings per share for both continuing operations and net income are presented on the face of the income statement. Entities with an extraordinary item also must present EPS data for those line items.	Basic and diluted earnings per share for both continuing operations and net income are presented on the face of the income statement.
7. Accompanied financial information	A financial and operational review not required. SEC registrants must include a management discussion and analysis section.	A financial and operational review is encouraged, but not required.
8. Changes in estimates	Handled prospectively.	Handled prospectively.
9. Changes in methods	Accounting policy changes are accounted for retrospectively by adjusting opening equity and comparatives, unless impracticable.	Accounting policy changes are accounted for retrospectively by adjusting opening equity and comparatives, unless impracticable.
10. Error corrections	Error corrections are accounted for retrospectively by adjusting opening equity and comparatives, without regard to practicable.	Error corrections are accounted for retrospectively by adjusting opening equity and comparatives, unless impracticable.
11. Long-term liabilities expected to be refinanced.	Classification may consider events after the reporting date (based on the entity's ability and intent).	Liabilities are classified according to their circumstances at the reporting date.

Although a single economic phenomenon can be faithfully represented in multiple ways, permitting alternative accounting methods for the same economic phenomenon diminishes comparability and, therefore, may be undesirable.[4]

Research and development costs are handled differently between IFRS and U.S. GAAP. In the United States, all R&D expenditures are expensed as incurred (with the exception of software development costs). Under IFRS, development costs are capitalized once the product becomes technically and economically feasible. This means that in addition to technological feasibility, the firms must demonstrate a clear intention to complete, a clear intention and ability to use or sell the product, an ability to generate future benefits and to reliably measure the expenditure, and adequate resources to complete the development.

One potentially large difference concerns valuations of property, plant, and equipment (PPE). In the United States, PPE is accounted for on a historical cost basis. Revaluations are not allowed, unless the asset has become impaired. Under IFRS rules, the firm can elect to revalue each class of PPE. Common examples of asset classes are land, machinery, furniture and fixtures, and land and buildings. However, this revaluation cannot be a one-time event. Once a firm has chosen to revalue the assets, the assets must be revalued regularly so that the carrying amount is not materially different from the fair value of the asset.

Impairment tests for long-lived assets must be performed at each reporting date under IFRS, while in the United States impairment testing is only performed if events cause a change in circumstance that indicates that the carrying value of the asset may not be recovered. Under IFRS, a one-step approach is used to determine the impairment loss. The impairment loss is the excess of the carrying amount over the asset's recoverable amount. The recoverable amount is the higher of the fair value less any costs to sell the asset or the present value of the future cash flows generated by the asset less disposal costs. Currently, IFRS uses a different definition of fair value than U.S. GAAP.

Depreciation of long-lived assets under IFRS must be based on component deprecation. Consider the following example from paragraph 44 of IAS 16. Suppose that an entity purchases an aircraft for $12 million, comprising the airframe ($6 million), the engine ($4 million), and remaining components ($2 million). Suppose that straight-line depreciation is used, the salvage value is zero, and that the useful lives of the components are:

Aircraft frame	20 years
The engine component	16 years
Other components	8 years

The useful life of the entire aircraft is 20 years. Under U.S. GAAP and IFRS, the following entries would be made to record the purchase:

U.S. GAAP:		
Asset	12,000,000	
Cash		12,000,000
IFRS:		
Aircraft–Airframe	6,000,000	
Aircraft–Engine	4,000,000	
Aircraft–Other	2,000,000	
Bank/Liability		12,000,000

[4] IASB Exposure Draft, "An improved conceptual framework for financial reporting," and FASB Exposure Draft, "Conceptual framework for financial reporting," September 29, 2008.

The entry to record depreciation expense would be:

U.S. GAAP:		
Depreciation ($12 million/20)	600,000	
Accumulated Depreciation		600,000
IFRS:		
Depreciation Aircraft–Airframe ($6 mil/20)	300,000	
Depreciation Aircraft–Engine ($4 mil/16)	250,000	
Depreciation Aircraft–Other ($2 mil/8)	250,000	
Accumulated Depreciation–Airframe		800,000

The amount of deprecation expense can vary significantly between IFRS and the United States.

Contingent liabilities, under IFRS, are defined as 'possible' obligations that will be confirmed by uncertain future events. Contingent liabilities are not recognized in the financial statements under IFRS. In the United States, contingent liabilities are recognized in the financial statements if they are probable and can be reasonably estimated. U.S. GAAP defines probable as "likely," and interprets this definition as implying a higher threshold than "more likely than not." IFRS does require, however, that present obligations be recorded if probable and estimable, and probable is defined here to mean "more likely than not." One of the most important distinctions between U.S. GAAP and IFRS is that IFRS allow reduced disclosure in certain situations. For instance, if the disclosure would severely prejudice the entity's position with another party to the obligation, the firm is allowed to reduce its disclosure under IFRS.

Illustration 11-3 provides comparisons on various issues. Related party disclosures, earnings per share, and capitalization of interest are similar between IFRS and U.S. GAAP. IFRS does require that the compensation of key employees be disclosed in the financial statements, while this is not required under U.S. GAAP.

Changes in accounting principles are handled retrospectively under both systems and changes in accounting estimates are performed prospectively. Under IFRS, error corrections are done retrospectively unless impractical, while under U.S. GAAP, the errors must be corrected regardless of practicality.

Finally, in the United States, certain obligations that are due within the year and expected to be refinanced can be excluded from current liabilities if the firm can demonstrate the ability and intent to refinance the obligation. Under IFRS, the liability is classified according to the obligation's circumstance at the reporting date.

IFRS Financial Statements Illustrated

In Illustrations 11-4, 11-5, and 11-6, examples of IFRS-based financial statements are provided. We do not provide an example of the statement of changes in equity. Notice on the balance sheet in Illustration 11-4, that the firm has chosen to classify assets and liabilities between current and noncurrent. In addition, the order of the assets and liabilities is in order of liquidity (i.e., the least liquid asset and liability is listed first). Long-lived assets would be listed first on the balance sheet with the current asset section listed second. On the liability and equity side of the balance sheet, equity is generally listed first with long-term liabilities listed second, followed by current liabilities.

In Illustration 11-4, there is an account listed as a noncurrent asset called 'investment in an associate.' In the United States, this is an investment accounted for using the equity method of accounting. In addition, issued capital refers to common shares and share premium refers to additional paid in capital. Provisions listed under current liabilities are the same as estimated liabilities in the United States.

ILLUSTRATION 11-4

Consolidated Balance Sheet (IFRS)
at December 31, 2010
(in *000* euros)

	2010	*2009*
Noncurrent assets		
Property, Plant, and Equipment	64,566	40,891
Intangible Assets	7,496	2,978
Investment in an Associate	924	824
Available-for-Sale Investments	7,294	4,224
Deferred Tax Asset	463	442
	80,743	49,358
Current assets		
Inventories	30,099	30,842
Trade and Other Receivables	33,483	29,391
Prepayments	336	200
Cash and Short-term Deposits	20,101	18,233
Total Current Assets	84,019	78,666
Total Assets	164,762	128,024
Equity attributable to equity holders of the parent		
Issued Capital	26,654	23,538
Share Premium	7,687	163
Treasury Shares	(937)	(937)
Other Capital Reserves	1,254	231
Retained Earnings	46,205	37,389
	80,863	60,385
Minority Interests	863	895
Total Equity	81,726	61,280
Noncurrent liabilities		
Interest-bearing Loans and Borrowings	18,244	23,666
Convertible Preference Shares	3,361	3,199
Provisions	2,360	93
Other Liabilities	5,693	2,915
Deferred Tax Liability	5,584	2,239
	35,242	32,112
Current liabilities		
Trade and Other Payables	23,450	25,750
Interest-bearing Loans and Borrowings	18,255	3,358
Other Financial Liabilities	534	549
Income Tax Payable	5,011	4,856
Provisions	545	119
Total Current Liabilities	47,794	34,631
Total Liabilities	83,036	66,744
Total Equity and Liabilities	164,762	128,024

The income statement prepared under IFRS is presented in Illustration 11-5. IAS 1.88 requires expenses be listed by nature of the expense or by their function within the entity, whichever provides information that is reliable and more relevant. In the illustration, the expenses are listed by nature (i.e., raw materials used, depreciation expense, etc.). In many IFRS income statements, revenues may be referred to as 'turnover.' This is simply a terminology difference and not a requirement of IFRS.

ILLUSTRATION 11-5

Consolidated Income Statement (IFRS)—disclosed by nature for the year ended December 31, 2010 (in *000* euros)

	2010	*2009*
Continuing operations		
Sale of goods	232,440	210,738
Rendering of services	20,729	20,010
Rental income	1,699	1,666
Revenue	254,867	232,414
Other income	1,918	3,083
Changes in inventories of finished goods and work in progress	(1,371)	(4,587)
Raw materials used	(179,802)	(159,024)
Employee benefits expense	(53,263)	(53,062)
Depreciation and amortization expense	(4,619)	(3,548)
Other expenses	(1,316)	(1,218)
Finance costs	(1,969)	(1,889)
Finance revenue	950	876
Share of profit of an associate	100	98
Profit before tax	15,495	13,143
Income tax expense	(4,489)	(3,911)
Profit for the year from continuing operations	11,006	9,232
Discontinued operation:		
Loss after tax for the year from a discontinued operation	266	(227)
Profit for the year	11,272	9,005
Attributable to:		
Equity holders of the parent	11,105	8,716
Minority interests	167	289
	11,272	9,005
Earnings per share attributable to ordinary equity holders of the parent		
basic	0.52	0.46
diluted	0.52	0.43
Earnings per share for continuing operations attributable to ordinary equity holders of the parent		
basic	0.52	0.47
diluted	0.50	0.44

RELATED CONCEPTS

In discussions between the FASB and IASB on developing a joint conceptual framework, they agreed that general purpose financial statements should not necessarily provide information useful to managers, since management is able to demand their own reports.

IFRS allows firms to choose either the direct or the indirect approach in computing cash from operations. In Illustration 11-6, the indirect approach is used. IFRS allows firms to start with either income before tax or income after-tax income in the reconciliation to cash from operations (income before tax is used in the illustration). In the United States, cash interest paid is classified as an operating cash flow, while under IFRS, the firm can choose to classify the cash outflow for interest as either operating or financing depending on which classification is more relevant to the entity.

LONG-TERM CONVERGENCE ISSUES FASB AND IASB

We address three long-term convergence issues between the FASB and the IASB. These issues are:

1. Accounting for leases by the lessee.
2. Revenue recognition.
3. Financial statement presentation.

ILLUSTRATION 11-6

Consolidated Statement of Cash Flows (IFRS)
for the year ended December 31, 2010

	2010	*2009*
Operating activities		
Profit before tax from continuing operations	15,495	13,143
Profit/(Loss) before tax from discontinued operations	258	(234)
Profit before tax	15,753	12,909
Adjustment to reconcile profit before tax to net cash flows		
Non-cash:		
Depreciation	4,594	4,093
Amortization and impairment of intangible assets	151	211
Gain on disposal of property, plant and equipment	(644)	(2,428)
Other gains and losses	801	889
Interest income	(950)	(876)
Interest expense	1,969	1,889
Share of net profit of associate	(100)	(98)
Movements in provisions	(592)	128
Working capital adjustments:		
Increase in trade and other receivables	(10,586)	(2,615)
Decrease in inventories	3,168	2,644
Increase in trade and other payables	3,260	3,054
Income tax paid	(4,334)	(4,006)
Net cash flows from operating activities	12,490	15,794
Investing activities		
Proceeds from sale of property, plant and equipment	2,408	2,806
Purchase of property, plant and equipment	(9,263)	(8,863)
Purchase of investment properties	(1,471)	(1,442)
Purchase of available-for-sale investments	(687)	(272)
Other	(770)	(574)
Net cash flows used In investing activities	(9,783)	(8,345)
Financing activities		
Proceeds from borrowings	3,315	3,200
Repayment of borrowings	(180)	(2,159)
Interest paid	(1,716)	(1,889)
Dividends paid to equity holders of the parent	(2,386)	(1,936)
Dividends paid to minority interests	(36)	(59)
Other	111	150
Net cash flows used in financing activities	(892)	(2,692)
Net increase in cash and cash equivalents	1,816	4,757
Net foreign exchange difference	52	23
Cash and cash equivalents at 1 January	18,233	13,453
Cash and cash equivalents at 31 December	20,101	18,233

LEASE ACCOUNTING CONVERGENCE

Currently, the guidance for leases is provided in *FASB Statement No. 13* **[Topic 840]** under U.S. GAPP and in IAS 17 under IFRS. Before we consider the guidance, there is one important terminology difference. For lessees in the United States, there are two types of leases: operating and capital. Under IAS 17, capital leases are referred to as financing leases. In this chapter we will use the terms capital lease and financing lease as equivalent.

A lease is a capital lease if *any one* of the following are met

U.S. GAAP (FASB 13)	*IFRS (IAS 17)*
1. Transfers title by the end of the lease.	**1.** Transfers title by the end of the lease.
2. Lease contains a bargain purchase option.	**2.** Lease contains a bargain purchase option.
3. Lease term is ***greater than 75%*** of the economic life of asset.	**3.** Lease term is for a ***major part*** of the economic life of asset.
4. The present value of the minimum lease payments is ***greater than or equal to 90% of the fair value*** of the leased asset at the inception of the lease.	**4.** The present value of the minimum lease payments is ***equal to substantially all of the fair value*** of the leased asset at the inception of the lease.
	5. The leased asset is a specialized asset that only the lessee can use.

Under IASB, there are three additional conditions that if met might indicate that a lease is capital lease (losses from lease cancelation reimbursed by the lessee, renewal periods covered by bargain rentals, and rental rebates at the end of the lease based on changes in fair value of the asset). The differences between FASB and IFRS in the table above are noted in bold and italics. These differences are often used to illustrate the difference between a 'rules-based' approach and a principals-based approach. Notice that under U.S. GAAP, there are bright-line rules, such as if the lease term is greater than 75%. Under IFRS, the lease is a capital lease if the lease term is for a major part of the economic life of the asset. Thus under IFRS, different companies might classify leases differently with similar characteristics. But it places the burden on the managers to determine the substance of the lease. On the other hand, the 'bright line' rules often result in managers manipulating the conditions of the lease to achieve a certain reporting objective. They know that if the lease term is greater than 75%, the lease will be classified as a capital lease.

Lessee Convergence Project Plan

The IASB and the FASB are working on a project to develop a new model for the recognition of assets and liabilities arising under lease contracts. It is intended that the final document will be issued by 2011.

Preliminary indications suggest that the boards are going to make a fundamental change in lease accounting that would eliminate these classification criteria and treat all leases (longer than a year) as a transfer of property rights and debt obligations, thus requiring capitalization of most leases on the balance sheet. The boards decided that a lessee should initially measure both its right-of-use asset and its lease obligation at the present value of the expected lease payments. The lessee should discount the lease payments using the lessee's incremental borrowing rate for all leases. Then, at each reporting date, the lessee would be required to reassess the lease term and its lease obligation using its current assumptions. Under existing rules, the lessee only considers these assumptions at the inception of the lease.

There are still major areas regarding leases upon which the two boards have not agreed. For instance, in presenting the lease information on the balance sheet, the FASB believes that there are important differences between leases that convey the right to use versus an in-substance purchase. The IASB believes the asset should be classified according to the nature of the asset. This difference also affects income statement presentation. For instance, does the lease payment include an interest portion and a principal portion with an additional charge for depreciation of the leased asset? The FASB believes that if the lease represents a right to use, then income statement presentation might vary from that required if the asset is in-substance a purchase.

While the major change will be the requirement that all leases extending beyond a year are capitalized, the financial statement presentation and the potential changes in lease assumptions have yet to be determined. The boards are not considering accounting for lessors at this time and hope to address accounting for subleases after a discussion paper is released.

REVENUE RECOGNITION CONVERGENCE

The IASB and the FASB are working on a project to develop a single statement on revenue recognition for both U.S. GAAP and IFRS. In particular, the project is intended to improve financial reporting by: (a) converging U.S. and international revenue recognition standards, (b) eliminating inconsistencies in existing revenue recognition standards and practices, (c) providing clearer principles for addressing future revenue recognition issues, and (d) filling voids in existing revenue recognition guidance.

The standard would apply to all contracts to provide goods and services to customers and would apply to all industries (but this could be relaxed in the future). It is hoped that the final document will be issued by 2011.

The boards have reached some preliminary views in developing a revenue recognition model. This section summarizes those views. The proposed model would apply to contracts with customers where a contract is an agreement between two or more parties that creates enforceable obligations (does not need to be in writing). A customer is a party that has contracted with an entity to obtain an asset (such as a good or a service) that represents an output of the entity's ordinary activities. The boards are considering a 'customer-consideration (allocation)' model.

Customer Consideration (Allocation) Model

LO4 Three major convergence topics for IFRS and FASB.

Three new terms are introduced in the customer consideration model: contract rights, performance obligations, and net contract asset/liability. To recognize a contract, an entity measures its rights and its performance obligations in the contract. The measurement of the rights would be based on the amount of the transaction price (that is, the promised consideration the customer would pay). Initially, the performance obligations would also be measured at the transaction price. A performance obligation is a promise to transfer an asset (such as goods or services) to the customer. A performance obligation can only be satisfied by transferring the promised good or service to the customer. If a contract comprises more than one performance obligation, an entity would allocate the transaction price to the performance obligations on the basis of the relative stand-alone selling prices of the goods and services underlying those performance obligations. Thus at the inception of the contract, the contract rights and the performance obligations would be equal and the net contract asset/liability would be zero.

Subsequent measurement of the performance obligations should measure the decrease in the entity's obligation to transfer goods and services to the customer. When a performance obligation is satisfied, the amount of revenue recognized is the amount of the transaction price that was allocated to the satisfied performance obligation at contract inception. Consequently, the total amount of revenue that an entity recognizes over the life of the contract is equal to the transaction price.

Under the customer consideration model, revenue is recognized from "increases" in the net contract position. Specifically, revenue is recognized when there is an *increase* in the ***contract asset*** or a decrease in the ***contract liability*** from satisfying ***performance obligations.*** Revenue is only recognized when a performance obligation is satisfied by transferring goods or services.

Performance obligations are considered satisfied when the customer controls the asset (i.e., when the inventory is the customer's inventory) or when then customer has received the service. Thus when a performance obligation is satisfied, revenue will be recognized in the amount of the transaction price allocated to that performance obligation.

To measure the contract asset or liability, (1) The underlying rights are measured at inception based on the customer consideration (the amount the customer is willing to pay); and (2) The rights are allocated to the separate performance obligations based on the sales price of the goods or services. Because of this, at inception, the sum of the performance obligations and the measure of rights are equal.

Consider the following example of the sale of refrigerators. Suppose that a retailer normally sells a refrigerator for $4,050 and a two-year warranty for $450. Suppose that the retailer, as part of a year-end promotion, contracts for delivery and includes the warranty for $4,300. The cost of refrigerators is $3,200. Warranty work is estimated to occur equally over time.

The initial allocation to the individual performance obligations (providing the refrigerator and the warranty) would be:

	Stand Alone Sales Price	*Percentage*	*Measurement of Performance Obligations*
Refrigerator	4,050	0.90	3,870
Two-year warranty	450	0.10	430
Total	4,500	1.00	4,300

If stand-alone prices are not available, management estimates might be acceptable. Suppose that on January 1, 2010, Frigid-R-Us (FRU) received $4,300 from the customer. The following entry would be recorded.

Cash	4,300	
Contract Liability–refrigerator		3,870
Contract Liability–warranty		430

On January 10, 2010, the refrigerator is delivered to the customer. FRU makes the following entry.

Contract liability–refrigerator	3,870	
Revenue		3,870
Cost of goods sold	3,200	
Inventory		3,200

During 2010, FRU incurred $200 of direct and indirect costs of servicing the refrigerator. Current practice recognizes these costs as expenses when incurred. The following entries would be made over this period.

Contract liability–warranty (1/2 of $430)	215	
Revenue		215
Warranty expense	200	
Cash		200

In this example, warranty revenue is recognized on a straight-line basis, but if the retailer had more specific estimates concerning the servicing of contracts, they could also be used. Under existing practice, in order for revenue to be recognized, revenue must be realized or realizable and earned (the earnings process must be complete or substantially complete). In this example, the customer consideration model would be similar to exiting practices.

FINANCIAL STATEMENT PRESENTATION

In 2004, the FASB and the IASB initiated a joint project on financial statement presentation. The purpose of this joint project between the FASB and the IASB is to establish a standard that will guide preparers of the financial statements in presenting financial information. The results of this project will directly affect how the management communicates financial statement information to users of financial statements. The primary goal of the joint project is to improve the usefulness of the information for capital providers. The project applies to private and public entities, but not to non-business organization.

This project is to be released in three phases. Phase A is to address which statements constitute a complete set of financial statements and the periods that the statements are required to be presented. Currently the FASB does not determine the number of years of financial statements that should be presented. The SEC generally requires three years for the income statement and the statement of cash flows along with two years for the statement of financial position. Phase B would address fundamental issues relating to presentation and display of information in the financial statements, including aggregating and disaggregating information in each primary financial statement, defining totals and subtotals, and reconsidering the use of a direct or an indirect method of presenting operating cash flows. Phase C is expected to address the presentation and display of interim financial information in U.S. generally accepted accounting principles (GAAP).

In October 2008, the boards released a joint discussion paper outlining their preliminary views. In this discussion paper, the boards developed three objectives for financial statement presentation based on the objectives of financial reporting and the input the boards received from users of financial statements and from members of their advisory groups. Those proposed objectives state that information should be presented in the financial statements in a manner that:

- **Portrays a cohesive financial picture of an entity's activities.** A cohesive financial picture means that the relationship between items across financial statements is clear and that an entity's financial statements complement each other as much as possible.
- **Disaggregates information so that it is useful in predicting an entity's future cash flows.** Financial statement analysis aimed at objectives such as assessing the amount, timing, and uncertainty of future cash flows requires financial information that is disaggregated into reasonably homogeneous groups of items. If items differ economically, users may wish to take that into account differently in predicting future cash flows.
- **Helps users assess an entity's liquidity and financial flexibility.** Information about an entity's liquidity helps users to assess an entity's ability to meet its

financial commitments as they become due. Information about financial flexibility helps users to assess an entity's ability to invest in business opportunities and respond to unexpected needs.

HOW THE FINANCIAL STATEMENTS MIGHT CHANGE

Statement of Comprehensive Income

It has been proposed that items will be classified into operating, investing, and financing categories rather than simply income and expense. Furthermore, an entity should disaggregate those items on the basis of their function within those categories. Then, within the function, the company would disaggregate its income and expense items by their nature. *Function* refers to the primary activities in which an entity is engaged, such as selling goods, providing services, manufacturing, advertising, marketing, business development, or administration. *Nature* refers to the economic characteristics or attributes that distinguish assets, liabilities, and income and expense items that do not respond equally to similar economic events. Examples of disaggregation by nature include disaggregating total revenues into wholesale revenues and retail revenues or disaggregating total cost of sales into materials, labor, transport, and energy costs.

The proposed presentation model eliminates the existing choice of presenting components of income and expense in an income statement and a statement of comprehensive income (two-statement approach) or, alternatively, of presenting information about other comprehensive income in its statement of changes in equity (U.S. generally accepted accounting principles only). All entities would present a *single statement of comprehensive income,* with items of other comprehensive income presented in a separate section. This statement would include a subtotal of profit or loss or net income and a total for comprehensive income for the period.

It is expected that the new presentation model would include more subtotals than are currently presented in an income statement or a statement of comprehensive income. Those additional subtotals will allow easier comparisons of effects across the financial statements. For example, users will be able to assess how changes in operating assets and liabilities generate operating income and cash flows. In Illustration 11-7, we provide an example of a one-year statement of comprehensive income prepared according to these guidelines (generally two years of comparable data would be required).

Statement of Financial Position

The statement of financial position would be grouped by major activities (operating, investing, and financing), not by assets, liabilities, and equity. See Illustration 11-8 for an example. Notice that the presentation of assets and liabilities in the business and financing sections clearly separate which net assets management uses in its business and financing activities.

Assets and liabilities are disaggregated into short-term and long-term subcategories within each category. Preparers could present assets and liabilities in order of liquidity if this presentation would provide more relevant information.

ILLUSTRATION 11-7

Proposed Financial Statement Presentation
Statement of Comprehensive Income
for the year ended 2012

		2012
Business		
Operating		
Sales		$ 800,000
Cost of Goods Sold		
Direct Materials	90,000	
Direct Labor	75,000	
Overhead—Depreciation	185,000	
Total Cost of Goods Sold		350,000
Gross Margin		450,000
Selling Expenses:		
Bad Debt Expense	18,000	
Commission Expense	40,000	
Total Selling Expense		58,000
General and Administration Expenses:		
Rent Expense	90,000	
Depreciation Expense	10,000	
Other Expenses	12,000	
Total General and Administration Expense		112,000
Operating Income		**280,000**
Investing		
Equity Income	14,000	
Investment Income		14,000
Business Income		**294,000**
Financing		
Interest Expense	36,000	
Financing Expenses		36,000
Income Taxes		
Current Income Tax Expense	40,000	
Deferred Income Tax Expense	14,000	
Income Tax Expense		54,000
Net Income		**204,000**
Other Comprehensive Income		
Unrealized Gain on Available for Sale Securities		4,000
Total Comprehensive Income		**$ 208,000**

Statement of Cash Flows

There would be fewer changes to the statement of cash flows since the major categories already include operating, investing, and financing. The boards are debating whether to require the direct format rather than allow preparers a choice of the direct versus indirect approach in preparing the operating section of the statement of cash flows. The direct method is more consistent with the proposed objectives of financial statement presentation than an indirect method. Presenting cash receipts and cash payments in the operating category provides a more useful disaggregation of cash flow information. In addition, a direct method presentation helps users relate information about operating assets and liabilities and operating income and expenses to operating cash receipts and payments.

ILLUSTRATION 11-8

Proposed Financial Statement Presentation
Statement of Financial Position
at December 31, 2011 and 2012

	December 31, 2011	*December 31, 2012*
Business		
Operating assets and liabilities		
Short-term		
Accounts Receivable	81,000	75,500
Allowance for doubtful accounts	(12,000)	(10,500)
Inventory	432,000	469,000
Prepaid insurance	20,500	18,000
Short-term assets	521,500	552,000
Accounts Payable–trade	(163,000)	(149,000)
Accrued interest payable	(9,500)	(14,000)
Short-term liabilities	(172,500)	(163,000)
Long-term		
Plant & equipment	613,000	650,000
Accumulated depreciation	(100,000)	(105,000)
Net long-term assets	513,000	545,000
Net operating assets	862,000	934,000
Investing assets		
Long-term		
Investment (equity method)	14,000	15,000
Investments (available for sale)	14,000	17,000
Net long-term assets	28,000	32,000
Net business assets	890,000	966,000
Financing		
Financing assets		
Short-term		
Cash	41,000	34,000
Financing liabilities		
Short-term		
Dividend payable	(20,000)	(16,000)
Short-term loan payable	(55,000)	(70,000)
Short-term liabilities	(75,000)	(86,000)
Long-term		
Bond payable	(100,000)	(145,000)
Net financing liabilities	(134,000)	(197,000)
Income Taxes		
Short-term		
Income taxes payable	(16,000)	(11,000)
Long-term		
Deferred tax liability	(55,000)	(38,000)
Net income tax liability	(71,000)	(49,000)
Net Assets	$ 685,000	$ 720,000
Equity		
Common Stock & paid in capital	220,000	220,000
Retained Earnings	485,000	505,000
Accumulated other Comprehensive Income	(20,000)	(5,000)
Total Equity	$ 685,000	$ 720,000
Accounts Payable—trade	$ 163,000	$ 139,000
Dividend Payable	20,000	16,000
Accrued Interest Payable	9,500	14,000
Accrued Taxes Payable	16,000	11,000
Short-term Loan Payable	55,000	65,000
Bond Payable	100,000	140,000
Deferred Taxes	55,000	38,000
Common Stock ($2 par, 45,000 & 55,000 shares)	90,000	90,000
Capital-in-Excess-of-Par	130,000	130,000
Retained Earnings	485,000	505,000
Less: Treasury Stock (6,000 & 10,000 shares)	(20,000)	(5,000)
Total Liabilities & Equity	$1,103,500	$1,163,000

New Reconciliation Schedule

The proposed presentation model includes a new schedule (to be included in the notes to financial statements) that reconciles cash flows to comprehensive income. This reconciliation schedule disaggregates income into its cash, accrual other than remeasurements, and remeasurement components (such as changes in fair values). Users analyze those components separately because the components often differ in their ability to help users predict future cash flows and assess earnings quality.

Ratios

The change in presentation coupled with the separation of business and financing activities in the statements of comprehensive income and cash flows should make it easier for users to calculate some key financial ratios for an entity's business activities or its financing activities. Ratios computed using working capital amounts now include a mixture of operating, investing, and financing items. The new format would allow a clearer distinction of amounts between operating and nonoperating.

INTERNATIONAL CONVERGENCE ISSUES

There are many obstacles that will need to be overcome before IFRS becomes the standard for accounting in the United States. In the following section, we discuss some of the relevant issues.

LIFO Inventories

There are usually fewer choices allowed in valuing inventory for companies under IFRS than in the United States. For instance, LIFO is not acceptable under international standards. The IASC issued *IAS 2* on inventories recommending specific cost. If specific cost is not determinable, the benchmark is FIFO or weighted average. Also, in the United States, the LIFO conformity rule, established in 1939, requires that taxpayers using LIFO for tax purposes must also use it for financial reporting purposes. Thus one important issue that the SEC must face is the potential costs incurred by firms to switch from LIFO to another method.

Accounting Trends and Techniques, in its survey of 600 largest companies in the United States, reported that 38% of the companies used LIFO for some portion of their inventory (FIFO was used by 64% of the firms). If IFRS were adopted and firms were required to switch to another method, such as FIFO, the LIFO reserve would become taxable. ExxonMobil's LIFO reserve at the end of 2008 was $10 billion (it was $25.4 billion in 2007), while GE's LIFO reserve at the end of 2008 was $706 million dollars. Using a 35% marginal tax rate, this would increase Exxon's and GE's tax by $3.5 billion and $247 million, respectively. It is unlikely that the SEC would allow such large costs to be incurred by firms to switch to international rules. Potential solutions might be for Congress to change the law to either eliminate the LIFO conformity rule or to modify it. Firms currently using LIFO could be significantly affected by a mandatory switch to IFRS.

The House Ways and Means Committee reported that a provision to repeal LIFO for U.S. tax purposes would raise approximately $106 billion over ten years.[5]

Political Process—Avoiding 'National GAAP' On February 15, 2006, the Ministry of Finance of the People's Republic of China announced the issuance of the Accounting Standards for Business Enterprises ("ASBEs") which consist of a new Basic Standard and 38 Specific ASBEs. The ASBEs cover nearly all the topics under the current International Financial Reporting Standards and became mandatory for listed Chinese enterprises on January 1, 2007. These standards include *substantially* all the IFRS with certain exceptions that reflect China's unique circumstances and environment. The first exception is the disclosure requirements for related parties. For instance, under Chinese rules, state enterprises are not by definition considered related parties simply because they are state controlled. These enterprises are thus exempted from related party disclosure provisions. One reason for this exemption is the dominance of government enterprises, making such disclosures particularly cumbersome. The IASB is considering changing the related party disclosure requirements to conform more closely to China's unique characteristics. A second difference is that China allows only the cost method for measuring fixed assets and intangibles. *IAS 16* allows revaluations and recoveries of impairment losses. Chinese officials felt that revaluations allowed firms to manipulate the numbers and therefore did not adopt the revaluation provisions. One other difference is that Chinese rules only allow the equity method of accounting for jointly controlled entities, while *IAS 31* also allows proportionate consolidation. Thus, significant differences remain between IFRS and Chinese GAAP.

The issue facing the IASB is to find a way to encourage individual countries to adopt all provisions of IFRS without 'carving out' selected sections. If each country tweaks the rules, a single global set of accounting standards will not emerge, but rather a jumble of 'national IFRS-like' rules. The SEC, in removing the reconciliation to U.S. GAAP requirement on Form 20-F, requires foreign registrants to adopt IFRS ***as promulgated by the IASB*** in order to avoid the reconciliation. If the firms do not adopt IFRS as promulgated by the IASB, they will still be required to reconcile to U.S. GAAP.

Political Process—Avoiding 'National Pressure' An event occurred in October 2008 which could cause the SEC to reconsider adopting IFRS. On this date, the European Commission met with leaders from Germany, France, Italy, and Britain to discuss the economic crisis. They were concerned that European banks might be at a disadvantage relative to U.S. banks. This concern arose because of the assumed ability of U.S. firms to reclassify assets expected to be traded (carried at fair value) into 'held to maturity' (carried at amortized cost) and avoid fair value measurements (permitted in only rare cases in the United States). IFRS rules did not allow such transfers. The European Commission threatened the IASB to change the rules or the EC would introduce legal changes to override the international rules. The IASB had four days to decide, and ultimately changed the rules and abandoned its own due process. Typically, such changes would require months of work, if not years, by the IASB. This change in the international rules allowed firms to 'backdate' the accounting to the beginning of July 2008. Thus the IASB was significantly

[5] House Ways and Means Committee, "H. R. 3970, Tax Reduction and Reform Act of 2007, October 29, 2007.

swayed by the European Commission toward this rule change due to political pressure. Undoubtedly, this event did not go unnoticed by the SEC. Ultimately, the SEC must determine how independent and credible the IASB is in setting accounting policy. Whereas in the United States the SEC serves to shield the FASB from political pressures, the IASB has no such protector. Thus, this event could play an important role in the SEC's decision regarding the adoption of IFRS, as well as in the decisions of other countries planning to adopt IFRS over the next several years. Further, the event could serve to trigger changes in the IASB to prevent such occurrences in the future.

Private Companies

It is unclear at this point which accounting policies will be required for private companies. The IASB is currently developing IFRS for private entities, while in the United States, it remains likely that U.S. GAAP, or some variant of U.S. GAAP, will continue to be applied for some time to smaller private companies. A current advantage for these companies is the flexibility of electing to report using a tax (or cash) basis. This is unlikely to change. It is too early to predict which direction accounting for private companies will take in the future.

SEC Registration and U.S. Listing for Non-U.S. Companies

In this section, we consider how international firms may issue securities in the United States. A registration with the SEC under the 1934 Securities Act is mandatory for non-U.S. companies that intend to list on a U.S. stock market. Such a registration can be achieved for firms that intend to do only a listing by filing a form *20-F* with the SEC. However, if non-U.S. companies issue securities in the United States along with the U.S. listing, then the sale of these securities must be registered under the 1933 Securities Act, typically through the filing of an *F-1* statement. This registration must be declared effective subsequent to the actual listing or the offering of securities for sale in the event of an equity capital acquisition program. The informational requirements of a *20-F* and an *F-1* are reasonably similar. Foreign companies are required to comply with the SEC continuous reporting requirements in a manner very similar to that of U.S.-listed companies. Annual reporting requirements for U.S. companies involve filing a form *10-K*, and in the case of non-U.S. companies, involve filing a form *20-F* with the SEC. Under the Securities Act of 1934, a non-U.S. company that registered with the SEC and listed its shares on a U.S. exchange would have to file *annual* reports on forms *20-F* and *interim* reports on forms *6-K* in order to keep the registration "current."

LO6 The role of form 20-F.

20-F Statement The *20-F* filing is similar to the *10-K* filing required of any publicly held domestic U.S. company, but the *20-F* allows the non-U.S. company to use IFRS as promulgated by the IASB or to retain its local GAAP reporting. If a company chooses to use its local GAAP (not IFRS), it can do so, as long as it meets one of two alternative conditions for explaining any differences between the reported numbers and numbers derived under U.S. GAAP. The firm may either (1) reconcile net income and the shareholders' equity, thus showing earnings based on U.S. GAAP; or (2) fully disclose all financial information required of U.S. firms, including such detailed information as segmental disclosures. However, if the company chooses to report under IFRS, these conditions are waived, effective November 2007.

The *20-F* is comprised of various subsections, each of which provides detailed information on the company and its securities issues within the United States. The key information provided in the *20-F* includes:

- A description of the firm's business model, its legal structure, regulatory framework, its management, shareholders, management discussion and analysis (MD&A) statement, and information on the structure of the company's outstanding securities and the markets on which those securities are traded.
- A detailed description of the securities that are being registered for U.S. public trading, including definitions of the rights of the shareholders.
- A description of the company's financial structure and the issuer's financial statements (audited two-year comparative balance sheets and three-year comparative income statements and statements of cash flows).
- If the firm adopts IFRS as promulgated by the IASB, the firm is not required to reconcile to U.S. GAAP; otherwise, the firm must provide a reconciliation to U.S. GAAP.

F-1 Statement A first-time offer of securities by any non-U.S. company that comes under the definition of a "foreign private issuer" requires filing an *F-1* statement as the principal registration statement. To qualify as a "foreign private issuer," a non-U.S. company must meet certain conditions of ownership, location of assets, and location of executive officers. The *F-1* forms are typically used only in a first-time offer by non-U.S. issuers, and on subsequent issuance, as long as the company has met certain periodic reporting requirements, a shorter *F-2* or *F-3* form may be used. Though the content and the structure of the registration statement of a non-U.S. issuer can vary from case to case depending on the nature of the offering, there are a few basic characteristics that are common across all types of statements.

In a study of the reconciliation differences between U.S. GAAP and national GAAP, examined over the period 2002–2007, a recent research study found that the sign of income reversed in over 5% of the 724 reconciliations examined (positive using one form of GAAP and negative using the alternative GAAP). The study found that income was higher using U.S. GAAP in 64% of the cases examined, while equity was higher 61% of the time under U.S. GAAP.[6] It should be noted that recent convergence efforts between the FASB and IASB should eliminate many of the differences. For instance, both boards now treat in-process R&D in a similar manner.

The most important component of a registration statement is the offer prospectus. The prospectus contains all information deemed necessary by the SEC for investors to make an informed investing decision. In addition to the financial statements, the prospectus also contains detailed nonfinancial information about the company, such as a description of the business, regulatory structure, management structure, capital structure, shareholding patterns, and shareholder rights. The financial statements may alternatively be presented in accordance with U.S. GAAP, in accordance with IFRS as promulgated by the IASB, or include an audited reconciliation of the home country GAAP numbers to U.S. GAAP. In addition to the prospectus, the *F-1* statement has information about the articles of association of the

[6] 'The market reaction to the reconciliation requirement elimination,' by P. Chaney, D. Jeter, and R. Willis, working paper, Vanderbilt University, 2009.

company, the registrant's bylaws, and significant legal and contractual obligations of the company. Such information is available on request by any related party.

AMERICAN DEPOSITORY RECEIPTS (ADRS): AN OVERVIEW

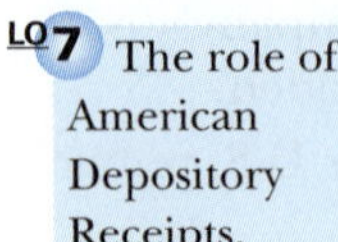

With the globalization of equity markets, both investors and issuers are going beyond their geographical boundaries to look for investments and sources of capital. The complexities in the mechanics of the resulting cross-border investing and capital raising may serve to explain, at least in part, the popularity of the *Depository Receipt (DR)*. A DR is a derivative instrument that usually represents a certain fixed number of publicly traded shares of a non-U.S. corporation. A DR that is traded in the United States is called an *American Depository Receipt (ADR)*, while one that is traded globally (outside the United States) is called a *Global Depository Receipt (GDR)*. An ADR is identical to a GDR in terms of its structure, operation, and legal perspective. ADRs may trade freely, subject to some conditions, like any U.S. security on one of the major exchanges like the *New York Stock Exchange (NYSE)* or NASDAQ, or trade *over-the-counter (OTC)* in the "pink sheet" market. The ADR is treated similarly to a domestic security for the purposes of clearance, settlement, transfer, and ownership.

An intermediary known as the Depository Bank (DR bank) creates ADRs, usually with the consent of the issuing company. The major DR banks are the Bank of New York, J. P. Morgan, and Citibank, who together account for the clear majority of the existing ADR programs. The DR bank is central to the creation and maintenance of the ADR market, providing the interface between the non-U.S. company and the U.S. investors who purchase ADRs. The creation of an ADR involves the purchase of shares of a non-U.S. company from its home markets by the brokers of the DR bank and placement with its custodian. Afterwards, the bank issues ADRs (denominated in U.S. dollars) in the United States equivalent to the shares that were deposited with the home market custodians. This results not only in the transfer of the trading location of the shares from a home country to the United States, but also in the creation of a dollar-denominated U.S. security that represents the shares of a non-U.S. company. In addition to this type of transfer, during the event of a new public offering, U.S. issuers can create ADRs that represent the newly issued shares, which then can be sold directly to the U.S. investors as a part of the offering.

Types of ADR Programs

ADRs may be classified as follows based on their characteristics. *Unsponsored ADRs:* As discussed in the previous section, the DR banks, with consent from the issuer, create most of the ADR programs. However, it is possible for a DR bank to create a DR program without a formal agreement with the issuing non-U.S. company. Such ADR programs, called unsponsored ADRs, usually arise due to existence of a great demand for the company's securities in the U.S. market. However, unsponsored programs are becoming obsolete. *Sponsored ADRs:* Sponsored programs account for over 98% of existing ADR programs in the United States. A sponsored program requires an exclusive agreement between the issuing company and its depository bank prior to the creation of the DR program. The bank agrees to issue ADRs to U.S. investors and to undertake ongoing tasks in providing information, as well as disbursements of various payouts (dividends, rights, etc.) that the company may make from time to time. Sponsored ADRs may be of four types, depending on whether the company registers the ADRs with the SEC and/or whether there is a capital campaign concomitant with the creation of the ADR program. It must be understood here that registration with the SEC is mandatory for a company that wants to list its ADRs on a U.S. stock exchange like the NYSE, NASDAQ, or AMEX. If a company chooses not to register with the SEC, it could still raise capital from private equity markets comprised of large institutional investors, and could thus trade the ADRs on the OTC markets. The following table is useful in understanding the various types of ADRs that exist in the markets today.

Types of Sponsored ADR Programs

	No SEC Registration	*SEC Registration*
Not Issuing Capital	Level I	Level II
Issuing Capital	Rule 144 A	Level III

Level I This method is the simplest way for non-U.S. companies to access the U.S. markets. Under this method, depository banks create an ADR program based on the underlying shares that already trade on the home markets. There is *no* capital raised, and the ADRs are *not* listed on the U.S. markets. Companies must file an *F-6* with the SEC, which requires them to disclose some preliminary information about their operations and their finances. There is no need for a U.S. GAAP reconciliation, and Level I issuers are exempt from continuous reporting with the SEC (as required by publicly traded U.S. companies). Level I programs are often used by non- U.S. companies as a method to familiarize themselves with U.S. equity markets and also to evaluate potential interest in their stock. As of year-end 1998, there were over 800 outstanding Level I programs.

These issues are not traded publicly on U.S. exchanges. Until April 1998, Level I issues were traded on electronic bulletin boards that were part of the OTC market, but subsequent to an SEC rule change, trading in these issues is now confined to the "pink sheet" market.

Level II These types of ADRs are similar to Level I since they do not involve raising new capital, but in contrast to Level I, Level II issues are registered with the U.S. SEC and listed on a major U.S. stock exchange. A U.S. SEC registration and an exchange listing require the company to file with the SEC an *F-6* registration of their ADRs and a *20-F* registration statement listing certain financial disclosures. Level II ADRs have greater visibility because of their public listing.

The following information concerning GlaxoSmithKline's Level II ADR was reported by the firm's depository bank, the Bank of New York.

Symbol:	GSK
CUSIP:	37733W105
Exchange:	NYSE
Ratio:	1 ADR / 2 Ordinary Shares
Country:	United Kingdom
Industry:	Pharmaceuticals-Healthcare
Depository:	Bank of New York
Level of program:	Level II
Effective date:	Dec, 27, 2000

Last price	Opening price	High price	Low price
\$54.19	\$54.45	\$54.60	\$54.12

As of 10/12/06

Level III Firms that want to raise capital from the public equity markets in the United States and also to list on a major U.S. stock exchange use the Level III ADRs. These programs comply with various rules and regulations of the SEC and with the requirements of the stock exchange on which they are traded. Level III ADRs are a part of a capital program and are accompanied by a full SEC registration. At the time of the equity offering, a non-U.S. company files a form *F-1* in order to register the shares underlying the Level III ADRs. Investors are informed of all material aspects of the firm and its business. Financial statements are prepared and firms agree to meet annual reporting requirements by filing form *20-F* and other annual financial disclosures.

Rule 144A Public offerings in the United States by non-U.S. issuers require a registration of their securities under the Securities Act of 1934. However, there are exemptions from such registration requirements for private placements. Rule 144A ADRs are those ADRs that are placed privately among large institutional buyers with over 100 million dollars under management (known as QIB firms) with restrictions on the subsequent trading of these securities. Rule 144A ADRs are neither publicly traded nor listed on any U.S. stock exchanges and can be exchanged only among QIBs. Firms, especially those from emerging markets, have favored the use of this 144A market for raising capital from the private placement market since they can do so without reporting the detailed disclosures that are required for an SEC registration.

SUMMARY

1. *Describe how the changing world environment is leading to an increased focus on international accounting standards (IFRS).* A dramatic rise in cross-border financial activity and the resulting internationalization of equity markets since the late 1980s have transformed the investor profiles of many companies. The movement has been away from a primarily debt-financed business world, in which a relatively informal flow of information between companies and creditors sufficed, to a primarily equity-financed environment in which more financial communication is demanded.

2. *Explain some of the major differences between IFRS and U.S. GAAP.* Some of the areas in which important differences arise include the fact the LIFO inventory is not permitted under IFRS, expenses on the income statement can be listed either by nature or function under IFRS, balance sheet items are generally listed in order of increasing liquidity, extraordinary items are not allowed under IFRS, property, plant and equipment can be revalued on a regular basis under IFRS, reversal of previously written down assets are allowed under IFRS, and development costs are capitalized under IFRS.

3. *List the seven milestones that must be achieved before the SEC will require adoption of IFRS. The seven milestones are:* (1) improvements in accounting standards; (2) the accountability and funding of the IASC Foundation; (3) the improvement in the ability to use interactive data for IFRS reporting; (4) education and training relating to IFRS; (5) limited early use of IFRS where this would enhance comparability for U.S. investors; (6) the anticipated timing of future rulemaking by the Commission; and (7) the implementation of the mandatory use of IFRS by U.S. issuers.

4. *Describe three major joint convergence topics between the IFRS and FASB.* Three of the major convergence topics include accounting for leases, financial statement presentation, and revenue recognition.

5. *List the steps that a non-U.S. company must follow to list its shares on a U.S. stock market.* A registration with the

SEC under the 1934 Securities Act is mandatory for non-U.S. companies that intend to list on a U.S. stock market. Such a registration can be achieved for firms that intend to do only a listing by filing a form *20-F* with the SEC. However, if non-U.S. companies issue securities in the United States along with the U.S. listing, then the sale of these securities must be registered under the 1933 Securities Act, typically through the filing of an *F-1* statement. This registration must be declared effective subsequent to the actual listing or the offering of securities for sale in the event of an equity capital acquisition program.

6. *Explain the role of form* 20-F *filed with the Securities and Exchange Commission.* The *20-F* allows the non-U.S. company to retain its local GAAP reporting and still be able to list on a U.S. stock exchange, so long as it meets one of two alternative conditions for explaining any differences between the reported numbers and numbers derived under U.S. GAAP. The firm may (1) use IFRS as promulgated by the IASB; (2) reconcile net income and shareholders' equity, thus showing earnings based on U.S. GAAP; or (3) fully disclose all financial information required of U.S. firms, including such detailed information as segmental disclosures.
7. *Indicate the role of American Depository Receipts in the issuing of securities of non-U.S. companies in the United States.* A depository receipt (DR) is a derivative instrument usually representing a certain fixed number of publicly traded shares of a non-U.S. corporation. A DR that is traded in the United States is called an American Depository Receipt (ADR). ADRs may trade freely, subject to some conditions, like any U.S. security on one of the major exchanges like the New York Stock Exchange (NYSE), NASDAQ, or the American Stock Exchange (AMEX), or trade over the counter (OTC) in the "pink sheet" market. The ADR is treated similarly to a domestic security for the purposes of clearance, settlement, transfer, and ownership.

APPENDIX A

List of Current International Financial Reporting Standards, Issued by IASC and IASB

IFRS 1	First-time Adoption of International Financial Reporting Standards
IFRS 2	Share-based Payment
IFRS 3	Business Combinations
IFRS 4	Insurance Contracts
IFRS 5	Noncurrent Assets Held for Sale and Discontinued Operations
IFRS 6	Exploration for and Evaluation of Mineral Resources
IFRS 7	Financial Instruments: Disclosures
IFRS 8	Operating Segments (replaces IAS 14 on segment reporting)
IAS 1	Presentation of Financial Statements
IAS 2	Inventories
IAS 7	Cash Flow Statements
IAS 8	Accounting Policies, Changes in Accounting Estimates and Errors
IAS 10	Events After the Balance Sheet Date
IAS 11	Construction Contracts
IAS 12	Income Taxes
IAS 14	Segment Reporting
IAS 16	Property, Plant, and Equipment
IAS 17	Leases
IAS 18	Revenue
IAS 19	Employee Benefits
IAS 20	Accounting for Government Grants and Disclosure of Government Assistance
IAS 21	The Effects of Changes in Foreign Exchange Rates
IAS 23	Borrowing Costs

IAS 24	Related Party Disclosures
IAS 26	Accounting and Reporting by Retirement Benefit Plans
IAS 27	Consolidated and Separate Financial Statements
IAS 28	Investments in Associates
IAS 29	Financial Reporting in Hyperinflationary Economies
IAS 30	Disclosures in the Financial Statements of Banks and Similar Financial Institutions
IAS 31	Interests in Joint Ventures
IAS 32	Financial Instruments: Disclosure and Presentation
IAS 33	Earnings per Share
IAS 34	Interim Financial Reporting
IAS 36	Impairment of Assets
IAS 37	Provisions, Contingent Liabilities, and Contingent Assets
IAS 38	Intangible Assets
IAS 39	Financial Instruments: Recognition and Measurement
IAS 40	Investment Property
IAS 41	Agriculture

QUESTIONS

LO1 1. As mentioned in Chapter 1, the project on business combinations was the first of several joint projects undertaken by the FASB and the IASB in their move to converge standards globally. Nonetheless, complete convergence has not yet occurred, and there are those who believe it to be a poor idea. Discuss the reasons for and against global convergence.

LO4 2. In recent months, virtually every topic that has come to the attention of the standard setters has been undertaken as a joint effort of the FASB and the IASB rather than as an individual effort by one of the two boards. List and discuss some of the joint projects that fall into this category.

LO1 3. What is the rationale for the harmonization of international accounting standards?

LO6 4. Why is the SEC, once so reluctant to accept IAS, now very willing to allow firms using IFRS to issue securities in the U.S. stock market without reconciling to U.S. GAAP?

LO7 5. Discuss the types of ADRs that non-U.S. companies might use to access the U.S. markets.

LO1 6. Describe the attitude of the FASB toward the IASB (International Accounting Standards Board).

LO3 7. How does the FASB view its role in the development of an international accounting system? Currently, two members of the IASB board were affiliated with the FASB. Comment on what effect this might have on the likelihood that the U.S. standard setters will accept the new IASB statements, if any?

 8. List some of the major differences in accounting between IFRS and U.S. GAAP.

Business Ethics

A vice president of marketing for your company has been charged with embezzling nearly $100,000 from the company. The vice president allegedly submitted fraudulent vendor invoices in order to receive payments. As the vice president of marketing for the company, the vice president is authorized to approve the payment of invoices submitted by third-party vendors who did work for the company. After the activities were uncovered, the company responded by stating: "All employees are accountable to our ethics guidelines and procedures. We do not tolerate violations of our ethics policy and will consistently enforce these policies and procedures."

1. How would you evaluate the internal controls of the company?
2. Do you think there are companies that develop comprehensive ethics and compliance programs for mid- and lower-level employees and ignore upper-level executives and managers?
3. Is it an ethical issue if companies are not forthcoming concerning fraudulent activities of top executives in an effort to minimize negative publicity?

EXERCISES

EXERCISE 11-1 **Component Depreciation** LO2

SMC Company purchases a building for $100,000. Included in this cost are $12,000 for electrical systems and $15,000 for the roof. The building is expected to have a 40 year useful life, but the electrical system will last for 20 years and the roof will last 15 years.

Required:

Part A: Assuming that straight-line depreciation is used, compute depreciation expense assuming that U.S. GAAP is used.

Part B: Assuming that straight line depreciation is used, compute depreciation expense for year one assuming IFRS is used (assume component depreciation).

EXERCISE 11-2 **Current International Issues** LO2 LO4

The International Accounting Standards Board (IASB) web address is www.iasb.org. On this web page, there is a section labeled "news." List some of the recent issues concerning the IASB.

EXERCISE 11-3 **Opinions: International Federation** LO2 LO4

The International Federation of Accountants' web address is www.ifac.org. On this page is a section labeled "media center." Next, choose 'articles.' Choose one of the items on this page and write a brief description.

EXERCISE 11-4A **IFRS Balance Sheet** LO2

Air France reports the following balance sheet for the year ended March 31, 2007.

Consolidated Balance Sheets

	March 31, 2007	*March 31, 2006*
		In € millions
Assets		
Goodwill	204	208
Intangible assets	424	428
Flight equipment	11,551	11,017
Other property, plant and equipment	2,007	1,955
Investments in equity associates	228	204
Pension assets	2,097	1,903
Other financial assets (*which includes €835 million of deposits related to financial leases as of March 31, 2007, €895 million as of March 31, 2006*)	1,095	1,182
Deferred tax assets	26	7
Other non-current assets	604	1,082
Total non current assets	18,236	17,986
Other short term financial assets (*which includes €631 million of deposits related to financial leases and investments between 3 months and 1 year as of March 31, 2007, €889 million as of March 31, 2006*)	689	932
Inventories	360	340
Trade accounts receivable	2,610	2,518
Income tax receivables	7	1
Other current assets	1,271	1,756

	March 31, 2007	*March 31, 2006*
		In € millions
Cash and cash equivalents	3,497	2,946
Total current assets	8,434	8,493
Total assets	26,670	26,479
Liabilities and equity		
Issued capital	2,375	2,290
Additional paid-in capital	539	430
Treasury shares	(30)	(58)
Reserves and retained earnings	5,415	5,072
Equity attributable to equity holders of Air France-KLM	8,299	7,734
Minority interest	113	119
Total Equity	8,412	7,853
Provisions and retirement benefits	1,387	1,453
Long-term debt	7,419	7,826
Deferred tax	891	839
Other non-current liabilities	401	417
Total non-current liabilities	10,098	10,535
Provisions	225	192
Current portion of long-term debt	1,098	1,260
Trade accounts payable	2,131	2,039
Deferred revenue on ticket sales	2,217	2,062
Current tax liabilities	21	167
Other current liabilities	2,335	2,269
Bank overdrafts	133	102
Total current liabilities	8,160	8,091
Total liabilities	18,258	18,626
Total liabilities and equity	26,670	26,479

Required:

A. What order are assets listed on the balance sheet?

B. Comment on other differences (IFRS relative to U.S. GAAP) that you might notice on the balance sheet.

C. What is the current ratio for the year's ending March 31, 2006 and 2007?

D. What is the ratio of long-term debt to equity for the year's ending March 31, 2006 and 2007?

E. Are there any typical balance sheet ratios that can't be computed using the IFRS-based financial statement?

PROBLEMS

PROBLEM 11-1 

British Petroleum's income statement was prepared using IFRS is presented below (in $ millions).

Group Income Statement
for the year ended 31 December

	2008	*2007*
Sales and other operating revenues	361,143	284,365
Earnings from jointly controlled entities—after interest and tax	3,023	3,135
Earnings from associates—after interest and tax	798	697
Interest and other revenues	736	754
Total revenues	365,700	288,951

Gains on sale of businesses and fixed assets	1,353	2,487
Total revenues and other income	367,053	291,438
Purchases	266,982	200,766
Production and manufacturing expenses	29,183	25,915
Production and similar taxes	6,526	4,013
Depreciation, depletion and amortization	10,985	10,579
Impairment and losses on sale of businesses and fixed assets	1,733	1,679
Exploration expense	882	756
Distribution and administration expenses	15,412	15,371
Fair value (gain) loss on embedded derivatives	111	7
Profit before interest and taxation from continuing operations	35,239	32,352
Finance costs	1,547	1,393
Net finance income relating to pensions and other post-retirement benefits	(591)	(652)
Profit before taxation from continuing operations	34,283	31,611
Taxation	12,617	10,442
Profit from continuing operations	21,666	21,169
Loss from Innovene operations	—	—
Profit for the year	21,666	21,169
Attributable to		
BP shareholders	21,157	20,845
Minority interest	509	324
	21,666	21,169
Earnings per share—cents		
Profit for the year attributable to BP shareholders		
Basic	112.59	108.76
Diluted	111.56	107.84
Profit from continuing operations attributable to BP shareholders		
Basic	112.59	108.76
Diluted	111.56	107.84

ExxonMobil Corporation's income statement was prepared using U.S. GAAP is presented below (in $ million).

Consolidated Statement of Income

	2008	*2007*
	(millions of dollars)	
Revenues and other income		
Sales and other operating revenue *(1)*	$459,579	$390,328
Income from equity affiliates	11,081	8,901
Other income *(2)*	6,699	5,323
Total revenues and other income	$477,359	$404,552
Costs and other deductions		
Crude oil and product purchases	$249,454	$199,498
Production and manufacturing expenses	37,905	31,885
Selling, general and administrative expenses	15,873	14,890
Depreciation and depletion	12,379	12,250
Exploration expenses, including dry holes	1,451	1,469
Interest expense	673	400
Sales-based taxes *(1)*	34,508	31,728
Other taxes and duties	41,719	40,953
Income applicable to minority interests	1,647	1,005
Total costs and other deductions	$395,609	$334,078

	2008	2007
Income before income taxes	$ 81,750	$ 70,474
Income taxes	36,530	29,864
Net income	$ 45,220	$ 40,610
Net income per common share (dollars)	$ 8.78	$ 7.36
Net income per common share—assuming dilution (dollars)	$ 8.69	$ 7.28

Required:

A. Are expenditures reported on BP's income statement reported by function or by nature of the expense? Be specific. Do you think that this format is more or less useful for users of the financial statements?

B. On the BP income statement, what is the earnings from affiliates usually referred to in the United States?

C. On ExxonMobil's income statement, are the expenses listed by function or by nature.

D. Compare the performance of BP relative to ExxonMobil? Is it easy to compare the numbers from companies using IFRS versus companies using U.S. GAAP?

E. Does it matter that BP using FIFO and ExxonMobil using LIFO for inventory? The LIFO reserve decreased by $15.4 billion dollars in 2008.

PROBLEM 11-2 **IFRS Income Statement and Terminology Differences** LO2

The first two lines of Unilever Group's 2008 consolidated income statement (using IFRS) reports the following amounts (in euros millions):

Income Statement

Continuing Operations	2008	2007
Turnover	40,523	40,187
Operating profit	7,167	5,245
Footnotes		
In footnote 3, the following is disclosed:		
Turnover	40,523	40,187
Cost of sales	21,342	20,558
Gross profit	19,181	19,629
Distribution and selling costs	9,309	9,429
Administration expenses	2,705	4,895
Operating profit	7,167	5,245

Required:

A. On the income statement, the first two lines in Unilever's income statement are Turnover and then Operating profit. What does the term 'Turnover' mean? Which costs are typically reported between 'Turnover' and operating profit?

B. How useful is Unilever's income statement presentation considering the information that is disclosed in footnote 3 rather than being reported on the face of the income statement?

PROBLEM 11-3 **IFRS Illustrated Financial Statements** LO2

Each of the Big 4 auditors along with Grant Thornton and BDO International provide illustrative financial statements on their Web pages.

http://www.pwc.com
http://www.grantthornton.com
http://www.kpmgifrg.com
http://www.bdointernational.com
http://www.iasplus.com/fs/fs.htm
http://www.ey.com/global

Required:

Using one of the Web pages, find an example of a financial statement prepared using IFRS.

A. Provide a Web search and provide a summary of differences between the IFRS income statement and a typical income statement prepared using U.S. GAAP.

B. Provide a Web search and provide a summary of differences between the IFRS balance sheet and a typical balance sheet prepared using U.S. GAAP.

C. Provide a Web search and provide a summary of differences between the IFRS statement of cash flows and a cash flow statement prepared using U.S. GAAP.

PROBLEM 11-4 **Financial Statement Presentation—Statement of Financial Position** LO4

Balance Sheet
at December 31, 2011 and 2010

	December 31, 2010	*December 31, 2011*
Cash	$ 49,200	$ 40,800
Trading Investments	16,800	20,400
Accounts Receivable	97,200	90,600
Allowance for doubtful accounts	(14,400)	(12,600)
Inventory	518,400	562,800
Prepaid insurance	24,600	21,600
Plant & equipment	735,600	780,000
Accumulated depreciation	(120,000)	(126,000)
Investment in Found Inc. (equity method)	16,800	18,000
Total assets	$1,324,200	$1,395,600
Accounts Payable—trade	$ 195,600	$ 178,800
Dividend payable	24,000	19,200
Accrued interest payable	11,400	16,800
Accrued taxes payable	19,200	13,200
Short-term loan payable	66,000	84,000
Bond payable	135,000	186,000
Discount on bond payable	(15,000)	(12,000)
Deferred taxes	66,000	45,600
Common Stock ($2 par)	108,000	108,000
Capital-in-excess-of-par	156,000	156,000
Retained Earnings	582,000	606,000
Less: Treasury Stock	(24,000)	(6,000)
Total Liabilities & Equity	$1,324,200	$1,395,600

Required:

Prepare a statement of financial position using the proposed new format as described in the chapter.

PROBLEM 11-5 **Financial Statement Presentation—Statement of Comprehensive Income** LO4

Income Statement
for year ended 2011

Sales		$ 800,000
Cost of Goods Sold		350,000
Gross margin		$ 450,000
Expenses:		
Bad debt expense	18,000	
Depreciation expense	40,000	
Interest expense	36,000	
Wage expense	90,000	
Loss on sale of equipment	10,000	
Other expenses	12,000	(206,000)

Other Income:		
Gain on bond retirement	14,000	
Equity income	7,000	21,000
Income before taxes		$265,000
Income tax expense (40%)		106,000
Net Income		159,000

In the statement of stockholders' equity, the following information was available.

Net income	159,000
Loss on available for sale securities	11,000
Comprehensive income	148,000

Required:

Prepare a statement of comprehensive income using the proposed new format as described in the chapter.

PROBLEM 11-6 Operating and Capital Leases LO4

The following footnote was disclosed at the beginning of 2011 (January 1, 2011).

At January 1, 2011

Year	*Capital Lease Payment*	*Operating Lease Payment*
2011	$ 5,000	$ 6,000
2012	5,000	6,000
2013	5,000	6,000
2014	5,000	
2015	5,000	
Total payments	$25,000	$18,000
Interest (10%)	6,046	
Present value	$18,954	

The capital lease began on January 1, 2010 when the fair value of the capital lease was $21,776 (with a six-year life). The operating lease began on January 1, 2011 when the fair value of the operating lease at the inception of the lease was $14,921 (with a three-year lease term). Straight-line depreciation is used for all assets. Each lease requires equal annual payments to be made at year-end.

Required:

1. Under existing U.S. GAAP, what is the amount of lease liability recorded on the balance sheet at January 1, 2011?
2. If the proposed changes in accounting for leases become authoritative, what would be the amount of lease liability recorded on the balance sheet at January 1, 2011?
3. Which approach (part 1 or part 2) do you think provides more relevant information to the users of the financial statements?

12

ACCOUNTING FOR FOREIGN CURRENCY TRANSACTIONS AND HEDGING FOREIGN EXCHANGE RISK

LEARNING OBJECTIVES

1. Distinguish between the terms "measured" and "denominated."
2. Describe what is meant by a foreign currency transaction.
3. Understand some of the more common foreign currency transactions.
4. Identify three stages of concern to accountants for foreign currency transactions, and explain the steps used to translate foreign currency transactions for each stage.
5. Describe a forward exchange contract.
6. Explain the use of forward contracts as a hedge of an unrecognized firm commitment.
7. Identify some of the common situations in which a forward exchange contract can be used as a hedge.
8. Describe a derivative instrument and understand how it may be used as a hedge.
9. Explain how exchange gains and losses are reported for fair value hedges and cash flow hedges.

American International Group Inc. (AIG) owes Wall Street firms over $10 billion for speculative trades classified as 'credit protection instruments.' AIG's financial products unit put billions of dollars at risk through speculative bets on the direction of pools of mortgage assets and corporate debt. The bailout package that AIG received does not cover these trades and the company is trying to raise funds to pay off its partners.[1]

Many companies in the United States engage in international activities such as exporting or importing goods, establishing a foreign branch, or holding an equity investment in a foreign company. Recording and reporting problems are encountered when transactions with a foreign company or the financial statements of a foreign branch or investee are measured in a currency other than U.S. currency.

[1] *WSJ*, December 10, 2008, AIG Faces $10 Billion in Losses on Bad Debts, page c1.

Transactions to be settled in a foreign currency must be translated—that is, expressed in dollars—before they can be aggregated with the domestic transactions of the U.S. firm. When a foreign branch or investee maintains its accounts and prepares its financial statements in terms of the currency of the country in which it is domiciled, the accounts must be translated from the foreign currency into dollars before financial statements for the combined entity are prepared. Translation is necessary because useful financial reports cannot be prepared until all transactions and account balances are stated in a common unit of currency.

In addition, the receivables or payables denominated in foreign currencies are subject to gains and losses because of changes in exchange rates. Also, firms make commitments or have budgeted forecasted transactions denominated in foreign currencies that are also subject to gains and losses from changes in exchange rates. Many companies resort to hedging strategies using derivatives to minimize the impact of these exchange rate changes on their financial statements. Derivative instruments can be characterized by volatile market values, and the firm's exposure to risk is usually not adequately represented by the amount reported in the books (carrying value) because of the great potential for future losses (and gains). Thus the accounting for these instruments is an important but difficult task.

Because of the widespread involvement of U.S. companies in foreign activities, accountants must be familiar with the problems associated with accounting for these activities. The expansion of international business has been of particular concern to accountants because of developments in the worldwide monetary system. These developments, coupled with the existence of a number of acceptable methods of translating foreign financial statements and reporting gains or losses on foreign currency fluctuations, have drawn the attention of the FASB at various times.[2] This chapter includes a discussion of the nature and use of exchange rates in the translation process, as well as the accounting standards applied in the translation of transactions measured in a foreign currency. Also, an introduction to hedge accounting is provided. The translation of accounts maintained in a foreign currency is discussed in the next chapter.

EXCHANGE RATES—MEANS OF TRANSLATION

Transactions that are to be settled in a foreign currency and financial statements of an affiliate maintained in a foreign currency are translated (converted) into dollars by multiplying the number of units of the foreign currency by a direct exchange rate. Thus, ***translation*** is the process of expressing monetary amounts that are stated in terms in a foreign currency into the currency of the reporting entity by using an appropriate exchange rate. An ***exchange rate*** is the ratio between a unit of one currency and the amount of another currency for which that unit can be exchanged at a particular time.

[2] The discussion in this chapter is based primarily on the accounting prescribed in *SFAS No. 52*, "Foreign Currency Translation" (Norwalk, CT: FASB, 1981), and *SFAS No. 133*, "Accounting for Derivative Instruments and Hedging Activities" (Norwalk, CT: FASB, 1998) [ASC 830 and 815].

"The yen fell against the dollar during Friday morning trading in New York. However, the Japanese currency gained ground versus the pound and euro. The move came amid the release of Japanese industrial production and consumer price data."[3]

A ***direct exchange quotation*** is one in which the exchange rate is quoted in terms of how many units of the domestic currency can be converted into ***one unit of foreign currency***. For example, a direct quotation of U.S. dollars for one British pound of 1.517 means that $1.517 could be exchanged for one British pound. To translate pounds into dollars, the number of pounds is multiplied by the direct exchange rate expressed in dollars per pound. Exchange rates are also often stated in terms of converting ***one unit of the domestic currency*** into units of a foreign currency, which is called an ***indirect quotation***. In the preceding example, one U.S. dollar could be converted into .6592 pound (1.00/1.517). To translate pounds into dollars, the number of pounds could also be divided by the indirect exchange rate (pounds per dollar).

Exchange rates may be quoted as either a spot rate or a forward rate. The ***spot rate*** is the rate at which currencies can be exchanged today, whereas the ***forward*** or ***future rate*** is the rate at which currencies can be exchanged at some future date. The forward rate is an exchange rate established at the time a forward exchange contract is negotiated. A ***forward exchange contract*** is a contract to exchange at a specified rate (the ***forward rate***) currencies of different countries on a stipulated future date. Before the currencies are exchanged, the spot rate may move above or below the contracted forward exchange rate, but this has no effect on the forward rate established when the forward exchange contract was negotiated. In both the spot and forward markets, a foreign exchange trader provides a quotation for buying (the ***bid rate***) and a quotation for selling (the ***offer rate***) foreign currency. The trader's buying rate will be lower than the quoted selling rate, and the spread between the two rates is profit for the trader. Exchange rates are reported daily in terms of both direct and indirect quotations (see Illustration 12-1) in the financial section of many newspapers.

The relationship between major currencies is determined largely by supply and demand factors, called **floating rates**. Floating rates increase the risk to companies doing business with a foreign company[4] because after a rate change occurs, all transactions are conducted at the new rate until the next change occurs. Because the amount to be received or paid is affected by a change in exchange rates, there is a direct economic impact on a company's operations. For example, a payable to be settled in 100,000 yen has a dollar equivalent value of $434 when the direct exchange rate is $.00434. An increase in the value of the yen to $.00625 would result in an increase in the payable to $625.

The selection of an exchange rate to be used in the translation process is complicated by the fact that some countries maintain multiple exchange rates. The government of a country may maintain official rates that differ from the market-determined rate, depending on the nature of the transaction. For example, a government may establish a set exchange rate for "essential goods and services" and allow the exchange rate for nonessential goods and services to float.

---

[3] Quote.com, 9/26/06.

[4] The concepts of economic exposure and accounting exposure are not identical. A company's economic exposure may be broadly defined as the uncertainty associated with the effect of exchange rate changes on the expected cash flows of the reporting entity. Accounting exposure, in contrast, is directly related to accounts that are translated at the current exchange rate.

ILLUSTRATION 12-1

Currencies **February 26, 2009**
U.S.-dollar foreign-exchange rates

	—Thurs—		US$ vs,		—Thurs—		US$ vs,
Country/currency	*in US$*	*per US$*	*YTD chg (%)*	*Country/currency*	*in US$*	*per US$*	*YTD chg (%)*
Americas				**Europe**			
Argentina peso	.2813	3.5549	**2.9**	**Czech Rep.** Koruna	.04519	22.129	**15.1**
Brazil real	.4245	2.3557	**1.8**	**Denmark** krone	.1710	5.8480	**9.8**
Canada dollar	.7980	1.2531	**3.0**	**Euro area** euro	1.2739	.7850	**9.7**
1-mos forward	.7979	1.2533	**3.0**	**Hungary** forint	.004233	236.24	**24.3**
3-mos forward	.7983	1.2527	**3.0**	**Norway** krone	.1439	6.9493	**–0.1**
6-mos forward	.7995	1.2508	**3.0**	**Poland** zloty	.2696	3.7092	**24.9**
Chile peso	.001676	596.66	**–6.5**	**Russia** ruble	.02803	35.676	**16.8**
Colombia peso	.0003919	2551.67	**13.5**	**Sweden** krona	.1114	8.9767	**14.7**
Ecuador US dollar	1	1	**unch**	**Switzerland** franc	.8591	1.1640	**9.1**
Mexico peso	.0668	14.9745	**9.1**	1-mos forward	.8595	1.1635	**9.1**
Peru new sol	.3082	3.245	**3.5**	3-mos forward	.8609	1.1616	**9.0**
Uruguay peso	.04290	23.31	**–4.4**	6-mos forward	.8632	1.1585	**9.0**
Venezuela b. fuerte	.465701	2.1473	**unch**	**Turkey** lira	.5912	1.6915	**9.8**
Asia-Pacific				**UK pound**	1.4307	.6990	**2.0**
				1-mos forward	1.4306	.6990	**1.9**
Australian dollar	.6493	1.5401	**9.6**	3-mos forward	1.4306	.6990	**1.8**
China yuan	.1463	6.8366	**0.2**	6-mos forward	1.4308	.6989	**1.8**
Hong Kong dollar	.1290	7.7538	**unch**				
India rupee	.01986	50.353	**3.6**	**Middle East/Africa**			
Indonesia rupiah	.0000835	11976	**9.8**	**Bahrain** dinar	2.6529	.3769	**unch**
Japan yen	.010168	98.35	**8.4**	**Eqypt** pound	.1787	5.5950	**1.7**
1-mos forward	.010172	98.31	**8.4**	**Israel** shekel	.2392	4.1806	**10.6**
3-mos forward	.010188	98.15	**8.4**	**Jordan** dinar	1.4104	.7090	**0.1**
6-mos forward	.010217	97.88	**8.3**	**Kuwait** dinar	3.4071	.2935	**6.2**
Malaysia ringgit	.2724	3.6711	**6.3**	**Lebanon** pound	.0006664	1500.60	**–0.5**
New Zealand dollar	.5085	1.9666	**15.3**	**Saudi Arabia** riyal	.2666	3.7509	**–0.1**
Pakistan rupee	.01252	79.872	**1.0**	**South Africa** rand	.1009	9.9108	**5.5**
Philippines peso	.0207	48.263	**1.7**	**UAE** dirham	.2723	3.6724	**unch**
Singapore dollar	.6502	1.5380	**7.4**				
South Korea won	.0006591	1517.22	**20.1**				
Taiwan dollar	.02870	34.843	**6.3**				
Thailand baht	.02781	35.958	**13.4**				
Vietnam dong	.00005720	17482	**unch**				

Note: Based on trading among banks of $1 million and more, as quoted at 4 p.m. ET by Reuters.

The yen sank sharply against the dollar and the euro Thursday as month-end flows intensified the pressure on a currency already being sold in response to more fundamental concerns.[5]

MEASURED VERSUS DENOMINATED

LO 1 Measured versus denominated.

Transactions are normally ***measured*** and recorded in terms of the currency in which the reporting entity prepares its financial statements. This currency is usually the

[5] 'Yen sinks against dollar, euro' by Don Curren WSJ ,c10, February 27, 2009.

domestic currency of the country in which the company is domiciled and is called the ***reporting currency***. In subsequent illustrations, the U.S. dollar is assumed to be the reporting currency of U.S.-based firms. Assets and liabilities are ***denominated*** in a currency if their amounts are fixed in terms of that currency. Thus a transaction between two U.S. companies requiring payment of a fixed number of dollars is both measured and denominated in dollars. In a transaction between a U.S. firm and a foreign company, the two parties usually negotiate whether the settlement is to be made in dollars or in the domestic currency of the foreign company. If the transaction is to be settled by the payment of a fixed amount of foreign currency, the U.S. firm measures the receivable or payable in dollars, but the transaction is denominated in the specified foreign currency. To the foreign company, the transaction is both measured and denominated in its domestic currency.

FOREIGN CURRENCY TRANSACTIONS

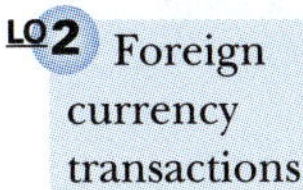

A transaction that requires payment or receipt (settlement) in a foreign currency is called a ***foreign currency transaction***. A transaction with a foreign company that is to be settled in dollars is not a foreign currency transaction to a U.S. firm because the number of dollars to be received or paid to settle the account is fixed and remains unaffected by subsequent changes in the exchange rate. Thus a transaction of a U.S. firm with a foreign entity to be settled in dollars is accounted for in the same manner as if the transaction had been with a U.S. company.

A foreign currency transaction will be settled in a foreign currency, and the U.S. firm exposed to the risk of unfavorable changes in the exchange rate that may occur between the date the transaction is entered into and the date the account is settled. For example, assume that a U.S. firm purchased goods from a French firm and the U.S. firm is to settle the liability by the payment of 20,000 euros. The French firm would measure and record the transaction as normal because the billing is in its reporting currency. Because the billing is in a foreign currency (denominated in euros), the U.S. firm must translate the amount of the foreign currency payable into dollars before the transaction is entered in its accounts. An increase (decrease) in the direct exchange rate will increase (decrease) the number of dollars required to buy the fixed number of euros needed to settle the foreign currency liability.

The ***direct exchange rate*** is often said to be increasing, or the foreign currency unit to be strengthening, if more dollars are needed to acquire the foreign currency units. If fewer dollars are needed, then the foreign currency is weakening or depreciating in relation to the dollar (the direct exchange rate is decreasing). Consider the following information.

	Direct Exchange Rates	
	Yen Strengthens $ Weakens	*Yen Weakens $ Strengthens*
Beginning of year	$1 = 1 yen	$1 = 1 yen
End of year	$2 = 1 yen	$.5 = 1 yen

Would a U.S. company holding a 10,000 *receivable* denominated in yen prefer the yen to strengthen or weaken? In this case, the company prefers a strengthened yen because the equivalent of more dollars would be received and an exchange gain would be incurred. If the transaction involved a *payable* denominated in yen, the firm would have incurred an exchange rate loss because more dollars would have to be paid. As will be shown later, because firms cannot perfectly predict changes in exchange rates, the U.S. firm may ***hedge***, that is, protect itself against an unfavorable change in the exchange rate by using derivatives.

In this chapter, we discuss the accounting for importing or exporting goods. Then we provide an introduction to hedging the risk of foreign currency rate changes.

Some currencies have undergone major changes in comparison to the U.S. dollar. Consider the changes in the following direct exchange rates between the U.S. dollar and the Brazilian real and the Australian dollar:

	U.S. Dollars to Convert to Foreign Currency			
	1/1/2000	*8/28/2001*	*10/12/06*	*Total % Change*
Australian dollar	$0.6565	$0.5293	$0.7509	14.4%
Brazilian real	$0.5435	$0.3907	$0.4647	(14.5%)

In both cases, from 2000 to 2001, the U.S. dollar strengthened relative to the other currencies. However, since 2001, both currencies have strengthened relative to the dollar. In general, over the time period reported, the U.S. dollar has strengthened relative to the real but weakened relative to the Australian dollar. One way to consider whether a currency has strengthened or weakened is to consider the direct exchange rate as the cost of the foreign currency. For instance, when the direct exchange rate increases, the currency is more valuable, so the currency has strengthened relative to the U.S. dollar.

Importing or Exporting of Goods or Services

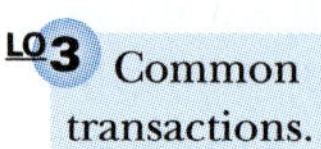

Probably the most common form of foreign currency transaction is the exporting or importing of goods or services. In each unsettled foreign currency transaction, there are three stages of concern to the accountant. These stages and the appropriate exchange rate to use in translating accounts denominated in units of foreign currency (except for forward exchange contracts) are as follows:

LO4 Three stages of concern.

1. ***At the date the transaction is first recognized in conformity with GAAP.*** Each asset, liability, revenue, expense, gain, or loss arising from the transaction is measured and recorded in dollars by multiplying the units of foreign currency by the current direct exchange rate. (The ***current exchange rate*** is the spot rate in effect on a given date.)
2. ***At each balance sheet date that occurs between the transaction date and the settlement date.*** Recorded balances that are denominated in a foreign currency are adjusted using the spot rate in effect at the balance sheet date, and the transaction gain or loss is recognized currently in earnings.
3. ***At the settlement date.*** In the case of a foreign currency payable, a U.S. firm must convert U.S. dollars into foreign currency units to settle the account, whereas foreign currency units received to settle a foreign currency receivable will be converted into dollars. Although translation is not required, a transaction gain or loss is recognized if the number of dollars paid or received upon conversion does not equal the carrying value of the related payable or receivable.

Using the spot rate to translate foreign currency receivables and payables at each measurement date ***provides an estimate of the number of dollars to be received or to be paid to settle the account.*** Note that both gains and losses result in adjustments to the receivable or payable, approximating a form of current value accounting. The increase or decrease in the expected cash flow is generally reported as a foreign currency ***transaction gain or loss***, sometimes referred to as an ***exchange gain or loss***, in determining net income for the current period.[6]

Importing Transaction To illustrate an importing transaction, assume that on December 1, 2007, a U.S. firm purchased 100 units of inventory from a French firm for 500,000 euros to be paid on March 1, 2008. The firm's fiscal year-end is December 31. Assume further that the U.S. firm did not engage in any form of hedging activity. The spot rates for euros ($/euro) at various times are as follow:

	Spot Rate
Transaction date—December 1, 2007	$1.25
Balance sheet date—December 31, 2007	1.28
Settlement date—March 1, 2008	1.27

The U.S. firm would prepare the following journal entry on December 1, 2007:

Dec. 1	Purchases	625,000	
	Accounts Payable (500,000 euros × $1.25/euro)		625,000

At the balance sheet date, the accounts payable denominated in foreign currency is adjusted using the exchange rate (spot rate) in effect at the balance sheet date. The entry is

Dec. 31 Transaction Loss	15,000	
Accounts Payable		15,000

Accounts payable valued at 12/31 (500,000 euros × $1.28/euro)	$640,000
Accounts payable valued at 12/1 (500,000 euros × $1.25/euro)	625,000
Adjustment to accounts payable needed	$ 15,000
or	
[500,000 euros × ($1.28 − $1.05) = $15,000]	

If the exchange rate had declined below $1.25,[7] for example to $1.23, the U.S. firm would have recognized a gain of $10,000 since it would have taken only $615,000 (500,000 euros × $1.23) to settle the $625,000 recorded liability.

Before the settlement date, the U.S. firm must buy euros in order to satisfy the liability. With a change in the exchange rate to $1.27, the firm must pay $635,000 on March 1, 2008, to acquire the 500,000 euros. The journal entry to record the

[6] One exception to this treatment of transaction gains and losses would involve intercompany transactions that are of a long-term financing or capital nature between an investor and an investee that are consolidated, combined, or accounted for by the equity method. These are accounted for as a component of stockholders' equity.

[7] Throughout this chapter, we often state the exchange rate simply in dollars; thus, a rate of $1.25 means $1.25 per unit of foreign currency (euro in this case).

settlement is:

Mar. 1	Accounts Payable	640,000	
	Transaction Gain		5,000
	Cash (500,000 euros × $1.27/euro)		635,000

Over the three-month period, the decision to delay making payment cost the firm $10,000 (the $635,000 cash paid less the original payable amount of $625,000). This net amount was recognized as a loss of $15,000 in 2007 and a gain of $5,000 in 2008.

Note in the preceding example that at December 31, the balance sheet date, a transaction loss was recognized on the open account payable. Such a loss is considered unrealized because the account has not yet been settled or closed. When an account payable (or receivable) is settled or closed, a transaction gain or loss on the settlement is considered realized. The FASB reasoned that users of financial statements are best served by reporting the effects of exchange rate changes on a firm's financial position in the accounting period in which they occur, even though they are unrealized and may reverse or partially reverse in a subsequent period, as in the illustration above. This procedure is criticized, however, because under GAAP, gains are not ordinarily reported until realized and because the recognition of unrealized gains and losses results in increased earnings volatility.

Exporting Transaction Now assume that the U.S. firm sold 100 units of inventory for 500,000 euros to a French firm. All other facts are the same as those for the importing transaction. The journal entries to record this exporting transaction on the books of the U.S. company are:

December 1, 2007—Date of Transaction

Accounts Receivable (500,000 euros × $1.25)	625,000	
Sales		625,000

December 31, 2007—Balance Sheet Date

Accounts Receivable ($640,000−$625,000)	15,000	
Transaction Gain		15,000
The receivable valued at 12/31: 500,000 euros × $1.28 =	$640,000	
The receivable valued at 12/1: 500,000 euros × $1.25 =	$625,000	
Change in the value of the receivable	$ 15,000	

March 1, 2008—Settlement Date

Cash (500,000 euros × $1.27)	635,000	
Transaction Loss	5,000	
Accounts Receivable		640,000

A comparison of the entries to record the exporting transaction with those prepared to record an importing transaction reveals that a movement in the exchange rate has an opposite effect on the company's reported income. That is, the increase in the exchange rate from $1.25 to $1.28 resulted in a transaction gain in the case of a foreign currency receivable, whereas a transaction loss was reported in the case of a foreign currency payable. When the exchange rate decreased from $1.28 to $1.27, a transaction loss was reported on the exposed receivable, whereas a transaction gain was reported on the exposed payable. Thus one tool available to management to hedge a potential loss on a foreign currency receivable is to enter into a transaction to establish a liability to be settled in the same foreign currency. Similarly, a liability to be settled in units of a foreign currency can be hedged by entering into a receivable transaction denominated in the same foreign currency. These relationships are summarized in the following chart.

	Balance Sheet		
	Exposed Account	*Effect on Balance Reported*	*Income Statement Effect*
Increase in Direct Exchange Rate			
Importing Transaction	Payable	Increase	Transaction loss
Exporting Transaction	Receivable	Increase	Transaction gain
Decrease in Direct Exchange Rate			
Importing Transaction	Payable	Decrease	Transaction gain
Exporting Transaction	Receivable	Decrease	Transaction loss

How should a transaction gain or loss be reported? In the previous examples, the dollar amount recorded in the Sales account and the Purchases account was determined by the exchange rate prevailing at the transaction date. Adjustments to the foreign-currency-denominated receivable or payable were recorded directly to transaction gain or loss. Under this approach, referred to as the ***two-transaction approach***, the sale or purchase is viewed as a transaction separate and distinct from the financing arrangement. Thus the transaction gain or loss does not result from an operating decision to buy or sell goods or services in a foreign market but from a financial decision to delay the payment or receipt of foreign currency and not to hedge the exposed receivable or payable against possible unfavorable currency rate changes.

An alternative view that was rejected by the FASB considers the initial transaction and settlement to be one transaction. Supporters of this method contend that the initial transaction is incomplete and the amounts recorded are estimates until such time as the total sacrifice from the purchase (units of domestic currency paid) or the total benefits from the sale (units of domestic currency received) are known. Under this view, transaction gains or losses should be accounted for as an adjustment to the cost of the asset purchased or to the revenue recorded in a sales transaction. There is an obvious implementation problem with this method when the sale or purchase is recorded in one fiscal period and the receipt or payment occurs in another period.

Bunge, an agribusiness and food company, reported foreign exchange gains and losses ranging from a 92 million dollar gain to a 22 million dollar loss between 2003 and 2005 on its 2005 annual report. Lands' End reported in its fiscal 2000 annual report that foreign currency transaction gains and losses are reported in "other income and expenses." It also stated that $3.8 million of losses were reported as "other expense" on the income statement in fiscal 1998, while the amounts of losses in fiscal years 1999 and 2000 were $1.9 million and $0.8 million, respectively.

TEST YOUR KNOWLEDGE

NOTE: Solutions to ***Test Your Knowledge*** questions are found at the end of each chapter before the end-of-chapter questions.

Multiple Choice

On December 1, 2009, SMC entered into a transaction to import raw materials from a foreign country. The account is to be settled March 1 with the payment of 50,000 euros. The spot rate for euros on December 1 was $1.4/euro and on March 1 was $1.44/euro.

1. If SMC does not hedge the payable, raw materials will be recorded on the books on March 1, 2010 at what amount?
   a. 50,000 euros
   b. $72,000
   c. $70,000
   d. None of the above
2. What is the total amount of the transaction gain or loss to be included in net income?
   a. $2,000 gain
   b. $2,000 loss
   c. No gain or loss is recognized until the raw materials are sold
   d. There is no gain or loss. The change in the value of the raw materials offsets the change in the payable.

Hedging Foreign Exchange Rate Risk

Derivative Instruments After the issuance of *SFAS No. 52* on foreign currency translation, the FASB became aware that firms were using creative instruments with increasing frequency to accomplish their desired hedging, many of which were not included in the scope of *SFAS No. 52.* Consequently, the FASB issued another standard, *SFAS No. 133* **[ASC 815]**, which expanded the scope of accounting for hedges. Under these newer guidelines, certain designated hedges are accounted for using ***hedge accounting***. This will be elaborated upon later.

RELATED CONCEPTS

Many assets and liabilities do not have readily observable market values and measurement often relies on *present values*. The use of simplifying assumptions aims for present value measurements that are sufficiently *reliable* and more *relevant* than undiscounted measurements.

A ***derivative instrument*** may be defined as a financial instrument that, by its terms at inception or upon occurrence of a specified event, provides the holder (or writer) with the right (or obligation) to participate in some or all of the price changes of another *underlying* value of measure, but does not require the holder to own or deliver the underlying value of measure. Thus its value is *derived* from the underlying value of measure. The underlying value of measure may be one or more referenced financial instruments, commodities, or other assets, or other specific items to which a rate, an index of prices, or another market indicator is applied. In most cases, derivatives differ from traditional instruments (stocks and bonds, for example) in that the eventual dollar amount of the performance is dependent upon subsequent value changes, rather than upon a static measure, and the eventual outcome is necessarily favorable to one of the parties involved and unfavorable to the other. The cash payments involved are made at the end of the contract rather than at its inception for the most part, and the instruments have consequently been treated in the past in many cases as a type of off-balance sheet agreement.

In *SFAS No. 133* **[ASC 815]**, the FASB identified the following as keystones for the accounting for derivative instruments:

- Derivative instruments represent rights or obligations that meet the definitions of assets or liabilities and should be reported in financial statements.
- Fair value is the most relevant measure for financial instruments and the only relevant measure for derivative instruments.
- Only items that are assets or liabilities should be reported as such in the balance sheet.
- Special accounting for items designated as being hedged should be provided only for qualifying items, as demonstrated by an assessment of the expectation of effective offsetting changes in fair values or cash flows during the term of the hedge for the risk being hedged.

"We view them [derivatives and the trading activities that go with them] as time bombs, both for the parties that deal in them and the economic system.

Essentially, these instruments call for money to change hands at some future date, with the amount to be determined by one or more reference items, such as interest rates, stock prices, or currency values. If, for example, you either long or short an S&P 500 futures contract, you are a party to a very simple derivatives transaction—with your gain or loss derived from movements in the index. Unless derivatives contracts are collateralized or guaranteed, their ultimate value also depends on the creditworthiness of the counterparties to them. In the meantime, though, before a contract is settled, the counterparties record profits and losses—often huge in amount—in their current earnings statements without so much as a penny changing hands.

The range of derivatives contracts is limited only by the imagination of man (or sometimes, so it seems, madmen). At Enron, for example, newsprint and broadband derivatives, due to be settled many years in the future, were put on the books. Or say you want to write a contract speculating on the number of twins to be born in Nebraska in 2020. No problem—at a price, you will easily find an obliging counterparty."[8]

Although over a thousand different types of derivative instruments have been created, they are sometimes separated into the following two broad categories:

- Forward-based derivatives, such as forwards, futures, and swaps, in which either party can *potentially* have a favorable or an unfavorable outcome but not both simultaneously (e.g., both will not simultaneously have favorable outcomes).
- Option-based derivatives, such as interest rate caps, option contracts, and interest rate floors, in which only *one* specified party can potentially have a favorable outcome and it agrees to a premium at inception for this potentiality. The other party is paid the premium, and it can potentially have only an unfavorable outcome.

[8] *Fortune*, "Avoiding a Mega-Catastrophe," by Warren Buffett, March 17, 2003.

Derivatives are recognized in the balance sheet at their fair value. Determination of that value is based on the changes in the underlying value of measure (commodity, financial instrument, index, etc.) and on assessment of the expected future cash flows. The result is a payable position for one of the involved parties and a receivable position for the other.

Forward Exchange Contracts

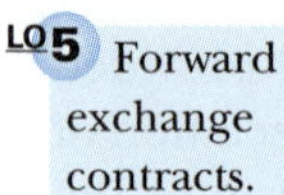

LO5 Forward exchange contracts.

Although hedging can be accomplished with many different types of derivatives, in this chapter we focus mainly on hedging with the use of forward contracts. Later in this chapter, we illustrate the use of options as a hedging device.

A forward exchange contract (forward contract) is an agreement to exchange currencies of two different countries at a specified rate (the forward rate) on a stipulated future date. At the inception of the contract, the forward rate normally varies from the spot rate. ***The difference between the two rates is referred to as a discount (premium) if the forward rate is less than (greater than) the spot rate***, as shown here.

	Exchange Rate	
Forward rate	$.175	} .007 premium
Spot rate	.168	} .006 discount
Forward rate	.162	

Which Kind of Forward Contract to Choose?

If the item being hedged is a foreign currency *account payable*, the firm should use a **forward contract to purchase the foreign currency** on the date the payable becomes due. This implies that the firm can lock in the cost of acquiring the foreign currency on the date the forward contract is acquired, and subsequent changes in the exchange rate will not affect the amount the firm has to pay. On the other hand, if the item being hedged is a foreign currency *accounts receivable*, the firm should use a ***forward contract to sell the foreign currency*** on the date the receivable is expected to be collected.

The valuation of a forward contract (intrinsic versus time value): Forward contracts are valued on a net basis. For example, consider the following. Suppose on January 1, 2009, you obtain a one-year forward contract to sell 10,000 Canadian dollars using the December 31, 2009, forward rate of $0.90. This forward rate is the best guess to estimate what the spot rate will be on December 31, 2009. Therefore on January 1, 2009, you believe that 10,000 Canadian dollars will be worth $9,000. The forward contract locks in the amount of cash you will receive, $9,000. But since on January 1 this is also the expected cost to obtain Canadian dollars, the value of the forward contract is zero on this date, and it will remain zero until the forward rate for December 31, 2009, settlement changes. Assume the following additional information:

Date	*Spot Rate*	*Forward Rate for 12/31/09 Settlement*	*Premium*
1/1/2009	$0.80	$0.90	$0.10
7/1/2009	$0.83	$0.88	$0.05
12/31/2009	$0.84	$0.84	$0.00

With this forward contract, the amount of dollars to be received is fixed at $9,000, but the amount paid to acquire the foreign currency alters with changes in the exchange rate. What conditions will cause the contract to be beneficial to the firm? If the future spot rate falls below the forward rate on the forward contract, the firm will benefit. Looking at the data in retrospect, this is a valuable forward contract for the firm because the forward contract locks in the cash received at the $0.90 rate, but the firm can purchase the currency on the settlement date at a spot rate of $0.84. In other words, the firm pays $0.84 to get $0.90. But on the date the forward contract is acquired, there is no guarantee that the firm will benefit from the contract (i.e., the spot rate on the settlement date might increase above $0.90).

As the settlement date for the forward contract approaches, the forward rate converges to the *settlement date* spot rate. Also, note that the premium changes over time but eventually will become zero on the settlement date. What is the ***value of the forward*** on July 1, 2009? The amount of cash received from the forward is fixed at $9,000, but now the forward rate for December 31 settlement has changed to $0.88. This implies that we could enter into a contract to purchase the 10,000 Canadian dollars for $8,800. Thus the value of the forward has increased by $200 (the change in the forward rate). Similarly, on the settlement date, the forward rate drops to $0.84. Now the 10,000 Canadian dollars can be purchased for $8,400, and the forward contract has increased in value by another $400. The ***total change in value of the forward contract*** from the inception to the settlement date can be computed by taking the difference between the original forward rate of $0.90 and the spot rate on the settlement date ($0.84). In this example the forward contract increased in value by $600 or [($0.90 – $0.84) (10,000)].

Notice that the initial premium is $0.10 and that the spot rate increased over the year by $0.04. The difference between these two equals the change in the value of the forward contract over the forward contract. (In this case the premium represents a gain, and the change in the spot rate is a loss.) Since the premium will eventually be zero on the settlement date, the change in the premium (or discount) is known as the *time element* of the change in value of the forward contract. The change in the spot rate is considered the change in the *intrinsic value* of the forward. Thus the total change in value is equal to the sum of the intrinsic value and the time value. (Keep in mind that each of these changes in value can be positive or negative.) This is summarized in the following chart.

		Forward Rate for 12/31/09		*Change in Value(a)*		
Date	*Spot Rate*	*Settlement*	*Premium*	*Total Value*	*Intrinsic Value*	*Time*
1/1/2009	$0.80	$0.90	$0.10			
7/1/2009	$0.83	$0.88	$0.05	$0.02	($0.03)	$0.05
12/31/2009	$0.84	$0.84	$0.00	$0.04	($0.01)	$0.05
Total change in rates and premium				$0.06	($0.04)	$0.10
Foreign currency (Canadian dollars)				10,000	10,000	10,000
Total change in value in dollars[a]				$600	($400)	$1,000

[a] *Definitions*

The total change in the value of the forward contract = the change in the forward rates multiplied by the foreign currency.

The change in the intrinsic value of the forward contract = the change in the spot rate multiplied by the foreign currency.

The change in the time value of the forward contract = the change in the premium multiplied by the foreign currency.

Why Do Forward Rates Differ from Spot Rates?

Forward rates for the purchase or sale of foreign currency, on some future date, can be higher, lower, or equal to the current spot rate on that currency. For instance, if the current spot rate for the exchange of pesos and dollars is $0.95, the forward rate to exchange pesos for dollars in one year might be higher or lower than $0.95 (it is unlikely to be equal). Why do these rates differ? The answer to this question involves differences in interest rates between the two countries. Suppose that the one-year forward rate and the current spot rate are equal but that in the United States the cost of borrowing money for one year is 5% while in Mexico the cost of borrowing is 10%. A U.S. company could take $9,500 and convert this amount into 10,000 pesos (at today's spot rate) and invest this amount in Mexico at 10% for one year. This would accumulate to 11,000 pesos. At the same time, the firm could buy a forward contract to sell 11,000 pesos at the forward rate of $0.95 for $10,450. Assuming investments in the United States and Mexico had equal risks and tax characteristics, this would amount to a risk-free 5% return (a 10% return in Mexico less 5% that could have been earned in the United States). Investors would commit large sums of money to this investment. In our example, this process would tend to drive up U.S. interest rates, drive down Mexican interest rates, and lower the forward rate. The equilibrium is known as ***interest rate parity.*** Therefore,

$$\textit{Forward rate} = \frac{(1 + i^{US})}{(1 + i^{Mexico})}\,(\textit{spot rate})$$

where *i* represents the interest rate and the superscript represents the country. Therefore, the forward rate that guarantees interest rate parity is $0.9068, or

Forward rate = (1.05/1.10)($0.95) = $0.9068.

Then in this example, the 11,000 pesos could only be converted into $9,975, enabling the U.S. company to earn only 5% interest. Therefore, if the interest rate in the foreign country is ***higher*** than the rates in the United States, the forward rate will be ***below*** the current spot rate. If the interest rate in the foreign country is ***lower*** than the rates in the United States, the forward rate will be ***above*** the current spot rate.

There are a number of business situations in which a firm may desire to acquire a forward exchange contract. The uses of forward contracts include the following:

1. **Hedges**
   a. Forward contracts used as a hedge of a ***foreign currency transaction.*** These include importing and exporting transactions denominated in foreign currency. These hedges do not qualify for hedge accounting under *SFAS No. 133* **[ASC 815]** because the foreign exchange gains and losses are already reported in earnings under *SFAS No. 52,* and the payables and receivables are reported at market value on the balance sheet.
   b. Forward contracts used as a hedge of an ***unrecognized firm commitment*** **(a fair value hedge).** An example of an unrecognized firm commitment is when a firm enters into a contract to purchase an asset in two months for a fixed amount of foreign currency. Since the exchange rate may change over the next two months, the firm might use a forward contract to hedge the potential change in value of the purchased asset. Hedge accounting rules apply. Both the change in value of the hedge and the value of the hedged item are reported in earnings (before the contract is reported on the books). This is illustrated later.
   c. Forward contract used as a hedge of a ***foreign-currency-denominated "forecasted" transaction*** (a cash flow hedge). A forecasted transaction is a situation where the firm has planned sales receipts (expected to occur in the near future) and uses the forward contract as a means to hedge the cash flow risk. Initially, foreign ex-

change gains and losses are reported in comprehensive income, while no offsetting amount is reported for the hedged item. Eventually, the exchange gains and losses will be reported in earnings in the period the hedged item affects earnings (i.e., if the item being hedged is a forecasted purchase of inventory, the gains and losses on the hedge will be reclassified into earnings when the inventory is sold).

d. Forward contracts as a hedge of a ***net investment in foreign operations.***

2. **Speculation**

Forward contracts used to speculate changes in foreign currency.

These classifications are important because the accounting for a particular type of forward contract depends on the purpose for which it was obtained. The difference in accounting relates primarily to two questions.

1. How is a transaction gain or loss on the forward contract computed, and when should the gain or loss be reported?
2. What value should be reported for the forward contract in the financial statements over the life of the contract?

Hedges of forecasted foreign currency transactions may include some intercompany transactions. The hedging of foreign currency intercompany cash flows with foreign currency options is not uncommon. Because of its belief that the accounting for all derivative instruments should be the same, the FASB broadened the scope of hedges that are eligible for hedge accounting (as specified in *SFAS No. 138* **[ASC 815–20–25–4]**). If an *intercompany* foreign currency derivative is created, it can only be a hedging instrument in the *consolidated* financial statements *if* the other member enters into an offsetting contract with an outside (unaffiliated) party to hedge its exposure. This restriction applies because the standards require that some component with foreign currency exposure must be a party to the hedging transaction. In the stand-alone statements of the subsidiary, however, the intercompany derivative could be designated as a hedge in the absence of third-party involvement. Therefore intercompany derivatives can be classified as either fair value or cash flow hedges if they meet the definition for that particular hedge and if the member of the consolidated group *not using the intercompany derivative* as a hedge enters into a derivative with an unrelated party to offset the original exposure from the intercompany hedge.

The euro failed to gain on news of a stabilization package for Central and Eastern Europe. Markets have been juggling the potential impact of several government initiatives throughout the world this week, leading to swings in risk appetite.[9]

USING FORWARD CONTRACTS AS A HEDGE

Hedge of a Foreign Currency Exposed Liability

Consider the following importing example.

Importing transaction with a forward contract used as a hedge

1. On December 1, 2007, a U.S. firm purchased inventory for 500,000 euros payable on March 1, 2008 (i.e., the transaction is denominated in euros).

[9] Euro Slides to Session Lows, by Riva Froymovich, WSJ, February 27, 2009.

2. The firm's fiscal year-end is December 31.
3. The spot rate for euros ($/euro) and the forward rates for euros on March 1, 2008, at various times are as follows:

	Spot Rate	*Forward Rate (for 3/1/2008 euros)*
Transaction date—December 1, 2007	$1.05	1.052
Balance sheet date—December 31, 2007	1.055	1.059
Settlement date—March 1, 2008	1.07	

4. On December 1, 2007, the U.S. firm entered into a forward contract to buy 500,000 euros on March 1, 2008, for $1.052.

LO7 Forward contracts as a hedge.

On December 1, 2007, the firm entered a contract to purchase inventory for 500,000 euros (the spot rate was $1.05 on that date). If the exchange rate did not change over the payment period, the firm would owe $525,000 to settle the payable. However, if the exchange rate increased to $1.07, the firm would have to pay $535,000 to settle the debt (500,000 × $1.07). On the other hand, if the exchange rate dropped to $1.02, the firm would only need to pay $510,000 (or 500,000 × $1.02). Because the firm cannot perfectly estimate the change in the exchange rate, the company might prefer to eliminate this risk by entering into a forward contract *to buy euros* on March 1, 2008. Since the forward rate on December 1, 2007, to purchase euros on March 1, 2008, is $1.052, the company can buy 500,000 euros on March 1 for a guaranteed price of $526,000. This fixed price means that the firm has determined in advance the maximum (and exact) amount of loss it will suffer—in this case $1,000. Thus the firm is protected from future increases in the exchange rate above $1.052. By locking into a set price, the firm gains if the spot rate on March 1, 2008, increases above $1.052 and loses if the spot rate decreases below $1.052. The important point to note about the hedge is that the firm knows with certainty on December 1, 2007, the amount of cash needed to purchase the asset.

The entries to record the purchase and forward exchange contract are as follows.

December 1, 2007—Transaction Date

(1) Purchases	525,000	
Accounts Payable (500,000 euros × $1.05)		525,000
To record purchase of goods on account using the spot rate on December 1, 2007.		

The accounts payable for the inventory purchase is recorded using the spot rate on the transaction date (on December 1, 2007):

(2) Foreign Currency (FC) Receivable from Exchange Dealer	526,000	
Dollars Payable to Exchange Dealer (500,000 euros × $1.052)		526,000
To record forward contract to buy 500,000 euros using the forward rate.		

At the date of the transaction, the U.S. firm records the forward contract by recognizing a payable and a receivable of $526,000 for the number of dollars to be paid (units of foreign currency to be purchased multiplied by forward rate) to the exchange dealer when the forward contract matures.[10] The net value of the forward contract is zero since the payable and the receivable are exactly offset. The value of the receivable from the dealer and the accounts payable for the purchase of inventory are subject to changes in exchange rate, but the gains and losses generally offset each other since the terms and the amounts are equal.

On December 31, 2007, the spot rate increases from $1.05 to $1.055, resulting in an increase of $2,500 to accounts payable. The spot rate is used for accounts payable since that is the amount needed to settle the liability.

December 31, 2007—Balance Sheet Date

(3) Transaction Loss	2,500	
Accounts Payable		2,500
To record a loss on the liability denominated in foreign currency		
Current value of accounts payable (500,000 euros × $1.055) =		$527,500
Less: Recorded value of accounts payable =		$525,000
Adjustment needed to accounts payable		$ 2,500
or [500,000 euros × ($1.055 − $1.05)] = $2,500		

On the other hand, the value of the forward contract is determined using the change in the forward rates. The forward rate increased to $1.059 from $1.052. This results in an increase of $3,500 to the receivable from the exchange dealer. Recall that the payable to the foreign exchange dealer is fixed by the forward contract. Thus the forward contract has a positive $3,500 value at this point (December 31).

(4) FC Receivable from Exchange Dealer	3,500	
Transaction Gain		3,500
To record a gain on foreign currency to be received from exchange dealer [(500,000 euros × $1.059 = $529,500) − $526,000].		

If the financial statements are prepared on December 31, 2007, the value of the forward contract is as follows:

FC Receivable from Exchange Dealer (500,000 × 1.059)	$529,500
Dollars Payable to Exchange Dealer (500,000 × 1.052)	526,000
Net Receivable from Exchange Dealer	$ 3,500

This net value would be reported on the balance sheet. In addition, accounts payable would be recorded at the spot rate, or $527,500. The income statement would report an exchange loss of $2,500 and an exchange gain of $3,500.

> Note that even though the forward contract and the accounts payable cover similar terms (December 1 to March 1) and amounts (500,000 euros), the amount of the transaction loss on the payable does not equal the transaction gain on the FC receivable. They are not equal because accounts payable is valued using changes in the spot rate, while the value of the forward contract is determined using changes in the forward rates. On the settlement date, the forward rate and the spot rate become equal. Thus the total transaction gain or loss on the contract will eventually equal the guaranteed gain or loss determined on the date the forward contract is acquired.

[10] In practice, a journal entry may not be made to record a forward contract when the contract was negotiated because it represents an executory contract. Although arguments can be made either for or against recording such contracts, in this chapter forward contracts are recorded because it is easier to analyze the subsequent adjustments required to report the effects of a forward contract on the firm's reported income.

On March 1, 2008, the spot rate increases to $1.07 from $1.055, resulting in an increase in accounts payable of $7,500 [($1.07 − $1.055) × 500,000]. Since on the settlement date, the forward rate on this date and the spot rate are identical, the change in the March 1 forward rate on December 31 to the spot rate on March 1, 2007, is $0.011, or ($1.059 to $1.07). This results in an increase to the foreign currency (FC) receivable of $5,500, or [($1.07 − $1.059) × 500,000]. The journal entries to record these events are as follows:

March 1, 2008—Settlement Date

	Debit	Credit
(5) Transaction Loss	7,500	
Accounts Payable		7,500
To record a loss from 12/31/07 to 3/1/08 on liability denominated in foreign currency. The current value of the payable $535,000 (500,000 euros × $1.07) less the recorded value of the payable on December 31 of $527,500 is $7,500: [(500,000 euros × $1.07, or $535,000) − $527,500].		
(6) FC Receivable from Exchange Dealer	5,500	
Transaction Gain		5,500
To record a gain from 12/31/07 to 3/1/08 on foreign currency to be received from exchange dealer. The change in the 12/31 forward rate to the spot rate on March 1, 2008, times 500,000 euros, or [(500,000 euros × $1.07, or $535,000) − $529,500].		

The recorded balances in both accounts payable and the FC receivable are $535,000, reflecting the spot rate on March 1, 2007. The dollars payable to the dealer remain fixed at $526,000, the original contracted amount. Entry (7) records the cash payment of $526,000 and the reduction of the FC payable. Also, the receivable is converted to the Investment in FC representing the 500,000 euros acquired in the forward contract. In entry (8), the euros are used to settle the accounts payable.

	Debit	Credit
(7) Dollars Payable to Exchange Dealer	526,000	
Investment in FC (500,000 euros)	535,000	
FC Receivable from Exchange Dealer		535,000
Cash		526,000
To record payment to exchange dealer and receipt of 500,000 euros (500,000 euros × $1.07 = $535,000).		
(8) Accounts Payable	535,000	
Investment in FC		535,000
To record payment of liability upon transfer of 500,000 euros.		

By obtaining the forward contract, the firm was able to establish at the transaction date the amount of dollars ($526,000) that it would take to acquire the 500,000 euros needed to settle the account with the foreign firm. Note, however, that the cost of the inventory of $525,000 was established on December 1 [entry (1)]. If the forward contract had not been obtained, the firm would have had to pay $535,000 to settle the account and would have reported a net loss of $10,000 on the exposed liability position. The net gain from entering into the forward contract, however, largely canceled out the net loss on the exposed liability position.

These transactions can be summarized in the following table.

Hedged Item	*Balance*	*Transaction Gain/(Loss)*	*Hedge*	*Balance*	*Transaction Gain/(Loss)*
Accounts Payable			**FC Receivable**		
12/1/2007	$ 525,000		12/1/2007	$ 526,000	
12/31/2007	527,500	(2,500)	2/31/2007	529,500	3,500
3/1/2007	535,000	(7,500)	3/1/2007	535,000	5,500
Total gain/(loss)		(10,000)			9,000

Thus the net effect is a $1,000 loss when the forward contract is used.

Hedge of a Foreign Currency Exposed Asset

LO 7 Forward contract as a hedge.

In the preceding example, the U.S. firm entered into a forward purchase contract to hedge an exposed liability position at a time when the forward rate was at a premium. Accounting for a forward contract entered into as a hedge of an exposed receivable position is based on similar analysis. However, because the U.S. firm will be receiving foreign currency in settlement of the exposed receivable balance, it will enter into a forward contract *to sell* foreign currency for U.S. dollars. In this case, the receivable from the dealer is denominated in a fixed number of dollars, the amount of which is based on the contracted forward rate, whereas the obligation to the dealer is denominated in a foreign currency, which is translated into dollars using the current spot rate.

TEST YOUR KNOWLEDGE

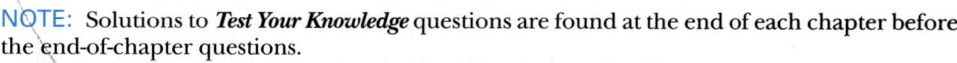

NOTE: Solutions to ***Test Your Knowledge*** questions are found at the end of each chapter before the end-of-chapter questions.

Multiple Choice

On December 1, 2009, SMC entered into a transaction to import raw materials from a foreign country. The account is to be settled March 1 with the payment of 50,000 euros. The spot rates and the forward rates on various dates are as follows:

Date	Spot Rate $ per euro	Forward Rate (March 1 Settlement)
Dec. 1	$1.00	$1.03
March 1	$1.04	$1.04

1. To hedge the company's accounts payable position, SMC should:
   a. Buy a forward contract to purchase 50,000 euros on March 1
   b. Buy a forward contract to sell 50,000 euros on March 1
   c. None of the above
2. If SMC uses a forward contract to hedge the payable, what is the overall transaction gain or loss on the company from using the hedge?
   a. $2,000 gain
   b. $1,500 loss
   c. $1,500 gain
   d. $2,000 loss
   e. $500 gain

Fair Value Hedge—Hedging an Unrecognized Foreign Currency Commitment

In the preceding discussion of the importing and exporting of goods, the purchase or sale of an asset was recorded on the transaction date. This date is considered the point at which title to the goods is transferred, which is consistent with the recording of a transaction with another domestic company. However, if the U.S. firm at a date earlier than the transaction date made a commitment to a foreign company to sell goods or buy goods, and the price was established in foreign currency at the commitment date, changes in the exchange rate between the commitment date and transaction date would be reflected in the cost or sales price of the asset. For example, assume that a U.S. firm made an agreement on June 1 to buy goods from a Swiss company for 500,000 Swiss francs. At this date, the spot rate was $.20, but on the transaction date, when title to the goods transferred and a journal entry was recorded, the spot rate was $.22. The entry to record the purchase is

Purchases (500,000 francs × $.22)	110,000	
Accounts Payable		110,000

Thus the change in the exchange rate that occurred between the commitment and the transaction dates becomes part of the cost of inventory rather than being reported as a separate gain or loss item. The company, however, may still acquire a forward contract to hedge against the unfavorable change in the fair value of the asset that may occur after the commitment date.

Such a forward contract is referred to as a **fair value hedge**, a derivative designed to hedge exposure to either a recognized asset or liability or, in this case, an unrecognized foreign currency commitment. In the case of an unrecognized foreign currency commitment, a fair value hedge is applicable only if there is an identifiable foreign currency commitment that specifies all significant terms (such as quantity and price) and performance is probable. ***A gain or loss on this type of forward contract as well as the offsetting gain or loss on the hedged item are recognized currently in earnings.*** The gain or loss (the change in the fair value of the forward contract) is an adjustment of the carrying value of the forward contract. Similarly, the change in value of the firm commitment is recorded as such on the balance sheet (even though the commitment has not yet been recorded). The measurement of hedge effectiveness is beyond the scope of this chapter, but since the forward contracts are for similar terms and amounts, they are assumed to be highly effective.

Fair Value Hedge Illustration To illustrate the accounting for a forward contract acquired to hedge an identifiable foreign currency commitment (a fair value hedge), the following facts are assumed:

Fair Value Hedge Example

1. On March 1, 2007, a U.S. firm contracts to sell equipment to a foreign customer located in Argentina for 200,000 pesos. The equipment is expected to cost $60,000 to manufacture and is to be delivered, and the account is to be settled one year later on March 1, 2008. Thus the transaction date and the settlement date are both March 1, 2008.
2. On March 1, 2007, the U.S. firm enters into a forward contract to sell 200,000 pesos in 12 months at the forward rate of $.39.

3. Spot rates and the forward rates for pesos on selected dates are

Date	*Spot Exchange Rate*	*3/1/2008 Forward Rate*
March 1, 2007	$.40	$.39
December 31, 2007	.397	.382
March 1, 2008	.38	

The journal entry to record the forward contract on March 1, 2003, is:

March 1, 2007

(1) Dollars Receivable from Exchange Dealer (200,000 pesos × $.39)	78,000	
FC Payable to Exchange Dealer		78,000
To record the forward contract to sell 200,000 pesos.		

Nine months later, on the balance sheet date (12/31/07), the FC payable needs to be adjusted to fair value using the *change in the forward rates.* Also, since this is a fair value hedge, the change in the fair value of the hedged item must also be recorded. This is computed using the change in the forward rate. These entries are as follows:

December 31, 2007

(2) FC Payable to Exchange Dealer	1,600	
Exchange Gain		1,600
To record gain on foreign currency to be delivered to exchange dealer using the change in forward rates (200,000 pesos × ($.39 − $.382)).		
(3) Exchange Loss	1,600	
Firm Commitment		1,600
To record loss on firm commitment using the change in the forward rate (200,000 pesos × ($.39 − $.382)).		

Note that the firm commitment has not been recorded on the books as of December 31, 2007. On the December 31, 2007, balance sheet, the value of the forward contract is as follows:

Dollars Receivable from Exchange Dealer (fixed) (200,000 × .39)	$78,000
FC Payable to Exchange Dealer (200,000 × .382)	76,400
Net Receivable	$ 1,600

On the balance sheet, the firm commitment would be reported as a $1,600 liability. On the Income Statement, the exchange gain of $1,600 is reported, as well as an exchange loss of $1,600.

On March 1, 2008 (the transaction date and the settlement date), the journal entries are:

March 1, 2008

(4) FC Payable to Exchange Dealer	400	
Exchange Gain		400
To record gain on forward contract from 12/31/07 to 3/1/08 [200,000 pesos × ($.38 − $.382)] = $400.		
(5) Exchange Loss	400	
Firm Commitment		400
To record loss on forward contract from 12/31/07 to 3/1/08 [200,000 pesos × ($.38 − $.382)] = $400.		

Entries (4) and (5) adjust the values of the FC payable and the change in the fair value of the firm commitment. Note that since the transaction date occurs on the settlement date, the change in value is computed as the change in the forward rate on 12/31/2007 to the spot rate on March 1, 2008 (i.e, .382 to .38).

		Debit	Credit
(6)	Investment in FC (200,000 × .38)	76,000	
	Firm Commitment	2,000	
	Sales (200,000 pesos × $.39)		78,000
	To record sale of equipment to foreign customer.		
(7)	Cost of Goods Sold	60,000	
	Inventory		60,000
	To record cost of equipment sold.		
(8)	Cash (200,000 × $.39)	78,000	
	FC Payable to Exchange Dealer (200,000 × $.38)	76,000	
	Investment in FC		76,000
	Dollars Receivable from Exchange Dealer		78,000
	To record settlement of forward contract.		

Because of the forward contract, the amount of sales recorded in entry (6) is equal to the forward rate on the forward contract multiplied by 200,000 pesos, or $78,000 (i.e., 200,000 × $.39). The firm commitment account is eliminated on this date. In entry (8), the firm sells 200,000 pesos for $78,000.

The effect of these transactions on the firm's profitability is as follows:

Sales ($76,000 + $2,000)	$78,000
Cost of Goods Sold	60,000
Gross Profit	$18,000

The number of dollars to be received was locked in by the forward contract at $78,000, and the equipment was expected to cost $60,000. Thus the forward contract permitted the U.S. firm to lock in an expected profit of $18,000 on the sales contract. If the forward contract had not been obtained, the profit earned on the contract would have depended on the exchange rate in effect when payment was received from the Argentinean customer. Without the hedge, the amount of sales recorded would have been $76,000 (200,000 pesos × $.38) and the gross profit would have been $16,000. And if the exchange rate had dropped below $.38, the amount of sales recorded would have been even lower. For example, at an exchange rate of $.30, the amount of sales recorded would have equaled the amount of cost of goods sold, thus eliminating any gross profit on the contract.

Discounting the Fair Value of the Forward Contract

As stated earlier, the change in the forward contract was computed using the change in the forward rate. According to *SFAS 133* **[ASC 815]**, these amounts should be discounted to a present value basis. For example, in entry (2), the exchange gain on the FC Payable was computed to be $1,600 by taking the change in the forward rates and multiplying by the amount of foreign currency in the forward contract [200,000 pesos × ($.39 − $.382)]. If this amount were discounted using an interest rate of 12% for two months (until the settlement date), the $1,600 would be recorded on the books at $1,600 less $32, or $1,568. Similarly, the firm commitment in entry (3) would be recorded on the books at its discounted amount of $980. These entries are repeated as entries (3a) and (4a).

(2a)	FC Payable to Exchange Dealer	1,568	
	Exchange Gain		1,568
	To record gain on forward contract from 12/31/07 to 3/1/08		
	[200,000 pesos × ($.39 − $.382)] =	$1,600	
	Less: ($1,600) (2/12) (12%) =	32	
	Total Discounted Gain	$1,568	
(3a)	Exchange Loss	1,568	
	Firm Commitment		1,568
	To record loss on forward contract from 12/31/07 to 3/1/08		
	[200,000 pesos × ($.39 − $.382)] less $32 = $1,568		

Then on March 1, 2008, the total gain over the life of the forward contract is $2,000 [or 200,000 × ($.39 − $.38)]. But since $1,568 was already recognized, entry (4) would be for $432 rather than simply the change since December 31.

(4a)	FC Payable to Exchange Dealer	432	
	Exchange Gain		432
	To record gain on forward contract from 12/31/07 to 3/1/08		
	plus the discount already recognized ($20)		
	[200,000 pesos × ($.382 − $.38)] = $400 + $32 = $432		
(5b)	Exchange Loss	432	
	Firm Commitment		432
	To record loss on forward contract from 12/31/07 to 3/1/08		
	plus the discount already recognized ($32)		
	[200,000 pesos × ($.382 − $.38)] = $400 + 32 = $432		

In the remainder of this chapter, we ignore the complication of discounting to simplify the already complex accounting for derivatives. We note also that, in many cases, the impact of discounting is not material.

Cash Flow Hedge—Hedge of a Forecasted Transaction

Firms may also be concerned about hedging the cash flows for future transactions that have not yet occurred or for which there are no firm commitments. Forward contracts in such circumstances are known as **cash flow hedges**. For instance, on January 26, 2007, Lands' End reported carrying $77 million of forward contracts and $16 million of options on the balance sheet. Lands' End anticipated selling products to subsidiaries in the United Kingdom, Japan, and Germany over the next year and planned to purchase various inventory items from European suppliers. Even though they might not have a specific contract, Lands' End may decide, because of the high probability of occurrence of these transactions, to hedge this foreign currency exchange risk by using a cash flow hedge.

LO7 Fair value hedge vs. cash flow hedge.

Unlike the treatment of fair value hedges, cash flow hedges may defer the Income statement recognition of the gains and losses on forecasted transactions if certain criteria are met. Like other gains and losses that are excluded from the income statement, they must be included as components of "other comprehensive income" and reported in the stockholders' equity section of the balance sheet. The criteria for this treatment include:

- The forecasted transaction is specifically identifiable at the time of the designation as a single transaction or a group of individual transactions.
- The forecasted transaction is probable, and it presents exposure to price changes that are expected to affect earnings and cause variability in cash flows.
- The forecasted transaction involves an exchange with an outside (unrelated) party. (An exception is allowed for intercompany foreign exchange transactions. See the previous discussion in this chapter.)
- The forecasted transaction does not involve a business combination.

Amounts in accumulated other comprehensive income are reclassified into earnings in the same period or periods during which the hedged forecasted transaction affects earnings. For example, if the forecasted hedged item is inventory, the reclassification from accumulated other comprehensive income into earnings occurs when the inventory is sold. If the forecasted hedged item is the purchase of a fixed asset, the reclassification occurs when the equipment is depreciated.

We next present an illustration of the accounting for a forecasted transaction meeting the criteria identified by the FASB for deferral of the gains or losses into comprehensive income.

Cash Flow Hedge Illustration—Forward Contracts To illustrate the hedge of a forecasted foreign currency transaction with the use of an option, assume the following:

1. On December 1, 2007, a U.S. firm estimates that at least 5,000 units of inventory will be purchased from a company in the United Kingdom during January of 2008 for 500,000 euros. The transaction is probable, and it is to be denominated in euros. Sales of the inventory are expected to occur in the six months following the purchase.
2. The company enters into a forward contract to purchase 500,000 euros on January 31, 2008, for $1.01.
3. Spot rates and the forward rates at the January 31, 2008, settlement were as follows (dollars per euro):

	Spot Rate	*Forward Rate for 1/31/08*
December 1, 2007	$1.03	$1.01
Balance Sheet Date (12/31/07)	$1.00	$0.99
January 31, 2008	$0.98	

By using the forward contract, the firm is assured of paying $505,000 regardless of changes in the exchange rate. If the exchange rate were to drop below $1.01 the firm would lose, but if the exchange rate were to exceed $1.01, the firm would be better off using the forward contract.

The entry on December 1, 2007, to record the forward exchange contract to purchase 500,000 euros on January 31, 2008, for $1.01 is:

December 1, 2007

		Debit	Credit
(1)	FC Receivable from Exchange Dealer (500,000 euros × $1.01)	505,000	
	Dollars Payable to Exchange Dealer		505,000

One month later on the balance sheet date (December 31, 2007), the change in the value of the forward contract is $10,000 [500,000 × ($1.01 − $0.99)]. Therefore, on December 31, 2007, the following entry is made:

December 31, 2007—Balance Sheet Date

(2) Foreign Exchange Loss—Other Comprehensive Income (Balance Sheet)	10,000	
FC Receivable from Exchange Dealer		10,000
To record a loss on the change in forward contract [500,000 × ($1.01 − $0.99)]		

Notice that unlike the fair value hedge, there is no offsetting firm commitment entry since this is a forecasted transaction. The exchange gain or loss is reported in comprehensive income and will affect the income statement when the inventory is eventually sold. On the balance sheet, the forward contract is reported as a liability at its fair value of $10,000, and the offsetting amount is reported in stockholders' equity in accumulated other comprehensive income (as a loss).

January 31, 2008—Transaction and Settlement Date

(3) Foreign Exchange Loss—Other Comprehensive Income (Balance Sheet)	5,000	
FC Receivable from Exchange Dealer		5,000
To adjust the forward contract to its market value of $20,000. The change in value of the forward contract [($.99 12/31 forward rate less $.98 January 31, 2008, spot rate) × 500,000 euros] is $5,000.		

Note that the balance in the FC Receivable account is $490,000 after entry (3). The entry to record the settlement of the forward contract is as follows:

(4) Investment in FC (500,000 euros)	490,000	
Dollars Payable to Exchange Dealer	505,000	
FC Receivable from Exchange Dealer		490,000
Cash		505,000
To settle with the trader.		

Now suppose that the forecasted transaction occurs and the 5,000 units of inventory are purchased on January 31, 2008, for 500,000 euros. The journal entry to record the purchase is:

(5) Inventory (at the 1/31/08 spot rate)	490,000	
Investment in FC (500,000 euros)		490,000

Suppose that in February, the inventory is sold for $600,000. The entries to record the sale and to reclassify the amounts from Other Comprehensive Income (a $15,000 loss, including $10,000 loss at December 31, 2007, plus the $5,000 additional loss at January 31, 2008) into earnings are as follows:

February 2008—Inventory Sales Date

(6) Cash	600,000	
Cost of goods sold	490,000	
Sales		600,000
Inventory		490,000

(7) Cost of goods sold (Income Statement)	15,000	
Foreign exchange loss—Other Comprehensive Income (Balance Sheet)		15,000
To reclassify the amounts from accumulated other comprehensive income into earnings (cost of goods sold).		

In entry (7), the amounts recorded in accumulated other comprehensive income are reclassified into earnings. The FASB does not specify where on the income statement this amount should be reported. Many companies include this gain or loss as part of cost of goods sold, as shown above.

TEST YOUR KNOWLEDGE

NOTE: Solutions to ***Test Your Knowledge*** questions are found at the end of each chapter before the end-of-chapter questions.

Multiple Choice

On October 1, 2008, Short Company ordered some equipment from a supplier for 200,000 euros. Delivery and payment is to occur on November 30, 2009. The spot rates on October 1 and November 30 are $1.50 and $1.30.

1. If the company does not hedge the commitment, at what amount is the equipment recorded on the books on November 30, 2009?
   a. $300,000
   b. $260,000
   c. $200,000
   d. None of the above
2. If the company acquires a forward contract to hedge any unfavorable changes in fair value of the equipment, at what amount is the equipment recorded on the books on November 30, 2009? The forward rate for November 30 settlement is $1.35.
   a. $300,000
   b. $260,000
   c. $270,000
   d. None of the above
3. If the forward contract is acquired, what is the overall exchange gain or loss?
   a. $0
   b. $10,000 gain
   c. $10,000 loss
   d. $30,000 gain

Economic Hedge of a Net Investment in a Foreign Entity

A U.S. firm that maintains an equity investment in a foreign company may enter into a foreign currency transaction or a nonderivative financial instrument in an effort to minimize or offset the effects of currency fluctuations on the net investment. A foreign currency transaction is considered a hedge of a net investment in a foreign entity if the forward contract is designated as, and is effective as, a hedge of the net investment. The gain or loss on the hedging instrument is reported in the same manner as the translation adjustment (under *SFAS No. 52*) **[ASC 815–35–35–1]**, that is, reported in the cumulative translation adjustment section of other comprehensive income.

For example, assume that a U.S. firm holds an investment in the net assets of a French company that conducts its business primarily in francs and accounts for the investment using the current rate method. As will be shown in Chapter 13, the investor company applying the equity method to a less than 50%-owned investee will record its share of the effect of a change in the exchange rate on the net assets of the foreign investee. To hedge against the exposure to exchange rate changes, the U.S. firm may enter into an agreement to borrow euros from a French bank. Assume further that the loan is designated as, and is effective as, a hedge of the net investment in the French company. On subsequent balance sheet dates, both the net assets of the foreign company and the loan denominated in euros are adjusted to reflect the current exchange rate. A gain (loss) from the adjustment of the liability will offset a loss (gain) from the adjustment of the net investment in the foreign company, and a hedge results. Both adjustments are reported as a component of stockholders' equity (accumulated other comprehensive income) rather than reported currently in income. However, if the net adjustment to the loan balance exceeds the adjustment of the balance of the investment, the excess is reported in the determination of net income as a transaction gain or loss. The gains or losses accumulated in a separate component of stockholders' equity remain there until part or all of the investment in the foreign company is sold.

Forward Contracts Acquired to Speculate in the Movement of Foreign Currencies

LO3 Common transactions.

A forward contract may be acquired for speculative purposes in anticipation of realizing a gain. For example, assume that on December 1, 2007, the spot rate for the British pound is $1.85 and that the 90-day futures rate is $1.86. Further assume that a company expecting the exchange rate to increase to, say, $1.93, enters into a contract on December 1 to acquire £100,000 on March 1, 2008. (A forward contract to sell foreign currency would be negotiated if the firm expected the future spot rate to be lower than the forward rate.) The firm's fiscal year ends on December 31, and on that date the futures rate for pounds to be purchased on March 1, 2008, is $1.87. The spot rate is $1.92 on March 1, 2008. The journal entries to record the transactions are:

December 1, 2007

(1) FC Receivable from Exchange Dealer	186,000	
Dollars Payable to Exchange Dealer		186,000
To record the forward contract (£100,000 × $1.86).		

This entry recognizes that the U.S. firm has contracted to buy £100,000 in 90 days when the payment of $186,000 is made to the exchange dealer. Both the debit and credit related to a forward contract are measured by multiplying the £100,000 by the forward rate of $1.86. The FASB reasoned that the forward rate should be used because a firm speculating in foreign currency changes is exposed to the risk of movements in the forward rate. Since both accounts are based on the forward rate, there is no separate accounting for any discount or premium on the forward contract.

December 31, 2007

(2) FC Receivable from Exchange Dealer	1,000	
Transaction Gain		1,000
To record gain on foreign currency to be received from exchange dealer [£100,000 × $1.87 = $187,000 − $186,000] or [£100,000 × ($1.87 − $1.86)].		

The foreign currency receivable is adjusted at the financial statement date since it is denominated in foreign currency units. The amount of the adjustment is computed by multiplying the units of foreign currency to be received by the difference between the forward rate available for the remaining life of the forward contract and the rate last used to value the contract. The transaction gain (or loss) is reported currently in income.

March 1, 2008

(3) FC Receivable from Exchange Dealer	5,000	
Transaction Gain		5,000
To record gain on foreign currency to be received from exchange dealer [(£100,000 × \$1.92 = \$192,000 − \$187,000)].		
(4) Dollars Payable to Exchange Dealer	186,000	
Investment in FC	192,000	
Cash		186,000
FC Receivable from Exchange Dealer		192,000
To record payment to exchange dealer and receipt of foreign currency.		
(5) Cash	192,000	
Investment in FC		192,000
To record conversion of pounds into cash.		

On March 1, the firm records any gain or loss as a result of changes in the exchange rate from the last valuation date to the date of the transaction. Upon payment of \$186,000 to the exchange dealer, the firm will receive £100,000, which can be converted into \$192,000. The total gain of \$6,000 recognized over the life of the contract is the difference between the value of the foreign currency received (\$192,000) when the forward contract was exercised and the amount paid (\$186,000) to the exchange dealer. If the firm had entered into a forward contract to sell foreign currency, the accounting would be similar to that above, except the debit in entry (1) is for a fixed amount of dollars to be received; the credit records the obligation to buy foreign currency units for delivery to the exchange dealer. The estimated cost of units to be delivered will vary as the exchange rate fluctuates.

Disclosure Requirements of the Various Hedges

SFAS No. 133 **[ASC 815–20–50]** specifies certain minimal disclosures for derivative instruments and nonderivative instruments designated as qualifying hedging instruments. The disclosures include the objectives of the instruments, the strategies for achieving those objectives, the context needed for understanding them, and the risk management policy. In addition, a description of transactions or items that are hedged must be disclosed for each category.

The following specific disclosures are required:

1. **Fair value hedges** (such as hedges of the foreign currency exposure of unrecognized firm commitments)
   - **a.** A description of where the amount of the gain or loss is reported on the income statement.
   - **b.** The amount of the gain or loss recognized in earnings when the hedged item no longer qualifies as a fair value hedge.
2. **Cash flow hedges** (includes forecasted transactions)
   - **a.** A description of where the amount of the gain or loss is reported on the income statement.

b. A description of the transactions or other events that will result in the reclassification into earnings of gains and losses that are reported in accumulated other comprehensive income, and the estimation of the net amount of the existing gains or losses at the reporting date expected to be reclassified into earnings within the next 12 months.

c. The maximum length of time over which the firm is hedging its exposure to the variability in future cash flows for forecasted transactions.

d. The amount of the gain or loss reclassified into earnings as a result of the discontinuance of cash flow hedges because it is probable that the transaction will not occur.

3. **Hedges of the net investment** in a foreign operation

The net amount of gains or losses is included in the cumulative translation adjustment during the reporting period. All derivative instruments not designated as hedges must be identified as to their purpose, and qualitative disclosures about the use of derivatives are encouraged.

Finally, the amount of net gains or losses from cash flow hedges on derivative instruments included in "other comprehensive income" must be shown as a separate classification. The disclosures should include beginning and ending accumulated gains or losses from derivative instruments, the net change during the period from hedging activities, and the net amount reclassified to earnings.

Using Options to Hedge Foreign Currency Changes

LO8 Derivatives used as a hedge.

So far in this chapter, forward contracts have been used as hedging items. With the use of a forward contract, the firm will report either a gain or a loss. For example, if an accounts payable of 10,000 euros is hedged using a forward rate of $1.30, the firm is guaranteed to pay only $13,000. If the spot rate on the date of settlement is higher than $1.30, the firm gains, but if the spot rate falls below $1.30, the firm would have been better off not using the forward contract. While a forward contract is costless to acquire, upon entering into such a contract the firm must eventually deliver the specified amount of currency regardless of the gain or loss.

Conversely, suppose the firm wanted to hedge against only the upside or downside risk from changes in the exchange rate. To accomplish this, the firm could use an **option**, which gives the holder the advantage of ***right*** but not the obligation to buy or sell the currency. Thus, if the exchange rate changes in a negative manner, the firm can simply let the option lapse without a loss. In other words, the holder of the option does not have to exercise the option. When using options, a call option is appropriate to hedge against downside risk. A ***call option*** is an option to purchase the foreign currency at a specified rate, referred to as the exercise price. A ***put option*** is an option to sell the foreign currency at a specified rate. The advantage of using options is that the option gives the holder the *right* to buy or sell the currency, but if the exchange rate changes in a negative manner, the firm can simply let the option lapse. In other words, the holder of the option does not have to exercise the option. The disadvantage of the option is that there is an initial cost (i.e., a premium) to acquire the option. For instance, in the preceding example, the firm could purchase an option for $600[11] that

---

[11] The seller of the option would use some option pricing model, such as Black-Scholes, for determining the amount of the premium paid.

would allow the firm to purchase 10,000 euros at an exercise price of $1.295. If the spot rate on the settlement date exceeds $1.295, the firm will exercise the option; if the spot rate is less than $1.295, the firm will let the option expire.

An "in the money" option is an option where the firm benefits if the option is exercised. If on the date the call option was purchased, the spot rate of $1.295 was equal to the exercise price of $1.295, the option would be out of the money at that point. This means that the entire value of the option is due to the "time value" of the option. The option has value because, over time, the spot rate may exceed the exercise price of the call option (or the spot rate may be less than the exercise price for a put option).

Continuing our example, suppose that one month later the spot rate increased to $1.31. For a call option, this means that the firm can exercise the option and obtain 10,000 euros for $1.295 when the current exchange rate is $1.31. Thus the option has an intrinsic value of $150 [the difference between the spot rate and exercise price multiplied by the amount of currency ($1.31 – $1.295) (10,000 euros)]. Thus, if the call option had a current market price of $700, $150 would be treated as the intrinsic value and $550 would be treated as the time value of the option. Thus "in the money" options contain both an intrinsic and time value element. If the spot rate drops to $1.28 (after the option was acquired), the firm would be better off not exercising the option and purchase the needed euros on the market at $1.28.

The following chart helps illustrate when a call or a put option might be used and when the option is in the money.

Item Hedged	*Option Used*	*Exercise Price Exceeds Spot Rate*	*Exercise Price Is Less Than the Spot Rate*
Payable	Call Option	"Out of the Money"	"In the Money"
Receivable	Put Option	"In the Money"	"Out of the Money"

Thus a call option is used when a foreign currency is needed to pay a liability in the future, and a put option is used when foreign currency received in the future needs to be sold and converted into dollars.

Cash Flow Hedge Using Options: An Illustration To illustrate the hedge of a forecasted foreign currency transaction with the use of an option, assume the following:

1. On December 1, 2007, a U.S. firm estimates that inventory will be sold to a company in Germany during January of 2008 for 500,000 euros. The cost of the inventory sold is estimated to be $300,000.
2. Spot rates were as follows (dollars per euro):

December 1, 2007	$1.03
Balance sheet date (12/31/07)	$1.00
February 1, 2008	$0.98

3. The transaction is to be denominated in euros.
4. On December 1, 2007, the company purchases a put option for $5,000 to hedge any changes that may occur in the receivable denominated in euros. This option allows the firm to sell 500,000 euros at $1.02 with an expiration date of February 1, 2008. The spot rate was $1.03 on this date so the option is out of the money. At year-end (the balance sheet date), the value of the option increased to $14,000. On the option expiration date, the option only has an intrinsic value (the difference between the exercise price and the spot rate). Therefore on February 1, the value of the option is $20,000.

The rationale for use of the option is as follows. Because the sale is expected to occur in the future (next January) and because the exchange rate may change unfavorably, the company buys an option to sell 500,000 euros at $1.02 or $510,000. When the sale of inventory occurs and the company receives the euros, the firm is subject to any exchange losses. However, because the firm now has an option to sell euros, the company can use the euros that it receives from the sale to deliver on the option. Therefore, if the exchange rate drops below the exercise rate ($1.02), the firm is covered (i.e., the firm exercises the option and sells the 500,000 euros for $510,000). If the exchange rate exceeds the exercise rate, the option will not be exercised.

The entries to record the purchase and forward exchange contract are:

December 1, 2007—Transaction Date

(1) Option to sell euros	5,000	
Cash		5,000
To record purchase of a put option.		

On the balance sheet date (December 31, 2007), the option is adjusted to its market value of $14,000. Therefore on December 31, 2007, the following entry is made.

December 31, 2007—Balance Sheet Date

(2) Option to sell euros	9,000	
Foreign exchange gain—Other Comprehensive Income (balance sheet equity)		9,000
To record a gain on the change in option value ($14,000 − $5,000).		

The recognition of the gain is reported in other comprehensive income because it qualifies under the criteria designated in *SFAS No. 133* **[ASC 815-30-35-9]**. For example, the forecasted transaction is probable, and it presents exposure to price changes that are expected to affect earnings and cause variability in cash flows. Amounts deferred from earnings are reported in other comprehensive income and are reclassified into earnings in the period during which the hedged forecasted transaction "affects earnings" (for example, when a forecasted sale actually occurs).[12]

February 1, 2008—Option Expiration Date

(3) Option to sell euros	6,000	
Foreign exchange gain—Other Comprehensive Income (balance sheet equity)		6,000
To adjust the option value to its market value of $20,000. The value of the option [($1.02 exercise price less $0.98 spot rate) × 500,000 euros] is $20,000 less the carrying value of the option ($14,000).		

Technically, since the forecasted transaction occurred on this date, the gain recorded in entry (3) could also be reported in earnings immediately. We chose to initially record the gain using the balance sheet account (other comprehensive income) and then immediately reclassify the total exchange gain into earnings (see entry 6 below).

(4) Investment in FC (500,000 euros)	490,000	
Revenues		490,000
Cost of goods sold	300,000	
Inventory		300,000
To sell the inventory (complete the forecasted transaction).		

[12] *SFAS No. 133*, "Accounting for Derivative Instruments and Hedging Activities" (Norwalk, CT: FASB, 1998), par. 31 **[ASC 815-30-35]**.

(5) Cash (exercise price $1.02 × 500,000 euros)	510,000	
Option to sell euros (intrinsic value on option date)		20,000
Investment in FC (500,000 euros @ $0.98)		490,000
To exercise the option and settle with the trader.		
(6) Foreign exchange gain—Other Comprehensive Income	15,000	
Revenue ($9,000 from entry 2 and $6,000 from entry 3).		15,000
To reclassify the total exchange gains into earnings.		

Note that in entry (4), revenue is recorded at the spot rate. However, entry (6) adjusts revenue to recognize the benefit of the option. Entry (6) is required because the amount recognized in other accumulated income is reclassified into earnings in the period the hedged item affects earnings. Thus the total amount of revenue recognized is $505,000, which represents the revenue recognized at the spot rate ($490,000) plus the net benefit of the option $15,000 ($1.02 exercise rate over the spot rate $0.98 multiplied by 500,000 euros less the initial cost of the option of $5,000).

Split Accounting—Intrinsic and Time Value Elements In order to qualify for "hedge accounting" under *SFAS No. 133* **[ASC 815–20–25–72 through 87]**, the hedges must be effective. Firms are required to measure the effectiveness of their hedges quarterly. If the hedge is not highly effective, hedge accounting can no longer be used. Therefore, firms must determine how they measure hedge effectiveness. This usually means that the changes in value of the hedge (e.g., the forward contract or option) should be approximately equal to the changes in value of the hedged item. In the examples used in this chapter, we have used the change in the forward rate to measure the change in value of the forward contracts and the total change in the value of the option to measure the change in value of the option. The FASB allows split accounting for derivatives. This means that the intrinsic value of the derivative and the part of the option value related to time can be separated and accounted for differently. For instance, firms can use the total change in value of the option to measure gains and losses *or* the change in the intrinsic value to measure the change in value of the derivative. The change in the time value element would be taken immediately into earnings. Although it is important to know that these complicating factors exist, in this chapter we measure the change in value of the derivative using the total value of the derivative. Also, we assume that all hedges are highly effective.

Other Forms of Foreign Borrowing or Lending

Earlier in the chapter, we illustrated the exporting or importing of inventory. Accounting for other types of foreign borrowing or lending transactions is similar; that is, the two-transaction approach is followed in which the cost of an asset acquired or revenue recognized is accounted for independently from the method of settlement. For example, if a fixed asset is acquired from a foreign company on credit, the cost of the asset is the number of foreign currency units that would be paid in a cash transaction multiplied by the exchange rate at the transaction date. The cost of the asset is not adjusted for subsequent changes in the exchange rate, but the liability is adjusted at each balance sheet date on the basis of the exchange rate in effect at that date. The adjustment to the liability is reported currently in income. The amount recorded for interest expense is the equivalent number of U.S. dollars needed to make the interest payment.

SUMMARY

1. *Distinguish between the terms* measured *and* denominated. Transactions are normally ***measured*** and recorded in terms of the currency in which the reporting entity prepares its financial statements. Assets and liabilities are ***denominated*** in a currency if their amounts are fixed in terms of that currency.
2. *Describe what is meant by a foreign currency transaction.* A foreign currency transaction is a transaction that requires settlement in a foreign currency, not in U.S. dollars (for a U.S. firm).
3. *Understand some of the more common foreign currency transactions.* Some common transactions include: (1) importing or exporting goods or services on credit with the receivable or payable denominated in a foreign currency; (2) borrowing from or lending to a foreign company with the amount payable or receivable denominated in the foreign currency; (3) engaging in a transaction with the intention of hedging a net investment in a foreign entity; and (4) entering into a forward contract to buy or sell foreign currency.
4. *Identify three stages of concern to accountants for foreign currency transactions and explain the steps used to translate foreign currency transactions for each stage.* At the initial date, the transaction is recognized (in conformity with GAAP), the account (balance sheet or income statement) arising from the transaction is measured and recorded in dollars by multiplying the foreign currency unit by the current exchange rate. At each subsequent balance sheet date until settlement, recorded balances that are denominated in a foreign currency are adjusted to reflect the current exchange rate in effect at the balance sheet date. At the settlement date, the treatment depends on whether the balance to be settled is a foreign currency payable or receivable. If a foreign currency payable is being settled, a U.S. firm must convert U.S. dollars into foreign currency units to settle the account. At the settlement of a foreign currency receivable, the foreign currency units received are converted into dollars.
5. *Describe a forward exchange contract.* A forward exchange contract is an agreement to exchange currencies of two different countries at a specified rate (the forward rate) on a stipulated future date. At the inception of the contract, the forward rate is usually different from the spot rate.
6. *Explain the use of forward contracts as a hedge of an unrecognized firm commitment.* In many cases, the firm enters into an agreement to purchase or sell goods where the transaction is denominated in a foreign currency. Because the exchange rate might change before the payable is paid or the receivable is collected, a firm can use a forward contract to lock in the amount of cash paid or the amount of cash received.
7. *Identify some of the common situations in which a forward exchange contract can be used as a hedge.* Hedges may be used to hedge a foreign currency exposed receivable or payable position, to hedge a net investment in a foreign subsidiary, to hedge an identifiable foreign currency commitment, or to hedge a forecasted transaction.
8. *Described a derivative instrument and understand how it may be used as a hedge.* A derivative is an executory contract between two parties to be executed at a later date, with the resulting future cash flows dependent on the change in some other underlying measure of value. The eventual dollar amount of the performance is determined by subsequent value changes, and the eventual outcome is necessarily favorable to one of the parties involved and unfavorable to the other.
9. *Explain how exchange gains and losses are reported for fair value hedges and cash flow hedges.* The FASB allows deferral of the exchange gain and loss on cash flow hedges (a forecasted transaction). Like other gains and losses that are excluded from the income statement, they are included as components of "other comprehensive income" and reported in the stockholders' equity section of the balance sheet. On the other hand, exchange gains and losses on fair value hedges (unrecognized firm commitments) are reported in current periods earnings along with the exchange gain or loss on the hedged item.

TEST YOUR KNOWLEDGE SOLUTIONS

12-1 1. c
2. b
12-2 1. a
2. b
12-3 1. b
2. c
3. a

QUESTIONS

LO2 1. Define currency exchange rates and distinguish between "direct" and "indirect" quotations.

LO3 2. Explain why a firm is exposed to an added risk when it enters into a transaction that is to be settled in a foreign currency.

LO4 3. Name the three stages of concern to the accountant in accounting for import–export transactions. Briefly explain the accounting for each stage.

LO4 4. How should a transaction gain or loss be reported that is related to an unsettled receivable recorded when the firm's inventory was exported?

LO4 5. A U.S. firm carried a receivable for 100,000 yen. Assuming that the direct exchange rate declined from $.009 at the date of the transaction to $.006 at the balance sheet date, compute the transaction gain or loss. What balance would be reported for the receivable in the firm's balance sheet?

LO4 6. Explain what is meant by the "two-transaction method" in recording exporting or importing transactions. What support is given for this method?

LO5 7. Describe a forward exchange contract.

LO7 8. Explain the effects on income from hedging a foreign currency exposed net asset position or net liability position.

LO6 9. What criteria must be satisfied for a foreign currency transaction to be considered a hedge of an identifiable foreign currency commitment?

LO5 10. The FASB classifies forward contracts as those acquired for the purpose of hedging and those acquired for the purpose of speculation. What main differences are there in accounting for these two classifications?

LO9 11. How are foreign currency exchange gains and losses from hedging a forecasted transaction handled?

LO8 12. What is a put option, and how might it be used to hedge a forecasted transaction?

LO8 13. Define a derivative instrument, and describe the keystones identified by the FASB for the accounting for such instruments.

LO8 14. Differentiate between forward-based derivatives and option-based derivatives.

LO9 15. List some of the criteria laid out by the FASB that are required for a gain or loss on forecasted transactions (a cash flow hedge) to be excluded from the income statement. If these criteria are satisfied, where are the gains or losses reported, and when (if ever) are they shown in the income statement? What is the rationale for this treatment?

Business Ethics

Executive stock options (ESOs) are used to provide incentives for executives to improve company performance. ESOs are usually granted "at-the-money," meaning that the exercise price of the options is set to equal the market price of the underlying stock on the grant date. Clearly, executives would prefer to be granted options when the stock price (and thus the exercise price) is at its lowest.

Backdating options is the practice of choosing a past date when the market price was particularly low. Backdating has not, in the past, been illegal if no documents are forged, if communicated to the shareholders, and if properly reflected in earnings and in taxes.

1. Since backdating gives the executive an "instant" profit, why wouldn't the firm simply grant an option with the exercise price lower than the current market price?
2. Suppose the executive was not involved in backdating the ESOs. Does the executive face any ethical issues?[13]

Note: Students are encouraged to read the WSJ referenced above.

[13] *WSJ*, "Options Study Becomes Required Reading," by Steve Stecklow, 5/30/06.

EXERCISES

EXERCISE 12-1 **Importing and Exporting Journal Entries** LO4

Selco, a U.S. Company, imports and exports tools, shop equipment, and industrial construction supplies. The company uses a periodic inventory system. During April the company entered into the following transactions. All rate quotations are direct exchange rates.

April 3 Purchased power tools from a wholesaler in Japan, on account, at an invoice cost of 1,600,000 yen. On this date the exchange rate for the yen was $.0072.

5 Sold hand tools on credit that were manufactured in the U.S. to a retail outlet located in West Germany. The invoice price was $2,800. The exchange rate for marks was $.5829.

9 Sold electric drills on account to a retailer in New Zealand. The invoice price was 16,800 U.S. dollars and the exchange rate for the New Zealand dollar was $.576.

11 Purchased drill bits on account from a manufacturer located in Belgium. The billing was for 801,282 francs. The exchange rate for francs was $.0312.

16 Paid 1,000,000 yen on account to the wholesaler for purchases made on April 3. The exchange rate on this date was $.0067.

18 Settled the accounts payable with the Belgium manufacturer. The exchange rate was $.0368.

22 Received full payment from the New Zealand retailer. The exchange rate was $.568.

30 Completed payment on the April 3 purchase. The exchange rate was $.0078.

Required:

Prepare journal entries on the books of Selco to record the transactions listed above.

EXERCISE 12-2 **Importing and Exporting Journal Entries** LO4

During December of the current year, Teletex Systems, Inc., a company based in Seattle, Washington, entered into the following transactions:

Dec 10 Sold seven office computers to a company located in Colombia for 8,541,000 pesos. On this date, the spot rate was 365 pesos per U.S. dollar.

12 Purchased computer chips from a company domiciled in Taiwan. The contract was denominated in 500,000 Taiwan dollars. The direct exchange spot rate on this date was $.0391.

Required:

A. Prepare journal entries to record the transactions above on the books of Teletex Systems, Inc. The company uses a periodic inventory system.

B. Prepare journal entries necessary to adjust the accounts as of December 31. Assume that on December 31 the direct exchange rates were as follows:

Colombia peso	$.00268
Taiwan dollar	$.0351

C. Prepare journal entries to record settlement of both open accounts on January 10. Assume that the direct exchange rates on the settlement dates were as follows:

Colombia peso	$.00320
Taiwan dollar	$.0398

D. Prepare journal entries to record the December 10 transaction, adjust the accounts on December 31, and record settlement of the account on January 10, assuming that the transaction was denominated in dollars rather than pesos. Assume the same exchange rates as those given.

EXERCISE 12-3 **Multiple Choice—Importing Transactions** LO6

On December 1, 2008, Tuscano Corp. entered into a transaction to import raw materials from a foreign company. The account is to be settled on February 1 with the payment of 60,000 foreign currency units (FCU). On December 1, Tuscano also entered into a forward contract to hedge the exposed position resulting from the import transaction. The forward rate is $.71 per unit of foreign currency. Tuscano Corp. has a December 31 fiscal year-end. Spot rates and the forward rates on relevant dates were:

Date	*Spot Rate per Unit of Foreign Currency*	*Forward Rate (Feb. 1 Settlement)*
December 1	$.69	$.71
December 31	.72	.715
February 1	.73	.73

Required:

Use the data given to select the best answer to each question.

1. The forward contract entered into on December 1 is an example of
   - **(a)** A hedge of an exposed receivable position.
   - **(b)** A hedge of a foreign currency commitment.
   - **(c)** A contract entered into for speculation.
   - **(d)** A hedge of an exposed payable position.

2. The entry to record the forward contract is

(a) Dollars Receivable	41,400	
FCU Payable		41,400
(b) FCU Receivable	41,400	
Dollars Receivable		41,400
(c) Dollars Receivable	42,600	
FCU Payable		42,600
(d) FCU Receivable	42,600	
Dollars Payable		42,600
(e) None of the above		

3. On December 31, what will be the adjusted balance in the Accounts Payable account and how much gain or loss was recorded as a result of the adjustment?

	Payable Balance	*Gain or Loss Recorded*
(a)	$43,200	$1,800 gain
(b)	40,800	2,400 loss
(c)	40,800	2,400 gain
(d)	43,200	1,800 loss

4. What amount of net transaction gain or loss from the transactions should be included in the determination of the 2008 net income?
   - **(a)** $1,500 loss.
   - **(b)** $1,800 loss.
   - **(c)** $—0—Because a gain or loss on the forward contract is offset by a loss or gain on the exposed position.
   - **(d)** $2,400 gain.

5. Which of the following statements is ***not*** true?
   - **(a)** Assuming the account payable is to be settled on February 1, Tuscano Corp. was able to reduce its cash outflow for the purchases as a result of entering into the forward contract.
   - **(b)** During 2009, a transaction loss of $600 was recorded on the forward contract.

(c) Tuscano Corp. paid $42,600 to complete the forward contract.

(d) During 2009 a transaction loss of $600 was recorded on the exposed payable.

EXERCISE 12-4 **Multiple Choice** LO2 LO4 LO6

Select the best answer for each of the following.

1. A forward contract is a hedge of an identifiable foreign currency commitment if
   - **(a)** The forward contract is designated as, and is effective as, a hedge of a foreign currency commitment.
   - **(b)** The foreign currency commitment is firm.
   - **(c)** The amount of the forward contract is equal to the amount of the commitment.
   - **(d)** Both (a) and (b).
   - **(e)** Both (a) and (c).
2. The Carnival Company has a receivable from a foreign customer that is payable in the local currency of the foreign customer. The account receivable for 800,000 local currency units (LCU) has been translated into $280,000 on Carnival's December 31, 2008, balance sheet. On January 15, 2009, the receivable was collected in full when the exchange rate was 4 LCU to $1. What journal entry should Carnival make to record the collection of this receivable?

(a) Cash	200,000	
Accounts Receivable		200,000
(b) Cash	200,000	
Transaction Loss	80,000	
Accounts Receivable		280,000
(c) Cash	200,000	
Deferred Transaction Loss	80,000	
Accounts Receivable		280,000
(d) Cash	280,000	
Accounts Receivable		280,000

3. A foreign currency transaction to a company domiciled in the United States is a transaction in which the amount is
   - **(a)** Measured in a foreign currency.
   - **(b)** Denominated in U.S. dollars.
   - **(c)** Denominated in a foreign currency.
   - **(d)** Measured in U.S. dollars.
4. A direct exchange quotation is one in which the exchange rate is quoted
   - **(a)** In terms of how many units of the domestic currency can be converted into one unit of foreign currency.
   - **(b)** In terms of how many units of the foreign currency can be converted into one unit of the domestic currency.
   - **(c)** For the future delivery of currencies exchanged.
   - **(d)** For the immediate delivery of currencies exchanged.

EXERCISE 12-5 **Multiple Choice** LO4

Select the best answer for each of the following.

1. A sale of goods by a U.S. company was denominated in a foreign currency. The sale resulted in a receivable that was fixed in terms of the amount of foreign currency that would be received. Exchange rates between the dollar and the currency in which the transaction was denominated changed so that a loss was incurred. This loss should be included as a(n)
   - **(a)** Extraordinary item in the income statement.
   - **(b)** Component of income from continuing operations.

(c) Separate component of stockholders' equity.
(d) Deferred item in the balance sheet.

2. On September 1, 2008, Change Corp. received an order for equipment from a foreign customer for 300,000 units of foreign currency when the U.S. dollar equivalent was $96,000. Change shipped the equipment on October 15, 2008, and billed the customer for 300,000 units of foreign currency when the U.S. dollar equivalent was $110,000. Change received the customer's remittance in full on November 16, 2008, and sold the 300,000 foreign currency units for $105,000. In its income statement for the year ended December 31, 2008, Change should report a foreign exchange loss of
   (a) $9,000
   (b) $5,000
   (c) $14,000
   (d) $—0—

3. McNeil, a U.S. corporation, bought inventory items from a supplier in Denmark on November 5, 2008, for 100,000 krones, when the spot rate was $.4395. At McNeil's December 31, 2008, year-end, the spot rate was $.4345. On January 15, 2009, McNeil bought 100,000 krones at the spot rate of $.4445 and paid the invoice. How much should McNeil report in its income statement for 2008 and 2009 as transaction gain or loss?

	2008	*2009*
(a)	$—0—	$ 500 loss
(b)	$500 loss	$—0—
(c)	$500 loss	$1,000 gain
(d)	$500 gain	$1,000 loss

4. During 2008 a U.S. firm sold inventory to a foreign customer. The transaction was denominated in the local currency of the buyer. The direct exchange rate decreased from the date of the transaction to the end of the fiscal period; the rate increased from the end of the fiscal year to the date the account was settled in 2009. A transaction gain or loss should be recognized

	2008	*2009*
(a)	Loss	Loss
(b)	Gain	Loss
(c)	Loss	Gain
(d)	Gain	Gain

(AICPA adapted)

EXERCISE 12-6 **Transaction Gain or Loss** LO4

Agentel Corporation is a U.S.-based importing-exporting company. The company entered into the following transactions during the month of November.

Nov. 6 Purchased merchandise from AGT, a Swiss firm, for 600,000 francs.
5 Sold merchandise to SLS, Inc., a firm located in Rio De Janeiro, for $200,000.
18 Sold merchandise to TNT, Ltd., a British firm, for 130,000 pounds.
20 Purchased merchandise from SDS, Ltd., a British firm, for $160,000.

All the transactions were unsettled at December 31, Agentel's fiscal year-end. Spot rates are as follows:

		Currency	
Date	*Franc*	*Real*	*Pound*
November 6	$.490	$.412	$1.520
November 15	.487	.409	1.509
November 18	.476	.414	1.506
November 20	.468	.405	1.498
December 31	.460	.398	1.482

Required:

A. Compute the amount that Agentel would report for each unsettled receivable and payable in its balance sheet prepared at December 31.

B. Compute the transaction gain or loss on each unsettled receivable and payable that would be reported in the income statement prepared for the year ended December 31.

EXERCISE 12-7 Journal Entries, Income Effect, and Amount of Cash Received LO6

ASI recently completed the development and installation of an accounting information system for a company located in Rio De Janeiro, Brazil. The company considered that all revenue realization criteria were satisfied and accordingly recorded on October 2, 2008, a receivable from the foreign company. The receivable is to be settled in 120 days on February 1 by the delivery of 300,000 Real. To hedge against an unfavorable change in the foreign exchange rate, ASI acquired a forward contract to sell 300,000 real on February 1 for $.4730 per real. The following exchange rates were quoted:

Date	*Spot Rate*	*Forward Rate (Delivery on 2/1)*
October 2	$.4737	$.4730
December 31	.4895	.4810
February 1	.4950	—

ASI is a calendar-year company.

Required:

A. Prepare the journal entries to record the transactions, adjust the accounts on December 31, and settle the receivable and forward contract on February 1.

B. **(1)** Based on the data given above, complete the following table.

	2008	*2009*
Revenue	______	______
Transaction gain (loss) related to the exposed receivable balance	______	______
Transaction gain (loss) related to the forward contract	______	______
Effect on net income	______	______

(2) What was the cumulative effect on net income (i.e., 2008 plus 2009)?

(3) How much cash was received when the account was settled?

EXERCISE 12-8 Fair Value Hedge (Unrecognized Firm Commitment) LO6

Vanderbilt Clothing Company placed a clothing order with a company located in Taiwan. The order was placed on November 1, 2008, for delivery on May 1, 2009. Vanderbilt agreed to pay for the goods on May 1, 2009, with the delivery of 5,000,000 Taiwan dollars. To protect against fluctuations in the exchange rate, the company entered into a forward contract on November 1, 2008, to buy 5,000,000 Taiwan dollars on May 1, 2009, for $.02634 per unit.

Direct exchange rates per Taiwan dollar on specific dates are as follows:

Date	*Spot Rate*	*Forward Rate—Maturity May 1*
November 1, 2008	$.02631	$.02634
December 31, 2008	.02740	.02735
May 1, 2009	.02591	—

Required:

Prepare the journal entries to be made by Vanderbilt Clothing Company during 2008 and 2009 to account for the transactions described above.

EXERCISE 12-9 Journal Entries—Speculation Using a Forward Contract LO5

Sharon Myers, chief finance officer for Sitco Products, convinced the president of the company to enter into a 90-day forward contract *to sell* 900,000 Swedish kronas as a speculative venture. When the forward contract was acquired on November 1, 2008, the spot rate for the krona was $.5045 and the 90-day future rate was $.5085. At December 31, 2008, the end of the firm's fiscal year, the spot rate was $.4981 and the future rate for kronas to be sold on January 30, 2009, was $.4996. On January 30, 2009, the spot rate was $.4826.

Required:

Prepare all necessary journal entries in regard to the forward contract.

EXERCISE 12-10 Journal Entries—Speculation Using a Forward Contract LO5

Use the data given in Exercise 12-9, except assume that on November 1, Sitco Products entered into a 90-day forward contract *to buy* 900,000 Swedish kronas on January 30 for $.5085 per krona.

Required:

Prepare all necessary journal entries in regard to the forward contract.

EXERCISE 12-11 Equipment Purchase, Issuance of a Note LO4

Roland Brothers, Inc. purchased equipment from a British firm for £120,000 on April 1, 2008. To finance the purchase of the equipment, the president of the company signed a note for £120,000 with a British bank. The loan is denominated in pounds, matures on March 31, 2009, and bears interest at 12% per annum payable on June 30, September 30, December 31, and March 31. Spot rates for the British pound are as follows:

April 1, 2008	$1.574
June 30, 2008	1.560
September 30, 2008	1.526
December 31, 2008	1.498
March 31, 2009	1.538

Required:

Prepare journal entries to record the purchase of the equipment, the interest payments, the adjustment of the accounts on December 31 (the fiscal year-end), and the payment of the note at maturity.

EXERCISE 12-12 Forward Contract Hedge of an Importing Transaction LO6

On November 15, 2008, Solanski Inc. imported 500,000 barrels of oil from an oil company in Venezuela. Solanski agreed to pay 50,000,000 bolivars on January 15, 2009. To ensure that the dollar outlay for the purchase will not fluctuate, the company entered into a forward contract *to buy* 50,000,000 bolivars on January 15 at the forward rate of $.0269. Direct exchange rates on various dates were:

	Spot Rate	*Forward Rate 1/15 Delivery*
November 15	$.0239	$.0269
December 31	.0224	.0254
January 15	.0291	

Solanski Inc. is a calendar-year company.

Required:

Compute the following:

1. The dollars to be paid on January 15, 2009, to acquire the 50,000,000 bolivars from the exchange dealer.

2. The dollars that would have been paid to settle the account payable had Solanski not hedged the purchased contract with the forward contract.
3. The discount or premium on the forward contract.
4. The transaction gain or loss on the exposed liability related to the oil purchase in 2008 and 2009.
5. The transaction gain or loss on the forward contract in 2008 and 2009.

EXERCISE 12-13 Cash Flow Hedge Illustration LO9

Consider the following information:

1. On December 1, 2008, a U.S. firm *plans* to purchase a piece of equipment (with an asking price of 100,000 francs) in Switzerland during January of 2009. The transaction is probable, and the transaction is to be denominated in euros.
2. On December 1, 2008, the company enters into a forward contract to buy 100,000 francs for $1.01 on January 31, 2009.
3. Spot rates and the forward rates for January 31, 2009, settlement were as follows (dollars per franc):

	Spot Rate	*Forward Rate for 1/31/09*
December 1, 2008	$0.99	$1.01
Balance sheet date (12/31/08)	$1.01	$1.02
January 31 and February 1, 2009	$1.04	

4. On February 1, the equipment was purchased for 100,000 francs.

Required:

A. Prepare all journal entries needed on December 1, December 31, January 31, and February 1 to account for the forecasted transaction, the forward contract, and the transaction to buy the equipment.

B. When should the company reclassify any amounts reported in other accumulated comprehensive income as a result of the cash flow hedge?

EXERCISE 12-14 Fair Value Hedge Illustration—Forward Contract LO6

Consider the following information:

1. On December 1, 2008, a U.S. firm *contracts* to sell equipment (with an asking price of 1,000,000 pesos) in Mexico. The firm will take delivery and will pay for the equipment on March 1, 2009.
2. On December 1, 2008, the company enters into a forward contract to sell 1,000,000 pesos for $0.0948 on March 1, 2009.
3. Spot rates and the forward rates for March 1, 2009, settlement were as follows (dollars per peso):

	Spot Rate	*Forward Rate for 3/1/09*
December 1, 2008	$0.0954	$0.0948
Balance sheet date (12/31/08)	0.0949	0.0944
March 1, 2009	0.0947	

4. On March 1, the equipment was sold for 1,000,000 pesos. The cost of the equipment was $40,000.

Required:

Prepare all journal entries needed on December 1, December 31, and March 1 to account for the forward contract, the firm commitment, and the transaction to sell the equipment.

EXERCISE 12-15 Fair Value Hedge Illustration—Options LO8

1. On June 1, 2008, a U.S. firm *contracts* to sell equipment (with an asking price of 2,000,000 krona) in Sweden. The firm will take delivery and will pay for the equipment on August 1, 2008.
2. Spot rates were as follows (dollars per krona):

	Spot Rate
June 1, 2008	$0.107
August 1, 2008	0.102

3. On August 1, the equipment was sold for 2,000,000 krona. The cost of the equipment was $100,000.

Suppose that on June 1, 2008, the firm believes, based on recent changes in the economy, that there is a high probability of exchange rate losses from the transaction. If the firm acquires an option to hedge the transaction, answer the following questions.

Required:

A. Does the firm believe that the krona is strengthening or weakening relative to the U.S. dollar?

B. What kind of option should the firm use: a put or a call option?

C. Suppose the following options are available. Each option can only be exercised on August 1. Choose the option that should be used to hedge the transaction and prepare all journal entries needed to record the hedge and the transaction to sell the equipment.

Option Type	*Amount*	*Exercise Rate*	*Cost to Acquire*
Call Option	2,000,000 krona	$0.1035	$ 8,000
Put Option	2,000,000 krona	$0.1035	$15,000

PROBLEMS

PROBLEM 12-1 Journal Entries—Exporting Transactions LO4

GAF manufactures electrical cells at its St. Louis facility. The company's fiscal year-end is September 30. It has adopted the perpetual inventory cost flow method to control inventory costs. The company entered into the following transactions during the month of September. All exchange rates are direct quotations.

Date		*Transaction*	*Billing Amount*	*Rate of Exchange*
2008				
Sept.	5	Exported 10 electrical cells to a company located in Argentina. Cost per unit, $950.	17,341 pesos	$1.1291
	9	Received raw materials ordered from a British company. The goods were shipped FOB destination and had not been recorded on the books of GAF, Inc.	12,200 Pounds	1.6821
	14	Exported 12 electrical cells to a company domiciled in Norway. Cost per unit, $970.	160,274 Krone	.1450
	30	End of fiscal year-end.		
		Peso		1.1091
		British pound		1.6911
		Krone		.1530

Date		Transaction	*Billing Amount*	*Rate of Exchange*
Oct.	5	Received full payment for the 10 units sold on September 5.		1.1190
	9	Paid British company in full for raw materials purchased September 9.		1.5948
	30	Received full payment for 12 units sold on September 14.		.1440

Required:

A. Prepare the journal entries required on the books of GAF to record the transactions and year-end adjustments. Round all computations to the nearest dollar.

B. Based on the two exporting transactions listed above, complete the following table.

	Transaction	
	Sept. 5	*Sept. 14*
September 30, 2008, year-end:		
1. Sales	_______	_______
2. Transaction gain (loss)	_______	_______
September 30, 2009, year-end:		
3. Sales	_______	_______
4. Transaction gain (loss)	_______	_______
5. Net effect on income for both years (Sum lines 1–4)	_______	_______
6. Cash received on settlement date	_______	_______

PROBLEM 12-2 **Importing/Exporting Transactions with a Forward Contract Hedge** LO6

Crystal Exporting Co. is a U.S. wholesaler engaged in foreign trade. The following transactions are representative of its business dealings. The company uses a periodic inventory system and is on a calendar-year basis. All exchange rates are direct quotations.

Dec. 1 Crystal Exporting purchased merchandise from Chang's Ltd., a Hong Kong manufacturer. The invoice was for 210,000 Hong Kong dollars, payable on April 1. On this same date, Crystal Exporting acquired a forward contract to buy 210,000 Hong Kong dollars on April 1 for $.1314.

Dec. 29 Crystal Exporting sold merchandise to Zintel Retailers for 120,000 Hong Kong dollars, receivable in 90 days. No hedging was involved.

April 1 Crystal Exporting received 120,000 Hong Kong dollars from Zintel Retailers.

1 Crystal Exporting submitted full payment of 210,000 Hong Kong dollars to Chang's, Ltd., after obtaining the 210,000 Hong Kong dollars on its forward contract.

Spot rates and the forward rates for the Hong Kong dollar were as follows:

	Spot Rate	*Forward Rate for April 1 Delivery*
Dec. 1	$.1265	$.1314
Dec. 29	.1240	.1305
Dec. 31	.1259	.1308
April 1	.1430	

Required:

A. Prepare journal entries for the transactions including the necessary adjustments on December 31.

B. Explain the income statement treatment given to any transaction gains and losses recognized at December 31.

PROBLEM 12-3 **Foreign Trade Journal Entries and Forward Contract Hedge** LO6

On December 1, 2008, King Company exported equipment that had cost $210,000 to a Brazilian company for 1,000,000 Real. The account is to be settled on January 31, 2009. King Company is a calendar-year company and uses a perpetual inventory system. Direct exchange rates were:

	Spot Rate
December 1	$.4441
December 31	.3690
January 31	.4421

Required:

A. Prepare journal entries to record the exporting transaction, adjust the accounts on December 31, and settle the account on January 31.

B. What effect did changes in the exchange rate have on income in 2008 and 2009?

C. Assume the facts given above, except that on December 1, King Company entered into a forward contract to sell 1,000,000 Real on January 31 for $.4451 per Real. Prepare the journal entries needed in 2008 and 2009 to record the forward contract and settle the accounts. The forward rate on December 31 for January 31 delivery was $.3810.

D. What is the combined effect on income in 2008 and 2009 from the exporting transaction and the forward contract?

PROBLEM 12-4 **Journal Entries—Exporting Transactions with Forward Contract Hedges** LO6

Centennial Exchange of St. Louis, Missouri, imports and exports grains. The company has a September 30 fiscal year-end. The periodic inventory system and the weighted-average cost flow method are used by the company to account for inventory cost. The company negotiated the following transactions during 2008 (assume forward contracts exist for the Krone and Forint).

Sept. 1 Sold 1,000,000 bushels of wheat to a Norwegian company for 16,500,000 Krone. The account is to be settled on October 30.

Sept. 1 The management of Centennial was concerned that the Krone would decline in value. They therefore entered into a forward contract to sell 16,500,000 Krone on October 30 for $.1442 per Krone.

Sept. 5 Sold 1,000,000 bushels of wheat to a Tokyo company for $5,300,000. The account is to be settled on November 5.

Sept. 15 Purchased grain from an exporting company that operates in Hungary. The contract provides for the payment of 20,000,000 forint on October 15.

Sept. 15 Entered into a forward contract to buy 20,000,000 forint on October 15 for $.006490 per Forint.

Sept. 18 Sold 500 tons of soybean meal to Able & Born, Ltd., a Toronto company, for 48,000 Canadian dollars. The account is to be settled on December 17.

Oct. 15 Completed the forward contract to buy 20,000,000 forint and then submitted payment to pay for the grain purchased on September 15.

Oct. 30 Received 16,500,000 Krones from the Norwegian customer and settled forward contract.

Nov. 5 Received payment in full for the wheat sold on September 5 to the Tokyo company.

Dec. 17 Received payment from Able & Born, Ltd. for the September 18 sale.

Direct exchange quotations for specific dates are presented below:

	Norway—Krone	*Japan—Yen*	*Hungary—Forint*	*Canada—Dollar*
September 1	$.1480	$.00738	$.006427	$.8250
September 5	.1458	.00740	.006428	.8248
September 15	.1456	.00741	.006430	.8246
September 18	.1456	.00737	.006431	.8245
September 30	.1455	.00736	.006433	.8243
October 15	.1458	.00734	.006435	.8241
October 30	.1457	.00732	.006370	.8241
November 5	.1456	.00730	.006439	.8244
December 17	.1453	.00731	.006438	.8250

On September 30, the forward rate for Krone (with an October 30 settlement) was $.1450 and the forward rate for Forints (with an October 15 settlement) was $.00640.

Required:

Prepare journal entries, including year-end adjustments, to record the above transactions.

PROBLEM 12-5 **Various Hedging Cases** LO5 LO9

Apple Company was incorporated in Delaware in 2006. On November 2, 2008, the controller of the company entered into a forward contract to sell 50,000 British pounds for $1.5920 on March 1, 2009. The following exchange rates were quoted on the indicated dates:

	Spot Rate	*Forward Rate March 1 Delivery*
November 2, 2008	$1.6021	1.5920
December 31, 2008	1.5820	1.58
March 1, 2009	1.6543	

Apple Company's fiscal year-end is December 31.

Required:

A. Assume that the forward contract was entered into as a hedge against an exposed foreign currency receivable balance in the amount of £50,000. Prepare the journal entries that would be made by Apple Company on

(1) November 2—to record the sale of the goods on account for £50,000 and to record the forward contract.

(2) December 31—to adjust the accounts related to the exposed asset and forward contract at fiscal year-end.

(3) March 1—to adjust the accounts related to the exposed asset and forward contract and to record the settlement of the receivable and delivery of the pounds to the exchange dealer.

B. Assume that the controller indicated on November 2 that the forward contract was acquired as a hedge of a future foreign currency transaction that is a commitment of Apple to sell inventory for £50,000 on March 1. Apple Company designates this hedge as a fair value hedge of an unrecognized firm commitment. Prepare the journal entries related to the forward contract and commitment to sell inventory that would be made by Apple Company on November 2, December 31, and March 1.

C. Assume that the contract was entered into to speculate in future exchange rate fluctuations. Prepare the journal entries that would be made by Apple Company on November 2, December 31, and March 1.

D. Compute the effect of the transactions in (A), (B), and (C) on the net income for the fiscal years ended December 31, 2008, and December 31, 2009. Indicate how the balance sheet accounts related to the forward contract would be reported in the December 31, 2008, balance sheet.

PROBLEM 12-6 **Hedge of an Unrecognized Foreign Currency Commitment – Fair Value Hedge** LO6

Citron Company is a U.S.-based citrus grower. On October 1, 2008, the company entered into a contract to ship 25,000 boxes of grapefruit on January 28 to Japan. Payment of 50,100,000 yen is to be received on March 29, 2009. On October 1, Citron also entered into a forward contract to sell 50,100,000 yen on March 29 at the forward rate of $.007412. The forward contract is considered a hedge of the unrecognized foreign currency commitment. The direct exchange rate and forward rate for the yen were as follows:

	October 1	*December 31*	*January 28*	*March 29*
Spot rate	$.007235	$.007879	$.007623	$.007640
Forward rate available for the remaining period of the forward contract	.007412	.007910	.007674	No appl.

Required:

A. Prepare the necessary journal entries to record the following transactions and events:

Oct. 1 Entered into the contract to sell the grapefruit and negotiated the forward contract.

Dec. 31 Fiscal year-end of Citron Company.

Jan. 28 The grapefruit were shipped FOB shipping point. The grapefruit cost Citron $7.50 per box. Citron uses a perpetual inventory system.

Mar. 29 Received the payment and delivered the yen to the exchange broker to settle the forward contract.

B. Compute the increase or decrease in income for each fiscal year as a result of the transactions above.

C. Compute the increase or decrease in income each period that would have occurred if Citron had not entered into the forward contract.

PROBLEM 12-7 **Foreign Currency Risk** LO2 LO5

During her first quarter review of the financial statements, Debra Bell, the CFO of HAL Computer Corporation, was distressed to notice the company's transaction loss had been steadily increasing each month. HAL is a publicly held manufacturer of "PC clone" personal computers. Like most manufacturers of its kind, HAL does not manufacture domestically but utilizes lower cost offshore suppliers for components and subcontractors for assembly. As it is HAL's policy to denominate foreign contracts in U.S. dollars whenever possible, the increase in transaction losses was particularly puzzling.

Subsequent conversations with HAL's controller, Tom Stewart, revealed all new contracts had been denominated in foreign currencies (primarily the South Korean won and Taiwanese dollar) in order to obtain more favorable purchase terms. Further, Mr. Stewart believed that the U.S. dollar would strengthen due to it being an election year. Since these contracts specify delivery and payment at various dates over the next 12 months, tremendous potential for exposure exists for the company if the dollar continues to decline against the major foreign currencies.

Required:

A. Mr. Stewart executed all new foreign contracts in foreign currencies in the belief it would help the company.

(1) Do you think he was justified in his actions given the company policy?

(2) On what basis did you decide if the controller was justified or not?

(3) Was the loss a factor in your decision? Is this appropriate?

B. A substantial amount of foreign denominated contracts already exist for goods and services not yet received.

(1) What actions may HAL take to minimize potential losses?

(2) What are the advantages and disadvantages of these actions?

(3) What implication does each of these scenarios have for financial statement disclosure?

C. Assume that you are Ms. Bell, and you are concerned about how the Board of Directors and the stockholders may react. Additionally, you are about to purchase a new home and are planning to sell some HAL stock for the down payment.

(1) After carefully considering all of your options, what action do you decide to take?

(2) Did concern over the Board, stockholders, or HAL's stock price enter into your decision? Why or why not?

PROBLEM 12-8 **Hedge of a Forecasted Sale Using a Foreign Currency Option** LO8

A U.S. company estimated that, in the first two months of 2010, its export sales to a Swiss company would generate 400,000 francs. On December 1, 2009, in an effort to protect against the weakening franc, the company purchased an option (out of the money) to sell 400,000 Swiss francs at an exchange rate of $0.60 with an expiration date of February 25, 2010. The cost of the option was $6,000. The spot rates on the following dates were:

December 1, 2009	$0.62
December 31, 2009	$0.60
February 25, 2010	$0.57

The option's value in the options market on December 31, 2009, was $9,000. December 31 is also an interim reporting date. The option was exercised on February 25, 2006.

Required:

Prepare all journal entries needed on December 1, December 31, and February 25 to account for the option.

PROBLEM 12-9 **Cash Flow Hedge Illustration—Forward Contract** LO9

Consider the following information:

1. On December 1, 2005, a U.S. firm *plans* to sell a piece of equipment [with an asking price of 200,000 units of a foreign currency (FC)] during January of 2006. The transaction is probable, and the transaction is to be denominated in euros.
2. The company enters into a forward contract on December 1, 2005 to sell 200,000 FC on February 1, 2006, for $1.02.
3. Spot rates and the forward rates for January 31, 2006, settlement were as follows (dollars per euro):

	Spot Rate	*Forward Rate for 2/1/06*
December 1, 2005	$1.04	$1.02
Balance sheet date (12/31/05)	$1.01	$1.00
January 31 and February 1, 2006	$0.99	

4. On January 31, the equipment was sold for 200,000 FC. The cost of the equipment was $170,000.

Required:

A. Prepare all journal entries needed on December 1, December 31, January 31, and February 1 to account for the forecasted transaction, the forward contract, and the transaction to sell the equipment.

B. Prepare any entry needed on February 1 to reclassify amounts from other accumulated comprehensive income into earnings.

PROBLEM 12-10 Fair Value Hedge of an Unrecognized Firm Commitment LO6

On October 1, 2008, Fairchange Corporation ordered some equipment from a supplier for 300,000 euros. Delivery and payment are to occur on November 15, 2008. The spot rates on October 1 and November 15, 2008, are $1.20 and $1.30, respectively.

Required:

A. Assume that Fairchange entered into a forward contract on October 1, 2008, to hedge the firm commitment. The forward rates for euros for November 15 delivery were

October 1	$1.23
November 15	$1.30

Furthermore, assume the equipment was purchased and paid for on November 15. Prepare all journal entries needed to record and settle the hedge and to record the purchase of the equipment.

B. If the forward contract was not acquired, record the journal entry to purchase the equipment.

PROBLEM 12-11 Fair Value Hedge of an Unrecognized Firm Commitment LO6

(This is a more complicated version of Problem 12-10.)

On October 1, 2008, Fairchange Corporation ordered some equipment from a supplier for 300,000 euros. Delivery is to occur on November 15, 2008, while payment is expected to occur on December 15, 2008. The spot rates on October 1, November 15, and December 15, 2008, are $1.20, $1.30, and $1.28, respectively.

Required:

A. Assume that Fairchange entered into a forward contract on October 1, 2008, to hedge the firm commitment. The forward rates for euros for December 15 delivery were

October 1	$1.23
November 15	$1.30
December 15	$1.28

Furthermore, assume the equipment was purchased on November 15 and was paid for on December 15, 2008. Prepare all journal entries needed to record and settle the hedge and to record the purchase and payment of the equipment.

B. If the forward contract was not acquired, record the journal entries to purchase and pay for the equipment.

PROBLEM 12-12 Fair Value Hedge of an Unrecognized Firm Commitment LO6

(This is the same as Problem 12-10 except that an option is used to hedge the commitment.)

On October 1, 2008, Fairchange Corporation ordered some equipment from a supplier for 300,000 euros. Delivery and payment are to occur on November 15, 2008. The spot rates on October 1 and November 15, 2008, are $1.20 and $1.30, respectively.

Required:

A. Assume that Fairchange purchased an option for $4,000 on October 1, 2008, to hedge 300,000 euros. The call option has an exercise price of $1.24. The values of the option on various dates are as follows:

October 1	$ 4,000
November 15	$ 18,000

Furthermore, assume the equipment was purchased and paid for on November 15. Prepare all journal entries needed to record and settle the hedge and to record the purchase of the equipment.

B. If the option was not acquired, record the journal entry to purchase the equipment.

13

TRANSLATION OF FINANCIAL STATEMENTS OF FOREIGN AFFILIATES

LEARNING OBJECTIVES

1. Distinguish between the current exchange rate and the historical exchange rate.
2. Understand the objectives of financial statement translation.
3. Identify the functional currency of a foreign entity.
4. Compare the two methods used to convert the financial statements of a foreign entity into U.S. dollars.
5. Distinguish between the circumstances under which each of the two methods is appropriate under current GAAP.
6. Explain the factors involved in translating the statements of a foreign entity operating in a highly inflationary economy.
7. Translate the statements of a foreign entity when the functional currency is the local currency.
8. Translate the statements of a foreign entity when the functional currency is the U.S. dollar.
9. Understand the concept of comprehensive income in the context of foreign currency translation.
10. Identify the disclosure requirements for firms with foreign entities.

"Quarterly corporate earnings will be even more important than usual to a stock market looking for clues about how fast the economy is slowing down. But first, investors will have to separate the wheat from the chaff. The chaff is the dollar, which this year has gone through convulsions not seen in years. The story varies, however, depending on which countries a firm operates in and the degree to which the company hedges against currency swings."[1]

In the preceding chapter, the translation of various types of foreign currency transactions entered into by a U.S. company was described. A U.S. company also may be involved in foreign activities through the operations of a branch, a subsidiary, or an investee company in a foreign country. If the foreign entity maintains its books in a

[1] *WSJ*, "Dollar to Play a Central Role in Profit Data," by Michael Gonzalez, 4/17/95, p. C1.

foreign currency, its accounts must be restated into dollars so that the accounts of the U.S. company and the foreign entity are stated in a common currency before the accounts are combined or consolidated or the equity method of accounting is applied. The concepts underlying the restatement of the accounts of a foreign entity are discussed in this chapter.

"The US dollar is the world's premiere currency, with approximately two thirds of world official foreign-exchange holdings being dollars. Moreover, many countries appear willing to run sustained trade surpluses with the US, supplying everything from t-shirts to Porsches in return for additional dollar holdings."[2]

The dollar has not been alone in its troubles. The yen has struggled, too, and the ratio between the two has fluctuated dramatically.

The rise in gold prices and fall of the dollar have begun to unsettle investors. In the short term, a weaker dollar means higher prices for imports and more expensive trips abroad. In the long run, a falling dollar could reduce the demand for U.S. debt. This could cause interest rates to increase, have a negative impact on the economy, and perhaps bring an end to the dollar as the world's premier currency.[3]

ACCOUNTING FOR OPERATIONS IN FOREIGN COUNTRIES

A U.S. firm may maintain branch offices or hold equity interests in companies that are domiciled in foreign countries. As a general rule, a foreign subsidiary is consolidated if the parent company owns, directly or indirectly, a controlling interest in the voting stock of the subsidiary. The exceptions to the general rule are as follows:

1. The intent to control is likely to be temporary.
2. Control does not actually rest with the parent company. For example, some governments restrict the withdrawal of assets from the country or impose exchange restrictions. Thus, a foreign entity may operate under conditions of foreign exchange restrictions, controls, or other government-imposed regulations that are of a type that raise significant doubt as to the parent company's ability to control the subsidiary.[4]

APB Opinion No. 18 [ASC 810–10–15–10] extended the equity method of accounting to an investment in common stock of a foreign company in which the investor can exert significant influence (generally holds a 20 to 50% interest in the voting stock) over the investee, unless the investee operates under conditions of exchange restrictions, controls, or other uncertainties that would affect the ability to influence the policies of the foreign investee. In other words, the APB considered it

[2] *YaleGlobal*, "Why Dollar Hegemony Is Unhealthy," Yale Global Online by Thomas I. Palley, 6/20/06.

[3] *USA Today*, "Beaten-up Dollar Unsettles Investors in USA and Abroad," by John Waggoner, 6/22/2006, p. B.1

[4] *Opinions of the Accounting Principles Board No. 18*, "The Equity Method of Accounting for Investments in Common Stock" (New York: AICPA, 1971), par. 17 [paragraph 323–10–15–6].

misleading to include in operations the investor's equity interest in the investee's net income if the income might not be distributed because of government restrictions. Investments in common stock not accounted for using the equity method are reported at fair value or at cost.

Accounting for a foreign entity is further complicated when there are significant differences between accounting principles in the United States and those in the other country. When such differences in accounting concepts exist, it is difficult to compare the results of operations and the financial position of companies operating in different countries. To aid statement users in making comparisons, foreign statements that are not in conformity with generally accepted accounting standards in the United States must be adjusted to conform to U.S. standards before conversion into U.S. dollars.

TRANSLATING FINANCIAL STATEMENTS OF FOREIGN AFFILIATES

A foreign entity will generally measure and record its transactions in terms of the currency of the country in which it is located, called the ***local currency***. A U.S. company maintaining a branch office in a foreign country or holding an equity interest in a foreign company must convert the account data expressed in a foreign currency into dollars before the financial statements can be combined or consolidated. Furthermore, if the equity method of accounting is used to account for an investment in a foreign investee company, the financial statements of the affiliate must be converted into dollars before the investor's share of the investee's reported net income or loss is properly determinable. The conversion from another currency into the currency of the parent company is frequently called "translation." Because the term is popularly used in this manner and because the FASB used the term "translation" in this way in the definitive standard (*SFAS No. 52*) on which much of this chapter is based, we too use the term to refer to the conversion process. Note, however, that the word has a dual meaning as used in the context of foreign currency conversion, and some users may prefer to restrict their use of the term to one of the following two definitions: (1) a generic term to apply to any restatement of foreign currency units into the currency of the parent (as used heretofore in this text) and (2) a specific term that applies only to one of the two methods of conversion described in the following sections (i.e., to the "current method" rather than to the "temporal method"). The FASB uses the term in both ways, as do we.

LO1 Current versus historical exchange rates.

In the process of translation, all accounts of the foreign entity stated in units of foreign currency are converted into the reporting currency by multiplying the foreign currency amounts by an exchange rate. The development of translation procedures is complicated by the fact that the rate of exchange between two currencies is not stable. There has been considerable controversy as to which foreign currency accounts should be translated using the current exchange rate and which accounts should be converted using historical exchange rates. The ***current exchange rate*** is the spot rate in effect at the end of the accounting period (i.e., the balance sheet date). The ***historical exchange rate*** is the spot rate in effect on the date a transaction takes place. Another controversial area relates to how to report the adjustment that is needed to balance the accounts that result when there are changes in the exchange rate.

"This isn't a German or American thing," according to Robert Eaton, one of the co-chairmen of DaimlerChrysler. He and the other co-chairman, Juergen Schrempp, portrayed the combination as a "merger of equals" and kept dual headquarters in Stuttgart, Germany, and Auburn Hills, Michigan. They recognized the riskiness of their juncture, and did their own analysis of international mergers' success rates, finding that 70% failed to achieve the level of success that was anticipated.[5]

Translation Adjustment or Translation Gain or Loss

The translation of some accounts using the current exchange rate and others using the historical exchange rate will result in an inequality between the total of the debit account balances and the total of the credit account balances. This difference may be referred to as a ***translation adjustment*** or ***translation gain or loss.*** As will be shown in a later section of this chapter, the amount of the translation adjustment is affected by an entity's accounting exposure to changes in the exchange rate. In an accounting sense, an entity's exposure to exchange risk is related to the set of accounts translated at the current rate. Current accounting standards require that the translation adjustment (gain or loss) be reported currently in income ***or*** deferred as a component of stockholders' equity, depending on the method used to translate the accounts. The appropriate method is not a free choice, but rather is dictated by the circumstances as described in *SFAS No. 52* [ASC 830–30–45–12]. If the adjustment is reported as a component of equity, it is not included in current earnings ***but*** is nonetheless a component of ***comprehensive income.***

The dollar fell sharply in thin trading Friday afternoon to a one-week low against the euro and a two-session low versus the yen. The turnaround reversed the dollar's gains through much of the week on mounting concerns over Europe and Japan's economies. Analysts say the selloff began when the euro hit $1.2650, a key technical level at which many traders and hedge funds had orders to buy the euro. In thin trading at the end of the week, particularly with much of the market going into the session betting on the dollar, this led to a volatile, sharp drive up in the euro, which had carry-through implications on the dollar versus yen as well.[6]

OBJECTIVES OF TRANSLATION—*SFAS No. 52* [ASC 830-30]

Functional Currency Concept

In *Statement of Financial Accounting Standards (SFAS) No. 52* **[ASC 830–30]**, the board determined that the objectives of translation are to:[7]

1. Provide information that is generally compatible with the exposed economic effects of an exchange rate change on an enterprise's cash flows and equity [par. 4(a)].
2. Reflect in consolidated statements the financial results and relationships of the individual consolidated entities as measured in their ***functional currencies*** in conformity with U.S. generally accepted accounting principles [par. 4(b)].

---

[5] Associated Press, "Management Shakeup Rocks DaimlerChrysler," by Justin Hyde, 9/25/99.

[6] February 20, 2009, Dow Jones Newswires.

[7] *Statement of Financial Accounting Standards No. 52*, "Foreign Currency Translation" (Norwalk, CT: FASB, 1981) [ASC 830–30].

LO2 The objectives of translation.

RELATED CONCEPTS

The functional currency approach was adopted to provide information compatible with the expected economic effects of a change in the exchange rate on the enterprise's *cash flows and equity*, consistent with the *objective of financial reporting* as specified in FASB Concept No.1.

With respect to the first objective, compatibility in terms of effect on equity is achieved if, for example, an entity is in an exposed asset position and the translation process results in an increase in stockholders' equity when there is a favorable change in the exchange rate. (An entity's exposed asset position is the excess of assets that are translated at the current exchange rate over liabilities that are translated at the current exchange rate.) An unfavorable change in the exchange rate should result in a reduction in stockholders' equity. Compatibility in terms of cash flow consequences is achieved if favorable (unfavorable) rate changes that are reasonably expected to affect cash flows are *reflected* as gains (losses) in determining net income for the period, and the effect of rate changes that have only remote and uncertain implications for realization are *excluded* from determining net income for the period.

In objective 2, the Board moved from a single-enterprise perspective of consolidation of a foreign entity to a multiple-enterprise perspective. The Board reasoned that foreign operations are often conducted in economic and currency environments that differ from those of the U.S. parent. Thus, a foreign entity is viewed as a separate business entity that generates its earnings in its local economic, legal, and political environment. The Board believes that the operating performance and financial condition of a foreign entity are best measured by expressing its accounts in the currency of the economic environment in which it primarily conducts its operations and generates and expends its cash, its ***functional currency.*** The determination of an entity's functional currency is discussed in a later section of this chapter. Also see Illustration 13-1 for a list of indicators to help in identifying the functional currency. Under the Board's view of a foreign entity, the translation of accounts expressed in the functional currency should retain the financial results and relationships that were created in the economic environment of the foreign operations rather than as if the operations had been conducted in the economic environment of the reporting currency.

TRANSLATION METHODS

LO4 Two methods of conversion.

To accomplish the objectives of translation, two translation methods are used depending on the functional currency of the foreign entity:

Current rate method. When using the current rate method, all assets and liabilities are translated using the current exchange rate. Revenue and expense transactions are translated at the exchange rate prevailing on the date each underlying transaction occurred. Since separate translation of each transaction is usually impractical, an appropriate average rate can be used to approximate the results that would be obtained from translation of each transaction.

Temporal method. Under this method, monetary assets and liabilities such as cash, receivables, and payables are translated at the current exchange rate. Assets and liabilities carried at historical cost are translated at historical exchange rates. Assets and liabilities carried at current values (such as inventory carried at market when applying the lower of cost or market rule) are translated at the current exchange rate. Thus, the temporal method places emphasis on whether an account is measured in terms of historical cost or current values.

ILLUSTRATION 13-1

Functional Currency Indicators

Economic Indicator	*Indicators Pointing to Local Currency as Functional Currency*	*Indicators Pointing to U.S. Dollar as Functional Currency*
Cash flows	Primarily in the local currency and do not directly affect parent's cash flows.	Directly affect the parent's cash flows on a current basis and are readily available for remittance to the parent.
Sales prices	Are not primarily responsive in the short term to exchange rate changes; determined primarily by local conditions.	Are primarily responsive in the short term to exchange rate changes; determined primarily by worldwide competition.
Sales market	Active local market although there may be significant amounts of exports.	Sales are mostly in the United States, or sales contracts are denominated in dollars.
Expenses	Production costs and operating expenses are determined primarily by local conditions.	Production costs and operating expenses are obtained primarily from U.S. sources.
Financing	Primarily denominated in the local currency, and foreign entity's cash flow from operations is sufficient to service existing and normally expected obligations.	Primarily from parent or other dollar-denominated obligations, or parent company is expected to service the debt.
Intercompany transactions	Low volume of intercompany transactions and there is not an extensive interrelationship between operations of the foreign entity and those of the parent. However, foreign entity may rely on parent's or affiliates' competitive advantages such as patents and trademarks.	High volume of intercompany transactions; there is an extensive interrelationship between operations of the parent and those of the foreign entity, or the foreign entity is an investment or financing device for the parent.

Source: Statement of Financial Accounting Standards No. 52, par. 42, [ASC 830–10–55–5].

Revenue and expense transactions, except those related to assets and liabilities translated at historical rates, are translated at exchange rates in effect on the dates the underlying transaction occurred. An appropriate average rate can be used to approximate the results that would be obtained from translation of each transaction. Revenues and expenses that relate to assets and liabilities translated at historical rates (such as depreciation expense, amortization expense, and the cost of sales) are translated at the historical rates used to translate the related assets and liabilities.

"You have to separate out the effect of the currency and ask yourself, How would the company have done in local currency?" says Terry Bivens, food, tobacco, and beverage analyst for Argus Research. "If you see a company that has done badly because of currency translations, but is going strong in local terms, then you're more reassured."[8]

[8] *WSJ*, "Dollar to Play a Central Role in Profit Data," by Michael Gonzalez, 4/17/95, p.C1.

IDENTIFYING THE FUNCTIONAL CURRENCY

The functional currency may be (1) the currency of the country in which the foreign entity is located (the local currency), (2) the U.S. dollar, or (3) the currency of another foreign country. Often, the functional currency is the local currency of the country in which the entity is located and in which the accounting records are maintained. For example, a French subsidiary with operations that are relatively self-contained and integrated in France would have the euro as its functional currency. In this example, the French subsidiary primarily generates and expends francs.

LO3 Identifying the functional currency.

In other cases, the dollar may be identified as the functional currency when a foreign subsidiary is a direct extension or an integral component of the reporting U.S. parent company. For example, the dollar would ordinarily be the functional currency for a subsidiary domiciled in Mexico that is financed by a U.S. parent company, that acquires significant assets by expending dollars, and whose only business is to assemble components that are manufactured in the United States and are returned to the United States to be sold by the parent company. In this case, the dollar may be the functional currency even though transactions of the subsidiary are recorded in pesos in the subsidiary's books.

RELATED CONCEPTS

One objective not considered in *FASB Statement No. 52,* the appropriateness of using a single *unit of measure* for the financial statements essentially requiring the U.S. dollar to be the monetary unit. This requirement ignores the fact that foreign operations are often entirely conducted in the currency of another country.

In still other cases, the identification of the functional currency will not be as clear as in these two examples. For example, a Mexico City subsidiary might manufacture a component for a product, a significant number of which are sold in Mexico or to companies domiciled in other foreign countries, in addition to providing some units for the U.S. parent, or a foreign entity might conduct significant amounts of business in two or more currencies. In such situations the functional currency could be a currency other than the dollar, such as the local currency of the foreign entity or the currency of a third country. To provide some guidance in selecting the functional currency, the FASB identified six economic indicators for management to consider. These indicators are listed in Illustration 13-1. The order in which the indicators are listed does not suggest any priority; rather, the indicators are to be considered both individually and collectively. When the indicators are mixed and the functional currency cannot be clearly identified, *SFAS No. 52* [ASC 830–10–45–6] indicates that management's judgment is required to assess the facts and circumstances in identifying the functional currency.

A foreign entity may operate and generate cash flows through more than one distinct and separable operation. Each of these operations may be identified as an entity and may have a different functional currency if conducted in different economic environments.

TEST YOUR KNOWLEDGE

NOTE: Solutions to ***Test Your Knowledge*** questions are found at the end of each chapter before the end-of-chapter questions.

Multiple Choice

1. Indicators that the local currency is also the functional currency include all of the following *except*:
   a. The majority of the cash flows are in the local currency.
   b. Sales prices are determined by local market conditions.
   c. Financing is generally from the parent or guaranteed by the parent.
   d. Production costs and expenses are determined by local conditions.

2. Indicators that the local currency is also the functional currency for a foreign subsidiary include:
   a. Sales are mostly in the United States.
   b. There is a high volume of intercompany transactions.
   c. Financing is primarily from the parent.
   d. Sales prices are not primarily responsive to short-term exchange rates.

TRANSLATION OF FOREIGN CURRENCY FINANCIAL STATEMENTS

The method used to translate a foreign entity's financial statements and the disposition of the resulting translation adjustment depends on the determination of the functional currency. As indicated earlier, the functional currency of the foreign entity might be (1) the local currency of the foreign entity, (2) the U.S. dollar, or (3) the currency of a third country (i.e., a country other than the country in which the subsidiary is located or the United States). The translation process and the disposition of the translation adjustment for these three situations, assuming that the books are kept in the local currency of the foreign entity and that the accounting conforms to U.S. generally accepted accounting principles, are summarized in a flow chart in Illustration 13-2. As shown in Illustration 13-2, an exception is made when the foreign economy is highly inflationary. In this case, the functional currency (as defined here) is not used to determine the appropriate accounting. Also, if the books of the foreign entity are kept in U.S. dollars, translation is not necessary. Further, if the books of the foreign entity are not kept in accordance with U.S. generally accepted accounting principles, the accounts must be adjusted to conform to U.S. GAAP, preferably before translating the account balances.

LO4 Which methods of conversion to use.

Note in Illustration 13-2 that the terms ***remeasurement*** and ***translation*** are used when the accounts stated in one currency are converted into another currency. The distinction between the two is as follows:

> ***Remeasurement.*** If a foreign entity does not maintain its records in its functional currency, the local currency accounts are remeasured into the functional currency using the temporal method. ***Remeasurement*** is the process of translating the accounts of a foreign entity into its functional currency when they are stated in another currency.
>
> ***Translation.*** Accounts measured in the functional currency are translated into the reporting currency using the current rate method.

As explained later, remeasurement is a change in the unit of measure, whereas translation retains the functional currency as the unit of measure and simply changes the form in which the accounts are stated. Recall that the term ***translation*** is used in two different ways: (1) as a generic term to apply to any restatement of foreign currency units into dollars and (2) more specifically to apply to the restatement of foreign currency units that are already measured in the functional currency into dollars (current rate method). Thus, "translation" may be used synonymously with the current method, while "remeasurement" is used synonymously with the temporal method. The first step in the translation process is to determine if the foreign entity is operating in a highly inflationary economy.

ILLUSTRATION 13-2

Summary of Translation Process and Disposition of Translation Gain or Loss

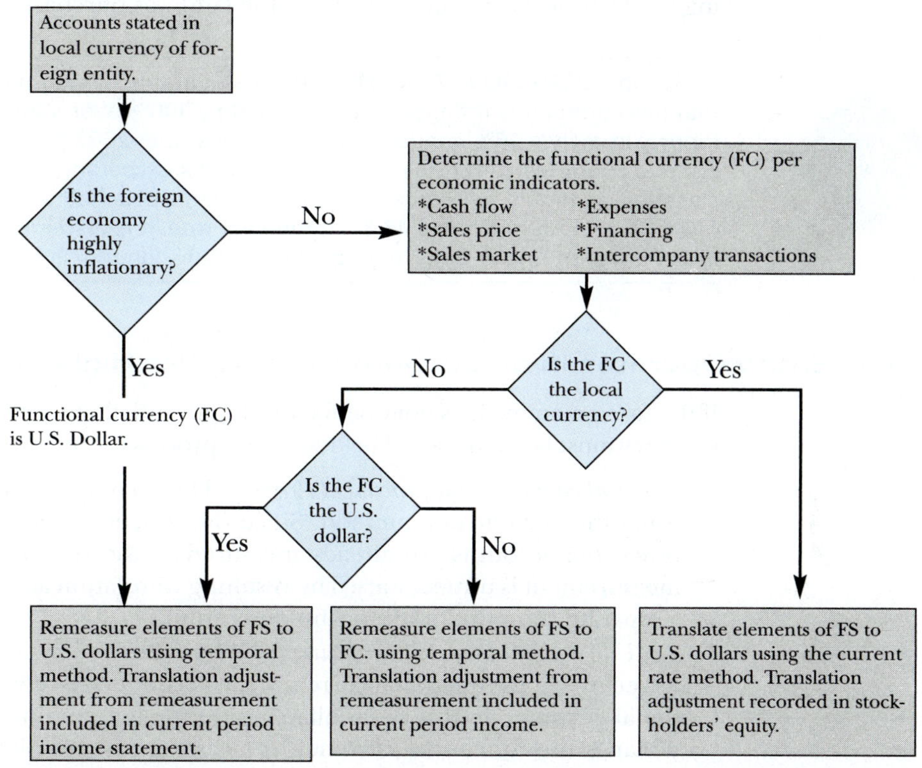

Source: Adapted from Dahli Gray, "Functional Currency Concept—Flexibility and Comparability Effects," *The Woman CPA*, January 1983, p. 22.

Foreign Entity Operates in a Highly Inflationary Economy

LO 6 Factors in a highly inflationary economy.

RELATED CONCEPTS

Under the *historical cost principle,* a stable *monetary unit* is important for reporting the financial position and operations over time. In a highly inflationary economy, historical cost numbers measured in nominal currency amounts lose *relevance.*

The relative rate of inflation between two countries is an important contributing factor to changes in exchange rates. Often, the currency of a country experiencing high inflation will weaken (i.e., one unit of that country's currency can be purchased with less domestic currency) substantially against the currency of a more stable economy. Thus, using the current rate method to translate inventories and fixed assets of foreign operations in highly inflationary economies often results in a substantial reduction in the translated amounts.

To illustrate, assume that a foreign subsidiary acquired land for 100,000 foreign currency units (FCU) when the exchange rate was \$1 per FCU. In subsequent years, the foreign country experienced significant inflation and the exchange rate decreased to \$.20 per FCU. If the current exchange rate is used, the land would translate to \$20,000 (100,000 FCU × \$.20) and a cumulative translation loss of \$80,000 is reported.

It is the Board's belief that the currency of a country that has a highly inflationary economy has lost its utility as a store of value and cannot be a functional measuring unit. As a practical solution to the problem, the Board prescribed that the financial statements of a foreign entity operating in a highly inflationary economy shall be remeasured as if the functional currency were the reporting currency (U.S. dollar). For such entities this means that the foreign financial statements should be translated using the ***temporal method***. According to the foregoing illustration, the land account would be translated to $100,000 (100,000 FCU × $1.00) using the historical exchange rate when the land was purchased.

SFAS No. 53 **[ASC 830–10–45–11]** states that a highly inflationary economy is one that has cumulative inflation of approximately 100% over a three-year period (approximately a 26% annual rate). As of December 2007, Myanmar and Zimbabwe are two countries with three-year inflation rates exceeding 100% and would be classified as highly inflationary economies. Venezuela had a three-year inflation rate of 60.6% and Angola had a 46.3% three-year rate. It is also important to watch trends in the inflation rate in determining whether the economy is highly inflationary.

Foreign Entity Operates in an Economy That Is Not Highly Inflationary

If the foreign entity does not operate in a highly inflationary economy, the functional currency must be identified. The translation process for the three possibilities follows:

1. *The local currency is the functional currency.* The accounts are translated into dollars using the current rate method. Since the functional currency is the local currency, the accounts are already measured in the functional currency, and remeasurement is unnecessary. The resulting translation adjustment is recorded as a separate component of stockholders' equity.
2. *The U.S. dollar is the functional currency.* When the foreign entity does not maintain its records in its functional currency, the accounts are remeasured into the functional currency, in this case dollars, using the temporal method. Since the U.S. dollar is the functional currency, remeasurement translates the accounts into dollars and no further translation is necessary. The resulting translation adjustment is reported in the current period's income statement.
3. *The functional currency is the currency of a third country.* The local currency accounts are first (a) remeasured in the functional currency (the currency of the third country) using the temporal approach, and then (b) the remeasured functional currency amounts are translated into dollars using the current rate approach. The translation gain or loss from using the temporal method is reported in income, while the adjustment resulting from use of the current rate approach is reported in a separate component of owners' equity.

The steps in the translation process may be diagrammed as shown in Illustration 13-3. Identification of the functional currency is the key step in the translation process as it determines the method to be used to translate the foreign currency accounts.

The approach outlined is consistent with the objective of preserving the financial results and relationships of an individual consolidated entity as measured in its functional currency. That is, when the local currency is identified as the functional currency, use of the current rate method retains the local currency as the unit of measure. A translation method preserves the financial results if a net income or loss reported in the functional currency statements is retained in the translated income statement. Maintaining relationships as measured in their functional currency is achieved when, for example, the current ratio is 2 : 1 when computed from the functional currency balance sheet and the ratio is also 2 : 1 when computed from the translated statements. The current rate method retains the financial results and relationships as measured in their functional currency by translating the assets and

ILLUSTRATION 13-3
Diagram of Translation Process

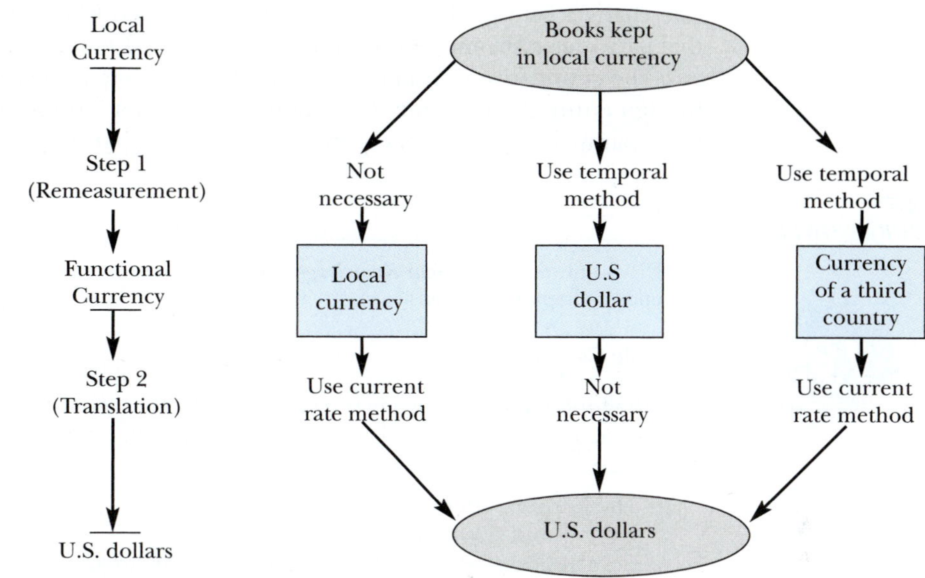

liabilities at one constant rate (the current rate) and the income statement items at one constant rate (the average rate).

Remeasurement using the temporal method when the functional currency is the U.S. dollar is consistent with a single-enterprise perspective of consolidation. In this case, the operations of the foreign entity are viewed as a direct extension or an integral component of the parent's domestic operations. That is, the parent and subsidiary are viewed as if they were a single company. The objective of translation is to change the unit of measure from that of the local currency to the reporting currency of the parent company, the functional currency. The translation process should then reflect all transactions of the subsidiary as if they were conducted or measured in one currency only, the parent's reporting currency. The use of historical exchange rates to translate accounts carried at historical cost preserves the original cost of the accounts in conformity with the historical cost concept. In effect, the accounts are restated as if dollars had been used to measure and record the assets and liabilities on the transaction dates.

When the functional currency is that of a third country, the accounts of the foreign entity maintained in its local currency are remeasured (translated) into the functional currency using the temporal method. The relationships as measured in the functional currency are retained by translating the functional currency balances into the reporting currency using the current rate method.

The reporting of the translation adjustment is also dependent on the selection of the functional currency. When the foreign entity's accounts are remeasured (temporal method) to the functional currency, either the U.S. dollar or the currency of a third country, the resulting adjustment is reported in the current period's income statement. When translating the accounts from the functional currency into dollars (current rate method), translation adjustments are accumulated and reported as a separate component of stockholders' equity. In the latter case, the Board regarded translation adjustments associated with a foreign investment as unrealized and considered their effect on cash flow to be uncertain and remote. As discussed earlier, one objective of translation is to provide information that is compatible with the expected economic effects of rate changes on cash flow. Compatibility is achieved when the effect of rate changes that have uncertain and remote implications for realization are excluded from income.

The cumulative translation adjustment is carried in the accounts until sale of the foreign entity. At that time, the amount attributable to that entity is removed from the separate component of equity and reported as part of the gain or loss on the sale.

TEST YOUR KNOWLEDGE

NOTE: Solutions to ***Test Your Knowledge*** questions are found at the end of each chapter before the end-of-chapter questions.

Multiple Choice

1. If the functional currency is the currency of a third country (not the parent's and not the local currency), the appropriate approach to converting the account balances into U.S. dollars is:
   a. The temporal approach.
   b. The current approach.
   c. Both approaches, with the accounts first converted into the functional currency using the temporal approach and then into U.S. dollars using the current approach.
   d. Both approaches, with the accounts first converted into the functional currency using the current approach and then into U.S. dollars using the temporal approach.

TRANSLATION OF FOREIGN FINANCIAL STATEMENTS ILLUSTRATED

To illustrate the translation process, assume that on January 2, 2009, P Company, a U.S.-based company, acquired for 2,000,000 francs an 80% interest in SFr Company, a Swiss company. SFr maintains its books in francs, and they are in conformity with GAAP in the United States. The translation process will be illustrated under two different assumptions: (1) the Swiss franc is the functional currency, and (2) the U.S. dollar is the functional currency.

Exchange rates for the franc for the 2009 fiscal year are as follows:*

Date	*Spot Rate*
January 2 (date of acquisition)	$.150
September 1	.160
December 31	.170
Average for the fourth quarter	.165
Average for the year	.156

In translating the income statement accounts, it is assumed that revenues were generated and expenses were incurred evenly during the year. It is also assumed that the company uses the FIFO cost flow assumption, and that the ending inventory was acquired during the last quarter.

* The exchange rate for Swiss francs is currently around $0.80.

Entries made on the books of P Company to account for the investment and the preparation of a consolidated statements workpaper based on the translated account balances are illustrated in the appendix to this chapter.

Functional Currency Is the Local Currency—Current Rate Method

Year-end financial statements at December 31 in francs for the subsidiary and the translation of the account balances into dollars using the current rate method are presented in Illustration 13-4. The translation rules are as follows:

Functional Currency Is Local Currency (Swiss Franc)—Current Rate Method

ILLUSTRATION 13-4
SFr Company
Workpaper to Translate Account Balances of Foreign Subsidy
December 31, 2009

Combined Statement of Income and Retained Earnings	*Adjusted Trial Balance (Francs)*	*Current Rate Method* *Translation Rate*		*Adjusted Trial Balance (Dollars)*
Sales	3,020,000	(A)	$.156	471,120
Cost of Goods Sold	1,850,000	(A)	.156	288,600
Depreciation Expense	100,000	(A)	.156	15,600
Other Expenses	655,000	(A)	.156	102,180
Income Tax Expense	82,000	(A)	.156	12,792
Net Income	333,000			51,948
1/1 Retained Earnings	480,000	(1)		72,000
	813,000			123,948
Less: 9/1 Dividends Declared	300,000	(H)	.16	48,000
12/31 Retained Earnings	513,000			75,948
Balance Sheet				
Cash	930,000	(C)	.17	158,100
Accounts Receivable (net)	608,000	(C)	.17	103,360
Inventories (FIFO cost)	830,000	(C)	.17	141,100
Land	500,000	(C)	.17	85,000
Buildings (net)	650,000	(C)	.17	110,500
Equipment (net)	430,000	(C)	.17	73,100
Total	3,948,000			671,160
Accounts Payable	640,000	(C)	.17	108,800
Short-Term Notes Payable	635,000	(C)	.17	107,950
Bonds Payable	900,000	(C)	.17	153,000
Common Stock	960,000	(H)	.15	144,000
Additional Paid-in Capital	300,000	(H)	.15	45,000
Retained Earnings	513,000			75,948
Total	3,948,000			634,698
Cumulative Translation Adjustment—Credit Balance*		(B/A)		36,462
Total				671,160

* Include as a component of stockholders' equity
(1) Retained earnings in dollars on January 2.
(A) Average exchange rate used to approximate the rate on the date these elements were recognized.
(H) Historical exchange rate.
(C) Current exchange rate.
(B/A) Balancing amount.

1. All assets and liabilities are translated from the local currency into the reporting currency using the current exchange rate (i.e., the spot rate on the balance sheet date).
2. Paid-in capital accounts are translated using the historical rate, but the date to which the historical rate pertains depends on whether the acquisition was accounted for as a purchase or a pooling of interests. In a ***purchase transaction***, the accounts are translated using the historical rate on the date the acquisition of the equity interest occurred. In the case of a ***pooling of interests***, these accounts are translated using the historical rate(s) that existed on the date(s) that the foreign entity's capital transaction(s) occurred.
3. Components of the ending retained earnings are translated as follows:
   a. The beginning retained earnings balance is set equal to the ending balance of last year. In this case, since this is the first year of acquisition, the balance is set equal to the January 2 balance of $72,000 (480,000 francs × $.15).
   b. As a component of equity, dividends are translated into dollars using the exchange rate in effect when the dividend was declared.
   c. Net income or loss is carried forward from the translated income statement as discussed later.
   d. The cumulative translation adjustment is a balancing amount in the balance sheet. (The adjustment is discussed in more detail in the next section.)
4. Revenue and expense accounts (including cost of goods sold and depreciation), gains, and losses are translated using the exchange rate when the elements were recognized during the period. Because separate translation of numerous transactions is usually impractical, the use of an appropriate average to translate revenue and expense accounts is permitted.

An Analysis of the Translation Adjustment When some accounts in a trial balance are translated using one rate and other accounts are translated using a different rate, an inequality will result between the total of the debit account balances and the total of the credit account balances. For example, in Illustration 13-4 the 608,000 francs debit balance in the accounts receivable account is translated to $103,360 using the current exchange rate of $.17, and the 608,000 franc credit included in the sales account balance is translated to $94,848 (608,000 francs × $.156) using the average exchange rate for the period. On these transactions there is a translation adjustment credit of $8,512, since the accounts receivable could be converted into $103,360 at the balance sheet date, as opposed to $94,848 at the time of the sale. A translation adjustment will also result when items that are translated at the current rate are included in two successive trial balances and the exchange rate changes.

LO7 The functional currency is the local currency.

In Illustration 13-4 the translation adjustment is a balancing amount that reconciles the total debit balances with the total credit balances after the individual accounts have been translated and is reported as a component of stockholders' equity. The translation adjustment for the period results from an entity's accounting exposure to exchange risk, which in an accounting sense is related to the set of accounts that are translated at the current rate. Fluctuations in the exchange rate have no effect on the translated amount of an account translated at a historical rate on two balance sheets.

The translation adjustment under the current rate method may be verified by a direct computation as in Illustration 13-5. Since all assets and liabilities are translated at the current rate under the current rate method, only net assets (assets minus liabilities) are exposed to currency fluctuations and thus result in a translation gain or loss. This net investment view of the firm recognizes that functional

ILLUSTRATION 13-5

Verification of the Translation Adjustment
Current Rate Method Functional Currency—Swiss Franc

	Francs	*Translation Rate*	*Reporting Currency (Dollars)*
1/1 Exposed net asset position	1,740,000*	$.15	261,000
Adjustments for changes in net asset position during year			
Net income for year	333,000	.156	51,948
Dividends declared	(300,000)	.16	(48,000)
Net asset position translated using rate in effect at date of each transaction			264,948
12/31 Exposed net asset position	1,773,000	.17	301,410
Change in cumulative translation adjustment during year—net increase			36,462
1/1 Cumulative translation adjustment†			—0—
12/31 Cumulative translation adjustment			36,462

* A condensed balance sheet for SFr Company on January 2, 2009 was as follows:

	Francs		*Francs*
Monetary Assets	1,100,000	Monetary Liabilities	1,800,000
Nonmonetary Assets		Common Stock	960,000
Inventory	760,000	Additional Paid-in Capital	300,000
Fixed Assets	1,680,000	Retained Earnings	480,000
Total	3,540,000	Total	3,540,000

1/1 Net assets = 3,540,000 francs − 1,800,000 francs = 1,740,000 francs.
† The beginning balance is zero since this was the first year the investment was held.

currency assets produce revenues in a foreign currency and can be an effective hedge of liabilities that require payment in the same foreign currency. Thus, equal amounts of functional currency assets and liabilities hedge one another and only net assets are exposed to exchange risk. Most firms will be in a net asset position, which results in a transaction gain (loss), when the direct exchange rate increases (decreases). Note that the steps shown in Illustration 13-5 provided a check for the current period change in the cumulative translation adjustment. To reconcile with the amount reported in the stockholders' equity section of the balance sheet, it is necessary to add (subtract) the cumulative translation adjustment reported in the prior period. To the extent that the adjustment is sometimes a gain and sometimes a loss, the cumulative amount may remain near zero. On the other hand, a series of adjustments in the same direction may result in a relatively large credit (debit) balance. Credit balances may be viewed as net cumulative gains, while debit balances reflect net cumulative losses.

The first column in Illustration 13-5 reconciles the net asset position at the beginning of the year to the net asset position at the end of the year. Note that only the transactions that affected stockholders' equity will cause a change in the net asset position. The Swiss francs balances in column 1 are translated into dollars using different exchange rates as follows. The beginning exposed net asset position is translated using the exchange rate in effect at the beginning of the period. The increases and decreases in the net asset position are translated using the exchange rate at the date the transactions were assumed to occur. The ending exposed net asset position is translated using the current exchange rate.

"International operations constitute about 15% of our 1998 consolidated operating profit, excluding unusual impairment and other items. As currency exchange rates change, translation of the income statements of our international businesses into U.S. dollars affects year-over-year comparability of operating results. We do not generally hedge translation risks because cash flows from international operations are generally reinvested locally. We do not enter into hedges to minimize volatility of reported earnings because we do not believe it is justified by the exposure or the cost."[9]

RELATED CONCEPTS

In *Concept No. 3, comprehensive income* is defined as the change in equity during a period from transactions with nonowners. Because a change in the exchange rate does not affect the net cash flows generated by the foreign operations (when the functional currency is not the U.S. dollar), the translation adjustment is reported separately from income; it is reported as a component of other comprehensive income.

Interpretation of Results In the preceding illustration, the current rate method was used to translate the foreign currency financial statements when the francs, as opposed to the dollar, was identified as the functional currency. As noted earlier, one of the objectives of translation is to retain in the translated statements the financial results and relationships of the financial statements as measured in the functional currency. With respect to financial results, a net income is reported in both the functional currency statements and the translated statements. A few selected financial ratios are computed here to show that the current rate method retains the financial relationships:

	Swiss Francs	*Dollars*
Current ratio	$\frac{2{,}368{,}000}{1{,}275{,}000} = 1.86$	$\frac{402{,}560}{216{,}750} = 1.86$
Debt to equity	$\frac{2{,}175{,}000}{1{,}773{,}000} = 1.23$	$\frac{369{,}750}{301{,}410} = 1.23$
Gross profit percentage	$\frac{1{,}170{,}000}{3{,}020{,}000} = 38.7\%$	$\frac{182{,}520}{471{,}120} = 38.7\%$
Net income to sales	$\frac{333{,}000}{3{,}020{,}000} = 11.0\%$	$\frac{51{,}948}{471{,}120} = 11.0\%$

Another objective of translation is to provide information that is generally compatible with the expected economic effects of a change in exchange rates. In the illustration, the exchange rate increased from $.15 to $.17 during the period, a favorable change for a U.S. parent company holding an investment in an exposed net asset position.

LO7 Comprehensive income and foreign currency translation.

Translation of the foreign currency financial statements using the current rate approach resulted in a $36,462 increase in stockholders' equity.

Statement of Comprehensive Income and Statement of Shareholders' Equity

Opinions remain divided as to the appropriateness of excluding currency translation adjustments from net income, as currently done under the "current" method. These adjustments represent one of several items of concern to the FASB because of their frequency of occurrence and relative importance, coupled with their exclusion from reported earnings. The FASB labeled such items as "other comprehensive income." In the early 1980s, the FASB defined comprehensive income as including ***all*** changes in equity during a period except those resulting from investments by owners and distributions to owners. Thus, comprehensive income consists of net income plus other

[9] Pepsi Company's Annual Report, 1998.

ILLUSTRATION 13-6

Functional Currency	**SFr Company**
Is Local Currency	**Comprehensive Income Statement**
(Franc)—Current	**for the Year Ended**
Rate Method	**December 31, 2009**
Net income	$51,948
Other comprehensive income:	
Currency translation adjustment	36,462
Comprehensive income	$88,410

SFr Company
Statement of Shareholders' Equity
for the Year Ended December 31, 2009

	Common Stock	*Additional Paid-in Capital*	*Retained Earnings*	*Accumulated Other Comprehensive Income*	*Total*
Balance, 1/1/09	$144,000	$45,000	$72,000	0	$261,000
Comprehensive income:					
Net income			51,948		51,948
Other comprehensive income:					
Currency translation adjustment				36,462	36,462
Total comprehensive income					*88,410*
Dividends declared			(48,000)		(48,000)
Balance, 12/31/09	$144,000	$45,000	$75,948	$36,462	$301,410

items such as unrealized gains (losses) on available-for-sale securities and certain pension costs related to minimum pension liability that are excluded from net income under current GAAP. More recently, the FASB added the requirement that a statement of comprehensive income must be included in a complete set of financial statements.

In Illustration 13-6, we show the statement of comprehensive income and the reconciliation of changes in all shareholders' equity accounts for the year 2009 for SFr Company in dollars. Of course, these amounts would be added to the parent's balances for preparation of a consolidated statement of comprehensive income (and a consolidated statement of shareholders' equity).

Functional Currency Is the U.S. Dollar—Temporal Method

LO8 The functional currency is the U.S. dollar.

The temporal method is used to remeasure the accounts of a foreign entity when the entity operates in a highly inflationary economy or its books are maintained in a currency other than its functional currency. The objective of the remeasurement process is to produce the same results as if the transactions of the foreign entity had been recorded initially in its functional currency. To accomplish this, the historical exchange rate is used to translate accounts carried at historical cost, while the current exchange rate is used to translate other accounts. The remeasurement process is as follows:

1. Monetary assets and liabilities (for example, cash, receivables, and most liabilities) that are expressed in the balance sheet at current values are translated using the current rate. (An asset or a liability is monetary if it represents a claim to a fixed amount of dollars. All other assets and liabilities are nonmonetary.)

2. Nonmonetary assets and liabilities carried at past exchange prices (historical cost) are translated at historical exchange rates, which results in translating these amounts to the equivalent number of dollars on the date the transaction took place.
3. Nonmonetary assets and liabilities carried at current or future exchange prices (for example, marketable securities or inventory carried at replacement cost) are translated at the current exchange rate.
4. Paid-in capital accounts are translated using the historical exchange rate at the date of acquisition, or at the date the original capital transaction(s) occurred if subsequent to acquisition.
5. The components that make up the ending retained earnings balance are translated as follows:
   a. The beginning balance is set equal to the ending balance of the last period.
   b. Dividends are translated at the rate existing on the date of the declaration.
   c. Net income or loss is carried forward from the translated income statement.
6. Revenues and expenses related to assets and liabilities translated at historical rates (primarily inventory cost and depreciation) are translated at the respective historical rates used to translate the related asset or liability.
7. Other revenue and expense accounts are translated in a manner that produces approximately the same results as if the individual transactions were translated at the rate in effect when the transaction occurred; generally a weighted average rate is used for all transactions for simplicity's sake.
8. The translation gain or loss is reported in the income statement.

A list of some common nonmonetary items that should be remeasured using the historical rate is presented in Illustration 13-7. Remeasurement of the nonmonetary accounts using historical exchange rates normally requires that the foreign entity maintain detailed records identifying the purchase date and the exchange rate.

The December 31 trial balance of SFr Company in francs and the remeasurement of the accounts using the temporal method are shown in Illustration 13-8.

ILLUSTRATION 13-7

Nonmonetary Items Remeasured Using the Historical Rate

Balance Sheet Items

Equity securities carried at cost (use current rate for those carried at fair value)
Inventories carried at cost (use current rate for those carried at fair value)
Prepaid expenses such as insurance, advertising, and rent
Property, plant, and equipment
Accumulated depreciation on property, plant, and equipment
Patents, trademarks, licenses, and formulas
Goodwill
Other intangible assets
Deferred charges and credits, except deferred income taxes and policy acquisition costs for life insurance companies
Common stock
Preferred stock carried at issuance price

Income Statement Items

Cost of goods sold
Depreciation of property, plant, and equipment
Amortization of intangible items such as patents, licenses, etc.
Amortization of policy acquisition costs for life insurance companies.

Source: Statement of Financial Accounting Standards No. 52, par. 48 [ASC 830–10–45–15].

Functional Currency
Is U.S. Dollar—
Temporal Method

ILLUSTRATION 13-8
SFr Company
Workpaper to Translate Account Balances of Foreign Subsidiary
December 31, 2009

Balance Sheet	*Adjusted Trial Balance (Francs)*	*Exchange Rate* (Temporal Method)		*Adjusted Trial Balance (Dollars)* (Temporal Method)	
Cash	930,000	(C)	.17	158,100	
Accounts Receivable (net)	608,000	(C)	.17	103,360	
Inventories (FIFO cost)	830,000	Sch. 1		136,950	
Land	500,000	(H)	.15	75,000	
Buildings (net)	650,000	(H)	.15	97,500	
Equipment (net)	430,000	(H)	.15	64,500	
Total	3,948,000			635,410	
Accounts Payable	640,000	(C)	.17	108,800	
Short-Term Notes Payable	635,000	(C)	.17	107,950	
Bonds Payable	900,000	(C)	.17	153,000	
Common Stock	960,000	(H)	.15	144,000	
Additional Paid-in Capital	300,000	(H)	.15	45,000	
Retained Earnings	513,000	(B/A)		76,660	
Total	3,948,000			635,410	
Combined Statement of Income and Retained Earnings					
Sales	3,020,000	(A)	.156	471,120	① Carry down retained earnings
Cost of Goods Sold	1,850,000	Sch. 1		276,570	
Depreciation Expense	100,000	(H)	.15	② 15,000	
Other Expenses	655,000	(A)	.156	102,180	
Income Tax Expense	82,000	(A)	.156	12,792	
Translation (Remeasurement) Loss	—	(B/A)		④ 11,918	
Net Income	333,000			52,660	
1/2 Retained Earnings	480,000	(1)		72,000	
	813,000			③ 124,660	
Less: 9/1 Dividends Declared	300,000	(H)	.16	48,000	
12/31 Retained Earnings	513,000			76,660	

(1) Retained earnings in dollars on January 2.
(A) Average exchange rate used to approximate the rate on the date these elements were recognized.
(H) Historical exchange rate.
(C) Current exchange rate.
(B/A) Balancing amount.

Schedule 1
Translation of cost of goods sold

	Francs	*Exchange Rate*	*Dollars*
Beginning inventory (assumed)	760,000	.15	114,000
Purchases (assumed)	1,920,000	.156	299,520
	2,680,000		413,520
Less: Ending inventory	830,000	.165	136,950
Cost of goods sold	1,850,000		276,570

Steps to determine translation (remeasurement) gain or loss using "plug" technique:
① Carry down retained earnings.
② Complete income statement down to translation gain or loss.
③ Beginning with ending retained earnings, work back to net income.

Ending Retained Earnings	+	Dividends	−	Beginning Retained Earnings	=	Net Income
\$76,660	+	\$48,000	−	\$72,000	=	\$52,660

④ Compute translation gain or loss in dollars:
Translation gain (loss) = Net Income − (Sales − Expenses)
= \$52,660 − (\$471,120 − \$406,542) = (\$11,918)

The first step is to translate the individual accounts, except for the ending retained earnings balance of 513,000 francs, using the appropriate exchange rate. The ending retained earnings balance of $76,660 is computed as a balancing amount required to equate the firm's liabilities and stockholders' equity with the total assets. Next, the ending retained earnings is carried to the combined statement of income and retained earnings where the translation loss of $11,918 is the balancing amount in the combined statement.

An Analysis of the Translation Gain or Loss The translation loss in the temporal method of translation is derived by a direct calculation in Illustration 13-9. Procedurally, the approach is based on the same underlying concept as that used to verify the translation adjustment reported when the current rate method was used. That is, the translation loss is related to those accounts translated at the current exchange rate. However, in applying the temporal method, in general, monetary items only are translated at the current rate while most nonmonetary items are translated at

ILLUSTRATION 13-9

Verification of the Translation (Remeasurement) Loss
Temporal Method
Functional Currency—U.S. Dollar

	Francs	*Exchange Rate*	*Reporting Currency (U.S. Dollar)*
1/1 Exposed net monetary liability position	700,000*	$.15	105,000
Adjustments for changes in net monetary position during the year:			
Less: Increase in cash and receivables from sales	(3,020,000)	.156	(471,120)
Add: Decrease in monetary assets or increase in monetary liabilities:			
Purchases	1,920,000	.156	299,520
Other expenses	655,000	.156	102,180
Income taxes	82,000	.156	12,792
Dividends declared	300,000	.16	48,000
Net monetary liability position translated using rate in effect at date of each transaction			96,372
12/31 Exposed net monetary liability position	637,000†	.17	108,290
Translation (remeasurement) gain (loss)			(11,918)

* The January 2, 2009, condensed balance sheet is given in Illustration 13-5.

	Francs
Monetary liabilities	1,800,000
Less: Monetary assets	1,100,000
Net monetary liability position	700,000

†See Illustration 13-8.

	Francs
Monetary liabilities (640,000 + 635,000 + 900,000)	2,175,000
Less: Monetary assets (930,000 + 608,000)	1,538,000
Net monetary liability position	637,000

historical rates. Accordingly, the dollar value of monetary items is affected by variations in the exchange rate, giving rise to a gain or loss. On the other hand, nonmonetary items will not result in a gain or loss because each item is translated in successive balance sheets using its respective historical exchange rate. As a result, as long as these items are reported in the balance sheet, they will retain their original translated dollar amounts (less accumulated amortization), even though the exchange rate may have changed.

A translation loss results from application of the temporal method, as opposed to the credit translation adjustment calculated on the exposed assets using the current rate method, because SFr Company maintained a net monetary liability position throughout the year. An increasing exchange rate will produce a translation loss on an exposed net monetary liability position.

Comparison of the Two Methods

In translating the balance sheet, the differences and similarities between the temporal and current rate methods are highlighted in the following schedule:

	Balance Sheet Translation Rates	
	Current Rate Method	*Temporal Method*
Monetary asset	Current	Current
Nonmonetary asset carried at historical cost	Current	Historical
Nonmonetary asset carried at market value	Current	Current
Monetary liability	Current	Current
Nonmonetary liability	Current	Historical

The two methods differ primarily in terms of the appropriate rate to use for nonmonetary items carried at historical cost. In the income statement, a net income of $51,948 resulted when the Swiss franc was the functional currency (Illustration 13-4), whereas a net income of $52,660 was reported when the U.S. dollar was the functional currency (Illustration 13-8). There are two reasons for this difference. First, when the foreign currency is strengthening against the dollar, cost of goods sold and depreciation expense are usually greater when the current rate method of translation is used. Second, a translation loss of $11,918 is reported in the dollar functional currency income statement, whereas a credit adjustment of $36,462 is reported in stockholders' equity in the franc functional currency statement.

The Chinese yuan showed strength against the US dollar and the European currency during early Asian deals on Thursday. The yuan thus climbed from a 2-day low against the euro. The Chinese economy expanded by 9.0 percent in 2008, the National Bureau of Statistics said today, coming in slightly below analyst expectations for 9.2 percent growth. Gross domestic product was up 13 percent in 2007.[10]

[10] RTTNews, February 2009.

FINANCIAL STATEMENT DISCLOSURE

Companies are required to disclose certain items, as follows:

1. The aggregate translation gain or loss included in the determination of net income for the period, including gains or losses related to forward contracts, should be disclosed in either the financial statements or notes thereto.
2. An analysis of the cumulative translation adjustment equity account should be provided in a separate statement or note or as part of a statement of changes in equity. The analysis should include:
   a. The beginning and ending cumulative translation adjustment amounts.
   b. The aggregate adjustment for the period resulting from the translation of foreign currency statements and gains and losses from certain hedging activities and intercompany long-term investment transactions.
   c. The amount of income taxes for the period allocated to the cumulative translation adjustment equity account.
   d. The amounts transferred from the cumulative translation adjustment equity account and included in the determination of net income for the period as a result of the sale of part or all of an investment in a foreign entity.
3. Exchange rate changes that occur after the balance sheet date and their effect on unsettled foreign currency transactions, if significant.

LO 10 Required disclosures.

U.S. companies must also comply with the provisions of the Foreign Corrupt Practices Act (FCPA). The FCPA was enacted in 1977 in response to disclosures by more than 400 U.S. corporations of questionable or improper payments made to foreign officials to elicit their support for business arrangements with the U.S. firms. An extensive investigation by the SEC revealed that in a significant number of cases, the foreign payments had been made to appear in the corporate records as a normal operating expense and that inadequate documentation precluded the verification of the purpose of the payment.

RELATED CONCEPTS

This presentation is believed to improve the *comparability* of financial statements because all entities will present the components of comprehensive income in a similar manner.

The FCPA contains two major sections: an antibribery section and an accounting standards section. The antibribery provision makes it a criminal offense to offer a bribe to a foreign government official or foreign political official. The accounting standards section of the Act is intended to help prevent the concealment of foreign corrupt payments.

In February 1978 the SEC issued *Accounting Series Release No. 242*, which emphasized the importance of the provisions of the Act and the need to comply with its requirements. In the release the SEC stated that although the Act imposed new requirements with respect to the maintenance of internal accounting controls and outlawed certain foreign corrupt practices, it did not alter the existing obligation to adequately disclose questionable and illegal corporate payments and practices. The SEC went on to state that "registrants have a continuing obligation to disclose all material information and all information necessary to prevent other disclosures made from being misleading with respect to such transactions."

In one of the current joint projects of the FASB and the IASB, the Boards are proposing a single statement of comprehensive income (in place of the current alternatives for presenting comprehensive income—in the statement of owners'

equity, in a statement separate from the income statement, or as part of the income statement). Further, the Boards propose that an entity should present foreign currency transaction gains and losses, including the components of any net gain or loss arising on remeasurement into the functional currency, in the same section and category as the assets and liabilities that give rise to the gains or losses. Also see Chapter 11 for an expanded discussion of the proposed changes in financial statement presentation.

TEST YOUR KNOWLEDGE

NOTE: Solutions to ***Test Your Knowledge*** questions are found at the end of each chapter before the end-of-chapter questions.

Multiple Choice

1. Under the current method of currency translation, which of the following balance sheet accounts is translated at historical exchange rates?
   a. Cash
   b. Accounts Receivable
   c. Bonds Payable
   d. Common Stock

HISTORICAL DEVELOPMENTS OF ACCOUNTING STANDARDS

The expansion of international business has been of particular concern to accountants because of developments in the worldwide monetary system during the 1970s. These developments, coupled with the existence of a number of acceptable methods of translating foreign financial statements and reporting gains or losses on foreign currency fluctuations, led the FASB to place the topic on its agenda in 1973. The result was the issuance in October 1975 of *Statement of Financial Accounting Standards No. 8*, "Accounting for the Translation of Foreign Currency Transactions and Foreign Currency Financial Statements."

One objective of *Statement No. 8* was to provide uniform accounting standards for the translation of foreign financial statements. A second objective was to fill the gap in authoritative literature on accounting for transactions with foreign companies. The *Statement* was not well received; it proved to be one of the most controversial statements issued by the FASB. Major criticism of the statement focused on the following points:

1. Reporting translation gains and losses in current income often resulted in unnecessary fluctuations in reported income.
2. Translation required by the statement sometimes resulted in reporting a loss when the economic effects of a rate change were expected to be favorable, and a gain when the economic effects were expected to be unfavorable.
3. Certain effective hedges of foreign exchange risk were ignored.

Concerned with the increasing criticism leveled against *Statement No. 8*, the Board added to its agenda a project to reconsider it in January 1979. As a result of this project, an exposure draft entitled "Foreign Currency Translation" was issued in August 1980. On the basis of more than 360 comment letters and views expressed in a public hearing, the Board issued a revised exposure draft. These series of developments culminated in the issuance of *SFAS No. 52*, which was discussed in this and the previous chapter. Although few would contend that the accounting as prescribed under *SFAS No. 52* is flawless, it has met with generally less criticism than *SFAS No. 8*.

Because of the euro, there are fewer instances where it is necessary to use both remeasurement and translation for a single subsidiary (i.e., the approach used when the functional currency is the currency of a third country). Currently, at least 12 European nations are using the euro—Austria, Belgium, Finland, France, Germany, Greece, Ireland, Italy, Luxembourg, the Netherlands, Portugal, and Spain. However, euros are accepted in England, Sweden, and Denmark. Figure 13-1 lists the spot rates for the euro against 35 other currencies.

To prepare for trade under the European Union (EU), U.S. companies must update their information systems, their internal and external financial reporting, and assess the impact of the *euro* on all business functions. CFOs, controllers, and CPAs will all play a role in helping businesses manage the complexities of currency conversion, as well as ensuring that reporting requirements are met and tax strategies are optimal.[11]

FIGURE 13-1

Spot Rates on February 27, 2009

US dollar	1.2644	Turkish lira	2.1558
Japanese yen	123.23	Australian dollar	1.9891
Bulgarian lev	1.9558	Brazilian real	3.0093
Czech koruna	28.090	Canadian dollar	1.5985
Danish krone	7.4504	Chinese yuan renminbi	8.6482
Estonian kroon	15.6466	Hong Kong dollar	9.8053
Pound sterling	0.89310	Indonesian rupiah	15147.51
Hungarian forint	300.46	Indian rupee	64.5730
Lithuanian litas	3.4528	South Korean won	1950.91
Latvian lats	0.7095	Mexican peso	19.1416
Polish zloty	4.7030	Malaysian ringgit	4.6852
New Romanian leu [1]	4.3025	New Zealand dollar	2.5275
Swedish krona	11.4524	Philippine peso	61.580
Swiss franc	1.4841	Singapore dollar	1.9559
Norwegian krone	8.8860	Thai baht	45.714
Croatian kuna	7.4334	South African rand	12.8146
Russian rouble	45.4977		

Source: European Central Bank

[11] *Journal of Accountancy*, "Are You Euro-Fluent?" by Anette Estrada and Sander Wechsler, June 1999, p. 22.

SUMMARY

1. *Distinguish between the current exchange rate and the historical exchange rate.* The current exchange rate is the spot rate in effect at the end of the accounting period (i.e., the balance sheet date). The historical exchange rate is the spot rate in effect on the date a transaction takes place.
2. *Understand the objectives of financial statement translation.* The objectives are to provide information that is compatible with the exposed economic effects of an exchange rate change on a firm's cash flows and equity, and to reflect in the consolidated statements the financial results and relationships of the individual entities as measured in their functional currencies in conformity with U.S. GAAP.
3. *Identify the functional currency of a foreign entity.* The functional currency is the currency of the primary economic environment in which the foreign entity conducts its operations and generates and expends its cash.
4. *Compare the two methods used to convert the financial statements of a foreign entity into U.S. dollars.* Under the ***current method***, all assets and liabilities are translated using the current exchange rate on the balance sheet date. For income statement accounts (revenues and expenses),a weighted-average exchange rate is used to approximate the results that would be obtained from translation of each transaction. Under the ***temporal method***, monetary assets and liabilities are translated at the current exchange rate. Assets and liabilities carried at historical cost are translated at historical exchange rates. Assets and liabilities carried at current values (such as inventory carried at market under the lower of cost or market rule) are translated at the current exchange rate. Revenues and expenses that relate to assets and liabilities translated at historical rates (such as depreciation expense, amortization expense, and the cost of sales) are translated at the historical rates used for the related assets and liabilities. Other revenues and expenses are converted using a weighted-average rate.
5. *Distinguish between the circumstances under which each of the two methods is appropriate under current GAAP.* The temporal method (also referred to as remeasurement) is appropriate when the functional currency is the U.S. dollar or when the foreign environment is highly inflationary. The current method (also referred to as translation) is appropriate when the functional currency is the local currency. If the functional currency is the currency of a third country, it is necessary to remeasure the accounts *first* into the functional currency using the temporal method and *then* to translate the accounts into U.S. dollars (the reporting currency) using the current method.
6. *Explain the factors involved in translating the statements of a foreign entity operating in a highly inflationary economy.* The currency of a country experiencing high inflation will weaken substantially against the currency of a more stable economy. Thus, using the current rate method to translate inventories and fixed assets of foreign operations in highly inflationary economies often results in a substantial reduction in the translated amounts. Because the currency of the country has lost its utility as a store of value and cannot be a functional measuring unit, the Board prescribed that the financial statements be remeasured as if the functional currency were the reporting currency (U.S. dollar).
7. *Translate the statements of a foreign entity when the functional currency is the local currency.* The accounts are translated into dollars using the current rate method. The resulting translation adjustment is recorded as a separate component of stockholders equity.
8. *Translate the statements of a foreign entity when the functional currency is the U.S. dollar.* When the foreign entity does not maintain its records in its functional currency, the accounts are remeasured into the functional currency (dollars) using the temporal method. The resulting translation adjustment is reported in the current period's income statement.
9. *Understand the concept of comprehensive income in the context of foreign currency translation.* The currency translation adjustment under the "current" method represents one of several items of concern to the FASB because of their frequency of occurrence and relative importance, coupled with their exclusion from reported earnings. These items are, however, included in comprehensive income, defined as *all* changes in equity during a period except those resulting from investments by owners and distributions to owners. A statement of comprehensive income must be included in a complete set of financial statements.
10. *Identify the disclosure requirements for firms with foreign entities.* Companies must disclose: (1) the aggregate translation gain or loss included in earnings for the period, including gains or losses related to forward contracts; (2) an analysis of the cumulative translation adjustment equity account; and (3) the effect of any significant exchange rate changes that occur after the balance sheet date.

APPENDIX

Accounting for a Foreign Affiliate and Preparation of Consolidated Statements Workpaper Illustrated

To illustrate the accounting for a foreign affiliate and the preparation of a consolidated statements workpaper, the illustration of the 80% interest in SFr Company will be continued. Since SFr Company maintains its books in francs, the trial balance in dollars is based on the translated balances contained in Illustrations 13-4 and 13-8.

DATE OF ACQUISITION

Recall that on January 2, 2009, P Company acquired for 2,000,000 francs an 80% interest in SFr. Company. The direct exchange rate for francs on January 2, 2009, was $.15. Thus it would have taken $300,000 (2,000,000 francs × $.15) to buy the 2,000,000 francs needed for the purchase price. The entry to record the acquisition is

Investment in SFr Company	300,000	
Cash		300,000

On the date of acquisition, since the business combination must be accounted for using the purchase method of accounting (cash was used to acquire the voting stock), assets, liabilities, and stockholders' equity accounts are translated from francs into dollars using the spot rate of $.15. Any difference between implied and book value interest acquired is allocated to individual assets and liabilities of a foreign subsidiary using essentially the same approach as that illustrated in Chapter 5. On January 2, SFr Company reported common stock of 960,000 francs, additional paid-in capital of 300,000 francs, and retained earnings of 480,000 francs for a net asset balance of 1,740,000 francs. The difference between implied and book value in francs and dollars is allocated to land and buildings in Illustration 13-10. When an acquisition qualifies as a purchase transaction, all accounts of the subsidiary are translated at the date of acquisition using the then-current exchange rate whether the current rate method or the temporal method is used in the translation process. Thus, the computation of the difference and its allocation is the same for both methods.

ILLUSTRATION 13-10

Allocation of Difference between Implied and Book Value

	Francs	*Translation Rate*	*Dollars*
Implied value (2,000,000/80%)	2,500,000**	$.15	375,000
Book value of SFr equity	1,740,000	.15	261,000
Difference between implied and book value interest acquired	760,000		114,000
Allocated to:			
Land	(385,000)*	.15	(57,750)
Buildings—10 year-remaining life	(375,000)*	.15	(56,250)
Unallocated balance	—0—		—0—

* Amounts are assumed.

** NCI = 2,500,00 × 20% = 500,000 at acquisition.

Translated NCI at acquisition is $75,000 (or 500,000 × .15).

ACCOUNTING FOR AN INVESTMENT IN A FOREIGN AFFILIATE—AFTER ACQUISITION

After the initial entry to record the purchase of the equity interest in SFr Company, P Company will make a book entry to record the declaration and receipt of cash dividends. P Company accounts for its investment by the cost method. In this case, SFr Company declared and paid a 300,000 franc dividend on September 1 when the direct exchange rate was $.16. The book entry to record the dividend receipt is:

Cash	38,400	
Dividend Income		38,400
300,000 francs × $.16 = $48,000 × .80 = $38,400		

Before consolidated financial statements are prepared, the subsidiary's financial statements must be translated into dollars using either the current rate method (Illustration 13-4) or the temporal method (Illustration 13-8). A workpaper to consolidate P Company and SFr Company is presented in Illustration 13-11 assuming that the current rate method was appropriate for translating the subsidiary's accounts (i.e., the functional currency of the subsidiary was its local currency). Workpaper entries in general journal form are given here:

Consolidated Statements Workpaper Entries—December 31, 2009

(1)	Dividend Income	38,400	
	Dividends Declared—SFr Company		38,400
	To eliminate intercompany dividends.		
(2)	Beginning Retained Earnings—SFr Company	72,000	
	Common Stock—SFr Company	144,000	
	Additional Paid-in Capital—SFr Company	45,000	
	Difference between Implied and Book Value	114,000	
	Investment in SFr Company		300,000
	NCI in equity		75,000
	To eliminate the investment account.		
(3)	Cumulative Translation Adjustment—SFr Company	29,170	
	Cumulative Translation Adjustment—P Company		29,170
	To recognize P Company's interest in the increase in stockholders' equity resulting from a change in exchange rates.		
(4)	Depreciation Expense	5,850	
	Land	65,450	
	Buildings	57,375	
	Cumulative Translation Adjustment—P Company		14,675
	Difference between Implied and Book Value		114,000
	To allocate the difference between implied and book value and to recognize the related translation adjustment.		

The major differences between the foregoing entries for the current rate method and those prepared in Chapter 5 are as follows:

1. Using the current rate method to translate the accounts of the subsidiary resulted in a cumulative translation adjustment of $36,462. The $36,462 increases stockholders' equity and translated net assets of the subsidiary. Since this amount is not reported in the income statement, a workpaper entry [entry (3)]

is made to recognize the parent's interest therein ($36,462 × .80 = $29,170). The remaining portion ($36,462 × .20 = $7,292) is extended to the noncontrolling interest column.

2. The difference between implied and book value at the date of acquisition was allocated to specific assets and translated into dollars using the exchange rate in effect on the purchase date. The amounts allocated to land and buildings at the end of the year are not the same amounts reported on the computation and allocation scheduled created on the date of acquisition. On the date of acquisition, these items were translated using the spot rate on that date (0.15). At the end of the year, they are translated using the exchange rate at the end of the year (0.17). Also, because depreciation expense is translated using the average exchange rate for the year of 0.156, there will be a translation adjustment of $14,675 needed to balance journal entry (4).

Subsequent to the Year of Acquisition

In years after the year of acquisition, an entry to establish reciprocity is made based on the undistributed net income. In this case the entry for the next year is:

Investment in SFr Company	3,158	
Beginning Retained Earnings—P Company		3,158
Retained Earnings—12/31/2009	$75,948	
Retained Earnings—Date of acquisition	72,000	
Undistributed net income	$ 3,948	
$3,948 × .80 = $3,158		

The other workpaper entries are similar to those illustrated before.

CONSOLIDATION WHEN THE TEMPORAL METHOD OF TRANSLATION IS USED

In completing the remeasurement process using the temporal method, a consolidated statements workpaper would be similar to the one previously illustrated for the current rate method. The major differences between the workpapers are as follows:

1. Under the temporal method, the translation gain or loss is included in the subsidiary's income statement and becomes a part of its ending retained earnings balance. The controlling interest in the gain or loss is recognized as part of consolidated net income in the current period. In subsequent periods the gain or loss is included in consolidated retained earnings as part of the reciprocity entry. Thus, a separate entry is not needed to recognize the parent's share of the translation gain or loss such as was done in entry (3) when the current rate method of translation was used.

2. The unamortized portion of the difference assigned to land and buildings and the amortization for the current period retain their historical dollar values since such nonmonetary assets are translated using historical rates.

Cost Method	ILLUSTRATION 13-11
80% Owned Foreign Subsidiary	**Consolidated Statements Workpaper**
Current Rate Method of Translation	**P Company and Foreign Subsidiary**
Year of Acquisition	**for the Year Ended December 31, 2009**

Income Statement	*P Company*	*SFr Company*	*Eliminations Dr.*	*Eliminations Cr.*	*Noncontrolling Interest*	*Consolidated Balances*
Sales and Other Revenue	4,200,000	471,120				4,671,120
Dividend Income	38,400		(1) 38,400			-
Total Revenues	4,238,400	471,120				4,671,120
Cost of Goods Sold	2,720,000	288,600				3,008,600
Depreciation Expense	210,000	15,600	(4) 5,850			231,450
Other Expenses	914,000	102,180				1,016,180
Income Tax Expense	100,000	12,792				112,792
Total Cost and Expense	3,944,000	419,172				4,369,022
Consolidated Net Income	294,400	51,948				302,098
Noncontrolling Interest in Net Income					9,220*	(9,220)
Net Income to Retained Earnings	294,400	51,948	44,250	—0—	9,220	292,878
Retained Earnings Statement						
1/1 Retained Earnings						
P Company	450,000					450,000
SFr Company		72,000	(2) 72,000			
Net Income from above	294,400	51,948	44,250		9,220	292,878
Dividends Declared						
P Company	(200,000)					(200,000)
SFr Company		(48,000)		(1) 38,400	(9,600)	
12/31 Retained Earnings to Balance Sheet	544,400	75,948	116,250	38,400	(380)	542,878
Balance Sheet						
Current Assets	1,324,400	402,560				1,726,960
Investment in SFr Company	300,000			(2) 300,000		—
Land	450,000	85,000	(4) 65,450			600,450
Buildings (net)	720,000	110,500	(4) 57,375			887,875
Equipment (net)	390,000	73,100				463,100
Difference between IV and BV	—		(2) 114,000	(4) 114,000		—
Total Assets	3,184,400	671,160				3,678,385
Current Liabilities	840,000	216,750				1,056,750
Bonds Payable	700,000	153,000				853,000
Common Stock						
P Company	800,000					800,000
SFr Company		144,000	(2) 144,000			
Additional Paid in Capital						
P Company	300,000					300,000
SFr Company		45,000	(2) 45,000			
Cumulative Translation adjustment:				(3) 29,170		
P Company	-			(4) 14,675		
						43,845
SFr Company		36,462	(3) 29,170		7,292	
Retained Earnings from above	544,400	75,948	116,250	38,400	(380)	542,878
1/1 Noncontrolling Interest in Net Assets				(2) 75,000	75,000	
12/31 Noncontrolling Interest in Net Assets					81,912 81,912	81,912
Total Liabilities and Owners' Equity	3,184,400	671,160	571,245	571,245		3,678,385

* ($51,948 − 5,850) × .20 = $9.220.

(1) To eliminate intercompany dividends.

(2) To eliminate the investment account and create noncontrolling interest account.

(3) To recognize interest in cumulative translation adjustment.

(4) To assign difference between implied and book value.

ILLUSTRATION 13-12

Verification of Cumulative Translation Adjustment

	Francs	*Translation Rate*	*Dollars*
Undervalued net assets at beginning of year	760,000	$.15	114,000
Amortization this period	(37,500)	.156	(5,850)
Net asset position translated using rate in effect at date of transaction			108,150
Unamortized balance at end of year*	722,500	.17	122,825
Current year change in cumulative translation adjustment			14,675

	Francs		*Dollars*
* Land	385,000	.17	65,450
Buildings less depreciation	337,500	.17	57,375
Total	722,500		122,825

REMEASUREMENT AND TRANSLATION OF FOREIGN CURRENCY TRANSACTIONS

SFAS No. 52 **[ASC 830–20–20]** defines a foreign currency transaction as one that is denominated in a currency other than the entity's functional currency. As discussed in Chapter 12, at the transaction date, the current exchange rate is used to measure and record a foreign currency transaction in the functional currency of the recording entity. At subsequent balance sheet dates, recorded balances that are denominated in a currency other than the functional currency are adjusted to the functional currency using the current exchange rate. Any transaction gain or loss resulting from this procedure is recognized currently in income. Although a thorough discussion and illustration of the effects on the financial statements of affiliated companies and on consolidated statements is beyond the scope of this text, two examples are presented to illustrate the procedures.

Assume that a Swiss subsidiary has a $100,000 loan payable to a U.S. bank. The loan is denominated in dollars and the franc is the functional currency of the subsidiary. Thus, this is a foreign currency transaction to the subsidiary but not to the U.S. bank. The current exchange rate was $.20 on the transaction date and $.16 on the balance sheet date. The subsidiary would compute a gain or loss as follows at the balance sheet date:

	Francs
Transaction date	$100,000 ÷ .20 = 500,000
Balance sheet date	$100,000 ÷ .16 = 625,000
Transaction loss reported in income	125,000

The U.S. bank would not record a gain or loss on its books because the payable is denominated in dollars.

Before consolidation, the accounts of the subsidiary are translated into dollars (the reporting currency) using the current rate method. In this illustration the payable of 625,000 francs as measured in the functional currency is translated to $100,000 (625,000 francs × $.16) to reflect the dollar denominated amount of the loan. In the income statement, the transaction loss of 125,000 francs is translated using the average exchange rate. When the current rate method is used, the adjustment resulting from translating the accounts into dollars is made to stockholders' equity.

If, in the foregoing illustration, the loan were denominated in francs (the functional currency of the subsidiary), the transaction would not be a foreign currency transaction to the subsidiary. The loan is a foreign currency transaction, however, to the U.S. bank. The bank will measure the 500,000 franc receivable into dollars at the transaction and balance sheet dates using the current rate. A transaction loss is computed at the balance sheet date as follows:

Transaction date	500,000 francs × $.20 =	$100,000
Balance sheet date	500,000 francs × $.16 =	$ 80,000
Transaction loss reported in income		$ 20,000

In the trial balance of the subsidiary, the payable is already measured in francs. Thus, a transaction gain or loss is not recognized currently in income. Note, however, that the payable is a component of the subsidiary's net asset position and will affect the translation gain or loss reported in the stockholders' equity section of the balance sheet when the payable is translated into U.S. dollars for consolidation purposes.

If the dollar is identified as the foreign entity's functional currency, then a dollar-denominated transaction is not a foreign currency transaction to either party. In the dollar trial balance of the subsidiary, the payable is restated to $100,000 at both the transaction date and the balance sheet date. Finally, if the functional currency is the dollar and the loan is denominated in francs, it is a foreign currency transaction to both parties, and the 500,000 franc loan is remeasured to $80,000 at the balance sheet date by both.

INTERCOMPANY RECEIVABLES AND PAYABLES

SFAS No. 52 **[ASC 830–20–35–1]** requires that transaction gains and losses on intercompany receivables and payables be recognized in the period that the exchange rate changes. The procedures for doing so are similar to those discussed in the preceding section. However, a company is required to distinguish between transactions that are of a long-term investment nature and other transactions. Intercompany transactions for which settlement is not planned or intended in the foreseeable future are considered a part of the net investment in the foreign entity. Accordingly, transaction gains or losses on the receivable or payable, whether denominated in dollars or in the local currency of the foreign entity, are deferred and accumulated with the translation adjustment in a separate component of stockholders' equity. A transaction gain or loss attributable to other intercompany accounts is reported currently in the determination of net income because it is expected to affect functional currency cash flows.

ELIMINATION OF INTERCOMPANY PROFIT

Profits and losses attributable to intercompany sales or transfers are eliminated on the basis of the exchange rate at the date of each sale or transfer. Here again, the use of averages or reasonable approximations of specific rates in effect on the due date of each transaction is permitted. To illustrate, the following assumptions are made:

1. Exchange rates: date of sale, $.14; balance sheet date, $.17.
2. The intercompany sale and profit in dollars and francs is:

	Dollars	Francs
Sales price to foreign subsidiary	14,000	100,000
Cost to parent company	10,500	75,000
Intercompany profit	3,500	25,000

3. None of the inventory was sold by the subsidiary during the current period.
4. The franc is the functional currency of the foreign entity.

At year-end, the inventory balance of 100,000 francs is translated to $17,000 using the current rate at the balance sheet date. In the consolidated balance sheet, the intercompany profit of $3,500 is eliminated from the inventory, which results in a carrying value for the inventory of $13,500. As shown below, this process includes $750 in the inventory carrying value that is related to the effect of the exchange rate change on the intercompany profit element.

	Francs	Translation Rate	Dollars
Inventory cost	75,000	.17	12,750
Intercompany profit	25,000	(.17 − .14)	750
Carrying value of ending inventory	100,000		13,500

The Board reasoned that intercompany profit occurs at the date of sale and that is the amount that should be eliminated. The $750 results from a subsequent change in the exchange rate, an event considered independent from the sale.

LIQUIDATION OF A FOREIGN INVESTMENT

Upon the sale of part or all of an investment in a foreign entity, a pro-rata share of the amount included in the accumulated translation adjustment equity account associated with that foreign investment is removed and reported as part of the gain or loss from the disposition of the investment. For example, if a company disposed of 50% of its interest in a foreign entity, 50% of the related accumulated translation adjustment would be removed from stockholders' equity and recognized in measuring the gain or loss on the sale.

TEST YOUR KNOWLEDGE SOLUTIONS

13-1 1. c

2. d

13-2 1. c

13-3 1. d

QUESTIONS

(The letter A or B after a question, exercise, or problem refers to the Appendix.)

LO2 1. What requirements must be satisfied if a foreign subsidiary is to be consolidated?

LO3 2. What is meant by an entity's functional currency and what are the economic indicators identified by the FASB to provide guidance in selecting the functional currency?

LO5 3. The __________ is the functional currency of a foreign subsidiary with operations that are relatively self-contained and integrated within the country in which it is located. In such cases, the __________ method of translation would be used to translate the accounts into dollars.

LO5 4. The __________ is the functional currency of a foreign subsidiary that is a direct and integral component or extension of a U.S. parent company. In such cases, the __________ method of translation is used to translate (remeasure) the accounts into dollars.

LO6 5. Which method of translation is used to convert the financial statements when a foreign subsidiary operates in a highly inflationary economy?

LO4 6. Define remeasurement.

LO4 7. Under the current rate method, how are assets and liabilities that are stated in a foreign currency translated?

LO4 8. Under the current rate method, describe how the various balance sheet accounts are translated (including the equity accounts) and how this translation affects the computation of various ratios (such as debt to equity or the current ratio). In particular, discuss whether or not the ratios will change when computed in local currencies and compared to their calculations (after translation) using the parent's currency.

LO4 9. What is the objective of the temporal method of translation?

LO4 10. Assuming that the temporal method is used, how are revenue and expense items in foreign currency financial statements converted?

LO7 11. A translation adjustment results from the process of translating financial statements of a foreign subsidiary from its functional currency into dollars. Where is the translation adjustment reported in the financial statements if the current rate method is used to translate the accounts?

Business Ethics

The Shady Tree Company is preparing to announce their quarterly earnings numbers. The company expects to beat the analysts' forecast of earnings by at least 5 cents a share. In anticipation of the increase in stock value and before the release of the earnings numbers, the company issued stock options to the top executives in the firm, with the option price equal to today's market price.

1. This type of executive stock option is often referred to as "spring-loading." Do you think this practice should be allowed? Does it provide information about the integrity of the firm or is this just good business practice?
2. Do you think this practice violates the insider trading rules?

EXERCISES

EXERCISE 13-1 Identifying the Exchange Rate LO5

Accounts are listed below for a foreign subsidiary that maintains its books in its local currency. The equity interest in the subsidiary was acquired in a purchase transaction. In the space provided, indicate the exchange rate that would be used to translate the accounts into dollars assuming that the functional currency was identified (a) as the U.S. dollar and (b) as the foreign entity's local currency. Use the following letters to identify the exchange rate:

H—historical exchange rate
C—current exchange rate
A—average exchange rate for the current period

	Exchange Rate if the Functional Currency Is:	
Account	*U.S. Dollar*	*Local Currency*
Cash	____	____
Accounts receivable	____	____
Inventory carried at cost	____	____
Inventory carried at market	____	____
Prepaid rent	____	____
Property, plant, and equipment	____	____
Goodwill	____	____
Accounts payable	____	____
Bonds payable	____	____
Unamortized premium on bonds payable	____	____
Preferred stock carried at issuance price	____	____
Common stock	____	____
Sales	____	____
Cost of goods sold	____	____
Depreciation expense	____	____

EXERCISE 13-2 Multiple Choice LO3 LO5 LO7 LO8

Select the best answer for each of the following items:

1. Golf Company acquired 80% of the outstanding stock of Ping Company, a foreign company, in an acquisition accounted for as a purchase transaction. In preparing consolidated statements, the paid-in capital of Ping Company should be translated into dollars at the
   (a) Current exchange rate in effect at the balance sheet date.
   (b) Exchange rate in effect at the date the capital transactions of the subsidiary took place.
   (c) Exchange rate in effect at the date Golf Company purchased the Ping Company stock.
   (d) Exchange rate effective when Ping Company was organized.

2. The account balances of a foreign entity are required by *SFAS No. 52* to be measured using that entity's functional currency. The functional currency of an entity is defined as
   (a) The currency in which the entity's transactions are recorded.
   (b) The currency of the primary economic environment in which the entity operates.
   (c) The U.S. dollar.
   (d) The local currency of the country in which the entity is physically located.

3. When translating foreign currency financial statements for an entity whose functional currency is the local currency of the country in which it is physically located, which of the following accounts is translated using current exchange rates?

	Bonds Payable	*Inventories Carried at Market*
(a)	No	No
(b)	Yes	No
(c)	No	Yes
(d)	Yes	Yes

4. A translation adjustment (or translation gain) that is a consequence of translation of a functional currency that is different from the reporting currency should be
   (a) Deferred and amortized over a period not to exceed 40 years.
   (b) Deferred until a subsequent year when a loss occurs and offset it against that loss.
   (c) Included as a separate item in the equity section of the balance sheet.
   (d) Included in net income in the period in which it occurs.

5. A wholly owned foreign subsidiary of Import Corporation has certain expense accounts for the year ended December 31, 2008, stated in local currency units (LCU) as follows:

	LCU
Amortization of patent (patent was acquired January 1, 2006)	40,000
Provision for doubtful accounts	40,000
Rent	120,000

The exchange rates at various dates are as follows:

	Dollar Equivalent of 1 LCU
December 31, 2008	$.20
Average for the year ended December 31, 2008	.24
January 1, 2006	.25

The subsidiary's operations were an extension of the parent company's operations. What total dollar amount should be included in Import's income statement to reflect the foregoing expenses for the year ended December 31, 2008?

(a) $48,000.

(b) $40,000.

(c) $48,400.

(d) $42,000.

(*AICPA adapted*)

EXERCISE 13-3 **Multiple Choice** LO3 LO4 LO5 LO7 LO8

Select the best answer choice for each of the following items.

1. Perez Company's operations are unrelated to the operations of its subsidiary. Certain balance sheet accounts of the foreign subsidiary at December 31, 2008, have been translated into U.S. dollars as follows:

	Translated at:	
	Current Rates	*Historical Rates*
Accounts receivable, current	$200,000	$220,000
Accounts receivable, long-term	130,000	140,000
Prepaid insurance	50,000	55,000
Goodwill	100,000	110,000

If the accounting is in accordance with *SFAS No. 52*, what total should be included in Perez's balance sheet at December 31, 2008, for the foregoing items?

(a) $480,000.

(b) $490,000.

(c) $495,000.

(d) $580,000.

2. When the functional currency of a foreign operation is the U.S. dollar, translation gains and losses resulting from translating (remeasuring) foreign currency financial statements into U.S. dollars should be included as

(a) An extraordinary item in the income statement for the period in which the rate changes.

(b) An ordinary item in the income statement for losses but deferred for gains in accordance with the conservatism convention.

(c) An ordinary item in the income statement for the period in which the rate changes.

(d) A deferred item in the balance sheet.

3. Pal Company is translating account balances of its foreign subsidiary into dollars for its December 31, 2008, balance sheet and its 2008 income statement. The functional currency was identified as the local currency of the foreign subsidiary. The average exchange rate for 2008 should be used to translate
   (a) Retained earnings at January 1, 2008.
   (b) Equipment purchased in 2008.
   (c) Sales for 2008.
   (d) Cash at December 31, 2008.
4. One of the first steps in translating the financial statements of a foreign subsidiary is the identification of the functional currency of that entity. Which of the following indicates that the functional currency is the local currency of the foreign entity?
   (a) There is a high volume of intercompany transactions.
   (b) Financing is primarily denominated in the local currency.
   (c) Sales are mostly in the United States, or sales contracts are denominated in dollars.
   (d) Sales prices are primarily responsive in the short term to exchange rate changes.
5. When the foreign operations are conducted in a highly inflationary economy, at what translation rates should the goodwill and accounts receivable accounts in foreign statements be translated into U.S. dollars?

	Goodwill	*Accounts Receivable*
(a)	Current	Average for year
(b)	Historical	Current
(c)	Historical	Historical
(d)	Current	Current

(*AICPA adapted*)

EXERCISE 13-4 **Foreign Currency Translation—Current Rate Method** LO7

On January 1, 2008, Trenten Systems, a U.S.-based company, purchased a controlling interest in Grant Management Consultants located in Zurich, Switzerland. The acquisition was treated as a purchase transaction. The 2008 financial statements stated in Swiss francs are given below.

GRANT MANAGEMENT CONSULTANTS
Comparative Balance Sheets
January 1 and December 31, 2008

	Jan. 1	*Dec. 31*
Cash and Receivables	20,000	55,000
Net Property, Plant, and Equipment	40,000	37,000
Totals	60,000	92,000
Accounts and Notes Payable	30,000	32,000
Common Stock	20,000	20,000
Retained Earnings	10,000	40,000
Totals	60,000	92,000

GRANT MANAGEMENT CONSULTANTS
Consolidated Income and Retained Earnings Statement
for the Year Ended December 31, 2008

Revenues	75,000
Operating Expenses including Depreciation of 3,000 francs	30,000
Net Income	45,000
Dividends Declared and Paid	15,000
Increase in Retained Earnings	30,000

Direct exchange rates for Swiss franc are:

	Dollars per Franc
January 1, 2008	$.5987
December 31, 2008	.5321
Average for 2008	.5654
Dividend declaration and payment date	.5810

Required:

A. Translate the year-end balance sheet and income statement of the foreign subsidiary using the current rate method of translation.

B. Prepare a schedule to verify the translation adjustment.

EXERCISE 13-5 **Foreign Currency Remeasurement—Temporal Method** LO8

Use the information provided in Exercise 13-4.

Required:

A. Convert (remeasure) the financial statements of the foreign subsidiary using the temporal method of translation.

B. Prepare a schedule to verify the translation gain or loss.

EXERCISE 13-6 **Local Currency Is a Foreign (Non-U.S.) Currency** LO7

Refer to Exercise 13-4. Using the same information, assume that the Brazilian real is identified as the functional currency of the subsidiary.

Required:

A. Remeasure the account balances that are expressed in Swiss francs into Brazilian reals, Direct exchange rates for the real are:

	Real per Franc
Beginning of current year	1.3940
End of current year	1.2899
Average for current year	1.3445
Dividend payment date	1.2438

B. Translate the remeasured accounts that are now stated in Reals into dollars using the current rate method. Direct exchange rates for the real are:

	Dollars per Real
Beginning of current year	$.4891
End of current year	.4630
Average for current year	.4751
Dividend payment date	.4740

EXERCISE 13-7 **Current Rate Method** LO7

Dorsey Corporation purchased 90% of the common stock of Lansing Company on January 1, 2002. The cost of the investment was equal to the book value interest acquired. Lansing Company operates two retail stores and an exporting business in London that specializes in buying and selling British tweeds. The subsidiary provided the following financial statements in pounds to the parent company:

LANSING COMPANY
Consolidated Income and Retained Earnings Statement
for the Year Ended December 31, 2008

Sales	2,900,000
Cost of Goods Sold	(1,400,000)
Depreciation Expense	(300,000)
Other Expenses	(400,000)
Net Income	800,000
1/1 Retained Earnings	900,000
	1,700,000
Less: Dividends Declared and Paid, December 31	(325,000)
12/31 Retained Earnings	1,375,000

LANSING COMPANY
Balance Sheet
December 31, 2008

Cash and Receivables	1,275,000
Merchandise Inventory	490,000
Property, Plant, and Equipment	3,450,000
Total	5,215,000
Current Liabilities	640,000
Long-Term Notes Payable	1,200,000
Capital Stock	2,000,000
Retained Earnings	1,375,000
Total	5,215,000

Lansing Company was incorporated on January 1, 2000, at which time all the property, plant, and equipment was purchased. The long-term notes were issued to partially finance the purchase of the fixed assets.

Direct exchange rates for the British pound are as follows:

January 1, 2000	$1.8996
January 1, 2002	1.8365
Average for the last quarter 2007	1.5300
January 1, 2008	1.4919
December 31, 2008	1.4730
Average for 2008	1.4788
Average for August–December 2008	1.4950

The January 1, 2008, retained earnings balance of Lansing in dollars was $1,593,408, and the cumulative translation adjustment was a debit balance of $939,898. The beginning inventory of £420,000 was acquired during the last quarter of 2007 and the ending inventory was acquired during the last five months of 2008. Sales were made and purchases and other expenses were incurred evenly during the year.

Required:

Translate the December 31, 2008, account balances of Lansing Company into dollars assuming that the pound is the functional currency of Lansing Company.

EXERCISE 13-8 **Temporal Method (Remeasurement)** LO8

Refer to the data provided in Exercise 13-7 for Dorsey Corporation and Lansing Company.

Required:

Translate (remeasure) the account balances of Lansing into dollars assuming that the dollar is the functional currency of Lansing Company. The beginning retained earnings balance of Lansing Company in dollars was $1,791,324.

EXERCISE 13-9 **Translation Assuming Various Functional Currencies** LO7 LO8

Slocome Travel owns a travel agency that operates in London. Account balances in pounds for the subsidiary are summarized below:

	2008	
	January 1	*December 31*
Cash and Receivables	32,000	35,000
Office Supplies	1,500	900
Land, Building, and Equipment	70,000	65,000
Accounts Payable	(15,500)	(6,900)
Long-Term Note Payable	(25,000)	(15,000)
Common Stock	(40,000)	(40,000)
Retained Earnings	(23,000)	(23,000)
Dividends—Declared and Paid on December 31	—	4,000
Revenues	—	(40,000)
Operating Expenses	—	20,000
Totals	—0—	—0—

Exchange rates for 2008 were as follows:

January 1	$1.5403
December 31	1.5961
Average for year	1.5532

The subsidiary did not make any purchases of office supplies or plant assets during the year. Revenues were earned and operating expenses, other than depreciation and supplies used, were incurred evenly throughout the year.

Required:

A. Prepare a schedule to compute the translation adjustment for the year, assuming the foreign entity's functional currency is the pound.

B. Prepare a schedule to compute the translation gain or loss, assuming the foreign entity's functional currency is the U.S. dollar.

C. Explain why your results differ under the two methods.

EXERCISE 13-10A **Consolidated Workpaper**

A U.S. company owns an 80% interest in a company located on Mars. Martian currency is called the Martian Credit. During the year the parent company sold inventory that had cost $24,000 to the subsidiary on account for $30,000 when the exchange rate was $.5192. The subsidiary still held one-half of the inventory and had not paid the parent company for the purchase at the end of the fiscal period. The unsettled account is denominated in dollars. The exchange rate at the fiscal year-end was $.4994.

Required:

A. **(1)** Compute the amounts that would be reported for the inventory and accounts payable in the subsidiary's translated balance sheet. The entity's functional currency is the Martian Credit.

(2) Compute the subsidiary's transaction gain or loss on the accounts payable denominated in dollars.

(3) How is the transaction gain or loss reported in the foreign entity's financial statements?

B. Compute the amount of the intercompany profit to be eliminated in the consolidated statements workpaper prepared for the current year.

C. **(1)** Assuming that the transaction had been denominated in 50,204 Martian Credits rather than dollars, compute the transaction gain or loss that would be reported by the parent company.

(2) How is the gain or loss reported in the consolidated financial statements?

(3) How would your answer differ if the loan to the foreign subsidiary was considered to be of a long-term investment nature?

PROBLEMS

PROBLEM 13-1 **Translation—Local Currency Is the Functional Currency** LO7

On January 1, 2008, a U.S. company purchased 100% of the outstanding stock of Ventana Grains, a company located in Latz City, New Zealand. Ventana Grains was organized on January 1, 1994. All the property, plant, and equipment held on January 1, 2008, was acquired when the company was organized. The business combination was accounted for as a purchase transaction. The 2008 financial statements for Ventana Grains, prepared in its local currency, the New Zealand dollar, are given here.

VENTANA GRAINS
Comparative Balance Sheets
January 1 and December 31, 2008

	Jan. 1	*Dec. 31*
Cash and Receivables	500,000	880,000
Inventories	600,000	500,000
Land	400,000	400,000
Buildings (net)	650,000	605,000
Equipment (net)	465,000	470,000
Totals	2,615,000	2,855,000

	Jan. 1	*Dec. 31*
Short-Term Accounts and Notes	295,000	210,000
Long-Term Notes (600,000 issued September 1, 2000, 80,000 issued July 1, 2008)	600,000	680,000
Common Stock	800,000	800,000
Additional Paid-in Capital	200,000	200,000
Retained Earnings	720,000	965,000
Total	2,615,000	2,855,000

VENTANA GRAINS
Consolidated Income and Retained Earnings Statement
for the Year Ended December 31, 2008

Revenues		3,225,000
Cost of Goods Sold:		
Beginning Inventory	600,000	
Purchases	2,100,000	
Goods Available for Sale	2,700,000	
Less: Ending Inventory	500,000	
Cost of Goods Sold		2,200,000
Gross Profit on Sales		1,025,000
Depreciation Expense	140,000	
Other Expenses	540,000	680,000
Net Income		345,000
Jan. 1 Retained Earnings		720,000
Total		1,065,000
Less: Dividends Paid		100,000
Dec. 31 Retained Earnings		965,000

The account balances are computed in conformity with U.S. generally accepted accounting standards.

Other information is as follows:

1. Direct exchange rates for the New Zealand dollar on various dates were:

Date	*Exchange Rate*
January 1, 1994	$.8011
September 1, 2004	.5813
January 1, 2008	.7924
July 1, 2008	.7412
December 31, 2008	.7298
Average for 2008	.7480
Average for the last four months of 2008	.7476

2. Ventana Grains purchased additional equipment for 100,000 New Zealand dollars on July 1, 2008, by issuing a note for 80,000 New Zealand dollars and paying the balance in cash.
3. Sales were made and purchases and "Other Expenses" were incurred evenly throughout the year.
4. Depreciation for the period in New Zealand dollars was computed as follows:

Building	45,000
Equipment—Purchased before 1/1/2008	85,000
Equipment—Purchased July 1, 2008	10,000

5. The inventory is valued on a FIFO basis. The beginning inventory was acquired when the exchange rate was $.7480. The ending inventory was acquired during the last four months of 2008.
6. Dividends of 50,000 New Zealand dollars were paid on July 1 and December 31.

Required:

A. Translate the financial statements into dollars assuming that the local currency of the foreign subsidiary was identified as its functional currency.

B. Prepare a schedule to verify the translation adjustment determined in requirement A. Describe how the translation adjustment would be reported in the financial statements.

PROBLEM 13-2 **Remeasurement—U.S. Dollar Is the Functional Currency** LO8

Refer to the information given in Problem 13-1.

Required:

A. Remeasure the financial statements into dollars assuming that the U.S. dollar was identified as the functional currency of the foreign subsidiary.

B. Prepare a schedule to verify the translation gain or loss determined in requirement A. Describe how the translation gain or loss would be reported in the financial statements.

PROBLEM 13-3 **Translation—Local Currency Is the Functional Currency** LO7

(This problem is a continuation of the illustration presented in the chapter.)

On January 2, 2008, P Company, a U.S.-based company, acquired for 2,000,000 francs an 80% interest in SFr Company, a Swiss company. On January 2, 2008, SFr Company reported a retained earnings balance of 480,000 francs. SFr's books are maintained in francs and are in conformity with U.S. generally accepted accounting principles. Trial balances of the two companies as of December 31, 2009, are presented here:

Debits	*P Company (Dollars)*	*SFr Company (Francs)*
Cash	500,200	962,500
Accounts Receivable	516,400	660,000
Inventories (FIFO cost)	627,800	1,037,500
Investment in SFr Company	300,000	—
Land	450,000	500,000
Buildings (net)	610,000	550,000
Equipment (net)	290,000	405,000
Dividends Declared	200,000	375,000
Cost of Goods Sold	2,720,000	2,312,500
Depreciation Expense	210,000	125,000
Other Expense	914,000	818,750
Income Tax Expense	100,000	102,500
Totals	7,438,400	7,848,750

Credits	*P Company (Dollars)*	*SFr Company (Francs)*
Accounts Payable	540,000	800,000
Short-term Notes Payable	300,000	650,750
Bonds Payable	700,000	850,000
Common Stock	800,000	960,000
Additional Paid-in Capital	300,000	300,000
Retained Earnings, 1/1	544,400	513,000
Sales	4,200,000	3,775,000
Dividend Income	54,000	—
Totals	7,438,400	7,848,750

Other information related to the subsidiary follows:

1. Beginning inventory of 830,000 francs was acquired when the exchange rate was $.165.
2. Purchases made uniformly throughout 2009 were 2,520,000 francs.
3. The franc is identified as the subsidiary's functional currency.
4. The subsidiary's beginning (1/1/09) retained earnings and cumulative translation adjustment (credit) in dollars were $75,948 and $36,462, respectively.
5. All plant assets were acquired before the parent obtained a controlling interest in the subsidiary.
6. Sales are made and all expenses are incurred uniformly throughout the year.
7. The ending inventory was acquired during the last quarter.
8. The subsidiary declared and paid dividends of 375,000 francs on September 2.
9. The following direct exchange rate quotations were available:

Date of subsidiary acquisition	$.15
Average for 2008	.156
January 1, 2009	.17
September 2, 2009	.18
December 31, 2009	.19
Average for the 4th quarter, 2009	.185
Average for 2009	.176

Required:

A. Prepare a translated balance sheet and combined statement of income and retained earnings for the subsidiary.

B. Prepare a schedule to verify the translation adjustment.

C. Compute the following ratios based on the franc and the U.S. dollar financial statements.
 (1) Current ratio.
 (2) Debt to equity.
 (3) Gross profit percentage.
 (4) Net income to sales.

PROBLEM 13-4 **Remeasurement—U.S. Dollar Is the Functional Currency** LO8
Use the information provided in Problem 13-3 for P Company and SFr Company.

Required:

A. Convert the accounts of the foreign subsidiary, assuming that the U.S. dollar is the functional currency of both companies. For this problem assume that the subsidiary's beginning (1/1/09) retained earnings balance in the translated balance sheet is $76,660.

B. Prepare a schedule to verify the translation gain or loss, assuming a 637,000 franc net exposed liability position at the beginning of the year.

PROBLEM 13-5 **Temporal Method** LO8
Pasquale Company is a manufacturer of oil drilling equipment located in Canada. The company is 90% owned by a U.S. parent company. The accounting department of Pasquale Company accumulated the following 2008 information for the company's auditor.

Equipment

1. The equipment account contained the following items:

Description	*Cost (Can. $)*	*Useful Life*	*Acquisition Date*	*Exchange Rate on Acquisition Date*
Drill press	30,000	5 years	July 15, 2004	$.8430
Stamping press	80,000	4 years	January 2, 2006	.7360
Fork lift	42,000	6 years	September 1, 2007	.6998

2. Pasquale Company depreciates assets by the straight-line method and assumes a zero residual value.

3. Its policy is to take a full year's depreciation on all depreciable assets acquired before July 1 and no depreciation on all depreciable assets required after July 1.

Inventory

1. The beginning inventory of 60,000 Canadian dollars was acquired during the last quarter of 2007.

2. Inventory purchases of 400,000 Canadian dollars were made uniformly during the year.

3. The ending inventory of 60,000 Canadian dollars was acquired during November and December, 2008.

Marketable Securities

1. Marketable securities, carried at cost, were acquired for 30,000 Canadian dollars when the direct exchange rate was $.9320.

Direct Exchange Rates

Average for the last quarter of 2007, $.7322
January 1, 2008, $.7080
Average for November and December, 2008, $.6845
Average for 2008, $.7140
December 31, 2008, $.6960

Required:

A. Compute the account balances that would be reported for equipment, inventory, and marketable securities in the December 31, 2008, balance sheet expressed in U.S. dollars, assuming that the temporal method was used to translate the accounts.

B. Compute the depreciation expense and cost of goods sold for 2008 in U.S. dollars, assuming that the temporal method was used to translate the accounts.

C. Repeat requirements A and B, assuming that the current rate method was used to translate the accounts.

D. Contrast the effects on income from using the current rate method and the temporal method to translate cost of goods sold and depreciation expense. Explain why net income is increased or decreased when the accounts were translated using the current rate method.

PROBLEM 13-6A Cost Method Workpaper—Current Rate Method LO7

For this problem, refer to the information provided in Problem 13-3 for P Company and SFr Company. Ignore deferred income taxes in the assignment of the difference between implied and book value.

Required:

A. If you have not already done so, prepare a workpaper to translate the trial balance of the subsidiary into dollars using the current rate method.

B. Prepare the journal entries made on the books of P Company during 2009 to account for its investment in SFr Company. P Company uses the cost method to record its investment in SFr Company. At the date of acquisition, the 760,000 franc difference between implied and book value interest acquired was allocated as follows:

Asset	*Francs*	*Translation Rate*	*Dollars*
Land	385,000	$.15	57,750
Building	375,000	.15	56,250
Total	760,000		114,000

The building is depreciated over a 10-year remaining life using the straight-line method of amortization.

C. Prepare a consolidated statement's workpaper at December 31, 2009.

PROBLEM 13-7A Cost Method Workpaper—Temporal Method LO8

COMPREHENSIVE

P Company holds an 80% interest in SFr Company, a Swiss company. A trial balance for P Company and SFr Company at December 31, 2009, and other data are given in Problems 13-3 and 13-4. Ignore deferred income taxes in the assignment of the difference between implied and book value.

Required:

A. If you have not already done so (Problem 13-4), prepare a workpaper to translate the trial balance of the subsidiary into dollars using the temporal method of translation. The subsidiary's beginning retained earnings balance in the translated balance sheet is $76,660.

B. Prepare the journal entries made on the books of P Company during 2009 to account for the investment in SFr Company. P Company uses the cost method to record its investment in SFr Company. At the date of acquisition, the 760,000 franc difference between implied and book value interest acquired was allocated as follows:

Asset	*Francs*	*Translation Rate*	*Dollars*
Land	385,000	$.15	57,750
Building	375,000	.15	56,250
Total	760,000		114,000

The building is depreciated over a 10-year remaining life using the straight-line method of amortization.

C. Prepare a consolidated statements workpaper at December 31, 2009.

PROBLEM 13-8A Cost Method Workpaper—Local Currency Is the Functional Currency LO7

COMPREHENSIVE

Babbit, Inc., a multinational corporation based in the United States, owns an 80% interest in Nakima Company, which is located in Sydney, Australia. The acquisition occurred on January 1, 2008. The difference between the implied value of 810,625 Australian dollars and the book value of Nakima equity was attributed to specific assets of Nakima Company as follows:

	100% Difference between MV and BV (Australian Dollars)
Equipment that has a 5-year remaining life	73,875
Land	54,063
Inventories—Nakima uses the FIFO cost flow assumption in pricing its inventory	27,187
Amount attributed to patents (10 year remaining life)	150,000
Total difference in Australian dollars	305,125

Ignore deferred income taxes in the assignment of the difference between implied and book value. The adjusted trial balances for the two companies on December 31, 2008 are presented here:

Debits	*Babbit Inc. (U.S. Dollars)*	*Nakima Company (Australian Dollars)*
Cash	65,885	95,250
Accounts Receivable	150,116	106,250
12/31 Inventory	115,000	83,250
Investment in Nakima Company	514,585	—0—
Land	59,400	187,500
Buildings and Equipment	200,000	250,000
Cost of Goods Sold	425,000	121,500
Other Expenses	75,000	51,750
Dividends Declared	50,000	31,250
Totals	1,654,986	926,750
Credits		
Accumulated Depreciation	125,000	93,750
Accounts Payable	14,750	62,500
Notes Payable	25,000	15,000
Capital Stock	600,000	340,500
1/1 Retained Earnings	325,000	165,000
Sales	545,475	250,000
Dividend Income	19,761	—0—
Totals	1,654,986	926,750

Additional Information:

1. Sales, purchases, and other expenses were incurred evenly during the year.
2. Dividends of 15,625 Australian dollars were paid on April 30 and October 31.
3. The accounts are presented in conformity with U.S. generally accepted accounting principles.
4. Direct rates of exchange.

1/1/08	$.7935
4/30/08	.7899
10/31/08	.7910
12/31/08	.7575
Average for 2008	.7962

5. The Australian dollar is identified as the functional currency of Nakima Company.

Required:

A. Prepare a workpaper to translate the trial balance of the subsidiary into U.S. dollars.

B. Prepare a schedule to verify the translation adjustment.

C. Prepare journal entries on the books of the parent company to record the purchase of the 80% interest in the subsidiary and to apply the cost method of accounting.

D. Prepare a consolidated statements workpaper at December 31, 2008. Journal entries made in requirement C that are not reflected in the trial balance of Babbit, Inc. are to be made as adjusting entries in the elimination columns of the workpaper.

PROBLEM 13-9 **Local Currency Is the Functional Currency, Equity Method for Investment** LO7

On January 2, 2008, P Company, a U.S.-based company, acquired for 2,000,000 francs an 80% interest in SFr Company. On January 2, 2008, SFr Company reported a retained earnings balance of 480,000 francs. SFr's books are maintained in francs and are in conformity with U.S. generally accepted accounting principles. Trial balances of the two companies as of December 31, 2009, are presented below.

Debits	*P Company (Dollars)*	*SFr Company (Francs)*
Cash	500,200	962,500
Accounts Receivable	516,400	660,000
Inventories (FIFO cost)	627,800	1,037,500
Investment in SFr Company	297,806	—
Land	450,000	500,000
Buildings (net)	610,000	550,000
Equipment (net)	290,000	405,000
Dividends Declared	200,000	375,000
Cost of Goods Sold	2,720,000	2,312,500
Depreciation Expense	210,000	125,000
Other Expense	914,000	818,750
Income Tax Expense	100,000	102,500
Totals	$7,436,206	7,848,750
Credits		
Accounts Payable	540,000	800,000
Short-Term Notes Payable	300,000	650,750
Bonds Payable	700,000	850,000
Common Stock	800,000	960,000
Additional Paid-in Capital	300,000	300,000
Retained Earnings, 1/1	542,878	513,000
Sales	4,200,000	3,775,000
Equity Income	53,328	—
Totals	$7,436,206	7,848,750

Other information related to the subsidiary follows:

1. Beginning inventory of 830,000 francs was acquired when the exchange rate was $.165.
2. Purchases made uniformly throughout 2009 were 2,520,000 francs.
3. The franc is identified as the subsidiary's functional currency.
4. The subsidiary's beginning (1/1/09) retained earnings and cumulative translation adjustment (credit) in dollars were $75,948 and $36,462, respectively.
5. All plant assets were acquired before the parent obtained a controlling interest in the subsidiary.
6. Sales are made and all expenses are incurred uniformly throughout the year.
7. The ending inventory was acquired during the last quarter.
8. The subsidiary declared and paid dividends of 375,000 francs on September 2.
9. The following direct exchange rate quotations were available:

Date of subsidiary acquisition	$.15
Average for 2008	.156
January 1, 2009	.17
September 2, 2009	.18
December 31, 2009	.19
Average for the fourth quarter, 2009	.185
Average for 2008	.176

Required:

A. Prepare a translated balance sheet and combined statement of income and retained earnings for the subsidiary.

B. Prepare a schedule to verify the translation adjustment.

C. Compute the following ratios based on the franc and the U.S. dollar financial statements:

(1) Current ratio.
(2) Debt to equity.
(3) Gross profit percentage.
(4) Net income to sales.

PROBLEM 13-10 **U.S. Dollar Is the Functional Currency, Equity Method for Investment** LO8

Use the information provided in Problem 13-9 for P Company and SFr Company.

Required:

A. Convert the accounts of the foreign subsidiary, assuming that the U.S. dollar is the functional currency of both companies. For this problem assume that the subsidiary's beginning (1/1/09) retained earnings balance in the translated balance sheet is $76,660.

B. Prepare a schedule to verify the translation gain or loss, assuming a 637,000 franc net exposed liability position at the beginning of the year.

PROBLEM 13-11A **Complete Equity Workpaper—Current Rate Method** LO7

COMPREHENSIVE

For this problem, refer to the information provided in Problem 13-9 for P Company and SFr Company. Ignore deferred income taxes in the allocation of the difference between implied and book value.

Required:

A. If you have not already done so, prepare a workpaper to translate the trial balance of the subsidiary into dollars using the current rate method.

B. Prepare the journal entries made on the books of P Company during 2009 to account for its investment in SFr Company. P Company uses the complete equity method to record its investment in SFr Company. At the date of acquisition, the 760,000 franc difference between implied and book value interest acquired was allocated as follows:

Asset	*Francs*	*Translation Rate*	*Dollars*
Land	385,000	$.15	57,750
Building	375,000	.15	56,250
Total	760,000		114,000

The building is depreciated over a 10-year remaining life using the straight-line method of amortization.

C. Prepare a consolidated statements workpaper at December 31, 2009.

PROBLEM 13-12A **Complete Equity Workpaper—Temporal Method** LO8

COMPREHENSIVE

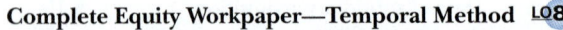

P Company holds an 80% interest in SFr Company, a Swiss company. A trial balance for P Company and SFr Company at December 31, 2009, and other data are given in Problems 13-9 and 13-10. The following numbers should change, however, from the amounts stated in Problem 13-9: In the P Company trial balance as of December 31, 2009, Investment in SFr Company is 307,256; Retained Earnings, 1/1 is 543,628; and Equity Income is 62,028. Ignore deferred income taxes in the allocation of the difference between implied and book value.

Required:

A. If you have not already done so (Problem 13-10), prepare a workpaper to translate the trial balance of the subsidiary into dollars using the temporal method of translation. The subsidiary's beginning retained earnings balance in the translated balance sheet is $76,660.

B. Prepare the journal entries made on the books of P Company during 2009 to account for the investment in SFr Company. P Company uses the complete equity method to record its investment in SFr Company. At the date of acquisition, the 760,000 franc difference between implied and book value interest acquired was allocated as follows:

Asset	*Francs*	*Translation Rate*	*Dollars*
Land	385,000	$.15	57,750
Building	375,000	.15	56,250
Total	760,000		114,000

The building is depreciated over a 10-year remaining life using the straight-line method of amortization.

C. Prepare a consolidated statements workpaper at December 31, 2009.

14 REPORTING FOR SEGMENTS AND FOR INTERIM FINANCIAL PERIODS

LEARNING OBJECTIVES

1. Understand the need for disaggregated financial data.
2. Describe the basic requirements of public companies in reporting segmental data.
3. Determine an operating segment.
4. Define a reportable segment.
5. Describe how common costs are handled in segmental reporting.
6. Identify the information to be presented for each reportable segment.
7. Explain when and what types of geographic data must be reported.
8. Explain when information about major customers must be reported.
9. Compare the international accounting standards for segmental reporting with the U.S. requirements.
10. Describe current requirements for companies to report interim information.
11. Indicate some problems with interim reporting and the authoritative position on the issue.

Given the current economic uncertainties, investors want answers to some old-fashioned, fundamental questions: What is the business today, and how did it perform this year? Where is the cash, and where are the profits? What drives the value of the company, what risks affect its businesses, and how flexibly can the company respond to change?

We think registrants can best answer these questions if they start with good disclosure responsive to *FASB Statement No. 131* about operating segments and major lines of products and services, and then build upon that framework to discuss the important risks affecting those businesses. Because Regulation S-K Items 101 (Description of Business) and 303 (MD&A) build upon segment disclosures, a registrant's comprehensive identification of operating segments and product and service lines is a critical part of every SEC filing.

The staff also has focused on the *Statement 131* [ASC 280] disclosures because, frankly, we are concerned that too many companies have not responded adequately to *Statement 131*'s mandate to present separately financial information for those business components that are regularly reviewed by the chief operating decision maker. It's difficult to believe that chief operating decision makers review as little disaggregated information as some company's segment disclosure would have us believe.[1]

In previous chapters we have dealt with the process of aggregating the financial data relating to the activities of an affiliated group of companies. Investors and lenders holding equity or creditor interests are aware of the importance of consolidated statements in reporting the financial position and results of operations of a group of companies under common control. At the same time, investors, creditors, and other users of financial statements also need disaggregated data that provide information about the various segments of an enterprise or affiliated group of companies.

NEED FOR DISAGGREGATED FINANCIAL DATA

LO1 The need for disaggregated financial data.

Research studies conducted by various organizations such as the Financial Executives Research Foundation, the Financial Analysts Federation, and the National Association of Accountants concluded that financial statement users want disaggregated information to aid them in evaluating prospective investments. If return on investment is computed on the basis of expected cash flows, the evaluation of risk requires an assessment of the uncertainty surrounding both the timing and the amount of these expected cash flows. Major uncertainty results from (1) factors unique to individual companies, (2) factors related to the industries and geographical areas in which those companies operate, and (3) related national and international economic and political factors.

Users need financial statement information to determine conditions, trends, and ratios that assist in predicting cash flows of firms. These factors are often compared with those of other firms, as well as with industry-wide data, and general national and international economic information is considered in making an overall evaluation of the risk involved. When a firm engages in activities in several industries or geographic areas, analysis and the process used to predict future cash flows become more complex. Different industries or geographic areas may have different rates of profitability, opportunities for growth, and types of risk. Thus, most users agree that, although consolidated financial information is important, it is more useful if supplemented with disaggregated information to assist in analyzing the uncertainties surrounding the timing and amounts of expected cash flows.

STANDARDS OF FINANCIAL ACCOUNTING AND REPORTING

Recognizing the importance of "segment" data and the necessity of establishing standards for disclosure, the Financial Accounting Standards Board issued *Statement of Financial Accounting Standards (SFAS) No. 14*, "Financial Reporting for Segments of a Business Enterprise." *SFAS No. 14* was subsequently amended by *SFAS No. 21*, and

[1] Excerpts from a speech by Robert A. Bayless, Chief Accountant, Division of Corporation Finance, U.S. Securities & Exchange Commission, "Debits and Credits in the New Economy," Meeting of the Silicon Valley Chapter of Financial Executives International, San Jose, California, September 18, 2001.

RELATED CONCEPTS

The FASB felt that the industry approach previously required in SFAS No. 14 did not provide the needed information required by users. Defining segments based on the enterprise's internal organization better defines the risks and opportunities that management deems important, and thus better meets the criterion of *usefulness*.

later superseded by *SFAS No. 131*, "Disclosures about Segments of an Enterprise and Related Information [ASC 280]." Segmental disclosures have limitations as well as strengths. The primary benefit is the unveiling of information that has been merged and possibly buried in the consolidated data. For example, specific information about a declining or growing product line or unstable geographic area may be useful in projecting future cash flows or in assessing risk. The arguments *against* segmental disclosures include the following:

- Segmental information may be misleading or meaningless due to inherent accounting classification and allocation problems, to lack of user knowledge, or to variation in the measurement techniques applied by different companies.
- Disclosures to competing firms, labor unions, and so on could have adverse effects and could discourage management from taking on desirable but risky projects in order to avoid the disclosures.
- Users are already bombarded with an excessive amount of accounting detail, and segmental disclosures merely add to the burden.

Nonetheless, most people believe the advantages outweigh the disadvantages. In addition, the increased pace of merger activity and the increase in foreign operations have led to greater importance being attached to segmental disclosures. Thus, the FASB issued *SFAS No. 131*, requiring all public companies to report information about the revenues earned in different countries and hold assets, about major customers, and about revenues for each product and service, even when *some* of the information is not used by the firm in its operating decisions.

"Get ready. Your disclosure will be cracking up. Cracking up and breaking open into new segment reporting, that is. As of year-end 1998 and for quarterly periods beginning thereafter, public companies have to start new segment reporting. Companies also have to restate their financials going back three years."[2]

LO2 Basic disclosure requirements.

In general, SFAS No. 131 [ASC 280–10–05–03] implemented a management approach, focusing on the way in which management organizes segments internally to make operating decisions and to assess performance. The objective of this approach is to facilitate consistency between internal and external reporting. Information may be segmented by product or service, by geographic area, by customer type, or by legal entity. For each operating segment, firms must report segmental profit or loss, certain items of revenue and expense, segmental assets, and other items.

Although there was concern that segment reporting would "give away the farm," many analysts and other users believed the previous rules, under *SFAS No. 14*, did not work well because the information reported didn't reflect management's internal accounting. Companies presented segmental information that didn't "relate to reality," leading to bad communications. The new rule should be a win-win for management and analysts, says one expert, making it easier for investor relations officials to talk to analysts and to communicate internally. "They might even learn a few new things about their companies."[3]

[2] *Investor Relations Business*, "Cracking Up: Segment Reporting Disclosure Is Coming," by Matthew Greco, 6/22/98, p. 1.
[3] Ibid.

LO3 Operating segment.

SFAS No. 131 [ASC 280] does not limit segmental reporting to financial data only. It also requires a discussion of the firm's rationale or method for categorizing its operations into segments, as well as any difference in measurement techniques between periods being reported or between the segment and the entire entity. The standard became effective for years beginning after December 15, 1997. If statements are presented for more than one period, the required information must be presented for each period. The information required should be a disaggregation of ***consolidated financial information*** where the firm has consolidated subsidiaries, and a disaggregation of the individual firm data if it has no consolidated subsidiaries.

We next define some terms that have been given specific connotations for purposes of segmental reporting. The terms and their definitions are as follows:

LO4 Reportable segments.

RELATED CONCEPTS

Providing segment data based on the enterprise's internal organization may make the segment data less *comparable* between similar firms if each firm is organized differently. *Relevance*, however, remains the overriding rather than comparability in this setting.

a. ***Operating segment.*** A component of an enterprise that may earn revenues and incur expenses, about which separate financial information is evaluated regularly by the chief operating decision maker in deciding how to allocate resources and in assessing performance.

b. ***Reportable segment.*** A segment considered to be significant to an enterprise's operations; specifically, one that has passed one of three 10% tests or has been identified as being reportable through other criteria (aggregation, for example).

c. ***Chief operating decision maker.*** A person whose general function (not specific title) is to allocate resources to, and assess the performance of, the segments of an enterprise.

d. ***Segment revenue.*** The revenue from sales to unaffiliated customers and from intersegment sales or transfers.

e. ***Segment operating profit or loss.*** All of a segment's revenue minus all operating expenses, including any allocated revenues or expenses (e.g., common costs).

f. ***Common costs.*** Operating expenses incurred by the enterprise for the benefit of more than one segment.

g. ***Segment assets.*** Those tangible and intangible assets directly associated with, or used by, a segment, including any allocated portion of assets used jointly by more than one segment. If portions of assets are allocated internally and used by the chief operating decision maker, then those amounts should be allocated on a reasonable basis and disclosed for external reporting purposes as well.

h. ***Corporate assets.*** Assets maintained for general corporate purposes and not used in the operations of any segment.

i. ***General corporate expense.*** An expense incurred for the benefit of the corporation as a whole, which cannot be reasonably allocated to any segment.

j. ***Transfer pricing.*** The pricing of products or services between operating segments or geographic areas.

Two of the most difficult tasks in applying the segment disclosure requirements are those of determining (1) an appropriate basis for the allocation of common costs and (2) appropriate operating segments.

Common Cost Allocation

LO5 Handling common costs.

The emphasis here is on ***operating*** expenses, as general corporate expenses are not allocated. Common costs should be allocated to a segment for external reporting purposes only if they are included in the segment's profit or loss calculations that are used internally by the chief operating decision maker (as defined above).

Although judgment must be used, prior research contains recommendations concerning common cost allocation methods. Probably the most extensive study on appropriate allocation methods was conducted by the Cost Accounting Standards Board, and its recommendations were issued in *Cost Accounting Standard No. 403*. Although *Standard No. 403* concerns the problem of allocating common home office expenses to segments of an organization involved in defense contracts, the general guidelines developed should be useful in applying the allocation provisions across other industries. In essence, *Cost Accounting Standard No. 403* suggests that, where possible, joint costs should be accumulated into logical and relatively homogeneous expense pools. The pools are then allocated to segments on the basis of beneficial or causal relationships as measured by activity or output of the segments.

For example, common data-processing expenses might be allocated on the basis of machine time or number or reports, joint personnel administration expenses on the basis of number of personnel or total labor hours, and joint centralized warehouse expenses on the basis of square footage, value of materials, or volume of transactions. Any remaining expenses that cannot be logically included in any of the homogeneous expense pools are allocated proportionately under a three-factor formula based on payroll costs, revenue, and assets of the segments. That is, the percentage of the residual expenses to be allocated to any segment is the arithmetical average of the following three percentages:

1. The segment's payroll dollars to the total payroll dollars of all segments.
2. The segment's operating revenue to the total operating revenue of all segments.
3. The average net book value of the sum of the segment's tangible capital assets plus inventories to the total average net book value of such assets of all segments.

Determining Operating Segments

SFAS No. 131 [ASC 280–10–50–1] provides that *operating segments* of the firm are to be determined using a modified management approach. An operating segment is a component that exhibits all of the following characteristics:

- It engages in business activities that may earn revenues and incur expenses (including transactions with other components of the entity).
- The entity's chief operating decision maker (may be one individual or a group of executives) regularly reviews the component's operating results to assess its performance and make decisions about resources to be allocated to it.
- Discrete financial information is available.

"Many companies boast in their annual reports about the myriad businesses they participate in—then, in their financials [under the old rules] reported as though they operated in a single industry. Patricia McConnell, accounting analyst for Bear, Stearns & Co., says, 'I don't think there's any more important information about a company than its businesses broken down into segments. Dividing the information along the same lines that management looks at is a fairly reasonable request—and should prevent companies from claiming they're in only one line of business.' "[4]

[4] *Institutional Investor*, "Dilutions of Grandeur," by Mary Lowengard, January 1988, p. 34.

Disclosures are required for each operating segment, subject to the quantitative thresholds and aggregation criteria presented next. Because the aggregation can occur before performing the quantitative tests, we present those criteria first.

Aggregation Criteria An entity is permitted (but not required) to aggregate operating segments that have similar economic characteristics if the segments are also similar in ***all*** the following areas:

- The nature of their products or services.
- The nature of the production processes.
- The types or class of customers.
- The methods used to distribute products or provide services.
- The nature of the regulatory environment (banking, for example).[5]

Quantitative Thresholds Each operating segment that is significant to the enterprise as a whole must be identified as a *reportable* segment. A segment is considered to be significant if it meets ***one or more*** of the following tests, the tests being applied separately for each fiscal year for which financial statements are prepared:

- Its combined external and internal revenue is ***10% or more*** of the combined external and internal revenue of all reportable segments.
- The absolute amount of its reported profit or loss is ***10% or more*** of the *greater* absolute amount of:
  - The combined reported profit of all operating segments not reporting a loss
  - The combined reported loss of all operating segments that reported a loss
- Its assets are ***10% or more*** of the combined assets of all operating segments.

RELATED CONCEPTS

The FASB rejected the requirement that a secondary definition of segments be disclosed if the internal organization is not segmented by products and services or geography. This requirement was rejected because of the cost of providing this alternative information (*cost-benefit considerations*).

Entities are permitted to present operating segments separately that fall below the quantitative thresholds, or such operating segments may be combined with other segments not meeting the quantitative thresholds if the segments share a *majority* of the aggregation criteria.

An example of the application of these tests for Papco, Inc. is presented in Illustration 14-1. In this example the information of Papco is segmented by its products. The results of the tests should be evaluated from the standpoint of ***comparability***. Thus, a segment that has been significant in the past and is expected to be significant in the future should be treated as a reportable segment even though it fails to meet a test in the current year. Further, if the structure of the organization changes so that the reportable segments are redefined, the information presented from prior periods should be ***restated*** so that it is comparable with the current structure (if practical). In such cases, the firm should explicitly disclose the fact that the earlier periods have been restated and why. Also, if a particular segment that was previously not considered significant becomes significant in the current period, then segmental data should be presented for that segment for the prior periods as well as the current one.

---

[5] See par. 17 of *SFAS No. 131* [ASC 280–10–50–11] for more details on the regulatory environment.

ILLUSTRATION 14-1

Significance Tests
Year Ended December 31, 2007
(Thousands of Dollars)
Papco, Inc.

	Segments					
Revenue Test	*Lumber*	*Paper*	*Printing*	*Furniture*	*Leather*	*Combined*
Sales to Unaffiliated Customers	$16,000	$ 3,000	$2,000	$1,500	$1,000	$23,500
Intersegment Sales	5,000	2,000	500	500	—0—	8,000
Total Revenue	$21,000	$ 5,000	$2,500	$2,000	$1,000	$31,500
Percentage of Total Revenue	67%	16%	8%	6%	3%	100%

The lumber and paper segments are reportable segments under the revenue test because their total revenues are at least 10% of combined total revenue of $31,500, whereas the other segments are not reportable segments under this test.

Operating Profit Test

Operating Profit (Loss)	$ 2,500	$ 600	$(300)	$ 150	$ (100)	$ 2,850
Percentage of $3,250*	77%	18%	9%	5%	3%	

The lumber and paper segments are reportable segments under the operating profit test because the absolute amounts of their operating profit or loss are each ***at least 10% of the greater of*** (1) the combined profit of all segments that did not incur a loss* ($2,500 + $600 + $150 = $3,250), or (2) the combined loss of all segments that incurred a loss ($300 + $100 = $400). The other segments are not reportable segments under this test.

Assets Test

Segment Assets	$25,000	$12,000	$8,000	$3,000	$4,000	$52,000
Percentage of Total Assets	48%	23%	15%	6%	8%	100%

The lumber, paper, and printing segments are reportable segments because their assets are at least 10% of combined identifiable assets of $52,000. The furniture and leather segments are not reportable segments under this test.

Reportable Segments (still subject to the 75% Combined Revenue Test)
1) Lumber (met all three tests above)
2) Paper (met all three tests above)
3) Printing (met the asset test above)

75% Combined Revenue Test

Sales to Unaffiliated Customers	$16,000	$ 3,000	$2,000	$1,500	$1,000	$23,500
Percentage of Total Sales	**68.1%**	**12.8%**	**8.5%**	6.4%	4.3%	100.0%
Combined Percentage		89.4%				

The three reportable segments have combined revenue in excess of 75% of total unaffiliated revenue; therefore, no additional segments need be identified. The furniture and leather segments would be combined when reported.

Seventy-Five Percent Combined Revenue Test

In addition to the tests described above, the reportable segments taken together must represent a substantial portion of the firm's total operations. To determine whether a substantial portion of a firm's operations are explained by its segment information, ***the combined revenue from sales to unaffiliated customers of all reportable segments must constitute at least 75% of the combined revenue from sales to unaffiliated customers of all operating segments.*** If the 75% test is not satisfied, additional segments must be identified until the test is met. The test is applied separately for each fiscal period for which financial statements are prepared.

Application of this 75% test to the situation presented in Illustration 14-1 produces the following:

$$\frac{\text{Combined sales to } \textit{unaffiliated} \text{ customers by the lumber, paper, and printing segments}}{\text{Combined sales to unaffiliated customers by all segments}} =$$

$$\frac{1\$16{,}000 + \$3{,}000 + \$2{,}0002}{\$23{,}500} = 89\%$$

Thus, the 75% test is met, and the lumber, paper, and printing segments will be reported individually and the furniture and leather segments combined into one unit. If the 75% test had not been met, one or more of the segments that did not qualify as reportable segments under the previous tests would have to be included as reportable segments.

Information to Be Presented The following types of information must be presented for each of a firm's reportable segments, and in the aggregate for the segments that are not separately reported.

LO6 Reportable segment information to be presented.

- ***General information.*** *SFAS No. 131* [ASC 280–10–50–21] requires an explanation of how management identified its reportable segments, as well as whether any segments have been aggregated. A description is also required of the types of products or services from which each segment obtains its revenues.
- ***Information about segment operating profit or loss.*** Rather than specifying a strict definition of profit or loss for segmental purposes, the standard designates that a management approach focusing on internal decision making be used to determine the measurement of segmental profit or loss. Thus, the following items are disclosed only *if* they are included in the measures reviewed by the chief operating decision maker: revenues from external customers, revenues from other segments, interest revenue and expense, depreciation, depletion and amortization expense, income tax expense, equity income from investments, extraordinary items, other unusual items, and other significant noncash items. The absence of specific rules in calculating segment profit or loss leaves room for possible departures from GAAP as applied at the consolidated level. For example, pension expense may not be allocated to segments if not reviewed by the decision maker for that segment. The possibility of departures from GAAP for segmental disclosures is addressed further in a later section of this chapter, in comparison to recommended international standards.
- ***Information about segment assets.*** Firms are required to disclose those assets that are evaluated by the chief operating decision maker for the segment, including the following information *if* such information is reviewed by the officer: expenditures for most long-lived assets and the carrying basis of "influential" investments, or those measured using the equity method.
- ***Information about the bases for measurement.*** Differences in measurement between segments and the consolidated entity must be disclosed for: income before tax, discontinued operations, extraordinary items, and for segment profit or loss. Similarly, differences in measurement between segment assets and the consolidated assets must be disclosed, if any. For example, information on how jointly used assets are allocated to segments may be needed to understand the segment information. The basis should be disclosed for any transactions between

RELATED CONCEPTS

***Verifiability* is a component of reliability. Segment data do not have the same degree of verifiability as other financial data. The tradeoff for lessened verifiability is the relevance of the segment data for users' decisions.**

segments, and any asymmetrical allocations to segments should be explained. Finally, any changes from the measurement methods used in prior periods must be disclosed, and their effects on segment profit or loss.

- ***Reconciliation of segment amounts and consolidated amounts for revenue, profit or loss, assets, and other significant items.*** Differences occur for a variety of reasons, including the following: Some segments not meeting the quantitative thresholds are presented as "all other." Some items are not allocated to segments if there is no reasonable basis for doing so, or because the information is not used by the chief operating decision maker. Transactions between segments may give rise to "intersegment" revenue, profit, or loss amounts that are eliminated from the consolidated totals. Because the focus in segmental reporting is a management approach, it may result in different accounting methods from those used for external reporting for the consolidated entity. A reconciliation of such items must be presented in sufficient detail to explain the differences. It should include:
  - Revenue to revenue reported in the consolidated income statement.
  - Operating profit or loss to pretax income from continuing operations in the consolidated income statement.
  - Segment assets to consolidated total assets.

  Illustration 14-5, presented later in this chapter, illustrates a reconciliation of the above items.
- ***Interim disclosures.*** Unlike the previous standard on segmental reporting, *SFAS No. 131* [ASC 280–10–50–32] requires that segmental disclosures be included in interim reports. The extent of the disclosures depends on whether the firm presents a complete set of financial statements for the interim period, or condensed financial statements. If the firm presents a complete set of statements, the interim disclosures are the same as presented above for reportable segments. If condensed statements are presented for interim periods, they should include the following for each reportable segment: revenues, including intersegment sales; profit or loss; disclosures of any changes in measurement bases for segmentation or components of profit or loss since the most recent annual report; any material changes in assets since the most recent annual report; and a reconciliation of income from continuing operations for the consolidated entity and for the total of the reportable segments.
- ***Enterprisewide Disclosures.*** Because of the choice allowed in designating reportable segments, a given firm may report its segmental information based on products or services, geographic areas, and so on. Thus other information about the bases not chosen is not provided as part of the above disclosures. *SFAS No. 131* [ASC 280–10–55] requires that such information be presented if practicable. If not practicable, the reason for not including the disclosures should be stated. These additional disclosures are made on an enterprisewide basis rather than a segmental basis, and are required even if a firm has only a single reportable segment. They include:

  —***Product or service disclosures***: revenues from external customers for each ***product or service*** or group of products or services, on the same basis as the general-purpose financial statements. This disclosure is not required if the reportable segments are structured around products or services.

—***Geographic area disclosures***: revenues from external customers and long-lived assets for the firm's country of domicile and for all the other countries in total, also on the same basis as the general-purpose financial statements; *and* revenues from external customers and long-lived assets for *each foreign country or group of foreign countries*, if material, along with the basis for allocating revenues (location of customer, where shipped, etc.). These disclosures are generally not required if the company's reportable segments have been organized around ***geographic area***. [ASC 280–10–50–41]

—***Major customer disclosures***: information about ***major customers*** for each customer representing ***10% or more*** of total enterprise revenues, including the amount of revenues and the segment(s) to which the revenue is traceable. A group of customers under common control is treated as a single customer, as are the various agencies of a government. [ASC 280–10–50–42]

Methods of Presentation Information about the reportable segments of a firm may be included in its financial statements in any of the following ways:

- Within the body of the financial statements, with appropriate explanatory disclosures in the footnotes to the financial statements.
- Entirely in the footnotes to the financial statements.
- In a separate schedule that is included as an integral part of the financial statements.

Financial information such as revenue, operating profit or loss, and identifiable assets must be presented in dollar amounts; related percentages may be shown if desired.

As an illustration of segment reporting, assume the segment data presented in Illustration 14-1. In addition, assume that the consolidated income statements and balance sheets for 2006 and 2007 for Papco, Inc. are as shown in Illustration 14-2. Disclosure of segmental information organized by products/services might take the form of the supporting schedules and footnotes as shown in Illustration 14-3. This illustration also serves to reconcile the segmental data to the totals for the consolidated entity.

ILLUSTRATION 14-2

Papco Inc.
Consolidated Income Statement
(Thousands of Dollars)

	Year Ended December 31	
	2007	*2006*
Sales	$23,500	$22,100
Cost of Goods Sold	16,400	15,300
Selling, General, and Administrative Expense	4,530	4,380
Interest Expense	600	570
Total Cost and Expense	21,530	20,250
Operating Income	1,970	1,850
Equity in Income of B Company	150	120
Income before Income Taxes	2,120	1,970
Income Taxes	1,020	980
Net Income	$ 1,100	$ 990

Papco Inc.
Consolidated Balance Sheet
(Thousands of Dollars)

	December 31	
	2007	*2006*
Cash	$ 1,870	$ 1,785
Receivables	2,640	2,860
Inventories	6,400	6,345
Investment in B Company	700	600
Plant and Equipment (net of accumulated depreciation of $17,500 in 2007 and $16,200 in 2006)	41,500	40,400
Other Assets	690	970
Total Assets	$53,800	$52,960
Current Liabilities	$ 2,400	$ 2,320
Bonds Payable	12,000	12,000
Common Stock, $50 par value	30,000	30,000
Additional Paid-in Capital	3,000	3,000
Retained Earnings	6,400	5,640
Total Liabilities and Stockholders' Equity	$53,800	$52,960

ILLUSTRATION 14-3

Papco Inc.
Segmental Disclosures by Product/Service
(Thousands of Dollars)

Year Ended December 31, 2007	*Lumber*	*Paper*	*Printing*	*Other*	*Total*
Revenues from external customers	$16,000	$ 3,000	$2,000	$2,500	$23,500
Intersegment revenues	5,000	2,000	500	500	8,000
Depreciation and amortization	640	290	190	100	1,220
Interest expense	200	100	80	100	480
Segment operating profit	2,500	600	(300)	50	2,850
Segment assets	25,000	12,000	8,000	7,000	52,000
Capital expenditures	1,540	420	30	210	2,200
Year Ended December 31, 2006	*Lumber*	*Paper*	*Printing*	*Other*	*Total*
Revenues from external customers	$15,200	$ 2,800	$2,100	$2,000	$22,100
Intersegment revenues	4,800	1,700	300	460	7,260
Depreciation and amortization	600	290	175	125	1,190
Interest expense	190	90	75	90	445
Segment operating profit	2,460	580	(430)	70	2,680
Segment assets	24,460	11,500	7,900	7,520	51,380
Capital expenditures	1,280	360	20	240	1,900

Note A—Product and Service Segments.

The Company operates in three main areas of product/service: lumber products, paper products, and printing. More detailed information about specific products and services is included in the "Business Operations" section of this report.

Intersegment sales are made at the same prices as sales to nonaffiliates.

Geographic Areas

LO7 Reporting on geographical areas

As mentioned in the preceding section, *SFAS No. 131* [ASC 280–10–50–22, 41] requires enterprises to report revenues from external customers and long-lived assets attributable to their domestic operations and foreign operations. Foreign operations are defined as those located outside the United States (or other "home country") that produce revenue from sales to unaffiliated customers or from intra-enterprise sales or transfers between countries or geographic areas. Foreign operations do ***not***,

ILLUSTRATION 14-4

Papco Inc.
Enterprisewide Disclosures
(Thousands of Dollars)

Geographic Information

	Year Ended December 31	
Revenue	*2007*	*2006*
United States	$18,000	$17,500
Foreign Countries		
Canada	4,000	3,500
Mexico	1,500	1,100
Total Revenue from Foreign Countries	5,500	4,600
Total Consolidated Revenue	$23,500	$22,100
Long-Lived Assets		
United States	$28,827	$28,180
Foreign Countries		
Canada	9,375	9,193
Mexico	4,688	4,597
Total Assets in Foreign Countries	14,063	13,790
Total Consolidated Assets	$42,890	$41,970

Major Customers
We do not provide information on major customers because no single external customer represented 10% or more of total revenues.

however, include unconsolidated subsidiaries and investees. If operations are conducted in two or more foreign countries or geographic areas, information must be presented separately for each significant foreign country or geographic area and in the aggregate for all other foreign operations. Where the operations in some foreign countries are grouped into geographic areas, the groupings should be made on the basis of a consideration of (1) proximity, (2) economic affinity, (3) similarities of business environments, and (4) the nature, scale, and degree of interrelationship of the operations in the various countries.

To illustrate, foreign operations information for Papco, Inc. might be presented as shown in Illustration 14-4, assuming that the company conducts operations in the United States, Canada, and Mexico.

Information about Major Customers

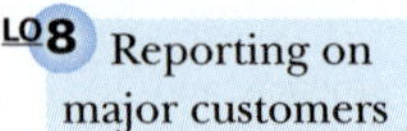
LO8 Reporting on major customers

To provide information about the potential effects of dependency on one or more major customers, if ***10% or more*** of the revenue of a firm is derived from sales to any *single customer,* that fact and the amount of revenue from each such customer must be disclosed, as stated previously. Also, if ***10% or more*** of the revenue is derived from sales to the *federal government, a state government, a local government, or a foreign government,* that fact and the amount of revenue must be disclosed. Disclosure should include the amount of sales to each customer and the reportable segment making the sales. Customers' names, however, need not be disclosed. These disclosures are required even if the firm has only one reportable segment.

Reconciliation

A reconciliation of major segmental data presented in earlier illustrations and the consolidated data in the income statement for Papco, Inc. is presented in Illustration 14-5.

ILLUSTRATION 14-5

Papco Inc.
Reconciliation of Major Segment Information
(Thousands of Dollars)

	Year Ended December 31	
Revenue	*2007*	*2006*
Total revenue for reportable segments	$28,500	$26,900
Revenue for other segments aggregated	3,000	2,460
Elimination of intersegment revenue	(8,000)	(7,260)
Total consolidated revenue	$23,500	$22,100
Profit and Loss		
Total profit and loss for reportable segments	$ 2,800	$ 2,610
Other profit and loss	50	70
Elimination of intersegment profits	(680)	(630)
Unallocated amounts relating to corporate headquarters:		
Interest expense	(120)	(125)
Depreciation	(80)	(75)
Equity in income of B Company	150	120
Income before taxes	$ 2,120	$ 1,970
Assets	*2007*	*2006*
Total assets for reportable segments	$45,000	$43,860
Other assets	7,000	7,520
Corporate investment in B Company	700	600
General corporate assets	1,100	980
Total consolidated assets	$53,800	$52,960
Other Significant Items		
Segment depreciation and amortization	$ 1,120	$ 1,065
Other depreciation and amortization	100	125
Adjustment for depreciation on corporate assets	80	75
Consolidated totals	$ 1,300	$ 1,265
Segment interest expense	$ 380	$ 355
Other interest expense	100	90
Adjustment for interest on corporate borrowing	120	125
Consolidated totals	$ 600	$ 570
Segment capital expenditures	$ 1,990	$ 1,660
Other capital expenditures	210	240
Adjustment for acquisition of corporate assets	200	150
Consolidated totals	$ 2,400	$ 2,050

INTERNATIONAL ACCOUNTING STANDARDS BOARD (IASB) POSITION ON SEGMENT REPORTING

Segmenting consolidated financial information (along product and service lines and along geographic lines) has proved highly relevant for assessing the profitability, risks, and prospects of a diversified or multinational enterprise. Investors, financial analysts, and credit grantors say segment information is indispensable.[6]

[6] *Accountancy*, "Segment Reporting Strengthened," by Paul Pacter, April 1997, p. 66.

LO 9 IAS versus U.S. GAAP.

The International Accounting Standards Board (and previously the IASC) has required segment information since around 1982. ***IAS No. 14*** (Revised), "Reporting Financial Information by Segmentation" was issued in 1998.

However, in January 2009, **IFRS 8** became effective. In this standard the basic management approach described in *SFAS No. 131* was adopted both in defining segments and in the information to be disclosed.

IFRS 8 applies to the separate or individual financial statements of an entity (and to the consolidated financial statements of a group with a parent) whose debt or equity instruments are traded in a public market, or that files its consolidated financial statements with a securities commission or other regulatory organization for the purpose of issuing any class of instruments in a public market.

Differences between IFRS 8 and *SFAS No. 131*

Under IFRS 8, the segments must include intangible assets when disclosing non-current assets attributable to the segment, while under *SFAS No. 131*, intangible assets are not disclosed. In addition, under IFRS 8, segmental liabilities must be disclosed if such a measure is provided to the chief operating decision maker. Under *SFAS No. 131* [ASC 280–10–50–22], liabilities are not disclosed. *SFAS 131* [ASC 280–10–50] requires an entity with a 'matrix' form of organization to determine operating segments based on products and services. IFRS 8 requires such an entity to determine its operating segments in accordance with the core principle.

For its primary operating segments, Wal-Mart reports two line-of-business segments, Wal-Mart Stores and Sam's, and one geographical segment, international, based on the three company divisions reporting to the chief decision-maker.[7]

TEST YOUR KNOWLEDGE

NOTE: Solutions to ***Test Your Knowledge*** questions are found at the end of each chapter before the end-of-chapter questions.

Short Answer

Nash Consolidated is involved in four operating segments, A,B,C, and D (there are no intersegment sales). The following information is available.

Segment	*Operating Profit (Loss)*	*Nonaffiliate Sales*	*Identifiable Assets*
A	(500)	1,600	4,000
B	100	400	600
C	900	2,000	5,000
D	90	1,000	1,000

[7] *Accountancy*, "A New Era of Segment Reporting," by S. Gray, D. Street, and N. Nichols, April 1999, pp. 76–78.

1. Using the revenue test, determine which of the operating segments are reportable segments.
2. Using the operating profit test, determine which of the operating segments are reportable segments.
3. Using the asset test, determine which of the operating segments are reportable segments.
4. Using your answer to parts 1 through 3 and using the 75% combined revenue test, determine the number of reportable segments.

In order to be admitted to, or retain membership in, the AICPA, practitioners who are engaged in the practice of public accounting are required to be enrolled in an AICPA approved practice-monitoring program under certain conditions.

In a document listing reporting deficiencies uncovered during the peer reviews, the following item was noted: Failure to disclose, in the accountant's or auditor's report, a material departure from professional standards [an example includes the omission of a significant income tax provision on interim financial statements].[8]

INTERIM FINANCIAL REPORTING

LO 10 Current interim reporting requirements.

In a dynamic business environment, financial information must be available on a timely basis if sound investment decisions are to be made. Although businesses have historically considered the fiscal year to be the primary reporting period, interim financial statements have been presented frequently to provide information concerning financial status and progress for time periods of less than one year. The normal time period for interim reporting is a quarter of a year (such reports are generally called quarterly reports), but other periods such as a month might be used. These interim statements are generally prepared for the most recent interim period, as well as on a cumulative or year-to-date basis; they may consist of statements of financial position, income, and cash flows. The primary focus, however, has been on the presentation of interim income information, and some companies present only interim income statements.

Publicly owned companies are generally required to file some type of quarterly report as part of the agreement with the stock exchanges that list their stock. In addition, the SEC requires public companies to file Form 10-Q with the Commission within 40 days after the end of each of the first three quarters of the fiscal year if the firm is considered an accelerated filer (45 days otherwise). The financial information disclosure portion of Form 10-Q requires that condensed financial statements include (1) comparative income statements for the quarter and year-to-date for the current and preceding year, (2) comparative statements of financial position at the end of the most recent quarter for the current and preceding year, and (3) comparative statements of cash flows for the current and preceding year. Most public companies also issue these reports required by the SEC to their stockholders and to other interested parties.

[8] www.AICPA.org, 7/7/06.

Problems in Interim Reporting

LO 11 Problems in interim reporting.

Although the SEC established disclosure requirements for the financial information included in Form 10-Q, the development of accounting practices to be followed in preparing interim financial reports for external reporting purposes was left to the accounting profession. No official guide or pronouncement on the practices to be used was issued until the Accounting Principles Board issued *Opinion No. 28*, "Interim Financial Reporting," in May 1973 [ASC 270]. Thus, before *APB Opinion No. 28* was issued, the form and content of interim reports and the accounting practices to be used in their preparation were left to the discretion of the reporting companies. In addition, interim reports are essentially unaudited reports. As a result, several problems evolved in the preparation of interim reports.

The seasonal nature of operations in many industries can cause wide fluctuations in revenues, expenses, and net income from one interim period to another. The relatively short time period available to determine interim results and the added cost of determining accurate figures for accruals, deferrals, and inventories encouraged the use of a variety of estimation techniques, some of which proved to be highly inaccurate. In fact, many firms used a wider variety of accounting practices and estimation procedures for interim reports than they did for year-end reports. In addition, two essentially conflicting views of the nature of interim periods exist among accountants. Some accountants hold that each interim period should ***stand alone*** as a basic accounting period; they conclude, therefore, that the results of operations for each interim period should be determined in the same manner as if the interim period were an annual period. Under this ***discrete*** view of an interim period, deferrals, accruals, and estimations at the end of each interim period are determined by following essentially the same principles and judgments that apply to annual periods.

Other accountants view each interim period as essentially an ***integral*** part of the annual period. Under this view, deferrals, accruals, and estimations at the end of each interim period are affected by judgments made at the interim date as to results of operations for the balance of the annual period. Thus, an expense item that might be considered as falling wholly within an annual accounting period could be allocated among interim periods on the basis of estimated time, sales volume, productive activity, or some other basis.

As a result of the problems just described, some companies issued interim financial statements reporting significant quarterly and year-to-date income for the first three quarters, but full-year statements that reported substantial net losses. The SEC filed complaints against several companies for failure to make adequate adjustments for accruals and deferrals of revenue and expenses on an interim basis and for failing to make appropriate adjustments on an interim basis for amortization, depreciation, and inventory obsolescence. In response to SEC complaints and general pressure from the financial and investing community, the APB issued *APB Opinion No. 28* [ASC 270] in May 1973.

APB Opinion No. 28

In *Opinion No. 28*, [ASC 270–10–05–1] the Board indicated that its basic objective was "to clarify the application of accounting principles and reporting practices to interim financial information, including interim financial statements and summarized interim financial data of publicly traded companies issued for external reporting purposes." The Board also concluded that "***each interim period should be viewed primarily as an integral part of an annual period*** " [ASC 270–10–45–1]. The Board also took the position that financial statements for each interim period should be based on the same accounting practices that are used for the preparation of annual financial statements. The *Opinion* presents guidelines for the presentation of revenue, costs associated with revenue, all other costs and expenses, and income tax provisions.

Revenue Revenue from products sold or services performed should be recognized as earned during an interim period on the same basis as that used for the full year. In addition, business with material seasonal variations should disclose the seasonal nature of their activities.

Costs Associated with Revenue Costs and expenses that are associated directly with or allocated to the products sold or to the services rendered for annual reporting purposes should be similarly treated for interim reporting purposes. However, the following are acceptable alternatives for inventory costing:

1. Estimated gross profit rates may be used by some companies to determine the cost of goods sold during interim periods, or they may use methods other than those used for year-end inventories. Companies using these methods should disclose the method used in the interim report and any significant adjustments that result from reconciliations with the annual physical inventory.
2. Companies using the LIFO method may encounter a liquidation of base period inventories at an interim date that is expected to be replaced by the end of the annual period. In these cases, cost of goods sold should be charged with the expected replacement cost of the liquidated LIFO base.
3. Inventory losses from market declines should be recognized in the interim period in which the decline occurs. Subsequent recoveries of these losses in interim periods should be recognized as gains to the extent of losses previously recognized in interim periods of the same fiscal period. However, market declines that are expected to be temporary within the fiscal year need not be recognized.

To illustrate, assume that Drex Company, which uses the FIFO inventory method, had 18,000 units in inventory at the beginning of the year at a FIFO cost per unit of $6. No purchases were made during the year. Information concerning quarterly sales and end-of-quarter replacement cost follows:

Quarter	*Sales in Units*	*End-of-Quarter Units on Hand*	*End-of-Quarter Replacement Cost*
1	3,000	15,000	$6.30
2	3,500	11,500	5.80
3	2,500	9,000	6.10
4	5,000	4,000	5.50
Total	14,000		

Assuming that the market decline in the second quarter was not expected to be temporary, cost of sales for the four quarters would be:

Quarter	Computation of Cost of Goods Sold		Cost of Goods Sold Quarter	Cumulative
1	Sold 3,000 units @ $6		$18,000	$18,000
2	Sold 3,500 units @ $6	$21,000		
	Plus write-down of ending inventory of 11,500 units to market [11,500 × ($6.00 – $5.80)]	+2,300	23,300	41,300
3	Sold 2,500 units @ $5.80	14,500		
	Less write-down recovery on ending inventory of 9,000 units [9,000 × ($6.00 – $5.80)]	(1,800)	12,700	54,000
4	Sold 5,000 units @ $6	30,000		
	Plus write-down of ending inventory of 4,000 units to market [(4,000 × ($6.00 – $5.50)]	+2,000	32,000	86,000

Because each interim period is considered an integral part of an annual period, the cumulative cost of goods sold ($86,000) should equal the amount that would be computed if the lower-of-cost-or-market method were applied on an annual basis. Thus, we can verify as follows:

Units Sold During Year		*FIFO Cost/Unit*	*Amount*
14,000	×	$6.00	$84,000
Add: Write-down of ending inventory to the lower of cost or market (4,000 × $.50)			2,000
Total cost of goods sold for the year			$86,000

This procedure also has the effect of determining the cumulative cost of goods sold at the end of any quarter within the year.

4. Companies that use standard cost for determining inventory and product cost should generally follow the procedures in reporting variances that are used for the fiscal year. Purchase price and volume variances that are expected to be absorbed by the end of the annual period should ordinarily be deferred at interim reporting dates. Unplanned purchase price and volume variances, however, should be reported at the end of the interim period by the procedures used at the end of the fiscal year.

All Other Costs and Expenses The Board concluded that, in accounting for costs and expenses that are not allocated to products sold or to services rendered, the following standards should apply:

1. Costs and expenses other than product costs should be charged to income in interim periods as incurred, or be allocated among interim periods based on an estimate of time expired, benefit received or activity associated with the periods. Procedures adopted for assigning specific cost and expense items to an interim period should be consistent with the bases followed by the company in reporting results of operations at annual reporting dates. However, when a specific cost or expense item charged to expense for annual reporting purposes benefits more than one interim period, the cost or expense item may be allocated to those interim periods.
2. Some costs and expenses incurred in an interim period cannot be readily identified with the activities or benefits of other interim periods and should be charged to the interim period in which incurred. Disclosure should be made as to the nature and amount of such costs unless items of a comparable nature are

included in both the current interim period and in the corresponding interim period of the preceding year.

3. Arbitrary assignment of the amount of such costs to an interim period should not be made.
4. Gains and losses that arise in any interim period similar to those that would not be deferred at year-end should not be deferred to later interim periods within the same fiscal year.[9]

In a study examining the predictive ability of *SFAS No. 131* versus *SFAS No. 14,* the predictive ability of the geographic sales reported by *SFAS No. 131* exceeds that of *SFAS No. 14.* In addition, the requirement that companies report revenues for the country of domicile and for each "material" country has enhanced the predictive ability of the segment data.[10]

Provision for Income Taxes Accounting for income taxes in interim financial statements can be very complex for a company with such items as operating loss carrybacks or carryforwards, extraordinary gains and losses, capital gains and losses, and other similar items. Our treatment here will cover the basic issue of interim provision of income taxes. The reader is referred to *FASB Interpretation No. 18,* "Accounting for Income Taxes in Interim Periods," which discusses complicating issues in detail and presents numerous examples of appropriate treatment.

The basic technique for computing income tax provisions for interim financial statements is described in *APB Opinion Nos. 28, 23,* and *24,* and in *SFAS No. 109* [ASC 740–270]. At the end of each interim period the company should make its best estimate of the effective tax rate expected to be applicable for the full fiscal year. The rate so determined should be used in providing for income taxes on a current year-to-date basis. The effective rate should reflect anticipated tax credits, foreign tax rates, percentage depletion, and other available tax planning alternatives. However, in arriving at this effective tax rate no effect should be included for the tax related to significant unusual or extraordinary items that will be separately reported or reported net of their related tax effect in reports for the interim period or for the fiscal year.

To illustrate the basic procedures, assume that during 2009 Drex Company had actual first-quarter earnings of $150,000 and expected to have full-year earnings of about $500,000. On the basis of its full-year earnings projection, Drex Company estimated that its combined state and federal tax rate would be 30%. Assume further that Drex Company estimated that it would have permanent differences between accounting income and taxable income during the year of $20,000 for penalties for environmental violations and a dividend exclusion of $50,000. On the basis of this information, Drex Company would compute its estimated effective income tax rate for the year as follows:

Estimated income before taxes	$500,000
Add: Nondeductible penalties	20,000
Less: Dividends exclusion	(50,000)
Estimated taxable income	$470,000
Estimated combined income tax payable ($470,000 × 30%)	$141,000
Estimated effective combined tax rate ($141,000/$500,000)	28.2%

[9] *Opinion of the Accounting Principles Board No. 28,* "Interim Financial Reporting" (New York: AICPA, May 1973), par. 15, [ASC 270–10–45–8].

[10] *Journal of International Accounting Research,* "The Predictive Ability of Geographic Segment Disclosures by U.S. Companies: SFAS No. 131 versus SFAS No. 14, by Bruce Behn, Nancy Nichols, and Donna Street, vol. 1, 2002, pp. 31–44.

This estimated rate is used to determine the income tax provision for the first quarter. Drex Company would, therefore, make the following entry:

Income Tax Expense ($150,000 × 28.2%)	42,300	
Income Tax Payable		42,300

Now assume that during the second quarter of 2009 Drex Company had actual earnings of $170,000, and that estimated total income for the year is $600,000. Estimated permanent differences remain the same as projected during the first quarter. Using this new information, Drex Company would again compute an estimated combined federal and state tax rate for the year.

Estimated income before taxes	$600,000
Less: Net permanent differences ($50,000 − $20,000)	(30,000)
Estimated taxable income	$570,000
Estimated combined income tax payable ($570,000 × 30%)	$171,000
Estimated effective combined tax rate ($171,000/$600,000)	28.5%

The new estimated tax rate is used to compute the estimated year-to-date income tax provision, and the provision required for the second quarter as indicated here:

Cumulative income for the first two quarters ($150,000 + $170,000)	$320,000
Estimated effective tax rate	28.5%
Cumulative tax provision needed	91,200
Less: Tax provided in first quarter	42,300
Tax provision for second quarter	$ 48,900

Drex Company would make the following tax provision entry for the second quarter:

Income Tax Expense	48,900	
Income Tax Payable		48,900

Note that the new estimated effective tax rate is ***not*** applied retroactively; that is, the first-quarter results are not restated. Tax expense reported in the second-quarter interim income statement would be $48,900, and the year-to-date tax expense and tax payable would be reported in the year-to-date income statement and statement of financial position at $91,200. The procedures for the third-quarter would duplicate those followed for the second quarter, taking new information and estimates into consideration. It should also be noted that the treatment provided in *APB Opinion No. 28* [ASC 250–10–45–13], and just illustrated, is entirely consistent with the normal treatment afforded a change in estimate under the provisions of *SFAS No. 154*, para. 19, "Accounting Changes and Error Corrections" [ASC 250–10–45–17]; that is, changes in estimates are treated currently and prospectively, not retroactively.

The preceding illustration assumed that there were no temporary differences. If temporary differences existed, they would have no effect on the computation of the combined effective tax rate, but would affect the tax expense and the tax liability recorded. For example, if there were an excess of tax depreciation over book depreciation during the first quarter amounting to $40,000, the first-quarter tax entry would be modified as follows:

Income Tax Expense	42,300	
Income Tax Payable [.282($150,000 − $40,000)]		31,020
Deferred Income Tax Liability (.282 × $40,000)		11,280

Interim Operating Losses When an interim operating loss gives rise to an expected income tax benefit, an asset is created to recognize the benefit. For example, if the loss for the interim or year-to-date period is expected to be offset by operating profit later in the same fiscal period, a tax benefit is traceable to the interim or year-to-date loss. *SFAS No. 109* [ASC 740–10–30–17], however, requires that the asset be reduced by a valuation allowance if it is "more likely than not" that some or all of the benefit may not be realized. Clearly this criterion is one of the more subjective the FASB has required, and its implementation is thus subject to managerial discretion (and auditor review).

Accounting Changes in Interim Periods

Change in Estimate A change in estimate should be accounted for in the interim period in which the change is made. No restatement of previously reported interim information should be made, but the effect on earnings of a change in estimate made in a current interim period should be reported in the current and subsequent interim periods, if material in relation to any period presented, and should continue to be reported as long as necessary to avoid misleading comparisons.

FASB Statement No. 154 [ASC 250], Accounting Changes and Error Corrections, replaces *FASB Statement No. 3* (Reporting Accounting Changes in Interim Financial Statements). The accounting changes addressed in this statement include all voluntary accounting changes and accounting changes where a new accounting pronouncement does not include specific transition provisions. *SFAS No. 154* requires retrospective application to financial statements of prior periods where practical. If not practical, the statement requires that the new statement be applied to the earliest period that is practical. If one of the prior year's financial statements being presented cannot be adjusted, an adjustment should be made to the beginning balance of retained earnings and not included in income.

Minimum Disclosures in Interim Reports

Because the amount of financial information disclosed in interim reports varies widely, the APB [ASC 270–10–50–1] established minimum disclosure standards relating to the following:

a. Sales or gross revenues, provision for income taxes, extraordinary items (including related income tax effects), and net income.

b. Basic and diluted earnings-per-share data for each period presented determined in accordance with the provisions of *SFAS No. 128* [ASC 260].

c. Seasonal revenue, costs, or expenses.

d. Significant changes in estimates or provisions for income taxes.

e. Disposal of a segment of a business and extraordinary, unusual, or infrequently occurring items.

f. Contingent items.

g. Changes in accounting principles or estimates.

h. Significant changes in financial position.

Overall, the APB and FASB have made a significant effort to improve the quality of interim financial reports. However, considerable controversy still exists and appears to center around the APB's assumption that an interim period should be accounted for as an integral part of the annual period.

International Issues in Interim Reporting

Some companies are still reporting only the minimum amount of information in their interim reports, despite publication of the Accounting Standards Boards' guidance in November 1996. For example, clothing manufacturer Albion, in its interim statement for the half-year ended March 31, 1998, reported only a one-page sheet of the minimum information required by the London Stock Exchange's Listing Rules. It did not say that the interim reports were prepared in a basis consistent with the policies used in the last reported annual period, though presumably this was the case. The ASB guidance statement recommends that interim reports use the same measurement and recognition bases and accounting methods as used in the annual reports, and that this should be stated in the interim report.[11]

IAS 34, "Interim Financial Reporting", does not state which entities should prepare and publish interim financial statements. The standard determines the minimum content of the interim reports if the entity elects or is required to prepare interim financial statements. IAS 34 generally requires that the interim period be a discrete reporting period.

IAS 34 applies when an entity publishes an interim financial report in accordance with International Financial Reporting Standards (IFRS). An *interim financial report* refers here to a financial report containing either a complete set of financial statements (described in IAS 1, *Presentation of Financial Statements*) or a set of condensed financial statements (described in this Standard) for an interim period; an *interim period* refers to any financial reporting period shorter than a full year. For the sake of timeliness and cost considerations, as well as to avoid repetition of information reported previously, an entity may provide less information at interim dates than in its annual financial statements. This Standard defines the ***minimal*** content of an interim financial report as containing *condensed financial statements* and *selected explanatory notes.* The purpose of the interim financial report is to provide an update to the latest complete set of annual financial reports. Accordingly, it focuses on ***new*** activities, events, and circumstances rather than duplicating information already reported.

The Standard is not, however, intended to prohibit or discourage an entity from publishing a complete set of financial statements (as described in IAS 1) in its interim financial report if it chooses to do so. *If such a complete set of financial statements is reported in the interim reports, the form and content of those statements should conform to the requirements of IAS 1.*

An interim financial report should, at a minimum, include:

(a) condensed income statement;
(b) condensed balance sheet;
(c) condensed statement showing either (i) all changes in equity or (ii) changes in equity except for those arising from capital transactions with owners and distributions to owners;
(d) condensed cash flow statement; and
(e) selected explanatory notes.

If an entity chooses to publish condensed financial statements in its interim financial report, those condensed statements must include each of the headings and subtotals that were included in its most recent annual financial statements and the selected explanatory notes as required by this Standard. Furthermore, additional line items or notes should be included if their omission would make the condensed interim financial statements misleading for any reason.

[11] *Accountancy*, "Gradual Acceptance of ASB Guidelines," vol. 122, September 1998, p. 78.

Materiality with respect to measurement, classification, and disclosure should be assessed in relation to the interim period financial data. In making assessments of materiality, it should be recognized that interim measurements may rely on estimates to a larger degree than annual measurements do.

The same accounting policies should be applied in interim financial statements that are used in a firm's annual financial statements, with the possible exception of any accounting policy changes made after the date of the most recent annual financial statements that are to be reflected in the *next* annual financial statements. Thus measurements for interim reporting purposes are made on a year-to-date basis. The measurement procedures for interim reporting are designed to ensure that the resulting information is *reliable* and that all material financial information *relevant* to an understanding of the financial position or performance of the entity is disclosed.

Differences between IFRS and US GAAP—Interim Reporting

The view of an interim period is conceptually quite different under U.S. GAAP and under IFRS. Under IFRS, the interim period is defined as a discrete reporting period, with certain exceptions. Recall that discrete reporting treats each interim period as a basic accounting period to be evaluated as if it were an annual period. Thus, end of period adjustments and deferrals are determined using the same principles as the annual report. Under U.S. GAAP, an interim period is an integral part of the full year (again, with certain exceptions). Thus, the adjustments and deferrals may be affected by judgment about the expected results for the entire year.

Disclosures for changes in accounting policy also differ significantly between U.S. GAAP and current IFRS. IFRS require the disclosure of any differences between accounting policies in the current interim period compared to the most recent annual financial statements as well as, at a minimum, a description of the nature and effect of the change. In contrast, U.S. GAAP require disclosure of any changes in accounting policies in the current interim period in comparison to: a) the comparable interim period of the previous year, 2) the preceding interim periods in the current year, and 3) the previous annual report.

"The Committee does agree that determination of what needs to be included in the notes to the interim financial statements about unusual events should be based on the stand-alone interim data. However, as users of financial statements, the Committee would find the 'accordion effect' associated with the discrete approach both disruptive and confusing . . . the Committee believes the most useful and practical approach to dealing with interim accounting is the integral approach."[12]

SUMMARY

1. *Understand the need for disaggregated financial data.* To aid in evaluating prospective investments and particularly the risk of those investments, financial statement users must assess the uncertainty surrounding both the timing and the amounts of expected cash flows. Major uncertainty results from factors unique to individual companies, factors related to the industries and geographical areas in which those companies operate, and related national and international economic and political factors. When a firm engages in activities in several industries or geographic areas, analysis and the prediction of future cash flows become somewhat more complicated because different segments may have different rates of profitability, growth opportunities, and types of risk.

[12] *Management Accounting*, "Interim Reporting," vol. 79, February 1998, p. 59.

2. *Describe the basic requirements of public companies in reporting segmental data.* In *SFAS No. 131* [ASC 280], the FASB requires all public companies to report information about the countries in which they earn revenues and hold assets, about major customers, and about revenues for each product and service, even when *some* of the information is not used by the firm in its operating decisions. In general, *SFAS No. 131* implemented a management approach, focusing on the way in which management organizes segments internally to make operating decisions and to assess performance.

3. *Determine an operating segment.* An operating segment is a component of an enterprise that may earn revenues and incur expenses, about which the chief operating decision maker regularly evaluates separate financial information in deciding how to allocate resources and in assessing performance. Discrete financial information is available about the segment.

4. *Define a reportable segment.* A reportable segment is a segment considered to be significant to an enterprise's operations; specifically, one that has passed one of three 10% tests or has been identified as being reportable through other criteria (aggregation, for example). The three 10% tests relate to combined external and internal revenues, reported profit or loss, and assets.

5. *Describe how common costs are handled in segmental reporting.* Common costs should be allocated to a segment for external reporting purposes only if they are included in the segment's profit or loss calculations that are used internally by the chief operating decision maker. The emphasis here is on operating expenses, as general corporate expenses are not allocated.

6. *Identify the information to be presented for each reportable segment.* The information presented includes: general information; information about segment operating profit or loss; information about segment assets; information about the bases for measurement; a reconciliation of segment amounts to the consolidated amounts for revenue, profit or loss, assets, and other significant items; interim disclosures; and enterprisewide disclosures regarding products or services, geographic areas, and major customers.

7. *Explain when and what types of geographic data must be reported.* Geographic disclosures are required on an enterprisewide basis unless the company's reportable segments have been defined based on geographic area. When required, firms must report revenues from external customers and long-lived assets attributable to their domestic operations and foreign operations. If operations are conducted in two or more foreign countries or geographic areas, information must be presented separately for each significant foreign country or geographic area and in the aggregate for all other foreign operations.

8. *Explain when information about major customers must be reported.* If 10% or more of the revenue of a firm is derived from sales to any single customer, that fact and the amount of revenue from each such customer must be disclosed. Also, if 10% or more of the revenue is derived from sales to the federal government, a state government, a local government, or a foreign government, that fact and the amount of revenue must be disclosed. These disclosures are required even if the firm has only one reportable segment.

9. *Compare the international accounting standards for segmental reporting with the U.S. requirements.* Whereas the U.S. standard focuses on the data reported and used internally by a chief operating decision maker, the IASC states its objective as providing insight into how the diversity of products and services and geographic operations affects an enterprise's overall risks and returns. The differences between the two standards include segment definition, measurement differences, uniformity across companies, and asymmetry allowed/disallowed in measurement.

10. *Describe current requirements for companies to report interim information.* Publicly owned companies are generally required to file some type of quarterly report as part of the agreement with the stock exchanges that list their stock. In addition, the SEC requires public companies to file Form 10-Q with the Commission within 45 days after the end of each of the first three quarters of the fiscal year.

11. *Indicate some problems with interim reporting and the authoritative position on the issue.* The seasonal nature of operations in many industries can cause wide fluctuations in revenues, expenses, and net income from one interim period to another. The relatively short time period available to determine interim results and the added cost of determining accurate figures for accruals, deferrals, and inventories encouraged the use of a variety of estimation techniques, some of which proved to be highly inaccurate. Two conflicting views of the nature of interim periods are: each period is *discrete* and should *stand alone* as a basic accounting period; or each interim period is an *integral* part of the annual period. In *APB Opinion No. 28* [paragraph 270-10-45-1], the Board supported the integral view.

APPENDIX

GE Segmental Disclosures, 2005 Annual Report (partial)

Operating Segments

Revenues

	Total Revenues			Intersegment Revenues			External Revenues		
[In millions]	*2005*	*2004*	*2003*	*2005*	*2004*	*2003*	*2005*	*2004*	*2003*
Infrastructure	$ 41,803	**$ 37,373**	**$ 36,569**	$ 405	**$ 481**	**$ 449**	$ 41,398	**$ 36,892**	**$ 36,120**
Industrial	32,631	**30,722**	**24,988**	702	**493**	**308**	31,929	**30,229**	**24,680**
Healthcare	15,153	**13,456**	**10,198**	9	—	**2**	15,144	**13,456**	**10,196**
NBC Universal	14,689	**12,886**	**6,871**	—	—	—	14,689	**12,886**	**6,871**
Commercial Finance	20,646	**19,524**	**16,927**	204	**279**	**197**	20,442	**19,245**	**16,730**
Consumer Finance	19,416	**15,734**	**12,845**	52	**33**	**23**	19,364	**15,701**	**12,822**
Corporate Items and Eliminations	5,364	**4,786**	**4,488**	[1,372]	**[1,286]**	**[979]**	6,736	**6,072**	**5,467**
Total	$149,702	**$134,481**	**$112,886**	$ —	**$ —**	**$ —**	$149,702	**$134,481**	**$112,886**

	Assets[a] at December 31			Property, Plant, and Equipment Additions[b] for the Years Ended December 31			Depreciation and Amortization for the Years Ended December 31		
[In millions]	*2005*	*2004*	*2005*	*2005*	*2004*	*2003*	*2005*	*2004*	*2003*
Infrastructure	$ 89,555	**$ 82,798**	**$ 76,185**	$ 4,188	**$ 3,938**	**$ 3,540**	$ 2,436	**$ 2,162**	**$ 2,077**
Industrial	41,556	**42,040**	**40,359**	4,367	**4,111**	**2,205**	3,292	**3,292**	**2,288**
Healthcare	24,661	**24,871**	**10,816**	460	**1,590**	**289**	617	**565**	**278**
NBC Universal	31,196	**34,206**	**11,619**	275	**1,189**	**121**	339	**273**	**117**
Commercial Finance	190,546	**184,388**	**172,471**	5,426	**4,573**	**5,141**	2,648	**2,772**	**2,444**
Consumer Finance	158,829	**151,255**	**106,530**	189	**217**	**191**	393	**334**	**276**
Corporate Items and Eliminations	136,999	**230,949**	**229,848**	199	**194**	**252**	208	**245**	**373**
Total	$673,342	**$750,507**	**$647,828**	$15,104	**$15,812**	**$11,739**	$ 9,933	**$ 9,643**	**$ 7,853**

Revenues originating from operations based in the United States were $89,887 million, $82,148 million and $69,998 million, in 2005, 2004, and 2003, respectively. Revenues originating from operations based outside the United States were $59,815 million, $52,333 million, and $42,888 million in 2005, 2004, and 2003, respectively. Property, plant, and equipment associated with operations based in the United States were $26,140 million, $25,219 million, and $20,591 million at year-end 2005, 2004, and 2003, respectively. Property, plant, and equipment associated with operations based outside the United States were $41,388 million, $37,884 million, and $32,560 million at year-end 2005, 2004, and 2003, respectively.

Basis for presentation

Our operating businesses are organized based on the nature of markets and customers.

	General Electric Company and Consolidated Affiliates				
[In millions]	*2005*	*2004*	*2003*	*2002*	*2001*
Revenues					
Infrastructure	$ 41,803	**$ 37,373**	**$ 36,569**	**$ 40,119**	**$ 36,419**
Industrial	32,631	**30,722**	**24,988**	**26,154**	**26,101**
Healthcare	15,153	**13,456**	**10,198**	**8,955**	**8,409**
NBC Universal	14,689	**12,886**	**6,871**	**7,149**	**5,769**
Commercial Finance	20,646	**19,524**	**16,927**	**15,688**	**14,610**
Consumer Finance	19,416	**15,734**	**12,845**	**10,266**	**9,508**
Total segment revenues	144,338	**129,695**	**108,398**	**108,331**	**100,816**
Corporate items and eliminations	5,364	**4,786**	**4,488**	**5,525**	**6,742**
CONSOLIDATED REVENUES	$149,702	**$134,481**	**$112,886**	**$113,856**	**$107,558**
SEGMENT PROFIT					
Infrastructure	$ 7,769	**$ 6,797**	**$ 7,362**	**$ 9,178**	**$ 7,869**
Industrial	2,559	**1,833**	**1,385**	**1,837**	**2,642**
Healthcare	2,665	**2,286**	**1,701**	**1,546**	**1,498**
NBC Universal	3,092	**2,558**	**1,998**	**1,658**	**1,408**
Commercial Finance	4,290	**3,570**	**2,907**	**2,170**	**1,784**
Consumer Finance	3,050	**2,520**	**2,161**	**1,799**	**1,602**
Total segment profit	23,425	**19,564**	**17,514**	**18,188**	**16,803**
Corporate Items and eliminations	(968)	**(327)**	**50**	**2,016**	**1,155**
GE interest and other financial charges	(1,432)	**(979)**	**(941)**	**(569)**	**(817)**
GE provision for income taxes	(2,750)	**(1,973)**	**(2,857)**	**(3,837)**	**(4,193)**
Earnings from continuing operations before accounting changes	18,275	**16,285**	**13,766**	**15,798**	**12,948**
Earning (loss) from discontinued operations, net or taxes	(1,922)	**534**	**2,057**	**(616)**	**1,130**
Earnings before accounting changes	16,353	**16,819**	**15,823**	**15,182**	**14,078**
Cumulative effect of accounting changes	—	**—**	**(587)**	**(1,015)**	**(287)**
CONSOLIDATED NET EARNINGS	$ 16,353	**$ 16,819**	**$ 15,236**	**$ 14,167**	**$ 13,791**

Our Businesses

A description of operating segments for General Electric Company and consolidated affiliates as of December 31, 2005, and the basis for presentation in this report, follows.

Infrastructure

Jet engines and replacement parts and repair and maintenance services for all categories of commercial aircraft; for a wide variety of military aircraft, including fighters, bombers, tankers and helicopters; and for executive and regional aircraft. Products and services are sold worldwide to airframe manufacturers, airlines and government agencies. Rail systems products and maintenance services including diesel electric locomotives, transit propulsion equipment, motorized wheels for off-highway vehicles, and railway signaling communications systems.

Financial products to airlines, aircraft operators, owners, lenders and investors including leases, aircraft purchasing and trading, loans, engine/spare parts financing, pilot training, fleet planning and financial advisory services.

Power plant products and services, including design, installation, operation and maintenance services sold into global markets. Gas, steam and aeroderivative turbines, generators, combined cycle systems, controls and related services, including total asset optimization solutions, equipment upgrades and contractual services, are sold to power generation and other industrial customers.

Renewable energy solutions including wind turbines and hydro turbines and generators. Advanced turbomachinery products and related services for the oil and gas market, including total pipeline integrity solutions. Substation automation, network solutions and power equipment sold to power transmission and distribution customers. Also includes portable and rental power plants, nuclear reactors, fuel and nuclear support services.

Chemical water treatment program services and equipment including mobile treatment systems and desalination processes. Financial products to the global energy industry including structured equity, leveraged leasing, partnerships, project finance and broad-based commercial finance.

Industrial

Major appliances and related services for products such as refrigerators, freezers, electric and gas ranges, cooktops, dishwashers, clothes washers and dryers, microwave ovens, room air conditioners and residential water system products. These products are distributed to both retail outlets and direct to consumers, mainly for the replacement market, and to building contractors and distributors for new installations. Lighting products include a wide variety of lamps and lighting fixtures. Electrical distribution and control equipment includes power delivery and control products such as transformers, meters and relays. Also includes:

GE Supply, a network of electrical supply houses. Products and services are sold in North America and in global markets under various GE and private-label brands.

High-performance engineered plastics used in a variety of applications such as automotive parts, computer enclosures, telecommunications equipment and construction materials. Products also include structured products, silicones and high-purity quartzware. Products and services are sold worldwide to a diverse customer base consisting mainly of manufacturers.

Rentals, leases, sales and asset management services of commercial and transportation equipment, including tractors, trailers, railroad rolling stock, modular space units, intermodal shipping containers and, primarily through an associated company, marine containers.

Measurement and sensing equipment (products and subsystems for sensing temperature, flow rates, humidity, pressure and detection of material defects); security equipment and systems (including card access systems, video and sensor monitoring equipment, integrated facility monitoring systems and explosive detection systems); a broad range of automation hardware and software. Markets are extremely diverse. Products and services are sold to commercial and industrial end-users, including utilities; original equipment manufacturers; electrical distributors; retail outlets; airports; railways; and transit authorities. Increasingly, products and services are developed for and sold in global markets.

Healthcare

Medical imaging systems such as magnetic resonance (MR) and computed tomography (CT) scanners, x-ray, nuclear imaging and ultrasound, as well as diagnostic cardiology and patient monitoring devices; related services, including equipment monitoring and repair, computerized data management and customer productivity services. Diagnostic imaging agents used in medical scanning procedures, protein separations products including chromatography purification systems used in the manufacture of biopharmaceuticals, and high-throughput systems for applications in genomics, proteomics and bioassays. Products and services are sold worldwide to hospitals, medical facilities, pharmaceutical and biotechnology companies and to the life science research market.

NBC Universal

Principal businesses are the furnishing of U.S. network television services to 230 affiliated stations, production of television programs, the production and distribution of motion pictures, operation of 30 VHF and UHF television broadcasting stations, operation of cable/satellite networks around the world, operation of theme parks, and investment and programming activities in multimedia and the Internet.

Commercial Finance

Loans, leases and other financial services to customers, including manufacturers, distributors and end-users for a variety of equipment and major capital assets. These assets include industrial related facilities and equipment; commercial and residential real estate; vehicles; corporate aircraft; and equipment used in many industries, including the construction, manufacturing, telecommunications and healthcare industries.

Consumer Finance

Private-label credit cards; bank cards; Dual Cards™; corporate travel and purchasing cards; personal loans; auto loans; leases and inventory financing; residential mortgages; home equity loans; debt consolidation loans; current and savings accounts and insurance products for customers on a global basis.

TEST YOUR KNOWLEDGE SOLUTIONS

14-1 1. Segments A, C, and D
2. Segments A and C
3. Segments A and C
4. Segments A, C, and D

QUESTIONS

LO1 1. For what types of companies would segmented financial reports have the most significance? Why?

LO1 2. Why do financial statement users (financial analysts, for example) need information about segments of a firm?

LO3 LO4 3. Define the following:

(a) Operating segment.

(b) Reportable segment.

LO4 4. Describe the guidelines to be used in determining (a) what constitutes an operating segment, and (b) whether a specific operating segment is a significant segment.

LO6 5. List the three major types of enterprisewide information disclosures required by *SFAS No. 131* [ASC 280], and explain how the firm's designation of reportable segments affects these disclosures.

LO6 6. What segmental disclosures are required, if any, for interim reports?

LO2 7. What type of disclosure is required of a firm when the major portion of its operations takes place within a single reportable segment?

LO6 8. List the types of information that must be presented for each reportable segment of a company under the rules of *SFAS No. 131* [ASC 280].

LO6 9. Describe the methods that might be used to disclose reportable segment information.

LO7 10. What types of information must be disclosed about foreign operations under *SFAS No. 131* [ASC 280–10–50–40]?

LO7 11. How are foreign operations defined under *SFAS No. 131* [ASC 280]?

LO7 12. If the operations of a firm in some foreign countries are grouped into geographic areas, what factors should be considered in forming the groups?

LO8 13. When must a firm present segmental disclosures for major customers? What is the reason for this requirement?

LO5 14. How are common costs distinguished from general corporate expenses for segmental purposes?

LO11 15. What is the purpose of interim financial reporting?

LO11 16. Some accountants hold the view that each interim period should stand alone as a basic accounting period, whereas others view each interim period as essentially an integral part of the annual period. Distinguish between these views.

LO11 17. Describe the basic procedure for computing income tax provisions for interim financial statements.

LO11 18. Describe how changes in estimates should be treated in interim financial statements.

LO10 19. What are the minimum disclosure requirements established ASC 270 for interim financial reports?

LO11 20. What is the general rule regarding the treatment of costs and expenses associated directly with revenues for interim reporting purposes?

Business Ethics

SMC Inc. operates restaurants based on various themes, such as Mex-delight, Chinese for the Buffet, and Steak-it and Eat-it. The Steak-it and Eat-it restaurants have not been performing well recently, but SMC prefers not to disclose these details for fear that competitors might use the information to the detriment of SMC. The restaurants are located in various geographical locations, and management currently measures profits and losses and asset allocation by restaurant concept. However, when preparing the segmental disclosures under *SFAS No. 131* [ASC 280], the company reports the segment information by geographical location only. The company recently hired you to review the financial statements.

1. What disclosures should the company report for segment purposes?
2. The company's CEO believed that the rules in *SFAS No. 131* [ASC 280] are vague and that the company could easily support its decision to disclose the segment data by geographic regions. What would you recommend to the CEO and how would you approach the issues?

Analyzing Financial Statements
AFS 14-1 Segmental Disclosures

In the Appendix to this chapter, the partial segmental disclosures for General Electric (GE) are provided.

1. How does GE organize and present its segment data?
2. Compute the following ratios for 2003, 2004, and 2005 for each segment reported.
   a. Segment profit percentage = (segment profit/segment revenue)
   b. Segment asset turnover = (segment revenue/segment assets)
3. Compute the growth rate for each segment for revenues and assets from 2003 to 2005. For example, the formula for revenue growth rate is:

$$\text{Growth rate in revenues} = \frac{\text{Revenues for 2005}}{\text{Revenues for 2003}} - 1$$

4. Evaluate each segment's performance using the computations from questions 2 and 3. Which segment performed the best and which segment performed the worst?
5. What percentage of GE's total revenues and assets are based outside the United States? Can you determine from the disclosures whether the trend is toward more or less globalization? Comment on the trend to the extent feasible.

EXERCISES

EXERCISE 14-1 Operating Profit Test LO4

Pong Industries' operations involve four operating segments, A, B, C, and D. During the past year, the operating profit (loss) of each segment was

Segment	*Operating Profit (Loss)*
A	$(600)
B	100
C	900
D	(700)

Required:

Applying the operating profit or loss test, determine which of the segments are reportable segments.

EXERCISE 14-2 **Revenue Test** LO4

Mane Company operates in five identifiable segments, V, W, X, Y, and Z. During the past year, sales to unaffiliated customers and intersegment sales for each segment were as follows:

Segment	*Sales to Nonaffiliates*	*Intersegment Sales*	*Total Sales*
V	$2,000	$ 400	$2,400
W	280	20	300
X	100	600	700
Y	1,100	—0—	1,100
Z	350	25	375
Total	$3,830	$1,045	$4,875

Required:

Applying the revenue test, determine which of the segments are reportable segments.

EXERCISE 14-3 **Significance Tests** LO4

Twodor Company is involved in four separate industries. Selected financial information concerning Twodor's involvement in each of the four industries is presented below:

	Industry Segment				
	A	*B*	*C*	*D*	*Total*
Sales to nonaffiliates	$ 80,000	$20,000	$24,000	$12,200	$136,200
Intersegment sales	130,000	84,000	12,000	3,800	229,800
Total revenue	210,000	104,000	36,000	16,000	366,000
Operating profit (loss)	(17,400)	12,000	1,500	(600)	(4,500)
Identifiable assets	222,000	110,500	28,000	26,000	386,500

Required:

Using all tests, determine which of the industry segments are reportable segments and explain how nonreportable segments (if any) should be reported.

EXERCISE 14-4 **Allocating Common Costs to Segments** LO5

The following information concerns the operations of Blane Company for the year ended December 31, 2008.

	(In Thousands of Dollars)		
	General Office	*Segment A*	*Segment B*
Net sales (operating revenue)		$60,000	$99,000
Cost of goods sold		27,200	35,600
Allocable expenses		12,600	10,800
General corporate expenses	$15,000		
Payroll dollars	9,200	34,800	18,200
Average net book value of tangible capital assets and inventories	5,200	70,000	54,500

Required:

Determine the operating profit (loss) for each of Blane's two segments for 2008.

EXERCISE 14-5 **Provision for Taxes—Interim** LO11

LAX Inc. has the following income before income tax and estimated effective annual income tax rates for the first three quarters of 2008.

Quarter	*Income Before Income Tax Provision*	*Estimated Effective Annual Tax Rate at End of Quarter*
1st	$70,000	32%
2nd	50,000	32%
3rd	40,600	38%

Required:

What should be LAX's income tax provision in the third-quarter income statement? (*AICPA adapted*)

EXERCISE 14-6 **Amounts on Quarterly Reports** LO11

The following information is available for Bailey Company for 2008:

1. On January 2, 2008, Bailey paid property taxes amounting to $60,000 on its plant and equipment for the calendar year 2008. In late March 2008 Bailey made major repairs to its machinery amounting to $66,000. These repairs will benefit the remainder of the calendar year's operations.
2. An inventory loss of $150,000 from market decline occurred in August 2008. Bailey recorded this loss in August 2008 after its June 30 quarterly report was issued. None of this loss had been recovered by the end of 2008.
3. At the end of July 2008, Bailey sold some equipment with a book value of $22,000 for $32,500.

Required:

State the dollar amounts that should appear in Bailey Company's March 31, June 30, September 30, and December 31, 2008, quarterly financial statements to report:

A. Property taxes.

B. Major repairs to machinery.

C. Inventory loss from market decline.

D. The gain or loss on sale of equipment. (*AICPA adapted*)

EXERCISE 14-7 **Inventory and Quarterly Reports** LO11

Day Company, which uses the FIFO inventory method, had 254,000 units in inventory at the beginning of the year at a FIFO cost per unit of $30. No purchases were made during the year. Quarterly sales information and two sets of end-of-quarter replacement cost figures follow:

		End-of-Quarter Replacement Cost	
Quarter	*Unit Sales*	*Case A*	*Case B*
1	100,000	$29	$25
2	30,000	22	27
3	42,500	18	19
4	30,500	22	27

The market decline in the first quarter under Case A was expected to be temporary, whereas under Case B the decline was expected to be nontemporary. Declines in other quarters were expected to be permanent.

Required:

Determine cost of goods sold for the four quarters under each case and verify the amounts by computing cost of goods sold using the lower-of-cost-or-market method applied on an annual basis.

EXERCISE 14-8 **Provision for Taxes—Quarterly Entries** LO11

Spur Company's actual earnings for the first two quarters of 2008 and its estimate during each quarter of its annual earnings are:

Actual first-quarter earnings	$ 400,000
Actual second-quarter earnings	510,000
First-quarter estimate of annual earnings	1,350,000
Second-quarter estimate of annual earnings	1,420,000

Spur Company estimated its permanent differences between accounting income and taxable income for 2008 as:

Environmental violation penalties	$ 25,000
Dividend income exclusion	180,000

These estimates did not change during the second quarter. The combined state and federal tax rate for Spur Company for 2008 is 42%.

Required:

Prepare journal entries to record Spur Company's provisions for income taxes for each of the first two quarters of 2008.

EXERCISE 14-9 **Multiple Choice** LO4 LO5 LO6 LO11

Select the best answer for each of the following.

1. Which of the following is ***not*** a consideration in segment reporting for diversified companies?

- **(a)** Consolidation policy.
- **(b)** Defining the segments.
- **(c)** Transfer pricing.
- **(d)** Allocation of joint costs.

2. Cream Company operates in three different industries, each of which is appropriately regarded as a reportable segment. Segment No. 1 contributed 60% of Cream Company's total sales. Sales for Segment No. 1 were $450,000 and traceable costs were $200,000. Total common costs for Cream were $300,000. Cream allocates common costs on the basis of the ratio of a segment's sales to total sales, an appropriate method of allocation. What should be the operating profit presented for Segment No. 1 for the year?

- **(a)** $270,000.
- **(b)** $70,000.
- **(c)** $180,000.
- **(d)** $250,000.

3. The profitability information that should be reported for each reportable segment of a business enterprise consists of

- **(a)** An operating profit or loss figure consisting of segment revenues less traceable costs but ***not*** allocated common costs.
- **(b)** An operating profit or loss figure consisting of segment revenues less allocated common costs but ***not*** traceable costs.
- **(c)** An operating profit or loss figure consisting of segment revenues less traceable costs and allocated common costs.
- **(d)** Segment revenues only.

4. In financial reporting for segments of a business enterprise, the operating profit or loss of a segment should include

- **(a)** Revenue from other segments.
- **(b)** Federal income taxes.
- **(c)** Interest expense even though the segment's operations are ***not*** principally of a financial nature.
- **(d)** Any of the above, *if* it is included in the measures reviewed by the chief operating decision maker.

5. A company that uses the LIFO method of inventory pricing finds at an interim reporting date that there has been a partial liquidation of the base period inventory level. The decline is considered temporary and the partial liquidation will be replaced before year-end. The amount shown as inventory at the interim reporting date should
   (a) Be shown at the actual level, and cost of sales for the interim reporting period should reflect the decrease in the LIFO base period inventory level.
   (b) *Not* give effect to the LIFO liquidation, and cost of sales for the interim reporting period should reflect the decrease in the LIFO base period inventory level.
   (c) *Not* give effect to the LIFO liquidation, and cost of sales for the interim reporting period should include the expected cost of replacement of the liquidated LIFO base.
   (d) Be shown at the actual level, and the decrease in inventory level should ***not*** be reflected in the cost of sales for the interim reporting period.
6. Which of the following is an inherent difficulty in determination of the results of operations on an interim basis?
   (a) Costs expended in one interim period may benefit other periods.
   (b) Depreciation on an interim basis is a partial estimate of the actual annual amount.
   (c) Cost of sales reflects only the amount of product expense allocable to revenue recognized as of the interim date.
   (d) Revenues from long-term construction contracts accounted for by the percentage-of-completion method are based on annual completion, and interim estimates may be incorrect.
7. In considering interim financial reporting, how did the Accounting Principles Board conclude that such reporting should be viewed?
   (a) As useful only if activity is evenly spread throughout the year so that estimates are unnecessary.
   (b) As a "special" type of reporting that need ***not*** follow generally accepted accounting principles.
   (c) As reporting of an integral part of an annual period.
   (d) As reporting of a basic accounting period.
8. Which of the following methods of inventory valuation is allowable at interim dates but ***not*** at year-end?
   (a) Estimated gross profit rates.
   (b) Retail method.
   (c) Specific identification.
   (d) Weighted average. *(AICPA adapted)*

PROBLEMS

PROBLEM 14-1 **Significance Tests—Segmental Reporting** LO4

Bacon Industries operates in seven different segments. Information concerning the operations of these segments for the most recent fiscal period follows:

Operating Segment	*Revenue* *Total*	*Intersegment*	*Operating Profit (Loss)*	*Identifiable Assets*
1	$ 4,200	$ 800	$ (600)	$ 7,000
2	6,000	1,200	2,000	8,800
3	51,000	7,000	2,100	35,400
4	48,000	—0—	8,800	37,600
5	13,000	—0—	3,200	14,000
6	64,500	3,400	4,000	52,000
7	12,000	2,000	(3,000)	16,400

Required:

Determine which of the segments must be treated as reportable segments.

PROBLEM 14-2 Significance Tests—Segmental Reporting LO4 LO5

Pacheco Industries is comprised of four separate profit centers, which are distributed throughout the United States. Relevant data for each profit center are summarized for 2008:

	Profit Center (in Thousands)				
	A	*B*	*C*	*D*	*Total*
Sales to nonaffiliates	$3,600	$ 8,700	$1,500	$1,200	$15,000
Intersegment sales	1,500	2,400	300	3,000	7,200
Operating profit (loss) before joint expense allocation	840	1,500	240	(60)	2,520
Identifiable assets	7,200	18,000	2,400	2,400	30,000
Labor hours worked	2,700	5,700	1,500	2,100	12,000

You determine that intersegment sales are distributed as follows:

	Buyer				
Seller	*A*	*B*	*C*	*D*	*Total*
A	$—0—	$1,200	$150	$150	$1,500
B	1,200	—0—	600	600	2,400
C	150	150	—0—	—0—	300
D	1,800	1,050	150	—0—	3,000
Total	$3,150	$2,400	$900	$750	$7,200

Common costs of $2,400,000 were incurred during 2008. Management believes that total labor hours worked during the year provides a reasonable basis for allocation of these costs.

In each situation described below, an operating segment is comprised of different combinations of profit centers. Thus, the "AB" operating segment consists of profit centers "A" and "B." Consider the following five combinations of operating segments:

1. AB, CD
2. AB, C, D
3. A, B, CD
4. A, B, C, D
5. A, BD, C

Required:

A. For each combination listed, determine which operating segments are reportable segments. Apply all required tests and indicate the results of each test separately.

B. For each combination given, indicate if the reportable segments determined in (A) above collectively represent a "substantial portion" of Pacheco Industries' total operations, applying the 75% revenue test.

PROBLEM 14-3 Issues in Segmental Reporting LO1 LO4

Perez Industries, a publicly held corporation, consists of several companies, each of which provides an array of products and services to unaffiliated customers. In your opinion, each of these companies qualifies as a separate operating segment.

The corporation is in the process of completing its first-year financial statements. Although the directors of Perez Industries wish to comply with the provisions of *SFAS No. 131* [ASC 280], they believe that disclosing each individual segment would result in an unwieldy and cumbersome set of financial statements. For this reason, they request that when you prepare these statements, you keep the identified segments to the minimum number that would ensure compliance with *SFAS No. 131* [ASC 280].

Required:

A. To what extent does the management of Perez Industries have a choice in deciding whether an operating segment must be reported?

B. The directors of Perez Industries presumably feel that too much disclosure of financial information will impair the overall utility of the financial statements. What are the arguments against segmental disclosures? What flexibility, if any, does the FASB allow that could invalidate this criticism? Explain.

C. Explain the needs for segment reporting. Why do consolidated financial statements fail to meet these needs?

D. Relate the concept of comparability to the required accounting treatment for intersegment transactions. What arguments would favor ***excluding*** the effect of intersegment transfers?

PROBLEM 14-4 **Comprehensive Segmental Reporting** LO4 LO6

Branson Industries conducts operations in five major industries, A, B, C, D, and E. Financial data relevant to each industry for the year ending December 31, 2008, are as follows:

(In Thousands)

	United States			*Canada*	
	A	*B*	*C*	*D*	*E*
Sales	$57,000	$120,000	$880,000	$50,000	$ 83,000
Cost of goods sold	20,000	75,000	400,000	9,400	49,000
Administrative expenses	18,000	26,000	152,000	12,000	8,000
Selling expenses	7,000	44,000	172,000	12,600	20,000
Total cost and expense	45,000	145,000	724,000	34,000	77,000
Operating profit	$12,000	$(25,000)	$156,000	$16,000	$ 6,000
Identifiable assets	$50,000	$95,000	$600,000	$98,000	$240,000
Depreciation and amortization expense	6,400	10,700	76,000	12,200	26,400
Capital expenditures	5,600	8,000	39,000	20,000	25,000

Included in the sales of segments C and E are intersegment sales of $120,000 and $40,000, respectively. Corporate offices have assets of $95,000 and incurred general corporate expenses of $76,000. All corporate assets are located in the United States and depreciation on corporate assets was $10,000. No single customer represents more than 10% of sales. There is no intercompany inventory in beginning or ending inventory. The intersegment sales are included in the measures reviewed by the chief operating decision maker, as are the capital expenditures and depreciation and amortization.

Required:

A. Which industry segments should be separately reported in the segment report, assuming that Branson defines its operating segments based on major industry (product/services)? Justify your answer.

B. Prepare a report to disclose required segment information under *SFAS No. 131* [ASC 280]. Include the enterprisewide disclosures.

PROBLEM 14-5 **Segmental Reconciliation** LO4 LO6

Bismac Industries is a diversified company whose operations are conducted in five product lines, L, M, N, O, and P. Segmented financial information is to be included with the December 31, 2008 annual report. Financial information pertaining to each segment for 2008 is as follows:

	L	*M*	*N*	*O*	*P*
Sales	$40,000	$ 85,000	$600,000	$50,000	$48,000
Cost of sales	15,000	45,000	275,000	22,000	29,000
Interest expense	4,000	11,000	50,000	4,000	1,000
Depreciation expense	5,000	8,000	54,000	6,000	5,000
Selling expense	8,000	32,000	140,000	9,000	10,000
Total cost and expense	32,000	96,000	519,000	41,000	45,000
Operating profit (loss)	$ 8,000	$(11,000)	$ 81,000	$ 9,000	$ 3,000
Identifiable assets	$30,000	$ 48,000	$320,000	$45,000	$95,000

Additional Information:

1. In addition to the identifiable assets listed, the general corporate office has assets of $90,000 on December 31, 2008, and incurred unallocated amounts related to corporate headquarters of: interest expense $1,000, depreciation expense $2,000.
2. Included in the sales of segment P are $15,000 of sales made to segment N during the year. None of these goods remains in the ending inventory of segment N on December 31, 2008. There were no capital expenditures during the year.
3. No single customer represented more than 10% of sales.

Required:

A. Determine which of the five segments must be treated as reportable segments and indicate the basis for your decision. Assume segments are defined based on product line.
B. Prepare a financial report by segments that is reconciled to consolidated data.

PROBLEM 14-6 Quarterly Income Tax Entries LO 11

Actual quarterly earnings and quarterly estimates of annual earnings for Sloan Company for the year ended December 31, 2008 are as follows:

Quarter	*Actual Quarterly Earnings*	*Quarterly Estimates of Annual Earnings*
1	$95,000	$400,000
2	85,000	370,000
3	92,000	370,000
4	96,000	N/A

The combined state and federal tax rate for 2008 is 30%. Sloan Company estimated it would have permanent differences between accounting income and taxable income during 2008. Each quarter's estimate of these annual differences is provided in the following table:

	Estimated Permanent Differences	
Estimate at End of Quarter	*Penalty for Pollution*	*Dividend Exclusion*
1	$14,000	$40,000
2	14,000	40,000
3	14,000	50,000

The actual amount of permanent differences for 2008 were environmental penalties, $14,000 dividend exclusion, $55,000.

Required:

Prepare journal entries to record Sloan Company's 2008 quarterly income tax provisions.

PROBLEM 14-7 **Various Interim Reporting Cases** LO11

The following statement is an excerpt from ASC 270–10–45–1, 2 [paragraphs 9 and 10 of *APB Opinion No. 28*, "Interim Financial Reporting"]:

> Interim financial information is essential to provide investors and others with timely information as to the progress of the enterprise. The usefulness of such information rests on the relationship that it has to the annual results of operations. Accordingly, the Board has concluded that each interim period should be viewed primarily as an integral part of an annual period.
>
> In general, the results for each interim period should be based on the accounting principles and practices used by an enterprise in the preparation of its latest annual financial statements unless a change in an accounting practice or policy has been adopted in the current year. The Board has concluded, however, that certain accounting principles and practices followed for annual reporting purposes may require modification at interim reporting dates so that the reported results for the interim period may better relate to the results of operations for the annual period.

Required:

Listed below are six independent cases on how accounting facts might be reported on an individual company's interim financial reports. For each case, state whether the method proposed to be used for interim reporting would be acceptable under generally accepted accounting principles applicable to interim financial data. Support each answer with a brief explanation.

A. Reed Company wrote inventory down to reflect lower of cost or market in the first quarter of 2005. At year-end the market value exceeds the original acquisition cost of this inventory. Consequently, management plans to write the inventory back up to its original cost as a year-end adjustment.

B. Greenfield Company realized a large gain on the sale of investments at the beginning of the second quarter. The company wants to report one-third of the gain in each of the remaining quarters.

C. Dole Company has estimated its annual audit fee. They plan to prorate this expense equally over all four quarters.

D. Fur Company was reasonably certain they would have an employee strike in the third quarter. As a result, they shipped heavily during the second quarter but plan to defer the recognition of the sales in excess of the normal sales volume. The deferred sales will be recognized as sales in the third quarter when the strike is in progress. Fur Company management thinks this is more nearly representative of normal second- and third-quarter operations.

E. Rexx Company takes a physical inventory at year-end for annual financial statement purposes. Inventory and cost of sales reported in the interim quarterly statements are based on estimated gross profit rates, because a physical inventory would result in a cessation of operations. Rexx Company does have reliable perpetual inventory records.

F. Shelley Company is planning to report one-fourth of its pension expense in each quarter.
(*CMA adapted*)

15

PARTNERSHIPS: FORMATION, OPERATION, AND OWNERSHIP CHANGES

LEARNING OBJECTIVES

1. Describe the characteristics of a general partnership, a limited partnership, and a joint venture.
2. List some important items to be included in the partnership agreement.
3. Understand the differences between partnerships' and corporations' equity accounts in the balance sheet.
4. Explain the purpose of the partners' drawing accounts and capital accounts.
5. Prepare journal entries to form a partnership using the bonus and the goodwill methods.
6. Describe some common agreements used to allocate partnership net income or loss.
7. Explain why salary allowances and interest allowances are used in allocating partnership profits and losses.
8. Describe the methods used to record partnership changes when a new partner is admitted or when a partner withdraws from the partnership.
9. Describe the rationale behind the goodwill method in accounting for changes in partnership membership.

"Sustainability can be a 2 + 2 = 5 (or even 50) game. To achieve outstanding triple bottom line performance, new types of economic, social, and environmental partnership are needed. Long-standing enemies must shift from mutual subversion to new forms of symbiosis. The resulting partnerships will help each partner perform traditional tasks more efficiently, while providing a platform from which to reach toward goals that none of the partners could hope to achieve on his own."[1]

The next two chapters deal exclusively with accounting and reporting problems associated with the partnership form of business organization. These chapters cover the complete life cycle of a partnership from its formation and operation to its liquidation. Partnerships are covered in this text because they are a common form of

[1] *Environmental Quality Management*, "Partnerships from Cannibals with Forks: The Triple Bottom Line of 21st-Century Business," by John Elkington, Autumn 1998, p. 37.

business organization. They are popular because they permit the pooling of limited resources, are easy to form (no special governmental approval is required), and may have certain tax advantages. Because partnerships are common, accountants are often called on to account for, and serve in, an advisory capacity to partnerships. Although many of the accounting concepts applicable to a sole proprietorship or a corporation are also applicable to partnerships, some aspects of partnership formation, operation, and liquidation require additional consideration. The unique aspects of accounting for a partnership are the focus of these chapters. Figure 15-1 presents a summary of statistics for partnerships in the United States from 2002 and 2003.

Accounting for a partnership is influenced by the agreement made among the partners and by the appropriate state statutes. Partnerships operate within the legal framework of the state in which they are organized and the statutes may vary from state to state. In order to illustrate statutory provisions, the Uniform Partnership Act (UPA) is integrated throughout the partnership chapters because it, or some modification thereof, is the partnership law that has been adopted by the majority of the

FIGURE 15-1

Partnership Statistics, 2002–2003

	Number of Partnerships				*Number of Partners*			
	2002		*2003*		*2002*		*2003*	
Industry Grouping	*Number*	*% of All Industries*	*Number*	*% of All Industries*	*Number*	*% of All Industries*	*Number*	*% of All Industries*
All industries	**2,242,169**		**2,375,375**		**14,328,108**		**14,108,458**	
Agriculture, forestry, fishing	117,667	5.2%	121,878	5.1%	441,697	3.1%	395,971	2.8%
Mining	29,549	1.3%	28,060	1.2%	508,417	3.5%	476,196	3.4%
Utilities	2,507	0.1%	2,491	0.1%	46,806	0.3%	55,072	0.4%
Construction	134,114	6.0%	140,495	5.9%	400,966	2.8%	415,581	2.9%
Manufacturing	38,364	1.7%	40,347	1.7%	207,357	1.4%	206,374	1.5%
Wholesale trade	37,800	1.7%	43,715	1.8%	139,856	1.0%	142,129	1.0%
Retail trade	122,013	5.4%	127,303	5.4%	348,663	2.4%	414,185	2.9%
Transportation and warehousing	26,007	1.2%	29,886	1.3%	557,404	3.9%	577,150	4.1%
Information	28,580	1.3%	31,804	1.3%	239,398	1.7%	369,701	2.6%
Finance and insurance	263,024	11.7%	258,990	10.9%	3,139,228	21.9%	3,089,160	21.9%
Real estate, rental, and leasing	999,786	44.6%	1,081,354	45.5%	6,328,546	44.2%	5,877,816	41.7%
Professional, scientific, and technical services	145,612	6.5%	151,076	6.4%	545,059	3.8%	541,138	3.8%
Holding companies	18,773	0.8%	21,579	0.9%	280,643	2.0%	236,675	1.7%
Administrative and support and waste management	44,405	2.0%	43,647	1.8%	106,975	0.7%	131,483	0.9%
Educational services	6,269	0.3%	9,084	0.4%	31,125	0.2%	26,755	0.2%
Health care and social assistance	47,468	2.1%	54,161	2.3%	238,773	1.7%	300,042	2.1%
Arts, entertainment, and recreation	42,691	1.9%	43,303	1.8%	269,175	1.9%	318,415	2.3%
Accommodation and food services	77,698	3.5%	81,341	3.4%	345,916	2.4%	374,520	2.7%
Other services	57,121	2.5%	62,667	2.6%	145,695	1.0%	154,705	1.1%
Nature of business not allocable	2,724	0.1%	2,193	0.1%	6,407	0.0%	5,390	0.0%

Adapted from *Statistics of Income Bulletin, Partnership Returns, 2003.* Fall 2005, U.S. Internal Revenue Service.

states. An in-depth study of the legal aspects of partnerships is generally contained in the typical business law course.

PARTNERSHIP DEFINED

A partnership is defined by the UPA as "an association of two or more persons to carry on as co-owners a business for profit."[2] Persons in this definition include individuals, partnerships, corporations, and other associations. Not only are corporations sometimes partners, but also partnerships can be shareholders in a corporation.

EToys Inc. is betting that a lot of American parents want to buy Barbie, Arthur and other favorite playthings without visiting the mall, let alone chasing screaming children down toy store aisles. "We're benefiting from eToys' success and are happy to be their partner", says a Mattel spokesman. If the eToys' offering is completed as planned, it will mean big gains for the firm's top management and a small squad of venture capitalists. The company's biggest shareholders are various partnerships affiliated with Idealab!, a business incubator and venture-capital firm run by inventor Bill Gross.[3]

In some cases, it may be difficult to determine whether a partnership has been formed or whether an individual is a partner in a business arrangement. To determine the existence of a partnership, it may be helpful to look for the following three attributes: (1) there must be an agreement, either expressed or implied, between two or more persons; (2) the business must be operated for the purpose of making a profit; and (3) members of the firm must be co-owners of the business. Co-ownership involves the right of each partner to share in the profits of the business, to participate in the management of the business, and to hold an interest in properties conveyed to the partnership. These rights are shared equally unless agreed to otherwise in the partnership agreement.

REASONS FOR FORMING A PARTNERSHIP

The prospective owner(s) of a business should consider the various attributes of the different forms of business organizations before selecting the one that they believe best meets their organizational objectives and personal goals. A form suitable for one set of business objectives may not be appropriate for another. It is possible for a firm to start as a proprietorship and, as the business and personal environments change, to move to a partnership form, and ultimately, to incorporate.

One of the major advantages of a partnership is that it permits the pooling of capital and other resources without the complexities and formalities of a corporation. A partnership is easier and less costly to establish than a corporation and is generally not subject to as much governmental regulation. Furthermore, the partners may be able to operate with more flexibility because they are subject neither to

[2] UPA, Section 6.

[3] *WSJ*, "EToys Plans to Join Web-Retailer Parade with Its Own IPO," by George Anders and Lisa Bannon, 4/6/99, p. B1.

the control of a board of directors nor to outside shareholders. There may also be certain tax advantages to a partnership, discussed later.

Chip Bell, senior partner with Performance Research Associates in Dallas, compares partnering to dancing. He suggests six steps to great partnerships:

- ***Focus***, or prepare to partner. There should be a clear commitment to some purpose.
- ***Audition***, or pick great partners. Auditions are about discovery and disclosure. Be open for warning cues.
- ***Rehearse***, or get the partnership in shape. Work the plan, ignoring opposition or objections.
- ***Dance***, or keep the magic in motion. Great partnerships keep going and growing.
- ***Hurt***, or manage the pain. Great dances are rarely flawless, and the capacity to bend and continue in the face of adversity makes for resilience.
- ***Bow out***, or know when to call it curtains.[4]

CHARACTERISTICS OF A PARTNERSHIP

LO1 Characteristics of a general partnership.

Some partnership characteristics may make it more difficult for a partnership to raise capital than for a corporation. Partnerships are thus most common in comparatively small businesses, professional organizations, such as medical clinics or an accounting practice, and some limited projects undertaken to accomplish a single goal, such as an oil and gas exploration project or the purchase of a parcel of real estate for investment purposes. However, there is no limit to the size or number of partners in a firm. For example, in the large international CPA firms, the number of partners is in the thousands and revenue is in the millions of dollars.

One distinctive characteristic of a partnership is its advantageous federal income tax treatment. A partnership is treated as a "flow through" entity from a federal income tax perspective and as such, income is not subject to taxation at the partnership level. A partnership must file an information return with the IRS in which income or loss is allocated to the individual partners. A partner's respective share of the income or loss is then reported on his or her individual income tax return, whether distributed by the partnership or not.

General Partnership

In a general partnership, each member is a general partner within the firm. That is, there is no "limited partner" in the organization. The following are characteristics of a general partnership.

Mutual Agency Every general partner is an agent of both the partnership and every other partner. Thus, a partner can bind the other partners to a contract if he or she is acting within the apparent scope of the business. Outside parties transacting business with a partner can assume the partner has the power to bind the partnership unless they are informed otherwise. Outside parties should be aware, however, that for certain acts, such as the assignment of partnership property, unanimous consent of the partners is required.

[4]Adapted from *Dance Lessons: Six Steps to Great Partnerships in Business and Life*, by Chip Bell and Heather Shea (St. Paul, MN: Highbridge Company, 1998). Also see *Executive Excellence*, "Steps to Great Partnerships," by Chip Bell and Heather Shea, March 1999, pp. 5–6.

Right to Dispose of a Partnership Interest A capital interest in a general partnership is a personal asset of the individual partner that can be sold or disposed of in any legal way. However, the UPA, recognizing the highly personal relationship of the partners, provides that a purchaser of another partner's interest does not have the right to participate in management unless he or she is accepted by all the partners. The new partner is entitled to the profit allocation acquired and, in the event of liquidation, to receive whatever assets the selling partner would have received had he or she continued in the partnership.

Unlimited Liability In a ***general partnership***, each partner is jointly and severally liable for the debts and obligations of the partnership. This means that in the case of liquidation, the creditors of the partnership, if not satisfied from assets of the partnership, can look to each partner's personal resources for recovery of unsatisfied claims. Jointly and severally means that a creditor can seek recovery from all the partners or can proceed against one or more of them separately.

Limited or Uncertain Life A general partnership may be dissolved for a number of reasons, including the death of a partner, the bankruptcy of an individual partner, the withdrawal of a partner from the partnership, or a judgment by a court that a partner is unsound of mind and incapable of performing his or her partnership duties.

The characteristics just discussed underline the importance of careful selection of the individuals to be associated in a general partnership. In particular, mutual agency and unlimited liability are distinctive features of a general partnership that could result in extensive personal liability resulting from the acts of other partners.

Recently, state laws have authorized the existence of a popular new form of general partnership known as a ***limited liability partnership (LLP)***. An LLP addresses the issue of unlimited liability by granting partners personal protection from partnership obligations arising from the actions of other partners. However, partners are still held personally liable for their own actions and those of others under their authority.

"Partnerships aren't for everyone. They require an investment of energy and demand vulnerability. And partnerships diminish the protection of anonymity. They are poor associations in which to hide. Partnership means working onstage, not backstage. Done well, partnerships work at amplifying disclosure and enhancing exposure."[5]

Limited Partnership

LO1 Characteristics of a limited partnership.

In a ***limited partnership***, one or more of the partners are general partners and one or more are limited partners. While general partners manage the firm and are personally liable for obligations of the partnership, limited partners invest capital only and limit their liability for partnership obligations to the amount of their investment.

[5] *Executive Excellence*, "Steps to Great Partnerships," by Chip Bell and Heather Shea, March 1999, pp. 5–6.

In return, limited partners give up the right to participate in the management of the firm.

The limited partnership form of organization is selected when the general partners want to raise capital without giving up management control of the business. It is also an attractive form when the tax benefits associated with a partnership are desired, but the investors do not want to assume personal liability for the obligations of the partnership. For these reasons, the limited partnership form is often used for professional sports franchises and offerings of partnership interests made to the public for the purpose of carrying out a specific business plan, such as real estate ventures or oil and gas exploration projects.

"Gene Phillips was at the helm when a now-defunct real estate partnership firm called Southmark sank into bankruptcy. His investors lost heavily. Phillips lived lavishly in Texas. . . . They say on Wall Street of limited partnerships: In the beginning, the limited partners have the money and the general partner has the experience. In the end the roles are reversed, especially if Gene Phillips is in the picture."[6]

Joint Ventures

LO1 Characteristics of a joint venture.

A ***joint venture*** is an arrangement entered into by two or more parties to accomplish a single or limited purpose for the mutual benefit of the members of the group, often to earn a profit. For example, a firm in one country may enter into an agreement with a firm of another country to pool their resources to construct an automobile manufacturing plant, or two or more firms may enter into an arrangement to develop a new product that requires complementary technological knowledge. Thus, the life of the joint venture is limited to that of the undertaking, which may be of short- or long-term duration.

The relationship between the parties in the arrangement is generally governed by a written agreement. A distinguishing characteristic of the agreement is that each joint venturer participates directly or indirectly in the overall management of the resources. Accordingly, major decisions require the consent of the ownership group.

Joint ventures are commonly organized as corporations or partnerships. If organized as a corporation, the investment in the joint venture generally must be accounted for using the equity method in accordance with the provisions of *Accounting Principles Board Opinion No. 18*.[7] As a corporation, a joint venture is governed by corporate law. If the arrangement is a partnership joint venture, interpretations of *Opinion No. 18* indicate that many of the provisions of that opinion are appropriate in accounting for the investment.[8] In general, partnership law applies to a partnership joint venture, but the authority of a joint venturer is limited to a greater extent than that of a general partner. For example, as a general rule, one party to the arrangement is not an agent of the other parties.

[6] *Forbes*, "The Old Double Dip," by Gretchen Morgenson, 7/7/97, pp. 54–56.

[7] *Opinion of the Accounting Principles Board No. 18*, "The Equity Method of Accounting for Investments in Common Stock" (New York: AICPA, 1971). [ASC 323]

[8] *Accounting Interpretations of APB Opinion No. 18* (New York: AICPA, 1972), par. 2. [ASC 323-30-15-3]

PARTNERSHIP AGREEMENT

LO2 Important items in a partnership agreement.

A partnership is a voluntary association based on the contractual agreement between or among legally competent persons. The contract between the parties is called the ***partnership agreement, partnership contract***, or ***articles of partnership***. The partnership agreement generally contains provisions related to the nature of the business, operating policies, and the relations between the partners in operating and terminating the business. In the contract, the partners should clearly express their intention, and the document should cover all aspects of operating the partnership. If there are subsequent disputes and the partners are unable to reach a satisfactory agreement, it may be necessary to resort to litigation.

The partnership agreement should reflect fully the precise intentions of the parties and be as unambiguous as possible. The agreement should include the following important points:

1. The name of the firm and identity of the partners.
2. The nature, purpose, and scope of the business.
3. The effective date of organization.
4. The length of time the partnership is to operate.
5. Location of the place of business.
6. Provision for the allocation of profit and loss.
7. Provision for salaries and withdrawals of assets by partners.
8. The rights, duties, and obligations of each partner such as the amount of time each partner will spend on business activities, and whether each partner is a general or limited partner.
9. Authority of each partner in contract situations.
10. Procedures for admitting a new partner.
11. Provisions that specify how operations are to be conducted and how the various partners' interests are to be satisfied on the withdrawal or the death of a partner.
12. Procedures for the arbitration of disputes.
13. Fiscal period of the partnership.
14. Identification and valuation of initial asset investments and the specification of capital interest that each partner is to receive.
15. Situations that may cause the dissolution of the partnership and provisions for terminating or continuing the business.
16. Accounting practices to be followed, such as depreciation policies, the sequence of closing procedures, and whether the cash or accrual basis is to be used in measuring net income.
17. Whether or not an audit is to be performed.

Some of the items listed will be discussed in more detail in later sections.

The law does not specify the form of the agreement. Although it may be oral, it is good business practice to have the agreement in writing for the protection of the individual partners. A written agreement tends to reduce the number of disagreements resulting from misunderstandings and "loss of memory."

Legally, the partners have a great deal of flexibility in drafting an agreement among themselves, but they must recognize that the UPA specifies certain rights of and obligations to outside parties that may not be avoided by the individual partners. For example, as noted previously, the UPA (Section 15) imposes unlimited liability on each general partner for partnership debts and obligations. A provision in a partnership agreement that exempts a general partner from this obligation would be superseded by the provision in the UPA.

In drafting the agreement, the partners should seek both legal and accounting assistance to assure that their rights are protected and to help anticipate and avoid as many points of conflict as possible. If there are later disputes related to the relations among the partners, most provisions set out in the UPA control only if the partners have failed to make an express agreement, or if the partners are unable to reach a mutually satisfying agreement. For example, in the absence of an agreement concerning how to share profits, the UPA provides that profits are to be shared equally. Differences arising from ordinary matters may be decided by a majority vote of the partners [UPA, Section 18(H)].

The Greatest Show on Earth

William Cameron Coup organized a show in 1869 that staged simultaneous performances in two rings. He later formed a partnership with P.T. Barnum, and in 1871 they opened "The Greatest Show On Earth" in Brooklyn, N.Y. About ten years later, Barnum went into partnership with James Anthony Bailey, another American showman and one of the best organizers in the business, and with two other impresarios. Eventually, however, Barnum and Bailey became sole partners, with their circus giving simultaneous shows in three rings.[9]

Capital Interest versus Profit Interest

In preparing the partnership agreement, the partners must recognize that there is a distinction between a partner's capital interest and his or her interest in income and losses subsequently reported by the partnership. A partner's ***capital interest*** is a claim against the net assets of the partnership as shown by the balance in the partner's capital account; an ***interest in income and loss*** determines how the partner's capital interest will increase or decrease as a result of subsequent operations. The partners may agree that an individual partner is to receive a one-third capital interest in the partnership, but the same partner's interest in income and loss may be equal to, greater than, or less than one-third.

ACCOUNTING FOR A PARTNERSHIP

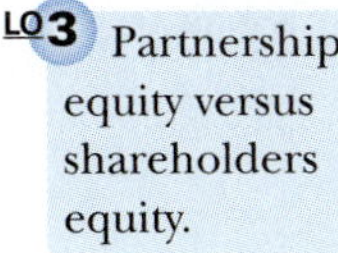

For accounting purposes, a partnership is considered a separate economic and accounting entity. The assets, liabilities, and residual capital interest, as well as the transactions and events that affect the accounts of the partnership, are areas of interest that require a separate accounting to provide information to the partners and other interested parties. Separation of these activities from the personal transactions of the individual partners is necessary in order to evaluate the performance of the partnership. This does not mean that other forms of statements cannot be prepared for other purposes. For example, a general partner has unlimited liability to the creditors of the partnership. Accordingly, the creditors may require information

[9] From *Funk and Wagnalls' New Encyclopedia*, Cambridge, MA: Funk and Wagnalls, Corp., 1996. *Infopedia*, SoftKey Multimedia Inc., 1996.

concerning the personal assets and debt position of individual partners, as well as the financial statements of the firm.

There is significantly more freedom in choosing a partnership accounting method than for other types of organizations, such as a corporation. While it is generally assumed that accounting for a partnership basically adheres to the same generally accepted accounting principles as accounting for a proprietorship or a corporation, it should be noted that small or specialized partnerships may utilize either cash basis or tax basis accounting as opposed to GAAP. Since partnerships are required to submit informational returns to the IRS that help determine individual partners' federal income tax, tax-based accounting may provide these partnerships with added convenience over GAAP-based accounting. While these varying methods are acceptable, this text will assume GAAP-based partnership accounting.

The primary difference in accounting for the different forms of organization is in the recording and reporting of capital transactions. A corporation's equity section reports the different sources of capital (for example, the issue of capital stock, additional paid-in capital from various sources, and retained earnings). Because each share of common stock has the same proportional interest in net income, dividends, voting rights, and assets in liquidation as any other share of the same class of stock, a separate capital account for each shareholder is not needed. However, in the case of a partnership, the capital interest in assets of each partner can vary. In addition, the partners' interest in net income or loss can vary and may not be proportional to their respective capital interests. As a result, the relationship of the partners' capital interest will change over time. To report the interest of each partner, a partnership's equity section normally consists of two accounts for each partner: one capital account and one drawing account.

LO4 Drawing and capital accounts.

Practice varies as to which of the two accounts is changed by capital transactions. Generally, investments and withdrawals of assets considered to be other than temporary are recorded in the capital account. The drawing account is typically debited to record withdrawals of assets in anticipation of profitable operations or payments of personal expenses of a partner from partnership assets. It is common practice to close the income summary account to either the drawing account or the capital account. The drawing account may be closed periodically to the capital account. The various sources of capital may thus be combined into one account. In this text, the income summary account and each partner's drawing account will be closed to the appropriate partners' capital accounts.

To illustrate the entries, assume that Ed Bell and Jane Peters operate a partnership in which they each originally contributed $25,000 cash. In the current year, income of $60,000 is to be allocated equally and each partner withdraws $1,000 per month or $12,000 a year. The entries follow:

At the beginning of the partnership:

Cash	50,000	
Bell, Capital		25,000
Peters, Capital		25,000
To form the partnership.		

Each month to record withdrawals:

Bell, Drawing	1,000	
Peters, Drawing	1,000	
Cash		2,000
To record monthly withdrawals.		

At the end of the period:

Income Summary	60,000	
Bell, Capital		30,000
Peters, Capital		30,000
To close the income summary account.		
Bell, Capital	12,000	
Peters, Capital	12,000	
Bell, Drawing		12,000
Peters, Drawing		12,000
To close the partners' drawing accounts.		

Generally, the same accounting concepts are used to determine net income for proprietorships, partnerships, and corporations. There are, however, several differences. First, because a partnership is not subject to income tax, no income tax expense is reported in the income statement. Second, interest on capital investment and salaries to partners have traditionally been treated as allocations of net income, rather than as expenses of the business. This practice is considered appropriate under the proprietary theory view of the firm in which all transactions with the owners are viewed as capital transactions. In other words, no revenue or expense should be recognized in transactions with the partners. Also, since the partners are owners of the business, the interest and salaries may not represent objectively determined amounts.

In addition to the transactions discussed before that affect a partner's capital interest, an individual partner may also lend cash to the partnership that may be accounted for as a liability of the partnership. A partner may also borrow cash from the partnership with the intention of repaying the loan to the partnership. In contrast to capital transactions, such as the withdrawal of assets as part of a profit allocation, an advance to a partner is accounted for as a receivable of the partnership, provided that the receivable satisfies the normal tests of collectibility. Generally accepted accounting standards should also be followed in accounting for, and disclosing, receivables from officers or members of a firm.

Recording the Formation of a Partnership

Assets invested in the partnership, any debts assumed by the partnership, and the capital interest each partner is to receive should be specified in the partnership agreement. A listing of partnership assets is important, because creditors of the partnership must satisfy their claims from partnership assets before seeking recovery of unpaid claims from the personal assets of individual partners.

Assets invested in the partnership can be either cash or noncash assets, such as a patent, land, or equipment. Noncash assets invested in the partnership are properly recorded at fair values on the date of investment.[10] Liabilities assumed by the partnership should also be recorded at their fair values.

Once the partners agree as to the identification and valuation of assets being invested, liabilities being assumed by the partnership, and the capital interest that each partner is to receive, the assets, liabilities, and equities are recorded on the

[10] *Accounting Principles Board Opinion No. 29*, "Accounting for Nonmonetary Transactions" (New York: AICPA, 1973), par. 18. Recall that the assets contributed retain their original *tax* basis [ASC 845–10–30–1].

books of the partnership. To illustrate, assume that the following items are being invested to form WY Partnership:

	Agreed Fair Values	
	Investment by Wright	*Investment by Young*
Cash	$10,000	$10,000
Inventory	10,000	—
Land	—	20,000
Building	—	40,000
Equipment	20,000	—0—
Totals	40,000	70,000
Mortgage on building assumed by the partnership	—0—	20,000
Net assets invested	$40,000	$50,000

The journal entry to record the initial investment, assuming that Wright and Young agree that each partner is to receive a capital credit equal to the fair value of the net assets each partner invested, is as follows:

Cash	20,000	
Inventory	10,000	
Land	20,000	
Building	40,000	
Equipment	20,000	
Mortgage Payable		20,000
Wright, Capital		40,000
Young, Capital		50,000

LO5 Recording the formation of a partnership.

A problem results if the sum of the agreed net asset values does not equal the negotiated capital interest or if the agreement is unclear. For example, there are several possible interpretations of an agreement that each partner is to receive an equal capital interest. Two possible types of entries, the bonus method and the goodwill method, might be used to record the formation. Assuming the facts in the preceding paragraph, these entries are as follows:

	I		*II*	
	Bonus Method		*Goodwill Method*	
Cash	20,000		20,000	
Inventory	10,000		10,000	
Land	20,000		20,000	
Building	40,000		40,000	
Equipment	20,000		20,000	
Intangible Asset*	—		10,000	
Mortgage Payable		20,000		20,000
Wright, Capital		45,000		50,000
Young, Capital		45,000		50,000

* Generally referred to as partnership goodwill.

Under the ***bonus*** method, there is a capital interest transfer of $5,000 from Young to Wright to equalize the capital balances. Such an entry is made if Young recognizes that Wright is contributing something to the firm other than tangible assets, but the partners are reluctant to recognize an intangible asset, or a value for it cannot be determined objectively. Under the ***goodwill*** method, if equal capital interests are to be given to each partner, Wright's capital is increased by $10,000. This is accomplished by recognizing an intangible asset of $10,000 with a corresponding increase in the credit to the capital account of Wright. It is assumed that Wright is contributing something of value to the partnership that is intangible in nature, and which could not be specifically identified. The value assigned to the intangible asset could have been more than $10,000. Young may also be contributing an intangible asset to the partnership in addition to the tangible assets identified and valued. Unless the intangible is specifically identifiable, such as a patent, it should probably ***not*** be recognized. It is difficult to justify the recognition of an unspecified intangible such as goodwill on the books of a ***new*** partnership that does not have an established earnings record.

Allocation of Net Income or Net Loss

The partners should include in the articles of partnership a provision indicating how income and losses are to be allocated. The profit and loss agreement determines how much each partner's interest in the firm increases or decreases as a result of operations. Often one of the major problems of accounting for a partnership is to determine the intent of the partners as indicated in the partnership agreement. The partners have much flexibility in the area. However, to avoid disagreement and potential litigation, the profit and loss agreement should be explicitly stated. In the absence of an agreement, courts have generally concluded that the intent of the parties was to allocate profits and losses equally. If a provision for profits, but not losses, is included in the agreement, the courts have generally concluded that losses should be allocated in the same ratio that profits are allocated. Therefore, the partnership agreement should state whether losses are to be allocated differently than profits.

The objective of the profit and loss agreement should be to reward the individual partners for their contributions of resources to the partnership. Some of the more common agreements are based on some combination of the following:

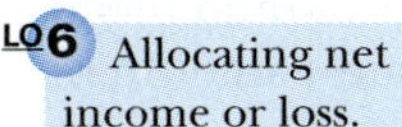
LO6 Allocating net income or loss.

1. A fixed ratio.
2. A ratio based on capital balances.
3. Interest on capital investment.
4. An allocation for time or managerial talent devoted to the partnership operation, either in the form of a fixed salary allocation or a bonus as a percentage of income.

Partnerships have a number of allocation possibilities and sometimes use several of the following strategies to allocate income or losses. Unless otherwise stated, income for the period is assumed to be $20,000 in the following examples.

Fixed Ratio One of the simplest agreements is for each partner to be allocated profit or loss each period on the basis of an equal percentage or some other specified ratio. For example, Adams and Brown may agree that profit and loss are to be allocated in the ratio 7:3. A profit of $20,000 would be allocated $14,000 to Adams and $6,000 to Brown. The entry to close the Income Summary account would take the following form:

Income Summary	20,000	
Adams, Capital		14,000
Brown, Capital		6,000

Note that the allocation determines the increase in each partner's interest in net assets resulting from operations. It has nothing to do with the withdrawals of assets by partners, which are recorded as debits to the capital or drawing accounts.

Unless stated otherwise, a loss of $20,000 would also be allocated using a 7:3 ratio. If this is not the intent of the partners, a separate loss agreement should be stipulated.

Capital Balances Assets invested in the partnership are important resources. The allocation of profits on the basis of the ratio of capital balances may result in an equitable allocation of profits when the operation of the partnership requires little of the partners' time, such as the operation of an apartment building in which there is a hired manager. To avoid conflicts, the capital ratio should be based upon the capital balance at a specific point in time, such as the amount of original investment, beginning-of-year balances, on average, or end-of-year balances. Allocations based on beginning and ending balances could be inequitable. For example, if the allocation ratio is based on ending balances, a partner could make a large capital investment at the end of the year. To avoid such abuse, partners may want to specify restrictions or use a weighted-average capital balance.

Assuming that the ratio is based on beginning capital balances and that Adams and Brown had balances of $60,000 and $40,000, respectively, the net income of $20,000 would be allocated as follows:

Capital Investment		*Net Income Allocation*
Adams	$ 60,000	($60,000/$100,000) × $20,000 = $12,000
Brown	40,000	($40,000/$100,000) × $20,000 = 8,000
	$100,000	$20,000

Net income allocation based on a weighted-average capital investment ratio is computed in Illustration 15-1. The weighted average is computed by multiplying the various capital balances that each partner maintained during the year by the fraction of the year that a particular capital balance was maintained. The $20,000 net income is allocated on the basis of the ratio of the weighted-average capital investment.

The allocation of a loss on the basis of the ratio of capital balances would mean that Adams, who has invested the most capital, would absorb the greatest amount of

ILLUSTRATION 15-1

Computation of Weighted-Average Capital Balances

Adams, Capital	(A) *Increase (Decrease) in Capital*	(B) *Cumulative Capital Balance*	(C) *Fraction of Year in Months*	(D) *Weighted Average (B) × (C)*
January 1 Beginning Balance		$60,000	3/12	$15,000
April 1 Added $30,000 Investment	$ 30,000	90,000	3/12	22,500
July 1 Withdrew $10,000	(10,000)	80,000	6/12	40,000
Weighted-Average Capital Balance				$77,500
Brown, Capital				
January 1 Beginning Balance		40,000	9/12	$30,000
October 1 Withdrew $10,000	$(10,000)	30,000	3/12	7,500
Weighted-Average Capital Balance				$37,500

Weighted-Average Investment		*Net Income Allocation*	
Adams	$ 77,500	($77,500/$115,000) × $20,000 =	$13,478
Brown	37,500	($37,500/$115,000) × $20,000 =	6,522
	$115,000		$20,000

the loss, which may be considered an unreasonable allocation. If this is the case, the partners may want to stipulate a different ratio for the allocation of losses.

Interest on Capital Investment Using the ratio of capital balances as the basis for allocation of profit assumes that invested capital is the most important resource of the partnership. However, in many profit-making organizations, other important resources should also be recognized. To accomplish this and still provide an equitable allocation, the partners may want to provide for interest on capital investment and allocate the remaining income on some other basis. Such a provision may also provide an incentive for additional capital to be invested, if necessary. The agreement should specify a minimum:

1. The interest rate,
2. The proper capital balance (beginning, ending, or average),
3. How remaining profits should be allocated, and
4. Whether or not interest should still be allocated in case of loss or in case profits are less than the agreed interest allocation.

LO7 Using interest allowances in allocating profits and losses.

Frequently, the interest allocation is based on weighted-average capital investment. To illustrate, assume the average investment in Illustration 15-1. Interest is then computed on this amount. Assuming a net income of $20,000, an 8% rate of interest, and that any remaining profit is to be divided equally, the profit (or loss, if negative) is allocated as follows:

Interest Allocation	*Adams*	*Brown*	*Total*
$77,500 × .08 =	$ 6,200		$ 6,200
37,500 × .08 =		$3,000	3,000
Total interest allocated	6,200	3,000	9,200
Remainder shared equally	5,400	5,400	10,800
Total to be allocated	$11,600	$8,400	$20,000

LO7 Using Salary allowance in allocating profits and losses.

Salary The partners may provide, as part of the profit and loss formula, a salary allowance in recognition of personal services rendered by a partner. The amount by which net income exceeds the salary allowances may then be divided by any ratio agreed upon by the partners. For example, if Adams devotes full time to the business activity and Brown spends a limited amount of time, the partnership agreement may specify that Adams is allowed a salary of $1,000 per month and that the remaining income is to be divided on the basis of the ratio of the beginning capital balances ($60,000 and $40,000, respectively). The allocation would be as follows:

	Adams	*Brown*	*Total*
Salary allowance	$12,000	$—0—	$12,000
Remainder			
($60,000/$100,000) × $8,000	4,800		
($40,000/$100,000) × $8,000		3,200	8,000
	$16,800	$3,200	$20,000

A salary agreement is considered part of the profit and loss allocation formula and may be made independent of the agreement between the partners as to the right to withdraw cash or other assets from the partnership. The withdrawal of cash reduces the partner's capital interest (debit to the drawing account) but plays no part in the allocation of net income. Since the term ***salary*** is normally understood to mean a cash payment for services received, it is important that the partners specify their intentions as to an allocation of profit or permission to withdraw assets.

Bonus Instead of basing the salary allocation on a fixed amount, the partners may provide for a bonus arrangement as a percentage of income or some other basis. Since a number of interpretations can result, the partners should explicitly state the basis to be used in calculating the bonus. Some possibilities based on net income are:

1. Net income before any allocation of income to partners (for example, before interest on capital, salaries to partners, and any bonus).
2. Net income after other income allocations, but before subtracting the bonus.
3. Net income after subtracting the bonus, but before subtracting the other allocations.
4. Net income after subtracting the bonus and other allocations from net income.

Calculation of the bonus in the first two alternatives is straightforward. To illustrate alternatives 3 and 4, assume that net income is $24,000, and a bonus of 20% is to be paid to Adams. Also, interest of $4,000 and $2,000 is to be allocated to Adams and Brown, respectively, and any remainder is to be allocated equally. The bonus and a proof of the calculation are as follows:

Alternative 3			*Alternative 4*		
Bonus	=	.2($24,000 − Bonus)	Bonus	=	.2($24,000 − $6,000 − Bonus)
Bonus	=	$4,800 − .2Bonus	Bonus	=	.2($18,000 − Bonus)
1.2 Bonus	=	$4,800	Bonus	=	$3,600 − .2Bonus
Bonus	=	$4,000	1.2 Bonus	=	$3,600
			Bonus	=	$3,000

Proof:

	Alternative 3	*Alternative 4*
Net income	$24,000	$24,000
Bonus	4,000	3,000
Interest		6,000
Income subject to bonus	$20,000	$15,000
	Bonus = .2($20,000)	Bonus = .2($15,000)
	Bonus = $4,000	Bonus = $3,000

Insufficient Income to Cover Allocation

In some cases, the partnership net income may be less than the interest and/or salary provided for in the partnership agreement. If the partners fail to provide for such an occurrence in the profit and loss formula, the established practice is to allocate the interest and/or salary as if sufficient income had been earned. The amount by which the salary and/or interest exceeds the net income is allocated to the individual partners in their agreed ratio for allocating residual income. For example, assume that Adams and Brown agree to divide profits as follows:

1. Salary: Adams, $4,000; Brown, $2,000.
2. Interest: 8% on average capital balances (see Illustration 15-1).
3. Remainder: To be divided equally.

A net income of $11,000 would be allocated as follows:

	Adams	Brown	Total
Salary	$ 4,000	$ 2,000	$ 6,000
Interest	6,200	3,000	9,200
	10,200	5,000	15,200
Excess allocation ($11,000 − $15,200)	(2,100)	(2,100)	(4,200)
Income allocation	$ 8,100	$ 2,900	$11,000

The entry to close the Income Summary account is:

Income Summary	11,000	
Adams, Capital		8,100
Brown, Capital		2,900

As will be shown in the next section, this procedure produces the same results as if each partner's salary and interest had been treated as an expense in the determination of the partnership net income or loss.

In the case of a loss of $20,000, the allocation would be as follows:

	Adams	Brown	Total
Salary	$ 4,000	$ 2,000	$ 6,000
Interest	6,200	3,000	9,200
	10,200	5,000	15,200
Excess allocation (−$20,000 − $15,200)	(17,600)	(17,600)	(35,200)
Loss allocation	$ (7,400)	$(12,600)	$(20,000)

To avoid such an allocation, the partners may elect to state an alternative allocation in the articles of partnership. Once again, this situation indicates the need for careful planning in drafting the partnership agreement.

TEST YOUR KNOWLEDGE

NOTE: Solutions to ***Test Your Knowledge*** questions are found at the end of each chapter before the end-of-chapter questions.

Multiple Choice

1. Bob and Tom form a partnership on January 1, 2008. Bob contributes $50,000, while Tom contributes $100,000 cash and a building worth $200,000. The building is subject to a mortgage of $40,000, which is assumed by the partnership. They agree to share profits and losses equally. Tom's capital account on January 1, 2008, should be:
   a. $300,000
   b. $280,000
   c. $155,000
   d. $260,000

SPECIAL PROBLEMS IN ALLOCATION OF INCOME AND LOSS

Salaries and Interest as an Expense

In the foregoing illustrations, salaries and interest were accounted for as an allocation of net income, rather than as an expense in the determination of net income. However, the partners may find the income statement more useful for evaluating the operating performance of the partnership if either or both salary and interest allocations were treated as an expense in the determination of net income. If the salary levels and interest rates are reasonable for the resources provided, the income statement for the partnership may be more comparable to income statements of nonpartnership forms of organization. To illustrate, assume that the partnership reported net income of $11,000 before the interest and salaries of the partners. The partners are to be allocated salaries and interest as follows:

	Adams	*Brown*
Salary	$4,000	$2,000
Interest	6,200	3,000

The partners agree to allocate residual income and loss evenly. Journal entries to record the salaries and interest would be:

Salary Expense	6,000	
Adams, Capital		4,000
Brown, Capital		2,000
Interest Expense	9,200	
Adams, Capital		6,200
Brown, Capital		3,000

Net loss for the period after salaries and interest would be $4,200, computed as follows:

Net income before salaries and interest		$11,000
Less: Salary expense	$6,000	
Less: Interest expense	9,200	15,200
Net loss		$ 4,200

After the revenue and expense accounts are closed, Income Summary would have a debit balance of $4,200, which would be allocated evenly to the partners as agreed. The following entry would be recorded to close the income summary account:

Adams, Capital	2,100	
Brown, Capital	2,100	
Income Summary		4,200

Changes in the capital accounts are presented here:

Adams, Capital

From Income Summary	2,100	Salary entry	4,000
		Interest entry	6,200
		Net change in capital	8,100

Brown, Capital

From Income Summary	2,100	Salary entry	2,000
		Interest entry	3,000
		Net change in capital	2,900

This procedure results in the same change in the capital accounts as if the salaries and interest were considered an allocation of profit. (See the previous illustration where profits were insufficient to cover salary and interest allocations.) The method of reporting that is selected should be the one that provides the most useful information to the partners. Since the normal practice is to recognize salaries and interest as an allocation of profit, any such amounts treated as an expense should be adequately disclosed so the statement reader can properly evaluate the operating performance of the firm.

Adjustment of Income of Prior Years

Errors may occur in accounting for partnership operations, such as failure to accrue or defer expenses or revenue, errors in the inventory count or pricing, or errors in the calculation or amortization of fixed assets. Problems in the allocation of profit and loss can result if (1) errors are discovered that occurred in specific prior years, and (2) the partners have altered the profit and loss agreement since the period in which the error occurred. In a corporation, an error correction is accounted for as an adjustment to the beginning retained earnings balance. However, in a partnership the correction is allocated to the individual partners' capital accounts. The allocation should be based on the profit and loss agreement in effect during the period of the error.

Other allocation problems may arise, such as market changes in assets being held for investment purposes that occur before a change in the allocation formula, or an adjustment for bad debts that cannot be attributed to any specific period. There is no clear-cut answer to such problems. Litigation can be avoided by providing for the treatment of such potential problems in the partnership agreement.

FINANCIAL STATEMENT PRESENTATION

The income statement, balance sheet, and statement of cash flows for a partnership presented in conformity with GAAP are prepared in much the same manner as they are for a corporation. The following is a list of some of the differences in partnership reporting:

1. On the balance sheet or in a supplementary schedule, changes in partner's equity during the year should be disclosed.[11]
2. Partners' salary allowances are generally recognized as an allocation of net income, not as an expense in the determination of net income.
3. There is no income tax expense. The partners report their share of the partnership income or loss for the period on their individual income tax returns.
4. Interest paid to a partner on a loan balance is recognized as an expense. Interest allowance on capital investment is considered an allocation of profit.

A statement of changes in partners' capital is prepared to disclose changes in the interest of each partner during the year as shown in Illustration 15-2. For some

[11] This disclosure is usually not made when the number of partners is very large. For example, some accounting firms have thousands of partners.

ILLUSTRATION 15-2
AB Partnership
Statement of Partners' Capital
for the Year Ended December 31, 2004

	Adams	*Brown*	*Total*
Capital Balance, January 1	$ 60,000	$40,000	$100,000
Add: Additional Investment	30,000	—0—	30,000
Net Income Allocation	16,800	3,200	20,000
	106,800	43,200	150,000
Less Withdrawals	10,000	10,000	20,000
Capital Balance, December 31	$ 96,800	$33,200	$130,000

external reporting purposes, such detail may not be considered necessary. The partnership capital, for example, may be reported as one amount, and the capital balance of each partner may be disclosed in a supplementary schedule or not disclosed at all.

CHANGES IN THE OWNERSHIP OF THE PARTNERSHIP

The UPA (Section 29) defines ***dissolution*** as "the change in the relation of the partners caused by any partner ceasing to be associated in the carrying on as distinguished from the winding up of the business." The partnership dissolution may be voluntary (for example, mutual agreement by the partners) or involuntary (for example, bankruptcy of an individual partner or the partnership itself). Although dissolution means the end of a specific relationship among the partners, it does not automatically result in the termination of business activity. For example, in some forms of dissolution, such as the bankruptcy of the partnership, the partnership operations are eventually terminated and the partnership ceases to exist. In other cases of dissolution the partnership may be dissolved, but the remaining partners may continue the normal operations of the partnership without any visible interruptions of the firm's operations.

In this chapter we consider the accounting problems associated with changes in the ownership of a continuing partnership. The changes that will be considered result from (1) admission of a new partner by the purchase of an interest directly from one or more current partners, which is frequently referred to as an assignment of a partnership interest, (2) admission of a new partner by investing assets in the partnership, and (3) withdrawal of a partner as a result of retirement or death. Unless precluded from doing so in the partnership agreement, generally a partner may insist on liquidation of the partnership in these forms of dissolutions. Because the going-concern value of the business is usually greater than its liquidation value, the partners may provide in the partnership agreement that such changes in the relations of the partners do not dissolve the partnership. Dissolution of the partnership in which operations are eventually terminated will be covered in the next chapter.

Valuation—A Central Issue

When there is a change in the membership of the partnership, the problem of assigning a fair value to the firm arises. For example, if a partner withdraws from the partnership and there are no express provisions in the partnership agreement for determining the settlement, an equitable payment for his or her interest must be negotiated among the existing partners. Similarly, before admission, an incoming partner must negotiate with the existing partners an equitable purchase price for the interest he or she acquires. The settlement or purchase price is based on a number of factors, one of which is the fair values of the partnership assets. However, the fair values of the partnership assets are generally not reflected on the partnership books. In accordance with generally accepted accounting standards, partnership assets are recorded at cost, and subsequent increases in their market value are not recognized.

LO9 Rationale behind the goodwill method.

One approach is to first revalue assets and liabilities to their fair values and record any identifiable unrecorded assets and liabilities before recording the admission or withdrawal of a partner. In addition, the settlement price paid to a withdrawing partner or the purchase price paid by a new partner may be used to infer a value for the firm as a whole. Any difference between the value of the firm implied by the payment and the fair value of the net assets may be assigned to an intangible asset frequently referred to as partnership goodwill. An increase or decrease in net assets is allocated to the appropriate partners in their profit or loss ratio. Under this approach, the use of fair values provides an equitable measure of each partner's capital interest in the partnership. Furthermore, when a new partner is admitted, failure to recognize fair values will result in unrecorded value changes realized later being allocated in the profit- and loss-sharing ratio unless a separate provision is made. An unrecorded increase in value would benefit the new partner, whereas an unrecorded decrease would be a detriment. Revaluation of assets and liabilities is supported on the basis that, in dissolution, the old partnership is dissolved and a new entity is formed.

In practice, some accountants are reluctant to recognize a change in the value of an asset, even though there may be objective evidence that a specific asset is undervalued. They argue that recording an increase in fair value for external reporting purposes is not in accordance with generally accepted accounting practice and that economic substance should take precedence over legal form. That is, even though the partnership may be legally dissolved, the economic substance of some types of dissolution is that the business activity continues without interruption. Proponents of this method would retain the historical cost carrying value, and either prescribe in the agreement that unrecorded changes in value will not be shared with a new partner when realized, or will require a disproportionately high capital investment in relation to the new partner's income-sharing percentage. In this chapter, the revaluation of assets is shown as one of the approaches to recording changes in ownership because it is commonly advocated as an acceptable alternative and its use has some merit.

Methods of Recording Changes in the Membership of the Partnership

Two methods are frequently used to record changes in partnership membership:

LO8 Recording partnership changes.

1. ***The bonus method.*** When this method is used, the assets of the partnership are increased by the amount of the assets invested by the partner being admitted. Any difference between the assets invested and the credit to the new partner's capital account is adjusted to the capital accounts of the other partners involved in the negotiations. If a partner withdraws from a partnership, the partners may agree

to settle his or her capital interest by permitting the withdrawal of partnership assets. If the bonus method is used to record the withdrawal, the difference between the recorded value of the assets withdrawn and the debit to the withdrawing partner's capital account is adjusted to the capital accounts of the remaining partners.

2. ***The goodwill method.*** When this method is used, a new asset is recorded that is based on the difference between the value implied by the amount of consideration negotiated in the admission or withdrawal of a partner and the values reported in the partnership books.

Whether the bonus method or goodwill method is used, unrecorded changes in the value of existing assets and liabilities that are objectively determinable may be recorded before the change in membership is recorded.

As will be demonstrated, if certain limited conditions related to the profit and loss agreement are satisfied, the bonus and goodwill methods will produce the same result. If these conditions are met, the use of the bonus method precludes the problem of recording an intangible asset.

The bonus and goodwill methods are used for either ***admission of a new partner*** or the ***withdrawal of a partner***, described in the following sections A and B.

SECTION A: ADMISSION OF A NEW PARTNER

An individual may acquire an interest in a partnership: (1) by purchasing all or part of an interest directly from one or more existing partners (this transaction occurs outside the partnership and represents a transfer of assets between individuals), or (2) by being admitted as an additional partner on the investment of assets in the firm. Generally, the individual invests cash and/or other assets (for example, land, patent rights, equipment, marketable securities). A new partner could be admitted, however, by contributing a resource such as managerial talent. Because accountants ordinarily do not record such assets, unless the partners agree to transfer capital to the new partner's account, he or she will begin with a zero capital balance.

Assignment of an Interest by an Existing Partner

LO8 Methods to record partnership changes.

A partner is entitled to sell his or her interest in the firm, but no partner can be forced to accept a new member to the partnership. The UPA (Section 27) provides that the purchasing party acquire only the right to receive profits and assets in the event of liquidation to which the selling partner would otherwise be entitled. The purchaser does not acquire the right to participate in management unless all remaining partners agree to grant this right. The mere act of selling an interest does not dissolve the partnership, because the overall relation of the partners is not changed.

In the following illustrations, it is assumed that the partnership currently consists of two partners, Alan Adams and Bill Brown, with respective capital interests of $60,000 and $40,000. Adams and Brown share income and losses in the ratio of 6:4. Both partners agree to the admission of a new partner.

Acquisition of Interest by Payment to One Partner If an individual acquires an interest in a partnership by making payment directly to an existing partner, the interest acquired is recorded in a new capital account by transferring a corresponding amount equal to the percentage interest acquired from the selling partner's capital account. For example, assume that Adams sold one-half of his interest in the firm to Carol Call for $36,000. The only entry necessary on the partnership books is to record the transfer of capital interest from the selling partner to the capital account established for the new partner. The entry is:

Adams, Capital (.50 × $60,000)	30,000	
Call, Capital		30,000

The following should be noted:

1. Since this is a personal transaction between the two individuals, the entry is the same regardless of the amount paid by Call directly to Adams.
2. Net assets and equities of the firm are not changed as a direct result of the transaction, since the sale was negotiated outside the partnership. However, as noted earlier, the partners may choose to revalue assets and liabilities.
3. The amount of capital transferred to Call is equal to Adams' recorded capital multiplied by the percentage interest in Adams' capital acquired by Call.
4. Call now has a capital interest of 30% ($30,000 of total interest of $100,000), but her profit interest does not have to equal this percentage.

A simplified balance sheet after the admission of Call would be as follows:

Net assets	$100,000	Adams, Capital	$ 30,000
		Brown, Capital	40,000
		Call, Capital	30,000
Total	$100,000	Total	$100,000

Acquisition of an Interest by Payment to More Than One Partner If Call had purchased a 30% interest from each partner for $36,000, the entry would be:

Adams, Capital (.30 × $ 60,000)	18,000	
Brown, Capital (.30 × $ 40,000)	12,000	
Call, Capital (.30 × $100,000)		30,000

The observations outlined before when the purchase was made from one partner apply in this case as well. Furthermore, this entry has no effect on how the cash payment made by Call is to be distributed to Adams and Brown outside the partnership. The amount and distribution of cash is a negotiated transaction between individuals and does not affect the partnership accounts unless the amount is used as a basis for the revaluation of the firm.

Goodwill Implied by the Purchase Price In the foregoing examples, the amount paid by Call to gain admission to the firm was ignored in recording the transfer of interest. This procedure is often referred to as the bonus method. Some argue that the payment of $36,000 for a $30,000 interest in the partnership indicates that the firm has assets that are unrecorded or undervalued. The assumption is that the negotiated purchase price took into consideration such factors as the fair values of the firm's assets, the present value of the firm's liabilities, and the valuation of the firm on the basis of future prospects. Thus, the payment can be used to approximate the value of the firm. If Call is willing to pay $36,000 for a 30% interest in the firm, then

ILLUSTRATION 15-3

Schedule of Account Balances

	Net Assets	+	*Goodwill*	=	*Capital* *Adams*	+	*Capital* *Brown*	+	*Capital* *Call*
Book Values	$100,000	+	$—0—	=	$(60,000)	+	$(40,000)	+	$ —0—
Record Goodwill			20,000		(12,000)		(8,000)		—0—
	100,000	+	20,000	=	(72,000)	+	(48,000)	+	—0—
Transfer of Capital					21,600		14,400		(36,000)
Balance after Admission of Call	$100,000	+	$20,000	=	$(50,400)	+	$(33,600)	+	$(36,000)

the implied value of the partnership net assets is $120,000 ($36,000 ÷ .30). Net assets and capital should be increased $20,000 from the recorded amounts of $100,000. Since this represents an unrecorded increase in the value of the firm's assets, the increase in assets of $20,000 is allocated to Adams and Brown in their profit-sharing ratio. To the extent that the excess cannot be assigned to specific identifiable recorded assets, the remaining amount is recorded as partnership goodwill. Assuming that the book values of assets and liabilities equal their fair values, the entries to record the increase in assets and admission of Call are as follows:

Goodwill	20,000	
Adams, Capital (.60 × $20,000)		12,000
Brown, Capital (.40 × $20,000)		8,000
Adams, Capital (.30 × $ 72,000)	21,600	
Brown, Capital (.30 × $ 48,000)	14,400	
Call, Capital (.30 × $120,000, also equal to cash paid)		36,000

This results in account balances as presented in Illustration 15-3.

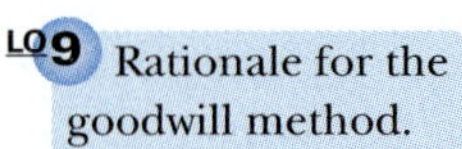

Rationale for the goodwill method.

Comparison of Bonus and Goodwill Methods In the illustration, Call is credited with a 30% interest in the firm under the bonus and the goodwill methods. To assist the partners in making a decision between the two methods, it may be helpful to demonstrate the effects of the two methods on their respective capital balances. If the firm were forced to liquidate, the goodwill would probably be of no value and, therefore, would represent a loss to the partnership.

The bonus and goodwill methods will yield the same result if two conditions related to the new profit and loss agreement are met. These are:

1. The new partner's profit-sharing percentage must be equal to his or her initial percentage interest in capital. In this illustration, Call received a capital interest of 30%. Her profit-sharing ratio must be 30%.
2. The old partner's profit-sharing ratio in the new partnership must be relatively the same as it was in the old partnership. Thus, if Call is to receive 30% of the profit in the new partnership, Adams and Brown must receive the remaining 70%. To be in the same relative ratio of 6:4, Adams must receive 42% (.6 ×.70) of profits, and Brown must receive 28% (.4 ×.70). The two methods are equivalent if, after recording goodwill impairment, the account balances are the same as they would be under the bonus method. The balances for each method are presented in Illustration 15-4.

ILLUSTRATION 15-4

Schedule of Account Balances

					Capital				
Goodwill Method	*Net Assets*	+	*Goodwill*	=	*Adams*	+	*Brown*	+	*Call*
Balances after recording goodwill and admitting Call	$100,000	+	$ 20,000	=	$(50,400)	+	$(33,600)	+	$(36,000)
Impairment of goodwill									
$20,000 × .42			(20,000)		8,400				
20,000 × .28							5,600		
20,000 × .30									6,000
Totals	$100,000	+	$—0—	=	$(42,000)	+	$(28,000)	+	$(30,000)
Bonus Method									
Balances after recording admission of Call	$100,000	+	$—0—	=	$(42,000)	+	$(28,000)	+	$(30,000)

The two methods will also yield the same results if the bonus method is used and the unrecorded assets ($20,000) are ultimately realized and allocated to the partners in the ratio of 42:28:30.

Acquisition of an Interest by Investing Assets

An individual may obtain a partnership interest in capital and future income by investing something of value to the firm. If assets are invested, the admission is recorded by debiting the assets invested and adjusting the net capital interest in the firm by a corresponding amount. It is important that the assets invested be fairly valued. Any gain or loss recognized on sales subsequent to recording the admission will be allocated on the basis of the new profit and loss formula.

Three situations can exist when an individual invests assets in a firm:

1. Book value of the capital interest acquired is equal to the fair value of the assets invested.
2. Book value of the capital interest acquired is less than the fair value of the assets invested.
3. Book value of the capital interest acquired is greater than the fair value of the assets invested.

The book value of the capital interest acquired is computed as follows:

$$\left(\text{Capital balances of existing partners} + \text{Investment of new partner}\right) \times \text{Percentage interest acquired by new partner} = \text{Book value of capital interest acquired}$$

To illustrate the three situations, assume that Adams and Brown have capital interests of $40,000 and $30,000, respectively. Assume further that, unless stated otherwise, the book values of the recorded assets and liabilities of the firm equal their fair values. Profits are shared in the ratio of 6:4. Call is to be admitted to the partnership, after which the profit ratio is to be 4:4:2. For simplicity, we will assume in all cases that Call invests cash.

Case 1: Book Value Acquired Is Equal to Assets Invested Assume that Adams, Brown, and Call agree that Call is to invest \$35,000 for a one-third capital interest in the partnership. The book value of Call's interest is equal to the assets invested and is computed as follows:

$$(\$70{,}000 + \$35{,}000) = \$105{,}000 \times (1/3) = \$35{,}000$$

The entry to record the admission of Call is simply:

Cash	35,000	
Call, Capital		35,000

Adams' and Brown's capital accounts remain unchanged at \$70,000, which represents the remaining two-thirds interest in the firm. Call's capital account properly reflects a one-third interest of \$35,000. It should be noted that the ratio of the capital balance of 40:30:35 does not equal the agreed profit and loss ratio 4:4:2.

Case 2: Book Value Acquired Is Less Than Assets Invested Assume now that Call is to invest \$50,000 for a one-third capital interest in the firm. Book value of the interest acquired is:

$$(\$70{,}000 + \$50{,}000) = \$120{,}000 \times (1/3) = \$40{,}000$$

In this case, the amount invested exceeds the book value interest acquired by \$10,000. There could be a number of explanations for Call's willingness to pay this \$10,000 excess. It could be that, as a result of a profitable and favorable outlook for the firm's operations, Adams and Brown are in a strong bargaining position.

The accounting problem is to record the admission of Call in accordance with the negotiated intentions of the parties involved. Obviously, if Call's capital account is credited with \$50,000, her interest would exceed one-third of the partnership's total capital. Either the bonus method or the goodwill method can be used to record the admission so that Call will end up with a one-third capital interest.

Bonus Method When the bonus method is used, the excess of the amount invested over the book value interest received is considered a bonus to the existing partners. In this example, Call invested \$10,000 more than the capital interest received. The \$10,000 bonus is allocated to the old partners on the basis of their profit and loss ratio, since this is an increase in partnership assets. The entry to admit Call is:

Cash	50,000	
Adams, Capital (.6 × \$10,000)		6,000
Brown, Capital (.4 × \$10,000)		4,000
Call, Capital ((1/3) × \$120,000)		40,000

Adams and Brown now have capital balances of \$46,000 and \$34,000 for a total capital interest of \$80,000, which is a two-thirds interest in total capital of \$120,000. Call has the remaining one-third interest of \$40,000.

The assets of the partnership may have been revalued before the admission of a new partner was recorded. The bonus method is frequently used when the parties do not want to record an intangible asset. Notice in the entry to record the admission that the assets are increased only by the amount invested. Any difference between the capital credit for Call and the cash invested is an adjustment to the capital accounts of Adams and Brown.

Goodwill Method Call may negotiate that she is to receive a capital credit equal to her investment. If Call is to receive a capital credit of $50,000 for a one-third interest, the total capital interest implied by this contract is $150,000. Adams and Brown must have the remaining two-thirds interest, or $100,000. Since their current balances of $70,000 represent their interest in the net assets, assets and capital appear to be understated by $30,000.[12] Assuming that the specific assets and liabilities are fairly valued, this understatement is recognized as goodwill attributable to the old partners and is allocated to Adams and Brown on the basis of their current profit and loss ratios. The journal entry is:

Goodwill	30,000	
Adams, Capital (.60 × $30,000)		18,000
Brown, Capital (.40 × $30,000)		12,000

The entry to record the admission of Call is:

Cash	50,000	
Call, Capital		50,000

Net Assets Undervalued Had the net assets not been fairly valued as assumed here, the excess payment by Call could mean that specific assets of the firm are undervalued, or that partnership liabilities are overstated. If so, the specific assets (whether tangible or identifiable intangible assets) and liabilities of the partnership could be adjusted instead of creating a goodwill account. However, the specific accounts should not be adjusted in the absence of objective evidence that there are unrecorded changes in value.

Case 3: Book Value Acquired Is Greater Than Assets Invested Assume that Call is to invest $20,000 for a one-third capital interest in the firm. Book value of the interest acquired is:

$$(\$70,000 + \$20,000) = \$90,000 \times (1/3) = \$30,000$$

In this case, the book value interest acquired exceeds the value of the assets invested by Call, which could imply that assets are overvalued ((1/3) (company value) = $20,000; or, company value = $60,000), or that for some reason, Adams and Brown are willing to grant Call a capital credit greater than the amount of assets she is investing. In some cases, for example, a partnership may be in need of operating capital and the partners may be willing to sacrifice their interest in existing assets to acquire the cash; or it could be that Call is bringing some particularly needed talent or reputation to the partnership.

In this case, as in Case 2, the admission could be recorded either by the bonus method or by the goodwill method. Under either method, Call will end up with a one-third interest in the net assets of the firm.

Bonus Method When the bonus method is used, assets are not increased above what the new partner is investing. If Call is to receive a $30,000 capital credit on investment of $20,000, then a bonus of $10,000 is being granted to Call. This bonus is

[12] An alternate way to calculate goodwill is: Net value of firm implied by contract of $150,000 minus (capital balances of Adams and Brown plus Call's investment) of $120,000 equals goodwill of $30,000.

allocated to reduce Adams' and Brown's capital in their agreed profit and loss ratio. The following entry reflects the bonus to Call and a resulting one-third interest in the total capital of $90,000:

Cash	20,000	
Adams, Capital (.60 × $10,000)	6,000	
Brown, Capital (.40 × $10,000)	4,000	
Call, Capital		30,000

Adams and Brown now have capital balances of $34,000 and $26,000, respectively, for a total of $60,000, or a two-thirds interest.

Goodwill Method If Adams and Brown are unwilling to reduce their capital accounts on the admission of Call, then an alternative to the bonus method is to compute and record the goodwill implicit in the agreement. Since Adams' and Brown's capital interests are to remain unchanged, the old partners' capital balances are used as the base to compute the value of the firm. If their interest represents a two-thirds interest in the net assets of the new partnership, then a three-thirds interest in the firm is $105,000 (or $70,000 ÷ 2/3), of which Call is to receive a capital credit of $35,000 ((1/3) × $105,000). The $15,000 difference between the capital credit of $35,000 and Call's investment of $20,000 is goodwill. The entry to record the admission of Call is:

Cash	20,000	
Goodwill	15,000	
Call, Capital		35,000

The entry recognizes that the new partner is investing cash and is bringing an intangible asset to the partnership. The amount recorded is based on the value implied by the partners' agreement.

Net Assets Overvalued The payment of $20,000 by Call for a larger capital interest may provide evidence that the recorded value of the firm's net assets does not reflect fair values and that the use of the bonus method or the creation of a goodwill account is an effort to avoid a reduction in net assets. The $20,000 invested by Call for a one-third interest could be used to impute a value for the partnership net assets after the admission of Call of only $60,000.[13] The journal entries to revalue the assets and admit Call are as follows:

Adams, Capital	18,000	
Brown, Capital	12,000	
Assets ($70,000 + $20,000 − $60,000)		30,000
Cash	20,000	
Call, Capital		20,000

Account balances that result from the admission of Call for the three alternatives discussed are given in Illustration 15-5. Subsequent events alone can indicate which method should have been used to record the admission. An examination of

[13] The implied value of $60,000 compared to the total *recorded* value of net assets of $90,000 ($40,000 + $30,000 + $20,000), including Call's investment, suggests that recorded assets are overvalued by $30,000.

ILLUSTRATION 15-5

Schedule of Account Balances

Debit	*Bonus Method*	*Goodwill Method*	*Overvalued Net Assets*
Net Assets	$90,000	$105,000	$60,000
Credits			
Adams, Capital	$34,000	$ 40,000	$22,000
Brown, Capital	26,000	30,000	18,000
Call, Capital	30,000	35,000	20,000
Totals	$90,000	$105,000	$60,000

one of a number of events that could result will emphasize the importance of the initial asset valuation. Assume that the bonus method was used to record the admission of Call and that the assets were overvalued and subsequently sold at a loss of $30,000. The agreed profit and loss ratio is 4:4:2. After this transaction, the partners' capital balances are as follows:

	Adams	*Brown*	*Call*
Balance after admission of Call	$(34,000)	$(26,000)	$(30,000)
Share of $30,000 loss	12,000	12,000	6,000
	$(22,000)	$(14,000)	$(24,000)

The selection of the bonus method as opposed to reducing overvalued assets results in a gain in Call's capital relative to Brown's. Additional comparisons of the three methods assuming various other subsequent events could be developed.

TEST YOUR KNOWLEDGE

NOTE: Solutions to ***Test Your Knowledge*** questions are found at the end of each chapter before the end-of-chapter questions.

Karl, Dave, and Luke have been operating a magazine stand for several years. They share profits and losses equally, and each has a $50,000 capital balance. They decided to admit a new partner, Craig. Craig is to receive a 25% interest in the partnership.

1. Determine the amount of cash that Craig must pay if the partners do not wish to recognize any goodwill or bonus.
2. Determine Craig's initial capital balance if he contributes $60,000 cash and the bonus method is applied.
3. Determine Craig's initial capital balance if he contributes $60,000 cash and the goodwill method is applied.

SECTION B: WITHDRAWAL OF A PARTNER

A partner cannot be prevented from withdrawing from a partnership by the other partners. Although some complex legal issues are involved, the partnership agreement may specify conditions for withdrawal and provisions for computing the settlement. If a settlement is not specifically provided for in the partnership agreement, Section 42 of the UPA states that "he or his legal representative. . . may have the value of this interest ascertained and shall receive as an ordinary creditor an amount equal to the value of this interest."

A buy/sell agreement can mandate that the exiting partner or heirs, in the case of death, sell his or her interest to the remaining owners, who are legally bound to buy the interest according to an agreed-upon method of valuation. It can also designate which partner becomes the buyer and which the seller if it comes to that end.[14]

If a partner withdraws in violation of the partnership agreement and without approval of the remaining partners, he is entitled only to his interest in the firm without consideration of goodwill. In such a case, the withdrawing partner is liable for damages sustained by the remaining parties for his breach of the partnership agreement. A partner who is forced to withdraw from a partnership is entitled to compensation for his full interest including goodwill.

LO8 Changes in partnership.

In the following examples, it is assumed that the partners mutually agree to the withdrawal such that: (1) the withdrawing partner may elect to sell his interest to an outside party; (2) the withdrawing partner may elect to sell his interest to one or more of the remaining partners; or (3) the partners may mutually agree to transfer partnership assets to the withdrawing partner for his interest in the firm. Case 1 has been discussed earlier and need not be reviewed again. The same considerations apply to Case 2, if negotiated outside the partnership. In Case 3 the partnership agreement may include requirements for determining the settlement price. In most cases the capital account does not reflect the current value of the partner's interest. To be equitable the fair values of the assets and liabilities need to be determined. It may be necessary to recognize unrecorded assets, correct the accounts for errors, or reflect changes in estimates such as the book value of depreciable assets. In the absence of a specific agreement, the partners may have to negotiate a settlement price at the date of withdrawal. Determination of an equitable value may be very difficult. The agreed settlement price may be equal to, greater than, or less than the book value interests of the withdrawing partner.

To illustrate the accounting for the withdrawal of a partner by transferring firm assets, assume a partnership consisting of three partners, Adams, Brown, and Call, with capital balances of $30,000, $40,000, $30,000, and a profit and loss ratio of 5:3:2. Any agreed asset and liability revaluations have already been recorded.

Bad things can happen if an outsider makes a bid for a piece of the company—the lead partner's share, say, but not everyone else's. You don't want to be forced to work alongside an incompetent heir or a crook. Solution: The buy/sell agreement dictates that an outsider cannot buy a majority interest without offering to buy out everyone else on the same terms. Alternatively, it might provide that the remaining partners have a right of first refusal on any shares being sold.[15]

Payment to a Retiring Partner

Payment in Excess of Book Value to a Withdrawing Partner Assume now that Adams is withdrawing from the partnership and the partners have mutually agreed that he is to receive payment of $40,000. The partners may agree to use the bonus method or the goodwill method to record the withdrawal.

[14] *Forbes*, "Planning for Divorce," by Leigh Gallagher, 3/22/99, pp. 94–95.

[15] *Forbes*, "Planning for Divorce," by Leigh Gallagher, 3/22/99, pp. 94–95.

Bonus Method If the bonus method is used, the remaining partners are charged with the amount of the payment that exceeds the book value of the retiring partner's capital balance. The amount of the bonus paid to the retiring partner is commonly allocated to the remaining partners on the basis of their relative profit and loss ratio (in this case the relative ratio of Brown to Call is 3:2). Support for this method is based on the cost principle. The bonus method may also be justified when the remaining partners are simply anxious to get rid of a partner for various reasons. Any recognition of goodwill is difficult to justify in the absence of an arm's-length transaction. The entry to record the withdrawal would be as follows:

Adams, Capital	30,000	
Brown, Capital	6,000	
Call, Capital	4,000	
Liability to Adams		40,000

RELATED CONCEPTS

The rationale for the bonus method is the *historical cost principle* and the absence of an arm's-length transaction. The rationale for the goodwill method is that formation of a new entity should be based on fair values.

Goodwill Method The goodwill method is used if (1) Brown and Call will not agree to a reduction in their capital balances; (2) the partners made specific provisions in the partnership agreement on how the withdrawal is to be recorded; or (3) the partners agree that an intangible asset should be recognized. If the partnership has been profitable, the firm as a whole may be worth more than the fair value of the net assets. Once again, the goodwill method is supported on the basis that a new entity is being formed and the accounts of the new entity should be based on fair values. One alternative is to calculate the implied goodwill from the price paid to the retiring partner. In our example, Adams receives a $10,000 excess payment over his capital balance. Since Adams' capital account is increased by 50% of any increase in assets, then a $10,000 excess payment implies a total goodwill of $20,000. The entries are:

Goodwill	20,000	
Adams, Capital		10,000
Brown, Capital		6,000
Call, Capital		4,000
Adams, Capital	40,000	
Liability to Adams		40,000

Some argue that, in accordance with the cost basis, only the goodwill of $10,000 that has been purchased should be recorded (called the partial goodwill method) and the entry should be:

Goodwill	10,000	
Adams, Capital		10,000
Adams, Capital	40,000	
Liability to Adams		40,000

Others would contend that the basis for recognizing goodwill should be "all or nothing at all."

It is probably difficult to justify recognition of any goodwill. If the goodwill is related to Adams, it will not exist if he withdraws. However, as discussed before, if the goodwill is based on past operations, the withdrawal may provide the objective evidence necessary to recognize it in the partnership accounts.

Payment of Less Than Book Value to a Withdrawing Partner A partner who is anxious to dispose of his or her interest in the partnership may agree to accept less than his or her book value interest in the partnership. The partner may do so for a number of reasons, such as (1) he or she may view the future of the company negatively,

(2) he or she may need operating capital for personal reasons, or (3) the business association may no longer be acceptable to the partner and, in his or her opinion, a forced liquidation of the firm might be detrimental to his or her interest. In such cases, use of the bonus method is justified, since the settlement may not be based on the economic value of the firm.

To illustrate, assume that Adams withdraws from the ABC Partnership and agrees to settle his $30,000 interest for $25,000. A bonus of $5,000 accrues to the remaining partners. The common practice is to allocate the bonus on the basis of their relative profit and loss ratio of 3:2. The entry would be:

Adams, Capital	30,000	
Brown, Capital		3,000
Call, Capital		2,000
Liability to Adams		25,000

A payment to Adams that is less than his capital interest may be an indication that assets are overvalued. Assets should be written down to fair values if it is determined that they are overvalued and that the settlement price is based on the net assets' fair value. In particular, if goodwill was previously recorded, an agreement to accept a payment that is less than the partner's book value interest may provide evidence that the intangible is overstated. Accordingly, the intangible should be reduced by the difference between the settlement price and the capital interest being retired. Assuming that assets are overvalued by $10,000, the sequence of entries becomes:

Adams, Capital	5,000	
Brown, Capital	3,000	
Call, Capital	2,000	
Asset		10,000
Adams, Capital	25,000	
Liability to Adams		25,000

Reducing the assets to fair value provides an equitable starting point for the new partnership formed by Brown and Call. As long as Brown and Call share profits in the same relative ratio, they will be indifferent as to the method used. However, it is more informative and conceptually preferred for the recorded asset values to reflect fair values if such values can be determined.

Death of a Partner

While historically under the UPA a partnership was dissolved by the death of a partner, recent changes now allow the partnership to continue operating by mandating a buyout of the deceased partner's interest.

Determining a partner's equity interest in the firm can result in disagreements between the surviving partners and the executor of the estate. To avoid litigation, the articles of partnership should contain procedures for determining a deceased partner's current equity in the partnership and the method of settlement. In the absence of specific provisions, the surviving partners and the executor of the estate must negotiate a settlement. To determine a partner's equity interest at the time of death, the assets and liabilities normally are adjusted to current values and the accounts are closed to determine the net income or loss earned since the end of the last fiscal period.

The partnership agreement may provide that the interest is to be settled by distributing partnership assets to the estate or the estate may receive payment by selling the interest to an outside party or to one or more of the surviving partners as individuals. Entries to record both types of settlements were presented in earlier sections of this chapter.

SUMMARY

1. *Describe the characteristics of a general partnership, a limited partnership, and a joint venture.* In a general partnership, the partners can bind the partnership into contracts, and the partnership interest is similar to a personal asset that can be sold. The primary difference between a general partnership and a limited partnership is that general partners are personally liable for the debts of the partnership, while a limited partner is only liable for the amount invested in the partnership. A joint venture occurs when two or more parties (agents) enter into an arrangement to pursue a specific purpose. When joint ventures are structured as partnerships, they follow the partnership laws. One exception is that one party cannot act (enter into a contract) on behalf of the joint venture without the consent of the other agents.

2. *List some important items to be included in the partnership agreement.* Important items to include in the partnership agreement are the name of the partnership, the identity of the partners, the effective date and the length of operations, the provision for allocating profits and losses, provisions for salaries and withdrawals, contracting authorities, procedures for admitting a new partner, and procedures for dissolution of the partnership.

3. *Understand the differences between partnerships' and corporations' equity accounts in the balance sheet.* In a corporation, amounts contributed by the owners (i.e., stockholders) are recorded in capital stock accounts. In addition, any income or loss earned by the corporation is reported in retained earnings. Dividends are considered a distribution of earnings and thus reduce retained earnings. In a partnership, amounts contributed by the owners (i.e., partners) are recorded in the partners' capital accounts. Any income or loss earned by the partnership is allocated to the partners' capital accounts. If a partner takes money out of the partnership, a drawing account is often used.

4. *Explain the purpose of the partners' drawing accounts and capital accounts.* In general, the partners' capital accounts are for permanent investments and should be updated periodically for withdrawals. Drawing accounts are often used in anticipation of earnings or to pay for personal expenses. Drawing accounts record withdrawals during the year and are closed to the partners' capital accounts at year-end.

5. *Prepare journal entries to form a partnership using the bonus and the goodwill methods.* A choice between the bonus and the goodwill methods for recording the formation of a partnership is needed if the amounts contributed by each partner do not agree with the amount of capital to be credited to each partner (for example, one partner contributes 40% of the assets but is to be given a 50% interest). For example, suppose that Bob and Ed enter into a partnership. Bob contributes $40 cash and Ed contributes $60. Yet each is to be given an equal interest. The journal entries under the bonus and goodwill methods are as follows:

Bonus Method		
Cash	$100	
Bob, Capital		$50
Ed, Capital		$50
Goodwill Method		
Cash	$100	
Intangible Asset	$ 20	
Bob, Capital		$60
Ed, Capital		$60

Under the bonus method, the total amount contributed is allocated to all partners in accordance with their agreed-upon capital share (equally in this illustration, resulting in a transfer of $10 from Ed to Bob). Under the goodwill method, Bob is assumed to be contributing an intangible asset to the firm. Since Ed contributed $60 and Bob only $40, an intangible asset of $20 is recorded to increase Bob's capital to $60.

6. *Describe some common agreements used to allocate partnership net income or loss.* Common agreements to allocate partnership net income or loss include using (1) fixed ratios, (2) a ratio based on the partners' capital balances, (3) an implicit interest rate based on the partners' capital accounts (such as 10% of the year-end capital balance), and (4) various amounts that represent salaries or bonuses. In addition, the agreement must specify how any excess or deficit after an original allocation is divided among the partners.

7. *Explain why salary allowances and interest allowances are used in allocating partnership profits and losses.* Interest allowances are often used as an incentive for capital to be invested and stay invested in the partnership. If a partner withdraws money from

the partnership, that partner will receive a lower amount of interest and thus a smaller allocation of total profits. If the partner contributes more funds, that partner will receive a higher allocation. Similarly, a salary allowance is a common method to reward partners providing services to the partnership for their efforts.

8. *Describe the methods used to record partnership changes when a new partner is admitted or when a partner withdraws from the partnership.* When a new partner is admitted, the new partner can purchase the interest from an existing partner or the new partner can contribute additional assets to the partnership. As when a partnership is formed, either the bonus or the goodwill method may be used if the amount contributed does not agree with the amount of capital to be credited to the new partner. Upon the withdrawal of a partner, the same procedures are applied. If the amount paid to the withdrawing partner is more or less than the partner's existing capital balance, either the bonus or the goodwill method can be used. In this case, the withdrawing partner's final capital balance must equal the amount paid. Under the bonus method, this is achieved by a transfer from (to) the remaining partners' capital accounts to (from) the withdrawing partner's capital balance. Under the goodwill method, the firm is revalued using the amount paid to the withdrawing partner. All partners' capital accounts are adjusted.

9. *Describe the rationale behind the goodwill method in accounting for changes in partnership membership.* Under the goodwill method of accounting for changes in partnership membership, the capital interest assigned to the new or withdrawing partner implies a certain value for the firm. Since records are maintained on historical cost, differences in net asset values are likely. In addition, significant intangible assets may have been created by the partnership over time. The goodwill method assumes that the assigned capital interest provides a basis for total firm valuation.

TEST YOUR KNOWLEDGE SOLUTIONS

15-1 1. d

15-2

1. (150,000 ÷ .75) = 200,000 less existing capital of 150,000 = $50,000 cash contribution.
2. (150,000 + 60,000) = 210,000 × 0.25 = $52,500 capital balance.
3. ($60,000 ÷ 0.25) = $240,000 total capital implied × 0.25 = $60,000 capital balance.

QUESTIONS

LO1 **1.** Describe the tax treatment of partnership income.

LO4 **2.** Distinguish between a partner's interest in capital and his interest in the partnership's income and losses. Also, make a general distinction between a partner's capital account and his drawing account.

LO1 **3.** Explain why a partnership is viewed in accounting as a "separate economic entity."

LO6 **4.** What are some of the methods commonly used in allocating income and losses to the partners?

LO7 **5.** Explain the distinction between the terms "withdrawals" and "salaries."

LO5 **6.** List some of the alternative methods of calculating a bonus that may appear in a partnership agreement.

LO8 **7.** What is meant by dissolution and what are its causes?

LO8 **8.** Discuss the methods used to record changes in partnership membership.

LO8 **9.** Differentiate between the admission of a new partner through assignment of an interest and through investment in the partnership.

LO8 **10.** Under what two conditions will the bonus and goodwill methods of recording the admission of a partner yield the same result?

LO8 **11.** Describe the circumstances where neither the goodwill nor the bonus method should be used to record the admission of a new partner.

LO8 **12.** How might a partner withdrawing in violation of the partnership agreement and without the consent of the other partners be treated? What about a partner who is forced to withdraw?

Business Ethics

Many companies with defined benefit plans are curtailing or eliminating the plans altogether. With a defined benefit plan, the company guarantees some set amount (or formula-determined payment) when the employee retires. Because most pension assets are invested in the stock market, whether a pension plan is fully funded often depends on the strength of the stock market. Because of this volatility, companies often find themselves unexpectedly in a position where they must either increase funding or disclose significant underfunding. Because of this, many companies simply reduce or eliminate the plan. Consider the pension plan of Golden Years Company (GYC). Historically, GYC has been a great company to work for, with strong employee benefits. GYC's pension liability is approximately $15 million. However, recently the company has been experiencing minor financial troubles in a decreasing stock market and, consequently, announced the termination of the pension plan in an effort to save costs. However, the pension plan was fully funded by $9 million (the fair value of assets exceeded the expected liability).

1. How does the firm reconcile the trade-off between financial performance and the responsibility to its employees?

EXERCISES

EXERCISE 15-1 **Partnership Formation: Bonus and Goodwill Methods** LO5

John, Jeff, and Jane decided to engage in a real estate venture as a partnership. John invested $100,000 cash and Jeff provided office equipment that is carried on his books at $82,000. The partners agree that the equipment has a fair value of $110,000. There is a $30,000 note payable remaining on the equipment to be assumed by the partnership. Although Jane has no physical assets to invest in the partnership, both John and Jeff believe that her experience as a real estate appraiser is a valuable skill needed by the partnership and is a basis for granting her a capital interest in the partnership.

Required:

Assuming that each partner is to receive an equal capital interest in the partnership,

A. Record the partnership formation under the bonus method.

B. Record the partnership formation under the goodwill method, and assume a total goodwill of $90,000.

C. Discuss the appropriateness of using either the bonus or goodwill methods to record the formation of the partnership.

EXERCISE 15-2 **Partnership Transactions and Capital Statements** LO5 LO6

Tom and Julie formed a management consulting partnership on January 1, 2008. The fair value of the net assets invested by each partner follows:

	Tom	*Julie*
Cash	$13,000	$12,000
Accounts receivable	8,000	6,000
Office supplies	2,000	800
Office equipment	30,000	—
Land	—	30,000
Accounts payable	2,000	5,000
Mortgage payable	—	18,800

During the year, Tom withdrew $15,000 and Julie withdrew $12,000 in anticipation of operating profits. Net profit for 2008 was $50,000, which is to be allocated based on the original net capital investment.

Required:

A. Prepare journal entries to:

(1) Record the initial investment in the partnership.

(2) Record the withdrawals.

(3) Close the Income Summary and Drawing accounts.

B. Prepare a statement of changes in partners' capital for the year ended December 31, 2008.

EXERCISE 15-3 **Allocation of Income or Loss** LO6

Jones, Silva, and Thompson form a partnership and agree to allocate income equally after recognition of 10% interest on beginning capital balances and monthly salary allowances of $2,000 to Jones and $1,500 to Thompson. Capital balances on January 1 were as follows:

Jones	$40,000
Silva	25,000
Thompson	30,000

Required:

Calculate the net income (loss) allocation to each partner under each of the following independent situations.

1. Net income for the year is $99,500.
2. Net income for the year is $38,300.
3. Net loss for the year is $15,100.

EXERCISE 15-4 **Allocation of Net Loss** LO6

Mary and Nancy invested $80,000 each to form a partnership. Mary has been authorized a salary of $20,000, while Nancy's salary is $25,000. Each partner is to receive 10% on the original capital investment. The profit and loss agreement stipulates that any remaining income or loss is to be divided equally. The partnership had a net loss of $20,000 this year.

Required:

Prepare the journal entry to record the allocation of the net loss for the year. Show supporting computations.

EXERCISE 15-5 **Bonus Agreement** LO6

On January 1, 2008, Tony and Jon formed T&J Personal Financial Planning with capital investments of $480,000 and $340,000, respectively. The partners wanted to draft a profit and loss agreement that would reward each individual for the resources invested in the partnership. Accordingly, the partnership agreement provides that profits are to be allocated as follows:

1. Annual salaries of $42,000 and $66,000 are granted to Tony and Jon, respectively.
2. In addition to the salary, Jon is entitled to a bonus of 10% of net income after salaries and bonus but before interest on capital investments is subtracted.
3. Each partner is to receive an interest credit of 8% on the original capital investment.
4. Remaining profits are to be allocated 40% to Tony and 60% to Jon.

On December 31, 2008, the partnership reported net income before salaries, interest, and bonus of $188,000.

Required:

Calculate the 2008 allocation of partnership profit.

EXERCISE 15-6 **Profit Distribution and Capital Statements** LO6

Hill, Jones, and Vose have been partners throughout 2008. Their average balances for the year and their balances at the end of the year before closing the nominal accounts are as follows:

Partner	Average Balances	Balances 12/31/08
Hill	$97,500	$70,000
Jones	27,300	21,800
Vose	14,250	11,700*

* Debit balance.

The income for 2008 is $108,000 before charging partners' salary allowances and before payment of interest on average balances at the agreed rate of 5% per annum. Annual salary allocations are $12,000 to Hill, $9,600 to Jones, and $8,800 to Vose. The balance of income is to be allocated at the rate of 60% to Hill, 10% to Jones, and 30% to Vose.

It is intended to distribute cash to the partners so that, after credits and allocations have been made as indicated in the preceding paragraph, the balances in the partners' accounts will be proportionate to their residual profit-sharing ratios. None of the partners is to invest additional cash, but they wish to distribute the lowest possible amount of cash.

Required:

Prepare a schedule of partners' accounts, showing balances at the end of 2008 before closing, the allocations of the net income for 2008, the cash distributed, and the closing balances. (*AICPA adapted*)

EXERCISE 15-7 Partner Admission LO8

Phil Phoenix and Tim Tucson are partners in an electrical repair business. Their respective capital balances are $90,000 and $50,000, and they share profits and losses equally. Because the partners are confronted with personal financial problems, they decided to admit a new partner to the partnership. After an extensive interviewing process they elect to admit Don Dallas into the partnership.

Required:

Prepare the journal entry to record the admission of Don Dallas into the partnership under each of the following conditions:

1. Don acquires one-fourth of Phil's capital interest by paying $30,000 directly to him.
2. Don acquires one-fifth of each of Phil's and Tim's capital interests. Phil receives $25,000 and Tim receives $15,000 directly from Don.
3. Don acquires a one-fifth capital interest for a $60,000 cash investment in the partnership. Total capital after the admission is to be $200,000.
4. Don invests $40,000 for a one-fifth interest in partnership capital. Implicit goodwill is to be recorded.

EXERCISE 15-8 Adjusting Entries for Partner Admission LO8

Bill and Jane share profits and losses in a 70:30 ratio. Mike is to be admitted into a partnership upon the investment of $14,000 for a one-third capital interest. Account balances for Bill and Jane on June 30, 2008 just before the admission of Mike are as follows:

COMPREHENSIVE

	Debit	Credit
Cash	$ 6,000	
Accounts Receivable	9,000	
Notes Receivable	2,000	
Merchandise Inventory	12,000	
Prepaid Insurance	500	
Accounts Payable		$ 9,500
Bill, Capital		12,000
Jane, Capital		8,000
	$29,500	$29,500

It is agreed that for purposes of establishing the interests of the former partners, the following adjustments shall be made:

1. An allowance for doubtful accounts of 2% of the accounts receivable is to be established.
2. The merchandise inventory is to be valued at $10,000.
3. Accrued expenses of $600 are to be recognized.
4. Prepaid insurance is to be valued at $300.
5. The goodwill method is to be used to record the admission of Mike.

Required:

Prepare the entries to adjust the account balances in establishing the interests of Bill and Jane and to record the investment by Mike.

EXERCISE 15-9 **Partner Admission** LO8

Beth, Steph, and Linda have been operating a small gift shop for several years. After an extensive review of their past operating performance, the partners concluded that the business needed to expand in order to provide an adequate return to the partners. The following balance sheet is for the partnership prior to the admission of a new partner, Mary.

Cash	$160,000
Other Assets	640,000
	$800,000
Liabilities	$200,000
Beth, Capital (40%)	265,000
Steph, Capital (40%)	215,000
Linda, Capital (20%)	120,000
	$800,000

Figures shown parenthetically reflect agreed profit-and-loss sharing percentages.

Required:

Prepare the necessary journal entries to record the admission of Mary in each of the following independent situations. Some situations may be recorded in more than one way.

1. Mary is to invest sufficient cash to receive a one-sixth capital interest. The parties agree that the admission is to be recorded without recognizing goodwill or bonus.
2. Mary is to invest $160,000 for a one-fifth capital interest.
3. Mary is to invest $160,000 for a one-fourth capital interest.
4. Mary is to invest $160,000 for a 40% capital interest.

EXERCISE 15-10 **Multiple Choice** LO6 LO8

Select the best answer for each of the following.

1. Jon and Joe formed a partnership on July 1, 2008, and invested the following assets:

	Jon	*Joe*
Cash	$65,000	$125,000
Realty		250,000

The realty was subject to a mortgage of $25,000, which was assumed by the partnership. The partnership agreement provides that Jon and Joe will share profits and losses in the ratio of one-third and two-thirds, respectively. Joe's capital account at July 1, 2008, should be

(a) $375,000
(b) $366,667
(c) $285,000
(d) $350,000

2. On July 1, 2008, Mary and Jane formed a partnership, agreeing to share profits and losses in the ratio of 4:6, respectively. Mary invested a parcel of land that cost her $40,000. Jane invested $50,000 cash. The land was sold for $60,000 on July 1, 2008, four hours after formation of the partnership. How much should be recorded in Mary's capital account on formation of the partnership?
   (a) $8,000
   (b) $24,000
   (c) $60,000
   (d) $20,000

3. The partnership agreement of Tami, Julie, and Kim provides for annual distribution of profit or loss in the following order:

   Tami, the managing partner, receives a bonus of 15% of profit.

   Each partner receives 10% interest on average capital investment.

   Residual profit or loss is divided equally.

   The average capital investments for 2008 were:

Tami	$100,000
Julie	200,000
Kim	300,000

   How much of the $94,500 partnership profit for 2008 should be allocated to Tami?
   (a) $10,000
   (b) $20,000
   (c) $30,950
   (d) $14,175

4. Tom and Jim are partners who share profits and losses in the ratio of 3:2, respectively. On August 31, 2008, their capital accounts were as follows:

Tom	$ 80,000
Jim	50,000
	$130,000

   On that date they agreed to admit John as a partner with a one-third interest in the capital and profits and losses, for an investment of $50,000. The new partnership will begin with a total capital of $180,000. Immediately after John's admission, what are the capital balances of the partners?

	Tom	*Jim*	*John*
(a)	$60,000	$60,000	$60,000
(b)	$73,333	$46,667	$60,000
(c)	$74,000	$46,000	$60,000
(d)	$80,000	$50,000	$50,000

5. On June 30, 2008, the balance sheet for the partnership of Al, Carl, and Paul, together with their respective profit and loss ratios, were as follows:

Assets, at Cost	$180,000
Al, Loan	$ 9,000
Al, Capital (20%)	42,000
Carl, Capital (20%)	39,000
Paul, Capital (60%)	90,000
Total	$180,000

Al has decided to retire from the partnership. By mutual agreement, the assets are to be adjusted to their fair value of $220,000 at June 30, 2008. It was agreed that the partnership would pay Al $61,200 cash for Al's partnership interest, including Al's loan, which is to be repaid in full. No goodwill is to be recorded. After Al's retirement, what is the balance of Carl's capital account?

- **(a)** $36,450.
- **(b)** $39,000.
- **(c)** $46,450.
- **(d)** $47,000.

(AICPA adapted)

EXERCISE 15-11 Multiple Choice LO1 LO2 LO6

Select the best answer for each of the following.

1. Which of the following is ***not*** a characteristic of a partnership?
   - **(a)** Limited life.
   - **(b)** Mutual agency.
   - **(c)** Limited liability.
   - **(d)** Right to dispose of partnership interest.
2. The articles of partnership need not include which of the following?
   - **(a)** Location of the place of business.
   - **(b)** Allocation of profit/loss.
   - **(c)** Procedures for admitting a new partner.
   - **(d)** Fiscal period of the partnership.
   - **(e)** All of the above should be included.
3. The High and Low partnership agreement provides special compensation to High for managing the business. High receives a bonus of 15% of partnership net income before salary and bonus, and also receives a salary of $45,000. Any remaining profit or loss is to be allocated equally. During 2008, the partnership had net income of $50,000 before the bonus and salary allowance. As a result of these distributions, Low's equity in the partnership would
   - **(a)** Increase.
   - **(b)** Not change.
   - **(c)** Decrease the same as High's.
   - **(d)** Decrease.
4. The allocation of an error correction should be based on the profit and loss agreement in effect when
   - **(a)** The error was made.
   - **(b)** The error was corrected.
   - **(c)** The error was discovered.
   - **(d)** The allocation should always be made equally.
5. If there is a provision for allocation of profits but not losses in the partnership agreement, courts have generally concluded that
   - **(a)** Losses should not be allocated to the capital accounts, but matched against future earnings.
   - **(b)** Losses should be allocated using the same approach as allocation of profits.
   - **(c)** Losses should be allocated equally.
   - **(d)** Losses should be allocated according to the ratio of balances in the capital accounts.
6. Partners E and F share profits and losses equally after each has been credited in all circumstances with annual salary allowances of $15,000 and $12,000, respectively. Under this agreement, E will benefit by $3,000 more than F in which of the following circumstances?

(a) Only if the partnership has earnings of $27,000 or more for the year.
(b) Only if the partnership does not incur a loss for the year.
(c) In all earnings or loss situations.
(d) Only if the partnership has earnings of at least $3,000 for the year.

EXERCISE 15-12 Income Allocation with Bonus LO6

The partnership agreement of ABC Associates provides that income should be allocated in the following manner:

1. Each partner receives interest of 20% of beginning capital.
2. Sue receives a salary of $25,000 and Josh receives a salary of $21,000.
3. Josh also receives a bonus of 10%.
4. Residual—divided equally.

The partnership's net income for 2008 was $90,000. Beginning capital balances were Sue, $30,000; Josh, $40,000.

Required:

Prepare a schedule to allocate the net income under each of the following independent situations:

A. Bonus is to be based on income before any profit allocation to partners for interest and salary.
B. Bonus is to be based on income after subtracting the bonus, but before allocation to partners for interest and salary.
C. Bonus is to be based on income after subtracting the bonus, interest, and salary.

EXERCISE 15-13 Partner Withdrawal LO8

Kazma, Folkert, and Tucker are partners with capital account balances of $30,000, $75,000, and $45,000, respectively. Income and losses are divided in a 4:4:2 ratio. When Tucker decided to withdraw, the partnership revalued its assets from $225,000 to $252,000, which represented an increase in the value of inventory of $8,000 and an increase in the value of land of $19,000. Tucker was then given $15,000 cash and a note for $40,000 for his withdrawal from the partnership.

Required:

A. Prepare the journal entry to record the revaluation of the partnership's assets.
B. Prepare the journal entry to record the withdrawal using the following independent methods.
   (1) Bonus.
   (2) Partial goodwill.
   (3) Full goodwill amount.

PROBLEMS

PROBLEM 15-1 Profit Allocation LO6

Day and Night formed an accounting partnership in 2008. Capital transactions for Day and Night during 2008 are as follows:

Date	*Transaction*	*Amount*
Day		
1/1	Beginning balance	$75,000
4/1	Withdrawal	18,750
6/1	Investment	37,500
11/1	Investment	18,750
Night		
1/1	Beginning balance	$37,500
7/1	Investment	18,750
10/1	Withdrawal	9,375

Partnership net income for the year ended December 31, 2008; is $68,400 before considering salaries or interest.

Required:

Determine the amount of profit that is to be allocated to Day and Night in accordance with each of the following independent profit-sharing agreements:

1. Day and Night failed to provide a profit-sharing arrangement in the articles of partnership and fail to compromise on an agreement.
2. Net income is to be allocated 60% to Day and 40% to Night.
3. Net income is to be allocated in the ratio of ending capital balances.
4. Net income is to be allocated in the ratio of average capital balances.
5. Interest of 15% is to be granted on average capital balances, salaries of $15,000 and $8,250 are to be allocated to Day and Night, respectively, and the remainder is to be divided equally.

PROBLEM 15-2 **Income Allocation and Capital Statements** LO6

Dave, Brian, and Paul are partners in a retail appliance store. The partnership was formed January 1, 2008, with each partner investing $45,000. They agreed that profits and losses are to be shared as follows:

1. Divided in the ratio of 40:30:30 if net income is not sufficient to cover salaries, bonus, and interest.
2. A net loss is to be allocated equally.
3. Net income is to be allocated as follows if net income is in excess of salaries, bonus, and interest.

   (a) Monthly salary allowances are:

Dave	$3,500
Brian	2,500
Paul	1,500

   (b) Brian is to receive a bonus of 8% of net income before subtracting salaries and interest, but after subtracting the bonus.

   (c) Interest of 10% is allocated based on the beginning-of-year capital balances.

   (d) Any remainder is to be allocated equally.

   Operating performance and other capital transactions were as follows.

		Capital Transactions					
	Net Income	*Dave*		*Brian*		*Paul*	
Year-End	*(Loss)*	*Investment*	*Withdrawals*	*Investment*	*Withdrawals*	*Investment*	*Withdrawals*
12/31/08	$(5,400)	$15,000	$17,000	$15,000	$7,000	$6,000	$3,200
12/31/09	27,000	—0—	17,000	—0—	7,000	6,000	3,200
12/31/10	120,000	—0—	19,000	—0—	9,000	6,000	3,200

Required:

A. Prepare a schedule of changes in partners' capital accounts for each of the three years.

B. Prepare the journal entry to close the income summary account to the partners' capital accounts at the end of each year.

PROBLEM 15-3 **Conversion from Cash to Accrual Basis** LO8

The partnership of Cain, Gallo, and Hamm engaged you to adjust its accounting records and convert them uniformly to the accrual basis in anticipation of admitting Kerns as a new partner. Some accounts are on the accrual basis and some are on the cash basis. The partnership's books were closed at December 31, 2008, by the bookkeeper, who prepared the general ledger trial balance that appears as follows:

Cain, Gallo, and Hamm
General Ledger Trial Balance
December 31, 2008

	Debit	*Credit*
Cash	$ 15,000	
Accounts Receivable	40,000	
Inventory	30,000	
Land	9,000	
Buildings	50,000	
Allowance for Depreciation of Buildings		$ 6,000
Equipment	56,000	
Allowance for Depreciation of Equipment		6,000
Goodwill	5,000	
Accounts Payable		56,000
Allowance for Future Inventory Losses		8,000
Cain, Capital		37,000
Gallo, Capital		60,000
Hamm, Capital		32,000
Totals	$205,000	$205,000

Your inquiries disclose the following:

1. The partnership was organized on January 1, 2007. No provision was made in the partnership agreement for the allocation of partnership profits and losses. During 2007, profits were allocated equally among the partners. The partnership agreement was amended, effective January 1, 2008, to provide for the following profit and loss ratio: Cain, 40%; Gallo, 40%; and Hamm, 20%. The amended partnership agreement also stated that the accounting records were to be maintained on the accrual basis and that any adjustments necessary for 2007 should be allocated according to the 2007 profit allocation agreement.
2. The following amounts were not recorded as prepayments or accruals.

	December 31	
	2008	*2007*
Prepaid insurance	$700	$ 800
Advances from customers	900	1,500
Accrued interest expense	—	450

   The advances from customers were recorded as sales in the year the cash was received.
3. In 2008, the partnership recorded a provision of $8,000 for anticipated declines in inventory prices. You convinced the partners that the provision was unnecessary and should be removed from the books.
4. The partnership charged equipment purchased for $4,400 on January 1, 2008, to expense. This equipment has an estimated life of 10 years and an estimated salvage value of $400. The partnership depreciates its capitalized equipment using the declining balance method at twice the straight-line depreciation rate.
5. The partners agreed to establish an allowance for doubtful accounts at 2% of current accounts receivable and 5% of past-due accounts. At December 31, 2007, the partnership had $54,000 of accounts receivable, of which only $4,000 was past due. At December 31, 2008, 20% of accounts receivable was past due, of which $4,000 represented sales made in 2007 and was considered collectible. The partnership had written off uncollectible accounts in the year the accounts became worthless as follows:

	Accounts Written Off In	
	2008	*2007*
2008 accounts	$ 800	—
2007 accounts	1,000	$250

6. Goodwill was recorded on the books in 2008 and credited to the partners' capital accounts in the profit and loss ratio in recognition of an increase in the value of the business resulting from improved sales volume. The partners agreed to write off the goodwill before admitting the new partner.

Required:

Prepare a worksheet showing the adjustments and the adjusted trial balance for the partnership on the accrual basis at December 31, 2008. All adjustments affecting income should be made directly to partners' capital accounts. Supporting computations should be in good form. (Do not prepare formal financial statements or formal journal entries.)

(*AICPA adapted*)

PROBLEM 15-4 **Partner Admission** LO8

Brown and Coss have been operating a tax accounting service as a partnership for five years. Their current capital balances are $92,000 and $88,000, respectively, and they share profits in a 60:40 ratio. Because of the growth in their tax business, they decide that they need a new partner. Moore is admitted to the partnership, after which the partners agree to share profits 40% to Brown, 35% to Coss, and 25% to Moore.

Required:

Prepare the necessary journal entries to admit Moore in each of the following independent conditions. If the information is such that both the bonus and goodwill methods are appropriate, record the admission using both methods.

1. Moore invests $90,000 in cash and receives a one-third capital interest.
2. Moore invests $120,000 cash for a 45% capital interest. Total capital after his admission is to be $300,000.
3. Moore agrees to invest $120,000 cash for a one-third capital interest, but will not accept a capital credit for less than his investment.
4. Moore invests $40,000 cash for a one-fourth capital interest. The partners agree that assets and the firm as a whole should not be revalued.
5. Moore invests $35,000 cash for a one-fifth capital interest. The partners agree that total capital after the admission of Moore should be $225,000.
6. Moore invests land in the partnership as a site for a new office building. The land, which originally cost Moore $90,000, now has a current market value of $150,000. Moore is admitted with a one-third capital interest.
7. Moore is admitted to the partnership by purchasing a 30% capital interest from each partner. A payment of $35,000 is made outside the partnership and is split between Brown and Coss.

PROBLEM 15-5 **Adjusting Entries for Partner Admission** LO8

The CAB Partnership, although operating profitably, has had a cash flow problem. Unable to meet its current commitments, the firm borrowed $34,000 from a bank giving a long-term note. During a recent meeting, the partners decided to obtain additional cash by admitting a new partner to the firm. They feel that the firm is an attractive investment, but that proper management of their liquid assets will be required. Meyers agrees to invest cash in the firm if her chief accountant can review the accounting records of the partnership.

The balance sheet for CAB Partnership as of December 31, 2008, is as follows:

Assets	
Cash	$ 8,000
Accounts Receivable	33,600
Inventory (at cost)	35,750
Land	27,000
Building (net of depreciation)	41,600
Equipment (net of depreciation)	27,250
Total	$173,200

Liabilities and Capital	
Accounts Payable	$ 32,450
Other Current Liabilities	6,750
Long-Term Note (8% due 2008)	34,000
Cox, Capital	37,500
Andrews, Capital	25,000
Bennet, Capital	37,500
Total	$173,200

The review of the accounts resulted in the accumulation of the following information:

1. Approximately 5% of the accounts receivable are uncollectible. The old partnership had been using the direct write-off method of accounting for bad debts.
2. Current replacement cost of the inventory is $41,250.
3. The market value of the land based on a current appraisal is $65,000.
4. The partners had been using an unreasonably long estimated life in establishing a depreciation policy for the building. On the basis of sound value (current replacement cost adjusted for use), the value of the building is $32,750.
5. There are unrecorded accrued liabilities of $3,275.

The partners agree to recognize the foregoing adjustments to the accounts. Cox, Andrews, and Bennet share profits 40:30:30. After the admission of Meyers, the new profit agreement is to be 30:20:30:20. Meyers is to receive a 25% capital interest in the partnership after she invests sufficient cash to increase the total capital interest to $150,000. Because of the uncertainty of the business, no goodwill is to be recognized before or after Meyers is admitted.

Required:

A. Prepare the necessary journal entries on the books of the old partnership to adjust the accounts.

B. Record the admission of Meyers.

C. Prepare a new balance sheet giving effect to the foregoing requirements.

PROBLEM 15-6 **Adjusting Entries for Partner Withdrawal** LO8

The December 31, 2008, balance sheet of the Datamation Partnership is shown below.

Datamation Partnership
Balance Sheet
December 31, 2008

Assets	
Cash	$ 80,000
Accounts Receivable	80,000
Inventory	62,000
Equipment	290,000
Total Assets	$512,000

Liabilities and Partners' Equity	
Accounts Payable	$ 60,000
Notes Payable to Dave, 8% dated September 1, 2008	22,000
Dave, Capital	220,000
Allen, Capital	110,000
Matt, Capital	100,000
Total Liabilities and Partners' Equity	$512,000

Dave, Allen, and Matt share profits and loses in the ratio of 50:30:20. The inventory on December 31 has a fair value of $68,000; accrued interest on the note payable to Dave is to be recognized as of December 31. The book values of all the other accounts are equal to their fair values. Allen withdrew from the partnership on December 31, 2008.

Required:

Prepare the journal entry or entries to record the withdrawal of Allen, given each of the following situations. Assume that the ***bonus*** method is used to account for the withdrawal.

1. Allen receives $36,624 cash and a $75,000 note from the partnership for his interest.
2. Matt purchases Allen's interest for $110,000.
3. The partnership gives Allen $35,000 cash and equipment with a book value and a fair value of $90,000 for his interest.
4. The partnership gives Allen $100,000 cash for his interest.
5. Allen sells one-fourth of his interest to Dave for $40,000 and three-fourths to Matt for $90,000.

PROBLEM 15-7 **Partner Withdrawal and New Profit-Loss Ratio** LO6 LO8

Neal, Palmer, and Ruppe are partners in a real estate company. Their respective capital balances and profit-sharing ratios are as follows:

As of December 31, 2008

Partners	*Capital Balance*	*Profit-Sharing Ratio*
Neal	$250,000	4
Palmer	150,000	3
Ruppe	100,000	3

Neal wishes to withdraw from the partnership on January 1, 2009, Palmer and Ruppe have agreed to pay Neal $300,000 from the partnership assets for his 50% capital interest. This settlement price was based on such factors as capital investments, sales performance, and earning capacity.

Palmer and Ruppe must decide whether to use the bonus method or the goodwill method (recognize total goodwill implied by the payment) to record the withdrawal, and they wish to compare the results of using the two methods.

Required:

Prepare a comparison of capital balances using the bonus and goodwill methods (and writing off goodwill implied due to subsequent impairment), assuming that

1. The new profit and loss ratio is in the same relative ratio as that existing before Neal's withdrawal.
2. The profit and loss ratio is changed to 3:2. Palmer is particularly interested in these results, because he feels that his present contribution of time and capital is better reflected by this new profit and loss ratio.

PROBLEM 15-8 **Comprehensive Partnership Problem** LO5 LO6 LO8

COMPREHENSIVE

Brian Snow and Wendy Waite formed a partnership on July 1, 2007. Brian invested $20,000 cash, inventory valued at $15,000, and equipment valued at $67,000. Wendy invested $50,000 cash and land valued at $120,000. The partnership assumed the $40,000 mortgage on the land.

On June 30, 2008, the partnership reported a net loss of $24,000. The partnership contract specified that income and losses were to be allocated by allowing 10% interest on the original capital investment, salaries of $15,000 to Brian and $20,000 to Wendy, and the remainder to be divided in the ratio of 40:60.

On July 1, 2008, Alan Young was admitted into the partnership with a $70,000 cash investment. Alan was given a 30% interest in the partnership because of his special skills. The partners elect to use the bonus method to record the admission. Any bonus should be divided in the old ratio of 40:60.

On June 30, 2009, the partnership reported a net income of $150,000. The new partnership contract stipulated that income and losses were to be divided in a fixed ratio of 20:50:30.

On July 2, 2009, Brian withdrew from the partnership for personal reasons. Brian was given $40,000 cash and a $60,000 note for his capital interest.

Required:

Prepare journal entries for each of the following events. Show computations.

1. Formation of the partnership.
2. Distribution of the net loss for the first year.
3. Admission of Alan into the partnership.
4. Distribution of the net income for the second year.
5. Withdrawal of Brian from the partnership.

PROBLEM 15-9 **Various Changes in Partnership Composition** LO6 LO8

The partnerships of Up & Down and Back & Forth started in business on July 1, 2005; each partnership owns one retail appliance store. It was agreed as of June 30, 2008, to combine the partnerships to form a new partnership to be known as Discount Partnership. Trial balances of the two original partnerships as of June 30, 2008 follow.

	Up & Down Trial Balance June 30, 2008		*Back & Forth Trial Balance June 30, 2008*	
Cash	$ 25,000		$ 20,000	
Accounts Receivable	90,000		140,000	
Allowance for Doubtful Accounts		$ 2,000		$ 6,000
Merchandise Inventory	180,000		115,000	
Land	25,000		35,000	
Buildings and Equipment	80,000		125,000	
Allowance for Depreciation		24,000		61,000
Prepaid Expenses	6,000		8,000	
Accounts Payable		42,000		54,000
Notes Payable		65,000		74,000
Accrued Expenses		34,000		44,000
Up, Capital		95,000		
Down, Capital		144,000		
Back, Capital				65,000
Forth, Capital				139,000
Totals	$406,000	$406,000	$443,000	$443,000

The following additional information is available.

1. The profit- and loss-sharing ratios for the former partnerships were 40% to Up and 60% to Down; 30% to Back and 70% to Forth. The profit- and loss-sharing ratio for the new partnership will be Up, 20%; Down, 30%; Back, 15%; and Forth, 35%.
2. The opening capital ratios for the new partnership are to be the same as the profit- and loss-sharing ratios for the new partnership. The capital assigned to Up & Down will total $225,000. Any cash settlements among the partners arising from capital account adjustments will be a private matter and will not be recorded on the partnership books.

3. The partners agreed that the allowance for bad debts for the new partnership is to be 4% of the accounts receivable balances.
4. The opening inventory of the new partnership is to be valued by the FIFO method. The inventory of Up & Down was valued by the FIFO method and the Back & Forth inventory was valued by the LIFO method. The LIFO inventory represents 80% of its FIFO value.
5. Depreciation is to be computed by the double-declining balance method with a 10-year life for the depreciable assets. Depreciation for three years is to be accumulated in the opening balance of the Allowance for Depreciation account. Up & Down computed depreciation by the straight-line method, and Back & Forth used the double-declining balance method. All assets were obtained on July 1, 2005.
6. After the books were closed, an unrecorded merchandise purchase of $4,000 by Back & Forth was discovered. The merchandise had been sold by June 30, 2008.
7. The accounts of Up & Down include a vacation pay accrual. It was agreed that Back & Forth should make a similar accrual for their 10 employees, who will receive a two-week vacation of $200 per employee per week.

Required:

A. Prepare a worksheet to determine the opening balances of a new partnership after giving effect to the information above. Formal journal entries are not required. Supporting computations, including the computation of goodwill, should be in good form.

B. Prepare a schedule computing the cash to be exchanged between Up & Down and between Back & Forth, in settlement of the affairs of each original partnership.

(*AICPA adapted*)

16

PARTNERSHIP LIQUIDATION

LEARNING OBJECTIVES

1. Describe the steps used to distribute available partnership assets in liquidation under the Uniform Partnership Act (UPA).
2. List the order of priority for each class of creditors in partnership liquidation under the UPA.
3. Prepare a liquidation schedule to settle debts and allocate assets.
4. Prepare a "safe payment approach" liquidation schedule.
5. Describe the four steps in the preparation of an advance plan for the distribution of cash in a partnership liquidation.
6. Prepare the journal entries to incorporate a partnership.

In an article entitled "How to Achieve a Productive Partnership—Accounting Firms," suggestions are provided on how to avoid or resolve problems in a partnership. One suggestion is to have clear agreements about the business relationship. For instance, focusing on the partnership's goal is more practical than attempting to change someone's personality. The key to managing personality differences is respect. Respect is shown by listening to partners and trying to understand them.[1]

In the preceding chapter, dissolution of a partnership in which the business affairs were continued without interruption was discussed. In this chapter, we will consider dissolutions in which the partnership is terminated. The phase of partnership operations that begins after dissolution and ends with the termination of partnership activities is referred to as "winding up the affairs." During this period the partnership's unfinished business is completed, some of the firm's noncash assets may be converted into cash (realization), liabilities are settled to the extent possible, and any remaining assets are distributed to the partners in settlement of their residual interest. These events may occur over a relatively short period of time (for example, there may be a lump-sum sale of the assets, and the liabilities may be assumed by the purchaser or discharged with the cash received), or over a period of several years if the assets are sold individually as the business affairs are gradually terminated.

In the first part of this chapter, we will assume that all noncash assets are converted into cash before any assets are distributed to creditors and partners; this procedure is referred to as a ***simple liquidation***. In the second part of the chapter,

[1] *Journal of Accountancy*, "How to Achieve a Productive Partnership—Accounting Firms," by David Coleman, May 1992.

we assume instead that noncash assets are sold in installments and cash is distributed to the various equity interests as it becomes available.

During the liquidation process, the accountant can provide service to the partners in a number of areas. He or she may assist in preparing financial statements and providing guidance to the partners to ensure that the liquidation proceeds in accordance with legal requirements and the partnership agreement. Much of the accounting for partnership liquidations depends on interpretation of the partnership agreement and the legal provisions governing partnership liquidation. The accountant needs to be familiar with pertinent statutory provisions, which may include the UPA and federal and state bankruptcy laws. In addition, for the protection of all parties concerned, it is advisable to seek legal counsel.

"Long before your business partnership is dissolved, the handling of the breakup or transfer of ownership should be planned. Astonishingly, 80% of new businesses fail to spell out the mechanism for a divorce. Why? The very idea introduces a seed of suspicion into an otherwise happy union."[2]

STEPS IN THE LIQUIDATION PROCESS

LO 1 Steps in the liquidation process.

The first step in the liquidation process is to compute any net income or loss up to the date of dissolution. The closing process should be completed and, as part of it, any net income or loss should be allocated to the partners in accordance with their profit and loss agreement.

In the next step of the liquidation process, assets that are not acceptable for distribution in their present form are converted into cash. If the sales price of an asset is greater than (less than) the recorded book value, there is a gain (loss) from the sale. Procedurally, gains and losses on the realization of assets may be collected in one account and then closed to the capital accounts of the individual partners. The allocation of realization gains or losses should be based on the residual profit and loss ratio, unless specific provisions for such allocation are made in the partnership agreement.[3] The rationale for this procedure is that since the changes in asset values are the result of risk assumed by the partnership, the gain or loss should be shared in the agreed profit and loss ratio. In addition, it may be difficult to separate gains and losses that result from liquidation from the under- or overstatement of book values that results from accounting policies followed in prior years. For example, a gain on the sale of an item of equipment could reflect the fact that the firm had used a conservative depreciation policy and recorded excessive depreciation in prior years. Other adjustments could result from the failure to recognize changes in market values in the appropriate year. Furthermore, any agreement as to interest and salaries in the income allocation formula is ignored when allocating realization gains and losses. The use of the residual ratio is justified, since interest and salaries

[2] *Forbes*, "Planning for Divorce," by Leigh Gallagher, 3/22/99, pp. 94–95.

[3] Section 18 of the UPA provides a list of rights and duties of partners, "subject to any agreement between them." Section 18(a) provides that "each partner must contribute toward the losses, whether of capital or otherwise, sustained by the partnership according to his share in the profits."

are income allocations for time and resources devoted to the normal operating activities of a going concern and are not directly associated with changes in fair values of assets.

The last step is to distribute the available assets to creditors and partners. Section 40(b) of the Uniform Partnership Act (UPA) provides that

> The liabilities of the partnership shall rank in order of payment, as follows:
> (I) Liabilities to creditors other than partners,
> (II) Liabilities to partners other than for capital and profits (such as loans),
> (III) Liabilities to partners in respect of capital,
> (IV) Liabilities to partners in respect of profits.

According to this ranking, firm creditors are the first to be paid from partnership assets. In determining the rights of various creditors to payment, liabilities are classified as those that are secured, partially secured, and unsecured, with some unsecured having priority. Bankruptcy laws dictate which of the partnership creditors are to be paid as cash becomes available. However, since this decision would have no impact on the total unpaid claims of the partnership, we will view the pool of creditors as if it were one unsecured obligation and will treat any cash payment as a reduction in total liabilities.

The UPA then provides for an order of payment that ranks partnership obligations to a partner ahead of asset distribution to a partner for capital investment. However, if a partner has a debit capital balance and has lent money to the partnership, it is legally permissible to offset the loan balance against the debit capital balance. The courts have recognized that this "right of offset" is necessary in order to avoid the potential inequity of distributing cash to a partner to satisfy an outstanding loan balance when the partner has either a debit capital balance, or potential for a debit capital balance. A debit capital balance is considered an asset of the partnership.[4] If the partner is unable to honor this obligation to the partnership by contributing additional assets, and for some reason cannot be forced to do so, the debit capital balance is allocated as a realization loss to the remaining partners in their relative profit and loss ratio. The residual claims of the remaining partners are reduced, as is the amount of cash they will receive.

Items III and IV are generally combined into one balance because of the practical problem of separating them. In other words, after several years of operation, a partner's capital investments, withdrawals, and income and loss elements may become combined into one balance and difficult to separate if the income summary account is closed to the capital accounts of each partner. In settling a partner's claim against the partnership, the partners may agree to the distribution of noncash assets. If so, the carrying value of the asset should be adjusted to fair value and the amount of the adjustment allocated to all the partners in accordance with the partnership agreement. The fair value of the distributed asset is then charged against the proper capital account.

---

[4] Section 40(a) of the UPA defines the assets of a partnership as including not only the partnership property, but also the contributions of partners necessary for the payment of all liabilities specified in section 40(b). Section 40(b) specifies that amounts owing to creditors and to partners for loans, capital, and profits are liabilities of a partnership.

"If a farm family partnership is not salvageable, the best procedure may be to negotiate a business 'divorce' as quickly as possible. Dissolution will require a mediator or attorney and, unfortunately, it won't be cheap. Competent lawyers and mediators cost money. Still the family members' desire to save on professional fees shouldn't lock them into a waltz toward inevitable financial and emotional ruin."[5]

PRIORITIES OF PARTNERSHIP AND PERSONAL CREDITORS

LO2 Order of priority for each class of creditors.

The UPA (Section 15) provides that partners are jointly liable for all contracts and other obligations of the partnership. This means that creditors of a partnership that are not paid in full from distribution of partnership assets must bring legal action against all the partners together to enforce their unsettled claims. Partners are jointly and severally liable for obligations that arise out of a tort and breach of trust committed by a partner while acting within the scope of the partnership business. ***Joint and several*** means that legal action may be brought against all the partners together or against any one or more of the partners in separate suits. A number of states have enacted legislation eliminating the distinction, and in those jurisdictions both contract and tort actions are joint and several. This latter approach, which permits suits against all (joint) or less than all (several) of the partners, is followed in this chapter. Conversely, personal creditors of an individual partner can seek recovery of payment from personal assets of the respective partner, and under certain conditions from partnership assets. Recognition of the rights of these two groups of creditors and the classification of assets into personal and partnership categories is referred to as ***marshaling of assets***. The order of priority concerning the availability of assets for each class of creditors in states that have adopted the UPA is as follows:

A. Partnership assets
   1. Partnership creditors.
   2. Personal creditors that did not recover their claims in full from personal assets. Recovery from partnership assets is limited to the extent that the partner has a credit interest in the partnership assets.

B. Personal assets
   1. Personal creditors.
   2. Partnership creditors who were not satisfied from partnership assets. Such claims may be made against an individual partner regardless of whether the partner has a debit or credit equity interest in the partnership.
   3. Claims of the partnership against the partner by nature of a deficit equity interest.

Because of the foregoing rules, the reader should recognize the importance of properly recording all partnership assets, liabilities, and capital interest of each partner.

[5] *Successful Farming*, Iowa edition, "Can Their Problem Be Solved?" by Donald Jonovic, May/June 1997, p. 65, copyright Meredith Corporation.

To illustrate the marshaling of assets rules, assume that ABCD Partnership reports the following balance sheet after the sale of all noncash assets:

Debits		*Credits*	
Cash	$ 50,000	Liabilities	$ 75,000
Bill Baker, Capital	15,000	Alice Amos, Capital	15,000
Carol Carter, Capital	35,000	Don Davis, Capital	10,000
Total	$100,000		$100,000

The partners share profits and losses equally. The personal and partnership status of each partner is as follows:

	Personal			*Partnership*
Partner	*Assets*	*Liabilities*	*Assets Greater Than (Less Than) Liabilities*	*Capital Balance (Cr.) Dr.*
Alice Amos	$20,000	$50,000	$(30,000)	($15,000)
Bill Baker	33,000	30,000	3,000	15,000
Carol Carter	90,000	40,000	50,000	35,000
Don Davis	40,000	10,000	30,000	(10,000)

The personal assets of each partner must be applied to the settlement of his or her personal liabilities before personal assets can be used to satisfy any partnership claims. Thus, the maximum amount that the partnership creditors and other partners could recover from the personal assets is $83,000 ($3,000 + $50,000 + $30,000). Because the personal liabilities of Amos exceed her personal assets, partnership claims cannot be enforced against her personal assets even though she has a credit interest in the partnership. However, her unsettled personal creditors in the amount of $30,000 can look for full or partial settlement of their claims from final distribution of partnership assets in settlement of her capital interest. At this time, the partnership has a claim of $15,000 and $35,000 against Baker and Carter, respectively. Baker, however, will have only $3,000 left for investment in the partnership to reduce his capital deficit. Carter has sufficient personal assets to satisfy her personal liabilities and invest in the partnership to cover her share of partnership losses. Davis is personally solvent and has a credit capital interest in the partnership.

The liquidation of the partnership is summarized in Illustration 16-1. Although formal journal entries are not shown, they would be recorded in a journal in accordance with the tabular arrangement summarized in the liquidation schedule. The steps in the liquidation process may proceed in any order as long as the rights of the partners, partnership creditors, and personal creditors are recognized. In this example, the following sequence of events occurs.

1. Baker invests $3,000 in the partnership and his remaining deficit of $12,000 is a liquidation loss that is allocated to the remaining partners in their relative profit and loss ratio, one-third each. (Note that because Carter has sufficient assets to cover her share of additional losses, $4,000 loss is allocated to her, even though she currently has a deficit capital balance.)

Marshaling of Assets

ILLUSTRATION 16-1
Schedule of Partnership Liquidation

			Capital and Loan Balances			
	Cash	*Liabilities*	*Amos 1/4*	*Baker 1/4*	*Carter 1/4*	*Davis 1/4*
Balance before cash distributions	50,000	(75,000)*	(15,000)	15,000	35,000	(10,000)
Investment by Baker	3,000			(3,000)		
	53,000	(75,000)	(15,000)	12,000	35,000	(10,000)
Allocation of Baker's deficit			4,000	(12,000)	4,000	4,000
	53,000	(75,000)	(11,000)	—0—	39,000	(6,000)
Payment to creditors	(53,000)	53,000				
	—0—	(22,000)	(11,000)	—0—	39,000	(6,000)
Investment by Carter	39,000				(39,000)	
	39,000	(22,000)	(11,000)	—0—	—0—	(6,000)
Payment to creditors	(22,000)	22,000				
	17,000	—0—	(11,000)	—0—	—0—	(6,000)
Payment to partners	(17,000)		11,000			6,000
	—0—	—0—	—0—	—0—	—0—	—0—

* In this chapter, () means that an account has a credit balance or a credit posted to an account.

2. Cash of $53,000 is distributed to the creditors.
3. The partnership creditors obtain judgment against Carter. (The creditors could have proceeded to recover their claims from any solvent partner individually, including Davis, who has a credit capital interest, or from the partners jointly.) Since Carter has a personal net asset position of $50,000, she will invest an additional $39,000 in the partnership, $22,000 of which will go to partnership creditors and $17,000 to the other partners.
4. The cash is distributed first to liquidate partnership liabilities and then to satisfy partner's capital interests.

Observe that the cash distribution to partners is based on their capital balances, not their profit and loss ratio. The unpaid personal creditors of Amos have a claim against her $11,000 partnership distribution.

If, in the illustration above, Carter was able to invest only $20,000 from her personal assets and Davis as well as Amos are personally insolvent, then the creditors and partners Amos and Davis would have unrecoverable losses of $19,000 as shown next.

	Cash	*Liabilities*	*Amos*	*Baker*	*Carter*	*Davis*
From Illustration 16-1	—0—	(22,000)	(11,000)	—0—	39,000	(6,000)
Investment by Carter	20,000				(20,000)	
Payment to creditors	(20,000)	20,000				
	—0—	(2,000)	(11,000)	—0—	19,000	(6,000)

SIMPLE LIQUIDATION ILLUSTRATED

In a simple liquidation, all of a partnership's noncash assets are converted into cash and the resulting gain or loss allocated before any distribution is made to the creditors and to the partners. To illustrate the accounting for a simple liquidation, assume that the condensed balance sheet of ABC Partnership that follows was prepared just before the liquidation:

LO 3 Preparing a liquidation schedule.

Assets, Liabilities, and Capital

Cash	$ 20,000	Liabilities	$ 70,000
Noncash Assets	180,000	Carter, Loan	10,000
		Alice Amos, Capital (50%)	80,000
		Bill Baker, Capital (30%)	30,000
		Carol Carter, Capital (20%)	10,000
Total	$200,000	Total	$200,000

The profit and loss ratio is in parentheses. Personal assets and liabilities of the partners are

	Assets	*Liabilities*	*Net Assets*
Amos	$50,000	$30,000	$20,000
Baker	40,000	12,000	28,000
Carter	20,000	25,000	(5,000)

The liquidation of the ABC Partnership is summarized in the schedule presented in Illustration 16-2. The following sequence of events recorded in Illustration 16-2 is based on the concepts previously discussed.

1. Noncash assets of $180,000 are sold for $52,000 and the resulting realization loss of $128,000 is allocated to the partners according to their profit and loss ratio.
2. Partnership liabilities, other than to partners, are paid before assets are distributed to partners.
3. The right of offset is exercised where a partner with an outstanding loan has a debit capital balance.
4. In transactions (4) and (5), the principles concerning the marshaling of assets are applied to determine if additional investments can be expected. In this case,

Simple Liquidation

ILLUSTRATION 16-2

Schedule of Partnership Realization and Liquidation

					Capital Balances		
	Cash	*Noncash Assets*	*Liabilities*	*Carter Loan*	*Amos .5*	*Baker .3*	*Carter .2*
Account balances before realization	20,000	180,000	(70,000)	(10,000)	(80,000)	(30,000)	(10,000)
(1) Sale of assets and allocation of $128,000 loss	52,000	(180,000)			64,000	38,400	25,600
	72,000	—0—	(70,000)	(10,000)	(16,000)	8,400	15,600
(2) Payment to creditors	(70,000)		70,000				
	2,000	—0—	—0—	(10,000)	(16,000)	8,400	15,600
(3) Offset loan against debit capital balance				10,000			(10,000)
	2,000	—0—	—0—	—0—	(16,000)	8,400	5,600
(4) Allocate debit capital balance of insolvent partner					3,500	2,100	(5,600)
	2,000	—0—	—0—	—0—	(12,500)	10,500	—0—
(5) Investment by Baker	10,500					(10,500)	
	12,500	—0—	—0—	—0—	(12,500)	—0—	—0—
(6) Payment to Amos	(12,500)				12,500		
	—0—	—0—	—0—	—0—	—0—	—0—	—0—

Carter with a deficit capital interest is also personally insolvent. Thus, her deficit is allocated to the other partners on the basis of their relative loss-sharing ratio: to Amos, to Baker.

5. Baker invests $10,500 in the partnership to eliminate his deficit after his personal assets were applied to the settlement of his personal liabilities.
6. Cash is distributed to Amos to satisfy her capital claim against the partnership assets.

TEST YOUR KNOWLEDGE

NOTE: Solutions to ***Test Your Knowledge*** questions are found at the end of each chapter before the end-of-chapter questions.

The trial balance for the ABC Partnership before bankruptcy is as follows:

Cash	*Noncash Assets*	*Liabilities*	*A Capital*	*B Capital*	*C Capital*
$20,000	$200,000	$30,000	$100,000	$60,000	$30,000

The partners share profits and losses in the ratio 40:40:20.

1. If the noncash assets are sold for $100,000 cash, determine the amount of cash, if any, that partner A will receive upon liquidation.
2. If the noncash assets are sold for $50,000 cash and assuming that partners with a deficit balance cannot contribute additional assets, determine the amount of cash, if any, that partner A will receive upon liquidation.

INSTALLMENT LIQUIDATION

Instead of the immediate conversion of noncash partnership assets to cash under a simple liquidation, it is sometimes advantageous for a partnership to extend the conversion over several months. For example, in certain types of businesses, such as land development, more cash may be generated if a company completes construction projects it has started. In other situations, the partnership may receive a greater cash price for the noncash assets if they are not sold at a forced liquidation. If the liquidation extends over a period of time, the partners will probably prefer that cash be distributed as it becomes available. If partners are to receive cash in installments before the total liquidation losses and the total cash available are known, safeguards must be taken to protect the interests of the creditors and the respective interest of each partner. In addition, the individual in charge of the liquidation must use safeguards to avoid potential liability for wrongful distributions. The remainder of this chapter focuses on the problems associated with a liquidation in installments and the general rules governing such liquidations. Once again, many of the procedures followed are necessary to satisfy legal requirements and to protect the person in charge of the liquidation and the residual partners' interests.

Safe Payment Approach

In computing how cash is to be distributed to the partners before all assets are disposed of, care must be taken to ensure that the partners' remaining capital balances will be adequate to absorb any potential loss. However, at this point, the amount of cash to be generated from the sale of noncash assets and the resulting gain or loss is not known. Therefore, the partners should view each cash distribution as if it were the final distribution.

One approach used to calculate a safe cash distribution is based on three assumptions:

1. A loan to or from an individual partner will be combined with the respective partner's capital account to determine his or her net interest in the partnership assets.
2. The remaining noncash assets will not provide any additional cash. In other words, the maximum potential loss is equal to the book value of noncash assets. (This assumption will be modified later in the chapter.)
3. A partner with a debit balance in his or her capital account will be unable to pay amounts owed to the partnership (that is, each partner is personally insolvent).

LO4 Safe payment approach.

The result of applying these assumptions is that cash will not be distributed to a partner whose capital account balance (including loan balance and drawing account) is insufficient to absorb his or her share of potential losses either from the write-off of assets or from the failure of a deficit partner to cover a debit capital balance. Of course, no partner should receive cash until the liabilities have been liquidated or provided for through the retention of adequate cash.

Computation of Safe Payment before Each Distribution To illustrate the safe payment approach when a partnership is liquidated in installments, assume that the following condensed balance sheet was prepared before the partners' agreement to liquidate the partnership.

Cash	$ 10,000	Liabilities	$ 28,000
Noncash Assets	100,000	Alice Amos, Capital (30%)	34,000
		Bill Baker, Capital (50%)	30,000
		Carol Carter, Capital (20%)	18,000
Total	$110,000	Total	$110,000

The partners' income- and loss-sharing percentages are stated in parentheses. The noncash assets were converted into cash over a period of time as follows:

	Sales Price	*Book Value*	*(Loss)*
Sale No. 1	$20,000	$30,000	(10,000)
Sale No. 2	15,000	25,000	(10,000)
Sale No. 3	10,000	30,000	(20,000)
Sale No. 4	2,000	10,000	(8,000)
Sale No. 5	—0—	5,000	(5,000)

The realization of the partnership assets and liquidation of the partnership are summarized in Illustration 16-3. A safe payment schedule is prepared *each time cash is to be distributed.* After the first sale of assets and all creditors have been paid, $2,000 cash remains to be distributed to partners. Schedule I in Illustration 16-3 demonstrates how the $2,000 will be distributed. In this case, the assumption that the remaining noncash assets of $70,000 are worthless results in a debit balance in Baker's capital account. Another assumption is that all partners are personally insolvent. Therefore, the hypothetical deficit is allocated to the remaining partners with credit balances on the basis of their relative profit and loss ratio: 3/5 to Amos, 2/5 to Carter. This allocation results in a hypothetical debit balance in Carter's capital account, which is assigned to Amos. Thus, if $2,000 is paid to Amos, this will leave her with a capital balance sufficient to absorb her share of the potential remaining losses. Amos will not be required to make an additional investment in the partnership unless significant amounts of unrecorded liabilities are discovered or significant amounts of liquidation expenses are incurred. But if it became necessary for Amos to make an additional investment, the other two partners would also be required to do so.

After the second sale of assets, $15,000 cash is available for distribution. The allocation of the $15,000 is shown in schedule II of Illustration 16-3. Note that, if the fair value of the remaining assets is zero, Baker's capital balance of $20,000 would be inadequate to absorb his share of the losses, which would be $22,500 ($45,000 × .50). Accordingly, at this time, Baker does not receive any of the cash to be distributed, since he could end up with a debit capital balance. After the third cash distribution, the partners'/capital balances are in their profit and loss ratio of 3:5:2. Once their capital interests are in accordance with the profit and loss ratio, any subsequent distribution of assets will be based on the profit and loss ratio. Note that each partner's capital account is now sufficient to absorb the final potential loss of $5,000.

A safe payment schedule is prepared to compute the amount of cash to be distributed and to determine which partner(s) will receive cash. The series of computations is not recorded in the accounts, since they are based upon certain assumed events that have not yet occurred. Only the actual transactions as they occur, such as the sale of assets and distribution of cash, are recorded in the accounts.

Additional Losses, Discovery of Liabilities, and Liquidation Expense Up to this point in this chapter, all available cash was distributed to (1) the partnership's creditors who were recorded on the partnership books or (2) the partners. In the calculation of a safe payment, it was assumed that the potential loss was equal to the book value of the remaining noncash assets. In addition, no liquidation expenses were incurred. As the liquidation proceeds, some liabilities that had not been recorded previously may be reported. These creditors have claims that must be satisfied from the available cash before payments are made to partners for their capital interest.

Certain expenses, such as the reasonable cost of carrying out the liquidation, have priority over payments to creditors. Furthermore, the disposal cost of assets may exceed the proceeds from the sale of the assets so that the resulting loss is greater than the assets' recorded book value. Such items can be considered in the safe payment schedule by adding the estimated liquidation expenses, disposal cost, and unrecorded liabilities to the book value of noncash assets. To illustrate, assume the facts presented in Illustration 16-3 except that it is estimated that added expenses of $1,000 will be incurred in completing the liquidation. The safe payment calculation for the first cash distribution would be modified as follows:

ILLUSTRATION 16-3

Schedule of Partnership Realization and Liquidation

Installment Liquidation

	Cash	Other Assets	Liabilities	Capital and Loan Balances Amos .3	Baker .5	Carter .2
Balance before realization	10,000	100,000	(28,000)	(34,000)	(30,000)	(18,000)
Sale of assets	20,000	(30,000)		3,000	5,000	2,000
	30,000	70,000	(28,000)	(31,000)	(25,000)	(16,000)
Payment to creditors	(28,000)		28,000			
	2,000	70,000	—0—	(31,000)	(25,000)	(16,000)
Payment to partners						
Safe payment Schedule I (below)	(2,000)			2,000		
	—0—	70,000	—0—	(29,000)	(25,000)	(16,000)
Sale of assets	15,000	(25,000)		3,000	5,000	2,000
	15,000	45,000	—0—	(26,000)	(20,000)	(14,000)
Payment to partners						
Safe payment Schedule II (below)	(15,000)			11,000		4,000
	—0—	45,000	—0—	(15,000)	(20,000)	(10,000)
Sale of assets	10,000	(30,000)		6,000	10,000	4,000
	10,000	15,000	—0—	(9,000)	(10,000)	(6,000)
Payment to partners						
Safe payment Schedule III (below)	(10,000)			4,500	2,500	3,000
	—0—	15,000	—0—	(4,500)	(7,500)	(3,000)
Sale of assets	2,000	(10,000)		2,400	4,000	1,600
	2,000	5,000	—0—	(2,100)	(3,500)	(1,400)
Payment to partners	(2,000)			600	1,000	400
	—0—	5,000	—0—	(1,500)	(2,500)	(1,000)
Write-off of assets		(5,000)		1,500	2,500	1,000
	—0—	—0—	—0—	—0—	—0—	—0—

Schedule I

Computation of Safe Payments

	Amos .3	Baker .5	Carter .2
Capital and loan balances	(31,000)	(25,000)	(16,000)
Allocation of potential loss—$70,000	21,000	35,000	14,000
	(10,000)	10,000	(2,000)
Allocation of Baker's potential deficit	6,000	(10,000)	4,000
	(4,000)	—0—	2,000
Allocation of Carter's potential deficit	2,000		(2,000)
Safe payment	(2,000)	—0—	—0—

Schedule II

Computation of Safe Payments

	Amos .3	Baker .5	Carter .2
Capital and loan balances	(26,000)	(20,000)	(14,000)
Allocation of potential loss—$45,000	13,500	22,500	9,000
	(12,500)	2,500	(5,000)
Allocation of Baker's potential deficit	1,500	(2,500)	1,000
Safe payment	(11,000)	—0—	(4,000)

Schedule III

Computation of Safe Payments

	Amos .3	Baker .5	Carter .2
Capital and loan balances	(9,000)	(10,000)	(6,000)
Allocation of potential loss—$15,000	4,500	7,500	3,000
Safe payment	(4,500)	(2,500)	(3,000)

	Amos	Baker	Carter
Capital and loan balances	(31,000)	(25,000)	(16,000)
Allocation of potential losses ($70,000 + $1,000)	21,300	35,500	14,200
Balances	(9,700)	10,500	(1,800)
Allocation of Baker's potential deficit	6,300	(10,500)	4,200
Balances	(3,400)	—0—	2,400
Allocation of Carter's potential deficit	2,400		(2,400)
Safe payment	(1,000)	—0—	—0—

As can be seen, the effect of the adjustment is to hold back cash equal to the estimated expenses, which results in a corresponding reduction in the cash distributed to Amos.

Advance Plan for the Distribution of Cash

LO5 Four steps in an advance plan.

In the preceding illustration, a safe payment to each partner was calculated before each cash distribution. This process was necessary until the capital accounts were in the profit- and loss-sharing ratio. Although this method is feasible, it is more informative and efficient to prepare an advance schedule that specifies the order in which each partner will participate and the amount of cash each partner will receive as it becomes available for distribution. For example, from such a schedule, the personal creditors of an insolvent partner would be able to compute how much cash would have to be generated from the sale of the partnership assets before any cash is distributed to the insolvent partner.

To illustrate the procedures for the preparation of an advance cash distribution plan, assume the set of facts employed in Illustration 16-3. The objective of the procedure is to derive the order and the amount of cash that should be distributed to each partner such that no partner receiving a cash distribution will have to make an additional investment in the firm. Such a distribution plan will bring the balances of the partners' capital accounts into their profit and loss ratio as soon as possible. The rationale for this procedure is that once the capital balances are in the profit and loss ratio, no one partner is in any better position than any other partner to absorb losses.

Steps in the development of an advance cash distribution plan are presented in Illustration 16-4 and explained below.

Step 1 Determine the net capital interest of each partner by combining the balance in the partner's capital account with obligations to or receivables from the partner.

	Amos	Baker	Carter
Capital balance	$34,000	$30,000	$18,000
Loan balance	—0—	—0—	—0—
Net capital interest	$34,000	$30,000	$18,000

Step 2 Determine the order in which the partners are to participate in cash distributions. The objective of this step is to provide an order of cash distribution in which the ratio of the partners' capital interest will eventually be equal to their

ILLUSTRATION 16-4

Preparation of an Advance Plan for the Distribution of Cash

Step 1	*Amos*	*Baker*	*Carter*
Capital balances	$ 34,000	$ 30,000	$18,000
Loan balances	—	—	—
Net capital interest	$ 34,000	$ 30,000	$18,000
Profit and loss ratio	.30	.50	.20

Step 2			
Loss necessary to reduce net capital balance to zero	$113,333	$ 60,000	$90,000
Order of cash distribution	1	3	2

	Loss Absorption Potential			*Asset Distribution*		
Step 3	*Amos*	*Baker*	*Carter*	*Amos*	*Baker*	*Carter*
Profit and loss ratio	.30	.50	.20	.30	.50	.20
Loss absorption potential	$113,333	$60,000	$90,000			
Net capital interest				$34,000	$30,000	18,000
Distribution to Amos to reduce her capital interest so that her loss absorption potential is the same as Carter's	23,333					
($113,333 − $90,000 = $23,333) × .30				7,000		
Balances after distribution to Amos	90,000	60,000	90,000	27,000	30,000	18,000
Distribution to Amos and Carter to reduce their capital interest so that their loss absorption potential is the same as Baker's	30,000		30,000			
($90,000 − $60,000 = $30,000) × .30				9,000		
($90,000 − $60,000 = $30,000) × .20						6,000
Balances after distribution to Amos and Carter	60,000	60,000	60,000	18,000	30,000	12,000
Remainder of asset distributions				.30	.50	.20

Step 4

Cash Distribution Plan

Order of Cash Distribution	*Liabilities*	*Amos* .3	*Baker* .5	*Carter* .2
1. First $28,000	100%			
2. Next $7,000		100%		
3. Next $15,000		60%		40%
4. Remainder		30%	50%	20%

profit and loss ratio. Once this is accomplished, all partners will have an equal ability to absorb their share of partnership losses. Several approaches can be used to accomplish this objective. One systematic approach is to determine the loss absorption potential of each partner by dividing the net capital interest of each partner by his or her respective profit and loss ratio.

	Amos	*Baker*	*Carter*
Net capital interest	$ 34,000	$30,000	$18,000
Profit and loss ratio	.30	.50	.20
Loss absorption potential	$113,333	$60,000	$90,000
Order of cash distribution	1	3	2

This computation determines the maximum amount of loss each partner is capable of absorbing and provides a basis for ranking the partners in terms of each partner's capital interest relative to his or her loss ratio. The partner with the largest loss absorption potential has the ability to absorb a greater share of losses before his or her capital account would be reduced to a zero balance. Thus, Amos will receive the first distribution of assets after the creditors' claims have been satisfied. The partner with the lowest loss absorption potential (Baker) will be the last partner to participate in the distribution of assets from the partnership.

Step 3 In Step 2, the order in which each partner is to participate in cash distributions was determined. The next step is to compute the amount of cash each partner is to receive as it becomes available for distribution. The objective is to determine the ***amount*** of cash to distribute to each partner to bring the ratios of their capital interests in the partnership into alignment with their profit and loss ratios. One way to do this is to consider the loss absorption potential computed in Step 2. It was determined in Step 2 that Amos is in the strongest position relative to the other partners and is to receive the first cash distribution. Amos is capable of absorbing her share of $113,333 in losses, which is $23,333 greater than the loss potential of Carter ($113,333 − $90,000), who is the next partner to participate in cash distributions. However, Amos must absorb only 30% or $7,000 ($23,333 × .30) of such potential losses. Thus, a payment to Amos of $7,000 reduces her loss absorption potential to Carter's (the next closest loss potential) level ($34,000 − $7,000 = $27,000/.30 = $90,000). Amos and Carter now have the same absorption potential for future losses. Also, note that a payment of $7,000 to Amos brings her capital interest into a ratio of 3:2 to that of Carter ($27,000:$18,000), which is the same as their relative profit and loss ratio.

The next step in the process is to bring the loss absorption potential of Amos and Carter into balance with that of Baker, who is the last partner to participate in the distribution of cash. Using the same rationale, Amos and Carter are now capable of absorbing losses of $30,000 ($90,000 − $60,000) greater than Baker. Since they must absorb 30% and 20% of the losses, respectively, the distribution to each partner is computed as follows:

To Amos: $30,000 × .30 = $9,000
To Carter: $30,000 × .20 = $6,000

Of the next $15,000, Amos is to receive $9,000 and Carter is to receive $6,000. Now all partners' capital balances are in the same ratio as their profit and loss sharing ratio.[6]

[6] An alternative method of determining the amount to be distributed at each level is to compute the capital account balances needed by each partner so as to bring the partners' capital balances into their agreed profit- and loss-sharing ratio. This approach is simpler in certain cases, but the approach in the text is more systematic when there are numerous partners. The alternative works by bringing the ratio of the partners' capital account balances into their profit- and loss-sharing ratio in the order in which the partners are to participate in the distribution. In this case, the first step is to compute what the capital account balance of Amos should be so that her capital balance is in the profit- and loss-sharing ratio with that of Carter (3:2). This can be computed as follows:

(Continues next page)

Step 4 A cash distribution plan is then prepared as follows:

Order of Cash Distribution	*Liabilities*	*Amos*	*Baker*	*Carter*
1. First $28,000	100%			
2. Next $7,000		100%		
3. Next $15,000		60%		40%
4. Remainder		30%	50%	20%

The first $28,000 available is, of course, paid to the creditors. Cash may be held back from distribution if it is anticipated that unrecorded liabilities will be discovered or if additional liquidation expenses will be incurred. The distribution of cash in excess of this reserve amount proceeds as determined. Amos will receive all of any additional cash up to $7,000. Additional cash in excess of $7,000 and up to $22,000 is distributed 60:40 to Amos and Carter. After $22,000 ($15,000 + $7,000) has been distributed to the partners, the capital accounts are in the desired profit and loss ratio of 3:5:2. Any further distributions to the partners are made according to the profit and loss ratio.

The advance distribution plan developed before will yield the same cash distribution as the process of computing a safe payment each time cash is available. As proof, in Illustration 16-5, the advance plan for distributing cash as developed in Illustration 16-4 is applied to determine the cash distribution in Illustration 16-3. Even though both methods produce the same results, the advance plan is more informative to both personal and partnership creditors, and to the partners. Interested parties now know the order in which individual partners will receive cash and the amounts that each may receive at each stage of the distribution process.

One requirement that must be satisfied in the development of the advance plan is that the partners must share income in the same ratio that they share losses. If this were not the case, the potential amount of a new loss would need to be computed after every allocation to the partners' capital accounts. This occurs because the

---

Let X = desired capital balance

$$\frac{\text{Loss ratio of Amos}}{\text{Loss ratio of Carter}} = \frac{X}{\text{Capital balance of Carter}}$$

$$\frac{3}{2} = \frac{X}{\$18{,}000}$$

$$2X = \$54{,}000$$

$$X = \$27{,}000$$

Since Amos has a capital balance of $34,000, it would take a distribution of $7,000 to reduce the balance to $27,000. The next level of payments should reduce the capital balances of Amos and Carter in such a way that their capital balances will be in the loss ratio to that of Baker, which is 3:5 and 2:5, respectively.

$$\frac{3}{5} = \frac{X}{\$30{,}000} \qquad \frac{2}{5} = \frac{X}{\$30{,}000}$$

$$5X = \$90{,}000 \qquad 5X = \$60{,}000$$

$$X = \$18{,}000 \qquad X = \$12{,}000$$

A distribution of $9,000 to Amos ($27,000 − $18,000) and $6,000 to Carter ($18,000 − $12,000) will produce capital balances in the ratio of 3:5:2 ($18,000: $30,000: $12,000).

ILLUSTRATION 16-5

Cash Distribution per Advance Plan

	Liabilities	*Amos*	*Baker*	*Carter*	*Total*
First Distribution: $30,000					
First—$28,000	$28,000				$28,000
Next—$2,000		$2,000			2,000
	$28,000	$2,000	—	—	$30,000
Second Distribution: $15,000					
First—$5,000					
(Remainder of $7,000 level)		$ 5,000			$ 5,000
Next—$10,000		6,000		$4,000	10,000
	—	$11,000	—	$4,000	$15,000
Third Distribution: $10,000					
First—$5,000					
(Remainder of $15,000 level)		$ 3,000		$2,000	$ 5,000
Next—$5,000		1,500	$2,500	1,000	5,000
	—	$ 4,500	$2,500	$3,000	$10,000
Last Distribution: $2,000					
First—$2,000	—	$ 600	$1,000	$ 400	$ 2,000

allocation of liquidation gains alters the order of cash distribution computed in the advance plan. To illustrate, assume that Amos, Baker, and Carter, with capital balances of $45,000, $24,000, and $20,000, respectively, share losses in the ratio of 5:3:2, but share income in the ratio of 3:5:2. The order of cash distribution based on the ratio of losses would be as follows:

	Amos	*Baker*	*Carter*
Net capital interest	$45,000	$24,000	$ 20,000
Loss ratios	.50	.30	.20
Loss absorption potential	$90,000	$80,000	$100,000
Order of cash distribution	2	3	1

Now assume that the partnership realizes a $50,000 gain. The allocation of the gain in the ratio of 3:5:2 and computation of the order of cash distribution follow:

	Amos	*Baker*	*Carter*
Net capital interest	$(45,000)	$(24,000)	$(20,000)
Allocation of $50,000 gain	(15,000)	(25,000)	(10,000)
Net capital interest	$(60,000)	$(49,000)	$(30,000)
Loss ratios	.50	.30	.20
New loss absorption potential	$120,000	$163,333	$150,000
New order of cash distribution	3	1	2

In this illustration an allocation of the $50,000 gain moved Baker from being the last partner to receive cash to being the first partner to receive cash.

It is also necessary to recompute an advance plan if a certain classification of losses is shared in a different ratio from the one used in preparing the advance plan, or if adjustments are made to the capital balances in other than the loss ratio.

For example, assume that it has been discovered that a cash withdrawal by a partner had been expensed instead of debited to his drawing account. The correction of the error would modify the loss absorption potential of that partner. If such adjustments occur frequently, then the computation of a safe payment may be less time-consuming and easier to use than the development of an advance cash distribution plan.

TEST YOUR KNOWLEDGE

NOTE: Solutions to ***Test Your Knowledge*** questions are found at the end of each chapter before the end-of-chapter questions.

Short Answer

1. The capital balances for partners A and B are $120,000 and $60,000, respectively. They share profits and losses in the ratio 60:40. The partnership has $15,000 in liabilities. Prepare a cash distribution plan.

INCORPORATION OF A PARTNERSHIP

LO6 Incorporation of a partnership.

After a partnership has been operating for a period of time, the partners may find that the partnership form of business is no longer satisfactory. The corporation, with its limited liability, continuity of existence, and ability to raise needed resources, may become more attractive. Upon incorporation, the assets and liabilities are transferred to the corporation and the partners receive capital stock in settlement of their interests. The partnership accounts should be restated to fair values to assure that the partners receive an equitable distribution of stock for their interests.

The partnership books may be retained for use by the corporation, or a new set of books may be established.

Retention of Partnership Books by Corporation

Assuming that the partnership books are used by the corporation, the steps to record the incorporation are as follows:

1. Assets and liabilities are adjusted to fair value. Frequently, a valuation adjustment account is created to accumulate the gains and losses.
2. The valuation adjustment account is closed to the partners' capital accounts in accordance with their profit and loss ratio.
3. The partners' capital accounts are closed upon the transfer of capital stock. Since the books are retained, offsetting credits are made to Capital Stock at par value for the number of shares issued. If the debit to partners' capital accounts exceeds the credit to Capital Stock, the difference is a credit to Additional Paid-in Capital.

To illustrate, assume that AB Partnership is to incorporate. The new corporation is authorized to issue 5,000 shares of $10 par value stock. Book values of the partnership accounts and fair values for the assets are determined to be:

	Book Value		
	Debit	*Credit*	*Fair Values*
Cash	$ 5,000		$ 5,000
Accounts Receivable	4,000		3,600
Inventory	5,000		7,000
Land	10,000		15,000
Equipment (net of depreciation)	6,000		5,000
Accounts Payable		$ 7,000	
Notes Payable		10,000	
Art, Capital		8,000	
Beck, Capital		5,000	
Total	$30,000	$30,000	

Other facts are: (1) Liabilities are assumed to be fairly valued; (2) Art and Beck share profits equally; (3) Art and Beck are to receive par value stock equal to their adjusted ending capital balances. The journal entries to incorporate are:

	Debit	Credit
(1) Inventory	2,000	
Land	5,000	
Equipment		1,000
Accounts Receivable		400
Valuation Adjustment		5,600
(2) Valuation Adjustment	5,600	
Art, Capital		2,800
Beck, Capital		2,800
(3) Art, Capital	10,800	
Beck, Capital	7,800	
Capital Stock—$10 par		18,600

New Books Established by Corporation

If the corporation establishes a new set of books, then all accounts on the partnership books will end with a zero balance. The only difference as compared to the illustration above is that on receipt of the stock, asset and liability accounts are closed on the partnership books and transferred to the corporation. To balance the entry, an asset account is created for the capital stock received in the amount of $18,600. This balance should also equal the sum of the balances in the remaining capital accounts. The entry to record the distribution of the capital stock is:

	Debit	Credit
Art, Capital	10,800	
Beck, Capital	7,800	
Capital Stock (from Corporation)		18,600

The corporation records the assets received and the liabilities assumed on the new books at the net cost of the stock issued ($18,600), which is also equal to the adjusted value of the net assets on the partnership books. A credit of $18,600 to balance the entry is made to capital stock issued.

SUMMARY

1. *Describe the steps used to distribute available partnership assets in liquidation under the Uniform Partnership Act (UPA).* The first step in the liquidation process is to compute any net income or loss up to the date of dissolution. The closing process should be completed and any net income or loss allocated to the partners in accordance with their profit and loss agreement. Next the assets that are not acceptable for distribution in their present form are converted into cash, and any gains or losses realized are allocated as specified in the partnership agreement (usually according to the profit and loss ratio). Finally, the available assets are distributed to creditors and partners.
2. *List the order of priority for each class of creditors in partnership liquidation under the UPA.* The liabilities are settled in the following order: (1) those owing to creditors other than partners, (2) those owing to partners other than for capital and profits, (3) those owing to partners in respect to capital, and (4) those owing to partners in respect to profits.
3. *Prepare a liquidation schedule to settle debts and allocate assets.* The liquidation schedule begins with a listing, generally in columns, of the partnership's assets, liabilities, and partners' capital balances. Any additional investments made by individual partners are recorded first, including those made by partners with debit balances and those resulting from a judgment of partnership creditors against individual partners. Cash is distributed first to liquidate partnership liabilities and then to satisfy partners' capital interests. The cash distribution is based on the partners' capital balances, not their profit and loss ratios.
4. *Prepare a "safe payment approach" liquidation schedule.* To calculate a safe cash distribution, the following three assumptions may be made: (1) A loan to or from an individual partner is combined with the partner's capital balance to determine his or her interest in the partnership assets. (2) The remaining noncash assets will not provide any additional cash (the worst-case scenario). (3) Any partner with a debit balance is assumed unable to pay the amounts owed to the partnership. The result of applying these assumptions is that cash will not be distributed to any partner whose capital balance is insufficient to absorb his or her share of potential losses.
5. *Describe the four steps in the preparation of an advance plan for the distribution of cash in a partnership liquidation.* Determine the net capital interest of each partner by combining the balance in the partner's capital account with any obligations to, or receivables from, that partner. Determine the order in which the partners are to participate in cash distributions. Compute the amount of cash each partner is to receive as it becomes available for distribution. Prepare a cash distribution plan. This plan will yield the same distribution as a safe payment plan computed each time cash becomes available, but it is more informative to both creditors and partners, as they know the plan in advance.
6. *Prepare the journal entries to incorporate a partnership.* Assets and liabilities are adjusted to fair values, often using a valuation adjustment account to accumulate gains and losses. The valuation adjustment account (or gains/losses) is closed to the partners' capital accounts in accordance with their profit and loss ratios. The partners' capital accounts are closed upon the transfer of capital stock. Since the books are retained, offsetting credits are made to the capital stock account at par for the number of shares issued. If the debit to partners' capital accounts is greater than the credit to the capital stock account, the difference is credited to additional paid-in capital.

TEST YOUR KNOWLEDGE SOLUTIONS

16-1 1. Partner A will receive $60,000 cash.
2. Partner A will receive $40,000 cash.

16-2

Order of Cash Distribution	*Liabilities*	*A (.6)*	*B (.4)*
1. First $15,000	100%		
2. Next $30,000		100%	
3. Remainder		60%	40%

QUESTIONS

LO1 1. Why are realization gains or losses allocated to partners in their profit and loss ratios?

LO3 2. In what manner should the final cash distribution be made in partnership liquidation?

LO2 3. Why does a debit balance in a partners' capital account create problems in the UPA order of payment for a partnership liquidation?

LO2 4. Is it important to maintain separate accounts for a partner's outstanding loan and capital accounts? Explain why or why not.

LO5 5. Discuss the possible outcomes in the situation where the equity interest of one partner is inadequate to absorb realization losses.

LO3 6. During a liquidation, at which point may cash be distributed to any of the partners?

LO3 7. What is "marshaling of assets"?

LO3 8. To what extent can personal creditors seek recovery from partnership assets?

LO4 9. In an installment liquidation, why should the partners view each cash distribution as if it were the final distribution?

LO4 10. Discuss the three basic assumptions necessary for calculating a safe cash distribution. How is this safe cash distribution computed?

LO4 11. How are unexpected costs such as liquidation expenses, disposal costs, or unrecorded liabilities covered in the safe distribution schedule?

LO5 12. What is the objective of the procedures used for the preparation of an advance cash distribution plan?

LO5 13. What is the "loss absorption potential"?

LO2 14. In what order must partnership assets be distributed?

Business Ethics

You and two of your former college friends, Freeman and Oxyman, formed a partnership called FOB, which builds and installs fabricated swimming pools. The business has been operating for 15 years and has become one of the top swimming pool companies in the area. Typically, you have been providing the on-site estimates for the pools, while your partners do most of the on-site construction. While visiting one of the sites, you hear a conversation between one of your partners and a customer. Your partner is explaining that the cost will increase by $10,000 because of unexpected rock removal. You are a bit surprised by this, since you had tested the area for rocks. Later, back at the office, you review the core-sample results done on that job, which did not reveal any rock. You decide to talk to the partner when he returns to the office. When the partner returns to the office, he is arguing with someone from a local bank concerning an outstanding personal loan.

1. What do you see as your duty with respect to the partnership?
2. What should you do? Explain your reasoning.

EXERCISES

EXERCISE 16-1 **Simple Liquidation** LO3

The CPA Partnership operated by Cook, Parks, and Argo is being liquidated. A balance sheet prepared at this stage in their liquidation process is presented below.

Cash	$40,000	Liabilities	$25,000
Other Assets	50,000	Parks, Loan	10,000
		Cook, Capital	30,000
		Parks, Capital	10,000
		Argo, Capital	15,000
Total	$90,000	Total	$90,000

The partners share profits and losses 30% (Cook), 50% (Parks), and 20% (Argo). The partners are all personally insolvent.

Required:

A. The partners wish to distribute the $40,000 in cash. Record in journal entry form the distribution of the available cash.

B. Record in journal entry form the completion of the liquidation process, assuming that the other assets of $50,000 are sold for $15,000.

EXERCISE 16-2 **Simple Liquidation** LO3

John, Jake, and Joe are partners with capital accounts of $90,000, $78,000, and $64,000 respectively. They share profits and losses in the ratio of 30:40:30. When the partners decide to liquidate, the business has $70,000 in cash, noncash assets totaling $260,000, and $98,000 in liabilities. The noncash assets are sold for $270,000, and the creditors are paid.

Required:

A. Prepare a schedule of partnership liquidation.

B. Prepare journal entries to record each of the following transactions.

(1) The sale of the noncash assets.

(2) The payment to the creditors.

(3) The distribution of cash to the partners.

EXERCISE 16-3 **Cash Distribution Schedule** LO3

The unsuccessful partnership of the Jones Brothers is about to undergo liquidation. They have asked you to estimate the amount of cash that each brother will receive. They share profits and losses equally.

Cash	$ 22,000	Liabilities	$ 35,000
Noncash Assets	110,000	Doug, Capital	55,000
		Dave, Capital	50,000
		Dan, Capital	(8,000)
	$132,000		$132,000

Both Doug and Dave are personally solvent, but Dan is not. They estimate that they will receive $65,000 from the sale of the noncash assets.

Required:

Prepare a schedule to estimate the amount of cash each brother will receive.

EXERCISE 16-4 **Cash Distribution Schedule** LO3

The ABC Partnership is in the process of liquidation. The account balances prior to liquidation are given below:

Debits		*Credits*	
Cash	$ 72,000	Liabilities	$ 40,000
Amos, Drawing	10,000	Boone, Loan	8,000
Boone, Drawing	15,000	Childs, Loan	25,000
Childs, Drawing	20,000	Amos, Capital	49,000
Operating Loss	21,000	Boone, Capital	18,000
Liquidation Loss	12,000	Childs, Capital	10,000
	$150,000		$150,000

The partners share profits in the following ratio: Amos, 1/5; Boone, 2/5; Childs, 2/5.

Required:

Prepare a schedule showing the calculations of the distribution of cash under the Uniform Partnership Act, assuming that all three partners have personal liabilities in excess of their personal assets.

EXERCISE 16-5 **Partnership Liquidation—Safe Payment Approach** LO4

Following is the balance sheet of the BDO Partnership:

Cash	$ 10,000	Liabilities	$ 18,000
Accounts Receivable	40,000	Brink, Capital	45,000
Inventory	30,000	Davis, Capital	27,000
Equipment	60,000	Olsen, Capital	50,000
	$140,000		$140,000

The partners share income 40:40:20, respectively. Assume that 70% of the receivables are collected and that inventory with a book value of $15,000 is sold for $10,000. All cash available at this time is to be distributed.

Required:

Determine the proper distribution of cash, using the safe payment approach.

EXERCISE 16-6 **Partnership Liquidation with Personal Asset Information** LO3

Pete, Tom, and Zack have operated a laundromat for 10 years. The partners, who share profits 4:3:3, respectively, decide to liquidate the partnership. The firm's balance sheet just before the partners sell the other assets for $30,000 is as follows:

Assets		*Liabilities and Capital*	
Cash	$ 15,000	Liabilities	$ 42,000
Other Assets	110,000	Pete, Capital	55,000
		Tom, Capital	14,000
		Zack, Capital	14,000
	$125,000		$125,000

The personal status of each partner just before liquidation is as follows:

	Personal Assets	*Personal Liabilities*
Pete	$55,000	$80,000
Tom	30,000	10,000
Zack	30,000	50,000

The partnership operates in a state that has adopted the Uniform Partnership Act.

Required:

A. Determine the amount of cash each partner will receive in liquidation and how much cash each partner must invest in the firm, given their personal positions.

B. Determine the amounts that the personal creditors will receive from personal assets and any distribution from the partnership.

EXERCISE 16-7 **Multiple Choice** LO3 LO4

Select the best answer for each of the following items:

1. In accordance with the marshaling of assets provision of the Uniform Partnership Act, rank the following liabilities of a partnership in order of payment.

(1) $20,000 loan from B. Barry who is a partner.

(2) $30,000 of profits from the last year of operations.

(3) $3,000 payable to a supplier.

(4) $100,000 in capital balances of the partners.

(a) 2,3,4,1.

(b) 4,2,1,3.

(c) 3,1,4,2.

(d) 3,1,2,4.

2. Personal assets are first allocated to partnership creditors and then to personal creditors.

(a) This statement is true.

(b) True if partner has debit balance in his/her capital account.

(c) This statement is false.

3. The following condensed balance sheet is presented for the partnership of Lisa, Lori, and Lucy, who share profits and losses in the ratio of 5:3:2, respectively:

Cash	$ 80,000	Liabilities	$140,000
Other Assets	280,000	Lisa, Capital	100,000
		Lori, Capital	100,000
		Lucy, Capital	20,000
Total	$360,000	Total	$360,000

The partners agreed to liquidate the partnership after selling the other assets. If the other assets are sold for $160,000, how much should Lisa receive upon liquidation?

(a) $37,500
(b) $38,500
(c) $40,000
(d) $100,000

Questions 4 and 5 are based on the following balance sheet for the partnership of Allen, Bob, and Cecil:

Cash	$ 20,000	Liabilities	$ 50,000
Other Assets	180,000	Allen, Capital (40%)	37,000
		Bob, Capital (30%)	65,000
		Cecil, Capital (30%)	48,000
	$200,000		$200,000

Figures shown parenthetically reflect agreed profit and loss sharing percentages.

4. If the firm, as shown on the original balance sheet, is dissolved and liquidated by selling assets in installments, the first sale of noncash assets having a book value of $90,000 realizes $50,000, and all cash available after settlement with creditors is distributed, the respective partners would receive (to the nearest dollar)
   (a) Allen, $8,000; Bob, $6,000; Cecil, $6,000.
   (b) Allen, $6,667; Bob, $6,667; Cecil, $6,666.
   (c) Allen, $0; Bob, $10,000; Cecil, $10,000.
   (d) Allen, $0; Bob, $18,500; Cecil, $1,500.
5. If the facts are as in item 4 above except that $3,000 cash is to be withheld, the respective partners would then receive (to the nearest dollar)
   (a) Allen, $6,800; Bob, $5,100; Cecil, $5,100.
   (b) Allen, $5,667; Bob, $5,667; Cecil, $5,666.
   (c) Allen, $0; Bob, $8,500; Cecil, $8,500.
   (d) Allen, $0; Bob, $17,000; Cecil, $0.

(AICPA adapted)

EXERCISE 16-8 **Multiple Choice** LO2 LO3 LO6

Select the best answer for each of the following items. Questions 1 and 2 are based on the following condensed balance sheet for the partnership of Caine, Davis, and Jones.

Cash	$ 90,000	Accounts Payable	$220,000
Other Assets	820,000	Jones, Loan	40,000
Caine, Receivable	40,000	Caine, Capital	300,000
		Davis, Capital	200,000
		Jones, Capital	190,000
Total	$950,000	Total	$950,000

The partners share income and loss in the ratio of 5:3:2, respectively.

1. Assume that the assets and liabilities are fairly valued in the balance sheet and the partnership decides to admit Kuman as a new partner with a one-fourth capital interest. No goodwill or bonus is to be recorded. How much should Kuman invest in cash or other assets?
   - **(a)** $172,500.
   - **(b)** $175,000.
   - **(c)** $230,000.
   - **(d)** $233,333.
2. Assume that instead of admitting a new partner, the partners decide to liquidate the partnership. If the other assets are sold for $600,000, how much of the available cash should be distributed to Caine?
   - **(a)** $170,000.
   - **(b)** $150,000.
   - **(c)** $190,000.
   - **(d)** $300,000.
3. A, B, C, and D are partners sharing profits and losses equally. The partnership is insolvent and is to be liquidated. The status of the partnership and each partner is as follows:

	Partnership Capital Balance	*Personal Assets (Exclusive of Partnership Interest)*	*Personal Liabilities (Exclusive of Partnership Interest)*
A	$15,000 Credit	$100,000	$40,000
B	10,000 Credit	30,000	60,000
C	20,000 Debit	80,000	5,000
D	30,000 Debit	1,000	28,000

   Assuming the Uniform Partnership Act applies, the partnership creditors
   - **(a)** Must first seek recovery against C because he is personally solvent and he has a negative capital balance.
   - **(b)** Will not be paid in full regardless of how they proceed legally because the partnership assets are less than the claims of the partnership creditors.
   - **(c)** Will have to share B's interest in the partnership on a pro-rata basis with B's personal creditors.
   - **(d)** Have first claim to the partnership assets before any partner's personal creditors have rights to the partnership assets.
4. If a partner with a debit capital balance during liquidation is insolvent, the following results:
   - **(a)** The partner must borrow money to invest in the partnership.
   - **(b)** The partnership will give the partner cash to the extent of the partners' debit balance.
   - **(c)** The partner's debit balance will be allocated to the other partners.
   - **(d)** None of the above.
5. If a partnership is undergoing a transformation to a corporation, which of the following is a result?
   - **(a)** Assets and liabilities are adjusted to fair value.
   - **(b)** The net assets are distributed to the partners in their profit and loss ratio.
   - **(c)** The partners receive stock in the new corporation.
   - **(d)** Both (a) and (c) are correct.

EXERCISE 16-9 **Rights of Various Parties** LO3

Q, R, S, and T are partners, sharing profits and losses 40%:20%:20%:20%, respectively. After sale of firm assets and payment of the available cash to the partnership creditors, a partnership trial balance and the personal status of each partner are as follows:

	Partnership Trial Balance		*Personal Status Exclusive of Partnership Interest*		
	Debit	*Credit*	*Partner*	*Assets*	*Liabilities*
Creditors		$ 2,000			
Q, Capital		500	Q	$15,000	$10,000
R, Capital		7,500	R	8,000	20,000
S, Capital	$ 6,000		S	15,000	4,000
T, Capital	4,000		T	6,000	8,000
	$10,000	$10,000			

The partnership operates in a state that has adopted the Uniform Partnership Act.

Required:

A. What are the rights of the partnership creditors on the unpaid balance of $2,000?

B. What are the rights of the individual creditors of each partner?

C. Assuming that Q pays the partnership creditors, prepare a schedule to show how the settlement by the partners will be completed.

D. Indicate the amount of assets that will be available to the personal creditors of R after the settlement by the partners.

E. Indicate the amount of assets that will be available to the personal creditors of T after the settlement by the partners.

EXERCISE 16-10 **Rights of Various Parties** LO3

The trial balance for the MAD Partnership is as follows just before declaring bankruptcy.

Cash	*Other Assets*		*Liabilities*	*Matt Loan*	*Matt Capital*	*Allen Capital*	*Dave Capital*
$20,000	$100,000	=	$18,000	$10,000	$44,000	$30,000	$18,000

Partners share profits in the ratio 45:30:25.

Required:

A. Prepare a schedule to show how available cash would be distributed to the partners after creditors are paid in full. State which partner would receive the first cash available and at what point and to what degree each of the remaining partners would participate in cash distributions.

B. Cash of $30,000 is available to partners after the creditors have been paid in full. Prepare the general journal entry to record the distribution of $30,000.

PROBLEMS

PROBLEM 16-1 **Simple Liquidation** LO3

The Discount Partnership is being liquidated. The current balance sheet is shown here.

Discount Partnership
Balance Sheet
January 14, 2008

Assets	
Cash	$ 25,000
Other assets	120,000
Total assets	$145,000
Liabilities and Partners' Equity	
Accounts payable	$ 40,000
Dawson, capital	31,000
Feeney, capital	65,000
Hardin, capital	9,000
Total liabilities and partners' equity	$145,000

Dawson, Feeney, and Hardin share profits and losses in a 30:40:30 ratio.

Required:

A. Prepare a schedule of partnership liquidation for each of the following three independent cases.

(1) The noncash assets are sold for $60,000, and any partner with a deficit is unable to eliminate any of the deficit.

(2) The noncash assets are sold for $60,000, and any partner with a deficit is able to invest cash equal to the amount of the deficit.

(3) The noncash assets are sold for $50,000, and any partner with a deficit is able to invest up to $8,000 cash in the partnership.

B. Prepare all necessary journal entries for case 2 above.

PROBLEM 16-2 **Installment Liquidation** LO4

Nelson, Parker, and Rice are partners who share profits 4:3:3, respectively. Parker decides that it would be more profitable for him to operate as a sole proprietor. Nelson and Rice are in agreement that life would be more rewarding if Parker were to enter into direct competition with them. Nelson and Rice make repeated attempts to acquire Parker's interest in the partnership. Unable to reach an agreement, the partners mutually agree that their association should be dissolved. A condensed balance sheet before realization of assets shows the following balances:

Assets		*Liabilities and Capital*	
Cash	$ 5,000	Liabilities	$20,000
Other Assets	60,000	Nelson, Capital	20,000
		Parker, Capital	12,000
		Rice, Capital	13,000
Total	$65,000	Total	$65,000

Asset realization is accomplished in four stages as follows:

Stage	*Sales Price*	*Book Value*
1	$16,000	$12,000
2	12,000	10,000
3	10,000	20,000
4	2,000	18,000

The partners prefer that cash be distributed as soon as it is available.

Required:

Prepare a summary in columnar form of the partnership realization and liquidation. You should prepare supporting schedules of safe payments before each cash distribution.

PROBLEM 16-3 **Installment Liquidation** LO4

Hann, Murphey, and Ryan have operated a retail furniture store for the past 30 years. Their business has been unprofitable for several years, since several large discount furniture stores opened in their sales territory. The partners recognize that they will be unable to compete with the larger chain stores and decide that since all the partners are near retirement, they should liquidate their business before it is necessary to declare bankruptcy. Account balances just before the liquidation process began were as follows:

Cash	$ 10,000	Liabilities	$110,000
Other Assets	218,000	Hann, Capital	50,000
		Murphey, Capital	42,000
		Ryan, Capital	26,000
	$228,000		$228,000

The partners share profits in the ratio of 5:3:2, respectively.

Rather than selling all the assets in a forced liquidation and incurring selling expenses, the partners agree that some of the noncash assets may be withdrawn in partial settlement of their capital interest. The partners agree that if the market value of a withdrawn asset is less than book value, the difference should be allocated to all partners in their loss ratio. If market value is greater than book value, the asset is to be adjusted to its market value before recording the withdrawal. All the partners are personally solvent and can make additional cash investment in the partnership up to $20,000 each. The following is a schedule of transactions that occurred during 2008 in the liquidation process.

March 15, 2008	During liquidation sale, noncash assets with a book value of $90,000 were sold for $80,000.
March 16, 2008	Sold accounts receivable with a book value of $30,000 to a factory for $26,000.
March 16, 2008	Paid all recorded partnership creditors.
March 18, 2008	Distributed all but $1,000 of available cash to partners.
March 19, 2008	Murphey withdrew from inventory furniture with a book value of $10,000 and a market value of $13,000 to satisfy part of his capital interest.
March 21, 2008	Sold remainder of inventory with a book value of $50,000 to a discount furniture store for $30,000 cash.
March 25, 2008	Assigned for $12,000 cash the remaining term of the lease on the warehouse. The lease was accounted for as an operating lease.
March 25, 2008	Distributed all available cash to partners.
April 1, 2008	Hann agreed to accept two vehicles with a book value of $10,000 and a market value of $8,000 in partial settlement of his capital interest.
April 5, 2008	All remaining assets were sold for $4,000.
April 6, 2008	Received additional cash from partners with debit capital balances.
April 6, 2008	Distributed available cash to partners.

Required:

Prepare a schedule of partnership realization and liquidation in accordance with the sequence of the foregoing events. Compute a safe payment to support your cash distribution to partners.

PROBLEM 16-4 Simple Liquidation with Personal Asset Information LO3

Mary, Paula, and Ray have operated a retail store for 20 years. The partners share profits and losses in the ratio of 4:3:3, respectively. The partnership is unable to meet its obligations and the partners decide to liquidate the partnership. The firm's balance sheet just before the partners sell the other assets for $20,000 is as follows.

Assets		*Liabilities and Partners' Equities*	
Cash	$ 10,000	Liabilities	$ 40,000
Other Assets	100,000	Mary, Capital	50,000
		Paula, Capital	10,000
		Ray, Capital	10,000
	$110,000		$110,000

After the sale of the noncash assets, the personal assets and liabilities of each partner are determined to be the following:

	Personal Assets	*Personal Liabilities*
Mary	$50,000	$80,000
Paula	30,000	10,000
Ray	30,000	50,000

The partnership operates in a state that has adopted the Uniform Partnership Act.

Required:

A. Determine the amount of cash each partner will receive in liquidation and how much cash each partner must contribute to the firm, given their personal positions.

B. Determine the amounts that the personal creditors will receive from personal assets and any distribution from the partnership.

PROBLEM 16-5 Advance Cash Distribution Plan LO5

Part A

Baker, Strong, and Weak have called on you to assist them in winding up the affairs of their partnership. You are able to gather the following information.

1. The trial balance of the partnership at June 30, 2008, is as follows.

	Debit	*Credit*
Cash	$ 6,000	
Accounts Receivable	22,000	
Inventory	14,000	
Plant and Equipment (net)	99,000	
Baker, Advance	12,000	
Weak, Advance	7,500	
Accounts Payable		$ 17,000
Baker, Capital		67,000
Strong, Capital		45,000
Weak, Capital		31,500
Total	$160,500	$160,500

2. The partners share profits and losses as follows: Baker, 40%; Strong, 40%; and Weak, 20%.
3. The partners are considering an offer of $100,000 for the accounts receivable, inventory, and plant and equipment as of June 30. The $100,000 would be paid to the partners in installments, the number and amounts of which are to be negotiated.

Required:

Prepare an advance cash distribution plan as of June 30, 2008. Prepare a schedule to show how the potential cash ($106,000) would be distributed as it becomes available.

Part B

Assume the facts in Part A except that the partners liquidate in stages instead of accepting the offer of $100,000. Cash is distributed to the partners at the end of each month.

A summary of the liquidation transactions follows.

July

$16,500—collected on accounts receivable; balance is uncollectible.

$10,000—received for the entire inventory.

$ 1,000—liquidation expenses paid.

$ 8,000—cash retained in the business at the end of the month.

August

$ 1,500—liquidation expenses paid.

As part payment of his capital interest, Weak accepted a piece of special equipment that he developed that had a book value of $4,000. The partners agreed that a value of $10,000 should be placed on the machine for liquidation purposes.

$ 2,500—cash retained in the business at the end of the month.

September

$75,000—received on sale of remaining plant and equipment.

$ 1,000—liquidation expenses paid.

No cash retained in the business.

Required:

Prepare a schedule of cash payments as of September 30, 2008, showing how the cash was actually distributed. Use the advance cash distribution plan developed in Part A where appropriate.

(*AICPA adapted*)

PROBLEM 16-6 **Statement of Changes in Partners' Capital and Liquidation** LO3

Mark Malone, Pete Patton, and Sally Spencer formed a partnership on January 1, 2008. Their original capital investments (all cash) were $140,000, $160,000, and $100,000, respectively. During the first year of operations, Mark withdrew $30,000, and the partnership reported a net income of $60,000. The partnership agreement stipulates that all income and losses are to be divided in the ratio of the original capital investments.

At the beginning of the second year, the partners decided to liquidate the business because of a disagreement. The assets and liabilities on January 2, 2009, were as follows: Cash, $37,000; Accounts Receivable, $129,000; Inventory, $188,000; Land, $85,000; Building (net), $180,000; Furniture and Fixtures (net), $30,000; Accounts Payable, $74,000; and Mortgage Payable, $145,000. The inventory was sold for three-quarters of its book value, the furniture and fixtures brought in $10,000, and $92,000 of the accounts receivable were collected. The remaining receivables were uncollectible. After the losses were allocated according to the partnership agreement and the accounts payable were paid in full, Pete accepted the land and building at book value and assumed the mortgage payable at book value as partial settlement of his capital interest. The cash balance was then distributed to the partners.

Required:

A. Prepare a statement of changes in partners' capital for the year ended December 31, 2008.

B. Prepare the journal entries to close the Drawing and Income Summary accounts for 2008.

C. Prepare a schedule of partnership liquidation.

D. Prepare the journal entries to record the liquidation activities.

PROBLEM 16-7 Incorporation of a Partnership LO6

Jan and Sue have engaged successfully as partners in their law firm for a number of years. Soon after their state's incorporation laws are changed to allow professionals to incorporate, the partners decide to organize a corporation to take over the business of the partnership.

The after-closing trial balance for the partnership is as follows:

After-Closing Trial Balance
December 31, 2008

	Debit	*Credit*
Cash	$15,000	
Accounts Receivable	32,400	
Allowances for Uncollectibles		$ 2,000
Prepaid Insurance	800	
Office Equipment	30,200	
Accumulated Depreciation		12,600
Jan, Loan (outstanding since 2000, at 5%)		6,400
Jan, Capital (50%)		29,400
Sue, Capital (50%)		28,000
	$78,400	$78,400

Figures shown parenthetically reflect agreed profit- and loss-sharing ratios.

The partners have hired you as an accountant to adjust the recorded assets and liabilities to their market values and to close the partners' capital accounts to the new corporate capital stock. The corporation is to retain the partnership's books, and the assets of the partnership should be taken over by the corporation in the following amounts:

Cash	$15,000
Accounts receivable	32,400
Allowance for uncollectibles	2,900
Prepaid insurance	800
Office equipment	16,000

Jan's loan is to be transferred to her capital account in the amount of $6,600.

Required:

A. Prepare the necessary journal entries to express the agreement described.

B. Prepare the entries to record the issuance of shares to Jan and Sue, assuming the issuance of 400 shares (par value $100) of stock to Jan and Sue.

PROBLEM 16-8 Discussion Case with Ethical Issue LO6

Alan Norwood is currently a senior associate with the law firm of Butler, Starns, and Madden (BSM). His compensation currently includes a salary of $155,000, and benefits valued at $5,000. BSM is considered among the strongest of local firms, with assets of $10 million (cash $2,000,000, and accounts receivables $8,000,000), liabilities of $7.5 million, and 11 partners.

Alan anticipates admission to the partnership on July 1 of this year. The senior managing partner, Jane Butler, has had preliminary discussions with Alan in which the senior partner proposed the following:

1. A 5% interest in BSM capital and profits in recognition of Alan's commitment to the firm and in exchange for a capital investment by Alan of $150,000. This 5% interest would be acquired from the other partners.
2. Alan's compensation will consist of a monthly withdrawal of $18,000 and benefits valued at $5,000 annually. Monthly withdrawals approximate firm profits, but any unpaid profits will be distributed as a bonus to Alan after the end of each partnership year.

On March 1, only one month prior to Alan's final negotiation meeting for entry into the partnership, Mary, one of the junior associates, discreetly informed Alan that the firm was drawing up documents for Hugh Starns' retirement. Hugh has a 5% interest in the firm's capital and profits with a book value of $125,000. The partners have agreed upon a $75,000 cash settlement of the interest held by Mr. Starns. (Of the other 10 partners, numbers 1 through 9 hold 10% interests, and number 10 holds a 5% interest).

Required:

A. Assume Mr. Starns retires with his $75,000 settlement, and Alan is admitted to the partnership as proposed.

(1) Prepare journal entries to record the retirement and admission.

(2) Discuss the factors Alan needs to consider in evaluating whether he has improved his annual compensation from the firm. Although this is not a tax course, include a discussion of the various tax issues.

(3) Should Alan be concerned regarding the impending retirement and settlement of Mr. Starns' capital account assuming Alan is confident that he will be able to match the revenue-generating ability of Mr. Starns?

B. Assume instead that Alan is so disturbed by the impending departure of Mr. Starns that he decides to join Mary, the junior associate, in leaving the firm to form their own law partnership. Both Alan and Mary feel confident that during their tenures at BSM they have developed such good working relationships with their clients that the majority of their clients will follow them to the new firm.

(1) Should Alan and Mary have any hesitation in quietly recruiting BSM clients to "follow them" to the new law firm?

(2) Can the partners of BSM prevent such recruiting of clients based on the claim that these clients are BSM "property"?

C. Assume instead that the firm encounters difficulties from which it is unable to recover, and in April, the decision is made to liquidate the firm. It is discovered that Mr. Starns has (in violation of the partnership agreement) taken draws which reduced firm cash and his capital account by $130,000. However, BSM owes Mr. Starns $10,000 for a separate loan made to the firm some 10 years ago. As of May 1, the firm had unallocated profits of $25,000, and cash had also increased by $25,000.

(1) Assuming that the provisions of UPA Section 40(b) are adhered to strictly, prepare entries to record the distributions. Assume that Mr. Starns is insolvent.

(2) If the other 10 partners are aware that Starns' capital account will take on a debit balance, can they rightfully hold repayment of the balance due to Starns for the $10,000 loan contingent on his reimbursement of his capital account's debit balance? Does this violate UPA Section 40(b)? On what basis can the partners justify their action (if challenged)?

INTRODUCTION TO FUND ACCOUNTING

LEARNING OBJECTIVES

1. Distinguish between a nonbusiness organization and a profit-oriented enterprise.
2. Explain the role of fund accounting.
3. Distinguish among the concepts of revenues, expenses, and expenditures as used in profit-oriented entities and as used for expendable fund entities.
4. Understand the classification of revenues and other resource inflows for fund accounting.
5. Understand the classification of expenditures and other resource outflows for fund accounting.
6. Describe the critical events in the use of financial resources of an expendable fund.
7. Explain how capital expenditures are recorded in an expendable fund.
8. Understand the role of a general fund.
9. Contrast the consumption and the purchases methods of accounting for inventories (and other prepaid items).

The 2005 Financial Report of the United States Government provides the president, Congress, and the American public information about the federal government's financial results and position. This report is prepared in accordance with GAAP and is subject to audit by the Government Accountability Office (GAO). For fiscal years ended 2004 and 2005, the GAO was unable to express an opinion on the U.S. government's consolidated financial statements due to material deficiencies in financial reporting. Of the 24 agencies that are consolidated in this report, only 18 received unqualified audit opinions. Four agencies, including the Department of Defense and the Department of Homeland Security, received disclaimers of opinion because of material deficiencies in financial reporting or because they had limited the scope of the auditor's work. These agencies represented 58% of the government's total assets.[1]

Accounting for nonbusiness organizations is referred to as **fund accounting.** Nonbusiness organizations are economic entities that are organized to provide a socially desirable service without regard to financial gain. In contrast, business enterprises are designed to earn a return on investment for equity investors, operate in a competitive market, and face liquidity concerns.

[1] *Financial Report of the United States* (with a forward by Representative Jim Cooper), Nelson Current, 2006.

The purpose of this chapter is to introduce the reader to fund accounting concepts and procedures. However, it is first necessary to present a brief introduction to the types and characteristics of organizations that use fund accounting concepts.

CLASSIFICATIONS OF NONBUSINESS ORGANIZATIONS

Nonbusiness organizations may be separated into five major classifications, as follows:

1. *Governmental units.* Governmental units include federal, state, and local governmental entities. Local governmental units include counties, townships, municipalities, school districts, and special districts. Special districts include organizational units such as port authorities, industrial development districts, sanitation districts, and soil and water conservation districts.
2. *Hospitals and other health care providers.*
3. *Colleges and universities.*
4. *Voluntary health and welfare organizations.* Voluntary health and welfare organizations are organizations that derive their revenue from voluntary contributions of the general public to be used for purposes connected with health, welfare, or community services. Examples of such organizations include heart associations, family planning councils, mental health associations, and foundations for the blind.
5. *All other nonbusiness organizations.* Other nonbusiness organizations take a variety of forms. They include such organizations as trade associations (Electrical Contractors Association), professional associations (State Society of Certified Public Accountants), performing arts organizations (the Tennessee Performing Arts Center), museums, religious organizations, and research and scientific organizations.

"With the United States officially in a recession, state and federal funding sources on which charitable organizations rely are drying up. . . Colleges and universities are seeing a marked increase in requests for financial aid, while hospitals are challenged by having to provide more charity care. These financial struggles have led many organizations to seek alternative revenue sources that are outside their charitable mission and, therefore, are taxable."[2]

DISTINCTIONS BETWEEN NONBUSINESS ORGANIZATIONS AND PROFIT-ORIENTED ENTERPRISES

LO1 Nonbusiness organizations versus profit-oriented enterprises.

The most obvious characteristic that distinguishes a *nonbusiness* organization from a *profit-oriented* enterprise is the absence of a primary goal to earn a profit. The services performed by nonbusiness organizations are based on social need rather than on the profit motive. Thus, their financial statements are sometimes referred to as ***not-for-profit***, or ***nonprofit, financial statements.*** Other characteristics of nonbusiness organizations also distinguish them from profit-oriented enterprises. For example, persons who contribute resources to a nonbusiness organization do not receive equity interests in the net assets of the organization. Nonbusiness organizations seldom finance their operations through charges to the individuals benefiting from the service. Thus, they must rely on political action (for example, tax levies) or fund-raising campaigns to sustain their activities and replenish their financial resources.

[2] "Reporting Unrelated Business Income," by Travis Patton and Jocelyn Bishop, *Journal of Accountancy*, February 2009, p. 52.

GASB CONCEPTUAL FRAMEWORK

The GASB has issued five statements on the conceptual framework:

Concepts Statement No. 1: "Objectives of Financial Reporting"

Concepts Statement No. 2: "Service Efforts and Accomplishments Reporting"

Concepts Statement No. 3: "Communication Methods in General Purpose External Financial Reports That Contain Basic Financial Statements"

Concepts Statement No. 4: Elements of Financial Statements

Concepts Statement No. 5: Service Efforts and Accomplishments Reporting—an amendment of *GASB Concepts Statement No. 2*

In the first concepts statement, the stated objectives of financial reporting are:

a. To assist in meeting the government's duty to be publicly accountable by providing information for users to assess if current-year revenues are sufficient to pay for current-year services.

b. To determine if the government's resources are obtained and used in accordance with legal or contractual requirements.

Financial reporting should allow users to evaluate operating results by providing information about the sources and uses of resources and how the government's activities are financed. In addition, information needs to be provided about the impact of operations on the financial position of the government.

Concepts Statement No. 2 develops the objective of clarifying the reporting of service efforts and accomplishments (SEA); it also identifies its elements and characteristics. The objective of SEA reporting is to provide more complete information about a governmental entity's performance than can be provided by the traditional financial statements. The elements of SEA reporting include categories of output and outcome indicators as well as efficiency and cost-outcome indicators. SEA information should focus primarily on measures of service accomplishments and measures of the relationships between service efforts and service accomplishments. SEA information also should meet the characteristics of relevance, understandability, comparability, timeliness, consistency, and reliability.

In *Concepts Statement No. 3*, a conceptual basis for determining the methods to present information within general-purpose external financial reports is provided.

Communication methods might include recognition in basic financial statements, disclosure in the footnotes, and presentation of supplementary information (whether required or not).

This Concepts Statement also addresses the necessary elements for the effective communication of relevant and reliable messages within financial reports. This includes a clarification of the roles and responsibilities of the preparer, the user, and the GASB for the effective communication of information.

In *Concepts Statement No. 4*, seven elements of *Statements of Financial Position* are defined. These are:

- *Assets*—resources with present service capacity that the entity presently controls
- *Liabilities*—present obligations to sacrifice resources or future resources that the entity has little or no discretion to avoid
- A *deferred outflow of resources*—a consumption of net resources by the entity that is applicable to a future reporting period
- A *deferred inflow of resources*—an acquisition of net resources by the entity that is applicable to a future reporting period
- *Net position*—the residual of all other elements presented in a statement of financial position
- *Outflow of resources*—a consumption of net resources by the entity that is applicable to the reporting period
- *Inflow of resources*—an acquisition of net resources by the entity that is applicable to the reporting period

In *Concepts Statement No. 5*, four sections of *Concept Statement No. 2* were modified and one section was deleted. *Concept No. 2* deals with service efforts and accomplishment reporting.

"The government is like a baby's alimentary canal, with a healthy appetite at one end and no responsibility at the other." —*Ronald Reagan*[3]

In addition, tax levies and voluntary contributions cannot be justified based on the value of the nonbusiness organization's services to the individuals contributing the money. Those who contribute resources to nonbusiness organizations do not necessarily benefit proportionately or at all from the services provided by such organizations. Because of these characteristics, the net income concept cannot be used to measure the effectiveness of the management of resources dedicated to nonbusiness objectives. Therefore, the income determination model of accounting is generally not applicable to such organizations.

In profit-oriented enterprises, net income functions as an implicit regulator in the sense that (1) in the long run, the organization must operate profitably to survive and (2) in the short run, failure to operate profitably will affect management's decisions and actions and perhaps whether management will be replaced. In the absence of this implicit regulator, stringent controls are often imposed to regulate the allocation and utilization of the financial resources of nonbusiness organizations. Such controls may be legally imposed (as in the case of governmental activities) or they may be imposed through formal action of the governing board.

Restrictions or limitations on the use of resources may be directly imposed by the individuals or groups that contribute such resources. For example, most nonbusiness organizations receive gifts, grants, or endowments that are only used for specific purposes designated by the donor, such as construction of buildings, research activities, scholarships, operation of parks, recreation programs, or the acquisition of land. In addition, the donor may stipulate that the principal of the gift remain intact and that only the income on the invested principal can be used for the purposes designated by the donor.

In order to account for these legally imposed, externally imposed, and self-imposed restrictions or limitations on the utilization of their resources, nonbusiness organizations have generally adopted the concepts of fund accounting. *In essence, an organization that uses fund accounting separates the assets, liabilities, and residual equity (known as a fund balance) into distinct funds organized for specific activities or objectives. In fund accounting, each fund consists of a self-balancing set of accounts and constitutes a separate accounting entity created and maintained for a specific purpose. Accounting for the inflow and outflow of resources of each fund is designed so that they can be compared with the approved or stipulated resource flows for that fund.*

FINANCIAL ACCOUNTING AND REPORTING STANDARDS FOR NONBUSINESS ORGANIZATIONS

The potential users of the financial reports of nonbusiness organizations include taxpayers, contributors, grantors, creditors, employees, managers, directors and trustees, service beneficiaries, financial analysts and advisers, brokers, underwriters, economists, taxing authorities, regulatory authorities, legislators, the financial press and reporting agencies, labor unions, trade associations, researchers, teachers, and students.

[3] Quoted in *New York Times Magazine.* From *The Merriam-Webster Dictionary of Quotations,* Merriam-Webster, Inc.: 1996. *Infopedia,* SoftKey Multimedia Inc., 1996.

"It was once said that the moral test of government is how that government treats those who are in the dawn of life, the children; those who are in the twilight of life, the elderly; and those who are in the shadows of life—the sick, the needy and the handicapped." —*Hubert H. Humphrey*[4]

Unlike for-profit organizations and depending on the type of nonbusiness organization, the accounting standards are not established by one unique standard-setting body.

Until 1980, the Financial Accounting Standards Board (FASB) and its predecessor bodies gave little, if any, attention to standards of reporting for nonbusiness organizations. In 1980, however, the FASB issued *Statement of Financial Accounting Concepts No. 4*, "Objectives of Financial Reporting by Nonbusiness Organizations." In that statement, the Board identified providers such as members, taxpayers, contributors, and creditors as the most important users for purposes of establishing external financial reporting objectives for nonbusiness organizations.

In 1984, the Governmental Accounting Standards Board (GASB) was created. Like those of the FASB, the operations and financing of the GASB are overseen by the Financial Accounting Foundation. The GASB is responsible for establishing financial accounting standards for all state and local governmental bodies, and the FASB is responsible for establishing financial accounting standards for all other nonbusiness organizations. Accounting and reporting standards for governmental units are described and illustrated in this chapter and in Chapter 18. Accounting and reporting standards for nongovernment nonbusiness organizations are described and illustrated in Chapter 19.

Illustration 17-1 indicates the standard-setting body (the GASB or the FASB) primarily responsible for determining the accounting standards for various types of nonbusiness organizations. Having two separate bodies establishing accounting standards can be confusing for users of the financial statements. For instance, the financial statements of a state university, such as the University of Tennessee, are prepared using

ILLUSTRATION 17-1

Financial Accounting Standards for Nonbusiness Organizations

GASB	FASB	Primary body establishing accounting standards
Governmental Units 1. Federal units • Veterans hospitals 2. State units • State hospitals • State universities 3. Local governments • Country government • School districts • Municipalities • Port authorities	*Nongovernmental Units* 1. Private colleges, universities, and community colleges 2. Private hospitals and voluntary health and welfare organizations 3. Other nongovernmental units • Private elementary schools • Professional organizations • Labor unions • Civic organizations • Trade associations	Nonbusiness organizations

[4] Excerpt from a 1977 speech. From *The Merriam-Webster Dictionary of Quotations*, Merriam-Webster, Inc.: 1996. *Infopedia*, SoftKey Multimedia Inc., 1996.

GASB rules, while a private university, such as Vanderbilt University, prepares its financial statements under the guidance of the FASB. Currently, there are significant accounting differences in rules between the FASB and the GASB. It is important for users of not-for-profit financial statements to have an understanding of the standards provided by both the GASB and the FASB. In this chapter and Chapter 18, the GASB rules are illustrated for governmental units; in Chapter 18, the hierarchy of generally accepted reporting standards for governmental entities is described; and in Chapter 19, the FASB's standards for other nonbusiness organizations are presented.

FUND ACCOUNTING

LO2 The role of fund accounting.

Fund accounting is designed primarily to meet internal reporting and control objectives; thus fund accounting may not be sufficient in itself to meet the objectives of financial reporting by nonbusiness organizations. Nevertheless, it does provide a basis for determining the fiscal responsibility and status of the organization and the compliance of administrators with the approved or stipulated receipt and utilization of financial resources. Therefore, fund accounting is an important means of meeting several of the accounting, control, and reporting objectives of most nonbusiness organizations.

Fund entities may be classified in a number of different ways. For example, they may be classified as expendable fund entities, fiduciary fund entities, and proprietary fund entities. ***Expendable fund entities*** are the funds most closely associated with basic fund accounting concepts, while ***proprietary fund entities*** are the nonbusiness funds that are most similar to business entities. ***Fiduciary funds entities*** are used to follow the activities in which the government acts as an agent or trustee for resources that belong to others, such as employee pension plans.

Expendable Fund Entities

Expendable fund entities consist of net ***financial resources*** that are dedicated to a specified use. Thus, separate expendable fund entities are established based on the purpose for which financial resources may or must be used. Examples of funds set up for specific purposes include a capital projects fund created to account for new highway construction or a debt service fund created to account for interest and principal payments on long-term debt. Thus within a government, many funds are established.

LO3 Differences in applications of revenues, expenses, and expenditures.

Financial resources consist of cash and claims to cash such as receivables and investments in marketable securities. The difference between the financial resources of an expendable fund entity and claims against those resources is referred to as the fund balance. Thus, the statement of financial position, or balance sheet, for an expendable fund entity reflects the financial resources of the fund, the claims against those resources, and the fund balance. Typically, assets and liabilities are not subdivided into current and noncurrent assets and liabilities. At a particular time the fund balance represents the net financial resources that are available for expenditure for the specified purposes or objectives for which the fund was created.

The financial resources of an expendable fund entity are not intended to be maintained intact. Ordinarily it is intended that they will be expended annually or over some other specified time period in order to carry out the objectives for which the fund was created. The measurement focus is on the flow of current financial resources in contrast to proprietary fund accounting, where the measurement focus is on the flow of economic resources.

The relevant measures of the operations of expendable fund entities are not, therefore, revenue, expense, and net income, but rather increases in fund resources, decreases in fund resources, and the change in the fund balance. The accounting model for the operating statement of an expendable fund entity is:

Financial resources inflows (by source)
− Financial resources outflows (by function)
= Change in fund balance

Thus, increases in fund resources include not only revenues, but also items such as proceeds from debt issuances and transfers from other funds. Decreases in fund resources include expenses, other expenditures, and transfers to other funds. However, the term "expense" as defined under GAAP is typically not used with fund accounting. Instead the term "expenditure" includes expenses as well as other items giving rise to cash (or other resource) outlays, without regard to timing or the matching with revenue that is an integral part of income determination under GAAP. Conversely, expenses may include items that are not current expenditures because of the timing of the outlay. The operating results of expendable fund entities are thus measured in terms of inflow, outflow, and balances of net current financial resources assigned to the fund. The appropriate operating statement for such entities is essentially a statement of changes in net financial resources. To provide a basis for comparison, both budgeted and actual resource flows may be presented in the operating statement or in related schedules. Later in this chapter, we describe the modified accrual basis commonly used in fund accounting, and the need for accrual-based reporting under *GASB Statement No. 34.*

In summary, in accounting for expendable funds, the emphasis is changed from matching revenues and expenses to a comparison of the *actual* inflows and outflows of financial resources with *stipulated* or *approved* resource flows. The objective in accounting for expendable fund entities is to measure the extent to which management has *complied* with the regulations or restrictions that govern the use of expendable fund resources. A secondary objective is to assist management with such compliance.

Restricted and Unrestricted Fund Entities

Expendable fund entities may be further classified as restricted or unrestricted. This classification is usually applicable to nonbusiness organizations other than governmental units. The unrestricted expendable fund entity includes the net current financial resources of the nonbusiness organization that are available to carry out the primary or general activities of the organization at the discretion of the governing board. Current financial resources that are restricted by donors or other outside agencies for specific current operating purposes are included in restricted expendable fund entities. The term "restricted" refers to *resources that bear a legal restriction as to use imposed by parties outside the organization.* The primary purpose of this distinction is to assist in the determination of the current financial resources that are available for use at the discretion of the governing board and those over which the governing board has little, if any, discretion as to use because of *externally* imposed restrictions. As illustrated in Chapter 19, most nonbusiness organizations other than governmental units have one unrestricted fund and one or more restricted funds.

Proprietary Fund Entities

Proprietary fund entities are used to account for the activities of nonbusiness organizations that are similar to those of business enterprises. Many nonbusiness organizations engage in quasi-commercial activities. The operation of an electric or water utility by a municipality and the rental of real estate by a religious organization are examples of such activities. Accordingly, even though these activities are accounted for in separate fund entities, relevant accounting measurements and reports are similar to those applicable to profit-oriented enterprises and focus on the determination of net income, financial position, and cash flows.

The accounting model for the statement of financial position of a proprietary fund entity is similar to a for-profit firm and is represented as follows:

Assets	=	Liabilities	+	Equity
Current and Noncurrent		Current and Noncurrent		Net Assets

The accounting model for the statement of revenues, expenses, and changes in fund net assets of a proprietary fund entity is presented as follows using the all-inclusive format:

Operating revenues
Less: operating expenses
= Operating income
Plus (minus): nonoperating revenues and expenses
= Income before other revenue, expenses, gains and losses, and transfers
Other revenue, expenses, etc.: capital contributions, additions to permanent and term endowments, special and extraordinary items
= Increases (decreases) in net assets
Plus: net assets—beginning of period
= Net assets—end of period

Fiduciary Fund Entities

Fiduciary funds include both trust and agency funds. Trust funds are funds where the government acts as trustee for an individual or organization. An example of a trust fund might be a pension trust fund in which the fund accounts for the accumulation of resources for pension benefit payments to employees, police, and firefighters of the city. An agency fund accounts for resources of various taxes, bonds, and other receipts held for individuals, outside organizations, and/or other funds.

Budgetary Fund Entities (Governmental Funds)

In the traditional compliance model of reporting on the operations of governmental units, actual and approved (or stipulated) inflows and outflows of resources are compared. Approved resource flows are incorporated into annual budgets. In some instances the budget for an expendable fund entity is so important (often because of legal requirements) to management control of fund resources that entries for budgeted revenues and expenditures are recorded in the books. Fund entities in which the budget is formally incorporated into the accounting records are sometimes referred to as ***budgetary funds***. (This is illustrated later in the chapter.)

The preparation, use, and importance of budgets for governmental units cannot be overemphasized. The annual budget for a governmental unit is usually prepared by the executive branch of the governmental unit. It is then presented to the legislative branch for consideration and enactment. In the case of annually levied taxes such as property taxes, adoption of budgeted revenue amounts may require the enactment of enabling legislation. In the case of continually levied taxes such as sales taxes and income taxes, no new legislation authorizing the tax is ordinarily required for the adoption of the budgeted amounts of revenue.

When budgeted expenditures are enacted into law, they are referred to as ***appropriations.*** Appropriations represent the maximum expenditures that are authorized by the legislature. As such, they represent (by budget category) amounts that cannot be legally exceeded unless subsequently amended by the legislative body. Accordingly, the accounting system must provide administrators of governmental units with timely information as to actual expenditures and allowable expenditures (appropriations) by budget category. In addition, financial reports must be prepared in such a way that the legislature or its representatives can determine that the spending limits authorized by it have not been exceeded. The approved budget may, therefore, be formally recorded in the accounting records of the appropriate fund(s). Such formal budgetary account integration is useful in assisting in the control and administration of fund resources.

Basis of Accounting

The basic financial statements of a government include two sections; government-wide financial statements and fund financial statements. Government-wide financial statements report on all the nonfiduciary activities of the government and provide both short- and long-run information about the financial status of the government. In addition to reporting the government funds statements on a modified accrual basis, a ***government-wide Statement of Activities*** and a ***government-wide Statement of Net Assets*** are required.[5] The government-wide financial statements are prepared using the economic resources measurement concept and the accrual basis of accounting (this is also appropriate for proprietary and fiduciary fund entities.).

Governmental fund (expendable funds) financial statements are reported using the current financial resources concept and the **modified accrual basis** of accounting. Financial resources of an expendable fund entity include cash, receivables, and securities that can be converted into cash. Revenues are recognized when they are measurable and available. Revenues are available when they are collectible within the current period or soon enough to pay liabilities of the current period. Governments are required to disclose the length of time used to define "available for use" for purposes of defining revenues. The cash basis of accounting is not appropriate. Under the modified accrual approach, it is not sufficient for an economic event to occur to affect the operating statement. ***Instead, the related cash flow must occur within a period short enough to have an effect on current spendable resources.*** In other words, revenues must be both measurable and available to liquidate liabilities of the current period.

[5] Governmental Accounting Standards Board (GASB), *GASB Statement No. 34*, "Basic Financial Statements—and Management's Discussion and Analysis—for State and Local Governments" (Norwalk, CT: June 1999).

The term "expenditure" rather than "expense" is used for governmental funds. Expenditures are recorded when a liability is incurred, similar to accrual accounting. However, because governments generally do not attempt to allocate costs to periods benefited and because some expenditures of the expendable fund entities are not recognized in the period in which they are incurred, the term **modified accrual accounting** is also used. Therefore, expenditures are recognizable when an event is expected to use current spendable resources (rather than future resources).

Before proceeding further, it is useful to contrast the concepts of revenue, expense, and expenditure as they are used in relation to profit-oriented entities and to expendable fund entities.

RELATED CONCEPTS

Government-wide financial statements are now presented on an accrual basis. One reason for the change is that accrual accounting better assists users in assessing whether the costs of services were shifted to future periods. Also, this information will assist users in determining whether a government's *financial position* has improved or deteriorated.

Profit-Oriented Entities (Income Determination)

Revenues—increases in net assets resulting from the sale of goods or services.

Expenses—costs of resources used to produce current period revenues.

Unusual, Infrequent, and Extraordinary Items—Extraordinary items are items that are *both* unusual in nature and infrequent of occurrence; they are reported net of taxes. Items that are either unusual or infrequent, but not both, are shown on a separate line, if material, but are not shown net of taxes.

Expendable Fund Entities

Revenues—any increase in (source of) net current financial resources ***other than*** increases from *other financing sources* (as defined below).

Expenditures—any decrease in (use of) net current financial resources ***other than*** decreases from *other financing uses* (as defined below); or the amount of financial resources expended during the period to carry out the operations and activities of the fund entity.

Other Financing Sources and Uses (and Transfers)—proceeds from debt issuances and transfers of financial resources to and from other funds.

Special and Extraordinary Items—Extraordinary items are both unusual in nature and infrequent of occurrence. Special items are significant transactions within the control of management that are either unusual or infrequent.

In the remainder of this chapter, fund accounting concepts are developed within the framework of state and local governmental units.

When President Barack Obama signed the American Recovery and Reinvestment Act of 2009 into law, the largest deficit in American history is almost guaranteed (doubling the deficit of 2008). In January, the Congressional Budget Office projected that the deficit this year would be $1.2 trillion before the stimulus package. That's more than the entire GDP of all but a handful of countries, and more, in nominal dollars, than the entire United States national debt in 1982.[6]

Classification of Revenues

LO4 Classification of revenues.

Revenues are classified by fund and by major revenue source. Major sources of revenue for state and local governmental units are summarized in Illustration 17-2. As shown, the number of sources of revenue available to governmental units is impressive when compared with those available to business enterprises.

[6] WSJ, February 17, 2009, "A Short History of the National Debt" by John Gordon.

ILLUSTRATION 17-2

Major Sources of Revenue for State and Local Governmental Units

Property taxes	Grants from federal, state, or local government units
Income taxes	Shared revenues from federal, state, or local government units
Sales and excise taxes	Payments in lieu of taxes from federal, state, or local government units
Gift and inheritance taxes	Interest earned on loans and investments
Fines and penalties	
Gifts and donations	
Forfeits	
Licenses and permits	
Sales of property	
Charges for services	

Other Financing Sources

Debt Issue Proceeds Governmental units may finance their operations through the issuance of bonds or other debt instruments. Although debt issue proceeds are sometimes classified as revenue of a particular fund entity, they are *not revenue* from the point of view of the issuing governmental unit because of the offsetting debt. Accordingly, debt issue proceeds should be classified separately from revenue for purposes of financial reporting. Debt issue proceeds are accounted for as "other financing sources."

Transfers of Resources from Other Funds Transfers of resources from other fund entities within an organization do not represent an increase in the expendable financial resources of the organization as a whole. Accordingly, even though they represent an increase in the financial resources of the recipient fund entity, they should ordinarily *be classified separately from revenue* for financial reporting purposes. Interfund operating transfers are accounted for as "other financing sources," or "uses."

Recognition of Revenue

In accounting for profit-oriented enterprises, revenue is ordinarily not recognized until (1) a transaction has taken place (that is, the amount of revenue can be objectively measured) and (2) the earnings process is complete or substantially complete. Criterion 2 is not applicable to expendable fund entities. The revenue-recognition criteria for expendable fund entities can be stated as follows: ***In accounting for expendable fund entities, revenue is ordinarily not recognized until (1) it can be objectively measured and (2) it is available to finance expenditures of the current period.***

Many sources of fund revenue do not meet the criteria of measurability and availability until they are received in cash. On the other hand, significant amounts of revenue (for example, property taxes, pledges, regularly billed charges for routine services, and some types of grants) meet both criteria and are recognized as revenue prior to the receipt of cash. The application of these criteria to several significant sources of revenue of governmental units may be illustrated as follows.

Property Taxes Property taxes usually meet both criteria when levied. The amount of property tax is precisely determinable when levied and the amount of uncollectible taxes ordinarily can be reasonably estimated on the basis of previous experience. Thus, the amount of property tax revenue is objectively determinable at the time the taxes are levied. Ordinarily, taxes are also considered to be ***available*** in the period levied, even though they are collectible in a period subsequent to the levy, because (1) they provide a basis for obtaining cash resources through the issuance of tax anticipation notes[7] and (2) they are usually collectible early in the subsequent period and thus are available to finance current period operations.

Income Tax and Sales Tax Self-assessed taxes such as the income tax and the sales tax usually are not objectively measurable or available until the tax returns are filed with payment. Where the tax returns have been filed but payment is delayed, revenue should be recognized when the returns are filed, assuming that a reasonable estimate can be made of noncollectible amounts, if any. In addition, sales taxes held by merchants may be recognized as revenue before they are received by the fund entity if the measurability and availability criteria are met.

Fines and Forfeits The amounts of fines, forfeits, inspection charges, parking meter receipts, and so on, are not objectively determinable or available until assessed or collected and are, therefore, not normally recognized as revenue until collected.

Sales of Property The entire amount of proceeds from the sale of property is treated as revenue at the time of sale because expendable assets are increased and are available to finance current expenditures in the same manner as any other revenues.

Pledges and Grants A pledge to contribute resources is considered revenue at the time it is made, so long as a reasonable estimate of uncollectible pledges can be made and there is no restriction on the time period in which the pledged resources can be expended. Grants may or may not be recognized as revenue at the time the grant is authorized. If the grant is dependent on the performance of services, or if the expenditure of funds is the prime factor for determining the eligibility for the grant funds, revenue should not be recognized until the time the services are performed or the expenditures are made. Grants that are not dependent on performance or expenditure of funds should be recognized in the period in which they are authorized.

Did the U.S. deficit increase or decrease in 2005? The answer to this question depends on how you measure the deficit. The commonly used definition (and the one used by President Bush) is based on cash accounting and is often quoted as being $318.5 billion. Under this measure the deficit decreased for 2005. However, using the accrual basis (which is required of private-sector firms), the deficit was $760 billion, which was significantly worse than the $600 billion deficit in the prior year.[8]

[7] Tax anticipation notes are notes or warrants issued in anticipation of the collection of taxes and are usually retirable only from the proceeds of the tax levy whose collection they anticipate.

[8] *Financial Report of the United States* (with a foreword by Representative Jim Cooper), Nelson Current, 2006.

Classification of Expenditures and Other Resource Outflows

LO5 Classification of expenditures.

As mentioned earlier, an expenditure is any decrease in net current financial resources other than transfers to other funds. Thus expenditures are not matched to the production of current revenues as are expenses for profit-seeking enterprises. Expenditures may be classified by fund, by function and/or activity, by organizational unit, by character (nature of the expenditure), or by object class. Since different classifications serve different purposes, multiple classification of expenditures is usually recommended. For example, the various classifications might be illustrated as follows:

Function—Public Safety
Organizational Unit—Fire Department or Police Department
Activity—Drug Control
Character—Current Operating
Object Class—Supplies or Salaries

Classification by Function and Activity Typical functional classifications of expenditures for state and local governmental units are presented in Illustration 17-3. Classification by function refers to the broad purposes for which expenditures are made. Classification by activity refers to the specific types of work performed to accomplish such purposes. For example, public safety is a major function of a municipality. The ***function*** of public safety may be divided into ***subfunctions*** such as police protection, fire protection, and protective inspection. The subfunction of police protection can be classified into ***activities*** such as criminal investigation, vice control, patrol, custody of prisoners, and crime laboratory.

Functional and activity classifications are particularly important and are the classifications ordinarily recommended for published financial reports. In addition, as noted by the National Council on Governmental Accounting:

> ***Activity*** classification is particularly significant because it facilitates evaluation of the economy and efficiency of operations by providing data for calculating expenditures per unit of activity. That is, the expenditure requirements of performing a given unit of work can be determined by classifying expenditures by activities and providing for performance

ILLUSTRATION 17-3

Functional Classification of Expenditures for State and Local Governmental Units

General Government
- Legislative
- Judicial
- Executive
- Elections
- Financial administration

Public Safety
- Police
- Fire
- Inspection

Public Works
- Highways and streets
- Sanitation

Health and Welfare

Recreation—Cultural
- Playgrounds
- Swimming pools
- Golf courses
- Parks
- Libraries

Urban Redevelopment and Housing

Economic Development and Assistance

> measurement where such techniques are practicable. These expenditure data, in turn, can be used in preparing future budgets and in setting standards against which future expenditure levels can be evaluated. Further, activity expenditure data provide a convenient starting point for calculating total and/or unit expenses of activities where desired, e.g., for "make or buy" and "do or contract out" decisions. Current operating expenditures (total expenditures less those for capital outlay and debt service) may be adjusted by depreciation and amortization data . . . to determine activity expense.[9]

Classification by Organizational Unit and by Object Class Classification of expenditures by organizational unit is important for management, control, and internal reporting purposes including responsibility accounting. Classification of expenditures by organizational unit is based on the departments, divisions, bureaus, or other administrative units that make expenditures to carry out their designated functions. Examples include police department, attorney general's office, corporation commission, city planning, and the like. Each organizational unit may have responsibility for several functions or activities. In some instances a function or activity may cross organizational unit lines.

Classification of expenditures by object class identifies what is acquired in return for the expenditure (i.e., the types of items purchased or services obtained). Typical object classifications are presented in Illustration 17-4. Classification by object is useful primarily for internal management and may be omitted from published financial reports.

ILLUSTRATION 17-4

Classification of Expenditures by Object Class

Personal Services
- Salaries
- Employee health and retirement benefits
- Payroll taxes, etc.

Supplies
- Office supplies
- Operating supplies
- Small tools

Other
- Professional services
- Telephone and telegraph
- Travel
- Rental (equipment, buildings, machinery)
- Postage and shipping
- Printing and publications
- Repairs and maintenance
- Insurance
- Miscellaneous

Capital Expenditures
- Land
- Buildings
- Improvements
- Machinery and equipment
- Motor vehicles
- Furniture and furnishings
- Office machines

---

[9] National Council on Government Accounting, *Statement 1: Governmental Accounting and Financial Reporting Principles* (Chicago: Municipal Finance Officers Association of the United States and Canada, 1979), pp. 16–17.

Transfers to Other Funds

Transfers of resources to other fund entities within an organization do not represent decreases in the expendable financial resources of the organization as a whole. Accordingly, even though they represent a decrease in the financial resources of a particular fund, they ordinarily should be classified separately from expenditures for financial reporting purposes.

Recognition of Expenditures

LO6 Critical events in the use of financial resources.

An expenditure is one of four critical events in the use of the financial resources of an expendable fund entity. The sequence of events is as follows:

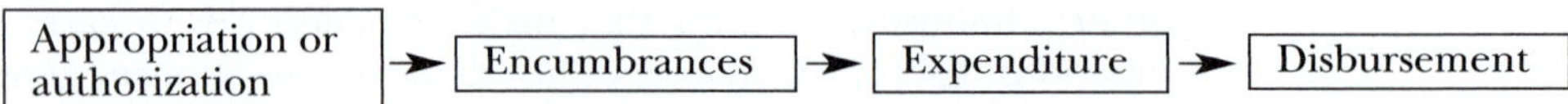

Appropriation Appropriations represent the maximum amount of expenditures that entities are authorized to spend. Administrators are responsible for expending fund resources only in the amounts and for the purposes prescribed in the appropriations act. In the case of governmental units, administrators are held strictly accountable for the provisions of the appropriation act, and stiff penalties are provided by law for those who fail to follow them. Thus, an important function of financial statements is to let administrators know how they stand relative to their appropriation authority. Furthermore, accounting safeguards must be in place to prevent the misuse of fund resources.

Encumbrance Since the amount of an appropriation cannot be legally exceeded, the placing of purchase orders and the signing of contracts are critical events in controlling the expenditures of expendable fund entities. The financial resources of a fund are said to be encumbered when a transaction is entered into that requires performance by another party before the governmental unit becomes liable to perform its part of the transaction by spending financial resources. An encumbrance reduces the remaining portion of appropriations encumbered and is formally recorded in the accounting records. Thus, at any particular time the accounting records will reflect management's remaining available appropriation authority as follows:

Appropriations − (Encumbrances + Expenditures) = Unencumbered balance

The unencumbered balance is the amount of resources that can still be obligated or expended without exceeding the legal or authorized limit.

Encumbrances are recorded as follows:

Purchase Order (Encumbrance)

(1) Encumbrance (appropriately classified)	10,000	
Reserve for Encumbrance		10,000
To record an order for goods in the amount of $10,000.		

Expenditures An expenditure is a decrease in fund resources or an increase in fund liabilities that occurs when the vendor or supplier performs on a contract or purchase order and goods or services are received. Expenditures are recognized in the accounting period in which the fund liability is incurred, except for unmatured interest on long-term debt, which is recognized when due, and certain compensated absences and claims and judgments, which are recognized when obligations are expected to be liquidated with expendable available resources. Thus, an expenditure and a corresponding liability or cash disbursement is recorded at the time goods or services are received or at the time funds are granted to an authorized recipient. When the goods ordered in (1) above are received, the following entries are made:

Receipt of Goods (Expenditure)

(2)	Expenditures (appropriately classified)	12,000	
	Vouchers Payable		12,000
	To record the receipt of goods invoiced at $12,000.		
(3)	Reserve for Encumbrance	10,000	
	Encumbrance		10,000
	To remove the encumbrance recorded in (1) for goods received and recorded as an expenditure in (2).		

In this case, the goods cost $2,000 more than was estimated when the order was placed.

Disbursements Disbursements represent the payment of cash for expenditures. Such payments may precede the expenditure (an advance), coincide with the expenditure (a direct payment), or follow the expenditure (the payment of a liability). The payment for the goods purchased in (2) above is recorded as follows:

Payment of Goods

(4)	Vouchers Payable	12,000	
	Cash		12,000
	To record payment of vouchers payable.		

Encumbrances and expenditures are classified on the same basis (by fund, function, organizational unit, activity, character, or object class) as appropriations. The effect on appropriation control of incorporating appropriations, encumbrances, and expenditures into the accounting records is demonstrated in Illustration 17-5 for an imaginary budget line item number 103.

In Illustration 17-5, it is assumed that the appropriation for budget category 103 is $50,000 and that the amount of expenditures in this category prior to the entries illustrated above was $15,000. The effects of entries (1), (2), (3), and (4) on the subsidiary ledger card for budget category 103 are to reduce the unencumbered balance by $12,000 (the amount of the actual expenditure). The most important thing to note is that at any particular time, information is available to administrators concerning their unexpended and uncommitted appropriation authority.

ILLUSTRATION 17-5

Subsidiary Ledger Control Card for One Budget Category
Function: Sanitation; Activity: Sanitary Sewer Cleaning; Object: Operating Supplies

Budget Line 103	*(A) Appropriation*	*(B) Encumbrance*	*(C) Expenditure*	*(D) Total (B) + (C)*	*(E) Unencumbered Balance (A) − (D)*
Prior Balance	$50,000	$ —	$15,000	$15,000	$35,000
Purchase Order [entry (1)]		10,000		10,000	(10,000)
Balance	50,000	10,000	15,000	25,000	25,000
Expenditure [entries (2) & (3)]		(10,000)	12,000	2,000	(2,000)
Balance	$50,000	$ —	$27,000	$27,000	$23,000

LO7 Capital expenditures.

Capital Expenditures In accounting for profit-oriented enterprises, capital expenditures are recorded as assets and are distinguished from expenses. The costs of such assets are recognized in the operating statements (income statement) of such enterprises through depreciation.

In accounting for an expendable fund entity, capital expenditures, like other expenditures, are treated as an outflow of financial resources. The assets acquired do not represent expendable financial resources but rather reflect the purposes for which financial resources have been used. Thus, they are not recorded or reported as assets of the fund entity. This treatment is consistent with the primary purpose of fund accounting, which is to provide accounting control over the collection and expenditure of financial resources and to assure that no violations of authorized limits on expenditures occur. The operating statements of expendable fund entities are therefore designed to reflect ***all*** the sources and uses of its financial resources. The position statement of the expendable fund entity is designed to present the status of its ***financial resources***, the related liabilities, and the ***net financial resources*** available for subsequent appropriation and expenditure. This emphasis on the status and flow of net financial resources requires that capital expenditures be treated the same as any other classification of expenditures and that they not be reflected as assets of the fund entity. This is not to say that controls are not maintained over fixed assets acquired by means of expendable fund resources. The organization establishes records and controls beyond the records of the expendable fund entity. Accounting for and reporting on fixed assets is illustrated in Chapter 18 for governmental units and in Chapter 19 for nongovernment nonbusiness organizations. General capital assets are assets associated with and arising from governmental activities. Although they are not reported as assets in government funds, they are reported as assets in government-wide statements required under *GASB Statement No. 34* (illustrated in the next chapter).

Depreciation is not accounted for in the records of an expendable fund entity for the same reason that fixed assets are excluded from the records of such entities. However, depreciation is recognized in the government-wide statement of assets and statement of activities. As stated previously, expenditures, not expenses, are generally measured in accounting for expendable fund entities. Acquisitions of fixed assets require the ***use*** of financial resources and are accounted for as expenditures. Proceeds from the sale of fixed assets ***provide*** financial resources and are accounted for as revenues. Depreciation expense is neither a source nor a use of the financial resources of an expendable fund entity, and thus is not properly recorded in the accounts of such entities. Inclusion of depreciation expense in the operating statement of an expendable fund entity would confuse two fundamentally different measurements—expenditures and expense—and would result in misleading inferences relative to the operating activities of the expendable fund entity. This does not mean that the concept or measurement of depreciation is not important from the point of view of the organization as a whole. Indeed, if meaningful cost/benefit analysis is to be attempted for a particular activity, the operating expenditures of the activity must be adjusted for depreciation to determine total activity cost. For this reason, depreciation expense is required on the government-wide statements (see Chapter 18). However, the primary objective of fund accounting is not to provide information relative to the costs and benefits of activities but to control the collection and expenditure of financial resources. Accounting for and reporting on depreciation are further discussed in Chapter 18 for state and local governmental units and in Chapter 19 for nongovernment nonbusiness organizations.

Recording Budgeted and Actual Revenue and Expenditures

Consider an expendable fund with a beginning balance of $100,000 in the fund balance. For the year, revenues and appropriations for expenditures were estimated to be $800,000 and $780,000, respectively. During the year, commitments for expenditures were $775,000 and revenues were $850,000. Notice that commitments were within the appropriation limit of $780,000 and that commitments were less than the expected revenues. However, for the year, actual expenditures were $600,000. (These expenditures were related to $605,000 worth of commitments for expenditures.) The following six journal entries reflect the information recorded in the fund. The statement of changes in unreserved fund balance for the expendable fund entity are presented in Illustration 17-6.

		Debit	Credit
(1)	Estimated Revenue (classified)	800,000	
	Appropriations (classified)		780,000
	Unreserved Fund Balance		20,000
	To record budgeted revenues and expenditures adopted by legislative body or governing board.		

In the first journal entry, the difference between budgeted revenue ($800,000) and budgeted expenditures ($780,000 of appropriations) is recorded as an increase or decrease in the unreserved fund balance ($20,000). In this case, since estimated revenues exceed estimated expenditures, the difference increases the fund balance by $20,000.

		Debit	Credit
(2)	Receivables or Cash	850,000	
	Revenue (classified)		850,000
	To record revenues recognized during the year.		
(3)	Encumbrances (classified)	775,000	
	Reserve for Encumbrances		775,000
	To record commitments made against appropriations (***$775,000 is an assumed amount***).		

ILLUSTRATION 17-6

Condensed Financial Statements of Expendable Fund Entity

Balance Sheet—January 1, 2008

Net Financial Resources (Assets minus Liabilities)	$100,000
Fund Balance (Unreserved)	$100,000

Statement of Changes in Unreserved Fund Balance
for Period Ended December 31, 2008

	Budget	*Actual*	*Actual Over (Under) Budget*
Unreserved Fund Balance—1/1	$100,000	$100,000	$ 0
Revenue	800,000	850,000	50,000
Total Resources Available	$900,000	$950,000	$ 50,000
Appropriations	780,000		
Expenditures (current year)		600,000	
Encumbrances (outstanding at 12/31)		170,000	
Total Resources Expended or Committed	780,000	770,000	(10,000)
Unreserved Fund Balance—12/13	$120,000	$180,000	$60,000

Balance Sheet—December 31, 2008

Net Financial Resources (Assets minus Liabilities)		$350,000
Fund Balance		
Unreserved	$180,000	
Reserved for Encumbrances (Outstanding Commitments)	170,000	$350,000

The second journal entry records the revenue recognized for the year. As commitments are made, encumbrances are recorded. The third journal entry records encumbrances. These amounts would then be posted to the various appropriation expenditure subsidiary accounts. This posting provides information as to the amount of each appropriation category that remains available for encumbrance or expenditure (see Illustration 17-5).

(4a)	Expenditures (classified)	600,000	
	Vouchers Payable or Cash		600,000
	To record receipt of encumbered goods and services.		
(4b)	Reserve for Encumbrances	605,000	
	Encumbrances		605,000
	To remove encumbrances on goods and services that have been recorded as expenditures (***$605,000 is an assumed figure***).		

Two journal entries are required to record expenditures for goods or services that have been previously encumbered. One entry is needed to record the actual expenditure amount and one entry is needed to reverse the encumbrance made when the commitment was recorded. Since the amount expended will not necessarily equal the amount encumbered, the dollar amounts in the two entries may not be the same. The reversal of the encumbrance is for the amount of the original encumbrance, which is assumed to be $605,000 in this example. The amount of expenditure is for the approved invoice price of the goods or services received.

(5)	Revenue	850,000	
	Estimated Revenue		800,000
	Unreserved Fund Balance		50,000
	To close budgeted and actual revenue accounts.		

Two closing entries are needed. The first closing entry is used to close actual revenues and estimated revenues against the unreserved fund balance. The excess of actual revenue over (under) budgeted revenue is recorded as an increase (decrease) in the unreserved fund balance. (Note that all subsidiary revenue and expenditure accounts would also be closed.)

(6)	Appropriations	780,000	
	Expenditures		600,000
	Encumbrances ($775,000 − $605,000)		170,000
	Unreserved Fund Balance		10,000
	To close appropriations, expenditures, and encumbrances accounts.		

The second closing entry is to close the appropriations account against expenditures and the amount of outstanding commitments remaining in the encumbrance account. The excess of appropriations over (under) expenditures plus encumbrances is recorded as an increase (decrease) in the unreserved fund balance. The balance of encumbrances at year-end is matched against appropriations because, although they are not expenditures, encumbrances do represent commitments made against the current year's appropriations and therefore represent the use of the appropriation authority of the current year. Notice that the balance in the reserve for encumbrance account is carried forward to the next year. The change in the reserve for encumbrance account is equal to the amount closed for encumbrances in entry (6).

After entries (5) and (6) are posted, all account balances except assets, liabilities, the unreserved fund balance, and the reserve for encumbrances have been closed. The balances in the unreserved fund balance and reserve for encumbrances accounts may be calculated as follows:

Reserve for encumbrances—January 1, 2008	$ —0—
Total amounts encumbered during 2008—entry (3)	775,000
Total encumbrances expended—entry (4)	(605,000)
Reserve for encumbrances—December 31, 2008	$ 170,000
Unreserved fund balance—January 1, 2008	$ 100,000
Excess of estimated revenue over appropriations—entry (1)	20,000
Excess of actual revenue over estimated revenue—entry (5)	50,000
Excess of appropriations over expenditures and encumbrances—entry (6)	10,000
Unreserved fund balance—December 31, 2008	$ 180,000

The $ 170,000 balance in the reserve for encumbrances account at December 31, 2008, represents the estimated amount of the net financial resources of the fund entity needed in the next year to pay the obligations authorized in the current year's appropriation. Thus, it represents a restriction on the availability of fund resources for future appropriation rather than a liability and is properly considered as a reserved portion of the total fund balance. The concept that the year-end balance in the Reserve for Encumbrances account is in reality a reserved fund balance would perhaps be clearer if an analysis of the change in the total fund balance were presented in the following form:

Total fund balance—January 1	$ 100,000
Add actual revenue	850,000
Deduct actual expenditures	(600,000)
Total fund balance—December 31	350,000
Less amount reserved for commitments	(170,000)
Unreserved fund balance—December 31	$ 180,000

Note that the increase in the ***total*** fund balance ($100,000 to $350,000, or $250,000 in this example) is always equal to the excess of ***actual*** revenues ($850,000; inflows of net financial resources) over ***actual*** expenditures ($600,000; outflows of net financial resources).

In the next year, the balance of the reserve for encumbrances will be charged by means of a separate expenditures account with the actual expenditures arising from the year-end commitments that are incurred in the subsequent year. A difference between the amount encumbered at the end of the year and the actual amount of the related expenditures that are incurred in the subsequent year is debited or credited to the unreserved fund balance.

Suppose that in the next year, the fund incurs $160,000 of expenditures on these commitments. The entries to record the expenditures would be:

Expenditures—2008	160,000	
Cash		160,000

There is not a second entry to reverse the encumbrance account, since the encumbrance account for 2008 was closed at the end of 2008. Thus at the end of 2009, this expenditure account is closed against the reserve for encumbrances account of $170,000. This closing entry is:

Reserve for encumbrance—2008	170,000	
Expenditure—2008		160,000
Unreserved fund balance		10,000

TEST YOUR KNOWLEDGE

NOTE: Solutions to ***Test Your Knowledge*** questions are found at the end of each chapter before the end-of-chapter questions.

Short Answer

1. On January 1, 2009, Stale City reported an unreserved fund balance of $50,000. During the year, estimated revenues were $400,000 and actual revenues were $425,000. Appropriations for the year were $350,000, while expenditures were $250,000 and encumbrances outstanding at December 31, 2009, were $80,000. Compute the unreserved fund balance at December 31, 2009.

In 2009, the U.S. will have its second "trillion-dollar deficit," with 2008's deficit being the first. However, the budget deficit for 2008 was officially reported as being $455 billion. How is this possible? Just borrow money from the Social Security trust fund, record it as an "intragovernmental transfer" and exclude it from the calculation of the deficit. Corporate managers have gone to jail for less than this.[10]

Lapsing of Appropriations

The treatment illustrated in this chapter for encumbrances outstanding at the end of the period was based on the assumption (and generally followed practice) that encumbered appropriations do not lapse at the end of the fiscal year. It is possible, however, for the legislative body or governing board to impose a provision that causes unexpended appropriations to lapse at the end of the year. In this case, the reserve for encumbrances must be closed out at the end of the year, and if the encumbered items are to be purchased in the next year, the appropriation for the next year must contain authority for such expenditures.

If appropriations lapse, the closing entry for appropriations at the end of the year takes the following form:

Reserve for Encumbrances	191,000	
Appropriations	1,744,000	
Expenditures		1,510,000
Encumbrances		191,000
Unreserved Fund Balance		234,000

The subsequent year's appropriation should include authorization for the purchase of the encumbered items. Therefore, the reserve for encumbrances would be reestablished at the beginning of the next year by a debit to encumbrances, and subsequent expenditures for the items would be accounted for the same as any other expenditures in that year.

Comprehensive Illustration—General Fund

LO8 Understanding the general fund.

The General Fund of Model City is now used to illustrate the principles of fund accounting developed in this chapter.

The general fund of a municipality is used to account for most of the current operations of a municipality other than those required to be accounted for in other

[10] WSJ, February 17, 2009, "A Short History of the National Debt" by John Gordon.

funds. It is established at the inception of the municipality and is continued as long as the municipality exists. A government never reports more than one general fund. Other government funds are established to account for specific municipality activities, such as a capital projects fund to build new highways or a debt services fund to service debt and interest payments. The general ledger trial balance of the General Fund of Model City on January 1, 2008, is as follows:

Model City
The General Fund
General Ledger Trial Balance
January 1, 2008

Cash	$ 45,000
Certificates of Deposit	100,000
Property Tax Receivable	190,000
Total Debits	$335,000
Estimated Uncollectible Taxes	$ 20,000
Vouchers Payable	65,000
Unreserved Fund Balance	95,000
Reserve for Encumbrances—2007	155,000
Total Credits	$335,000

The budget adopted by the City Council for the General Fund for the fiscal year ending December 31, 2008, is presented in summary form below.

Model City
The General Fund
2008 Fiscal-Year Budget

Estimated Revenue	
Licenses and Permits	$ 188,250
Property Tax	1,158,750
State Grant—Education	300,000
Charges for Services	135,000
Proceeds from Sales of Equipment	78,000
Total	$1,860,000
Appropriations	
Public Safety	516,000
General Government	293,500
Highways and Streets	135,500
Sanitation	75,000
Health	148,500
Cultural—recreation	88,500
Education	687,000
Total	$1,944,000
Excess of Appropriations over Estimated Revenue	($84,000)
Transfer from Enterprise Fund	150,000
Less Transfers to: Debt Service Fund	(96,000)
Excess (deficiency) of Revenue and Transfers from Other Funds over Appropriations and Transfers to Other Funds	($30,000)

Summary entries to record the activities and transactions of the General Fund during 2008 are presented below. Remember, each entry to these general ledger control accounts also requires detailed postings by appropriate classifications to the related subsidiary accounts. The assignment to specific subsidiary accounts of amounts credited to revenue or appropriations and of amounts debited to encumbrances, expenditures, or estimated revenue is shown in parentheses for these summary entries.

		Debit	Credit
(1)	Estimated Revenue	1,860,000	
	Unreserved Fund Balance	84,000	
	Appropriations		1,944,000
	To record budgeted revenue and expenditures.		
(2)	Due from Enterprise Fund	150,000	
	Transfers from Other Funds		150,000
	To record authorization for transfer of resources from other fund entities incorporated in budget adopted by City Council.		

For financial reporting purposes, transfers of resources from other fund entities of the same organization are distinguished from revenue of the recipient fund entity. Interfund transfers are properly recognized (accrued) in the period in which they are authorized. Control over authorized transfers from other fund entities may be achieved by recording them as a receivable at the beginning of the year for which they are authorized (budgeted).

		Debit	Credit
(3)	Transfer to Other Funds	96,000	
	Due to Debt Service Fund		96,000
	To record authorization for transfer of resources to another fund entity incorporated in budget adopted by city council.		

Although authorized transfers to other fund entities may be viewed as appropriation expenditures from the point of view of the General Fund entity, for purposes of financial reporting they are distinguished from expenditures. Control over authorized transfers to other fund entities may be achieved by recording them as liabilities at the beginning of the period for which they are authorized (budgeted).

		Debit	Credit
(4)	Property Tax Receivable	1,287,500	
	Estimated Uncollectible Taxes		128,750
	Revenue		1,158,750
	To record property taxes at time they are levied.		

The estimate for uncollectible taxes is determined on the basis of collection policy and prior years' experience. It is recorded as a direct reduction of revenue, however, rather than as an expenditure, since the failure to collect taxes is not an outflow of net financial resources. Accordingly, there is no appropriation for the amount of estimated uncollectible taxes and it is, therefore, properly accounted for as a reduction of revenue rather than as an expenditure.

		Debit	Credit
(5)	Other Receivables	80,000	
	Revenue		80,000
	To record billings for routine services.		
(6)	Expenditures—2007	148,000	
	Vouchers Payable		148,000
	To record receipt of goods and services ordered in 2007 and originally authorized for $155,000.		

A separate expenditure control account (and subsidiary ledger) is used to record expenditures during the current year that were encumbered (authorized) in the prior year. At the end of the year, this expenditure account will be closed out against Reserve for Encumbrances—2007 and any difference taken to the unreserved fund balance [see entry (26) below].

		Debit	Credit
(7)	Encumbrances	1,291,000	
	Reserve for Encumbrances—2008		1,291,000
	To record encumbrances (commitments) on goods and services ordered during current year.		

		Debit	Credit
(8)	Cash	1,281,000	
	Property Tax Receivable		1,201,000
	Other Receivables		80,000
	To record collection of $170,500 of property taxes levied in 2003 and $1,030,500 of property taxes levied in 2008, and to record collection of $80,000 in other receivables.		
(9)	Estimated Uncollectible Taxes	19,500	
	Property Tax Receivable		19,500
	To record write-off of uncollected 2003 property taxes authorized by City Council ($190,000 − $170,500 = $19,500).		
(10)	Cash	221,000	
	Revenue		221,000
	To record collection of licenses, permits, fees, service charges, etc.		
(11)	Expenditures	1,050,000	
	Vouchers Payable		1,050,000
	Reserve for Encumbrances—2008	1,100,000	
	Encumbrances		1,100,000
	To record receipt of goods and services that had been previously encumbered [entry (7) above] in the amount of $1,100,000.		
(12)	Expenditures	210,000	
	Vouchers Payable		210,000
	To record receipt of goods and services that had ***not*** been previously encumbered.		

Not all expenditures go through the encumbrance process. Encumbrances are formally recognized in the accounts only when there is an extended period of time between the date the commitment is made and the date the expenditure is incurred. For example, routine payroll expenditures are not encumbered.

		Debit	Credit
(13)	Receivable from State Government	275,000	
	Revenue		275,000
	To record municipal education grant authorized by state legislature.		

The amount of revenue recognized is based on an approved grant application filed with the Department of Education and is not dependent on the future performance of specific services or specified expenditures of financial resources.

		Debit	Credit
(14)	Encumbrances	250,000	
	Reserve for Encumbrances—2008		250,000
	To record a contract to acquire office furnishings and equipment.		
(15)	Cash	100,000	
	Due from Enterprise Fund		100,000
	To record receipt of a cash transfer from the Enterprise Fund.		
(16)	Expenditures	250,000	
	Vouchers Payable		250,000
	Reserve for Encumbrances—2008	250,000	
	Encumbrances		250,000
	To record receipt of office equipment and furnishings and to remove encumbrance.		

Capital expenditures, like other expenditures, represent the approved utilization of the financial resources of the General Fund and therefore are recorded as expenditures and not as assets in the records of the General Fund. However, general capital assets (and related depreciation expense) are required to be reported in the government-wide financial statements.

	Debit	Credit
(17) Vouchers Payable	1,650,000	
Cash		1,650,000
To record payment of liabilities.		
(18) Cash	87,250	
Revenue		87,250
To record proceeds from sale of used furniture and equipment.		

Since the proceeds from the sale of Model City assets constitute expendable financial resources, they are recorded as revenue by the recipient general fund.

Under *GASB Statement No. 34*, a government-wide Statement of Activities prepared on an accrual basis is required, in addition to the funds statements prepared on the modified accrual basis. One entry that is affected is the sale of an asset such as entry (18) above. The proceeds from the sale of an asset are not reported as revenue; instead the difference between the carrying value of the asset (after considering depreciation) and the cash received is reported as a gain or loss on the government-wide statement of activities.[11]

	Debit	Credit
(19) Cash	275,000	
Receivable from State Government		275,000
To record collection of grant from state legislature.		
(20) Due to Debt Service Fund	96,000	
Cash		96,000
To record authorized transfers of cash to other Model City fund entities.		
(21) Certificates of Deposit	6,000	
Revenue		6,000
To record interest earned on certificates of deposit that has been reinvested in the certificates.		
(22) Estimated Uncollectible Taxes	76,000	
Property Tax Receivable		76,000
To record write-off of 2008 property taxes authorized by City Council.		
(23) Expenditures	200,000	
Cash (to internal service fund)		200,000
To record interfund services provided by the internal service fund.		

Summary of Expendable Fund Entries

1. At the beginning of the period, estimated revenues are debited against appropriations (estimated expenditures), with the difference recorded to Unreserved Fund Balance.
2. At the beginning of the period, transfers to and from other funds are recorded against "due from" or "to other funds."
3. During the period, revenues are recorded against an increase in assets (i.e., against receivables, cash, etc.).
4. During the period, when the firm makes a commitment for goods or services, the account encumbrances is debited and reserve for encumbrances is credited. (Encumbrances are future expenditures.)

[11] Governmental Accounting Standards Board (GASB), *GASB Statement No. 34*, "Basic Financial Statements—and Management's Discussion and Analysis—for State and Local Governments" (Norwalk, CT: June 1999).

5. During the period, when goods that have been ordered (and encumbered) are received or contracted services are performed, two entries are prepared:
   a. Expenditures are debited against a decrease in assets or an increase in liabilities. This may or may not equal the amount of the original encumbrance.
   b. When the expenditure is recorded, the entry to record the encumbrance (item 4 above) is reversed. (This may or may not be equal to the actual expenditure.) Therefore, the amount remaining in the reserve for encumbrances represents the amount of funds that have been committed in the current period, but that are expected to be paid in the next period.
6. Purchases of capital assets are recorded in the same manner as any expenditure. An expenditure is debited and either cash or a liability is credited.
7. Gross proceeds from the sale of capital assets are recorded as revenues.

In 2004, GASB issued *Statement 45*, "Accounting and Financial Reporting for Post-Employment Benefits Other Than Pensions" (OPEB). This statement requires that local governments report OPEB on an accrual basis rather than on a "pay-as-you-go" basis. OPEB might include such health benefits (including spouses) as dental, vision, or life insurance. The dollar amount of the liability included on the financial statements can be incredibly significant and underlies the potential cost to local governments. For instance, in one extreme example, for the city of Duluth, this liability amounted to $180 million, which was twice the total annual budget of the city.[12]

Preclosing Trial Balance The transactions summarized in the journal entries above are reflected in the December 31, 2008, general ledger trial balance for the General Fund of Model City presented below.

Model City
The General Fund
General Ledger Trial Balance
December 31, 2008

	Dr.	*Cr.*
Cash	$ 63,250	
Certificates of Deposit	106,000	
Property Taxes Receivable	181,000	
Due from Enterprise Fund	50,000	
Estimated Revenue	1,860,000	
Expenditures	1,710,000	
Encumbrances	191,000	
Transfers to Other Funds (debt service)	96,000	
Expenditures—2007	148,000	
Estimated Uncollectible Taxes		$ 53,250
Vouchers Payable		73,000
Unreserved Fund Balance		11,000
Reserve for Encumbrances		191,000
Reserve for Encumbrances—2007		155,000
Appropriations		1,944,000
Revenue		1,828,000
Transfer from Other Funds (enterprise fund)		150,000
Total	$4,405,250	$4,405,250

[12] *FedGazette*, Federal Reserve Bank of Minneapolis, May 2006.

Closing Entries December 31, 2008, closing entries for the General Fund are as follows:

		Debit	Credit
(24)	Unreserved Fund Balance	32,000	
	Revenue	1,828,000	
	Estimated Revenue		1,860,000
	To close out actual and budgeted revenue accounts.		

		Debit	Credit
(25)	Appropriations	1,944,000	
	Expenditures (for 2008)		1,710,000
	Encumbrances		191,000
	Unreserved Fund Balance		43,000
	To close out appropriations and current year's expenditures and encumbrances accounts.		

Note that the reserve for encumbrances also has a credit balance of $191,000.

		Debit	Credit
(26)	Reserve for Encumbrances—2007	155,000	
	Expenditures—2007		148,000
	Unreserved Fund Balance		7,000
	To close out expenditures for goods and services ***ordered*** and encumbered in prior year. See entry (6).		

		Debit	Credit
(27)	Transfers from Other Funds	150,000	
	Unreserved Fund Balance		54,000
	Transfers to Other Funds		96,000
	To close out interfund transfers to the unreserved fund balance.		

Summary of Closing Entries for Expendable Funds

1. Revenues are closed against estimated revenues. The difference is recorded in unreserved fund balance.
2. Recall that appropriations are approved expenditures for the year. Appropriations are closed against expenditures (actual for the current year) and encumbrances (current year commitments). Any difference is reported in the unreserved fund balance. Recall that the expenditures made for prior year's encumbrances are closed against the reverse for encumbrances for that specific year.
3. Transfers to and from other funds are closed against the unreserved fund balance.

Financial Statements

The two basic statements prepared for expendable fund entities are (1) a balance sheet and (2) a statement of revenue, expenditures, and changes in fund balance. Revenue should be classified by major sources and expenditures by major functions in the statement of revenue, expenditures, and changes in fund balance. In addition, comparative information for the prior year should be presented both in that statement and in the balance sheet. For the general fund, these statements are presented in Illustrations 17-7 and 17-8.

ILLUSTRATION 17-7

Model City
The General Fund
Balance Sheet
December 31, 2008 and 2007

Assets	*2008*	*2007*
Cash	$ 63,250	$ 45,000
Certificate of Deposit	106,000	100,000
Property Tax Receivable (less allowance for uncollectible amounts, 2008—$53,250; 2007—$20,000)	127,750	170,000
Due from Other Funds	50,000	—
Total	$347,000	$315,000
Liabilities and Fund Balance		
Vouchers Payable	$ 73,000	$ 65,000
Fund Balance		
Unreserved	83,000	95,000
Reserved for Encumbrances	191,000	155,000
Total Fund Balance	274,000	250,000
Total Liabilities and Fund Balances	$347,000	$315,000

LLUSTRATION 17-8

Statement of Revenues, Expenditures, and Changes in Fund Balance
The General Fund
for Years Ended December 31, 2008, and December 31, 2007

	2008	*2007*
Revenues		
Property Taxes	1,158,750	1,105,000
Licenses and Permits	170,500	175,000
State Grant—education	275,000	250,000
Charges for Services	130,500	130,000
Interest	6,000	—
Total Revenue	1,740,750	1,660,000
Expenditures		
Public Safety	480,000	360,000
General Government	289,000	175,000
Highways and Streets	128,000	130,000
Sanitation	70,000	71,000
Health	141,000	132,000
Cultural—recreation	80,000	82,000
Education	670,000	640,000
Total Expenditures	1,858,000	1,590,000
Excess (deficiency) of Revenues over Expenditures	(117,250)	70,000
Other Financing Sources (Uses)		
Operating Transfers In—Enterprise Fund	150,000	—
Operating Transfers Out—Debt Service Fund	(96,000)	(60,000)
Total Other	54,000	(60,000)
Special Items		
Proceeds from Sales of Equipment	87,250	—
Net Change in Fund Balance	24,000	10,000
Fund Balance—Beginning	250,000	240,000
Fund Balance—Ending	274,000	250,000

ACCOUNTING AND FINANCIAL REPORTING FOR POLLUTION REMEDIATION OBLIGATIONS

GASB Statement No. 49 requires that a government report a liability related to pollution remediation under five key circumstances. The standard requires that information about pollution clean-up efforts be disclosed in the financial statements along with the liabilities, expenses, and expenditures which are estimated using an "expected cash flows" measurement technique. According to GASB Chairman Robert Attmore: "Today's proposal intends to improve financial reporting by fostering more transparent and more consistent accounting that encourages comparability."[*]

[*] GASB News Release 1/31/06.

For budgetary fund entities, a financial statement that compares budgeted and actual operating results should also be prepared. Budgeted comparison statements should be presented as required supplementary information (RSI). The purpose of budgetary comparison reporting is to show whether resources were obtained and used in accordance with the entity's legally adopted budget. Since amounts encumbered (encumbrances) against the current year's appropriation authority (budget) must be treated in the same manner as expenditures in budgeted statements, the "actual" data may be different from those presented in accordance with generally accepted accounting principles in the statement of revenue, expenditures, and other changes in fund balance. In that case, the difference between the budgetary basis and generally accepted accounting principles should be explained in the notes to the financial statements. An example of the Budgetary Comparison Schedule is shown in Illustration 17-9 and the Budget-to-GAAP Reconciliation schedule is shown in Illustration 17-10.

Analysis of the Financial Statements The balance sheet of the General Fund can be used to assess the short-term financing needs of the government and perhaps the ability to meet these needs. In Illustration 17-7, note that total assets equal $347,000 and that payables related to expenditures are $73,000. However, the fund balance is composed of $191,000 in the reserve for encumbrances. This is the amount of the fund balance set aside for commitments made by the government prior to the end of the year. Thus only $83,000 is available for general purposes for the next year ($347,000 − 73,000 − 191,000 = $83,000).

The statement of revenues, expenditures, and changes in fund balance (Illustration 17-8) focuses on cash and other current resources that flow in and out of the government. Both revenues and expenditures are listed by function. Approximately 66.5% of revenues come from property taxes. The largest expenditure is due to education, which comprises about 36% of total expenditures.

Note that even though the fund balance increased during the year, expenditures exceeded revenues by $117,250. After considering other transfers and financing sources, you can see that the deficit is still $63,250. The only reason that the fund balance increased during the year is because the government sold equipment. Is this a cause for concern? Keep in mind that the timing of cash flows is very important for these statements. Recall that purchased assets are expenditures and that these purchases may be financed from activities in previous years.

ILLUSTRATION 17-9

Model City
Budgetary Comparison Schedule
General Fund
for the Year Ended December 31, 2008

	Budgeted Amounts			
	Original	*Final*	*Actual Amounts*	*Variance with Final Budget Favorable (Unfavorable)*
Budgetary Fund Balance, January 1	$ 250,000	$ 250,000	$ 250,000	—
Resources				
Property Tax	1,158,750	1,158,750	1,158,750	—
Licenses and Permits	190,000	188,250	170,500	(17,750)
Grants	300,000	300,000	275,000	(25,000)
Charges for Services	131,000	135,000	130,500	(4,500)
Sale of Equipment	83,000	78,000	87,250	9,250
Interest	6,000	6,000	6,000	—
Transfers from Other Funds	150,000	150,000	150,000	—
Amounts Available for Appropriations	$2,268,750	$2,266,000	$2,228,000	$(38,000)
Charges to Appropriations				
Public Safety	510,000	516,000	480,000	36,000
General Government	290,000	293,500	289,000	4,500
Highways and Streets	135,000	135,500	128,000	7,500
Sanitation	73,000	75,000	70,000	5,000
Health	140,000	148,500	141,000	7,500
Cultural—recreation	90,000	88,500	80,000	8,500
Education	690,000	687,000	670,000	17,000
Transfers to Other Funds	96,000	96,000	96,000	—
Total Charges to Appropriations	2,024,000	2,040,000	1,954,000	86,000
Budgetary Fund Balance, December 31	$ 244,750	$ 226,000	$ 274,000	$ 48,000

ILLUSTRATION 17-10

Model City
Budgetary Comparison Schedule
Budget-to-GAAP Reconciliation

	General Fund
Sources/inflows of resources:	
Actual amounts (budgetary basis) "available for appropriation" from the Budget to Actual Comparison Statement (see Illustration 17-9)	$2,228,000
Differences—budget to GAAP	
The fund balance at the beginning of the year is a budgetary resource and is not a current year revenue for financial reporting purposes	(250,000)
Transfers from other funds are inflows of budgetary resources but are not revenues for financial reporting purposes	(150,000)
The proceeds from the sale of equipment are budgetary resources but are regarded as a special item, rather than revenue, for financial reporting purposes	(87,250)
Total revenues as reported on the Statement of Revenues, Expenditures, and Changes in Fund Balances—General Fund (see Illustration 17-8)	$1,740,750
Uses/outflows of resources:	
Actual amounts (budgetary basis) total charges to appropriation from the Budget to Actual Comparison Statement (see Illustration 17-9)	$1,954,000
Differences—budget to GAAP	
Transfers to other funds are outflows of budgetary resources but are not expenditures for financial reporting purposes	(96,000)
Total expenditures as reported on the Statement of Revenues, Expenditures, and Changes in Fund Balance—General Fund (See Illustration 17-8)	$1,858,000

REPORTING INVENTORY AND PREPAYMENTS IN THE FINANCIAL STATEMENTS

Inventory

LO9 Consumption and purchases Methods.

There are two methods of accounting for and reporting inventory in the financial statements of expendable fund entities: the ***consumption method*** and the ***purchases method.*** Under *GASB Statement No. 34,* the consumption method is consistent with the government-wide approach, and the purchases method is not acceptable. Both are acceptable for fund purposes, however, and are illustrated here. Under the consumption method, inventory is considered to be a financial resource (asset), and expenditures for inventory are reported on the operating statement in the period in which the inventory is used. Under the purchases method, inventory is not considered to be a financial resource (asset) and expenditures are recognized in the period the inventory is purchased whether it is used or not.

To illustrate, assume that $20,000 in inventory is on hand at the beginning of the period, that $50,000 in inventory is purchased during the period, and that inventory at the end of the period is $24,000. Entries under each method are as follows:

	Consumption Method			*Purchases Method*		
When Purchased:	Expenditures	50,000		Expenditures	50,000	
	Cash		50,000	Cash		50,000
End of Year:	Inventory	4,000		NO ENTRY		
	Expenditures		4,000			

The entry at the end of the year under the consumption method adjusts the inventory account from its beginning of year balance, $20,000, to the correct ending inventory amount, $24,000. If inventory decreases, expenditures would be debited and inventory credited. Under this method, inventories are automatically reported as an asset in the financial statements. As compared to the purchases method, the current year's financial statements prepared under the consumption method reflect $4,000 less expenditures and result in a $ 24,000 larger fund balance.

Reserve for Inventory

Purchases Method Material amounts of inventory should be disclosed in the financial statements either by footnote or by reporting an asset in the balance sheet with a contra account (Reserve for Inventory) reported as part of the total fund balance. To illustrate the reporting of inventory as both an asset and an expenditure under the purchases method, assume that the balance sheet at the beginning of the period was as shown here:

Inventory	$ 20,000
Other Financial Resources (net)	400,000
Net Assets	$420,000
Fund Balance	
Reserve for Inventory	$ 20,000
Unreserved Fund Balance	400,000
Total Fund Balance	$420,000

In addition to the purchases method entry illustrated above, another entry is necessary at the end of the year to record the $4,000 increase in inventory as follows:

Purchases Method

End of Year		
Inventory	4,000	
Reserve for Inventory		4,000

If inventory decreases, Reserve for Inventory is debited and Inventory is credited. Assuming net financial resources (excluding inventory) increase by $100,000 during the period, the amounts that would be reported in the balance sheet at the end of the period are as follows:

Inventory	$ 24,000
Other Financial Resources (net)	500,000
Net Assets	$524,000
Fund Balance	
Reserve for Inventory	$ 24,000
Unreserved Fund Balance	500,000
Total Fund Balance	$524,000

When a reserve for inventory is created under the purchases method, the amounts reported for inventory and the ***total*** fund balance are the same as those reported under the consumption method. However, the amount of expenditures reported in the operating statement will still differ (in this case by $4,000).

Consumption Method In some cases it is considered desirable to both (1) use the consumption method and (2) report a reserve for inventory. If the consumption method is used, the reserve for inventory is created and adjusted by debiting or crediting the "unreserved fund balance." For example, using the above illustration and assuming the balance in Reserve for Inventory was $20,000 at the beginning of the year, another entry in addition to those illustrated under the consumption method above would be made at the end of the year as follows:

Consumption Method

End of Year		
Unreserved Fund Balance	4,000	
Reserve for Inventory		4,000

Prepayments

Prepayments for items such as insurance or rent that cover more than one accounting period may also be reported using the consumption or purchases methods. Under the purchases method the cost is reported as an expenditure in the period when the insurance premium or rent is paid without regard to the period benefited (there is no allocation among accounting periods). Under the consumption method, a prepaid asset would be recorded and expenditures reduced to the extent that the premium or rent payment is for a subsequent period.

According to a University of Tennessee study, the state of Tennessee lost $34 million in 1999 in tax revenue to e-commerce. The reason? Sales tax is not collected on most Internet sales, and Tennessee (currently with no state income tax) is among those states that rely heavily upon sales tax revenue. Although both Congress and President Clinton have been reluctant to take any steps toward inhibiting the growth of e-commerce, many believe that the Internet tax panel should recommend an approach to Congress that ensures that states get what they are entitled to in tax revenue.[13]

GASB STATEMENT No. 56, "CODIFICATION OF ACCOUNTING AND FINANCIAL REPORTING GUIDANCE CONTAINED IN THE AICPA STATEMENTS ON AUDITING STANDARDS"

The GASB issued *Statement No. 56* in 2009 to incorporate into its authoritative literature certain accounting and financial reporting guidance presented in the AICPA's *Statements on Auditing Standards.* This statement addresses three issues not included in the authoritative literature that establishes accounting principles—related party transactions, going concern considerations, and subsequent events. This statement did not establish new accouting standards but rather incorporated the existing guidance (to the extent appropriate in a governmental environment) into the GASB standards. The goal of this statement was to improve financial reporting by contributing to the GASB's efforts to codify all sources of GAAP for state and local governments so that they derive from a single source, bringing the authoritative accounting and financial reporting literature together in one place. The guidance was intended to be modified as needed to appropriately recognize the governmental environment and the needs of governmental financial statement users.

Unless otherwise specified, pronouncements of the GASB apply to financial reports of all state and local governmental entities, including general purpose governments; public benefit corporations and authorities; public employee retirement systems; and public utilities, hospitals and other healthcare providers, and colleges and universities.

SUMMARY

1. *Distinguish between a nonbusiness organization and a profit-oriented enterprise.* The primary goal of a profit-oriented enterprise is to earn a profit. Nonbusiness organizations provide services based on social need. Persons who contribute to nonbusiness organizations receive no equity in the organization and do not necessarily benefit proportionally or at all from the services provided.

2. *Explain the role of fund accounting.* Resources received by nonbusiness organizations typically have restrictions or are limited by use. In many cases, the nonbusiness organization has self-imposed restrictions on the use of resources. In order to account for these restrictions, nonbusiness organizations use fund accounting. In essence, the organization separates the assets, liabilities, and

[13] *The Leaf-Chronicle*, "State Is Losing Out on Revenue," by the editorial board of *The Leaf-Chronicle*, 2/12/00, p. A6.

residual equity into distinct funds organized for specific objectives. Each fund is treated as a separate accounting entity consisting of a self-balancing set of books.

3. *Distinguish among the concepts of revenues, expenses, and expenditures as used in profit-oriented entities and as used for expendable fund entities.* Profit-oriented entities recognize revenues on an accrual basis and expenses using the matching principle. Expendable fund entities typically treat any increase in financial resources as revenues, such as from property taxes or sales of equipment (except debt issuances and transfers from other funds). Also, expendable funds treat any decrease in resources as an expenditure (except transfers to other funds).
4. *Understand the classification of revenues and other resource inflows for fund accounting.* Revenues are classified by source, such as property taxes, fines and penalties, and licenses and permits.
5. *Understand the classification of expenditures and other resource outflows for fund accounting.* Expenditures are classified by function, by activity, by organizational unit, by object, or by character (nature of the item). For government-wide reporting, the statement of activities classifies expenses by function.
6. *Describe the critical events in the use of financial resources of an expendable fund.* Before resources can be spent, they must follow a series of events. First, the amount must be authorized (appropriated) by proper authorities. Second, since the amounts spent cannot exceed the appropriations, when a purchase order is placed (or a contract is signed), an encumbrance is recorded against a reserve for encumbrance. Any unencumbered balance indicates the amount of resources not yet committed. When a contract is performed or a service received, an expenditure is recorded and the encumbrance and the reserve for encumbrance are reduced. At year-end, appropriations, encumbrances, and expenditures are closed to fund balance. The reserve for encumbrances carries over to the next period.
7. *Explain how capital expenditures are recorded in an expendable fund.* In profit-oriented firms, capital expenditures are recorded as assets and depreciated over their useful lives. In an expendable fund, capital expenditures are treated as expenditures (as an outflow of resources), but are not depreciated. Funds are set up to properly account for the source and use of resources during a particular period and to ensure that the fund does not spend more than its limit (appropriation).
8. *Understand the role of a general fund.* The general fund is used to account for all externally *unrestricted* financial resources. In other words, the general fund is used to account for all resources that have not been set aside for specific activities. Funds typically divide governments into categories based on the restrictions of the resources.
9. *Contrast the consumption and the purchases methods of accounting for inventories (and other prepaid items).* The consumption method treats inventory as an asset until used, while the purchases method treats all inventory purchases as expenditures of the period. Therefore, inventory is not recorded on the balance sheet if the purchases method is used. Both methods are acceptable for fund purposes, but in the government-wide statements, only the consumption method is acceptable.

TEST YOUR KNOWLEDGE SOLUTION

Beginning unreserved fund balance	$ 50,000
Excess of estimated revenue over appropriations	50,000
Excess of actual revenue over estimated revenue	25,000
Excess of appropriations over expenditures and encumbrances	20,000
Unreserved fund balance—December 31	$145,000

APPENDIX

City of Atlanta Partial Financial Statements

City of Atlanta, Georgia
Balance Sheet
Governmental Funds
December 31, 2004

(in thousands)	*General Fund*	*Other Governmental Funds*	*Total Governmental Funds*
Assets			
Cash and cash equivalents	$ 181	$ 29,525	$ 29,706
Investments	104,943	254,549	359,492
Receivables	38,071	4,456	42,527
Due from other governments		7,848	7,848
Due from others	64,573	2,697	67,270
Investments in escrow	22,026	4,304	26,330
Total Assets	**$229,794**	**$303,379**	**$533,173**
Liabilities and Fund Balances			
Liabilities			
Accounts payable	$ 8,617	$ 2,447	$ 11,064
Accrued liabilities	10,410	421	10,831
Other		448	448
Due to other funds	48,123	34,209	82,332
Deferred revenue	4,942	1,378	6,320
Total Liabilities	**$72,092**	**$38,903**	**$110,995**
Fund Balances (Deficit)			
Reserved for:			
Encumbrances	$ 6,353	$ 39,394	$ 45,747
Special programs		69,511	69,511
Capital improvements		139,431	139,431
Debt service		37,556	37,556
Unreserved:			
General fund	151,349		151,349
Other funds		(21,416)	(21,416)
Total Fund Balances	**$157,702**	**$264,476**	**$422,178**
Total Liabilities and Fund Balances	**$229,794**	**$303,379**	**$533,173**

City of Atlanta, Georgia
Statement of Revenues, Expenditures, and Changes in Fund Balances
Governmental Funds
for the Year Ended December 31, 2004

(in thousands)	*General Fund*	*Other Governmental Funds*	*Total Governmental Funds*
Revenues			
Property taxes	$147,597	$ 45,330	$192,927
Local option sales taxes	83,518		83,518
Public utility, alcoholic beverage & other taxes	106,449		106,449
Licenses & permits	54,327		54,327

(in thousands)	*General Fund*	*Other Governmental Funds*	*Total Governmental Funds*
Charges for current services	8,894	15,867	24,761
Fines, forfeitures & penalties	1,112	17,392	18,504
Investment income	1,985	2,949	4,934
Intergovernmental revenues & contributions	542	48,650	49,192
Building rentals & concessions	10,394		10,394
Other	1,689	7,968	9,657
Total Revenues	**$416,507**	**$138,156**	**$554,663**
Expenditures			
Current			
General government	$ 57,047	$ 55,832	$112,879
Police	138,765	4,193	142,958
Fire	60,794	217	61,011
Corrections	34,355	928	35,283
Public Works	26,951	7,555	34,506
Parks, Recreation & Cultural Affairs	24,365	8,641	33,006
Nondepartmentals	39,440	20,708	60,148
Capital Outlays		15,330	15,330
Debt Service:			
Principal payments	4,500	8,848	13,348
Interest payments	4,417	21,229	25,646
Bond issue costs		31	31
Total Expenditures	**$390,634**	**$143,512**	**$534,146**
Excess (deficiency) of revenues over expenditures	$ 25,873	$ (5,356)	$ 20,517
Other Financing Sources (Uses)			
Proceeds from long-term debt	$ 3,053	$ 55,500	$ 58,553
Premium on bonds sold		3,576	3,576
Transfers in (out)	10,851	(7,529)	3,322
Net change in fund balances	**$ 39,777**	**$ 46,191**	**$ 85,968**
Fund Balance—Beginning of the year	117,925	218,285	336,210
Fund Balance—End of Year	**$157,702**	**$264,476**	**$422,178**

QUESTIONS

(The letter A indicated for a question, exercise, or problem refers to the appendix.)

LO1 1. What characteristics distinguish nonbusiness organizations from profit-oriented enterprises?

LO2 2. Define a fund as the term is applied in accounting for the activities of governmental units and other nonbusiness organizations.

LO6 3. What is the significance of the "unreserved fund balance" of an expendable fund entity?

LO4 LO5 4. What are the major classifications of increases and decreases in expendable fund resources?

LO3 5. What are the revenue-recognition criteria for expendable fund entities? How do these criteria differ from revenue-recognition criteria for profit-oriented enterprises?

LO5 6. Expenditures may be classified by function, activity, object, or organizational unit. Give an example of each classification for a municipality. Which classification is the most appropriate for external financial reporting?

LO3 7. Distinguish between an appropriation, an encumbrance, an expenditure, and a disbursement.

LO3 8. Distinguish between an expense and an expenditure.

LO3 9. Explain and justify the difference between the treatment of estimated uncollectible taxes in fund accounting and the treatment of estimated bad debts in commercial accounting.

LO6 10. Explain the purposes of encumbrance accounting. Might encumbrance accounting be used by commercial enterprises?

LO6 11. Is the year-end balance in the Reserve for Encumbrances account a liability? Explain.

LO6 12. What columns would you suggest for a subsidiary ledger account in order that it might be a subsidiary not only to the "appropriations" control account but also the "encumbrances" and the "expenditures" control accounts?

LO7 13. Why is depreciation on fixed assets not recorded in the records of expendable fund entities?

LO8 14. How does the adoption of a budget for a general fund entity differ from the adoption of a budget by a commercial unit?

LO8 15. Describe the principal financial statements used to report on the activities and status of expendable fund entities.

LO5 16. Why may it be difficult or impossible for a governmental unit to determine the total cost of performing a particular activity or function?

Business Ethics

At State College, where football has long reigned as king and fans are near fanatical in their attendance, the frenzy for football tickets has recently reached an all-time high. With requests for home game tickets at an unprecedented level, prices on everything from parking passes to hotel rooms to home rentals have soared beyond belief. Parking passes were going for $500 on eBay, and hotel rates have doubled—and in some cases nearly tripled—reaching as high as $650 per night at some hotels.

1. What are the moral or ethical issues in charging what people will pay for rooms and tickets to attend a State College football game?
2. Why not let the economic forces of supply and demand determine prices in our capitalistic system?

ANALYZING FINANCIAL STATEMENTS (AFS)

AFS 17-1 Balance Sheet

In the appendix to this chapter, the balance sheet for the General Fund for the City of Atlanta is reported.

1. How is the format used on the balance sheet for the general fund different from the format used by for-profit organizations? Which categories of the balance sheet seem to be missing for government funds?
2. What is the largest asset reported in the General Fund? Is this surprising?
3. For the General Fund, the reserve for encumbrances is $6,353 (thousand). What does this balance represent?

AFS 17-2 Statement of Revenues, Expenditures, and Changes in Fund Balances

In the appendix to this chapter, the Statement of Revenues, Expenditures, and Changes in Fund Balances for the General Fund for the City of Atlanta is reported.

1. How is the format used on the Statement of Revenues, Expenditures, and Changes in Fund Balances for the general fund different from the format on Income Statements used by for-profit organizations? Which items appear on the government fund's statements that do not appear on Income Statements used by for-profit companies?
2. What is the largest expenditure of the General Fund on the Statement of Revenues, Expenditures, and Changes in Fund Balances?
3. What is the largest source of revenue for the General Fund on the Statement of Revenues, Expenditures, and Changes in Fund Balances?
4. Evaluate the performance of the General Fund using the Statement of Revenues, Expenditures, and Changes in Fund Balances.

EXERCISES

EXERCISE 17-1 **General Fund Journal Entries** LO8

Several independent financial activities of a governmental unit are given below.

1. Revenue from the sale of licenses and permits for the first two months totaled $15,000.
2. Land that had been donated previously was sold for $100,000.
3. An order was placed for the purchase of a new fire engine at a price of $130,000.
4. Bonds with a face value of $500,000 were issued at par value to finance a new park.
5. A $250,000 grant was received from the federal government to help improve the local schools.
6. The new fire engine was received and accepted. The approved price, however, was $140,000 rather than $130,000.

Required:

Prepare the journal entries needed to account for each transaction in the General Fund.

EXERCISE 17-2 **General Fund Journal Entries** LO8

Listed are typical financial activities of a local governmental unit.

1. The legislative unit approved the budget for the general operating fund. Estimated revenues are $4,000,000, and appropriations for expenditures are $3,800,000.
2. Statements of property tax assessments totaling $3,000,000 were mailed to property owners. It is estimated that 4% of the assessed taxes will be uncollectible.
3. Notification was received from the state that this unit's share of sales tax revenues from the fourth quarter of the previous year will be $500,000.
4. The manager signed a contract to purchase equipment costing $250,000.
5. The equipment ordered above was received and paid for.
6. Employees were paid their biweekly wages of $36,000.
7. Property taxes in the amount of $2,050,000 were collected.

Required:

Prepare the necessary journal entries to record the transactions listed above in the records of the General Fund.

EXERCISE 17-3 **General Fund Journal Entries** LO8

Listed are transactions of the Town of Jackson.

1. A budget consisting of estimated revenues of $1,950,000 and appropriations for expenditures of $1,800,000 was passed by the town council.
2. Property taxes of $1,150,000 were assessed; $1,115,000 are expected to be collectible.
3. Property taxes in the amount of $1,080,000 were collected.
4. Equipment costing $200,000 was purchased, and the old equipment was sold at the end of its estimated useful life for $24,000.
5. A contract was signed with an independent company to do the trash collecting for the year. The contract price was $96,000.
6. The first monthly bill of $8,000 was received from the trash collector.
7. The $8,000 bill was paid.

Required:

Prepare the journal entries needed in the records of the General Fund to account for these transactions.

EXERCISE 17-4 **General Fund Closing Entries** LO8

Following is the preclosing trial balance for the General Fund of the City of Doyle.

Doyle City
The General Fund
General Ledger Trial Balance
December 31, 2009

Cash	$ 400,000	
Certificates of Deposit	350,000	
Due from State Government	112,000	
Due from Other Funds	30,000	
Taxes Receivable	774,000	
Estimated Revenue	3,110,000	
Expenditures	1,960,000	
Encumbrances	734,000	
Transfers to Other Funds	90,000	
Expenditures—2008	55,000	
Estimated Uncollectible Taxes		$ 30,000
Vouchers Payable		64,000
Due to Other Funds		27,000
Unreserved Fund Balance		760,000
Reserve for Encumbrances		734,000
Reserve for Encumbrances—2008		50,000
Appropriations		2,700,000
Revenue		3,210,000
Transfers from Other Funds		40,000
	$7,615,000	$7,615,000

Required:

Prepare in general journal form the closing entries for the General Fund of Doyle City.

EXERCISE 17-5 **General Fund Closing Entries** LO8

The preclosing trial balance for the General Fund of the City of Springfield is presented below.

City of Springfield
The General Fund
General Ledger Trial Balance
December 31, 2008

Cash	$ 90,000	
Certificates of Deposit	120,000	
Property Taxes Receivable	175,000	
Estimated Revenue	1,690,000	
Expenditures	1,310,000	
Expenditures—2007	32,000	
Encumbrances	165,000	
Estimated Uncollectible Taxes		$ 51,000
Vouchers Payable		65,000
Unreserved Fund Balance		41,000
Reserve for Encumbrances		165,000
Reserve for Encumbrances—2007		35,000
Appropriations		1,550,000
Revenue		1,675,000
	$3,582,000	$3,582,000

Required:

Prepare the closing entries for the General Fund.

EXERCISE 17-6 **Accounting for Supplies** LO9

In 2008, Bay City purchased supplies valued at $350,000. At the end of the year, $65,000 of the supplies were still in the inventory. No supplies were on hand at the beginning of the year. The city uses the purchases method to account for supplies.

Required:

A. Prepare the journal entry necessary to report the supplies as an asset in the balance sheet of Bay City.

B. What amount of expenditures for supplies will be shown in the statement of revenues, expenditures, and changes in fund balance?

EXERCISE 17-7 **Purchases versus Consumption Methods** LO9

At the beginning of 2008, the City of Fairview reported an Unreserved Fund Balance of $555,000 and a supplies inventory balance of $175,000. During the year, Fairview purchased $225,000 in supplies and used $220,000 worth. The city will report a reserve for supplies inventory.

Required:

A. Prepare the necessary journal entries under the purchases method.

B. Prepare the journal entries needed to account for the supplies under the consumption method.

C. What would the 12/31/08 balance in the Unreserved Fund Balance be under each method, assuming that the only transactions of the fund are those involving the supplies?

EXERCISE 17-8 **Journal Entries** LO8

During 2008, the City of Greenfield engaged in the following financial activities:

1. The City Council approved the budget for the general operating fund. The budget shows estimated revenues of $1,900,000 and appropriations for expenditures of $1,850,000.
2. Property tax assessments for 2008 were compiled and statements mailed to property owners. Assessments total $955,000. Past collection experience indicates that approximately 5% of assessed property taxes are delinquent or uncollectible during the year of billing.
3. A low bid of $15,000 was accepted for a new vehicle for the fire chief. A purchase order was issued providing for additional costs for painting and ancillary equipment (negotiated after the bid) prior to delivery. The estimate of additional costs is $1,400.
4. Additional purchase orders placed during the year amount to $140,000.
5. City employees are issued paychecks for the month of April. The total payroll amounts to $90,000.
6. The City received a statement from the State Treasurer that the City's portion of the state sales tax for the first half-year is $375,000.
7. Vouchers for expenditures totaling $135,000 are approved for payment. Encumbrances against these vouchers were recorded at a total of $137,000.
8. The vehicle for the fire chief was delivered and accepted. The invoice in the amount of $16,200 was approved for payment.
9. Property tax collections for the month of June amounted to $450,000.
10. The City Treasurer issued checks in payment of the vouchers totaling $135,000 and for the invoice for the fire chief's vehicle.
11. A purchase order previously issued for an electric typewriter (estimated price $650) was canceled when the vendor indicated a three-month delay in delivery.

Required:

Prepare journal entries to record and account for the foregoing transactions.

EXERCISE 17-9 General Fund Journal Entries LO8

The following events relate typical activities in a municipality that affect the General Fund.

1. The Meadville City Council passed an ordinance approving a general operating budget of $580,000 for fiscal year 2008. The city's only source of revenue is from property taxes. For 2001, these revenues are estimated at $565,000.
2. A property tax levy of $1 per $100 assessed valuation (total assessed valuation equals $60,000,000) is billed to property owners. Taxes are due in the current fiscal year. Experience indicates that 3% of taxes billed will be uncollectible.
3. A motorcycle for the Department of Public Safety is ordered by the purchasing department on the basis of a low bid of $4,200.
4. The motorcycle in (3) above is received and the invoice is approved for payment. Extra accessories not included in the bid price amount to $425.
5. Salaries and wages in the amount of $20,000 are paid by check to city employees for the two-week period ending on May 15.
6. The property division sold used typewriters and other office equipment at a public auction. Total receipts were $8,225.
7. Property taxes in the amount of $540,000 were collected.

Required:

Prepare the necessary journal entries to record each event in the accounts of the General Fund.

EXERCISE 17-10 Multiple Choice LO2 LO6 LO8 LO9

Select the best answer for each of the following items:

1. When used in fund accounting, the term "fund" usually refers to
   (a) A sum of money designated for a special purpose.
   (b) A liability to other governmental units.
   (c) The equity of a municipality in its own assets.
   (d) A fiscal and accounting entity having a set of self-balancing accounts.
2. Authority granted by a legislative body to make expenditures and to incur obligations during a fiscal year is the definition of an
   (a) Appropriation.
   (b) Authorization.
   (c) Encumbrance.
   (d) Expenditure.
3. What type of account is used to earmark the fund balance to liquidate the contingent obligations of goods ordered but not yet received?
   (a) Appropriations.
   (b) Encumbrances.
   (c) Obligations.
   (d) Reserve for encumbrances.
4. A city's General Fund budget for the forthcoming fiscal year shows estimated revenues in excess of appropriations. The initial effect of recording this will result in an increase in
   (a) Taxes receivable.
   (b) Fund balance.
   (c) Reserve for encumbrances.
   (d) Encumbrances.
5. The Reserve for Encumbrances account is properly considered to be a
   (a) Current liability if payable within a year; otherwise, a long-term debt.
   (b) Fixed liability.
   (c) Floating debt.
   (d) Reservation of the fund's equity.

6. In preparing the General Fund budget of Dover City for the forthcoming fiscal year, the City Council appropriated a sum greater than expected revenues. This action of the Council will result in
   (a) A cash overdraft during that fiscal year.
   (b) An increase in encumbrances by the end of that fiscal year.
   (c) A decrease in the fund balance.
   (d) A necessity for compensatory offsetting action in the Debt Service Fund.
7. What would be the effect on the General Fund balance in the current fiscal year of recording a $150,000 purchase for a new fire truck out of General Fund resources, for which a $146,000 encumbrance had been recorded in the General Fund in the previous fiscal year?
   (a) Reduce the General Fund balance by $150,000.
   (b) Reduce the General Fund balance by $146,000.
   (c) Reduce the General Fund balance by $4,000.
   (d) Have no effect on the General Fund balance. *(AICPA adapted)*

PROBLEMS

PROBLEM 17-1 Journal Entries, Closing Entries, and Trial Balance LO8

The general ledger trial balance of the General Fund of the City of Bedford on January 1, 2008, shows the following:

	Dr.	*Cr.*
Cash	$100,000	
Taxes Receivable	75,000	
Allowance for Uncollectible Taxes		$ 35,000
Unreserved Fund Balance		110,000
Reserve for Encumbrances—2007		30,000
Total	$175,000	$175,000

A summary of activities and transactions for the General Fund during 2008 is presented here:

1. The City Council adopted a budget for the General Fund with estimated revenues of $1,560,000 and authorization for appropriated expenditures of $1,400,000. The budget authorized the transfer of $50,000 from the Water Fund to the General Fund for operating expenses as a payment in lieu of taxes. Cash for the payment of interest due for the year on the $1,000,000, 8% bond issue for the Civic Center is approved for transfer from the General Fund to the Debt Service Fund.
2. The annual property tax levy of 10% on assessed valuation ($11,000,000) is billed to property owners. Two percent is estimated to be uncollectible.
3. Goods and services amounting to $1,150,000 were ordered during the year.
4. Invoices for all goods ordered in 2007 amounting to $29,000 were approved for payment.
5. Funds for bond interest on Civic Center bonds were transferred to the Debt Service Fund.
6. Invoices for goods and services received during the year totaling $1,155,000 were recorded. These were encumbered previously [see (3) above].
7. Transfer of funds from the Water Company was received in lieu of taxes.
8. Taxes were collected from property owners in the amount of $1,050,000.
9. Past-due tax bills of $17,000 were charged off as uncollectible.
10. Checks in payment of invoices for goods and services ordered in 2007 and 2008 were issued [see items (4) and (6) above].
11. Revenues received from miscellaneous sources, other than property taxes, of $455,000 were recorded.
12. Purchase order for two trash collection vehicle systems complete with residence trash containers for automatic pickup of trash was issued. Bid price per system was $120,000.

Required:

A. Prepare journal entries to record the summary transactions. You may find it necessary or convenient to post journal entries to ledger t-accounts before the preparation of the required trial balances.
B. Prepare a preclosing trial balance.
C. Prepare closing entries.
D. Prepare a postclosing trial balance.

PROBLEM 17-2 Unreserved Fund Balance—Adjusting and Closing Entries LO6

The following account balances, among others, were included in the preclosing trial balance of the General Fund of the City of Lynchburg on December 31, 2009.

Estimated Revenue	$630,000
Expenditures	468,000
Encumbrances	120,000
Expenditures—2008	43,000
Reserve for Encumbrances (Note 1)	162,000
Appropriations	672,000
Revenue	696,000
Reserve for Supplies Inventory (Note 2)	72,000
Supplies Inventory (Note 2)	72,000
Unreserved Fund Balance	24,000

Note 1: The balance in this account was $42,000 on January 1, 2009. Purchase orders outstanding on December 31, 2009, total $120,000.
Note 2: Supplies on hand on December 31, 2009, amount to $60,000.

Required:

A. What was the balance in the Unreserved Fund Balance account on December 31, 2008? What was the total Fund Balance on December 31, 2008?
B. Prepare the necessary adjusting and closing entries for the year ended December 31, 2009. Supplies inventory is accounted for using the purchases method.
C. Prepare a schedule to calculate the Unreserved Fund Balance and the total Fund Balance on December 31, 2009.

PROBLEM 17-3 Computing Unreserved Fund Balance and Closing Entries LO6

The following account balances, among others, were included in the preclosing trial balance of the General Fund of the City of Madison on December 31, 2009.

Appropriations	$3,488,000
Cash	270,000
Due to Other Funds	100,000
Due from Other Funds	250,000
Encumbrances	382,000
Estimated Revenue	3,720,000
Expenditures	3,020,000
Expenditures—2008	296,000
Reserve for Encumbrances	382,000
Reserve for Encumbrances—2008	310,000
Revenue	3,656,000
Taxes Receivable	600,000
Transfers from Other Funds	300,000
Transfers to Other Funds	520,000
Unreserved Fund Balance	422,000
Vouchers Payable	400,000

Required:

A. Prepare the necessary closing entries on December 31, 2009.

B. Calculate the amount of both the unreserved fund balance and the total fund balance in the balance sheet (1) on December 31, 2008 and (2) on December 31, 2009.

C. Prepare a schedule reconciling the December 31, 2008, total fund balance with the December 31, 2009, total fund balance by reference to actual inflows and outflows of financial resources.

PROBLEM 17-4 **Entries, Balance Sheet, Statement of Revenues, Expenditures, and Changes in Fund Balance** LO8

The trial balance for the General Fund of the City of Monte Vista as of December 31, 2008, is presented here:

	Debit	*Credit*
Cash	$300,000	
Supplies Inventory	75,000	
Unreserved Fund Balance		$300,000
Reserve for Supplies Inventory		75,000
	$375,000	$375,000

Transactions of the General Fund for the year ended December 31, 2009, are summarized as follows:

1. The City Council adopted the following budget for 2009:

Estimated revenue	$1,600,000
Transfer from trust fund	50,000
Appropriations	1,530,000
Transfer to debt service fund	80,000

2. Property taxes of $1,500,000 were levied, of which it is estimated that $30,000 will not be collected.

3. Purchase orders in the amount of $1,400,000 were placed with suppliers and other vendors.

4. Property taxes in the amount of $1,450,000 were collected.

5. Cash was received from the Trust Fund in the amount of $50,000.

6. Invoices in the amount of $1,380,000 were approved for payment. The amount originally encumbered for these invoices was $1,360,000. The invoices included $25,000 net of trade-in allowance for the purchase of a new minicomputer and $400,000 for supplies. The City received a trade-in-allowance of $4,000 on its old minicomputer, which had been purchased three years earlier for $16,000. At the time the old minicomputer was purchased, it was estimated that it would have a useful life of four years. The new minicomputer is expected to last at least six years. The City of Monte Vista uses the purchase method to account for supplies inventory.

7. Licenses and fees in the amount of $48,000 were collected.

8. Vouchers in the amount of $1,300,000 were paid.

9. Cash in the amount of $80,000 was transferred to the Debt Service Fund.

10. Supplies on hand at the end of the year amount to $100,000.

Required:

A. Prepare entries in general journal form to record the transactions of the General Fund for the year ended December 31, 2009.

B. Prepare a preclosing trial balance for the General Fund as of December 31, 2009.

C. Prepare the necessary closing entries for the General Fund for the year ended December 31, 2009.

D. Prepare a balance sheet and a statement of revenues, expenditures, and changes in fund balance for the General Fund for the year ended December 31, 2009.

PROBLEM 17-5 **Balance Sheet, Statement of Revenues, Expenditures, and Changes in Fund Balance** LO8

The trial balance for the General Fund of the City of Fairfield as of December 31, 2008, is presented here:

City of Fairfield
The General Fund
Adjusted Trial Balance
December 31, 2008

	Debit	*Credit*
Cash	$430,000	
Property Tax Receivable	45,000	
Estimated Uncollectible Taxes		$ 20,000
Due from Trust Fund	50,000	
Vouchers Payable		60,000
Reserve for Encumbrances		30,000
Unreserved Fund Balance		415,000
	$525,000	$525,000

Transactions for the year ended December 31, 2009, are summarized as follows:

1. The City Council adopted a budget for the year with estimated revenue of $735,000 and appropriations of $700,000.
2. Property taxes in the amount of $590,000 were levied for the current year. It is estimated that $24,000 of the taxes levied will prove to be uncollectible.
3. Proceeds from the sale of equipment in the amount of $35,000 were received by the General Fund. The equipment was purchased 10 years ago with resources of the General Fund at a cost of $150,000. On the date of purchase, it was estimated that the equipment had a useful life of 15 years.
4. Licenses and fees in the amount of $110,000 were collected.
5. The total amount of encumbrances against fund resources for the year was $642,500.
6. Vouchers in the amount of $455,000 were authorized for payment. This was $15,000 less than the amount originally encumbered for these purchases.
7. An invoice in the amount of $28,000 was received for goods ordered in 2008. The invoice was approved for payment.
8. Property taxes in the amount of $570,000 were collected.
9. Vouchers in the amount of $475,000 were paid.
10. Fifty thousand dollars was transferred to the General Fund from the Trust Fund.
11. The City Council authorized the write-off of $30,000 in uncollected property taxes.

Required:

A. Prepare entries in general journal form to record the transactions for the year ended December 31, 2009.

B. Prepare a preclosing trial balance for the General Fund as of December 31, 2009.

C. Prepare the necessary closing entries for the year ended December 31, 2009.

D. Prepare a balance sheet and a statement of revenues, expenditures, and changes in fund balance for the General Fund for the year ended December 31, 2009.

PROBLEM 17-6 **Balance Sheet, Statement of Revenues, Expenditures, and Changes in Fund Balance** LO8

Hunnington Township's adjusted trial balance for the General Fund at the close of its fiscal year ended June 30, 2009, is presented here:

Hunnington Township
General Fund Trial Balance
June 30, 2009

Cash	$ 11,000	
Property Tax Receivable—current (Note 1)	82,000	
Estimated Uncollectible Taxes—current		$ 1,500
Property Tax Receivable—delinquent	25,000	
Estimated Uncollectible Taxes—delinquent		16,500
Accounts Receivable (Note 1)	40,000	
Allowance for Uncollectible Accounts		4,000
Due from Internal Service Fund (Note 5)	50,000	
Expenditures (Note 2)	755,000	
Encumbrances	37,000	
Revenue (Note 3)		60,000
Due to Enterprise Fund (Note 5)		10,000
Vouchers Payable		20,000
Reserve for Encumbrances—prior year		44,000
Reserve for Encumbrances		37,000
Surplus Receipts (Note 4)		7,000
Appropriations		720,000
Unreserved Fund Balance		80,000
	$1,000,000	$1,000,000

Note 1: The current tax roll and accounts receivable, recorded on the accrual basis as sources of revenue, amounted to $500,000 and $200,000, respectively.
Note 2: Includes $42,500 paid during the fiscal year in settlement of all purchase orders outstanding at the beginning of the fiscal year.
Note 3: Represents the difference between the budgeted (estimated) revenue of $700,000 and the actual revenue realized during the fiscal year.
Note 4: Represents the proceeds from the sale of equipment damaged by fire. The equipment originally cost $40,000 and had been held for 80% of its useful life prior to the fire.
Note 5: The interfund payable and receivable resulted from cash advances (loans) to and from the respective funds.

Required:

A. Prepare a statement of revenues, expenditures, and changes in fund balance.
B. Prepare a balance sheet for the General Fund at June 30, 2009. (*AICPA adapted*)

PROBLEM 17-7 **Complete Accounting Cycle—General Fund** LO8
The January 1, 2008, trial balance, the calendar-year 2008 budget, and the 2008 transactions of the City of Roseburg are presented here:

City of Roseburg
Trial Balance
January 1, 2008

	Debit	*Credit*
Cash	$155,450	
Certificates of Deposit	200,000	
Accounts Receivable	28,675	
Supplied Inventory	37,600	
Due from Federal Government	58,000	
Property Taxes Receivable	75,600	
Allowance for Uncollectible Taxes		$ 32,150
Vouchers Payable		181,000
Unreserved Fund Balance		226,075
Reserve for Inventory		37,600
Reserve for Encumbrances		78,500
	$555,325	$555,325

City of Roseburg
Budget for General Fund
Calendar Year 2008

Estimated Revenue	
City vehicle and retail license fees	$ 252,000
Property taxes	1,448,000
City sales tax	327,000
Collections for trash service	153,000
Sale of city-owned property	88,000
Total estimated revenue	2,268,000
Appropriations	
General government	261,000
Public safety and security	875,000
Health and welfare	434,000
Recreation and parks	126,000
Street maintenance	367,000
Sanitation	162,000
Total appropriations	2,225,000
Excess of Revenues over Appropriations	43,000
Transfer from Water and Sewer Fund	118,000
Less Payments (transfers) to Debt Service Funds	(55,000)
Excess of Revenue and Fund Transfers to General Fund over Appropriations and Fund Transfers out of General Fund	$ 106,000

Transactions of the City of Roseburg that affected the General Fund during the year are summarized below:

1. The City Council approved the budget and it was recorded.
2. Orders for goods and services were issued for a total of $1,202,000 during the year.
3. Goods and services were delivered against all orders placed with a total invoice amount of $1,165,600. Of this, $80,000 was for orders placed in the prior year.
4. The City accepted a low bid of $78,000 for a new street sweeper for the sanitation department. A purchase order was issued.
5. The City received $92,500 from the sale of an old street sweeper and one obsolete fire engine at public auction. The street sweeper cost $60,000 7 years ago, at which time it was estimated to have a useful life of 10 years. The fire engine cost $200,000 8 years ago, at which time it was estimated to have a useful life of 12 years.
6. Property tax statements were issued. The tax levy was 8% of the assessed valuation of $18,500,000. An estimated 2% of the tax levy will be uncollectible.
7. Payment was received from the federal government. This was a grant to be used for upgrading sanitation department equipment.
8. The amount of $55,000 was transferred to the Debt Service Fund for the payment of interest on the outstanding bond issue.
9. The city billed residents for trash service. Total billings amounted to $155,675.
10. Property taxes totaling $1,438,455 were collected, of which $34,200 was past-due collections from the prior year; $18,250 of past-due taxes was charged off as uncollectible.
11. Wages paid to employees during the year amounted to $998,765.
12. City retail establishments remitted a total of $333,650 in sales tax collections for the year.

13. Other cash receipts during the year were:

Vehicle license fees and parking fines	$ 98,682
Retail license fees	130,000
For trash services (including $28,675 due at end of prior year)	148,720
Transfer from Water and Sewer Fund	118,000

14. Cash purchases of printed forms and other office supplies for the year amounted to $57,680.

15. The street sweeper was delivered and an invoice for $78,000 plus freight charges of $1,280 was received. The invoice was approved for payment and a check issued.

16. Checks were issued in payment of outstanding vouchers totaling $1,207,100.

17. End-of-year activities: (adjustments)

Supplies Inventory 12/31/08: $38,250
Accrued interest on CDs at 5%

The city uses the purchases method to account for supplies expenditures.

Required:

A. Enter the opening trial balance data in t-accounts.

B. Prepare journal entries for the year's transactions. Do not include entries for year-end adjustments. Post entries to t-accounts.

C. Prepare a preclosing trial balance.

D. Prepare journal entries to adjust the Supplies Inventory and record the interest on the CDs.

E. Prepare journal entries to close the revenue, expenditures, and encumbrance accounts.

F. Prepare a comparative balance sheet for 2007–2008.

G. Prepare a statement of revenues, expenditures, and changes in fund balance for 2008.

PROBLEM 17-8 Reconstructing Journal Entries LO8

The following summary of transactions was taken from the accounts of the Madras School District General Fund before the books were closed for the fiscal year ended June 30, 2009:

	Postclosing Balances June 30, 2008	*Preclosing Balances June 30, 2009*
Cash	$400,000	$ 700,000
Property tax receivable	150,000	170,000
Estimated uncollectible taxes	(40,000)	(70,000)
Estimated revenue		3,000,000
Expenditures		2,842,000
Expenditures—prior year		
Encumbrances		91,000
	$510,000	$6,733,000
Vouchers payable	$ 80,000	$ 408,000
Due to other funds	210,000	142,000
Reserve for encumbrances	60,000	91,000
Unreserved fund balance	160,000	182,000
Revenue from taxes		2,800,000
Miscellaneous revenue		130,000
Appropriations		2,980,000
	$510,000	$6,733,000

Additional Information:

1. Property taxes in the amount of $2,870,000 were assessed for the year. Taxes collected during the year totaled $2,810,000.
2. An analysis of the transactions in the vouchers payable account for the year ended June 30, 2009, follows:

	Debit (Credit)
Current expenditures	$(2,700,000)
Expenditures for prior year	(58,000)
Vouchers for payment to other funds	(210,000)
Cash payments during year	2,640,000
Net change	$ (328,000)

3. During the year the General Fund was billed $142,000 for services performed on its behalf by other city funds.
4. On May 2, 2009, commitment documents were issued for the purchase of new textbooks at a cost of $91,000.

Required:

On the basis of the data presented, reconstruct the original detailed journal entries that were required to record all transactions for the fiscal year ended June 30, 2009, including the recording of the current year's budget. Do not prepare closing entries at June 30, 2009.

(*AICPA adapted*)

18

INTRODUCTION TO ACCOUNTING FOR STATE AND LOCAL GOVERNMENTAL UNITS

LEARNING OBJECTIVES

1. Identify the issues involved in developing standards for nonprofit organizations.
2. Describe the broad categories of government fund entities.
3. Distinguish between a general fund and a special revenue fund.
4. Explain the use of a capital projects fund.
5. Describe the purpose of a debt service fund.
6. Explain the use of a permanent fund.
7. Distinguish proprietary funds from government funds.
8. Describe where capital assets and long-term obligations are reported in government financial statements.
9. Describe the changes in reporting requirements under *GASB Statement No. 34.*
10. Explain the benefits of government-wide statements.
11. Describe the types of interfund activities.

"I don't make jokes—I just watch the government and report the facts."
—*Will Rogers*[1]

The lifestyles and well-being of all people are significantly affected by the activities of both profit-oriented enterprises and nonbusiness organizations. Of these, probably none is more important and pervasive in its impact on our daily lives than government. Today there are more than 70 thousand state and local governmental units, which employ more than 20 million people and collect annual revenues in excess of 500 billion dollars. The well-publicized problems of some city governments have attracted great interest and concern in the past. These problems focused attention

[1] Quoted in *Saturday Review.* From *The Merriam-Webster Dictionary of Quotations,* Merriam-Webster, Inc., 1996; *Infopedia,* SoftKey Multimedia Inc., 1996.

on the need for (among other things) adequate accounting and financial reporting practices by cities and other governmental units as a basis for evaluating the extent of such problems and potential solutions.

Governments traditionally have focused their reporting on groupings of 'funds' rather than on the government 'taken as a whole.' The newer financial reporting model retains this traditional focus on funds, but at the same time insists that fund financial statements be accompanied for the first time by financial statements that focus on the overall government (i.e., 'government-wide' financial statements)."[2]

As a consequence, the Governmental Accounting Standards Board (GASB) has reexamined the methods of accounting for state and local governments with significant changes being implemented. The GASB's *Statement No. 34*, "Basic Financial Statements—and Management's Discussion and Analysis—for State and Local Governments,"[3] issued in June 1999, affects all governmental units and is considered to be one of the most important statements issued by a governing accounting body. The rules require governments to provide basic financial statements using a government-wide (entity-wide) approach. This does not eliminate traditional fund accounting because governments are required to report statements emphasizing their major funds.[4] In addition, for the first time, financial managers are required to provide a management's discussion and analysis (MD&A) that gives readers an objective and easily readable analysis of the government's financial performance for the year. Thus, MD&A provides an analysis of the government's overall financial position and the results of the previous year's operations to assist users in assessing whether the government's finances have improved or deteriorated. Each analysis includes a comparison of the current year to the prior year based on the government-wide statements. In addition, the analysis explains significant variations in fund-based financial results and budgetary information, and describes capital assets and long-term debt activity during the year. The MD&A concludes with a description of currently known facts, decisions, or conditions that are expected to have a material impact on the government's future financial position and operations.

The Government Finance Officers Association's (GFOA) position regarding the Government Accounting Standards Board (GASB) *Statement No. 34* was to encourage its members not to implement the infrastructure provisions of *GASB Statement No. 34*, to threaten to withhold GFOA's funding to GASB if GASB proceeded with the implementation of *Statement No. 34*, and to allow governments not complying with the provisions to continue to participate in the GFOA's Certificate of Achievement for Excellence in Financial Reporting Program.[5]

---

[2] "The GASB's New Financial Reporting Model: An Overview for Finance Officers," July 1999, Government Finance Officers Association.

[3] Governmental Accounting Standards Board, *Statement No. 34*, "Basic Financial Statements—and Management's Discussion and Analysis—for State and Local Governments." (Financial Accounting Foundation and Government Accounting Standards Board: Norwalk, CT, 1999).

[4] Major funds as defined by the GASB are discussed later in this chapter.

[5] *The Government Accountants Journal*, Spring 2000, "GFOA Missed the Mark" by Edward Gomeau, p. 21.

Generally, fund accounting rules in the past have followed a ***flow of current financial resources*** concept. Basically, this implies that each year is treated as a distinct event and the principal measurement of importance is the source and use of funds (where funds are usually defined on a modified accrual basis). The simplicity of this concept, unfortunately, leaves room for inadequacies. For example, a city that borrows to balance a current period budget deficit, as in the Washington, D.C., example above, must consider the future financial consequences of this decision. This example raises such questions as: Does fund accounting information alone provide users of governmental statements with sufficient information to evaluate the government? Therefore, *GASB Statement No. 34* requires "full accrual" accounting for all government-wide statements (i.e., ***flow of economic resources approach***). Under this approach, governments would not be able to defer payment of expenses into the future and avoid recognition in the current year (e.g., avoiding payment of pension obligations). Under accrual accounting, the accountability of politicians for economic decisions made during the current period may be more readily assessed. The fund-based reports will still maintain the flow of current financial resources concept showing the short-term performance of the individual funds (as opposed to the long-term focus of the *full accrual-based government-wide statements*).

Until the mid-1990s, agencies' financial management systems were designed to keep track of how money was spent, much as consumers do with their checkbooks. But now, under a collection of new financial management laws, the requirements are much broader. Not only must agencies keep track of spending, but they must also account for the value and depreciation of assets, account for and justify inventory levels, plan for capital purchases, assess environmental liabilities, and estimate future costs such as postretirement health care benefits. In short, it is no longer enough to simply track spending. Agencies must manage their finances.[6]

In Figure 18-1, the reporting requirements are listed for the financial reporting model, along with the illustration number used in this chapter.

THE HISTORY OF GENERALLY ACCEPTED GOVERNMENTAL ACCOUNTING STANDARDS

Like generally accepted accounting standards for profit-oriented enterprises, standards of accounting and reporting for governmental units are in a constant state of evolution and change. The pioneer organization in promulgating standards of accounting and reporting for state and local governmental units was the Municipal Finance Officers Association (MFOA). Such standards were formulated by its National Committee on Governmental Accounting, which in 1974 was reconstituted as the National Council on Governmental Accounting (NCGA). In 1979 the NCGA issued *Statement 1: Government and Financial Reporting Principles.* Until 1984 this and subsequent statements and interpretations of the NCGA, along with the AICPA Industry Audit Guide: *Audits of State and Local Governmental Units* (1974) as amended by subsequently issued AICPA Statements of Position, constituted the primary sources of generally accepted governmental accounting standards.

[6] *Government Executive,* Vol. 31:2, "Money Matters," by Katherine McIntire Peters, February 1999, pp. 31–34.

FIGURE 18-1

Financial Reporting Model: Minimum Information Required for Fair Presentation in Conformity with Generally Accepted Accounting Principles (GAAP)

Government-wide Financial Statements	*Fund Financial Statements*
Statement of net assets (Illustration 18-16) Statement of activities (Illustration 18-17)	*Governmental funds*: Balance sheet (Illustration 18-13) Statement of revenues, expenditures, and changes in fund balances (Illustration 18-14) Reconciliation to government-wide statements (Illustration 18-15 and 18-16) *Proprietary funds*: Balance sheet or statement of net assets (Illustration 18-9) Statement of revenues, expenses, and changes in net assets (Illustration 18-10) Statement of cash flows—direct format *Fiduciary funds*: Statement of fiduciary net assets Statement of changes in fiduciary net assets

Notes to the Financial Statements
1. Schedule of changes in capital assets (Illustration 18-11)
2. Schedule of changes in long-term liabilities (Illustration 18-12)

Required Supplemental Information (RSI)
1. Management's Discussion and Analysis
2. Budgetary Comparison schedules (see Chapter 17)

In 1984 the GASB was established as a separate board under the oversight of the Financial Accounting Foundation (FAF), the same foundation that oversees the activities of the Financial Accounting Standards Board (FASB). The GASB is composed of two full-time and three part-time members supported by an administrative, technical, and research staff. Funding for the GASB is separate from that of the FASB.

The GASB is the body responsible for establishing financial accounting and reporting standards for governments. With its first pronouncement, *Authoritative Status of NCGA Pronouncements and AICPA Industry Audit Guide*, the GASB endorsed prior statements and interpretations of the NCGA, as well as the accounting and financial reporting standards embodied in the 1974 *AICPA Industry Audit Guide* as amended. Pronouncements of the GASB include GASB Statements (GASBS), GASB Interpretations (GASBI), GASB Concept Statements (GASBCS), and GASB Technical Bulletins (GASBTB). Pronouncements of the GASB are codified in the GASB's *Codification of Governmental Accounting and Financial Reporting Standards* (cited as *GASB Cod.*). This codification is updated annually.

Hierarchy of Generally Accepted Reporting Standards for Governmental Entities

The hierarchy used to establish generally accepted reporting standards for all state and local governmental-owned entities, including government-owned colleges and universities, health care providers, and utilities, is included in *GASB Statement No. 55*, "The Hierarchy of Generally Accepted Accounting Principles for State and Local Governments." The GAAP hierarchy governs what constitutes GAAP for all state and local governmental entities. It lists the order of priority of pronouncements that a governmental entity should look to for accounting and financial reporting guidance. The sources of accounting principles that are generally accepted are categorized as follows:

(a) Officially established accounting principles–Governmental Accounting Standards Board (GASB) Statements and Interpretations.
(b) GASB Technical Bulletins and, if specifically made applicable to state and local governmental entities by the American Institute of Certified Public Accountants (AICPA) and cleared by the GASB, AICPA Industry Audit and Accounting Guides, and AICPA Statements of Position.
(c) AICPA Practice Bulletins if specifically made applicable to state and local governmental entities and cleared by the GASB, as well as consensus positions of a group of accountants organized by the GASB that attempts to reach consensus positions on accounting issues applicable to state and local governmental entities.
(d) Implementation guides (Q&As) published by the GASB staff, as well as practices that are widely recognized and prevalent in state and local government.

If the accounting treatment for a transaction or other event is not specified by a pronouncement in category (a), a governmental entity should consider whether the accounting treatment is specified by an accounting principle from *a source in another category*. In such cases, if categories (b)–(d) contain accounting principles that specify accounting treatments for a transaction or other event, the governmental entity should follow the accounting treatment specified by the accounting principle from the source in the highest category—for example, follow category (b) treatment over category (c) treatment.

If the accounting treatment for a transaction or other event is not specified by a pronouncement or established in practice in *any* of the above categories ((a)–(d)), then the governmental entity should consider accounting principles for *similar transactions or other events* within categories (a)–(d) and may consider other accounting literature. A governmental entity should *not* follow the accounting treatment specified in accounting principles for similar transactions or other events in those cases where accounting principles either *prohibit* the application of the accounting treatment to the particular transaction or event or where they indicate that the accounting treatment should not be applied by analogy.

This hierarchy distinguishes the authority of the GASB and the FASB with regard to state and local governmental entities and implements the FAF trustees' jurisdictional determination of the respective roles of the two boards. The GASB and the FASB each has primary responsibility for setting standards for entities under its jurisdiction, but pronouncements of one Board should not be mandatory for entities under the jurisdiction of the other Board *unless designated as such by the primary Board.*

THE STRUCTURE OF GOVERNMENTAL ACCOUNTING

A governmental unit, although a separate *legal* entity, consists of a number of separate fund and other *accounting* entities. There are eleven broad categories of fund entities and two account group entities. The eleven categories of fund entities fall under three subheadings: (I) governmental funds, (II) proprietary funds, and (III) fiduciary funds, as shown below.

Fund Entities

(I) Governmental Funds (expendable)—reporting focuses on the sources, use, and balances of current financial resources. The accounting and reporting emphasis for these types of funds is on the inflow, outflow, and unexpended balance of net financial resources and on compliance with detailed legal provisions that specify the types of revenue to be raised and the purposes for which financial resources may be expended (the flow of current financial resources measurement basis). The different types of governmental funds are distinguished by the sources of their financial resources or the types of activities financed by the resources of the fund.

RELATED CONCEPTS

GASB Statement 45 **is expected to provide a better foundation for** ***decision making*** **about the level and types of benefits and the financing of those benefits.**

(1) ***General Fund***—to account for all financial resources except those required to be accounted for in another fund.

(2) ***Special Revenue Funds***—to account for the proceeds of specific revenue sources (other than trusts for individuals, private organizations, or other governments or for major capital projects) that are legally restricted to expenditures for specified purposes. This category includes items reported as expendable trust funds under the former rules.

(3) ***Capital Projects Funds***—to account for financial resources to be used for the acquisition or construction of major capital facilities (other than those financed by proprietary funds or in trusts for individuals, private organizations, or other governments). Capital outlays financed by general obligation proceeds should be accounted for through a capital projects fund.

(4) ***Debt Service Funds***—to account for the accumulation of resources for, and the payment of, general long-term debt principal and interest. Debt service funds are required if they are legally mandated and/or if financial resources are being accumulated for principal and interest payments maturing in future years.

(5) ***Permanent Funds***—to account for resources that are legally restricted to the extent that only earnings, and not principal, may be used for purposes that support the government's programs—that is, for the benefit of the government or its citizenry. An example is a cemetery perpetual care fund, which provides resources for the ongoing maintenance of a public cemetery.

(II) **Proprietary Funds (nonexpendable)**—reporting focuses on the determination of operating income, changes in net assets, financial position, and cash flows. Government operations that are similar to commercial business operations such as a water utility, an electric utility, or a central garage or central computer facility are accounted for in the *proprietary fund* category. Financial accounting and reporting for these entities closely parallel accounting and reporting for profit-oriented enterprises. Thus both current and fixed assets and current and noncurrent liabilities are accounted for in the records of proprietary funds. In addition, revenue, expenses (including depreciation and amortization expense), and net income are determined and reported for these fund entities.

(6) ***Enterprise Funds***—to account for any activity for which a fee is charged to external users for goods or services.

(7) ***Internal Service Funds***—to report any activity that provides goods or services to other funds, departments, or agencies of the primary government and its component units, or to other governments, on a cost-reimbursement basis.

(III) **Fiduciary Funds**—reports assets held in a trustee or agency capacity for others and that cannot be used to support the government's own programs. Fiduciary fund reporting focuses on net assets and changes in net assets. These include:

(8) ***Pension (and Other Employee Benefit) Trust Funds***—used to report resources that are required to be held in trust for the members and beneficiaries of

defined benefit pension plans, defined contribution plans, other postemployment benefit plans, or other employee benefit plans.

(9) ***Investment Trust Funds***—used to report the external portion of investment pools reported by the sponsoring government.

(10) ***Private-Purpose Trust Funds***—used to report escheat property and to report all other trust agreements under which principal and income benefit individuals, private organizations, or other governments.

(11) ***Agency Funds***—used to report resources held by the reporting government in a purely custodial capacity (assets equal liabilities). Agency funds typically involve only the receipt, temporary investment, and remittance of fiduciary resources to individuals, private organizations, or other governments.

With the implementation of *GASB Statement No. 45,* many governments are reporting, for the first time, the cost of annual other post-employment benefits (OPEB) and unfunded liabilities for past service costs. Before this statement, governments followed a 'pay as you go' approach, with the costs not reported until after the employees retired.[7]

GOVERNMENTAL FUND ENTITIES

General Fund

All revenues and expenditures of a governmental unit not accounted for in other governmental or proprietary funds are accounted for in the general fund. The variety of revenue sources available to the general fund and the variety of functions and activities financed by the resources of the general fund are ordinarily more numerous than are those for any other fund. Accounting entries and reports for the general fund of a governmental unit were illustrated in Chapter 17.

Special Revenue Funds

RELATED CONCEPTS

Because nonprofit organizations are typically not self-sustaining or profit oriented, and because they rely heavily on its resource providers, stewardship information is very important for *full disclosure*.

Special revenue funds are used to account for the proceeds of specific revenue sources that are required by statute, charter provisions, or local ordinance to be used to finance particular functions or activities of the governmental unit. Examples of special revenue funds are those established to finance the operations of special facilities, such as parks or museums, or of particular activities, such as the licensing and regulation of professions. Although the sources of revenue for special revenue funds in general are similar to those for the general fund, a typical special revenue fund will have only a single revenue source such as a single tax, or specified portion thereof, or a license fee, the proceeds of which are legally restricted to be expended for a specific purpose, function, or activity.

Accounting entries and financial reports for special revenue funds are analogous in all respects to the accounting entries and financial reports for the general fund illustrated in Chapter 17, and no further illustration is presented here beyond

[7] GASB, "GASB Statement 45 on OPEB Accounting by Governments, A Few Basic Questions and Answers."

a brief summary. In special revenue funds, as in the general fund, the following steps are taken:

1. A budget is established and recorded in the accounts.
2. Encumbrances are used to control budgeted expenditures.
3. Fixed assets acquired by the expenditure of special revenue fund resources are not reported as assets of the special revenue fund but rather are recorded on a schedule of capital assets and reported on the government-wide statement of net assets.
4. Depreciation of fixed assets is not recorded or reported by the special revenue fund. (Depreciation expense on these assets is reported on the government-wide statements.)
5. The liability for long-term debt of the specific revenue fund is not recorded or reported as a liability of the special revenue fund but is reported as a liability on the government-wide statement of net assets. The proceeds are recorded in the special revenue fund.

Under *GASB Statement No. 34,* expendable trust funds are reported with special revenue funds. Assume, for example, that Model City has an ordinance that requires all licensed contractors to deposit funds with the city to guarantee performance on their contracts. The deposits must be returned to the contractors when they relinquish their licenses. When a deposit is received, cash is debited and the fund balance is credited. When deposits are refunded, the fund balance is debited and cash is credited. Since the deposits may be held by the city for substantial periods of time, the resources of the trust fund are usually invested, and modest amounts of revenue may be earned.

Capital Projects Funds

Capital projects funds are established to account for the *resources* used by a governmental unit to acquire or construct major capital facilities (i.e., permanent assets with long lives). Major capital facilities include assets such as buildings, streets and highways, and storm drain systems. The primary purpose of accounting for the acquisition of major capital facilities in a separate capital projects fund is to show that the resources designated for such purposes were used for authorized purposes only and that any unexpended balances of such resources or resource deficits have been treated properly. *Resources* for the acquisition of major capital facilities include (1) proceeds of long-term debt issues, (2) grants or payments from other governmental units and agencies, (3) funds from private sources, (4) transfers of current revenues from other governmental funds, (5) special assessments (to be discussed later), and (6) other sources.

Not all major capital facilities acquisitions are accounted for in capital project funds. Construction and acquisition of capital facilities financed by enterprise funds are accounted for in the enterprise fund. In addition, in some instances the resources of the general fund or a special revenue fund are appropriated for the acquisition of a major capital facility. So long as such acquisitions do not involve the issuance of general obligation long-term debt securities, they may be accounted for in the fund that appropriates the resources rather than in a separate capital projects fund.

The operations of a capital projects fund may extend over several accounting periods. Separate capital projects funds are ordinarily created for each major capital project. When the project is completed, the associated capital projects fund is closed out.

Capital Projects Fund Example To illustrate accounting and reporting procedures for a capital projects fund, assume that Model City authorizes the construction of a combination library and civic center that will be financed from the following sources (one from within the local government and one from the state):

General obligation bonds (par value)	$2,000,000
State government grant	1,000,000
Total authorized for construction	$3,000,000

Construction is to begin on September 1, 2008, and the bonds are to be issued on October 1, 2008.

Entries—2008 Entries to record the transactions of the capital projects fund during 2008 are summarized and explained as follows:

(1) Due from State Government	1,000,000	
Grant Revenue		1,000,000
To open Capital Projects Fund.		

There is no budget entry to record estimated revenue and appropriations into the accounting records. Sources of estimated revenues for a capital project are few and predictable in amount. Thus, it serves no useful purpose to record them. Likewise, an appropriation account is not required as a formal control device, since the funds can be expended only for the single authorized project. Thus, the fund balance itself serves as an adequate measure of, and control over, unexpended appropriation authority.

(2) Cash	2,100,000	
Bond Issue Proceeds—Other Financing Sources		2,100,000
To record receipt of proceeds from issuance of long-term debt securities. The bonds were issued at a market rate of 6.787%.		

The Bond Issue Proceeds account is closed to the Fund Balance at the end of the year.

EFFECT OF A TRANSACTION ON DIFFERENT FUNDS

Each fund is a set of self-balancing accounts. The previous entry, to record the issuance of the bond, is a source of funds for the capital projects fund. Yet, the debt is not recorded as a liability of the fund. This transaction illustrates that one transaction can, and often does, affect several other funds at the same time. The liability will be reported on the government-wide statement of net assets.

When bonds are issued at a premium, the difference between the bond issue proceeds and the par value of the bonds represents an interest adjustment and is usually transferred to the debt service fund that is used to service the principal and interest on the debt.

(3) Transfer to Debt Service Fund	100,000	
Cash		100,000
To record transfer of cash in amount of bond premium to Debt Service Fund.		

TRANSFERS BETWEEN FUNDS

It is not unusual for resources to be transferred between funds. Most transfers, like the one in Entry (3), are recurring nonreciprocal transfers (also known as operating transfers) and are reported separately from revenues and expenditures on the statement of revenues, expenditures, and changes in fund balance as "other financing sources and uses." Transfers are discussed later in the chapter.

		Debit	Credit
(4)	Certificates of Deposit	1,000,000	
	Cash		1,000,000
	To record investment of excess cash in temporary investments.		
(5)	Encumbrances	2,500,000	
	Reserve for Encumbrances		2,500,000
	To record encumbrance created by signing construction contract with Lloyd-Jones Construction Company.		
(6)	Cash	750,000	
	Due from State Government		750,000
	To record collection of part of grant from State Government.		
(7)	Expenditures	200,000	
	Vouchers Payable		200,000
	To record unencumbered expenditures for architect and legal fees. Payment is recorded in entry (9).		
(8)	Reserve for Encumbrances	1,300,000	
	Encumbrances		1,300,000
	Expenditures	1,300,000	
	Contracts Payable		1,300,000
	To record approved contract billings on construction completed to date and to remove encumbrance thereon.		
(9)	Vouchers Payable	150,000	
	Contracts Payable	1,300,000	
	Cash		1,450,000
	To record payment of liabilities (includes a portion of (7) and all of (8)).		
(10)	Interest Receivable	12,500	
	Interest Revenue		12,500
	To record interest earned on certificate of deposit to December 31, 2008.		

The treatment of interest income on temporary investments depends on legal provisions or established policy. One alternative is to transfer such earnings to the debt service fund. A second alternative is to treat such earnings as revenue of the capital projects fund. The latter treatment is justified on the grounds that resources allocated to the project are restricted exclusively to that project and, accordingly, any earnings on such resources are also restricted resources and should not be diverted to any other use.

December 31, 2008, Trial Balance The December 31, 2008, trial balance for the capital projects fund presented below reflects the transactions recorded in 2008.

	Debit	*Credit*
Cash	$ 300,000	
Interest Receivable	12,500	
Certificates of Deposit	1,000,000	
Due from State Government	250,000	
Encumbrances	1,200,000	
Expenditures	1,500,000	
Vouchers Payable		$ 50,000
Contracts Payable		—0—
Reserve for Encumbrances		1,200,000
Unreserved Fund Balance		—0—
Grant Revenue		1,000,000
Interest Revenue		12,500
Bond Issue Proceeds—Other Financing Sources		2,100,000
Transfer to Debt Service Fund—Other Financing Use	100,000	
	$4,362,500	$4,362,500

Closing Entries—December 31, 2008

		Debit	Credit
(11)	Bond Issue Proceeds	2,100,000	
	Grant Revenue	1,000,000	
	Interest Revenue	12,500	
	Transfer to Debt Service Fund		100,000
	Unreserved Fund Balance		3,012,500
	To close revenue and related accounts to unreserved fund balance.		
(12)	Unreserved Fund Balance	2,700,000	
	Encumbrances		1,200,000
	Expenditures		1,500,000
	To close expenditures and encumbrances accounts to unreserved fund balance.		

Since no budget accounts were formally recorded in the accounting records, there are no budget accounts to be closed at year-end. Hence, the nominal accounts are closed directly to the unreserved fund balance. As in the general fund, the closing of the encumbrances account against the unreserved fund balance has the same effect as if an entry were made at year-end to reclassify an equal amount of the unreserved fund balance to a reserve for encumbrances.

At the end of each year, the cost of construction in progress represented by expenditures incurred by the capital projects fund during the year will be reported on the government-wide statement of net assets.

Completion of Project Entries in 2009 to record the completion of the project are presented and explained below.

		Debit	Credit
(13)	Encumbrances	1,200,000	
	Unreserved Fund Balance		1,200,000
	To reestablish the contract encumbrance closed out at end of previous year.		

Since capital projects funds are project oriented rather than period oriented, there is no need, as there is in accounting for the general fund or a special revenue fund, to identify expenditures with appropriation authority of a particular year. Thus, expenditures for amounts encumbered in prior years are not segregated from other expenditures of the current year. Entry (13) reestablishes the encumbrance equal to the beginning of year balance in the reserve for encumbrances account).

		Debit	Credit
(14)	Expenditures	225,000	
	Vouchers Payable		225,000
	To record unencumbered expenditures.		
(15)	Cash	250,000	
	Due from State Government		250,000
	To record receipt of cash payment from State Government.		
(16)	Cash	1,020,000	
	Certificate of Deposit		1,000,000
	Interest Receivable		12,500
	Interest Revenue		7,500
	To record redemption of certificate of deposit.		
(17)	Reserve for Encumbrances	1,200,000	
	Encumbrances		1,200,000
	Expenditures	1,200,000	
	Contracts Payable		1,200,000
	To record approved final contract billings on completed construction and to remove remaining contract encumbrance.		

		Debit	Credit
(18)	Contracts Payable	1,200,000	
	Contracts Payable—Retained Percentage		125,000
	Cash		1,075,000
	To record payment of contract except for retention of 5% of the contract price pending inspection of completed project.		
(19)	Vouchers Payable	275,000	
	Cash		275,000
	To record payment of liabilities.		

December 31, 2009, Trial Balance The preclosing trial balance of the capital projects fund on December 31, 2009, is presented below:

	Debit	*Credit*
Cash	$ 220,000	
Expenditures	1,425,000	
Contracts Payable—Retained Percentage		$ 125,000
Unreserved Fund Balance		1,512,500
Interest Revenue		7,500
	$1,645,000	$1,645,000

Closing Entry—December 31, 2009

		Debit	Credit
(20)	Unreserved Fund Balance	1,417,500	
	Interest Revenue	7,500	
	Expenditures		1,425,000
	To close nominal accounts to unreserved fund balance.		

Financial Statements A comparative balance sheet and a comparative statement of revenues, expenditures, and changes in fund balance for the years ended December 31, 2009, and December 31, 2008, are presented in Illustrations 18-1 and 18-2.

ILLUSTRATION 18-1

Library and Civic Center Capital Projects Fund
Balance Sheet at December 31, 2009, and December 31, 2008

Assets	*2009*	*2008*
Cash	$220,000	$ 300,000
Interest Receivable	—	12,500
Certificates of Deposit	—	1,000,000
Due from State Government	—	250,000
Total Assets	$220,000	$1,562,500
Liabilities and Fund Balance		
Vouchers Payable	$ —	$ 50,000
Contracts Payable—Retained Percentage	125,000	—
Total Liabilities	$125,000	$ 50,000
Fund Balance		
Unreserved	95,000	312,500
Reserve for Encumbrances	—	1,200,000
Total Fund Balance	95,000	1,512,500
Total	$220,000	$1,562,500

ILLUSTRATION 18-2

Library and Civic Center Capital Projects Fund
Statement of Revenues, Expenditures, and Other Changes in Fund Balance for Years Ended December 31, 2009, and December 31, 2008

	2009	*2008*	*Cumulative*
Revenues			
Grant Revenue	$ —	1,000,000	1,000,000
Interest Revenue	7,500	12,500	20,000
Total Revenue	7,500	1,012,500	1,020,000
Expenditures			
Capital Asset/Construction	1,425,000	1,500,000	2,925,000
Total Expenditures	1,425,000	1,500,000	2,925,000
Excess (deficiency) of Revenues over Expenditures	(1,417,500)	(487,500)	(1,905,000)
Other Financing Sources (Uses)			
Proceeds of Long-Term Capital-related Debt	—	2,100,000	2,100,000
Operating Transfer Out	—	(100,000)	(100,000)
Total Other Financing Sources (Uses)	—	2,000,000	2,000,000
Net Change in Fund Balance	(1,417,500)	1,512,500	95,000
Fund Balance—January 1	1,512,500	—	—
Fund Balance—December 31	$ 95,000	$1,512,500	$ 95,000

Closing Out a Capital Projects Fund Although the cost of a capital project should equal the resources provided for its acquisition, actual expenditures normally do not equal the project authorization. If an unexpended fund balance remains after the completion of the project, it should be distributed to the contributors of project resources in proportion to their contribution. For example, unless legal or policy decisions dictate otherwise, the capital projects fund of Model City illustrated above would be closed out as follows:

		Debit	Credit
(21)	Contracts Payable—Retained Percentage	125,000	
	Cash		125,000
	To record final payment on contract.		
(22)	Transfer to Debt Service Fund—Other Financing Use	(1) 63,333	
	Expenditures	(2) 31,667	
	Cash		95,000
	To record distribution of Fund Balance.		

(1) ($2,000,000/$3,000,000) × $95,000 = $63,333 to another governmental fund.

(2) ($1,000,000/$3,000,000) × $95,000 = $31,667 to the state government.

For financial reporting purposes, transfers to other funds within a governmental unit are distinguished from expenditures. The return of $31,667 to the state government is treated as an expenditure because it reduces the financial resources of Model City.

When construction is completed, the assets acquired with capital projects fund resources are recorded at cost in the government activities column in the government-wide statement of net assets. No assets are recorded in the capital projects fund.

Debt Service Funds

Debt issued by the government is separated into two categories: general obligation long-term debt that supports the activities of the government as a whole, and debt that is issued by proprietary funds to support specific activities of the fund. Long-term liabilities directly related to, and expected to be paid from, fiduciary funds should be reported in the statement of fiduciary net assets. General obligation long-term debt consists of bonds, notes, or warrants that are secured by the general credit and revenue-raising powers of the governmental unit as a whole, rather than by the resources of a specific fund. Two funds are involved in accounting for general obligation long-term debt. The debt is recorded on the statement of net assets while *the funds* used to meet the principal and interest payments are accumulated in the ***debt service fund***. Since the principal is not reported as a liability of the debt service fund, payments of bond principal and interest are *expenditures* of (rather than reduction of liabilities of) the debt service fund.[8] On the other hand, long-term debt that is the specific obligation of an enterprise fund (a proprietary fund) is a liability of that fund, and the accumulation of resources for its payment will be accounted for in that fund, rather than in a debt service fund.

General obligation bonds may be serial bonds or term bonds. The principal of a term bond is repaid in one lump sum at a specified maturity date. The total principal of serial bonds is repaid in a specified number of annual (and usually equal) installments.

Debt service funds are usually financed by one or more of the following sources of revenue:

General property tax
Sales tax or other specified tax revenues
Transfers of other governmental fund revenues
Special assessments (to be discussed later)
Revenue from the investment of debt service fund resources

For purposes of illustrating the difference between the debt service for serial bonds and for term bonds, two debt service funds—Land Acquisition Serial Bonds Debt Service Fund and Library and Civic Center Term Bonds Debt Service Fund—are illustrated for Model City. In reality both these funds might be collapsed into a single debt service fund.

Serial Bonds Accounting for the accumulation of resources and payment of annual installments of principal and interest on serial bonds is relatively simple. To illustrate, assume that in 2005, Model City issued \$1,800,000 in 8% serial bonds at par, \$300,000 of which come due on July 1 of each year beginning July 1, 2006. On January 1, 2008, there is \$1,200,000 in principal on these bonds outstanding, and \$300,000 in principal and \$96,000 in interest will come due on July 1, 2008. Annual installments of principal are financed from general property tax revenues, and annual interest payments are financed by the appropriation of resources of the general fund. At the beginning of 2008, the debt service fund had cash and receivables

[8] Matured long-term debt that has not yet been redeemed with the resources of the debt service fund may be recorded as a liability of the debt service fund.

of $5,000 available to make debt payments. The trial balance of the Land Acquisition Serial Bonds Debt Service Fund on January 1, 2008, is as follows:

Trial Balance—January 1, 2008

	Debit	*Credit*
Cash	$3,000	
Taxes Receivable Property	2,000	
Fund Balance		$5,000
Total	$5,000	$5,000

Transactions of the fund for 2008 are summarized in general journal form below.

A. Budgeting Revenue and Appropriations

		Debit	Credit
(1)	Estimated Revenue	315,000	
	Authorized Transfer from the General Fund	96,000	
	Appropriations (300,000 + 96,000)		396,000
	Fund Balance		15,000
	To record budgeted revenue, transfers, and appropriations for current year.		

B. Revenue Generation and Fund Transfers

		Debit	Credit
(2)	Property Tax Receivable	320,000	
	Allowance for Uncollectible Taxes		4,000
	Revenue (net)		316,000
	To record general property tax levy earmarked for debt service on serial bonds.		
(3)	Due from the General Fund	96,000	
	Transfer from General Fund—Other Financing Source		96,000
	To record amount of resources authorized for transfer from General Fund during current period.		
(4)	Cash	316,000	
	Property Tax Receivable		316,000
	To record collection of property taxes.		
(5)	Cash	96,000	
	Due from the General Fund		96,000
	To record receipt of cash transfer from General Fund.		

C. Debt Expenditure

		Debit	Credit
(6)	Expenditures—Principal	300,000	
	Expenditures—Interest	96,000	
	Cash		396,000
	To record payment of interest and principal on July 1.		

D. Year-End Entries

		Debit	Credit
(7)	Revenue	316,000	
	Estimated Revenue		315,000
	Fund Balance		1,000
	Transfer from General Fund—Other Financing Source	96,000	
	Authorized Transfer from General Fund		96,000
	Appropriations	396,000	
	Expenditures—Principal		300,000
	Expenditures—Interest		96,000
	To close nominal and budget account balances at year-end.		
(8)	Allowance for Uncollectible Taxes	4,000	
	Property Tax Receivable		4,000
	To record write-off of taxes authorized by City Council.		

The postclosing trial balance for this fund on December 31, 2008, is as follows:

Trial Balance—December 31, 2008

	Debit	*Credit*
Cash	$21,000	
Fund Balance		$21,000
Total	$21,000	$21,000

A statement of revenues, expenditures, and changes in fund balance is presented in Illustration 18-3. for the Land Acquisition Serial Bonds Debt Service Fund.

Term Bonds Accounting for the debt service of term bonds is more complicated than accounting for serial bonds. Debt service funds for term bonds require annual additions to fund resources that, with compound interest, will provide the total amount of bond principal by the maturity date of the bonds. In addition, the debt service fund for a term bond issue must provide for the payment of periodic interest on the bonds.

To illustrate, assume that the $2,000,000 in bonds issued on October 1, 2008, to finance the construction of the Library and Civic Center of Model City were 8% bonds that mature five years after their issue date. (These bonds were issued in the capital projects fund earlier in this chapter. The bonds have a stated interest rate of 8% and an original market rate of 6.787%.) The calculation of the required annual additions to the debt service fund is presented in Illustration 18-4. It is assumed that funds can be invested at an average annual return of 10%. The required annual principal addition of $327,595 is calculated by dividing the term bond principal of $2,000,000 by the amount of an ordinary annuity of $1.00 for five periods at 10% ($2,000,000/6.1051 = $327,595). Alternatively, it can be calculated by first getting the present value $2,000,000 discounted back for five periods at 10% ($2,000,000 × 0.62092 = $1,241,840). Then divide $1,241,840 by the present value of an ordinary annuity for five periods at 10% ($1,241,840/3,79079 = $327,595). See Appendix Tables A1 and A2 for present value table factors. In addition, $160,000 is needed to cover the interest payments ($2,000,000 × .08).

ILLUSTRATION 18-3

Land Acquisition Serial Bonds Debt Service Fund
Statement of Revenues, Expenditure, and Changes in Fund Balance
for Year Ended December 31, 2008

Revenues	
General Property Taxes	$316,000
Expenditures	
Principal Payments on Serial Bonds	300,000
Interest on Bonds	96,000
Total Expenditures	396,000
Other Financing Sources (Uses)	
Transfers in (from General Fund)	96,000
Net Change in Fund Balance	$ 16,000
Fund Balance—January 1	5,000
Fund Balance—December 31	$ 21,000

ILLUSTRATION 18-4

Debt Service Fund—Term Bonds
Required Annual Additions and Required Earnings for
$2,000,000 Library and Civic Center Bond Issue

Year	*Required Principal Additions (1)*	*Required Earnings (2)*	*Required Increase in Fund Balance (3)*	*Required Fund Balance (4)*
2009	$ 327,595		$ 327,595	$ 327,595
2010	327,595	$ 32,760	360,355	687,950
2011	327,595	68,795	396,390	1,084,340
2012	327,595	108,434	436,029	1,520,369
2013	327,595	152,036	479,631	2,000,000
	$1,637,975	$ 362,025	$2,000,000	

Required Principal Addition (1)	$ 327,595
Required Interest Addition (0.08 × $2,000,000)	160,000
Required Annual Addition	$ 487,595

(1) The required principal addition equals ($2,000,000 × 0.62092)/3.79079 or $327,595
(2) Required earnings equals 10% times the previous year's required fund balance (column (4))
(3) The required increase in fund balance equals the sum of column (1) and column (2)
(4) The required fund balance equals the cumulative sum of the required increase in fund balance, column (3)

These calculations do not take into account the $100,000 premium on the issue of the bonds that is transferred by the capital projects fund to the debt service fund in 2008. However, if the fund balance of a debt service fund exceeds actuarial requirements, the excess is ordinarily carried forward without adjustment until the final addition to the fund is made. It is assumed that annual additions to the Library and Civic Center Term Bonds Debt Service Fund are derived from an earmarked portion of the general property tax assessment.

Transactions—2008 Transactions of the fund in 2008 are summarized in general journal form as follows:

	Debit	Credit
(1) Cash	100,000	
Transfer from Capital Projects Fund—Other Financing Use		100,000
To record transfer of cash from Capital Projects Fund for the premium received on bond issue proceeds.		

Note that for fund accounting purposes, the premium on the bond issued is not amortized to expense over the life of the bond, but is considered an operating transfer-in that increases the fund balance. However, on the government-wide financial statements (illustrated later in the chapter), the premium needs to be amortized to expense.

Without a transfer of cash to the debt service fund by the capital projects fund, no entries would have been required in the debt service fund until the 2009 fiscal year.

	Debit	Credit
(2) Investments	100,000	
Cash		100,000
To record investment of cash in a certificate of deposit.		

	Debit	Credit
(3) Interest Receivable	4,000	
Interest Income		4,000
To accrue interest receivable from the certificate of deposit on December 31, 2008.		
(4) Interest Income	4,000	
Transfer from Capital Projects Fund	100,000	
Fund Balance		104,000
To close nominal accounts to Fund Balance.		

The postclosing trial balance on December 31, 2008, is as follows:

Trial Balance—December 31, 2008

	Debit	*Credit*
Investments	$100,000	
Interest Receivable	4,000	
Fund Balance		$104,000
Total	$104,000	$104,000

Transactions—2009 Revenue and expenditure transactions for 2009 are summarized later in Illustration 18-6. At the end of 2009, the postclosing trial balance for the fund is as follows:

Trial Balance—December 31, 2009

	Debit	*Credit*
Cash	$ 33,000	
Interest Receivable	4,000	
Property Tax Receivable	6,000	
Investments	400,000	
Allowance for Uncollectible Taxes		$ 1,000
Fund Balance		442,000
Total	$443,000	$443,000

Transactions—2010 Transactions for 2010 (also shown later in Illustration 18-6) are summarized in general journal form as follows:

A. Budget Additions, Appropriations, and Estimated Revenues

	Debit	Credit
(1) Required Additions ($327,595 + $160,000)	487,595	
Required Earnings	32,760	
Fund Balance		520,355
To record budgeted additions and budgeted income on invested resources of fund for current year (see Illustration 18-4).		

The amounts reported in the required additions and the required earnings accounts are determined (actuarially) to meet the current and future years' interest and principal payments. For example, $160,000 is needed to meet the current year's interest payment. An additional $327,595 is needed for the fund to accumulate to meet future payments. In addition, existing funds must earn some minimum rate to accumulate to the desired amount. The required earnings amount is $32,760 during the current year. If the actual amount of additions and earnings equals these budgeted amounts, the fund balance will equal the present value of the remaining interest and principal payments at the assumed interest rate.

		Debit	Credit
(2)	Fund Balance	160,000	
	Appropriations		160,000
	To record budgeted expenditures for bond interest for current year.		
(3)	Property Tax Receivable	503,000	
	Allowance for Uncollectible Taxes		15,000
	Revenue (net of uncollectible accounts)		488,000
	To record property tax levy earmarked for debt service on Library and Civic Center term bonds.		

B. Collection of Receivables, Investment Income, and Purchase of Investments

		Debit	Credit
(4)	Cash	485,000	
	Property Tax Receivable		485,000
	To record collection of property taxes.		
(5)	Investments	360,000	
	Premium on Investments	15,000	
	Cash		375,000
	To record investment of fund resources.		

Debt service fund investments are closely regulated by law and are usually restricted to quality government and municipal securities. When such investments are expected to be held to maturity, they are recorded at their par value and premium or discount is recorded in a *separate* account and amortized by reducing or increasing investment income over the remaining life of the investment.

		Debit	Credit
(6)	Cash	26,000	
	Interest Receivable		4,000
	Interest Income		22,000
	To record receipt of interest on investments.		
(7)	Allowance for Uncollectible Taxes	13,000	
	Property Tax Receivable		13,000
	To record write-off of property taxes authorized by City Council.		
(8)	Interest Receivable	21,000	
	Interest Income		21,000
	To record interest accrued on investments to December 31, 2006.		
(9)	Interest Income	1,200	
	Premium on Investments		1,200
	To record current year's amortization of premium on investments.		

C. Expenditure for Interest

		Debit	Credit
(10)	Expenditures	160,000	
	Interest Payable		160,000
	To record expenditures for current year's interest on bonds.		
(11)	Interest Payable	160,000	
	Cash		160,000
	To record payment of interest.		

D. Closing Entries

		Debit	Credit
(12)	Revenue	488,000	
	Required Additions		487,595
	Fund Balance		405
	Interest Income	41,800	
	Required Earnings		32,760
	Fund Balance		9,040
	Appropriations	160,000	
	Expenditures		160,000
	To close budgeted and nominal account balances at year-end.		

Comparative financial statements for the Library and Civic Center Term Bonds Debt Service Fund are presented in Illustrations 18-5 and 18-6. Two things should be noted about these statements, as follows:

ILLUSTRATION 18-5

Model City
Library and Civic Center Term Bonds Debt Service Fund
Balance Sheet at December 31, 2010, December 31, 2009, and December 31, 2008

Assets	*2010*	*2009*	*2008*
Cash	$ 9,000	$ 33,000	$ —
Interest Receivable	21,000	4,000	4,000
Taxes Receivable (less allowance for uncollectible taxes, 2010—$3,000; 2009—$1,000)	8,000	5,000	
Investment (at maturity value)	760,000	400,000	100,000
Unamortized Premium on Investments	13,800	—	—
Total Assets	$811,800	$442,000	$104,000
Liabilities and Fund Balance			
Fund Balance:			
Reserved for Debt Service	$811,800	$442,000	$104,000

Disclosure

The actuarial requirements in the fund balance are $687,950 in 2010 and $327,595 in 2009. See Illustration 18-4.

ILLUSTRATION 18-6

Library and Civic Center Term Bonds Debt Service Fund
Statement of Revenues, Expenditures, and Changes
In Fund Balance for Years Ended December 31, 2010, 2009, and 2008

	2010	*2009*	*2008*
Revenues			
General Property Tax	$488,000	$488,000	$ —
Interest on Investments (net of amortization)	41,800	10,000	4,000
Total Revenues	529,800	498,000	4,000
Expenditures			
Redemption of Term Bonds	—	—	—
Interest on Bonds	160,000	160,000	—
Total Expenditures	160,000	160,000	—
Excess (Deficiency) of Revenues over Expenditures	369,800	338,000	4,000
Other Financing Sources (Uses)			
Transfers In	—	—	100,000
Net Change in Fund Balance	369,800	338,000	104,000
Fund Balance—January 1	$442,000	$104,000	—
Fund Balance—December 31	$811,800	$442,000	$104,000

Note: The actuarial requirements in the fund balance are $687,950 in 2010, $327,595 in 2009, and $—0— in 2008. See Illustration 18-4.

(1) There is no interest payable accrual on general obligation long-term debt. For fund accounting, there are no entries to record the accrual of interest payable on the bonds from the last interest payment date (July 1 for the serial bonds and October 1 for the term bonds) to the end of the fiscal year. This action is justified because financial resources that are appropriated by the debt service fund are usually appropriated in the period the interest on the debt must be paid. To accrue the debt service fund expenditure and liability in one year, but record the transfer or collection of the financial resources appropriated for this purpose in a later year, would be confusing and would result in an overstatement of fund liabilities and expenditures and an understatement of the fund balance. Thus, for fund purposes it is considered appropriate and more informative to treat interest payable on general obligation long-term debt at the end of the year as an expenditure in the year of payment. *However, on the accrual-based government-wide statements, this interest must be accrued regardless of the period that the interest will be paid.* On the government-wide statement of net assets, accrued interest of $76,000 ($36,000 from the serial bond and $40,000 from the term bond) is included in liabilities, while no accrued interest is included on the governmental fund statements.

(2) Actuarial requirements must be disclosed. An essential disclosure in the financial statements of debt service funds for term bonds is the amount, actuarially determined, of resources that is necessary on the financial statement date for the accumulation of sufficient resources to redeem the debt on its maturity date. The actuarial requirements shown in Illustrations 18-5 and 18-6 are those determined in the "Required Fund Balance" column of Illustration 18-4.

Closing Out the Debt Service Fund Assume the following trial balance for the Library and Civic Center Term Bonds Debt Service Fund on September 15, 2013:

Trial Balance—September 15, 2013

	Debit	*Credit*
Cash	$2,220,000	
Fund Balance		$2,220,000
Total	$2,220,000	$2,220,000

Entries to close the fund are as follows:

		Debit	Credit
(1)	Expenditures—Principal	2,000,000	
	Expenditures—Interest	160,000	
	Cash		2,160,000
	To record redemption of matured bonds and payment of interest.		
(2)	Transfer to X Fund—Other Financing Use	60,000	
	Cash		60,000
	To record transfer of unexpected fund resources to another governmental fund.		

The unexpended balance of the fund after the final payment of interest and principal on the matured bonds should be disposed of in accordance with legal or bond indenture requirements. Usually the unexpended balance is transferred to another debt service fund, but legal requirements may specify an alternative disposition. The accounts of the fund being terminated should be closed in such a way as to reflect compliance with applicable legal requirements.

(3) Fund Balance	2,220,000	
Expenditures—Principal		2,000,000
Expenditures—Interest		160,000
Transfer to X Fund—Other Financing Use		60,000
To close out Debt Service Fund.		

After these entries are posted, the balance of all accounts would be zero and the Debt Service Fund would effectively cease to exist.

The Montana Senate supported a bill to prohibit benefits for people who retire early in an effort to offset the declining value of the state's pension funds. Previously, full benefits were awarded to anyone retiring after 30 years of service.[9]

Credit Suisse estimated that state and local governments owed more than $1.5 trillion in unfunded health-care and non-pension benefits. Boston's College's Center for Retirement Research has estimated that the recent market meltdown has eliminated $1 trillion from municipal pension funds. The fear is that many municipalities might have to follow the city of Vallejo, California and declare bankruptcy. The city was spending 74 percent of its general fund budget on public sector salaries and benefits. New York City added $63 billion in liabilities in order to comply with GASB 45.[10]

Permanent Funds

Nonexpendable Trust Funds Nonexpendable trust funds are generally reported as permanent funds. There are two types of nonexpendable trust funds: those in which the principal must be retained intact but earnings may be expended, and those in which both the principal and the earnings of the fund must be retained intact. An example of the latter type of nonexpendable trust funds is the *revolving loan fund*, in which interest collected on loans outstanding increases the funds available for subsequent loans.

Nonexpendable trust funds may be established as a result of a gift, a bequest, or some other action that requires the governmental unit to act in a fiduciary capacity and to maintain and conserve cash or other assets that it does not own. Trust funds must be accounted for in accordance with the terms of the trust agreement or the applicable provisions of statutory and common law. Accounting procedures must result in a clear distinction between nonexpendable fund resources and expendable resources resulting from the earnings of the fund. Appropriate procedures are also necessary to ensure that the expenditure of expendable resources is made in accordance with the trust agreement or other applicable legal provisions.

Where the earnings of a trust fund may be expended, they are generally transferred to a special revenue fund (expenditures restricted to specified use). To illustrate, assume that a private donor granted Model City $300,000 for the purpose of financing the purchase of rare editions of the classics for the public library. As a result of this grant, two funds were created:

1. The Classics Endowment Fund to account for the nonexpendable fund principal and the investment (this fund is classified as a permanent fund).

[9] Senate nixes early retirement to plug pension gap, Associate Press, February 25, 2009.

[10] The Great GASB, City Journal, February 24, 2009.

2. The Classics Acquisition Fund to account for the expenditure of the earnings of the endowment fund (this fund is classified as a special revenue fund).

The general ledger trial balances for each fund on January 1, 2008, are presented below.

Classics Endowment Fund

(Permanent Fund)	*Debit*	*Credit*
Cash	$ 2,000	
Certificates of Deposit	300,000	
Interest Receivable (accrued)	7,500	
Due to Classics Acquisition Fund		$ 9,500
Fund Balance		300,000
Total	$309,500	$309,500

Classics Acquisition Fund

(Special Revenue Fund)		
Cash	$ 8,000	
Due from Classics Endowment Fund	9,500	
Fund Balance		$ 17,500
Total	$ 17,500	$ 17,500

Transactions for 2008 for each fund are summarized below in general journal form.

Classics Endowment Fund

(1)	Cash	30,000	
	Interest Receivable		7,500
	Interest Income		22,500
	To record interest collected on certificate of deposit.		
(2)	Interest Receivable	7,500	
	Interest Income		7,500
	To accrue interest on certificate of deposit.		
(3)	Transfer to Classics Acquisition Fund	30,000	
	Due to Classics Acquisition Fund		30,000
	To record amount of 2008 income transferable to Classics Acquisition Fund.		
(4)	Due to Classics Acquisition Fund	32,000	
	Cash		32,000
	To record cash payment to Classics Acquisition Fund.		

For purposes of simplification, it is assumed that the trust agreement requires that the entire endowment principal be invested in a savings account earning 10% interest. Usually, the principal of an endowment fund is invested in various securities. If the securities are purchased at a premium or discount, such amounts should ordinarily be amortized to interest income, and only the net amount of investment income would accrue to the recipient Classics Acquisition Fund. Accounting procedures for an endowment fund are complicated further if the endowment includes depreciable income-producing assets such as rental properties. In that case, earnings accruing to the recipient expendable fund must also be reduced by depreciation if the trust principal is to be maintained "intact."

Classics Acquisition Fund

(1)	Due from Classics Endowment Fund	30,000	
	Fund Balance		30,000
	To record expendable earnings due from endowment fund.		

(2) Cash	32,000	
Due from Classics Endowment Fund		32,000
To record receipt of cash from endowment fund.		
(3) Fund Balance	18,000	
Cash		18,000
To record acquisition of rare books.		

Financial statements for these funds are presented in Illustrations 18-7 and 18-8.

ILLUSTRATION 18-7

Classics Endowment Fund
Balance Sheet
December 31, 2008 and December 31, 2007

Assets	*2008*	*2007*
Cash	$ —	$ 2,000
Interest Receivable	7,500	7,500
Investments	300,000	300,000
Total Assets	$307,500	$309,500
Liabilities and Fund Balance		
Due to Classics Acquisition Fund	$ 7,500	$ 9,500
Fund Balance	300,000	300,000
Total	$307,500	$309,500

Statement of Revenues, Expenditures, and Changes In Fund Balances for Years Ended December 31, 2008, and December 31, 2007

	2008	*2007*
Revenues		
Interest Income	$ 30,000	$ 30,000
Expenditures	—	—
Excess (Deficiency) of Revenues over Expenditures	30,000	30,000
Other Financing Sources (Uses)		
Transfers to Classics Acquisitions Fund	(30,000)	(30,000)
Net Change in Fund Balance:	—	—
Fund Balance—January 1	300,000	300,000
Fund Balance—December 31	$300,000	$300,000

According to government accounting standards, the U.S. government's responsibilities to make future payments for social insurance and certain other programs are not reported as liabilities on the U.S. government's balance sheet, even though they will have a significant claim on budgetary resources in the future. The U.S. government's 2005 balance sheet shows liabilities of $9,915 billion. What it does not show is the net present value of all responsibilities (for current participants over a 75-year period), including Medicare and Social Security payments and pensions and benefits for federal employees and veterans, amounting to $49,403 billion.[11]

[11] *Financial Report of the United States* (with a foreword by Representative Jim Cooper), Nelson Current, 2006.

ILLUSTRATION 18-8

Classics Acquisition Fund
Balance Sheet
December 31, 2008, and December 31, 2007

Assets	*2008*	*2007*
Cash	$22,000	$ 8,000
Due from Classics Endowment Fund	7,500	9,500
Total Assets	$29,500	$17,500
Liabilities and Fund Balance		
Fund Balance	$29,500	$17,500

Statement of Revenues, Expenditures, and Changes In Fund Balances for Years Ended December 31, 2008, and December 31, 2007

	2008	*2007*
Revenues	$ —	$ —
Expenditures	18,000	20,000
Excess (Deficiency) of Revenues over Expenditures	(18,000)	(20,000)
Other Financing Sources (Uses)		
Transfers from Endowment Trust Fund	30,000	30,000
Excess (Deficiency) to Fund Balance	12,000	10,000
Fund Balance—January 1	17,500	7,500
Fund Balance—December 31	29,500	$17,500

PROPRIETARY FUNDS

In *GASB Statement No. 34*, the proprietary fund operating statement requirements were changed from a capital maintenance approach to a change in net assets approach. Under a capital maintenance approach, certain resource flows such as contributions of capital assets and permanently restricted contributions of financial assets were excluded from the operating or income statement "bottom line" and were reported as direct charges to equity or net assets. In other words, they were not considered revenues or expenses, but "balance-sheet only" transactions. The board concluded that the change in net assets approach, which is already required in the government-wide statement of activities, is also appropriate for proprietary funds. Under the change in net assets approach, ***all*** changes in net assets are included somewhere in the "statement of activities" and are included in the "bottom-line" total in the change in net assets for the year. There are no "direct to equity" transactions and no mandatory reporting distinction between capital transactions and operating transactions. No additional change in net assets is reported between the beginning and ending net assets, as would be needed under the capital maintenance approach.

Proprietary fund reporting focuses on the determination of operating income, changes in net assets (or cost recovery), financial position, and cash flows. The cash flow statement is to be prepared using the direct basis. Proprietary funds include Enterprise and Internal Service Funds, as illustrated in the following sections.

Enterprise Funds

Enterprise Funds may be used to report any activity for which a fee is charged to external users for goods and services. The most common examples of governmental enterprises are public utilities that provide such services as water or electricity. Other activities of governmental units that are accounted for in Enterprise Funds include airports, transportation systems, parking lots and garages, and recreational facilities such as swimming pools. Activities are required to be reported as Enterprise Funds if any one of the following is met:

- The activity is financed with debt that is secured solely by a pledge of the net revenues from fees and charges of the activity.
- Laws or regulations require that the activity's costs of providing services including capital costs (such as depreciation or debt service) be recovered with fees and charges, rather than with taxes or similar revenues.
- The pricing policies of the activity establish fees and charges designed to recover its costs, including capital costs (such as depreciation and debt service).

The resources to establish an enterprise fund may come from contributions or from the proceeds of long-term debt issues or both. Contributions may be obtained from other governmental units, resources of the General Fund of the same governmental unit, property owners, subdivision developers, or customers.

A balance sheet of the proprietary funds (both the Enterprise and the Internal Service Funds) is presented in Illustration 18-9, and several features of the enterprise fund are pointed out. Some assets are restricted in use by bond provisions or other arrangements and are classified on the balance sheet as ***restricted assets.*** Restricted assets are generally reported between current assets and capital assets. In Illustration 18-9, the Restricted Assets consist of assets segregated in compliance with the sinking fund requirements of the revenue bonds,[12] and the Current Liabilities (Payable from Restricted Assets) consist of the current interest and principal installments due on the revenue bonds.

Under *GASB Statement No. 34*, proprietary funds no longer report "equity accounts" on the statement of net assets. Under the proposal, net assets will be reported externally as either (1) invested in capital assets, net of related debt, (2) unrestricted net assets, or (3) restricted net assets. Internally, the government may keep separate the sources of capital as in the past. In this case, contributions would be classified by source and segregated from retained earnings. Finally, both fixed assets and long-term debt are accounted for and reported as specific assets and liabilities of the Enterprise Fund.

Internal Service Funds

Internal Service Funds are used to account for any activity that provides goods or services to ***other funds, departments, or agencies of the primary governmental unit and its component units, or to other governments***, on a cost reimbursement basis. Internal service

[12] Revenue bonds are long-term obligations, where the principal and interest are paid from the earnings of self-supporting enterprises on which the bond proceeds were spent.

ILLUSTRATION 18-9
Model City
Proprietary Funds
Balance Sheet at December 31, 2008*

	Business-Type Activities—Enterprise Fund	*Governmental Activities*
	Sewer Fund	*Internal Service Fund*
Assets		
Current Assets:		
Cash	$ 100,000	$ 22,500
Receivables	451,000	100,000
Total Current Assets	$ 551,000	$122,500
Noncurrent Assets:		
Restricted Assets	509,000	—
Capital Assets (net of accumulated depreciation)	10,000,000	420,000
Construction in Progress	40,000	—
Total Noncurrent Assets	10,549,000	420,000
Total Assets	$11,100,000	$542,500
Liabilities		
Current Liabilities:		
Current Liabilities (payable from current assets)	$ 361,000	$ 27,500
Current Liabilities (payable from restricted assets)	282,000	—
Total Current Liabilities	643,000	27,500
Revenue Bonds Payable	4,200,000	—
Total Liabilities	$ 4,843,000	$ 27,500
Net Assets		
Invested in capital assets, net of related debt	5,558,000	420,000
Restricted	500,000	
Unrestricted	199,000	95,000
Total Net Assets	$ 6,257,000	$515,000
Total Liabilities and Net Assets	$11,100,000	$542,500

* An alternative to the balance sheet format shown here is a statement of net assets format, which presents the same information but is organized slightly differently.

funds should be used only if the reporting government is the predominant participant in the activity. Otherwise, the activity should be reported as an Enterprise Fund.

Typical examples of activities accounted for in Internal Service Funds include the operations of central computer facilities, central garages and motor pools, central purchasing and stores departments, and central printing departments.

Internal Service Funds are established with resources obtained from contributions from other funds, proceeds from the sale of general obligation bonds, or long-term advances from other funds. If an Internal Service Fund obtains resources from the proceeds of the issuance of general obligation bonds, the bond liability is ***not*** accounted for in the records of the Internal Service Fund. Rather a Debt Service Fund is established, and the bond liability is accounted for on the statement of net assets. Upon the receipt of the bond issue proceeds, the entry in the records of the Internal Service Fund is a debit to Cash and a credit to Capital Contributions—General Obligation Bonds. A balance sheet and the statement of revenues, expenses, and changes in fund balance for an Internal Service Fund are included as part of the proprietary fund statements as shown in

ILLUSTRATION 18-10

Model City
Proprietary Funds
Statement of Revenues, Expenses, and Changes in Fund Net Assets
for the Year Ended December 31, 2008

	Business-Type Activities—Enterprise Fund	*Governmental Activities*
	Sewer Fund	*Internal Service Fund*
Operating Revenues		
Charges for Services	$1,500,000	$200,000
Total Operating Revenues	1,500,000	200,000
Operating Expenses		
Personal Services	675,000	185,000
Utilities	105,000	20,000
Depreciation Expense	500,000	15,000
Total Operating Expenses	1,280,000	220,000
Operating Income (loss)	220,000	(20,000)
Nonoperating Revenue (Expenses)		
Interest Expense (10%)	(42,000)	—
Total Nonoperating Revenue (expenses)	(42,000)	—
Income Before Contributions and Transfers	178,000	(20,000)
Transfers Out—General Fund	(150,000)	—
Change in Net Assets	28,000	(20,000)
Total Net Assets—beginning of year	6,229,000	535,000
Total Net Assets—end of year	6,257,000	515,000

Illustrations 18-9 and 18-10. As indicated, fixed assets acquired with the resources of the Internal Service Fund and depreciation thereon are recorded in the accounting records of that fund.

FIDUCIARY FUNDS

Trust and Agency Funds

As stated earlier, trust and agency funds focus on reporting net assets and changes in net assets. Fiduciary funds are used to report assets held in a trustee or agency capacity for others and therefore cannot be used to support the government's own programs. Fiduciary funds include pension trust funds, investment trust funds, private-purpose trust funds, and agency funds. The three types of *trust* funds should be used to report resources held and administered by the reporting government when it is acting in a fiduciary role. These funds are distinguished from *agency* funds generally by the existence of a trust agreement that affects the degree of management involvement and the length of time that the resources are held. Accounting procedures for agency funds and most trust funds are quite similar and are relatively simple. The disclosures under *GASB Statement No. 34* require a separate statement of fiduciary responsibilities with a statement of net assets and a statement of changes in net assets. The statement of net assets and the statement of changes in net assets may be presented in a "layered" approach or presented as separate statements.

Agency Funds For example, assume that Model City collects property taxes on behalf of a legally separate governmental unit such as a water improvement district. The following entries are made to record the amount of taxes to be collected and their remittance to the water improvement district.

(1)	Property Tax Receivable	250,000	
	Due to Water Improvement District		250,000
	To record levy of taxes earmarked for Valley Water Improvement District.		
(2)	Cash	250,000	
	Property Tax Receivable		250,000
	To record collection of taxes earmarked for Valley Water Improvement District.		
(3)	Due to Water Improvement District	250,000	
	Cash		250,000
	To record remittance to Valley Water Improvement District of taxes collected on its behalf.		

Agency funds are purely custodial, and assets always equal liabilities (no fund balance exists or if a fund balance is recorded, it is reported as a liability). These funds do not involve revenues or expenditures, nor do they require the preparation of a statement of revenues, expenditures, and changes in fund balance.

Quebec's pension fund announced that the value of its assets fell by $39.8 billion in 2008. The 25% decline in the value of assets has retirees worried. The fund underperformed other funds (Ontario's fund suffered a 15.3% loss) because of aggressive investments in novel financial instruments such as nonbank asset-backed commercial paper.[13]

CAPITAL ASSETS AND LONG-TERM DEBT

Under *GASB Statement No. 34*, governments report all capital assets, including infrastructure assets, and unmatured general long-term debt on a government-wide basis and report depreciation expense as a charge to operations in each period. General fixed assets of a governmental unit are the fixed assets that are not accounted for in proprietary (enterprise, internal service, and nonexpendable trust) funds.

General long-term debt of a governmental unit is the unmatured principal of general obligation indebtedness that is not accounted for in a proprietary fund or trust fund. Such debt is reported on the government-wide statement of net assets. *Governments must maintain amortization schedules for all debt issued since the effective interest expense is reported on the government-wide statement of activities and the amortized debt is reported on the statement of net assets.*

Capital Assets

General fixed assets may be acquired through gift or foreclosure, or they may be acquired through the expenditure of resources of the general fund, special revenue funds, or capital project funds.

[13] Quebec pension fund loses 25%, theStar.com, February 26, 2009.

INFRASTRUCTURE ASSETS

How should a government account for streets, sidewalks, bridges and other immovable assets? Prior to the issuance of *GASB Statement No. 34* on reporting for state and local governments, most governments ignored accounting for these assets. Using the former rules, if the majority of a city's bridges needed repairs, there was no information provided in statements. Under the new rules, governments will be required to show the historical cost of these assets on the government-wide statement of net assets and include depreciation expense on the government-wide statement of activities. Although this topic is a controversial issue, the GASB felt that capitalization and depreciation of infrastructure assets is important to assist users in:

1. Determining whether current-year revenues are sufficient to pay for current-year services.
2. Assessing the service efforts and costs of programs.
3. Determining whether the government's financial position improved or deteriorated as a result of the year's operations.
4. Assessing the government's financial position and condition.

Governments are required to capitalize and report major general infrastructure assets that were acquired (purchased, constructed, or donated) in fiscal years ending after June 30, 1980. The initial capitalization amount should be based on historical cost. If determination of historical cost is not practical because of inadequate records, estimated historical cost may be used.

The valuation of constructed or purchased general fixed assets is determined using the cost basis. Donated assets, intended for use by the city, would not be recorded in the government funds as assets or revenue. However, donated assets would be recorded as an asset and as revenue on the government-wide financial statements. Donated assets are recorded at their estimated fair value at the time they are received. Consider the following classifications of general fixed assets and the sources of the funds:

Classification of Assets	*Classification of Sources of Assets*
Land	Investments in general fixed assets from:
Buildings	Capital projects funds
Improvements other than buildings	General obligation bonds
Machinery and equipment	Special assessment debt with government commitment
Construction in progress	Federal grants
Infrastructure assets	State grants
	Local grants
	General fund revenues
	Special revenue fund revenues
	Contributions from property owners
	Private gifts

Prior to *GASB Statement No. 34*, governments maintained a set of self-balancing account groups called the General Fixed Asset Account Group and the General Long-Term Obligation Account Group. In place of these account groups, information on capital assets and long-term debt is reported in the statement of net assets, in addition to detailed schedules for both in the footnotes (illustrated later in the chapter). The following journal entries reflect how the capital asset transactions would be reported on the statement of net assets.

Accounting events in 2008 that affect the capital assets of Model City are summarized below in general journal form:

Purchase of a Fixed Asset

		Debit	Credit
(1)	Machinery and Equipment	250,000	
	Cash		250,000
	To record expenditure for office equipment made by General Fund in 2004 (see Chapter 17).		

Sale of a Fixed Asset

		Debit	Credit
(2)	Cash	87,250	
	Accumulated Depreciation	140,000	
	Machinery and Equipment		225,000
	Gain on sale		2,250
	To record sale of used office equipment.		

Equipment, which was purchased five years ago for $225,000, was sold for $87,250. Accumulated depreciation on the asset was $140,000. The proceeds of the sale were accounted for as revenue of the General Fund (see Chapter 17). When a general fixed asset is sold, both its original cost and accumulated depreciation are removed from the records. Under *GASB Statement No. 34,* the difference between the book value of the asset ($85,000) and the cash received ($87,500) is reported as a gain (loss) on sale and reported on the government-wide statement of activities. In this case, the gain is $2,250.

During 2008, $1,500,000 was spent on construction of Model City's Library and Civic Center. (Of the amount incurred, recall that $50,000 was still owed.) Thus the impact on the government-wide statement of net assets is:

	Debit	Credit
Construction in Progress	1,500,000	
Cash		1,450,000
Vouchers payable		50,000
Depreciation Expense (321,000 − 15,000)	306,000	
Accumulated Depreciation—Buildings		120,000
Accumulated Depreciation—Machinery and equipment		55,000
Accumulated Depreciation—Improvements		131,000

Total depreciation expense of $321,000 includes $15,000 of depreciation expense already recorded in the Internal Service Fund.

As previously explained, depreciation of general fixed assets is not measured or reported in the accounts of governmental funds. Since depreciation is now required on government-wide statements, accumulated depreciation is deducted from the related assets in the statement of net assets. Notice that the recognition of accumulated depreciation does ***not*** result in the recording or reporting of depreciation expense in any governmental fund type. ***It is reported only on the government-wide statements.***

The required disclosures about capital assets are presented in Illustration 18-11. The primary difference between past disclosures (pre-*GASB 34*) and the new disclosures is that the capital assets of the Internal Service Fund and infrastructure assets are included in the new disclosures for *governmental activities.*

Long-Term Dept

General long-term obligations of a governmental unit include the unmatured principal on bonds, warrants, notes, and other long-term general obligations, including special assessment debt for which the government is obligated in some manner. It is not limited to liabilities arising from debt issues, but may include noncurrent

ILLUSTRATION 18-11

Disclosure of Information About Capital Assets for the Year Ending December 31, 2008

	Primary Government			
Governmental Activities	*Beginning Balance*	*Additions*	*Retirements*	*Ending Balance*
Land	$ 500,000			$ 500,000
Building*	4,760,000			4,760,000
Improvements	2,795,000			2,795,000
Machinery and Equipment*	950,000	250,000	(225,000)	975,000
Construction in Progress		1,500,000		1,500,000
Infrastructure	5,000,000			5,000,000
Total at historical cost	$14,005,000	1,750,000	225,000	$15,530,000
Less accumulated depreciation				
Building*	(1,490,000)	(130,000)		(1,620,000)
Improvements	(600,000)	(31,000)		(631,000)
Machinery and Equipment*	(235,000)	(60,000)	140,000	(155,000)
Infrastructure	(1,000,000)	(100,000)		$(1,100,000)
Total accumulated depreciation	$(3,325,000)	(321,000)	140,000	$(3,506,000)
Governmental activities capital assets, net	$10,680,000	1,429,000	(85,000)	$12,024,000
Business-Type Activities:				
Utility Plant	12,000,000			12,000,000
Construction in Progress	—	40,000		40,000
Totals at historical cost	12,000,000	40,000		12,040,000
Less accumulated depreciation				
Utility Plant	(1,800,000)	(200,000)		(2,000,000)
Business-type Activities Capital Assets, Net	$10,200,000	$(160,000)		$10,040,000

Depreciation Expense Charged to Governmental Activities as Follows:

Public Safety	$ 36,612
General Government	18,210
Highways and Streets	12,332
Sanitation	6,745
Health	13,585
Cultural—recreation	153,963
Education	64,553
In addition, depreciation on capital assets held by the Internal Service Fund is charged to the various functions based on usage	15,000
	$ 321,000

* Includes, in ending balances, the capital assets of the Internal Service Fund ($360,000 and $200,000 in buildings and equipment, respectively, with $100,000 and $50,000 in accumulated depreciation).

liabilities arising from lease agreements and similar commitments. It does not include long-term debt that is the specific liability of proprietary funds. However, where the full faith and credit of the governmental unit is pledged as additional assurance that specific proprietary fund liabilities will be paid, the contingent liability should be disclosed in the notes to the financial statements.

The following journal entries reflect now the following events affect the statement of net assets of Model City:

Cash	2,100,000	
Term Bond Payable		2,000,000
Premium on Bond Payable		100,000
Interest Expense	96,000	
Serial Bond Payable	300,000	
Cash		396,000

To meet the reporting requirements, amortization schedules are needed. The following amortization schedules are prepared for the serial and the term bonds.

Term Bond Amortization Schedule

Effective interest rate = 6.7875%. Coupon rate = 8%

Date	*Interest Expense*	*Cash*	*Premium Amortization*	*Unamortized Premium*	*Term Bond Balance*
				100,000	$2,100,000
10/1/09	142,537	160,000	17,463	82,537	2,082,537
10/1/10	141,352	160,000	18,648	63,889	2,063,889
10/1/11	140,086	160,000	19,914	43,975	2,043,975
10/1/12	138,734	160,000	21,266	22,709	2,022,709
10/1/13	137,291	160,000	22,709	0	2,000,000

Serial Bond Amortization Schedule

Effective interest rate = 8%. Coupon rate = 8%

Date	*Interest Expense*	*Cash*	*Principal Payment*	*Serial Bond Balance*
				1,200,000
7/1/08	96,000	396,000	300,000	900,000
7/1/09	72,000	372,000	300,000	600,000
7/1/10	48,000	348,000	300,000	300,000
7/1/11	24,000	324,000	300,000	—

If the serial bonds were issued at a premium or discount, the amortization schedule would adjust interest expense to the historical market rate (effective interest rate), similar to the term bond illustrated above.

The total effective interest expense is $119,634 (or 50% of $96,000 plus 50% of $72,000 plus 25% of $142,537). Accrued interest payable is $76,000 (or 25% of $160,000 plus 50% of $72,000). An example of the disclosure requirements concerning long-term liabilities is presented in Illustration 18-12.

ILLUSTRATION 18-12

Model City

Schedule of General Long-Term Obligations
December 31, 2008, and December 31, 2007

Governmental Activities	*Beginning Balance*	*Additions*	*Reductions*	*Ending Balance*	*Amounts Due within One Year*
Term Bonds	$ —	$2,100,000	$ 4,366	$2,095,634	$ —
Serial Bonds	1,200,000	—	300,000	900,000	300,000
Governmental Activities Long-Term Liabilities	$1,200,000	$2,100,000	$304,366	$2,995,634	$300,000
Business-Type Activities					
Revenue Bonds Payable	$4,200,000	$ —	$ —	$4,200,000	$ —
Business-Type Activities Long-Term Liabilities	$4,200,000	$ —	$ —	$4,200,000	$ —

TEST YOUR KNOWLEDGE

NOTE: Solutions to ***Test Your Knowledge*** questions are found at the end of each chapter before the end-of-chapter questions.

True or False

1. Are the following statements concerning fixed assets true or false?
   a. _________ Infrastructure assets need to be disclosed on the government-wide statement of net assets.
   b. _________ Accrued interest is reported as a liability on the statement of net assets.
   c. _________ Depreciation expense does not have to be recorded for either government-wide or governmental fund balance reports.

EXTERNAL REPORTING REQUIREMENTS (*GASB STATEMENT No. 34*)

The following statements and disclosures are required:[14]

Reporting Governmental Fund Financial Statements

1. Balance sheet (Illustration 18-13)
2. Statement of revenues, expenditures, and changes in fund balances (Illustration 18-14)
3. Reconciliation to the government-wide statements (Illustrations 18-15 and 18-16)

Reporting Proprietary Fund Financial Statements

1. Balance sheet (Illustration 18-9) or a statement of net assets (not shown); either format is acceptable
2. Statement of revenues, expenses, and changes in fund net assets (Illustration 18-10)
3. Statement of cash flows (not shown)—direct format

Reporting Fiduciary Funds (and Similar Component Units) Financial Statements

1. Statement of fiduciary net assets (not shown)
2. Statement of changes in fiduciary net assets (not shown)

Reporting Government-wide Statements

1. Statement of net assets (Illustration 18-16)
2. Statement of activities (Illustration 18-17)

Combining Statements for Major Component Units

1. Statement of net assets (not shown)
2. Statement of activities (not shown)

[14] The focus of the governmental and proprietary fund statements is on major funds. Nonmajor funds are aggregated and displayed in a single column. Combining statements, showing the details of the non-major funds, are not required but may be presented as supplementary information.

Notes to the Financial Statements

1. Schedule of changes in capital assets (Illustration 18-11)
2. Schedule of changes in long-term liabilities (Illustration 18-12)

Required Supplementary Information (RSI)

1. Management's discussion and analysis (MD&A)
2. Budgetary comparison schedules (see Chapter 17, Illustration 17-9), accompanied by information reconciling the budget-to-GAAP (see Chapter 17, Illustration 17-10)

GOVERNMENT FUND-BASED REPORTING

Earlier in the chapter, several individual fund financial statements were illustrated. In this section, we discuss the reporting requirements for the governmental funds aggregated. See Illustrations 18-13 and 18-14 for the fund balance sheets

ILLUSTRATION 18-13

Model City
Governmental Funds*
Balance Sheets at December 31, 2008

		Capital Projects Fund	*Debt Service Funds*		*Special Revenue Fund*	*Permanent Fund*	*Total Governmental Funds*
Assets	*General Fund*	*Library and Civic Center*	*Library and Civic Center Term Bond*	*Land Acquisition Serial Bond*	*Classics Acquisitions*	*Classics Endowment*	
Cash	$ 63,250	$ 300,000	$ —	$21,000	$22,000	$ —	$ 406,250
Interest Receivable		12,500	4,000			7,500	24,000
Investments	106,000	1,000,000	100,000			300,000	1,506,000
Property Tax Receivable	127,750						127,750
Due from Other Funds	50,000				7,500		57,500
Due from State Government		250,000					250,000
Total Assets	$347,000	$1,562,500	$104,000	$21,000	$29,500	$307,500	$2,371,500
Liabilities and Fund Balance							
Vouchers Payable	$ 73,000	$ 50,000					$ 123,000
Due to Other Funds						7,500	7,500
Total Liabilities	$ 73,000	$ 50,000	$ —	$ —	$ —	$ 7,500	$ 130,500
Fund Balances:							
Unreserved	83,000	312,500					395,500
Reserved for							
Encumbrances	191,000	1,200,000					1,391,000
Debt Services			104,000	21,000			125,000
Other					29,500	300,000	329,500
Total Fund Balances	274,000	1,512,500	104,000	21,000	29,500	300,000	2,241,000
Total Liabilities and Fund Balances	$347,000	$1,562,500	$104,000	$21,000	$29,500	$307,500	$2,371,500

* Because Model City does not have very many funds, all of which were considered important to readers, the city reported on all funds rather than focusing on only the major funds, as defined by percentage cutoffs.

ILLUSTRATION 18-14

Model City
Governmental Funds*
Statement of Revenues, Expenditures, and Changes in Fund Balances
for the Year Ended December 31, 2008

		Capital Projects Fund	*Debt Service Funds*		*Special Revenue Fund*	*Permanent Fund*	*Total Governmental Funds*
	General Fund	*Library and Civic Center*	*Library and Civic Center Term Bond*	*Land Acquisition Serial Bond*	*Classics Acquisitions*	*Classics Endowment*	
Revenues							
Property Taxes	$1,158,750		$316,000				$1,474,750
Licenses and Permits	170,500						170,500
State Grant—education	275,000						275,000
Intergovernmental		$1,000,000					1,000,000
Charges for Services	130,500						130,500
Interest	6,000	12,500		$ 4,000		$ 30,000	52,000
Total Revenue	$1,740,750	$1,012,500	$316,000	$ 4,000		$ 30,000	$3,103,250
Expenditures							
Public Safety	$ 480,000						$ 480,000
General Government	289,000						289,000
Highways and Streets	128,000						128,000
Sanitation	70,000						70,000
Health	141,000						141,000
Cultural—recreation	80,000				$ 18,000		98,000
Education	670,000						670,000
Debt Service							
Principal			$300,000				300,000
Interest			96,000				96,000
Capital Outlay		$1,500,000					1,500,000
Total Expenditures	$1,858,000	$1,500,000	$396,000	—	$ 18,000	—	$3,772,000
Excess (deficiency) of revenues over expenditures	$ (117,250)	$ (487,500)	$(80,000)	$ 4,000	$(18,000)	$ 30,000	(668,750)
Other Financing Sources (Uses)							
Proceeds from long-term capital debt		$2,100,000					$2,100,000
Transfers in	$ 150,000		$ 96,000	$100,000	$ 30,000		376,000
Transfers out	(96,000)	(100,000)				$(30,000)	(226,000)
Total other	$ 54,000	$2,000,000	$ 96,000	$100,000	$ 30,000	$(30,000)	$2,250,000
Special Items							
Proceeds from sale of equipment	$ 87,250						$ 87,250
Net change in fund balance	24,000	$1,512,500	$ 16,000	$104,000	$ 12,000	$ —	$1,668,500
Fund balance—beginning	250,000	—	5,000	—	17,500	300,000	572,500
Fund balance—ending	$ 274,000	$1,512,500	$ 21,000	$104,000	$ 29,500	$300,000	$2,241,000

* Because Model City does not have very many funds, all of which were considered important to readers, the city reported on all funds rather than focusing on only the major funds, as defined by percentage cutoffs. In addition, $250,000 of capital expenditures made by the general fund are included in the following governmental activities: Public Safety, $100,000, Cultural–recreation, $50,000, and Education, $100,000.

and the statement of revenues, expenditures, and changes in fund balances for the governmental funds. Fund information is important because funds are created to account for financial resources and the activities that they support and to aid management in decision making. Because much of the government's activities is managed and accounted for in a limited number of funds, the governmental fund reporting is designed to report the government's ***major funds***. For example, in Illustration 18-13, each of the funds is reported in separate columns. Governments are required only to report the ***major funds*** in separate columns, but have flexibility to report more funds separately if desired. *Individual governmental funds and proprietary funds are major funds if the total assets, liabilities, revenues, or expenditure/ expenses of that individual fund are at least 10% of the corresponding total for the relevant fund category (governmental or enterprise funds) and at least 5% of the corresponding total for all governmental and enterprise funds combined.* In addition, any fund that may be important to financial statement users should be reported as a major fund. Internal Service Funds are exempt from major fund reporting. Therefore to avoid double counting (revenue to the internal service fund is an expenditure of the government funds), the net effects of internal service transactions are eliminated.

Reconciliation between Government Fund Balances and Government-wide Net Assets

The primary difference between the disclosure requirement for capital assets (Illustration 18-11) and prior disclosures relates to the assets of the Internal Service Funds and infrastructure assets. On the statement of net assets, the Internal Service Fund's assets and liabilities are reported in governmental activities along with infrastructure assets. To assist the users of the financial statements, governments must reconcile the change in fund balances in the governmental funds (see Illustration 18-14) with the changes in fund balance reported on the government-wide statements (see Illustration 18-17 later in the chapter). This reconciliation is reported in Illustration 18-15. In addition, governments must reconcile the fund balance in the governmental funds (see Illustration 18-13) with the fund balance reported in the statement of net assets prepared on a government-wide basis (from Illustration 18-16). This reconciliation is reported at the bottom of Illustration 18-16. These reconciliations highlight the major differences between fund accounting and accrual accounting. For instance, in the governmental funds, amounts spent to acquire capital assets are expenditures; while under accrual accounting, these assets are capitalized on the balance sheet and depreciated on the statement of activities. Similarly, when bonds are issued, the total proceeds increase financial resources on the statement of revenues, expenditures, and changes in fund balance, whereas under accrual accounting, bond issues increase liabilities on the balance sheet. Total proceeds from the sale of an asset are also included on the statement of revenues, expenditures, and changes in fund balance, whereas under accrual accounting only the difference between the carrying value of the asset and the cash received is reported on the statement of activities. Similarly, in the governmental funds, only the amount of cash interest paid is treated as an expenditure; in the government-wide statements, the effective interest expense is recorded on the statement of activities with accrued interest payable reported on the balance sheet.

ILLUSTRATION 18-15

Model City
Reconciliation of the Statement of Revenues, Expenditures, and Changes in Fund Balances of Governmental Funds to the Statement of Activities
for the Year Ended December 31, 2008

Net change in fund balances—total governmental funds (Illustration 18-14)	**$1,668,500**
Governmental funds report capital outlays as expenditures while governmental activities report depreciation expense to allocate those expenditures over the life of the asset. This is the amount by which capital outlays exceeded depreciation in the current period. (a)	1,444,000
In the statement of activities, only the gain on the sale of equipment is reported, while in the governmental funds, the proceeds from the sale increase financial resources. Thus, the change in net assets differs from the change in fund balance by the book value of the asset sold.	(85,000)
Bond proceeds provide current financial resources to governmental funds, but issuing debt increases long-term liabilities in the statement of net assets.	(2,100,000)
Repayment of bond principal is an expenditure in the government funds, but reduces long-term liabilities in the statement of net assets.	300,000
Some expenses reported on the statement of activities do not require the use of current financial resources and therefore are not reported as expenditures in government funds (in this case, accrued interest). (b)	(23,634)
Internal service funds are used by management to charge the cost of certain activities to individual funds. The net revenue (expense) of the internal service fund is reported with governmental activities. (c)	(20,000)
Change in Net Assets of Governmental Activities (see Illustration 18-17)	**$1,183,866**

(a) Total capital expenditures from the capital projects fund ($1,500,000) plus purchases by the General Fund ($250,000) less depreciation expense, excluding depreciation from the Internal Service Fund ($321,000 − $15,000).
(b) Total interest expense using the accrual basis is $119,634 but only $96,000 is recognized as an expenditure. (The $119,634 includes $84,000 from the serial bond and $35,634 from the term bond.)
(c) The $20,000 is charged equally to public safety and to the general government.

GOVERNMENT-WIDE REPORTING

As stated previously, the primary financial statements under *GASB Statement No. 34* are prepared on a government-wide basis. These statements are prepared on the accrual basis using the flow of economic resources concept. These primary statements include:

1. The statement of net assets.
2. The statement of activities.

Note that a governmental-wide statement of cash flows is *not* required. Cash flow statements are required for proprietary funds.

Statement of Net Assets

The statement of net assets reports both financial and capital resources. The statement of net assets is prepared using the accrual basis and a government-wide format (formerly called entity-wide basis). Under the prior rules, the balance sheet listed

ILLUSTRATION 18-16

Model City
Statement of Net Assets—Government-wide Basis At December 31, 2008

	Primary Government		
Assets	*Total Government Activities*	*Business-Type Activities*	*Total*
Cash	$ 428,750	$ 100,000	$ 528,750
Interest Receivable	24,000		24,000
Investments	1,506,000		1,506,000
Receivables	227,750	451,000	678,750
Internal Balances	50,000	(50,000)	—
Due from State Government	250,000		250,000
Restricted Assets		509,000	509,000
Capital Assets (net)	12,024,000	10,040,000	22,064,000
Total Assets	$14,510,500	$11,050,000	$25,560,500
Liabilities			
Payables	$ 226,500	$ 593,000	$ 819,500
Long-term Liabilities			
Due within One Year	300,000		300,000
Due in More Than One Year	2,695,634	4,200,000	6,895,634
Total Liabilities	3,222,134	4,793,000	$ 8,015,134
Net Assets			
Invested in Capital Assets, Net of Related Debt	9,028,366	5,558,000	14,586,366
Unrestricted	1,805,500	199,000	2,004,500
Restricted for			
Debt Service	125,000	500,000	625,000
Other	329,500		329,500
Total Net Assets	$11,288,366	$ 6,257,000	$17,545,366

Reconciling the Statement of Net Assets with Governmental Fund Reporting

Fund balance for governmental activities (see Illustration 18-13)	**$ 2,241,000**
Capital assets used in governmental activities are not financial resources and are not reported in the funds ($12,024,000 less internal service fund assets of $420,000)	11,604,000
Internal service funds are used by management to charge the costs of certain activities to individual funds. The assets and liabilities of the internal service fund are included in the governmental activities in the statement of net assets. (Note: this line item includes capital assets.)	515,000
Some liabilities are not due in the current period and are not recognized in the funds ($40,000 and $36,000 accrued interest on the serial and term bonds)	(76,000)
Long-term liabilities (plus unamortized premium) are not due and payable in the current period and therefore are not reported in the funds.	(2,995,634)
Net assets in governmental activities (see Illustration 18-17)	$11,288,366

each fund's assets and liabilities with no overall government totals. Under the current format, governments are encouraged to present the statement that displays assets less liabilities equaling net assets, rather than the traditional balance sheet format. While permitted, no distinction between current and long-term is required under the proposal for government-wide assets and liabilities. However, if no distinction is made, the items should be listed in the order of liquidity. In Illustration 18-16, we show the "net asset format" with items listed in the order of liquidity rather than the classified version of the statement of net assets. If the classified format is used and there are liabilities with maturities longer than one year, the current portion should be listed separately from the amount due later than one year.

The statement of net assets is divided into two categories: the primary government and its discretely presented component units. The *primary government* columns include the governmental funds, the business-activities (proprietary) funds, and a total column.[15] *Component units* are governmental units that are legally independent of the reporting government, but within the reporting unit's control. Control means either appointing a majority of the unit's governing body members or being fiscally dependent (e.g., the budget is approved by the primary government). An example of a component unit is a school district that receives funding from the county. Because the school district is financially accountable to the county, it is considered a component unit. No component units are shown in Illustration 18-16.

At a minimum, assets, liabilities, and net assets should be disclosed for each of the following four categories:

A. Primary Government[16]
   1. Government activities
   2. Business-type activities
   3. Total primary government activities (total of 1 and 2)

B. Discretely Presented Component Units
   4. "Discretely presented" component units (discretely presented, as opposed to blended, means reporting the data in a separate column as if it were a separate fund).

Under previous guidelines, long-term debt was reported as one amount. Under the new rules, the current portion of long-term debt must be listed separately from the noncurrent portion. In addition, a footnote is required for the governmental, business-type, and component units activities showing the additions and reductions to the long-term liability account for the year, including the current portion.

Similar to the requirements for long-term debt, a footnote is required showing the additions and reductions to the capital asset account. The amount of depreciation charged to governmental activities is required. This information is disclosed for the government, business-type, and component units activities.

Net Assets Net assets are displayed in three components as follows:

1. *Invested in capital assets, net of related debt.* This component consists of capital assets including restricted capital assets, net of accumulated depreciation and reduced by the outstanding balances of any bonds, mortgages, notes, or other borrowings attributable to the acquisition, construction, or improvement of those assets.
2. *Restricted* (listed by major categories of restrictions such as capital projects, debt service, etc.). Net assets are reported as restricted when constraints placed on

[15] Fiduciary activities whose resources are not available to finance the government's programs should be excluded from the government-wide statements and should be reported only in the fund financial statements.

[16] Component units that meet the criteria for blending should be reported in the primary government columns (GASB Codification 2600.115).

net asset use are either: (a) externally imposed by creditors (such as through debt covenants), grantors, contributors, or laws and regulations of other governments, or (b) imposed by law. When permanent endowments or permanent fund principal amounts are included, "restricted net assets" should be displayed in two components—expendable and nonexpendable. Nonexpendable net assets are those that are required to be retained in perpetuity.

3. *Unrestricted.* Unrestricted net assets consist of net assets that do not meet the definition of *restricted* or *invested in capital assets, net of related debt.*

Infrastructure Asset Reporting Issues One of the more controversial rules of *GASB Statement No. 34* is that infrastructure assets such as roads, bridges, storm sewers, water systems, and so on are reported as assets in the governmental-wide statements at historical cost (or estimated historical cost at transition). In addition, governments are required to report depreciation on these assets.[17]

TEST YOUR KNOWLEDGE

NOTE: Solutions to ***Test Your Knowledge*** questions are found at the end of each chapter before the end-of-chapter questions.

Multiple Choice

1. In reconciling the fund balance for government activities to net assets in government activities (government-wide basis), which of the following items is *not* a reconciling item?
   a. Capital assets used in government activities
   b. Accrued interest on debt
   c. Long-term liabilities
   d. All of the above are reconciling items
   e. Two of the above are reconciling items.

Statement of Activities

The statement of activities presented in Illustration 18-17 is prepared on a government-wide basis and is presented using a *net cost* format. This format separates revenues into program revenues and general revenues. Then expenses are reduced by program revenues resulting in "net (expense) revenue." General revenues, extraordinary items and special items, and transfers are reported separately. ***Program revenues*** include three categories: charges for services; program-operating grants and contributions; and capital grants and contributions. (In the illustration only two of the three categories are used.) Charges for services include revenues attributable to a specific program because they result from exchange transactions, such as charges

[17] Governments may elect not to report depreciation expense for infrastructure assets if two conditions are met. First, a government must use an asset management system that contains up-to-date inventories of the assets, be able to assess the condition of the assets, and be able to estimate the amounts needed to preserve the network at a level established by the government. Second, the government must be able to document that the network of infrastructure assets is being preserved at a level established and disclosed by the government.

ILLUSTRATION 18-17

Model City
Statement of Activities—Government-wide
for the Year Ended December 31, 2008

		Program Revenues		Net (Expense) Revenue and Changes in Net Assets — Primary Government		
Functions/Programs	*Expenses*	*Charges for Services*	*Grants and Contributions*	*Governmental Activities*	*Business-type Activities*	*Total*
Primary Government						
Government Activities						
Public Safety	$ 426,612			$ (426,612)		$ (426,612)
General Government	317,210	$ 192,000	$1,000,000	874,790		874,790
Highways and Streets	140,332	94,000		(46,332)		(46,332)
Sanitation	76,745			(76,745)		(76,745)
Health	154,585			(154,585)		(154,585)
Cultural—recreation	201,963	15,000		(186,963)		(186,963)
Education	634,553		275,000	(359,553)		(359,553)
Interest on Long-term Debt	119,634			(119,634)		(119,634)
Total Governmental Activities	2,071,634	301,000	1,275,000	(495,634)		(495,634)
Business-type Activities						
Sewer	1,322,000	1,500,000			$ 178,000	178,000
Total Business-type Activities	1,322,000	1,500,000			178,000	178,000
Total Primary Government	$3,393,634	$1,801,000	$1,275,000	$ (495,634)	$ 178,000	$ (317,634)

	Governmental Activities	Business-type Activities	Total
General Revenues			
Taxes:			
Property taxes, levied for general purposes	$ 1,158,750		$ 1,158,750
Property taxes, levied for debt service	316,000		316,000
Interest and investment earnings	52,500		52,500
Special item—gain on sale of equipment	2,250		2,250
Transfers	150,000	(150,000)	—
Total general revenues, special items, and transfers	1,679,500	(150,000)	1,529,500
Change in Net Assets	1,183,866	28,000	1,211,866
Net assets—beginning (assumed)	10,104,500	6,229,000	16,333,500
Net assets—ending	$11,288,366	$6,257,000	$17,545,366

to customers. Licenses and permits would generally be reported as charges for services under program revenues since the users benefit directly from the services provided. In Illustration 18-17, the $170,500 of revenue from licenses and permits from Illustration 18-14 is included as charges for services: highways and streets ($94,000), cultural and recreation ($15,000), and general government ($61,500, along with an additional $130,500 from Illustration 18-14). "All" taxes are considered ***general revenue.*** In Illustration 18-17, columns are used to distinguish between governmental and business-type activities of the primary government. A total column for the primary government should be presented.[18]

[18] Discretely presented component units are shown in a separate column and not included in the totals for the primary government.

The statement of activities might actually change how governments do business, according to one expert, who claims that these net cost statements by departments and functions might give governments a lot of heartburn as the numbers for certain funds may look bad. Other funds, however, could look better. He gives the example of a police department being funded from an ad valorem tax collected for general purposes. Since the government specifically dedicates the revenue from the ad valorem tax for the police department, the net cost would no longer be as big a negative on the Statement of Activities since there would now be revenue directly associated with the function.[19]

MANAGEMENT'S DISCUSSION AND ANALYSIS (MD&A)

Management's Discussion and Analysis (MD&A) is an integral part of the annual reporting of a government entity, as required by *GASB Statement No. 34.* This discussion should provide an objective and easily readable analysis of the government's financial activities based on currently known facts, decisions, or conditions. It provides financial managers with the opportunity to present both a short-term and a long-term analysis of the government's activities. MD&A should discuss the current-year results in comparison with the prior year. This comparison should include a discussion of both the positive and the negative aspects of the current year changes. The focus of the MD&A is on the primary government (i.e., it should distinguish between the primary government and its component units). The MD&A requirements are general, rather than specific, to encourage financial managers to report effectively only the most relevant information. At a minimum, MD&A should include:

a. A brief discussion of the basic financial statements including interrelationships among the statements and significant differences in the information provided.

b. Condensed financial information derived from government-wide financial statements comparing the current year to the prior year.

c. An analysis of the government's overall financial position and results of operations to assist users in assessing whether financial position has improved or deteriorated as a result of the year's operations. The analysis should address both governmental and business-type activities as reported in the government-wide financial statements and the *reasons* for significant changes from the prior year.

d. An analysis of balances and transactions of individual funds. This analysis should address the reasons for significant changes in fund balances or fund net assets and whether restrictions, commitments, or other limitations significantly affect the availability of fund resources for future use.

e. An analysis of significant variations between original and final budget amounts and between final budget amounts and actual results for the general fund (or its equivalent).

f. A description of significant capital asset and long-term debt activity during the year, including a discussion of commitments made for capital expenditures, changes in credit ratings, and debt limitations that may affect the financing of planned facilities or services.

---

[19] *Practical Accountant,* Vol. 32, "New Look for Government Statements," by Howard Wolosky, August 1999, pp. 47–50.

g. A discussion by governments that use the modified approach to report some or all of their infrastructure assets including significant changes in the assessed condition of eligible infrastructure assets from previous condition assessments, how the current assessed condition compares with the condition level the government has established, and any significant differences from the estimated annual amount to maintain/preserve eligible infrastructure assets compared with the actual amounts spent during the current year.

h. A description of currently known facts, decisions, or conditions that are expected to have a significant effect on financial position (net assets) or results of operations (revenues, expenditures, and other changes in net assets).

SPECIAL ASSESSMENTS

Some capital improvements or services provided by a municipality are undertaken for the primary benefit of a particular property owner or groups of property owners rather than for the general public. In such cases, the costs of providing the capital improvements or services are often charged in whole or in part to the property owners who receive the benefit. In some cases, the municipality may share in the cost of an improvement in recognition of the public benefits that result from the project. Special assessments that are levied against the benefited property owners for services are referred to as ***service-type special assessments***. Special assessments that are levied against the benefited property owners for capital improvements are referred to as ***capital improvement special assessments***.

Examples of service-type special assessment projects include street lighting, street cleaning, and snow plowing. Although financing for the routine provision of such services usually comes from general revenues, when such services are extended or provided at more frequent intervals, special assessments are sometimes levied. In such cases only the affected property owners are charged for the additional services.

More frequently, special assessments are levied for capital improvement projects. Examples of such improvements include the paving or widening of residential streets or the construction of sidewalks or storm sewers. Although the affected property owners may be deemed the primary beneficiary of such projects, the projects often improve or add to the general fixed assets or infrastructure of the municipality as well. In some cases, such as the construction of water or sewer mains, such projects may provide capital assets that become an integral part of the government's enterprise activities.

Unlike service-type special assessment projects, capital improvement special assessment projects have two distinct and functionally different phases. The first phase consists of financing and constructing the project. Generally, this phase is completed over a period of two months to two years depending on the nature of the project.

The second phase consists of collecting the assessment principal and interest levied against the benefited properties and repaying the cost of financing the construction. Typically, capital improvement special assessment projects are financed by the issuance of long-term debt in the form of serial bonds, the principal and interest of which are repaid from the installment collection of special assessments. Thus, the collection of special assessment principal and interest and the repayment of the special assessment debt usually extend over a substantially longer period than the period it takes to complete the construction of the related project.

Reporting Service-type Special Assessments

Under *GASB Statements No. 6* and *No. 34,* transactions of a ***service-type special assessment*** are reported in the general fund, a special revenue fund, or an enterprise fund as best reflects the nature of the transactions. Service-type special assessments are recognized as revenue in the period the services are provided, regardless of when the assessment is billed or collected. Expenditures (or expenses) for which the assessments are levied are recognized on the same basis as other expenditures or expenses of the fund type used to account for the service assessment.

Reporting Capital Improvement Special Assessments

Where capital improvements are financed by special assessments, the transactions are recorded differently depending on whether the government is obligated in some way to assume the payment of related debt service in the event of default by property owners. The extent of the government's liability for debt related to a special assessment capital improvement can vary significantly. However, for purposes of financial reporting, a government is considered to be obligated in some manner for the repayment of special assessment debt unless (1) the government is prohibited by constitution, charter, statute, ordinance, or contract from assuming the debt in the event of default by the property owner, or (2) the government is not legally liable for assuming the debt and makes no statement, or gives no indication, that it will, or may, honor the debt in the event of default.

Where the government is obligated in some manner for the repayment of special assessment debt, all transactions related to capital improvements financed by special assessments are recorded like any other capital improvement and financing transactions. Transactions of the construction phase of the project are accounted for in a ***capital projects fund.*** Transactions of the *debt service phase* are accounted for in a ***debt service fund.*** The fixed assets constructed or acquired (other than those related to an enterprise fund) and the long-term debt are reported in the government-wide statement of net assets.

For the debt service transactions, such debt is reported in an ***agency fund*** rather than a debt service fund, to reflect the fact that the government's duties are limited to acting as an agent for the assessed property owners and the bondholders. The construction phase is still accounted for in a capital projects fund but the source of revenue is described as "contribution from property owners." The fixed assets constructed or acquired are recorded in the government-wide statement of net assets or an enterprise fund as appropriate. Recording this type of capital improvement special assessment project in this manner recognizes that the construction or acquisition is a governmental activity that results in the addition of a governmental asset but that the acquired asset is not financed by government debt.

To illustrate, assume that a municipality undertakes a street-widening project that will provide additional shop-front parking. Cash for the project will be provided by the proceeds of a \$10 million issue of 8% special assessment debt and \$2 million in general fund revenues. One-tenth of the debt plus interest is payable each July 1. A \$10 million 8% special assessment levy against the benefiting property owners will provide most of the funds to service the debt and retire the bonds. However, since special assessments will be due on June 1, the city will make a one-time payment out of general fund revenues of one month's interest on the entire special assessment debt on June 1 of the first year.

Financed by Bonds for Which Government Is Obligated in Some Manner			*Financed by Bonds for Which Government Is Not Obligated in Any Manner*		

Transactions

(1) $10 million in 8% special assessment serial bonds are issued and $2 million is transferred to the capital projects fund from the general fund:

Capital Projects Fund			*Capital Projects Fund*		
Cash	10,000,000		Cash	10,000,000	
Bond Issue Proceeds		10,000,000	Contributions from Property Owners		10,000,000
To record proceeds from bond issue.					

General Fund			*General Fund*		
Transfer to Capital Projects Fund	2,000,000		Same entry as on left		
Cash		2,000,000			

Capital Projects Fund			*Capital Projects Fund*		
Cash	2,000,000		Same entry as on left		
Transfer from General Fund		2,000,000			
To record transfer of funds from general fund to capital projects fund.					

(2) Construction is completed at a cost of $12 million:

Capital Projects Fund			*Capital Projects Fund*		
Expenditures	12,000,000		Same entry as on left		
Cash		12,000,000			
To record the cash outlay for capital projects.					

(3) The first installment of the special assessment levy is billed and collected (11 months' interest is included in the billing) and an amount equal to one month's interest is transferred to the debt service fund or an agency fund from general fund revenues:

Debt Service Fund					
Special Assessments Receivable	1,733,333		No entry		
Special Assessment Revenue		1,733,333			
To record billing of special assessment due June 1.					

General Fund			*General Fund*		
Transfer to Debt Service Fund	66,667		Expenditures	66,667	
Cash		66,667	Cash		66,667

Debt Service Fund			*Agency Fund*		
Cash	66,667		Cash	66,667	
Transfer from General Fund		66,667	Amount Held for Debt Service		66,667
Cash	1,733,333		Cash	1,733,333	
Special Assessments Receivable		1,733,333	Amount Held for Debt Service		1,733,333
To record cash collections from general fund revenues and from property owners.					

(4) Twelve months' interest and principal is paid on the special assessment bonds on July 1:

Debt Service Fund			*Agency Fund*		
Expenditure—Principal	1,000,000		Amount Held for Debt Service	1,800,000	
Expenditures—Interest	800,000		Cash		1,800,000
Cash		1,800,000			

Special assessment levies including interest are not recognized as revenue until the period in which payment is due from the assessed property owners. In particular, no revenue is recognized for unbilled but accrued interest on special assessments. Special assessment debt service expenditures for principal and interest are recognized in the period that the debt service payments are due. In particular, no expenditure is recognized for interest accrued, but not yet due, on special assessment debt. Nonrecognition of accrued interest receivable or payable on special assessments is based on the conclusion that the effect on the debt service fund balance would represent merely a timing difference rather than a true fund equity.

INTERFUND ACTIVITY

Interfund activity within and among the three fund categories (governmental, proprietary, and fiduciary) should be classified and reported as follows:

Interfund Activity

a. *Reciprocal interfund activity*—internal counterpart to exchange and exchange-like transactions. It includes:

1. *Interfund loans*—Interfund loans should be reported as interfund receivables in the lender fund and as an interfund payable in the borrower fund.
2. *Interfund services provided and used*—sales and purchases of goods and services between funds for a price approximating their external exchange value. Interfund services provided and used should be reported as revenues in seller funds and expenses or expenditures in the purchaser funds. Unpaid amounts should be reported as interfund receivables and payables in the fund balance sheet or the statement of net assets.

b. *Nonreciprocal interfund activity*—the internal counterpart to nonexchange transaction.

1. *Interfund transfers*—flows of assets without an equivalent flow of assets in return and without a requirement for repayment. In government funds, transfers should be reported as "other financing uses" in the funds and as "other financing sources" in the funds receiving the transfer. In proprietary funds, transfers should be reported after nonoperating revenues and expenses.
2. *Interfund reimbursements*—repayments *from the funds* responsible for the particular expenditure or expense *to the funds* that initially paid for them. Reimbursements should not be displayed in the financial statements.

Illustration of Reciprocal Interfund Activity—Interfund Loans

Assume that the general fund advances $4,000 as a temporary loan to a special revenue fund. Corresponding entries to record the advance are

General Fund		
Due from Special Revenue Fund	4,000	
Cash		4,000

Special Revenue Fund		
Cash	4,000	
Due to General Fund		4,000

Interfund Services Provided and Used

Interfund services provided and used are interfund transactions that would be treated as revenue, expense, or expenditures if they were entered into with organizations outside the governmental unit. Contributions in lieu of taxes from an enterprise fund to the general fund and internal service fund billings to government departments for services rendered are examples of interfund services provided and used. Interfund services provided and used are accounted for as revenue, expense, or expenditures of the funds involved. Accounting for interfund services provided and used in this manner is necessary for the determination of the operating results (net income) of proprietary funds.

To illustrate, assume that the internal service fund bills the Police Department for $3,000 for services rendered. The corresponding entries to record this billing are

Internal Service Fund		
Due from General Fund	3,000	
Revenue		3,000

General Fund		
Expenditures	3,000	
Due to Internal Service Fund		3,000

Illustration of Nonreciprocal Interfund Activity—Interfund Transfers

Some nonreciprocal interfund transfers represent nonrecurring transfers between funds. Examples include nonrecurring contributions from the general fund to proprietary funds, the return of part or all of such contributions to the general fund, and transfers of the residual balances of discontinued funds to the general fund or to debt service funds.

To illustrate, assume that an enterprise fund transfers $150,000 of excess resources to the general fund. Corresponding entries to record the transfer are

Enterprise Fund		
Transfer to General Fund	150,000	
Cash		150,000

General Fund

Cash	150,000	
Transfer from Enterprise Fund		150,000

Nonreciprocal transfers should be reported as other financing sources or uses in the governmental funds. Nonreciprocal transfers to or from proprietary funds should be reported after nonoperating revenues and expenses.

In other cases, nonreciprocal transfers consist of recurring transfers between funds for the purpose of shifting resources from the fund legally required to record the revenue to the fund legally required to expend the revenue. An example of this type of transfer is the annual transfer of revenue from an endowment trust fund to an expendable trust fund. To illustrate, the net effect of the entries to record the transfer of revenue from the Classics Acquisition Endowment Trust Fund of Model City to the Classics Acquisition Expendable Trust Fund may be summarized as follows.

Endowment Trust Fund

Transfer to Expendable Trust Fund	30,000	
Cash		30,000

Expendable Trust Fund

Cash	30,000	
Transfer from Endowment Trust Fund		30,000

As stated earlier, nonreciprocal transfers should be reported as other financing sources or uses in the governmental funds. Nonreciprocal transfers to or from proprietary funds should be reported after nonoperating revenues and expenses.

Interfund Reimbursements

Interfund reimbursements are transactions that involve the transfer of resources from one fund to another in order to reimburse the recipient fund for expenditures made by it that are properly expenditures of the reimbursing fund. The recipient fund should record the transaction as a credit to expenditures, and the reimbursing fund should record the transaction as a debit to expenditures.

For example, assume that the general fund performs services in the amount of $10,000 for a special revenue fund. The corresponding entries to record the reimbursement are

Special Revenue Fund

Expenditures	10,000	
Due to General Fund (or cash)		10,000

General Fund

Due from Special Revenue Fund (or cash)	10,000	
Expenditures		10,000

SUMMARY

1. *Identify the issues involved in developing standards for nonprofit organizations.* Currently both the GASB and the FASB are responsible for setting standards for nonprofit organizations. The GASB is involved in establishing standards for governments, while the FASB has been responsible since 1979 for setting standards for all other nonbusiness organizations. Because of the dual nature of standard setting, public universities and hospitals follow different rules from private universities and hospitals. Therefore, it is important to the users of financial statements to understand the differences between the standards of public and private organizations.
2. *Describe the broad categories of government fund entities.* Government entities are composed of a set of separate self-balancing funds. The eight categories of funds fall under three primary groups. **Government funds** include the general fund, special revenue funds, capital projects funds, debt service funds, and permanent funds. Government funds report on current period resources and focus on inflows, outflows, and unexpended resources. In addition, they are designed to determine compliance with legal provisions specifying how revenues are raised and resources spent. The funds in this group are organized by the types of activities each fund is designed to carry out. The second primary group includes the **proprietary funds**, which in turn include the enterprise funds and the internal service funds. These funds are used to account for the business-type activities of the government. Since these funds operate similarly to for-profit organizations, the accounting also parallels for-profit organizations. The statements issued by proprietary funds include cash flow statements, balance sheets, and accrual-based income statements. The last group includes **fiduciary funds**. These funds, which include trust and agency funds, account for assets held by the government for others, and these funds cannot be used to support the government's own programs.
3. *Distinguish between a general fund and a special revenue fund.* Special revenue funds are used to account for resources that are legally restricted for some specific expenditure (other than capital projects or debt service). If resources are unrestricted, then they will be accounted for in a general fund.
4. *Explain the use of a capital projects fund.* Capital projects funds are used to account for resources used to acquire permanent assets with long lives, such as buildings, streets and highways, and sewer systems. The purpose of this type of fund is to show that funds designated for capital projects are used for authorized purposes only and that any unexpended amounts are treated properly. Long-term assets acquired by proprietary funds are accounted for in the proprietary fund accounts.
5. *Describe the purpose of a debt service fund.* Governments issue two kinds of debt: general long-term debt that supports the activities of the government as a whole, and debt that is issued by a proprietary fund to support that fund's activities. The debt service fund accounts for the funds used to meet principal and interest payments for general long-term debt. The principal amounts of the general long-term debt are recorded in the government-wide statement of net assets. Therefore, payments of interest and principal are expenditures of the debt service fund. It should be noted that accrued interest is not recorded in the debt service fund (even though it is required on the government-wide statements).
6. *Explain the use of a permanent fund.* Permanent funds include nonexpendable trust funds. These are funds in which the principal must remain intact and the earnings either spent or retained also, as specified. The resources in these funds must be accounted for according to law or trust provisions.
7. *Distinguish proprietary funds from government funds.* Proprietary funds account for the activities of governments that are similar to for-profit enterprises. For example, cities often provide water to the public and recover all or most of the cost through charges to the public. These funds are accounted for using the accrual basis of accounting, and all assets (including fixed assets) and liabilities (including long-term debt) are accounted for. The cash flow statement is prepared using the direct format, and accrual-based revenues and expenses are reported on the income statement. Government funds operate using a flow of financial resources concept where each year is treated as a distinct event, and the important measurements are the current period's sources and uses of funds.

8. *Describe where capital assets and long-term obligations are reported in government financial statements.* Fixed assets and long-term obligations are not reported for governmental activities. Instead, these items are reported on the government-wide Statement of Net Assets and for proprietary funds. In addition, schedules of capital assets showing both cost and accumulated depreciation are required to be disclosed. Similarly, a schedule of long-term obligations highlighting the additions and reductions in debt is required. In addition, accrued interest is reported on the Statement of Net Assets.

9. *Describe the changes in reporting requirements under GASB Statement No. 34.* Two additional statements are the statement of net assets and the statement of activities, both prepared on a government-wide basis using accrual accounting. Fund-based statements are still required, but only major funds are required to be shown separately (minor funds can be combined). Additional statements reconciling the differences between the government-wide statement and the fund statements are required. In addition, disclosures relating to capital assets and long-term liabilities are added. Proprietary fund reports must include a direct-based statement of cash flows. Also, net assets are displayed by three categories: invested in capital assets, net of related debt; restricted; and unrestricted. Another important change is that infrastructure assets (i.e., roads, bridges, etc.) are reported on the government-wide basis.

10. *Explain the benefits of government-wide statements.* The new government-wide statements help users assess the extent to which the government has invested in capital assets. Also, users can assess whether the public paid for services they received during the year or if the costs are shifted to other periods. The government-wide statement of activities focuses on the net cost of each of the government's functions. The expenses of the individual functions are compared to the revenues generated directly by that function. This helps users assess whether each program provides a benefit or a burden to the public.

11. *Describe the types of interfund activities.* Reciprocal interfund activity is similar to exchanges or exchange-like transactions. It includes interfund loans and interfund services provided and used. Interfund loans should be reported as interfund receivables in the lender fund and as an interfund payable in the borrower fund. Interfund services provided and used are sales or purchases of goods and services between funds for a price approximating their external exchange value. Interfund services provided and used should be reported as revenues in the seller funds and expenses or expenditures in the purchaser funds. Unpaid amounts should be reported as interfund receivables and payables in the fund balance sheet or the statement of net assets.

Nonreciprocal interfund activity is similar to nonexchange transactions. This includes interfund transfers (e.g., outflows of assets without an equivalent inflow of assets in return and without a requirement for repayment) and interfund reimbursements (repayments from the funds responsible for a particular expenditure or expense to the funds that initially paid for them). In government funds, interfund transfers should be reported as "other financing uses" in the funds initiating the transfer and as "other financing sources" in the funds receiving the transfer. In proprietary funds, interfund transfers should be reported after no operating revenues and expenses. Reimbursements should not be displayed in the financial statements.

TEST YOUR KNOWLEDGE SOLUTIONS

18.1 1. a. T

b. T

c. F Depreciation expense is reported on the government-wide statement of net activities.

18.2 1. d

APPENDIX A

Government-Wide Financial Statements
City of Atlanta

City of Atlanta, Georgia Statement of Activities for the Year Ended December 31, 2004 (in thousands)

		Program Revenues		
Functions/Programs	*Expenses*	*Charges for Services*	*Operating Grants and Contributions*	*Capital Grants and Contributions*
Primary Government				
Governmental Activities:				
General Government	$ 104,383	$ 77,014	$43,037	$ —
Police	134,950	19,135	—	—
Fire	63,714	416	1	—
Corrections	35,107	8,068	17	—
Public Works	68,675	3,876	164	—
Parks, Recreation, and Cultural Affairs	32,739	1,622	4,975	—
Nondepartmental	62,691	—	—	—
Interest on Long-term Debt	22,101	—	—	—
Total Governmental Activities	524,360	110,131	48,194	—
Business-type Activities				
Watershed Management	228,554	252,007	—	—
Aviation	303,703	273,575	—	229,610
Sanitation	47,536	47,219	—	—
Parks and Recreational Facilities	969	539	—	—
Underground Atlanta	10,895	2,651	—	—
Civic Center	1,427	1,347	—	—
Total Business-type activities	593,085	577,338	—	229,610
Total Primary Government	$1,117,445	$687,469	$48,194	$229,610
Component Units-	$ 67,003	$ 42,435	$ 6,044	$ 1,444

General revenues:
Taxes:
Property taxes levied for general purposes
Property taxes levied for debt service
Local option sales tax
Public utility franchise taxes
Business taxes
Federal and state aid not restricted for specific purposes
Investment income
Other:
Total general revenues
Transfers
Total general revenues and transfers
Change in net assets
Net assets—beginning of year, as previously stated
Correction of prior year errors
Net assets—beginning of year, as restated
NET ASSETS—END OF YEAR

Net (Expenses) Revenues and Changes in Net Assets			
Government Activities	*Business-type Activities*	*TOTALS*	*Component Units*
$ 15,668		$ 15,668	
(115,815)		(115,815)	
(63,297)		(63,297)	
(27,022)		(27,022)	
(64,635)		(64,635)	
(26,142)		(26,142)	
(62,691)		(62,691)	
(22,101)		(22,101)	
(366,035)		(366,035)	
	$ 23,453	23,453	
	199,482	199,482	
	(317)	(317)	
	(430)	(430)	
	(8,244)	(8,244)	
	(80)	(80)	
	213,863	213,863	
(366,035)	213,863	(152,172)	
			$(17,080)
198,875	20,449	219,324	—
—	—	—	—
83,518	—	83,518	6,867
46,809	—	46,809	—
38,262	—	38,262	—
542	—	542	—
5,022	44,452	49,474	361
9,657	—	9,657	3,832
382,685	64,901	447,586	11,060
4,208	(4,208)	—	—
386,893	60,693	447,586	11,060
20,858	274,556	295,415	(6,020)
870,639	3,392,989	4,263,628	68,351
(130,682)	17,654	(113,008)	—
739,977	3,410,643	4,150,620	68,351
$760,835	$3,685,199	$4,446,035	$62,331

City of Atlanta, Georgia Statement of Net Assets, December 31, 2004 (in thousands)

	Governmental Activities	*Business-type Activities*	*Total*	*Component Units*
Assets				
Current Assets:				
Cash and cash equivalents	$ 29,706	$ 12,693	$ 42,399	$ 7,015
Restricted cash	—	285,250	285,250	3,675
Investments in pooled investment fund	67,560	592,948	660,508	—
Investments	210,520	—	210,520	7,094
Receivables (net of allowances for uncollectibles)	60,321	60,410	120,731	14,558
Due from other governments	7,848	14,041	21,889	723
Internal balances	103,154	(103,154)	—	—
Inventories	—	12,720	12,720	279
Other restricted assets	—	35,544	35,544	—
Prepaid expenses and other assets	—	2,011	2,011	486
Total current assets	479,109	912,463	1,391,572	33,830
Noncurrent assets:				
Restricted cash	—	—	—	16,721
Restricted investments	—	3,102,739	3,102,739	21,814
Capital assets:				
Land and construction in progress	90,440	2,606,689	2,697,129	30,211
Other capital assets, net of depreciation	325,604	2,734,467	3,060,071	247,119
Infrastructure, net of depreciation	534,469	—	534,469	—
Investments in joint venture	—	73,079	73,079	—
Investments in escrow	26,330	—	26,330	—
Other assets	—	218,731	218,731	7,183
Long-term receivable	—	—	—	9,526
Total noncurrent assets	976,843	8,735,705	9,712,548	332,574
Total Assets	1,455,952	9,648,168	11,104,120	366,404
Liabilities				
Current liabilities				
Accounts payable	46,296	44,977	91,273	8,724
Accrued expenses, vacations, and compensatory pay	30,695	19,638	50,333	40
Claims payable	—	9,600	9,600	—
Contract retentions	368	1,952	2,320	—
Due to other governments	80	450	530	—
Other liabilities	—	3,263	3,263	7,916
Deferred revenues	372	6,635	7,007	682
Liabilities payable from restricted assets	—	168,015	168,015	2,634
Current portion of long-term debt	24,663	67,258	91,921	26,830
Current portion of workers' compensation	3,573	—	3,573	—
Current portion of capital leases	—	2,756	2,756	—
Total current liabilities	106,047	324,544	430,591	46,826
Noncurrent liabilities				
Noncurrent portion of long-term debt	557,409	5,524,767	6,082,176	257,247
Noncurrent portion of capital leases	—	22,760	22,760	—
Other long-term liabilities	31,661	90,898	122,559	—
Total Liabilities	695,117	5,962,969	6,658,086	304,073
Net Assets				
Invested in capital assets, net of related debt	368,441	2,269,963	2,638,404	31,719
Restricted for:				
Debt service	37,556	651,610	689,166	—
Programs	69,511	—	69,511	20,972
Capital projects	139,431	—	139,431	—
Unrestricted	145,896	763,626	909,522	9,640
Total Net Assets	$ 760,835	$3,685,199	$ 4,446,033	$ 62,331

City of Atlanta, Georgia
Reconciliation of Governmental Fund Balance Sheet to the Government-wide Statement of Net Assets
December 31, 2004
(in thousands)

Total fund balances		$422,178
Amounts reported for governmental activities in the Statement of Net Assets are different because:		
Accounts receivable used in governmental activities represents amounts that are not financial resources and, therefore, are not reported in the above funds:		
Taxes receivable	$ 14,214	
Accounts receivable	5,445	
Allowance for uncollectible receivables	(5,112)	14,547
Other liabilities are not recognized as current year revenues and, therefore, are classified as deferred in the above funds		5,948
Capital assets used in governmental activities are not financial resources and, therefore, are not reported in the above funds:		
Land and construction in progress	90,440	
Cost of capital assets	2,292,457	
Less: Accumulated depreciation	(1,432,384)	950,513
Internal service funds are used by management to charge the costs of automotive services and management information systems activities as well as transactions related to the provision of life, accident, and medical insurance benefits through outside insurance companies for permanent employees and retirees. The assets and liabilities of the internal service funds are included in governmental activities in the statement of net assets.		
Net assets for internal service fund	4,301	4,301
Long-term liabilities, including capital leases, are not due and payable in the current period and therefore are not reported in the above funds.		
General obligation and annual bonds	(290,365)	
SWMA revenue refunding bonds	(23,965)	
Limited obligation bonds	(90,935)	
Section 108 loans	(11,250)	
Certificates of participation	(165,557)	
Vacation pay	(21,626)	
General claims payable	(15,699)	
Workers' compensation	(17,255)	(636,652)
NET ASSETS OF GOVERNMENTAL ACTIVITIES		$760,835

QUESTIONS

(The letter A indicated here for a question, exercise, or problem refers to the appendix.)

LO2 **1.** Eleven funds are recommended to account for the various activities and resources of a governmental unit. Identify these funds by title and type and briefly state (in two sentences or less) the basic purpose of each fund.

LO10 **2.** Why are governments required to prepare financial statements on a government-wide basis using full accrual accounting?

LO7 **3.** What is the difference between a governmental fund and a proprietary fund?

LO2 **4.** Are fiduciary funds governmental funds or proprietary funds? Explain.

LO11 **5.** A disbursement by the general fund to another fund may be recorded as a receivable, an expenditure, or a fund transfer. Explain the circumstances that would result in each of these different treatments.

LO2 LO8 **6.** In what funds would you expect bonds payable to be included?

LO2 LO8 **7.** In what funds might property and other nonfinancial resources be recorded?

LO3 LO4 **8.** Why are budgeted revenues and expenditures formally recorded in the records of the general fund but not in the records of a capital projects fund?

LO4 **9.** Are all major capital facilities acquisitions accounted for in a capital projects fund? Explain.

LO5 **10.** What exception to the normal expenditure recognition criteria is associated with debt service funds and what is the justification for this exception?

LO11 **11.** Identify and describe four types of interfund activities.

LO2 **12.** The following funds and account groups are recommended for use in accounting for state and municipal governmental financial operations:

A. General Fund.

B. Special Revenue Fund.

C. Debt Service Fund.

D. Capital Projects Fund.

E. Agency Fund.

F. Enterprise Fund.

G. Internal Service Fund.

H. Trust Fund.

I. Government-wide Statement of Activities.

J. Government-wide Statement of Net Assets.

Identify, by the letters given above, the funds and account groups in which each of the account titles below might properly appear.

(1) Bonds Payable.

(2) Reserve for Encumbrances.

(3) Equipment.

(4) Appropriations.

(5) Estimated Revenue.

(6) Property Taxes Receivable.

(7) Construction Work in Progress.

(8) Accumulated Depreciation.

(9) Depreciation Expense.

(10) Required Earnings.

LO9 **13.** Describe some of the major reconciling items between a government fund and the government-wide financial statements.

Business Ethics

GASB 45 requires that the expected future costs of retiree health costs be recognized in the current period. Prior to this, governments used a pay-as-you-go plan in which only the current year's actual payments affected the financial statements.

Suppose you are working for a government prior to the issuance of *GASB 45*. As part of the collective bargaining agreement, the government offers employees increased health benefits.

1. Prior to the issuance of *GASB 45*, what would be the impact on the government's financial statements?
2. Under *GASB 45*, what are the financial statement implications?
3. Why might the current governmental leaders agree to offer such a benefit?
4. What are the ethical issues involved in this decision?

ANALYZING FINANCIAL STATEMENTS (AFS)

AFS 18-1 Type of Government Fund LO5

Part A: The following departments of activities are recorded in the City of Atlanta's Comprehensive Annual Financial Report in the appendix to this chapter. Indicate the type of fund that most likely would be used for each department by placing a G for governmental, P for proprietary, or F for fiduciary by each department.

1. __________ Department of Aviation (Airport Authority)
2. __________ Police and Fire Departments
3. __________ Water and Wastewater System
4. __________ Agency Funds
5. __________ Sanitation
6. __________ Public Works
7. __________ Pension and Retirement Trust Funds
8. __________ Internal Service (e.g., Information Technology)
9. __________ Payment of General Obligation Debt

Part B: What is the main factor that causes some of the above departments to be classified in the proprietary fund?

AFS 18-2 Statement of Net Assets

Examine the financial statements for the City of Atlanta in the appendix to this chapter.

1. The balance in unrestricted net assets can be positive or negative. A negative balance would indicate that the government owes more than it owns. What is the balance in unrestricted net assets for the governmental activities?
2. Does the balance in the unrestricted net assets indicate that the city has cash available to spend? Examine the amount of cash and cash equivalents on the statement of net assets. Does the city have enough cash to spend? If not, what would the city need to do to have cash available?
3. Net assets are considered restricted if their use is constrained for a specific purpose. What is the largest purpose listed for restricted net assets?

AFS 18-3 Reconciling the Governmental Fund Balance with the Government-Wide Statement of Net Assets

Examine the appendixes in both Chapter 17 and this chapter (specifically the reconciliation between the Governmental Fund Balance Sheet and the Government-wide Statement of Net Assets.

1. What are the top two categories of reconciling differences between the two statements? Is this to be expected? Why or why not?
2. Discuss one of the other reconciling items. Why did the item appear in one, but not the other?

AFS 18-4 Statement of Activities

Examine the Statement of Activities in the appendix to this chapter.

1. For each of the six governmental activities listed (from general government to Parks, Recreation, and Cultural Activities), did the program revenue exceed program expenses? List the excess or deficit for each activity.
2. For each of the six business-type activities listed (from Watershed Management to Civic Center), did the program revenue exceed program expenses? List the excess or deficit for each activity.

3. For the total primary government, did the City of Atlanta have an excess or a deficit before considering general revenues? After considering general revenues, did net assets increase or decrease? List the amount of the change.

EXERCISES

EXERCISE 18-1 **Identify the Fund** LO2

The following transactions take place:

1. A cement mixer was purchased with resources of the general fund.
2. A contract was signed for the construction of a new civic center.
3. Bonds were issued to finance the construction of the new civic center.
4. Construction of the civic center was completed.

Required:

Indicate the name of the fund(s) in which each of the transactions or events should be recorded.

EXERCISE 18-2 **Identify the Fund** LO2

The following transactions take place:

1. A commitment was made to transfer general revenues to the entity in charge of providing transportation for all government agencies.
2. Construction bonds were issued at a premium. The premium is to be included in funds accumulated to retire the debt.
3. Police salaries were paid.
4. Interest and principal were paid on general obligation serial bonds.

Required:

Indicate the name of the fund(s) in which each of the transactions or events should be recorded.

EXERCISE 18-3 **Identify the Interfund Activity** LO11

The following events take place:

1. The Special Revenue Fund transfers $8,000 to the Internal Service Fund as a temporary loan.
2. The Internal Service Fund bills the Special Revenue Fund $20,000 for services performed.
3. Interest payments in the amount of $14,000 that are the responsibility of the Debt Service Fund are paid by the General Fund.
4. The unexpended balance of the Capital Projects Fund, which is $65,000, is transferred to the General Fund.
5. Current expendable revenues of the Trust Fund in the amount of $35,000 are transferred to the Special Revenue Fund.
6. The General Fund transfers $100,000 to start an Internal Service Fund.

Required:

A. Identify the interfund activity as a loan, services provided and used, interfund transfer, or interfund reimbursement and prepare entries in general journal form to record the transactions on the records of the funds involved.
B. Why is it important to distinguish residual equity transfers from operating transfers?

EXERCISE 18-4 **Journal Entries** LO2 LO8

The following events take place:

1. Hector Madras died and left 100 acres of undeveloped land to the city for a future park. He acquired the land at $100 an acre, but at the date of his death the land was appraised at $8,000 an acre.
2. The city authorized the transfer of $100,000 of general revenues and the issuance of $1,000,000 in general obligation bonds to construct improvements on the donated land. The bonds were sold at par.
3. The improvements were completed at a cost of $1,100,000, and the operation of the park was turned over to the City Parks Department.

Required:

Prepare entries in general journal form to record these transactions in the proper fund(s). Designate the fund in which each transaction is recorded. If the transaction did not result in a journal entry to a government fund, record the journal entry needed to reflect the information in the government-wide Statement of Net Assets.

EXERCISE 18-5 **Journal Entries** LO2 LO8

The following transactions take place:

1. The General Fund repaid the Special Revenue Fund a loan of $10,000 plus $900 in interest on the loan.
2. On January 1, the city issued 9% general obligation bonds with a face value of $2,000,000 payable in 10 years to finance the construction of city offices. Total proceeds were $2,300,000.
3. On December 20, construction was completed and occupancy taken of the city offices. The full cost of $1,960,000 was paid to the contractor, and appropriate closing entries were made with regard to the project.

Required:

Prepare entries in general journal form to record these transactions in the proper fund(s). Designate the fund in which each entry is recorded.

EXERCISE 18-6 **Journal Entries** LO5

On January 1, 2008, Allentown issued $800,000 of 9% serial bonds at par. Semiannual interest is payable on January 1 and July 1 and principal of $80,000 matures each January 1 starting in 2009. The debt will be serviced through a special tax levy designed especially for this purpose. Therefore, transfers will be provided as needed from the Special Revenue Fund.

The following transactions occurred relating to the Debt Service Fund.

2008	
June 29	A transfer of $36,000 was received from the Special Revenue Fund.
July 1	The semiannual interest payment was made.
Dec. 18	A Special Revenue Fund transfer of $20,000 was received.
2009	
Jan. 1	A payment on bond principal and semiannual interest was made.
2019	
Jan. 2	Accumulations in the Debt Service Fund amounted to $55,000 in investments and $40,000 in cash. The investments were liquidated at face value and the final interest and principal payment was made.
Jan. 4	Having served its purpose, the Debt Service Fund's remaining assets were transferred to the Special Revenue Fund.

Required:

Prepare the journal entries necessary to record the foregoing transactions.

EXERCISE 18-7 **Multiple Choice** LO2 LO8

Select the best answer for each of the following:

1. The City of Apache should use a Capital Projects Fund to account for
   - (a) Structures and improvements constructed with the proceeds of a special assessment.
   - (b) Special Revenue funds set aside to acquire land for city parks.
   - (c) Construction in progress on the city-owned electric utility plant, financed by an issue of revenue bonds.
   - (d) Assets to be used to retire bonds issued to finance an addition to the City Hall.
2. Activities of a central print shop offering printing services at cost to various city departments should be accounted for in
   - (a) The General Fund.
   - (b) An Internal Service Fund.
   - (c) A Special Revenue Fund.
   - (d) An Agency Fund.
3. Adams County collects property taxes for the benefit of the state government and the local school districts and periodically remits collections to these units. These activities should be accounted for in
   - (a) An Agency Fund.
   - (b) The General Fund.
   - (c) An Internal Service Fund.
   - (d) A Special Revenue Fund.
4. In order to provide for the retirement of general obligation bonds, the City of Globe invests a portion of its receipts from general property taxes in marketable securities. This investment activity should be accounted for in
   - (a) A Capital Projects Fund.
   - (b) A Debt Service Fund.
   - (c) A Trust Fund.
   - (d) The General Fund.
5. The transactions of a municipal police retirement system should be recorded in
   - (a) The General Fund.
   - (b) A Special Revenue Fund.
   - (c) A Trust Fund.
   - (d) An Internal Service Fund.

(*AICPA adapted*)

EXERCISE 18-8 **Multiple Choice** LO2 LO8

Select the best answer for each of the following:

1. The activities of a municipal golf course that receives three-fourths of its total revenue from a special tax levy should be accounted for in
   - (a) An Enterprise Fund.
   - (b) The General Fund.
   - (c) A Trust Fund.
   - (d) A Special Revenue Fund.
2. Equipment in general governmental service that had been constructed 10 years before with resources of a Capital Projects Fund was sold. The receipts were accounted for as unrestricted revenue. Entries are necessary in the
   - (a) General Fund and Capital Projects Fund.
   - (b) General Fund.

(c) General Fund, Capital Projects Fund, and Enterprise Fund.

(d) General Fund, Capital Projects Fund, and Debt Service Fund.

3. An account for expenditures does not appear in which fund?

   (a) Capital Projects.

   (b) Enterprise.

   (c) General.

   (d) Special Revenue.

4. Part of the general obligation bond proceeds from a new issuance was used to pay for the cost of a new City Hall as soon as construction was completed. The remainder of the proceeds was transferred to repay the debt. Entries are needed to record these transactions in the

   (a) General Fund and Proprietary Fund.

   (b) General Fund, Agency Fund, and Debt Service Fund.

   (c) Trust Fund and Debt Service Fund.

   (d) Debt Service Fund, Capital Projects Fund.

5. Cash secured from property tax revenue was transferred for the eventual payment of principal and interest on general obligation bonds. The bonds had been issued when land was acquired several years ago for a city park. Upon the transfer, an entry would be made in which of the following?

   (a) Debt Service Fund.

   (b) Enterprise Fund.

   (c) Agency Fund.

   (d) General Fund.

(*AICPA adapted*)

EXERCISE 18-9 **Multiple Choice** LO2 LO8

Select the best answer for each of the following:

1. Premiums received on general obligation bonds are generally transferred to what fund or group of accounts?

   (a) Debt Service.

   (b) General.

   (c) Special Revenue.

2. Of the items listed below, those most likely to have parallel accounting procedures, account titles, and financial statements are

   (a) Special Revenue Funds and Internal Service Funds.

   (b) Internal Service Funds and Debt Service Funds.

   (c) The General Fund and Special Revenue Funds.

3. Recreational facilities run by a governmental unit and financed on a user-charge basis would be accounted for in which fund?

   (a) General.

   (b) Trust.

   (c) Enterprise.

   (d) Capital Projects.

4. Taylor City should record depreciation as an expense in its

   (a) Enterprise Fund and Internal Service Fund.

   (b) Internal Service Fund and the General Fund.

(c) General Fund and Enterprise Fund.

(d) Enterprise Fund and Capital Projects Fund.

5. A performance budget relates a governmental unit's expenditures to

(a) Objects of Expenditure.

(b) Expenditures of the preceding fiscal year.

(c) Individual months within the fiscal year.

(d) Activities and programs.

(*AICPA adapted*)

EXERCISE 18-10 **Identify the Fund** LO2 LO8

Write the name of the fund(s) in which each of the following transactions or events would be recorded.

1. Bonds, the proceeds of which were to be used for the construction of a new City Hall, were issued.
2. A sum of money was appropriated, to be advanced from monies on hand, to finance the establishment of a City Garage for servicing city-owned transportation equipment.
3. A contribution was received from a private source. The use of the income earned on the investment of this sum of money was specifically designated by the donor.
4. Proceeds received from a bond issue were used for the purchase of the privately owned water utility in the city.
5. Property taxes designated to be set aside for the eventual retirement of the City Hall building bonds were collected.
6. Real estate and personal property taxes, which had not been assessed or levied for any specific purpose, were collected.
7. Payment was made to the contractor for progress made in the construction of the new City Hall.
8. Interest was paid on the bonds issued for the purchase of the water utility.
9. Bonds, the proceeds of which are to be used to pay for the improvement of streets in the residential district, were issued. The debt is to be serviced by assessments on the property benefited. The government is obligated to the bondholders to assure the timely payment of principal and interest on the debt.
10. Salaries of personnel in the office of the mayor were paid.
11. Interest was paid on the City Hall building bonds.
12. Installment payments were received from the property owners assessed for the street improvement project.
13. Interest was paid on bonds issued for the payment of the improvement of streets in the residential district.
14. Interest was received on the investment of moneys set aside for the retirement of the City Hall building bonds.
15. Sums of money were received from employees by payroll deductions to be used for the purchase of United States government bonds for those employees individually.
16. City motor vehicle license fees, to be used for general street expenditures, were collected.
17. Materials to be used for the general repair of the streets were purchased.
18. The City Garage was reimbursed for services on the equipment of the fire and police departments.
19. Excess funds were transferred from the water utility to the General Fund.

(*AICPA adapted*)

EXERCISE 18-11 **Capital Projects Fund—Journal Entries** LO4

On June 1, 2008, the City of Cape May authorized the construction of a police station at an expected cost of $250,000. Financing will be provided through transfers from a Special Revenue Fund.

The following transactions occurred during the fiscal year beginning June 1, 2008, relating to the Capital Project Fund.

1. The $250,000 receivable from the Special Revenue Fund was recorded.
2. The Special Revenue Fund transferred $125,000 to the Capital Project Fund to begin construction on the police station.
3. The Capital Project Fund invested the transfer of monies in a six-month certificate, at 5%.
4. A contract in the amount of $250,000 was let to the lowest bidder.
5. Architect and legal fees in the amount of $3,125 were approved for payment. There was no encumbrance for these expenditures.
6. Contract billings in the amount of $250,000 were approved for payment on the completion of the police station and the encumbrance was removed.
7. The six-month certificate was redeemed at maturity with interest revenue.
8. The Special Revenue Fund transferred the final amount of $125,000 to the Capital Projects Fund.
9. All liabilities except for the retention of 5% of the contract price were paid.
10. All requirements and obligations were completed; the final payment of the contract price was made and all nominal accounts were closed.

Required:

Prepare the journal entries necessary in the Capital Projects Fund to record the transactions and events described above.

EXERCISE 18-12 **Capital Projects Fund—Journal Entries** LO4

The town of Aberdeen authorized a fire station to be built at an estimated cost of $150,000. On January 1, 2008, 6% bonds with a par value of $150,000 were authorized and issued. Any difference between the par value of the bonds and the proceeds from their sale is transferred to the Debt Service Fund.

The following transactions relating to the Capital Project Fund occurred during 2008.

1. Encumbrances were recorded on signing contracts in the amount of $150,000.
2. Proceeds from the bond issue were received in the amount of $155,000.
3. The premium on the bond issue was transferred to the Debt Service Fund.
4. Contract billings in the amount of $150,000 were approved for payment on the completion of the fire station.
5. The contractor was paid except for retention of 5% of the contract price.
6. The final contract price was paid on the completion of the requirements and obligations of the contract. The nominal accounts were closed.

Required:

Prepare the journal entries necessary in the Capital Projects Fund to record the transactions and events described above.

EXERCISE 18-13 **Determining a Government's Major Funds** LO2

Required:

Using Illustrations 18-9, 18-10, 18-13, and 18-14, determine which of Model City's funds qualify as major funds using the percentage cutoffs. Calculate aggregate amounts for all other nonmajor funds, and indicate how they would be presented.

EXERCISE 18-14 Determining Amounts to Report for Long-Term Liabilities LO5

On January 1, 2008, Metropolis City issued a 7%, 5-year, $100,000 general obligation bond for $96,007. The bond pays interest annually (on December 31) and was issued to yield 8%. The bond was issued in the capital projects fund, and the proceeds are to be used to build a giant ball that will drop twenty stories on New Year's Eve. No construction has occurred. A debt service fund was created to meet the interest and principal payments. The city prepares financial statements on December 31 of each year.

Required:

Determine how the above information will be reflected on each of the following statements for the year 2008.

1. The governmental funds' statement of revenue, expenditures, and changes in fund balances. List the governmental fund and then list the dollar amount within the appropriate heading on the statement (such as Revenues, Expenditures, or Other Financing Sources (Uses)).
2. The government-wide statement of net assets.
3. The government-wide statement of activities.

EXERCISE 18-15 Determining Amounts to Report for Capital Assets LO4

The following schedule of capital assets was prepared for Capital City.

Government Activities	*Beginning Balance*	*Additions*	*Retirements*	*Ending Balance*
Total Capital Assets (gross)	$500,000	100,000	(75,000)	$525,000
Less: Accumulated Depreciation	(200,000)	(30,000)	25,000	(205,000)
Net Capital Assets	$300,000	70,000	(50,000)	$320,000

All capital acquisitions were made in a capital projects fund (and paid for with cash). An asset was sold by the general fund for $65,000 cash.

Required:

Determine how the above information will be reflected on each of the following statements for the year 2008.

1. The governmental funds' statement of revenue, expenditures, and changes in fund balances. List the governmental fund and then list the dollar amount within the appropriate heading on the statement (such as Revenues, Expenditures, or Other Financing Sources (Uses)).
2. The government-wide statement of net assets.
3. The government-wide statement of activities.

EXERCISE 18-16 Reconciliation Schedule—Statement of Activities LO9

The following information is available about items that differ between the governmental funds and the government-wide statements. Assume that there are no internal service funds. The schedule of capital assets prepared for the year ended December 31, 2008, includes the following items:

Government Activities	*Beginning Balance*	*Additions*	*Retirements*	*Ending Balance*
Total Capital Assets (at gross)	$700,000	$50,000	$(25,000)	$725,000
Less: Accumulated Depreciation	(170,000)	(30,000)	17,500	(182,500)
Net Capital Assets	$530,000	$20,000	$ (7,500)	$542,500

The bond was issued at the beginning of the year, and the following amortization schedule is available.

Date	*Interest Expense*	*Cash Paid*	*Premium Amortization*	*Bond Balance*
1/1/2008				$104,213
12/31/2008	6,253	7,000	747	$103,466

The net change in fund balances—total governmental funds was $1,100,000.

Required:

Prepare the reconciliation of the statement of revenues, expenditures, and changes in fund balances to the statement of activities on a government-wide basis for the year ended December 31, 2008.

EXERCISE 18-17 Reconciliation Schedule—Statement of Net Assets LO9

The following information was available about items that differed between the governmental funds and the government-wide statements. Assume that there are no internal service funds. The schedule of capital assets prepared for the year ended December 31, 2008, included the following items:

Government Activities	*Beginning Balance*	*Additions*	*Retirements*	*Ending Balance*
Total Capital Assets (at gross)	$800,000	$60,000	$(30,000)	$830,000
Less: Accumulated Depreciation	(200,000)	(40,000)	22,500	(217,500)
Net Capital Assets	$600,000	$20,000	$ (7,500)	$612,500

The bond was issued at the beginning of the year and the following amortization schedule is available:

Date	*Interest Expense*	*Cash Paid*	*Premium Amortization*	*Balance*
1/1/2008				$104,213
12/31/2008	$6,253	$7,000	$747	$103,466

The total fund balances for governmental activities was $3,125,000 at the end of the year.

Required:

Prepare the reconciliation of the governmental fund balances to the net assets reported for governmental activities on the Statement of Net Assets as of December 31, 2008.

PROBLEMS

PROBLEM 18-1 Debt Service Fund LO5

On January 1, 2008, the City of Cape May authorized and issued $200,000 of 5%, three-year term bonds. Interest is payable annually on December 31. A debt service fund is established to accumulate the necessary resources to pay the annual interest on the bonds and to redeem the bonds when they mature. The required annual addition for principal and interest will be transferred annually to the debt service fund from the general fund. It is assumed that amounts received by the debt service fund for the payment of principal can be invested at an annual return of 8%.

Required:

A. Prepare a schedule to calculate the annual required additions and annual required earnings to repay the principal on the bonds assuming that the first installment for principal and interest is transferred to the debt service fund from the general fund on December 30, 2008.

B. Prepare the entries to be recorded by the debt service fund as follows:

(1) The 2009 budget entry.

(2) The entry to record the annual transfer from the general fund.

(3) The entry to record the annual payment of interest.

(4) The entry to record $4,929 in interest income for 2009.

(5) The entry(s) to close the accounts at the end of 2009.

PROBLEM 18-2 **Capital Projects Fund and Related Funds** LO4 LO8

The Town of Green River authorized a municipal building to be constructed at a cost of $175,000. The construction will be financed from the proceeds from the issue of $175,000 of 6% bonds. Any difference between the par value of the bonds and the proceeds from their sale is transferred to the Debt Service Fund.

Transactions and events relating to this project include the following:

1. The proceeds from the sale of the bonds were received and included a premium on the bond issue in the amount of $15,000. The premium was transferred to Debt Service Fund.
2. Encumbrances were recorded on signing of the construction contract in the amount of $175,000.
3. Contract billings in the amount of $85,000 were approved for payment.
4. Contract billings were paid in the amount of $85,000.
5. All nominal accounts were closed and construction in progress was recorded in the appropriate account group in anticipation of the preparation of financial statements.
6. Encumbrances that were closed in anticipation of the preparation of financial statements are reestablished in the Capital Projects Fund.
7. Contract billings in the amount of $90,000 were approved on the completion of the municipal building.
8. Contract billings of $90,000 less a retention of 5% were paid.
9. The building was accepted, all construction liabilities were paid, and the building was recorded as an asset in the appropriate account group.

Required:

Prepare the journal entries relating to the Capital Projects Fund and the Debt Service Fund for the transactions and events described above. Clearly identify the fund in which each entry is recorded.

PROBLEM 18-3 **Special Assessment Debt** LO5 LO8

The City of Dayville has undertaken a sidewalk construction project. The project is being financed by the proceeds from the issue on July 1, 2008, of $500,000 of 7% special assessment debt. One quarter of the principal plus interest is payable on June 30 of each year beginning June 30, 2009. Property owners are assessed to provide the funds to pay the principal and interest on the debt.

The following transactions occurred during the period July 1, 2008, through June 30, 2009.

1. The bonds for the construction of the sidewalks were issued at par value.
2. The sidewalks were completed at a cost of $500,000.
3. Property owners were assessed and billed for the first installment of principal and interest on the special assessment debt.

4. Assessments for the first installment of principal and interest on the special assessment debt were collected and the June 30, 2009, payment of principal and interest on the special assessment debt was made.

Required:

Prepare all journal entries for the above transactions that are necessary in the funds of the City of Dayville assuming that.

A. The City of Dayville has made a commitment to the holders of the special assessment debt to assure the timely and full payment of principal and interest on the appropriate due dates.

B. The City of Dayville has not obligated itself in any manner on the special assessment debt that was issued for the construction of the sidewalks.

PROBLEM 18-4 **Internal Service Fund** LO2

The administrators of the City of Lyons have obtained approval from the City Council to centralize the computer facility as of January 1, 2008. An internal service fund is created to account for the activities of the computer facility. The City Council has approved a contribution of $25,000 from the General Fund for use as working capital and an advance from the Electric Utility Fund of $355,000 for the purchase of equipment and facilities. The $355,000 advance will be repaid by the internal service fund in 20 equal annual installments.

The following transactions relate to the establishment and operation of the Internal Service Fund.

January 1	The computer facility received the contribution from the General Fund and the advance from the Electric Utility Fund.
January 4	Land and a building were purchased for $175,000 of which $25,000 was assigned to land. Hardware was purchased for $125,000 and equipment to protect the hardware was purchased for $55,000.
April 10	The computer facility billed the Electric Utility Fund for service provided. The service cost $200,000 and was billed at a mark-up of 25% on cost. (Direct costs of providing computer services are accumulated in the "Computer Service" account. When services are billed to departments, this account is credited and the "Cost of Service" account is debited for the cost of services billed.)
April 29	Administrative expenses totaling $10,000 were approved for payment.
May 1	Payment of $37,750 was received from the Electric Utility in partial payment of the April 10 billing.
May 1	The administrative expense was paid.
December 2	The first of 20 equal annual installments to the Electric Utility Fund was paid.
December 30	Depreciation expense was recorded for the year as administration expense. The building was estimated to have a remaining useful life of 25 years; the hardware was estimated to have a useful life of 5 years; the equipment to protect the hardware was estimated to have a useful life of 10 years.
December 31	The nominal accounts of the internal service fund were closed through a closing account, "Excess of Billings to Departments over Costs," which in turn was closed to unrestricted net assets.

Required:

Prepare the journal entries necessary in the Internal Service Fund to record the transactions and events described above. The chart of accounts presented below may be used as an aid.

The closing account, "Excess of Billings to Departments over Costs," is similar to the "Income Summary" account of a corporation.

PROBLEM 18-5 **Tax Agency Fund** LO2

An administrative section of the County Assessor's Office of Mecklenburg County serves as the billing and collection agency for all property taxes assessed in Mecklenburg County. A charge of 1% of taxes and penalties collected is apportioned among recipients of the taxes for this service. All property tax records—current and delinquent—are maintained in this administrative unit. The 1% charge is included as revenue in the General Fund budget of the county government.

Current Assets:	*Liabilities:*
Cash	Vouchers payable
Due from general fund	Advance from electric utility
Due from electric utility fund	
Computer service	*Net Assets:*
	Unrestricted net assets
Fixed Assets:	
Land	*Revenue:*
Building	Billing to departments
Equipment—hardware	Contribution from general fund
Equipment—protection	
Accumulated depreciation	*Costs and Expense:*
	Cost of computer service
	Administrative expense

Information relative to the collection of property taxes for fiscal year 2008 is as follows:

Assessed valuation	$5,826,300
Tax rates per $100 assessed:	
County government	$1.20
State government	.80
City of Midvale	2.80
Unified school district	3.20

Tax bills are issued on January 1; taxes are payable without penalty by April 30; taxes paid after April 30 are subject to a 5% penalty for late payment. Taxes not paid by June 30 are considered delinquent.

No delinquent taxes remain uncollected for years prior to 2008.

An estimated 3% of billed taxes for 2008 will be uncollectible.

A summary of the activities of the Tax Agency Fund for the period January 1, 2008, to June 30, 2008, includes the following:

January 1	Tax bills are mailed to property owners. Accounts are opened by the tax collection unit.
April 30	Taxes collected and deposited during first four months total $372,883. Distribution of taxes collected is made to the applicable governmental units.
June 30	Taxes collected and deposited during May and June including the 5% penalty total $73,412. Distribution of taxes and penalties collected is made to the applicable governmental units.

Required:

A. Prepare in general journal form entries to record the activities of the Tax Agency Fund from January 1 to June 30. Establish a Delinquent Account for taxes not collected.

B. Prepare a balance sheet for the Tax Agency Fund after adjusting the accounts on June 30.

PROBLEM 18-6 Journal Entries—Identify the Fund LO2 LO8

The following activities and transactions are typical of those that may affect the various funds used by a typical municipal government.

Required:

Prepare journal entries to record each transaction and identify the fund in which each entry is recorded.

A. The Greenville City Council passed a resolution approving a general operating budget of $5,000,000 for the fiscal year 2008. Total revenues are estimated at $4,900,000.

B. The Greenville City Council Passed an ordinance providing a property tax levy of $6.25 per $100 of assessed valuation for the fiscal year 2008. Total property valuation in Greenville City is $204,800,000. Property is assessed at 25% of current property valuation. Property tax bills are mailed to property owners. An estimated 3% will be uncollectible.

C. Reed City sold a general obligation term bond issue for $1,000,000 at 105 to a major brokerage firm. The stated interest rate is 5%. Proceeds are to be used for construction of a new Central Law Enforcement Building. (*Note:* Entries are required in the Capital Project Fund).

D. The premium on bond sale in (C) above is transferred to the Debt Service Fund.

E. At the end of fiscal year 2008, the Greenville City Council approves the write-off of $52,550 of uncollected 2007 taxes because of inability to locate the property owners. The tax bills have been referred to the legal department for further action.

F. The Reed City Central Law Enforcement Building [(C) above] is completed. Contracts and expenses total $989,000, and all have been paid and recorded in the Capital Project Fund. Prepare entries to close this project and record the completion of the project in all other funds or account groups affected. Any balance in the Capital Project Fund is to be applied to payment of interest and principal of the bond issue.

G. On May 1, 2008, Hopi City supervised the issue of 6% serial bonds at par to finance street curbing in an area recently incorporated in the city limits. The face amount of the bonds is $600,000; interest is payable annually, and bonds are to be retired in equal amounts over five years from collections from assessments against property owners. The City acts as a collection agent and has given assurances to the debt holders that it will guarantee payment of principal and interest even though it is not obligated to do so.

(1) Record the issuance of the bonds on May 1, 2008.

(2) Record the payment to bondholders on May 1, 2009.

H. The curbing project in (G) above was completed on November 30 at a total of $590,000. Record summary entries for expenditure transactions May 1–November 30, 2008, and on completion of the project.

PROBLEM 18-7 Journal Entries—Identify the Fund LO2 LO8

The following transactions take place.

1. Bond proceeds of $1,000,000 were received to be used in constructing a firehouse. An equal amount is contributed from general revenues.
2. $800,000 of serial bonds matured. Interest of $120,000 was paid on these and other serial bonds outstanding.
3. $8,000 was received as insurance proceeds from the accidental destruction of a four-year-old police car costing $24,000.
4. $120,000 in expendable funds was transferred from the City Parks Endowment Fund to the City Parks Special Revenue Fund.
5. Equipment purchased from general revenues at a cost of $200,000 was sold for $40,000.
6. The City Water Company (an enterprise fund) issued a bill for $800 for water provided to the street department's street cleaner.
7. The City Water Company transferred $400,000 in excess funds to the General Fund.

8. A central motor pool was established by a contribution of $120,000 from the General Fund, a long-term loan of $80,000 from the City Parks Special Revenue Fund, and general obligation bond issue proceeds of $200,000.
9. The Motor Pool Fund billed the General Fund $10,000 and the City Parks Fund $4,000 for the use of motor vehicles.
10. Special Assessment Bonds in the amount of $400,000 were retired. The city has indicated a willingness to guarantee the payment of principal even though it was not obligated to do so.
11. Customers' deposits of $8,000 for water meters were received by the City Water Company during the year. The monies are to be held in trust until the customers request that their services be disconnected and the final bills are collected.
12. It is determined that the Service Fund will require an annual contribution of $60,000 and earnings of $6,000 in the current year to accumulate the amounts necessary to retire general obligation term bonds.

Required:

Prepare entries in general journal form to record these transactions in the proper fund(s). Designate the fund in which each entry is recorded.

PROBLEM 18-8 **General Fund Journal Entries and Related Fund Adjustments** LO2 LO8

You have been engaged to examine the financial statements of the Town of Bridgeport for the year ended June 30, 2008. Your examination disclosed that, because of the inexperience of the town's bookkeeper, all transactions were recorded in the General Fund. The following General Fund trial balance as of June 30, 2008, was furnished to you.

General Fund Trial Balance
Town of Bridgeport
June 30, 2008

	Debit	*Credit*
Cash	$ 16,800	
Short-term Investments	40,000	
Accounts Receivable	11,500	
Taxes Receivable—current year	30,000	
Tax Anticipation Notes Payable		$ 50,000
Appropriations		400,000
Expenditures	382,000	
Estimated Revenue	320,000	
Revenues		360,000
General Property	85,400	
Bonds Payable	52,000	
Fund Balance		127,700
	$937,700	$937,700

Your audit disclosed the following additional information:

1. The accounts receivable of $11,500 includes $1,500 due from the town's water utility for the sale of scrap sold on its behalf. Accounts for the municipal water utility are maintained in a separate fund.
2. The balance in Taxes Receivable—Current Year is now considered delinquent, and the town estimates that $24,000 will be uncollectible.
3. On June 30, 2008, the town retired, at par value, 6% general obligation serial bonds totaling $40,000. The bonds were issued on July 1, 2003, at a face value of $200,000. Interest paid during the year ended June 30, 2008, was charged to Bonds Payable.
4. Expenditures for the year ended June 30, 2008, included $11,200 applicable to purchase orders issued to the prior year. Outstanding purchase orders at June 30, 2008, not recorded in the accounts amounted to $17,500.

5. On June 28, 2008, the State Revenue Department informed the town that its share of a state-collected, locally shared tax would be $34,000.
6. During the year, equipment with a book value of $7,900 was removed from service and sold for $4,600. In addition, new equipment costing $90,000 was purchased. The transactions were recorded in General Property.
7. During the year, 100 acres of land were donated to the town for use as an industrial park. The land had a value of $400,000. This donation has not been recorded.

Required:

A. Prepare the formal reclassification, adjusting, and closing journal entries for the General Fund as of June 30, 2008.

B. Prepare the formal adjusting journal entries for any other fund as of June 30, 2008.

(*AICPA adapted*)

PROBLEM 18-9 **Journal Entries—Various Funds** LO2 LO8

The Village of Oakridge, which was incorporated recently, began financial operations on July 1, 2008, the beginning of its fiscal year. The following transactions occurred during this first fiscal year, July 1, 2008, to June 30, 2009.

1. The Village Council adopted a budget for general operations during the fiscal year ended June 30, 2008. Revenues were estimated at $400,000. Legal authorizations for budgeted expenditures were $394,000.
2. Property taxes were levied in the amount of $390,000; it was estimated that 2% of this amount would prove to be uncollectible. These taxes are available as of the date of levy to finance current expenditures.
3. During the year, a resident of the village donated marketable securities valued at $50,000 to the village under the terms of a trust agreement. The terms of the trust agreement stipulated that the principal amount is to be kept intact; use of revenue generated by the securities is restricted to financing college scholarships for needy students. Revenue earned and received on these marketable securities amounted to $5,500 through June 30, 2009.
4. A General Fund transfer of $5,000 was made to establish an Internal Service Fund to provide for a permanent investment in inventory.
5. During the year the Internal Service Fund purchased various supplies at a cost of $1,900.
6. Cash collections recorded by the General Fund during the year were as follows:

Property taxes	$386,000
Licenses and permits	7,000

7. The Village Council decided to build a village hall at an estimated cost of $500,000 to replace space occupied in rented facilities. The village does not record project authorizations. It was decided that general obligation bonds bearing interest at 6.5% would be issued. On June 30, 2009, the bonds were issued at their face value of $500,000, payable June 30, 2026. No contracts have been signed for this project, and no expenditures have been made.
8. A fire truck was purchased for $150,000 and the voucher approved and paid by the General Fund. This expenditure was previously encumbered for $150,000.

Required:

Part A: Prepare journal entries to record each of the transaction above in the appropriate fund(s) of Oakridge Village for the fiscal year ended June 30, 2009. Use the following funds:

General Fund
Capital Projects Fund
Internal Service Fund
Permanent Fund
Special Revenue Fund

Each journal entry should be numbered to correspond with the transactions described above. Do ***not*** prepare closing entries for any fund. Present your answer in the following format:

			Amounts	
Transaction Number	*Fund*	*Account Title and Explanation*	*Debit*	*Credit*
1				
2				
.				
.				

Part B: For transactions 7 and 8, describe how the information would be reflected on the government-wide financial statements (if at all).

(*AICPA adapted*)

PROBLEM 18-10 Journal Entries—Various Funds LO2 LO8

The following transactions represent practical situations frequently encountered in accounting for municipal governments. Each transaction is independent of the others.

1. The City Council of Bernardville adopted a budget for the general operations of the government during the new fiscal year. Revenues were estimated at $695,000. Legal authorizations for budgeted expenditures were $650,000.
2. Taxes of $160,000 were levied for the special revenue fund of Millstown. One percent was estimated to be uncollectible.
3. **(a)** On July 25, 2009, office supplies estimated to cost $2,390 were ordered for the city manager's office of Bullersville. Bullersville, which operates on the calendar year, does not maintain an inventory of such supplies.

   (b) The supplies ordered July 25 were received on August 9, 2009, accompanied by an invoice for $2,500.
4. On October 10, 2009, the general fund of Washingtonville repaid to the utility fund a loan of $1,000 plus $40 interest. The loan had been made earlier in the fiscal year.
5. A prominent citizen died and left 10 acres of undeveloped land to Harper City for a future school site. The donor's cost of the land was $55,000. The fair value of the land was $85,000.
6. **(a)** On March 6, 2009, Dahlstrom City supervised the issue of 6% special assessment bonds payable March 6, 2014, at face value of $90,000. Interest is payable annually. Dahlstrom City, which operates on the calendar year, will supervise the use of the proceeds to finance a curbing project. The City has made no commitments and has not obligated itself in any manner with respect to the payment of principal and interest on the debt.

   (b) On October 26, 2009, the full $84,000 cost of the completed curbing project was recorded. Also, appropriate closing entries were made with regard to the project.
7. **(a)** Conrad Thamm, a citizen of Basking Knoll, donated common stock valued at $22,000 to the City under a trust agreement. Under the terms of the agreement, the principal amount is to be kept intact; use of revenue from the stock is restricted to financing college scholarships for needy students.

   (b) On December 14, 2009, dividends of $1,100 were received on the stock donated by Mr. Thamm.
8. **(a)** On February 23, 2009, the Town of Lincoln, which operates on the calendar year, issued 5% general obligation bonds with a face value of $300,000 payable February 23, 2019, to finance the construction of an addition to the City Hall. Total proceeds were $308,000.

(b) On December 31, 2009, the addition to the City Hall was officially approved, the full cost of $297,000 was paid to the contractor, and appropriate closing entries were made with regard to the project. (Assume that no entries have been made with regard to the project since February 23, 2009.)

Required:

For each transaction, prepare the necessary journal entries for all the funds involved. No explanation of the journal entries is required. Use the following headings for your workpaper.

Transaction Number	*Journal Entries*	*Dr.*	*Cr.*	*Fund*

In the far right column, indicate in which fund each entry is to be made, using the coding below:

Funds	
General	G
Special revenue	SR
Capital projects	CP
Debt service	DS
Enterprise	E
Internal service	IS
Permanent fund	P
Trust or agency	TA

(*AICPA adapted*)

PROBLEM 18-11 Capital Projects Fund LO4

The City of Minden entered into the following transactions during the year 2006.

1. A bond issue was authorized by vote to provide funds for the construction of a new municipal building, which it was estimated would cost $1,000,000. The bonds are to be paid in 10 equal installments from a Debt Service Fund, and payments are due March 1 of each year. Any premium on the bond issue, as well as any balance of the Capital Projects Fund, is to be transferred directly to the Debt Service Fund.
2. An advance of $80,000 was received from the General Fund to underwrite a deposit on the land contract of $120,000. The deposit was made.
3. Bonds of $900,000 were sold for cash at 102. It was decided not to sell all the bonds because the cost of the land was less than expected.
4. Contracts amounting to $780,000 were let to Standstone and Company, the low bidder, for construction of the municipal building.
5. The temporary advance from the General Fund was repaid and the balance on the land contract was paid.
6. On the basis of the architect's certificate, contract billings were approved for $640,000 for the work completed to date.
7. Contract billings paid in cash by the treasurer amounted to $620,000.
8. Because of changes in the plans, the contract with Sandstone and Company was revised to $880,000; the remainder of the bonds were sold at 101.
9. Before the end of the year, the building had been completed, and additional contract billings amounting to $230,000 approved. All contract billings were paid by the treasurer to the contractor in final payment for the work.

Required:

A. Prepare entries to record the foregoing transactions (excluding the entries necessary to close out the fund) of the Capital Projects Fund.

B. Prepare a preclosing trial balance for the Capital Projects Fund.

C. Prepare entries necessary to close out the Capital Projects Fund on the completion of construction.

D. Prepare a statement of revenues, expenditures, and changes in fund balance for the Capital Projects Fund.

E. Prepare preclosing trial balances at December 31, 2009, for the Debt Service Fund, considering only the proceeds, expenditures, and transfers resulting from transactions of the Capital Projects Fund.

(*AICPA adapted*)

PROBLEM 18-12 Determining a Government's Major Funds LO2 LO8

The following information is available about Gotham's City government funds.

Governmental Funds	*Assets*	*Liabilities*	*Revenues*	*Expenditures*
1 General Fund	$ 9,408	$ 7,753	$ 86,022	$ 88,717
2 HUD Programs	7,504	6,428	2,731	2,954
3 Community Development	13,616	440	549	2,664
4 Route 7 Construction	10,478	1,115	273	11,298
5 Impact Fees	371	61	35	755
6 Local Gas Tax	2,139	170	1,436	2,971
7 Historic District	194	4	60	47
8 Central City Development	1,618	151	4,783	6,804
9 Community Redevelopment	2,365	—	42	1,872
10 Culvert Project			1,471	1,974
11 Bridge	2,602	686	3	1,270
12 Cemetery Fund	1,405	—	72	—
	$51,700	$16,808	$ 97,477	$121,326
Proprietary Funds				
13 Water and Sewer	$12,149	$ 4,679	$11,329	$ 6,907
14 Parking Facilities	372	672	1,344	1,582
	12,521	5,351	12,673	8,489
Totals, All Funds	$64,221	$22,159	$110,150	$129,815

Required:

Using the information about the government's funds, determine which funds qualify as "major" funds using percentage cutoffs and would be required to be included in the governmental fund financial statements.

PROBLEM 18-13 Preparing Government-wide Financial Statements LO9

Circus City issued an 8%, 10-year $2,000,000 bond to build a monorail mass transit system. The city received $1,754,217 cash from the bond issuance on January 1, 2008. The bond yield is 10%. Interest is paid annually on December 31 of each year. Disclosure information about capital assets is reported below.

Disclosure of Information about Capital Assets for the Year Ending December 31, 2008

	Primary Government			
Governmental Activities	*Beginning Balance*	*Additions*	*Retirements*	*Ending Balance*
Land	$ 500,000			$ 500,000
Building	760,000			760,000
Machinery and Equipment	950,000		$(225,000)	725,000
Construction in Progress		$1,500,000		1,500,000
Infrastructure	450,000			450,000
Totals at historical cost	$2,660,000	$1,500,000	$(225,000)	$3,935,000
Less accumulated depreciation				
Building	(190,000)	(59,150)		(249,150)
Machinery and Equipment	(235,000)	(76,050)	140,000	(171,050)
Infrastructure	(50,000)	(33,800)		(83,800)
Total accumulated depreciation	$(475,000)	$(169,000)	$140,000	$(504,000)
Governmental activities capital assets, net	$2,185,000	$1,331,000	$ (85,000)	$3,431,000

Depreciation expense charged to governmental activities as follows:

Public Safety	$ 55,000
General Government	72,000
Highways and Streets	25,000
Sanitation	17,000
	$169,000

Circus City's governmental funds financial statements are as follows:

Circus City
Governmental Funds
Fund Balance Sheets at December 31, 2008

		Capital Projects Fund	*Debt Service Fund*	*Total Governmental Funds*
Assets	*General Fund*	*Monorail Fund*	*Term Bond Fund*	
Cash	$ 64,000	$ 300,000	$—	$ 364,000
Interest Receivable		12,000	4,000	16,000
Investments	100,000	1,250,500	100,000	1,450,500
Property Tax Receivable	183,000			183,000
Total Assets	$347,000	$1,562,500	$104,000	$2,013,500
Liabilities and Fund Balance				
Vouchers Payable	$ 73,000	$ 50,000		$ 123,000
Total Liabilities	$ 73,000	$ 50,000	$—	$ 123,000
Fund Balances:				
Unreserved	83,000	312,500		395,500
Reserved for Encumbrances	191,000	1,200,000		1,391,000
Debt Service			104,000	104,000
Total Fund Balance	274,000	1,512,500	104,000	1,890,500
Total Liabilities and Fund Balances	$347,000	$1,562,500	$104,000	$2,013,500

Circus City
Governmental Funds
Statement of Revenues, Expenditures, and Changes in Fund Balances for the Year Ended December 31, 2008

		Capital Projects Fund	*Debt Service Fund*	*Total Governmental Funds*
	General Fund	*Monorail Fund*	*Term Bond*	
Revenues				
Property Taxes	$ 525,000		$ 50,000	$ 575,000
Licenses and Permits*	150,000			150,000
State Grant—highways and streets	250,000			250,000
Intergovernmental—state grant		$1,000,000		1,000,000
Charges for Services (general government)	130,000			130,000
Investment Earnings	75,000			75,000
Total Revenue	$1,130,000	$1,000,000	$ 50,000	$2,180,000
Expenditures				
Public Safety	$ 500,000			$ 500,000
General Government	300,000			300,000
Highways and Streets	130,000			130,000
Sanitation	70,000			70,000
Debt Service				
Interest			$160,000	160,000
Capital Outlay		$1,500,000		1,500,000
Total Expenditures	$1,000,000	$1,500,000	$160,000	$2,660,000
Excess (deficiency) of revenues over expenditures	$ 130,000	$ (500,000)	$(110,000)	$ (480,000)
Other Financing Sources (Uses)				
Proceeds from long-term capital debt		$1,754,217		$1,754,217
Transfers in			$160,000	160,000
Transfers out	$ (160,000)			(160,000)
Total other	$ (160,000)	$1,754,217	$160,000	$1,754,217
Special Items				
Proceeds from sales of equipment	$ 115,000			$ 115,000
Net change in fund balance	85,000	1,254,217	50,000	1,389,217
Fund balance—beginning	189,000	258,283	54,000	501,283
Fund balance—ending	$ 274,000	$1,512,500	$104,000	$1,890,500

* Revenues from licenses and permits are assigned to highways and streets ($100,000) and to the general government ($50,000).

Required:

Using the information above, prepare the statement of activities and the statement of net assets on a government-wide basis (using full accrual accounting). The beginning fund balance in the government-wide Statement of Net Assets is $2,686,283.

PROBLEM 18-14 Reporting Information about Long-term Liabilities LO5 LO8

On January 1, 2000, the city of Nashvegas issued an 8% annual, 10-year, $10,000 bond for $11,472 (an effective yield of 6%). The bonds become due on December 31, 2009. On June 30, 2008, the city of Nashvegas issued an 8% annual, 10-year, $10,000 bond to yield 10% (the proceeds are $8,771).

Required:

A. Assuming that both bonds are general obligation bonds, prepare the schedule of long-term liabilities at December 31, 2008 (see Illustration 18-12 for an example).

B. Determine the amount of interest reported on the government-wide statement of activities for the year ending December 31, 2008.

C. Determine the amount of long-term liabilities reported on the government-wide statement of net assets at December 31, 2008.

D. Determine the total amount of interest expenditures included in the governmental statement of revenues, expenditures, and changes in net assets for the year ending December 31, 2008.

E. Determine the amount of debt (if any) reported on the governmental funds balance sheet.

19

ACCOUNTING FOR NONGOVERNMENT NONBUSINESS ORGANIZATIONS: COLLEGES AND UNIVERSITIES, HOSPITALS AND OTHER HEALTH CARE ORGANIZATIONS

LEARNING OBJECTIVES

1. Describe the source of accounting standards for nongovernment nonbusiness organizations (NNOs).
2. Identify the three basic statements for NNOs.
3. Describe the basic funds used by nongovernment nonbusiness organizations.
4. Distinguish between a current restricted fund and an unrestricted fund.
5. Explain the term "assets whose use is limited."
6. Distinguish between a mandatory and a nonmandatory transfer.
7. Explain how contributions are recorded by NNOs.
8. Understand how donated services are recorded.
9. Describe the funds used to account for property, plant and equipment.
10. Explain the basic accounting used by endowment funds.
11. Indicate how equity investments are reported in the financial statements.
12. Explain the change in accounting for loan funds brought about by new standards.
13. Understand the use of an annuity or life income fund.
14. Discuss the special reporting issues of hospitals.

The public's concern about executive pay is affecting academia. In an article in the *Wall Street Journal*, Vanderbilt University's chancellor came under fire for running up a tab of $700,000 for frequent parties at his Greek-revival university-owned mansion. In addition, Vanderbilt University's Board of Trust did not approve the $2.2 billion budget between 2000 and 2005 (which is larger than the revenues of all but the largest 800 public companies). The Board of Trust is creating a committee to monitor the chancellor's spending and his pay package. In addition, another committee is examining potential conflicts of interest.[1]

Nonbusiness organizations other than governmental units are referred to in this text as nongovernment nonbusiness organizations (NNOs). In this chapter, we describe the accounting for the following four major classifications of NNOs:

1. *Nonprofit institutions of higher education.* This category includes private colleges, universities, and community colleges.
2. *Hospitals and other health care providers.*
3. *Voluntary health and welfare organizations (VHWOs).* These are organizations that derive their revenue from voluntary contributions of the general public to be used for purposes connected with health, welfare, or community services. Examples of such organizations include heart associations, family planning councils, mental health associations, and foundations for the blind.
4. *Other nongovernment nonbusiness organizations (ONNOs).* ONNOs take a variety of forms and include a broad assortment of organizations such as cemetery organizations, civic organizations, fraternal organizations, labor unions, libraries, museums, other cultural institutions, performing arts organizations, political parties, private and community foundations, private elementary and secondary schools, professional associations, public broadcasting stations, religious organizations, social and country clubs, trade associations, and zoological and botanical societies.

The Justice Department attempted in 1989 to prevent a merger between nonprofit Carilion Health Systems and Roanoke Valley Town's one other hospital. The Department failed. Two decades later, the concerns over monopoly power appear to have been justified as the cost of health care soars even more than elsewhere. Health insurance rates in Roanoke went from being the lowest in the state to being the highest, with an example of a $4,727 colonoscopy being cited.[2]

SOURCES OF GENERALLY ACCEPTED ACCOUNTING STANDARDS FOR NONGOVERNMENT NONBUSINESS ORGANIZATIONS

Until the early 1970s, accounting and reporting practices for NNOs were developed under the auspices of various interested professional associations such as the American Hospital Association, the Hospital Financial Management Association, the American Council on Education, and the National Association of College and University Business Officers. In the early 1970s, the AICPA exhibited an interest in financial reporting problems in this area that resulted in the issuance of separate *Industry Audit Guides for Hospitals, Colleges and Universities,* and *Voluntary Health and Welfare Organizations.* These *Audit Guides* were developed by different committees over approximately the same time period.

Inevitably, there were differences in the practices and reporting standards recommended in the different *Audit Guides,* as well as differences between those

[1] *WSJ,* "Vanderbilt Reins in Lavish Spending by Chancellor," by Joann S. Lublin and Daniel Golden, 9/26/06, by p. A1.

[2] *WSJ,* "Nonprofit Hospital Flex Pricing Power," by John Carreyrou, August 28, 2009, p A1.

recommended in the *Audit Guides* and those recommended in the publications of the professional associations. Later, several *Statements of Position* issued by the Accounting Standards Division of the AICPA resulted in amendments to each of the *Audit Guides.* In addition, a *Statement of Position* was issued containing the recommendations of the AICPA on accounting and reporting standards for NNOs not covered under the three *Industry Audit Guides.* By the late 1970s, all significant differences between the financial accounting and reporting standards recommended in the *Audit Guides* and those recommended in the publications of the professional associations relating to hospitals and to colleges and universities had been resolved and the various professional association publications and *Audit Guides* had been amended accordingly. Unfortunately, there continue to be significant differences among the *Audit Guides* (as amended) themselves with regard to recommended accounting and reporting practices for different types of NNOs.

In 1979 the Financial Accounting Standards Board assumed responsibility for setting accounting and reporting standards for all nonbusiness organizations except governmental units. In preparation for addressing specific standards for NNOs, the Board first undertook to incorporate NNOs into its *Statements of Financial Accounting Concepts.* In 1980 the Board issued *FASB Concepts Statement No. 4,* "Objectives of Financial Reporting by Nonbusiness Organizations." In 1985, the Board amended *FASB Concepts Statement No. 2,* "Qualitative Characteristics of Accounting Information," to apply to NNOs as well as to business enterprises and issued *Concepts Statement No. 6,* "Elements of Financial Statements," which encompasses NNOs as well as business enterprises. The FASB has now issued four statements on nonprofit accounting, *SFAS Nos. 93, 116, 117,* and *124* [ASC 958]. These are discussed later in the chapter.

Hierarchy of Generally Accepted Reporting Standards for Nongovernment Nonbusiness Organizations

Not-for-profit organizations (such as colleges and universities and health care providers) that may be either government owned or privately owned are referred to herein as ***special entities.*** Government-owned special entities come under the jurisdiction of the Government Accounting Standards Board (GASB). The hierarchy used to establish generally accepted reporting standards for all state and local governmental-owned entities was presented in Chapter 18. Government-owned special entities come under that hierarchy. The hierarchy used to establish generally accepted reporting standards for NNOs other than government-owned special entities is the same as that for business organizations and is summarized below.

U.S. GAAP Hierarchy (*SFAS No. 168*)—effective September 2009

Authoritative: Included in the FASB Accounting Standards Codification

Non-Authoritative: Not-included in the FASB Accounting Standards Codification

NNOs in the private sector should look to this hierarchy for accounting and reporting guidance.

With different hierarchies for entities under the jurisdiction of the FASB and entities under the jurisdiction of the GASB, different accounting standards may apply to special entities depending on whether they are privately owned or government owned. For example, *SFAS No. 93*, issued in August of 1987, requires that all privately owned not-for-profit organizations record depreciation [ASC 958–360–35–1]. *GASB Statement No. 34* require governmental entities to begin recording depreciation in 2001. The issue of conflicts among multiple standard-setting bodies remains controversial.

Most of the guidance for NNOs other than government-owned special entities is found in *Audit and Accounting Guides* of the AICPA and in publications of industry associations.[3] Examples of industry association publications include:

Colleges and Universities

Audits of Colleges and Universities, second edition (AICPA, 1975)

Financial Accounting and Reporting Manual for Higher Education [National Association of College and University Business Officers (NACUBO), Loose Leaf]

Hospitals and Other Health Care Providers

Audits of Providers of Health Care Services (AICPA, 1989)

Voluntary Health and Welfare Organizations (VHWOs)

Audits of Voluntary Health and Welfare Organizations (AICPA, 1988)

Other Nongovernment Nonbusiness Organizations

Audits of Certain Nonprofit Organizations, second edition (AICPA, 1987).

GASB Statement No. 15 allows public colleges and universities to use either the AICPA/NACUBO model (described in this chapter) or the government model (described in Chapter 18). In the discussion that follows, all illustrations, including those for colleges and universities, are based on the hierarchy described in this chapter for NNOs other than government-owned special entities.

"In a survey comparing the financial reporting of colleges and universities to publicly held corporations, a number of differences in styles and formats between the two groups were discovered. For example, 100% of the colleges responding to the survey listed the statement of financial position as the first statement that appeared in the annual report, while 69% of corporations listed the income statement first. In addition, 82% of colleges used the term 'statement of financial position' to describe the balance sheet, while 94% of the corporations surveyed used the term 'balance sheet.' All the income statements for publicly held corporations were single-column statements (for each year), unless they were part of some consolidating statement; in contrast, 84% of the national liberal arts colleges presented the statement of activities in multiple columns (with headings for different types of net assets), and only 10 out of 120 colleges used a single-column format, stacking the various categories of net assets."[4]

---

[3] Exceptions include *SFAS No. 93, No. 116, No. 117,* and *No. 124.*

[4] *NACUBO Business Officer,* "Corporate-Like," by Frederick M. Weis, June 1999, pp. 28–33.

FROM CONCEPTUAL FRAMEWORK—
FINANCIAL ACCOUNTING STANDARDS BOARD

FASB Statement of Financial Concepts No. 4 "Objectives of Financial Reporting by Nonbusiness Organizations"

The purpose of this statement is to establish the objectives for external reporting by nonbusiness organizations. There are several major distinguishing characteristics of nonbusiness versus business organizations. Generally, nonbusiness organizations receive resources from providers who do not expect to receive anything or expect to receive amounts significantly less than the amounts given. This characteristic results in frequent transactions concerning grants and contributions, which are infrequent in business organizations. Nonbusiness organizations tend to operate for purposes other than profit. Finally, nonbusiness organizations tend not to have defined ownership interests that can be bought or sold, or tend not to have liquidation values.

Concepts Statement No. 4 identifies seven major objectives of financial reporting.

1. Because the users of the financial statements make decisions about whether to provide resources to the organization, the information provided by the nonbusiness organization should be useful for such decisions.
2. The information provided should help the resource providers and others assess the nonbusiness organization's service and its ability to provide the service.
3. The information provided should help the resource providers and others assess the nonbusiness organization's stewardship responsibilities.
4. Information about the economic resources, obligations, and net resources of an organization, and the effects of changes in these resources, should be provided.
5. Information about the performance of the organization should be provided. Performance should be measured periodically and information should be provided about the service efforts and accomplishments along with information to assess this performance.
6. Information should be provided concerning how the organization obtains and spends cash and how the organization repays borrowing.
7. Information should be provided to help users understand the financial information provided.

Financial Reporting for Not-for-Profit Organizations

In 1993, the FASB standardized much of the variability in reporting for nonprofit companies by issuing *SFAS No. 117,* "Financial Statements of Not-for-Profit Organizations" [ASC 958–205–05–1]. This statement requires far more aggregation of data than most organizations had previously reported. Three basic financial statements are required:

1. A statement of financial position (balance sheet).
2. A statement of activities.
3. A statement of cash flows.

Also, *SFAS No. 117* [ASC 958–205–45–2] requires that net assets (assets less liabilities) be presented in three principal categories in the statement of financial position as follows:

1. ***Unrestricted net assets.***
2. ***Temporarily restricted net assets***—These are resources that must be used for a specific purpose or in a specific time period where the restriction is donor imposed.

3. ***Permanently restricted net assets***—These are endowments, where the interest might be spent but the principal must not be used.

The categories of net assets under *SFAS No. 117* [ASC 958] replace the fund balances used in previous reports. The term *restricted net assets* should not be confused with a restricted fund or assets whose use is limited. For example, a governing board of a hospital might designate certain resources to be used for a specific purpose; such items would still be classified on the statement of financial position as unrestricted net assets.

The FASB did not specify precise formats for the statements, but did require that information about liquidity be disclosed. Organizations can meet this requirement by classifying assets and liabilities as current or noncurrent, or they may choose to list the assets and liabilities in the order of liquidity. The FASB also expressed a strong preference for the term "statement of financial position" rather than balance sheet.

On the statement of activities, revenues may result in an increase in any one of the three categories of net assets. However, *all expenses must be reported as decreases in unrestricted net assets.* Thus, all expenses are listed in one column.

In the appendix to this chapter, the three financial statements are illustrated for a private educational institution (Illustrations 19-4 through 19-7). Two formats are provided for the statement of financial position: one that displays a net asset desegregation (Illustration 19-4) and one that displays a fund group desegregation (Illustration 19-5). The statement of activities is shown in Illustration 19-6 and the statement of cash flows is presented in Illustration 19-7.

Financial Report for Public Colleges and Universities

During November of 1999, the GASB issued *Statement No. 35,* Basic Financial Statements—and Management's Discussion and Analysis—for Public Colleges and Universities—an amendment of *GASB Statement No. 34.* This statement established the standards for public colleges and universities using the reporting guidelines set out in *GASB Statement No. 34* (see Chapter 18). *Statement No. 35* allows public colleges and universities to apply the guidance designed for special-purpose governments. This means that colleges and universities, in separately issued financial statements, can follow the reporting requirements for such governments. Also, public institutions are required to include a management's discussion and analysis (MDA) section, as well as other supplemental disclosures.

FUND ACCOUNTING

Whereas in some instances the total resources of an NNO may be available to finance its functions and operating activities, in most cases restrictions are placed on certain of the organization's resources by donors, by law or contract, or by other external authorities. Donors, for example, often specify the specific purpose or program to which their contributions are to be applied, and sometimes the time period in which the resources contributed by them may be expended. To facilitate the observance of such restrictions, most NNOs use fund accounting for recordkeeping and reporting purposes.

ILLUSTRATION 19-1

Comparison of Fund Structures of Different Nonbusiness Organizations

	Names of the Funds Used by Different Nonbusiness Organizations			
Primary Purpose of Funds and Account Group	*State and Local Governmental Units*	*Colleges and Universities*	*Hospitals*	*Voluntary Health and Welfare Organizations and ONNOs*
Financing of Current Operations	General Fund Special Revenue Fund	Unrestricted Current Restricted Current	General Fund Specific Purpose	Unrestricted Current Restricted Current
Acquisition of and Accountability for Major Capital Assets and Related Long-term Obligations	Capital Projects Debt Service General Fixed Assets Account Group General Long-term Obligation Account Group	Plant: Unexpended For Renewals and Replacements For Retirement of Debt Investment in Plant	Plant Replacement and Expansion	Plant (Land, Building, and Equipment)
Fiduciary Responsibilities	Permanent Agency	Endowment Loan Agency Annuity Life Income	Endowment Agency	Endowment Loan Agency Annuity Life Income

The fund structure of different nonbusiness organizations is summarized in Illustration 19-1. The fund structure and terminology differ among NNOs primarily because of the separate development of accounting and reporting standards for the different organizations. There are six funds commonly used, each of which will be discussed in turn. They are:

1. ***Current Fund*** (restricted and unrestricted). The unrestricted fund is often referred to by hospitals as the general fund, and the restricted fund as a special purpose fund.
2. ***Plant Fund.*** Several subfunds may be used to account for different aspects of plant and equipment, including the debt to acquire them.
3. ***Endowment Fund.***
4. ***Loan Fund.***
5. ***Agency or Custodial Fund.***
6. ***Annuity and Life Income Fund.***

ACCRUAL BASIS OF ACCOUNTING

Generally accepted accounting standards require that financial statements for NNOs be prepared using the accrual basis of accounting. Thus, revenues are reported when earned and realized or realizable, and expenditures are reported when materials or services are received. Expenses incurred before the reporting date are accrued, and expenses applicable to future periods are deferred. Although accrual accounting is used, the primary emphasis in reporting for NNOs is the disclosure of the sources of the entity's resources and how they were used to accomplish the objectives of the organization, rather than the determination of net income.

CLASSIFICATION OF REVENUE AND EXPENSE

"Moody's Investors Service plans to make some changes in the way it rates the operating performance of colleges and universities, saying investors have been frustrated by accounting practices that can mask financial weaknesses. Most of the changes will be made in the ratings of private colleges and universities, which have widely divergent methods of reporting nonoperating revenues and expenses, rates of spending endowment funds, and participation in the private 'off-balance-sheet' financing of campus facilities, particularly dormitories."[5]

For external reporting purposes, revenues are classified by source (such as net patient service revenue), and expenses and expenditures are classified by function or activity (such as research). An example of major sources of revenue is presented in Illustration 19-2. As indicated, hospitals and colleges and universities distinguish revenues between operating and nonoperating, while VHWOs and ONNOs classify revenues based on the source of the revenue, such as public support. Typical functional classifications of expenditures and expenses for different types of NNOs are presented in Illustration 19-3.

ILLUSTRATION 19-2

Major Sources of Revenue for Different Classifications of Nongovernment Nonbusiness Organizations

Colleges and Universities	*Hospitals*	*Voluntary Health and Welfare Organizations and ONNOs*
Tuition and Fees	***Operating Revenue***	***Public Support***
Federal, State, or Local Appropriations	Patient Service Revenue (Gross) Less Deductions (charity allowances, courtesy allowances, policy discounts, contractual adjustments, etc.)	Public Contributions
Federal, State, or Local Grants and Contracts	Net Patient Service Revenue	Special Events
Private Gifts, Grants, and Contracts	Other Operating Revenue (tuition from schools, specific-purpose grants, revenue from auxiliary enterprises, etc.)	Legacies and Bequests
Endowment Income		Federated and Nonfederated Campaigns
Sales and Services of Educational Activities (film rentals, testing services, etc.)	***Nonoperating Revenue***	***Revenue***
Sales and Services of Auxiliary Enterprises (residence halls, food services, etc.)	Unrestricted Gifts and Grants	Membership Dues
	Unrestricted Income from Endowment Funds	Investment Income
	Donated Services	Realized Gains on Investment Activities
	Income from Board Designated Funds	

[5] *Chronicle of Higher Education,* Vol. 45:22, "Investment Service Plans to Change the Way It Evaluates Colleges' Finances," by Martin van der Werf, 2/5/99, p. A40.

ILLUSTRATION 19-3

Functional Classification of Expenditures and Expenses for Different Types of Nongovernment Nonbusiness Organizations

Colleges and Universities	*Hospitals*	*Voluntary Health and Welfare Organizations and ONNOs*
Instruction	Professional Care of Patients	***Program Services***
Academic Instruction	Dietary Services	Research
Community Education	General Services	Public Education
Research	Administrative Services	Professional Education and Training
Institutes and Centers	Employee Health and Welfare	Community Service
Project Research	Medical Malpractice Costs	Other
Public Service	Depreciation and Amortization	***Support Services***
Community Service	Interest	Management and General
Conferences and Institutes	Provision for Bad Debts	Fund Raising
Extension Service		
Academic Support		
Computer Services		
Libraries		
Student Services		
Admissions		
Counseling		
Financial Aid		
Health and Infirmary		
Intramural Athletics		
Student Organizations		
Registrar		
Remedial Instruction		
Institutional Support		
Operation and Maintenance of Plant		
Scholarships and Fellowships		
Auxiliary Enterprises		

ACCOUNTING FOR CURRENT FUNDS

NNOs distinguish between unrestricted funds and restricted funds (or, for hospitals, between the general fund and specific purpose funds) in accounting for current operations. See Illustration 19-1.

Current Unrestricted Funds

Current unrestricted funds include financial resources of the organization that may be *expended at the discretion of the governing board* to carry out the operations of the organization and to accomplish its objectives. The resources and operations of current unrestricted funds of NNOs are similar in many ways to the resources and operations of the general fund of a municipality.

Current Restricted Funds

In a sense, all resources of an NNO that are not accounted for as current unrestricted funds are restricted because of *legal, contractual, or external restrictions on their use.* Current restricted funds are distinguished from other funds (such as plant or endowment funds) in that current restricted funds consist of financial resources that are ***currently available*** for use in ***operations***, but which may be expended only for purposes specified by the donor, grantor, or other ***external*** party.

Thus, the resources of both current funds—restricted and unrestricted—may be used by the organization to carry out its current operations and activities. Current unrestricted resources may be expended at the discretion of the governing board, whereas current restricted resources may be expended only in accordance with externally imposed restrictions.

Accounting for Board Designated Funds

The governing board of an NNO may designate resources of the current unrestricted fund (general fund of hospitals) for specific purposes, projects, or investment. An example of a specific purpose might include research expenditures, while an addition to the plant would be an example of a specific project. Such designations are intended to aid in the planning and control of expenditures and to limit the discretion of management (as distinguished from the governing board) over expenditures of the designated resources. However, these designations do not constitute, and should not be confused with, donor or external restrictions on the use of resources. The governing board has the authority to reverse or modify such designations at will. Accordingly, *board designated funds should be accounted for as unrestricted funds* and the term "restricted" should ***not*** be used in connection with them. Such funds should never be included in the current restricted (specific purpose) funds.

Hospitals

Assets set aside by the governing board of a hospital for *board-designated purposes* are reported separately in the general funds portion of the statement of financial position as ***assets whose use is limited.***

To illustrate, assume that the governing board designated $200,000 of current unrestricted funds for future research grants and $50,000 for financing an addition to plant and equipment. Hospitals would report these items separately from other assets in the assets section of the general fund statement of financial position as follows:

General Funds	
Assets whose use is limited:	
By board for research grants	$200,000
By board for acquisition of equipment	50,000
Total assets whose use is limited	$250,000

Assets whose use is limited under terms of debt indentures, trust agreements, third-party reimbursement arrangements, or other similar arrangements are also presented in the statement of financial position as "assets whose use is limited."

Other Nonbusiness Nongovernmental Organizations (ONNOs)

ONNOs report the amounts and purposes of board designated funds either in the *footnotes* to the financial statements *or by reclassification* of an equivalent portion of the Current Unrestricted Fund Balance similar to an appropriation of retained earnings.

Using the information from the previous example and assuming reclassification of a portion of the Current Unrestricted Fund Balance, an entry is made as follows:

Current Unrestricted Fund

(1)	Fund Balance	250,000	
	Board Designated Reserve for Research Grants		200,000
	Board Designated Reserve for Plant Expansion		50,000
	To record designation of reserves by action of governing board.		

The reserves would be reported as part of the total Current Unrestricted Fund Balance as follows:

Current Unrestricted Fund Balance

Available for Current Expenditures	$1,500,000*
Board Designated Reserve for Research Grants	200,000
Board Designated Reserve for Plant Expansion	50,000
Total Current Unrestricted Fund Balance	$1,750,000

* This is an assumed amount.

Colleges and Universities

Unrestricted current funds of colleges and universities that are designated by the board for specific current operating purposes are accounted for in the same manner as board designated funds of ONNOs (by footnote or by reclassification of the Unrestricted Current Fund Balance). However, *some board-restricted current resources can be transferred to other funds.* The allowable transfers are resources designated by the governing boards for loans, investments, or plant expansion. These funds can be transferred to loan funds, endowment funds, or plant funds.

If in the preceding example, the governing board was the Board of Regents of a university, the entries recorded on the books of the university would be as follows:

Unrestricted Current Funds

(1)	Fund Balance—Unallocated	200,000	
	Fund Balance—Allocated for Research Grants		200,000
	To establish a reserve in Fund Balance for research grants.		
(2)	Nonmandatory Transfer to Plant Funds	50,000	
	Cash		50,000
	To record the transfer to Plant Funds for purposes of making additions to plant.		

Unexpended Plant Fund

(1)	Cash	50,000	
	Fund Balance—Unrestricted		50,000
	To record the receipt of cash from the Unrestricted Current Fund for the purpose of financing additions to plant.		

Mandatory and Nonmandatory Transfers

The terms ***mandatory transfer*** and ***nonmandatory transfer***, which are unique to accounting and reporting for colleges and universities, are described in the *Industry Audit Guide* as follows.[6]

[6] *Audits of Colleges and Universities*, second edition (New York: AICPA, 1975), p. 104.

Mandatory Transfers. This category includes ***transfers*** from the Current Funds group to other fund groups arising from (1) ***binding legal agreements*** related to the financing of educational plant, such as amounts for debt retirement, interest, and required provisions for renewals and replacements of plant not financed from other sources and (2) ***grant agreements*** with agencies of the federal government, donors, and other organizations to match gifts and grants to loan and other funds. Mandatory transfers may be specified to be made from unrestricted or from restricted current funds.

Nonmandatory Transfers. This category includes those ***transfers*** from the Current Funds group to other fund groups made ***at the discretion of the governing board*** to serve a variety of objectives, such as additions to loan funds, additions to quasi-endowment funds, general or specific plant additions, voluntary renewals and replacements of plant, and prepayments on debt principal. It also may include the retransfer of resources back to current funds.

The recording of a nonmandatory (board designated) transfer was illustrated in the preceding section. To illustrate a mandatory transfer, assume that a university is required by the terms of a mortgage agreement to transfer $340,000 of tuition and fees that have been recorded as revenue in the unrestricted current funds to pay principal and interest on long-term debt that is carried as a liability in the plant fund accounts. The transfer of funds is recorded as follows:

Mandatory Transfer

Unrestricted Current Funds

Mandatory Transfer to Plant Funds	340,000	
Cash		340,000
To record transfer of funds for payment of principal and interest on mortgage note carried as a liability in Plant Fund.		

Plant Fund (for Retirement of Indebtedness)

Cash	340,000	
Fund Balance—Restricted		340,000
To record receipt of mandatory transfer from Unrestricted Current Funds.		

Mandatory and nonmandatory transfers are shown separately in both the statement of changes in fund balances and in the statement of current funds revenues, expenditures, and other changes.

Revenue and Support from Fund-Raising Events

The costs incurred by VHWOs and ONNOs in carrying out public support fund-raising events, such as dinners, dances, theater parties, auctions, and so on, are deducted from gross contributions received; and only the net funds provided by the event are reported as support (revenue) in the financial statements.

CONTRIBUTIONS

In *SFAS No. 116* [ASC 958], "Accounting for Contributions Received and Contributions Made,"[7] the FASB adopted standards requiring all NNOs subject to its jurisdiction to recognize contributions, including unconditional promises to give, as ***revenue*** in the period received.[8] *SFAS No. 116* does not apply to tax exemptions, abatements, or incentives, or to transfers of assets from a government to a business enterprise. Contributions include gifts of cash, pledges (promises to give cash or other assets), donated services, and gifts of noncash assets. Conditional promises to give (where the contribution would be returned if the conditions are not met) are recognized when they become unconditional, that is, when the conditions are substantially met. Donors sometimes restrict unconditional contributions to be used for a specific purpose. Donor-restricted contributions are still reported as revenues and results in an increase in *restricted* net assets. Other contributions are reported as revenues resulting in increases in *unrestricted* net assets. Expiration of donor restrictions results in a transfer from restricted net assets to unrestricted net assets.

Pledges

RELATED CONCEPTS

The objectives of financial accounting for both business and nonbusiness organizations is to provide information that is *useful to decision makers.* However, the absence of traditional owners in a non-business organization generally means that information needs to be presented for current and potential *resource-providers* to make rational decisions regarding resource allocation for the organization.

Pledges are signed commitments to contribute specific amounts of money to an organization on a future date or in installments. Although resembling promissory notes, pledges generally are not enforceable contracts. Regardless, pledges are recorded as revenues when a promise to give is nonrevocable and unconditional, at the present value of the expected receipts.[9] All NNOs should establish an allowance for uncollectible pledges.

The recording of pledges may be illustrated by assuming that, as a result of a fund-raising campaign, an organization receives written and signed pledges to contribute $300,000 for unrestricted use by the organization in the current or future years. Experience indicates that about 15% of pledges from similar past campaigns were never collected. Entries to record the pledges using the accrual basis of accounting are as follows.

Current Unrestricted Fund

(1)	Pledges Receivable	300,000	
	Revenue—Contributions		300,000
	To record gross amount of campaign pledges.		
(2)	Expense—Provision for Uncollectible Pledges	45,000	
	Allowance for Uncollectible Pledges		45,000
	To record provision for estimated uncollectible pledges.		

Contributions are shown net of the Provision for Uncollectible Pledges in the operating statement, and Pledges Receivable are shown net of the Allowance for

[7] *SFAS No. 116*, "Accounting for Contributions Received and Contributions Made" (FASB: Norwalk, CT, June 1993). [ASC 958–605–25–8 through 13]

[8] ASC 958 defines an unconditional promise to give as a promise to give that depends only on the passage of time or demand by the promises for performance.

[9] Suppose an alumnus offered to give $10 million to the school *if* 90% of his fellow alumni contributed money to the school. This conditional promise would be disclosed in the footnotes and would not be recorded until the condition is met and the promise becomes unconditional.

Uncollectible Pledges in the statement of financial position. If the amounts pledged contain restrictions on their use, entries similar to those made in the current unrestricted fund (above) would be made in the current restricted fund or in a loan, endowment, or plant fund as appropriate. If the payments for unconditional promises to give are not received by year-end, the contribution should be discounted and recorded in temporarily restricted net assets.

Donated Services

Some of the operations and activities of NNOs may be carried out by volunteers who donate their time and expertise. Donated services may range from the limited participation of large numbers of volunteers in fund-raising activities to active and sustained involvement in the organization by a few dedicated individuals.

Contributions of services are *recognized* only *if* the services received:

1. Create or enhance nonfinancial assets, ***or***
2. **a.** Require specialized skills,
   b. Are provided by individuals possessing those skills, ***and***
   c. Would need to be purchased if not provided by donation.

To illustrate the first alternative, consider an architect who contributes services to construct a building. Since the service helps create a fixed asset, the service would be recognized. For example, if a building valued at $1,500,000 included an estimated value of $400,000 assigned to the architectural services, then revenue from donated services of $400,000 would be recognized.

If the first alternative is not met, then all three conditions of the second alternative (2 above) must be satisfied in order for the contribution to be recognized. Suppose that a retired tax partner from a Big Five firm offers to teach a tax course at a local college. Since the school would need to hire a qualified person possessing specialized skills to teach the course, the service would be recorded. These conditions generally prohibit organizations from recording the value of the services of volunteer solicitors and from recording the value of donated services received on a casual or intermittent basis.

When these conditions are met, NNOs record and report the value of the services received, net of incidental expenses reimbursed to the contributing personnel, as revenue or support in the current unrestricted fund (or the general fund for hospitals). In the same entry, an amount equal to the revenue or support recognized is recorded as an expense in the appropriate expense account (e.g., professional fees expense).

Example of Donated Service Assume that the necessary conditions are met and that the services of a CPA who audited the records of a heart association at no charge were valued at $15,000, and those of an attorney who provided necessary legal services to the organization at no charge had a value of $6,000. The entry to record the revenue and expense resulting from the donated services is:

Current Unrestricted Fund

(1)	Management and General Expense	21,000	
	Donated Services Revenue		21,000
	To record value of donated services.		

Had the organization incurred any costs for incidental expenses of the CPA or attorney, the value of the services recorded would be reduced by the amount of those costs.

Donated Collection Items

Contributions of works of art, historical treasures, and similar assets are not capitalized if (a) the donated items are added to collections held for public exhibition, education, or research in furtherance of public service rather than financial gain; (b) the donated items are protected, cared for, and preserved; and (c) organizational policy requires proceeds from any future sale of the items to be used to acquire other items for collections.

Donor-imposed Restricted Contributions

Donor-imposed restrictions limit the use of assets that are received. Some restrictions limit the organization's ability to sell the asset. Restrictions may be permanent or temporary. For instance, temporary restrictions may stipulate that the resource can only be used after a specified date, for a particular program or service, or to acquire buildings or equipment. In any case, the organization needs to distinguish between contributions received that increase permanently restricted net assets, contributions that increase temporarily restricted net assets, and those that increase unrestricted net assets. This separation provides users with important information such as: Were aggregate net assets maintained only because permanently restricted net assets made up for a decline in unrestricted net assets? The primary difference between a donor-imposed restriction and a conditional contribution is that a donor-imposed restriction limits the use of donated assets while a conditional contribution creates a barrier that must be overcome before assets transferred or promised become contributions received. Therefore, donor-imposed restricted assets are recorded as contribution revenues (also known as restricted support) in the period received, thus increasing either temporarily or permanently restricted net assets. Then, as the expenditures are made, or the restriction expires, the net assets are released from temporarily restricted net assets or permanently restricted net assets and are reported as unrestricted net assets on the Statement of Activities.

For example, suppose a university received $120,000 in contributions that were restricted for specific operating purposes and spent $80,000 in the current year, with the remaining $40,000 spent in the second year. The following entries would be recorded:

Restricted Current Funds

(1)	Cash	120,000	
	Contribution Revenue (restricted support)		120,000
	To record restricted contributions.		
(2)	Net Assets Released from Restrictions	80,000	
	Cash		80,000
	To release funds from restricted into unrestricted assets.		

Unrestricted Current Funds

(1)	Cash	80,000	
	Net Assets Released from Restrictions		80,000
	To receive funds into unrestricted from restricted assets.		
(2)	Expenses—educational	80,000	
	Cash		80,000
	To record expenditures of restricted assets for specified purposes.		

The effect of these transactions is reported in the following condensed statement of activities.

	Unrestricted	Temporarily Restricted
Revenues and Support		$120,000
Net Assets Released from Restrictions	$80,000	(80,000)
Total Revenues and Support	80,000	40,000
Expenses	(80,000)	
Changes in Net Assets	—0—	$ 40,000

In the next year, assuming that the money is spent as planned, the remaining $40,000 is released from restrictions and recorded as an expense.

TEST YOUR KNOWLEDGE

19.1

NOTE: **Solutions to *Test Your Knowledge*** questions are found at the end of each chapter before the end-of-chapter questions.

Short Answers

Determine how much of the following contributions should be treated as unrestricted revenue during the current year.

1. Mary contributed $40,000 cash to her alma mater. She did not impose any restrictions on the contribution.
2. David contributed $60,000 cash to State University. He stipulated that the money could not be used until Professor Lowgrade retired. Professor Lowgrade is not expected to retire for five years.
3. Betty pledged to give $10,000 to the University of Treetop by the end of the year.

ACCOUNTING FOR PLANT FUNDS

Most transactions involving property, plant and equipment are accounted for by NNOs other than hospitals in a plant fund. The plant fund is used to account for (1) the property, plant and equipment owned by the organization and the net investment, (2) the accumulation of financial resources for the acquisition or replacement of property, plant and equipment, (3) the acquisition and disposal of property, plant and equipment, (4) liabilities relating to the acquisition of property, plant and equipment, and (5) depreciation expense and accumulated depreciation.

Colleges and Universities

Colleges and universities also account for the accumulation of financial resources to service-related indebtedness in the plant fund. All types of NNOs are required by generally accepted accounting principles to record depreciation expense.

The combination of rapid change in technology and university capital budgeting procedures can result in what amounts to the university "capitalizing scrap." By the time the budgeting and purchasing procedures are implemented, and the equipment is delivered, it is not far from being obsolete, at which point the whole procedure has to start over. As an alternative, colleges can consider leasing equipment.[10]

The plant fund of colleges and universities is usually divided into four separate self-balancing subgroups:[11]

1. *Unexpended Plant Fund*: to account for resources used to purchase property, plant and equipment (similar to a capital projects fund of a municipality).
2. *Funds for Renewals and Replacements*: to account for resources used to renovate or replace existing property, plant and equipment (also similar to a capital projects fund of a municipality).
3. *Funds for Retirement of Indebtedness*: to account for resources to be used to retire or pay interest on debt incurred in the acquisition or replacement of property, plant and equipment (similar to the debt service fund of a municipality).
4. *Investment in Plant*: to account for the institution's property, plant and equipment, related debt, and net investment in plant.

Both board-designated funds and externally restricted funds are accounted for in the plant fund of colleges and universities; therefore, a distinction is made between restricted and unrestricted fund balances.

To illustrate the funds and the procedures used to account for transactions relating to property, plant and equipment by different NNOs, assume the following example.

PLANT FUND EXAMPLE

1. During the year, resources are obtained for the acquisition of property, plant and equipment as follows:

Loan proceeds	$500,000
Contributions restricted by donor for plant	200,000
Board designation of unrestricted funds	50,000
	$750,000

2. Land is acquired for a building site for $750,000.
3. Principal and interest of $200,000 and $20,000, respectively, are paid on long-term obligations relating to property, plant and equipment.
4. The amount of depreciation expense on all fixed assets for the year is $235,000.

[10] *Tax Adviser*, Vol. 29:11, "From Here to Technology in Less than an Eternity," by Corey Schou, K. Smith, and W. Stratton, November 1998, pp. 790–793.

[11] It is likely that most NNOs will reorganize the plant fund in the future to agree more readily with the new external reporting practices. For example, instead of using the four subfunds of the plant fund, they might collapse them all into one fund.

The transactions described above would be recorded by colleges and universities as follows (the journal entry numbers correspond to the information in the box above):

Unrestricted Current Fund

(1A)	Nonmandatory Transfer to Plant Funds (unexpended)	50,000	
	Cash		50,000
	To record transfer of board designated unrestricted funds to Plant Fund.		

Unexpended Plant Fund

(1B)	Cash	750,000	
	Notes Payable		500,000
	Revenue—Contributions—Restricted		200,000
	Fund Balance—Unrestricted		50,000
	To record receipt of resources to be used for additions to property, plant and equipment.		
(2A)	Land	750,000	
	Cash		750,000
	To record acquisition of land.		
(2B)	Fund Balance—Restricted	200,000	
	Fund Balance—Unrestricted	50,000	
	Notes Payable	500,000	
	Land		750,000
	To transfer assets and related liabilities to Investment in Plant Fund.		

Investment in Plant Fund

(2C)	Land	750,000	
	Notes Payable		500,000
	Net Investment in Plant		250,000
	To record acquisition of land and related indebtedness from the Unexpended Plant Fund.		

The construction of assets and related debt is accounted for in the *unexpended plant fund* until the construction is completed. On the completion of construction, the assets and related liabilities are transferred from the unexpended plant fund to the *investment in plant fund* using entries similar to those presented in (2B) and (2C) above.

Funds for Retirement of Indebtedness

(3A)	Fund Balance—Restricted	200,000	
	Cash (principal)		200,000
	Interest Expense	20,000	
	Cash		20,000
	To record payment of principal and interest on obligations related to property, plant and equipment.		

Investment in Plant Fund

(3B)	Notes Payable	200,000	
	Net Investment in Plant		200,000
	To record reduction in indebtedness related to property, plant and equipment.		
(4)	Depreciation Expense	235,000	
	Accumulated Depreciation		235,000
	To record annual depreciation on property, plant and equipment that is included in the assets of the Investment in Plant Fund.		

Prior to 1990, depreciation of assets was not required for colleges and universities (except in endowment funds and nonexpendable trust funds). *SFAS No. 93*, "Recognition of Depreciation by Not-for-Profit Organizations," as amended by *SFAS No. 99*, requires that all NNOs including colleges and universities measure and report depreciation and accumulated depreciation on all depreciable property, plant and equipment.

Hospitals

Most property, plant and equipment transactions of hospitals are accounted for in the General Fund and not in a Plant Fund. However, contributed resources that may be used only to acquire property, plant and equipment are accounted for in a *plant replacement and expansion (restricted) fund* until the expenditures that satisfy the donor's terms are made. At that time, the assets acquired and the related fund balance are recorded in (transferred to) the General Fund.

To illustrate, the transactions presented in the preceding example would be recorded by a hospital as follows:

Plant Replacement and Expansion Fund

		Debit	Credit
(1A)	Cash	200,000	
	Revenue—Contributions—Restricted		200,000
	To record receipt of contributions that may be used only to acquire property, plant and equipment.		

General Fund

		Debit	Credit
(1B)	Cash	500,000	
	Notes Payable		500,000
	To record proceeds from note authorized by governing board to be used for acquisition of property, plant and equipment.		

The hospital *may* also record a reclassification of the General Fund Balance and establish a Board Designated Reserve for Plant Expansion in an amount of unrestricted funds designated by the governing board for additions to property, plant and equipment. It is assumed here that such designations are not recorded but are simply disclosed in the footnotes to the financial statements.

Plant Replacement and Expansion Fund

		Debit	Credit
(2A)	Fund Balance	200,000	
	Cash		200,000

General Fund

		Debit	Credit
(2B)	Land	750,000	
	Cash		550,000
	Fund Balance		200,000

Taken together, entries (2A) and (2B) record the acquisition of land with $200,000 in externally restricted funds and $550,000 in unrestricted board designated funds.

General Fund

		Debit	Credit
(3)	Interest Expense	20,000	
	Notes Payable	200,000	
	Cash		220,000
	To record payment of principal and interest.		

		Debit	Credit
(4)	Depreciation Expense	235,000	
	Accumulated Depreciation		235,000
	To record annual depreciation expense on property, plant and equipment that is included in assets of the General Fund.		

Voluntary Health and Welfare Organizations and Other Nongovernment Nonbusiness Organizations

Voluntary health and welfare organizations and ONNOs use a single Plant Fund and report the fund balance in two classifications as "expended" or "unexpended." The Expended Fund Balance is equal to the organization's net investment in property, plant and equipment (gross assets less related liabilities and accumulated depreciation). The Unexpended Fund Balance represents the amount of resources available to replace or acquire additional property, plant and equipment.

These same transactions illustrated previously would be accounted for by VHWOs or ONNOs as follows:

Current Unrestricted Fund

		Debit	Credit
(1A)	Transfer to Plant Funds	50,000	
	Cash		50,000
	To record transfer of cash to Plant Fund.		

Plant Fund

		Debit	Credit
(1B)	Cash	750,000	
	Notes Payable		500,000
	Contributions—Revenue—Restricted		200,000
	Transfer from Current Unrestricted Fund		50,000
	To record receipt of resources to be used for additions to property, plant and equipment.		

While VHWOs classify contributions that are restricted for the acquisition of plant assets as Support, ONNOs classify such contributions in a separate section of the operating statement entitled Capital Additions.

Plant Fund

		Debit	Credit
(2)	Land	750,000	
	Cash		750,000
	To record acquisition of land.		
(3)	Notes Payable	200,000	
	Interest Expense	20,000	
	Cash		220,000
	To record payment of principal and interest on obligations related to property, plant and equipment.		
(4)	Depreciation Expense	235,000	
	Accumulated Depreciation		235,000
	To record annual depreciation expense on property, plant and equipment included in assets of the Plant Fund.		

As noted earlier, the Plant Fund Balance is classified as Expended Fund Balance and Unexpended Fund Balance. The Expended Fund Balance is analogous to the Net Investment in Plant recorded in the plant funds of a university. Before the financial statements are prepared, the Expended Fund Balance must be adjusted to reflect the change in the organization's net investment in plant resulting from the transactions above. The change in the net investment in plant is calculated as follows:

Increases:		
Purchase of Land	$750,000	
Reduction of Indebtedness	200,000	$950,000
Decreases:		
Issue Notes Payable	(500,000)	
Depreciation Expense	(235,000)	(735,000)
Net Increase in Investment in Plant		$215,000

Plant Fund

(5) Unexpended Fund Balance	215,000	
Expended Fund Balance		215,000

To recognize the effect on the Fund Balances of the increase in the organization's net investment in property, plant and equipment.

Nonexhaustible Assets of Other Nongovernment Nonbusiness Organizations

Prior to 1990, ONNOs were not required to recognize depreciation expense and accumulated depreciation on "nonexhaustible" assets such as landmarks, monuments, cathedrals, and historical treasures or on structures used primarily as houses of worship. In *SFAS No. 93*, the Board considered and rejected the assertions that such assets are nonexhaustible and that those assets and structures used primarily as houses of worship need not be depreciated. Thus depreciation concepts and measurement are applied to these as well as other depreciable assets of ONNOs. However, depreciation need not be recognized on historical treasures and works of art that have estimated useful lives that are extraordinarily long. To qualify, such assets must have cultural, historical, or esthetic value that is worth preserving perpetually, and the holder must have and exercise the financial and technological ability to protect and preserve the asset.

ACCOUNTING FOR ENDOWMENT FUNDS

Endowment funds are similar to the nonexpendable trust funds of governmental units described in Chapter 18. When the donated funds have been given in perpetuity, the endowment fund is referred to as a *pure endowment fund*. When the donor has specified a particular date or event after which the principal of the endowment fund may be expended, the endowment fund is referred to as a *term endowment fund*. Resources of an unrestricted fund that are designated by the governing board for endowment purposes are accounted for in the unrestricted fund by all NNOs except colleges and universities. Colleges and universities may transfer such resources from the unrestricted current fund to a separate fund referred to as a quasi-endowment fund. Since the establishment of a quasi-endowment fund may be rescinded at the discretion of the governing board, it is recorded as a non-mandatory transfer in the unrestricted current fund and as a credit to Fund Balance—Unrestricted in the quasi-endowment fund.

The income from endowment funds generally may be expended as earned either for specified purposes or at the discretion of the governing board. If there are no restrictions on the use of the endowment fund income, it is recognized as revenue in the organization's unrestricted or general fund. Otherwise, endowment fund income is recognized as a resource addition to current restricted (specific purpose) funds, loan funds, plant funds, or other funds as appropriate to the use of the endowment income specified by the donor.

To illustrate the recording of endowment fund income that may be used for restricted and unrestricted purposes, assume that dividends and interest on endowment fund investments amount to $400,000, of which $150,000 is restricted for research grants and the remainder is unrestricted. Suppose that $100,000 in research grants is awarded during the period. Entries to record the income on endowment fund investments are summarized here:

Endowment Fund

		Debit	Credit
(1)	Cash	400,000	
	Due to Unrestricted Fund		
	(General Fund of Hospital)		250,000
	Due to Restricted Fund		
	(Specific Purpose Fund of Hospital)		150,000
	To record receipt of dividends and interest.		

Current Unrestricted Fund

		Debit	Credit
(2)	Due from Endowment Fund	250,000	
	Unrestricted Income (Investment Income)		250,000
	To record unrestricted Endowment Fund income.		

Current Restricted Fund

		Debit	Credit
(3)	Due from Endowment Fund	150,000	
	Restricted Income (Investment Income)		150,000
	To record restricted Endowment Fund income.		
(4)	Research Expense	100,000	
	Cash		100,000
	To record payment of research grants.		

Accounting for Public Nonprofit Organizations For *public* nonprofits (governmental nonprofits), accounting for endowment funds differs from the external reports of *private* NNOs. This section illustrates the differences in accounting between governmental nonprofits (under GASB rules) and private nonprofits (under FASB rules). For governmental nonprofits, restricted endowment fund income is not reported as revenue until it is expended for the restricted purposes. Entries (3) and (4) above would be replaced with entries (3a), (4a), and (4b) below:

Current Restricted Fund

		Debit	Credit
(3a)	Due from Endowment Fund	150,000	
	Fund Balance (Deferred Income)		150,000
	To record availability of restricted income.		
(4a)	Expenditure	100,000	
	Cash		100,000
	To record payment of research grants.		
(4b)	Fund Balance (Deferred Income)	100,000	
	Income from Endowment Fund (Investment Income)		100,000
	To record revenue for restricted assets expended.		

Public hospitals would report the cash as a reduction of fund balance in the specific purpose fund, with the expenditure and the income offsetting each other in the General Fund.

ACCOUNTING FOR INVESTMENTS

SFAS No. 124 [ASC 958–320], "Accounting for Certain Investments Held by Not-for-Profit Organizations," requires that all not-for profit organizations report investments in equity securities with readily determinable fair values and all debt securities at fair value in the appropriate net asset category (unrestricted, temporarily restricted, or permanently restricted net assets). Unrealized gains and losses are to be recognized as well as realized gains and losses in the Statement of Activities. Investments accounted for using the equity method, as well as investments in consolidated subsidiaries, are excluded from this requirement.[12] Readily determined fair values are usually those quoted in a stock exchange.

To illustrate, suppose that Vanderbilt University receives an unrestricted cash gift of $800,000 and immediately purchases an equity investment with the same fair value. The following entries are made:

		Debit	Credit
(1)	Cash	800,000	
	Revenue—Contributions—Unrestricted		800,000
	To record unrestricted contribution.		
(2)	Equity Investments	800,000	
	Cash		800,000
	To record the purchase of marketable equity investments.		

There are no specific requirements for reporting investment income (such as dividends or interest) other than distinguishing among the net assets. Suppose that during the year, the investments earned dividend income of $30,000 and that at the end of the year, the investment was worth $820,000. The following entries would be made:

		Debit	Credit
(1)	Cash	30,000	
	Investment Income—Unrestricted		30,000
	To record the receipt of dividends from investment.		
(2)	Equity Investments	20,000	
	Unrealized Gain on Investment—Unrestricted		20,000
	To adjust the investment to market ($820,000 less $800,000).		

If the investment income is restricted by donors, the income would be classified as either temporarily or permanently restricted.

Investment Pools

To improve effectiveness and flexibility in investing, NNOs often pool the investments of different funds into a single investment portfolio. Once placed in the pooled investment portfolio, individual securities are no longer identified with the contributing fund. Rather, they are pooled with all other investments. Gains, losses, and income of the investment portfolio pool are allocated by maintaining a record of the percentage interest (equity) of each fund in the investment pool. Investments that are nonmarketable should generally not be included in the pool but should be kept separate.

The initial equity interest of each fund in the investment pool is based on the ***relative market value*** of the investments contributed. Revised percentage (equity)

[12] Real estate, mortgage notes, equity securities without a determinable fair value, and venture capital funds are also excluded.

interests in the investment pool must be calculated whenever additional resources are placed or removed from the investment pool. At the time securities are brought into, or removed from, the investment pool, the carrying values of the securities are usually adjusted to their fair market values on the records of the participating funds.

A spokesperson for Sacred Heart Medical Center in Spokane, Washington, said the hospital did not belong on a list of "Fifty Fastest Growing Hospitals" recently released because a change in accounting methods had resulted in a deceptive depiction of its growth. Similarly, Ron Anderson, M.D. and CEO of a Dallas hospital, said a change recommended by the FASB in how the hospital recognized its revenues had made the hospital "look like" it had suddenly grown by $80 to $90 million.[13]

ACCOUNTING FOR LOAN FUNDS

Loan funds are used to account for loans to students and staff of colleges and universities, for loans to employees of hospitals, and for loans to beneficiaries of the interests of certain ONNOs (for example, loans to music students by symphony orchestra societies). Loan funds are generally revolving (repayments of loan balances and interest are in turn loaned to other individuals).

Historically, loan funds did not use any revenue or expense accounts, and all transactions were recorded directly to the fund balance. It was assumed that any income earned would offset the costs of operating the fund and was netted against the fund balance. For internal reporting purposes, these same procedures might be followed. Currently, for external reporting purposes, all revenues and expenses must be recognized on an accrual basis. Therefore, for external reporting purposes, the following entries would be made:

(1)	Cash	200,000	
	Revenue—Contributions—Restricted		200,000
	To record contribution received for establishment of a Loan Fund.		
(2)	Loans Receivable	125,000	
	Cash		125,000
	To record loans to students.		
(3)	Bad Debt Expense	2,500	
	Allowance for Uncollectible Loans		2,500
	To record estimated allowance for uncollectible loans.		
(4)	Investments	75,000	
	Cash		75,000
	To record investment of excess funds in money market account.		
(5)	Allowance for Uncollectible Loans	500	
	Loans Receivable		500
	To record write-off of a loan to student severely disabled in automobile accident.		
(6)	Investments	5,000	
	Investment Income—Restricted		5,000
	To record income on money market account.		

[13] *Health Care Strategic Management,* Vol. 17:4, "Some on 'Fastest Fifty' List of Fast-Growing Hospitals Say They Don't Belong There," by Ed Egger, April 1999, pp. 17–19.

ACCOUNTING FOR AGENCY (CUSTODIAL) FUNDS

An agency (custodial) fund is the same as its counterpart in a governmental unit. It is used to account for the assets held by an NNO as a custodian for others. Unless significant amounts are involved, resources held by an NNO as an agent for others are often accounted for as assets and liabilities in the unrestricted or general fund rather than in a separate agency fund. When a separate agency fund is used, the balance in the fund is reported as a liability since the organization does not have any equity in the fund. To illustrate, assume that resources in the amount of $15,000 belonging to the Association of Volunteer Aids are deposited with an NNO. Entries to account for this agency relationship in the unrestricted fund are as follows:

Unrestricted Fund

(1)	Cash	15,000	
	Due to Volunteer Aids		15,000
	To record deposit of assets belonging to Association of Volunteer Aids.		
(2)	Due to Volunteer Aids	15,000	
	Cash		15,000
	To record distribution of assets to Association of Volunteer Aids.		

Similar entries are made in an agency fund if such a fund is used.

ACCOUNTING FOR ANNUITY AND LIFE INCOME FUNDS

An NNO may accept the contribution of assets to the organization on the condition that the organization make annuity payments to a specified recipient for a specified period of time (*annuity fund*) or that the organization pay the income earned on the contributed assets to a specified recipient during his or her lifetime (*life income fund*). The major distinction between the two funds is that the beneficiary of an annuity fund is assured of periodic payments of a ***stated amount***, whereas life income fund beneficiaries receive periodic payments of ***varying amounts*** depending on the earnings of the fund. At the end of the annuity or on the death of the life income beneficiary, the unexpended assets of the fund are transferred to the unrestricted fund or to an endowment fund, loan fund, plant fund, or other fund specified by the donor.

To illustrate transactions recorded in an Annuity Fund, assume that on January 1, 2008, an individual donated securities with a market value of $325,000 to an NNO on the condition that she be paid $40,000 a year for 10 years beginning December 31, 2008. At the end of the 10-year period, unexpended assets are to be placed in a permanent endowment fund. It is estimated that the investments in the Annuity Fund will yield at least 8% annually. Entries to account for the basic transactions of the Annuity Fund are presented here:

Annuity Fund

(1)	Investments	325,000	
	Annuity Payable		268,400
	Revenue—Contributions—Permanent Restriction		56,600
	To record establishment of an Annuity Fund with an Annuity Payable equal to the present value of an annuity of $40,000 discounted over 10 periods at 8% (6.71008 × $40,000 = $268,400).		

		Debit	Credit
(2)	Cash	26,000	
	Annuity Payable		26,000
	To record investment income for year at 8%.		
(3)	Annuity Payable	40,000	
	Cash		40,000
	To record annual annuity payment.		

Each year the Annuity Payable balance is reduced by annuity payments and by losses on investments and is increased by investment income and gains on investments. The reasoning is that if actual investment earnings equal expected investment earnings, the net decrease in the Annuity Payable balance each year will be equal to the decrease in its present value. If the actuarial assumptions change, an entry to Annuity Payable would be made with an offset to a Change in Annuity Payable—Permanent Restriction account. This account is reported on the Statement of Activities.

ISSUES RELATING TO COLLEGES AND UNIVERSITIES

Recognition of Service Fee Revenue: The full amount of university tuition and fees is recorded as revenue at standard rates even though the university does not intend to collect the full amount because of remissions or waivers for scholarships and fellowships. Amounts of tuition and fees that are waived are recorded as expenditures for scholarships and fellowships.

Operating versus Nonoperating Income: The FASB does not require that organizations disclose a measure of operating income. Therefore, if an organization has a 5% spending rate, any investment income earned above or below this rate might be classified as nonoperating. It will be important to users to understand the institution's policies and any relevant state laws.

ISSUES RELATING TO HOSPITALS

Hospital patient service revenue is recorded at established rates, regardless of whether the hospital expects to collect the full amount. Some exceptions and several other issues relating to hospital revenues are addressed below:

Charity Care: Hospitals are required by some federal grant programs to provide healthcare services to individuals who cannot pay. Charity care revenues are not included in net revenues reported on the income statement. If the revenue was recorded, an entry to Debit Revenue and Credit Accounts Receivable should be made to reverse it out.

Contractual Allowances: Contractual allowances result from agreements made with third-party payers. Hospitals have standard rates that they charge for specific procedures. However, third-party payers, such as Blue Cross/Blue Shield, stipulate amounts that they are willing to pay. Therefore, contractual allowances are used to reduce the hospital's gross revenue to revenues net of contractual allowances.

Capitation Revenues: Health care organizations may contract with groups (or individuals) to provide health care services for some defined period of time. The health care firms generally receive a fixed amount each month to provide any necessary services needed for that month. Thus revenues are easily budgeted, and cost control becomes an important issue if a large percentage of revenues comes from capitation contracts.

Malpractice: Potential losses from malpractice claims are enormous. Health care organizations are constantly monitoring and altering the controls needed to help prevent such claims. Current rules for malpractice follow *SFAS No. 5*, "Accounting for Contingencies [ASC 450]."

SUMMARY

1. *Describe the source of accounting standards for nongovernment nonbusiness organizations (NNOs).* Before 1970, there were several professional bodies that prescribed accounting practices for nongovernment nonbusiness organizations. During the 1970s, the AICPA developed audit guides for hospitals, colleges and universities, and voluntary health and welfare organizations. In 1979, the FASB assumed responsibility for setting accounting standards for all nonbusiness organizations except government units. Government units follow the direction of the GASB.
2. *Identify the three basic statements for NNOs.* The three basic financial statements include a statement of financial position (balance sheet), a statement of activities, and a statement of cash flows. Net assets are presented in three categories in the statement of financial position. These categories are unrestricted net assets, temporarily restricted net assets, and permanently restricted net assets.
3. *Describe the basic funds used by nongovernment nonbusiness organizations.* Basic funds used by NNOs include the following six funds. (1) Current funds (both restricted and unrestricted): These funds account for financial resources used in current period operations. Hospitals typically call these special purpose funds and general funds respectively. (2) Plant funds: These funds are used to account for different aspects of property, plant, and equipment, including the debt to acquire them. (3) Endowment funds: These funds are used to account for donated contributions that must be maintained permanently (pure endowment funds) or that must be maintained until a certain date (term endowment funds). (4) Loan funds: These funds are used to account for loans to students and staff of colleges and universities, for loans to employees of hospitals, and often to beneficiaries of other nongovernment nonbusiness organizations (ONNOs). (5) Agency or custodial funds: These funds are used to account for funds held for others. (6) Annuity or life income funds: Sometimes an NNO accepts a contribution on the condition that periodic payments be made to some recipient for a specific period of time (annuity fund) or that the earnings be paid to some recipient during his or her lifetime (life income fund).
4. *Distinguish between a current restricted fund and an unrestricted fund.* Current funds are used to account for current period resources. Current unrestricted funds include resources that may be expended at the discretion of the governing board, while current restricted funds account for resources that are restricted because of legal, contractual, or other external restrictions. Therefore, current restricted resources can only be expended in accordance with externally imposed restrictions.
5. *Explain the term "assets whose use is limited."* The governing board may designate resources of the current unrestricted fund for specific purposes, projects, or investments. Because the governing body can reverse such decisions, these funds should never be classified as restricted. These resources are typically reported separately on the statement of financial position.
6. *Distinguish between a mandatory and a nonmandatory transfer.* These terms are specific to accounting for colleges and universities. Mandatory transfers are interfund transfers made because of binding legal agreements or agreements made in receiving grants. For instance, if a debt agreement specifies

that a portion of tuition revenues be used to meet interest payments, a university would transfer resources from a current unrestricted fund to the appropriate fund. A nonmandatory transfer would include any other transfer from the current funds to other funds made at the *discretion* of the governing board.

7. *Explain how contributions are recorded by NNOs.* Contributions, including unconditional promises to give, are recognized as revenue in the period received. Conditional promises are recognized when they become unconditional. Conditional promises should be distinguished from donor-restricted contributions. If the contributions are unconditional (cannot be returned if the condition is not met), donor-restricted contributions are still recognized as revenue. Pledges are recognized as revenues at the present value of the expected receipts when a promise is nonrevocable and unconditional.
8. *Understand how donated services are recorded.* If certain conditions are met, donated services are recognized as both revenue and expense. Contributions of services are recognized only if the services received create a nonfinancial asset (such as a building) or if the services received require specialized skills, are provided by someone possessing those skills, and would have to be purchased if not provided by the donation. Donated collections of art, historical treasures, or other similar assets are generally not capitalized.
9. *Describe the funds used to account for property, plant and equipment.* Plant funds may include an unexpended plant fund (to account for resources used to purchase plant and equipment), funds for renewals and replacement, funds for retirement of indebtedness, and investment in plant (to account for the assets and the related debt).
10. *Explain the basic accounting used by endowment funds.* When an endowment fund receives interest or dividends on endowment investments, the cash is recorded against a "due to fund" account. When the appropriate fund receives the cash, it is recognized as income for that fund. Also, any expenditures paid with the income of the endowment is recognized as an expense of the fund that incurred the expenditure.
11. *Indicate how equity investments are reported in the financial statements.* Equity investments (less than 20% ownership) and all debt investments are reported at fair value with any unrealized gains and losses reported on the Statement of Activities. Equity investments with ownership over 20% are excluded from this requirement. If the income from the investment is restricted by donors, then the income would be classified as either temporarily or permanently restricted.
12. *Explain the change in accounting for loan funds brought about by new standards.* Loan funds are typically revolving in that repayments of loan balances and interest are usually loaned to other individuals. Therefore, historically no revenues or expenses have been recorded. For external reporting purposes, since accrual accounting must be used, all revenues and expenses of the loan fund must now be recorded on the Statement of Activities.
13. *Understand the use of an annuity or life income fund.* Sometimes donors give institutions money with the condition that either a stated amount (annuity fund) or a part of the earnings (life income fund) be paid to some beneficiary. The organization records the investment at market value. A payable is recorded at the present value of the estimated amount to be paid. Revenues are then recognized for the difference. As payments are made, the payable is reduced. As income is earned, no income is recorded but, instead, the Annuity Payable account is increased. Any adjustments to the actuarial assumptions result in an adjustment to the Payable account and to the statement of activities.
14. *Discuss the special reporting issues of hospitals.* Some of the issues related to hospitals include accounting for charity care, contractual allowances, and capitation revenues. Charity revenues should not be included in net revenues reported on the income statement. However, hospitals are free to disclose the amount of charity care that they provide. Contractual allowances result from agreements that hospitals have made with third-party payers. Some third-party payers, such as Blue Cross/Blue Shield, stipulate amounts that they are willing to pay. The contractual allowance equals the hospital's billing rate and the amount the third-party payer actually pays. Health care organizations often contract with groups to provide health care services for a fixed fee. Therefore, the capitation revenues are the amount the health care organization receives from this contract. Under a capitation system, revenues are fixed and the costs of providing the service and cost control are key factors in measuring the organization's performance.

APPENDIX

Sample Financial Statements for Private Educational Institutions

ILLUSTRATION 19-4

Private Educational Institution
Statement of Financial Position
Net Asset Class Desegregation

Assets	*Unrestricted*	*Temporarily Restricted*	*Permanently Restricted*	*Total*
Cash and Cash Equivalents	$ 22,368	$ 14,912	—	$ 37,280
Short-term Investments	55,920	37,280	—	93,200
Accounts Receivable	55,920	—	—	55,920
Accrued Interest Receivable	11,184	7,456	—	18,640
Contributions Receivable	41,490	33,552	8,388	83,880
Prepaid Expenses and Other Assets	55,920	—	—	55,920
Loans to Students and Faculty	93,200	74,560	18,640	186,400
Deposits with Trustees	37,280	—	—	37,280
Long-term Investments	97,860	78,288	19,572	195,720
Land, Buildings, and Equipment, Less Accumulated Depreciation	83,880	67,104	16,776	167,760
Total Assets	$555,472	$313,152	$63,376	$932,000
Liabilities and Net Assets				
Accounts Payable and Accrued Liabilities	$ 34,500	—	—	$ 34,500
Deferred Revenues	13,800	—	—	13,800
Other Liabilities	11,500	—	—	11,500
Amounts Held on Behalf of Others	20,700	—	—	20,700
Annuities Payable	36,800	—	—	36,800
Long-term Debt	82,800	—	—	82,800
U.S. Government Grants Refundable	29,900	—	—	29,900
Total Liabilities	$230,000	—	—	230,000
Net Assets:				
Unrestricted	325,472	—	—	325,472
Temporarily restricted	—	313,152	—	313,152
Permanently restricted	—	—	63,376	63,376
Total Net Assets	325,472	313,152	63,376	702,000
Total Liabilities and Net Assets	$555,472	$313,152	$63,376	$932,000

ILLUSTRATION 19-5

Private Educational Institution
Statement of Financial Position
Fund Groups Desegregation

Assets	*Current Funds*	*Loan Funds*	*Endowment & Similar Funds*	*Plant Funds*	*Total*
Cash and Cash Equivalents	$ 22,368	$ 5,592	—	$ 9,320	$ 37,280
Short-term Investments	55,920	13,980	—	23,300	93,200
Accounts Receivable	55,920	—	—	—	55,920
Accrued Interest Receivable	7,456	5,592	3,728	1,864	18,640
Contributions Receivable	50,328	—	12,582	20,970	83,880
Prepaid Expenses and Other Assets	55,920	—	—	—	55,920
Loans to Students and Faculty	—	186,400	—	—	186,400
Deposits with Trustees	—	—	—	37,280	37,280
Long-term Investments	—	—	195,720	—	195,720
Land, Buildings, and Equipment, Less Accumulated Depreciation	—	—	—	167,760	167,760
Total Assets	$247,912	$211,564	$212,030	$260,494	$932,000
Liabilities and Net Assets					
Accounts Payable and Accrued Liabilities	$ 20,700	—	—	$ 13,800	$ 34,500
Deferred Revenues	13,800	—	—	—	13,800
Other Liabilities	11,500	—	—	—	11,500
Amounts Held on Behalf of Others	20,700	—	—	—	20,700
Annuities Payable	—	—	36,800	—	36,800
Long-term Debt	—	—	—	82,800	82,800
U.S. Government Grants Refundable	—	29,900	—	—	29,900
Total Liabilities	$ 66,700	$ 29,900	$ 36,800	$ 96,600	$230,000
Net Assets:					
Unrestricted	$163,091	$ 18,166	$ 35,046	$ 24,584	$325,472
Temporarily restricted	18,121	54,499	43,808	32,779	313,152
Permanently restricted	—	108,999	96,376	106,531	63,376
Total Net Assets	$181,212	$181,664	$175,230	$163,894	$702,000
Total Liabilities and Net Assets	$247,912	$211,564	$212,030	$260,494	$932,000

ILLUSTRATION 19-6

Private Educational Institution
Statement of Activities
Multicolumn Format

	Unrestricted	*Temporarily Restricted*	*Permanently Restricted*	*Total*
Revenues and Gains:				
Tuition and Fees, Net of Scholarship Allowances	$ 90,400	—	—	$ 90,400
Contributions	74,580	40,680	20,340	135,600
Contracts and Other Exchange Transactions	45,200	—	—	45,200
Investment Income on Endowment	10,576	8,407	8,137	27,120
Other Investment Income	10,848	7,232	—	18,080
Net Realized Gains on Investments	27,120	24,327	16,353	67,800
Net Unrealized Appreciation on Investments	18,080	18,080	9,040	45,200
Auxiliary Services	22,600	—	—	22,600
Total Revenues and Gains	$299,404	$ 98,726	$53,870	$452,000
Net Assets Released from Restrictions	91,450	(91,450)	—	—
Total Revenues, Gains, and Other Support	$390,854	$ 7,276	$53,870	$452,000
Expenses and Losses:				
Educational and General:				
Instruction	$ 87,964	—	—	$ 87,964
Research	64,507	—	—	64,507
Public Service	29,321	—	—	29,321
Academic Support	32,253	—	—	32,253
Student Services	41,049	—	—	41,049
Institutional Support	8,796			8,796
Total Educational and General Expenses	263,890	—	—	$263,890
Auxiliary Enterprises	20,525	—	—	20,525
Total Expenses	284,415	—	—	$284,415
Fire Loss	8,796			8,796
Present Value Adjustment to Annuity Obligations	—	4,144	—	4,144
Total Expenses and Losses	$293,211	4,144	—	$297,355
Increase (Decrease) in Net Assets	**$ 97,643**	**$ 3,132**	**$53,870**	**$154,645**
Net assets at beginning of year	227,829	310,020	9,506	547,355
Net assets at end of year	$325,472	$313,152	$63,376	$702,000

ILLUSTRATION 19-7

Private Educational Institution
Statement of Cash Flows
Indirect Method

Cash Flows from Operating Activities:	
Changes in net assets	$154,643
Adjustments to reconcile change in net assets to net cash provided by (used for) operating activities:	
Depreciation	23,240
Amortization of discounts on investments	(10,315)
Amortization of discounts on indebtedness	9,860
Increase in accounts receivable	(7,680)
Decrease in contributions receivable	6,290
Increase in accounts payable and accrued expenses	4,513
Decrease in deferred revenues	(1,800)
Contributions restricted for long-term investment	(5,100)
Interest and dividends restricted for reinvestment	(1,400)
Net realized and unrealized gains from investments	(113,000)
Fire loss	8,796
Net cash provided by (used for) operating activities	$ 68,047
Cash Flows from Investing Activities:	
Proceeds from sales and maturities of investments	5,678
Purchases of investments	(19,049)
Purchases of land, building, and equipment	(65,867)
Disbursements of loans to students and faculty	(23,156)
Repayments of loans from students and faculty	19,880
Net cash provided by (used for) investing activities	$(82,514)
Cash Flows from Financing Activities:	
Proceeds from issuance of indebtedness	20,500
Repayments of principal of indebtedness	(10,500)
Receipts of interest and dividends restricted for reinvestment	4,200
Contributions received restricted for long-term investment	5,500
Payments to annuitants	(16,403)
Receipts of refundable governmental loan funds	12,600
Net cash provided by (used for) financing activities	$ 15,897
Net increase (decrease) in cash and cash equivalents	$ 1,430
Cash and cash equivalents at beginning of year	35,850
Cash and cash equivalents at end of year	$ 37,280

TEST YOUR KNOWLEDGE SOLUTION

19-1 1. $40,000

2. Zero, treated as restricted support

3. If the amount pledged is received by the end of the year, the revenue is unrestricted. Otherwise the revenue is considered restricted support.

QUESTIONS

LO1 1. What authoritative body(s) is (are) responsible for establishing financial accounting standards for NNOs?

LO1 2. Why do most NNOs use fund accounting?

LO4 3. NNOs distinguish between restricted and unrestricted funds. Why is this distinction important?

LO3 4. What is the major difference in accounting for the general fund of a hospital and the unrestricted fund of other NNOs?

LO7 5. What is the major difference in accounting between conditional and unconditional pledges? Give an example of each.

LO6 6. What is the relationship (if any) between board designated funds and nonmandatory transfers?

LO5 7. May board designated funds ever be accounted for in the unrestricted current fund? Explain.

LO8 8. When should an NNO record donated services in its accounting records?

LO8 9. The donated services of volunteer workers on fund-raising campaigns are usually not given accounting recognition. Why?

LO14 10. Universities and hospitals often reduce their standard service charge to students or patients. How are these reductions reflected in the statements of revenue and expenses of these organizations? Explain.

LO9 11. What fund is used to account for the library books owned by a university? How should depreciation of the library books be reflected in the financial statements of the university?

LO9 12. In which fund of a hospital are medical equipment and related long-term obligations recorded? Would your answer be the same for a voluntary health and welfare organization? Explain.

LO9 13. What capital assets (if any) of ONNOs need not be depreciated?

LO10 14. Identify three different types of endowment funds and explain how they differ.

LO13 15. Distinguish an annuity fund from a life income fund.

Business Ethics

On the first page of this chapter, an article is referenced describing the recent activities of the chancellor of Vanderbilt University. Comment on the pros and cons, from an ethical perspective, of allowing a university employee in such a position great flexibility in spending.

EXERCISES

EXERCISE 19-1 **Cash Gift to a College** LO3

A $36,000 cash gift was received by a college during the year.

Required:

A. In which fund should the gift be recorded if there were no restrictions on the use of the cash?

B. In which fund should the gift be recorded if the donor specified that the cash was to be used to replace obsolete and damaged equipment?

EXERCISE 19-2 **Donated Services** LO8

During 2008 volunteer pinstripers donated their services to General Hospital at no cost. The staff at General Hospital was in control of the pinstripers' duties. If regular employees had provided the services rendered by the volunteers, their salaries would have totaled $6,000.

While working for the hospital, the pinstripers received complimentary meals from the cafeteria, which normally would have cost $500.

Required:

Prepare the journal entry necessary in the General Fund to record the donated services on the books of General Hospital.

EXERCISE 19-3 **Journal Entries for a Library** LO3 LO7

The Franklin Public Library received a restricted contribution of $300,000 in 2008. The donor specified that the money must be used to acquire books of poetry written in the sixteenth century. As of December 31, 2008, only $100,000 of the restricted resources had been expended.

Required:

Prepare the journal entries necessary to record these events during 2008. Indicate the fund in which each journal entry is recorded.

EXERCISE 19-4 **University Loan Fund** LO12

The following events relate to Grearson University Loan Fund:

1. $100,000 is received from an estate to establish a faculty and student loan fund. Annual interest rates range from 8% for students to 10% for faculty.
2. Loans to students totaled $60,000, and $40,000 was disbursed to faculty members (of the total loans made, 10% are estimated to be uncollectible).
3. Grearson wrote off a $1,000 student loan as uncollectible.
4. The following loans were repaid.

	Principal	*Interest*
Faculty	$ 5,000	$500
Student	10,000	800

Required:

Prepare the journal entries necessary to record these transactions and indicate the fund(s) in which the transactions are recorded.

EXERCISE 19-5 **Pooled Investment Fund** LO3

Hastings College pooled the individual investments of three of its funds on December 31, 2007. The recorded value and the fair market value of the investments on December 31, 2007, are presented here:

	Recorded Value	*Fair Value*
Loan fund	$121,000	$105,000
Quasi-endowment fund	128,000	147,000
Life income fund	151,000	168,000
Total	$400,000	$420,000

During 2008 the investment pool earned dividends of $12,000 and interest of $18,000 and distributed cash in these amounts to the respective funds. Realized gains on transactions of the investment pool amounted to $20,000 and were reinvested in securities held in the pool.

Required:

Prepare the journal entries that are necessary in the records of each of the funds to account for the earnings of the investment pool during 2008.

EXERCISE 19-6 **Reporting Contributions** LO7

A well-known celebrity sponsored a telethon for the Help for the Blind Foundation on November 1, 2008. Pledges in the amount of $1,000,000 were called in. Using similar telethon campaigns as a basis, it is estimated that 25% of the pledges will be uncollectible.

During 2009, $700,000 of contributions from these pledges were collected. The remainder were uncollectible.

Required:

Identify the appropriate fund(s) and prepare the journal entries necessary in 2008 and 2009 to record these transactions.

EXERCISE 19-7 **Endowment and Related Funds** LO10

Jefferson Hospital received money from a donor to set up an endowment fund. The following information pertains to this contribution:

During 2008

1. $2,000,000 was received to establish the fund. The requirements were
   - (a) $100,000 of the endowment fund's income must be used for research grants each year.
   - (b) The remainder of income is under the discretion of the governing board.
   - (c) The principal is expendable after the donor's death. It shall be used to purchase equipment.
2. The cash received was invested in a number of securities.

During 2009

3. Dividends of $100,000 and interest of $300,000 were received.
4. The income was transferred to the appropriate funds.
5. Of the restricted income, only $80,000 was expended for its specified purpose during 2009.
6. The governing board specified that $200,000 of the income would be used for loans for deserving medical students.

During 2010

7. $180,000 was lent to medical students.
8. The donor died of cancer.

Required:

Set up headings for the following funds: Endowment, General, Specific Purpose, and Plant Replacement and Expansion. Prepare the entries necessary in each fund to record the events listed above.

EXERCISE 19-8 **Plant Fund** LO9

After the election of a prominent political figure, the principal from a term endowment fund was expendable by Crandall University. The official was elected this year. The fund was restricted to the construction of a Political Science building annex. The following transactions occurred because of this event:

1. A transfer of $3,000,000 is made from the Endowment Fund (Term) to the Unexpended Plant Fund.
2. Construction is begun on the Political Science annex. Costs of construction during the year amounted to $1,000,000, of which $30,000 remained unpaid at the end of the year. (The financial controller does not record transfers to the Investment in Plant subgroup until a project has been completed.)
3. By the end of the following year, the annex is completed at an additional cost of $2,100,000. All costs have been paid.
4. The completed building is recorded in the Investment in Plant subgroup.

Required:

Record the journal entries for each transaction and identify the fund or fund subgroup in which each entry is recorded.

EXERCISE 19-9 **Multiple Choice** LO4

Select the best answer for each of the following items:

1. Which of the following should be included in the current funds revenue of a not-for-profit private university?

	Tuition Waivers	*Unrestricted Bequests*
(a)	Yes	No
(b)	Yes	Yes
(c)	No	Yes
(d)	No	No

2. The current funds group of a not-for-profit private university includes which of the following subgroups?

	Term-Endowment Funds	*Life-Income Funds*
(a)	No	No
(b)	No	Yes
(c)	Yes	Yes
(d)	Yes	No

3. Tuition waivers for which there is ***no*** intention of collection from the student should be classified by a not-for-profit university as

	Revenue	*Expenditures*
(a)	No	No
(b)	No	Yes
(c)	Yes	Yes
(d)	Yes	No

4. Which of the following is utilized for current expenditures by a not-for-profit university?

	Unrestricted Current Funds	*Restricted Current Funds*
(a)	No	No
(b)	No	Yes
(c)	Yes	No
(d)	Yes	Yes

5. In the loan fund of a college or university, each of the following types of loans would be found except

(a) Student.

(b) Staff.

(c) Building.

(d) Faculty.

(*AICPA adapted*)

EXERCISE 19-10 Multiple Choice LO4

Select the best answer choice for each of the following items:

1. Which of the following receipts is properly recorded as unrestricted current funds on the books of a university?

(a) Tuition.

(b) Student laboratory fees.

(c) Housing fees.

(d) Research grants.

2. The current funds group of a not-for-profit private university includes which of the following?

	Annuity Funds	*Loan Funds*
(a)	Yes	Yes
(b)	Yes	No
(c)	No	No
(d)	No	Yes

3. On January 2, 2008, John Reynolds established a $500,000 trust, the income from which is to be paid to Mansfield University for general operating purposes. The Wyndham National Bank was appointed by Reynolds as trustee of the fund. What journal entry is required on Mansfield's books?

(a) Memo entry only		
(b) Cash	500,000	
Endowment Fund Balance		500,000
(c) Nonexpendable Endowment Fund	500,000	
Endowment Fund Balance		500,000
(d) Expendable Funds	500,000	
Endowment Fund Balance		500,000

4. For the fall semester of 2008, Cherry College assessed its students $2,300,000 for tuition and fees. The net amount realized was only $2,100,000 because of the following revenue reductions:

Refunds occasioned by class cancellations and student withdrawals	$ 50,000
Tuition remissions granted to faculty members' families	10,000
Scholarships and fellowships	140,000

How much should Cherry College report for the period for unrestricted current funds revenues from tuition and fees?

(a) $2,100,000.

(b) $2,150,000.

(c) $2,250,000.

(d) $2,300,000.

5. During the years ending June 30, 2007 and June 30, 2008, Schafer University conducted a cancer research project financed by a $2,000,000 gift from an alumnus. This entire amount was pledged by the donor on July 10, 2006, although he paid only $500,000 at that date. The gift was restricted to the financing of this particular research project. During the two-year research period, Schafer's related gift receipts and research expenditures were as follows:

	Year Ended June 30	
	2007	*2008*
Gift receipts	$700,000	$ 800,000
Cancer research restricted expenditures	900,000	1,100,000

How much gift revenue should Schafer University report in the temporarily restricted column of its statement of activities for the year ended June 30, 2008?

(a) $0.

(b) $800,000.

(c) $1,100,000.

(d) $2,000,000.

(*AICPA adapted*)

EXERCISE 19-11 Multiple Choice LO7 LO8

Select the best answer for each of the following items:

1. Cura Foundation, a voluntary health and welfare organization, supported by contributions from the general public, included the following costs in its statement of functional expenses for the year ended December 31, 2009.

Fund raising	$500,000
Administrative	300,000
Research	100,000

   Cura's functional expenses for 2009 program services included
   (a) $900,000.
   (b) $500,000.
   (c) $300,000.
   (d) $100,000.

2. Community Service Center is a voluntary welfare organization funded by contributions from the general public. During 2008 unrestricted pledges of $900,000 were received, half of which were payable in 2008 with the other half payable in 2009 for use in 2009. It was estimated that 10% of these pledges would be uncollectible. How much should Community report as net contribution revenue for 2008 with respect to the pledges?
   (a) $0.
   (b) $405,000.
   (c) $810,000.
   (d) $900,000.

3. Theresa Plato is a social worker on the staff of Community Service Center, a voluntary welfare organization. She earns $30,000 annually for a normal workload of 2,000 hours. During 2008 she contributed an additional 800 hours of her time to Community at no extra charge. How much should Community record in 2008 as contributed service expense?
   (a) $12,000.
   (b) $6,000.
   (c) $1,200.
   (d) $0.

4. The basis of accounting used by nonprofit organizations is the
   (a) Cash basis.
   (b) Modified accrual basis.
   (c) Accrual basis.
   (d) Modified cash basis.

(*AICPA adapted*)

EXERCISE 19-12 Multiple Choice LO3 LO7

Select the best answer for each of the following items:

1. Which NNOs must record depreciation on exhaustible assets?
   (a) Hospitals.
   (b) VHWOs.
   (c) ONNOs.
   (d) All of the above.

2. Which statement relating to VHWOs is most nearly correct?
   (a) Use modified accrual accounting practices.
   (b) Report expenditures on a functional basis.
   (c) Record pledges when they are received.
   (d) Recognize donated services as revenue if measurable.

3. Which of the following funds of a VHWO does not have a counterpart fund in governmental accounting?
   (a) Current Unrestricted Fund.
   (b) Land, Building, and Equipment Fund.
   (c) Agency Fund.
   (d) Endowment Fund.
4. A voluntary health and welfare organization received a pledge in 2007 from a donor specifying that the amount pledged be used in 2009. The donor paid the pledge in cash in 2008. The pledge should be accounted for as
   (a) A deferred credit in the balance sheet at the end of 2007, and as support in 2008.
   (b) A deferred credit in the balance sheet at the end of 2007 and 2008, and as support in 2009.
   (c) Support in 2009.
   (d) Support in 2008, and no deferred credit in the balance sheet at the end of 2007.
   (e) None of the above.
5. Which of the following should be used in accounting for nonprofit health agencies?
   (a) Fund accounting and accrual accounting.
   (b) Fund accounting but not accrual accounting.
   (c) Accrual accounting but not fund accounting.
   (d) Neither accrual accounting nor fund accounting.

(*AICPA adapted*)

EXERCISE 19-13 Multiple Choice LO4 LO7

Select the best answer for each of the following items:

1. Depreciation should be recognized in the financial statements of
   (a) Private sector proprietary (for profit) hospitals only.
   (b) Both private sector proprietary (for profit) hospitals and not-for-profit hospitals.
   (c) Both private sector proprietary (for profit) hospitals and not-for-profit hospitals, only when they are affiliated with a university.
   (d) All private sector hospitals, as a memorandum entry not affecting the statement of revenue and expenses.
2. Securities donated to a nonbusiness organization should be recorded at the
   (a) Donor's recorded amount.
   (b) Fair market value at the date of the gift.
   (c) Fair market value at the date of the gift or the donor's recorded value, whichever is lower.
   (d) Fair market value at the date of the gift or the donor's recorded value, whichever is higher.
3. The Charity Services ledger account of a nonprofit hospital is a(an)
   (a) Contra-asset account.
   (b) Expense account.
   (c) Contra-revenue account.
   (d) Loss account.
4. The restricted groupings recommended for hospitals do not include
   (a) Specific purpose funds.
   (b) Endowment funds.
   (c) Plant funds.
   (d) Plant replacement and expansion funds.

(*AICPA adapted*)

EXERCISE 19-14 Multiple Choice LO7 LO8

Select the best answer for each of the following items:

1. An unrestricted pledge from an annual contributor to a not-for-profit hospital made in December 2007 and paid in cash in March 2008 would generally be credited to
   (a) Nonoperating revenue in 2007.
   (b) Nonoperating revenue in 2008.
   (c) Operating revenue in 2007.
   (d) Operating revenue in 2008.
2. A gift to a not-for-profit hospital that is not restricted by the donor should be credited directly to
   (a) Fund balance.
   (b) Deferred revenue.
   (c) Operating revenue.
   (d) Nonoperating revenue.
3. During the year ended December 31, 2008, Melford Hospital received the following donations, stated at their respective fair values:

Employee services from members of a religious group.	\$100,000
Medical supplies from an association of physicians. These supplies were restricted for indigent care and were used for such purposes in 2008.	30,000

   How much revenue (both operating and nonoperating) from donations should Melford report in its 2008 statement activities?
   (a) \$0.
   (b) \$30,000.
   (c) \$100,000.
   (d) \$130,000.
4. On July 1, 2007, Lilydale Hospital's Board of Trustees designated \$200,000 for expansion of outpatient facilities. The \$200,000 is expected to be expended in the fiscal year ending June 30, 2010. In Lilydale's balance sheet at June 30, 2008, this cash should be classified as a \$200,000
   (a) Restricted current asset.
   (b) Restricted noncurrent asset.
   (c) Unrestricted current asset.
   (d) Asset whose use is limited.

(*AICPA adapted*)

PROBLEMS

PROBLEM 19-1 **Statement of Activities—Hospital** LO2

The following events were recorded on the books of Mercy Hospital for the year ended December 31, 2008.

1. Revenue from patient services totaled $16,000,000. The allowance for uncollectibles was established at $3,400,000. Of the $16,000,000 revenue, $6,000,000 was recognized under cost reimbursement agreements. This revenue is subject to audit and retroactive adjustment by third-party payers (estimated adjustments are included in the allowance account).
2. Patient service revenue is accounted for at established rates on the accrual basis.
3. Other operating revenue totaled $346,000, of which $160,000 was from specific purpose funds.
4. Mercy received $410,000 in unrestricted gifts and bequests. They are recorded at fair market value when received.
5. Endowment funds earned $160,000 in unrestricted income.
6. Board designated funds earned $82,000 in income.
7. Mercy's operating expenses for the year amounted to $13,370,000. This included $500,000 in straight-line depreciation.

Required:

Prepare a statement of activities for Mercy Hospital for the year ended December 31, 2008.

(*AICPA adapted*)

PROBLEM 19-2 **Various Funds—Hospital** LO3

On January 1, 2008, a new Board of Directors was elected for Bradley Hospital. The new board switched to a different accountant. After reviewing the hospital's books, the accountant decided that the accounts should be adjusted. Effective January 1, 2008, the board decided that

1. Separate funds should be established for the General Fund, the Bradley Endowment Fund, and the Plant Replacement and Expansion Fund (the old balances will be reversed to eliminate them).
2. The accounts should be maintained in accordance with fund accounting principles. The balances in the general ledger at January 1, 2008, are presented here:

Cash	$ 50,000	
Investment in U.S. treasury bills	105,000	
Investment in common stock	417,000	
Interest receivable	4,000	
Accounts receivable	40,000	
Inventory	25,000	
Land	407,000	
Building	245,000	
Equipment	283,000	
Allowance for depreciation		$ 376,000
Accounts payable		70,000
Bank loan		150,000
Endowment fund balance		119,500
Other fund balances		860,500
Total	$1,576,000	$1,576,000

The following additional information is available:

1. Under the terms of the will of J. Ethington, founder of the hospital, "The principal of the bequest is to be fully invested in trust forevermore in mortgages secured by productive real estate in Central City and/or in U.S. Government securities . . . and the income therefrom is to be used to defray current expenses."

2. The Endowment Fund consists of the following:

Cash received in 1898 by bequest from Ethington	$ 81,500
Net gains realized from 1956 through 1989 from the sale of real estate acquired in mortgage foreclosures	23,500
Income received from 1990 through 2007 from 90-day U.S. treasury bill investments	14,500
Balance per general ledger on January 1, 2008	$119,500

3. The land account balance is composed of

1900 appraisal of land at $10,000 and building at $5,000, received by donation at that time. The building was demolished in 1934.	$ 15,000
Appraisal increase based on insured value in land title policies issued in 1954.	380,000
Landscaping costs for trees planted.	12,000
Balance per general ledger on January 1, 2008	$407,000

4. The building balance is composed of

Cost of present hospital building completed in January 1961, when the hospital commenced operations	$ 300,000
Adjustment to record appraised value of building in 1971.	(100,000)
Cost of elevator installed in hospital building in January 1987.	45,000
Balance per general ledger on January 1, 2008	$ 245,000

The estimated useful lives of the hospital building and the elevator when new were 50 years and 20 years, respectively.

5. The hospital's equipment was inventoried on January 1, 2008. The costs shown in the inventory agreed with the equipment account balance in the general ledger. The allowance for depreciation account at January 1, 2008, included $158,250 applicable to equipment, and that amount was determined to be accurate. All depreciation is computed on a straight-line basis.

6. A bank loan was obtained to finance the cost of new operating room equipment purchased in 2004. Interest was paid to December 31, 2007.

7. Common stock with a market value of $417,000 was donated to Bradley Hospital with the stipulation that the proceeds from the sale of the stock must be used for facilities expansion. The hospital plans to undertake expansion of its facilities next year and to sell these securities at that time.

Required:

Using the workpaper form below, prepare the entries necessary to establish the correct balances as of January 1, 2008.

	Trial Balance		*Adjustments*		*General Fund*		*Endowment Fund*		*Plant Replacement Fund*	
Account Description	*Debit*	*Credit*	*Debit*	*Credit*	*Debit*	*Credit*	*Debit*	*Credit*	*Debit*	*Credit*

(*AICPA adapted*)

PROBLEM 19-3 **Various Funds—University** LO2 LO3

A partial statement of financial position of Century University is shown below.

Century University
Partial Statement of Financial Position
June 30, 2007

Assets	
Current Funds	
Unrestricted	
Cash	$210,000
Accounts Receivable (less allowance for doubtful accounts, $9,000)	341,000
State Appropriations Receivable	75,000
Total Unrestricted	626,000
Restricted	
Cash	7,000
Investments	60,000
Total Restricted	67,000
Total Current	$693,000

Liabilities and Fund Balances	
Current Funds	
Unrestricted	
Accounts Payable	$ 45,000
Deferred Revenues	66,000
Fund Balance	515,000
Total Unrestricted	626,000
Restricted	
Fund Balance	67,000
Total Restricted	67,000
Total Current	$693,000

During the fiscal year ended June 30, 2008, the following transactions occurred:

1. A gift of $100,000 was received from an alumnus on July 7, 2007. One-half of the gift was to be used for the purchase of books for the university's library and the rest was to be used to establish a scholarship fund per the alumnus's request. It was also requested that the income generated by the scholarship fund be awarded annually as a scholarship for a qualified disadvantaged student. The board decided that the funds for the new scholarship should be invested in savings certificates on July 20, 2007. These savings certificates were purchased on July 21, 2007.
2. Revenue for the fiscal period from student tuition and fees amounted to $1,900,000. During the fiscal year, $1,686,000 of this amount was collected; $66,000 had been collected in the prior year. The university had also received $158,000 by June 30, 2008, for fees for the session beginning July 1, 2008.
3. During the year ended June 30, 2008, the university collected $349,000 of the outstanding accounts receivable at the beginning of the year. The balance was determined to be uncollectible and was written off against the allowance account. At June 30, 2008, the allowance account was increased by $3,000.
4. Because of late student fee payments, $6,000 in interest charges were earned and collected.
5. The state appropriation was received. Another unrestricted appropriation of $50,000 was made by the state. This had not been paid to the university by the fiscal year-end.
6. An unrestricted gift of $25,000 cash was received from alumni of the university.

7. During the year, investments of $21,000 were sold for $26,000. Investment income amounting to $1,900 was received.
8. Unrestricted operating expenses were recorded at $1,777,000, $59,000 of which remains unpaid.
9. Restricted current funds of $13,000 were spent for authorized purposes during the year.
10. The accounts payable at June 30, 2007, were paid during the year.
11. During the year, $7,000 interest was earned and received on the savings certificates purchased in accordance with the board's resolution [in item (1)].

Required:

A. Prepare journal entries to record in summary form the transactions above for the year ended June 30, 2008. Each journal entry should be numbered to correspond with the transaction described above. Set up the following headings:

	Current Funds					
	Unrestricted		*Restricted*		*Endowment Fund*	
Accounts	*Dr.*	*Cr.*	*Dr.*	*Cr.*	*Dr.*	*Cr.*

B. Prepare a statement of activities for the year ended June 30, 2008.

C. Prepare a statement of activities for the current funds for the year ended June 30, 2008. Include more details about the revenues and expenses.

PROBLEM 19-4 **Journal Entries—University** LO3

The following transactions of Beltville College transpired during 2008. The funds necessary are the Endowment Fund, the Annuity Fund, the Plant Fund—Unexpended, the Plant Fund—Investment in Plant, the Loan Fund, the Unrestricted Current Fund, and the Restricted Current Fund.

January 1

1. A gift of $10,000 was received from Carl Brown. The principal was to be held intact and the income to be used for any purpose designated by the governing board.
2. David Gross donated $20,000. The principal was to be held intact and the income to be used for scholarships for worthy students.
3. Roxanne Norton donated $30,000, of which the principal was to remain intact while the interest was to be used for student loans. All income is to be relent; all losses from loans are to be charged against income.
4. A gift of $205,000 was received from Brian Carr. Semiannual payments of $10,000 are to be made to the donor during his lifetime. On his death the fund is to be used to purchase or construct a students' residence. Mr. Carr has a life expectancy of five years and investments are expected to earn 8% annually.
5. Kathy Jackson donated 1,000 shares of BIM stock, which had a market value of $150 per share on that date. All income received from the shares is to be held intact and the shares cannot be held for more than five years. Once the board sells the shares, all the proceeds are to be used to build a student hospital.
6. The assets of the Brown and Gross funds were consolidated into a pooled investment account by the governing board (in proportion to the principal accounts). Electric Power Bonds worth $30,000 were purchased. The 12% interest was payable on January 1 and July 1.
7. The Norton Fund cash is used to purchase Cravit Company 10% bonds at par for $30,000. January 1 and July 1 are the interest dates.

8. With the cash from the Carr Fund, $200,000 of 8% U.S. Treasury notes was purchased at par. The interest dates are January 1 and July 1.

July 1

9. The interest was received on all bonds and notes and was transferred to the proper funds. Dividends of $4,000 were received from BIM stock.
10. The stipulated payment is made to Mr. Carr from the Endowment Fund.
11. Electric Power Company bonds bought at par value for $20,000 are sold at 102. The gain is added to the principal.
12. A $300 student loan was made from the Norton Fund.

October 1

13. A notice of Brian Carr's death is received. There is no liability to his estate.
14. The Gross Scholarship Fund awards a $200 scholarship.
15. $200,000 par of U.S. Treasury notes are sold for $206,000.

December 31

16. Interest on bonds is received.
17. $100 of principal and $5 of interest were repaid on the student loan.
18. A building was purchased for $250,000 using the funds available from the Carr gift. The residence hall will have a 20-year mortgage payable to account for the balance.

Required:

Using the following format, record the journal entries necessary for each event.

Event	*Fund*	*Journal Entry*

(*AICPA adapted*)

PROBLEM 19-5 **Journal Entries—Financial Statements—Library** LO2

Preston Library, a nonprofit organization, presented the following statement of financial position and statement of activities for its fiscal year ended February 28, 2007.

Preston Library
Statement of Financial Position
February 28, 2007

Assets	*Unrestricted*	*Temporarily Restricted*
Current Assets		
Cash	$ 285,000	$80,000
Grants Receivable	80,000	
Prepaid Expenses	65,000	
Total	430,000	
Investments (at market)	1,020,000	
Land, Building, and Equipment (less accumulated depreciation of $50,000)	530,000	
Total Assets	$1,980,000	$80,000
Liabilities and Fund Balances		
Current Liabilities		
Accounts Payable and Accrued Expenses	$ 150,000	
Total	150,000	
Long-Term Debt	200,000	
Fund Balances	1,630,000	80,000
Total Liabilities and Fund Balances	$1,980,000	$80,000

Preston Library
Statement of Activities
for Year Ended February 28, 2007

Support and Revenue	*Unrestricted*	*Temporarily Restricted*
Support		
Grants	$ 70,000	$—0—
Gifts	300,000	80,000
Total	370,000	80,000
Revenue		
Service Fees	22,000	
Book Rentals and Fines	107,000	
Investment Income	71,000	
Total	200,000	—0—
Total Support and Revenue	$ 570,000	$80,000
Expenses		
Program Services		
Circulating library	$ 212,000	
Research library	86,000	
Exhibits	20,000	
Community services	10,000	
Total	328,000	—0—
Supporting Services		
General and administrative	175,000	
Fund raising	111,000	
Total	286,000	—0—
Total Expenses	614,000	—0—
Increase (decrease) in net assets	(44,000)	80,000
Fund Balances—beginning of year	1,674,000	—0—
Fund Balances—end of year	$1,630,000	$80,000

The following transactions occurred during the fiscal year ended February 28, 2008.

1. Fees were billed as follows:

Service fees	$30,000
Book rentals	43,000
Book fines	78,000

2. $40,000 of the Grant Receivable was received. Another grant in the amount of $20,000 was promised.

3. Contributions in the amounts summarized below were received:

Unrestricted	$215,000
Restricted	108,000

4. Investment income totaled $75,000 for the year.

5. Vouchers for the year were approved as follows:

Circulating library	$189,000
Research library	74,000
Exhibits	15,000
Community services	12,000
General and administrative	166,000
Fund raising	103,000
Total	$559,000

6. During the year, $500,000 worth of vouchers were paid.

Adjustment Data

7. Accounts Payable and Accrued Expenses at February 28, 2008, should be $217,000. The difference should be allocated to the following expenses:

Research library	$5,000
General and administrative	3,000

8. Additions to the research library in the amount of $68,000 that were approved in (5) above were made in accordance with the terms of a contribution that had been received earlier and that was restricted for that purpose.

9. The current market value of the investments is $1,035,000 (no investment transactions occurred).

10. Depreciation amounted to $9,000 for the year. It should be allocated as follows:

Circulating library	$3,500
Research library	2,900
General and administrative	2,600

11. Prepaid Expenses should be $60,000. The difference should be allocated to:

Exhibits	$3,700
General and administrative	1,300

Required:

A. Prepare journal entries to record the transactions.

B. Prepare the statement of financial position and the statement of activities for the year ended February 28, 2008.

(*AICPA adapted*)

PROBLEM 19-6 **Statement of Financial Position** LO2

The December 31, 2008, statement of financial position for the Blood Donors of America Foundation is presented below.

Statement of Financial Position
December 31, 2008

Assets	
Cash	$ 470,000
Accounts Receivable	160,000
Allowance for Doubtful Accounts	(30,000)
Pledges Receivable	930,000
Allowance for Doubtful Pledges	(130,000)
Inventories	400,000
Investments	19,300,000
Land	1,300,000
Buildings and Improvements	46,500,000
Equipment	2,700,000
Accumulated Depreciation	(13,500,000)
Other Assets	200,000
Total Assets	$58,300,000

Liabilities	
Accounts Payable	$ 700,000
Accrued Expenses	130,000
Deferred Revenue—Unrestricted	100,000
Deferred Capital Addition	1,600,000
Long-term Debt	7,350,000
Total Liabilities	9,880,000

Fund Balances	
Plant	29,000,000
Endowment	3,850,000
Restricted	7,300,000
Unrestricted	8,270,000
Total Fund Balances	48,420,000
Total Liabilities and Fund Balances	$58,300,000

Additional information concerning the statement of financial position is as follows:

1. Except for $70,000 of cash, the Endowment Fund is made up of investments only. There are no liabilities.
2. The Plant Fund has no current liabilities and includes some investments and $15,000 in cash.
3. In addition to investments, the Current Restricted Fund consists of the pledges receivable, $35,000 of accounts payable, and cash of $155,000.

Required:

Prepare a corrected statement of financial position for the Blood Donors of America Foundation at December 31, 2008, using the following columnar format:

	Current Unrestricted	*Current Restricted*	*Plant*	*Endowment*	*Total*
(Account Titles)	$	$	$	$	$

(*AICPA adapted*)

PROBLEM 19-7 **Investment Pool** LO11

Three funds of the Leukemia Foundation, a nonprofit welfare organization, began an investment pool on January 1, 2009. The costs and fair market values on this date were as follows:

	Cost	*Market Value*
Restricted fund	$ 55,000	$ 70,000
Lambert endowment fund	215,000	210,000
Plant fund	200,000	220,000
Total	$470,000	$500,000

During 2009 the investment pool reinvested $20,000 in realized gains and received interest of $15,000 and dividends of $10,000. Interest and dividend income was distributed to the respective funds. The Plant Fund withdrew from the investment pool on December 31, 2009, when the total current market value was $540,000. It distributed securities in the amount of its percentage share.

On January 3, 2010, the Fargot Annuity Fund entered the investment pool with investments costing $100,000 and having a current market value of $117,600. During 2010 the pool received interest of $25,000 and dividends of $15,000, which were distributed to the participating funds. Realized gains of $30,000 were reinvested in the pool.

Required:

A. Calculate the equity percentages of the contributing funds in the investment pool at January 1, 2009, and at January 3, 2010.

B. Using the format shown below, prepare entries necessary on the records of the funds that contributed securities to the investment pool to account for the earnings of the investment pool in 2009 and 2010.

Date	*Fund*	*Journal Entry*

GLOSSARY

Accretive Term applied to a business combination in which the acquirer's earnings per share increase as a result of the merger.

Accrual accounting The usual basis of accounting for profit-seeking enterprises under generally accepted accounting principles; revenues are recognized when earned, and expenses are matched against those revenues in the period of the benefit.

Acquisition accounting Method of accounting for business combinations in which the assets and liabilities of the acquired firm are valued at fair market values, including the recording of goodwill implied by any excess of purchase price over the net fair value. (Also called purchase method.)

Adjusting entries Journal entries needed to correct any accounts of the affiliates that may be incorrect at the financial statement date, or to recognize the effects of a transaction made by one party (such as the parent), but not recorded by another party (such as a subsidiary).

Advance plan for the distribution of cash A schedule that specifies the order in which each partner will participate in sharing profit and losses and the amount of cash each partner will receive as it becomes available for distribution.

Affiliate An entity that controls, is controlled by, or is under common control with, another entity, either directly or indirectly through one or more intermediaries.

Agency funds Funds used to report resources held by the reporting government in a purely custodial capacity (assets equal liabilities). Agency funds typically involve only the receipt, temporary investment, and remittance of fiduciary resources to individuals, private organizations, or other governments.

Agency or custodial fund of an NNO Funds used to account for the assets held by an NNO (nongovernment nonbusiness organization) as a custodian for others.

American depository receipt (ADR) A depository receipt that is traded in the United States. ADRs may be sponsored or unsponsored.

Amortization The transfer of the cost of an asset over its useful life from the balance sheet to the income statement. Amortization is required for intangible assets with a finite life.

Annuity and life income fund of an NNO An NNO may accept the contribution of assets to the organization on the condition that the organization make annuity payments to a specified recipient for a specified period of time (annuity fund) or that the organization pay the income earned on the contributed assets to a specified recipient during his or her lifetime (life income fund).

Appropriations The maximum expenditures that are authorized by the legislature when budgeted expenditures are enacted into law.

Articles of partnership See Partnership agreement.

Asset acquisition A business combination in which one corporation pays cash or issues stock or debt for the net assets of another company, and the acquired company no longer exists as a separate legal entity.

Bargain purchase A business combination in which the price paid to acquire another firm is lower than the fair value of identifiable net assets (assets minus liabilities).

Bonus method A method used when the composition of a partnership changes (such as admission of a new partner) to adjust the partners' capital accounts equitably to account for undervalued assets or the existence of implied goodwill. Under this method, the assets are not revalued (and goodwill is not recorded).

Budgetary funds Fund entities in which the budget is formally incorporated into the accounting records.

Capital improvement special assessments Assessments levied against property owners for capital improvements that benefit them.

Capital maintenance approach An approach under which some changes in net assets are excluded from the Statement of Activities, such as capital contributions and permanently restricted contributions of financial assets.

Capital projects fund A fund used to account for financial resources to be used for the acquisition or construction of major capital facilities.

Change in net assets approach An approach, required on all governmentwide financial statements, under which all changes in net assets are reported on the Statement of Activities. There are no "balance sheet-only" transactions.

Chief operating decision maker A person whose general function (not specific title) is to allocate resources to, and assess the performance of, the segments of an enterprise.

Common costs Operating expenses incurred by the enterprise for the benefit of more than one segment.

Complete equity method A variation of the equity method, in which the reported income (loss) of the investee is adjusted for excess depreciation, goodwill amortization, and other differences implied by the investor's purchase price, in measuring the investor's income from investment.

Component units of a government Legally independent units that are within the government's control. (A school district is funded by the county, but is independent of the county; therefore, the county includes the school district as a component unit.)

Comprehensive income All changes in net assets (or equity) or an entity during the current period except those arising from investments by the owners and distributions to the owners.

Computation and Allocation Schedule A schedule used to show how the cost of an acquisition (the purchase price) is allocated to specific assets and liabilities of the subsidiary.

Conglomerate A business combination among firms in unrelated industries.

Connecting affiliates A type of indirect ownership where the parent and the parent's subsidiary both have ownership interests in a third company.

Consolidated entity (affiliated group) A group of firms consisting of a parent and all subsidiaries for which consolidated financial statements are prepared.

Consolidated financial statements The combined financial statements of a parent and its subsidiaries as one economic entity, as though the separate companies were a single company with one or more divisions or branches.

Consolidated net income A number equal to the parent company's income from its independent operations plus (minus) reported subsidiary income (loss) plus or minus adjustments for the period relating to the amortization of the difference between implied and book value.

Consolidated retained earnings The retained earnings of the parent company, after reflecting any needed adjustments from the perspective of the consolidated entity. Under the complete equity method, the adjustments are already included in the books of the parent. Under the partial equity method, for example, the number is calculated as the parent company's recorded partial-equity basis retained earnings plus or minus the cumulative effect of the adjustments to date relating to the amortization of the difference between implied and book value.

Constructive retirement (of bond obligation) Extinguishment of debt from the perspective of the consolidated entity, occurring in situations such as when one affiliate purchases another affiliate's outstanding bonds from outsiders.

Consumption method for inventory Method of accounting for inventory in which the inventory is considered a financial resource (asset) and expenditures for inventory are reported on the operating statement in the period the inventory is used.

Control (effective control) The ability of an entity to direct the policies and management that guide the ongoing activities of another entity so as to increase its benefits and limit its losses from that other entity's activities. For purposes of consolidated financial statements, control involves decision-making ability not shared with others.

Controlling interest The interest of the parent company in a partially owned subsidiary. The term is also used to refer to the parent's interest in the combined profits of the parent and its subsidiary.

Corporate assets Assets maintained for general corporate purposes and not specifically used in the operations of any segment.

Cost method A method used to account for an investment in another company, in which the income from investment consists of dividends received. Under this method, the carrying value of the investment changes only when the percentage ownership changes, or when it is believed to be permanently impaired.

Current exchange rate The spot rate in effect at the end of the accounting period (i.e., the balance sheet date).

Current fund of an NNO (restricted and unrestricted). Current unrestricted funds include financial resources of an organization that may be expended at the discretion of the governing board. Current restricted funds consist of financial resources that are currently available for use in current operations, but which may be expended only for purposes specified by the donor, grantor, or other external party.

Current rate method A method of converting accounts from a foreign currency into the parent's reporting currency, in which all assets and liabilities are translated using the current exchange rate. This method is appropriate when the accounts are already measured in the functional currency. (Also called translation.)

Debt service fund A fund used to account for the accumulation of resources for the payment of general long-term debt principal and interest.

Deferred taxes Taxes resulting from temporary differences between taxable income and income reported under generally accepted accounting principles; deferred tax liabilities represent an increase in taxes payable in future years as a result of these differences, while deferred tax assets represent a resulting decrease in taxes payable in future years.

Depository receipt (DR) A derivative instrument usually representing a certain fixed number of publicly traded shares of a non-U.S. corporation.

Derivative Financial product whose value depends on another *underlying* value of measure, but whose terms do not require the holder to own or deliver the underlying value of measure. Thus its value is *derived* from the underlying value of measure (examples include options, swaps, forwards, and futures).

Dilutive Term applied to an acquisition in which the acquirer's earnings per share decrease as a result of the combination.

Direct exchange quotation A quotation in which the exchange rate is quoted in terms of how many units of the domestic currency can be converted into one unit of foreign currency.

Direct expenses Expenses incurred in a business combination, such as accounting and consulting fees, that would not have been incurred in the absence of the combination. These types of expenses are capitalized (charged to an asset account) under purchase accounting rules.

Dissolution The change in the relation of the partners that occurs when a partner ceases to be associated with a partnership, as distinguished from the winding up of the business.

Downstream sales Sales by a parent company to one or more of its subsidiaries.

Economic entity concept A concept that emphasizes control of the whole by a single management, so that the consolidated financial statements are intended to provide information about a group of legal entities—a parent company and its subsidiaries—operating as a single unit.

Eliminating entries Journal entries that are made only on the consolidated workpaper (and not on the parent's or subsidiary's books) to cancel the effects of intercompany transactions and accounts.

Encumbrance Term applied to the financial resources of a fund when a transaction is entered into that requires the performance on the part of another party before the government becomes liable to perform its part of the transaction. (For example, placing a purchase order creates an encumbrance, but the government is not liable until the goods are received.)

Endowment fund of an NNO Category of funds that includes both pure endowment funds and term endowment funds. Pure endowment funds require that the principal be kept in perpetuity, while term endowment funds allow the principal to be spent after a particular date or event.

Enterprise fund A fund used to account for any activity for which a fee is charged to external users for goods and services.

Equity allocation rule When the par (or stated) value of the shares issued by the issuing firm in a pooling of interests exceeds the total par or stated value of the combining company's stock, the excess should be deducted first from the combined other contributed capital and then from combined retained earnings.

Equity method A method used to account for an investment in another company, in which the income from investment consists of the investor's share of the profits (losses) of the investee. Under this method, the carrying value of the investments is adjusted continually to reflect the investee's profits, losses, and dividends.

Exchange rate The ratio between a unit of one currency and the amount of another currency for which that unit can be exchanged at a particular time.

Expendable fund entity A fund entity established to account for net financial resources dedicated for specific use(s).

Expenditure Decrease in the financial resources of a fund or incurrence of a fund liability.

Father–son–grandson affiliation A type of indirect ownership where the parent has ownership interests in a subsidiary that owns a controlling interest in a third firm.

Fiduciary funds Funds that hold assets in a trustee or agency capacity for others and that cannot be used to support the government's own programs.

Financial synergy Financial advantages or benefits arising from a business combination; for example, the opportunity to file a consolidated tax return may allow profitable corporations' tax liability to be reduced by the losses of unprofitable affiliates.

Also, when an acquisition is financed using debt, the interest payments are tax deductible, creating a financial synergy.

Floating rates The exchange rates between major currencies, largely determined by supply and demand factors.

Flow of current financial resources Concept under which each year is treated as a distinct event and the only measurement that is important is the source and use of funds (where funds are usually defined on a modified accrual basis). A charge to operations is generally made when goods and services are acquired rather than when the goods and services are consumed or used.

Flow of economic resources A concept or focus now required for government-wide financial statements, which requires the accrual basis and thus recognizes economic transactions and other events when they occur, rather than only when the related inflows and outflows of cash or other financial resources occur. A charge is made to operations in the period when goods and services are used or consumed rather than when goods and services are acquired.

Forecasted transaction Expected future transaction that does not bear severe penalties for nonperformance or that is not under contract.

Foreign currency exposure The loss potential that exists as a result of uncertainty about future changes in exchange rates.

Foreign currency transaction A transaction that requires settlement in a foreign currency.

Forward exchange contract An agreement to exchange currencies of two different countries at a specified rate (the forward rate) on a stipulated future date. At the inception of the contract, the forward rate normally differs from the spot rate.

Forward rate An exchange rate quoted for future delivery of currencies exchanged.

Functional currency The currency in which a company primarily conducts its operations and generates and expends cash.

Fund accounting A system of accounting for nonbusiness organizations where the entities' resources are accounted for by individual funds.

GASB See Government Accounting Standards Board.

General corporate expense Any expense incurred for the benefit of the corporation as a whole, which cannot be reasonably allocated to any segment.

General fund A fund used to account for unrestricted financial resources, especially those required to be accounted for in another fund.

General partnership A partnership in which all partners are general (rather than limited). Characteristics of general partnerships include mutual agency, unlimited liability, limited life, and the right to dispose of a partnership interest.

Global depository receipt (GDR) A depository receipt that is traded globally.

Goodwill (or excess of implied over fair value) The excess of the value implied by the acquisition cost over the fair value of the identifiable net assets of the subsidiary on the date of acquisition.

Goodwill method A method used when the composition of a partnership changes (such as admission of a new partner) to adjust the partners' capital accounts equitably to account for the existence of implied goodwill. Under this method, the goodwill is recorded, and the capital accounts of the partners responsible for creating the goodwill are credited.

Government Accounting Standards Board (GASB) The authoritative body responsible for establishing financial accounting standards for all state and local governmental bodies.

Government-wide financial statements The Statement of Activities and the Statement of Net Assets now required to be prepared on an accrual basis listing the total activities of the government.

Hedge A purchase or sale transaction entered into to counterbalance potential losses (profits) arising from price fluctuations; a way of transferring the risk of price fluctuations from one group to another (for example, from seller to purchaser).

Historical exchange rate The spot rate in effect on the date a transaction takes place.

Horizontal combination (horizontal integration) A business combination among companies within the same industry operating at the same basic level (competitors).

Horizontal sales Sales from one subsidiary to another subsidiary.

Impairment The decline in fair value of an asset below its recorded book value, resulting in a reported loss in the income statement. Goodwill and other intangible assets with indefinite lives must be reviewed at least annually for potential impairment.

Implied value The fair value of an acquired entity, as implied by its purchase (acquisition) price. Implied value may be calculated as the acquisition cost divided by the percentage acquired.

Indirect expenses Expenses related to business combinations that are ongoing in nature, such as those incurred to maintain a mergers and acquisitions department, and that would have continued in the absence of a specific acquisition. These expenses, which also include managerial or secretarial time and overhead allocated to the merger, are expensed as incurred.

Indirect ownership A relationship created when a parent owns a subsidiary that owns an interest in another firm; i.e., the parent indirectly owns an interest in the third firm.

Infrastructure assets Immovable assets of a government such as streets, sidewalks, bridges, drains, street lights, etc.

Installment liquidation A liquidation that extends over a period of time, in which partners receive cash in installments before the total liquidation losses and total cash available are known.

Intercompany accounts (reciprocal accounts) Accounts that are maintained in the separate books of a parent and its subsidiaries that reflect a single transaction and should be eliminated in preparing the consolidated reports; for example, an "account receivable from subsidiary" on the books of a parent is reciprocal to an "account payable to parent" on the books of the subsidiary.

Interfund activity Activity between funds that includes reciprocal and nonreciprocal transactions. Reciprocal interfund activities include interfund loans and interfund services provided and used. Nonreciprocal interfund activities include interfund transfers and interfund reimbursements.

Interfund transfers See Interfund activity.

Internal service fund A fund used to account for any activity that provides goods or services to other funds, departments, or agencies of the primary government on a cost-reimbursement basis.

International Accounting Standards Board (IASB) A committee whose missions are to formulate international accounting standards used in the presentation of financial statements and to promote their worldwide acceptance and observation.

International Federation of Accountants (IFAC) An organization of practicing international accountants that is responsible for appointing members to the IASC Board.

International Financial Reporting Standards (IFRS) Standards issued by the International Accounting Standards Board (IASB) as part of a drive toward the global harmonization of accounting practices.

Investee A corporation that issues (sells) voting stock held by an investor (buyer).

Investment trust funds Funds used to report the external portion of investment pools reported by the sponsoring government.

Investor A business entity that holds an investment in voting stock of another company.

Joint and severally liable Legal action may be brought against all the partners together or against any one or more of the partners in separate suits.

Joint venture An arrangement entered into by two or more parties to accomplish a single or limited purpose for the mutual benefit of the members of the group, often to earn a profit.

Leveraged buyout (LBO) The creation by a group of employees (generally a management group) and third-party investors of a new company to acquire all the outstanding common shares of their employer company. The management group contributes whatever stock they hold to the new corporation and borrows sufficient funds to acquire the remainder of the common stock.

Limited partnership A partnership in which one or more of the partners are general and one or more are limited. Limited partners invest capital only and limit their liability for partnership obligations to the extent of the amount invested.

Liquidating dividend In the context of business combinations, dividends declared by a subsidiary in excess of its cumulative earnings since acquisition.

Loan funds of an NNO Funds used to account for loans to students and staff of colleges and universities, to hospitals, and to beneficiaries of the interests of certain ONNOs (e.g., loans to music students by symphony orchestra societies). Loan funds are generally revolving (repayments of loan balances and interest are in turn lent to other individuals).

Local currency The currency in which a foreign entity will generally measure and record its transactions, usually the currency of the country in which it is located.

Major funds of a government Funds of a government that are required to be displayed separately on the balance sheet and the statement of revenues, expenditures, and changes in fund balances. Size percentage cutoffs are used to determine the major funds.

Majority-owned subsidiary A subsidiary in which a parent or the parent's other majority-owned subsidiaries hold more than 50% of the outstanding voting stock.

Modified accrual accounting A variation of accrual accounting used by expendable fund entities. Revenues must be both measurable and available to liquidate liabilities of the current period before they are recognized. Expenditures are recognizable when an event is expected to use current spendable resources, rather than future resources.

Monetary accounts Cash and other assets and liability accounts that are to be settled in cash.

Mutual agency One of the characteristics of a general partnership; each general partner is an agent of both the partnership and every other partner. Thus a partner can bind the other partners to a contract.

Net assets An entity's assets minus liabilities.

Net assets (not-for-profit) Term replacing the label "fund balance" as historically used in not-for-profit organizations under the authority of the FASB. Net Assets are categorized into unrestricted, temporarily restricted, and permanently restricted categories.

Net monetary position Monetary assets minus monetary liabilities.

Noncontrolling interest (minority interest) The interest in the profits (losses) or net assets of a partially owned subsidiary of all shareholders other than the parent.

Nongovernment nonbusiness organizations (NNOs) NNOs include nonprofit institutions of higher education, hospitals and other healthcare providers, voluntary health and welfare organizations (VHWOs), and other nongovernment nonbusiness organizations (ONNOs).

Operating segment A component of an enterprise that may earn revenues and incur expenses, about which separate financial information is evaluated regularly by the chief operating decision maker in deciding how to allocate resources and in assessing performance.

Option A legal right to buy or sell something at a specified price, usually within a specified time period (for example, in a foreign currency option contract, the holder has the right to buy or sell a specified amount of currency according to stipulated terms).

Other financing sources Proceeds from debt issuances and transfers of financial resources to and from other funds.

Other nongovernment nonbusiness organizations (ONNOs) Wide variety of organizations taking assorted forms, ranging from cemetery organizations, civic organizations, and labor unions to performing arts organizations, political parties, private and community foundations, private elementary and secondary schools, and zoological and botanical societies.

Parent A company that controls another company, usually achieved by direct or indirect ownership of some or all of its voting stock.

Parent company concept A concept that emphasizes the interests of the parent's shareholders in such a way that the consolidated financial statements reflect those stockholder interests in the parent itself, plus their undivided interests in the net assets of the parent's subsidiaries.

"Parent only" financial statements The unconsolidated financial statements of a parent company, in which its subsidiaries are shown as investments.

Partial equity method A variation of the equity method, in which the reported income (loss) of the investee is used to measure the investor's income from investment, without adjustment.

Partnership agreement A contractual agreement between or among legally competent persons to form a voluntary partnership (may also be called a partnership contract or articles of partnership).

Pension (and other employee benefit) trust funds Funds used to report resources that are required to be held in trust for the members and beneficiaries of defined benefit pension plans, defined contribution plans, other postemployment benefit plans, or other employee benefit plans.

Permanent fund A fund used to account for resources that are legally restricted to the extent that the earnings, and not principal, can be used to support the activities of the government.

Permanently restricted net assets Endowments in which the interest may be spent but the principal must not be used.

Plant fund of an NNO Fund used to account for (1) the property and equipment owned by the organization and the net investment, (2) the accumulation of financial resources for the acquisition or replacement of property and equipment, (3) the acquisition and disposal of property and equipment, (4) liabilities relating to the acquisition of property and equipment, and (5) depreciation expense and accumulated depreciation.

Pooling of interests method A method of accounting for business combinations, allowed prior to June 2001 in the U.S., in which the assets and liabilities of the combining firm are carried forward at their historical book values. This method, which requires the use of stock as the medium of exchange, is sometimes justified as the uniting of two or more groups of shareholders into a single "pooled" entity, with no group being dominant.

Primary government Part of the government including the government funds and the proprietary funds, but not including component units of the government.

Private-purpose trust funds Funds used to report escheat property. These funds should be used to report all other trust agreements under which principal and income benefits individuals, private organizations, or other governments.

Pro forma statements Financial statements prepared to show the effect of planned or contemplated transactions as if they had occurred during the period covered by the financial statements; sometimes called "as if" statements.

Profit or loss agreement An agreement that indicates how a partnership's profits or losses should be allocated. Common agreements are based on a fixed ratio, a ratio based on capital balances, interest on capital balances, an allocation based on time or managerial talent, or some combination of these.

Proprietary (nonexpendable) fund entities The activities of nonbusiness organizations that operate similar to those of business enterprises, such as water utilities. Proprietary funds include enterprise and internal service funds.

Purchase method See Acquisition accounting.

Purchases method for inventory Method of accounting for inventory in which the inventory is not considered a financial resource (asset), and all inventory purchases are recognized as expenditures whether the inventory is used or not.

Push down accounting The establishment of a new accounting and reporting basis for a subsidiary company in its separate financial statements based on the purchase price paid by the parent company to acquire a controlling interest in the outstanding voting stock of the subsidiary company.

Reciprocal stockholdings A relationship created when two or more affiliates have ownership interests in each other; for example, the parent owns shares in a subsidiary that also owns shares in the parent.

Relevance One of the primary qualities of accounting information identified in *SFAC No. 2*, referring to the characteristic of making a difference in a decision.

Reliability One of the primary qualities of accounting information identified in *SFAC No. 2*, incorporating the characteristics of verifiability, representational faithfulness, and reasonable freedom from error and bias.

Remeasurement The process of translating the accounts of a foreign entity into its functional currency when they are stated in another currency (often used to refer to the temporal method).

Remeasurement gain or loss Gain or loss arising from the application of the temporal method to convert accounts from a nonfunctional foreign currency into U.S. dollars.

Reportable segment A segment considered to be significant to an enterprise's operations; specifically one that has passed one of three 10% tests or has been identified as being reportable through other criteria (aggregation, for example).

Reporting currency The currency in which a company reporting entity prepares its financial statements, usually the domestic currency of the country in which the company is domiciled.

Reserve for inventory A fund balance account sometimes used under the purchases method for inventory to offset a debit to inventory.

Restricted fund entities An expendable fund whose current financial resources are limited as to use because of externally imposed restrictions.

Safe payment approach A schedule used in an installment liquidation that guarantees that before any cash is distributed to partners, the partners' remaining capital balances are sufficient to absorb any potential loss.

Segment assets Those tangible and intangible assets directly associated with, or used by, a segment, including any allocated portion of assets used jointly by more than one segment. If portions of assets are allocated internally and used by a chief operating decision maker, then those amounts should be allocated on a reasonable basis and disclosed for external reporting purposes as well.

Segment operating profit or loss All of a segment's revenue minus all operating expenses, including any allocated revenues or expenses (e.g., common costs).

Segment revenue The revenue from sales to unaffiliated customers and from intersegment sales or transfers.

Service-type special assessment An assessment levied against property owners for services that benefit them.

Settlement date Date at which a payable is paid or a receivable is collected.

Simple liquidation A procedure in which all noncash assets are converted into cash before any assets are distributed to creditors and partners.

Sound value The fair value of used assets in appraisal reports.

Special items Significant fund accounting transactions within the control of management that are either unusual or infrequent.

Special revenue fund A fund used to account for the proceeds of specific revenue sources that are legally restricted to expenditures for specified purposes.

Spot rate An exchange rate quoted for immediate delivery of a currency.

Statutory consolidation A consolidation resulting when a new corporation is formed to acquire two or more other corporations through an exchange of voting stock; the acquired corporations then cease to exist as separate legal entities.

Statutory merger A legal term referring to the loss of a subsidiary's corporate legal entity status by canceling its corporate charter. The parent takes title to the newly acquired subsidiary's assets and assumes responsibility for its liabilities, and the subsidiary ceases to exist as a separate legal entity, although it may be continued as a separate division of the acquiring company.

Stock acquisition A business combination in which one corporation pays cash or issues stock or debt for all or part of the voting stock of another company, and the acquired company remains intact as a separate legal entity.

Stock exchange ratio A ratio generally defined as the number of shares of the acquiring company to be exchanged for each share of the acquired company, thus constituting a negotiated price.

Subsidiary A company that is controlled by another company through direct or indirect ownership of some or all of its voting stock.

20-F statement A form filed annually with the Securities and Exchange Commission (SEC) by foreign firms that list in the U.S. stock exchanges.

Takeover premium The excess of the amount offered, or agreed upon, in an acquisition over the prior stock price of the acquired firm.

Temporal method A method of converting accounts from a foreign currency into the functional currency, in which monetary assets and liabilities are translated at the current exchange rate; assets and liabilities carried at historical cost are translated at historical exchange rates; and assets and liabilities carried at current values are translated at the current exchange rate (also called remeasurement).

Temporarily restricted net assets Resources that must be used for a specific purpose or in a specific time period where the restriction is donor imposed (rather than imposed by the governing board).

Tender offer An offer made directly to the shareholders of a company targeted by another company in a potential business combination. Usually published in a newspaper, a tender offer typically provides a price higher than the current market price for shares made available by a certain date.

Totally held subsidiary A subsidiary in which a parent or the parent's other majority-owned subsidiaries hold substantially all the subsidiary's outstanding equity securities and where the subsidiary is not materially indebted to any party other than the parent and/or the parent's other totally held subsidiaries.

Transaction gain or loss The gain or loss that arises from holding foreign currency receivables or payables and resulting from changes in exchange rates between the transaction date and the settlement date.

Transfer pricing The pricing of products or services between operating segments or geographic areas.

Translation Term is used in the two following ways: (1) as a generic term to apply to any restatement of foreign currency units into the reporting currency and (2) more specifically, to apply to the restatement of foreign currency units that are already measured in the functional currency into dollars (current rate method).

Translation adjustments Dual-meaning term referring either to: (1) any gains or losses resulting from the effects of converting financial statements from foreign currency into the parent's reporting currency; or (2) those gains and losses arising from the application of the current method to convert from the functional currency into U.S. dollars.

Treasury stock method An accounting method under which a reciprocal stockholding is presented as treasury stock on the consolidated balance sheet from the perspective of the parent firm, and the noncontrolling shareholders' interest in the parent is essentially ignored.

Undistributed subsidiary income The difference between the parent's share of the subsidiary's income, which is included in consolidated net income, and the amount of dividends received from the subsidiary, which is included in its taxable income if the affiliates file separate tax returns.

Unlimited liability A feature of a general partnership, establishing that each partner is jointly and severally liable for the debts and obligations of the partnership. Thus creditors, in a liquidation, can proceed against the personal assets for recovery of claims.

Unrealized intercompany profit (loss) Profit (loss) that has not been realized from the point of view of the consolidated entity through subsequent sales to third parties and must be eliminated in the preparation of consolidated financial statements.

Unrestricted net assets Net assets that do not meet the definition of temporarily or permanently restricted net assets and are designated to indicate their availability for general operations.

Upstream sales Sales by subsidiary companies to the parent company.

Vertical combination (vertical integration) A business combination among companies within the same industry operating at different levels (supplier and customer).

Voluntary health and welfare organizations (VHWOs) Organizations that derive their revenues from voluntary contributions of the general public to be used for purposes connected with health, welfare, or community services.

Wholly owned subsidiary A subsidiary in which all of the subsidiary's outstanding voting stock is owned by the parent and/or the parent's other wholly owned subsidiaries.

APPENDIX: TABLES OF PRESENT VALUES

TABLE A1 Present Value of 1

$$p^n = \frac{1}{(1+i)^n} = (1+i)^{-n}$$

(n) PERIODS	2%	2.5%	3%	4%	5%	6%	8%	9%	10%	12%	15%
1	.98039	.97561	.97087	.96154	.95238	.94340	.92593	.91743	.90909	.89286	.86957
2	.96117	.95181	.94260	.92456	.90703	.89000	.85734	.84168	.82645	.79719	.75614
3	.94232	.92860	.91514	.88900	.86384	.83962	.79383	.77218	.75132	.71178	.65752
4	.92385	.90595	.88849	.85480	.82270	.79209	.73503	.70843	.68301	.63552	.57175
5	.90573	.88385	.86261	.82193	.78353	.74726	.68058	.64993	.62092	.56743	.49718
6	.88797	.86230	.83748	.79031	.74622	.70496	.63017	.59627	.56447	.50663	.43233
7	.87056	.84127	.81309	.75992	.71068	.66506	.58349	.54703	.51316	.45235	.37594
8	.85349	.82075	.78941	.73069	.67684	.62741	.54027	.50187	.46651	.40388	.32690
9	.83676	.80073	.76642	.70259	.64461	.59190	.50025	.46043	.42410	.36061	.28426
10	.82035	.78120	.74409	.67556	.61391	.55839	.46319	.42241	.38554	.32197	.24719
11	.80426	.76214	.72242	.64958	.58468	.52679	.42888	.38753	.35049	.28748	.21494
12	.78849	.74356	.70138	.62460	.55684	.49697	.39711	.35554	.31863	.25668	.18691
13	.77303	.72542	.68095	.60057	.53032	.46884	.36770	.32618	.28966	.22917	.16253
14	.75788	.70773	.66112	.57748	.50507	.44230	.34046	.29925	.26333	.20462	.14133
15	.74301	.69047	.64186	.55526	.48102	.41727	.31524	.27454	.23939	.18270	.12289
16	.72845	.67362	.62317	.53391	.45811	.39365	.29189	.25187	.21763	.16312	.10687
17	.71416	.65720	.60502	.51337	.43630	.37136	.27027	.23107	.19785	.14564	.09293
18	.70016	.64117	.58739	.49363	.41552	.35034	.25025	.21199	.17986	.13004	.08081
19	.68643	.62553	.57029	.47464	.39573	.33051	.23171	.19449	.16351	.11611	.07027
20	.67297	.61027	.55368	.45639	.37689	.31180	.21455	.17843	.14864	.10367	.06110
21	.65978	.59539	.53755	.43883	.35894	.29416	.19866	.16370	.13513	.09256	.05313
22	.64684	.58086	.52189	.42196	.34185	.27751	.18394	.15018	.12285	.08264	.04620
23	.63416	.56670	.50669	.40573	.32557	.26180	.17032	.13778	.11168	.07379	.04017
24	.62172	.55288	.49193	.39012	.31007	.24698	.15770	.12641	.10153	.06588	.03493
25	.60953	.53939	.47761	.37512	.29530	.23300	.14602	.11597	.09230	.05882	.03038
26	.59758	.52623	.46369	.36069	.28124	.21981	.13520	.10639	.08391	.05252	.02642
27	.58586	.51340	.45019	.34682	.26785	.20737	.12519	.09761	.07628	.04689	.02297
28	.57437	.50088	.43708	.33348	.25509	.19563	.11591	.08955	.06934	.04187	.01997
29	.56311	.48866	.42435	.32065	.24295	.18456	.10733	.08216	.06304	.03738	.01737
30	.55207	.47674	.41199	.30832	.23138	.17411	.09938	.07537	.05731	.03338	.01510
31	.54125	.46511	.39999	.29646	.22036	.16425	.09202	.06915	.05210	.02980	.01313
32	.53063	.45377	.38834	.28506	.20987	.15496	.08520	.06344	.04736	.02661	.01142
33	.52023	.44270	.37703	.27409	.19987	.14619	.07889	.05820	.04306	.02376	.00993
34	.51003	.43191	.36604	.26355	.19035	.13791	.07305	.05340	.03914	.02121	.00864
35	.50003	.42137	.35538	.25342	.18129	.13011	.06763	.04899	.03558	.01894	.00751
36	.49022	.41109	.34503	.24367	.17266	.12274	.06262	.04494	.03235	.01691	.00653
37	.48061	.40107	.33498	.23430	.16444	.11579	.05799	.04123	.02941	.01510	.00568
38	.47119	.39128	.32523	.22529	.15661	.10924	.05369	.03783	.02674	.01348	.00494
39	.46195	.38174	.31575	.21662	.14915	.10306	.04971	.03470	.02430	.01204	.00429
40	.45289	.37243	.30656	.20829	.14205	.09722	.04603	.03184	.02210	.01075	.00373

TABLE A2 Present Value of an Ordinary Annuity of 1

$$P_{ni} = \frac{1 - \frac{1}{(1+i)^n}}{i} = \frac{1 - v^n}{i}$$

(n) PERIODS	2%	2.5%	3%	4%	5%	6%	8%	9%	10%	12%	15%
1	.98039	.97561	.97087	.96154	.95238	.94340	.92593	.91743	.90909	.89286	.86957
2	1.94156	1.92742	1.91347	1.88609	1.85941	1.83339	1.78326	1.75911	1.73554	1.69005	1.62571
3	2.88388	2.85602	2.82861	2.77509	2.72325	2.67301	2.57710	2.53130	2.48685	2.40183	2.28323
4	3.80773	3.76197	3.71710	3.62990	3.54595	3.46511	3.31213	3.23972	3.16986	3.03735	2.85498
5	4.71346	4.64583	4.57971	4.45182	4.32948	4.21236	3.99271	3.88965	3.79079	3.60478	3.35216
6	5.60143	5.50813	5.41719	5.24214	5.07569	4.91732	4.62288	4.48592	4.35526	4.11141	3.78448
7	6.47199	6.34939	6.23028	6.00205	5.78637	5.58238	5.20637	5.03295	4.86842	4.56376	4.16042
8	7.32548	7.17014	7.01969	6.73274	6.46321	6.20979	5.74664	5.53482	5.33493	4.96764	4.48732
9	8.16224	7.97087	7.78611	7.43533	7.10782	6.80169	6.24689	5.99525	5.75902	5.32825	4.77158
10	8.98259	8.75206	8.53020	8.11090	7.72173	7.36009	6.71008	6.41766	6.14457	5.65022	5.01877
11	9.78685	9.51421	9.25262	8.76048	8.30641	7.88687	7.13896	6.80519	6.49506	5.93770	5.23371
12	10.57534	10.25776	9.95400	9.38507	8.86325	8.38384	7.53608	7.16073	6.81369	6.19437	5.42062
13	11.34837	10.98319	10.63496	9.98565	9.39357	8.85268	7.90378	7.48690	7.10336	6.42355	5.58315
14	12.10625	11.69091	11.29607	10.56312	9.89864	9.29498	8.24424	7.78615	7.36669	6.62817	5.72448
15	12.84926	12.38138	11.93794	11.11839	10.37966	9.71225	8.55948	8.06069	7.60608	6.81086	5.84737
16	13.57771	13.05500	12.56110	11.65230	10.83777	10.10590	8.85137	8.31256	7.82371	6.97399	5.95424
17	14.29187	13.71220	13.16612	12.16567	11.27407	10.47726	9.12164	8.54363	8.02155	7.11963	6.04716
18	14.99203	14.35336	13.75351	12.65930	11.68959	10.82760	9.37189	8.75563	8.20141	7.24967	6.12797
19	15.67846	14.97889	14.32380	13.13394	12.08532	11.15812	9.60360	8.95012	8.36492	7.36578	6.19823
20	16.35143	15.58916	14.87747	13.59033	12.46221	11.46992	9.81815	9.12855	8.51356	7.46944	6.25933
21	17.01121	16.18455	15.41502	14.02916	12.82115	11.76408	10.01680	9.29224	8.64869	7.56200	6.31246
22	17.65805	16.76541	15.93692	14.45112	13.16300	12.04158	10.20074	9.44243	8.77154	7.64465	6.35866
23	18.29220	17.33211	16.44361	14.85684	13.48857	12.30338	10.37106	9.58021	8.88322	7.71843	6.39884
24	18.91393	17.88499	16.93554	15.24696	13.79864	12.55036	10.52876	9.70661	8.98474	7.78432	6.43377
25	19.52346	18.42438	17.41315	15.62208	14.09394	12.78336	10.67478	9.82258	9.07704	7.84314	6.46415
26	20.12104	18.95061	17.87684	15.98277	14.37519	13.00317	10.80998	9.92897	9.16095	7.89566	6.49056
27	20.70690	19.46401	18.32703	16.32959	14.64303	13.21053	10.93516	10.02658	9.23722	7.94255	6.51353
28	21.28127	19.96489	18.76411	16.66306	14.89813	13.40616	11.05108	10.11613	9.30657	7.98442	6.53351
29	21.84438	20.45355	19.18845	16.98371	15.14107	13.59072	11.15841	10.19828	9.36961	8.02181	6.55088
30	22.39646	20.93029	19.60044	17.29203	15.37245	13.76483	11.25778	10.27365	9.42691	8.05518	6.56598
31	22.93770	21.39541	20.00043	17.58849	15.59281	13.92909	11.34980	10.34280	9.47901	8.08499	6.57911
32	23.46833	21.84918	20.38877	17.87355	15.80268	14.08404	11.43500	10.40624	9.52638	8.11159	6.59053
33	23.98856	22.29188	20.76579	18.14765	16.00255	14.23023	11.51389	10.46444	9.56943	8.13535	6.60046
34	24.49859	22.72379	21.13184	18.41120	16.19290	14.36814	11.58693	10.51784	9.60858	8.15656	6.60910
35	24.99862	23.14516	21.48722	18.66461	16.37419	14.49825	11.65457	10.56682	9.64416	8.17550	6.61661
36	25.48884	23.55625	21.83225	18.90828	16.54685	14.62099	11.71719	10.61176	9.67651	8.19241	6.62314
37	25.96945	23.95732	22.16724	19.14258	16.71129	14.73678	11.77518	10.65299	9.70592	8.20751	6.62882
38	26.44064	24.34860	22.49246	19.36786	16.86789	14.84602	11.82887	10.69082	9.73265	8.22099	6.63375
39	26.90259	24.73034	22.80822	19.58448	17.01704	14.94907	11.87858	10.72552	9.75697	8.23303	6.63805
40	27.35548	25.10278	23.11477	19.79277	17.15909	15.04630	11.92461	10.75736	9.77905	8.24378	6.64178

INDEX

A
Accounting Industry Reform Act of 2002, 87
Accounting Principles Board (APB) Opinions:
No. 16, 47, 271
No. 18, 640–641, 729
No. 23, 190, 705
No. 24, 705
No. 28, 702–707
Accounting Research Bulletin (ARB):
No. 43, 524
No. 51, 46–47, 310, 334
Accounting Series Release No. 242 (SEC), 660
Accounting standards, international, *see* International accounting
Accounting Standards Codification (ASC), 558
Accounting Standards for Business Enterprises (ASBEs), 577
Accretion concept, 24–25
Accretive acquisitions, 25
Accrual accounting:
modified accrual accounting, 811
nongovernmental organizations and, 934–935
Accumulated depreciation, 267–269
Acquisition (purchase) accounting. *See also* Business combinations; Consolidated financial statements
acquisition date, 416, 664. *See also* Ownership interest
acquisition of interest, 744–751
contingent considerations, 61–65
cost methods and, 141–152
equity methods and, 154–161
explanation and illustration of, 56–60
interim acquisitions, 165–176
treatment of expenses, 52–53
Activity classifications, fund accounting and, 814–815
Adelphia Communications Corp., 526
Adjusted investment accounting, *see* Investments
Adjusting entries, 97
ADR, *see* American Depository Receipts
Affiliated companies. *See also* Business combinations; Consolidated financial statements
consolidated tax returns and, 189
definition of, 84
separate tax returns and, 188–193
Agency (custodial) fund accounting, 952
Agency funds, governmental, 857, 879, 895
Aggregation criteria, operating segments, 692
AICPA, *see* American Institute of Certified Public Accountants
Airline industry, 358
Allocation and depreciation of differences between implied and book values:
accumulated depreciation and, 267–270
acquisition cost less than fair value, 224–226
assets and liabilities of subsidiary and, 219–226
consolidated net income and, 226–230, 240–261
consolidated retained earnings and, 240–261
debt and, 261–264
depreciable assets used in manufacturing, 270
fair values less than book value, 264–266
implied value in excess of fair value, 221–224
push down accounting, 270–275
using complete equity method, 252–261
using cost method, 231–240
using partial equity method, 242–252
Allocation of constructive gain or loss, 456
Allocation problems, partnerships and, 738–741
Allstate Corp., 10
American Depository Receipts (ADR), 580–582
Level 11, 581
Level I, 581
Level III, 582
program types, 580–582
role of, 580
Rule 144A and, 582
sponsored, 580–581
unsponsored, 580
American Institute of Certified Public Accountants (AICPA), 524, 538, 558, 853–855, 929–931
American Recovery and Reinvestment Act of 2009, 811
Amortization:
of goodwill, 69–70
intangible assets and, 52, 221
schedules for bonds, 883
AMR Corp., 532
Angola, 648
Annuity fund accounting, 952–953
AOL Time Warner, 302

APB Opinions, see Accounting Principles Board Opinions
Appropriations, 810
  fund accounting and, 816
  lapsing of, 822
ASBEs (Accounting Standards for Business Enterprises), 577
ASC (Accounting Standards Codification), 558
Ashikaga Bank, 10
"As if" statements, *see* Pro forma statements
Assets:
  acquisition of, 84, 89
  contingent assets, 19–20
  definition of, 35
  marshaling of, 774
  stock acquisitions vs., 14–15
  transfers in reorganization, 524–525
  valuation of, 56–57
  voluntary assignment of, 517
Assumed liabilities, 19
AT&T, 5

B

BAE Systems PLC, 218
Bally Total Fitness Holding Corp., 7
Bank of America, 309
Bankruptcy, 518–521. *See also* Bankruptcy Reform Act; Insolvency
  dividends and, 520–521
  federal laws and, 518–519
  involuntary petitions and, 520
  and mergers, 2, 10
  secured and unsecured creditors and, 520–521
  and voluntary assignment of assets, 517
  voluntary petitions and, 519
Bankruptcy Abuse Prevention and Consumer Protection Act of 2005, 519
Bankruptcy Reform Act (1978), 515. *See also* Insolvency
  involuntary petitions and, 520
  liquidation (Chapter 7) and, 521
  provisions of, 518
  reorganization (Chapter 11) and, 522–523
  secured and unsecured creditors and, 520–521
  Statement of Affairs and, 530–532
  voluntary petitions and, 518
Bargain acquisitions, 57, 59–60, 101, 220–221
BASF AG, 6
Bayer AG, 6
BellSouth Corporation, 5
Beresford, Dennis, 32
Berkshire Hathaway, 83–84
Bid rates, 593
BlackRock, 138
Board designated funds, 937
Bonds, intercompany, *see* Intercompany bonds
Bond holdings, intercompany, *see* Intercompany bonds
Bonuses, partnerships and, 738
Bonus method, 734, 743–744, 748–750, 753
Book values, 29, 94, 434–438. *See also* Allocation and depreciation of differences between implied and book values; Consolidated financial statements
Budgetary fund entities, 809–810
Build-A-Bear Workshop, 25
Business combinations. *See also* Consolidated financial statements
  accretive acquisitions, 25
  allocation of expenses and, 20
  assumed liabilities and, 19
  avoiding pitfalls, 19–21
  book value and, 29
  CEO egos and, 20–21
  conglomerate mergers, 13
  consolidated balance sheet values and, 28–29
  consolidated financial statements and, 25–30
  consolidated net income and, 28
  contingent considerations in acquisitions, 61–65
  defense tactics and, 6–7
  deferred taxes in, 69–70
  definition of, 5
  deregulation and, 14
  dilutive acquisitions, 25
  diversification and, 9
  divestitures and, 10
  due diligence and, 19–21
  earnings accretion and, 24–25
  earnings dilution and, 24–25
  economic entity concept and, 26–27
  fair value and, 29
  financial synergy and, 9
  friendly combinations, 5, 6
  goodwill and, 22–25
  goodwill impairment test, 48–50
  historical perspective on, 11–14, 44–53
  horizontal integration, 11
  income tax consequences in, 59
  income tax laws and, 9
  intercompany profit and, 29
  international marketplace and, 9
  interpreting percentages, 19
  leveraged buyouts, 65–66
  merger mania, 11
  most active industries, 13
  nature of, 5–7
  negotiated price and, 22
  net asset and future earnings contributions, 22–25
  new disclosure requirements, 51–52
  noncontrolling interest and, 27–28
  nonrecurring items and, 20
  operating synergies and, 8, 13–14
  parent company concept and, 26, 27
  price and method of payment, 21–25

pro forma statements, 53–55
reasons for, 7–11
statutory consolidations, 16
statutory mergers, 15–16
stock acquisitions, 16
stock exchange ratio and, 22
stock vs. asset acquisitions, 14–15
strategic acquisitions, 13–14
takeover premiums, 17–18
treatment of acquisition expenses, 52–53
unfriendly (hostile) combinations, 5–6
vertical integration, 11

C
CAD Schedule, *see* Computation and Allocation Difference Schedule
Call options, 619–620
Call price, 483
Capital assets, governmental accounting and, 879–881
Capital balances, partnerships and, 736–737
Capital expenditures, fund accounting and, 818
Capital improvement special assessments, 894–897
Capital interest, partnership agreements and, 731
Capital investment, partnerships and, 736–737
Capital One Financial Corporation, 17
Capital project funds, 856, 858–863, 895
Capital transactions, partnerships and, 732–733
Capitation revenues, hospital, 953–954
Carilion Health Systems, 929
Carrying value, 432–434, 524–525
Cash distributions, partnership liquidation and, 782–787
Cash dividends, versus stock dividends, 478
Cash flow:
consolidated statement of, 177–184
hedges, 613–616, 618–622
year after acquisitions, 178–180
year of acquisition, 180–184
CBS Corp., 51
Chapter 7 (of Bankruptcy Reform Act), 519–521
Chapter 11 (of Bankruptcy Reform Act), 520, 522–523
Charity care, 953
Chief operating decision maker, 690
China, 577
Chinese yuan, 659
Chiron Corp., 8
Chrysler Corp., 6–7, 16, 517
Clinton Administration, 14
COGS, *see* Cost of Goods Sold
Colleges and university accounting:
current fund accounting and, 937–938
expenditure and expense classifications, 936
issues relating to, 953
mandatory transfers and, 938–939
nonmandatory transfers and, 938–939
operating vs. nonoperating income and, 953
plant funds and, 943–946
service fee revenue and, 953
Common cost allocation, in segment reporting, 690–691
Comparability, 34, 692
Complete equity method:
on books of investor, 138–140
constructive retirement of subsidiary bonds, 461–466, 469–471
downstream sales and, 307–309
implied and book values and, 260–261
intercompany sales and, 326–331
property and equipment disposal by purchasing affiliate and, 387–389
purchase and sale of subsidiary stock by parent, 424–428
recording investments in subsidiaries and, 153–163
separate tax returns and, 192–193
significant influence and, 133–136
subsidiary perferred stock outstanding, 490–492, 495
unrealized intercompany profit, 338–340
upstream sales and, 382–387
Component units, governmental, 890
Composition agreements, 516–517
Comprehensive income:
currency translations and, 654–655
distinguishing between earnings and, 34–36
statement of, 36
Computation and Allocation Difference (CAD) Schedule, 94, 98–100, 104–105, 143, 167, 173, 264, 265
Conglomerate mergers, 13
Congressional Budget Office, 811
ConocoPhillips, 261
Consistency, 34
Consolidated balances, intercompany sales and, 302–312
Consolidated balance sheets, 28–29
Consolidated financial statements, 25–30
accounting for investments, 133–141
accumulated depreciation as separate balance, 267–269
adjusting entries, 97, 107
allocation and depreciation of differences, 219–226
balance sheet values and, 28–29
cash flows, 177–184
consolidated net income, *see* Consolidated net income
controlling and noncontrolling interests, 240–242
cost and book value differences, 100–104
cost method after acquisition, 141–152
deferred taxes, 114–115, 188–193
discounted notes receivable, 476–477

Consolidated financial statements, *(continued)*
economic entity concept and, 26–27
equity method recording investments in subsidiaries, 153–163
expense item elimination, 163–164
implied and book value differences, 94, 96–98
intercompany bonds, 454–476
intercompany interest, rent, service fees, 389–392
intercompany profit, 29
intercompany revenue elimination, 163–164
intercompany sale of depreciable property, 362–370
intercompany sales and consolidated balances, 302–312
intercompany sales of land, 359–362
interim acquisition of subsidiary stock, 165–176
investment elimination and, 93–96
investment recorded using complete equity method, 252–260
investment recorded using cost method, 231–240
investment recorded using partial equity method, 242–249
letter notation, 97
limitations of, 110–111
more than one subsidiary, 108–110
noncontrolling interest and, 27–28, 98–100
number notation, 97
parent acquisition of subsidiary stock and, 416–420
parent company concept and, 26, 27
parent sale of subsidiary stock and, 415
paying more than book value, 103
preaffiliation profit, 332–333
purchase price below book value, 104–105
purpose of, 89–90
requirements regarding subsidiaries, 88–89
retained earnings analysis, 319
revenue recognition principle and, 93
separate tax returns, 188–193
stock dividends issued by subsidiary, 478–483
subsidiary treasury stock holdings, 106
subsidiary with preferred stock outstanding, 486–497
upstream sales, 312–320
workpapers and, 92–98
Consolidated net income:
calculations of, 397–398
cash flows and, 177
implied and book values and, 240–242, 250–252, 260–261
intercompany sale of inventory and, 318, 331
intercompany sale of property and equipment and, 379–382, 389
under parent company and economic entity concepts, 28
recording investments in subsidiaries and, 147, 158–159
subsidiary revenue and expense items and, 166
workpapers and, 144
Consolidated retained earnings:
calculations of, 397–398
implied and book values and, 226, 240–242, 250–252, 260–261
intercompany sale of inventory and, 319, 331
intercompany sale of property and equipment and, 379–382, 389
of parent, 228
Consolidation. *See also* Consolidated financial statements
consolidated sales, 299–306, 325
statutory, 16
when temporal method used, 666–668
Constructive gain or loss, 455–458
Consumption method, expendable fund entities and, 832–833
Consumption of benefit, 37
Contingent assets, 19–20, 66
Contingent considerations in acquisitions, 61–66
Contingent liabilities, 66
Contractual agreements composition agreements, 516–517
extension of payment periods, 516
formation of creditor's committee, 517
insolvency and, 516–517
voluntary assignment of assets, 517
Contractual allowances, hospitals, 953
Contributions, 940–943
donated collection items, 942
donated services, 941
donor-imposed restricted contributions, 942–943
pledges, 940–941
Control, definitions of, 85–88
Controlling interest. *See also* Noncontrolling interest
complete equity method analysis and, 260–261
in consolidated net income, 144, 158–159, 166
cost method analysis and, 240–242
partial equity method analysis and, 250–251
Convergys Corp., 10
Cost Accounting Standard No. 403, 691
Cost method:
conservative view and, 146
consolidated statements after acquisition and, 141–152
constructive retirement of subsidiary bonds, 460–461, 467–468
downstream sales and, 306–307
historical cost principle and, 143
implied and book values and, 235–242
intercompany sale of inventory and, 318–319
interim acquisitions and, 166–172
investments and, 133–137, 231–240

parent acquires subsidiary stock through several purchases, 416–420
parent sells subsidiary stock to third parties, 415
preferred stock outstanding, 493
property/ equipment disposal by purchasing affiliate, 378–379
separate tax returns and, 190–191
subsidiary preferred stock outstanding, 491–493
unrealized intercompany profit, 337–338
upstream sales and, 312–320, 370–378
workpaper format and, 142–148
Cost of Goods Sold (COGS), 234, 244, 254, 368
Cost of sales assuming downstream sales, 299–306
Creditor's committee formation, 517
Crooch, Michael, 4
Cumulative undistributed income, 154
Current exchange rate, 641
Current fund accounting accounting for board designed funds, 937
colleges and universities, 938
current restricted funds, 936–937
current unrestricted funds, 936
hospitals, 937
mandatory and nonmandatory transfers, 938–939
nongovernmental nonbusiness organizations and, 936–939
other nonbusiness nongovernmental organizations, 937–938
revenue and support from fund-raising events, 939
Current method, functional currency is local currency, 651–655
Current rate conversion method, 643
Current restricted funds, 936–937
Current unrestricted funds, 936
Customer consideration model, 570–572

D

Daimler-Benz, 16
DaimlerChrysler, 16
Dean Witter Discover & Co., 2, 10
Debt:
allocating difference between implied and book value to, 261–264
constructive retirement of, 453
Debt issue proceeds, fund accounting and, 812
Debtor-in-possession lending, 526, 532
Debt service funds, 856, 895
Defensive tactics, business combinations and, 6–7
Deferred taxes:
in business combinations, 69–70
consequences when affiliates file separate returns, 188–193
on date of acquisition, 114–115
and intercompany profit, 334, 337–340, 396
and intercompany sales of equipment, 394–396
Deficiency account, 530
Definitions of financial statement elements, 35
Dell Inc., 312
Depository Bank (DR bank), 580
Depository Receipt (DR), 580–582
Depreciable assets:
disposal by subsidiary, 269–270
at net and gross values, 267–269
used in manufacturing, 270
Depreciable property:
financial reporting objectives, 363
intercompany sale of, 362–370
realization through usage and, 362–363
Depreciation:
accumulated, 267–269
of differences, *see* Allocation and depreciation of differences
intangible assets and, 221
Derivative instruments, 600–602
Dilution, earnings, 24–25
DIP financing, 526, 532
Direct acquisition expenses, 53, 66
Direct exchange quotations, 593
Disaggregated financial data, 688. *See also* Segment reporting
Disbursements, fund accounting and, 818
Disclosure requirements for business combinations, 51–52
Disney, 261
Dissolution, partnerships, 742
Distributions to owners, 35
Diversification, 9
Divestitures, 10
Dividends, liquidating, 135, 137
Donated collection items, 942
Donated services, 941
Donor-imposed restricted contributions, 942–943
Downstream sales, 301
consolidated sales and, 299–306
cost method and, 319–320
cost of sales and, 299–306
inventory balances and, 299–306
DR, *see* Depository Receipt
Due diligence, business combinations and, 19–21
Due diligence reports, 19

E

Earnings. *See also* Consolidated retained earnings
dilution and accretion, 24–25
distinguishing from comprehensive income, 34–36
in establishing goodwill, 23
expense allocations and, 20
nonrecurring items boosting, 20
stock dividends and, 481–483
Eastman Kodak Company, 25

Economic entity concept, 26–27
 consolidated balance sheet values and, 29
 consolidated net income and, 27–28
 noncontrolling interest and, 27–28
 versus parent concept, 31–32
Edison Electric Institute, 115
Eliminating entries:
 after acquisition (equity method), 160
 basic workpaper eliminating entries, 164
 downstream sales and, 303–309
 expense items, 163–164
 intercompany dividends, 161
 intercompany revenue, 163–164
 investment carried at equity and, 155–157
 reasons for, 97
 summary for intercompany sales, 332
 year of acquisition (cost method), 144–146
Emerging Issue Task Force (EITF), 558
Encumbrances, fund accounting and, 816
Endowment fund accounting, 948–949
Enron Corp., 52, 86
Enterprise funds, 856, 876
Enterprisewide disclosures, segment reporting and, 695
Equipment:
 cost method and, 378–379
 disposal by purchasing affiliate, 378–379, 387–389
 intercompany sale of, 379–382, 389, 394–396
Equity:
 definition of, 35
 investments carried at, 154–161
Equity method, 184. *See also* Complete equity method; Partial equity method
Ernst & Young, 14
Esmark, 13
EToys Inc., 726
Euro, 662
European Commission, 577–578
Excess earnings approach, to estimating goodwill, 23
Exchange rates. *See also* Foreign currency transactions
 current exchange rate, 641
 definitions regarding, 592–593
 direct exchange rate, 595
 historical exchange rate, 641
 means of translation, 592–594
 sample, 594
Expendable fund entities, 807–808
Expenditures, fund accounting and, 814–821
Expenses:
 definition of, 35
 direct acquisitions and, 53
 impact of earnings on allocation of, 20
 interim financial reporting and, 704–705
 item elimination, 163–164
 matching to revenues, 37
Expense classification, nongovernment nonbusiness, 935–936
Exporting of goods and services, 596–599
Exporting transactions, 598–599
Exposed liability, forward contracts and, 605–609
External expansion, 7–8. *See also* Business combinations
Extraordinary gains, 60
ExxonMobil, 576

F

F-1 statement, 578–580
FAF, *see* Financial Accounting Foundation
Fair value, 67
 acquisition costs less than, 224–226
 hedges, 610–613, 618
 of net assets, 29
 reorganizations and, 525
Fair value accounting, 32, 45
FASB, *see* Financial Accounting Standards Board
FCPA (Foreign Corrupt Practices Act), 660
Federal Deposit Insurance Corporation (FDIC), 517
Federal-Mogul, 10
Federal Trade Commission, 14
Fiduciary funds, 809, 856–857, 878–879
FIFO (first in, first-out), 234, 244, 307, 576
Financial Accounting Foundation (FAF), 555, 854
Financial Accounting Standards Board (FASB):
 advanced accounting issues and, 33–34
 business combinations and, 2
 codification project of, 38–40
 comprehensive income and, 654–655
 Concepts Statement No. 2, 930
 Concepts Statement No. 4, 33, 806, 932
 Concepts Statement No. 5, 34–37, 249
 Concepts Statement No. 6, 34, 116, 930
 Concepts Statement No. 7, 33–34
 conceptual framework of, 30–37
 on contingent assets, 19–20
 earnings vs. comprehensive income, 34–36
 economic entity vs. parent concept, 31–32
 Interpretation No. 18, 705
 Interpretation No. 48, 115–117
 long-term convergence issues with IASB, 567–568
 Statement No. 3, 707
 Statement No. 5, 115
 Statement No. 8, 661–662
 Statement No. 12, 218
 Statement No. 13, 568–569
 Statement No. 14, 688, 689
 Statement No. 15, 516, 524
 Statement No. 21, 688
 Statement No. 52, 600, 616, 641, 642–643, 662, 669
 Statement No. 53, 648
 Statement No. 93, 931

Statement No. 109, 59, 70, 71, 115–117, 190, 334, 705
Statement No. 116, 940
Statement No. 117, 932–933
Statement No. 124, 950
Statement No. 128, 707
Statement No. 131, 687, 689–691, 694, 695, 697
Statement No. 133, 600–601, 612, 618, 622
Statement No. 138, 605
Statement No. 140, 87
Statement No. 141, 45–47, 51, 59–60
Statement No. 141R, 4, 20, 29, 45, 46, 54–55, 70–71, 416–417
Statement No. 142, 47, 48, 51
Statement No. 144, 50, 52
Statement No. 154, 707
Statement No. 157, 262
Statement No. 160, 4, 29, 38, 70, 420, 428–429
Statement No. 162, 33, 558, 559
Statement No. 167, 117–118
Statement No. 168, 38, 558, 559
Financial affiliates. *See also* Consolidated financial statements
accounting for investment after acquisition, 665–668
consolidated statements workpaper illustrated, 664–670
consolidation when temporal method of translation used, 666–668
date of acquisition and, 664
elimination of intercompany profit, 669–670
intercompany receivables and payables, 629
liquidation of foreign investment, 670
remeasurement and translation of foreign currency transactions, 668–669
Financial synergy, 9
Fines and forfeits, fund accounting and, 813
First-in, first-out (FIFO), 234, 244, 307, 576
Fixed ratio, in partnerships, 735
Flextronics Software Systems, 65
Floating rates, 593
Flow of current financial resources concept, 853
Flow of economic resources approach, 853
Ford Motor Company, 11
Forecasted transactions, hedging of, 613–616
Foreign affiliates. *See also* Translation of foreign financial statements
accounting for operations of, 640–641
financial statement disclosure, 660–661
functional currency identification, 645
high inflationary economies and, 647–648
objectives of translation (SFAS No. 52), 642–643
operating in economies not highly inflationary, 648–650
translating financial statements of, 641–642
translation adjustment, 642
translation gain or loss, 642
translation methods, 643–644
translation of foreign currency financial statements, 646–659
Foreign company exposed liability, 605–609
Foreign Corrupt Practices Act (FCPA), 660
Foreign currency exposed asset, 609
Foreign currency movements, forward contracts and, 617–618
Foreign currency transactions, 595–605. *See also* Exchange rates
Foreign currency translation of financial statements, 646–650
Foreign exchange rates, *see* Exchange rates
Form 10-K, 578
Form 10-Q, 701
Form 20-F, 578–579
Formation, partnership, 733–735
Forward-based derivatives, 601
Forward contracts. *See also* Hedging foreign exchange risk
cash flow hedges, 613–616
discounting fair value of, 612–613
economic hedges of net investment in foreign entities, 616–617
fair value hedge, 610–613
hedge of foreign company exposed liability, 605–609
hedge of foreign currency exposed asset, 609
speculation in foreign currency movement and, 617–618
Forward exchange contracts, 593, 602–605
Forward rates, 593, 604
Fresh start accounting, 524
Friendly combinations, 5, 6
Full-year reporting alternative:
cost method, 166–170
equity method, 172–173
Functional currency:
concept of, 642–643
economies not highly inflationary, 648–650
highly inflationary economies, 647–648
identification of, 645
indicators, 644
local currency as, 651–655
U.S. dollar as, 655–659
Function classifications, fund accounting and, 814–815
Fund accounting. *See also* Nonbusiness organizations
analysis of financial statements, 830
appropriations and, 816
basis for accounting, 810–811
budgetary fund entities (governmental funds), 809–810
capital expenditures and, 818
comprehensive illustration of, 822–828

Fund accounting. *(continued)*
debt issue proceeds and, 812
disbursements and, 817
encumbrances and, 816
expendable fund entities, 807–808
expenditure classification, 814–815
expenditures and, 816–817
fiduciary fund entities, 809
financial statements and, 828–831
fines and forfeits and, 813
function and activity classifications and, 814–815
income taxes and, 813
inventory and, 832–833
lapsing of appropriations and, 822
nongovernment nonbusiness organizations, 933–934, 936–939
object class classifications and, 815
organizational unit classifications and, 815
pledges and grants and, 813
prepayments and, 833
property taxes and, 812–813
proprietary fund entities, 809
recognition of expenditures, 816–818
recognition of revenue, 812–813
recording revenues and expenditures, 819–821
resource outflows, 814–815
restricted and unrestricted fund entities, 808
revenue classifications, 811
role of, 807
sales of property and, 813
sales taxes and, 813
transfer of resources from other funds, 812
transfers to other funds, 816
Fund-raising events, 939
Future earnings contributions, 22–25
Future rates, 593

G

GAAP, *see* Generally Accepted Accounting Principles
Gains, definition of, 35
GDR (Global Depository Receipt), 580
General Electric (GE), 111, 576
General funds, governmental, 856–857
Generally Accepted Accounting Principles (GAAP). *See also* U.S. GAAP
changes in ownership interest and, 415–416
and FASB codification project, 38–39
GAAP hierarchy, 33
minimum information required for fair presentation, 854
General partnerships, 727–728. *See also* Partnerships
limited or uncertain life, 728
mutual agency and, 727
right to dispose and, 728
unlimited liability and, 728
General revenues, governmental, 892
Geographic area disclosures, segment reporting and, 696–698
Global Depository Receipt (GDR), 580
Globalization, *see* International accounting
Golden West Financial Corp., 103
Goodwill, 66
amortization of, 69–70, 218
book vs. implied value and, 146
disclosures mandated by FASB, 51–52
estimation of value of, 22–25
excess earnings approach to estimating, 23
impairment of, 249
impairment tests, 48–50
measurement of, 216–217
negative, 60
recording in consolidated statements, 101
Goodwill method, partnerships and, 734, 744, 749–750, 753
Government Accounting Standards Board (GASB), 806–807, 930
Concepts Statement No. 1, 804
Concepts Statement No. 2, 804
Concepts Statement No. 3, 804
Concepts Statement No. 4, 804
Concepts Statement No. 5, 804
establishment of, 854
Statement No. 15, 931
Statement No. 34, 808, 810, 818, 826, 832, 852–853, 858, 875–876, 879–881, 884–885, 891, 931, 933
Statement No. 35, 933
Statement No. 45, 827, 857
Statement No. 46, 834
Statement No. 48, 834
Statement No. 49, 830
Governmental accounting, *see* State and local government
Governmental fund entities, 809–810, 855–875
capital project funds, 858–863
debt services funds, 864–872
general funds, 857
interfund activity, 897–899
interfund loans, 898
interfund reimbursements, 899
interfund services provided and used, 898
interfund transfers, 898–899
permanent funds, 872–874
special revenue funds, 857–858
Government Finance Officer's Association (GFOA), 852
Government fund balances, net assets and, 887–888
Government fund-based reporting, 885–888
Government-wide financial statements, 810–811. *See also* Fund accounting

Government-wide reporting:
 infrastructure asset reporting issues, 891
 statement of activities, 891–892
 statement of net assets, 810–811, 888–891
Grant of equity interest, 525
Greenmail, 7
Gross profit rate, intercompany sales and, 309
Guidant Corp., 60

H

Harris, Trevor, 48
Health care providers, 929. *See also* Nongovernment nonbusiness organizations
Hedging foreign exchange risk, 596, 600–601
 cash flow hedge, 613–616
 disclosure requirements of, 618–619
 economic hedge of net investment in foreign entity, 616–617
 fair value hedge, 610–613
 fair value vs. cash flow hedges, 613
 foreign currency exposed asset, 609
 foreign currency exposed liability, 605–609
 forward contracts and, 604–605
 options and foreign currency changes, 619–622
 split accounting and, 622
Hewlett-Packard, 7
Historical costs, 34, 143, 305, 521
Historical development of accounting standards, 661–662
Historical exchange rate, 641
Historical perspective on business combinations, 11–14
Horizontal integration, 11
Horizontal mergers, 8
Horizontal sales, 301, 310–311
Hospitals, 929. *See also* Nongovernment nonbusiness organizations
 capitation revenues, 953–954
 charity care and, 953
 contractual allowances and, 953
 current fund accounting and, 937
 expenditure and expense classifications, 936
 issues relating to, 953–954
 malpractice and, 954
 plant funds and, 946–947
House Ways and Means Committee, 577

I

IAS, see International Accounting Standards
IASB, *see* International Accounting Standards Board
IASC, *see* International Accounting Standards Committee
IASC Foundation, 555
IFRS, *see* International Financial Reporting Standard(s)
Implied values, *see* Allocation and depreciation of differences between implied and book values; Consolidated financial statements
Importing of goods and services, 596–599
Importing transactions, 596–598
Inco Ltd., 2
Income adjustment of prior years, partnerships and, 741
Income tax. *See also* Deferred taxes; Tax returns
 fund accounting and, 813
 interim financial reporting and, 705–706
Incorporation of partnership, 787–788
Indirect acquisition costs, 53
Indirect exchange quotations, 593
Inflationary economy, affiliates operating in, 647–648
Infrastructure assets, 880
Insolvency. *See also* Reorganizations accounting
 accounting for reorganizations, 524–526
 bankruptcy, 518–521
 composition agreements and, 516–517
 contractual agreements and, 516–517
 creditor's committee formation, 517
 definition of, 515
 extension of payment periods and, 516
 fresh start accounting, 524
 liquidation, 521
 quasi reorganization, 524
 realization and liquidation account, 535–539
 reorganization under Reform Act, 522–523
 Statement of Affairs and, 530–532
 trustee accounting and reporting, 532–535
 voluntary assignment of, 517
Installment liquidation, partnership, 778–787
Intangible assets, amortization of, 52
Intercompany bonds:
 accounting for bonds, 454–459
 book entry related to bond investment, 459–475
 constructive gain or loss on, 455–458
 constructive retirement of debt, 453
 interim purchase of, 475–476
 three-year comparison, 473–474
Intercompany dividends, elimination of, 146
Intercompany interest, 389–392
Intercompany pricing adjustments, 309–310
Intercompany profit:
 deferred tax consequences of, 334, 337–340, 396
 elimination of with foreign subsidiary, 669–670
 intercompany sales and, 309–310
 prior to affiliation, 332–333
Intercompany receivables and payables, international, 669
Intercompany rent, 389–392
Intercompany revenue elimination, 29, 163–164

Intercompany sales. *See also* Upstream sales
complete equity method and, 326–331
consolidated balances determination and, 302–312
cost method and, 312–320
deferred tax consequences of, 394–396
of depreciable property, 362–370
determination of intercompany profit and, 309
determination of noncontrolling interest and, 367–370
eliminating intercompany profit and, 310
financial reporting objectives and, 302–303
of inventories, 335–337
inventory pricing adjustments, 309–310
of land, 359–362
noncontrolling interest and, 310–311
of nondepreciable property, 359–362
partial equity method and, 321–325
property/equipment disposal by purchasing affiliate, 378–379
realization through usage and, 362–363
subsidiary stock and, *see* Subsidiary company(-ies)
summary of workpaper elimination entries, 332
Intercompany service fees, 389–392
Interest:
intercompany, 389–392
noncontrolling, 28–29
partnerships and, 737–741
Interfund activity, governmental, 897–899
interfund loans, 898
interfund reimbursements, 899
interfund services provided and used, 898
interfund transfers, 898–899
Interim acquisitions:
cost method full-year reporting, 166–170
cost method partial-year reporting, 170–172
equity method full-year reporting, 172–173
equity method partial-year reporting, 173–175
Interim disclosures, segment reporting and, 695
Interim financial reporting, 701–709
accounting changes in interim periods, 707
APB Opinion No. 28 and, 702–707
costs and expenses and, 704–705
costs associated with revenues and, 703–704
current requirements, 701
income tax provisions, 705–706
interim operating losses and, 706–707
international issues in, 708–709
minimum disclosures in interim reports, 707
problems in, 702
revenues and, 703
Internal expansion, 8
Internal service funds, 856, 876–878
International accounting. *See also* Foreign affiliates; Foreign currency transactions; Forward contracts
American depository receipts, 580–582
exchange rate translation, 592–594
financial statement disclosure, 660–661
foreign affiliate and preparation of consolidated workpaper, 664–670
foreign currency transactions, 595–605
functional currency is local currency, 651–655
functional currency is U.S. dollar, 655–659
hedging foreign exchange risk, 605–622
historical developments of accounting standards, 661–662
and increased focus on standards, 552–553
interim reporting and, 708–709
measured vs. denominated transactions, 594–595
objectives of translation, 642–643
operations of foreign affiliates, 640–641
segment reporting and, 699–700
translating financial statements of foreign affiliates, 641–642
translation of foreign currency financial statements, 646–650
International Accounting Standards (IAS), 539, 553, 583–584
No. 1, 560, 708
No. 8, 559
No. 14, 700
No. 16, 564
No. 17, 568–569
No. 34, 708
International Accounting Standards Board (IASB), 552, 553, 555, 559–560, 577
consolidated financial statements, 3
and FASB, 4, 31, 32, 45, 273, 569–570, 660–661
positions on segment reporting, 699–700
International Accounting Standards Committee (IASC), 553, 709
International Financial Reporting Standard(s) (IFRS), 3, 45, 66–67, 112, 184, 538, 552–557, 708, 709
implementation of mandatory use of, 557
list, 583–584
Intrinsic value of forward contracts, 603
Inventory(-ies):
downstream sales and, 299–306
fund accounting and, 832–833
intercompany sales of, 335–337
reserve for, 832–833
Investment accounting, nongovernment nonbusiness organizations, 950–951
Investment elimination in consolidated financial statements, 93–96
Investments in subsidiaries, 89, 133–141
carried at complete equity, 161–163
carried at equity year after acquisition, 159–161
carried at equity year of acquisition, 154–159
complete equity method for, 138–140, 153–163, 252–260

cost method for, 136–137, 231–240
partial equity method for, 137–138, 153–163, 242–249
Investment pools, 950–951
Investment trust funds, 857
Involuntary petitions, 521
Irvine Biomedical, Inc., 57

J
Johnson & Johnson, 101
Joint ventures, 729
J.P. Morgan Chase & Co., 84
Junk bond market, merger financing and, 10

K
Kmart Corp., 526
Kohlberg Kravis Roberts & Co., 65
KPMG Peat Marwick, 14, 19

L
Land, intercompany sale of, 359–362
Lands' End, 599, 613
Last-in, first-out (LIFO), 576
Lawsuit contingencies, 63–64
LBO, *see* Leveraged buyouts
Lease contracts, 569–570
Lehman Brothers, 10, 515
Leiner Health Products, 10
Letter notation of adjusting entries, 97
Level I ADR, 581
Level II ADR, 581
Level III ADR, 582
Leveraged buyouts (LBO), 7, 65–66
Liabilities, assumed, 19, 56–57
Liability, in general partnerships, 728
Life insurance fund accounting, 952–953
LIFO (last-in, first-out), 576
Limited liability partnerships (LLP), 728–729
Limited life, in general partnerships, 728
Limited partnerships, *see* General partnerships; Partnerships
Liquidation, 521
of dividends, 135, 137
of foreign investment, 670
involuntary petitions and, 521
of partnerships, *see* Partnership liquidation
trustee duties and, 521
LLP (limited liability partnerships), 728–729
Loan fund accounting, for nongovernment nonbusiness organizations, 951
Local governmental units, *see* Fund accounting; State and local government
Lockheed Martin Corp., 18
Long-term debt, governmental accounting and, 881–883
Losses, definition of, 35
Loss or lack of benefit, 37
Lucent Technologies Inc., 10
LukOil, 261

M
M&A, *see* Mergers and acquisitions
Major customer disclosures, segment reporting and, 696, 698
Majority-owned subsidiaries, 85, 87
Malpactice, hospital, 954
Management's discussion and analysis (MD&A), 852, 893–894
Mandatory transfers, 938–939
Manufacturing, depreciable assets used in, 270
Market value accounting, 32
MCI, 2
Measured vs. denominated transactions, 594–595
Measurement period, adjustments during, 62, 67
Mendecino Redwood, 10
Mergers and acquisitions (M&A), 1–2. *See also* Business combinations
from 1972 through 2008, 11–12
and bankruptcies, 2, 10
conglomerate mergers, 13
earning dilution and accretion and, 24–25
horizontal mergers, 8
junk bond market and, 10
merger mania, 11
mode of payment in, 21
planning for, 4–5
statutory merger, 15–16
stock prices and, 21
vertical mergers, 8
Merrill Lynch, 138
Method of payment in business combinations, 21–25
MFOA (Municipal Finance Officers Association), 853
Minimum disclosures, in interim reports, 707
Minority interest, 100
Modified accrual accounting, 811
Morgan Stanley, 2
Morgan Stanley Dean Witter, 48
Municipal Finance Officers Association (MFOA), 853
Mutual agency, in general partnerships, 727
Myanmar, 648

N
National Bureau of Statistics, 659
National City Corp., 84
National Council on Government Accounting (NCGA), 853
NBTY, 10
NCGA (National Council on Government Accounting), 853
Negative goodwill, 66

Negotiated price, in business combinations, 22
Net assets:
  government fund balances and, 887–888
  in price determination in business combinations, 22–25
Net income, *see* Consolidated net income
Net income or loss, allocation in partnerships, 735–738
Net investment hedges, 616–617, 619
News Corp., 14
NNO, *see* Nongovernment nonbusiness organizations
Nonbusiness organizations. *See also* Fund accounting
  classifications of, 803
  distinctions from profit-oriented enterprises, 803–805
  financial accounting for, 805–807
  reporting standards for, 805–807
Noncontrolling interest, 66. *See also* Controlling interest
  cash flows and, 177
  consolidated net income and, 147–148, 158–159
  cost method analysis and, 240–242
  definition of, 84
  determination in intercompany sales, 367–370
  partial equity method analysis and, 250–251
  subsidiary as intercompany seller and, 375
  for upstream sales, 310–311
Nondepreciable property, intercompany sale of, 359–362
Nonexhausitble assets, 948
Nongovernment nonbusiness organizations (NNO):
  accrual basis of accounting for, 934–935
  agency (custodial) fund accounting, 952
  annuity and life income fund accounting, 952–953
  classifications of, 929
  college and university issues, 953
  contributions and, 940–943
  current funds accounting, 936–939
  endowment fund accounting, 948–949
  financial reporting for not-for-profit organizations, 932–933
  financial reporting for public colleges and universities, 933
  fund accounting for, 933–934
  generally accepted accounting standards for, 929–933
  hospital issues, 953–954
  investment accounting, 950–951
  loan fund accounting, 951
  plant fund accounting, 943–948
  revenue and expense classification, 935–936
Nonmandatory transfers, 938–939
Nonoperating income, colleges and universities and, 953
Nonprofit institutions of higher learning, 929. *See also* Nongovernment nonbusiness organizations
Nonrecurring items boosting earnings, 20
North Fork Bancorporation, 17
Northrop Grumman Corp., 2
Norton-Simon, 13
Notes receivable, discounted, 476–477
Not-for-profit organizations, 932–933. *See also* Nonbusiness organizations
Novartis AG, 8
Number notation, eliminating entries and, 97

O

Obama, Barack, 14, 811
Object class classifications, 815
Offer rates, 593
ONNOs, *see* Other nongovernment nonbusiness organizations
Ontario, 879
OPEB (other post-employment benefits), 857
Operating income, colleges and universities and, 953
Operating losses, interim, 706–707
Operating segments, 690–693. *See also* Segment reporting
Operating synergies, 8, 13–14
Option-based derivatives, 601
Options, in hedging foreign currency changes, 619–622
Order for relief, 519
Organizational unit classifications, 815
Other nongovernment nonbusiness organizations (ONNOs), 929
  current fund accounting and, 937–938
  expenditure and expense classifications, 936
  nonexhaustible assets of, 948
  plant funds and, 947–948
Other post-employment benefits (OPEB), 857
Ownership changes, partnerships and, 742–744
Ownership interest:
  acquisition date determination and, 416
  and carrying value per share, 432–434
  and existing book value per share, 434–438
  parent acquires in stages, 415–420
  parent sells shares to third parties, 415
  parent sells subsidiary stock investment on open market, 420–424, 428–430
  subsidiary issuance of additional shares, 415

P

Pacific Lumber, 10
Pac-man defense, 7
Parent company concept, 26–29, 31–32, 84
Partial elimination, intercompany profit and, 29
Partial equity method:
  accounting for investments by, 133–138
  downstream sales and, 306–307
  implied and book values and, 250–252

intercompany sale of inventory and, 325–326
property/equipment disposal by purchasing affiliate and, 378–379
purchase and sale of subsidiary stock by parent, 424–428
recording investments in subsidiaries and, 153–163, 242–249
separate tax returns and, 192–193
unrealized intercompany profit, 337–338
upstream sales and, 370–378
Partial year reporting alternatives:
cost method, 170–172
equity method, 173–175
Partnerships. *See also* Partnership liquidation
accounting for, 731–739
acquisition of interest by investing assets, 747–751
acquisition of interest by payment to one partner, 744–745
adjustment of income of prior years and, 741
admission of new partner, 744–747
allocation of net income or loss, 735–738
bonuses and, 738
bonus method and, 734, 743–744, 748–750, 753
capital balances and, 736–737
capital interest and, 731
characteristics of, 727–729
death of partner, 754
definition of, 726
dissolution and, 742
drawing and capital accounts, 732–733
financial statement presentation, 741–742
fixed ratio and, 735
general partnerships, 727–728
goodwill implied by purchase price and, 745–746
goodwill method and, 734, 744, 748–750, 753
incorporation of, 787–788
insufficient income to cover allocation, 738–739
interest allowances and, 737–738
interest on capital investment and, 737–738
joint ventures, 729
limited partnerships, 728–729
ownership changes and, 742–744
partnership agreements, 730–731
partnership equity vs. shareholders equity, 731–732
payment to retiring partner, 752–754
profit interest and, 731
reasons for forming, 726–727
recording changes in, 743–744
recording formation of, 733–735
salaries and interest as an expense and, 739–741
salary allowances and, 737–738
statistics for partnerships in U.S., 725
steps for successful, 727
Uniform Partnership Act (UPA), 773
valuation and changes in ownership, 742–743
withdrawal of partner, 751–754
Partnership agreements, 730–731
Partnership equity, 731
Partnership liquidation. *See also* Partnerships
advance plan for cash distributions, 782–787
installment liquidation, 778–787
marshaling of assets, 774
preparing a schedule of, 777–778
priorities of partnership and personal creditors, 774–776
safe payment approach and, 779–782
simple liquidation illustrated, 776–778
steps in, 772–774
Payment methods in business combinations, 21–25
Payment period extensions, 516
PCAOB (Public Company Accounting Oversight Board), 87
Pension trust funds, 856–857, 879
Permanent funds, 856, 872–874
Personal creditors, partnership liquidation and, 774–776
Phelps Dodge, 2
Pitfalls, avoiding, before deal, 19–21
Plant funds, 943–948
colleges and universities, 943–946
hospitals, 946–947
other nongovernment nonbusiness organizations, 947–948
voluntary health and welfare organizations, 947–948
Pledges and grants, 813, 940–941
PNC Financial Services Group Inc., 84
Poison pills, 6–7
Pooling of interests, 34, 47
PPE (property, plant, and equipment), 564
Preaffiliation profit, 332–333
Premiums, takeover, 17–18
Prepayments, fund accounting and, 833
Presentation methods:
IASB vs. FASB, 572–573
in segment reporting, 696
Present value measurements, 600
Present values tables, A1–A3
Present value techniques, 454
Price, determining in business combinations, 21–25
Primestar, 14
Private-purpose trust funds, 857
Product of service disclosures, 695
Profit, intercompany:
about, 29
deferred tax consequences of, 334, 337–340, 396
Profit interest, partnership agreements and, 731
Pro forma statements, 53–55
Program revenues, governmental, 891–892

Property:
  depreciable, 362–370
  disposal by purchasing affiliate, 378–379, 387–389
  fund accounting and, 812–813
  intercompany sale of, 362–370, 379–382, 389
  nondepreciable, 359–362
  taxes, 812–813
Property, plant, and equipment (PPE), 564
Proportional consolidation, 27
Proprietary funds, 809, 875–878
  enterprise funds, 876
  governmental, 856
  internal service funds, 876–878
Public colleges and universities, financial reporting for, 933
Public Company Accounting Oversight Board (PCAOB), 87, 538
Public nonprofit organizations, accounting for, 949
Purchase in-process R&D, 67
Purchases method, expendable fund entities and, 832–833
Purchasing affiliate, 334
Pure endowment funds, 948–949
Push down accounting, 270–275
Put option, 620

Q

QIB firms, 582
Qualifying special purpose entities (QSPE), 87
Quantitative thresholds, operating segments, 692
Quasi-reorganization, 524
Quebec, 879

R

R&D, *see* Research and development
Realization and liquidation account, 535–539
Realization through usage, 362–363
Recession of 2008, 2
Reciprocity, 169
Reconciliation, segmental data, 698–699
Redemption price, 483
Reform Act, *see* Bankruptcy Reform Act
Remeasurement, foreign currency transactions, 646, 668–669
Rent, intercompany, 389–392
Reorganizations accounting, 524–529
  carrying value and, 524–525
  DIP financing and, 526, 532
  fair value and, 525
  grant of equity interest, 525
  modification of terms, 524–526
  restructuring illustration, 525–529
  transfer of assets, 524–525
Reorganization under Reform Act, 522–523
Replacement cost new, 267
Reportable segments, 690
Reported book value, 29
Reporting currency, 595
Reporting dates, 67
Required supplementary information (RSI), 830
Research and development (R&D):
  capitalization of, 56–57, 218
  expensing of, 221
  international differences, 564
  purchased in-process, 67
Reserve for inventory, 832–833
Resource outflows, fund accounting and, 814–815
Restricted fund entities, 808
Restructuring plans, 67
Retained earnings, *see* Consolidated retained earnings
Revenues:
  definition of, 35
  fund accounting and, 811, 819–821
  interim financial reporting and, 703–704
  matching expenses to, 37
  nongovernment nonbusiness organizations and, 935–936
  recognition, 93, 359, 570–572, 812–813
Revenue bonds, 876
Right to dispose, in general partnerships, 728
Rite Aid Corp., 14
Roanoke, Virginia, 929
RSI (required supplementary information), 830
Rule 144A, 582

S

Safe payment approach, partnership liquidation and, 779–782
St. Jude Medical, 57
Salaries, partnerships and, 737–741
Sales taxes, fund accounting and, 813
Schedule of partnership realization and liquidation, 777–778
Schering AG, 6
SEC, *see* Securities and Exchange Commission
Secured creditors, bankruptcy and, 520–521
Securities Act of 1934, 578
Securities and Exchange Commission (SEC), 552, 553–560, 576, 578, 660
Security issuance costs, 53
Segment reporting:
  aggregation criteria and, 692
  bases for measurement information and, 694–696
  basic disclosure requirements, 689
  common cost allocation, 690–691
  determining operating segments, 691–693
  enterprisewide disclosures, 695
  General Electric example, 711–714
  general information and, 694
  geographic area disclosures, 696

geographic area reporting, 697–698
interim disclosures, 695
International Accounting Standards Board positions on, 699–700
major customer disclosures, 696, 698
operating profit or loss, 690
presentation methods, 696
product or service disclosures, 695
quantitative thresholds and, 692
reconciliation of segmental data, 695, 698–699
reportable information to be presented, 694–696
revenue, 690
segment assets information and, 694
segment profit or loss information, 694
seventy-five percent combined revenue test, 693–697
standards of financial accounting for, 688–699
terminology regarding, 690
Selling affiliate, in intercompany sales, 311
Separate tax returns:
cost method and, 190–191
partial and complete equity methods and, 192–193
tax consequences of, 188–193
undistributed subsidiary income and, 189–192
Serial bonds, 864–866, 883
Service fees, intercompany, 389–392
Service fee revenue, 953
Service-type special assessments, 894–895
Settlement rate spot date, 603
Seventy-five percent combined revenue test, 693–697
SFAS, *see* Statement of Financial Accounting Standards
Shareholders equity, 731–732
SIC (Standing Interpretation Committee), 553
Significance tests, 693
SOCE (statement of changes in equity), 560
SORIE (statement of recognized income or expense), 560
Sound value, 267
Special assessments, governmental, 894–897
Special purpose entities (SPE), 66, 86
Special revenue funds, 856, 857–858
Speculation, forward contracts and, 605
Spin-offs, 10
Split accounting, intrinsic and time value elements, 622
Sponsored ADRs, 580–581
Spot rates, 593, 604, 662
Standing Interpretation Committee (SIC), 553
State and local government. *See also* Fund accounting
capital assets and, 879–881
capital improvement special assessments, 895–897
external reporting requirements, 884–885
fiduciary funds, 856–857, 878–879
fund entities, 855–857
generally accepted governmental accounting standards, 853–855
governmental funds, 855–875
government fund balances and government-wide net assets and, 887–888
government fund-based reporting, 885–888
government-wide reporting, 888–893
interfund activity, 897–899
long-term debt and, 881–883
management's discussion and analysis, 893–894
proprietary funds, 856, 875–878
service-type special assessments, 895
special assessments, 894–897
standards, 854–855
structure of governmental accounting, 855–857
Statement of activities, 891–892
Statement of Affairs, 519, 530–532
Statement of cash flows, 574
Statement of changes in equity (SOCE), 560
Statement of comprehensive income, 36, 573
Statement of financial position, 573–575
Statement of net assets, 888–891
Statement of recognized income or expense (SORIE), 560
Statement of Shareholders' Equity, 654–655
Statement on Auditing Standards (SAS) No. 69, 558
Statements of Financial Accounting Concepts (SFAC), 32–33
No. 2, 930
No. 4, 33, 806, 932
No. 5, 34–37, 249
No. 6, 34, 116, 930
No. 7, 33–34
Statements of Financial Accounting Standards (SFAS):
No. 3, 707
No. 5, 115
No. 8, 661–662
No. 12, 218
No. 13, 568–569
No. 14, 688–689
No. 15, 516, 524
No. 21, 688
No. 52, 600, 616, 641–643, 662, 669
No. 53, 648
No. 93, 931
No. 109, 59, 70, 71, 115–117, 190, 334, 705
No. 116, 940
No. 117, 932–933
No. 124, 950
No. 128, 707
No. 131, 687, 689–691, 694–695, 697
No. 133, 600–601, 612, 618, 622
No. 138, 605
No. 140, 87
No. 141, 45–47, 51, 59, 60

Statements of Financial Accounting Standards (SFAS): (continued)
- *No. 141R,* 4, 20, 29, 45, 46, 54–55, 70–71, 416–417
- *No. 142,* 47–48, 51
- *No. 144,* 50, 52
- *No. 154,* 707
- *No. 157,* 262
- *No. 160,* 4, 29, 38, 70, 420, 428–429
- *No. 162,* 33, 558, 559
- *No. 167,* 117–118
- *No. 168,* 38, 558, 559

Statutory consolidations, 16
Statutory mergers, 15–16
Step acquisitions, 67
Stock acquisitions:
- advantages of, 89
- versus asset acquisitions, 14–15
- consolidated financial statements and, 89–90
- firm valuation and, 21
- interim acquisitions, 165–176
- investments at date of acquisition, 91
- by parent, 416–420
- purchasing additional shares, 178
- push down accounting and, 270–275
- reasons for, 89
- recording investments in, 153–163
- requirements regarding consolidation of, 88–89
- stock exchange ratios, 22
- stock-for-stock swaps, 22
- subsidiaries and control, 85–88
- terminology regarding, 84
- treasury stock holdings, 106
- use of workpapers and, 92–98

Stock dividends:
- both preferred and common stock outstanding, 483–497
- versus cash dividends, 478
- consolidating subsidiary with preferred stock outstanding, 486–497
- determining equity interest by class, 483–485
- difference between cost of investment and book value of interest, 485
- issued by subsidiary, 478–483
- issued from postacquisition earnings, 481–482
- issued from preaquisition earnings, 482–483

Strategic acquisitions, 13–14
Subsidiary company(-ies), 26. *See also* Consolidated financial statements; Ownership interest; Stock acquisitions; Stock dividends
- asset valuation and classification, 90
- book value of, 94
- definition of, 84–88
- disposal of depreciable assets, 269–270
- implied value of, 94
- initial investment in, 89–90
- as intercompany seller, 310–311, 367–378
- issuance of stock by, 430–438
- more then one subsidiary company and, 108–110

Subsidiary dividends paid, 177
Synergies:
- financial, 9
- operating, 8

T

Tables of present values, A1–A3
Takeover premiums, 17–18
Tax Reform Act of 1986, 9
Tax returns. *See also* Deferred taxes; Income tax
- consolidated for affiliated companies, 189
- filing separate, 188–193
- undistributed subsidiary income and, 189–190

Temporal conversion method, 643–644, 648, 649, 655–659, 666–668
Tender offers, 5, 6
Term bonds, 866–867, 883
Term endowment funds, 948–949
Term modification, reorganizations and, 524–526
Texas Commerce Banc-shares Inc., 84
Thomson Reuters, 2
Thornwood Associates, 10
Thrifty PayLess Holdings Inc., 14
Time elements, in forward contracts, 603
Total elimination, 29
Totally held, definition of, 85
Transfer pricing, 690
Translation:
- exchange rate, 592–594
- foreign currency transactions, 668–669

Translation of foreign financial statements:
- adjustment, 642
- analysis of gain or loss, 658–659
- current rate method, 643
- economies not highly inflationary, 648–650
- of financial statements, 641–642
- functional currency concept, 642–643
- functional currency is local currency, 651–655
- functional currency is U.S. dollar, 655–659
- gain or loss, 642
- high inflationary economies, 647–648
- methods of, 643–644
- objectives of, 642–643
- process of, 646–650
- temporal method, 643–644

TransWorld Airlines, 532
Troubled debt restructurings, 524–529. *See also* Insolvency; Reorganizations accounting
Trustees:
- accounting and reporting, 532–535
- liquidations and, 521

Trust funds, 872–874, 878–879
TRW Inc., 2
Two-transaction approach, 599

U
Uncertain tax positions, accounting for, 115–117
Underlying value, in hedge accounting, 600
Undistributed subsidiary income:
 and separate tax returns, 189–192
 and unrealized intercompany profit, 396–397
Unfriendly (hostile) combinations, 5–6
Uniform Partnership Act (UPA), 773
United Kingdom, 461
United States:
 format differences with United Kingdom, 461
 partnerships in (2002 and 2003), 725
U.S. Department of Justice, 929
U.S. dollar, 655–659
U.S. GAAP:
 convergence of IFRS and, 553–557
 and FASB codification project, 38–39
 hierarchy, GAAP, 558–567
 IFRS vs., 3, 66–67, 112, 184, 557, 709
Unlimited liability, in general partnerships, 728
Unrealized intercompany profit, 302, 334, 337–340
Unrecognized foreign currency commitment, 610–613
Unrestricted fund entities, 808
Unsecured creditors, bankruptcy and, 520–521
Unsponsored ADRs, 580
UPA (Uniform Partnership Act), 773
Upstream sales, 301. *See also* Intercompany sales
 cost method and, 312–320
 noncontrolling interest and, 310–311, 367–370
 subsidiary as intercompany seller, 370–378

V
Valuation, changes in partnership ownership and, 742–743
Value of the forward contracts, 603
Variable interest entities (VIE), 46, 86, 117–118
Venezuela, 648
Verizon Communications, 10
Vertical integration, 11
Vertical mergers, 8
VisionAire Corp., 521
Vivendi Universal, 2
Voluntary health and welfare organizations, 929. *See also* Nongovernment nonbusiness organizations
 expenditure and expense classifications, 936
 plant funds and, 947–948

W
Wachovia Corp., 84
Wal-Mart Stores, 700
Walt Disney Co., 86
Washington Mutual, 84
Wells Fargo & Co., 84
White knight, 7
White squire, 7
Wholly owned, definition of, 85
WorldCom, 2, 519
Workpapers:
 accounting for foreign affiliates and, 664–670
 alternate workpaper formats, 186–188
 basic eliminating entries, 164
 bond investment and, 459–475
 cost method and, 144–152
 disposal of property and equipment by purchasing affiliate, 387–389
 downstream sales, 299–306
 entry adjustment prior to eliminating, 107–108
 equity method and, 153–163
 functional currency is local currency, 651–655
 functional currency is U.S. dollar, 657
 implied value and, 96–105
 intercompany balance sheet eliminations, 106–107
 intercompany sales, 321–331, 359–367
 interim acquisitions of subsidiary stock, 155–175
 investment costs and, 93–100, 231–249, 252–260
 more than one subsidiary company, 108–110
 preparing consolidated statements using, 92–111
 put down basis, 273–275
 separate tax returns and, 190–191
 stock dividends issued by subsidiary, 479–481
 subsidiary as intercompany seller, 370–378
 subsidiary with preferred stock outstanding, 486–497
 upstream sales, 312–318, 382–387
 workpaper-only entries, 96
Workpaper-only entries, 97

Z
Zimbabwe, 648